ARCHITECTURAL DETAILS

Classic Pages from
ARCHITECTURAL GRAPHIC STANDARDS
1940 – 1980

RAMSEY/SLEEPER

THE AMERICAN INSTITUTE OF ARCHITECTS

ARCHITECTURAL DETAILS

Classic Pages from
ARCHITECTURAL GRAPHIC STANDARDS
1940 – 1980

Edited by
DONALD WATSON, FAIA

JOHN WILEY & SONS, INC.

New York • Chichester • Weinheim • Brisbane • Toronto • Singapore

To order books or for customer service call (800)–CALL WILEY (225–5945).

Library of Congress Cataloging-in-Publication Data:

Ramsey, Charles George, 1884–1963.
    Architectural details for restoration and maintenance from Architectural graphic standards 4th through 7th editions / Donald Watson, editor.
        p. cm.
    Includes index.
    ISBN 0-471-41270-8
    1. Building—Details—Drawings. 2. Building—Details—Drawings—Standards. I. Watson, Donald. II. Ramsey, Charles George, 1884–1963. Architectural graphic standards. III. Title.

TH2031 .R34 2001
721'.028'4—dc21   2001017651

Printed in the United States of America
10 9 8 7 6 5 4 3 2 1

CONTENTS

PUBLISHER'S NOTE

THE ONGOING ENTERPRISE of publishing *Architectural Graphic Standards* resembles the building industry in New York City: the old and established edifices are regularly renovated or even demolished and replaced, in order to keep pace with changing needs within severe space constraints. As design and construction standards have changed over the decades, many details from *Architectural Graphic Standards* have been removed from the book, even as it grew from 233 pages in the 1932 first edition, to nearly 1,100 pages in the current tenth edition, published in 2000. However, most of the building stock that was constructed during the mid-to-late twentieth century still stands, and much of it requires repair, restoration, or renovation. Indeed, industry statistics suggest that a larger investment over the next few decades will be made in maintaining existing buildings than in new construction. This volume, *Architectural Details,* provides architects and construction professionals with thousands of pieces of essential architectural data that were published in *Architectural Graphic Standards* between roughly 1940 and 1980, but removed from subsequent editions due to space limitations and changing architectural standards. In his Preface, editor Donald Watson points out that his criteria for selecting specific pages for this volume include continuing relevance for work on existing buildings in restoration and maintenance, as well as compelling visual presentation of classic architectural data and standards. John Wiley & Sons are proud to present *Architectural Details* as must-have material for practicing professionals, and as adaptive reuse of classic architectural drawings.

ROBERT C. GARBER
Publisher
Professional/Trade Publishing
John Wiley & Sons, Inc.

ABOUT THE EDITOR

DONALD WATSON, FAIA, NCARB is a practicing architect. He is a noted author and editor of professional books in architecture and environmental design, including *Time-Saver Standards for Architectural Design Data* (7th edition) and *Time-Saver Standards for Building Materials and Systems* (1st edition). He served as Visiting Professor and Chair of the Environmental Design Program at Yale School of Architecture from 1970 to 1990. He is a former Dean of Architecture and currently Clinical Professor of Architecture, Rensselaer Polytechnic Institute, Troy, New York.

PREFACE

SINCE ITS INCEPTION in 1932, *Architectural Graphic Standards* has provided a record of standard architectural and construction details and has served as a widely accepted reference for architectural practice.

In the earlier editions, each page of *Architectural Graphic Standards* was essentially a hand-drawn plate devoted to a specific topic, reflecting a fairly straightforward, traditional approach to architectural design. Subsequent editions were revised to follow the increasing breadth of architectural practice and technological advances in construction. In keeping with its practical mission to be a single-volume reference work, many pages were dropped entirely or substantially changed with successive editions. Moreover, the content of prior pages was often condensed and represented in newly formatted pages. One can see in ensuing editions more text and additional numerical documentation. In recent editions, computer drawing and lettering have provided for more unified and detailed illustrations. Each edition has thus reflected the historical evolution of the topics as well as modes of representing the working knowledge of a practitioner of architecture.

Looking back through its seventy-year history of publication, the question posed by the publishers of *Architectural Graphic Standards* was: "Do some pages that have been 'left behind' in the process of revision contain something of value, either for current or for historical reference?"

This volume of *Architectural Graphic Standards* is the answer to that question. It is an affirmative, "Yes."

In reviewing more than 4,000 pages of past editions, a great many useful pages were identified that are worthy of scrutiny. Some useful pages had been eliminated due to the unenviable editorial task of reducing the number of pages to fit within one bound volume. Nonetheless, some of them contain useful and relevant information.

The result of the review of these pages is assembled here in this archival volume so that once again these "lost pages" are available to the contemporary architect and student of professional practice. Example pages reprinted in this volume include data for residential design; sitework and landscaping; stairs; fireplaces; energy related topics,

such as sun shading and solar control; and appendix sections, such as drawing methods, geometry, and metrication. Some topics, such as stonework and terra cotta, plank and beam framing, roofing systems, mill construction, and pneumatic tube conveyors, are of historical interest as references of systems no longer commonly used but which are still extant in buildings now subject to remodeling and adaptive reuse.

Other discontinued pages present data in a visually interesting and compelling way. In some cases, data may have been updated and is shown in more recent editions in some new format. In other cases, data is outdated or less relevant to current practice. Some examples of well presented visual data are included in this volume, for instance the entire set of masonry pages, and pages on wood framing, paneling and joints, roofing, flashing, hardware, fireplaces, geometry and classical architecture.

In successive editions, certain topics had evolved over many decades of publication. Such pages provide an overview of the historical evolution of architectural details and data. Seeing these pages side-by-side reveals how design and practice details have evolved over the past seventy years. These plates also show how *Architectural Graphic Standards* has been a collaborative and multigenerational endeavor in building the archival reference data of practice.

The following are highlights of pages included in this volume:

1 GENERAL PLANNING AND DESIGN DATA

The first pages in this volume [pages 3-5] are examples of pages that provide an overview of the evolution of architectural data. These plates depict increasingly diverse renditions of the human figure, including a plate drawn in the 1940s for *Architectural Record* magazine by Earnest Irving Freese and a plate from the Henry Dreyfuss *Measure of Man and Woman* (1956), first published in the seventh edition of *Architectural Graphic Standards.*

Other pages in Chapter 1, such as residential data [pages 6-15], are visually clear and easily referenced for residential and small commercial practice. Data for residential storage data [16-23] are painstaking in detail, resulting in a unique collection of detailed data for the residential and cabinet designer. Earthquake and wind resistance construction details [pages 24-26] are included here because they convey information in a particularly clear and unique way.

2 SITEWORK

Many of the sitework and landscaping pages reprinted here have been dropped in the process of prior revisions, although they remain useful. The editorial decision to drop them may have been made because landscape design is increasingly perceived to be a specialization, to be given over to the purview of a landscape architectural professional and therefore not essential for a volume devoted primarily to building. However, the pages on landscape design of many prior editions are reprinted here because they are visually attractive and informative and because all architects should be knowledgeable about landscape design. As a result, the entire set of pages in Chapter 2 [pages 27-84] can be considered a supplement to current publications.

3 MASONRY

Without masonry, there would not be architecture, at least, as we perceive it historically. Many of the pages reprinted in Chapter 3 [pages 85-118] are derived from the earliest editions of *Architectural Graphic Standards* as hand-drawn plates of architectural stone details. These pages have been dropped from recent editions because masonry is no longer so widely used, at least in some of the ways recorded here. These plates are of historical and archival value. They serve as a reference for the architectural historian and preservationist who may be remodeling structures that conform to these details.

4 METALS

Because architectural practices related to metals and expansion joints have greatly changed, there are few historical pages on this topic that remain of interest. The few pages reprinted in Chapter 4 [pages 120-126] are included in this volume because they record historical practice and details that can be found in the many extant buildings built in mid-twentieth century.

5 WOOD AND PLASTICS

It is often remarked that wood construction remains relatively the same as practiced in the American Colonial era. While this is not exactly the case, the plates reprinted in

Chapter 5 [pages 127-170] give evidence of the enduring handcraft of wood construction. The plates on pages 162-165 convey a way of building that is thoughtful and deliberate. Pages 166 and 167, "Multi-use Wood Frame Member," which were carried in *Architectural Graphic Standards* for only a few editions, show an unusual method of wood detailing that demands a cabinetmaker's skill to construct (as well as a very benign climate to endure). These and other plates in this part will be of historical interest to the enthusiast of residential wood construction and craft.

6 THERMAL AND MOISTURE PROTECTION

Chapter 6 contains pages included from prior editions for several different reasons. The pages on thermal comfort [pages 173-174] are no longer carried in current editions of *Architectural Graphic Standards* in their original format. They are the contribution of the late John Yellott whose mastery of these topics and clarity and conciseness of presentation are epochal and thus worth reprinting. Other plates, particularly those on roofing, illustrate now seldom used or out-of-date roofing systems, but are reprinted for archival reference, because many roofs are found in existing buildings that are represented by such details.

7 DOORS AND WINDOWS

The plates in Chapter 7 document now out-of-date window systems [pages 223-230] and are included for historical reference. The plates on nails and hardware [pages 231-244], while typical of architect and builders catalogue data, are exemplary of the visual lexicon represented in the archive of *Architectural Graphic Standards.*

8 INTERIOR STAIRS AND STAIRWELLS

The plates in Chapter 8 [pages 246-260] present data on stair design. In the regular editions of *Architectural Graphic Standards,* these plates are normally dispersed in many different sections (to conform to the MasterFormat classification system). It is therefore all the more useful to look at stair data as an entity, since stairs are one of the severe tests of an achitect's knowledge of detailing and also of human ergometrics. These pages are reprinted to provide a helpful supplement to contemporary sources on stair design.

9 SPECIALTIES

Fireplaces are common in houses and other residential scale facilities, more for their aesthetic character than their original function as heat sources, with the result that each edition of *Architectural Graphic Standards* has reduced the pages devoted to its detailing. The extensive number of pages reprinted here, including "Tower Clocks and Bells" [page 282] are historical plates that in some cases date to the earliest editions of the book.

10 CONVEYING SYSTEMS

The pages reprinted here of "Pneumatic Tubes" [pages 285-288] are no longer carried in current editions of *Architectural Graphic Standards.* Although electronic data transmission has rendered such systems obsolete, they remain in use in existing buildings for which these plates provide an historical reference.

11 ELECTRICAL

The plates reprinted here record the complete set of previously published pages on lightning protection and are now reduced to one page in the current *Architectural Graphic Standards.*

12 ENERGY AND ENVIRONMENTAL DESIGN

Due to the emergent nature of the topic, the *Architectural Graphic Standards* pages on topics related to solar orientation, sun control, climate, and environmental design have undergone a good deal of change in the past thirty years. This section reprints many original pages on these topics that have since been revised entirely. The data, however, is not obsolete. For example, several methods for the still-relevant design of sunshading systems are provided so that one can pick and choose amongst several equally useful methods. The work of the Olgyay Brothers, dating from the 1950s, remains in present editions of *Architectural Graphic Standards* but is here given in the original plates. There are also plates on warm-humid climate construction and natural ventilation by the late Arthur Bowen (pages 325-326) and on natural lighting by the late Ben Evans (pages 327-329). Each of these experts made important contributions to these topics, so their original plates are valuable for continuing reference.

APPENDIX

The Appendix carries valuable archival pages that are not otherwise carried in current publications. While drawing symbols and drawing methods are now given over to computer-aided design and drafting, the standards for manual drafting methods are, nonetheless, a valuable standard for reference. Modular coordination is still a relevant approach to building, for which prior *Architectural Graphic Standards* pages provide a lucid summary and reference. Further, geometry is a topic of architectural knowledge that has remained in the architect's lexicon since the earliest known books on architecture by Vitruvius and Alberti. Finally, the pages on metrication provide a complete reference on the topic for practitioners using the international system.

In recent decades, visualization of complex data has become recognized as critical to the understanding and practice of architecture. From its beginning, *Architectural Graphic Standards* has provided an invaluable collection of plates and pages that depict details, data, and knowledge required for architectural practice. This volume reveals this unique historical record and contribution.

DONALD WATSON, FAIA
Editor

December, 2000

PREFACE
TO THE FOURTH EDITION

THIS FOURTH EDITION of *Architectural Graphic Standards* is really a new book. The authors and the purpose remain the same as for the Third Edition, but the content is greatly changed. The new edition was delayed until the trend of new developments in all aspects of building became defined. Only 46 pages remain unchanged. The rest have been revised, and 368 entirely new pages have been added. In all, the Fourth Edition is 80 per cent larger than the Third.

Special care has been given to preparing the Index, since the usefulness of the book as a reference is so dependent on this feature. It has been expanded and worked over to make certain that the user can find the desired subject quickly. Each topic is indexed and cross-indexed so that there are now nearly 12,000 references. A handy classified table of contents has been added on the inside of front and back covers.

Suggestions from users of the earlier edition have been incorporated in the Fourth Edition. All material, new or old, has been checked with authorities, associations, manufacturers, and/or architects to insure its correctness.

It is impossible to thank each contributor and advisor. Acknowledgments are made at the foot of some of the pages. We are, moreover, most grateful to these men, who have done so much for this edition of our book by giving us their time, advice, and technical information:

Sullivan A. S. Patorno, Consulting Engineer (Mechanical Work)
Elwyn E. Seelye, Consulting Engineer (Structural Work)
Ralph Eberlin, Consulting Engineer (Site Engineering)
Leo Novick, Landscape Architect (Landscaping)
Andre Halasz, Architect
Prentice Bradley, Architect (Modular Coordination)
A. J. Amendola, Architect (Food Service Equipment)
E. R. Armengol (Steel Windows)
Daniel Schwartzman, Architect

The First Edition was mainly the work of our own hands, with some assistance. However, for the Fourth Edition, which is two and one half times larger than the First, we have depended more and more on our staff, which has labored for three years to complete the work. We thank them all, and in particular:

John J. Baron
William Chaplinsky
Robert J. Davis
Peter S. Hopf

Herbert Kass
George B. Kurtzke
Udell Stephen Madden
Madeline C. Scott

CHARLES G. RAMSEY
HAROLD R. SLEEPER

April, 1951

PREFACE
TO THE FIFTH EDITION

SINCE THE PUBLICATION of the Fourth Edition of *Architectural Graphic Standards* five years ago, the building industry has made great strides, new techniques have been developed, new standards have been made and others have been changed.

Our goal for the Fifth Edition was to include all these new developments as well as to bring standards up to date and to include such data, previously omitted, as now appears useful.

What this would entail was unknown until our staff had spent two and a half years of necessary research and work.

However, we do feel our goal has been achieved and the Fifth Edition of *Architectural Graphic Standards* is complete and ready for your use.

Every page of the Fourth Edition was first analyzed, then checked and reviewed. If no great change was indicated, pages were sent for comments and criticisms. Many pages were scrapped and new ones substituted. New pages were developed for added subjects with the help of various associations, manufacturers or individuals. When completed, every page was finally reviewed by the best qualified organization or person.

We have been greatly benefited in securing data, technical material and advice from persons and organizations for this edition because of the present wide acceptance of the book by the building industry.

The problem "how to keep the volume within bounds of usefulness in weight and size" was alleviated greatly by the publication late last year of *Building Planning and Design Standards* by Harold R. Sleeper. Pages relevant to specific types of building were revised and published in that book. These books may be used as companion volumes. Which volume to consult may be decided by asking:

Is it a question or item of a general nature that may occur in a variety of buildings? If so, consult *Architectural Graphic Standards.*

Is it a question pertaining to a specific type of building? Then use *Building Planning and Design Standards.*

In all, some 38 pages from the Fourth Edition were omitted, thus making room for new material. Our desire to limit the size and weight of this Edition has been further assisted by cutting the weight of paper. So, in spite of the additions of 161 pages of drawings, no noticeable increase in weight or size has occurred.

Although standards or data no longer currently used have generally been omitted, a few such pages have been retained; for instance, on the advice of our mechanical engineers, a page on an obsolete type of radiator has been retained for alteration work.

The entire order and make-up of the Fifth Edition have been rearranged. The contents have been grouped into twenty-three sections, each with its own table of contents. These groups are shown on the inside of the front and back covers for those who are interested in one entire subject rather than a specific item.

The index has been modified and clarified by a change in format that makes it more readily useful.

Besides adding new pages relative to new subjects, many old subjects have been redrawn in toto. For instance, the entire section on furring, lathing and plastering was deleted and re-created with many added pages.

The hundreds of companies, associations, consultants and advisors are given acknowledgment on the pages to which they contributed. We wish to thank them for their generous aid.

Special thanks are due the following consultants for their contribution and excellent advice:

Anthony J. Amendola, A.I.A. (Food Service Equipment)
Prentice Bradley, A.I.A. (Modular Coordination)
Ralph Eberlin, Consulting Engineer (Site Engineering)
Andre Halasz, A.I.A.
Leo Novick, Landscape Architect
Mongitore & Moesel, Consulting Engineers (Mechanical Work)
Daniel Schwartzman, A.I.A.
Elwyn E. Seelye, Consulting Engineer (Structural Work)
Frederic N. Whitley, P.E., Consulting Fireplace Engineer

We are grateful to the many architects who have suggested subject matter for inclusion in this Edition. The authors' most irksome duty, that of selection, was guided by such thoughtful advice. There is no limit to what might have been included except that of the size of the volume. We hope that our choice will prove useful and adequate.

The revision of this book, an immense task, has been possible because of a devoted task force working for two and a half years. This work could not have been done by the authors alone, as it was in the earlier Editions.

Our grateful thanks are due:

John D. Chase, for his excellent direction of this work, and to Laurel Anderson, Joanna Arfman, Warren E. Bendixon, Marian Dorr-Dorynek, Paul Hertgen, Robert J. Jacuruso, Edwin T. Kehrle, George Klett, Jane F. Patton, Fred Y. Senftleber, Francis J. Sheridan, Paula J. Treder.

CHARLES G. RAMSEY
HAROLD R. SLEEPER

June, 1956

PREFACE
TO THE SIXTH EDITION

FOR GENERATIONS of architects, engineers, draftsmen and builders, *Architectural Graphic Standards* will need no introduction. It has been their drafting room companion since 1932 when the 233-page First Edition, authored by Charles George Ramsey, AIA, and Harold Reeve Sleeper, FAIA, was published by Wiley. In the subsequent four editions, including the Fifth published in 1956, these authors revised, modernized, added new pages and dropped obsolete ones until the Fifth Edition contained 758 pages, and the work was established as the architects' and building industry's reference bible. With every edition, the task of updating required more and more time for research, analysis, and plate development and this activity became in essence Harold R. Sleeper's career and his major contribution to the architectural profession. During Sleeper's last years, and after work on the Sixth Edition had begun, he invited his publisher to carry on this work. He also expressed the hope that The American Institute of Architects would assume authorship and carry on his, Ramsey's, and his publisher's graphic standards philosophy for the benefit of future generations of practitioners.

In 1962, Walker G. Stone, an Architectural Engineering graduate of the University of Illinois, with a position at that time as Editor-in-Chief, Professional Publications, and later Vice President of Wiley, began discussion with William H. Scheick, Executive Director of the AIA, with the objective of carrying out Sleeper's expressed wish. The AIA responded favorably since a new edition of *Architectural Graphic Standards*, reflecting the rapidly changing techniques of contemporary building, was in keeping with the Institute's goal of serving its membership and the building industry with authoritative practice aids. In 1963, Wiley and the AIA jointly established an Advisory Board on *Architectural Graphic Standards* to advise both parties on the feasibility, contents and format of the project. The members of the ten man board were Walker G. Stone, Wiley, New York, New York; John C. Anderson, AIA, Minneapolis, Minnesota; Joseph N. Boaz, AIA, Atlanta, Georgia; Harold D. Hauf, FAIA, Los Angeles, California; Dean F. Hilfinger, FAIA, Bloomington, Illinois; Gershon Meckler, PE, Toledo, Ohio; Edwin T. Pairo, AIA, Washington, D.C.; F. Spencer Roach, AIA, Philadelphia, Pennsylvania; Harry E. Rodman, FAIA, Troy, New York, and Jack Train, FAIA, Chicago, Illinois.

Thus in July, 1964, on the basis of the Advisory Board's report, Wiley and the AIA agreed as publisher and author to produce this Sixth Edition. Joseph N. Boaz, AIA, former Professor of Architecture, School of Design, North Carolina State University and now with the architectural firm of Toombs, Amisano and Wells, Atlanta, Georgia, accepted the invitation to become its editor. His leave of absence was arranged through the willing support of the Dean of the School of Design, Henry Kamphoefner, FAIA. He immediately took up residence in New York City where the project became headquartered in space provided by Wiley.

The Advisory Board's recommendations had made it clear that the new edition would be a completely new book, not simply a revision. To assist the Editor in determining content, organization and format, a smaller Editorial Advisory Committee succeeded the earlier ten man board. The committee was composed of the following: Harold D. Hauf, FAIA, then with the architectural firm of Charles Luckman Associates of Los Angeles and later Professor of Architecture at the University of Southern California; Louis DeMoll, FAIA, partner of the Ballinger Company, Architects and Engineers of Philadelphia, Pennsylvania; Dean D. Kenneth Sargent, FAIA, School of Architecture, Syracuse University; and ex officio committee members Walker G. Stone, Project Director for Wiley, and myself, bearing project management responsibility for the AIA.

In the initial 14 months, Editor Boaz devoted full time to the project at Wiley's office in New York City and for the year and a half following his September, 1965, return to his teaching duties in North Carolina, he was able to continue direction of the work on a part-time basis. During the period February, 1965, to February, 1966, he was ably assisted by William Tashlick, AIA, Assistant to the Editor, now with the Rouse Co., Columbia, Maryland, and Wiley's architectural drafting staff, headed up by Chief Draftsman David Edward Miller, an architectural student of Rensselaer Polytechnic Institute. During this 20-month period, Editor Boaz undertook the staggering task of determining the detailed contents of the book, its organization, the graphic design of typical pages, including typography, and the meticulous research and assembly of definitive data sources and technical files for each subject. He worked closely with many authors of technical references, with trade associations, and with scholars with specialized knowledge. At the same time, he and his assistant supervised the Wiley drafting staff in the production of approximately 200 pages of the finished book.

The Editorial Advisory Committee, after several review sessions, concluded that the revision as initially planned would not meet the standards of the AIA in a period of rapidly changing technology unless the participation of many specially qualified members of the Institute were obtained.

In the new approach adopted by the Editorial Advisory Committee, 94 architectural and engineering firms were selected for their special interest and experience in the subjects assigned. The coordination of this selection process and the work of these firms was part of my own AIA management responsibilities. Beginning in 1968, I was assisted in this task by a new Coordinating Editor for Manuscript, Douglas S. Stenhouse, AIA, Washington, D.C. These firms, with the careful guidance of Editor Boaz and the Editorial Advisory Committee chaired by Harold Hauf, FAIA, contributed over 475 plates of this book. Their contributions are acknowledged on each of the pages they prepared.

In order for these firms, scattered all over the nation, to produce pages of technical excellence, a highly complex coordinating procedure was devised. Editor Boaz transmitted a data file for each subject ranging in size from one to thirteen pages. His transmittal included his own Editor's remarks, instructions for graphic make up of pages, sample completed pages and tracing paper forms. To assist him in this highly complex task, the AIA and Wiley employed Charles Fouhy, AIA, as Coordinating Editor for Production and Operations at Wiley's offices in New York. Charles Fouhy managed the complicated flow of pages and communications among all concerned and then supervised the preparation and accuracy of the final inked drawings prepared by Wiley's architectural drafting staff and the J. and R. Technical Services, Inc., New York, New York. They are to be commended for their adherence to the highest publishing standards.

Each of the contributing firms submitted a preliminary drawing for review by the Editorial Advisory Committee, followed by a final submission for editorial approval. Although the technical judgment of the individuals in firms who prepared the plates was given heaviest weighting, every page received review and critique at both stages by one member of the Committee, by Editor Boaz, and by Chairman Hauf, who resolved any ambiguities in the critiques and indicated final approval. The review was meticulous and often resulted in returns to the contributors for revision. It was a long and difficult task but it is believed that the results herein attest to a conscientious, scholarly, and thorough effort by all participants.

A parallel development in 1967 was the enlargement of the Editorial Advisory Committee which was then made a part of the regular national AIA Committee Structure. The new members were Bernard B. Rothschild, FAIA, of Finch, Alexander, Barnes, Rothschild and Paschal, Atlanta, Georgia; and Robert E. Walters, AIA, of Caudill, Rowlett and Scott, Houston, Texas. In 1968 the Committee was further augmented by the addition of Andrew Bustard, AIA, Havertown, Pennsylvania; Gordon Comb, AIA, St. Paul, Minnesota; and Jay S. Pettit, Jr., AIA, Detroit, Michigan.

Throughout this long history, the ultimate responsibility has been patiently borne by the successive Presidents of the AIA, the Board of Directors and, particularly the Chairmen of the Commission on Professional Practice. They are listed as follows:

	President	Chairman, Commission on Professional Practice
1964	Arthur G. Odell, Jr., FAIA Charlotte, North Carolina	Daniel Schwartzman, FAIA New York, New York
1965	Morris Ketchum, Jr., FAIA New York, New York	Dean F. Hilfinger, FAIA Bloomington, Illinois
1966	Charles M. Nes, Jr., FAIA Baltimore, Maryland	Victor C. Gilbertson, FAIA Minneapolis, Minnesota
1967	Robert L. Durham, FAIA Seattle, Washington	Bernard B. Rothschild, FAIA Atlanta, Georgia
1968	George E. Kassabaum, FAIA St. Louis, Missouri	Jack D. Train, FAIA Chicago, Illinois
1969-1970	Rex W. Allen, FAIA San Francisco, California	Joseph H. Flad, FAIA Madison, Wisconsin

When Victor Gilbertson completed his term on the AIA Board in 1966, he was asked to continue his policy direction on behalf of the Board, in recognition of the complexity of the project and the confusion caused by annual changes in assignment of responsibility. He deserves a note of thanks.

Those of us who have been associated with this project from its beginning feel strongly that two men of the AIA deserve particular thanks and recognition for their interest, patience and enthusiastic support. They are William H. Scheick, FAIA, Executive Director of the AIA from 1960-1969, and Morris Ketchum, Jr., FAIA, whose strong position of leadership reinforced the AIA and the project staff when problems of finance, staff, and the complexity of the project were discouraging.

Additionally, William L. Slayton, Executive Vice President of the AIA since December 1969, has enthusiastically supported the project.

So the efforts of hundreds of people, mostly volunteers, were combined to finally produce a document of technical excellence. Here, also, we wish to acknowledge the vitally important assistance of hundreds of organizations and individuals whose contributions have provided the data sources utilized by plate contributors. Their names are listed following the text. Without their technical output, this work would not have been possible.

Most important to any author is the encouragement and professional guidance of his publisher. Walker G. Stone, Vice President of Wiley, who has been deeply involved with *Architectural Graphic Standards,* played a continuous and decisive role in this entire project. For this, The American Institute of Architects extends its thanks.

It has been my privilege to work with all of these devoted and generous contributors from the inception of the AIA's authorship of *Architectural Graphic Standards.* The patience and fortitude of all participants has been an inspiration to me. They deserve the appreciation of the entire building industry.

ELLIOT CARROLL, FAIA
Deputy Executive Vice President
The American Institute of Architects

July 16, 1970

PREFACE
TO THE SEVENTH EDITION

THE SEVENTH EDITION of *Architectural Graphic Standards* is the second edition prepared by the American Institute of Architects. Published 49 years after the first edition, it carries on the work of the originating authors, Charles George Ramsey, AIA, and Harold Reeve Sleeper, FAIA. Their major contribution to the architectural profession in the first five sequentially updated editions established the book as the most widely recognized handbook reference in the construction industry. Sleeper expressed the hope that on his death the American Institute of Architects would assume his editorial responsibilities for updating the book. In 1964 John Wiley & Sons and the Institute entered into an agreement for this purpose. The sixth edition, published in 1970, was the first result of this agreement, and the present edition represents further development of this essential reference book.

Wiley representation on this project is centered on the staff of the Professional Group, John Wiley & Sons, headed by Michael Harris, Vice President and General Manager, and Robert B. Polhemus, Vice President. As had been true for many years, Walker G. Stone represented John Wiley's interest in the project during the early planning of the seventh edition. After Stone's retirement in 1976, Wiley named William Dudley Hunt, Jr., FAIA, as Wiley's editor for the Architectural Graphic Standards project. During the development of the seventh edition an excellent working relationship has been enjoyed between the Wiley staff and the AIA. Dudley Hunt's encouragement, guidance, and counsel was continuously supportive of the AIA staff effort. The book could not have been completed without the full cooperation of the Wiley production staff. Robert J. Fletcher, Manager of Production, has ably steered the project to completion with the skilled assistance of Jeramiah McCarthy in the graphic production and Valda Aldzeris whose careful copy editing helped pull the book together.

When, in 1976, the AIA Board approved preparation of a new edition, the AIA undertook a search for an editor for the new edition. William L. Slayton, Hon. AIA, Executive Vice President of the AIA until 1978, assigned the project to the Practice Department then headed by Edward G. Petrazio, FAIA. The Architectural Graphic Standards Task Force was named, and Robert T. Packard, AIA, named Editor by mid-1976. In the ensuing period the project was moved to the new AIA Department of Practice and Design administered by Michael B. Barker, AICP, reporting to the AIA Board Commission in this area and to Group Executive James A. Scheeler, FAIA. Continued enthusiastic support from David Olan Meeker, Jr., FAIA, Executive Vice President of the AIA since 1978, has provided excellent encouragement for completion of the project.

During the four-year preparation the AIA Presidents and Chairmen of the Commission of Practice and Design have monitored the development of the project. Listed below are those whose continued support has been essential to timely completion of the book:

Year	Presidents of AIA	Chairmen of Commission on Practice and Design
1976	Louis DeMoll, FAIA	Donald J. Stephens, FAIA
1977	John M. McGinty, FAIA	Adolph R. Scrimenti, FAIA
1978	Elmer E. Botsai, FAIA	Frank R. Mudano, FAIA
1979	Ehrman B. Mitchell, Jr., FAIA	Thomas H. Teasdale, FAIA
1980	Charles E. Schwing, FAIA	Donald L. Hardison, FAIA

The AIA Committee on Architectural Graphics Standards was reestablished to oversee the administration of the new edition, and its membership was constituted so as to combine the required continuity from previous editions, fresh insights of those not previously involved, and the interdisciplinary participation of representatives of other design professions. Elliot Carroll, FAIA, Assistant to the Architect of the Capitol who had, as AIA Deputy Executive Vice President, acted as Project Director for the sixth edition, has been its effective Chairman. The Committee organized an Editorial Review Board headed by Joseph A. Wilkes, FAIA, of Wilkes and Faulkner, Washington, D.C. Joseph A. Wilkes' long hours of voluntary service were a major contribution to the profession. Members included several persons who performed similar functions for the sixth edition, including Bernard B. Rothschild, FAIA, of FABRAP, Atlanta, Georgia, and Robert E. Walters, AIA, of CRS, Houston, Texas. Victor C. Gilbertson, FAIA, of Hills/Gilbertson/Fisher, Inc., Minneapolis, Minnesota, closely identified with the sixth edition, was also named to the new committee, as was William H. Scheick, FAIA, former AIA Executive Director who gave his good advice during 1976 and 1977.

Other members of the expanded committee include Jean Paul Carlhian, FAIA, of Shepley, Bulfinch, Richardson and Abbot, Boston, Massachusetts, Richard K. Dee, ASLA, Johnson and Dee of Avon, Connecticut, Porter Driscoll, AIA, of the National Bureau of Standards, Robert E. Fehlberg, FAIA, of CTA Architects-Engineers, Billings, Montana, Ian Grad, PE of Syska & Hennessey, New York, P. Richard Rittlemann, AIA of Burt, Hill, Kosar, Rittlemann Associates, Butler, Pennsylvania, and Adolph R. Scrimenti, FAIA of Scrimenti/Shriver/Spinelli/Peratoni Architects, Somerville, New Jersey.

Editorial offices were established at AIA Headquarters. To aid in the determination of the content of the new edition, Wiley conducted an extensive survey confirming the wide-ranging interests of the users of *Architectural Graphic Standards.* A detailed outline was developed and procedures established for acquiring drawings for what has become a 70 percent new edition. As work proceeded, AIA staff was enlarged with the joint support of Wiley and AIA. The editor, assistant editor John R. Hoke, Jr., AIA, and technical editor William G. Miner, AIA, have been augmented by a number of secretaries and draftspersons. Particular thanks should go to Lou Ellen Utermohle, who has worked on the project since its earliest days and has contributed so much to the smooth running of the project.

It has been the design professional offices that have prepared the bulk of material. The high quality contribution of the more than 140 professional firms (up from 100 firms participating in the sixth edition) involved indicates the scope of interest and involvement in this national cooperative venture. In addition, substantial contributions have been made by trade and professional associations and government agencies. The Center for Building Technology and the Solar Energy Research Institute have been particularly helpful. The increase in building technology and engineering, as well as renewed interest in energy efficient systems, has prompted some expansion of the book. Other areas of added material include more data on the design basis of regulations, as in seismic design, design for the handicapped, fire safety considerations, and energy conservation. A separate chapter has been added to introduce metric conversion concepts. The book has been expanded from 14 chapters to 17.

Firms that offered to assist in the work were provided with detailed instructions and were asked to submit rough pencil sketches for review before preparing final manuscript and pencil drawings. These in turn were processed and approved for preparation of inked drawings and typesetting by the publisher. This effort was supplemented by illustrators and the editorial staff in Washington. This time-consuming process is what gives *Architectural Graphic Standards* its far-reaching authoritative character.

Care has been taken to refer the readers of *Architectural Graphic Standards* to other sources for additional and current data. This book is a compilation of material available at the time of preparation and is a general guide to construction technology. Resources of the AIA Library have been most helpful to the editorial staff, as well as to the many publications generally available to the construction industry.

The members of the AIA editorial staff have enjoyed their part in the process. Our thanks to the architects, engineers, and other professionals who are the real authors of this book.

ROBERT T. PACKARD, AIA
Editor

ARCHITECTURAL DETAILS

Classic Pages from
ARCHITECTURAL GRAPHIC STANDARDS
1940 – 1980

1 GENERAL PLANNING AND DESIGN DATA

DIMENSIONS of THE HUMAN FIGURE

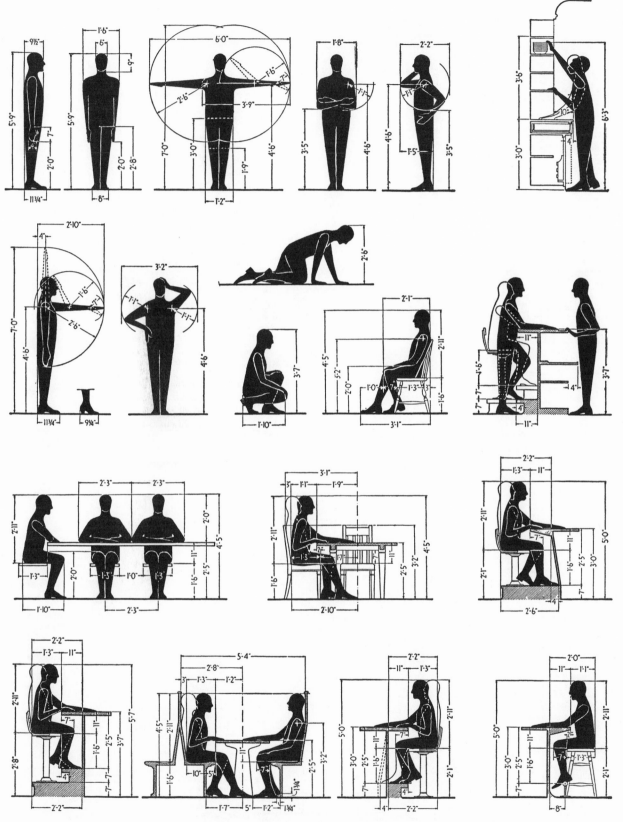

Scale of Human Figure 1/4" = 1'-0"

These dimensions are based on the average or normal adult. As clearances are minimum they should be increased when conditions will allow.

Table, desk, and other sitting work-top heights are shown 2'-5"; however some authorities prefer 2'-6" or 2'-6½". See sheets titled "Children's Furniture," for their size and furniture.

Drawings by Ernest Irving Freese

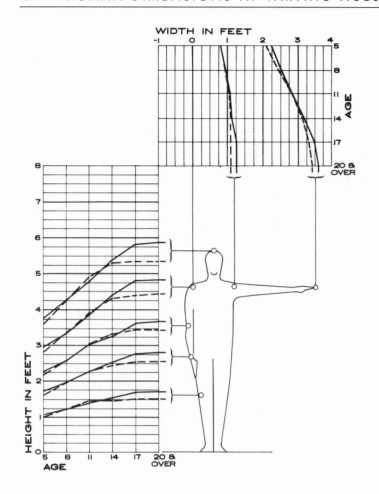

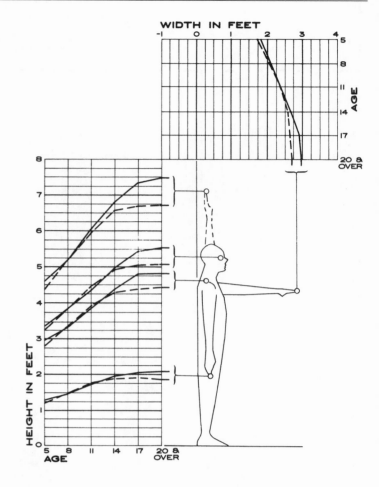

LEGEND
MALE ————————
FEMALE — — — — —

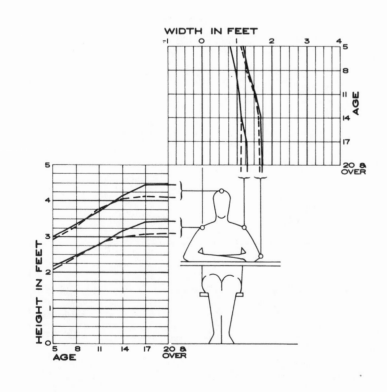

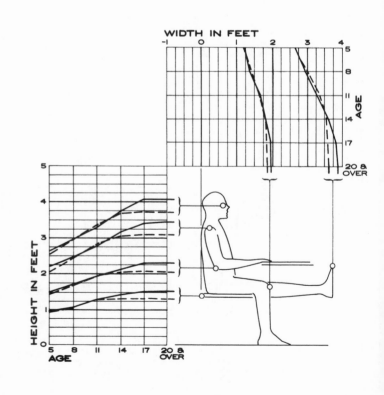

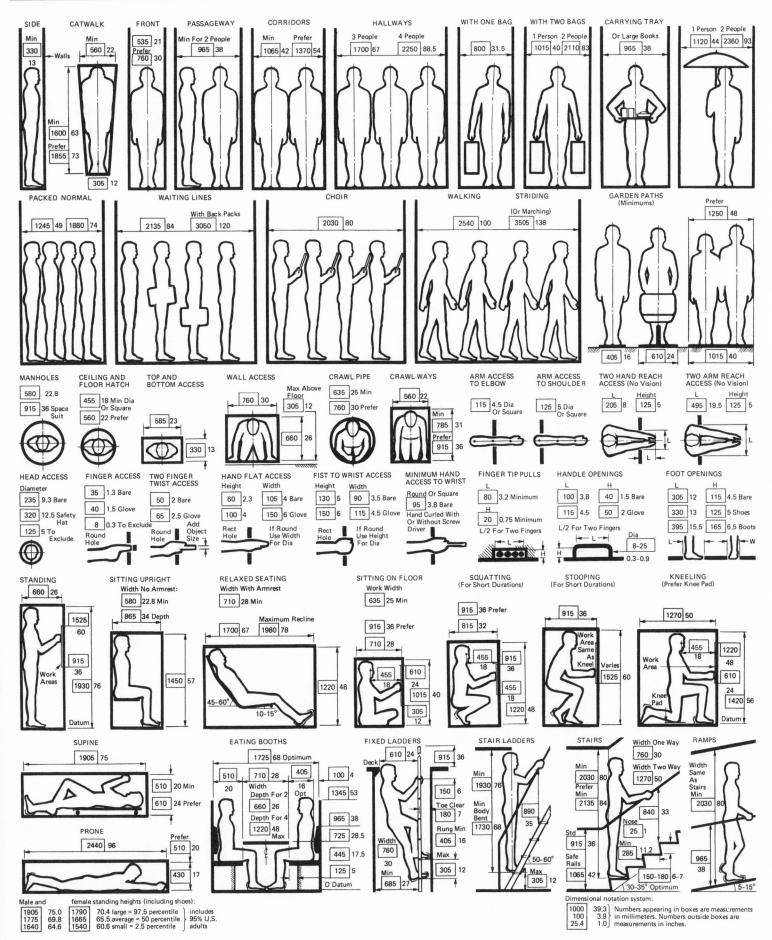

Niels Diffrient, Alvin R. Tilley; Henry Dreyfuss Associates; New York, New York

GENERAL NOTE:

Various methods listed below are applicable to different purposes, e.g. preliminary cost analysis, rental income appraisal, estimation of financial value for loan requirements, and design.

1. CALCULATION OF GROSS BLDG. AREA OR "ARCHITECTURAL AREA"

Total sq. ft. of basic areas of the several floors of a building including basements, mezzanine & intermediate floored tiers and penthouses of headroom height, added to total percentages of partial areas.

a. SUGGESTED STANDARDS FOR BASIC AREA

To calculate floor areas, include the full square foot area of spaces on all floors enclosed within the face of exterior wall surfaces of the building with the addition of dormers, bays, and chimneys, including tunnels 6'–0" wide w/slab.

b. PERCENTAGE OF PARTIAL AREAS

Garage	2/3 of area
Carport	1/2 of area
Unenclosed porch	1/2 of area
Enclosed porch	2/3 of area
Unfinished basement	1/2 of area
Covered walkways (paved)	1/2 of area
Open area under bldg. (paved)	1/2 of area
Canopies	1/4 of area
Two story room	1 1/2 of area
Penthouse (headroom height)	2/3 of area
Tunnels under 6'–0" wide w/slab	1/2 of "

c. EXCLUDE THE FOLLOWING:

Unfinished attics (finished attics are included where headroom is 5'–0" or over), crawl spaces and terraces, pipe trenches, roof overhangs, chimneys.

2. BREAKDOWN OF GROSS BLDG. AREA (SIMILAR TO G.S.A. STANDARDS)

a. NET ASSIGNABLE AREA OR "NET USABLE SPACE".

(Include interior columns or necessary projections)

b. CIRCULATION AREA

(1.) Horizontal—corridors, lobbies, ent. tunnels, & bridges.

(2.) Vertical—stairs, elev. shafts, & towers.

c. MECHANICAL AREA

(1.) Boiler rm. elec. vault, etc.

(2.) Cooling towers, enclosed shafts, duct-space.

(3.) Toilets & restroom lounge area.

d. CONSTRUCTION AREA (STRUCTURE, WALL THICKNESSES, ETC.)

e. PARTIAL AREAS (SEE 1.b.)

3. EXPLANATION OF FAMILIAR TERMS:

a. "GROSS INSIDE SPACE" equals net assignable area, plus horizontal circulation plus mechanical area.

b. "NET RENTABLE SPACE" equals net assignable plus horiz. circulation & mechanical services pertaining directly to rentable area.

c. "TOTAL NET AREA" (GSA standards) equals net assignable plus horizontal circulation area.

d. "BLDG. EFFICIENCY" equals percentage of net assignable in relation to "gross inside space."

4. STANDARD OF THE FEDERAL HOUSING ADMINISTRATION

Include areas of floors above basement, measured from outside surfaces of exterior walls; include bays, dormers, utility rooms, vestibules, hall & closets.

Do not include garage or finished attic spaces.

In a half story measure from outside surfaces of exterior walls or partitions enclosing the areas, except do not include areas where ceiling height is less than 5'–0".

Do not deduct for stairwells, interior light shafts, chimneys, fireplaces, thickness of partitions, or thickness of enclosing walls.

Porches, attached terraces, balconies and projecting fireplaces or chimneys, outside the exterior walls, are not included.

DEFINITIONS:

Half story: If finished as living area, must be 50% or greater than 50% of the calculated area of floor below.

Full story: Completely finished for living area, enclosed by exterior walls with a ceiling height 5'–0" min. at exterior walls.

Attic: Unfinished or partially finished as living area when the calculated area is less than 50% of floor below.

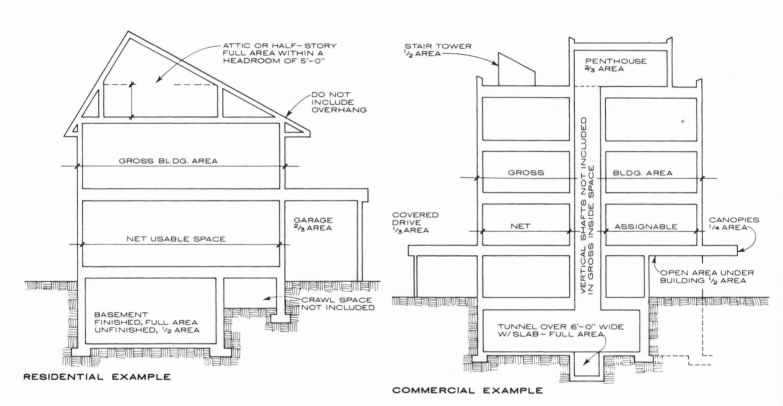

RESIDENTIAL EXAMPLE

COMMERCIAL EXAMPLE

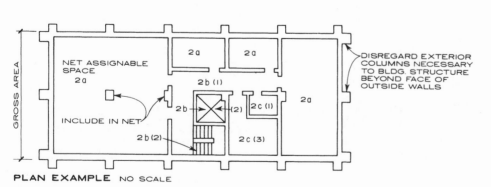

PLAN EXAMPLE NO SCALE

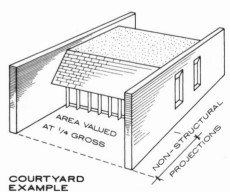

COURTYARD EXAMPLE

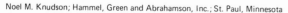

Noel M. Knudson; Hammel, Green and Abrahamson, Inc.; St. Paul, Minnesota

ARCHITECTURAL VOLUME OF BUILDINGS

The ARCHITECTURAL VOLUME (cube or cubage) of a building is the sum of the products of the areas defined on previous page (using the area of a single story for multi-story portions having the same area on each floor) and the height from the underside of the lowest floor construction system to the average height of the surface of the finished roof above for the various parts of the building.

From AIA Document D101, 1967

CUBAGE includes the following volumes, taken in full:

The cubic content of the actual space enclosed within the outer surfaces of the exterior or outer walls and contained between the outside of the roof and the bottom of the lowest floor; bays, oriels, dormers; penthouses; chimneys; walk through tunnels; tanks, vaults, pits and trenches, if made of building construction materials (not simple earth excavations); enclosed porches and balconies, including screened areas.

The CUBAGE includes the following volumes in part:

a) Two-thirds ($^2/_3$) volume for:
Non-enclosed porches, if recessed into the building and not having enclosing sash or screens.

b) One-half ($^1/_2$) volume for:
Non-enclosed porches built as an extension to the building, without enclosing sash or screens.

Areaways and pipe tunnels.

Patio areas that have building walls extended on two sides, roof over and paved surfacing.

The CUBAGE does not include the following features:

The cubage of outside steps, terraces, courts, garden walls; light shafts; parapets, cornices, roof overhangs; footings, deep foundations, piling, caissons, special foundations and similar features. Note: In making cubic foot cost analysis, as a matter of information and reference, it is recommended that cost items such as piling, caissons, deep foundations, unusual step construction and other non-typical features be listed as factors having an effect on the unit cost without being included in the cubage.

CUBIC FOOT COST

The CUBIC FOOT COST equals the net cost divided by the total cubage.

The NET COST in usual practice includes the following:

The building construction, including built-in cabinets and furniture, all finishes and hardware; mechanical work, including plumbing, heating, air conditioning and controls; electrical work, lighting fixtures, sound and signal systems; elevators; sprinklers; equipment provided for the operation of the building.

The NET COST usually excludes the following:

Furniture and furnishings, such as ranges, laundry and kitchen equipment, clocks, lockers, files; organs; draperies, shades, blinds, awnings; non-built in furniture; roads, walks, terraces, and other site development; landscaping; sewage disposal system; power plant; wells or other water supply; utilities to the building. Also fees for Architects, Engineers and specialty consultants.

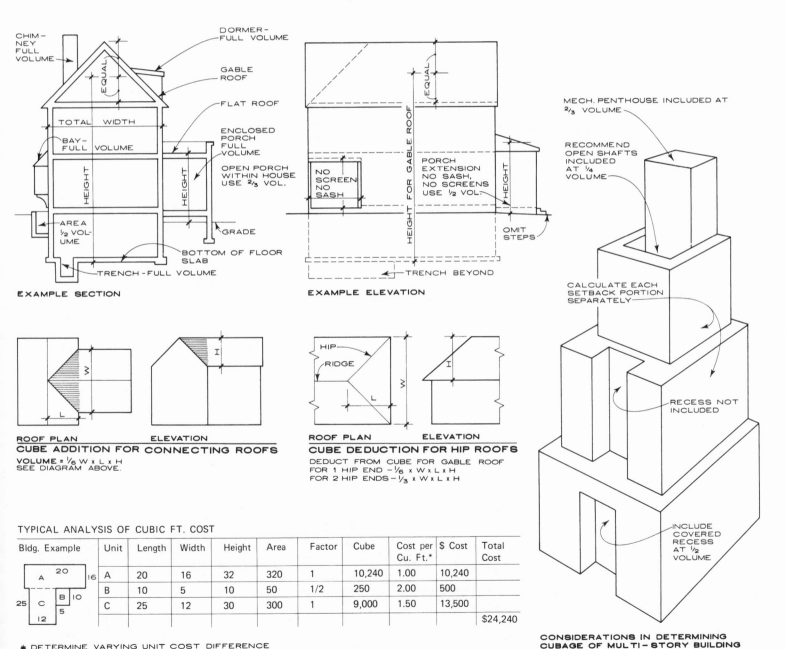

EXAMPLE SECTION

EXAMPLE ELEVATION

ROOF PLAN ELEVATION
CUBE ADDITION FOR CONNECTING ROOFS
VOLUME = $^1/_6$ W x L x H
SEE DIAGRAM ABOVE.

ROOF PLAN ELEVATION
CUBE DEDUCTION FOR HIP ROOFS
DEDUCT FROM CUBE FOR GABLE ROOF
FOR 1 HIP END — $^1/_6$ x W x L x H
FOR 2 HIP ENDS — $^1/_3$ x W x L x H

MECH. PENTHOUSE INCLUDED AT $^2/_3$ VOLUME

RECOMMEND OPEN SHAFTS INCLUDED AT $^1/_4$ VOLUME

CALCULATE EACH SETBACK PORTION SEPARATELY

RECESS NOT INCLUDED

INCLUDE COVERED RECESS AT $^1/_2$ VOLUME

CONSIDERATIONS IN DETERMINING CUBAGE OF MULTI-STORY BUILDING

TYPICAL ANALYSIS OF CUBIC FT. COST

Bldg. Example	Unit	Length	Width	Height	Area	Factor	Cube	Cost per Cu. Ft.*	$ Cost	Total Cost
	A	20	16	32	320	1	10,240	1.00	10,240	
	B	10	5	10	50	1/2	250	2.00	500	
	C	25	12	30	300	1	9,000	1.50	13,500	
										$24,240

✳ DETERMINE VARYING UNIT COST DIFFERENCE

Noel M. Knudson; Hammel, Green and Abrahamson, Inc.; St. Paul, Minnesota

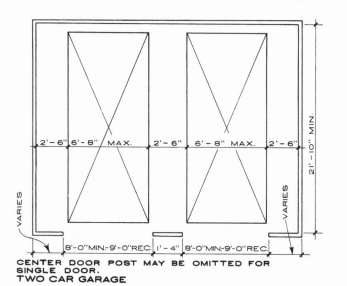

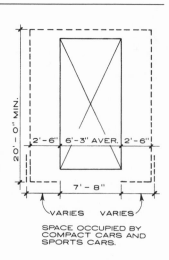

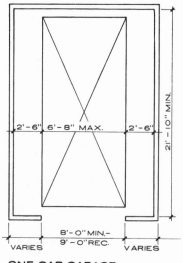

CENTER DOOR POST MAY BE OMITTED FOR SINGLE DOOR.
TWO CAR GARAGE

ONE CAR GARAGE

SPACE OCCUPIED BY COMPACT CARS AND SPORTS CARS.

NOTE: Garages may be enlarged to provide for work areas, photo labs, laundry rooms etc.

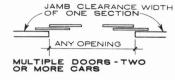

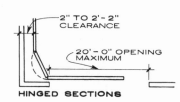

JAMB CLEARANCE - WIDTH OF DR.
SINGLE DOOR

MULTIPLE DOORS - TWO OR MORE CARS

HINGED SECTIONS

NOTE:

6 1/2" to 9" necessary from top of opening to ceiling (all sliding doors).

SLIDING DOORS

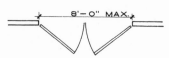

DOUBLE OR TRIPLE HINGED

MULTIPLE HINGED DOOR FOR TWO OR MORE CARS

OFFSET HINGE - MULTI - LEAVE

LOCATE SUPPORTS TO ALLOW FOR CAR DOOR SWINGS

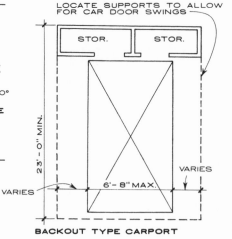

NOTE: For multiple and offset hinged doors, swinging to one or both sides, hinged in or out and used for 2 or more cars: 6 1/2" to 11" necessary from top of opening to ceiling.

HINGED DOORS

BACKOUT TYPE CARPORT

WIDTHS OF COMMONLY USED HINGED DOORS

A.   8'-0" opening 2 door—4'-0", 3 door—2'-8", 4 door—2'-0"
B.   8'-6" opening 2 door—4'-3", 3 door—2'-10", 4 door—2'-11 1/2"
C.   9'-0" opening 2 door—4'-6", 3 door—3'-0", 4 door—2'-3"

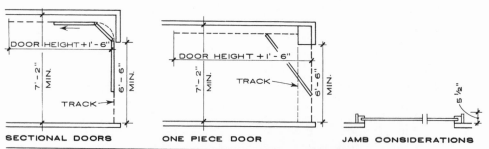

SECTIONAL DOORS   **ONE PIECE DOOR**   **JAMB CONSIDERATIONS**

LIFT DOORS—MOST WIDELY USED —AUTOMATIC OPTIONAL

NOTE:

Heights: 6'—6", 6'—10", 7'—0", 7'—6" and 8'—0".
Lift doors generally 4'—0" sections high, sometimes 2'—0" or 3'—0"

PASS THRU TYPE CARPORT
NO SCALE

R. E. Powe, Jr.; Hugh N. Jacobsen, AIA; Washington, D. C.

GARAGES and DRIVEWAYS

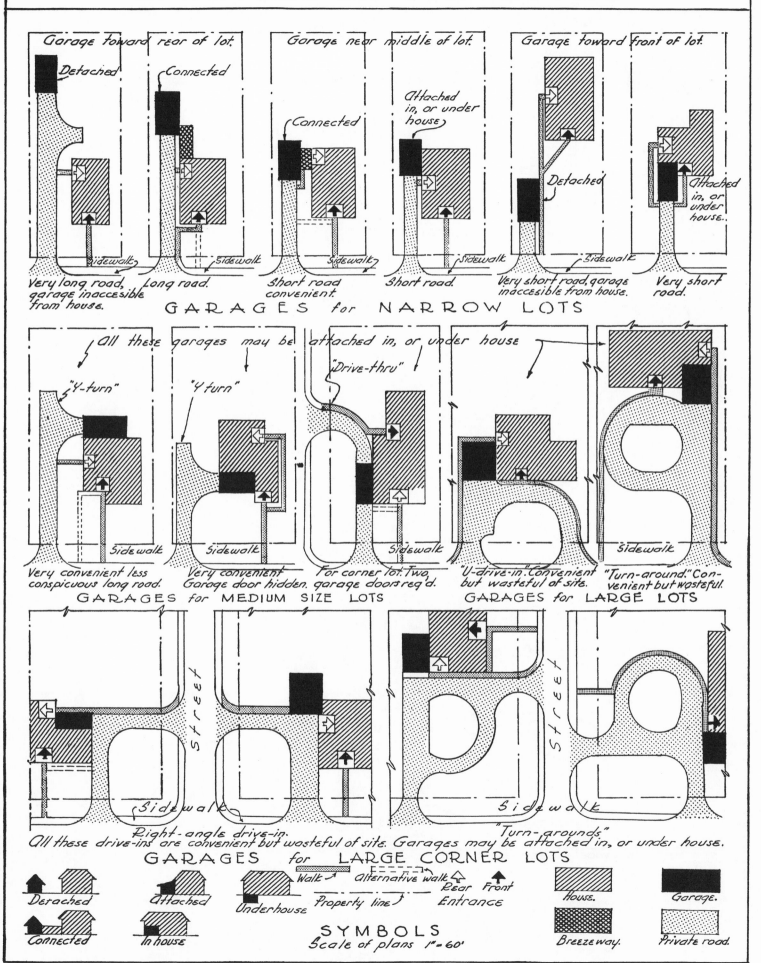

Garage toward rear of lot.

Detached Connected

Very long road, garage inaccessible from house. Long road.

Garage near middle of lot.

Connected

Attached in, or under house.

Short road convenient. Short road.

Garage toward front of lot.

Detached

Very short road, garage inaccessible from house.

Attached in, or under house.

Very short road.

GARAGES for NARROW LOTS

All these garages may be attached in, or under house

"Y-turn" "Y turn" "Drive-thru"

Very convenient less conspicuous long road. Very convenient Garage door hidden. For corner lot. Two garage doors req'd. "U-drive-in." Convenient but wasteful of site. "Turn-around." Convenient but wasteful.

GARAGES for MEDIUM SIZE LOTS GARAGES for LARGE LOTS

Right-angle drive-in. "Turn-arounds"

All these drive-ins are convenient but wasteful of site. Garages may be attached in, or under house.

GARAGES for LARGE CORNER LOTS

Detached Attached Underhouse Walk Alternative walk Rear Front Entrance House. Garage.

Connected In house Property line Breezeway. Private road.

SYMBOLS
Scale of plans 1"= 60'

PRIVATE ROADS & TURNS

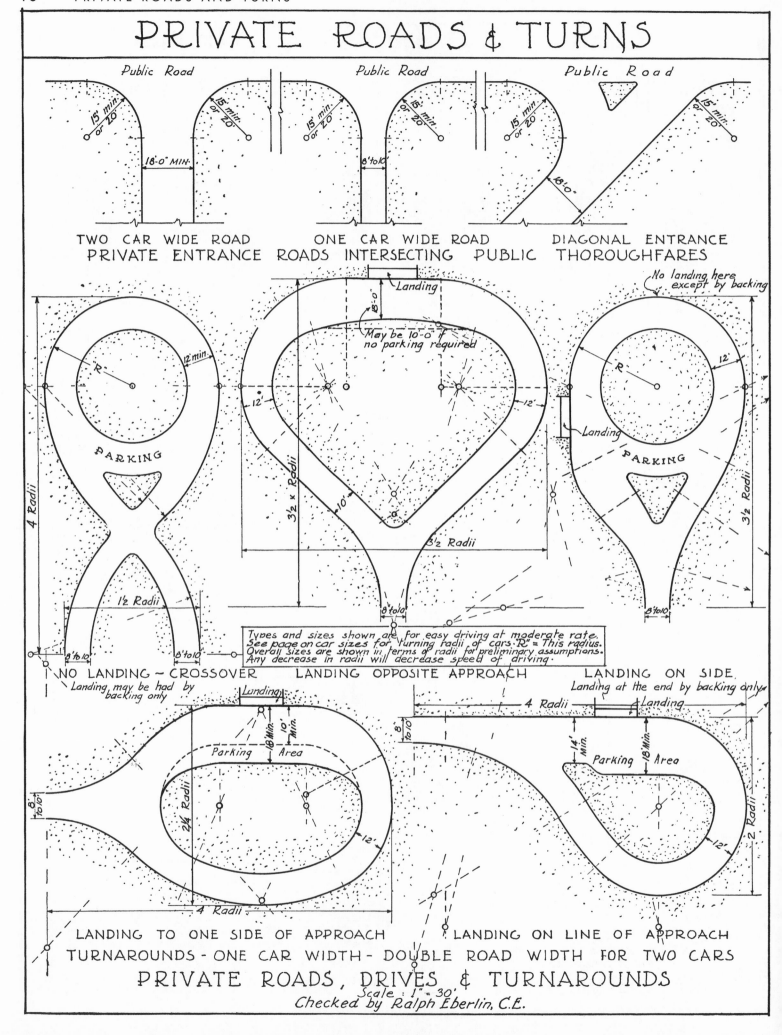

Public Road   Public Road   Public Road

15' min. or 20'   15' min. or 20'   15' min. or 20'   15' min. or 20'   15' min. or 20'

18'-0" MIN.   8'to10   18'-0"

TWO CAR WIDE ROAD   ONE CAR WIDE ROAD   DIAGONAL ENTRANCE

PRIVATE ENTRANCE ROADS INTERSECTING PUBLIC THOROUGHFARES

Landing

No landing here except by backing

May be 10'-0" if no parking required

R   12 min   R   12'

Landing

PARKING   PARKING

4 Radii   3½ × Radii   3½ Radii

18'-0

12'   12'

10'

3½ Radii

1½ Radii   8'to10   8'to10

8'to10   8'to10

Types and sizes shown are for easy driving at moderate rate.
See page on car sizes for turning radii of cars "R" = This radius.
Overall sizes are shown in terms of radii for preliminary assumptions.
Any decrease in radii will decrease speed of driving.

NO LANDING ~ CROSSOVER   LANDING OPPOSITE APPROACH   LANDING ON SIDE

Landing may be had by backing only   Landing at the end by backing only

Landing   4 Radii   Landing

10' Min.

18' Min.   8'to10

Parking   Area   14' Min.   Parking   Area

2½ Radii   18' Min.

12'   12'

8'to10

4 Radii

LANDING TO ONE SIDE OF APPROACH   LANDING ON LINE OF APPROACH

TURNAROUNDS - ONE CAR WIDTH - DOUBLE ROAD WIDTH FOR TWO CARS

PRIVATE ROADS, DRIVES & TURNAROUNDS

Scale: 1" = 30'
Checked by Ralph Eberlin, C.E.

GARAGE ROADS & TURNS

Garage

16'-0"   8'-0"
Min.

Garage placed here when space requirements are limited

18'-0"

16'-0"

24'-0"

10'-0"

8'-0" or 9'-0"

Backing

59'-0"

₵

forward

13'-0"

18'-0"

18'-0"R

4'-0"

1'-0"

8'-0" Min.
9'-0" Aver.
10'-0" wide

36'-0"

Entrance Road to Garage

Note:
All turns require 1'-6" clearance beyond road line shown. These turns are for easy driving with average size car. Larger radii will permit faster & easier driving. Smaller radii should be used for small cars only.

This dimension equals wheelbase—between 6'-8" & 12'-3" for most cars less than 11'-0"

Garage

1'-0"

8'-0" or 9'-0"

11'-0"

18'-0"

18'-0"R

Backing

19'-0"

8'-0"

56'-0 to 58'-0"

18'-0"

Forward

67'-0"±

18'-0"R

2'-0"

30'-0"

Entrance Road to Garage.

8'-0" Minimum
9'-0" Average
10'-0" Wide

"Y" TURN FOR BACKING IN
Dotted line shows route going in
Scale: 1/16" = 1'-0"

Employed only where space limitations demand its use.

Finish

3 x wheel base

Start

2 x wheel base

Wheelbase Minimum 6'-8"
do.   Maximum 12'-3"
normally under 11'-0"

MINIMUM TURNING SPACE—BACKING THREE TIMES

"Y" TURN FOR BACKING OUT
Dotted line shows route going out
Scale: 1/16" = 1'-0"

7'-10"

2'-6"   2'-10"   2'-6"
6" 2'-0"   2'-0" 6"

curb

Do not use curbs on narrower runways as trucks often have 5'-10" to 6'-0" wheel gauge

4'-10"
1'-6"   1'-10"   1'-6"

MINIMUM (only for Crosley)

1'-0"
2'-0"   3'-0"   2'-0"

AVERAGE

1'-6"
2'-6"   2'-6"   2'-6"

WIDE

5'-0" Average Gauge

CONCRETE RUNWAYS TO GARAGES
Widen for all turns

Garage

8'-0" or 9'-0"

3'-0"

Forward (in)

Back (out)

Forward (out)

28'-0"±

25'-0"±

Back (in)

Forward (in)

8'-0"
10'-0"

16'-0"±   20'-0"±

36'-0"±

DOUBLE 'Y' TURN REQUIRING BACKING BOTH WAYS
Exact size depends on car. This is for average car
Employed only where space limitations demand its use.

ROADS AND TURNS FOR PRIVATE GARAGES

TRUCK and TRAILER SIZES

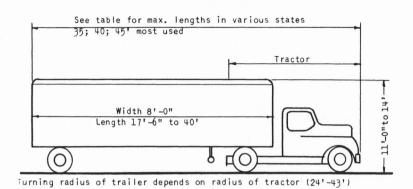

See table for max. lengths in various states
35; 40; 45' most used

Tractor

Width 8'-0"
Length 17'-6" to 40'

11'-0" to 14'

Turning radius of trailer depends on radius of tractor (24'-43')

Max. Length	States
45'	Ala. Conn. Ga. Ill. Iowa. Ky. Me. Mass. Minn. Miss. Mo. N.D. N.H. N.J. Ohio Tenn. Tex. Va. W.Va.
48'	N.C.
50'	Ark. D.C. Del. Fla. Ind. Kans. La. Nebr. N.Y. Okla. Ore. R.I. S.C. S.D. Vt. Wisc.
55'	Md. Mich.
60'	Calif. Colo. Idaho Mont. Utah. Wash. Wyo.
65'	Ariz. N.M. Nevada (no restriction)

SEMI-TRAILER & TRUCK TRACTOR

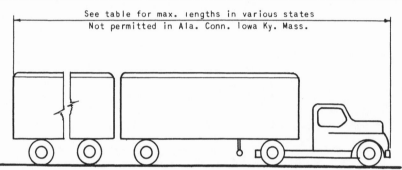

See table for max. lengths in various states
Not permitted in Ala. Conn. Iowa Ky. Mass.

Max. Length	States
45'	Ga. Ill. Me. Minn. Miss. Mo. N.D. N.H. Tenn. Tex. Va. W.Va.
48'	N.C.
50'	Ark. D.C. Fla. Ind. Kans. Nebr. N.J. N.Y. Okla. Pa. R.I. S.C. S.D. Oreg. Vt. Wisc.
55'	Md. Mich.
60'	Calif. Colo. Del. La. Mont. Ohio. Wash. Wyo. Utah.
65'	Ariz. Idaho N.M. Nevada (no restriction)

In many western states combinations of truck & full trailer and tractor
semi-trailer & full trailer are used to full legal length.

FULL TRAILER SEMI-TRAILER & TRUCK TRACTOR

DATA CHECKED BY OPERATIONS COUNCIL, AMERICAN TRUCKING ASSOCIATIONS INC.

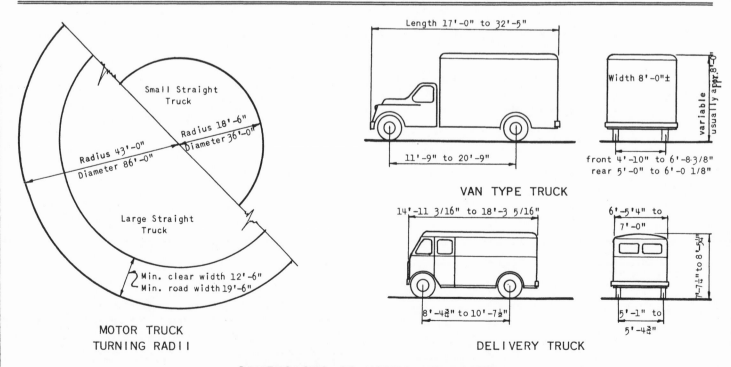

Small Straight Truck

Radius 18'-6"
Diameter 36'-0"

Radius 43'-0"
Diameter 86'-0"

Large Straight Truck

Min. clear width 12'-6"
Min. road width 19'-6"

MOTOR TRUCK TURNING RADII

Length 17'-0" to 32'-5"

11'-9" to 20'-9"

Width 8'-0"±

variable usually appr. 8'-0"

front 4'-10" to 6'-8 3/8"
rear 5'-0" to 6'-0 1/8"

VAN TYPE TRUCK

14'-11 3/16" to 18'-3 5/16"

8'-4 3/4" to 10'-7 1/2"

6'-5 1/4" to 7'-0"

7'-7 1/2" to 8'-5 1/4"

5'-1" to 5'-4 3/4"

DELIVERY TRUCK

DIMENSIONS OF MOTOR VEHICLES

TRUCKING DOCKS

Outside Single Doors:
Space between end of building and first door opening where there are stairs inside at dock 3'. No stairs a min. of 1'.

24" to 36" stairs inside at dock

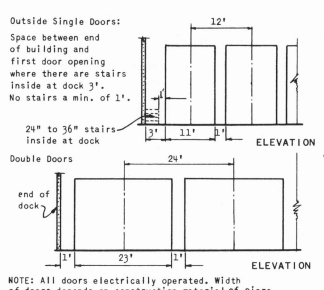

Double Doors

end of dock

ELEVATION

NOTE: All doors electrically operated. Width of doors depends on construction material of piers

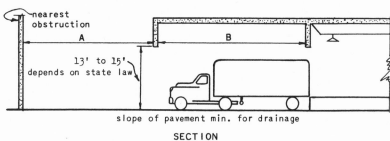

Size of Vehicle	A clearance outside of bldg. includ. street	B clearance inside bldg.
50'	50'	55'
30'	30'	35'
25'	25'	30'

nearest obstruction

13' to 15' depends on state law

slope of pavement min. for drainage

SECTION

CLOSED MOTOR CARRIER DOCK

Doors at Dock: Single Doors:
Space between end of bldg. & first door opening where there are no stairs min. 1'.

min. 1'

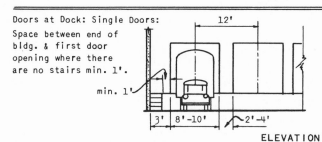

Size of vehicle	A clearance from dock to nearest obstruction
50'	100'
30'	60'
25'	50'

Double Doors:

end of dock

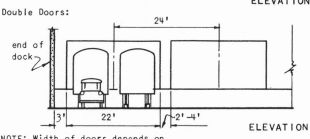

ELEVATION

NOTE: Width of doors depends on construction material of dock piers.

nearest obstruction   canopy or marquee

6' to 14'

13' to 15' depends on state law

slope of pavement min. for drainage

SECTION

OPEN MOTOR CARRIER DOCK

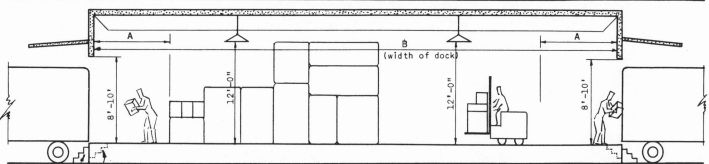

open stairs (preferred) prevents injury to dock workers

Recessed stairs

SECTION

Size of vehicle	Platform height
50'	52"±
30'	48"±
25'	44"±

	2 wheeled hand truck operation	Fork lift truck oper.	4 wheeled hand truck operation	Drag line operation
A	6'	10'	10'	10'
B	50'	60'	70'	80'

NOTE: These dimensions same for all types of Motor Carrier Docks

MOTOR CARRIER DOCK CLEARANCES

DATA SUPPLIED BY OPERATIONS COUNCIL, AMERICAN TRUCKING ASSOCIATIONS INC.

TRUCKING-CLEARANCES and DETAILS

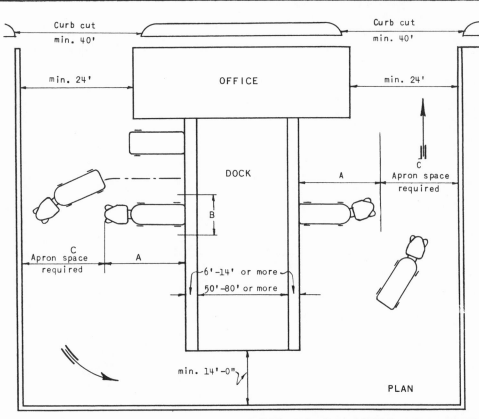

Curb cut — min. 40'

Curb cut — min. 40'

min. 24'

OFFICE

min. 24'

DOCK

Apron space required — A — C

B

Apron space required — C — A

6'-14' or more

50'-80' or more

min. 14'-0"

PLAN

Curb cut: used to prevent accident on swing into yard or gate.

Traffic flow #1
  Counter clockwise around dock, preferred since it permits backing from left (driver's side)

APRON SPACE required for maneuver into or out of position for tractor trailer

A	B	C
Tractor trailer length	Width of position	Apron space required
35'	10'	46'
	12'	43'
	14'	39'
40'	10'	48'
	12'	44'
	14'	42'
45'	10'	57'
	12'	49'
	14'	48'

LOADING OF MOTOR VEHICLES

DATA SUPPLIED BY OPERATIONS COUNCIL, AMERICAN TRUCKING ASSOCIATIONS INC.

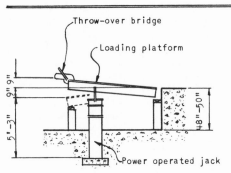

Throw-over bridge

Loading platform

9" 9"

5' 3"

48"-50"

Power operated jack

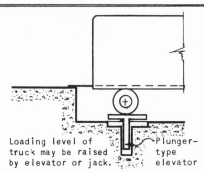

Loading level of truck may be raised by elevator or jack.

Plunger-type elevator

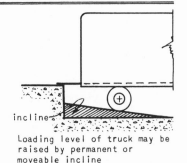

incline

Loading level of truck may be raised by permanent or moveable incline

Loading levels of trailer ("L") variable from 44" to 50" (48" to 54" for heavy-duty units). For van-type trucks 42" to 46" (44" to 46" average). For delivery trucks 25" to 31".

LOADING DOCK LEVELING DEVICES   SECTIONS

DATA CHECKED BY OPERATIONS COUNCIL AMERICAN TRUCKING ASSOCIATIONS INC.

Used for protection of door jams, walls, and corners. May be combined with corners & col. guards.
  Usually made of cast iron, ½" min. thickness. For heavy traffic, thicker metal is required.
  Other patterns available. Sizes given are made by most manufacturers, though given pattern may vary.

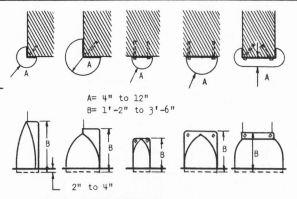

A= 4" to 12"
B= 1'-2" to 3'-6"

2" to 4"

WHEEL GUARDS

DATA FROM "ARCHITECTURAL METAL HANDBOOK" BY PERMISSION OF THE NATIONAL ASSOCIATION ARCHITECTURAL METAL MFRS.

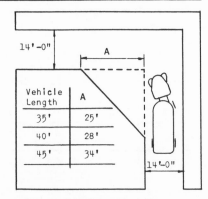

14'-0"

A

14'-0"

Vehicle Length	A
35'	25'
40'	28'
45'	34'

TURNING CLEARANCE FOR INSIDE DRIVEWAY

BUS DATA

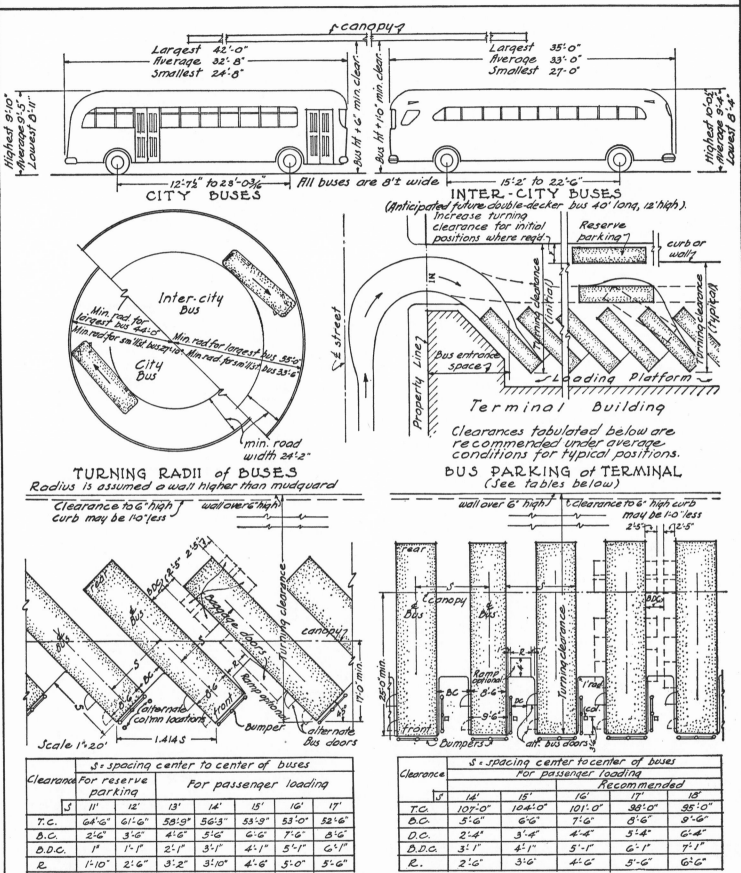

CITY BUSES

Largest 42'-0"
Average 32'-8"
Smallest 24'-8"

Highest 9'-10"
Average 9'-5"
Lowest 8'-11"

12'-7½" to 23'-0 3/16"

All buses are 8'± wide

canopy

Bus ht + 6" min. clear.
Bus ht +1'-0" min. clear.

INTER-CITY BUSES
(Anticipated future double-decker bus 40' long, 12' high).

Largest 35'-0"
Average 33'-0"
Smallest 27'-0"

Highest 10'-0"
Average 9'-4"
Lowest 8'-4"

15'-2" to 22'-6"

TURNING RADII of BUSES
Radius is assumed a wall higher than mudguard

Inter-city Bus

City Bus

Min. rad. for largest bus 44'-0"
Min. rad for sm'llst. bus 27'-10"
Min. rad for largest bus 55'-0"
Min. rad. for sm'llst. bus 33'-6"

min. road width 24'-2"

BUS PARKING at TERMINAL
(See tables below)

Increase turning clearance for initial positions where req'd.

Reserve parking
curb or wall

Turning clearance (initial)
Turning clearance (typical)

Property Line
₵ street
IN
Bus entrance space
Loading Platform

Terminal Building

Clearances tabulated below are recommended under average conditions for typical positions.

45° ANGLE BUS PARKING at TERMINAL

Clearance to 6" high curb may be 1'-0" less
wall over 6" high

Bus
Baggage doors
Turning clearance
canopy
Ramp optional
alternate column location
Bumper
alternate Bus doors
17'-0" min.

Scale 1" = 20'
1.414S

Clearance	S = spacing center to center of buses						
	For reserve parking		For passenger loading				
S	11'	12'	13'	14'	15'	16'	17'
T.C.	64'-6"	61'-6"	58'-9"	56'-3"	53'-9"	53'-0"	52'-6"
B.C.	2'-6"	3'-6"	4'-6"	5'-6"	6'-6"	7'-6"	8'-6"
B.D.C.	1"	1'-1"	2'-1"	3'-1"	4'-1"	5'-1"	6'-1"
R	1'-10"	2'-6"	3'-2"	3'-10"	4'-6"	5'-0"	5'-6"

90° ANGLE BUS PARKING at TERMINAL

wall over 6" high
Clearance to 6" high curb may be 1'-0" less

rear
₵ canopy
₵ Bus
Turning clearance
25'-0" min.
front
Bumpers
Ramp optional
8'-6"
9'-6"
att. bus doors
1' rad.

Clearance	S = spacing center to center of buses				
	For passenger loading				
			Recommended		
S	14'	15'	16'	17'	18'
T.C.	107'-0"	104'-0"	101'-0"	98'-0"	95'-0"
B.C.	5'-6"	6'-6"	7'-6"	8'-6"	9'-6"
D.C.	2'-4"	3'-4"	4'-4"	5'-4"	6'-4"
B.D.C.	3'-1"	4'-1"	5'-1"	6'-1"	7'-1"
R.	2'-6"	3'-6"	4'-6"	5'-6"	6'-6"

Buses shown here are 8'-6" × 40'-0" - 54 passenger, so that future facilities will accommodate the larger vehicles. T.C. = recommended minimum turning clearance to wall for typical conditions. Increase T.C. for initial positions and for special conditions; B.C. = clearance between buses; D.C. = door clearance; B.D.C. = baggage door clearance to adjacent bus; R = ramp width. Height of first step in bus from ground (loaded): city bus - 12" to 16", inter-city - 8" to 17".

DATA for RESIDENTIAL WORK

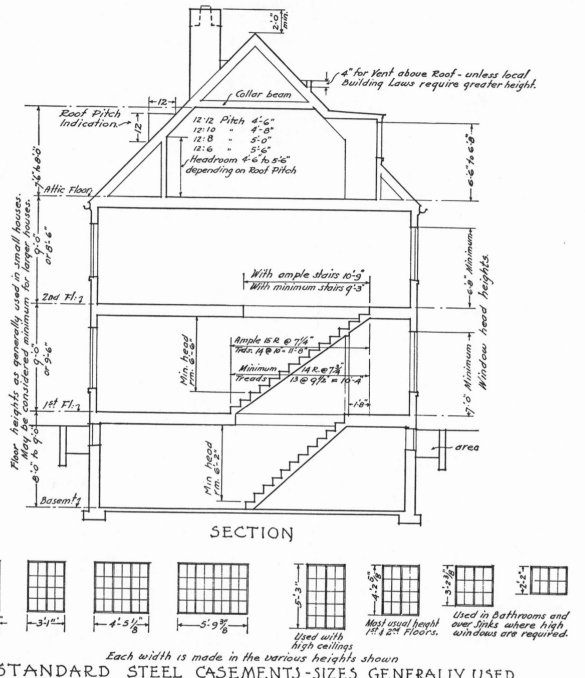

2'-0" min.

4" for Vent above Roof - unless local Building Laws require greater height.

Collar beam

—12—

Roof Pitch Indication.

—12—

12:12 Pitch 4'-6"
12:10 "   4'-8"
12:8   "   5'-0"
12:6   "   5'-6"

Headroom 4'-6" to 5'-6" depending on Roof Pitch

6'-6" to 6'-8"

Attic Floor.

7'-6" 8'-0"

Floor heights as generally used in small houses. May be considered minimum for larger houses.

9'-0" or 8'-6"

With ample stairs 10'-9"
With minimum stairs 9'-3"

6'-8" Minimum

2nd Fl.

9'-0" or 9'-6"

Min. head rm. 6'-6"

Ample 15 R @ 7 1/4"
Trds. 14 @ 10 = 11'-8"

Minimum Treads

14 R. @ 7 3/4"
13 @ 9 1/2" = 10'-4"

7'-0" Minimum   Window head heights.

1st Fl.

8'-0" to 9'-0"

1'-8"

Min. head rm. 6'-2"

area

Basem't.

SECTION

Each width is made in the various heights shown

1'-7 7/8"   3'-1"   4'-5 1/8"   5'-9 3/8"

5'-3"
Used with high ceilings

4'-2 5/8"
Most usual height 1st & 2nd Floors.

3'-2 1/8"
Used in Bathrooms and over Sinks where high windows are required.

2'-2"

STANDARD STEEL CASEMENTS - SIZES GENERALLY USED.

5'-6"
Used for First Floor Windows.

A

4'-6"
Most used height 1st & 2nd floors.

A

4'-2"
Usually Second Floor.

A

3'-6"
Used in Bathrooms and over Sinks etc.

B

3'-2"

B

Widths in intervals of 4" from 1'-4" to 4'-0" for Type A.
Widths in intervals of 4" from 1'-4" to 3'-4" for Type B.

Many other sizes are stock.
These sizes generally are carried as Stock.

2'-8 7/8"   1'-2 3/4"

2'-8 7/8"   1'-6 3/4"

2'-8 7/8"   1'-10 3/4"

STANDARD STEEL BASEMENT WINDOWS.

2'-8"
6'-8" or 7'-0"
Service.

2'-8"
6'-8" or Usually 7'-0"

3'-0"
Douglas Fir only - 2'-10" x 6'-10"

Front Doors.

USUAL SIZES of WOOD D-H-WINDOWS.   EXTERIOR DOORS.

MATERIAL for USE in SETTING UP APPROXIMATE SIZES and HEIGHTS on SKETCHES.

DATA for RESIDENTIAL WORK

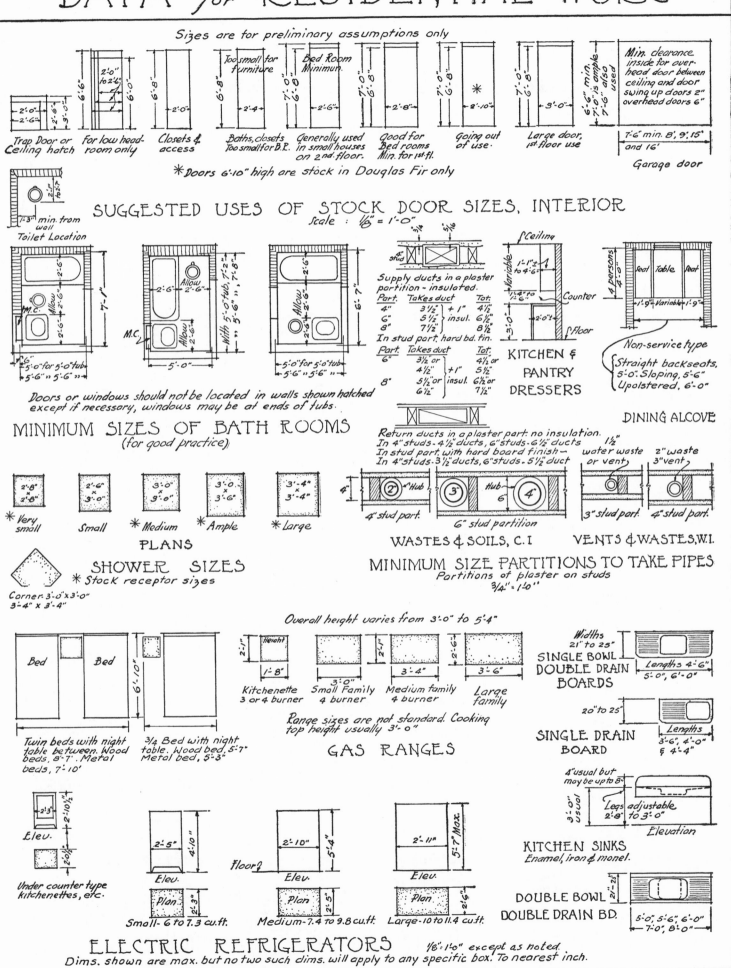

Sizes are for preliminary assumptions only

Too small for furniture | Bed Room Minimum. | Generally used in small houses on 2nd. floor. | Good for Bed rooms Min. for 1st fl. | Going out of use. | Large door, 1st floor use

Trap Door or Ceiling hatch | For low head-room only | Closets & access | Baths, closets Too small for B.R. |

Min. clearance inside for overhead door between ceiling and door swing up doors 2" overhead doors 6"

7-6 min. 8', 9', 15' and 16'

Garage door

* Doors 6'-10" high are stock in Douglas Fir only

SUGGESTED USES OF STOCK DOOR SIZES, INTERIOR
Scale : ⅛" = 1'-0"

Toilet Location

1'-3" min. from wall

Supply ducts in a plaster partition - insulated.

Part.	Takes duct		Tot.
4"	3½	+1" insul.	4½
6"	5½		6½
8"	7½		8½

In stud part. hard bd. fin.

Part.	Takes duct		Tot.
6"	3½ or 4½	+1" insul.	4½ or 5½
8"	5½ or 6½		6½ or 7½

KITCHEN & PANTRY DRESSERS

4 persons 4'-0"

Seat | Table | Seat

1'-9" | Variable | 1'-9"

Non-service type
Straight backseats, 5'-0". Sloping, 5'-6"
Upolstered, 6'-0"

DINING ALCOVE

Doors or windows should not be located in walls shown hatched except if necessary, windows may be at ends of tubs.

MINIMUM SIZES OF BATH ROOMS
(for good practice)

Return ducts in a plaster part. no insulation.
In 4" studs - 4½" ducts, 6" studs - 6½" ducts
In stud part. with hard board finish—
In 4" studs - 3½" ducts, 6" studs - 5½" duct

water waste or vent

2" waste
3" vent

2'-8" x 2'-8"	2'-6" x 3'-0"	3'-0" x 3'-0"	3'-0" x 3'-6"	3'-4" x 3'-4"
* Very small	Small	* Medium	* Ample	* Large

PLANS

2" Hub | 3 | Hub 4"

4" stud part. | 6" stud partition | 3" stud part. | 4" stud part.

WASTES & SOILS, C.I. | VENTS & WASTES, W.I.

SHOWER SIZES
* Stock receptor sizes

Corner- 3'-0" x 3'-0"
3'-4" x 3'-4"

MINIMUM SIZE PARTITIONS TO TAKE PIPES
Partitions of plaster on studs
¾" = 1'-0"

Bed | Bed

Overall height varies from 3'-0" to 5'-4"

Height

Kitchenette 3 or 4 burner | Small Family 4 burner | Medium family 4 burner | Large family

Range sizes are not standard. Cooking top height usually 3'-0"

Widths 21" to 25"

SINGLE BOWL DOUBLE DRAIN BOARDS

Lengths 4'-6" 5'-0", 6'-0"

Twin beds with night table between. Wood beds, 8'-7". Metal beds, 7'-10' | ¾ Bed with night table. Wood bed, 5'-7". Metal bed, 5'-3"

GAS RANGES

20" to 25"

SINGLE DRAIN BOARD

Lengths 3'-6", 4'-0" & 4'-4"

4" usual but may be up to 8"

Legs adjustable to 3'-0"

Elevation

KITCHEN SINKS
Enamel, iron & monel.

Elev.

Under counter type kitchenettes, etc.

Elev. | Plan
Small- 6 to 7.3 cu.ft.

Floor | Elev. | Plan
Medium- 7.4 to 9.8 cu.ft.

Elev. | Plan
Large-10 to 11.4 cu.ft.

DOUBLE BOWL DOUBLE DRAIN BD.

5'-0", 5'-6", 6'-0" 7'-0", 8'-0"

ELECTRIC REFRIGERATORS
⅛"=1'-0" except as noted.
Dims. shown are max. but no two such dims. will apply to any specific box. To nearest inch.

CLOSETS

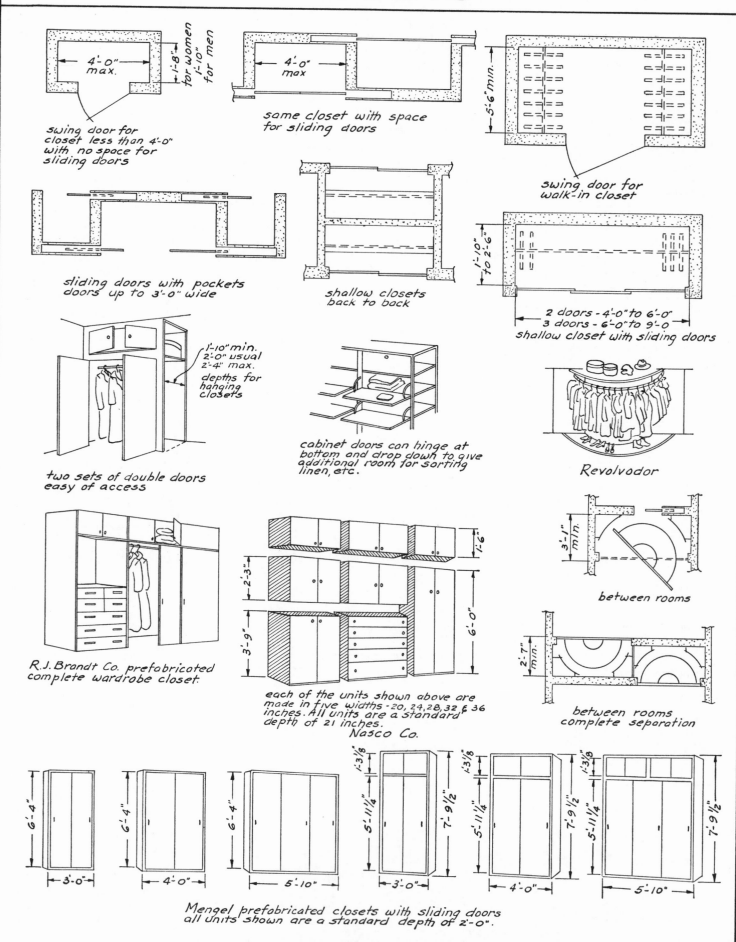

swing door for closet less than 4'-0" with no space for sliding doors

4'-0" max.

1'-8" for women 1'-10" for men

same closet with space for sliding doors

4'-0" max

5'-6" min.

swing door for walk-in closet

sliding doors with pockets doors up to 3'-0" wide

shallow closets back to back

1'-10" to 2'-6"

2 doors - 4'-0" to 6'-0"
3 doors - 6'-0" to 9'-0
shallow closet with sliding doors

1'-10" min.
2'-0" usual
2'-4" max.
depths for hanging closets

two sets of double doors easy of access

cabinet doors can hinge at bottom and drop down to give additional room for sorting linen, etc.

Revolvodor

3'-1" min.

between rooms

R.J. Brandt Co. prefabricated complete wardrobe closet.

1'-6"
2'-3"
3'-9"
6'-0"

each of the units shown above are made in five widths - 20, 24, 28, 32 & 36 inches. All units are a standard depth of 21 inches.
Nasco Co.

2'-7" min.

between rooms complete separation

6'-4"   6'-4"   6'-4"   1-3/8" 7'-9½" 5'-11¼"   1-3/8" 5'-11¼" 7'-9½"   1-3/8" 5'-11¼" 7'-9½"

3'-0"   4'-0"   5'-10"   3'-0"   4'-0"   5'-10"

Mengel prefabricated closets with sliding doors all units shown are a standard depth of 2'-0".

TRAYS & SHELVES

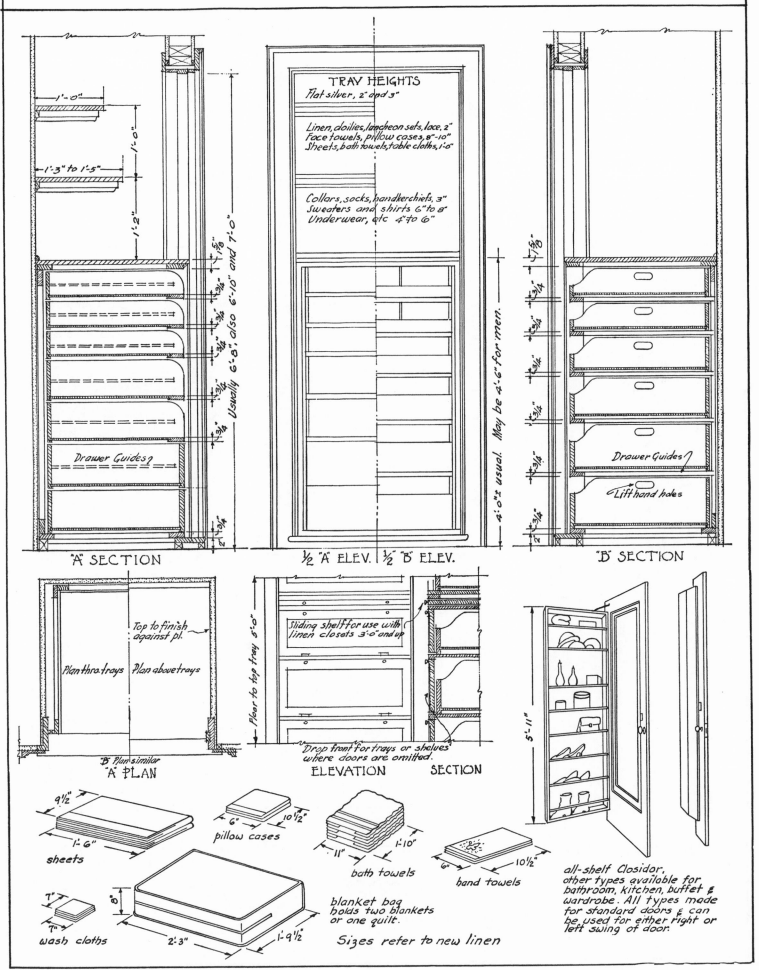

TRAY HEIGHTS

Flat silver, 2" and 3"

Linen, doilies, luncheon sets, lace, 2"
Face towels, pillow cases, 8"-10"
Sheets, bath towels, table cloths, 1'-0"

Collars, socks, handkerchiefs, 3"
Sweaters and shirts 6" to 8"
Underwear, etc. 4" to 6"

"A" SECTION

1'-0"
1'-3" to 1'-5"
1'-2"
Usually 6'-8", also 6'-10" and 7'-0"
Drawer Guides

½ "A" ELEV. ½ "B" ELEV.

4'-0"± usual. May be 4'-6" for men.

"B" SECTION

Drawer Guides
Lift hand holes

"A" PLAN

Top to finish against pl.
Plan thro. trays   Plan above trays
"B" Plan similar

ELEVATION   SECTION

Floor to top tray 5'-0"
Sliding shelf for use with linen closets 3'-0" and up
Drop front for trays or shelves where doors are omitted.

5'-11"

all-shelf Closidor, other types available for bathroom, kitchen, buffet & wardrobe. All types made for standard doors & can be used for either right or left swing of door.

9½"
1'-6"
sheets

6"   10½"
pillow cases

11"   1'-10"
bath towels

6"   10½"
hand towels

7"
7"
wash cloths

8"
2'-3"   1'-9½"
blanket bag holds two blankets or one quilt.

Sizes refer to new linen

APPAREL

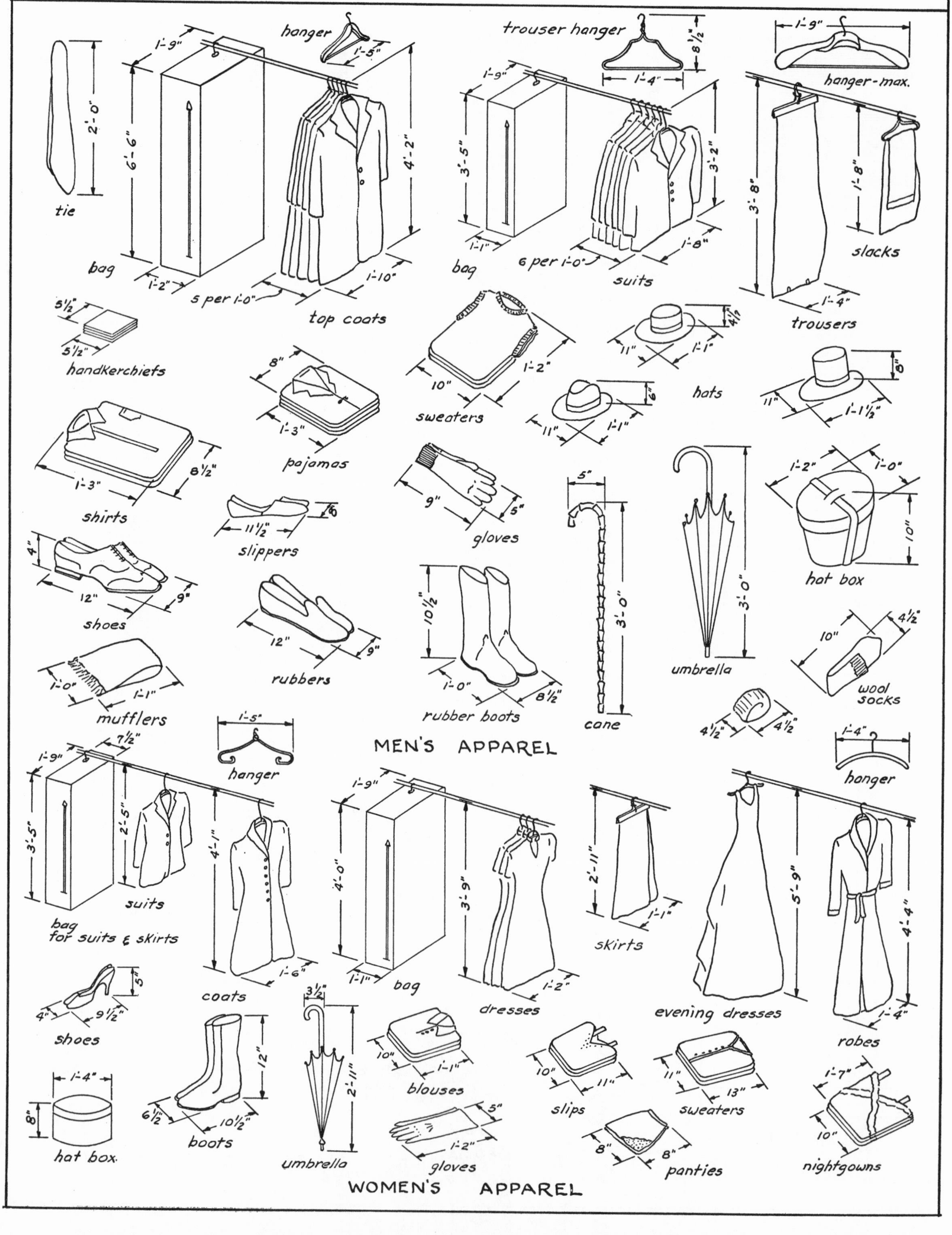

hanger

trouser hanger

hanger - max.

tie

bag

top coats

bag

suits

slacks

trousers

handkerchiefs

sweaters

hats

pajamas

shirts

slippers

gloves

hats

hat box

shoes

rubbers

rubber boots

cane

umbrella

wool socks

mufflers

hanger

MEN'S APPAREL

hanger

bag for suits & skirts

suits

coats

bag

dresses

skirts

evening dresses

robes

shoes

boots

umbrella

blouses

slips

sweaters

panties

nightgowns

hat box

gloves

WOMEN'S APPAREL

FURNISHINGS - RUGS - LINEN

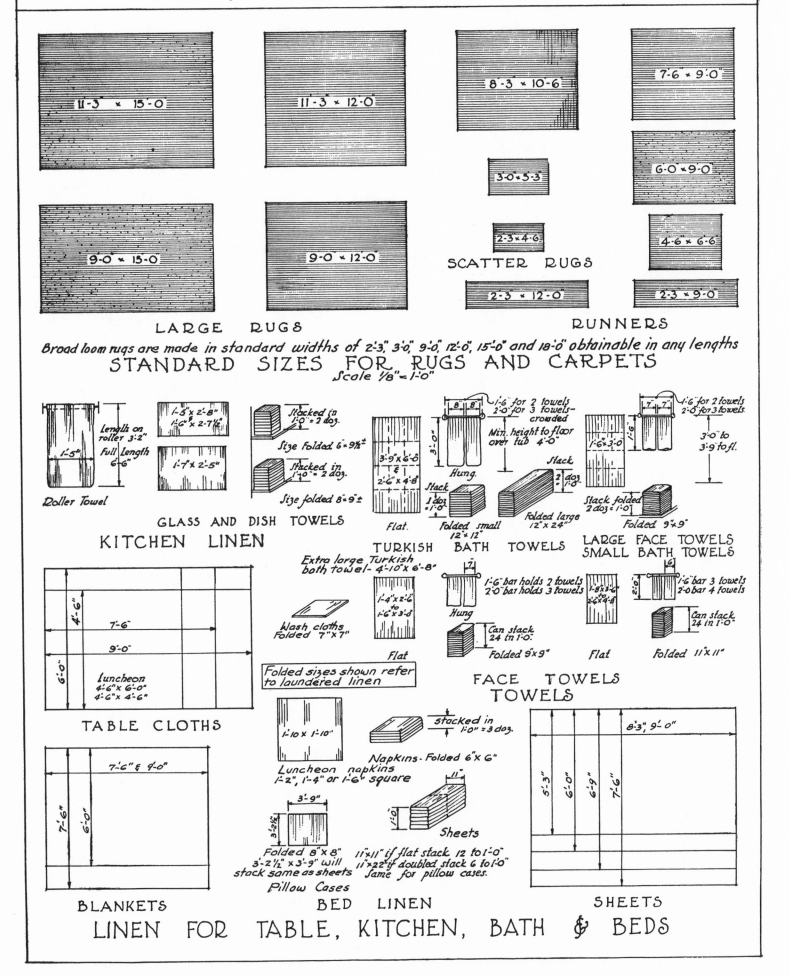

LARGE RUGS

11-3 × 15-0

11-3 × 12-0

9-0 × 15-0

9-0 × 12-0

SCATTER RUGS

8-3 × 10-6

3-0 × 5-3

2-3 × 4-6

RUNNERS

7-6 × 9-0

6-0 × 9-0

4-6 × 6-6

2-3 × 12-0

2-3 × 9-0

Broad loom rugs are made in standard widths of 2-3", 3-0", 9-0", 12-0", 15-0" and 18-0" obtainable in any lengths

STANDARD SIZES FOR RUGS AND CARPETS
Scale 1/8" = 1-0"

KITCHEN LINEN

Length on roller 3-2"
Full Length 6-6"
1-5"
Roller Towel

1-5" × 2-8"
1-6" × 2-7½"
1-7" × 2-5"

GLASS AND DISH TOWELS

Stacked in 1-0" = 2 doz.
Size Folded 6" × 9½"±
Stacked in 1-0" = 2 doz.
Size folded 8" × 9"±

TURKISH BATH TOWELS

3-9" × 6-0"
2-6" × 4-8"
Flat.

8 × 8
1-6 for 2 towels
2-0 for 3 towels — crowded
3-0"
Min. height to floor over tub 4-0"
Hung.

Stack 1 doz. = 1-0"
Folded small 12" × 12"

Stack 2 doz. = 1-0"
Folded large 12" × 24"

LARGE FACE TOWELS
SMALL BATH TOWELS

7 × 7
1-6 for 2 towels
2-0 for 3 towels.
1-6 × 3-0
1-6
3-0" to 3-9" to fl.

Stack folded 2 doz = 1-0"
Folded 9" × 9"

Extra large Turkish bath towel - 4-10" × 6-8"

1-4" × 2-6" to 1-6" × 3-8"
Flat

Wash cloths Folded 7" × 7"

Folded sizes shown refer to laundered linen

TABLE CLOTHS

4-6"
7-6"
9-0"
6-0"
Luncheon 4-6" × 6-0" 4-6" × 4-6"

FACE TOWELS
TOWELS

7
1-6" bar holds 2 towels
2-0" bar holds 3 towels
Hung

Can stack 24 in 1-0"
Folded 9" × 9"

1-8" × 3-6" 2-6" × 4-8"
Flat

6
2-0"
1-6" bar 3 towels
2-0" bar 4 towels

Can stack 24 in 1-0"
Folded 11" × 11"

BLANKETS

7-6" & 9-0"
7-6"
6-0"

BED LINEN

1-10" × 1-10"
stacked in 1-0" = 3 doz.
Napkins - Folded 6" × 6"
Luncheon napkins 1-2", 1-4" or 1-6" square

3-9"
3-2½"
Folded 8" × 8"
3-2½" × 3-9" will stack same as sheets
Pillow Cases

11
1-0"
Sheets
11" × 11" if flat stack 12 to 1-0"
11" × 22" if doubled stack 6 to 1-0"
Same for pillow cases.

SHEETS

8-3", 9-0"
5-3"
6-0"
6-9"
7-6"

LINEN FOR TABLE, KITCHEN, BATH & BEDS

CLOSET ACCESSORIES

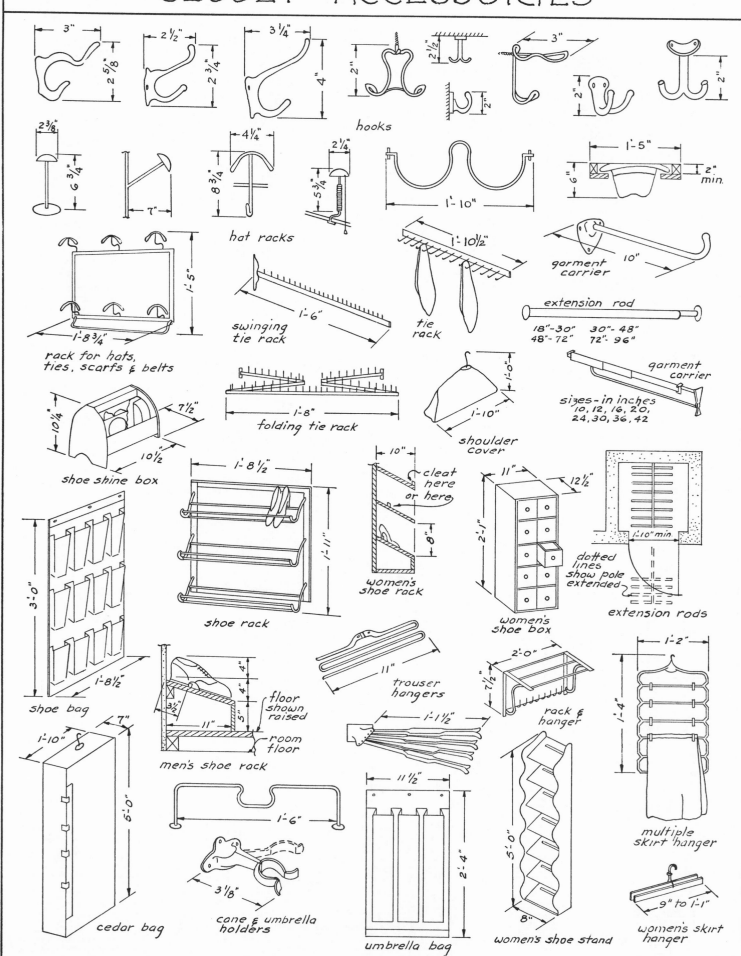

hooks

hat racks

garment carrier

extension rod
18"-30"   30"-48"
48"-72"   72"-96"

swinging tie rack

tie rack

rack for hats, ties, scarfs & belts

folding tie rack

shoulder cover

garment carrier
sizes- in inches
10, 12, 16, 20,
24, 30, 36, 42

shoe shine box

shoe rack

women's shoe rack

women's shoe box

extension rods

shoe bag

men's shoe rack

trouser hangers

rack & hanger

multiple skirt hanger

cedar bag

cane & umbrella holders

umbrella bag

women's shoe stand

women's skirt hanger

COAT ROOMS & EQUIPMENT and BED CLOSETS

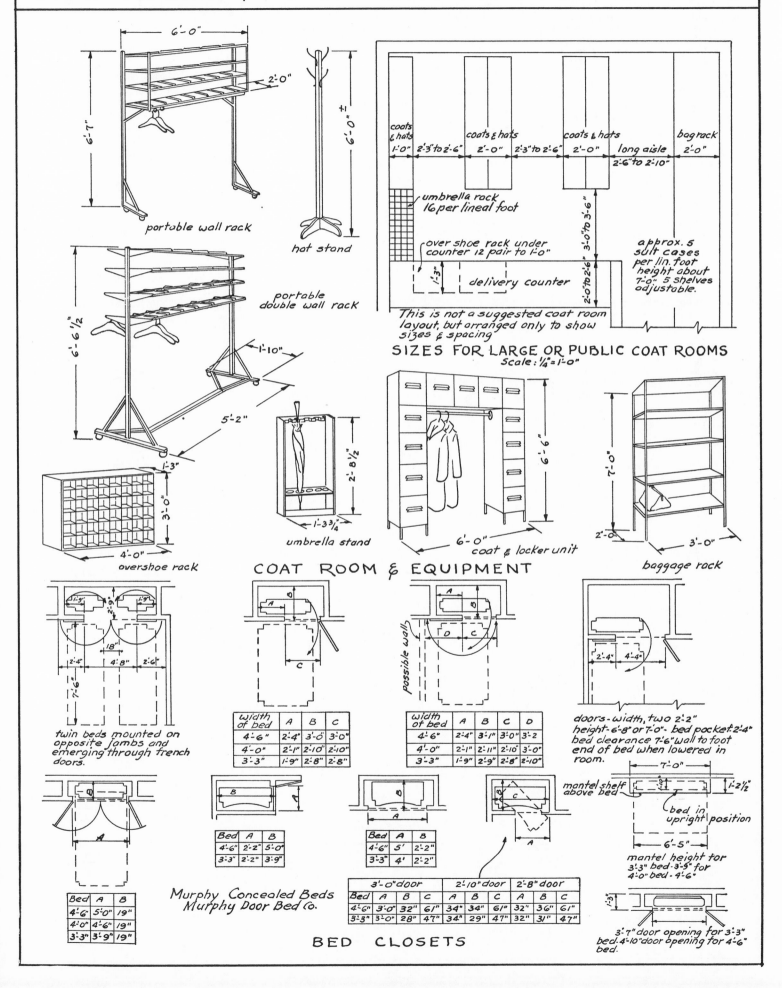

portable wall rack

hat stand

portable double wall rack

umbrella rack 16 per lineal foot

over shoe rack under counter 12 pair to 1'-0"

delivery counter

This is not a suggested coat room layout, but arranged only to show sizes & spacing

approx. 5 suit cases per lin. foot height about 7'-0" 5 shelves adjustable.

SIZES FOR LARGE OR PUBLIC COAT ROOMS
Scale: 1/4"=1'-0"

overshoe rack

umbrella stand

coat & locker unit

baggage rack

COAT ROOM & EQUIPMENT

twin beds mounted on opposite jambs and emerging through french doors.

doors-width, two 2'-2" height-6'-8" or 7'-0"- bed pocket 2'-4" bed clearance 7'-6" wall to foot end of bed when lowered in room.

width of bed	A	B	C
4'-6"	2'-4"	3'-0"	3'-0"
4'-0"	2'-1"	2'-10"	2'-10"
3'-3"	1'-9"	2'-8"	2'-8"

width of bed	A	B	C	D
4'-6"	2'-4"	3'-1"	3'-0"	3'-2"
4'-0"	2'-1"	2'-11"	2'-10"	3'-0"
3'-3"	1'-9"	2'-9"	2'-8"	2'-10"

mantel shelf above bed

bed in upright position

mantel height for 3'-3" bed-3'-5" for 4'-0" bed-4'-6"

Bed	A	B
4'-6"	2'-2"	5'-0"
3'-3"	2'-2"	3'-9"

Bed	A	B
4'-6"	5'	2'-2"
3'-3"	4'	2'-2"

Murphy Concealed Beds
Murphy Door Bed Co.

Bed	A	B
4'-6"	5'-0"	19"
4'-0"	4'-6"	19"
3'-3"	3'-9"	19"

	3'-0"door			2'-10"door			2'-8"door		
Bed	A	B	C	A	B	C	A	B	C
4'-6"	3'-0"	32"	61"	34"	34"	61"	32"	36"	61"
3'-3"	3'-0"	28"	47"	34"	29"	47"	32"	31"	47"

3'-7" door opening for 3'-3" bed-4'-10" door opening for 4'-6" bed.

BED CLOSETS

ASEISMIC DESIGN CONCEPT

Earthquake forces result from very erratic vertical and horizontal vibratory motion of the ground on which the structure rests. For the most part, the vertical forces are neglected by the codes owing to the combination of safety factors inherent in the vertical framing members. The horizontal forces may vary in direction, intensity and duration and are affected materially by geological conditions.

Seismic forces are assumed to act as static horizontal loads on a structure as a function of the mass multiplied by certain factors for different types of resisting elements. Resisting elements may be moment resisting frames or shear walls or a combination of both.

The configuration of a structure and its fundamental period affects its earthquake resistance considerably. Symmetry in plan is very desirable. Unusual shaped plans result in highstress concentration areas and must be specifically designed for. Structural elements must be tied together to make them respond to earthquake motion as a unit; or structural separations may be required.

Most building materials are adaptable to use as resisting elements. Brittle materials must be avoided, unless properly reinforced. Ductile materials are most desirable. Up-to-date codes require that all buildings over 160 feet high must have "ductile" moment resisting frames.

Earthquake resistant structures can be designed, however, to result in minimum structural damage and maximum safety within economic limits. Aseismic knowledge and design is being steadily improved, and there is no substitute for sound structural engineering experience and judgment.

The data set forth herewith is a very brief resume of "Recommended Lateral Force Requirements and Commentary" prepared by the Seismology Committee of the Structural Engineers Association of California, 1967. These requirements have been adopted by several codes.

DEFINITIONS

SPACE FRAME is a three dimensional structural system composed of interconnected members, other than bearing walls, laterally supported so as to function as a complete self-contained unit with or without the aid of horizontal diaphragms or floor bracing systems.

SPACE FRAME – VERTICAL LOAD-CARRYING: a space frame designed to carry all vertical loads.

SPACE FRAME – MOMENT RESISTING: a vertical load-carrying space frame in which the members and joints are capable of resisting design lateral forces by bending moments.

SPACE FRAME – DUCTILE MOMENT RESISTING: A space frame-moment resisting complying with special requirements for a ductile moment resisting space frame.

BOX SYSTEM is a structural system without a complete vertical load-carrying space frame. In this system, the required lateral forces are resisted by shear walls as hereinafter defined.

SHEAR WALL is a wall designed to resist lateral forces parallel to the wall. Braced frames subjected primarily to axial stresses shall be considered as shear walls for the purpose of this definition.

LATERAL FORCE RESISTING SYSTEM is that part of the structural system to which the lateral forces are assigned.

TOTAL LATERAL FORCE OR BASE SHEAR FORMULA

$V = ZKCW$

V = Total lateral force or shear at the base.

Z = Numerical coefficient dependent upon the zone as determined by the seismic zone map.

K = Numerical coefficient set forth in Table A.

C = Numerical coefficient dependent upon the fundamental period of vibration of the structure determined by properly substantiated technical data or by arbitrary code formula.

W = Total dead load. (Plus 25 percent of storage and warehouse live loads.)

HORIZONTAL FORCE FACTOR "K" FOR BUILDINGS OR OTHER STRUCTURES

TYPE OR ARRANGEMENT OF RESISTING ELEMENTS	K
All building framing systems except as hereinafter classified.	1.00
Buildings with a box system as defined	1.33
Buildings with a dual bracing system consisting of a ductile moment resisting space frame and shear walls designed with the following criteria: 1. The frames and shear walls shall resist the total lateral force in accordance with their relative rigidities considering the inraction of the shear walls and frames. 2. The shear walls acting independently of the ductile moment resisting space frame shall resist the total required lateral force. 3. The ductile moment resisting space frame shall have the capacity to resist not less than 25 percent of the required lateral force.	0.80
Buildings with a ductile moment resisting space frame designed in accordance with the following criteria: The ductile moment resisting space frame shall have the capacity to resist the total required lateral force.	0.67
Elevated tanks plus full contents, on four or more cross braced legs and not supported by a building.	3.00
Structures other than buildings.	2.00

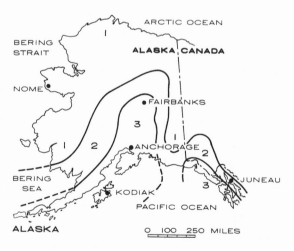

ALASKA

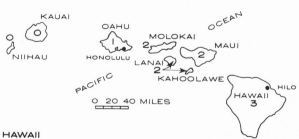

HAWAII

CONTIGUOUS STATES

0   200   400 MILES

SEISMIC PROBABILITY

ZONE	DAMAGE	"Z"
0	None	0
1	Minor	0.25
2	Moderate	0.50
3	Major	1.00

SEISMIC ZONE MAPS OF THE UNITED STATES

Harold P. King, CEC; King, Benioff, Steinmann, King; Sherman Oaks, California

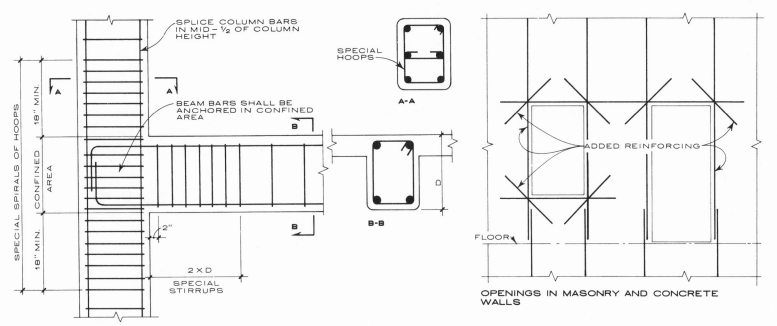

SPLICE COLUMN BARS IN MID – ½ OF COLUMN HEIGHT

SPECIAL HOOPS

A–A

BEAM BARS SHALL BE ANCHORED IN CONFINED AREA

SPECIAL SPIRALS OF HOOPS

18" MIN.

CONFINED AREA

18" MIN.

2"

2 × D

SPECIAL STIRRUPS

B–B

D

REINFORCING DETAIL FOR DUCTILE MOMENT RESISTING SPACE FRAME

ADDED REINFORCING

FLOOR

OPENINGS IN MASONRY AND CONCRETE WALLS

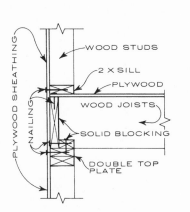

PLYWOOD SHEATHING

WOOD STUDS

2 × SILL

PLYWOOD

WOOD JOISTS

NAILING

SOLID BLOCKING

DOUBLE TOP PLATE

WOOD DIAPHRAGM WITH PLYWOOD SHEAR WALLS

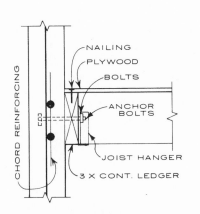

NAILING

PLYWOOD

BOLTS

CHORD REINFORCING

ANCHOR BOLTS

JOIST HANGER

3 × CONT. LEDGER

WOOD DIAPHRAGM WITH MASONRY OR CONCRETE SHEAR WALLS

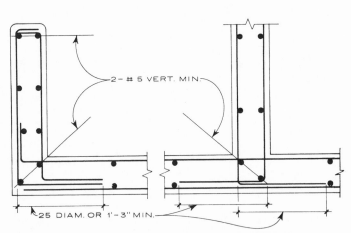

2 – # 5 VERT. MIN.

25 DIAM. OR 1'–3" MIN.

INTERSECTION OF CONCRETE OR REINFORCED MASONRY WALLS

PARAPET WALLS TO BE REINFORCED FOR 100% GRAVITY LATERAL LOAD

SLAB REINFORCING TO BE ANCHORED IN BEAM

EDGE BEAMS MUST SERVE AS CHORD OF DIAPHRAGM

CONCRETE DIAPHRAGM WITH CONCRETE FRAME

WELD

CONC. FILL

STEEL DECK

STEEL BEAM

STEEL DECK DIAPHRAGM WITH STEEL FRAME

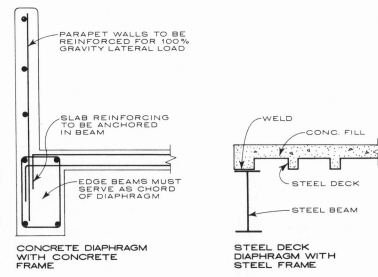

PLYWOOD SHEATHING

SOLID BLOCKING

TIE-DOWN

CONCRETE FOOTING

PLYWOOD SHEATHED SHEAR WALL WITH TIE-DOWNS

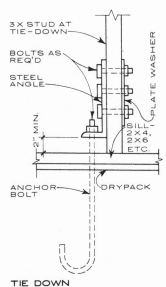

3 × STUD AT TIE-DOWN

BOLTS AS REQ'D

STEEL ANGLE

PLATE WASHER

SILL – 2 × 4, 2 × 6 ETC.

2" MIN.

ANCHOR BOLT

DRYPACK

TIE DOWN

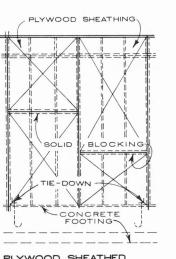

Harold P. King, CEC; King, Benioff, Steinmann, King; Sherman Oaks, California

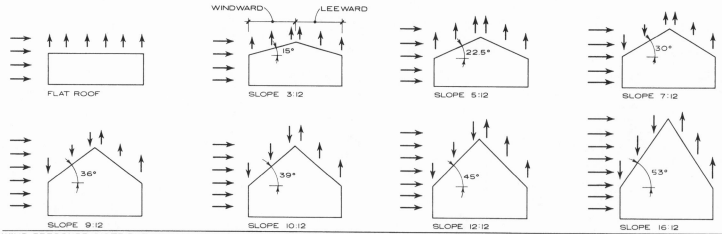

WIND PRESSURE DISTRIBUTION ON PITCHED, OR GABLE, ROOFS OF VARYING SLOPES

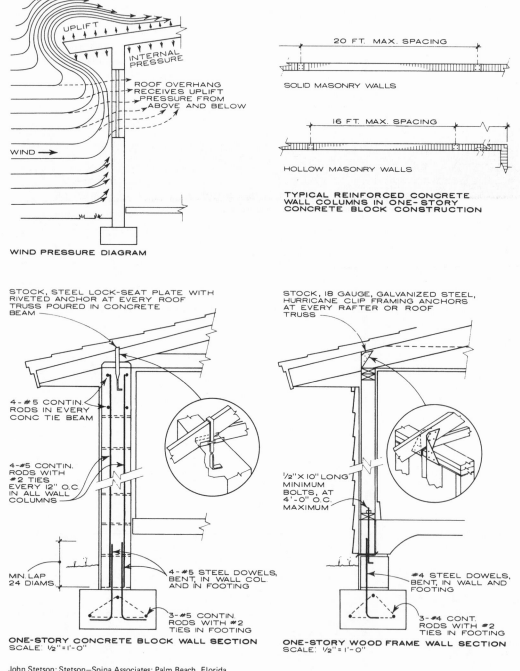

WIND PRESSURE DIAGRAM

TYPICAL REINFORCED CONCRETE
WALL COLUMNS IN ONE-STORY
CONCRETE BLOCK CONSTRUCTION

ISOMETRIC OF TYP. WALL COLUMN
WITH CONTINUOUS TOP TIE BEAM

ONE-STORY CONCRETE BLOCK WALL SECTION
SCALE: 1/2"=1'-0"

ONE-STORY WOOD FRAME WALL SECTION
SCALE: 1/2"=1'-0"

John Stetson; Stetson—Spina Associates; Palm Beach, Florida

MINIMUM DESIGN WIND LOAD FACTORS FOR VARIOUS HEIGHT ZONES ON VERTICAL PROJECTIONS OF BUILDINGS

Southern Std. Bldg. Code			Uniform Code	
Height Zone Feet	Horizontal Loads lbs. per sq.ft.		Height Zone Feet	Horizontal Loads lbs/sq.ft.
	inland region	coastal region		
0–30	10	25	0–60	15
31–50	20	35	60 up	20
51–99	24	45		
100–199	28	50	Coastal region is
200–299	30	50	that area lying
300–399	32	50	within 125 miles
over 400	40	50	of the coast.

MINIMUM REQUIRED WIND LOADS ON PITCHED, OR GABLE, ROOFS OF BUILDINGS

1. For roof slopes less than 30° designed to withstand loads acting outward normal to the surface equal to 1 1/4 times the horizontal loads specified for the corresponding height zone in which the roof is located.

2. For roof slopes greater than 30° designed to withstand loads acting inward normal to the surface equal to those specified for zone, load applied to windward slope.

2 SITEWORK

SOIL BEARING TEST

TESTING PROCEDURE

1. Make test on leveled but otherwise undisturbed portions of bearing material.
2. When tests are sufficiently below ground level, remove material immediately adjoining test location.
3. Test assembly consists of a vertical timber or post, with or without braced timber footing, resting upon soil to be tested and supporting a platform on which test loads are to be placed.
4. Exact area resting on soil may be not less than 1 sq. ft. for bearing materials of classes 1 thru 4 (see table "Soil Bearing Values") and not less than 4 sq. ft. for other bearing materials.
5. Platform to be symmetrical in respect to post and as close to soil as practicable.
6. Maintain post vertically by guys or wedges.
7. Load may be any convenient material which can be applied in required increments. EX: cement or sand in bags, pig iron or steel in bars.
8. Take all possible precautions to prevent jarring or moving post while applying load.
9. Take settlement readings at least once every 24 hours at a point which remains undisturbed during test.
10. Plot settlement against time.
11. Apply proposed allowable load per sq. ft. and allow to remain undisturbed until there has been no settlement for 24 hours.

NOTES FOR THE TEST ASSEMBLY SHOWN:

1. Load per sq. ft. on soil equals ¼ of load on platform times Y/Z, plus approximately 500 lbs. for the test assembly.
2. Establish bench mark before steel plate and 6"x8"s are in place, in order to include the weight of the test assembly.

CLASS	MATERIAL	Allowable bearing tons/sq. ft.	
	SOIL BEARING VALUES*		
1	Massive crystalline bed rocks (granite, gneiss, trap rock, etc.) in sound condition.	100	
2	Foliated rocks (bedded limestones; schist, slate) sound cond'n.	40	
3	Sedimentary rocks (hard shales, siltstones, sandstones, soft limestones), sound condition.	15	
4	Hard pan; gravel, sands, exceptionally compacted.	10	
5	Gravel, sand-gravel mixtures; compact.	6	
6	Gravel, loose; coarse sand, compact.	4	
7	Coarse sand, loose; sand-gravel mixtures, loose; fine sand, compact; coarse sand, wet, confined.	3	
8	Fine sand, loose; fine sand, wet, confined.	2	
9	Stiff clay.	4	
10	Medium stiff clay.	2	2.5**
11	Soft clay.	1	1.5**

*Based on data in N.Y. State Illustrated Code Manual (1953) and Nat'l Bldg Code (1949)

**Nat'l Bldg. Code recommendations

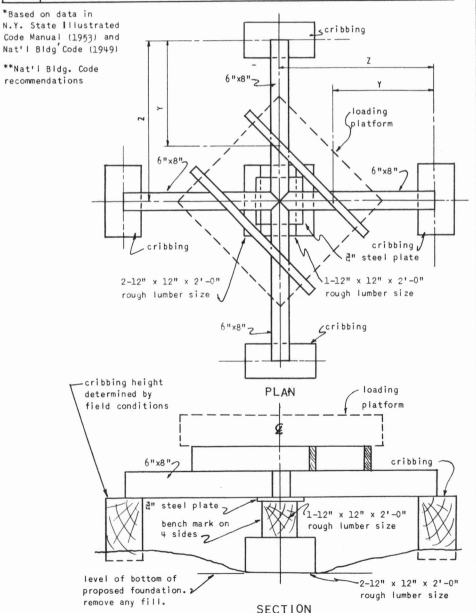

PLAN

SECTION

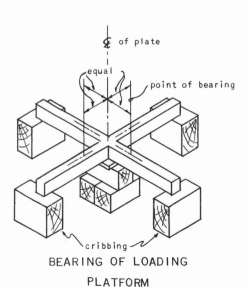

BEARING OF LOADING

PLATFORM

SLOPE SITE DEVELOPMENT RELATIONSHIP

AVERAGE % GRADE	DEVELOPMENT POTENTIAL	REMARKS
0–5%	Good for building sites, parking lots, play fields, roads.	Minimum necessity for grade changing devices. Minimum excavation for development.
5–10%	Good for building sites, roads, Fair for parking lots, play fields.	Minor necessity for grade changing devices. Minor excavation for development.
10–20%	Fair for building sites & roads. Difficult for parking lots, play fields.	Moderate use of grade changing devices. Moderate excavation for development.
20–40%	Difficult for building sites & roads. Very difficult for parking lots & play fields.	Considerable use of grade changing devices. Considerable excavation for development.
40%– OVER	Conservation area or buffer zone.	Extreme use of grade changing devices. Extreme excavation for development.

NOTE: Slope site development relationships may vary with local climate, topography and soil conditions.

SLOPE TERMINOLOGY :   % GRADE = 100 $\frac{V}{H}$

RATIO = H : V

EXAMPLE :

SLOPE-SURFACE TREATMENT RELATIONSHIPS

SURFACE TREATMENT	MAXIMUM SLOPE	DESIRABLE MAX. SLOPE	MINIMUM SLOPE	DESIRABLE MIN. SLOPE
CONCRETE SMOOTH FINISH	——	50% (1:1)	0.5%	1%
CONCRETE ROUGH FINISH	——	50% (1:1)	0.75%	1.5%
ASPHALT	——	50% (1:1)	1%	2%
BRICK	——	50% (1:1)	1%	2%
COBBLESTONES	——	50% (1:1)	1%	2%
LAWN	33.3% (3:1)	25% (4:1)	1%	2%
GROUND COVER PLANTS	50% (2:1)	33.3% (3:1)	2%	3%

GRADE CHANGE	V.C. LENGTH
3%	0
10%	4'
25%	6'
50%	10'

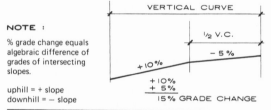

NOTE :

% grade change equals algebraic difference of grades of intersecting slopes.

uphill = + slope
downhill = – slope

DESIRABLE MINIMUM ROUNDING FOR CHANGES IN EARTH SLOPES

RELATIONSHIP OF SLOPE TO HORIZONTAL AND VERTICAL DISTANCES

GRADE	HORIZONTAL DISTANCES						
	100'	75'	50'	25'	10'	1'	0.1'
1%	1	0.75	0.5	0.25	0.1	0.01	0.001
2%	2	1.5	1.0	0.5	0.2	0.02	0.002
3%	3	2.25	1.5	0.75	0.3	0.03	0.003
4%	4	3.0	2.0	1.0	0.4	0.04	0.004
5%	5	3.75	2.5	1.25	0.5	0.05	0.005
6%	6	4.5	3.0	1.5	0.6	0.06	0.006
7%	7	5.25	3.5	1.75	0.7	0.07	0.007
8%	8	6.0	4.0	2.0	0.8	0.08	0.008
9%	9	6.75	4.5	2.25	0.9	0.09	0.009
10%	10	7.5	5.0	2.50	1.0	0.10	0.010
11%	11	8.25	5.5	2.75	1.1	0.11	0.011
12%	12	9.0	6.0	3.0	1.2	0.12	0.012
13%	13	9.75	6.5	3.25	1.3	0.13	0.013
14%	14	10.5	7.0	3.5	1.4	0.14	0.014
15%	15	11.25	7.5	3.75	1.5	0.15	0.015
20%	20	15.0	10.0	5.0	2.0	0.2	0.02
25%	25	18.75	12.5	6.25	2.5	0.25	0.025
50%	50	37.5	25.0	12.5	5.0	0.5	0.05

VERTICAL DISTANCES IN FEET

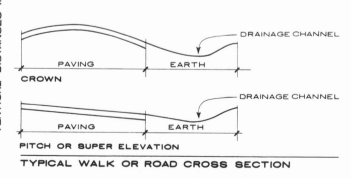

EARTH BANK   EARTH TERRACE   STONE RIPRAP

CRIBBING   WALL   COMBINATION

TYPICAL GRADE CHANGING DEVICES

DRAINAGE CHANNEL

PAVING   EARTH

CROWN

DRAINAGE CHANNEL

PAVING   EARTH

PITCH OR SUPER ELEVATION

TYPICAL WALK OR ROAD CROSS SECTION

Floyd Zimmerman; Sasaki, Dawson, DeMay Associates, Inc.; Watertown, Massachusetts

GENERAL INFORMATION

Before an architectural design can proceed a plot or site plan must be drawn to scale, showing the relevant available information about the construction area. This plan should show the relationship of the new building to property lines (and monuments), street lines above and below ground, and other features. It usually will also show the new contour lines and needed elevation information, such as special bench marks.

In simple building layout, key corner marks are placed on pegs or hubs, using the transit and steel tapes to ensure right angles and correct distances. The initial layout on the ground should be established in correct relationship to baselines, property lines, buildings, and so on. Once the building is laid out, diagonals shoud be measured and compared to make certain that all the building angles are square.

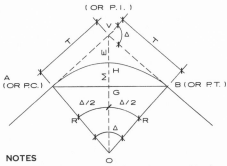

WATER TUBE LEVELING METHOD

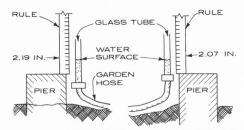

NOTES

The word tangent is used to signify the straight (not curved) portion of the building. From the plan some other relations that may be useful are also seen:

The long chord is c:
$$c = AB = AG + GB$$
$$= 2R \sin \tfrac{1}{2}\Delta$$

The mid-ordinate is M:
$$M = HG = OH - OG$$
$$= R - R\cos \tfrac{1}{2}\Delta$$

The external is E:
$$E = HV = OV - OH$$
$$= R/\cos \tfrac{1}{2}\Delta - R$$

A frequently used relationship, however, is the tangent (or semitangent) of the curve, which is T:
$$T = AV = BV$$
$$= R \tan \tfrac{1}{2}\Delta$$

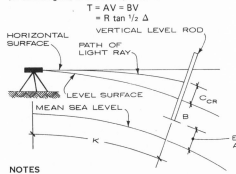

NOTES

Because of the curvature of the earth and the refraction or bending of light rays, the path of the ray of light departs both from the horizontal plane and from the level surface. In any situation employing fairly long sighting, a correction to the rod reading may be needed. The formula for the correction for curvature and refraction is

$$C_{CR} \text{ (ft)} = 0.572k^2$$

$$k = \text{sighted distance (miles)}$$

CURVATURE AND REFRACTION

Walter H. Sobel, FAIA and Associates; Chicago, Illinois

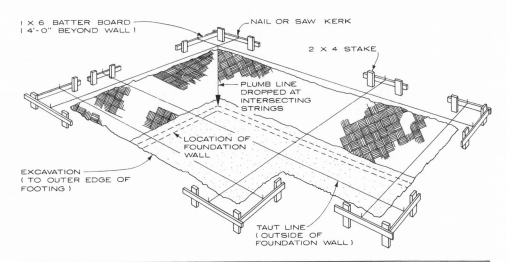

STAKING AND EXCAVATION (RESIDENTIAL)

NOTES

A transit or theodolite is basically an angle measuring instrument (it can also measure distances and elevations). It measures horizontal angles in the horizontal plane about an azimuth (vertical) axis, as well as vertical angles in a vertical plane about an elevation (horizontal) axis. To provide very great accuracy in setting a baseline at any angle to some existing reference line a technique is employed that involves repeated measuring of an angle. Essentially it consists of first laying out the angle, then measuring it carefully, and finally moving the newly set point as needed to achieve the proper angle. An engineer's level is used for surveying work of ordinary accuracy.

A   = ANGLE OF INTERSECTION
R   = RADIUS OF CURVE
P.I. = POINT OF INTERSECTION (V)
P.C. = POINT OF CURVATURE (A)
P.T. = POINT OF TANGENCY (B)

NOTES

On a construction site for a structure, it is important to place the project and its several components at the proper elevation. Control leveling will first be made to establish bench marks (BM) nearby to ensure this. Temporary bench marks for construction should be within 100 ft, at most 200 ft, of the location where they will be needed. Their location should be foreseen carefully enough to forstall any need to use a turning point between them and the constructed item (framework, pile, cap, etc.) that needs an elevation check.

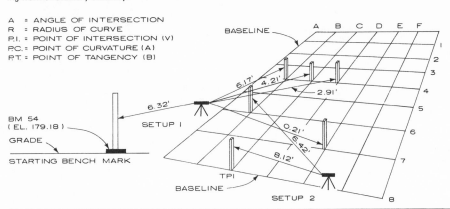

GRID SYSTEM

NOTES

A grid system is used for conveniently identifying the points whose elevation is required periodically. The level is set where both the bench mark and the desired points on the grid iron can be observed. Sighting on a known point (BM 54) gives the elevation of the instrument (H.I = 185.50), from which elevations of grid points can be found by sighting each point in turn. This method may very well be used to take readings on a concrete floor slab or grade to detect local settlements or to determine that it has been finished to specification.

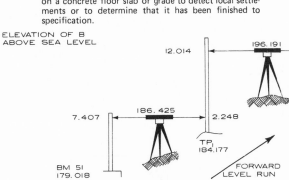

NOTES

When differential leveling is done, to set vertical control points one starts at a known elevation, sets up a transit or leveling device, reads a backsight on a level rod held on the known bench mark, and then reads a foresight on the rod held on a point whose elevation is needed. Temporarily, this new point becomes the known elevation. The instrument is then moved forward, and the process is begun anew to set a new point.

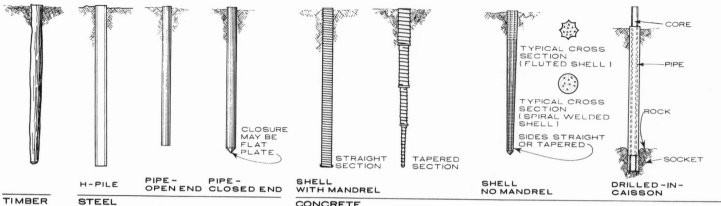

TIMBER   **STEEL**   **CONCRETE**   **DRILLED-IN-CAISSON**

NOTE: A mandrel is a member inserted into a hollow pile to reinforce the pile shell while it is driven into the ground.

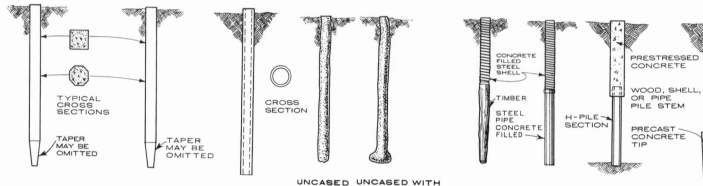

CONCRETE   **COMPOSITE**

GENERAL PILE DATA

PILE TYPE	MAXIMUM LENGTH (FT)	OPTIMUM LENGTH (FT)	SIZE (IN.)	MAXIMUM CAPACITY (TONS)	OPTIMUM LOAD RANGE (TONS)	USUAL SPACING
TIMBER	110	45-65	5-10 tip 12-20 butt	40	15-25	2'6'' to 3'0''
STEEL						
H-pile	250	40-150	8-14	200	50-200	2'6'' to 3'6''
Pipe—open end concrete filled	200	40-120	10-24	250	100-200	3'0'' to 4'0''
Pipe—closed end concrete filled	150	30-80	10-18	100	50-70	3'0'' to 4'0''
Shell—mandrel concrete filled straight or taper	100	40-80	8-18	75	40-60	3'0'' to 3'6''
Shell—no mandrel concrete filled	150	30-80	8-18	80	30-60	3'0'' to 3'6''
Drilled-in caisson concrete filled	250	60-120	24-48	3500	1000-2000	6'0'' to 8'0''
CONCRETE						
Precast	80	40-50	10-24	100	40-60	3'0''
Prestressed	200	60-80	10-24	200	100-150	3'0'' to 3'6''
Cylinder pile	150	60-80	36-54	500	250-400	6'0'' to 9'0''
Uncased or drilled	60	25-40	14-20	75	30-60	3'0'' to 3'6''
Uncased with enlarged base	60	25-40	14-20	150	40-100	6'0''
COMPOSITE						
Concrete—timber	150	60-100	5-10 tip 12-20 butt	40	15-25	3'0'' to 3'6''
Concrete—pipe	180	60-120	10-23	150	40-80	3'0'' to 4'0''
Prestressed concrete H-pile	200	100-150	20-24	200	120-150	3'6'' to 4'0''
Precast concrete tip	80	40	13-35	180	150	4'6''

NOTES

Timber piles must be treated with wood preservative when any portion is above permanent groundwater table.

Applicable material Specifications Concrete—ACL 318; Timber—ASTM D25: Structural Sections ASTM A36, A572 and A696.

For selection of type of pile consult foundation engineer.

Mueser, Rutledge, Johnston & DeSimone; New York, New York

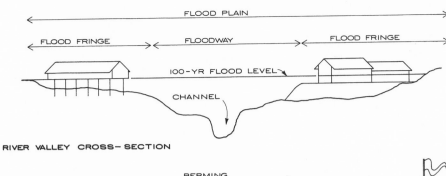

RIVER VALLEY CROSS-SECTION

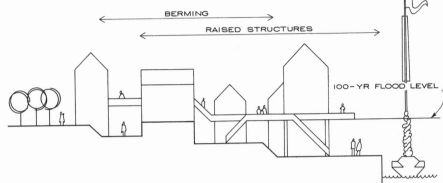

PROPOSED WHARF AREA DEVELOPMENT
FLOODWAY DEVELOPMENT

DUNE PROTECTION

Dunes provide a natural shoreline defense against storm wave and water level attack that is preferred above all other methods. Often termed a nonstructural coastal protection method, dunes supply short term surges of sediment to high energy wave attack. Material is usually deposited in offshore bars and returns onshore after storm passage to begin beach rebuilding.

Maintenance of existing dune fields should be performed through vegetation stabilization and sand fencing, which promote further dune growth and limit wind losses. The cutting of roadways or paths should be prohibited and timber crossovers used instead. In areas where no dunes exist and sufficient beach width is present, dune construction using successive tiers of sand fencing will promote further formation.

Dwellings should always be placed behind primary dunes. Construction atop or in front of dunes has historically shown structural damage from storms and should be prohibited.

ENCROACHMENT, FLOODWAY, AND COASTAL HIGH HAZARD ZONES

Development and encroachment, which restrict the flow of flood water has adverse effects. The flood level is raised upstream as well as locally, and the velocity downstream is increased, causing increased scouring and erosion. The floodway concept has been developed for riverine areas to permit local development within flood fringe areas without causing harm to others. The floodplain may be divided into two zones, one intended to carry the full cross section of the 100-yr flood and to be kept clear of obstruction; the other, the flood fringe, only to be developed with adequate precautions.

An analogous concept of the floodway is used for coastal areas. The 100-yr flood plain is divided into the coastal high hazard or velocity area and the general coastal flood plain. Construction may only occur within a coastal high hazard area if the structure is elevated on adequately anchored piles to the 100-yr flood level and if the space below the 100-yr flood level is left free of obstruction to minimize the impact from wave and wind driven water.

Care of the underside of floor deck in a building elevated above grade is one of the major maintenance considerations for building in the 100-yr flood plain. The material used to enclose floor spaces may be inundated by flood waters and thus should be resistant to water damage. Provision must also be made to allow water that may find its way into the floor sandwich to drain out and for the joist spaces to dry out.

Post and pile foundations are braced when it is determined that their size, number, spacing, and embedment condition will not be sufficient to resist lateral forces. 2 x 6 diagonal wood framing, threaded rods, and shear walls are different ways of bracing.

PIER CONSTRUCTION

Pier construction is a common technique for elevating structures in flood hazard areas. The special loading conditions associated with flooding make it essential that an architect or engineer be consulted for the design of pier foundations. Four factors determine pier footing depth: (1) frost depth, (2) flood or wind hazard loadings, (3) scour, (4) high volume change soils. The table below summarizes some of the major requirements for pier construction.

Good anchorage of posts or piles to the ground is essential for preventing wind and flood forces from overturning or uplifting elevated structures. In post construction the hole should be a minimum of 8 in. larger in diameter than the greatest dimension of a post section. This allows for alignment and backfilling. A clean well-consolidated backfill is necessary to ensure a structure of good lateral stability and resistance against wind and water uplifting.

The two critical areas are the connections between floor beams and piers and the connection between floor beams and floor joists in pier foundations designed to resist flood loading conditions. Floor beams can be anchored to piers with steel anchor bolts embedded in the pier and bolted through the beams with nuts and large diameter washers. The bolts should be embedded at least 12 in. in concrete, and 18 in. in masonry piers. Uplift and horizontal movements of joists can be avoided by securely anchoring joists to the beams by (1) metal framing plates and clips, (2) plywood sheating or wood siding, and (3) metal strapping.

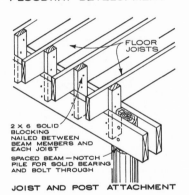

JOIST AND POST ATTACHMENT

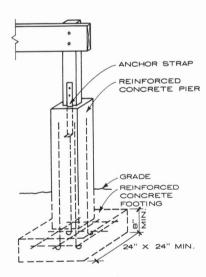

REINFORCED CONCRETE PIER AND FOUNDATION

PLYWOOD ANCHORAGE
CONSTRUCTION DETAILS

PIER TABLE

PIER MATERIAL	MIN. PIER SIZE	MIN. FOOTING	PIER SPACING RIGHT ANGLES TO JOIST	PARALLEL TO JOIST	HEIGHT RANGE
Brick	12" x 12"	24" x 24" x 8"	8' o.c.	12' o.c.	18" to 6'
Concrete masonry	12" x 12" or 8" x 16"	24" x 24" x 8" / 20" x 24" x 8"	8' o.c.	12' o.c.	18" to 8'
Poured-in-place concrete	12" dia. or 10" x 10"	20" x 20" x 8"	Dependant on type of framing and loading conditions		18" to 12' +

Wajeda J. Rab, RLA; Maryland National Capital Park and Planning Commission; Silver Spring, Maryland

Phillip Renfrow, AIA; Komatsu/Brown Architects; Washington, D.C.

GENERAL NOTES

Drainage systems are provided to intercept and dispose of the water flow to the degree necessary to prevent inordinate damage to an area or facility from seepage and direct runoff. Each of these two sources requires its own method of control and competent engineering design to ensure a degree of protection commensurate with the hazard potential.

Subsurface drainage systems are designed to lower the natural water table, intercept underground flow, and dispose of infiltration percolating downward through soils from surface sources. These systems are typically used under floors, around foundations, in planters, and under athletic fields and courts. Each system must be provided with a positive outfall either by pumped discharge or gravity drain above expected high water levels.

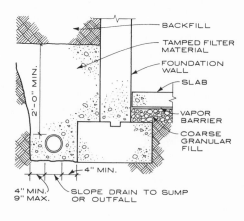

FOOTING DRAIN

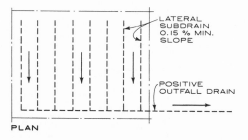

PLAN

Drain layout varies to meet need. May be grid, parallel, herringbone, or random pattern to fit topography.

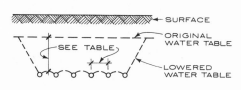

SECTION

Depths indicated in table below are minimum range. Greater depths may be required in order to prevent frost heave in colder climates or where soils have a high capillarity.

SUBSURFACE DRAINAGE SYSTEM

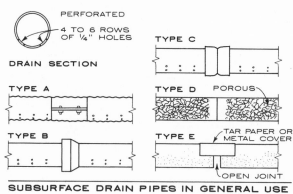

SUBSURFACE DRAIN PIPES IN GENERAL USE

DRAIN TYPE	MATERIAL	JOINT
A	CORRUGATED METAL FLEXIBLE PLASTIC	COLLARS
B	CONCRETE CLAY TILE	BELL AND SPIGOT
C	ASBESTOS CEMENT RIGID PLASTIC	SLEEVE SOCKET
D	POROUS CONCRETE	TONGUE AND GROOVE
E	UNPERFORATED CLAY TILE CONCRETE PLASTIC	BUTT

TYPICAL SECTION

If perforated drain is used, it should be installed with the holes facing downward.

When used to intercept sidehill seepage, bottom of trench should be cut into underlying impervious material a minimum of 6 in.

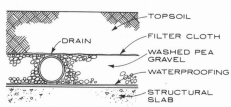

PLANTER DRAIN

DRYWALLS

Drywells are used to provide an underground means of disposal for surface runoff. Their effectiveness is in direct proportion to the porosity of surrounding soils, and they are efficient for draining only small areas. High rates of rainfall runoff cannot be absorbed at the considerably lower percolation rates of most soils, and the difference is temporarily stored in the drywell. Efficiency is reduced during extended periods of wet weather when receiving soils are saturated and the well is refilled prior to draining completely.

DEPTH AND SPACING OF SUBDRAINS RECOMMENDED FOR VARIOUS SOIL CLASSES

SOIL CLASSES	PERCENTAGE OF SOIL SEPARATES			DEPTH OF BOTTOM OF DRAIN (FT)	DISTANCE BETWEEN SUBDRAINS (FT)
	SAND	SILT	CLAY		
Sand	80-100	0-20	0-20	3-4	150-300
				2-3	100-150
Sandy loam	50-80	0-50	0-20	3-4	100-150
				2-3	85-100
Loam	30-50	30-50	0-20	3-4	85-100
				2-3	75-85
Silt loam	0-50	50-100	0-20	3-4	75-85
				2-3	65-75
Sandy clay loam	50-80	0-30	20-30	3-4	65-75
				2-3	55-65
Clay loam	20-50	20-50	20-30	3-4	55-65
				2-3	45-55
Silty clay loam	0-30	50-80	20-30	3-4	45-55
				2-3	40-45
Sandy clay	50-70	0-20	30-50	3-4	40-45
				2-3	35-40
Silty clay	0-20	50-70	30-50	3-4	35-40
				2-3	30-35
Clay	0-50	0-50	30-100	3-4	30-35
				2-3	25-30

Kurt N. Pronske, P. E.; Reston, Virginia

SURFACE DRAINAGE SYSTEMS: Designed to collect and dispose of rainfall runoff. There are two basic types. One, a ditch/swale and culvert, or open system, is generally used in less densely populated and more open areas where natural surfaces predominate. In urbanized areas where much of the land is overbuilt, the second type is used—the pipe, inlet/catchbasin and manhole, or closed system. Combinations of the two are quite common where terrain and density dictate.

SYSTEM NOTES: The location of the storm sewer in the street must be coordinated with other utilities, existing as well as proposed, which may have a priority position in the right-of-way. Detailed design is required in order to determine the most efficient combination of pipe size, slope, and material for a given system.

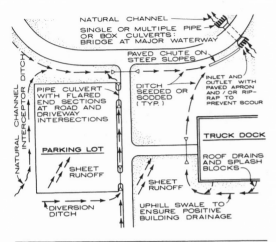

OPEN SYSTEM

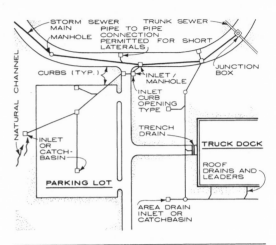

SHAPE	MATERIAL	SIZE RANGE
DIA.	PRECAST CONCRETE	1' TO 12' DIA.
	CORRUGATED METAL	
	· PIPE	1' TO 10' DIA.
	· PLATE PIPE	1' TO 21' DIA.
RISE / SPAN	PRECAST ✳ CONCRETE	18"X11" TO 168 3/4" X 106 1/2"
	CORRUGATED METAL	
	· PIPE ARCH (S X R)	18" X 11" TO 103" X 71"
	· PLATE PIPE ARCH (S X R)	6'-1" X 4'-7" TO 20'-7" X 13'-2"
RISE / SPAN	CORRUGATED METAL	
	· PLATE ARCH (S X R)	6'-0" X 1'-9 1/2" TO 25'-0" X 12'-6"
RISE / SPAN	PRECAST CONCRETE	23" X 14" TO 180" X 116"
	PRECAST ✳ CONCRETE	3' X 2' TO 12'X12'
	POURED IN PLACE CONCRETE BOX	VARIABLE - SUBJECT TO SPECIFIC DESIGN

✳ LIMITED AVAILABILITY

CULVERT SECTIONS

CLOSED SYSTEM

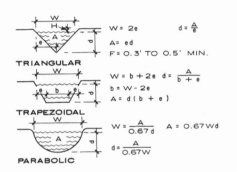

$W = 2e \qquad d = \dfrac{A}{e}$

$A = ed$

$F = 0.3'$ TO $0.5'$ MIN.

TRIANGULAR

$W = b + 2e \qquad d = \dfrac{A}{b + e}$

$b = W - 2e$

$A = d(b + e)$

TRAPEZOIDAL

$W = \dfrac{A}{0.67 \, d} \qquad A = 0.67 \, Wd$

$d = \dfrac{A}{0.67 \, W}$

PARABOLIC

CHANNEL / DITCH SECTIONS

NOTE

Choice of section depends on topography, soil type, and runoff quantities. The ability to withstand erosion is a function of soil type and flow velocity. Most ditches are at least seeded or sodded. Where ditch slopes exceed 4 to 5%, some type of lining pavement is usually required to prevent erosion.

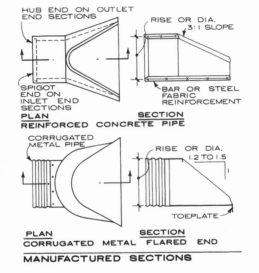

PLAN
SECTION
REINFORCED CONCRETE PIPE

PLAN
SECTION
CORRUGATED METAL FLARED END

MANUFACTURED SECTIONS

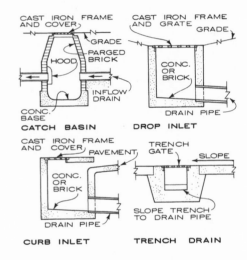

CATCH BASIN   **DROP INLET**

CURB INLET   **TRENCH DRAIN**

INLETS

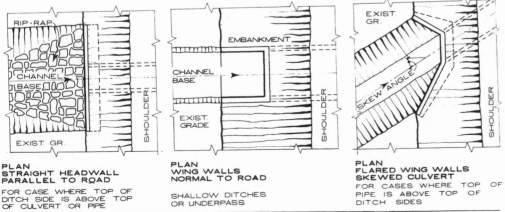

PLAN
STRAIGHT HEADWALL PARALLEL TO ROAD

FOR CASE WHERE TOP OF DITCH SIDE IS ABOVE TOP OF CULVERT OR PIPE

PLAN
WING WALLS NORMAL TO ROAD

SHALLOW DITCHES OR UNDERPASS

PLAN
FLARED WING WALLS SKEWED CULVERT

FOR CASES WHERE TOP OF PIPE IS ABOVE TOP OF DITCH SIDES

HEADWALL DESIGN AS CONTROLLED BY TOPOGRAPHY

MANHOLES: Provided at the upper end of sewers and at changes in sewer sizes, slope, or alignment. Maximum distance between manholes varies from 300 to 600 ft for inspection and maintenance depending on size of sewer and local standards and practice.

INLETS AND CATCHBASINS: Provided at low points and periodically along swales and gutters to intercept runoff. Spacing is a function of size and type of unit and slope of gutter or swale in relation to the amount of runoff anticipated. The choice of unit (i.e., drop inlet, curb inlet, grate inlet) is subject to local codes and practice. Catchbasins have a sump below the outlet pipe to trap debris and silt, and are used where storm sewers are expected to flow at less than self-cleaning velocity (2 fps minimum). Catchbasins should not be interconnected and must be cleaned periodically to maintain a proper trap.

INLET/MANHOLE: Combination units used to reduce number of structures in the system.

JUNCTION BOX: Used in lieu of manhole for joining larger sewers, 48 in. and up. Customized design is required for each juncture.

TRENCH DRAINS: Used at the base of truck docks, ramps, and stairs, i.e., wherever it is desirable to intercept runoff along a level plane.

Kurt N. Pronske, P. E.; Reston, Virginia

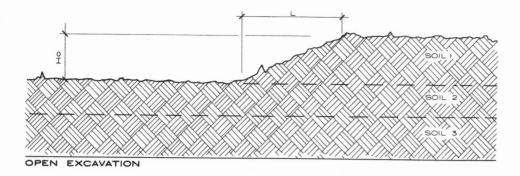

OPEN EXCAVATION

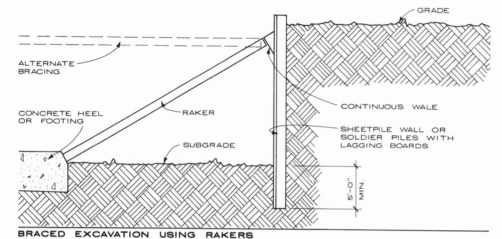

BRACED EXCAVATION USING RAKERS

- ALTERNATE BRACING
- CONCRETE HEEL OR FOOTING
- RAKER
- SUBGRADE
- GRADE
- CONTINUOUS WALE
- SHEETPILE WALL OR SOLDIER PILES WITH LAGGING BOARDS
- 5'-0" MIN.

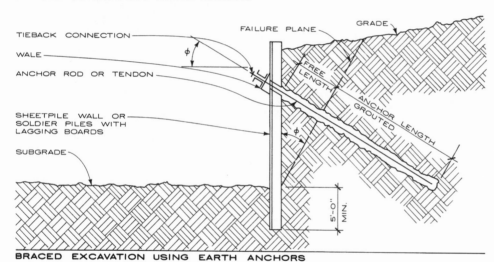

BRACED EXCAVATION USING EARTH ANCHORS

- TIEBACK CONNECTION
- WALE
- ANCHOR ROD OR TENDON
- SHEETPILE WALL OR SOLDIER PILES WITH LAGGING BOARDS
- SUBGRADE
- FAILURE PLANE
- GRADE
- FREE LENGTH
- ANCHOR LENGTH GROUTED
- 5'-0" MIN.

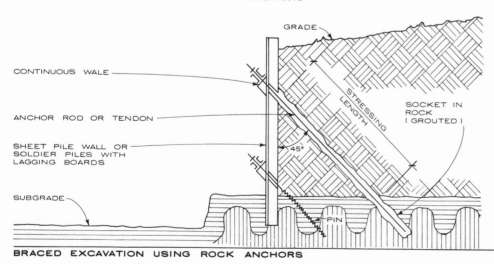

BRACED EXCAVATION USING ROCK ANCHORS

- CONTINUOUS WALE
- ANCHOR ROD OR TENDON
- SHEET PILE WALL OR SOLDIER PILES WITH LAGGING BOARDS
- SUBGRADE
- GRADE
- STRESSING LENGTH
- SOCKET IN ROCK (GROUTED)
- 45°
- PIN

Mueser, Rutledge, Johnston & DeSimone; New York, New York

EMBANKMENT STABILITY
CONSULT FOUNDATION ENGINEER

SOIL TYPES			L/HO	REMARKS
S1	S2	S3		
Fill	Rock		>1.5	Check sliding of S1
Soft clay	Hard clay	Rock	>1.0	Check sliding of S1
Sand	Soft clay	Hard clay	>1.5	Check lateral displacement of S2
Sand	Sand	Hard clay	>1.5	
Hard clay	Soft clay	Sand	<1.0	Check lateral displacement of S2

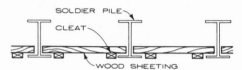

- SOLDIER PILE
- CLEAT
- WOOD SHEETING

TIMBER LAGGING

- TONGUE AND GROOVE BOARDS

TIMBER SHEETING

- INTERLOCKING Z SECTIONS

STEEL SHEETING

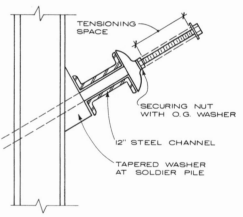

- TENSIONING SPACE
- SECURING NUT WITH O.G. WASHER
- 12" STEEL CHANNEL
- TAPERED WASHER AT SOLDIER PILE

CHANNEL WALER DETAIL

NOTES

1. For shallow depths of excavation cantilever sheeting may be used, if driven to sufficient depth.
2. For deep excavations, several tiers of bracing may be necessary.
3. If subgrade of excavation is used for installation of spreadfootings or mats, proper dewatering procedures may be required to avoid disturbance of bearing level.
4. At times it may be possible to improve the bearing stratum by excavation of compressible materials and their replacement with compacted granular backfill.
5. For evaluation of problems encountered with sheeting and shoring, a foundation engineer should be consulted.
6. Local codes and OSHA regulations must be considered.
7. Proximity of utilities and other structures must be considered in design.

Embankment stabilization is required where extremely steep slopes exist that are subject to heavy storm water runoff. The need for mechanical stabilization can be reduced by intercepting the runoff, or slowing the velocity of the runoff down the slope. Diversions are desirable at the tops of slopes to intercept the runoff. Slopes can be shelved or terraced to reduce the velocity of runoff to the point where a major erosion hazard is avoided. Use an armored channel or slope drain if concentrated runoff down a slope must be controlled.

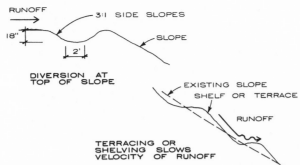

DIVERSION AT TOP OF SLOPE

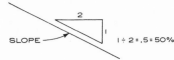

1 ÷ 2 = .5 = 50%

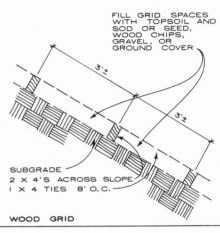

TERRACING OR SHELVING SLOWS VELOCITY OF RUNOFF

SOIL	GRADIENT	RATIO
Dry sand	33%	3:1
Loam	40%	2.5:1
Compacted clay	80%	1.25:1
Saturated clay	20%	5:1

MAXIMUM GRADIENTS FOR BARE SOILS

BASIC PRINCIPLES OF SLOPE EROSION CONTROL

For slopes up to 2:1 slope stabilization may be achieved using stone, broken concrete, or wood grid as shown. For slopes up to 1:1, set stone or broken concrete in mortar setting bed and joints. Use retaining walls for extremely steep slopes.

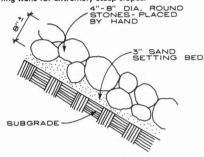

STONE

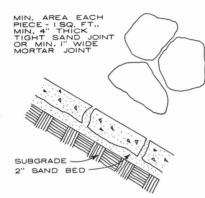

BROKEN CONCRETE

WOOD GRID

SLOPE STABILIZATION WITH RIPRAP

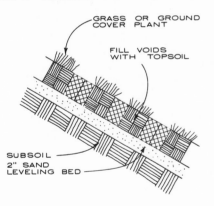

TYPICAL INSTALLATION SECTION

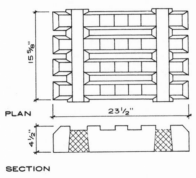

PLAN

SECTION

TYPICAL PRECAST UNITS

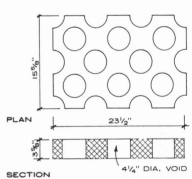

PLAN

SECTION

Precast concrete paving units may be used for slope stabilization up to 1:1 slope. Use retaining walls for steeper slopes.

PRECAST PERFORATED CONCRETE PAVING UNITS

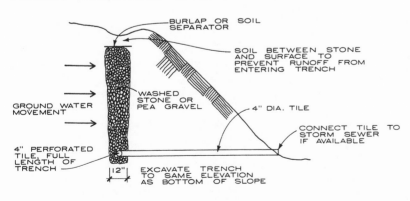

INTERCEPTOR DRAIN FOR WEEPING BANK

DIVERSION AT TOP OF SLOPE

TOP OF SLOPE

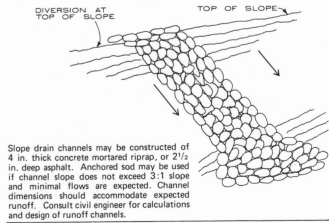

Slope drain channels may be constructed of 4 in. thick concrete mortared riprap, or 2¹/₂ in. deep asphalt. Anchored sod may be used if channel slope does not exceed 3:1 slope and minimal flows are expected. Channel dimensions should accommodate expected runoff. Consult civil engineer for calculations and design of runoff channels.

SLOPE DRAIN

John M. Beckett; Beckett, Raeder, Rankin, Inc.; Ann Arbor, Michigan

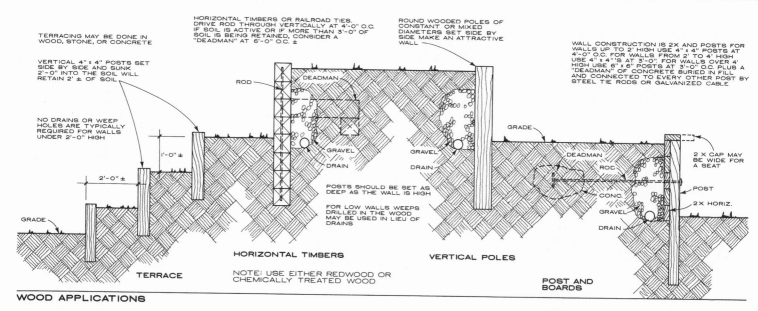

TERRACING MAY BE DONE IN WOOD, STONE, OR CONCRETE

VERTICAL 4" x 4" POSTS SET SIDE BY SIDE AND SUNK 2'-0" INTO THE SOIL WILL RETAIN 2' ± OF SOIL

NO DRAINS OR WEEP HOLES ARE TYPICALLY REQUIRED FOR WALLS UNDER 2'-0" HIGH

HORIZONTAL TIMBERS OR RAILROAD TIES. DRIVE ROD THROUGH VERTICALLY AT 4'-0" O.C. IF SOIL IS ACTIVE OR IF MORE THAN 3'-0" OF SOIL IS BEING RETAINED, CONSIDER A "DEADMAN" AT 6'-0" O.C. ±

ROUND WOODED POLES OF CONSTANT OR MIXED DIAMETERS SET SIDE BY SIDE MAKE AN ATTRACTIVE WALL

WALL CONSTRUCTION IS 2X AND POSTS FOR WALLS UP TO 2' HIGH USE 4" x 4" POSTS AT 4'-0" O.C. FOR WALLS FROM 2' TO 4' HIGH USE 4" x 4"'S AT 3'-0" O.C. FOR WALLS OVER 4' HIGH USE 6" x 6" POSTS AT 3'-0" O.C. PLUS A "DEADMAN" OF CONCRETE BURIED IN FILL AND CONNECTED TO EVERY OTHER POST BY STEEL TIE RODS OR GALVANIZED CABLE

ROD   DEADMAN   GRADE   DEADMAN   2 X CAP MAY BE WIDE FOR A SEAT

GRAVEL DRAIN   GRAVEL DRAIN   ROD   POST   2X HORIZ.

CONC.   GRAVEL   DRAIN

POSTS SHOULD BE SET AS DEEP AS THE WALL IS HIGH

FOR LOW WALLS WEEPS DRILLED IN THE WOOD MAY BE USED IN LIEU OF DRAINS

GRADE   1'-0" ±   2'-0" ±

GRADE

TERRACE   HORIZONTAL TIMBERS   VERTICAL POLES   POST AND BOARDS

NOTE: USE EITHER REDWOOD OR CHEMICALLY TREATED WOOD

WOOD APPLICATIONS

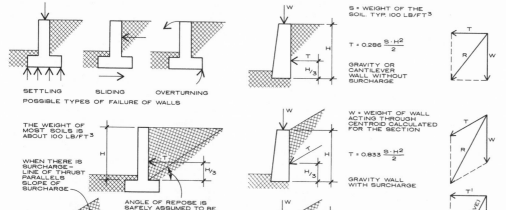

SETTLING   SLIDING   OVERTURNING

POSSIBLE TYPES OF FAILURE OF WALLS

THE WEIGHT OF MOST SOILS IS ABOUT 100 LB/FT³

WHEN THERE IS SURCHARGE - LINE OF THRUST PARALLELS SLOPE OF SURCHARGE

ANGLE OF REPOSE IS SAFELY ASSUMED TO BE 33° FOR MOST SOILS

ONLY SOIL ABOVE THE ANGLE OF REPOSE EXERTS ANY THRUST (T) ON THE WALL

GENERAL RELATIONSHIPS

S = WEIGHT OF THE SOIL. TYP. 100 LB/FT³

$$T = 0.286 \frac{S \cdot H^2}{2}$$

GRAVITY OR CANTILEVER WALL WITHOUT SURCHARGE

W = WEIGHT OF WALL ACTING THROUGH CENTROID CALCULATED FOR THE SECTION

$$T = 0.833 \frac{S \cdot H^2}{2}$$

GRAVITY WALL WITH SURCHARGE

$$T = 0.833 \frac{S(H+H^1)^2}{2}$$

CANTILEVER WALL WITH SURCHARGE

FORMULAS

FORCE DIAGRAMS

SLIDING

The thrust on the wall must be resisted. The resisting force is the weight of the wall times the coefficient of soil friction. Use a safety factor of 1.5. Therefore:

$$W(C.F.) \geq 1.5T$$

Average coefficients:

Gravel	0.6
Silt/dry clay	0.5
Sand	0.4
Wet clay	0.3

OVERTURNING

The overturning moment equals T(H/3). This is resisted by the resisting moment. For symmetrical sections, resisting moment equals W times (width of base/2). Use a safety factor of 2.0. Therefore:

$$M_R \geq 2(M_0)$$

SETTLING

Soil bearing value must resist vertical force. For symmetrical sections that force is W (or W')/bearing area. Use a safety factor of 1.5. Therefore:

$$S.B. \geq 1.5(W/A)$$

STRUCTURAL DESIGN CONSIDERATIONS

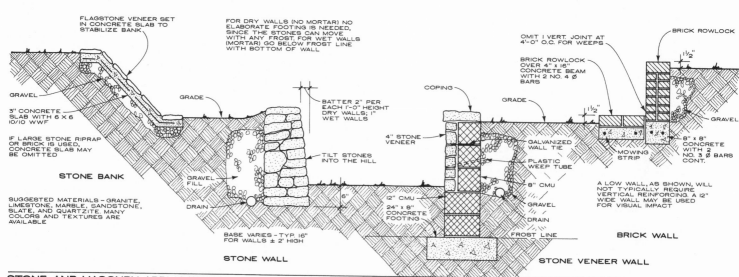

FLAGSTONE VENEER SET IN CONCRETE SLAB TO STABILIZE BANK

GRAVEL

3" CONCRETE SLAB WITH 6 x 6 10/10 WWF

IF LARGE STONE RIPRAP OR BRICK IS USED, CONCRETE SLAB MAY BE OMITTED

STONE BANK

SUGGESTED MATERIALS - GRANITE, LIMESTONE, MARBLE, SANDSTONE, SLATE, AND QUARTZITE. MANY COLORS AND TEXTURES ARE AVAILABLE

FOR DRY WALLS (NO MORTAR) NO ELABORATE FOOTING IS NEEDED, SINCE THE STONES CAN MOVE WITH ANY FROST. FOR WET WALLS (MORTAR) GO BELOW FROST LINE WITH BOTTOM OF WALL

GRADE

BATTER 2" PER EACH 1'-0" HEIGHT DRY WALLS; 1" WET WALLS

TILT STONES INTO THE HILL

GRAVEL FILL

DRAIN   6"

BASE VARIES - TYP. 16" FOR WALLS ± 2' HIGH

STONE WALL

COPING

4" STONE VENEER

GALVANIZED WALL TIE

PLASTIC WEEP TUBE

8" CMU

12" CMU

24" x 8" CONCRETE FOOTING

FROST LINE

OMIT 1 VERT. JOINT AT 4'-0" O.C. FOR WEEPS

BRICK ROWLOCK OVER 4" x 16" CONCRETE BEAM WITH 2 NO. 4 Ø BARS

GRADE

MOWING STRIP

A LOW WALL, AS SHOWN, WILL NOT TYPICALLY REQUIRE VERTICAL REINFORCING. A 12" WIDE WALL MAY BE USED FOR VISUAL IMPACT

BRICK ROWLOCK

1½"   1½"

GRAVEL

8" x 8" CONCRETE WITH 2 NO. 3 Ø BARS CONT.

GRAVEL   DRAIN

BRICK WALL

STONE VENEER WALL

STONE AND MASONRY APPLICATIONS

Charles R. Heuer, AIA; Washington, D.C.

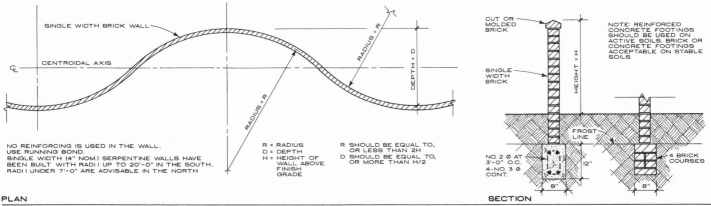

SINGLE WIDTH BRICK WALL

CENTROIDAL AXIS

RADIUS = R

RADIUS = R

DEPTH = D

R = RADIUS
D = DEPTH
H = HEIGHT OF WALL ABOVE FINISH GRADE

R SHOULD BE EQUAL TO, OR LESS THAN 2H
D SHOULD BE EQUAL TO, OR MORE THAN H/2

NO REINFORCING IS USED IN THE WALL.
USE RUNNING BOND.
SINGLE WIDTH (4" NOM.) SERPENTINE WALLS HAVE BEEN BUILT WITH RADII UP TO 20'-0" IN THE SOUTH.
RADII UNDER 7'-0" ARE ADVISABLE IN THE NORTH

PLAN

CUT OR MOLDED BRICK

SINGLE WIDTH BRICK

HEIGHT = H

NOTE: REINFORCED CONCRETE FOOTINGS SHOULD BE USED ON ACTIVE SOILS. BRICK OR CONCRETE FOOTINGS ACCEPTABLE ON STABLE SOILS

FROST LINE

NO. 2 Ø AT 3'-0" O.C.
4-NO. 3 Ø CONT.

12"

8"

4 BRICK COURSES

8"

SECTION

SERPENTINE GARDEN WALLS

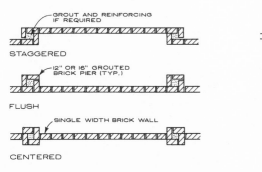

GROUT AND REINFORCING IF REQUIRED

STAGGERED

12" OR 16" GROUTED BRICK PIER (TYP.)

FLUSH

SINGLE WIDTH BRICK WALL

CENTERED

TYPICAL PLANS

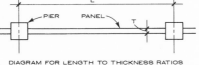

L

PIER   PANEL   T

DIAGRAM FOR LENGTH TO THICKNESS RATIOS

REINFORCING = .0005 CROSS-SECTIONAL AREA OF WALL
RUN HORIZ. AND VERT.

2 WIDTH BRICK PANEL

12" GROUTED PIER

FOOTING

PLAN

LENGTH TO THICKNESS RATIOS

WIND PRESSURE (LB/FT^2)	MAXIMUM L/T RATIO
5	35
10	25
15	20
20	18
25	16
30	14
35	13
40	12

PIER AND PANEL WALLS

WIND PRESSURE CHART

HEIGHT ZONE (FT)	WIND PRESSURE MAP AREAS (PSF)						
	20	25	30	35	40	45	50
Less than 30	15	20	25	25	30	35	40

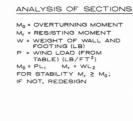

POUNDS PER SQUARE FOOT
20 25 30 35 40 45 50

ANALYSIS OF SECTIONS

M_o = OVERTURNING MOMENT
M_r = RESISTING MOMENT
W = WEIGHT OF WALL AND FOOTING (LB)
P = WIND LOAD (FROM TABLE) (LB/FT^2)
$M_o = PL_1$ $M_r = WL_2$
FOR STABILITY $M_r \geq M_o$;
IF NOT, REDESIGN

CANTILEVER FOOTINGS ARE OFTEN USED AT PROPERTY LINES OR TO INCREASE RESISTANCE TO OVERTURNING. BE SURE TO CHECK FOR WIND FROM EITHER DIRECTION

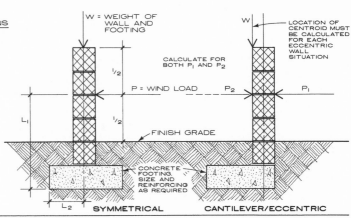

W = WEIGHT OF WALL AND FOOTING

CALCULATE FOR BOTH P_1 AND P_2

L_1

1/2

1/2

P = WIND LOAD P_2 P_1

FINISH GRADE

CONCRETE FOOTING. SIZE AND REINFORCING AS REQUIRED

L_2

SYMMETRICAL

W

LOCATION OF CENTROID MUST BE CALCULATED FOR EACH ECCENTRIC WALL SITUATION

CANTILEVER/ECCENTRIC

HORIZONTAL LOADING — FREESTANDING WALLS

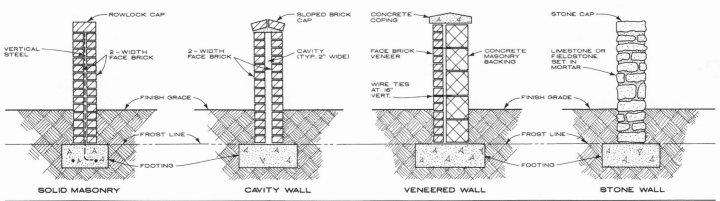

ROWLOCK CAP

VERTICAL STEEL

2-WIDTH FACE BRICK

FINISH GRADE

FROST LINE

FOOTING

SOLID MASONRY

SLOPED BRICK CAP

2-WIDTH FACE BRICK

CAVITY (TYP. 2" WIDE)

CAVITY WALL

CONCRETE COPING

FACE BRICK VENEER

CONCRETE MASONRY BACKING

WIRE TIES AT 16" VERT.

FINISH GRADE

FROST LINE

FOOTING

VENEERED WALL

STONE CAP

LIMESTONE OR FIELDSTONE SET IN MORTAR

STONE WALL

FREESTANDING WALL TYPES

Charles R. Heuer, AIA; Washington, D. C.

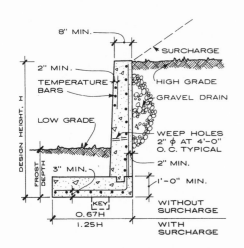

Place base below frost line. Dimensions are approximate.

CONCRETE OUTLINES FOR L TYPE RETAINING WALL

Soil pressure at toe equals 0.2 times the height in kips per square foot. Dimensions are preliminary.

H	B
3'-0''	1'-6''
4'-0''	2'-0''
5'-0''	2'-6''
6'-0''	3'-0''
7'-0''	3'-6''
8'-0''	4'-0''
9'-0''	4'-6''
10'-0''	5'-0''

MASS CONCRETE RETAINING WALL WITHOUT SURCHARGE

RETAINING WALL – VERTICAL CONTROL JOINT

RETAINING WALL – VERTICAL EXPANSION JOINT

NOTES

Provide control and/or construction joints in concrete retaining walls about every 25 ft and expansion joints about every fourth control and/or construction joint. Coated dowels should be used if average wall height on either side of a joint is different.

Consult with a structural engineer for final design of concrete retaining walls.

Use temperature bars if wall is more than 12 in. thick.

Keys shown dashed may be required to prevent sliding in high walls and those on moist clay.

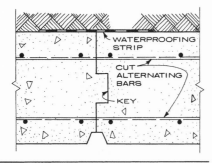

PRELIMINARY DIMENSIONS

BACKFILL SLOPING ϕ = 33° – 40' (1½ : 1)					BACKFILL LEVEL—NO SURCHARGE				
CONCRETE OUTLINES					CONCRETE OUTLINES				
HEIGHT OF WALL = H (FT)	B (FT)	a (FT)	b (FT)	c (FT)	HEIGHT OF WALL = H (FT)	B (FT)	a (FT)	b (FT)	c (FT)
3	2'-6''	0'-11''	0'-7''	1'-0''	3	1'-9''	0'-10½''	0'-4''	0'-6½''
4	3'-2''	1'-0''	0'-9''	1'-5''	4	2'-2''	0'-11''	0'-5''	0'-10''
5	3'-10''	1'-1''	1'-0''	1'-9''	5	2'-8''	0'-11''	0'-5''	1'-4''
6	4'-6''	1'-2''	1'-3''	2'-1''	6	3'-3''	1'-0''	0'-8''	1'-7''
7	5'-3''	1'-3''	1'-6''	2'-6''	7	3'-10''	1'-0''	1'-0''	1'-10''
8	5'-11''	1'-4''	1'-9''	2'-10''	8	4'-3''	1'-1''	1'-1''	2'-1''
9	6'-8''	1'-5''	2'-0''	3'-3''	9	4'-9''	1'-1''	1'-1''	2'-7''
10	7'-5''	1'-6''	2'-3''	3'-8''	10	5'-4''	1'-2''	1'-4''	2'-10''
11	8'-1''	1'-7''	2'-6''	4'-0''	11	5'-10''	1'-2''	1'-6''	3'-2''
12	8'-10''	1'-8''	2'-9''	4'-5''	12	6'-6''	1'-3''	1'-8''	3'-7''
13	9'-6''	1'-9''	3'-0''	4'-9''	13	7'-0''	1'-4''	1'-8''	4'-0''
14	10'-3''	1'-10''	3'-3''	5'-2''	14	7'-8''	1'-4''	2'-1''	4'-3''
15	11'-0''	1'-11''	3'-6''	5'-7''	15	8'-1''	1'-5''	2'-1''	4'-7''
16	11'-10''	2'-0''	3'-10''	6'-0''	16	8'-6''	1'-5''	2'-2''	4'-11''
17	12'-7''	2'-1''	4'-1''	6'-5''	17	9'-0''	1'-6''	2'-3''	5'-3''
18	13'-4''	2'-2''	4'-4''	6'-10''	18	9'-6''	1'-7''	2'-4''	5'-7''
19	14'-2''	2'-3''	4'-8''	7'-3''	19	10'-2''	1'-7''	2'-6''	6'-1''
20	15'-0''	2'-4''	5'-0''	7'-8''	20	10'-5''	1'-8''	2'-6''	6'-3''

Key shown dashed may be required to prevent sliding in high walls and those on moist clay.

CONCRETE OUTLINES FOR "T" TYPE RETAINING WALL WITH LEVEL AND SLOPING BACKFILL

Neubaur · Sohn, Engineers; Washington, D.C.

DIMENSIONS AND REINFORCEMENT

WALL	H	B	T	A	VERTICAL RODS IN THE WALL	HORIZONTAL RODS IN FOOTING
8 in. thickness	3'-4''	2'-4''	9''	8''	3/8'' @ 32''	3/8'' @ 27''
	4'-0''	2'-9''	9''	10''	1/2'' @ 32''	3/8'' @ 27''
	4'-8''	3'-3''	10''	12''	5/8'' @ 32''	3/8'' @ 27''
	5'-4''	3'-8''	10''	14''	1/2'' @ 16''	1/2'' @ 30''
	6'-0''	4'-2''	12''	15''	3/4'' @ 24''	1/2'' @ 25''

NOTE

These dimensions and reinforcement are for level backfill. Consult structural engineer for walls over 6 ft high, sloping fill, or vehicular loads.

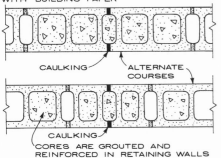

LINE ONE SIDE OF CORE WITH BUILDING PAPER

CAULKING — ALTERNATE COURSES

CAULKING — CORES ARE GROUTED AND REINFORCED IN RETAINING WALLS

SHEAR-RESISTING CONTROL JOINT

NOTE

Long retaining walls should be broken into panels 20 to 30 ft in length by means of vertical control joints. Joints should be designed to resist shear and other lateral forces while permitting longitudinal movement.

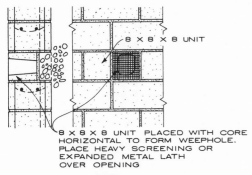

8 X 8 X 8 UNIT

8 X 8 X 8 UNIT PLACED WITH CORE HORIZONTAL TO FORM WEEPHOLE. PLACE HEAVY SCREENING OR EXPANDED METAL LATH OVER OPENING

ALTERNATE WEEPHOLE DETAIL

NOTE

Four inch diameter weepholes located at 5 to 10 ft spacing along the base of the wall should be sufficient. Place about 1 cu ft of gravel or crushed stone around the intake of each weephole.

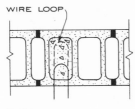

WIRE LOOP

PLAN VERTICAL ROD

NOTE

Place wire loop extending into core in mortar joints as wall is laid up. Loosen before mortar sets. After inserting bar, pull wire loop and bar to proper position and secure wire by tying free ends.

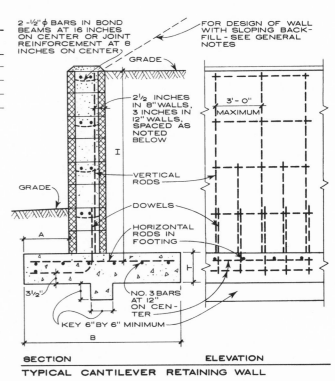

2 - 1/2'' φ BARS IN BOND BEAMS AT 16 INCHES ON CENTER OR JOINT REINFORCEMENT AT 8 INCHES ON CENTER

FOR DESIGN OF WALL WITH SLOPING BACK-FILL - SEE GENERAL NOTES

GRADE

2 1/2 INCHES IN 8'' WALLS, 3 INCHES IN 12'' WALLS, SPACED AS NOTED BELOW

VERTICAL RODS

GRADE

DOWELS

HORIZONTAL RODS IN FOOTING

3'-0'' MAXIMUM

A

3 1/2''

NO. 3 BARS AT 12'' ON CEN-TER

KEY 6'' BY 6'' MINIMUM

B

SECTION   **ELEVATION**

TYPICAL CANTILEVER RETAINING WALL

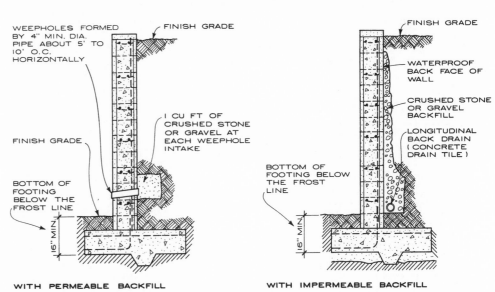

WEEPHOLES FORMED BY 4'' MIN. DIA. PIPE ABOUT 5' TO 10' O.C. HORIZONTALLY

FINISH GRADE

FINISH GRADE

1 CU FT OF CRUSHED STONE OR GRAVEL AT EACH WEEPHOLE INTAKE

BOTTOM OF FOOTING BELOW THE FROST LINE

16'' MIN.

WITH PERMEABLE BACKFILL

FINISH GRADE

WATERPROOF BACK FACE OF WALL

CRUSHED STONE OR GRAVEL BACKFILL

LONGITUDINAL BACK DRAIN (CONCRETE DRAIN TILE)

BOTTOM OF FOOTING BELOW THE FROST LINE

16'' MIN.

WITH IMPERMEABLE BACKFILL

BACKFILLING PROCEDURES AND DRAINAGE

GENERAL NOTES

1. Concrete for footings should be mixed in the following approximate proportions: 1 part portland cement, 2 3/4 parts sand, and 4 parts gravel. Gravel should be well graded and not exceed 1 1/2 in. in size. Amount of water used for each bag of cement should not exceed 5 1/2 gal unless the sand is very dry.
2. Use fine grout where grout space is less than 3 in. in least dimension. Use coarse grout where the least dimension of the grout space is 3 in. or more.
3. Steel reinforcement should be clean, free from harmful rust, and in compliance with applicable ASTM standards for deformed bars and steel wire.
4. Alternate vertical bars may be stopped at the midheight of the wall. Vertical reinforcement is usually secured in place after the masonry work has been completed and before grouting.

5. Designs herein are based on an assumed soil weight (vertical pressure) of 100 pcf. Horizontal pressure is based on an equivalent fluid weight for the soil of 45 pcf.
6. Walls shown are designed with a safety factor against overturning of not less than 2 and a safety factor against horizontal sliding of not less than 1.5. Computations in the table for wall heights are based on level backfill. One method of providing for additional loads due to sloping backfill or surface loads is to consider them as an additional depth of soil, that is, an extra load of 300 psf can be treated as 3 ft of extra soil weighing 100 psf.
7. Top of masonry retaining walls should be capped or otherwise protected to prevent the entry of water into unfilled hollow cells and spaces. If bond beams are used, steel is placed in the beams as the wall is constructed. If desired, horizontal

joint reinforcement may be placed in each joint (8 in. o.c.) and the bond beams omitted.
8. Allow 24 hr for masonry to set before grouting. Pour grout in 4 ft layers, 1 hr between each pour. Break long walls into panels of 20 to 30 ft in length with vertical control joints. Allow 7 days for finished wall to set before backfilling. Prevent water from accumulating behind wall by means of 4 in. diameter weepholes at a 5 to 10 ft spacing (with screen and graded stone) or by a continuous drain with felt covered open joints in combination with waterproofing.
9. Where backfill exceeds 6 ft in height, provide a key under the base of the footing to resist the tendency of the wall to slide horizontally.
10. Heavy equipment used in backfilling should not approach closer to the top of the wall than a distance equal to the height of the wall.

Stephen J. Zipp, AIA; Wilkes and Faulkner Associates; Washington, D.C.

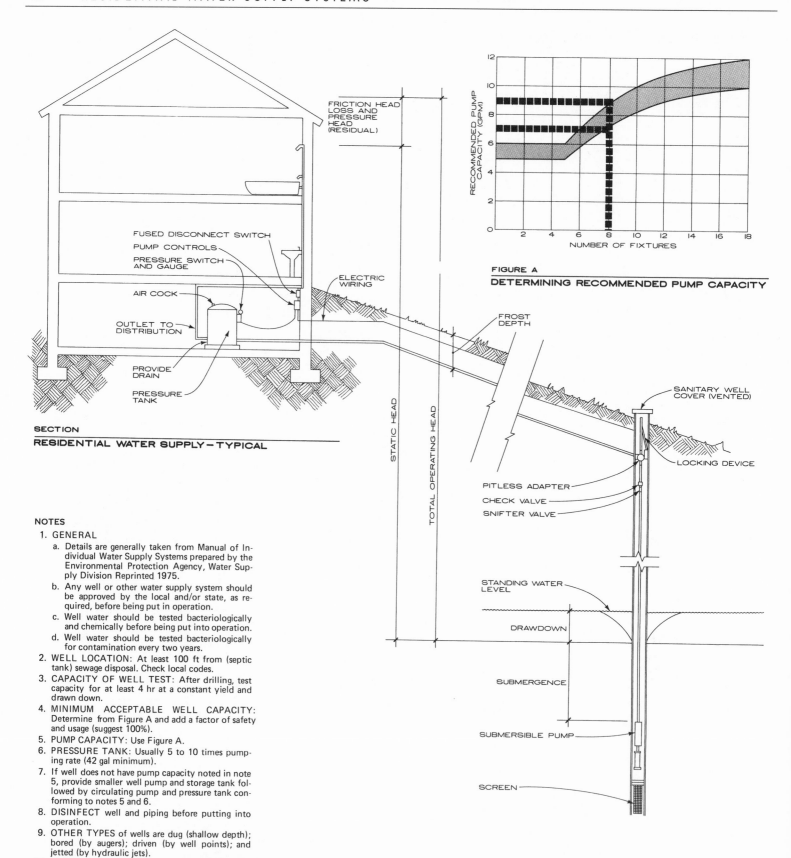

FRICTION HEAD
LOSS AND
PRESSURE
HEAD
(RESIDUAL)

FUSED DISCONNECT SWITCH
PUMP CONTROLS
PRESSURE SWITCH
AND GAUGE
AIR COCK
OUTLET TO
DISTRIBUTION
ELECTRIC
WIRING
PROVIDE
DRAIN
PRESSURE
TANK

SECTION

RESIDENTIAL WATER SUPPLY — TYPICAL

FIGURE A

DETERMINING RECOMMENDED PUMP CAPACITY

RECOMMENDED PUMP CAPACITY (GPM)

NUMBER OF FIXTURES

FROST
DEPTH

STATIC HEAD

TOTAL OPERATING HEAD

SANITARY WELL
COVER (VENTED)

LOCKING DEVICE

PITLESS ADAPTER
CHECK VALVE
SNIFTER VALVE

STANDING WATER
LEVEL

DRAWDOWN

SUBMERGENCE

SUBMERSIBLE PUMP

SCREEN

NOTES

1. GENERAL
   a. Details are generally taken from Manual of Individual Water Supply Systems prepared by the Environmental Protection Agency, Water Supply Division Reprinted 1975.
   b. Any well or other water supply system should be approved by the local and/or state, as required, before being put in operation.
   c. Well water should be tested bacteriologically and chemically before being put into operation.
   d. Well water should be tested bacteriologically for contamination every two years.
2. WELL LOCATION: At least 100 ft from (septic tank) sewage disposal. Check local codes.
3. CAPACITY OF WELL TEST: After drilling, test capacity for at least 4 hr at a constant yield and drawn down.
4. MINIMUM ACCEPTABLE WELL CAPACITY: Determine from Figure A and add a factor of safety and usage (suggest 100%).
5. PUMP CAPACITY: Use Figure A.
6. PRESSURE TANK: Usually 5 to 10 times pumping rate (42 gal minimum).
7. If well does not have pump capacity noted in note 5, provide smaller well pump and storage tank followed by circulating pump and pressure tank conforming to notes 5 and 6.
8. DISINFECT well and piping before putting into operation.
9. OTHER TYPES of wells are dug (shallow depth); bored (by augers); driven (by well points); and jetted (by hydraulic jets).
10. OTHER TYPES OF WELL PUMPING SYSTEMS:
    a. Centrifugal pump with motor above ground and below water level in well.
    b. Jet pump with pump and motor above ground.
    c. Direct or reciprocating pumps in the well with motor above ground.

Jack L. Staunton, P.E.; Staunton and Freeman, Consulting Engineers; New York, New York

FIGURE B

DRILLED WELL — SECTION

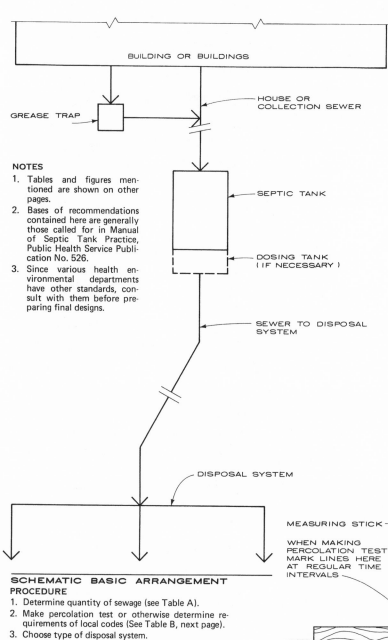

NOTES

1. Tables and figures mentioned are shown on other pages.
2. Bases of recommendations contained here are generally those called for in Manual of Septic Tank Practice, Public Health Service Publication No. 526.
3. Since various health environmental departments have other standards, consult with them before preparing final designs.

SCHEMATIC BASIC ARRANGEMENT

PROCEDURE

1. Determine quantity of sewage (see Table A).
2. Make percolation test or otherwise determine requirements of local codes (See Table B, next page).
3. Choose type of disposal system.
4. Layout disposal systems.
5. Design septic tank.
6. Use dosing tank, diversion box and/or trap where necessary.

MATERIALS

Piping may be salt glazed clay bell and spigot, tile pipe, asbestos cement or concrete bell and spigot. If near well or any other water supply, use cast iron.

Where trees or shrubs may cause root stoppage in clay pipe, use cast iron.

Use bituminous joints or rubber ring type joints for clay, concrete, or asbestos cement pipe; use lead for cast iron pipe.

SIZE

4 in. diameter for small installations; 6 in. is better in all cases.

GRADE

In northern latitudes, start sewer approximately 3 ft below grade. In southern latitudes, sewer may start just below grade.

PITCH

Pitch 4 in. sewer 1/4 in./ft minimum. Pitch 6 in. sewer 1/8 in./ft minimum.

Jack L. Staunton, P.E.; Staunton and Freeman Consulting Engineers; New York, New York

TABLE A   QUANTITIES OF SEWAGE FLOWS

TYPE OF ESTABLISHMENT	GALLONS PER PERSON PER DAY
Airports (per passenger)	5
Bathhouses and swimming pools	10
Camps	
Campground with central comfort stations	35
Day camps (no meals served)	15
Resort camp (night and day) with limited plumbing	50
Cottages and small dwelling with seasonal occupancy[1]	50
Country clubs (per resident member)	100
Country clubs (per nonresident member present)	25
Dwellings	
Boarding houses[1]	50
Multiple family dwellings (apartments)	60
Single family dwellings[1]	75
Factories (gallons per person, per shift, exclusive of industry wastes)	35
Hospitals (per bed space)	250+
Hotels with private baths (2 persons per room)[2]	60
Institutions other than hospitals (per bed space)	125
Laundries, self-service (gallons per wash, i.e., per customer)	50
Mobile home parks (per space)	250
Picnic parks (toilet wastes only, per picnicker)	5
Picnic parks with bathhouses, showers, and flush toilets	10
Restaurants (toilets and kitchen wastes per patron)	10
Restaurants (kitchen wastes per meal served)	3
Restaurants (additional for bars and cocktail lounges)	2
Schools	
Boarding	100
Day, with gyms, cafeteria, and showers	25
Service stations (per vehicle served)	10
Theaters	
Movie (per auditorium seat)	5
Drive-in (per car space)	5
Travel trailer parks with individual water and sewer hookups	100
Workers	
Day, at schools and offices (per shift)	15

NOTES

1. Two people per bedroom.
2. Use also for motels.

PROCEDURE

First soak hole by filling at least 12 in. over gravel with water and continue to refill with water so that hole is soaked for 24 hr. After 24 hr adjust the depth of water over the gravel to approximately 6 in. Now measure the drop in water level over a 30 min period.

MEASURING STICK

WHEN MAKING PERCOLATION TEST MARK LINES HERE AT REGULAR TIME INTERVALS

BATTER BOARD OR OTHER FIXED REFERENCE POINT

WATER SURFACE

4" OR LARGER DIAMETER (HOLE MAY BE MADE WITH AN AUGER)

THE LOCATION AND ELEVATION OF THIS HOLE ARE APPROXIMATELY THE SAME AS DISPOSAL FIELD

2" LAYER OF GRAVEL

6"

NOTE: THIS TEST IS RECOMMENDED BY THE ENVIRONMENTAL PROTECTION AGENCY. CHECK LOCAL REQUIREMENTS FOR OTHER TEST CONDITIONS.

METHOD OF MAKING PERCOLATION TEST

TABLE B.   ALLOWABLE RATE OF SEWAGE APPLICATION TO A SOIL ABSORPTION SYSTEM

PERCOLATION RATE [TIME (MIN) FOR WATER TO FALL 1 IN.]	MAXIMUM RATE OF SEWAGE APPLICATION (GAL/SQ FT/DAY)[1] FOR ABSORPTION TRENCHES,[2] SEEPAGE BEDS, AND SEEPAGE PITS[3]	PERCOLATION RATE [TIME (MIN) FOR WATER TO FALL 1 IN.]	MAXIMUM RATE OF SEWAGE APPLICATION (GAL/SQ FT/DAY)[1] FOR ABSORPTION TRENCHES,[2] SEEPAGE BEDS, AND SEEPAGE PITS[3]
1 or less	5.0	10	1.6
2	3.5	15	1.3
3	2.9	30[4]	0.9
4	2.5	45[4]	0.8
5	2.2	60[4, 5]	0.6

NOTES

1. Not including effluents from septic tanks that receive wastes from garbage grinders and automatic washing machines.
2. Absorption area is figured as trench bottom area and includes a statistical allowance for vertical sidewall area.
3. Absorption area for seepage pits is effective sidewall area.
4. Over 30 is unsuitable for seepage pits.
5. Over 60 is unsuitable for absorption systems.

If permissible, use sand filtration system. For subsurface sand filters use 1.15 gal/sq ft/day.

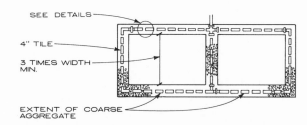

ABSORPTION TRENCH ARRANGEMENT FOR LEVEL GROUND FOR HOUSEHOLD DISPOSAL

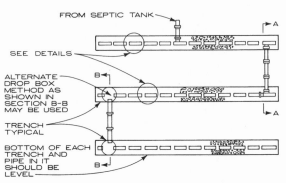

NOTE
INVERT OF THE OVERFLOW PIPE MUST BE AT LEAST 4" LOWER THAN INVERT OF THE SEPTIC TANK OUTLET

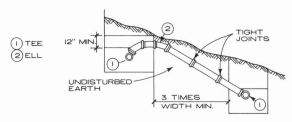

SECTION A-A

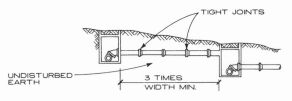

(ALTERNATE CONSTRUCTION)

SECTION B-B

ABSORPTION TRENCH ARRANGEMENT FOR HILLY SITE FOR HOUSEHOLD DISPOSAL

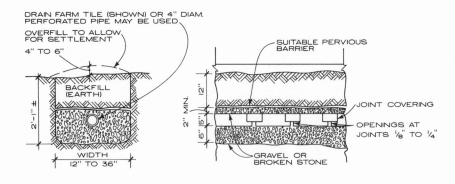

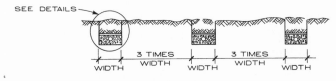

ABSORPTION TRENCH SYSTEM DETAILS

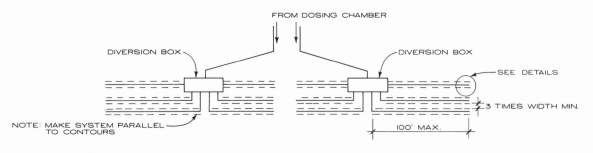

ABSORPTION TRENCH ARRANGEMENT FOR INSTITUTIONAL AND LIGHT COMMERCIAL DISPOSAL

Jack L. Staunton, P. E.; Staunton and Freeman, Consulting Engineers; New York, New York

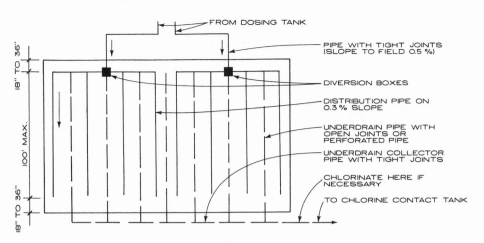

FROM DOSING TANK

PIPE WITH TIGHT JOINTS
(SLOPE TO FIELD 0.5 %)

DIVERSION BOXES

DISTRIBUTION PIPE ON
0.3 % SLOPE

UNDERDRAIN PIPE WITH
OPEN JOINTS OR
PERFORATED PIPE

UNDERDRAIN COLLECTOR
PIPE WITH TIGHT JOINTS

CHLORINATE HERE IF
NECESSARY

TO CHLORINE CONTACT TANK

18" TO 36"

100' MAX.

18" TO 36"

PLAN

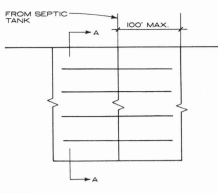

FROM SEPTIC
TANK

100' MAX.

PLAN

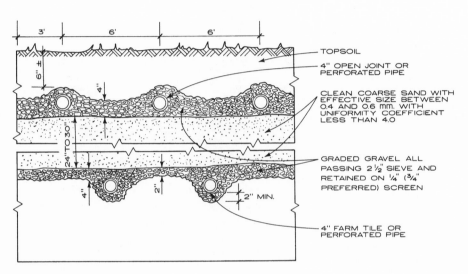

TOPSOIL

4" OPEN JOINT OR
PERFORATED PIPE

CLEAN COARSE SAND WITH
EFFECTIVE SIZE BETWEEN
0.4 AND 0.6 mm. WITH
UNIFORMITY COEFFICIENT
LESS THAN 4.0

GRADED GRAVEL ALL
PASSING 2½" SIEVE AND
RETAINED ON ¼" (¾"
PREFERRED) SCREEN

4" FARM TILE OR
PERFORATED PIPE

SECTIONAL ELEVATION

SUBSURFACE SAND FILTER

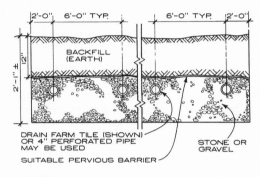

BACKFILL
(EARTH)

2'-0"   6'-0" TYP.   6'-0" TYP.   2'-0"

DRAIN FARM TILE (SHOWN)
OR 4" PERFORATED PIPE
MAY BE USED

SUITABLE PERVIOUS BARRIER

STONE OR
GRAVEL

SECTION A-A

SEEPAGE BED

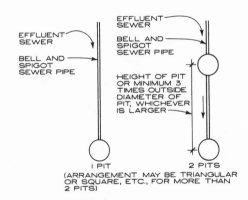

EFFLUENT
SEWER

BELL AND
SPIGOT
SEWER PIPE

EFFLUENT
SEWER

BELL AND
SPIGOT
SEWER PIPE

HEIGHT OF PIT
OR MINIMUM 3
TIMES OUTSIDE
DIAMETER OF
PIT, WHICHEVER
IS LARGER

I PIT

2 PITS
(ARRANGEMENT MAY BE TRIANGULAR
OR SQUARE, ETC., FOR MORE THAN
2 PITS)

ARRANGEMENT

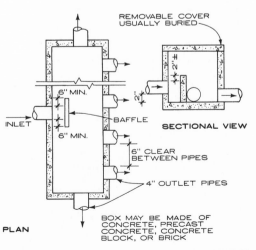

REMOVABLE COVER
USUALLY BURIED

6" MIN.

6" MIN.

INLET

BAFFLE

SECTIONAL VIEW

6" CLEAR
BETWEEN PIPES

4" OUTLET PIPES

BOX MAY BE MADE OF
CONCRETE, PRECAST
CONCRETE, CONCRETE
BLOCK, OR BRICK

PLAN

DIVERSION BOX

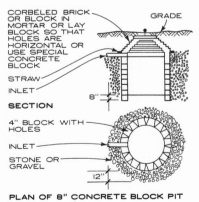

REINFORCED CONCRETE
COVER WITH
LIFTING RING

PRECAST REINF.
CONCRETE

INLET

SLOTS FOR
LEACHING

STONE OR
GRAVEL

GRADE

OUTLET

2'-0"

4" 7'-6" DIAM. 12"
USUALLY   4"

SECTION

CORBELED BRICK
OR BLOCK IN
MORTAR OR LAY
BLOCK SO THAT
HOLES ARE
HORIZONTAL OR
USE SPECIAL
CONCRETE
BLOCK

GRADE

STRAW

INLET

8"

SECTION

4" BLOCK WITH
HOLES

INLET

STONE OR
GRAVEL

12"

PLAN OF 8" CONCRETE BLOCK PIT

SEEPAGE PITS

Jack L. Staunton, P. E.; Staunton and Freeman, Consulting Engineers; New York, New York

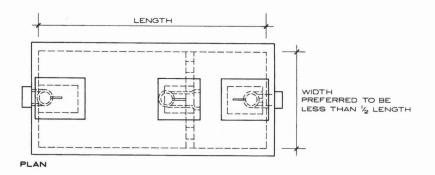

PLAN

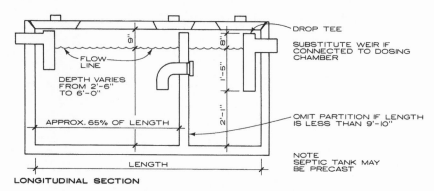

LENGTH

WIDTH PREFERRED TO BE LESS THAN ½ LENGTH

DROP TEE

SUBSTITUTE WEIR IF CONNECTED TO DOSING CHAMBER

FLOW LINE

DEPTH VARIES FROM 2'-6" TO 6'-0"

APPROX. 65% OF LENGTH

OMIT PARTITION IF LENGTH IS LESS THAN 9'-10"

NOTE SEPTIC TANK MAY BE PRECAST

LENGTH

LONGITUDINAL SECTION

SEPTIC TANK

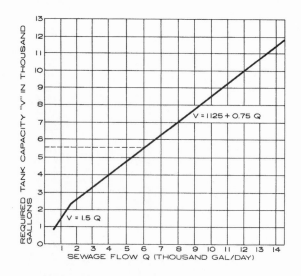

$V = 1125 + 0.75\ Q$

$V = 1.5\ Q$

DETERMINATION OF SEPTIC TANK VOLUME

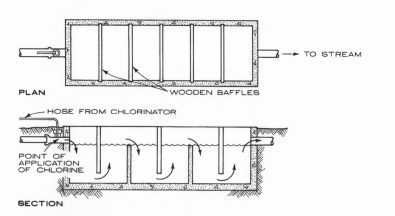

PLAN

WOODEN BAFFLES

TO STREAM

HOSE FROM CHLORINATOR

POINT OF APPLICATION OF CHLORINE

SECTION

CHLORINE CONTACT CHAMBER

Jack L. Staunton, P. E.; Staunton and Freeman, Consulting Engineers; New York, New York

NOTES
• DOSE FROM CHAMBER TO EQUAL ¾ OF FARM TILE OR PERFORATED PIPE IN ONE FIELD
• PIPES MAY BE SUBSTITUTED FOR SIPHONS IF CONDITION DICTATES

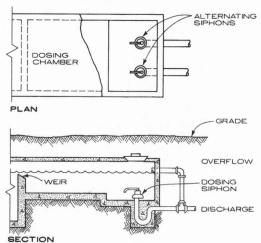

ALTERNATING SIPHONS

DOSING CHAMBER

PLAN

GRADE

OVERFLOW

WEIR

DOSING SIPHON

DISCHARGE

SECTION

DOSING CHAMBER WITH ALTERNATING SIPHONS

NOTE
GREASE TRAPS TO BE USED ONLY IF THEY ARE CLEANED DAILY

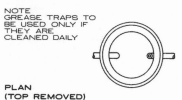

PLAN (TOP REMOVED)

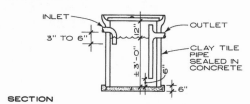

INLET

OUTLET

3" TO 6"

12"

±3'-0"

6"

6"

CLAY TILE PIPE SEALED IN CONCRETE

SECTION

PLAN (TOP REMOVED)

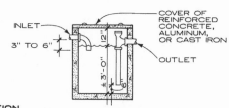

INLET

3" TO 6"

12"

±3'-0"

COVER OF REINFORCED CONCRETE, ALUMINUM, OR CAST IRON

OUTLET

SECTION CONCRETE BOX

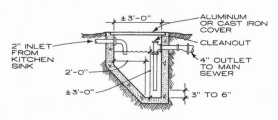

±3'-0"

2" INLET FROM KITCHEN SINK

2'-0"

±3'-0"

ALUMINUM OR CAST IRON COVER

CLEANOUT

4" OUTLET TO MAIN SEWER

3" TO 6"

TYPICAL GREASE TRAPS

EXTERIOR STEPS

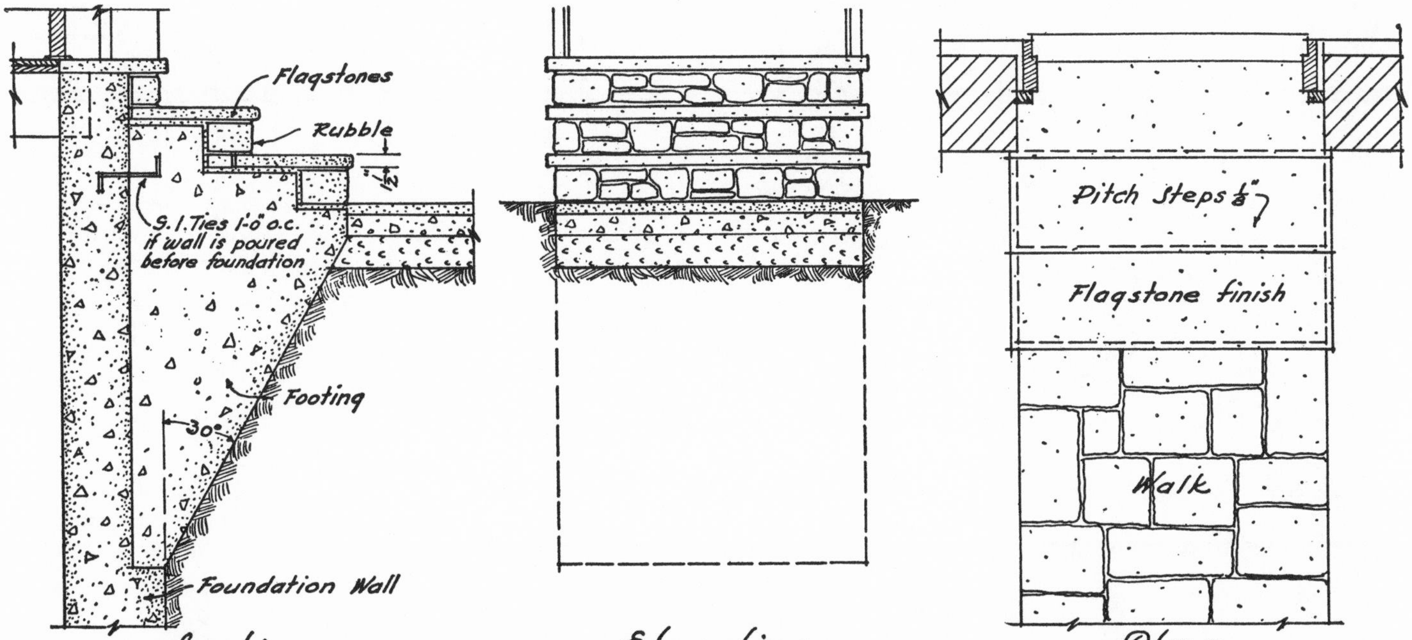
Flagstones
Rubble
½"
S.I. Ties 1'-0" o.c. if wall is poured before foundation
Footing
30°
Foundation Wall
Pitch Steps ⅛"
Flagstone finish
Walk

Section Elevation Plan

SLOPE-BACK FOUNDATION for ENTRANCE STEPS

This type of footing will stay in place, but becomes uneconomical when there are more than three or four steps.
½"=1'-0"

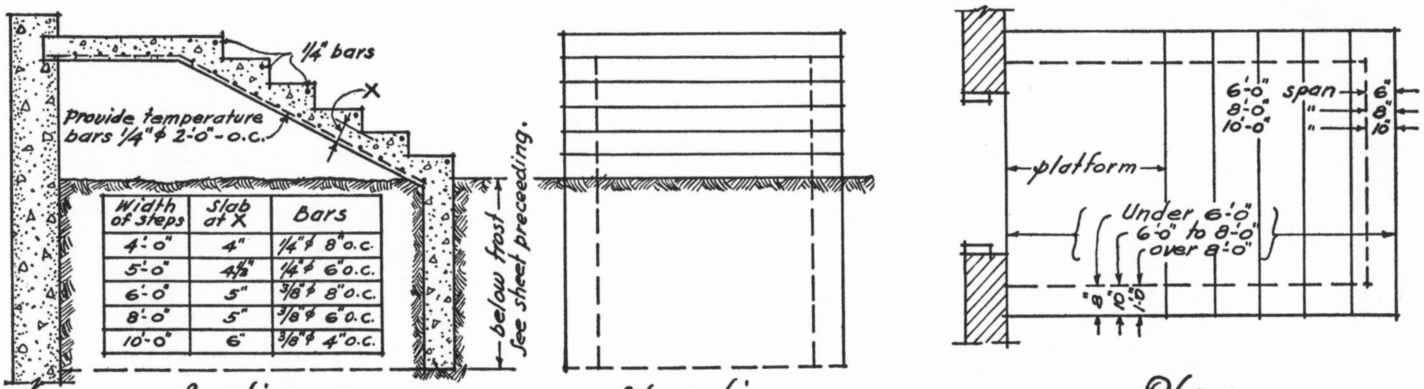
¼" bars
X
Provide temperature bars ¼"ϕ 2'-0" o.c.
below frost
See sheet preceeding.
6'-0" span 6"
8'-0" " 8"
10'-0" " 10"
platform
Under 6'-0"
6'-0" to 8'-0"
over 8'-0"
8" 10" 1'-0"

Width of steps	Slab at X	Bars
4'-0"	4"	¼"ϕ 8"o.c.
5'-0"	4½"	¼"ϕ 6"o.c.
6'-0"	5"	⅜"ϕ 8"o.c.
8'-0"	5"	⅜"ϕ 6"o.c.
10'-0"	6"	⅜"ϕ 4"o.c.

Section Elevation Plan

SELF SUPPORTING SLAB FOR STEPS AND PLATFORM

DIAGRAMS of CONCRETE STEPS for RESIDENTIAL WORK

Finish is not indicated but slabs will take slate, flag or other finish.
¼"=1'-0"

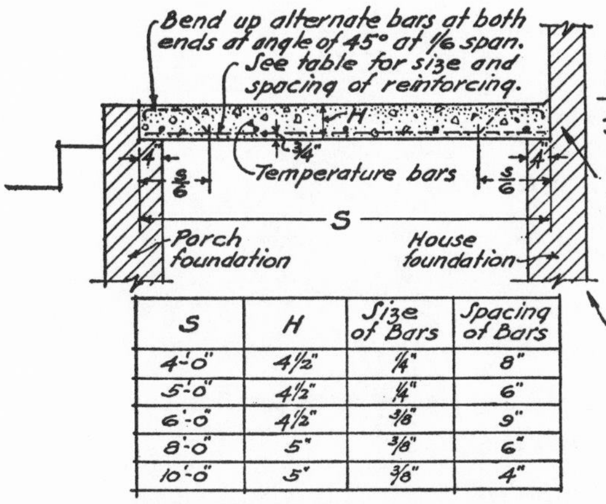
Bend up alternate bars at both ends at angle of 45° at ⅙ span. See table for size and spacing of reinforcing.
H
¾"
4"
S/6
Temperature bars
S
Porch foundation
House foundation

S	H	Size of Bars	Spacing of Bars
4'-0"	4½"	¼"	8"
5'-0"	4½"	¼"	6"
6'-0"	4½"	⅜"	9"
8'-0"	5"	⅜"	6"
10'-0"	5"	⅜"	4"

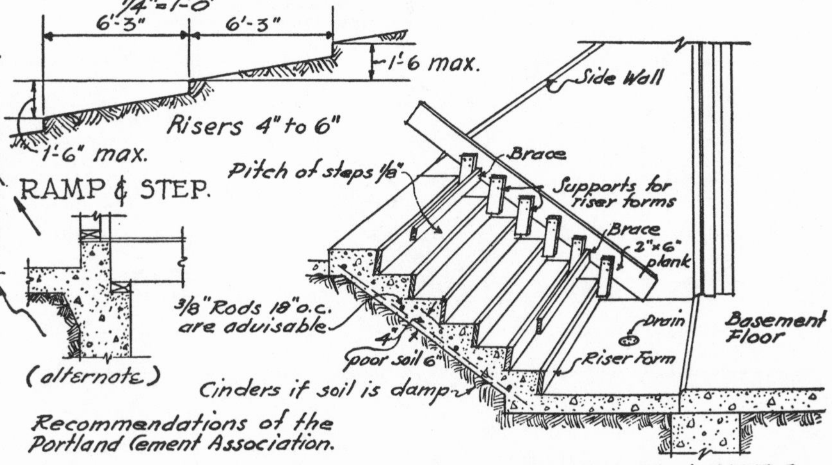
6'-3"
6'-3"
1'-6 max.
Risers 4" to 6"
1'-6" max.
RAMP & STEP.
(alternate)
Side Wall
Brace
Pitch of steps ⅛"
Supports for riser forms
Brace 2"x6" plank
⅜" Rods 18" o.c. are advisable
4"
Poor soil 6"
Drain
Basement Floor
Riser Form
Cinders if soil is damp

Recommendations of the Portland Cement Association.

REINFORCED CONCRETE PORCH FLOOR CONCRETE BASEMENT STEPS

STEPS ETC; CONCRETE, FLAGSTONE and BLUESTONE

Calculations checked by Elwyn E. Seelye, Structural Engineer.

BRICK PAVING

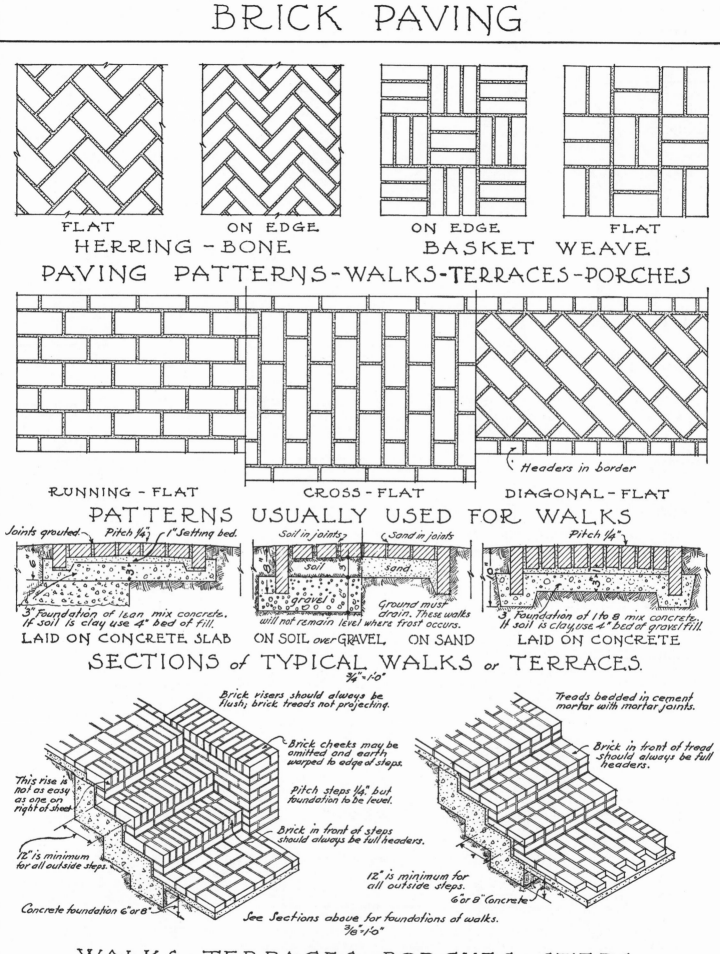

FLAT · ON EDGE · ON EDGE · FLAT

HERRING - BONE · BASKET WEAVE

PAVING PATTERNS - WALKS - TERRACES - PORCHES

RUNNING - FLAT · CROSS - FLAT · DIAGONAL - FLAT

Headers in border

PATTERNS USUALLY USED FOR WALKS

Joints grouted. · Pitch 1/4" · 1" Setting bed. · Soil in joints · Sand in joints · Pitch 1/4"

soil · sand

gravel

3" Foundation of lean mix concrete. If soil is clay use 4" bed of fill. · Ground must drain. These walks will not remain level where frost occurs. · 3 Foundation of 1 to 8 mix concrete. If soil is clay, use 4" bed of gravel fill.

LAID ON CONCRETE SLAB · ON SOIL over GRAVEL · ON SAND · LAID ON CONCRETE

SECTIONS of TYPICAL WALKS or TERRACES.

3/4"=1'-0"

Brick risers should always be flush; brick treads not projecting. · Treads bedded in cement mortar with mortar joints.

Brick cheeks may be omitted and earth warped to edge of steps. · Brick in front of tread should always be full headers.

This rise is not as easy as one on right of sheet · Pitch steps 1/4" but foundation to be level.

12" is minimum for all outside steps. · Brick in front of steps should always be full headers.

12" is minimum for all outside steps. · 6"or 8" Concrete

Concrete foundation 6"or 8" · See Sections above for foundations of walks. · 3/8"=1'-0"

WALKS - TERRACES - PORCHES - STEPS.
Recommendations of the Common Brick Manufacturers Association of America.

PAVING ~ WALKS, PATHS, PORCHES & TERRACES

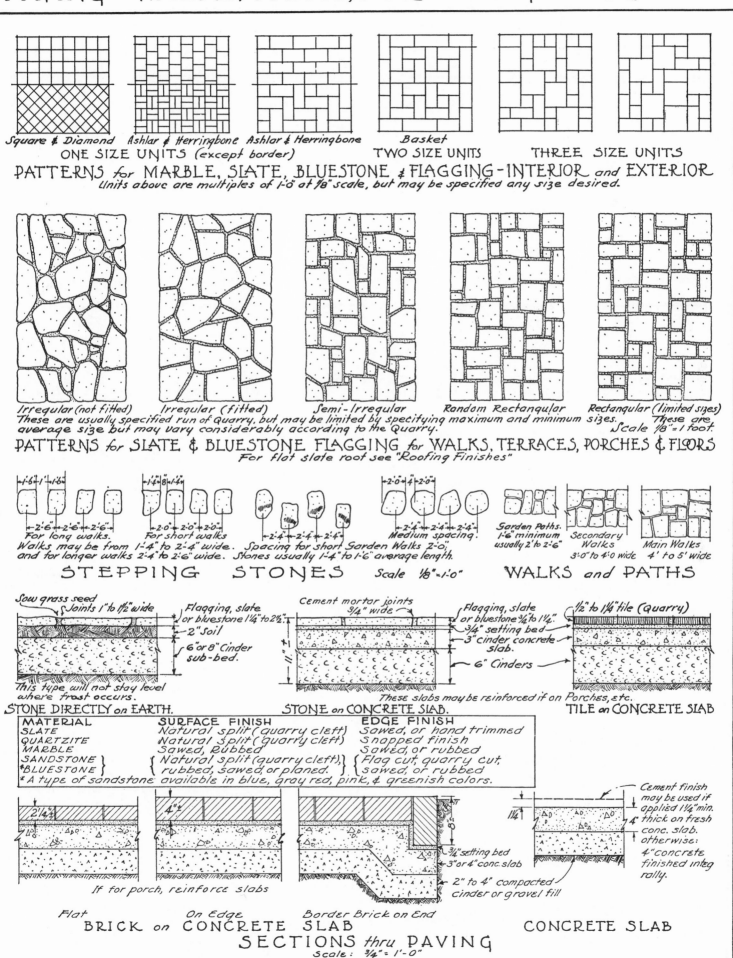

Square & Diamond   Ashlar & Herringbone   Ashlar & Herringbone   Basket

ONE SIZE UNITS (except border)   TWO SIZE UNITS   THREE SIZE UNITS

PATTERNS for MARBLE, SLATE, BLUESTONE & FLAGGING~INTERIOR and EXTERIOR
Units above are multiples of 1'-0" at 1/8" scale, but may be specified any size desired.

Irregular (not fitted)   Irregular (fitted)   Semi-Irregular   Random Rectangular   Rectangular (limited sizes)

These are usually specified run of Quarry, but may be limited by specifying maximum and minimum sizes.   These are
average size but may vary considerably according to the Quarry.   Scale 1/8" = 1 foot.

PATTERNS for SLATE & BLUESTONE FLAGGING for WALKS, TERRACES, PORCHES & FLOORS
For flat slate roof see "Roofing Finishes"

For long walks   For short walks   Spacing for short Garden Walks 2'-0".   Medium spacing.   Garden Paths.   Secondary   Main Walks
Walks may be from 1'-4" to 2'-4" wide,   Stones usually 1'-4" to 1'-6" average length.   1'-6" minimum   Walks   4' to 5' wide
and for longer walks 2'-4" to 2'-6" wide.   usually 2' to 2'-6"   3'-0" to 4'-0" wide

STEPPING STONES   Scale 1/8"=1'-0"   WALKS and PATHS

Sow grass seed   Flagging, slate   Cement mortar joints   Flagging, slate   1/2" to 1 1/4" tile (Quarry)
Joints 1" to 1 1/2" wide   or bluestone 1 1/4" to 2 1/2".   3/4" wide   or bluestone 3/4" to 1 1/4".
2" Soil   3/4" setting bed   3/4" setting bed
6" or 8" Cinder   Flagging, slate   3" cinder concrete   3" cinder concrete
sub-bed.   slab.   slab.
6" Cinders

This type will not stay level   These slabs may be reinforced if on Porches, etc.
where frost occurs.

STONE DIRECTLY on EARTH.   STONE on CONCRETE SLAB.   TILE on CONCRETE SLAB

MATERIAL	SURFACE FINISH	EDGE FINISH
SLATE	Natural split (quarry cleft)	Sawed, or hand trimmed
QUARTZITE	Natural split (quarry cleft)	Snapped finish
MARBLE	Sawed, Rubbed	Sawed, or rubbed
SANDSTONE }	{ Natural split (quarry cleft),	{ Flag cut, quarry cut,
*BLUESTONE }	rubbed, sawed, or planed. }	sawed, or rubbed

* A type of sandstone available in blue, gray, red, pink, & greenish colors.

Cement finish
may be used if
applied 1 1/4" min.
thick on fresh
conc. slab.
otherwise:
3/4" setting bed   4" concrete
3" or 4" conc. slab   finished integ-
2" to 4" compacted   rally.
cinder or gravel fill

If for porch, reinforce slabs

Flat   On Edge   Border Brick on End

BRICK on CONCRETE SLAB   CONCRETE SLAB

SECTIONS thru PAVING
Scale: 3/4" = 1'-0"

ROADS & PAVING

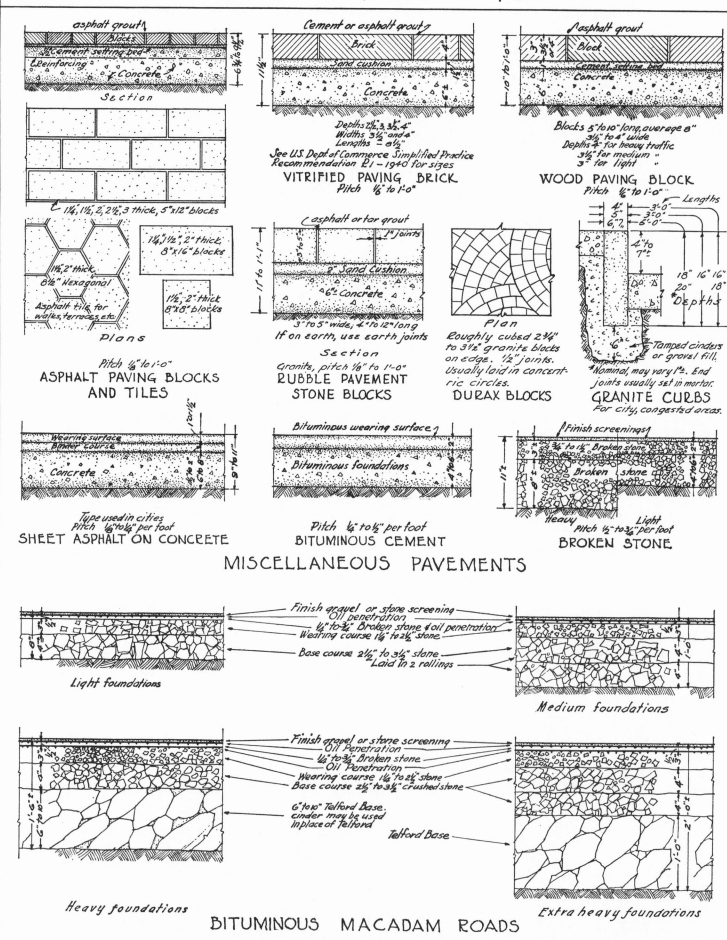

asphalt grout
Blocks
½ Cement setting bed
Reinforcing
Concrete
Section

1¼, 1½, 2, 2½, 3 thick, 5"x12" blocks

1¼,1½, 2" thick
8"x16" blocks

1½, 2" thick
8"x8" blocks

1½, 2" thick
6½" Hexagonal

Asphalt tile for walks, terraces, etc.

Plans

Pitch ⅛" to 1'-0"
ASPHALT PAVING BLOCKS
AND TILES

Cement or asphalt grout
Brick
Sand cushion
Concrete

Depths 2½, 3, 3½, 4"
Widths 3½" and 4"
Lengths – 8½"
See U.S. Dept. of Commerce Simplified Practice
Recommendation R.1 – 1940 for sizes
VITRIFIED PAVING BRICK
Pitch ⅛" to 1'-0"

asphalt or tar grout
1" joints
2" Sand Cushion
6" Concrete

3" to 5" wide, 4" to 12" long
If on earth, use earth joints
Section
Granite, pitch ⅛" to 1'-0"
RUBBLE PAVEMENT
STONE BLOCKS

Plan
Roughly cubed 2¾"
to 3½" granite blocks
on edge. ½" joints.
Usually laid in concentric circles.
DURAX BLOCKS

asphalt grout
Block
Cement setting bed
Concrete

Blocks 5" to 10" long, average 8"
3½" to 4" wide
Depths 4" for heavy traffic
3½" for medium "
3" for light "
WOOD PAVING BLOCK
Pitch ⅛" to 1'-0"

Lengths
4"   3'-0"
5"   4'-0"
6", 7"   5'-0"
4" to 7"±
18" 16" 16"
20" 18"
Depths
Tamped cinders
or gravel fill.
*Nominal, may vary 1"±. End
joints usually set in mortar.
GRANITE CURBS
For city, congested areas.

Wearing surface
Binder course
Concrete

Type used in cities
Pitch ⅛" to ¼" per foot
SHEET ASPHALT ON CONCRETE

Bituminous wearing surface
Bituminous foundations

Pitch ¼" to ½" per foot
BITUMINOUS CEMENT

Finish screenings
¾ to 1½" Broken stone
Broken stone
Heavy   Light
Pitch ½" to ¾" per foot
BROKEN STONE

MISCELLANEOUS PAVEMENTS

Finish gravel or stone screening
Oil penetration
¼" to ¾" Broken stone & oil penetration
Wearing course 1¼" to 2½" stone
Base course 2½" to 3½" stone
Laid in 2 rollings

Light foundations

Medium foundations

Finish gravel or stone screening
Oil Penetration
¼" to ¾" Broken stone
Oil Penetration
Wearing course 1¼" to 2½" stone
Base course 2½" to 3½" crushed stone
6" to 10" Telford Base.
cinder may be used
in place of Telford
Telford Base

Heavy foundations

Extra heavy foundations

BITUMINOUS MACADAM ROADS

NOTE: Small car dimensions should be used only in lots designated for small cars or with entrance controls that admit only small cars. Placing small car stalls into a standard car layout is not recommended. Standard car parking dimensions will accommodate all normal passenger vehicles. Large car parking dimensions make parking easier and faster and are recommended for luxury, a high turnover, and use by the elderly. When the parking angle is 60° or less, it may be necessary to add 3 to 6 ft to the bay width to provide aisle space for pedestrians walking to and from their parked cars. Local zoning laws should be reviewed before proceeding.

RECOMMENDED RANGE OF STALL WIDTHS (SW)

WIDTH (ft) — 8 — 9 — 10 — 11 — 12

- Small car use
- All day parker use
- Standard car use
- Luxury and elderly use
- Supermarket and camper use
- Handicapped use*

*Minimum requirements = 1 or 2 per 100 stalls or as specified by local, state, or federal law; place convenient to destination.

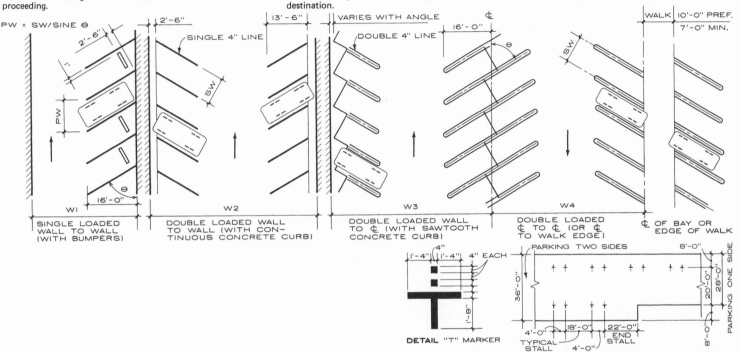

$PW = SW/SINE \theta$

SINGLE LOADED WALL TO WALL (WITH BUMPERS) — W1

DOUBLE LOADED WALL TO WALL (WITH CONTINUOUS CONCRETE CURB) — W2

DOUBLE LOADED WALL TO ₵ (WITH SAWTOOTH CONCRETE CURB) — W3

DOUBLE LOADED ₵ TO ₵ (OR ₵ TO WALK EDGE) — W4

₵ OF BAY OR EDGE OF WALK

DETAIL "T" MARKER

PARALLEL PARKING STALLS AND "T" MARKER DETAIL

PARKING DIMENSIONS IN FEET AND INCHES

	SW	W	45°	50°	55°	60°	65°	70°	75°	80°	85°	90°
Group I: small cars	8'-0"	1	25'-9"	26'-6"	27'-2"	29'-4"	31'-9"	34'-0"	36'-2"	38'-2"	40'-0"	41'-9"
		2	40'-10"	42'-0"	43'-1"	45'-8"	48'-2"	50'-6"	52'-7"	54'-4"	55'-11"	57'-2"
		3	38'-9"	40'-2"	41'-5"	44'-2"	47'-0"	49'-6"	51'-10"	53'-10"	55'-8"	57'-2"
		4	36'-8"	38'-3"	39'-9"	42'-9"	45'-9"	48'-6"	51'-1"	53'-4"	55'-5"	57'-2"
Group II: standard cars	8'-6"	1	32'-0"	32'-11"	34'-2"	36'-2"	38'-5"	41'-0"	43'-6"	45'-6"	46'-11"	48'-0"
		2	49'-10"	51'-9"	53'-10"	56'-0"	58'-4"	60'-2"	62'-0"	63'-6"	64'-9"	66'-0"
		3	47'-8"	49'-4"	51'-6"	54'-0"	56'-6"	59'-0"	61'-2"	63'-0"	64'-6"	66'-0"
		4	45'-2"	46'-10"	49'-0"	51'-8"	54'-6"	57'-10"	60'-0"	62'-6"	64'-3"	66'-0"
	9'-0"	1	32'-0"	32'-9"	34'-0"	35'-4"	37'-6"	39'-8"	42'-0"	44'-4"	46'-2"	48'-0"
		2	49'-4"	51'-0"	53'-2"	55'-6"	57'-10"	60'-0"	61'-10"	63'-4"	64'-9"	66'-0"
		3	46'-4"	48'-10"	51'-4"	53'-10"	56'-0"	58'-8"	61'-0"	63'-0"	64'-6"	66'-0"
		4	44'-8"	46'-6"	49'-0"	51'-6"	54'-0"	57'-0"	59'-8"	62'-0"	64'-2"	66'-0"
	9'-6"	1	32'-0"	32'-8"	34'-0"	35'-0"	36'-10"	38'-10"	41'-6"	43'-8"	46'-0"	48'-0"
		2	49'-2"	50'-6"	51'-10"	53'-6"	55'-4"	58'-0"	60'-6"	62'-8"	64'-6"	65'-11"
		3	47'-0"	48'-2"	49'-10"	51'-6"	53'-11"	57'-0"	59'-8"	62'-0"	64'-3"	65'-11"
		4	44'-8"	45'-10"	47'-6"	49'-10"	52'-6"	55'-9"	58'-9"	61'-6"	63'-10"	65'-11"
Group III: large cars	9'-0"	1	32'-7"	33'-0"	34'-0"	35'-11"	38'-3"	40'-11"	43'-6"	45'-5"	46'-9"	48'-0"
		2	50'-2"	51'-2"	53'-3"	55'-4"	58'-0"	60'-4"	62'-9"	64'-3"	65'-5"	66'-0"
		3	47'-9"	49'-1"	52'-3"	53'-8"	56'-2"	59'-2"	61'-11"	63'-9"	65'-2"	66'-0"
		4	45'-5"	46'-11"	49'-0"	51'-8"	54'-9"	58'-0"	61'-0"	63'-2"	64'-10"	66'-0"
	9'-6"	1	32'-4"	32'-8"	33'-10"	34'-11"	37'-2"	39'-11"	42'-5"	45'-0"	46'-6"	48'-0"
		2	49'-11"	50'-11"	52'-2"	54'-0"	56'-6"	59'-3"	61'-9"	63'-4"	64'-8"	66'-0"
		3	47'-7"	48'-9"	50'-2"	52'-4"	55'-1"	58'-4"	60'-11"	62'-10"	64'-6"	66'-0"
		4	45'-3"	46'-8"	48'-5"	50'-8"	53'-8"	57'-0"	59'-10"	62'-2"	64'-1"	66'-0"
	10'-0"	1	32'-4"	32'-8"	33'-10"	34'-11"	37'-2"	39'-11"	42'-5"	45'-0"	46'-6"	48'-0"
		2	49'-11"	50'-11"	52'-2"	54'-0"	56'-6"	59'-3"	61'-9"	63'-4"	64'-8"	66'-0"
		3	47'-7"	48'-9"	50'-2"	52'-4"	55'-1"	58'-4"	60'-11"	62'-10"	64'-6"	66'-0"
		4	45'-3"	46'-8"	48'-5"	50'-8"	53'-8"	57'-0"	59'-10"	62'-2"	64'-1"	66'-0"

θ ANGLE OF PARK

NOTE: θ angles greater than 70° have aisle widths wide enough for two-way travel.

William T. Mahan, AIA; Santa Barbara, California

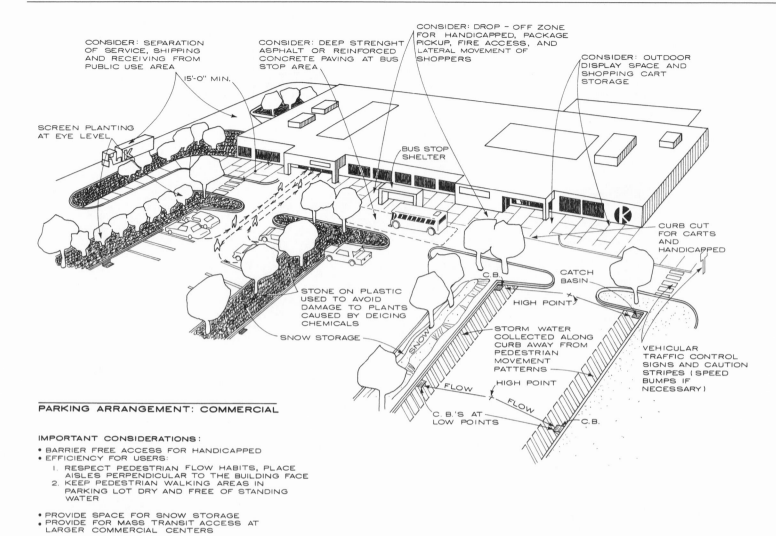

CONSIDER: SEPARATION OF SERVICE, SHIPPING AND RECEIVING FROM PUBLIC USE AREA

15'-0" MIN.

SCREEN PLANTING AT EYE LEVEL

CONSIDER: DEEP STRENGTH ASPHALT OR REINFORCED CONCRETE PAVING AT BUS STOP AREA

CONSIDER: DROP - OFF ZONE FOR HANDICAPPED, PACKAGE PICKUP, FIRE ACCESS, AND LATERAL MOVEMENT OF SHOPPERS

CONSIDER: OUTDOOR DISPLAY SPACE AND SHOPPING CART STORAGE

BUS STOP SHELTER

CURB CUT FOR CARTS AND HANDICAPPED

C.B.

CATCH BASIN

HIGH POINT

STONE ON PLASTIC USED TO AVOID DAMAGE TO PLANTS CAUSED BY DEICING CHEMICALS

SNOW STORAGE

SNOW

STORM WATER COLLECTED ALONG CURB AWAY FROM PEDESTRIAN MOVEMENT PATTERNS

HIGH POINT

FLOW

FLOW

C.B.'S AT LOW POINTS

C.B.

VEHICULAR TRAFFIC CONTROL SIGNS AND CAUTION STRIPES (SPEED BUMPS IF NECESSARY)

PARKING ARRANGEMENT: COMMERCIAL

IMPORTANT CONSIDERATIONS:

• BARRIER FREE ACCESS FOR HANDICAPPED
• EFFICIENCY FOR USERS:
  1. RESPECT PEDESTRIAN FLOW HABITS, PLACE AISLES PERPENDICULAR TO THE BUILDING FACE
  2. KEEP PEDESTRIAN WALKING AREAS IN PARKING LOT DRY AND FREE OF STANDING WATER

• PROVIDE SPACE FOR SNOW STORAGE
• PROVIDE FOR MASS TRANSIT ACCESS AT LARGER COMMERCIAL CENTERS

PLANTING CONSIDERATIONS

The distribution and placement of plants in parking areas can help to relieve the visually overwhelming scale of large parking lots. To maximize the impact of landscape materials, the screening capabilities of the plants must be considered. High branching canopy trees do not create a visual screen at eye level. When the landscaped area is concentrated in islands large enough to accommodate a diversified mixture of canopy and flowering trees, evergreen trees, and shrubs, visual screening via plants is much more effective. Planting low branching, densely foliated trees and shrubs can soften the visual impact of large parking areas. Consider the use of evergreens and avoid plants that drop fruit or sap.

DESIGN CONSIDERATIONS

While efficiency (number of spaces per gross acres) is the major practical consideration in the development of parking areas, several other important design questions exist. Barrier free design is mandatory in most communities. Parking spaces for the handicapped should be designated near building entrances. Curb cuts for wheelchairs should be provided at entrances. The lots should not only be efficient in terms of parking spaces provided, but should also allow maximum efficiency for pedestrians once they leave their vehicles.

Pedestrians habitually walk in the aisles behind parked vehicles. This should be recognized in the orientation of the aisles to building entrances. When aisles are perpendicular to the building face, pedestrians can walk to and from the building without squeezing between parked cars with carts and packages. Pedestrian movement areas should be graded to avoid creating standing water in the paths of pedestrians. Space should be provided for snow storage within parking areas, if required.

Johnson, Johnson & Roy, Inc.; Ann Arbor, Michigan

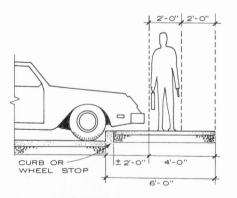

2'-0"   2'-0"

CURB OR WHEEL STOP

± 2'-0"   4'-0"

6'-0"

AUTOMOBILE OVERHANG REQUIREMENT

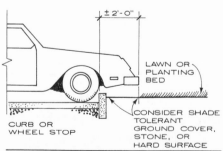

± 2'-0"

LAWN OR PLANTING BED

CURB OR WHEEL STOP

CONSIDER SHADE TOLERANT GROUND COVER, STONE, OR HARD SURFACE

OVERHANGS IN PLANTING AREA

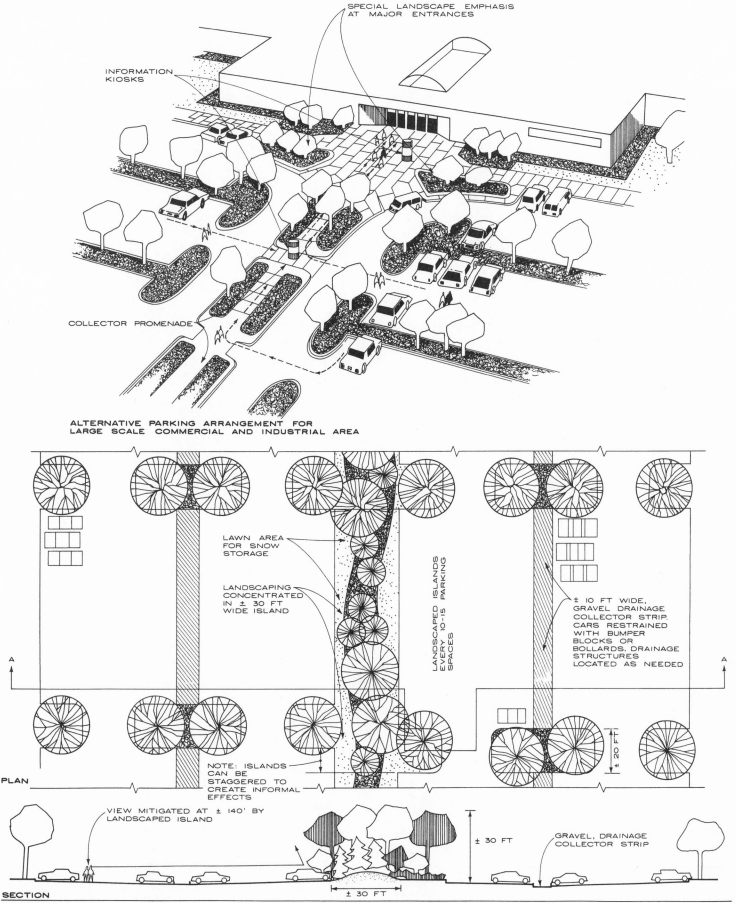

SPECIAL LANDSCAPE EMPHASIS
AT MAJOR ENTRANCES

INFORMATION
KIOSKS

COLLECTOR PROMENADE

ALTERNATIVE PARKING ARRANGEMENT FOR
LARGE SCALE COMMERCIAL AND INDUSTRIAL AREA

LAWN AREA
FOR SNOW
STORAGE

LANDSCAPING
CONCENTRATED
IN ± 30 FT
WIDE ISLAND

LANDSCAPED ISLANDS
EVERY 10-15 PARKING
SPACES

± 10 FT WIDE,
GRAVEL DRAINAGE
COLLECTOR STRIP.
CARS RESTRAINED
WITH BUMPER
BLOCKS OR
BOLLARDS. DRAINAGE
STRUCTURES
LOCATED AS NEEDED

A

A

± 20 FT

PLAN

NOTE: ISLANDS
CAN BE
STAGGERED TO
CREATE INFORMAL
EFFECTS

VIEW MITIGATED AT ± 140' BY
LANDSCAPED ISLAND

± 30 FT

GRAVEL, DRAINAGE
COLLECTOR STRIP

SECTION

± 30 FT

CONCENTRATED PLANTING FOR LARGE PARKING AREAS — SECTION A-A

Johnson, Johnson & Roy, Inc.; Ann Arbor, Michigan

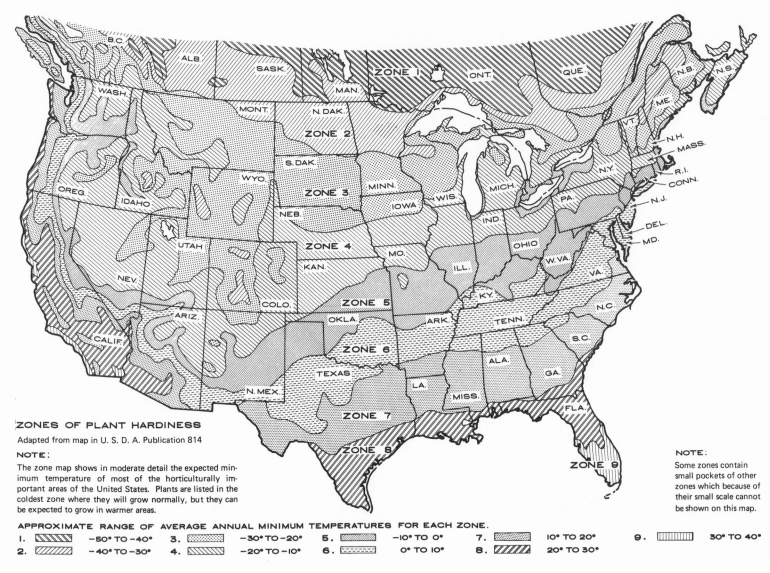

ZONES OF PLANT HARDINESS

Adapted from map in U. S. D. A. Publication 814

NOTE:
The zone map shows in moderate detail the expected minimum temperature of most of the horticulturally important areas of the United States. Plants are listed in the coldest zone where they will grow normally, but they can be expected to grow in warmer areas.

NOTE:
Some zones contain small pockets of other zones which because of their small scale cannot be shown on this map.

APPROXIMATE RANGE OF AVERAGE ANNUAL MINIMUM TEMPERATURES FOR EACH ZONE.

| 1. | −50° TO −40° | 3. | −30° TO −20° | 5. | −10° TO 0° | 7. | 10° TO 20° | 9. | 30° TO 40° |
| 2. | −40° TO −30° | 4. | −20° TO −10° | 6. | 0° TO 10° | 8. | 20° TO 30° | | |

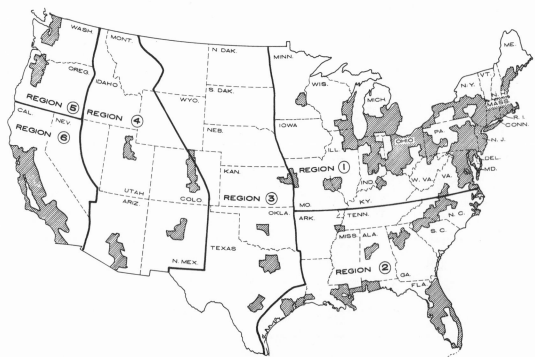

PLANT REGIONS

REGION ①   THE NORTHEAST
REGION ②   THE SOUTHEAST
REGION ③   THE PLAINS
REGION ④   THE ROCKIES
REGION ⑤   THE PACIFIC NORTHWEST
REGION ⑥   THE PACIFIC SOUTHWEST

AREA OF EMERGING URBANIZATION

NOTE:
Plant development is related to soil development and together are controlled by climate. The most commonly used ornamental trees and shrubs for a given area are related to the natural plant region and the hardiness zone of that area. No attempt is made here to show local conditions which would affect the selection of plant material.

RELATIONSHIP OF PLANT REGIONS TO URBAN AREAS

Laurence & Beatriz Coffin, Urban Planners & Landscape Architects; Washington, D. C.

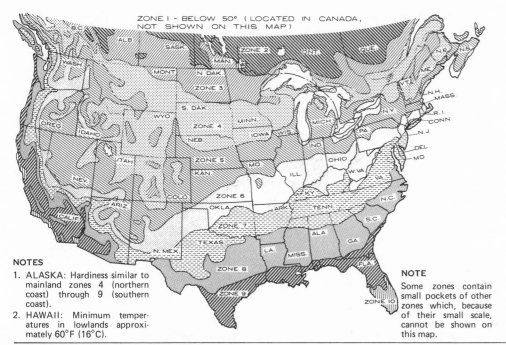

ZONE I – BELOW 50° (LOCATED IN CANADA, NOT SHOWN ON THIS MAP)

NOTE

The zone map shows in moderate detail the expected minimum temperature of most of the horticulturally important areas of the United States. Plants are listed in the coldest zone where they will grow normally, but they can be expected to grow in warmer areas.

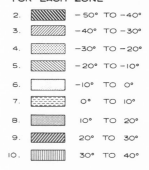

APPROXIMATE RANGE OF AVERAGE ANNUAL MINIMUM TEMPERATURES FOR EACH ZONE

Zone	Range
2.	−50° TO −40°
3.	−40° TO −30°
4.	−30° TO −20°
5.	−20° TO −10°
6.	−10° TO 0°
7.	0° TO 10°
8.	10° TO 20°
9.	20° TO 30°
10.	30° TO 40°

NOTES

1. ALASKA: Hardiness similar to mainland zones 4 (northern coast) through 9 (southern coast).
2. HAWAII: Minimum temperatures in lowlands approximately 60°F (16°C).

NOTE

Some zones contain small pockets of other zones which, because of their small scale, cannot be shown on this map.

ZONES OF PLANT HARDINESS
(ADAPTED FROM MAP IN U.S.D.A. PUBLICATION 814)

NEEDLE EVERGREENS—30 FT AND OVER

BOTANICAL NAME	COMMON NAME	SHAPE			RATE OF GROWTH			USE				FOLIAGE COLOR					CULTURAL CONDITIONS							HARDINESS ZONES									
		Columnar	Conical	Spreading	Slow	Medium	Fast	Urban	Seashore	Ornamental	Windbreak	Green	Light Green	Dark Green	Silver Green	Blue Green	Full Sun	Dry Soil	Moist Soil	Acid	Alkaline	Well Drained	Average	1	2	3	4	5	6	7	8	9	10
Abies concolor	White fir		•			•	•			•	•					•	•			•							•						
Araucaria excelsa	Norfolk Island pine		•	•					•	•				•			•			•													•
Cedrus atlantica glauca	Blue atlas cedar		•	•		•				•	•					•	•					•							•				
Cedrus deodara	Deodar cedar		•			•				•	•		•				•					•								•			
Cedrus libani stenocoma	Cedar of Lebanon		•	•		•				•				•			•					•						•					
Chamaecyparis lawsoniana	Lawson false cypress	•	•		•					•	•			•			•		•										•				
Chamaecyparis obtusa	Hinoki false cypress		•	•	•					•	•			•			•		•										•				
Chamaecyparis pisifera	Sawara false cypress	•	•		•					•	•	•		•			•		•								•						
Cryptomeria japonica	Cryptomeria	•	•		•				•					•			•		•	•									•	•			
Cunninghamia lanceolata	Common China fir			•	•					•	•	•			•			•		•				•						•			
Cupressus sempervirens 'stricta'	Italian pyramidal cypress	•			•					•	•			•			•	•				•								•			
Juniperus chinensis	Chinese juniper		•		•	•	•			•	•	•					•			•	•		•					•					
Juniperus scopulorum	Western red cedar	•		•						•	•	•			•	•	•			•	•		•					•					
Juniperus virginiana	Eastern red cedar	•	•		•			•		•	•	•					•			•	•		•		•								
Larix leptolepis	Japanese larch		•	•		•	•			•		•					•				•					•							
Libocedrus decurrens	California incense cedar	•	•			•				•				•			•					•						•					
Metasequoia glyptostroboides	Dawn redwood		•			•	•			•	•	•					•					•						•					
Picea*	Spruce										•																						
Pinus*	Pine										•																						
Podocarpus macrophyllus	Yew podocarpus	•				•				•				•			•													•			
Pseudolarix amabilis	Golden larch		•	•		•				•				•			•		•	•							•						
Pseudotsuga menziesii	Douglas fir		•	•		•	•			•	•			•			•										•						
Sciadopitys verticulata	Umbrella pine	•	•		•					•	•			•			•			•		•					•						
Sequoiadendron giganteum	Giant sequoia	•								•					•	•	•											•					
Taxodium distichum	Bald cypress	•					•		•				•				•		•				•				•						
Taxus Baccata	English yew		•	•	•					•	•			•					•	•	•	•						•				
Taxus Baccata stricta	Irish yew	•			•					•	•			•					•	•	•	•						•				
Thuja occidentalis	American arborvitae	•	•		•				•		•	•					•			•					•								
Thuja plicata	Giant arborvitae	•	•		•				•		•	•					•			•							•						
Tsuga canadensis	Canada hemlock		•	•		•				•	•			•					•	•	•	•				•							
Tsuga caroliniana	Carolina hemlock		•	•		•			•	•				•					•	•	•	•					•						

*See other references for local species and varieties.

A. E. Bye & Associates, Landscape Architects; Old Greenwich, Connecticut

PHYSICAL

CROWN: Trees increase each year in height and spread of branches by adding a new growth of twigs.

TRUNK: The tree trunk supports the crown and produces the bulk of the useful wood.

ANNUAL RINGS: Reveal age of tree by showing new growth added each year.

HEARTWOOD: This was once sapwood. It is now inactive wood giving strength and stiffness.

OUTER BARK: The outer bark protects tree from injuries.

ROOTS: The roots anchor the tree and help hold the soil against erosion.

PHYSIOLOGICAL

LEAVES: The leaves make food for the tree by combining carbon dioxide from the air and water from the soil in the presence of sunlight. Oxygen, a by-product, is released.

SAPWOOD: The sapwood, or xylem, carries the sap (water and nutrients) from roots to the leaves.

CAMBIUM: The cambium is a layer of cells between the bark and the wood. This is where growth in diameter occurs with the formation of annual rings of new wood inside and new bark outside.

INNER BARK: The inner bark, or phloem, carries food made in the leaves down to the branches, trunk, and roots.

ROOT HAIRS: The tiny root hairs absorb the minerals from soil moisture and send them up as nutrient salts in the sapwood to the leaves.

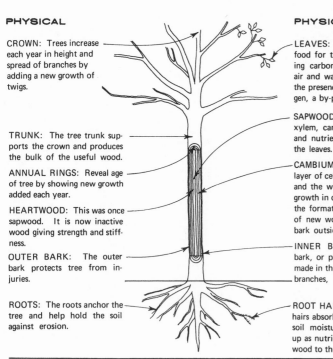

TREE FUNCTION

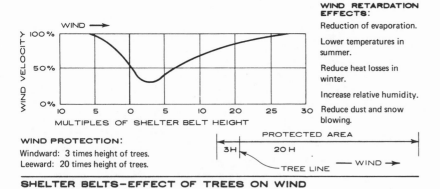

MULTIPLES OF SHELTER BELT HEIGHT

WIND RETARDATION EFFECTS:

Reduction of evaporation.

Lower temperatures in summer.

Reduce heat losses in winter.

Increase relative humidity.

Reduce dust and snow blowing.

WIND PROTECTION:

Windward: 3 times height of trees.
Leeward: 20 times height of trees.

PROTECTED AREA

3H | 20 H

TREE LINE — WIND →

SHELTER BELTS—EFFECT OF TREES ON WIND

EFFECTS OF CITY GREEN-BELTS:

Observations quoted here are for temperate regions and are approximate. Greater discrepancies will occur in tropical regions. All observations will change with particular local conditions. They are only given as a working tool for the planning of urban green spaces.

AIR TEMPERATURE

A	B
90°F	75°–80°F
75°F	65°–70°F
60°F	58°–60°F
45°F	44°–48°F
30°F	29°–31°F
15°F	17°F

FLOOR TEMPERATURE

A	B
70°F	60°F
50°F	45°F
30°F	33°F
Frozen ground	Frozen depth reduced to half

LIGHT INTENSITY %

A	B
Cloudless 100%	5–50%
Cloudy 100%	15–75%

RELATIVE HUMIDITY

A	B
85%	77%
70%	75%
60%	60%

RELATIVE TEMPERATURE, HUMIDITY AND LIGHT INTENSITY OUTSIDE VS. INSIDE FOREST

TREE GROWTH AND CITY CONDITIONS

REQUIRED FACTORS FOR TREE GROWTH	AVERAGE CITY CONDITIONS IN COMPARISON WITH SURROUNDING RURAL AREA	NECESSARY CHANGES TO FOSTER TREE GROWTH IN CITIES	EFFECT OF TREES ON CITY CONDITIONS
LIGHT	Less illumination Decrease overall solar radiation		Decrease light intensity under tree canopies
AIR	More air pollution Air stagnation Formation of wind canyons	Physical control of air pollution	Purified air Dust reducing effect Wind protection
HEAT	Higher night time temperature Downtown heat islands Periodic temperature inversion		Cooling and regulatory effects
WATER	Less rainfall Lower relative humidity	Irrigation	Water conservation Relative humidity regulation
SOIL Must be capable of absorbing moisture There must be aeration There must be a supply of nutrients Must be free of harmful concentration of salts	Ground severely compacted with poor permeability to air and water Soil low in organic matter Soil affected by concentration of harmful chemicals	Preparation of soil Tree feeding	Increase ground permeability to air and water Soil stability

Laurence & Beatriz Coffin, Urban Planners & Landscape Architects; Washington, D. C.

NOTES

Several factors should be considered when designing with plants:

1. The physical environment of the site:
   - Soil conditions (acidity, porosity).
   - Available sunlight.
   - Available precipitation.
   - Seasonal temperature range.
   - Exposure of the site (wind).
2. The design needs of the project:
   - Directing movement.
   - Framing vistas.
   - Moderating the environment of the site.
   - Creating space by using plants to develop the base, vertical, and overhead planes.
3. The design character of the plants chosen:
   - Height.
   - Mass.
   - Silhouette (rounded, pyramidal, spreading).
   - Texture (fine, medium, coarse).
   - Color.
   - Seasonal interest (flowers, fruit, fall color).
   - Growth habits (fast or slow growing).

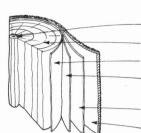

CROWN: THE HEAD OF FOLIAGE OF THE TREE LEAVES — THE FOLIAGE UNIT OF THE TREE THAT FUNCTIONS PRIMARILY IN FOOD MANUFACTURE BY PHOTOSYNTHESIS

HEARTWOOD: THE NONLIVING CENTRAL PART OF THE TREE GIVING STRENGTH AND STABILITY

ANNUAL RINGS: REVEAL AGE OF THE TREE BY SHOWING THE YEARLY GROWTH

SAPWOOD (XYLEM): CARRIES NUTRIENTS AND WATER TO THE LEAVES FROM THE ROOTS

CAMBIUM: LAYER BETWEEN THE XYLEM AND PHLOEM WHERE CELL GROWTH OCCURS, ADDING NEW SAPWOOD TO THE INSIDE AND NEW INNER BARK TO THE OUTSIDE

INNER BARK (PHLOEM): CARRIES FOOD FROM THE LEAVES TO THE BRANCHES, TRUNK, AND ROOTS

OUTER BARK: THE AGED INNER BARK THAT PROTECTS THE TREE FROM DESSICATION AND INJURY

ROOTS: THE ROOTS ANCHOR THE TREE AND HELP HOLD THE SOIL AGAINST EROSION

ROOT HAIRS: THE TINY ROOT HAIRS ABSORB THE MINERALS FROM THE SOIL MOISTURE AND SEND THEM AS NUTRIENT SALTS IN THE SAPWOOD TO THE LEAVES

PHYSICAL CHARACTERISTICS

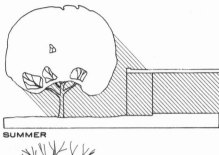

SUMMER

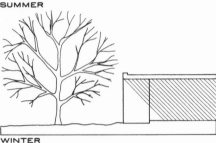

WINTER

RADIATION PROTECTION

In summer deciduous plants obstruct or filter the sun's strong radiation, thus cooling the area beneath them. In winter the sun penetrates through.

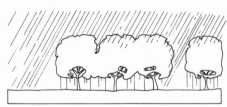

DIRECT SOUND   REFRACTED SOUND

NOISE SCREEN

SOUND SOURCE

SOUND ATTENUATION

Plantings of deciduous and evergreen materials reduce sound more effectively than deciduous plants alone. Planting on earth mounds increases the attenuating effects of the buffer.

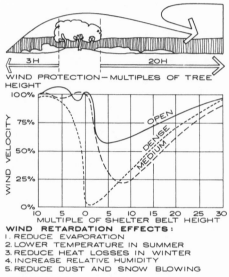

WIND PROTECTION — MULTIPLES OF TREE HEIGHT

WIND VELOCITY / MULTIPLE OF SHELTER BELT HEIGHT

WIND RETARDATION EFFECTS:
1. REDUCE EVAPORATION
2. LOWER TEMPERATURE IN SUMMER
3. REDUCE HEAT LOSSES IN WINTER
4. INCREASE RELATIVE HUMIDITY
5. REDUCE DUST AND SNOW BLOWING

DENSITY

The density of a planted wind buffer determines the area that is protected. Height and composition are also factors in wind protection.

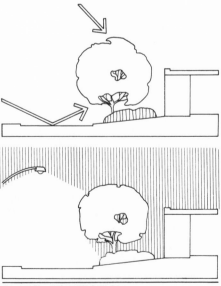

GLARE PROTECTION

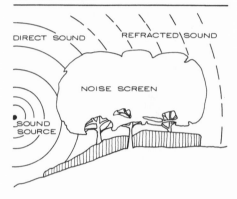

PARTICULATE MATTER TRAPPED ON THE LEAVES IS WASHED TO THE GROUND DURING A RAINFALL. GASEOUS AND OTHER POLLUTANTS ARE ASSIMILATED IN THE LEAVES

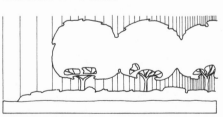

FUMES AND ODORS CAN BE MECHANICALLY MASKED BY FRAGRANT PLANTS AND CHEMICALLY METABOLIZED IN THE PHOTOSYNTHETIC PROCESS

AIR FILTRATION

Large masses of plants physically and chemically filter and deodorize the air to reduce air pollution.

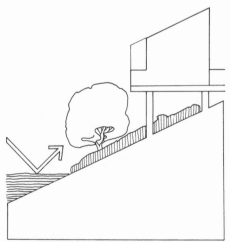

GLARE PROTECTION

The sun's vertical angle changes seasonally; therefore, the area subject to the glare of reflected sunlight varies. Plants of various heights screen glare from adjacent reflective surfaces (water, paving, glass, and building surfaces).

GLARE PROTECTION

Glare and reflection from sunlight and/or artificial sources can be screened or blocked by plants of various height and placement.

A. E. Bye and Associates, Landscape Architects; Old Greenwich, Connecticut

Robin Roberts; Washington, D.C.

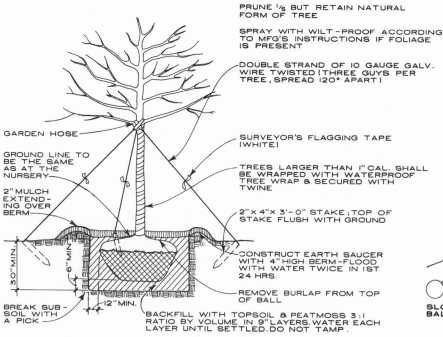

PRUNE 1/5 BUT RETAIN NATURAL FORM OF TREE

SPRAY WITH WILT-PROOF ACCORDING TO MFG'S INSTRUCTIONS IF FOLIAGE IS PRESENT

DOUBLE STRAND OF 10 GAUGE GALV. WIRE TWISTED (THREE GUYS PER TREE, SPREAD 120° APART)

GARDEN HOSE

GROUND LINE TO BE THE SAME AS AT THE NURSERY

2" MULCH EXTENDING OVER BERM

SURVEYOR'S FLAGGING TAPE (WHITE)

TREES LARGER THAN 1" CAL. SHALL BE WRAPPED WITH WATERPROOF TREE WRAP & SECURED WITH TWINE

2" x 4" x 3'-0" STAKE; TOP OF STAKE FLUSH WITH GROUND

CONSTRUCT EARTH SAUCER WITH 4" HIGH BERM-FLOOD WITH WATER TWICE IN IST 24 HRS.

REMOVE BURLAP FROM TOP OF BALL

BACKFILL WITH TOPSOIL & PEATMOSS 3:1 RATIO BY VOLUME IN 9" LAYER UNTIL SETTLED. DO NOT TAMP.

30" MIN. 6" MIN. 12" MIN.

BREAK SUB-SOIL WITH A PICK

PLANTING & GUYING DETAILS-FOR MINOR TREES 1 1/2" CALIPER AND SMALLER, BALLED & BURLAPPED.

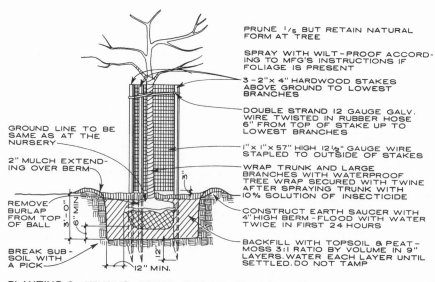

PRUNE 1/5 BUT RETAIN NATURAL FORM AT TREE

SPRAY WITH WILT-PROOF ACCORDING TO MFG'S INSTRUCTIONS IF FOLIAGE IS PRESENT

3 - 2" x 4" HARDWOOD STAKES ABOVE GROUND TO LOWEST BRANCHES

DOUBLE STRAND 12 GAUGE GALV. WIRE TWISTED IN RUBBER HOSE 6" FROM TOP OF STAKE UP TO LOWEST BRANCHES

1" x 1" x 57" HIGH 12 1/2" GAUGE WIRE STAPLED TO OUTSIDE OF STAKES

WRAP TRUNK AND LARGE BRANCHES WITH WATERPROOF TREE WRAP SECURED WITH TWINE AFTER SPRAYING TRUNK WITH 10% SOLUTION OF INSECTICIDE

CONSTRUCT EARTH SAUCER WITH 4" HIGH BERM-FLOOD WITH WATER TWICE IN FIRST 24 HOURS

BACKFILL WITH TOPSOIL & PEAT-MOSS 3:1 RATIO BY VOLUME IN 9" LAYERS. WATER EACH LAYER UNTIL SETTLED. DO NOT TAMP

GROUND LINE TO BE SAME AS AT THE NURSERY

2" MULCH EXTENDING OVER BERM

REMOVE BURLAP FROM TOP OF BALL

BREAK SUB-SOIL WITH A PICK

12" MIN.

PLANTING & STAKING DETAIL-FOR MAJOR TREES 2" CALIPER AND LARGER, BALLED AND BURLAPPED.

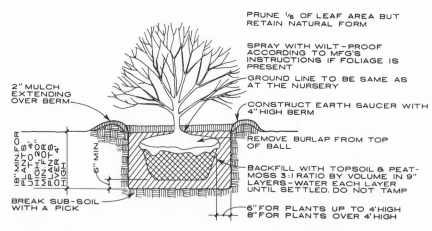

PRUNE 1/5 OF LEAF AREA BUT RETAIN NATURAL FORM

SPRAY WITH WILT-PROOF ACCORDING TO MFG'S INSTRUCTIONS IF FOLIAGE IS PRESENT

GROUND LINE TO BE SAME AS AT THE NURSERY

CONSTRUCT EARTH SAUCER WITH 4" HIGH BERM

REMOVE BURLAP FROM TOP OF BALL

BACKFILL WITH TOPSOIL & PEAT-MOSS 3:1 RATIO BY VOLUME IN 9" LAYERS-WATER EACH LAYER UNTIL SETTLED. DO NOT TAMP

2" MULCH EXTENDING OVER BERM

18" MIN. FOR PLANTS UP TO 4' HIGH, 20" MIN. FOR PLANTS OVER 4' HIGH

6" MIN.

BREAK SUB-SOIL WITH A PICK

6" FOR PLANTS UP TO 4' HIGH
8" FOR PLANTS OVER 4' HIGH

SHRUB PLANTING DETAIL-FOR ALL SHRUBS BALLED AND BURLAPPED

Laurence & Beatriz Coffin, Urban Planners & Landscape Architects; Washington, D. C.

PROPOSED GRADE

EXIST. GRADE

DEADMAN AT LEAST 8" DIAMETER 2'-0" LONG AND NOT LESS THAN 18" BELOW THE SURFACE

SLOPE PLANTING DETAIL-FOR MAJOR & MINOR TREES, BALLED & BURLAPPED

STANDARD SHADE TREES—BALLED AND BURLAPPED

*CALIPER	HEIGHT RANGE	MAXIMUM HEIGHTS	MINIMUM BALL DIAM.	MINIMUM BALL DEPTH
1/2 to 3/4 in.	5 to 6 ft.	8 ft.	12 inches	9 inches
3/4 to 1 in.	6 to 8 ft.	10 ft.	14 inches	10 inches
1 to 1 1/4 in.	7 to 9 ft.	11 ft.	16 inches	12 inches
1 1/4 to 1 1/2 in.	8 to 10 ft.	12 ft.	18 inches	13 inches
1 1/2 to 1 3/4 in.	10 to 12 ft.	14 ft.	20 inches	14 inches
1 3/4 to 2 in.	10 to 12 ft.	14 ft.	22 inches	15 inches
2 to 2 1/2 in.	12 to 14 ft.	16 ft.	24 inches	16 inches
2 1/2 to 3 in.	12 to 14 ft.	16 ft.	28 inches	19 inches
3 to 3 1/2 in.	14 to 16 ft.	18 ft.	32 inches	20 inches
3 1/2 to 4 in.	14 to 16 ft.	18 ft.	36 inches	22 inches
4 to 5 in.	16 to 18 ft.	22 ft.	44 inches	26 inches
5 to 6 in.	18 and up.	26 ft.	48 inches	29 inches

*In the selection of trees from commercial nurseries, caliper indicates the diameter of the trunk taken 6 inches above the ground level up to and including 4 inch caliper size and 12" inches above the ground level for larger sizes.

SHRUBS & MINOR TREES BALLED AND BURLAPPED

HEIGHT RANGE	MINIMUM BALL DIAM.	MINIMUM BALL DEPTH
1 1/2 to 2 ft.	10 inches	8 inches
2 to 3 ft.	12 inches	9 inches
3 to 4 ft.	13 inches	10 inches
4 to 5 ft.	15 inches	11 inches
5 to 6 ft.	16 inches	12 inches
6 to 7 ft.	18 inches	13 inches
7 to 8 ft.	20 inches	14 inches
8 to 9 ft.	22 inches	15 inches
9 to 10 ft.	24 inches	16 inches
10 to 12 ft.	26 inches	17 inches

NOTE FOR STD. SHADE TREES AND SHRUBS AND MINOR TREES Ball sizes should always be of a diameter to encompass the fibrous and feeding root system necessary for the full recovery of the plant.

2" MULCH INSTALLED BEFORE PLANTS

SUBSOIL TO BE BROKEN WITH A PICK AXE

6" DEEP PLANTING BED CONTAINING 3 PARTS TOP-SOIL TO ONE PART PEAT-MOSS

GROUND COVER PLANTING DETAIL
NOTE: GROUND COVERS SHOULD BE POT OR CONTAINER GROWN

Silhouettes indicate specimens of natural form, but varieties or forced forms possessing compact, spreading, columnar or pyramidal characteristics are available. The height at the ten year stage of development is given as an architectural design factor to be considered in the selection of tree sizes.

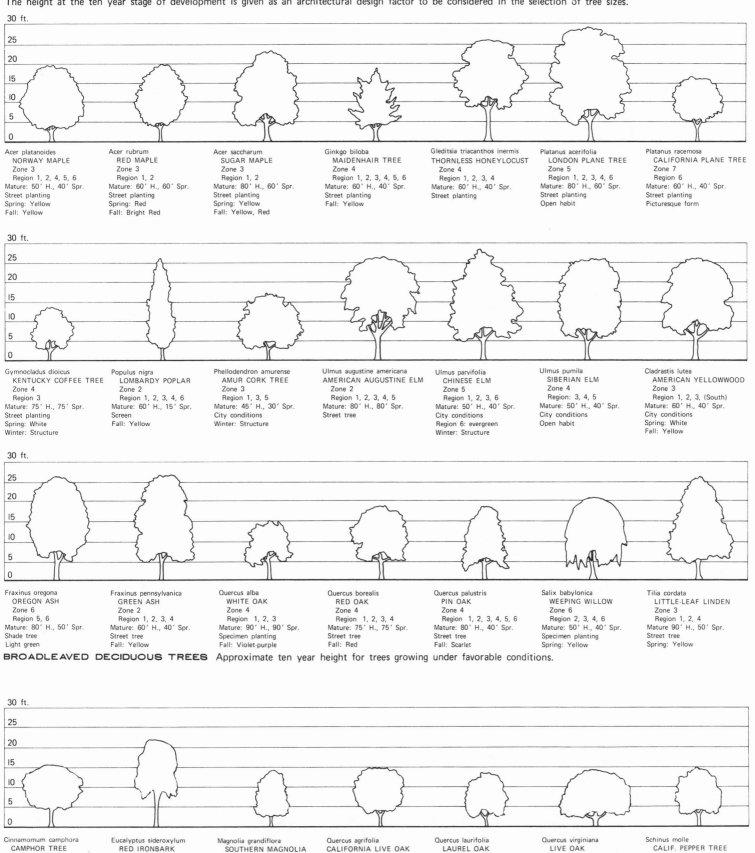

Acer platanoides
NORWAY MAPLE
Zone 3
Region 1, 2, 4, 5, 6
Mature: 50' H., 40' Spr.
Street planting
Spring: Yellow
Fall: Yellow

Acer rubrum
RED MAPLE
Zone 3
Region 1, 2
Mature: 60' H., 60' Spr.
Street planting
Spring: Red
Fall: Bright Red

Acer saccharum
SUGAR MAPLE
Zone 3
Region 1, 2
Mature: 80' H., 60' Spr.
Street planting
Spring: Yellow
Fall: Yellow, Red

Ginkgo biloba
MAIDENHAIR TREE
Zone 4
Region 1, 2, 3, 4, 5, 6
Mature: 60' H., 40' Spr.
Street planting
Fall: Yellow

Gleditsia triacanthos inermis
THORNLESS HONEYLOCUST
Zone 4
Region 1, 2, 3, 4
Mature: 60' H., 40' Spr.
Street planting

Platanus acerifolia
LONDON PLANE TREE
Zone 5
Region 1, 2, 3, 4, 6
Mature: 80' H., 60' Spr.
Street planting
Open habit

Platanus racemosa
CALIFORNIA PLANE TREE
Zone 7
Region 6
Mature: 60' H., 40' Spr.
Street planting
Picturesque form

Gymnocladus dioicus
KENTUCKY COFFEE TREE
Zone 4
Region 3
Street planting
Spring: White
Winter: Structure

Populus nigra
LOMBARDY POPLAR
Zone 2
Region 1, 2, 3, 4, 6
Mature: 60' H., 15' Spr.
Screen
Fall: Yellow

Phellodendron amurense
AMUR CORK TREE
Zone 3
Region 1, 3, 5
Mature: 45' H., 30' Spr.
City conditions
Winter: Structure

Ulmus augustine americana
AMERICAN AUGUSTINE ELM
Zone 2
Region 1, 2, 3, 4, 5
Mature: 80' H., 80' Spr.
Street tree

Ulmus parvifolia
CHINESE ELM
Zone 5
Region 1, 2, 3, 6
Mature: 50' H., 40' Spr.
City conditions
Region 6: evergreen
Winter: Structure

Ulmus pumila
SIBERIAN ELM
Zone 4
Region 3, 4, 5
Mature: 50' H., 40' Spr.
City conditions
Open habit

Cladrastis lutea
AMERICAN YELLOWWOOD
Zone 3
Region 1, 2, 3, (South)
Mature: 60' H., 40' Spr.
City conditions
Spring: White
Fall: Yellow

Fraxinus oregona
OREGON ASH
Zone 6
Region 5, 6
Mature: 80' H., 50' Spr.
Shade tree
Light green

Fraxinus pennsylvanica
GREEN ASH
Zone 2
Region 1, 2, 3, 4
Mature: 60' H., 40' Spr.
Street tree
Fall: Yellow

Quercus alba
WHITE OAK
Zone 4
Region 1, 2, 3
Mature: 90' H., 90' Spr.
Specimen planting
Fall: Violet-purple

Quercus borealis
RED OAK
Zone 4
Region 1, 2, 3, 4
Mature: 75' H., 75' Spr.
Street tree
Fall: Red

Quercus palustris
PIN OAK
Zone 4
Region 1, 2, 3, 4, 5, 6
Mature: 80' H., 40' Spr.
Street tree
Fall: Scarlet

Salix babylonica
WEEPING WILLOW
Zone 6
Region 2, 3, 4, 6
Mature: 50' H., 40' Spr.
Specimen planting
Spring: Yellow

Tilia cordata
LITTLE-LEAF LINDEN
Zone 3
Region 1, 2, 4
Mature 90' H., 50' Spr.
Street tree
Spring: Yellow

BROADLEAVED DECIDUOUS TREES Approximate ten year height for trees growing under favorable conditions.

Cinnamomum camphora
CAMPHOR TREE
Zone 9
Region 2, 6
Mature: 40' H., 60' Spr.
Street planting

Eucalyptus sideroxylum
RED IRONBARK
Zone 9
Region 6
Mature: 60' H., 40' Spr.
City conditions
Blue-gray

Magnolia grandiflora
SOUTHERN MAGNOLIA
Zone 7
Region 2, 6
Mature: 60' H., 70' Spr.
Specimen planting
Lustrous dark green

Quercus agrifolia
CALIFORNIA LIVE OAK
Zone 9
Region 6
Mature: 60' H., 70' Spr.
Street planting
Glossy dark green

Quercus laurifolia
LAUREL OAK
Zone 7
Region 2
Mature: 60' H., 60' Spr.
Specimen planting
Lustrous dark green

Quercus virginiana
LIVE OAK
Zone 7
Region 2
Mature: 60' H., 100' Spr.
Specimen planting
Fine texture

Schinus molle
CALIF. PEPPER TREE
Zone 9
Region 4, 6
Mature: 40' H., 30' Spr.
Street tree
Light green

BROADLEAVED EVERGREEN TREES Approximate ten year height for trees growing under favorable conditions.
Botanical name and Common name of trees given in this order. See Zones and Regions in given maps. H. = Height, Spr. = Spread

Laurence & Beatriz Coffin, Urban Planners & Landscape Architects; Washington, D. C.

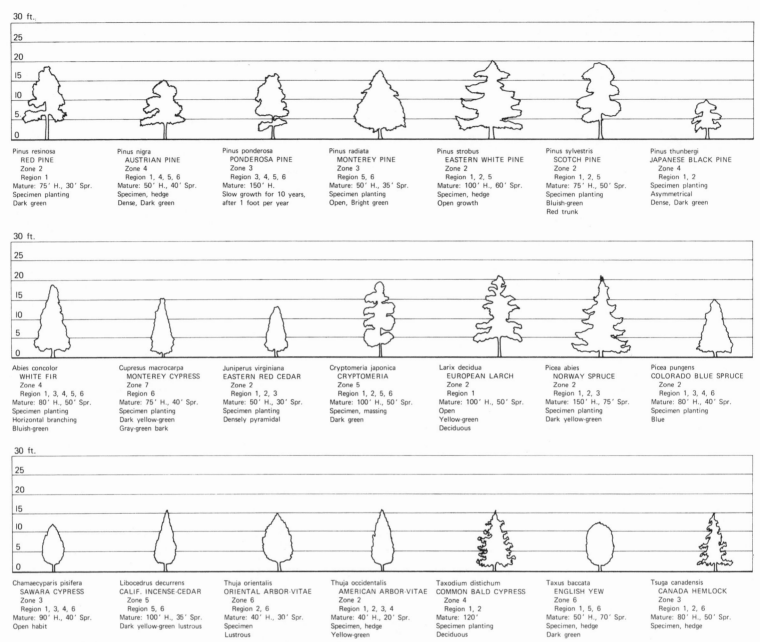

30 ft.
25
20
15
10
5
0

Pinus resinosa	Pinus nigra	Pinus ponderosa	Pinus radiata	Pinus strobus	Pinus sylvestris	Pinus thunbergi
RED PINE	AUSTRIAN PINE	PONDEROSA PINE	MONTEREY PINE	EASTERN WHITE PINE	SCOTCH PINE	JAPANESE BLACK PINE
Zone 2	Zone 4	Zone 3	Zone 3	Zone 2	Zone 2	Zone 4
Region 1	Region 1, 4, 5, 6	Region 3, 4, 5, 6	Region 5, 6	Region 1, 2, 5	Region 1, 2, 5	Region 1, 2
Mature: 75' H., 30' Spr.	Mature: 50' H., 40' Spr.	Mature: 150' H.	Mature: 50' H., 35' Spr.	Mature: 100' H., 60' Spr.	Mature: 75' H., 50' Spr.	Specimen planting
Specimen planting	Specimen, hedge	Slow growth for 10 years,	Specimen planting	Specimen, hedge	Specimen planting	Asymmetrical
Dark green	Dense, Dark green	after 1 foot per year	Open, Bright green	Open growth	Bluish-green	Dense, Dark green
					Red trunk	

30 ft.
25
20
15
10
5
0

Abies concolor	Cupresus macrocarpa	Juniperus virginiana	Cryptomeria japonica	Larix decidua	Picea abies	Picea pungens
WHITE FIR	MONTEREY CYPRESS	EASTERN RED CEDAR	CRYPTOMERIA	EUROPEAN LARCH	NORWAY SPRUCE	COLORADO BLUE SPRUCE
Zone 4	Zone 7	Zone 2	Zone 5	Zone 2	Zone 2	Zone 2
Region 1, 3, 4, 5, 6	Region 6	Region 1, 2, 3	Region 1, 2, 5, 6	Region 1	Region 1, 2, 3	Region 1, 3, 4, 6
Mature: 80' H., 50' Spr.	Mature: 75' H., 40' Spr.	Mature: 50' H., 30' Spr.	Mature: 100' H., 50' Spr.	Mature: 100' H., 50' Spr.	Mature: 150' H., 75' Spr.	Mature: 80' H., 40' Spr.
Specimen planting	Specimen planting	Specimen planting	Specimen, massing	Open	Specimen planting	Specimen planting
Horizontal branching	Dark yellow-green	Densely pyramidal	Dark green	Yellow-green	Dark yellow-green	Blue
Bluish-green	Gray-green bark			Deciduous		

30 ft.
25
20
15
10
5
0

Chamaecyparis pisifera	Libocedrus decurrens	Thuja orientalis	Thuja occidentalis	Taxodium distichum	Taxus baccata	Tsuga canadensis
SAWARA CYPRESS	CALIF. INCENSE-CEDAR	ORIENTAL ARBOR-VITAE	AMERICAN ARBOR-VITAE	COMMON BALD CYPRESS	ENGLISH YEW	CANADA HEMLOCK
Zone 3	Zone 5	Zone 6	Zone 2	Zone 4	Zone 6	Zone 3
Region 1, 3, 4, 6	Region 5, 6	Region 2, 6	Region 1, 2, 3, 4	Region 1, 2	Region 1, 5, 6	Region 1, 2, 6
Mature: 90' H., 40' Spr.	Mature: 100' H., 35' Spr.	Mature: 40' H., 30' Spr.	Mature: 40' H., 20' Spr.	Mature: 120'	Mature: 50' H., 70' Spr.	Mature: 80' H., 50' Spr.
Open habit	Dark yellow-green lustrous	Specimen	Specimen, hedge	Specimen planting	Specimen, hedge	Specimen, hedge
		Lustrous	Yellow-green	Deciduous	Dark green	

CONIFER TREES (EVERGREEN UNLESS OTHERWISE INDICATED)

Exposure and atmospheric conditions will greatly affect this group of trees. They are not recommended for street planting or for locations with heavy air pollution. Approximate ten year height for trees growing under favorable conditions.

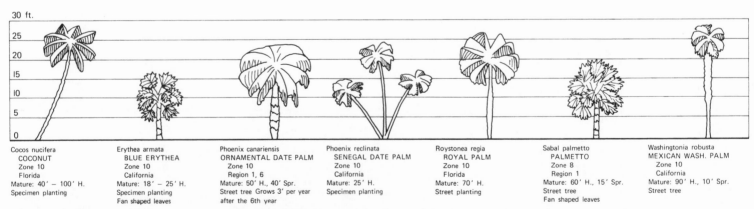

30 ft.
25
20
15
10
5
0

Cocos nucifera	Erythea armata	Phoenix canariensis	Phoenix reclinata	Roystonea regia	Sabal palmetto	Washingtonia robusta
COCONUT	BLUE ERYTHEA	ORNAMENTAL DATE PALM	SENEGAL DATE PALM	ROYAL PALM	PALMETTO	MEXICAN WASH. PALM
Zone 10	Zone 10	Zone 10	Zone 10	Zone 10	Zone 8	Zone 10
Florida	California	Region 1, 6	California	Florida	Region 1	California
Mature: 40' – 100' H.	Mature: 18' – 25' H.	Mature: 50' H., 40' Spr.	Mature: 25' H.	Mature: 70' H.	Mature: 60' H., 15' Spr.	Mature: 90' H., 10' Spr.
Specimen planting	Specimen planting	Street tree Grows 3' per year	Specimen planting	Street planting	Street tree	Street tree
	Fan shaped leaves	after the 6th year			Fan shaped leaves	

PALM TREES   APPROXIMATE TEN YEAR HEIGHT FOR TREES GROWING UNDER FAVORABLE CONDITIONS

Botanical name and Common name given in this order. See Zones and Regions in given maps. H. = Height Spr. = Spread.

Laurence & Beatriz Coffin, Urban Planners & Landscape Architects; Washington. D. C.

Betula populifolia
GREY BIRCH
Zone 2
Region 1, 2, 3, 4, 5
Mature: 30' H., 20' Spr.
White bark
Fall: Yellow

Cornus florida
FLOWERING DOGWOOD
Zone 4
Region 1, 2, 3(East)
Mature: 20' H., 25' Spr.
Spring: White or Pink
Fall: Red

Cornus nutalli
PACIFIC DOGWOOD
Zone 7
Region 5, 6
Mature: 30' H., 30' Spr.
Spring: White
Fall: Scarlet and Yellow

Cercis canadensis
EASTERN REDBUD
Zone 4
Region 1, 2, 4
Mature: 30' H., 30' Spr.
Spring: Purplish Pink
Fall: Yellow

Crataegus phaenopyrum
WASHINGTON HAWTHORN
Zone 4
Region 1, 2
Mature: 30' H., 30' Spr.
Spring: White
Fall: Orange

Ilex opaca
AMERICAN HOLLY
Zone 5
Region 1, 2
Mature: 40' H., 25' Spr.
Dark green, Red fruit
Evergreen

Lagerstroemia indica
CRAPE MYRTLE
Zone 7
Region 2, 6
Mature: 20' H., 20' Spr.
Spring: Pink, Bluish
Dense

Acer palmatum
JAPANESE MAPLE
Zone 5
Region 1, 2, 6
Mature: 20' H., 20' Spr.
Spring: Red
Fall: Red

Delonix regia
FLAME TREE
Zone 10
Florida
Mature: 40' H., 40' Spr.
Summer: Red flowers
Fern-like folliage

Myrica californica
CALIFORNIA BAYBERRY
Zone 7
Region 5, 6
Mature: 30' H., 15' Spr.
Bronze colored
Evergreen

Magnolia soulangeana
SAUCER MAGNOLIA
Zone 5
Region 1, 2, 6
Mature: 25' H., 25' Spr.
Spring: White - Pink
Coarse texture

Malus (species)
FLOWERING CRAB
Zone 4
Region 1, 2, 6
Mature: 20' H., 25' Spr.
Spring: White, Pink, Red
Dense

Prunus serrulata
ORIENTAL CHERRY
Zone 5, 6
Region 1, 2, 5, 6
Mature: 25' H., 25' Spr.
Spring: White, Pink
Glossy bark

Photinia serrulata
CHINESE PHOTINIA
Zone 7
Region 2, 6
Mature: 36' H., 25' Spr.
Spring: New growth Red
Lustrous evergreen

Botanical name and Common name of trees and shrubs given in this order. See Zones and Regions in given maps.
H. = Height   Spr. = Spread
MINOR TREES—ADAPTED TO CITY CONDITIONS, DECIDUOUS UNLESS OTHERWISE SPECIFIED.

SIZE	DECIDUOUS SHRUBS—WITHSTANDING CITY CONDITIONS				EVERGREEN SHRUBS—WITHSTANDING CITY CONDITIONS		
10' to 15' HIGH Scale 1" = 30'	Cornus racemosa **GRAY DOGWOOD** Zone 4 Region 1, 2 Red stalks Hedge	Hamamells virginiana **COMMON WITCH HAZEL** Zone 4 Region 1, 2, 3 Fall: Yellow	Ligustrum amurense **AMUR PRIVET** Zone 3 Region 1, 2, 3, 5, 6 Nearly evergreen Hedge or specimen	Syringa vulgaris **COMMON LILAC** Zone 3 Region 1, 4, 5 Spring: Lilac Massing	Juniperus chinensus columnaris **CHINESE JUNIPER** Zone 4 Region 1, 2, 3 Hedge specimen	Taxus cupidata capitata **JAPANESE YEW** Zone 4 Region 1, 2, 3, 4, 5, 6 Specimen Dark green	Rhododendron maximum **ROSEBAY RHODODENDRON** Zone 3 Region 1, 2, 5 Spring: Pink Dark green, dense
6' to 10' HIGH Scale 1" = 20'	Aronia arbutifolia **RED CHOKEBERRY** Zone 5 Region 1, 2 Spring: White Fall: Red	Fremontia californica **FLANNEL BUSH** Zone 7 California Spring: Yellow Massing	Spirea prunifolia plena **BRIDALWREATH SPIREA** Zone 4 Region 1, 2, 3 Spring: White	Viburnum tomentosum **DOUBLEFILE VIBURNUM** Zone 2 Region 1, 2, 3, 4, 5, 6 Spring: White Massing	Taxus cuspidata **JAPANESE YEW** Zone 4 Region 1, 2, 3, 4, 5, 6 Hedge Dark green	Myrtus communis **MYRTLE** Zone 8–9 Region 2, 6 Hedge, Specimen Massing	Nerium oleander **NERIUM** Zone 7–8 Region 2, 3, 4, 6 Bamboo-like Light green—white flower
2' to 6' HIGH Scale 1" = 20'	Berberis thunbergi **JAPANESE BARBERRY** Zone 5 Region 1, 2, 3, 4, 5, 6 Fall: Scarlet Hedge	Forsythia intermediaspetabilis **SHOWY BORDER FORSYTHIA** Zone 5 Region 1, 2, 3, 4, 5, 6 Spring: Yellow Massing	Euonymus alata **WINGED EUONYMUS** Zone 3 Region 1, 2, 5, 6 Fall: Scarlet Hedge: Massing	Rosa rugosa **RUGOSA ROSE** Zone 2 Region 1, 2 Fall: Orange Hedge	Juniperus chinensis pfitzeriana **PFITZER'S JUNIPER** Zone 4 Region 1, 2 Feathery texture	Buxus suffruticosa **DWARF BOX** Zone 5 Region 2, 3, 6 Dark lustrous	Pinus mugo mughus **MUGO PINE** Zone 2 Region 1, 2, 4, 5, 6 Bright green Specimen, Massing
6" to 24" HIGH Used as ground cover	 Cotoneaster horizontalis **ROCK SPRAY** Zone 4 Region 1, 2, 3, 4, 5, 6	Cytisus albus **PORTUGUESE BROOM** Zone 5 Region 1, 5 White flowers	Euonymus fortunei **WINTER CREEPER** Zone 2 Region 1, 2, 3, 4, 5, 6	 Juniperus sabina tamariscifolia **TAMARIX JUNIPER** Zone 4 Region 3, 4, 5, 6	Juniperus chinensis sargenti **SARGENT JUNIPER** Zone 4 Region 1, 2	Hedera helix vars. **ENGLISH IVY** Zone 4 Region 1, 2	Pachistima cambyi **CAMBYI PACHISTIMA** Zone 5 Region 1, 2 Fall: Bronze

Silhouettes indicate specimens of natural form. Shrubs are adaptable to different height and forms by pruning. A wide range of varieties and exotic shrubs
can be found throughout the plant regions. A few shrubs commonly used are listed here.

Laurence & Beatriz Coffin, Urban Planners & Landscape Architects; Washington, D. C.

BROAD LEAVED EVERGREENS

BOTANICAL NAME	COMMON NAME	HEIGHT					FLOWER COLOR				SEASON				CULTURAL CONDITIONS							USES				HARDINESS ZONES									
		Under 1 ft	1 to 3 ft	3 to 6 ft	6 to 10 ft	10 ft and over	White	Yellow-orange	Pink-red	Purple-blue	Spring	Summer	Fall	Winter	Partial sun	Full sun	Full shade	Moist soil	Dry soil	Acid soil	Alkaline soil	City	Seashore	Ornamental	Hedge	1	2	3	4	5	6	7	8	9	10
Abelia x grandiflora	Glossy abelia			•					•			•			•	•		•				•		•	•						•				
Azalea varieties*	Azalea varieties			•	•		•	•	•		•				•	•		•		•		•								•					
Buxus sempervirens	Common box			•											•	•		•						•						•					
Calliandra inaequilatera	Pink powder puff			•					•		•					•				•				•											•
Callistemon citrinus	Lemon bottle brush			•	•				•		•	•		•		•			•					•										•	
Calluna vulgaris	Heather		•				•		•	•		•	•			•		•	•					•						•					
Citrus sinensis	Sweet orange				•	•	•	•			•	•	•	•		•		•						•										•	•
Codiaeum variegatum	Croton			•											•	•		•						•	•										•
Cotoneaster species*	Cotoneaster species	•	•	•			•				•	•				•							•	•						•	•	•	•		
Daphne cneorum	Rose daphne	•							•		•				•	•		•	•	•			•							•					
Elaeagnus pungens	Thorny elaeagnus				•	•	•						•			•	•	•	•		•		•		•							•			
Enkianthus campanulatus	Redvein enkianthus				•		•		•		•				•	•		•		•				•						•					
Erica carnea	Spring heather	•					•		•		•					•		•	•					•							•				
Eriobotrya japonica	Loquat				•	•	•						•	•		•		•	•				•										•		
Euonymus japonica	Evergreen euonymus				•		•								•	•		•	•	•					•									•	
Euphorbia pulcherrima	Poinsetta		•	•					•					•	•		•		•				•												•
Fatsia japonica	Japanese fatsia				•	•	•						•				•		•				•	•									•		
Ficus benjamina	Weeping fig				•										•			•						•											•
Gardenia jasminoides	Gardenia			•			•				•	•	•		•	•		•		•				•									•		
Gaultheria shallon	Salal			•			•		•			•			•	•	•	•	•	•				•							•				
Hebe traversii	Traverse hebe			•			•					•				•	•							•	•								•		
Hibiscus rosa-sinensis	Chinese hibiscus				•			•	•			•				•							•	•										•	
Hypericum species*	Saint-John's-wort species	•							•			•	•			•	•						•									•			
Ilex (evergreen species)**	Holly (evergreen species)	•	•	•	•										•	•		•		•	•		•	•				•	•	•	•	•			
Ixora coccinea	Ixora				•	•		•	•		•	•	•	•	•	•	•	•		•				•											•
Jasminum mesnyi	Primrose jasmine				•			•			•	•				•		•	•	•				•									•		
Kalmia latifolia	Mountain laurel			•	•		•		•		•				•	•		•		•		•		•						•					
Laurus nobilis	Laurel				•	•					•					•		•	•	•				•								•			
Ligustrum japonicum	Japanese privet			•	•	•	•					•				•		•	•	•				•	•							•			
Mahonia aquifolia	Oregon holly-grape	•							•		•				•			•	•					•						•	•				
Myrtus communis 'compacta'	Compact Myrtle		•	•			•					•				•		•					•		•								•		
Nandina domestica	Nandina			•			•					•				•		•						•								•			
Nerium Oleander	Oleander				•	•	•	•	•	•	•	•				•		•	•	•			•	•								•			
Olea europarea	Common olive				•	•	•				•					•		•					•											•	
Osmanthus heterophyllus	Holly osmanthus				•	•	•					•				•		•					•	•								•			
Photinia serrulata	Chinese photinia				•	•	•				•				•			•					•									•			
Pieris floribunda	Mountain andromeda		•				•				•				•	•	•	•		•				•						•					
Pieris japonica	Japanese andromeda		•				•				•					•		•		•		•		•							•				
Pittosporum tobira	Japanese pittosporum			•			•				•					•		•	•	•				•	•								•		
Plumbago capensis	Cape plumbago	•								•	•	•	•	•		•		•						•										•	
Prunus laurocerasus 'schipkaenis'	Schipka cherry-laurel		•	•			•				•					•		•		•				•	•							•	•		
Pyracantha coccinea	Firethorn			•			•				•					•		•		•	•			•	•							•			
Rhododendron species*	Rhododendron species	•	•	•	•		•				•	•			•	•	•	•		•				•					•	•	•				
Schinus molle	California pepper tree				•		•		•							•		•	•	•	•			•										•	
Skimmia japonica	Japanese skimmia		•				•				•						•	•						•								•			
Ulmus parvifolia pendens	Evergreen elm				•											•		•	•	•	•			•											•
Viburnum rhytidophyllum	Leatherleaf viburnum			•	•	•	•				•			•		•	•							•							•				
Xylosma senticosa	Xylosma	•			•											•		•						•									•		

* See other references for local species and varieties.
** Also deciduous ilex available.

A. E. Bye & Associates, Landscape Architects; Old Greenwich, Connecticut

DECIDUOUS TREES—20 TO 50 FT

Botanical Name	Common Name	Rounded	Weeping	Spreading	Conical	Columnar	Oval	Slow	Medium	Fast	Shade Tree	Ornamental	Street Tree	Urban Tree	Seashore Tree	Flowers	Fruit	Leaf Color	Bark	Light Shade	Full Sun	Dry Soil	Moist Soil	Well Drained Soil	Acid Soil	Alkali Soil	1	2	3	4	5	6	7	8	9	10
Acer campestre	Hedge maple	●						●			●	●	●							●	●										●					
Acer ginnala	Amur maple	●								●	●	●	●			●		●	●	●	●							●								
Acer palmatum	Japanese maple	●						●			●		●					●		●	●		●	●							●					
Ailanthus altissima	Tree of heaven	●								●			●	●		●		●		●	●	●		●									●			
Albizia julibrissin	Hardy silk tree			●						●	●	●	●		●		●			●	●													●		
Amelanchier laevis	Allegany serviceberry	●								●		●		●	●	●	●	●	●	●	●	●	●	●							●					
Arbutus unedo	Strawberry tree			●				●				●				●	●		●		●			●											●	
Bauhinia variegata	Buddhist bauhinia	●								●	●	●	●	●		●				●	●		●		●											●
Betula populifolia	Gray birch			●			●			●		●							●	●	●	●	●							●	●					
Broussonetia papyrifera	Common paper mulberry	●		●						●		●		●			●	●		●	●	●	●										●		
Camellia japonica	Common camellia	●					●				●					●		●		●													●		
Carpinus caroliniana	American hornbeam	●					●				●	●	●					●	●	●	●						●									
Cassia fistula	Golden shower senna	●								●		●	●			●				●	●		●													●
Castanea mollissima	Chinese chestnut			●					●	●			●		●	●	●		●	●	●		●									●	●		
Cercis canadensis	Eastern redbud	●		●				●			●		●		●		●		●	●	●								●						
Chionanthus virginicus	Fringetree	●		●				●			●		●		●	●	●		●	●	●								●						
Cladastris lutea	American yellowwood	●						●		●	●	●	●		●	●		●	●		●			●				●							
Clethera barbinervis	Japanese clethera			●					●			●				●			●	●		●									●				
Cornus florida	Flowering dogwood	●	●	●					●		●		●		●	●	●		●	●	●		●							●					
Cornus kousa	Japanese dogwood			●					●		●		●		●	●	●		●	●	●		●							●					
Cornus mas	Cornelian cherry	●		●					●		●		●		●	●			●	●	●		●							●					
Crataegus species*	Hawthorne species	●		●				●	●	●		●	●	●	●	●	●		●	●	●	●		●	●					●					
Delonix regia	Royal poinciana			●				●	●	●	●		●	●					●	●	●														●
Elaeagnus angustifolia	Russian olive	●		●						●		●	●	●	●	●	●	●	●	●							●								
Firmiana simplex	Chinese parasol tree				●					●	●					●		●	●	●		●									●				●
Fraxinus holotricha	Moraine ash	●		●						●	●							●		●										●					
Fraxinus velutina glabra	Modesto ash	●								●	●		●					●		●	●	●								●					
Halesia carolina	Carolina silverbell	●			●			●			●		●		●		●		●			●								●					
Koelreuteria paniculata	Goldenrain tree			●						●	●	●	●	●	●	●	●		●											●					
Laburnum watereri	Waterer laburnum					●				●		●			●		●				●									●					
Magnolia species*	Magnolia	●								●		●			●	●	●		●	●		●	●	●						●	●	●	●	●	
Malus species*	Crab apple species	●		●					●			●		●		●	●			●		●		●			●	●	●	●					
Melia azedarach	Chinaberry	●		●						●	●			●		●	●			●	●	●		●						●				●	
Phellodendron amurense	Amur cork tree			●						●	●	●			●			●	●		●	●	●	●					●						
Prunus species*	Cherries, apricots, plums, peaches	●								●		●		●	●	●	●				●							●	●	●	●	●				
Pterocarya fraxinifolia	Caucasian wing nut			●						●			●				●			●		●								●					
Pyrus calleryana "Bradford"	Bradford pear				●			●			●	●	●	●		●	●	●		●										●					
Salix babylonica	Babylon weeping willow		●							●		●						●		●		●										●			
Salix elegantissima	Thurlow weeping willow		●							●		●						●		●		●								●					
Sapium sebiferum	Chinese tallow tree			●						●	●						●	●		●	●	●													●
Sorbus alnifolia	Korean mountain ash	●			●					●		●	●			●	●	●	●		●									●					
Sorbus aucuparia	Rowan tree	●		●						●		●				●	●	●		●										●					
Stewartia koreana	Korean stewartia				●				●			●				●		●	●	●	●									●					
Styrax japonica	Japanese snowbell	●		●			●				●		●		●	●		●	●	●										●					
Syringa amurensis japonica	Japanese tree lilac			●	●			●	●		●	●	●		●				●	●	●									●					
Ulmus parvifolia	Chinese elm		●							●		●		●	●	●	●	●	●	●	●									●					
Viburnum sieboldii	Siebold viburnum	●		●					●			●				●	●	●		●	●		●		●					●					

*See other references for local species and varieties.

A. E. Bye & Associates, Landscape Architects; Old Greenwich, Connecticut

LARGE DECIDUOUS TREES—50 FT AND OVER

Botanical Name	Common Name	Rounded	Weeping	Spreading	Conical	Columnar	Oval	Slow	Medium	Fast	Shade Tree	Ornamental	Street Tree	Urban Tree	Seashore Tree	Flowers	Fruit	Leaf Color	Bark	Light Shade	Full Sun	Dry Soil	Moist Soil	Acid Soil	Alkaline Soil	Well Drained Soil	1	2	3	4	5	6	7	8	9	10
Acacia decurrens dealbata	Silver wattle			•						•		•				•					•		•			•										•
Acer platinoides and varieties	Norway maple and varieties	•			•	•				•	•	•	•	•	•	•					•					•			•							
Acer rubrum	Red or swamp maple	•				•				•	•	•	•		•		•	•	•			•							•							
Acer saccharum	Sugar maple				•		•		•		•	•							•		•	•		•			•			•							
Aesculus hippocastanum	Horse chestnut	•				•					•	•				•	•	•			•	•		•						•							
Betula nigra	River birch			•						•	•	•	•				•	•	•		•	•		•	•						•						
Betula papyrifera	Canoe or paper birch			•	•					•	•	•					•	•	•		•	•	•	•					•								
Betula pendula	European birch		•		•	•					•	•					•	•	•		•	•							•								
Carpinus betulus	European hornbeam	•			•		•				•		•	•	•				•	•	•	•										•					
Cercidiphyllum japonicum	Katsura tree	•							•	•	•	•		•	•			•	•	•	•	•		•							•						
Cornus controversa	Giant dogwood			•					•				•				•	•			•			•								•					
Eucalyptus species*	Eucalyptus species	•								•	•	•	•	•				•	•	•	•															•	•
Fagus grandifolia	American beech	•					•				•	•			•			•	•	•	•			•					•								
Fagus sylvatica and varieties*	European beech and varieties	•	•	•			•				•	•			•			•	•	•	•			•						•							
Fraxinus americana	White ash	•								•	•	•			•			•			•									•							
Fraxinus oregona	Oregon ash				•					•	•	•		•				•			•												•				
Fraxinus pennsylvanica lanceolata	Green ash	•		•						•	•	•						•			•							•									
Ginkgo biloba	Ginkgo			•	•	•		•				•		•	•				•		•	•	•							•							
Gleditsia triacanthos and varieties*	Honey locust and varieties			•						•	•	•		•	•	•					•	•								•							
Gordonia lasianthus	Loblolly bay gordonia				•			•				•		•			•				•	•	•											•			
Liquidambar styraciflua	Sweet gum			•						•	•	•		•				•	•	•	•	•										•					
Liriodendron tulipifera	Tulip tree						•			•	•	•		•			•		•		•	•								•							
Magnolia grandiflora	Southern magnolia			•					•			•		•			•	•							•										•		
Nyssa sylvatica	Black tupelo			•					•			•			•			•			•	•		•	•							•					
Pittosporum rhombifolium	Diamond leaf pittosporum	•							•					•			•				•																•
Platanus acerifolium	London plane tree	•		•						•	•	•	•	•	•	•		•		•	•	•		•							•						
Populus alba	White poplar			•		•				•	•			•			•	•			•									•							
Populus tremuloides	Quaking aspen			•						•	•	•						•	•	•	•	•	•		•	•			•	•							
Prunus serotina	Black cherry			•					•		•	•		•			•	•			•								•								
Quercus alba	White oak	•		•			•				•	•			•			•			•	•	•							•							
Quercus borealis	Red oak	•		•					•		•			•	•			•			•									•							
Quercus coccinea	Scarlet oak	•		•					•		•			•				•			•									•							
Quercus falcata	Southern red oak	•		•					•		•			•				•			•											•					
Quercus imbricaria	Shingle oak	•			•		•				•	•						•			•											•					
Quercus kelloggii	California black oak	•		•					•		•							•			•	•		•											•		
Quercus laurifolia	Laurel oak	•									•			•				•			•		•												•		
Quercus palustris	Pin oak			•					•				•	•				•			•		•	•						•							
Quercus phellos	Willow oak	•		•						•		•	•	•				•			•		•	•								•	•			
Quercus robur and varieties*	English oak and varieties	•			•		•				•			•				•			•											•					
Quercus shumardii	Shumard oak		•						•		•			•				•			•		•								•						
Quercus virginiana	Live oak	•		•							•	•		•			•	•			•	•												•		
Salix alba tristis	Golden weeping willow		•							•	•	•			•			•		•	•			•				•									
Sassafras albidum	Sassafras			•					•		•						•	•	•	•	•	•	•							•							
Sophora japonica	Japanese pagoda tree	•		•					•	•	•	•		•	•		•				•	•	•							•							
Tilia cordata	Little leaf linden			•	•	•				•	•	•	•	•		•				•	•	•		•					•								
Tilia euchlora	Crimean linden			•						•	•	•	•	•	•	•	•				•	•		•							•						
Tilia tomentosa	Silver linden			•		•				•	•	•	•	•	•	•	•				•	•		•							•						
Zelkova serrata and varieties*	Japanese zelkova and varieties	•								•	•	•		•	•		•		•		•	•		•			•					•					

*See other references for local species and varieties.

A. E. Bye & Associates, Landscape Architects; Old Greenwich, Connecticut

DECIDUOUS SHRUBS

Botanical Name	Common Name	0 to 3 ft	3 to 6 ft	6 to 10 ft	10 ft and over	Flowers	Fruit	Foliage Color	Good Winter Appearance	Rapid Growth	Easy Maintenance	White	Yellow-orange	Pink-red	Blue-purple	Spring	Summer	Fall	Winter	Urban	Seashore	Hedges	Sun	Shade	Light Shade	Acid Soil	Alkaline Soil	Moist Soil	Dry Soil	Well drained Soil	1	2	3	4	5	6	7	8	9	10
Amelanchier stolonifera	Running serviceberry		●			●	●	●			●	●				●						●		●		●	●		●	●	●				●						
Aronia species*	Chokeberry species	●	●	●	●	●	●	●	●			●	●			●					●	●	●	●		●	●	●	●	●					●						
Berberis species*	Barberry species	●	●	●		●	●	●	●			●		●		●					●	●	●	●		●	●	●	●	●					●						
Calycanthus floridus	Sweet shrub		●	●		●		●				●			●		●						●		●	●	●	●	●						●						
Caragana arborescens	Siberian pea tree				●	●	●							●			●				●		●	●			●	●	●	●		●									
Cercis chinensis	Chinese redbud		●	●		●		●				●			●	●	●							●	●	●				●									●		
Chaenomeles species*	Quince species	●	●			●	●					●	●	●	●		●				●	●	●	●			●	●	●	●	●				●						
Clethra alnifolia	Summer sweet		●			●		●				●	●		●			●				●		●	●	●	●		●					●							
Cornus species*	Dogwood species	●	●	●	●	●	●	●	●	●	●	●	●		●		●				●		●	●		●	●		●	●		●									
Corylopsis species*	Winter hazel species	●	●	●	●	●		●				●		●		●							●	●	●	●	●		●									●			
Cotinus species*	Smoke tree species		●	●		●		●				●		●	●		●						●				●	●	●									●			
Cotoneaster species*	Cotoneaster species	●	●	●	●	●	●	●	●			●	●		●		●				●	●	●	●				●	●					●							
Cytisus species*	Scotch broom species	●	●	●		●			●	●		●	●		●	●					●		●			●		●	●					●							
Deutzia species*	Deutzia species	●	●			●						●	●		●	●				●		●			●			●	●					●							
Euonymus species*	Euonymus species		●	●	●		●	●	●		●					●				●	●	●	●	●		●			●	●			●								
Exochorda species*	Pearlbush species		●	●	●	●						●			●						●		●			●			●	●					●						
Forsythia species*	Forsythia species	●	●	●		●			●	●		●			●					●		●		●		●			●	●					●						
Fothergilla species*	Fothergilla species	●	●	●		●		●				●	●	●		●						●		●	●	●		●							●						
Hamamelis species*	Witch hazel species		●	●	●	●		●	●			●		●		●	●	●	●	●		●		●	●			●	●					●							
Hibiscus species*	Rose of Sharon species		●	●	●	●					●	●		●	●	●		●	●	●	●	●	●	●		●			●	●					●						
Ilex verticillata	Winterberry		●				●	●	●	●		●								●		●		●	●	●		●					●								
Jasminum nudiflorum	Winter jasmine	●	●	●	●	●			●					●			●			●		●		●		●				●					●						
Kerria japonica	Kerria		●	●		●		●	●			●			●		●	●	●		●		●		●			●	●					●							
Kolkwitzia amabilis	Beauty bush		●			●	●	●	●		●			●		●					●		●		●			●	●	●				●							
Lagerstroemia indica	Crape myrtle		●	●	●	●		●	●			●		●	●		●			●		●	●	●			●		●											●	
Lespedeza species*	Bush clover species	●	●			●						●			●		●	●					●			●	●	●					●								
Ligustrum species*	Privet species		●	●	●	●	●			●		●				●	●	●		●	●	●	●	●	●	●			●	●	●		●								
Lindera benzoin	Spicebush		●	●	●	●	●					●		●		●				●			●	●	●	●			●					●							
Myrica pensylvanica	Bayberry		●	●			●		●		●									●	●		●			●			●	●	●	●									
Photinia villosa	Oriental photinia			●	●	●	●	●	●			●	●			●							●		●	●			●	●				●							
Plumeria rubra	Frangipani			●	●	●			●			●	●	●	●		●	●	●			●		●		●			●	●	●										●
Potentilla species*	Bush cinquefoil species		●			●						●	●	●		●	●	●		●			●					●	●		●										
Rhamnus species*	Buckthorn species			●	●		●	●												●	●	●	●	●		●			●	●		●									
Rhododendron	Azalea	●	●	●	●	●						●	●	●	●	●	●				●			●	●	●	●	◦		●		●									
Rosa species*	'Shrub' rose species		●	●	●	●	●	●	●			●	●	●	●		●	●	●		●	●	●	●			●			●	●	●									
Spiraea species*	Spiraea species	●	●	●		●		●		●		●		●		●	●				●		●					●	●						●						
Stephanandra species*	Stephanandra species	●	●	●		●		●				●				●								●					●										●		
Stewartia species*	Stewartia species			●	●	●		●	●			●	●				●							●		●	●		●										●		
Symphoricarpos species*	Snowberry species	●	●				●		●										●		●	●	●	●		●			●	●	●		●								
Symplocos paniculata	Sapphireberry			●	●	●	●					●				●					●		●			●	●												●		
Syringa species*	Lilac species	●	●	●	●	●				●		●	●	●	●	●	●				●	●	●	●		●		●					●								
Vaccinium corymbosum	Highbush blueberry		●	●		●	●	●	●			●	●				●				●	●	●	●		●	●		●								●				
Viburnum species*	Viburnum species	●	●	●	●	●	●	●	●	●			●		●		●	●			●	●	●	●	●	●	●		●	●	●			●							

NOTES

*See other references for local species and varieties. Listings in this chart represent large genera of many species and varieties. Other sources need to be consulted to obtain detailed information. The hardiness zone notations indicate that most of the species within the family are hardy to that zone but there are a few that are not.

A. E. Bye & Associates, Landscape Architects; Old Greenwich, Connecticut

GROUND COVERS

Botanical Name	Common Name	Less than 6 in.	6 to 12 in.	12 to 18 in.	18 in. and over	Sun	Shade	Light Shade	Acid	Alkaline	Seashore	City	Moist Soil	Dry Soil	Well-drained Soil	Green	Dark Green	Blue Green	Gray Green	Purple Green	Flowers	Fruit	Mowable	Slopes	Rapid Growth	Easy Maintenance	1	2	3	4	5	6	7	8	9	10
DECIDUOUS																																				
Asperula odorata	Sweet woodruff		●				●		●				●		●						●				●	●			●							
Coronilla varia	Crown vetch			●	●	●		●	●	●			●	●		●						●			●	●	●		●								
Cotoneaster (spreading varieties)	Cotoneaster		●			●			●	●	●				●		●					●	●		●							●				
Gazania uniflora	Trailing gazania	●				●			●	●					●				●			●			●	●	●									●	
Phlox subulata	Ground pink	●				●								●	●	●						●			●	●			●							
Rosa wichuraiana	Memorial rose		●			●					●				●		●					●			●	●	●					●				
Trifolium repens	White clover	●				●							●			●						●		●		●	●			●							
Vaccinium angustifolium laevifolium	Low bush blueberry		●			●	●	●	●				●			●						●	●			●	●			●							
Veronica repens	Creeping speedwell	●				●	●	●					●			●						●				●	●										
Xanthorhiza simplicissima	Yellowroot			●	●			●					●			●						●				●	●				●						
BROAD LEAVED EVERGREENS																																				
Ajuga reptans	Bugleweed	●				●	●	●					●					●	●		●	●			●	●				●							
Anthemis nobilis	Chamomile	●	●			●									●						●		●		●				●							
Arabis albida	Wall rockcress	●				●							●						●		●								●							
Arctostaphylos uva-ursi	Bearberry		●			●		●	●					●		●						●	●		●		●		●								
Baccharis pilularis	Coyote bush			●	●	●			●			●	●			●						●			●	●	●								●		
Carissa macrocarpa 'green carpet'	Green carpet natal plum		●			●		●	●						●		●	●				●			●											●	
Carpobrotus edulis	Hottentot fig	●				●			●				●		●		●	●				●			●	●	●										●
Ceanothus griseus horizontalis	Carmel creeper			●	●			●				●		●		●						●			●									●		
Ceratostigma plumbaginoides	Leadwort		●			●		●					●	●		●	●					●				●	●							●			
Cornus canadensis	Bunchberry		●				●	●	●				●			●	●					●	●			●		●									
Cotoneaster dammeri	Bearberry cotoneaster		●			●		●	●	●	●	●	●			●						●	●		●		●					●					
Dichondra repens	Dichondra	●				●	●	●					●	●		●								●	●	●											●
Drosanthemum hispidum	Rosea ice plant		●			●						●			●					●		●			●	●	●									●	
Euonymus fortunei coloratus	Purple-leaf wintercreeper	●				●	●	●	●				●			●				●					●		●					●					
Fragaria chiloensis	Wild strawberry		●			●		●				●		●		●						●	●		●	●							●				
Galax aphylla	Galax	●	●				●	●	●				●			●										●	●				●						
Hedera helix	English ivy		●			●	●	●					●	●		●									●	●					●						
Hypericum calycinum	Aaronsbeard Saint-John's-wort		●			●		●							●		●					●			●	●								●			
Iberis sempervirens	Evergreen candytuft		●			●						●	●	●		●						●			●		●					●					
Leucothoe catesbaei	Drooping leucothoe		●	●	●	●	●	●	●				●			●						●			●	●						●					
Lotus bertholettii	Parrot's beak, coral gem	●	●			●								●	●		●					●			●	●									●		
Micromeria chamissonis	Yerba buena	●				●		●		●		●		●		●									●	●								●			
Pachistma canbyi	Canby pachistima		●	●		●	●	●					●			●									●		●					●					
Pachysandra terminalis	Japanese spurge		●				●	●	●				●			●						●	●			●						●					
Rosmarinus officinalis prostratus	Creeping rosemary			●	●	●						●	●		●		●					●			●									●			
Saxifraga stolonifera	Strawberry geranium	●						●					●			●				●	●	●			●									●			
Trachelospermum jasminoides	Star jasmine		●	●		●		●	●				●			●						●				●	●							●			
Vinca minor	Myrtle, periwinkle	●					●	●					●			●						●		●	●	●	●					●					
NEEDLE EVERGREENS																																				
Calluna vulgaris	Scotch heather	●	●	●	●	●		●	●			●				●						●				●					●						
Erica carnea	Spring heath		●			●		●	●						●				●		●	●										●				
Juniperus chinensis varieties	Varieties of Chinese juniper			●	●	●			●		●	●	●	●	●	●	●	●	●						●	●				●						
Juniperus conferta	Shore juniper		●			●					●		●				●								●						●					
Juniperus horizontalis douglasii	Waukegan juniper	●	●			●							●			●									●		●									
Juniperus horizontalis 'Bar Harbor'	Bar Harbor juniper		●			●					●		●	●	●			●	●						●		●									
Juniperus horizontalis 'wiltonii'	Wilton carpet juniper	●				●							●					●							●		●									
Juniperus horizontalis 'plumosa'	Andorra juniper		●			●							●	●	●				●	●					●				●							
Juniperus procumbens 'nana'	Japanese garden juniper	●	●			●							●					●							●		●									
Juniperus sabina tamariscifolia	Tamarix juniper		●			●						●	●	●	●		●								●	●	●				●					
Taxus baccata repandens	Spreading English yew			●	●	●	●	●					●		●		●								●					●						

A. E. Bye & Associates, Landscape Architects; Old Greenwich, Connecticut

PLANT CHARTS

The intent of the plant chart is to indicate the wide variety of plants available to the designer. There are many unusual trees, shrubs, and ground covers for every environmental and design situation. In using the charts, the designer will obtain a general perception of the plants listed. It is strongly recommended that more specific information be sought in botanic journals. The charts note the northernmost reaches of the plant listed, but some plants will not grow where winters are too warm. The southern reach of those particular plants has not been included in the charts because of conflicting and inadequate information. There are many regional variations in climate that should be considered when selecting plants. The designer is urged to consult a landscape architect to ensure the best selection for the design.

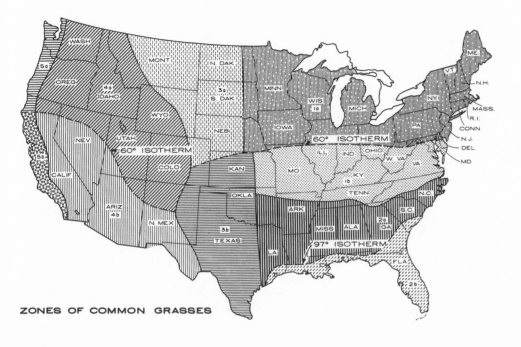

ZONES OF COMMON GRASSES

GRASSES

In selecting a type of grass for lawn development the designer must consider both environmental and use factors. The amount of available sunlight, the temperature range, rainfall, soil type, and drainage will determine the type of grass that will survive in a given location while additional consideration of tolerance to traffic and recuperative rates will ensure the best possible lawn. For example, different grasses are used for athletic fields depending on environmental factors: bluegrasses and fescues in the northern zones; Bermuda grasses and zoysias in the southern zones, and St. Augustine grass in the extreme south. All are rugged, but require different environments to grow well. Another example is bent grass. Although it requires high maintenance, it is desirable for golf courses because of its fine texture and thick growth.

Lawns can be installed by seed, sprigging, or sod at varying costs. Careful installation at the proper time of the year will ensure the health and beauty of the lawn. Proper soil preparation including aerating the soil, adding topsoil, fertilizer, lime, if necessary, good drainage, and the use of high quality certified weedfree seed is important for success. Frequently, mixtures of seeds are used, since growing conditions are rarely uniform throughout the lawn area. This practice can also mitigate the effects of lawn disease. More specific information is available from local agricultural agents.

GRASSES

Botanical Name	Common Name	Sun	Shade	Light Shade	Well-drained Soil	Moist	Dry	Acid	Alkaline	Cool	Warm	Coarse	Fine	Thick	Hairy	High	Moderate	Minimal	Green	Dark Green	Light Green	Blue Green	Gray Green	Brown (hot weather)	Brown (cold weather)	1a	1b	2a	2b	3a	3b	4a	4b	5a	5b
Agropyron	Wheat	●			●			●	●		●							●			●					●	●	●							
Agrostis	Bent	●	●		●		●	●	●	●	●		●			●		●	●							●	●			*		*		●	*
Ammophila	Beach	●			●			●	●	●			●					●			●					●	●	●						●	*
Axonopus	Carpet	●		●			●			●	●							●			●				●			●	●						
Bouteloua	Blue gamma	●			●			●	●				●					●					●	●						*	●	*	●		
Buchloë	Buffalo	●			●			●	●		●		●					●					●	●						●	●	*	*		
Cynodon	Bermuda	●		*	●		●	●			●		●			●		●		●					●			●	●	*		*			●
Eremochloa	Centipede	●		●	●	*		●			●		●				●			●					●			●	●	*		*			*
Festuca	Fescue	●	●	●	●	●	●	●	●	●			●				●			●						●	●	*		*		●	*	●	
Lolium	Rye	●		●	●			●	●	●		●				●		●	●							●	●	*	*			*		●	●
Paspalum notatum	Bahia	●		●	●	*		●			●	●					●		●						●			●	●						
Poa	Bluegrass	●		*	●	●		●		●	●		●			●				●						●	●			*		*		●	
Stenotaphrum	St. Augustine	●	●	●		●		●		●	●	●				●						●			●					*	●	*		*	*
Zoysia	Zoysia	●	●	●			●	●			●		●				●								●						*	*		*	●

*Will grow under special conditions: high altitude, proximity to water, or irrigation.

NOTES

1. Consult local agricultural agent, horticulturist, or nurseryman in your area for best grasses for slopes, maintenance concerns, and general planting instructions.
2. Planting slopes: (a) 3 to 1 is maximum for mowed banks. (b) 2 to 1 is maximum for unmowed banks.

A. E. Bye & Associates, Landscape Architects; Old Greenwich, Connecticut

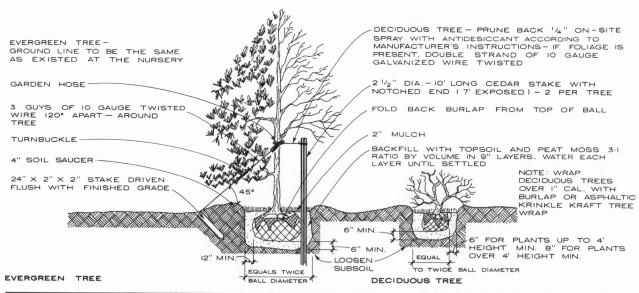

EVERGREEN TREE - GROUND LINE TO BE THE SAME AS EXISTED AT THE NURSERY

GARDEN HOSE

3 GUYS OF 10 GAUGE TWISTED WIRE 120° APART – AROUND TREE

TURNBUCKLE

4" SOIL SAUCER

24" X 2" X 2" STAKE DRIVEN FLUSH WITH FINISHED GRADE

EVERGREEN TREE

DECIDUOUS TREE – PRUNE BACK 1/4" ON-SITE SPRAY WITH ANTIDESICCANT ACCORDING TO MANUFACTURER'S INSTRUCTIONS – IF FOLIAGE IS PRESENT. DOUBLE STRAND OF 10 GAUGE GALVANIZED WIRE TWISTED

2 1/2" DIA. – 10' LONG CEDAR STAKE WITH NOTCHED END (7' EXPOSED) – 2 PER TREE

FOLD BACK BURLAP FROM TOP OF BALL

2" MULCH

BACKFILL WITH TOPSOIL AND PEAT MOSS 3:1 RATIO BY VOLUME IN 9" LAYERS. WATER EACH LAYER UNTIL SETTLED

NOTE: WRAP DECIDUOUS TREES OVER 1" CAL. WITH BURLAP OR ASPHALTIC KRINKLE KRAFT TREE WRAP

6" FOR PLANTS UP TO 4' HEIGHT MIN. 8" FOR PLANTS OVER 4' HEIGHT MIN.

45°

12" MIN.

EQUALS TWICE BALL DIAMETER

6" MIN.

6" MIN.

LOOSEN SUBSOIL

EQUAL

TO TWICE BALL DIAMETER

DECIDUOUS TREE

PLANTING DETAILS – TREES AND SHRUBS

SHRUBS AND MINOR TREES BALLED AND BURLAPPED

HEIGHT RANGE (FT)	MINIMUM BALL DIAMETER (IN.)	MINIMUM BALL DEPTH (IN.)
1 1/2 - 2	10	8
2-3	12	9
3-4	13	10
4-5	15	11
5-6	16	12
6-7	18	13
7-8	20	14
8-9	22	15
9-10	24	16
10-12	26	17

NOTE: Ball sizes should always be of a diameter to encompass the fibrous and feeding root system necessary for the full recovery of the plant.

STANDARD SHADE TREES—BALLED AND BURLAPPED

CALIPER* (IN.)	HEIGHT RANGE (FT)	MAXIMUM HEIGHTS (FT)	MINIMUM BALL DIAMETER (IN.)	MINIMUM BALL DEPTH (IN.)
1/2 - 3/4	5-6	8	12	9
3/4 - 1	6-8	10	14	10
1 - 1 1/4	7-9	11	16	12
1 1/4 - 1 1/2	8-10	12	18	13
1 1/2 - 1 3/4	10-12	14	20	14
1 3/4 - 2	10-12	14	22	15
2 - 2 1/2	12-14	16	24	16
2 1/2 - 3	12-14	16	28	19
3 - 3 1/2	14-16	18	32	20
3 1/2 - 4	14-16	18	36	22
4-5	16-18	22	44	26
5-6	18 and up	26	48	29

*Caliper indicates the diameter of the trunk taken 6 in. above the ground level up to and including 4 in. caliper size and 12 in. above the ground level for larger sizes.

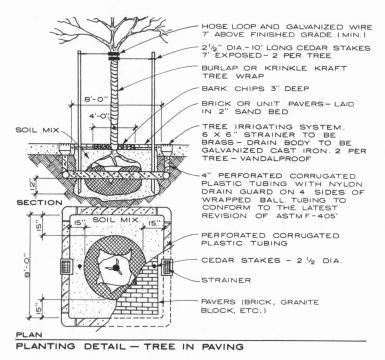

HOSE LOOP AND GALVANIZED WIRE 7' ABOVE FINISHED GRADE (MIN.)

2 1/2" DIA. – 10' LONG CEDAR STAKES 7' EXPOSED – 2 PER TREE

BURLAP OR KRINKLE KRAFT TREE WRAP

BARK CHIPS 3" DEEP

BRICK OR UNIT PAVERS – LAID IN 2" SAND BED

TREE IRRIGATING SYSTEM. 6 X 6" STRAINER TO BE BRASS – DRAIN BODY TO BE GALVANIZED CAST IRON. 2 PER TREE – VANDALPROOF

4" PERFORATED CORRUGATED PLASTIC TUBING WITH NYLON DRAIN GUARD ON 4 SIDES OF WRAPPED BALL. TUBING TO CONFORM TO THE LATEST REVISION OF ASTM F-405'

PERFORATED CORRUGATED PLASTIC TUBING

CEDAR STAKES – 2 1/2 DIA.

STRAINER

PAVERS (BRICK, GRANITE BLOCK, ETC.)

SOIL MIX

8'-0"

4'-0"

SECTION

SOIL MIX

15" 15"

15"

15"

8'-0"

PLAN

PLANTING DETAIL – TREE IN PAVING

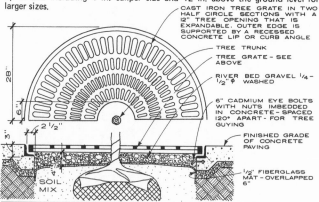

CAST IRON TREE GRATE IN TWO HALF CIRCLE SECTIONS WITH A 12" TREE OPENING THAT IS EXPANDABLE. OUTER EDGE IS SUPPORTED BY A RECESSED CONCRETE LIP OR CURB ANGLE

TREE TRUNK

TREE GRATE – SEE ABOVE

RIVER BED GRAVEL 1/4 - 1/2" φ WASHED

6" CADMIUM EYE BOLTS WITH NUTS IMBEDDED IN CONCRETE – SPACED 120° APART – FOR TREE GUYING

FINISHED GRADE OF CONCRETE PAVING

1/2" FIBERGLASS MAT – OVERLAPPED 6"

SOIL MIX

28"

6"

2 1/2"

3"

TREE GRATE DETAIL

2" MULCH INSTALLED BEFORE PLANTS

SUBSOIL TO BE BROKEN WITH A PICKAX

6" DEEP PLANTING BED CONTAINING 3 PARTS TOP SOIL TO ONE PART PEAT MOSS

GROUND COVER PLANTING DETAIL
NOTE: GROUND COVERS SHOULD BE POT OR CONTAINER GROWN

A. E. Bye & Associates, Landscape Architects; Old Greenwich, Connecticut

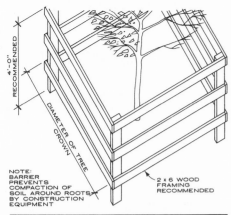

TREE PROTECTION BARRIER

NOTE:
BARRIER PREVENTS COMPACTION OF SOIL AROUND ROOTS BY CONSTRUCTION EQUIPMENT

2 x 6 WOOD FRAMING RECOMMENDED

4'-0" RECOMMENDED

DIAMETER OF CROWN

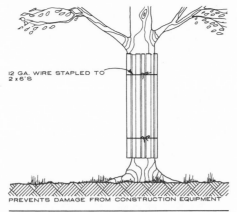

TREE TRUNK PROTECTION

12 GA. WIRE STAPLED TO 2 x 6'S

PREVENTS DAMAGE FROM CONSTRUCTION EQUIPMENT

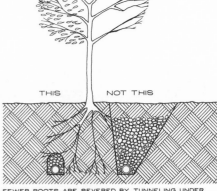

THIS   NOT THIS

FEWER ROOTS ARE SEVERED BY TUNNELING UNDER TREE THAN BY TRENCHING

UNDERGROUND UTILITIES NEAR EXISTING TREES

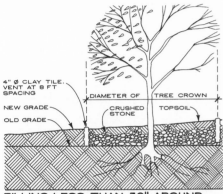

4" Ø CLAY TILE. VENT AT 8 FT SPACING

NEW GRADE
OLD GRADE

DIAMETER OF TREE CROWN
CRUSHED STONE   TOPSOIL

FILLING LESS THAN 30" AROUND EXISTING TREE

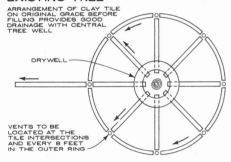

ARRANGEMENT OF CLAY TILE ON ORIGINAL GRADE BEFORE FILLING PROVIDES GOOD DRAINAGE WITH CENTRAL TREE WELL

DRYWELL

VENTS TO BE LOCATED AT THE TILE INTERSECTIONS AND EVERY 8 FEET IN THE OUTER RING

PLAN

FILLING OVER 30" AROUND EXISTING TREE

CUTTING AROUND EXISTING TREES

Extreme care should be taken not to compact the earth within the crown of the tree. Compaction can cause severe root damage and reduce the air and water holding capacity of the soil.

If no surrounding barrier is provided, care should be taken not to operate equipment or store materials within the crown spread of the tree. If this area should be compacted, it would be necessary to aerate the soil thoroughly in the root zone immediately following construction. Certain tree species are severely affected by manipulation of the water table, and great care should be exercised to minimize this condition.

SPECIAL USE OF TREES

Trees for special uses should be branched or pruned naturally according to type. Where a form of growth is desired that is not in accordance with a natural growth habit, this form should be specified. For example:

1. BUSH FORM: Trees that start to branch close to the ground in the manner of a shrub.
2. CLUMPS: Trees with three or more main stems starting from the ground.
3. CUT BACK OR SHEARED: Trees that have been pruned back so as to multiply the branching structure and to develop a more formal effect.
4. ESPALIER: Trees pruned and trained to grow flat against a building or trellis, usually in a predetermined pattern or design.
5. PLEACHING: A technique of severe pruning, usually applied to a row or bosque of trees to produce a geometrically formal or clipped hedgelike effect.
6. POLLARDING: The technique in which annual severe pruning of certain species of trees serves to produce abundant vigorous growth the following year.
7. TOPIARY: Trees sheared or trimmed closely in a formal geometric pattern, or sculptural shapes frequently resembling animals or flowers.

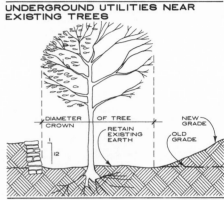

DIAMETER OF TREE   NEW GRADE
CROWN   RETAIN EXISTING EARTH   OLD GRADE

12

FILLING GRADE AROUND EXISTING TREE

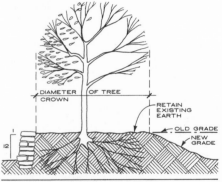

DIAMETER OF TREE
CROWN   RETAIN EXISTING EARTH

12   OLD GRADE
NEW GRADE

CUTTING GRADE AROUND EXISTING TREE

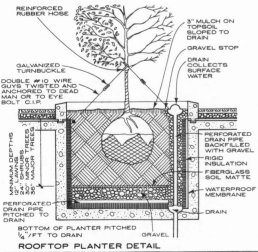

REINFORCED RUBBER HOSE

GALVANIZED TURNBUCKLE

DOUBLE #10 WIRE GUYS TWISTED AND ANCHORED TO DEAD MAN OR TO EYE BOLT C.I.P.

3" MULCH ON TOPSOIL SLOPED TO DRAIN
GRAVEL STOP
DRAIN COLLECTS SURFACE WATER

PERFORATED DRAIN PIPE BACKFILLED WITH GRAVEL
RIGID INSULATION
FIBERGLASS SOIL MATTE
WATERPROOF MEMBRANE
DRAIN

MINIMUM DEPTHS
12" LAWNS
24" SHRUBS
36" MAJOR TREES

PERFORATED DRAIN PIPE PITCHED TO DRAIN

BOTTOM OF PLANTER PITCHED 1/4"/FT TO DRAIN   GRAVEL

ROOFTOP PLANTER DETAIL

PLANTING ON STRUCTURES

SELECTING PLANTS FOR ROOFTOPS

WIND TOLERANCE

Higher elevations and exposure to wind can cause defoliation and increased transpiration rate. High parapet walls with louvers screen wind velocity and provide shelter for plants.

HIGH EVAPORATION RATE

Drying effects of wind and sun on soil around planter reduce available soil moisture rapidly. Irrigation, mulches, moisture holding soil additives (perlite, vermiculite and peat moss), and insulation assist in reducing this moisture loss.

RAPID SOIL TEMPERATURE FLUCTUATION

The conduction capacity of planter materials tends to produce a broad range of soil temperatures. Certain plant species suffer severe root damage because of cold or heat. Use of rigid insulation lining planter alleviates this condition.

TOPSOIL

Topsoil in planters should be improved to provide the optimum growing condition. A general formula would add fertilizer (as per soil testing) plus 1 part peat moss or vermiculite (high water holding capacity) to 3 parts topsoil. More specific requirements for certain varieties of plants or grasses should be considered.

ROOT CAPACITY

Plant species should be carefully selected to adapt to the size of the plant bed. If species with shallow fibrous roots are used instead of species with a tap root system consult with nurseryman. Consider the ultimate maturity of the plant species in sizing planter.

Jim E. Miller and David W. Wheeler; Saratoga Associates; Saratoga Springs, New York

Erik Johnson; Lawrence Cook and Associates; Falls Church, Virginia

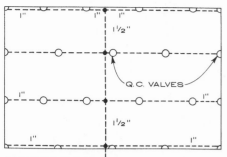

QUICK-COUPLING SYSTEM

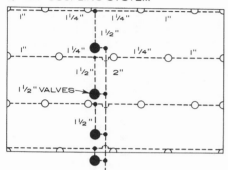

ROTARY POP-UP SYSTEM

TYPICAL LAYOUTS - AREA 1.15 ACRES

DESIGN FACTORS

a. Size of the supply line; b. length of supply line; c. available water pressure. These factors will govern the type of system, type of heads and pipe size to be used.

TYPES OF SYSTEMS

Uses	SPRAY SYSTEM		ROTARY POP-UP	IMPACT SYSTEM
Uses	Residential, light commercial		Commercial, recreational	Commercial, agricultural
Affects of wind/ evaporation	Low		Moderate	High
Pressure (psi)	15–30		30–100	25–100
Maximum operating radius (ft)	360°	30	97	117
	180°	15	97	77
	90°	12	97	77
Head spacing (ft)	10–24		30–100	70–100

TYPES OF PIPE

Polyvinyl chloride or polyethylene piping is commonly used, since it is easily cut and joined together. Steel and copper pipe is also used. Standard pipe is produced in 1/2 to 12 in. diameters and 20 or 40 ft lengths. Pipe sleeves should be preset under walks and through walls for future extension of the system.

TYPES OF CONTROL

QUICK COUPLER: This system is normally under pressure, and key is inserted where water is needed.

MANUAL: This system is turned on by use of a valve; all heads are in place.

AUTOMATIC: This system is operated from a central control unit. The valves are placed at remote locations with lines from the valves to the control unit. The control lines are buried with the pipe.

PRECIPITATION RATES

The amount of precipitation applied to lawn areas must be adjusted according to the species of grass, the traffic it receives, the subsoil conditions, and the gradient across its surface. Typical precipitation rates range from 1/10 in./hr for heavy, dense soils to 3/4 in./hr for light, sandy soils. Final calculations for lawn sprinkler system designs should be entrusted to expert consultants.

John Barclay; Seibert, Hunter, Shute & Plumley; Medford, Oregon

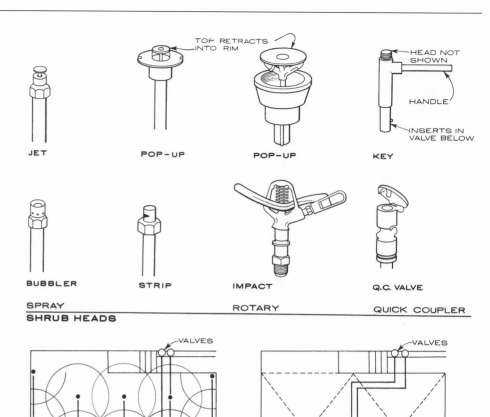

SHRUB HEADS

STANDARD SPRAY HEADS
(OVERTHROW NOT PERMITTED IN SOME AREAS)

OPTIONAL HEADS AVAILABLE

TYPICAL LAYOUT - RESIDENTIAL

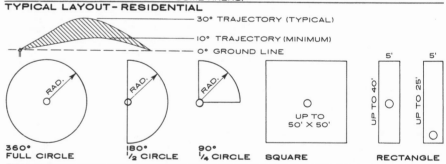

30° TRAJECTORY (TYPICAL)
10° TRAJECTORY (MINIMUM)
0° GROUND LINE

360° FULL CIRCLE   180° 1/2 CIRCLE   90° 1/4 CIRCLE   SQUARE   RECTANGLE

PRECIPITATION PATTERNS

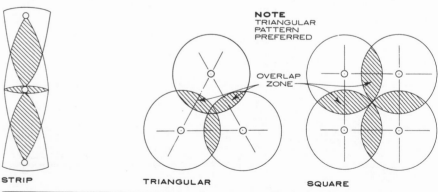

NOTE TRIANGULAR PATTERN PREFERRED

OVERLAP ZONE

STRIP   TRIANGULAR   SQUARE

PRECIPITATION COVERAGE

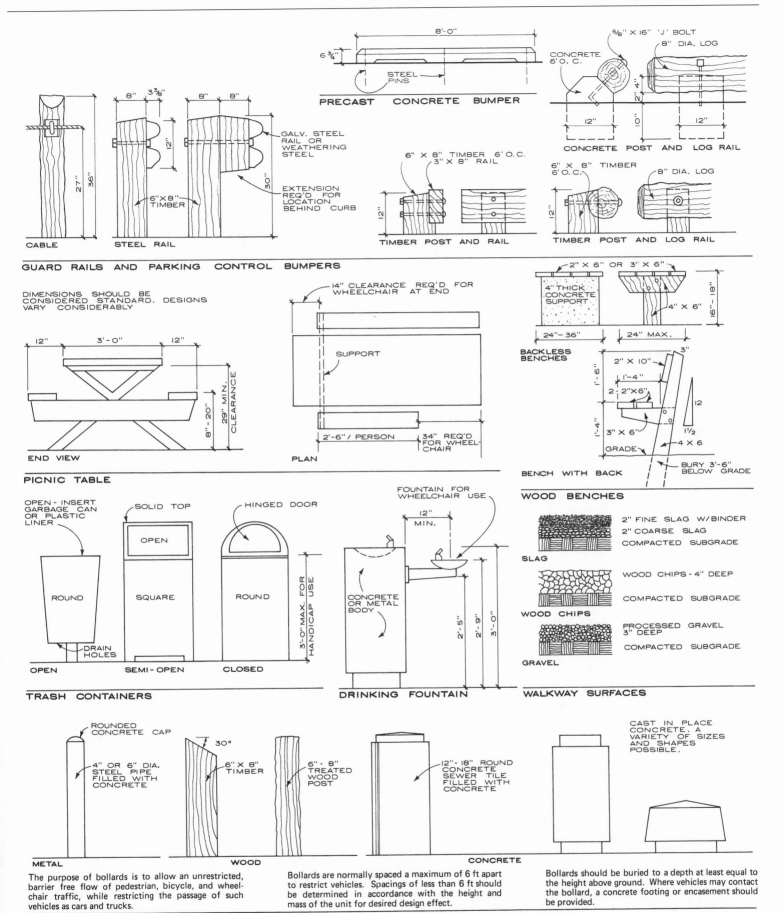

PRECAST CONCRETE BUMPER

CONCRETE POST AND LOG RAIL

CABLE

STEEL RAIL

TIMBER POST AND RAIL

TIMBER POST AND LOG RAIL

GUARD RAILS AND PARKING CONTROL BUMPERS

DIMENSIONS SHOULD BE CONSIDERED STANDARD. DESIGNS VARY CONSIDERABLY

END VIEW

PLAN

PICNIC TABLE

BACKLESS BENCHES

BENCH WITH BACK

WOOD BENCHES

OPEN

SEMI-OPEN

CLOSED

TRASH CONTAINERS

DRINKING FOUNTAIN

SLAG

2" FINE SLAG W/BINDER
2" COARSE SLAG
COMPACTED SUBGRADE

WOOD CHIPS

WOOD CHIPS - 4" DEEP
COMPACTED SUBGRADE

GRAVEL

PROCESSED GRAVEL 3" DEEP
COMPACTED SUBGRADE

WALKWAY SURFACES

METAL

WOOD

CONCRETE

The purpose of bollards is to allow an unrestricted, barrier free flow of pedestrian, bicycle, and wheelchair traffic, while restricting the passage of such vehicles as cars and trucks.

Bollards are normally spaced a maximum of 6 ft apart to restrict vehicles. Spacings of less than 6 ft should be determined in accordance with the height and mass of the unit for desired design effect.

Bollards should be buried to a depth at least equal to the height above ground. Where vehicles may contact the bollard, a concrete footing or encasement should be provided.

BOLLARDS

John M. Beckett; Beckett, Raeder, Rankin, Inc.; Ann Arbor, Michigan

PLAY ELEMENTS

Several basic activities constitute the activity play and concurrently several basic elements can be combined to create a play environment. The physical activities of jumping, climbing, swinging, sliding, crawling, hanging, running, building are essential to play and must be provided by a play area. The social and intellectual aspect of play must also be accommodated; imitation, role playing, interaction with others, and problem solving are essential to a child's growth. A playground must challenge children to maintain their interest and participation. The play equipment should allow the child to challenge himself or herself physically and to expand self-understanding.

GROWTH AND DEVELOPMENT

As children grow their physical abilities change, as does the scale of equipment that will challenge them. Physical growth is accommodated by social development resulting in different levels and types of interaction and activity. A child's play experience must be successful as well as challenging. Therefore play equipment should be designed and selected to meet the physical and intellectual requirements of groups that will use it. The height, distance between levels, and the ability and strength required to use the equipment should be scaled to the size and level of social and intellectual development of the child.

EQUIPMENT COMPONENTS

Several basic elements may be used to create play equipment. These elements are seen in the wide range of manufactured products available. The most commonly used and easily manipulated components are round, square, and rectangular timber, steel pipe and sheets, tires, drums, ladders, and landform, as illustrated below. The greater the variety of combinations to which these components are applied, the more options for play are available to the user.

SINGLE UNIT VS. INTEGRATED PLAY EQUIPMENT

Many types of play equipment are designed to stand alone as units. While they may often be linked to other equipment, they are generally single activity items. Where space or other conditions limit the scope of development such equipment is useful. However, since activity proceeds in a continuous flow, integrated play areas have proved to be more successful than arrangements of individual items. Linking of equipment and equipment that combines several activities on one structure increase the options available to the user and tend to increase the interest and challenge.

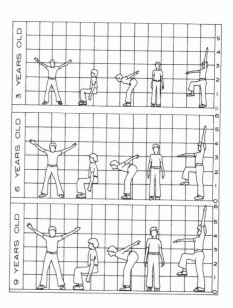

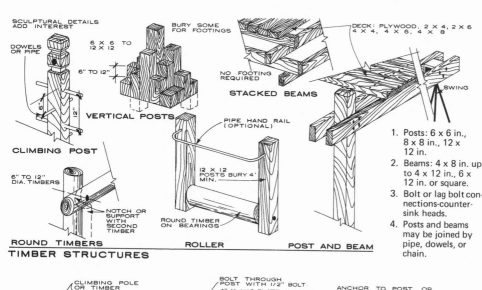

TIMBER STRUCTURES

1. Posts: 6 x 6 in., 8 x 8 in., 12 x 12 in.
2. Beams: 4 x 8 in. up to 4 x 12 in., 6 x 12 in. or square.
3. Bolt or lag bolt connections-countersink heads.
4. Posts and beams may be joined by pipe, dowels, or chain.

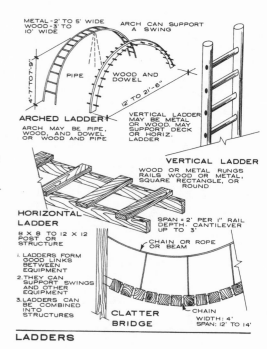

LADDERS

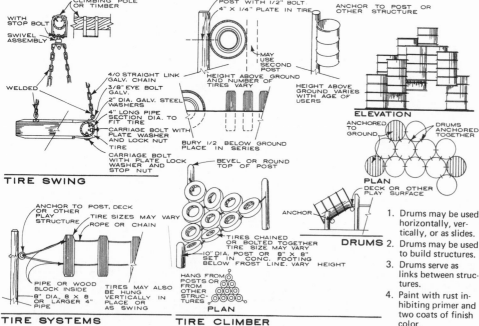

TIRE SWING

TIRE SYSTEMS

TIRE CLIMBER

DRUMS

1. Drums may be used horizontally, vertically, or as slides.
2. Drums may be used to build structures.
3. Drums serve as links between structures.
4. Paint with rust inhibiting primer and two coats of finish color.

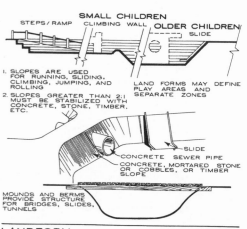

LANDFORM

Bruce A. Rankin; Beckett, Raeder, Rankin, Inc.; Ann Arbor, Michigan

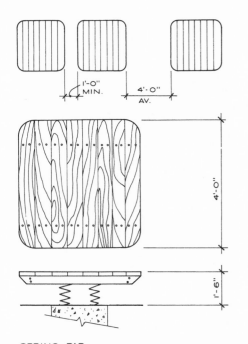

SPRING PAD

NOTE
SINGLE UNIT PLAY EQUIPMENT: Generally designed to provide one or two activities in a specific, controlled location. Where integrated systems are not possible, single units can be used, especially if they are located so that a sequence or sequences of activities can be followed by the users.

SINGLE UNIT PLAY EQUIPMENT

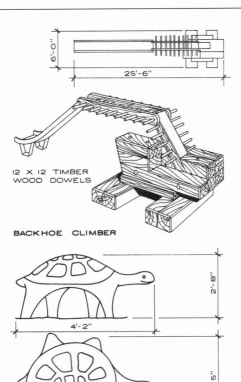

12 X 12 TIMBER
WOOD DOWELS

BACKHOE CLIMBER

TURTLE

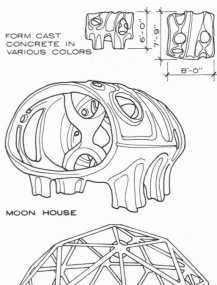

FORM CAST
CONCRETE IN
VARIOUS COLORS

MOON HOUSE

DIA.: 8'-17'; HEIGHT: 4'-7';
GALVANIZED 1⁵⁄₁₆" O.D. PIPE

DOME CLIMBER

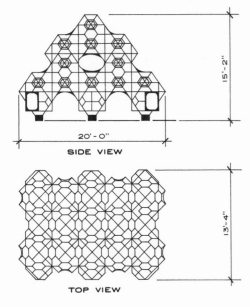

SIDE VIEW

TOP VIEW

³⁄₁₆" CLEAR LEXAN
CURVED SPACE SYSTEM

NOTE
MODULAR PLAY UNITS: Basic building blocks for a variety of structures through either combinations or juxtapositions. Such units can stand alone or be integrated into a system. They offer the designer considerable latitude in structuring a play area.

MODULAR UNIT PLAY EQUIPMENT

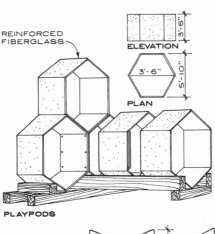

REINFORCED
FIBERGLASS

ELEVATION

PLAN

PLAYPODS

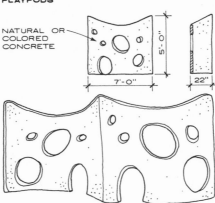

NATURAL OR
COLORED
CONCRETE

PLAYWALL

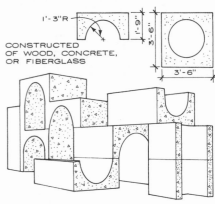

CONSTRUCTED
OF WOOD, CONCRETE,
OR FIBERGLASS

PRECAST BLOCKS

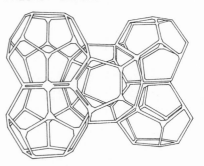

5'-6" DODECAHEDRON UNITS;
ENAMELED 1⁵⁄₈" O.D. STEEL PIPE

PLAY CLIMBERS

Bruce A. Rankin, Beckett Raeder & Rankin, Inc. Ann Arbor, Michigan

Robin Roberts; Washington, D.C.

INTEGRATED PLAY AREAS

Integrated play areas may be comprised of several types and sizes of elements. The goal of integrating equipment is to establish connections between activities and activity zones so that a continuous flow is maintained. The child may create his or her own sequence of events within a wide variety of options.

Structures that combine several activities stimulate and challenge the user by allowing imagination and interplay with others to determine how the piece of equipment is used. Combining materials on a structure creates further variety and interest.

Play areas should be treated as three-dimensional systems allowing movement of various kinds (swinging, climbing, sliding, etc.) vertically, horizontally, and diagonally at varying levels. They should be flexible and adaptable to the changes in individual growth.

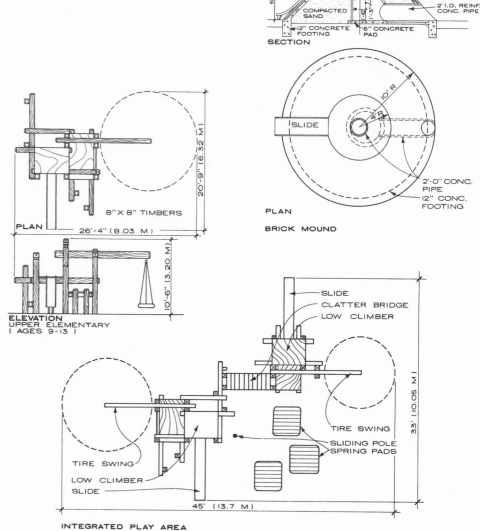

NOTES

Two methods of expanding the capabilities of an integrated playground are linking and juxtapositioning.

1. LINKING OF EQUIPMENT: Connecting activity centers with links that are in themselves play structures, thus multiplying the possible uses of all of the structures involved.
2. JUXTAPOSITIONING EQUIPMENT: Placing units close enough together to generate interaction from one to the other; also increases the play potential and interest of the area.

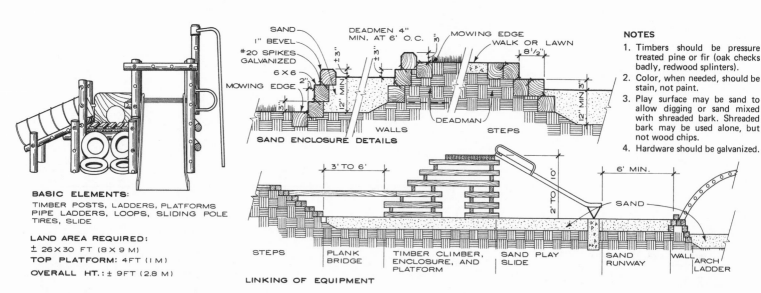

BASIC ELEMENTS:

TIMBER POSTS, LADDERS, PLATFORMS
PIPE LADDERS, LOOPS, SLIDING POLE
TIRES, SLIDE

LAND AREA REQUIRED:
± 26 × 30 FT (8 × 9 M)
TOP PLATFORM: 4FT (1M)
OVERALL HT.: ± 9FT (2.8 M)

NOTES

1. Timbers should be pressure treated pine or fir (oak checks badly, redwood splinters).
2. Color, when needed, should be stain, not paint.
3. Play surface may be sand to allow digging or sand mixed with shreaded bark. Shreaded bark may be used alone, but not wood chips.
4. Hardware should be galvanized.

Bruce A. Rankin; Beckett, Raeder, Rankin, Inc.; Ann Arbor, Michigan

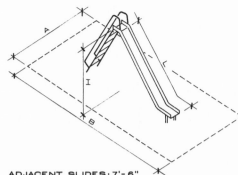

ADJACENT SLIDES: 7'- 6"
(CHUTES C.TO C.) OTHERS 10' O.C.

SLIDES

		NURSERY		STRAIGHT		RACER	
H	L	A	B	A	B	A	B
5	10	8	20				
6	12	8	22				
7	14	8	24				
8	16			12	30	20	30
10	20			12	35	20	35
12	24			15	40	25	40
13½	30			15	45	25	45

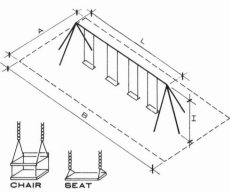

CHAIR   SEAT

SWINGS

NO SWINGS	CHAIR TYPE			SEAT TYPE						
	L	A	B	L	A	B	A	B	A	B
2	8	17	24	9	17	25	21	25	25	25
3	10	17	26	15	17	31	21	31	25	31
4	16	17	32	18	17	34	21	34	25	34
6	20,24	17	38	27,30	17	46	21	46	25	46
8				36	17	52	21	52	25	52
9				45	17	61	21	61	25	61
Height	8'			8',10',12'	8'		10'		12'	

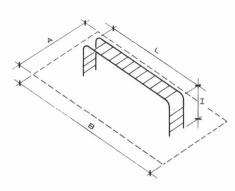

HORIZONTAL LADDER

HEIGHT	LENGTH	A	B
6	12	8	25
7½	16	8	30

GENERAL PLANNING INFORMATION

EQUIPMENT	AREA (SQ FT)	CAPACITY (NUMBER OF CHILDREN)
Slide	450	4-6
Low swing	150	1
High swing	250	1
Horizontal ladder	375	6-8
Seesaw	100	2
Junior climbing gym	180	8-10
General climbing gym	500	15-20

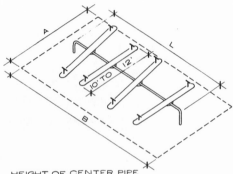

HEIGHT OF CENTER PIPE
1'-0" TO 3'-0" ABOVE GROUND

SEESAWS

BOARDS	1	2	3	4	6
L	3	6	9	12	18
A	20	20	20	20	20
B	5	10	15	20	25

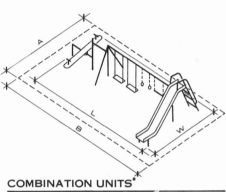

COMBINATION UNITS*

ENCLOSURE LIMITS
A = W + 12'-0''
B = L + 6'-0''

*Types and no. of units are variable.

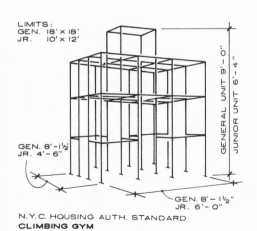

LIMITS:
GEN. 18' x 18'
JR. 10' x 12'

GENERAL UNIT 9'-0"
JUNIOR UNIT 6'-4"

GEN. 8'-1½"
JR. 4'-6"

GEN. 8'-1½"
JR. 6'-0"

N.Y.C. HOUSING AUTH. STANDARD
CLIMBING GYM

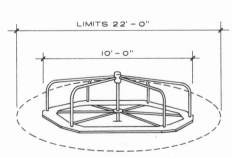

LIMITS:
A = 8'-0"
B = L +6'-0"

HORIZONTAL BARS

LIMITS 22'-0"
10'-0"

10 FT. DIAMETER IS CONSIDERED STAND-
ARD. OTHER DIAMETERS = 12',14'& 16'
LIMITS 24', 26'& 28' DIA.

MERRY - GO - ROUND

Vincent F. Nauseda; Sasaki, Dawson Associates, Inc.; Watertown, Massachusetts

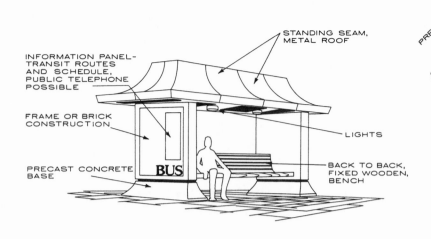

COMMUNITY TRANSIT SHELTER
MILD CLIMATE, OPEN ON TWO SIDES

URBAN TRANSIT SHELTER
COLD CLIMATE, OPEN VISUALLY ON
ALL SIDES FOR EASY SURVEILLANCE

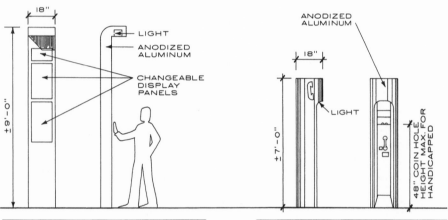

URBAN INFORMATION KIOSK

TELEPHONE KIOSK

URBAN AREA KIOSK

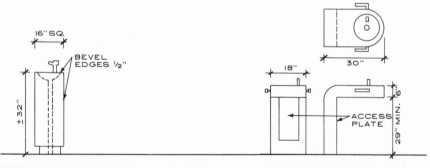

CONCRETE DRINKING FOUNTAIN

METAL DRINKING FOUNTAIN, ACCOMMODATES USERS IN WHEELCHAIRS

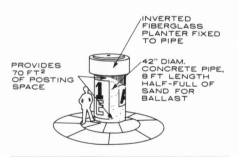

CAMPUS KIOSK

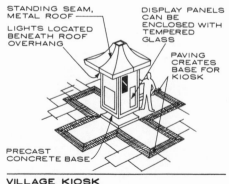

VILLAGE KIOSK

SITE DETAILS

The process of designing and detailing has changed significantly over the last decade with the increased availability of well-designed, cataloged site furnishings. The need for custom designed site furnishings, however, is still felt on many urban design projects. Because of this dual option, the designer is forced to choose the alternative that best serves the project's design objectives. In some cases, both cataloged and custom designed site furnishings are used, defining still a third option.

Among the many considerations in making site detailing decisions are the existing site furnishings in the development area, local codes, the availability of cataloged site furnishings, local maintenance concerns, and cost. Each area of site furnishing detailing emphasizes certain unique considerations. Such considerations involve user habits and needs, maintenance, safety, aesthetics, and construction feasibility. The emphasis of relevant considerations is noted on the above details.

Johnson, Johnson & Roy; Ann Arbor, Michigan

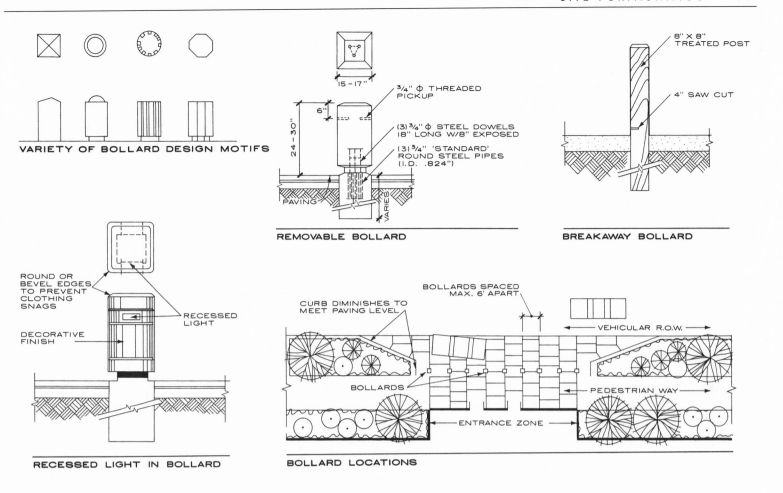

VARIETY OF BOLLARD DESIGN MOTIFS

REMOVABLE BOLLARD

15 – 17"

6"

24 – 30"

VARIES

PAVING

¾" Φ THREADED PICKUP

(3) ¾" Φ STEEL DOWELS 18" LONG W/8" EXPOSED

(3) ¾" 'STANDARD' ROUND STEEL PIPES (I.D. .824")

BREAKAWAY BOLLARD

8" X 8" TREATED POST

4" SAW CUT

RECESSED LIGHT IN BOLLARD

ROUND OR BEVEL EDGES TO PREVENT CLOTHING SNAGS

DECORATIVE FINISH

RECESSED LIGHT

BOLLARD LOCATIONS

CURB DIMINISHES TO MEET PAVING LEVEL

BOLLARDS SPACED MAX. 6' APART

VEHICULAR R.O.W.

BOLLARDS

PEDESTRIAN WAY

ENTRANCE ZONE

VARIETY OF BENCH DESIGN MOTIFS

MOLDED FIBERGLASS   DOUBLE BACK   CONTOURED WOOD

STONE OR MASONRY   WALL MOUNTED   WOOD WITH CONCRETE BASE

NOTE
BENCHES SHOULD BE LOCATED SO AS NOT TO CONFLICT WITH MAJOR PEDESTRIAN FLOW

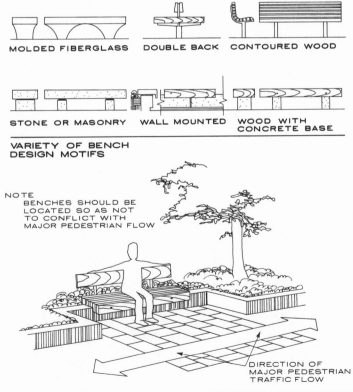

DIRECTION OF MAJOR PEDESTRIAN TRAFFIC FLOW

BENCH LOCATION

Johnson, Johnson & Roy; Ann Arbor, Michigan

WALL HUNG BENCH DETAIL

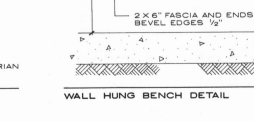

BRICK WALL W/CONCRETE FILL

¼" X 3" STEEL BAND, BENT TO SHAPE AND PAINTED FLAT BLACK

2 X 8", BEVEL ½" TOP AND BOTTOM

¼" Φ LAG SCREW W/NEOPRENE AND GALVANIZED WASHER

½" Φ GALVANIZED ROD, THREAD BOTH ENDS

3"

6 COURSES

WELD SECURELY GALVANIZED WASHER AND NUT

14 – 16"

2" Φ X ¼" NEOPRENE WASHERS

2 X 2 X ¼" STEEL ANGLE ± 3' O.C. PAINTED FLAT BLACK

2 X 4'S

2 X 6" FASCIA AND ENDS BEVEL EDGES ½"

1' – 0"

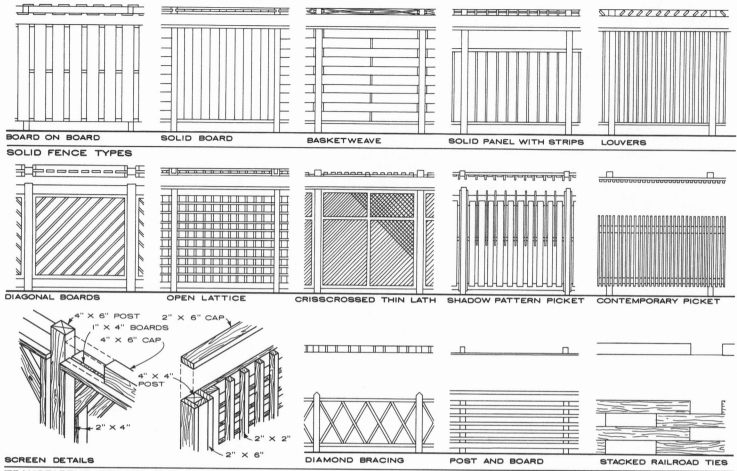

BOARD ON BOARD   SOLID BOARD   BASKETWEAVE   SOLID PANEL WITH STRIPS   LOUVERS

SOLID FENCE TYPES

DIAGONAL BOARDS   OPEN LATTICE   CRISSCROSSED THIN LATH   SHADOW PATTERN PICKET   CONTEMPORARY PICKET

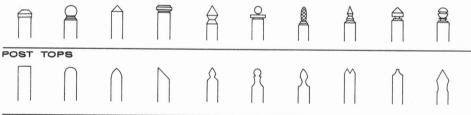

DIAMOND BRACING   POST AND BOARD   STACKED RAILROAD TIES

4" X 6" POST
1" X 4" BOARDS
4" X 6" CAP
2" X 6" CAP
4" X 4" POST
2" X 4"
2" X 2"
2" X 6"

SCREEN DETAILS

TRANSPARENT FENCES AND SCREENS

GENERAL NOTES

The following issues should be considered when selecting a wood fence pattern:

1. The topography of the site and the prevailing wind conditions.
2. The architectural style of surrounding buildings as well as the adjacent use of land.
3. The required height of the fence and the size of the property to be enclosed.

Wood fences can be constructed as solid walls and used near buildings for protection and privacy of outdoor spaces. A semitransparent wood screen is often used to enclose an outdoor room without totally obstructing views or restricting natural ventilation. Long open fence patterns are best used at the property line to define boundaries or limit access to a site.

MATERIALS

Wood posts and rails are usually made of red or white oak, western larch, many species of pine, eastern red cedar, or redwood. Wood or aluminum caps should be used wherever end grains are exposed to the weather.

Most heartwoods, especially cedar and redwood, have superior natural resistance to decay. Other exposed wood members should be treated with water soluble preservatives such as chromated copper arsenate (CCA) or pentachlorophenol dissolved in a volatile solvent. Creosote or pentachlorophenal in an oil solvent should be avoided, since they do not mix with stains or paints.

Uncoated wood rapidly weathers to a shade of gray. A broad range of colors are obtainable with standard paints, bleaches, and stains. Clear water repellents may be used with redwood and cedar. Natural finishes or penetrating stains allow more of the wood grain to show than paint and are preferable for severe weather exposures. Varnishes deteriorate rapidly in sunlight and water.

Fasteners should be of noncorrosive aluminum alloy or stainless steel. Top quality, hot dip galvanized steel is acceptable. Metal flanges, cleats, bolts, and screws are better than common nails.

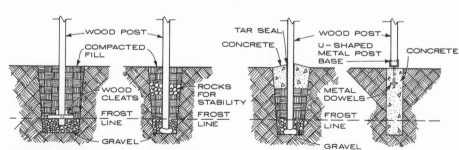

POST TOPS

PICKET TOPS

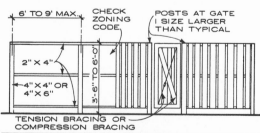

6' TO 9' MAX.
CHECK ZONING CODE
POSTS AT GATE 1 SIZE LARGER THAN TYPICAL
2" X 4"
4" X 4" OR 4" X 6"
3'-6" TO 6'-0"
TENSION BRACING OR COMPRESSION BRACING

TYPICAL FENCE DIMENSIONS

WOOD POST
COMPACTED FILL
WOOD CLEATS
FROST LINE
GRAVEL
ROCKS FOR STABILITY
FROST LINE
TAR SEAL
CONCRETE
WOOD POST
U-SHAPED METAL POST BASE
METAL DOWELS
FROST LINE
GRAVEL
CONCRETE

FOOTING DETAILS

Charles R. Heuer, AIA; Washington, D.C.

CONSIDERATIONS

The following factors must be considered when installing or renovating outdoor lighting systems:

1. In general, overhead lighting is more efficient and economical than low level lighting.
2. Fixtures should provide an overlapping pattern of light at a height of about 7 ft.
3. Lighting levels should respond to site hazards such as steps, ramps, and steep embankments.
4. Posts and standards should be placed so that they do not create hazards for pedestrians or vehicles.

NOTE

All exterior installations must be provided with ground fault interruption circuit.

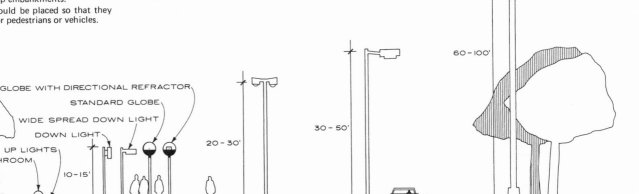

LOW LEVEL
- Heights below eye level
- Very finite patterns with low wattage capabilities
- Incandescent and fluorescent
- Lowest maintenance requirements but highly susceptible to vandals

MALL AND WALKWAY
- 10-15' heights average multiuse because of extreme variety of fixtures and light patterns
- Incandescent, mercury vapor
- Susceptible to vandals

SPECIAL PURPOSE
- 20-30' heights average
- Recreational, commercial, residential, industrial
- Metal halide, mercury vapor
- Fixtures maintained by gantry

PARKING AND ROADWAY
- 30-50' heights average
- Large recreational, commercial, industrial areas; highways
- Mercury vapor, high pressure sodium
- Fixtures maintained by gantry

HIGH MAST
- 60-100' heights average
- Large area lighting—parking, recreational, highway interchanges
- Mercury vapor, high pressure sodium
- Fixtures must lower for maintenance

DEFINITIONS

A lumen is a unit used for measuring the amount of light energy given off by a light source. A footcandle is a unit used for measuring the amount of illumination on a surface. The amount of usable light from any given source is partially determined by the source's angle of incidence and the distance to the illuminated surface. See Chapter 1 on illumination.

RECOMMENDED LIGHTING LEVELS IN FOOTCANDLES

	COMMERCIAL	INTERMEDIATE	RESIDENTIAL
PEDESTRIAN AREAS			
Sidewalks	0.9	0.6	0.2
Pedestrian ways	2.0	1.0	0.5
VEHICULAR ROADS			
Freeway*	0.6	0.6	0.6
Major road and expressway*	2.0	1.4	1.0
Collector road	1.2	0.9	0.6
Local road	0.9	0.6	0.4
Alleys	0.6	0.4	0.2
PARKING AREAS			
Self-parking	1.0	—	—
Attendant parking	2.0	—	—
Security problem area	—	—	5.0
Minimum for television viewing of important interdiction areas	10.0	10.0	10.0
BUILDING AREAS			
Entrances	5.0	—	—
General grounds	1.0	—	—

*Both mainline and ramps.

Johnson, Johnson & Roy; Ann Arbor, Michigan

MINIMUM MAINTAINED FOOTCANDLES, MEASURED ON GROUND SURFACE AT POINT OF LEAST ILLUMINATION

NOTE

The total intensity of two or more overlapping light patterns equals the sum of their individual intensities.

MEASURING LIGHT INTENSITY IN FOOTCANDLES

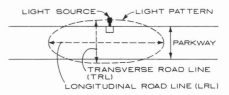

1. CUTOFF means that maximum of 10% of light source lumens fall outside of TRL area
2. SEMICUTOFF means that maximum of 30% of light source lumens fall outside of the TRL area
3. NONCUTOFF means that no control limitations exist

CUTOFF TERMINOLOGY
(NOTE: "CUTOFF" IS MEASURED ALONG TRL.)

NOTE

Degree of cutoff is determined by one of the following:

(a) design of fixture housing
(b) incorporation of prismatic lens over light source
(c) addition of shield to fixture on "house side"

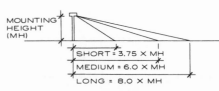

SHORT = 3.75 X MH
MEDIUM = 6.0 X MH
LONG = 8.0 X MH

TYPES OF DISTRIBUTION
(NOTE: "DISTRIBUTION" IS MEASURED ALONG LRL)

VEHICULAR CONSIDERATIONS

There are strong differences between the perceptual performance of the driver and that of the pedestrian. Increasing speed imposes five limitations on man:

1. MAN'S CONCENTRATION INCREASES: While stationary or walking, a person's attention may be widely dispersed. When moving in an automobile, however, he or she concentrates on those factors that are relevant to the driving experience.

2. THE POINT OF CONCENTRATION RECEDES: As speed or motion increases, a person's concentration is directed at a focal point increasingly farther away.

3. PERIPHERAL VISION DIMINISHES: As the eye concentrates on detail at a point of focus a great distance ahead, the angular field of vision shrinks. This shrinking process is a function of focusing distance, angle of vision, and distance of foreground detail.

4. FOREGROUND DETAIL FADES INCREASINGLY: While concentrating on more significant distant objects, a person perceives foreground objects to be moving and increasingly blurred.

5. SPACE PERCEPTION BECOMES IMPAIRED: As the time available for perceiving objects decreases, specific details become less noticeable, making spatial perception more difficult.

With an increasing rate of motion, it becomes more and more important that copy, including illustrations and symbols, be created specifically for out-of-doors use and not merely rescaled from other media of communication. The safety of the motorist and passengers can depend on the clarity of messages conveyed by signs.

VEHICLE SPEEDS VERSUS LETTER HEIGHT ON TRAFFIC SIGNS

INITIAL SPEED	DISTANCE TRAVELED WHILE READING	DISTANCE TRAVELED WHILE SLOWING	TOTAL DISTANCE	SIZE OF COPY AT 65 FT/IN.
30 mph	110 ft	200 ft	310 ft	4.8 in.
40 mph	147 ft	307 ft	454 ft	7.0 in.
50 mph	183 ft	360 ft	543 ft	8.4 in.
60 mph	220 ft	390 ft	610 ft	9.4 in.

NOTE: It is recommended that street name signs have 4 in. letters in area where vehicle speeds are 30-35 mph. For speeds of 40 mph and over, a 5 in. letter size is recommended.

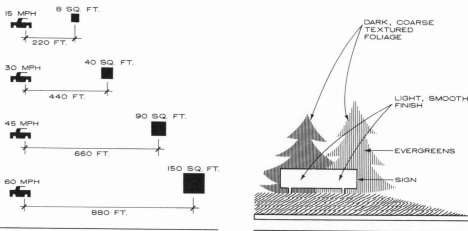

SPEED, SIGHT DISTANCE AND GRAPHIC SIZE RELATION SHIPS

NOTE: LETTERS SHOULD CONSTITUTE APPROXIMATELY 40% OF GRAPHIC'S AREA.

CONSIDER BACKGROUND WHEN CHOOSING COLOR AND MATERIALS

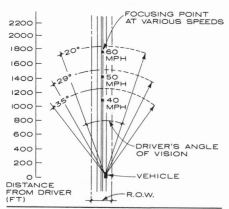

RELATIONSHIP BETWEEN DRIVER'S FOCUSING POINT AND ANGLE OF VISION   DOES NOT CONSIDER EFFECT OF PRECEDING TRAFFIC

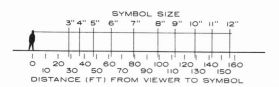

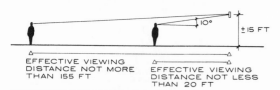

PEDESTRIAN CONSIDERATIONS

Johnson, Johnson & Roy; Ann Arbor, Michigan

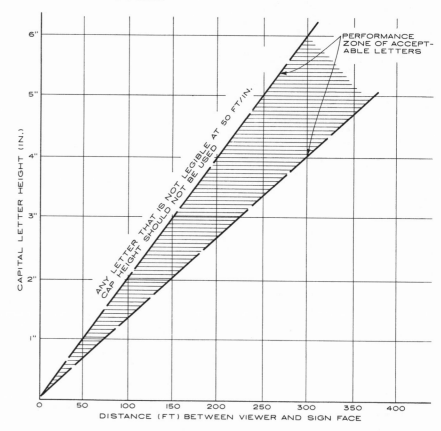

NOTE

Under normal daylight conditions, with normal vision, and an angular distortion of 0° approximately 50 ft/in. of capital height can be taken as a guideline for minimal legibility, as seen from the chart.

BIKE PATH CLASSIFICATIONS

Three bike path classifications have been generally accepted in the United States:

1. CLASS I: Completely separated right-of-way designated exclusively for bicycles. Through traffic, whether by motor vehicles or pedestrians, is not allowed. Cross flows by vehicles and pedestrians are allowed but minimized.
2. CLASS II: Restricted right-of-way designated exclusively or semiexclusively for bicycles. Through traffic by motor vehicles or pedestrians is not allowed. Cross flows by vehicles and pedestrians are allowed but minimized.
3. CLASS III: Shared right-of-way designated by signs or stencils. Any pathway that shares its through traffic right-of-way with either moving (but not parked) motor vehicles or pedestrians.

CLASS I: TOTAL SEPARATION / DIVIDING STRIP BETWEEN RIGHTS-OF-WAY ON SEPARATE SURFACES

CLASS II: TOTAL OR PARTIAL SEPARATION / ADJACENT, BUT SEPARATED RIGHTS-OF-WAY ON SAME SURFACE

CLASS III: NO SEPARATION / SHARED RIGHT-OF-WAY ON SAME SURFACE

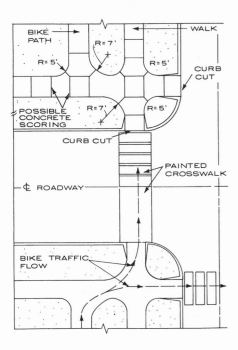

CLASS I: BIKE PATH, ON-GRADE INTERSECTION CONSIDERATIONS

Johnson, Johnson & Roy; Ann Arbor, Michigan

VERTICAL AND HORIZONTAL LAYOUT

The gradients of a bike path are directly related to the amount of use it will get. Extremes of steepness and flatness should be avoided if possible. The following gradients are recommended:

GRADIENT	LENGTH NORM	MAXIMUM
1.5%	1000 ft	—
3%	400 ft	800 ft
4.5%	150 ft	300 ft
10%	30 ft	60 ft

The following formula can be used to determine horizontal radii used on bike paths:

$$R = 1.528V + 2.2*$$

where R = the unbraked radius of curvature (ft) negotiated by a bicycle on a flat, dry, bituminous concrete surface and V = the velocity of bicycle (mph).

*Formula applicable to a maximum design speed of 18 mph. Using this formula, the minimum radius acceptable for a 10 mph design speed would be 17.5 ft. The radii used at the base of gradients in excess of 4.5% and running longer than 100 ft should be longer to accept higher design speeds (20-30 mph). Shorter radii can be used along approaches to on-grade intersections to slow cyclists down as they merge with pedestrians.

BIKE PATH INTERSECTIONS

One of the most dangerous elements of a bike path system is the on-grade intersection that brings bicycles, pedestrians, and automobiles together. If possible, Class I bike paths should include complete grade separations. Often this is not economically feasible; therefore, the following recommendations should be considered:

1. If possible, merge bicycles and pedestrians a minimum of 100 ft from the intersection using warning signs for both cyclists and pedestrians.
2. Provide warning signs for motorists indicating special caution at intersections.
3. Maintain adequate lighting (see Chapter 1 on illumination).
4. Install walk-don't walk, electronic crosswalk signals at busy intersections.
5. Control placement and maintenance of plant materials so as to maintain adequate site distance and visibility.

Confusion at intersections tends to increase at Class II and III bike paths. Warning signs are therefore recommended along approaches to intersections for all three types of users (distance from intersections for signs varies with speed of vehicular traffic).

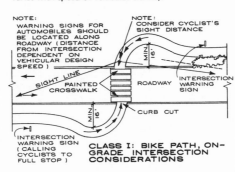

CLASS I: BIKE PATH, ON-GRADE INTERSECTION CONSIDERATIONS

BICYCLE SIZES

FRAME SIZE "W"	FRAME SIZE "F"
16"	12"
20"	13"
24"	16" boys 15" girls
26"	18", 19", 21", 23"
27"	19", 21", 23"

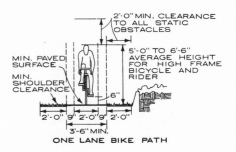

ONE LANE BIKE PATH

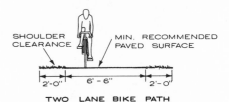

TWO LANE BIKE PATH

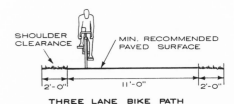

THREE LANE BIKE PATH

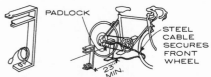

UPRIGHT, METAL BICYCLE RACK

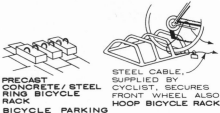

PRECAST CONCRETE/STEEL RING BICYCLE RACK / HOOP BICYCLE RACK
BICYCLE PARKING

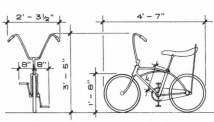

YOUTH'S SPORT W/"HIGHRISE" HANDLEBARS
FRAME SIZE (F) 13½", 14½"

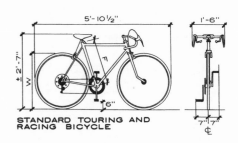

STANDARD TOURING AND RACING BICYCLE

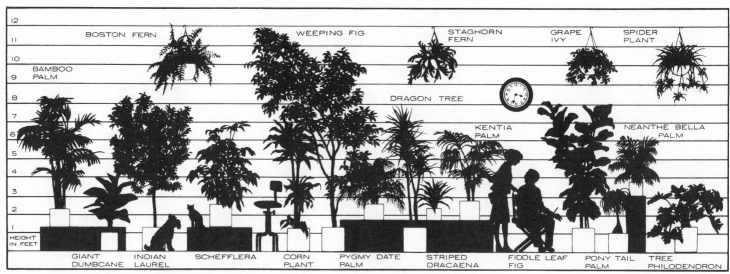

FORM, TEXTURE, AND SIZES OF SOME TYPICALLY USED INTERIOR PLANTS

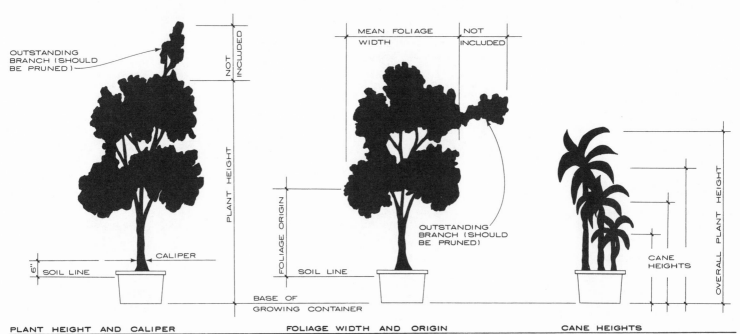

| PLANT HEIGHT AND CALIPER | FOLIAGE WIDTH AND ORIGIN | CANE HEIGHTS |

INTERIOR PLANT SPECIFICATIONS

NOTE

Plant height should be measured as overall height from the base of the growing container to mean foliage top. Isolated outstanding branches should not be included in height. (Since most plants are installed in movable planters, this overall height measurement should be utilized.)

NOTE

Foliage width should be measured across the nominal mean width dimension. Isolated outstanding branches should not be included in foliage width. Origin or start of foliage should be measured from the soil line.

NOTE

Many plant varieties are grown from rooted canes, with the plant being made up of one or more canes. The number of canes must be specified, if plant form is to be identified. Cane heights should always be measured from the base of the growing container.

OTHER PLANT SPECIFICATION FACTORS

1. Accurately describe plant form (e.g., multistem vs. standard tree form, clump form) and foliage spread desired. Indicate "clear trunk" measurements on trees, if desired. These measurements are from soil line to foliage origin point. Specify caliper, if significant.

2. Indicate lighting intensities designed or calculated for interior space where plants will be installed.

3. Indicate how plants will be used (i.e., in at-grade planter or in movable decorative planter). If movable decorative planters are used, indicate interior diameter and height of planter for each plant specified, since growing container sizes vary considerably.

4. Specify both botanical and common plant names.

5. Indicate any special shipping instructions or limitations.

6. Specify in-plant height column, whether plant height is measured as overall height or above-the-soil line height. Recommended height measurements:

   Interior plants: overall plant height (i.e., from bottom of growing container to mean foliage top).
   Exterior plants: above-the-soil line height.

7. Indicate whether plants are to be container grown or balled and burlapped (B & B) material.

8. Indicate location of all convenient water supply sources on all interior landscaping layouts.

Richard L. Gaines, AIA; Plantscape House; Apopka, Florida

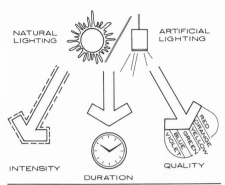

INTERIOR PLANT LIGHTING FACTORS

LIGHTING DURATION NEEDS

1. Adequate lighting is the product of intensity times duration to yield "footcandle-hours"; therefore, compensation between the two exists (e.g., 300 ft-c x 12 hr = 360 ft-c x 10 hr).
2. Recommended rule of thumb: 10-12 hr of continuous lighting on a regular basis, 7 days a week.
3. Generally, it is believed that continuous 24 hr lighting period might be detrimental to plants, but no research bears this out and many projects are under this regime with no apparent bad effects.

LIGHTING INTENSITY NEEDS

1. All plants desire good lighting, but many are tolerant and adaptable to lower light conditions.
2. Because most interior plants are native to areas with intensities of 10-14,000 ft-c, these plants must be "trained" through an acclimatization process of lowered light (2000-4000 ft-c), water and fertilizer levels for survival, and maintained appearance in the interior environment.
3. All plants have varying degrees of interior lighting intensity requirements, best understood as footcandle (lumens/square foot) requirements.
4. Lighting intensity for plants must be planned and is not simply a footcandle measurement after the building is complete (i.e., footcandle meters are "after the fact" instruments).
5. Intensity must always be above the individual light compensation point for each plant variety, for survival. (LCP is the intensity point at which the plant utilizes as much food as it produces; hence no food storage. Eventually, the plant could die with no food backup.)
6. Recommended rule of thumb: design for a MINIMUM of 50 ft-c on the ground plane for fixed floor type of planters and 75 ft-c at desk height for movable decorative floor planters.
7. Flowering plants and flowers require extremely high intensities (above 2000 ft-c) or direct sunlight to bud, flower, or fruit, as well as lighting high in red and far-red energy.

RECOMMENDED LIGHTING SOURCES FOR PLANTS

Lighting sources are listed in order of priority, based on plant growth efficiency, color rendition preference, and energy efficiency.

CEILING HEIGHT	RECOMMENDED LIGHT SOURCE
10 ft and less	Daylight—sidewall glazing Cool white fluorescent Natural light fluorescent Incandescent Plant growth fluorescent

10-15 ft	Daylight
	  Sidewall glazing
	  Major glazing
	  Skylights
	Metal halide lamp, phosphor coated
	Mercury lamp, deluxe white
	Mercury lamp, warm deluxe white
	High pressure sodium (if color rendition not a design factor)
	Quartz halogen lamp
	Incandescent

15 ft and greater	Daylight
	  Sidewall glazing
	  Major glazing
	  Skylights
	Metal halide lamp, clear
	Metal halide lamp, phosphor coated
	Mercury lamp, deluxe white
	Mercury lamp, warm deluxe white
	High pressure sodium (if color rendition not a design factor)
	Quartz halogen lamp
	Incandescent

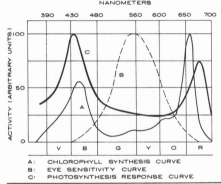

SPECTRAL ENERGY DISTRIBUTION CURVE SHOWING OPPOSING PLANT AND HUMAN EYE RESPONSES

A: CHLOROPHYLL SYNTHESIS CURVE
B: EYE SENSITIVITY CURVE
C: PHOTOSYNTHESIS RESPONSE CURVE

LIGHT QUALITY NEEDS

1. Natural lighting is about twice as efficient as cool white fluorescent lighting for plant growth, because of sunlight's broad range spectrum (i.e., 200 ft-c of CWF = 95 ft-c of natural light).
2. Chlorophyll is most responsive to blue and red wavelength energy in the production of food. The human eye is least responsive to blue and red energy and most responsive to the green-yellow region of the spectrum.
3. High blue energy emitting sources are best for overall plant maintenance (stockier growth, dark green color, little elongation).
4. High red energy emitting sources produce lighter colored foliage, elongated growth, stragglier growth.
5. Designer must be cognizant of color rendition of source, as well as light quality, if lighting is to be used for both plant lighting and illumination. (See Lamp Responses table.)
6. Ultraviolet energy is believed to be somewhat helpful to the photosynthesis process, but is not considered necessary as an integral segment of plant lighting.

Richard L. Gaines, AIA; Plantscape House; Apopka, Florida

LAMP RESPONSES ON INTERIOR PLANTS

BULB	ROOM APPEARANCE	COLORS STRENGTHENED	COLORS GREYED	PLANT RESPONSES
CW	Neutral to cool	Blue, yellow, orange	Red	Green foliage, stem elongates slowly, multiple side shoots, flower life long
WW	Yellow to warm	Yellow, orange	Blue, green, red	
GRO-PL	Purple to pink	Blue, red	Green, yellow	Deep green foliage, stem elongates very slowly, thick stems, multiple side shoots, late flowers on short stems
GRO-WS	Warm	Blue, yellow, red	Green	Light green foliage, stem elongates rapidly, suppressed side shoots, early flowering on long stems, plant matures and dies rapidly
AGRO	Neutral to warm	Blue, yellow, red	Green	
VITA	Neutral to warm	Blue, yellow, red	Green	
HG	Cool	Blue, green, yellow	Red	Green foliage expands, stem elongates slowly, multiple side shoots, flower life long
MH	Cool green	Blue, green, yellow	Red	
HPS	Warm	Green, yellow, orange	Blue, red	Deep green, large foliage, stem elongates very slowly, late flowers, short stems
LPS	Warm	Yellow	All except yellow	Extra deep green foliage, slow, thick stem elongation, multiple side shoots, some flowering, short stems. Some plants require supplemental sun
INC	Warm	Yellow, orange, red	Blue	Pale, thin, long foliage, stems spindly, suppressed side shoots early, short-lived flowers
INC-HG	Warm	Yellow, orange, red	Blue	

KEY

CW: cool white fluorescent.
WW: warm white fluorescent.
GRO-PL: Gro-Lux plant light.
GRO-WS: Gro-Lux wide spectrum.
AGRO: Agro-Lite.
VITA: Vita-Lite.

HG: mercury (all types).
MH: metal halide.
HPS: high pressure sodium.
LPS: low pressure sodium.
INC-HG: incandescent mercury.
INC-PL: incandescent plant light.

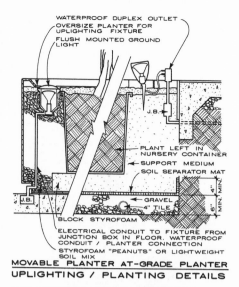

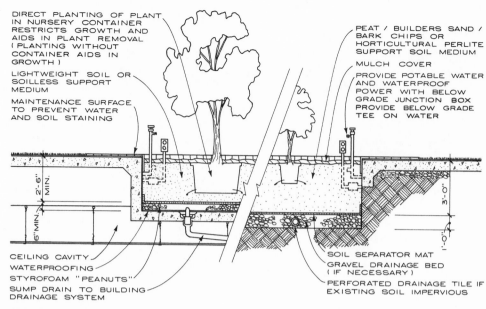

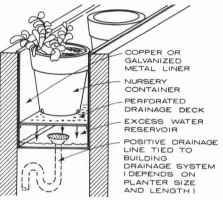

MOVABLE PLANTER AT-GRADE PLANTER
UPLIGHTING / PLANTING DETAILS

ABOVE–GRADE PLANTER   **AT – GRADE PLANTER**
FLOOR PLANTER DETAILS

RAILING PLANTER DETAIL

UPLIGHTING AND ELECTRICAL NEEDS

1. May be of some benefit to plants, but inefficient for plant photosynthesis because of plant physiological structure. Chlorophyll is usually in upper part of leaf.
2. Uplighting should never be utilized as sole lighting source for plants.
3. Waterproof duplex outlets above soil line with a waterproof junction box below soil line are usually adequate for "atmosphere" uplighting and water fountain pumps.

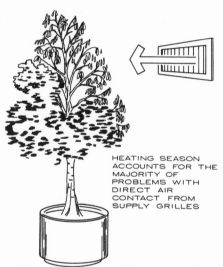

FOLIAGE BURN FROM DIRECT HEAT CONTACT

HVAC EFFECT ON PLANTS

1. Air-conditioning (cooled air) is rarely detrimental to plants, even if it is "directed" at plants. The ventilation here is what counts! Good ventilation is a must with plants; otherwise oxygen and temperatures build up. Heat supply, on the other hand, when "directed" at plants, can truly be disastrous. Plan for supplies directed away from plants, but maintain adequate ventilation.
2. Extended heat or power failures of sufficient duration can damage plant health. The lower limit of temperature as a steady state is 65°F for plant survival. Brief drops to 55°F (less than 1 hr) are the lower limit before damage. Temperatures up to 85°F for only 2 days a week can usually be tolerated.
3. The relative humidity should not be allowed to fall below 30%, as plants prefer a relative humidity of 50–60%.

Richard L. Gaines, AIA; Plantscape House; Apopka, Florida

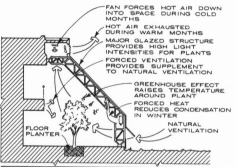

GREENHOUSE EFFECT RAISES NEED FOR ADEQUATE VENTILATION

TEMPERATURE REQUIREMENTS

1. Most plants prefer human comfort range: 70-75°F daytime temperatures and 60-65°F nighttime temperatures.
2. An absolute minimum temperature of 50°F must be observed. Plant damage will result below this figure. Rapid temperature fluctuations of 30-40°F can also be detrimental to plants.
3. "Q-10" phenomenon of respiration: for every 10°C rise in temperature, plants' respiration rate and food consumption doubles.
4. Both photosynthesis and respiration decline and stop with time, as temperatures go beyond 80°F. Beware of the greenhouse effect!

WATER SUPPLY REQUIREMENTS

1. Movable and railing planters are often watered by watering can. Provide convenient access to hot and cold potable water by hose bibbs and/or service sinks (preferably in janitor's closet) during normal working hours, with long (min. 24 in.) faucet-to-sink or floor distances. Provide for maximum of 200 ft travel on all floors.
2. At-grade floor planters are usually watered by hose and extension wand. Provide hose bibbs above soil line (for maximum travel of 50 ft) with capped "tee" stub-outs beneath soil line. If soil temperature is apt to get abnormally low in winter, provide hot and cold water by mixer-faucet type hose bibbs.
3. High concentrations of fluoride and chlorine in water supply can cause damage to plants. Provide water with low concentrations of these elements and with a pH value of 5.0-6.0. Higher or lower pH levels can result in higher plant maintenance costs.

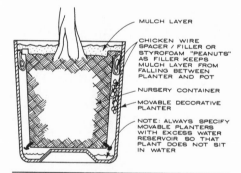

MOVABLE DECORATIVE PLANTER DETAIL

STORAGE REQUIREMENTS

Provide a secured storage space of approximately 30 sq ft for watering equipment and other maintenance materials. It may be desirable to combine water supply and janitor needs in the same storage area.

AIR POLLUTION EFFECTS ON PLANTS

Problems result from inadequate ventilation. Excessive chlorine gas from swimming pool areas can be a damaging problem, as well as excessive fumes from toxic cleaning substances for floor finishes, etc. Ventilation a must here!

3 MASONRY

CUT STONE

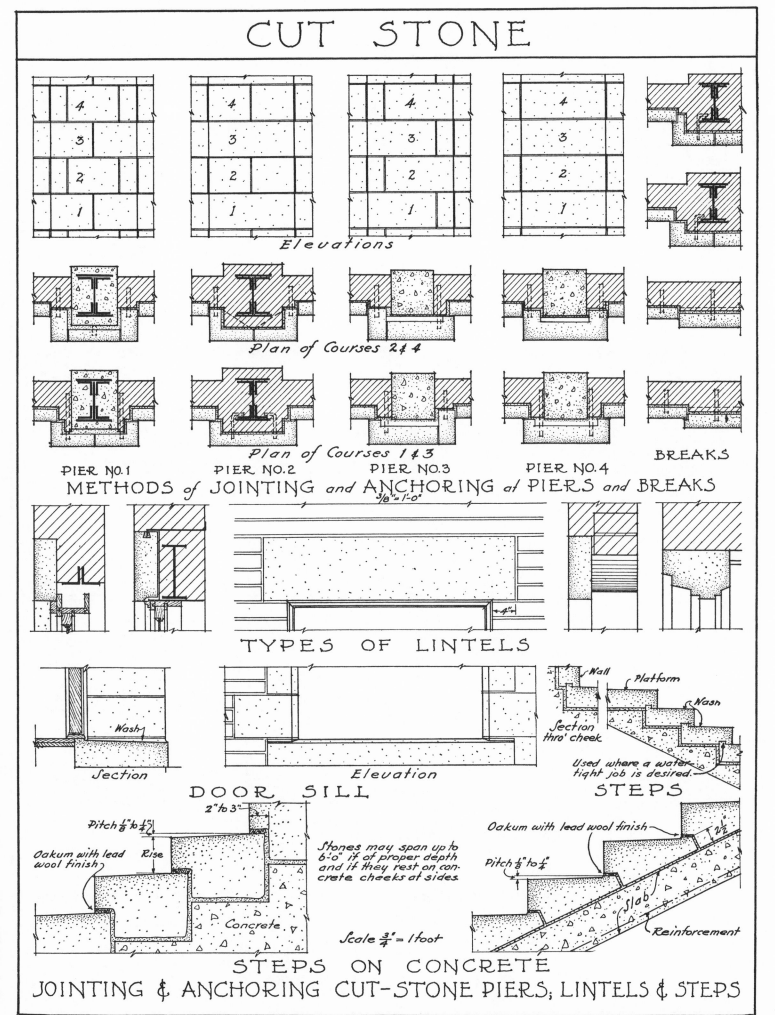

Elevations

Plan of Courses 2 & 4

Plan of Courses 1 & 3

BREAKS

PIER NO.1   PIER NO.2   PIER NO.3   PIER NO.4

METHODS of JOINTING and ANCHORING at PIERS and BREAKS

3/8" = 1'-0"

4"

TYPES OF LINTELS

Wash

Section

Elevation

DOOR SILL

Wall   Platform   Wash
Section thro' cheek
Used where a water tight job is desired.

STEPS

2" to 3"
Pitch 1/8" to 1/4"
Oakum with lead wool finish   Rise
Concrete
Stones may span up to 6'-0" if of proper depth and if they rest on concrete cheeks at sides.
Scale 3/4" = 1 foot

Oakum with lead wool finish   2 1/2"
Pitch 1/8" to 1/4"
Slab
Reinforcement

STEPS ON CONCRETE

JOINTING & ANCHORING CUT-STONE PIERS, LINTELS & STEPS

CUT STONE

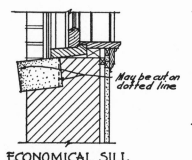

ECONOMICAL SILL
Made of a strip fitted to form wash

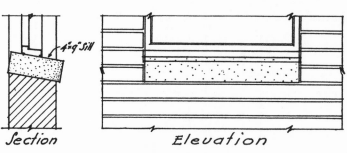

May be cut on dotted line

4"-9" Sill

Section

Elevation

SLIP SILL
Used for Factory and other economical construction

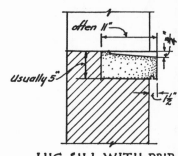

often 11"

Usually 5"

LUG SILL WITH DRIP

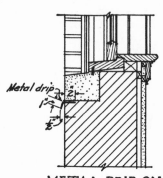

Metal drip

METAL DRIP ON FLUSH SILL.

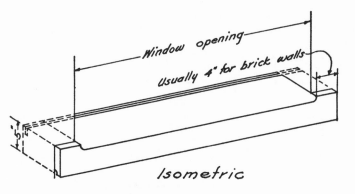

Window opening

Usually 4" for brick walls

Isometric

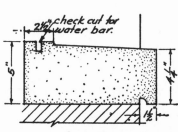

2½" check cut for water bar.

Section
Showing check for water bar.

Lug sill may be a true lug sill with throated wash like this or a plain bevelled sill 4" to 8" longer than opening.

LUG SILL
Recommended by "Stone Setting."

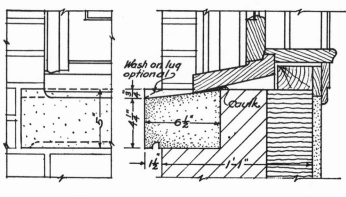

Wash or lug optional

Caulk.

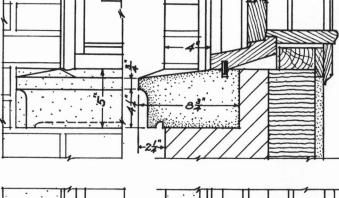

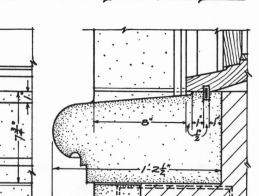

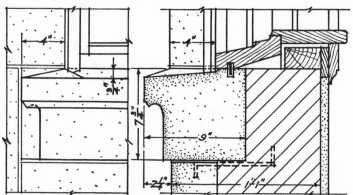

VARIOUS TYPES OF SILLS SHOWING DRIPS & WASHES.
Recommendations of the Indiana Limestone Co.

CUT STONE WINDOW SILLS

Scales ¾" & 1½" = 1'-0"

CUT STONE

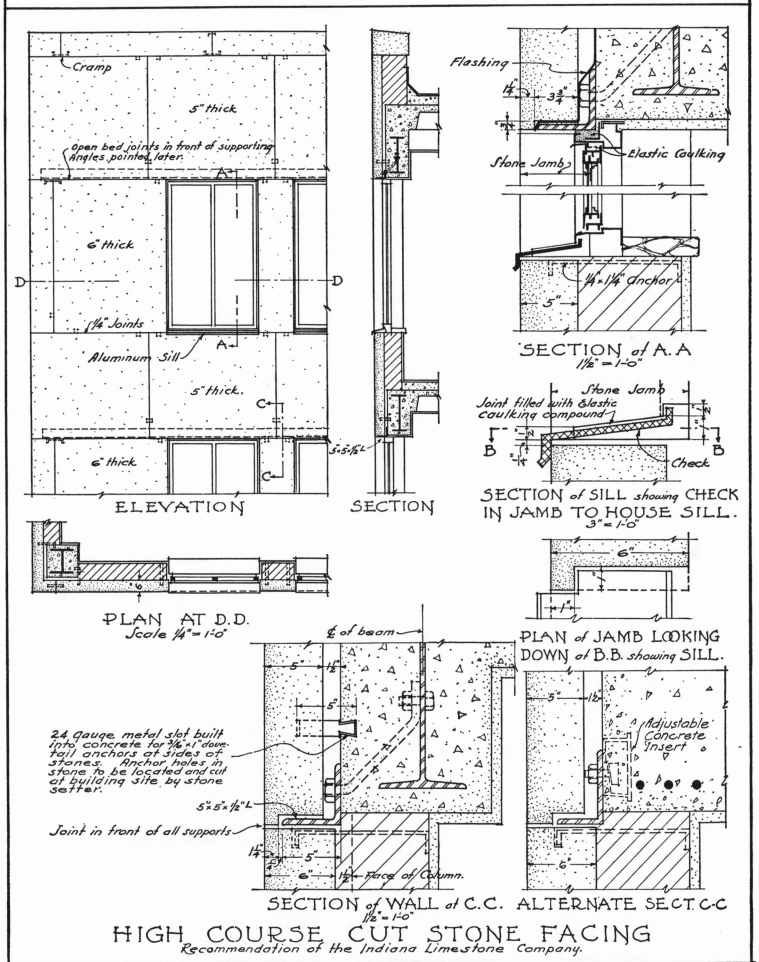

ELEVATION

SECTION

SECTION of A.A
1½" = 1'-0"

- Cramp
- 5" thick
- Open bed joints in front of supporting Angles, pointed later.
- 6" thick
- 1¼" Joints
- Aluminum Sill
- 5" thick.
- 6" thick
- 5"×5"×½" L

- Flashing
- Stone Jamb
- Elastic Caulking
- 1¼"×1¼" Anchor
- 1¼"
- 3¾"
- 5"

SECTION of SILL showing CHECK IN JAMB TO HOUSE SILL.
3" = 1'-0"

- Stone Jamb
- Joint filled with Elastic caulking compound
- Check

PLAN AT D.D.
Scale ¼" = 1'-0"

PLAN of JAMB LOOKING DOWN of B.B. showing SILL.
- 6"
- 1"

- 24 gauge metal slot built into concrete for ³⁄₁₆"×1" dove-tail anchors at sides of stones. Anchor holes in stone to be located and cut at building site by stone setter.
- Joint in front of all supports
- 5"×5"×½" L

SECTION of WALL at C.C.
1½" = 1'-0"
- ₵ of beam
- 5"
- 1½"
- 5"
- 1¼"
- 5"
- 6"
- 1½"
- Face of Column.

ALTERNATE SECT. C-C
- Adjustable Concrete Insert
- 5"
- 1½"
- 6"

HIGH COURSE CUT STONE FACING
Recommendation of the Indiana Limestone Company.

CUT STONE

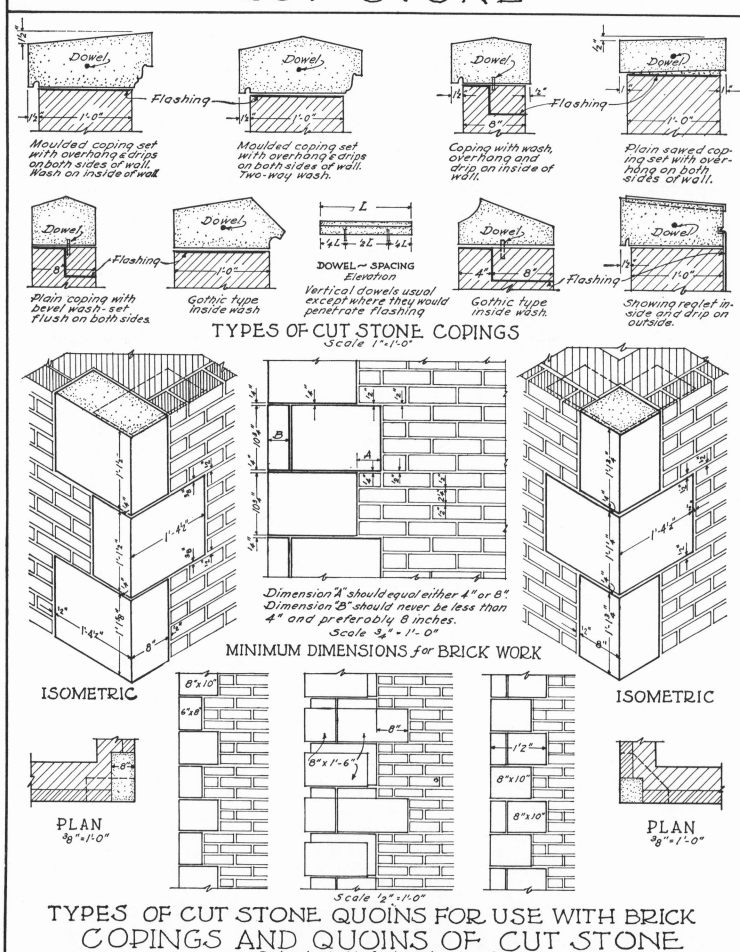

Moulded coping set with overhang & drips on both sides of wall. Wash on inside of wall.

Moulded coping set with overhang & drips on both sides of wall. Two-way wash.

Coping with wash, overhang and drip on inside of wall.

Plain sawed coping set with overhang on both sides of wall.

Plain coping with bevel wash-set flush on both sides.

Gothic type inside wash.

DOWEL ~ SPACING
Elevation
Vertical dowels usual except where they would penetrate flashing

Gothic type inside wash.

Showing reglet inside and drip on outside.

TYPES OF CUT STONE COPINGS
Scale 1" = 1'-0"

Dimension "A" should equal either 4" or 8".
Dimension "B" should never be less than 4" and preferably 8 inches.
Scale 3/4" = 1'-0"

MINIMUM DIMENSIONS for BRICK WORK

ISOMETRIC

ISOMETRIC

PLAN
3/8" = 1'-0"

PLAN
3/8" = 1'-0"

Scale 1/2" = 1'-0"

TYPES OF CUT STONE QUOINS FOR USE WITH BRICK
COPINGS AND QUOINS OF CUT STONE
Data checked by Indiana Limestone Co.

CUT STONE

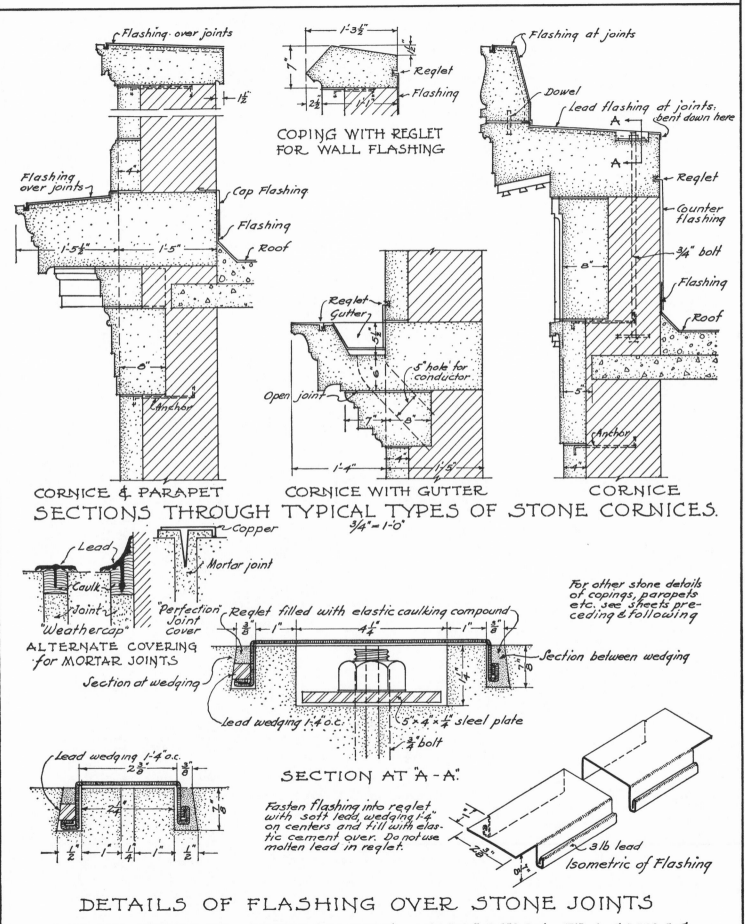

Flashing over joints

COPING WITH REGLET
FOR WALL FLASHING

1'-3½"
1"
Reglet
Flashing
2½"
1'-1"

Flashing at joints
Dowel
Lead flashing at joints:
bent down here
A
A
Reglet
Counter flashing
¾" bolt
Flashing
Roof
8"
5"
Anchor

Flashing over joints
Cap Flashing
Flashing
Roof
1'-5½"   1'-5"
8"
Anchor
1½"
4"

Reglet
Gutter
Open joint
5" hole for conductor
1'-4"   1'-5"
7"   8"
5½"

CORNICE & PARAPET   CORNICE WITH GUTTER   CORNICE
SECTIONS THROUGH TYPICAL TYPES OF STONE CORNICES.
¾"=1'-0"

Copper
Lead
Mortar joint
Caulk
Joint
"Weathercap"
"Perfection" Joint Cover

ALTERNATE COVERING
for MORTAR JOINTS

Reglet filled with elastic caulking compound
Section between wedging
Section at wedging
⅜" 1"   4¼"   1" ⅝"
⅞" ¼"
Lead wedging 1'-4" o.c.
5"x4"x¼" steel plate
¾" bolt

For other stone details of copings, parapets etc. see sheets preceding & following

Lead wedging 1'-4" o.c.
2⅜" ⅜"
2¼"
7" ⅞"
½" 1" ¼" 1" ½"

SECTION AT "A-A."

Fasten flashing into reglet with soft lead, wedging 1'-4" on centers and fill with elastic cement over. Do not use molten lead in reglet.

1"
2⅜"
¾"
3 lb lead
Isometric of Flashing

DETAILS OF FLASHING OVER STONE JOINTS
LIMESTONE CORNICES SHOWING FLASHING
Recommendations of the Indiana Limestone Co

STONE WORK

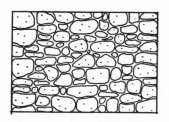

UNCOURSED FIELDSTONE ROUGH OR ORDINARY.

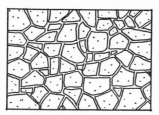

POLYGONAL, MOSAIC OR RANDOM.

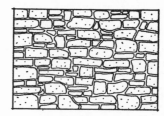

COURSED

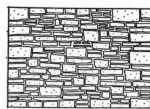

Laid of stratified stone fitted on job. It is between rubble & ashlar. Finish is quarry face, seam face or split. Called rubble ashlar in granite.

TYPES OF RUBBLE MASONRY

SQUARED-STONE MASONRY.

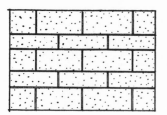

RANGE. Coursed

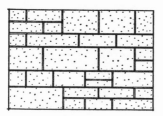

BROKEN RANGE.

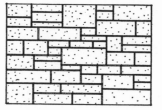

RANDOM RANGE. Interrupted coursed

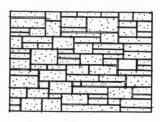

RANGE. Coursed (Long stones)

TYPES OF ASHLAR MASONRY
This is stone that is sawed, dressed, squared or Quarry faced.

ELEVATIONS SHOWING FACE JOINTING FOR STONE.

Draft line

For both hard and soft stones.
Rock or Pitch Face.

Smooth, but saw mark visible. All stones.
Sawed Finish (Gang).

More marked than sawed. Soft stones.
Shot Sawed (Rough).

Smooth finish with some texture. Soft stones.
Machine Finish (Planer).

Tooled margin

May be coarse, medium or fine. Usually on hard stones.
Pointed Finish.

After pointing on hard stones.
Pean Hammered.

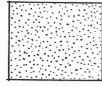

For soft stones
Bush-hammered.

All stones. Used much on granite. 4 to 8 cut in ⅛."
Patent Bush-hammer.

For soft stones.
Drove or Boasted.

Random

For soft stones.
Hand Tooled.

Tool marks may be 2 to 10 per inch.
Machine Tooled.

For soft stones
Tooth-chisel.

Random

For soft stones.
Crandalled.

Textured by machine For Limestone
Plucker Finish.

Very smooth.

For Limestone. Done by machine.
Carborundum Finish.

Smooth

All stones. May use sand or carborundum.
Rubbed (Wet).

Very Smooth

Marble, granite. For interior work. Soft stones.
Honed (rubbed first).

Very smooth Has high gloss.

Marble and Granite.
Polished (honed first).

STONE FINISHES.
Seam face and split face (or quarry face) not shown as they are not worked finishes.

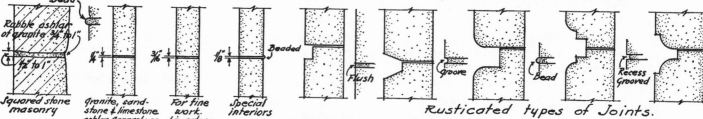

Bead

Rubble ashlar of granite ¾ to 1"

½ to 1"

Squared stone masonry

¼"

Granite, sand-stone & limestone ashlar. general use.

³⁄₁₆"

For fine work. Limestone

⅛"

Special interiors

Beaded

Flush

Groove

Bead

Recess Grooved

Rusticated types of Joints.

STONE JOINTS

TYPES, FINISH AND JOINTING OF STONE MASONRY.
A perch is nominally 16'-6" long, 1'-0" high & 1'-6" thick = 24¾ cu. ft. In some localities 16½ & 22 cu. ft. are used.

STONE WORK

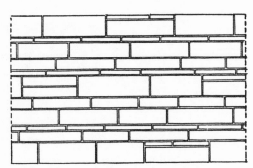

· FOUR UNIT, LONG TYPE RANGE WORK ·
Average length of Stones four times height.
· BROKEN RANGE ·

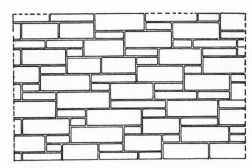

· TWO UNIT, MEDIUM TYPE RANDOM ASHLAR ·
Average length of larger Stones is three times height.

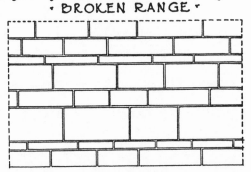

· FOUR UNIT, MEDIUM TYPE RANGE · WORK ·
Average length of Stones about 2½ times their height.
· RANGE ·

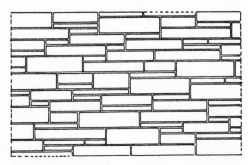

· THREE UNIT, LONG TYPE RANDOM ASHLAR ·
Average length of Stones 4 times height or more

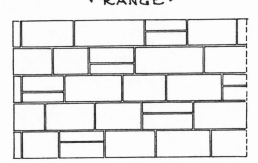

· EQUAL COURSE HEIGHTS ·
With occasional units divided by horizontal joints.
· BROKEN RANGE ·

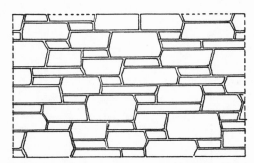

· THREE · UNIT · RANDOM · ASHLAR; ANGULAR · BROKEN · END ·
Average length of larger Stones 2 times their height.
Joints ¾" thick.

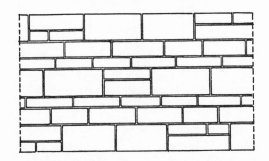

· · THREE UNIT RANGE WORK ·
With occasional Horizontal joints in the higher Courses.
· BROKEN · RANGE ·

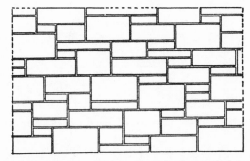

· THREE · UNIT · MEDIUM · TYPE · RANDOM · ASHLAR ·
· Average length of larger Stones about twice the height.

This type of Stone is delivered in strips & jointed to length at the job. Joints all ½" except where noted ¾" ~ ·

· RANGE & BROKEN RANGE ·   **· RANDOM · RANGE ·**

· Scale: ~ ¼" = 1'·0" ·

· JOINTING · OF · STRIP · LIMESTONE · ASHLAR ·

· ≈ Recommendations of the "Indiana Limestone Co." ≈ ·

STONE WORK and BACKING

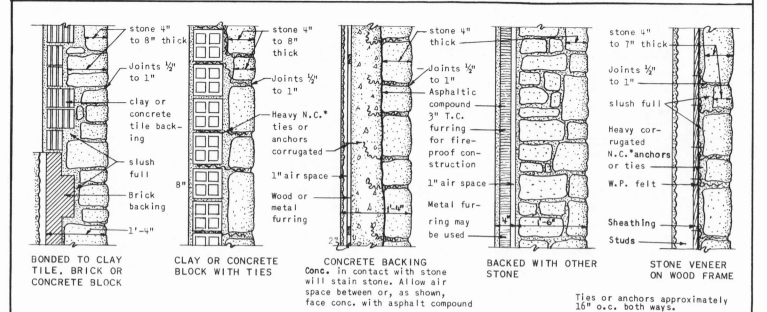

BONDED TO CLAY TILE, BRICK OR CONCRETE BLOCK

- stone 4" to 8" thick
- Joints ½" to 1"
- clay or concrete tile backing
- slush full
- Brick backing
- 1'-4"

CLAY OR CONCRETE BLOCK WITH TIES

- stone 4" to 8" thick
- Joints ½" to 1"
- Heavy N.C.* ties or anchors corrugated
- 1" air space
- Wood or metal furring
- 8"

CONCRETE BACKING
Conc. in contact with stone will stain stone. Allow air space between or, as shown, face conc. with asphalt compound

- stone 4" thick
- Joints ½" to 1"
- Asphaltic compound
- 3" T.C. furring for fire-proof construction
- 1" air space
- Metal furring may be used
- 2½"
- 1'-4"

BACKED WITH OTHER STONE

- 4"
- 1'-6"

STONE VENEER ON WOOD FRAME

- stone 4" to 7" thick
- Joints ½" to 1"
- slush full
- Heavy corrugated N.C.*anchors or ties
- W.P. felt
- Sheathing
- Studs

Ties or anchors approximately 16" o.c. both ways.

TYPICAL METHODS OF BACKING SQUARED-STONE OR GRANITE FACING

(Not recommended for buildings over two stories high)

DRESSING & FINISH FOR THIS TYPE OF STONE: Rough squared as to length & rise — Bed & joints split or pitched approximately square to face. Faces pitched out of wind. Finish: 1. Rock Face 2. Seam Face 3. Split or Quarry Face. — Joints ½'' to 1'' of 1 part cement (non-staining), 1 part lime & 1 part sand.

*N.C. = Non-corrosive

FRAME BACKING

- *N.C. spike bent into mortar bed
- Corrugated *N.C. wall ties bent to mortar bed.
- 2¼"
- 5"
- 7¾"
- 7¾"
- 2¼"
- ½" JTS

BRICK BACKING

- Corrugated *N.C. wall ties laid in mortar bed
- Bond stone

HOLLOW TILE BACKING

- Corrugated *N.C. Wall Tie laid in mortar bed
- Brick fillers
- METHOD OF ANCHORING WHERE STONE COURSES LEVEL UP WITH TOPS OF BACKING TILE
- 5"
- 2¼"
- 2¼"
- 2¼"
- 7¾"
- 5"
- ½" JTS
- Bond stone

METHOD OF ANCHORING WHERE TOPS OF STONE DO NOT LEVEL UP WITH TOPS OF BACKING BLOCKS

CONCRETE BLOCK BACKING

- Face of backing water proofed
- Brick filler
- Toggle bolt anchor & washer with #16 ga. corrugated *n.c. wall tie punched for toggle bolt and bent into mortar bed
- Bond stones

*non-corrosive

BACKING FOR CUT STONE

DATA BY INDIANA LIMESTONE INSTITUTE

ANCHORING of STONEWORK

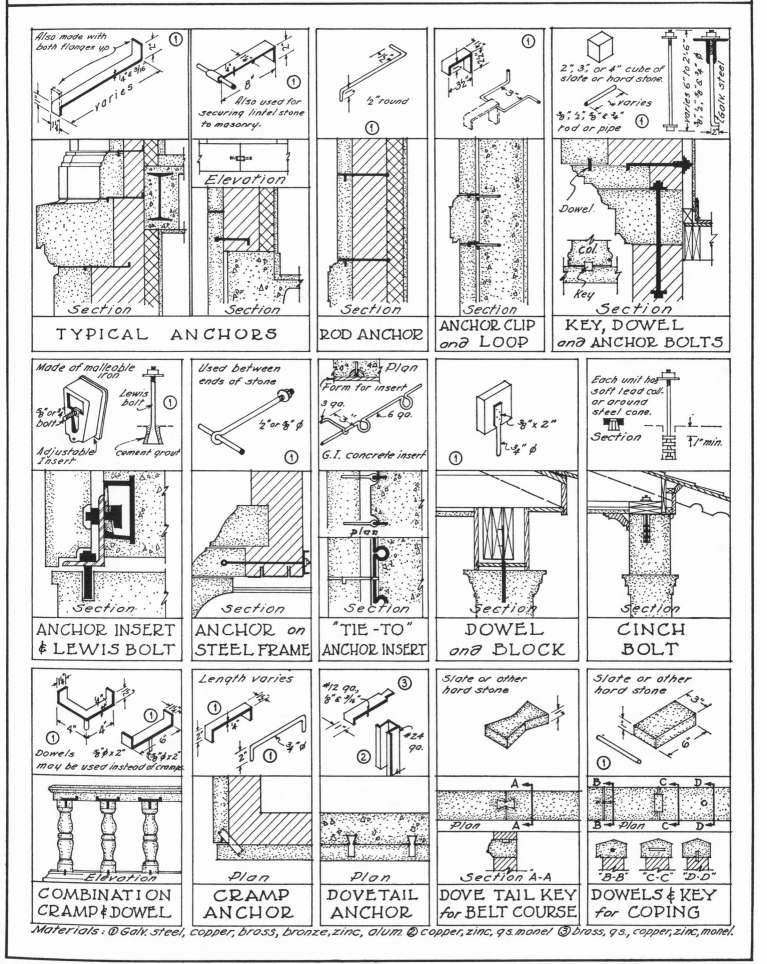

Also made with both flanges up

varies

Also used for securing lintel stone to masonry.

Elevation

½" round

Section

Section

Section

TYPICAL ANCHORS

ROD ANCHOR

ANCHOR CLIP and LOOP

2", 3", or 4" cube of slate or hard stone.

⅜", ½", ⅝" & ¾" rod or pipe   varies

varies 6' to 2'-6"   Calk steel

Dowel

Col.

Key

Section

KEY, DOWEL and ANCHOR BOLTS

Made of malleable iron

Lewis bolt

⅝" or ¾" bolt

Adjustable Insert   cement grout

Section

ANCHOR INSERT & LEWIS BOLT

Used between ends of stone

½" or ⅝" ∅

Section

ANCHOR on STEEL FRAME

Plan

Form for insert

3 ga.   6 ga.

G.I. concrete insert

plan

Section

"TIE-TO" ANCHOR INSERT

⅜" x 2"

¾" ∅

Section

DOWEL and BLOCK

Each unit has soft lead collar around steel cone.

Section   1" min.

Section

CINCH BOLT

Dowels ⅝" ∅ x 2" may be used instead of cramps.

Elevation

COMBINATION CRAMP & DOWEL

Length varies

¾" ∅

Plan

CRAMP ANCHOR

#12 ga., ⅜" & ⁹⁄₁₆"

#24 ga.

Plan

DOVETAIL ANCHOR

Slate or other hard stone

Plan

Section A-A

DOVE TAIL KEY for BELT COURSE

Slate or other hard stone

Plan

"B-B" "C-C" "D-D"

DOWELS & KEY for COPING

Materials: ① Galv. steel, copper, brass, bronze, zinc, alum. ② copper, zinc, g.s. monel. ③ brass, g.s., copper, zinc, monel.

GRANITE

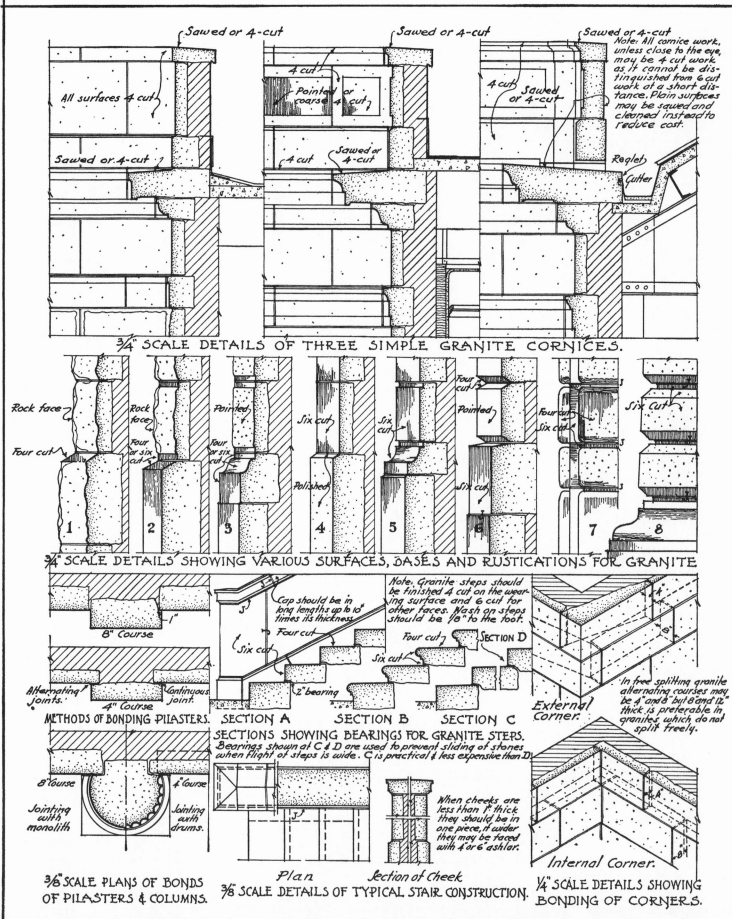

Sawed or 4-cut

Sawed or 4-cut

Sawed or 4-cut

Note: All cornice work, unless close to the eye, may be 4 cut work as it cannot be distinguished from 6 cut work at a short distance. Plain surfaces may be sawed and cleaned instead to reduce cost.

All surfaces 4 cut

4 cut

Pointed or coarse 4 cut

4 cut

Sawed or 4-cut

4 cut

Sawed or 4-cut

Sawed or 4-cut

Reglet

Gutter

¾" SCALE DETAILS OF THREE SIMPLE GRANITE CORNICES.

Rock face

Rock face

Pointed

Six cut

Six cut

Four cut

Pointed

Four cut Six cut

Six Cut

Four cut

Four or six cut

Four or six cut

Polished

Six cut

1   2   3   4   5   6   7   8

¾" SCALE DETAILS SHOWING VARIOUS SURFACES, BASES AND RUSTICATIONS FOR GRANITE

1"

8" Course

Cap should be in long lengths up to 10 times its thickness.

Four cut

Six cut

Note: Granite steps should be finished 4 cut on the wearing surface and 6 cut for other faces. Wash on steps should be ⅛" to the foot.

Four cut

SECTION D

Six cut

Alternating joints.

Continuous joint.

4" Course

Four cut

Six cut

2" bearing

In free splitting granite alternating courses may be 4" and 8" but 8 and 12" thick is preferable in granites which do not split freely.

External Corner.

METHODS OF BONDING PILASTERS.

SECTION A   SECTION B   SECTION C

SECTIONS SHOWING BEARINGS FOR GRANITE STEPS.
Bearings shown at C & D are used to prevent sliding of stones when flight of steps is wide. C is practical & less expensive than D.

8" Course

4" Course

Jointing with monolith.

Jointing with drums.

When cheeks are less than 1" thick they should be in one piece, if wider they may be faced with 4" or 6" ashlar.

Internal Corner.

⅜" SCALE PLANS OF BONDS OF PILASTERS & COLUMNS.

Plan   Section of Cheek

⅜" SCALE DETAILS OF TYPICAL STAIR CONSTRUCTION.

¼" SCALE DETAILS SHOWING BONDING OF CORNERS.

TYPICAL GRANITE DETAILS showing PRACTICAL METHODS of CONSTRUCTION.
Recommendations of the National Building Granite Quarries Association.

EXTERIOR MARBLE, SOAPSTONE & GRANITE VENEER

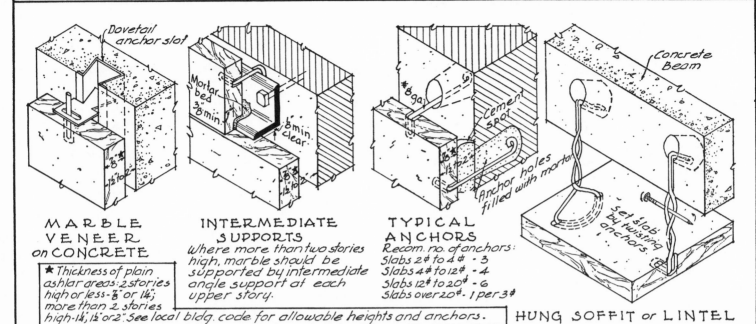

MARBLE VENEER on CONCRETE

Dovetail anchor slot

★ Thickness of plain ashlar areas: 2 stories high or less-¾" or 1¼"; more than 2 stories high-1¼", 1½" or 2". See local bldg. code for allowable heights and anchors.

INTERMEDIATE SUPPORTS

Mortar bed ⅜" min.   ⅜" min. clear.

Where more than two stories high, marble should be supported by intermediate angle support at each upper story.

TYPICAL ANCHORS

Cement spot

Anchor holes filled with mortar

Recom. no. of anchors:
Slabs 2# to 4# - 3
Slabs 4# to 12# - 4
Slabs 12# to 20# - 6
Slabs over 20# - 1 per 3#

HUNG SOFFIT or LINTEL

Concrete Beam

Set slab by twisting anchors

METHODS of ANCHORING EXTERIOR MARBLE VENEER

SUPPORT at SIDEWALK

Cement Spot
Continuous Shelf angle

SUPPORT at SPANDREL

Cement spot
Anchor
Angle
Window frame

MARBLE CAPS and COPINGS

Stainless metal flashg.
Marble cap
stainless metal coping
Marble coping
Flash

Joints for exterior marble or soapstone veneer usually ⅛" but may be less than ¹⁄₁₆"; use neat white Portland cement or non-staining pointing mastic with plastic or aluminum cushions spaced to support the weight. Use spots of non-staining Portland cement and accelerator or bonding cement behind slabs at or near anchors and also not spaced over 18" apart. Marble up to 2" thick may also be set with plasticized synthetic resin bonding cement without anchors. Use same number of these cement spots as number of anchors which would otherwise be required.

Scale of sections - 1½" = 1'·0"

EXTERIOR MARBLE and SOAPSTONE VENEER
Data by Marble Institute of America, Inc

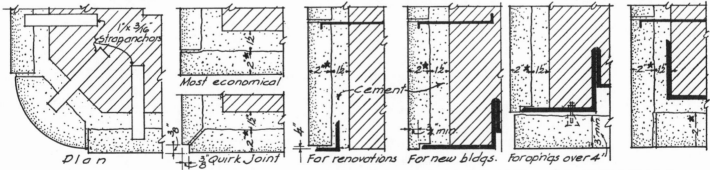

CORNER DETAILS

1"x ³⁄₁₆" Strap anchors
Most economical
Plan
⅜" Quirk Joint

LINTEL & SOFFIT SECTIONS

Cement
For renovations   For new bldgs.   For op'n'gs over 4"

¼" mortar joints usually used, but ³⁄₁₆" or ⅛" may be used for close work. Anchors to be galvanized or non-corroding (for sizes see page "Anchors for Stone Work"). 2 anchors to be used in top bed of each stone. ★ Thickness of granite veneer varies 1" to 2¼", but 2" is most commonly used. Granite veneer lintels should not be load bearing. Back may be parged or slushed full. See local bldg. code for allowable heights and anchors. Largest practical slab - 8' high x 12' wide.   Scale of details - 1½" = 1'·0"

EXTERIOR GRANITE VENEER

ARCHITECTURAL TERRA COTTA WALL BLOCKS

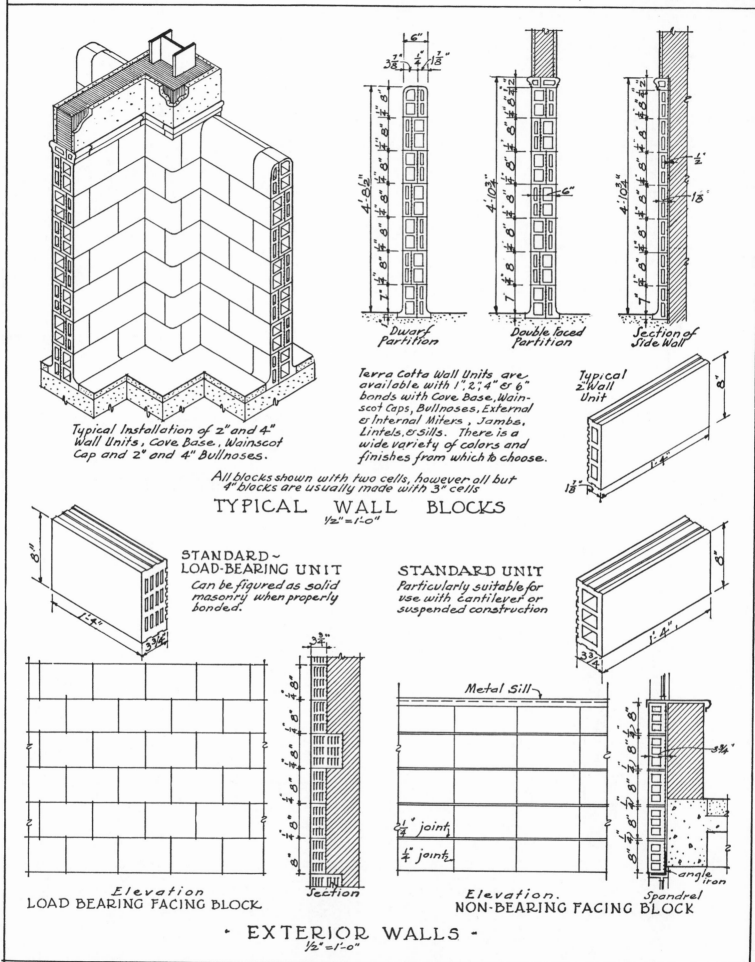

Typical Installation of 2" and 4"
Wall Units, Cove Base, Wainscot
Cap and 2" and 4" Bullnoses.

Dwarf Partition

Double Faced Partition

Section of Side Wall

Terra Cotta Wall Units are
available with 1", 2", 4" & 6"
bonds with Cove Base, Wainscot Caps, Bullnoses, External
& Internal Miters, Jambs,
Lintels, & Sills. There is a
wide variety of colors and
finishes from which to choose.

Typical 2" Wall Unit

All blocks shown with two cells, however all but
4" blocks are usually made with 3" cells

TYPICAL WALL BLOCKS
½" = 1'-0"

STANDARD~
LOAD-BEARING UNIT
Can be figured as solid
masonry when properly
bonded.

STANDARD UNIT
Particularly suitable for
use with cantilever or
suspended construction

Metal Sill

2¼" joint

¼" joint

Elevation
LOAD BEARING FACING BLOCK

Section

Elevation.
NON-BEARING FACING BLOCK

Spandrel

angle iron

· EXTERIOR WALLS ·
½" = 1'-0"

ARCHITECTURAL TERRA COTTA – EXTERIOR

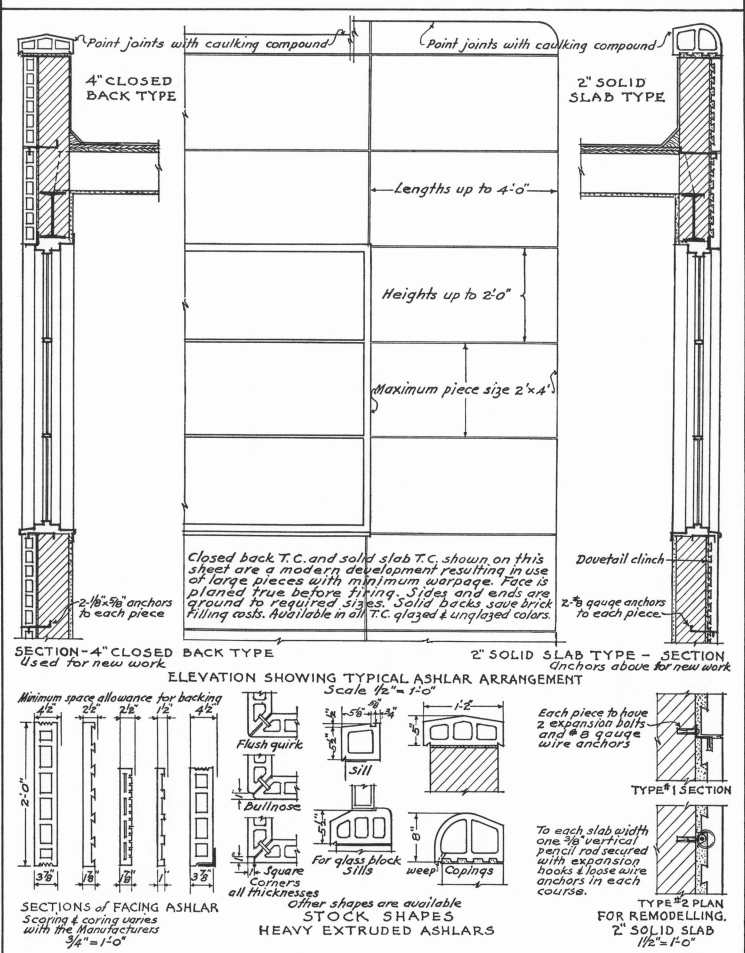

Point joints with caulking compound

Point joints with caulking compound

4" CLOSED BACK TYPE

2" SOLID SLAB TYPE

Lengths up to 4'-0"

Heights up to 2'-0"

Maximum piece size 2'×4'

Closed back T.C. and solid slab T.C. shown on this sheet are a modern development resulting in use of large pieces with minimum warpage. Face is planed true before firing. Sides and ends are ground to required sizes. Solid backs save brick filling costs. Available in all T.C. glazed & unglazed colors.

2-1/8"×5/8" anchors to each piece

Dovetail clinch

2-#8 gauge anchors to each piece

SECTION - 4" CLOSED BACK TYPE
Used for new work

2" SOLID SLAB TYPE – SECTION
Anchors above for new work

ELEVATION SHOWING TYPICAL ASHLAR ARRANGEMENT
Scale 1/2" = 1'-0"

Minimum space allowance for backing
4 1/2"   2 1/2"   2 1/2"   1 1/2"   4 1/2"

2'-0"

3 7/8"   7/8"   7/8"   1"   3 7/8"

SECTIONS of FACING ASHLAR
Scoring & coring varies with the Manufacturers
3/4" = 1'-0"

Flush quirk

Bullnose

Square Corners all thicknesses

sill

For glass block sills

weep   Copings

Other shapes are available
STOCK SHAPES
HEAVY EXTRUDED ASHLARS

Each piece to have 2 expansion bolts and #8 gauge wire anchors

TYPE #1 SECTION

To each slab width one 3/8" vertical pencil rod secured with expansion hooks & loose wire anchors in each course.

TYPE #2 PLAN
FOR REMODELLING.
2" SOLID SLAB
1 1/2" = 1'-0"

ARCHITECTURAL TERRA COTTA-EXTERIOR

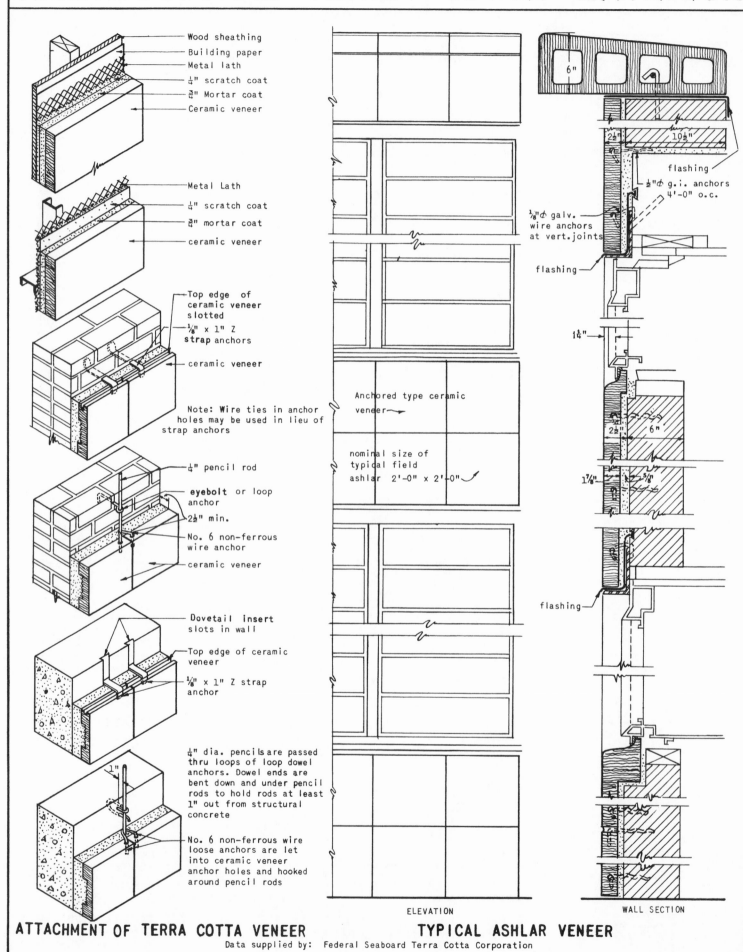

Wood sheathing
Building paper
Metal lath
¼" scratch coat
¾" Mortar coat
Ceramic veneer

Metal Lath
¼" scratch coat
¾" mortar coat
ceramic veneer

Top edge of ceramic veneer slotted
⅛" x 1" Z strap anchors
ceramic veneer

Note: Wire ties in anchor holes may be used in lieu of strap anchors

¼" pencil rod
eyebolt or loop anchor
2½" min.
No. 6 non-ferrous wire anchor
ceramic veneer

Dovetail insert slots in wall
Top edge of ceramic veneer
⅛" x 1" Z strap anchor

¼" dia. pencils are passed thru loops of loop dowel anchors. Dowel ends are bent down and under pencil rods to hold rods at least 1" out from structural concrete

No. 6 non-ferrous wire loose anchors are let into ceramic veneer anchor holes and hooked around pencil rods

Anchored type ceramic veneer

nominal size of typical field ashlar 2'-0" x 2'-0"

6"
2½"   10½"
flashing
½"⌀ g.i. anchors 4'-0" o.c.
⅛"⌀ galv. wire anchors at vert. joints
flashing
1¼"
2½"   6"
1⅞"   ⅝"
flashing

ATTACHMENT OF TERRA COTTA VENEER   **TYPICAL ASHLAR VENEER**

ELEVATION   WALL SECTION

Data supplied by: Federal Seaboard Terra Cotta Corporation

ARCHITECTURAL TERRA COTTA

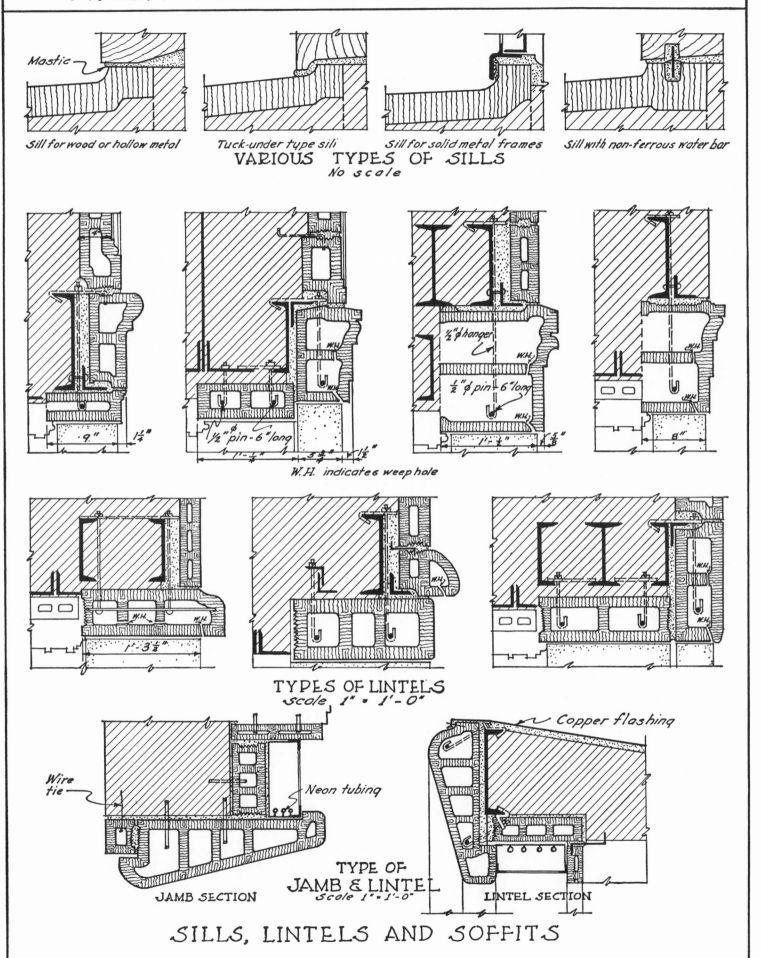

Mastic

Sill for wood or hollow metal

Tuck-under type sill

Sill for solid metal frames

Sill with non-ferrous water bar

VARIOUS TYPES OF SILLS
No scale

9" 1¼"

1½"ø pin-6"long 1'-¼" 5¾" 1½"

½"ø hanger

½"ø pin-6"long

W.H.

1'-¼" 5⅝"

8"

W.H. indicates weep hole

1'-3½"

TYPES OF LINTELS
scale 1" = 1'-0"

Wire tie

Neon tubing

Copper flashing

JAMB SECTION

TYPE OF
JAMB & LINTEL
Scale 1"=1'-0"

LINTEL SECTION

SILLS, LINTELS AND SOFFITS

ARCHITECTURAL TERRA·COTTA

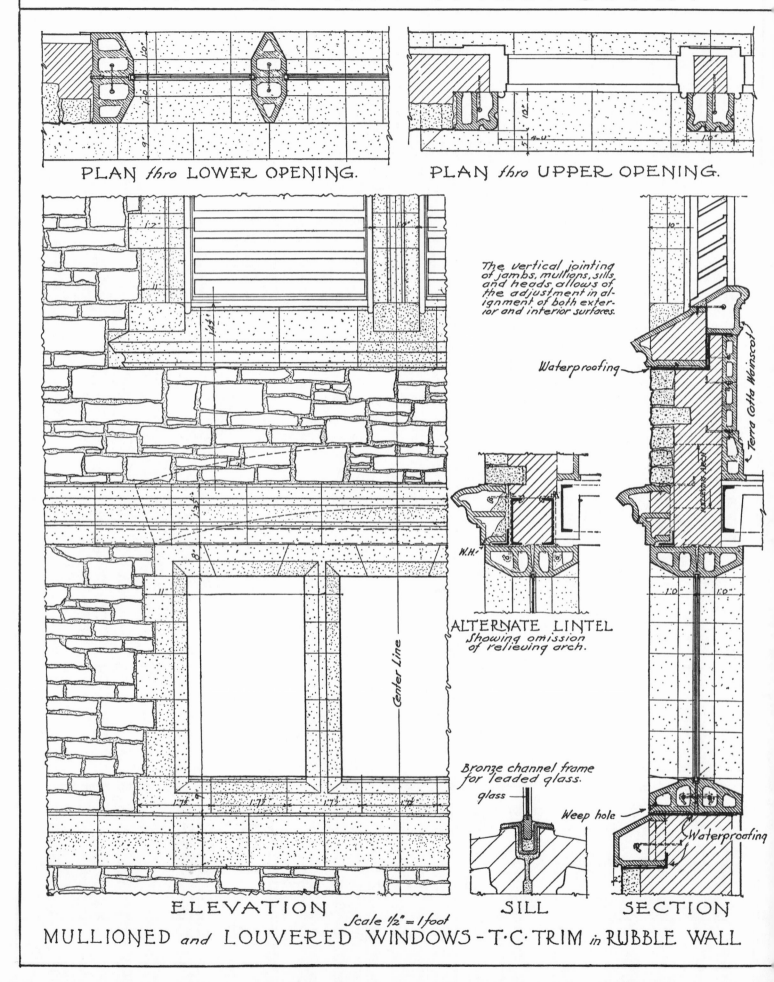

PLAN *thro* LOWER OPENING.

PLAN *thro* UPPER OPENING.

The vertical jointing of jambs, mullions, sills and heads allows of the adjustment in alignment of both exterior and interior surfaces.

Waterproofing

Terra Cotta Wainscot

ALTERNATE LINTEL
Showing omission of relieving arch.

Bronze channel frame for leaded glass.

glass

Weep hole

Waterproofing

Center Line

ELEVATION

Scale ½" = 1 foot

SILL

SECTION

MULLIONED *and* LOUVERED WINDOWS – T·C· TRIM *in* RUBBLE WALL

ARCHITECTURAL TERRA COTTA

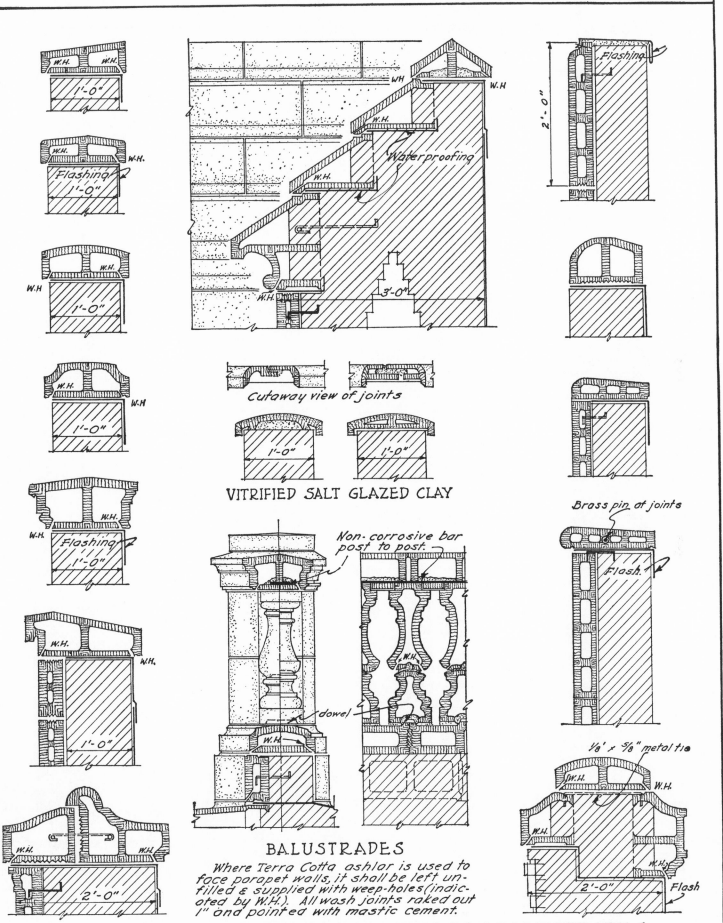

Waterproofing

Flashing

2'-0"

Cutaway view of joints

VITRIFIED SALT GLAZED CLAY

Brass pin at joints

Flash.

Non-corrosive bar post to post.

dowel

1/8" x 5/8" metal tie

Flash

BALUSTRADES

Where Terra Cotta ashlar is used to face parapet walls, it shall be left un-filled & supplied with weep-holes (indicated by W.H.). All wash joints raked out 1" and pointed with mastic cement.

T.C. JOINTING, ANCHORING COPINGS & BALUSTRADES

Scale 3/4" = 1'-0"

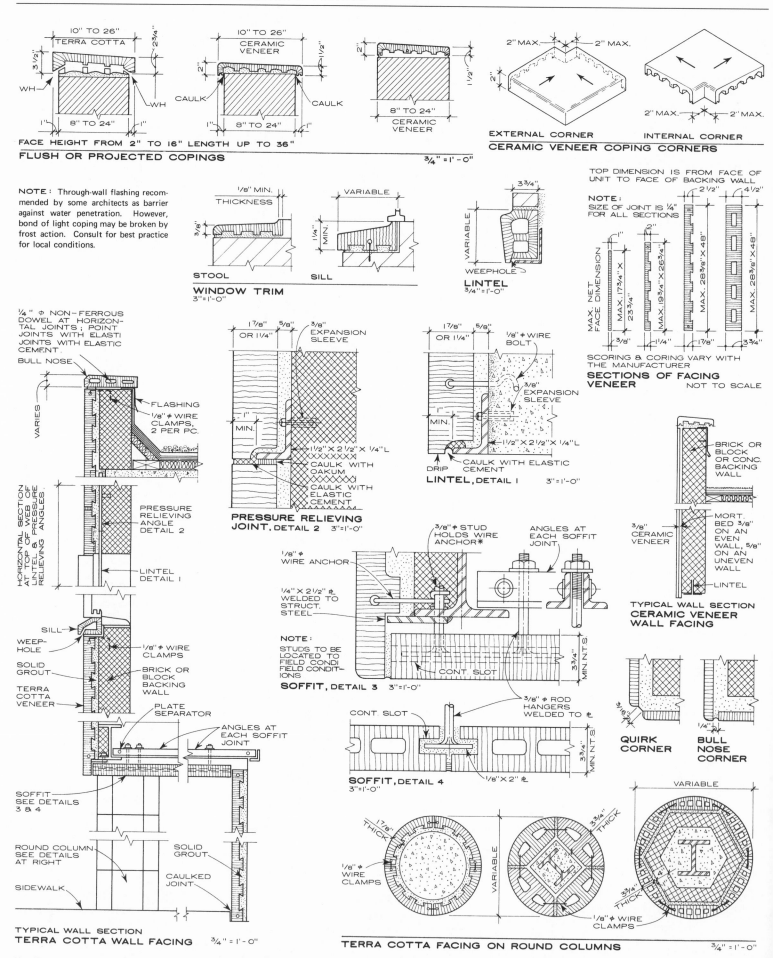

10" TO 26"
TERRA COTTA
2 3/4"
3 1/2"
WH
WH
1" 8" TO 24" 1"
FACE HEIGHT FROM 2" TO 16" LENGTH UP TO 36"
FLUSH OR PROJECTED COPINGS

10" TO 26"
CERAMIC VENEER
1 1/2"
2"
CAULK
CAULK
1" 8" TO 24" 1"

2"
1 1/2"
8" TO 24"
CERAMIC VENEER

2" MAX. 2" MAX.
2"
EXTERNAL CORNER

2" MAX.
2" MAX.
INTERNAL CORNER
CERAMIC VENEER COPING CORNERS

3/4" = 1'-0"

NOTE: Through-wall flashing recommended by some architects as barrier against water penetration. However, bond of light coping may be broken by frost action. Consult for best practice for local conditions.

1/8" MIN.
THICKNESS
3/8"
STOOL

VARIABLE
1 1/4" MIN.
SILL
WINDOW TRIM
3" = 1'-0"

3 3/4"
VARIABLE
VARIABLE
WEEPHOLE
LINTEL
3/4" = 1'-0"

TOP DIMENSION IS FROM FACE OF
UNIT TO FACE OF BACKING WALL

NOTE:
SIZE OF JOINT IS 1/4"
FOR ALL SECTIONS

2 1/2"   4 1/2"
1"   2"
MAX. NET FACE DIMENSION
MAX. 17 3/4" X 23 3/4"
MAX. 19 3/4" X 26 3/4"
MAX. 28 3/8" X 48"
MAX. 28 3/8" X 48"
3/8"   1 1/4"   1 7/8"   3 3/4"

SCORING & CORING VARY WITH
THE MANUFACTURER
SECTIONS OF FACING VENEER   NOT TO SCALE

1/4" Ø NON-FERROUS DOWEL AT HORIZONTAL JOINTS; POINT JOINTS WITH ELASTIC JOINTS WITH ELASTIC CEMENT.
BULL NOSE
VARIES
FLASHING
1/8" Ø WIRE CLAMPS, 2 PER PC.
PRESSURE RELIEVING ANGLE DETAIL 2
HORIZONTAL SECTION AT TOP OF WEB OF LINTEL & PRESSURE RELIEVING ANGLES.
LINTEL DETAIL I
SILL
WEEP-HOLE
SOLID GROUT
TERRA COTTA VENEER
1/8" Ø WIRE CLAMPS
BRICK OR BLOCK BACKING WALL
PLATE SEPARATOR
ANGLES AT EACH SOFFIT JOINT
SOFFIT SEE DETAILS 3 & 4
ROUND COLUMN SEE DETAILS AT RIGHT
SIDEWALK
SOLID GROUT
CAULKED JOINT
TYPICAL WALL SECTION
TERRA COTTA WALL FACING   3/4" = 1'-0"

Max Martin Nathan, Rogers, Butler & Burgun; New York, New York

1 7/8" OR 1 1/4"   5/8"   3/8"
EXPANSION SLEEVE
1" MIN.
1 1/2" X 2 1/2" X 1/4" L
CAULK WITH OAKUM
CAULK WITH ELASTIC CEMENT
PRESSURE RELIEVING JOINT, DETAIL 2   3" = 1'-0"

1 7/8" OR 1 1/4"   5/8"
1/8" Ø WIRE BOLT
3/8" EXPANSION SLEEVE
1" MIN.
1 1/2" X 2 1/2" X 1/4" L
DRIP
CAULK WITH ELASTIC CEMENT
LINTEL, DETAIL 1   3" = 1'-0"

1/8" Ø WIRE ANCHOR
1/4" X 2 1/2" L WELDED TO STRUCT. STEEL
3/8" Ø STUD HOLDS WIRE ANCHOR*
ANGLES AT EACH SOFFIT JOINT
NOTE:
STUDS TO BE LOCATED TO FIELD CONDITIONS
CONT. SLOT
3 3/4" MIN. N.T.S.
SOFFIT, DETAIL 3   3" = 1'-0"

CONT. SLOT
3/8" Ø ROD HANGERS WELDED TO L
1/8" X 2" L
3 3/4" MIN. N.T.S.
SOFFIT, DETAIL 4
3" = 1'-0"

BRICK OR BLOCK OR CONC. BACKING WALL
3/8" CERAMIC VENEER
MORT. BED 3/8" ON AN EVEN WALL, 5/8" ON AN UNEVEN WALL
LINTEL
TYPICAL WALL SECTION
CERAMIC VENEER WALL FACING

3/8"
1/4"
QUIRK CORNER   **BULL NOSE CORNER**

VARIABLE
1 7/8" THICK
1/8" Ø WIRE CLAMPS
3 3/4" THICK
VARIABLE
3 3/4" THICK
1/8" Ø WIRE CLAMPS
TERRA COTTA FACING ON ROUND COLUMNS   3/4" = 1'-0"

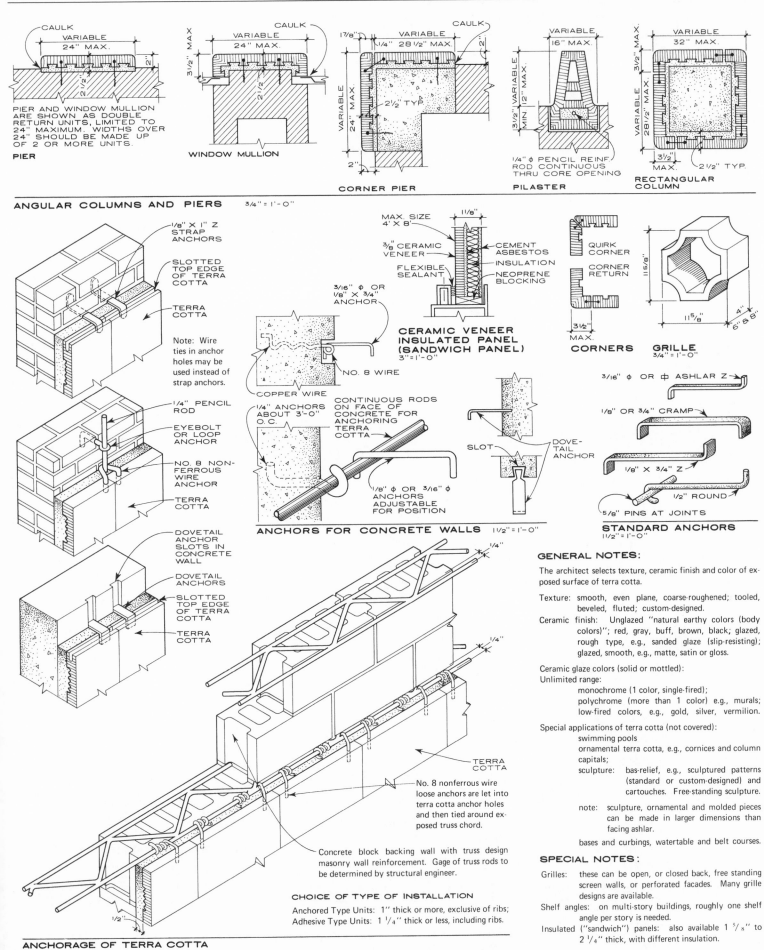

PIER AND WINDOW MULLION ARE SHOWN AS DOUBLE RETURN UNITS, LIMITED TO 24" MAXIMUM. WIDTHS OVER 24" SHOULD BE MADE UP OF 2 OR MORE UNITS.

PIER

WINDOW MULLION

CORNER PIER

PILASTER

RECTANGULAR COLUMN

ANGULAR COLUMNS AND PIERS   3/4" = 1'-0"

CERAMIC VENEER INSULATED PANEL (SANDWICH PANEL) 3" = 1'-0"

CORNERS   GRILLE   3/4" = 1'-0"

ANCHORS FOR CONCRETE WALLS 1 1/2" = 1'-0"

STANDARD ANCHORS 1 1/2" = 1'-0"

ANCHORAGE OF TERRA COTTA

Max Martin Nathan, Rogers, Butler & Burgun; New York, New York

CHOICE OF TYPE OF INSTALLATION

Anchored Type Units: 1" thick or more, exclusive of ribs;
Adhesive Type Units: 1 1/4" thick or less, including ribs.

GENERAL NOTES:

The architect selects texture, ceramic finish and color of exposed surface of terra cotta.

Texture: smooth, even plane, coarse-roughened; tooled, beveled, fluted; custom-designed.

Ceramic finish: Unglazed "natural earthy colors (body colors)"; red, gray, buff, brown, black; glazed, rough type, e.g., sanded glaze (slip-resisting); glazed, smooth, e.g., matte, satin or gloss.

Ceramic glaze colors (solid or mottled):
Unlimited range:
   monochrome (1 color, single-fired);
   polychrome (more than 1 color) e.g., murals;
   low-fired colors, e.g., gold, silver, vermilion.

Special applications of terra cotta (not covered):
   swimming pools
   ornamental terra cotta, e.g., cornices and column capitals;
   sculpture: bas-relief, e.g., sculptured patterns (standard or custom-designed) and cartouches. Free-standing sculpture.
   note: sculpture, ornamental and molded pieces can be made in larger dimensions than facing ashlar.
   bases and curbings, watertable and belt courses.

SPECIAL NOTES:

Grilles: these can be open, or closed back, free standing screen walls, or perforated facades. Many grille designs are available.

Shelf angles: on multi-story buildings, roughly one shelf angle per story is needed.

Insulated ("sandwich") panels: also available 1 5/8" to 2 1/4" thick, with different insulation.

STRUCTURAL CLAY TILE for COMBINATION BRICK & TILE WALLS

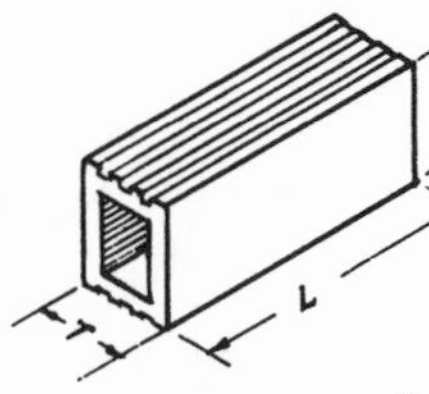
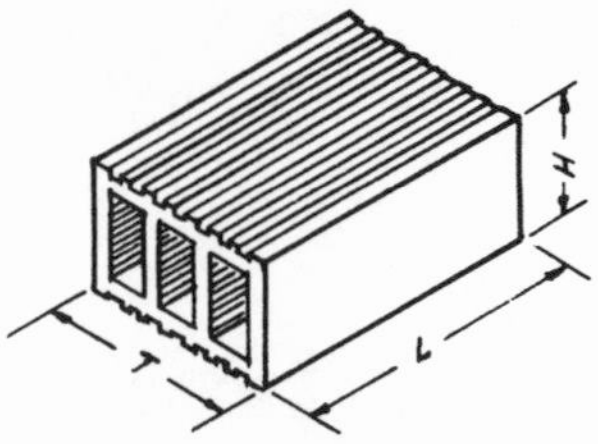

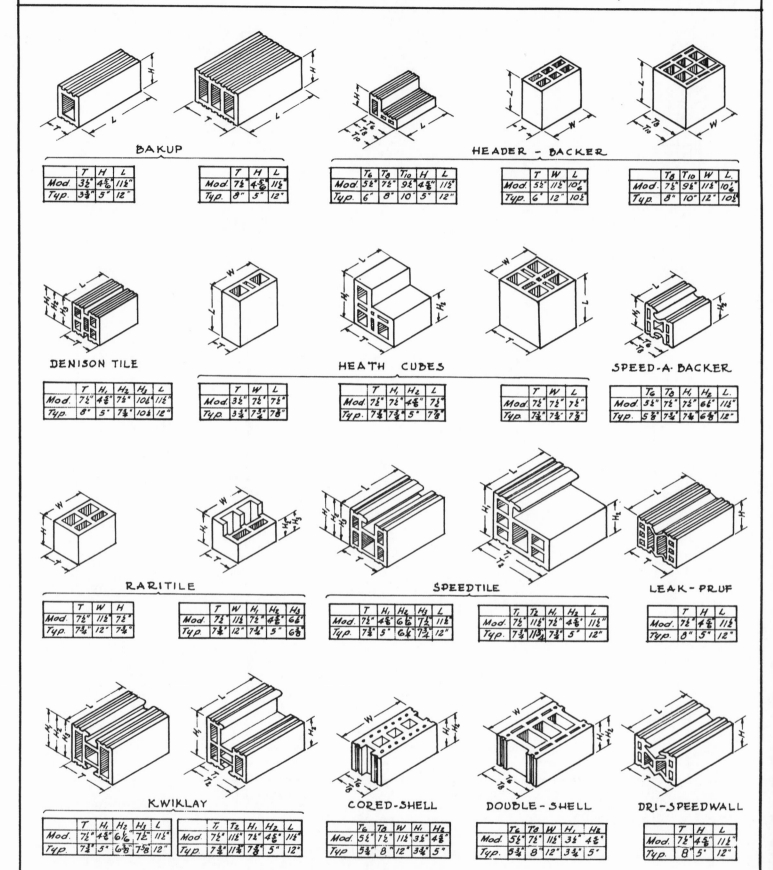

BAKUP

	T	H	L
Mod.	3 1/2"	4 5/6"	11 1/2"
Typ.	3 3/4"	5"	12"

	T	H	L
Mod.	7 1/2"	4 5/6"	11 1/2"
Typ.	8"	5"	12"

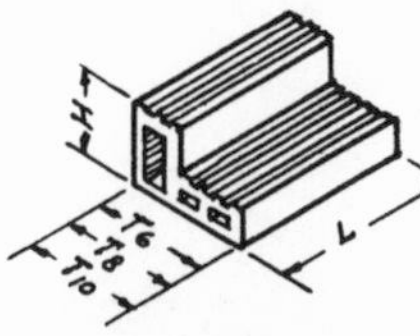
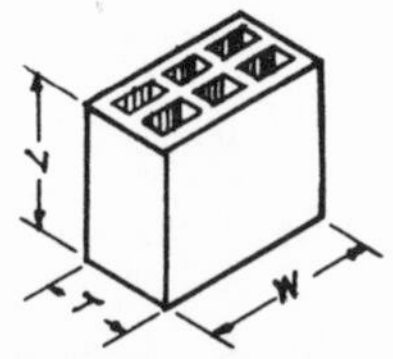
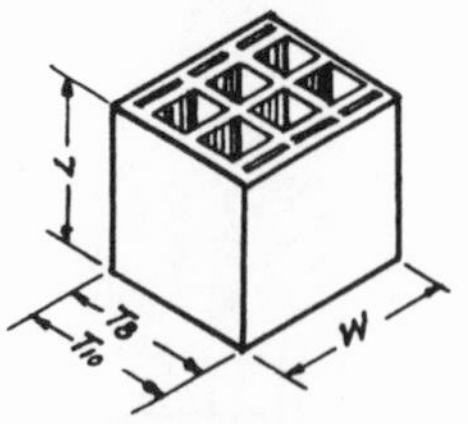

HEADER - BACKER

	T_6	T_8	T_{10}	H	L
Mod.	5 1/2"	7 1/2"	9 1/2"	4 5/6"	11 1/2"
Typ.	6"	8"	10"	5"	12"

	T	W	L
Mod.	5 1/2"	11 1/2"	10 1/6"
Typ.	6"	12"	10 1/2"

	T_8	T_{10}	W	L.
Mod.	7 1/2"	9 1/2"	11 1/2"	10 1/6"
Typ.	8"	10"	12"	10 1/2"

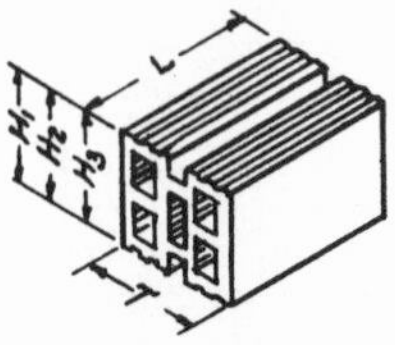

DENISON TILE

	T	H_1	H_2	H_3	L
Mod.	7 1/2"	4 5/6"	7 1/2"	10 1/6"	11 1/2"
Typ.	8"	5"	7 3/4"	10 1/2"	12"

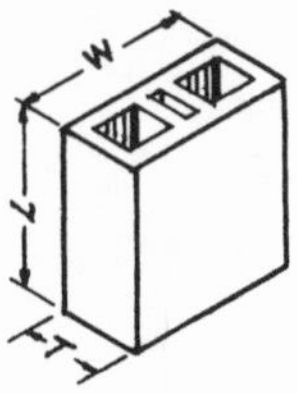
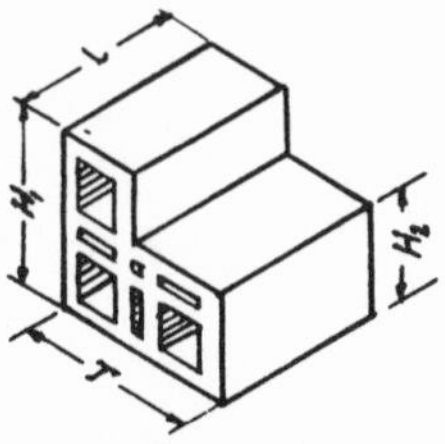
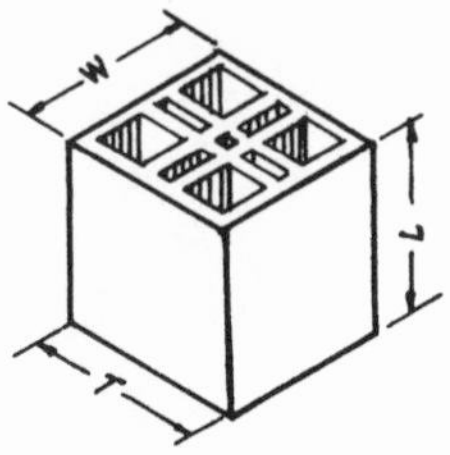

HEATH CUBES

	T	W	L
Mod.	3 1/2"	7 1/2"	7 1/2"
Typ.	3 3/4"	7 3/4"	7 7/8"

	T	H_1	H_2	L
Mod.	7 1/2"	7 1/2"	4 5/6"	7 1/2"
Typ.	7 3/4"	7 3/4"	5"	7 7/8"

	T	W	L
Mod.	7 1/2"	7 1/2"	7 1/2"
Typ.	7 3/4"	7 3/4"	7 7/8"

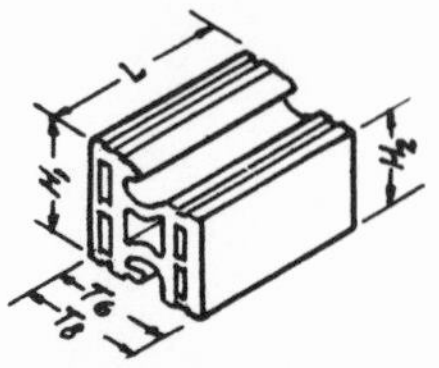

SPEED-A-BACKER

	T_6	T_8	H_1	H_2	L.
Mod.	5 1/2"	7 1/2"	7 1/2"	6 1/6"	11 1/2"
Typ.	5 7/8"	7 3/4"	7 3/4"	6 3/8"	12"

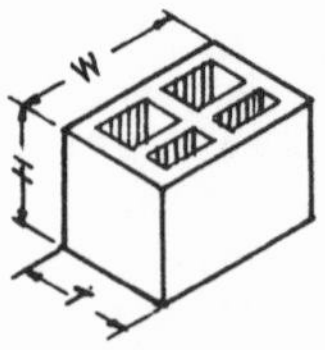
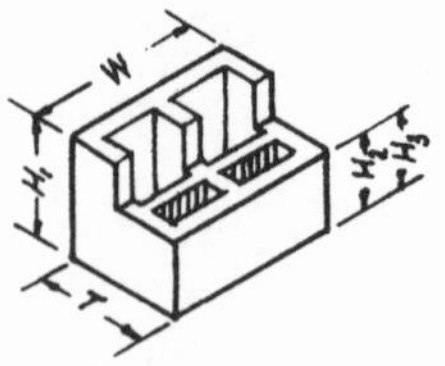

RARITILE

	T	W	H
Mod.	7 1/2"	11 1/2"	7 1/2"
Typ.	7 3/4"	12"	7 3/4"

	T	W	H_1	H_2	H_3
Mod.	7 1/2"	11 1/2	7 1/2"	4 5/6"	6 1/6"
Typ.	7 3/4"	12"	7 3/4"	5"	6 3/8"

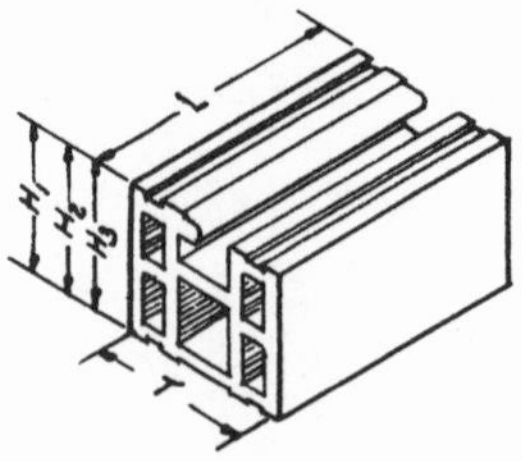
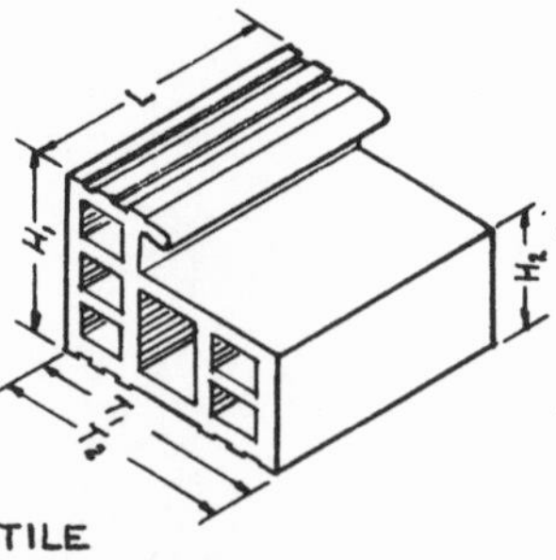

SPEEDTILE

	T	H_1	H_2	H_3	L
Mod.	7 1/2"	4 5/6"	6 1/6"	7 1/2"	11 1/2"
Typ.	7 3/4"	5"	6 1/4"	7 3/4"	12"

	T_1	T_2	H_1	H_2	L
Mod.	7 1/2"	11 1/2"	7 1/2"	4 5/6"	11 1/2"
Typ.	7 3/4"	11 3/4"	7 3/4"	5"	12"

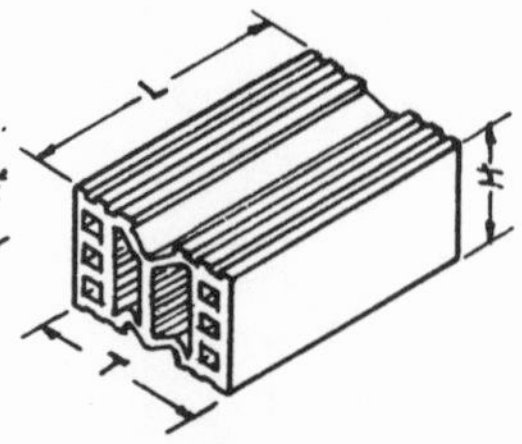

LEAK-PRUF

	T	H	L
Mod.	7 1/2"	4 5/6"	11 1/2"
Typ.	8"	5"	12"

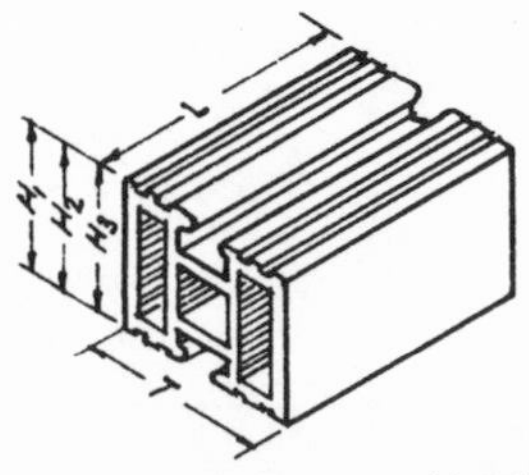
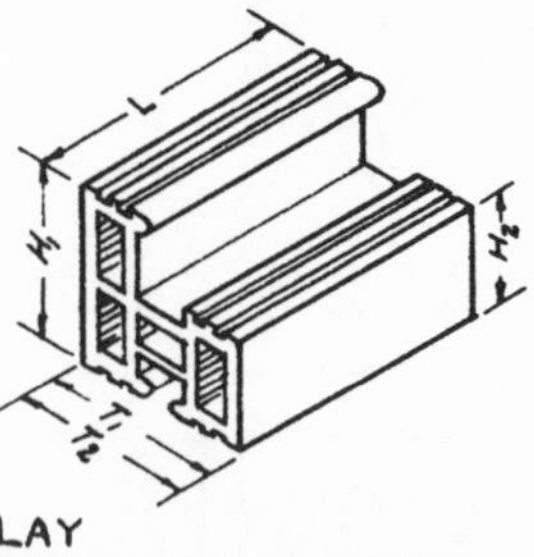

KWIKLAY

	T	H_1	H_2	H_3	L
Mod.	7 1/2"	4 5/6"	6 1/6"	7 1/2"	11 1/2"
Typ.	7 3/4"	5"	6 3/8"	7 5/8"	12"

	T_1	T_2	H_1	H_2	L
Mod.	7 1/2"	11 1/2"	7 1/2"	4 5/6"	11 1/2"
Typ.	7 3/4"	11 3/4"	7 5/8"	5"	12"

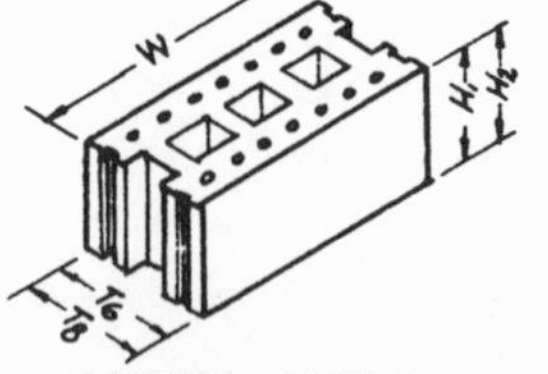

CORED-SHELL

	T_6	T_8	W	H_1	H_2
Mod.	5 1/2"	7 1/2"	11 1/2"	3 1/2"	4 5/6"
Typ	5 3/4"	8"	12"	3 3/4"	5"

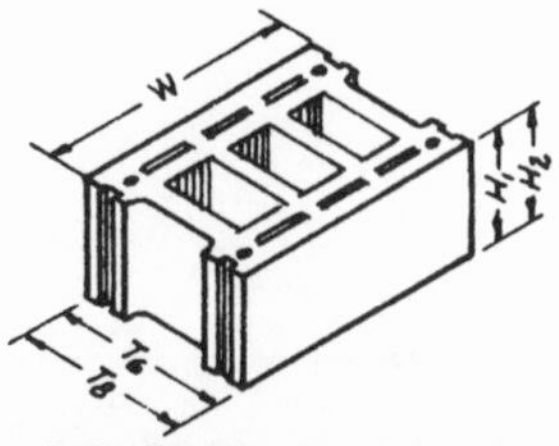

DOUBLE-SHELL

	T_6	T_8	W	H_1	H_2
Mod.	5 1/2"	7 1/2"	11 1/2"	3 1/2"	4 5/6"
Typ.	5 3/4"	8"	12"	3 3/4"	5"

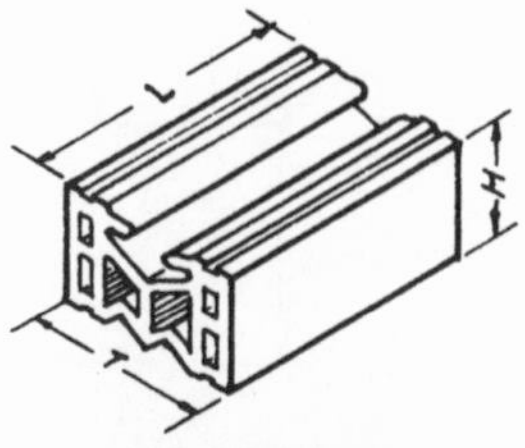

DRI-SPEEDWALL

	T	H	L
Mod.	7 1/2"	4 5/6"	11 1/2"
Typ.	8"	5"	12"

Mod.= actual modular size of tile. Typ.= actual typical (non-modular) size of tile. Standard mortar joint for structural clay tile is 1/2".

Recommendations of the Structural Clay Products Institute - 1956

STRUCTURAL CLAY TILE

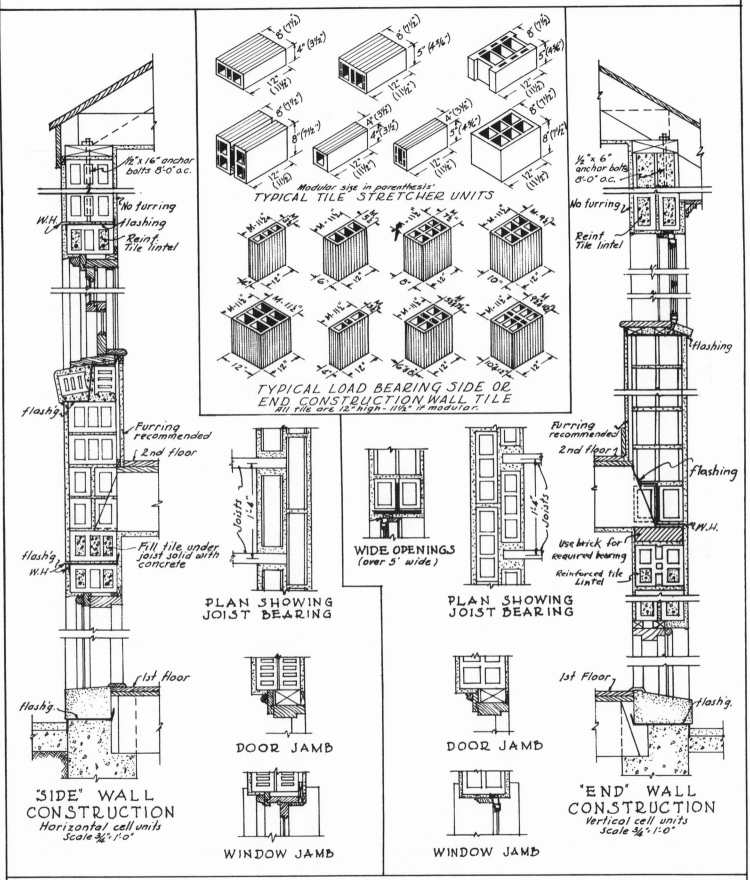

Modular size in parenthesis'
TYPICAL TILE STRETCHER UNITS

TYPICAL LOAD BEARING SIDE OR END CONSTRUCTION WALL TILE
All tile are 12" high - 11½" if modular.

½"x 16" anchor bolts 8'-0" a.c.

W.H.

No furring

flashing

Reinf. Tile lintel

flash'g.

Furring recommended

2nd floor

flash'g. W.H.

Fill tile under joist solid with concrete

Joists 14"

PLAN SHOWING JOIST BEARING

WIDE OPENINGS (over 5' wide)

14" Joists

PLAN SHOWING JOIST BEARING

½"x 6" anchor bolts 8'-0" O.C.

No furring

Reinf. Tile lintel

flashing

Furring recommended

2nd floor

flashing

W.H.

Use brick for required bearing

Reinforced tile Lintel

1st floor

flash'g.

"SIDE" WALL CONSTRUCTION
Horizontal cell units
Scale ¾"= 1'-0"

DOOR JAMB

WINDOW JAMB

DOOR JAMB

WINDOW JAMB

1st Floor

flash'g.

"END" WALL CONSTRUCTION
Vertical cell units
Scale ¾"= 1'-0"

All tile sizes figured for use with standard ½" mortar joint

EXTERIOR WALL CONSTRUCTION with STUCCO FINISH

Recommendations of the Structural Clay Products Institute. 1956

STRUCTURAL CLAY TILE

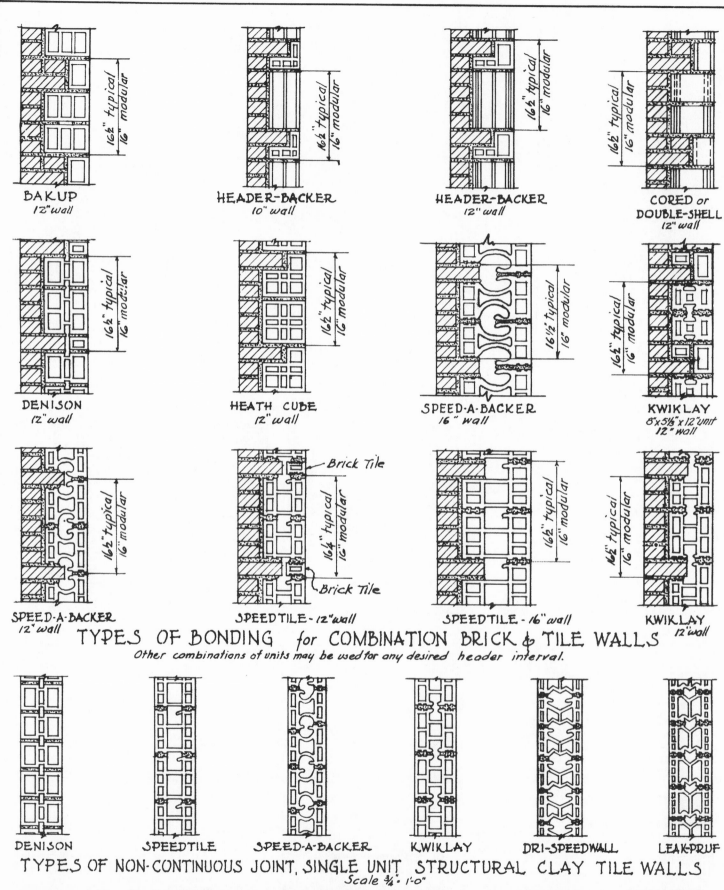

BAKUP
12" wall

HEADER-BACKER
10" wall

HEADER-BACKER
12" wall

CORED or DOUBLE-SHELL
12" wall

DENISON
12" wall

HEATH CUBE
12" wall

SPEED-A-BACKER
16" wall

KWIKLAY
8"x5⅓"x12" unit
12" wall

SPEED-A-BACKER
12" wall

SPEEDTILE - 12" wall
Brick Tile
Brick Tile

SPEEDTILE - 16" wall

KWIKLAY
12" wall

TYPES OF BONDING for **COMBINATION BRICK & TILE WALLS**
Other combinations of units may be used for any desired header interval.

DENISON   **SPEEDTILE**   **SPEED-A-BACKER**   **KWIKLAY**   **DRI-SPEEDWALL**   **LEAK-PRUF**

TYPES OF NON-CONTINUOUS JOINT, SINGLE UNIT STRUCTURAL CLAY TILE WALLS
Scale ¾": 1'-0"

Scoring not indicated on sections. Tile is made by most manufacturers to make combination walls 10", 12", 14", 16" thick. Mortar for both brick and back-up tile to be 1 part Portland Cement, 1 part lime, and 5 to 6 parts clean sharp sand. Mortar beds to be ½" thick; parging recommended back of brick or for face of tile.
Recommendations of the Structural Clay Products Institute - 1955

STRUCTURAL CLAY TILE

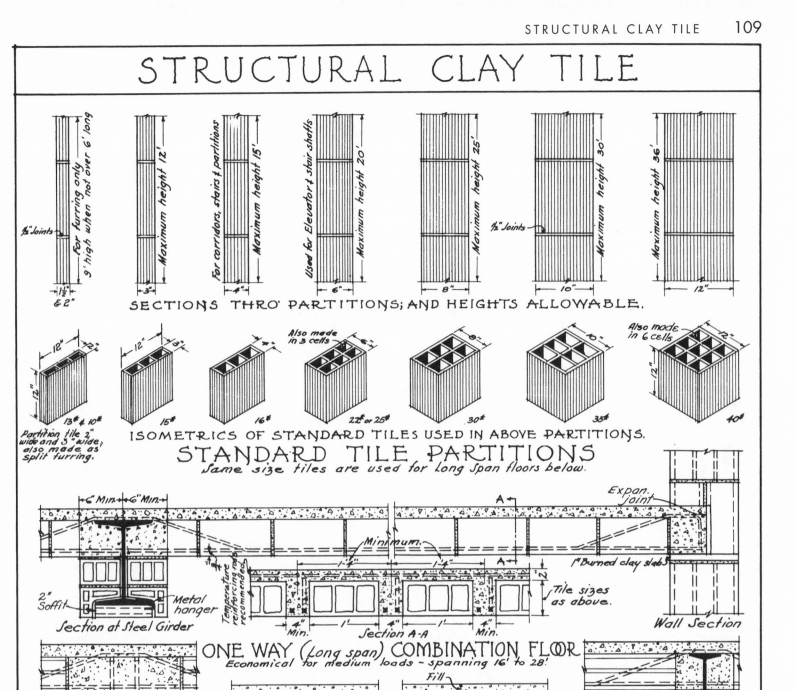

SECTIONS THRO' PARTITIONS; AND HEIGHTS ALLOWABLE.

½" Joints — For furring only 9' high when not over 6' long — 1½" & 2"

Maximum height 12' — 3"

For corridors, stairs & partitions — Maximum height 15' — 4"

Used for Elevator & stair shafts — Maximum height 20' — 6"

Maximum height 25' — 8" — ½" Joints

Maximum height 30' — 10"

Maximum height 36' — 12"

ISOMETRICS OF STANDARD TILES USED IN ABOVE PARTITIONS.

Partition tile 2" wide and 3" wide; also made as split furring. — 13# & 10#

15#

16#

Also made in 3 cells — 22# or 25#

30#

35#

Also made in 6 cells — 40#

STANDARD TILE PARTITIONS
Same size tiles are used for Long Span floors below.

ONE WAY (Long span) COMBINATION FLOOR
Economical for medium loads - spanning 16' to 28'

6" Min. — 6" Min. — 2" Soffit — Metal hanger — Section at Steel Girder — Temperature reinforcing rods recommended. — Minimum. — 1'-4" — 1'-4" — Section A-A — 4" Min. — 1' — 4" Min. — 1' — 4" Min. — Tile sizes as above. — Expan. joint — 1" Burned clay slabs — Wall Section

TWO WAY COMBINATION FLOOR (SCHUSTER)
Economical where bearing is had on four walls.

Section at Concrete girder — Min. 4" — 1' — 4" Min. — Fill — Min. 4" — 1' — 4" Min. — variable 3" to 12' — Clip tile — Section at I Beam

THICKNESS OF ONE-WAY SLABS - FOR PRELIMINARY ASSUMPTION ONLY.

Type of Building	Live Load	Span						Type of Building	Live Load	Span					
		8'	12'	16'	20'	24'	28'			8'	12'	16'	20'	24'	28'
Residence or Apartment	40	6	6	8	10	12	14	Public Assembly	100	8	8	10	12	14	—
Office Building	60	6	6	8	12	14	—	Heavy Duty Building	120	8	8	10	12	14	—
School or College	75	6	6	10	10	14	—	Side Walks	250	10	10	12	14	—	—

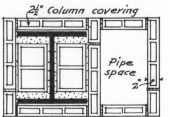

2½" Column covering — Pipe space 2" — **COLUMN & PIPE CHASE**

2½" Column covering — Clips may be used at intersections — 4" partition — Clips — Clips — 6" partition built in — Clips — **PARTITIONS JOINING COLUMN**

2½" Column covering — Keep all pipes and ducts 3" away from steel. — **PIPES at COLUMN**

In N.Y. City & East 2½"×8"×12" tile with 1" web is used, elsewhere 3"×12"×12" partition tile is also used; for exterior cols. use 4"×12"×12" tile.

COLUMN FIREPROOFING

Scale ¾" = 1'-0" *Recommendations of the Structural Clay Products Institute, 1956*

STRUCTURAL CLAY FACING TILE· GLAZED & UNGLAZED

Shapes are made in Series based on face dimensions of the stretcher unit.
The "standard depth" or bed of full shapes in all series is generally 3¾" and that of soaps 1¾".
A variety of shapes are available in all series. Series are lettered.

   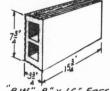

"4S" 2⅔"x8" Face   "4DC" 5⅓"x8" Face   "6PC" 4"x12" Face Not generally available   "6TC" 5⅓"x12" Face   "8W" 8"x16" Face

STRETCHERS OF STANDARD SERIES

SERIES "4S" (1 BRICK EQUIV.)   SERIES "4D" (2 BRICK EQUIV.)   SERIES "6P" (2¼ BRICK EQUIV.)   SERIES "6T" (3 BRICK EQUIV.)   SERIES "8W" (6 BRICK EQUIV.)

(All sizes shown are modular.)

STANDARD· FINISHES & COLORS

CERAMIC COLOR GLAZE			UNGLAZED	CLEAR GLAZE	SALT GLAZE
FINISH	Satin		FINISH - Smooth	FINISH · Glossy	FINISH · Glossy
SINGLE COLOR FIELD SHADES White Blue Light Gray Ivory Sunlight Yellow Light Green Coral Tan Ocular Green	MULTI-COLOR FIELD SHADES Gray mottle White mottle Green mottle Cream mottle	SINGLE COLOR TRIM SHADES Black	COLORS Light Gray Cream Light Buff Golden Buff Gray Manganese Spot Cream Manganese Spot	COLORS Clear Glaze	COLORS Cream Tone Buff Tone

TYPES OF UNITS

SOLID MASONRY UNITS: { Multi-cored or uncored unit whose NET cross-sectional area in every plane parallel to the Bearing surface is 75% or more of its GROSS cross-sectional area measured in the same plane.

HOLLOW MASONRY UNITS: A unit whose NET cross-sectional area in any plane parallel to the bearing surface is less than 75% of its gross cross-sectional area measured in the same plane.

Type & direction of scoring and coring are optional with each manufacturer. When intended for exterior use, the absorbtion of the body should be limited in accord with Facing Tile Institute Standard Specifications.

GRADING RULES

	CERAMIC GLAZED STRUCTURAL FACING TILE	CLEAR GLAZED STRUCTURAL FACING TILE	SALT GLAZED STRUCTURAL FACING TILE	SMOOTH UNGLAZED STRUCTURAL FACING TILE
First Quality	Select Quality	Select Quality	Select Quality	Select Quality
Second Quality	"B" Quality	Standard Quality	Standard Quality	

SERIES "6T", 5⅓"x12" (Three brick equivalent) SIMILAR SHAPES IN OTHER SIZES

   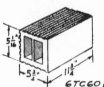 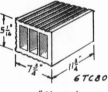

6T — Stretcher - scored or unscored backs   6TA — Soap Stretcher   6TCA — Soap Stretcher   6TC60 (Unglazed only) — 6" Stretcher   6TC80 — 8" Stretcher

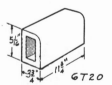 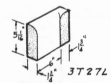 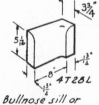

6T20 — Bullnose sill or cap 4" reveal, also square   6T20A — Soap Bullnose sill or cap, 2" reveal also square   3T27L — Bullnose sill or cap, internal square corner   5T24CR — Bullnose sill or cap, Bullnose corner, also soap, square corner   4T28L — Bullnose sill or cap, coved internal corner

(All shapes available in opposite hand)

Data from Handbook of Facing Tile Institute - Washington, D.C.

Continued on next page

STRUCTURAL CLAY FACING TILE - GLAZED & UNGLAZED

Continued from preceding page

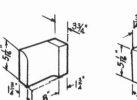

4T20BL
Bullnose coved
internal corner.
Sill or Cap.

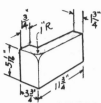

GT304R
Starter for bullnose
sill or jamb. Also use
with slope sills.

6T20B
Bullnose sill
or cap, 4" reveal.

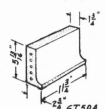

6T50A
Cove base
stretcher.

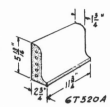

6T520A
Round top
cove base
stretcher.

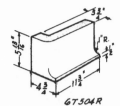

GT504R
Cove base,
bullnose jamb
or starter
4" return.

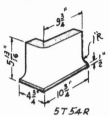

5T54R
Cove base bullnose
corner, 4" return.

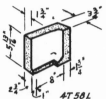

4T58L
Cove base, coved
internal corner.

4T59L
Cove base
octagonal
internal corner.

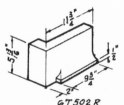

GT502R
Cove base starter,
also square jamb.

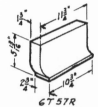

6T57R
Coped cove base
internal (square
corner).

5T4&6T4
5T4 = 9¾" length
6T4 = 11¾" length
Bullnose corner,
also jamb or
starter.

6T4A
Soap, bullnose
jamb or starter
2" return.

5T6
Octagonal
External
Corner.

5T4B&6T4B
5T4B = 9¾" length
6T4B = 11¾" length
Bullnose corner,
also jamb or
starter.

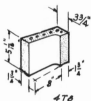

4T8
Coved
internal
corner.

4T9
Octagonal
internal
corner.

6T20D
Bullnose coping,
sill, cap or lintel.
4" wall.

5T5
Bullnose
full end,
4" wall.

6T260D
Bullnose coping,
sill, cap or lintel.
6" wall.

6T260
Bullnose cap
or sill.

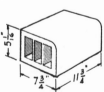

6T280
Bullnose coping,
sill, cap or lintel.
8" reveal.

6T70
Slope sill,
4" reveal.

6T780
Slope sill,
8" reveal.

6T760
Slope sill,
6" reveal.

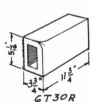

GT30R
Bullnose miter.

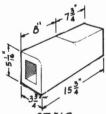

8T31R
Bullnose sill miter.

5T24X27R
Bullnose coping,
sill, cap or lintel.

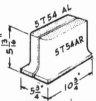

5T54 AL & AR
Cove base
bullnose end
4" wall.

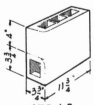

6T34R
Bullnose jamb
miter used with
sills and lintels.

(All sizes shown are modular)
(All shapes available in opposite hand)
SERIES "GT"- 5⅓"x12" (Three brick Equivalent) SIMILAR SHAPES IN OTHER SIZES
Data from Handbook of Facing Tile Institute - Washington, D.C.

STRUCTURAL CLAY FACING TILE-GLAZED & UNGLAZED

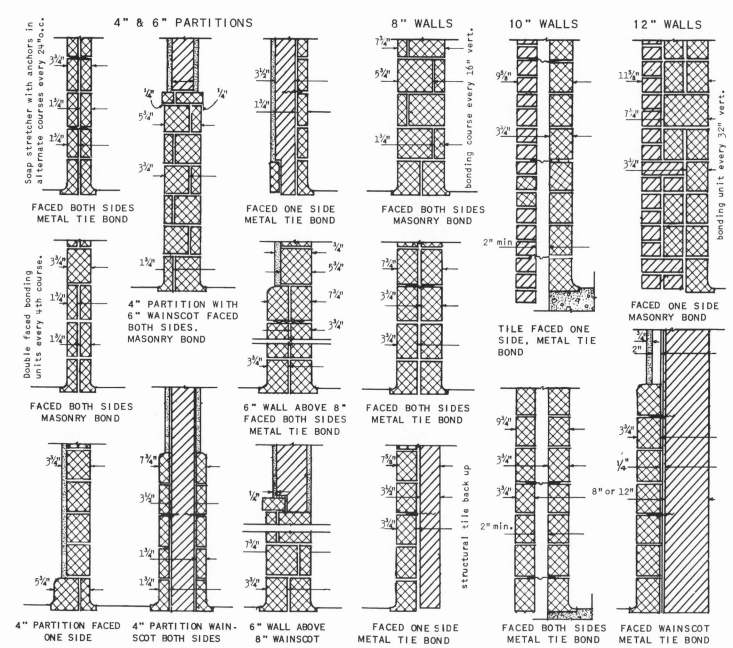

Soap stretcher with anchors in alternate courses every 24"o.c.

4" & 6" PARTITIONS

3¾"
1¾"
1¾"

FACED BOTH SIDES
METAL TIE BOND

Double faced bonding units every 4th course.

3¾"
1¾"

FACED BOTH SIDES
MASONRY BOND

3¾"
1¾"
5¾"

4" PARTITION FACED
ONE SIDE

¼"   ¼"
5¾"
3¾"
1¾"

4" PARTITION WITH
6" WAINSCOT FACED
BOTH SIDES.
MASONRY BOND

7¾"
3½"
1¾"
1¾"

4" PARTITION WAIN-
SCOT BOTH SIDES

3½"
1¾"

FACED ONE SIDE
METAL TIE BOND

¾"
5¾"
7¾"
3¾"
3¾"

6" WALL ABOVE 8"
FACED BOTH SIDES
METAL TIE BOND

¼"
7¾"
3¾"

6" WALL ABOVE
8" WAINSCOT

8" WALLS

7¾"
5¾"
1¾"

bonding course every 16" vert.

FACED BOTH SIDES
MASONRY BOND

7¾"
3¾"
3¾"

FACED BOTH SIDES
METAL TIE BOND

7⅝"
3½"
3¾"

FACED ONE SIDE
METAL TIE BOND

structural tile back up

10" WALLS

9⅝"
3¾"

2" min.

TILE FACED ONE
SIDE, METAL TIE
BOND

9¾"
3¾"
3¾"

2" min.

FACED BOTH SIDES
METAL TIE BOND

12" WALLS

11⅝"
7¾"
3¾"

bonding unit every 32" vert.

FACED ONE SIDE
MASONRY BOND

¾"
2"
3¾"
¼"

8" or 12"

FACED WAINSCOT
METAL TIE BOND

Where metal anchors are indicated space them not more than 16" vertically & 24" horizontally.

TYPICAL WALL SECTIONS - UNITS 5 1/3" HIGH

COURSES	HEIGHT	COURSES	HEIGHT	COURSES	HEIGHT
1	5⅓"	14	6'- 2⅔"	27	12'- 0"
2	10⅓"	15	6'- 8"	28	12'- 5⅓"
3	1'- 4"	16	7'- 1⅓"	29	12'-10⅔"
4	1'- 9⅓"	17	7'- 6⅔"	30	13'- 4"
5	2'- 2⅔"	18	8'- 0"	31	13'- 9⅓"
6	2'- 8"	19	8'- 5⅓"	32	14'- 2⅔"
7	3'- 1⅓"	20	8'-10⅔"	33	14'- 8"
8	3'- 6⅔"	21	9'- 4"	34	15'- 1⅓"
9	4'- 0"	22	9'- 9⅓"	35	15'- 6⅔"
10	4'- 5⅓"	23	10'- 2⅔"	36	16'- 0"
11	4'-10⅔"	24	10'- 8"	37	16'- 5⅓"
12	5'- 4"	25	11'- 1⅓"	38	16'-10⅔"
13	5'- 9⅓"	26	11'- 6⅔"	39	17'- 4"

WALLS, PARTITION & FURRING OF 5 1/3" UNITS

DATA FROM HANDBOOK OF THE FACING TILE INSTITUTE·WASHINGTON, D.C.

GLASS BLOCKS

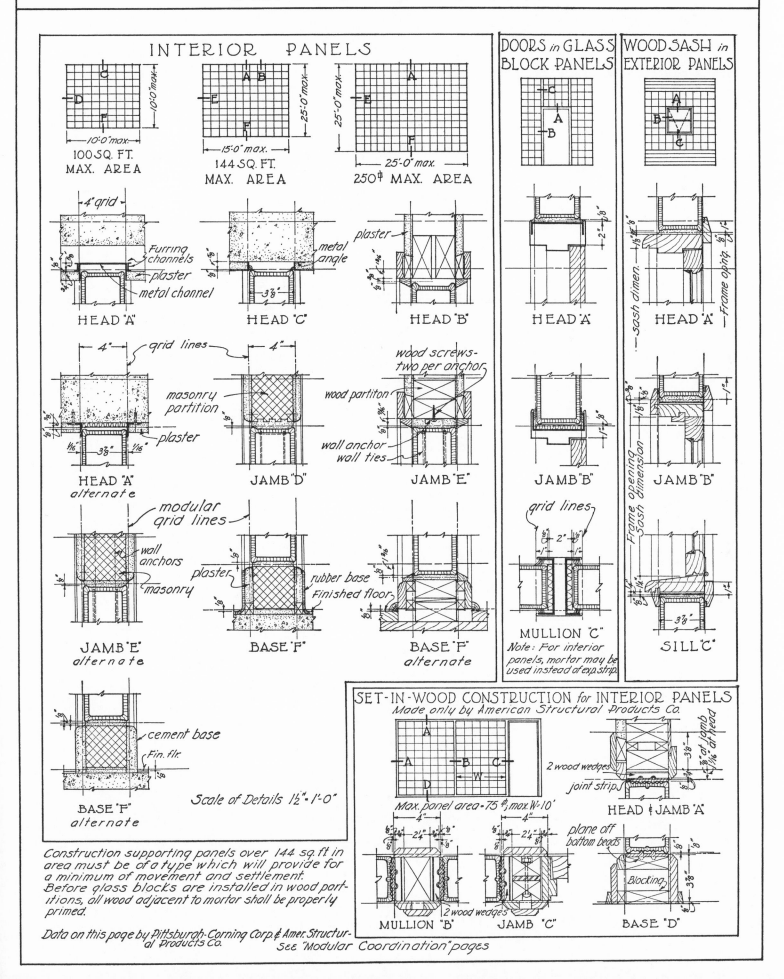

INTERIOR PANELS

100 SQ. FT. MAX. AREA — 10'-0" max. — 10'-0" max.

144 SQ. FT. MAX. AREA — 15'-0" max. — 25'-0" max.

250# MAX. AREA — 25'-0" max. — 25'-0" max.

4" grid — Furring channels — plaster — metal channel
HEAD "A"

metal angle — 3⅜"
HEAD "C"

plaster
HEAD "B"

4" — grid lines — masonry partition — plaster — 1/16 — 3⅜" — 1/16
HEAD "A" alternate

4" — masonry partition
JAMB "D"

wood screws - two per anchor — wood partiton — wall anchor — wall ties
JAMB "E"

modular grid lines — wall anchors — masonry
JAMB "E" alternate

plaster — rubber base — Finished floor
BASE "F"

BASE "F" alternate

cement base — Fin. flr.
BASE "F" alternate

Scale of Details 1½"=1'-0"

Construction supporting panels over 144 sq. ft in area must be of a type which will provide for a minimum of movement and settlement. Before glass blocks are installed in wood partitions, all wood adjacent to mortar shall be properly primed.

Data on this page by Pittsburgh-Corning Corp. & Amer. Structural Products Co.

DOORS in GLASS BLOCK PANELS

HEAD "A"

JAMB "B"

grid lines — 2"
MULLION "C"

Note: For interior panels, mortar may be used instead of exp. strip.

WOOD SASH in EXTERIOR PANELS

Sash dimen. — Frame opng.
HEAD "A"

Frame opening — Sash dimension
JAMB "B"

3⅜"
SILL "C"

SET-IN-WOOD CONSTRUCTION for INTERIOR PANELS
Made only by American Structural Products Co.

Max. panel area = 75#; max. W = 10'

4" — 2¼"
MULLION "B"
2 wood wedges

4" — 2¼"
JAMB "C"

2 wood wedges — joint strip
HEAD & JAMB "A"

plane off bottom beads — Blocking — 3⅜"
BASE "D"

See "Modular Coordination" pages

LAYOUT TABLE

NO. OF BLOCKS	6" $5\frac{3}{4} \times 5\frac{3}{4} \times 3\frac{7}{8}$	8" $7\frac{3}{4} \times 7\frac{3}{4} \times 3\frac{7}{8}$	12" $11\frac{3}{4} \times 11\frac{3}{4} \times 3\frac{7}{8}$
1	0'–6"	0'–8"	1'–0"
2	1'–0"	1'–4"	2'–0"
3	1'–6"	2'–0"	3'–0"
4	2'–0"	2'–8"	4'–0"
5	2'–6"	3'–4"	5'–0"
6	3'–0"	4'–0"	6'–0"
7	3'–6"	4'–8"	7'–0"
8	4'–0"	5'–4"	8'–0"
9	4'–6"	6'–0"	9'–0"
10	5'–0"	6'–8"	10'–0"
11	5'–6"	7'–4"	11'–0"
12	6'–0"	8'–0"	12'–0"
13	6'–6"	8'–8"	13'–0"
14	7'–0"	9'–4"	14'–0"
15	7'–6"	10'–0"	15'–0"
16	8'–0"	10'–8"	16'–0"
17	8'–6"	11'–4"	17'–0"
18	9'–0"	12'–0"	18'–0"
19	9'–6"	12'–8"	19'–0"
20	10'–0"	13'–4"	20'–0"
21	10'–6"	14'–0"	21'–0"
22	11'–0"	14'–8"	22'–0"
23	11'–6"	15'–4"	23'–0"
24	12'–0"	16'–0"	24'–0"
25	12'–6"	16'–8"	25'–0"

This table is based on Modular Coordination assuming $\frac{1}{4}$" mortar joints between glass blocks.

For minimum required opening height, find table dimension and add $\frac{3}{8}$".

For minimum required opening width, find table dimension and add $\frac{1}{2}$".

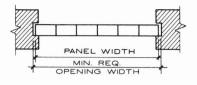
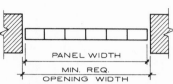

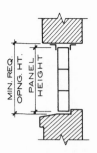

CHASE CONSTRUCTION

MAXIMUM PANEL AREA – 144 SQ. FT.
MAXIMUM HEIGHT – 20 FEET
MAXIMUM WIDTH – 25 FEET
MORTAR JOINTS = $\frac{1}{4}$ INCH

WALL ANCHOR CONSTRUCTION

MAXIMUM PANEL AREA – 100 SQ. FT.
MAXIMUM HEIGHT – 10 FEET
MAXIMUM WIDTH – 10 FEET
MORTAR JOINTS = $\frac{1}{4}$ INCH

ESTIMATING DATA
FOR 100 SQ. FT. OF PANEL $\frac{1}{4}$" MORTAR JOINTS

NOMINAL BLOCK SIZE	6"	8"	12"
NUMBER OF BLOCKS	400	225	100
PANEL WEIGHT, LBS.	2000	1800	1900
MORTAR VOLUME, CU. FT.	4.3	3.2	2.2

For design purposes, glass block panels weigh approximately 20 lbs. per sq. ft. installed. This applies to all sizes of blocks.

INSTALLATION

1. Sill area to be covered by mortar shall first have a heavy coat of asphalt emulsion and allowed to dry.

2. Adhere expansion strips to jambs and head with asphalt emulsion. Expansion strip must extend to sill.

3. When emulsion on sill is dry, place full mortar bed joint—do not furrow.

4. Set lower course of block. All mortar joints must be full and not furrowed. Steel tools must not be used to tap blocks in position. Mortar shall not bridge expansion joints. Visible width mortar joint shall be ¼" or as specified.

5. Install panel reinforcing in horizontal joints where required as follows:

(a) Place lower half of mortar bed joint. Do not furrow.

(b) Press panel reinforcing into place.

(c) Cover panel reinforcing with upper half of mortar bed and trowel smooth. Do not furrow.

(d) Panel reinforcing must run from end to end of panels and where used continuously must lap 6 inches. Reinforcing must not bridge expansion joints.

6. Place full mortar bed for joints not requiring panel reinforcing. Do not furrow.

7. Follow above instructions for succeeding courses. The number of blocks in successive lifts shall be limited to prevent squeezing out of mortar or movement of blocks.

8. Strike joints smoothly while mortar is still plastic and before final set. At this time rake out all spaces requiring caulking to a depth equal to the width of the spaces. Remove surplus mortar from faces of glass blocks and wipe dry. Tool joints smooth and concave, before mortar sets, so that exposed edges of blocks have sharp clean lines.

9. After final mortar set, pack oakum tightly between glass block panel and jamb and head construction. Leave space for caulking.

10. Caulk panels as indicated on details.

11. Final cleaning of glass block faces shall not be done until after final mortar set.

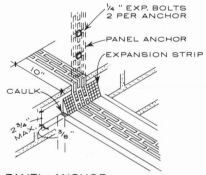

PANEL ANCHOR

Dotted lines show use on existing structure.

GLASS BLOCK IN EXISTING WINDOW OPENING

Glass blocks and modules will fit nearly any existing window opening.

The drawings show typical head, sill and jamb section details for conventional window and glass block replacement. Notice how simple it is to work glass block into existing construction. It makes no difference if the opening is oddly shaped. Arches and irregular openings can be easily rebuilt to accommodate the glass blocks or modules by employing standard masonry construction techniques.

Many standard ribbon windows and ventilator attachments are available. These can be easily combined with glass blocks and modules.

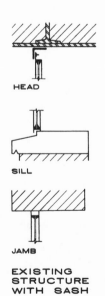

HEAD   HEAD

SILL   SILL

JAMB   JAMB

EXISTING STRUCTURE WITH SASH

SAME STRUCTURE WITH GLASS BLOCKS

Robert D. Livingstone; Holden, Yang, Raemsch & Corser; New York, New York

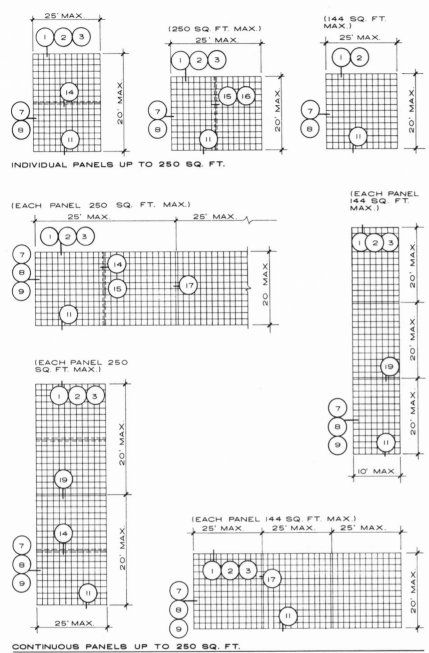

INDIVIDUAL PANELS UP TO 250 SQ. FT.

EXTERIOR PANELS UP TO 250 SQ. FT.

CONTINUOUS PANELS UP TO 250 SQ. FT.

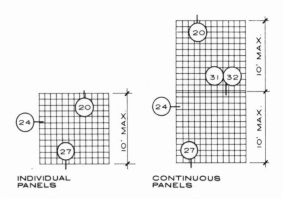

INDIVIDUAL PANELS

CONTINUOUS PANELS

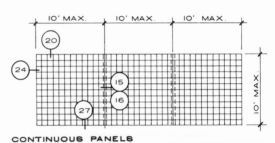

CONTINUOUS PANELS

EXTERIOR PANELS UP TO 100 SQ. FT.

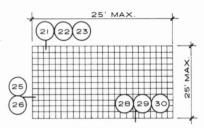

INDIVIDUAL PANELS 250 SQ. FT. MAXIMUM AREA

INTERIOR PANELS

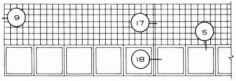

RIBBON WINDOWS

VENTILATORS

VERTICAL WINDOWS

Robert D. Livingstone; Holden, Yang, Raemsch & Corser; New York, New York

GLASS BUILDING UNITS

1. These pages show elevations and sections of typical glass block panels. The large scale sections are typical head, jamb and sill details to show principles of construction only.

2. Any structural members must be calculated for safe loading, and local building codes checked for any possible restrictions on panel sizes or detail.

3. While single panels of glass block are limited to a maximum of 144 square feet, panel and curtain wall sections up to a maximum area of 250 square feet may be erected if properly braced to limit movement and settlement.

4. If chase construction cannot be used, substitute the panel anchor construction. Panel anchors are used to give lateral support for glass block panels.

5. Any glass block installation that is made in a frame construction shall have the wood adjacent to the mortar properly primed with asphalt emulsion.

6. Underwriters' Listing: glass block panels may be used for window openings subject to light fire exposure (class F openings).

7. Other types available are ornamental, sculptured and colored blocks of various sizes. Solid glass blocks (glass bricks) $2 \frac{5}{16}$ " thick x $5 \frac{7}{8}$ " x $8 \frac{7}{8}$ " for installation in detention windows.

DAYLIGHTING NOMOGRAPH

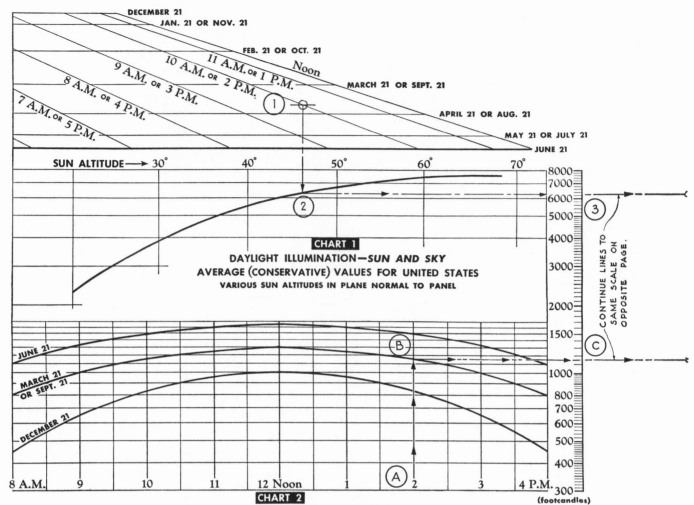

DECEMBER 21
JAN. 21 OR NOV. 21
FEB. 21 OR OCT. 21
11 A.M. or 1 P.M.   Noon
10 A.M. or 2 P.M.   MARCH 21 OR SEPT. 21
9 A.M. or 3 P.M.
8 A.M. or 4 P.M.   APRIL 21 OR AUG. 21
7 A.M. or 5 P.M.   MAY 21 OR JULY 21
JUNE 21

SUN ALTITUDE ⟶ 30°   40°   50°   60°   70°

CHART 1
DAYLIGHT ILLUMINATION—*SUN AND SKY*
AVERAGE (CONSERVATIVE) VALUES FOR UNITED STATES
VARIOUS SUN ALTITUDES IN PLANE NORMAL TO PANEL

8000
7000
6000
5000
4000
3000
2000
1500

CONTINUE LINES TO SAME SCALE ON OPPOSITE PAGE.

JUNE 21
MARCH 21 OR SEPT. 21
DECEMBER 21

8 A.M.   9   10   11   12 Noon   1   2   3   4 P.M.

1500
1000
800
700
600
500
400
300
(footcandles)

CHART 2
DAYLIGHT ILLUMINATION—*SKY ONLY*
AVERAGE (CONSERVATIVE) VALUES FOR UNITED STATES

"CHART 1" VALUES ARE BASED ON THE SUN BEING IN A PLANE NORMAL TO THE PANEL.
FOR OTHER CONDITIONS, MULTIPLY NOMOGRAPH VALUES BY THE FOLLOWING
FACTORS DEPENDING ON AMOUNT OF DEPARTURE FROM NORMAL : 0° TO 15° - 1;
16° TO 30° - 4/5; 31° TO 45° - 2/3; 46° TO 60° - 1/2; 61° TO 75° - 1/3; 76° TO 90° - USE VALUE
BASED ON "CHART 2" INSTEAD OF "CHART 1"

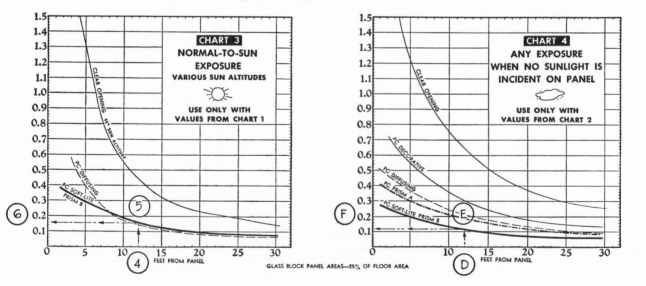

CHART 3
NORMAL-TO-SUN
EXPOSURE
VARIOUS SUN ALTITUDES

USE ONLY WITH
VALUES FROM CHART 1

1.5
1.4
1.3
1.2
1.1
1.0
0.9
0.8
0.7
0.6
0.5
0.4
0.3
0.2
0.1
0   5   10   15   20   25   30
FEET FROM PANEL

CLEAR OPENING 45° SUN ALTITUDE
PC DIFFUSING
PC SOFT-LITE PRISM B

GLASS BLOCK PANEL AREAS—25% OF FLOOR AREA

CHART 4
ANY EXPOSURE
WHEN NO SUNLIGHT IS
INCIDENT ON PANEL

USE ONLY WITH
VALUES FROM CHART 2

1.5
1.4
1.3
1.2
1.1
1.0
0.9
0.8
0.7
0.6
0.5
0.4
0.3
0.2
0.1
0   5   10   15   20   25   30
FEET FROM PANEL

CLEAR OPENING
PC DECORATIVE
PC DIFFUSING
PC PRISM A
PC SOFT-LITE PRISM B

FOR PC GLASS BLOCKS

**FOR ESTIMATING DAYLIGHT ILLUMINATION ON WORKING PLANES (30" ABOVE FLOOR)
PROVIDED BY PANELS OF PITTSBURGH CORNING GLASS BLOCKS**

FOR TWO EXAMPLES SHOWN, FOLLOW CONSECUTIVELY
EITHER STEPS ①,②,③, ETC. OR STEPS Ⓐ,Ⓑ,Ⓒ, ETC.

THE NOMOGRAPH IS BASED ON A RATIO OF PANEL AREA TO
FLOOR AREA OF 25%. VALUES READ FROM IT CAN BE
PROPORTIONED FOR OTHER PANEL TO FLOOR RATIOS AS FOLLOWS:

$$\text{CORRECT VALUE} = \text{NOMOGRAPH READING} \times 4 \times \frac{\text{PANEL AREA}}{\text{FLOOR AREA}}$$

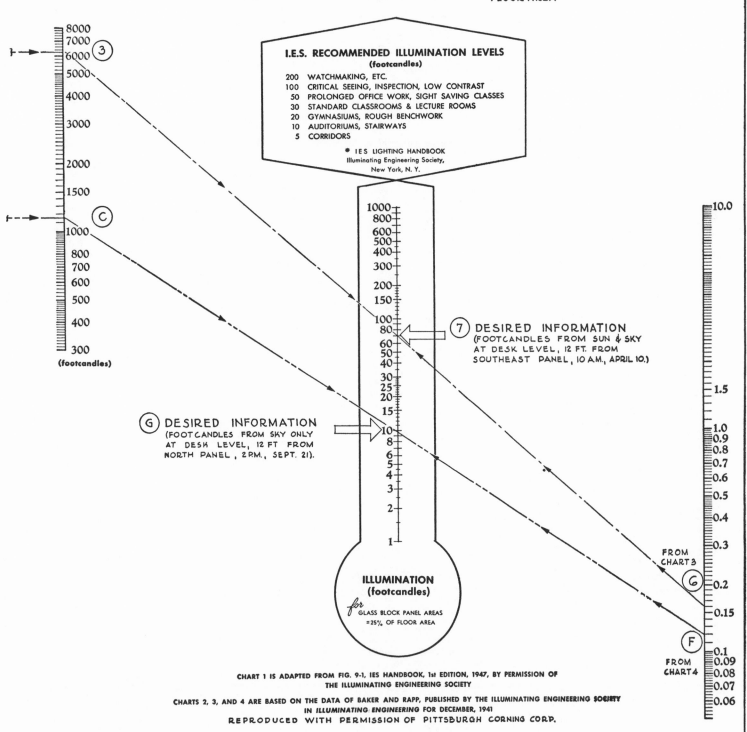

I.E.S. RECOMMENDED ILLUMINATION LEVELS
(footcandles)

200	WATCHMAKING, ETC.
100	CRITICAL SEEING, INSPECTION, LOW CONTRAST
50	PROLONGED OFFICE WORK, SIGHT SAVING CLASSES
30	STANDARD CLASSROOMS & LECTURE ROOMS
20	GYMNASIUMS, ROUGH BENCHWORK
10	AUDITORIUMS, STAIRWAYS
5	CORRIDORS

※ IES LIGHTING HANDBOOK
Illuminating Engineering Society,
New York, N. Y.

⑦ **DESIRED INFORMATION**
(FOOTCANDLES FROM SUN & SKY
AT DESK LEVEL, 12 FT. FROM
SOUTHEAST PANEL, 10 A.M., APRIL 10.)

Ⓖ **DESIRED INFORMATION**
(FOOTCANDLES FROM SKY ONLY
AT DESK LEVEL, 12 FT FROM
NORTH PANEL, 2 P.M., SEPT. 21).

ILLUMINATION
(footcandles)
for
GLASS BLOCK PANEL AREAS
=25% OF FLOOR AREA

(footcandles)

FROM CHART 3

FROM CHART 4

CHART 1 IS ADAPTED FROM FIG. 9-1, IES HANDBOOK, 1st EDITION, 1947, BY PERMISSION OF
THE ILLUMINATING ENGINEERING SOCIETY

CHARTS 2, 3, AND 4 ARE BASED ON THE DATA OF BAKER AND RAPP, PUBLISHED BY THE ILLUMINATING ENGINEERING SOCIETY
IN *ILLUMINATING ENGINEERING* FOR DECEMBER, 1941

REPRODUCED WITH PERMISSION OF PITTSBURGH CORNING CORP.

ADOBE DETAILS

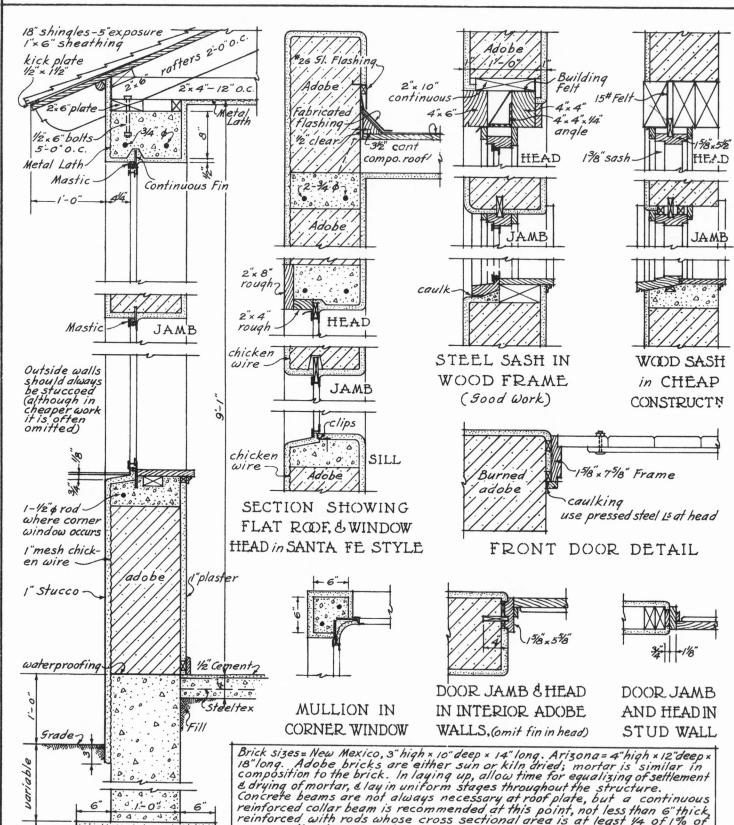

18" shingles-5" exposure
1"×6" sheathing
kick plate
½"×1½"
rafters 2'-0" o.c.
2"×6"
2"×4"-12" o.c.
2"×6" plate
½"×6" bolts
5'-0" o.c.
Metal Lath
Mastic
¾" φ
8"
Metal Lath
Continuous Fin
1'-0"
¼"

Mastic   JAMB

Outside walls should always be stuccoed (although in cheaper work it is often omitted)

1-½" φ rod where corner window occurs
1" mesh chicken wire
1" Stucco
adobe
1" plaster
waterproofing
½" Cement
Steeltex
Fill
Grade
variable
½ φ rods
1'-0"
6"   1'-0"   6"

WALL SECTION SHOWING PITCHED ROOF

#26 Sl. Flashing
Adobe
Fabricated flashing
½" clear
3½" cant compo. roof
2"×10" continuous
2"-¾" φ
Adobe
2"×8" rough
2"×4" rough   HEAD
chicken wire   JAMB
chicken wire   clips   SILL
Adobe
9'-1"

SECTION SHOWING FLAT ROOF, & WINDOW HEAD in SANTA FE STYLE

Adobe
1'-0"
Building Felt
4"×4"
4"×6"
4"×4"×¼" angle
HEAD
caulk   JAMB

STEEL SASH IN WOOD FRAME (Good Work)

Adobe
15# Felt
1⅝×5½
1⅜" sash   HEAD
JAMB

WOOD SASH in CHEAP CONSTRUCT'N

Burned adobe
1⅝"×7⅝" Frame
caulking
use pressed steel Ls at head

FRONT DOOR DETAIL

6"
6"

MULLION IN CORNER WINDOW

1⅝"×5⅝"

DOOR JAMB & HEAD IN INTERIOR ADOBE WALLS, (omit fin in head)

¾"   1⅛"

DOOR JAMB AND HEAD IN STUD WALL

Brick sizes = New Mexico, 3" high × 10" deep × 14" long. Arizona = 4" high × 12" deep × 18" long. Adobe bricks are either sun or kiln dried; mortar is similar in composition to the brick. In laying up, allow time for equalizing of settlement & drying of mortar, & lay in uniform stages throughout the structure. Concrete beams are not always necessary at roof plate, but a continuous reinforced collar beam is recommended at this point, not less than 6" thick, reinforced with rods whose cross sectional area is at least ¼ of 1% of cross sectional area of the course; when used as window lintel they are generally 8" deep & reinforced same as collar beam. 4" concrete beams are recommended under window sills; but not reinforced. One story walls 12" thick in Arizona; 10" in New Mexico & not to exceed 12' in height; two story not over 22' in height = 18" thick at 1st. floor & 12" at second. Interior partitions, non-bearing 8" min., bonded & toothed into side walls or with metal mesh bond of gal. wire mesh. Stud walls anchored to adobe walls with 3" perf. gal. strap anchors, with ends hooked 10" into adobe. Min. pitch for shingled roofs 4" rise to 12" min.

This sheet prepared with the assistance of Richard A. Morse & Arthur T. Brown, Architects., Tucson, Arizona.

4 METALS

EXPANSION JOINTS

THERMAL EXPANSION FACTORS of MATERIALS
(inches per degree)

METALS		MASONRY	
Aluminum (wrought)	.0000128	Brick	.0000031
Bronze	.0000101	Clay tile	.0000033
Copper	.0000098	Concrete	.0000065
Lead	.0000159	Granite	.0000040
Monel	.0000078	Limestone	.0000038
Steel (medium)	.0000067	Marble	.0000056
Zinc	.0000178	Plaster	.0000092

GLASS (common) .0000047

Width of expansion joint is generally assumed as 1" (one inch).
Actual amount of expansion may be determined as follows:

FORMULA

Multiply span (in inches) of material x 100° (average difference
in F. temperature between winter & summer) x the factor of
expansion of the material.   { Span" x 100° F. x Factor }

NOTES

A complete separation should be made between old & new construction by expansion joints. A complete frame of columns and
beams should be on both sides of the joint but no structural connections between the two frames. Because roofs expand more than walls, expansion joints are sometimes placed in roof slabs and top floor walls under 200 ft. Expansion
joints are used in cold storage plants, breweries, etc., where
the temperature is at an unusual degree. Steel trusses
with spans over 45 ft. should be free to move laterally at
one end. A slip joint should be provided between foundation & walls that contain transecting joints. (the foundation, being underground, is but little affected by the temperature of the air).

Joints should be installed around machinery foundations
to isolate vibration & permit differential settlement in floor.

FILLERS USED IN EXPANSION JOINTS
Premoulded

A. Composition (asphalt, vegetable fibre. B. Jute (rubber coated).
C. Sponge rubber. D. Cork & asphalt composition. E. Cork.
Standard thicknesses of premould. fillers ¼", ⅜", ½", ¾", 1".

Mastic

A. Asphalt compound
B. Rubberized asphalt comp'd. (various colors)

TABLE OF MAXIMUM ALLOWANCES

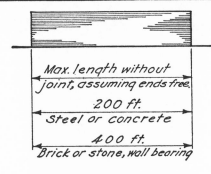

Max. length without
joint, assuming ends free.
200 ft.
Steel or concrete
400 ft.
Brick or stone, wall bearing

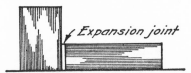

Expansion joint

A. New building adjoining existing bldg.
B. Long, low building abutting high bldg.
C. Wings adjoining main structure.

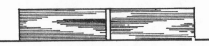

Long buildings

Expansion joints

Long, low building between high wings

LOCATIONS OF EXPANSION JOINTS
Diagrammatic Elevations
no scale

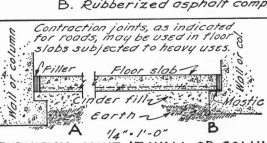

Contraction joints, as indicated
for roads, may be used in floor
slabs subjected to heavy uses.

Wall or column   Filler   Floor slab   Wall or col.
Cinder fill   Mastic
Earth

A   ¼" = 1'-0"   B

EXPANSION JOINT AT WALL OR COLUMN
Detail A used for heavy loads in 1 story bldgs.
where pressure is greater under floor slab
than under footing
Detail B used in multi-story bldgs. where
pressure is greater under footing than
under floor slab.

SPACING of JOINTS
in CONCRETE ROAD SLABS
Non-reinforced slabs - contraction joints from 15'-25' depending on
aggregate & climate. Expansion joints 90'-
120' depending on temp. ranges. Reinf. slabs
40'-60' depending on reinf. & climate. Contraction joints seldom used.

Suggested thicknesses of premoulded
filler for expansion joints spaced at intervals
of:

→ 15' to 20'	20' to 30'	30' to 50'	50' to 60'
Thickness of filler :→ ¼"	⅜"	½"	¾"

Approved by Elwyn E. Seelye, Consulting Engineer

Expansion
joints
Contraction
joints

JOINTS in
CONCRETE WALKS
½" joints spaced 30' c. to c.

¾" Ø x 16" dowel 18" o.c.   Deformed
Bitum. seal   metal

Construct'n.   Contract'n.   Longitudinal

JOINTS
⅜" = 1'-0"

¾" Ø x 16" dowel
12" c.c., greased
at cap end.

Premoulded
filler
Expan. joint

JOINTS in RETAINING WALLS

Paper or
felt optional   Joints 75 ft. max. c. to c.

Filler   Filler

Waterstop 20 oz. min.   Felt bond-break

½" = 1'-0"

②   ①
½" Ø dowels 4'-0" o.c.

Column
stubs
bolted
to beam
Flashing
Roof slab
¼" Ø
steel
rods
½" = 1'-0"
¼" Ø
steel
rods

Reinforcing parapet walls
against temp. strains
by the use of horizontal
steel rods & ① col. stubs
in steel structures. ② dowels in concrete construct.

EXPANSION JOINTS ~ FLOORS

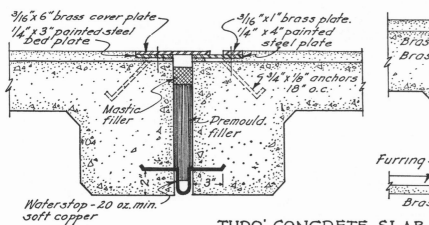

3/16"x 6" brass cover plate
1/4" x 3" painted steel bed plate
3/16"x1" brass plate.
1/4" x 4" painted steel plate
Mastic filler
Premould. filler
3/4"x 1/8" anchors 18" o.c.
Waterstop - 20 oz. min. soft copper
2"   3"   4"

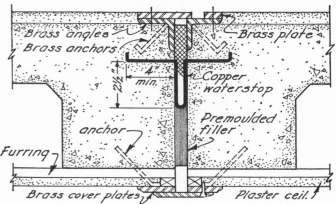

Brass angles
Brass anchors
Brass plate
4" min.
2 1/2"
Copper waterstop
Premoulded filler
anchor
Furring
Brass cover plates
Plaster ceil.

THRO' CONCRETE SLAB AT BEAM

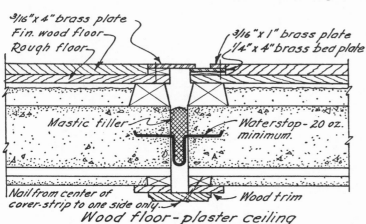

3/16"x 4" brass plate
Fin. wood floor
Rough floor
3/16"x 1" brass plate
1/4"x 4" brass bed plate
Mastic filler
Waterstop - 20 oz. minimum.
Nail from center of cover-strip to one side only.
Wood trim

Wood floor - plaster ceiling

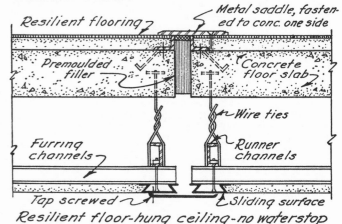

Resilient flooring
Metal saddle, fastened to conc. one side
Premoulded filler
Concrete floor slab
Wire ties
Furring channels
Runner channels
Tap screwed
Sliding surface

Resilient floor-hung ceiling-no waterstop

THRO' CONCRETE SLABS

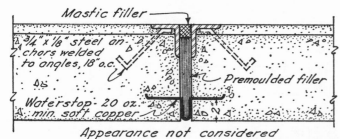

3/16"x 4" brass plate
Tap screwed
Brass angles
Brass anchors
Mastic filler
Waterproofing
Premoulded filler
Waterstop - 20 oz. min. soft copper

THRO' WATERPROOFED SLAB ON EARTH

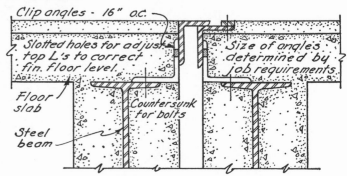

Clip angles - 16" o.c.
Slotted holes for adjust. top L's to correct fin. floor level.
Size of angles determined by job requirements
Floor slab
Steel beam
Countersunk for bolts

THRO' FLOOR SLAB ON STEEL BEAMS

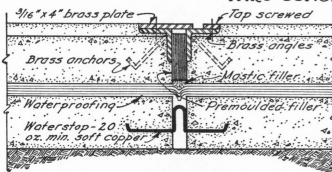

Mastic filler
3/4"x 1/8" steel anchors welded to angles, 18" o.c.
Premoulded filler
Waterstop- 20 oz. min. soft copper
Appearance not considered

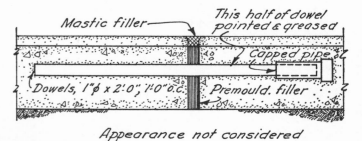

Mastic filler
This half of dowel painted & greased
Capped pipe.
Dowels, 1" ⌀ x 2'-0", 1'-0" o.c.
Premould. filler
Appearance not considered

THRO' UTILITY FLOOR SLABS
Scale 1 1/2" = 1'-0"

Waterstops - 20 oz. min. soft copper, 8'-0" lengths. Ends lapped 3/4" & soldered. Lead may be used to fill joints instead of mastic filler where traffic is severe. Deformed reinforcing bars should never pass through an expansion joint. Reinforcing not shown.

Data checked by the National Assoc. of Ornamental Metal Mfrs., & the Copper & Brass Research Assoc.

EXPANSION JOINTS - WALLS

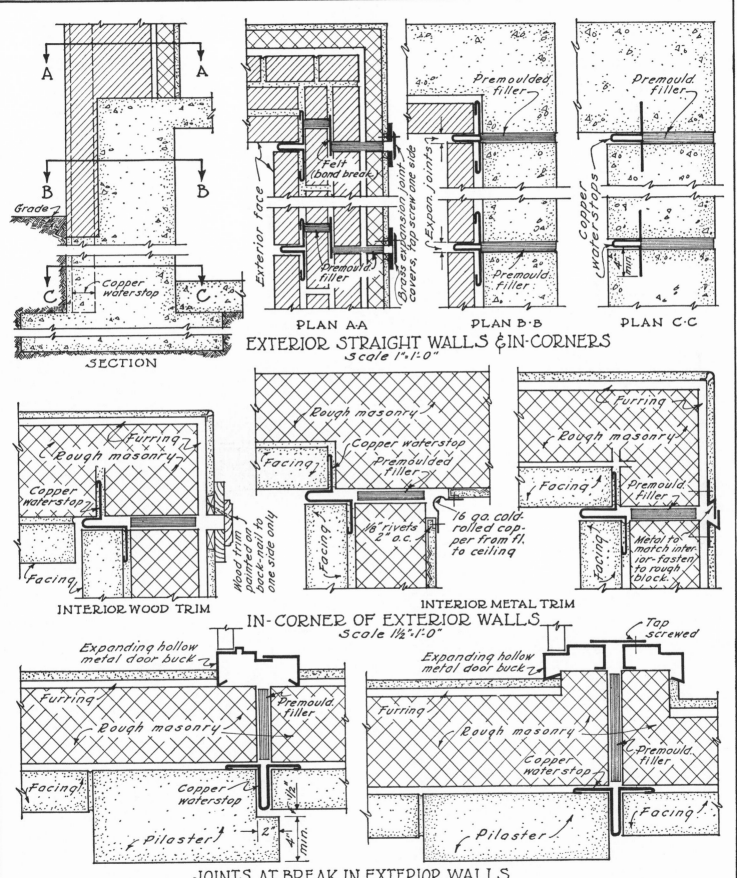

SECTION

Grade

Copper waterstop

A A

B B

C C

PLAN A·A

Exterior face

Felt (bond break)

Premould. filler

Brass expansion joint covers, tap screw one side

PLAN B·B

Premoulded filler

Expansion joints

Premould. filler

PLAN C·C

Premould. filler

Copper waterstops

4" min.

EXTERIOR STRAIGHT WALLS & IN-CORNERS
Scale 1"=1'-0"

INTERIOR WOOD TRIM

Furring

Rough masonry

Copper waterstop

Facing

Wood trim painted on back-nail to one side only

Rough masonry

Copper waterstop

Premoulded filler

Facing

⅛" rivets 2" o.c.

16 ga. cold-rolled copper from fl. to ceiling

INTERIOR METAL TRIM

Furring

Rough masonry

Facing

Premould. filler

Facing

Metal to match interior-fasten to rough block

IN-CORNER OF EXTERIOR WALLS
Scale 1½"=1'-0"

Expanding hollow metal door buck

Furring

Rough masonry

Facing

Premould. filler

Copper waterstop

Pilaster

1½"   2"   4" min.

Tap screwed

Expanding hollow metal door buck

Furring

Rough masonry

Copper waterstop

Premould. filler

Facing

Pilaster

JOINTS AT BREAK IN EXTERIOR WALLS
with hollow metal door bucks on interior. Scale 1½"=1'-0"

Diagrams show suggested schemes for expansion joints to be adapted to specific uses. Indicated facing and rough masonry may be of any material. Waterstops are 20 oz. minimum soft copper, 8'-0" lengths, from footing to eave or top of parapet wall. Above grade, lap end joints 4" unsoldered; below grade, end jts. soldered.
Data checked by the Copper & Brass Research Assoc., & the National Assoc. of Ornamental Metal Mfrs.

EXPANSION JOINTS ~ ROOFS & WALLS

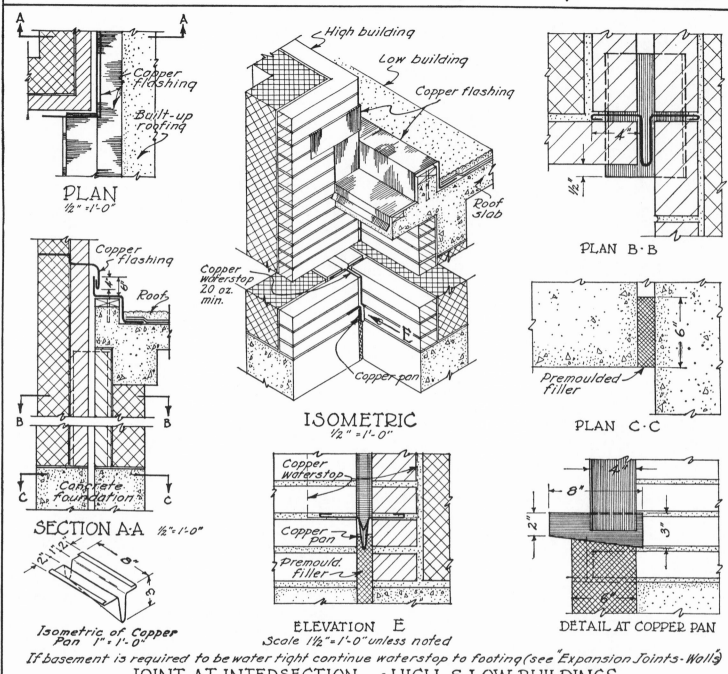

PLAN
1/2" = 1'-0"

Copper flashing
Built-up roofing

High building
Low building
Copper flashing
Roof slab

PLAN B·B

SECTION A·A   1/2"=1'-0"

Copper flashing
Roof
Concrete foundation

Copper waterstop 20 oz. min.
Copper pan

ISOMETRIC
1/2" = 1'-0"

Premoulded filler

PLAN C·C

Isometric of Copper Pan   1"=1'-0"

Copper waterstop
Copper pan
Premould. filler

ELEVATION E
Scale 1 1/2"=1'-0" unless noted

DETAIL AT COPPER PAN

If basement is required to be water tight continue waterstop to footing (see "Expansion Joints - Walls")

JOINT AT INTERSECTION of HIGH & LOW BUILDINGS

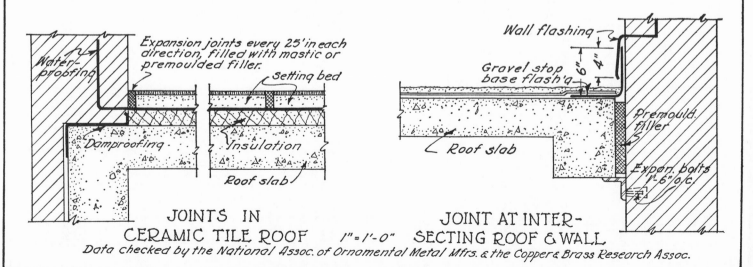

Waterproofing
Expansion joints every 25' in each direction, filled with mastic or premoulded filler.
Setting bed
Dampproofing
Insulation
Roof slab

Wall flashing
Gravel stop base flash'g
Roof slab
Premould. filler
Expan. bolts 1'-6" o.c.

JOINTS IN CERAMIC TILE ROOF   1"=1'-0"

JOINT AT INTERSECTING ROOF & WALL

Data checked by the National Assoc. of Ornamental Metal Mfrs. & the Copper & Brass Research Assoc.

EXPANSION JOINTS - ROOFS

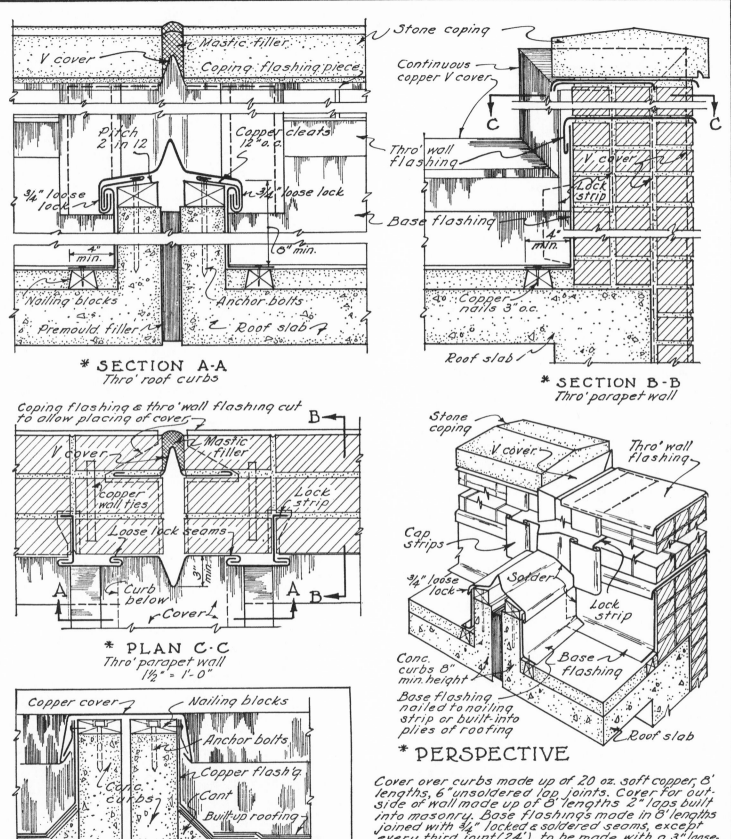

* SECTION A·A
Thro' roof curbs

V cover — Mastic filler
Coping flashing piece
Pitch 2 in 12 — Copper cleats 12" o.c.
¾" loose lock — ¾" loose lock
4" min. — 8" min.
Nailing blocks — Anchor bolts
Premould filler — Roof slab

* SECTION B·B
Thro' parapet wall

Stone coping
Continuous copper V cover
Thro' wall flashing
V cover
Lock strip
Base flashing
4" min.
Copper nails 3" o.c.
Roof slab

* PLAN C·C
Thro' parapet wall 1½" = 1'-0"

Coping flashing & thro' wall flashing cut to allow placing of cover
V cover — Mastic filler
copper wall ties — Lock strip
Loose lock seams
Curb below — Cover
3" min.

* PERSPECTIVE

Stone coping
V cover — Thro' wall flashing
Cap strips
¾" loose lock — Solder
Lock strip
Conc. curbs 8" min. height — Base flashing
Base flashing nailed to nailing strip or built-into plies of roofing
Roof slab

JOINT THRO' ROOF SLABS AT CURB
Scale 1" = 1'-0"

Copper cover — Nailing blocks
Anchor bolts
Copper flash'g
Conc. curbs — Cant
Built-up roofing
Premoulded filler — Roof slab

Cover over curbs made up of 20 oz. soft copper, 8' lengths, 6" unsoldered lap joints. Cover for outside of wall made up of 8' lengths 2" laps built into masonry. Base flashings made in 8' lengths joined with ¾" locked & soldered seams, except every third joint (24'), to be made with a 3" loose-lock filled with elastic cement or white lead. Cover piece, cap strings & lock strips made of 20 oz. soft copper. The rest of the metal made of 20 oz. cold rolled copper

*Data from the Copper & Brass Research Assoc.

CLASSIFICATION BY NATURE OF COMPONENTS

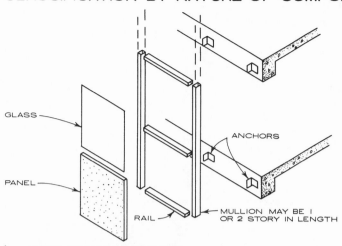

GLASS

PANEL

ANCHORS

RAIL

MULLION MAY BE 1 OR 2 STORY IN LENGTH

1. GRID SYSTEM (STICK)
FRAMING MEMBERS VISUALLY PROMINENT
COMPONENTS INSTALLED PIECE BY PIECE

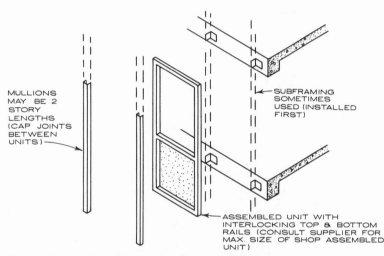

MULLIONS MAY BE 2 STORY LENGTHS (CAP JOINTS BETWEEN UNITS)

SUBFRAMING SOMETIMES USED (INSTALLED FIRST)

ASSEMBLED UNIT WITH INTERLOCKING TOP & BOTTOM RAILS (CONSULT SUPPLIER FOR MAX. SIZE OF SHOP ASSEMBLED UNIT)

2. GRID SYSTEM (PANEL AND MULLION)
FRAMING MEMBERS VISUALLY PROMINENT
PANEL PREASSEMBLED & INSTALLED AS SHOWN

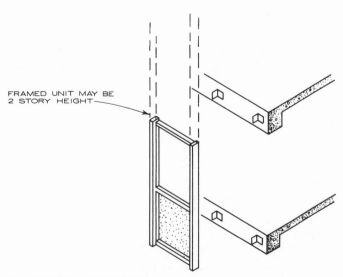

FRAMED UNIT MAY BE 2 STORY HEIGHT

3. PANEL SYSTEM
COMPLETELY PREASSEMBLED UNITS; MAY OR MAY NOT INCLUDE INTERIOR FINISH

CLASSIFICATION BY USAGE

A CUSTOM TYPE

Walls designed specifically for one project, using specially designed parts and details. Such walls may be used on buildings of any height, but are more typical of multistoried structures. Included in this category are the highly publicized (and often more expensive) walls which serve as design pacesetters.

B COMMERCIAL TYPE

Walls made up principally of parts and details standardized by the manufacturer and assembled either in the manufacturer's stock patterns or in accord with the architect's design. This type is offered by many manufacturers and is typically used on one and two story buildings, but may be used on taller structures. Commercial walls offer lower cost because of quantity production, and also offer the advantages of proven performance.

C INDUSTRIAL TYPE

Walls in which ribbed, fluted, or otherwise preformed metal sheets in stock sizes are used, along with standard metal sash, as the principal components. This type of metal curtain wall has a long history of satisfactory performance, and, in its insulated form, finds wide use in many important buildings outside the industrial field.

GENERAL NOTES:

1. Mullions which extend through the wall and are exposed on both exterior and interior of the building, should include a thermal break (especially if they are aluminum).

2. When mullions serve as guide rails for roof mounted window washing platforms or "rigs," mullions should be designed as a track and reinforced against thrust, using information on loads from cleaning equipment manufacturer.

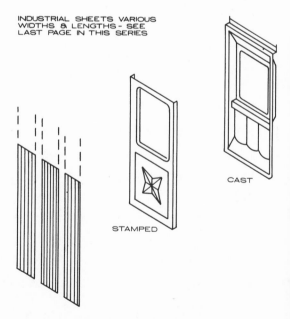

INDUSTRIAL SHEETS VARIOUS WIDTHS & LENGTHS - SEE LAST PAGE IN THIS SERIES

STAMPED

CAST

ALTERNATE PANEL TYPES

5 WOOD AND PLASTICS

BALLOON FRAMING

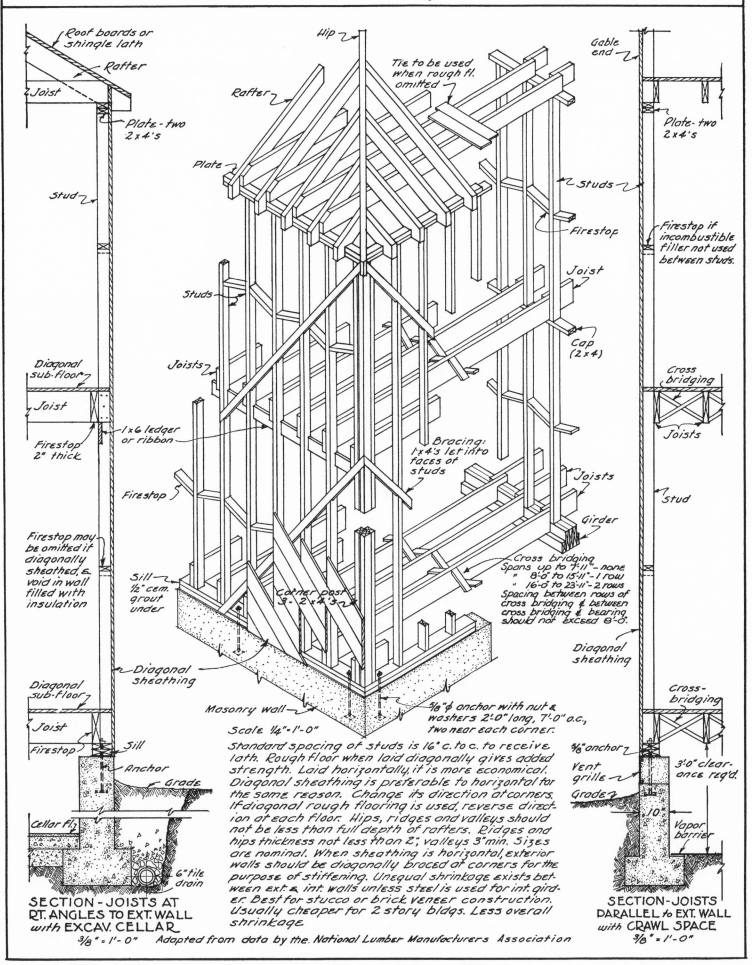

Roof boards or shingle lath

Rafter

Joist

Plate - two 2 x 4's

stud

Diagonal sub-floor

Joist

1 x 6 ledger or ribbon

Firestop 2" thick

Firestop

Firestop may be omitted if diagonally sheathed, & void in wall filled with insulation

Sill ½" cem. grout under

Diagonal sheathing

Diagonal sub-floor

Joist

Firestop

Sill

Anchor

Grade

Cellar Fl.

6" tile drain

SECTION - JOISTS AT RT. ANGLES TO EXT. WALL with EXCAV. CELLAR

3/8" = 1'-0"

Hip

Tie to be used when rough fl. omitted

Rafter

Plate

Studs

Firestop

Joist

Cap (2 x 4)

Bracing: 1 x 4's let into faces of studs

Joists

Girder

Corner post 3 - 2 x 4's

Cross bridging. Spans up to 7'-11" - none
" 8'-0" to 15'-11" - 1 row
" 16'-0" to 23'-11" - 2 rows
Spacing between rows of cross bridging & between cross bridging & bearing should not exceed 8'-0".

Masonry wall

5/8" ⌀ anchor with nut & washers 2'-0" long, 7'-0" o.c., two near each corner.

Scale ¼" = 1'-0"

Standard spacing of studs is 16" c. to c. to receive lath. Rough floor when laid diagonally gives added strength. Laid horizontally, it is more economical. Diagonal sheathing is preferable to horizontal for the same reason. Change its direction at corners. If diagonal rough flooring is used, reverse direction at each floor. Hips, ridges and valleys should not be less than full depth of rafters. Ridges and hips thickness not less than 2"; valleys 3" min. Sizes are nominal. When sheathing is horizontal, exterior walls should be diagonally braced at corners for the purpose of stiffening. Unequal shrinkage exists between ext. & int. walls unless steel is used for int. girder. Best for stucco or brick veneer construction. Usually cheaper for 2 story bldgs. Less overall shrinkage

Gable end

Plate - two 2 x 4's

Firestop if incombustible filler not used between studs.

Studs

Cross bridging

Joists

Stud

Diagonal sheathing

Cross-bridging

5/8" anchor

Vent grille

Grade

3'-0" clearance req'd.

10"

Vapor barrier

SECTION - JOISTS PARALLEL to EXT. WALL with CRAWL SPACE

3/8" = 1'-0"

Adapted from data by the National Lumber Manufacturers Association

BRACED FRAMING

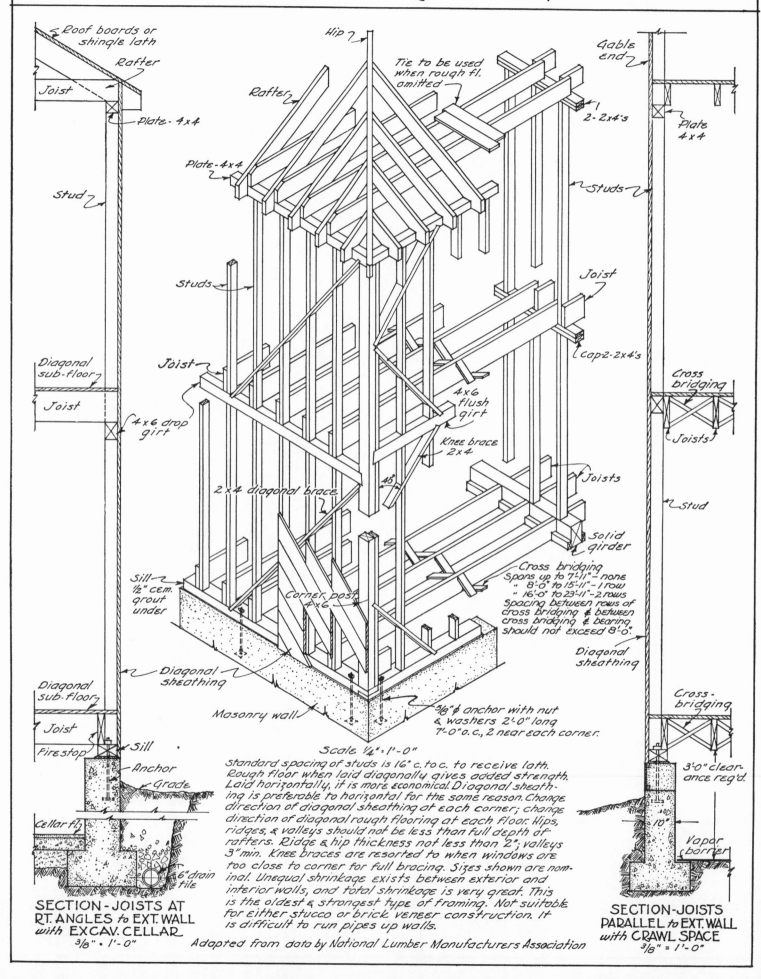

Roof boards or shingle lath

Rafter

Joist

Plate- 4 x 4

Stud

Hip

Tie to be used when rough fl. omitted

Rafter

Plate- 4 x 4

Gable end

1
2- 2x4's

Plate
4 x 4

Studs

Studs

Diagonal sub-floor

Joist

Joist

4 x 6 drop girt

Joist

Cap 2-2x4's

Joist

Cross bridging

Joists

4x6 flush girt

Knee brace 2x4

Stud

2 x 4 diagonal brace

45

Sill
½" cem. grout under

Corner post 4 x 6

Solid girder

Cross bridging
Spans up to 7'-11"- none
" 8'-0" to 15'-11"- 1 row
" 16'-0" to 23'-11"- 2 rows
spacing between rows of
cross bridging & between
cross bridging & bearing
should not exceed 8'-0".

Diagonal sheathing

Diagonal sheathing

Diagonal sub-floor

Joist

Firestop

Sill

Masonry wall

⅝"∅ anchor with nut
& washers 2'-0" long
7'-0" o.c., 2 near each corner.

Cross- bridging

Anchor

Grade

3'-0" clear-ance req'd.

Cellar fl.

6" drain tile

Scale ¼" = 1'-0"

Vapor barrier

standard spacing of studs is 16" c. to c. to receive lath.
Rough floor when laid diagonally gives added strength.
Laid horizontally, it is more economical. Diagonal sheathing is preferable to horizontal for the same reason. Change
direction of diagonal sheathing at each corner; change
direction of diagonal rough flooring at each floor. Hips,
ridges, & valleys should not be less than full depth of
rafters. Ridge & hip thickness not less than 2"; valleys
3" min. Knee braces are resorted to when windows are
too close to corner for full bracing. Sizes shown are nominal. Unequal shrinkage exists between exterior and
interior walls, and total shrinkage is very great. This
is the oldest & strongest type of framing. Not suitable
for either stucco or brick veneer construction. It
is difficult to run pipes up walls.

**SECTION-JOISTS AT
RT. ANGLES to EXT. WALL
with EXCAV. CELLAR**
⅜" = 1'-0"

Adapted from data by National Lumber Manufacturers Association

**SECTION-JOISTS
PARALLEL to EXT. WALL
with CRAWL SPACE**
⅜" = 1'-0"

WESTERN (or PLATFORM) FRAMING

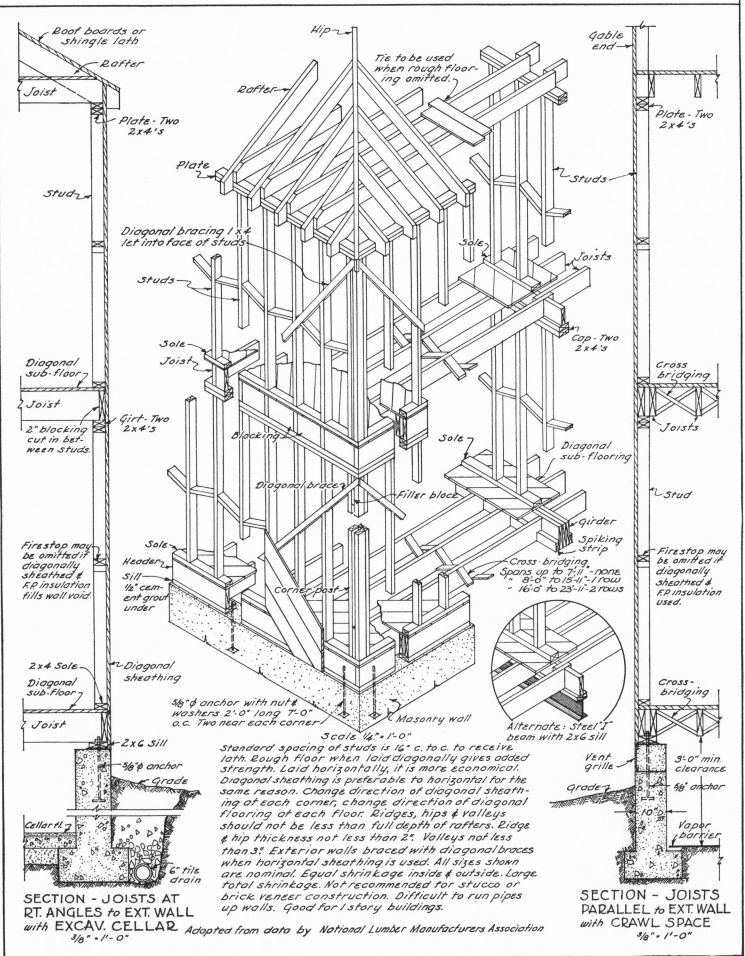

Roof boards or shingle lath

Rafter

Joist

Plate - Two 2x4's

Stud

Diagonal sub-floor

Joist

2" blocking cut in between studs.

Firestop may be omitted if diagonally sheathed & F.P. insulation fills wall void.

2x4 Sole

Diagonal sub-floor

Joist

2x6 Sill

5/8"⌀ anchor

Grade

Cellar fl.

6" tile drain

Hip

Tie to be used when rough flooring omitted.

Rafter

Plate

Diagonal bracing 1x4 let into face of studs

Studs

Sole

Joist

Blocking

Diagonal brace

Filler block

Girt - Two 2x4's

Sole

Header

Sill - 1/2" cement grout under

Corner post

Diagonal sheathing

5/8"⌀ anchor with nut & washers 2'-0" long 7'-0" o.c. Two near each corner

Masonry wall

Scale 1/4" = 1'-0"

Sole

Joists

Cap - Two 2x4's

Sole

Diagonal sub-flooring

Girder

Spiking strip

Cross-bridging. Spans up to 7'-11" - none
" 8'-0" to 15'-11" - 1 row
" 16'-0" to 23'-11" - 2 rows

Alternate: Steel "I" beam with 2x6 sill

Gable end

Plate - Two 2x4's

Studs

Cross bridging

Joists

Diagonal sub-flooring

Stud

Firestop may be omitted if diagonally sheathed & F.P. insulation used.

Cross-bridging

Vent grille

Grade

3'-0" min. clearance

5/8" anchor

10"

Vapor barrier

Standard spacing of studs is 16" c. to c. to receive lath. Rough floor when laid diagonally gives added strength. Laid horizontally, it is more economical. Diagonal sheathing is preferable to horizontal for the same reason. Change direction of diagonal sheathing at each corner, change direction of diagonal flooring at each floor. Ridges, hips & valleys should not be less than full depth of rafters. Ridge & hip thickness not less than 2". Valleys not less than 3". Exterior walls braced with diagonal braces when horizontal sheathing is used. All sizes shown are nominal. Equal shrinkage inside & outside. Large total shrinkage. Not recommended for stucco or brick veneer construction. Difficult to run pipes up walls. Good for 1 story buildings.

SECTION - JOISTS AT RT. ANGLES to EXT. WALL with EXCAV. CELLAR
3/8" = 1'-0"

Adopted from data by National Lumber Manufacturers Association

SECTION - JOISTS PARALLEL to EXT. WALL with CRAWL SPACE
3/8" = 1'-0"

MODERN BRACED FRAMING

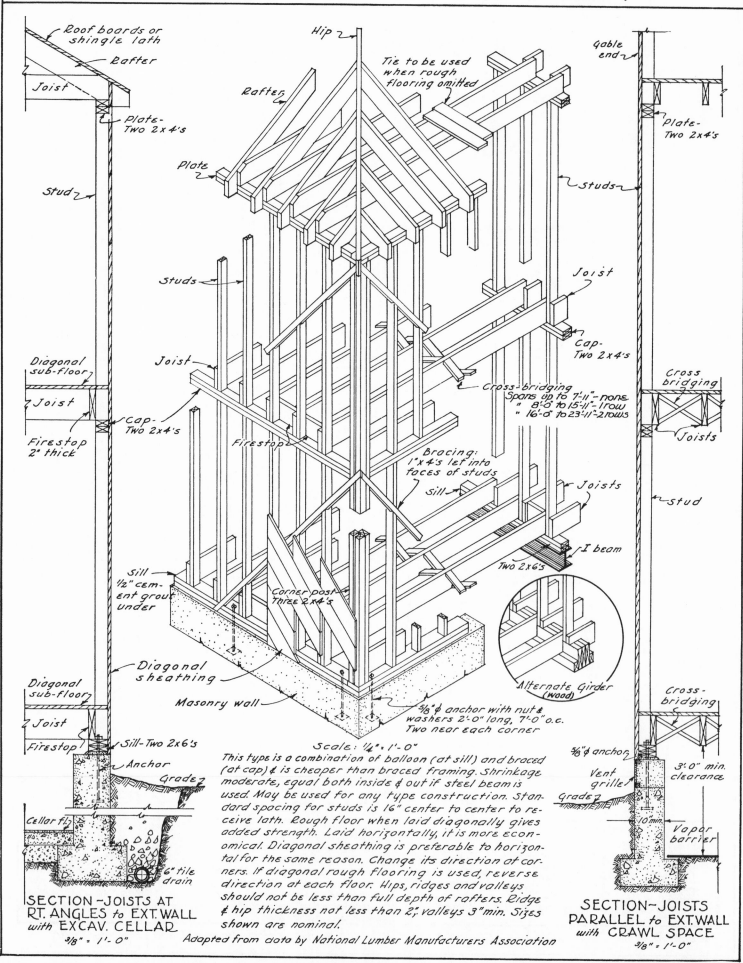

Roof boards or shingle lath

Rafter

Joist

Plate-Two 2x4's

Stud

Hip

Tie to be used when rough flooring omitted

Rafter

Plate

Studs

Joist

Studs

Cap-Two 2x4's

Cross-bridging
Spans up to 7'-11"-none
" 8'-0" to 15'-11"-1 row
" 16'-0" to 23'-11"-2 rows

Diagonal sub-floor

Joist

Cap-Two 2x4's

Firestop 2" thick

Joist

Firestop

Bracing: 1"x4's let into faces of studs

Sill

Joists

Joists

I beam

Two 2x6's

Sill ½" cement grout under

Corner post Three 2x4's

Stud

Cross bridging

Joists

Alternate Girder (wood)

Diagonal sheathing

Masonry wall

⅝"ø anchor with nut & washers 2'-0" long, 7'-0" o.c. Two near each corner

Gable end

Plate-Two 2x4's

Scale: ¼" = 1'-0"

Diagonal sub-floor

Joist

Firestop

Sill-Two 2x6's

Anchor

Grade

Cellar fl.

6" tile drain

This type is a combination of balloon (at sill) and braced (at cap) & is cheaper than braced framing. Shrinkage moderate, equal both inside & out if steel beam is used. May be used for any type construction. Standard spacing for studs is 16" center to center to receive lath. Rough floor when laid diagonally gives added strength. Laid horizontally, it is more economical. Diagonal sheathing is preferable to horizontal for the same reason. Change its direction at corners. If diagonal rough flooring is used, reverse direction at each floor. Hips, ridges and valleys should not be less than full depth of rafters. Ridge & hip thickness not less than 2"; valleys 3" min. Sizes shown are nominal.

⅝"ø anchor

Vent grille

Grade

10" min.

3'-0" min. clearance

Vapor barrier

Cross-bridging

SECTION–JOISTS AT RT. ANGLES to EXT. WALL with EXCAV. CELLAR
3/8" = 1'-0"

Adapted from data by National Lumber Manufacturers Association

SECTION–JOISTS PARALLEL to EXT. WALL with CRAWL SPACE
3/8" = 1'-0"

LIGHT WOOD FRAMING DETAILS

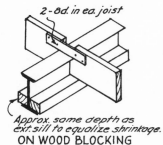
2-8d. in ea. joist
Approx. same depth as
ext. sill to equalize shrinkage.
ON WOOD BLOCKING

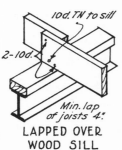
10d. TN to sill
2-10d.
Min. lap
of joists 4".
LAPPED OVER WOOD SILL

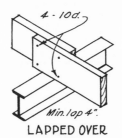
4 - 10d.
Min. lap 4".
LAPPED OVER GIRDER

2-8d. in ea. joist
ON STEEL ANGLES

2-8d. in ea. joist
ON LOWER FLANGE

WOOD JOISTS SUPPORTED on STEEL GIRDERS

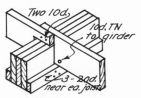
Two 10d.
10d. TN to girder
2-3 80d.
near ea. joist
OVERLAPPING JOISTS NOTCHED over GIRDER ✱
Bearing only on ledger, not on top of girder.

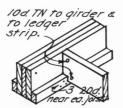
10d. TN to girder &
to ledger strip.
2-3 80d.
near ea. joist
JOIST NOTCHED OVER LEDGER STRIP ✱
Notching over bearing not recommend'd.

Girder & joist notched for hanger.
JOIST IN BRIDLE IRON
Also called joist hanger or stirrup

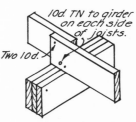
10d. TN to girder on each side of joists.
Two 10d.
JOISTS BEARING on GIRDER ✱
Min. lap 4" inches

Two 8d. in each joist
2-10d. TN to girder
3-20d. near ea. joist
JOISTS NOTCHED OVER GIRDER ✱
Bearing only on ledger, not on top of girdr.

WOOD JOISTS SUPPORTED on WOOD GIRDERS

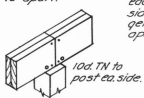
Two 10d. each end on one side, others stag. 16" apart.
10d. TN to post ea. side.
TWO PIECE GIRDER ✱
Girder joints only at supports.

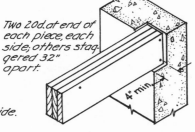
Two 20d. at end of each piece, each side; others staggered 32" apart.
4" min.
THREE PIECE GIRDER ✱
Four piece girder: add 1 pc. nailed with 20d. to three pc.

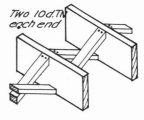
Two 10d. TN each end
1"x3" CROSS BR'G. 2"x3" REC'D. ✱
Lower ends not nailed until flooring is layed.

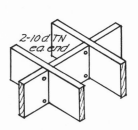
2-10d. TN ea. end
SOLID BRIDGING
Used for heavy loading; under partitions

GIRDERS   BRIDGING

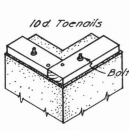
10d. Toenails
Bolt
2"x6" SILL ✱

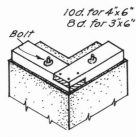
10d. for 4"x6"
8d. for 3"x6"
Bolt
3"x6, 4"x6" SILL
Halved at corners

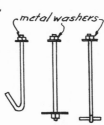
metal washers
TYPES OF SILL ANCHORS

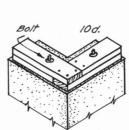
Bolt   10d.
4"x6" DOUBLE SILL ✱
Nails staggered along sill 24" on centers.

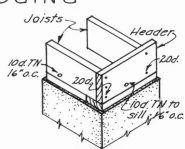
Joists
Header
10d. TN 16" o.c.
20d.
10d. TN to sill 16" o.c.
PLATFORM FRAMING ✱
Toenail to sill not required if diagonal sheathing used.

SILL DETAILS

3/8" = 1'-0"

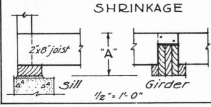
SHRINKAGE
2"x8" joist
"A"
Sill
Girder
1/2" = 1'-0"

Select joist-girder detail which has the approx. same shrinkage "A" as the sill detail used.

Steel Girders: Provide steel bearing plate on outside wall.
Anchor Bolts: 1/2" to 3/4" dia. 1'-6" to 2'-0" long, 6' to 8' o.c. Two at each corner (see Sill Details), two at each joint.
Sills: 3" thickness or more affords more nailing surface for sheathing & a better lap splice. Impregnate or creosote for long life. Lay on 1/2" cement mortar grout.
Wood Posts: Rest on C.I. plates or cement footing & keep at least 3" above floor to prevent rotting & termites.
All dimensions nominal.

✱ Data developed from "Technique of House Nailing," Nov. 1947, Housing & Home Finance Agency, Washington, D.C.

LIGHT WOOD FRAMING DETAILS

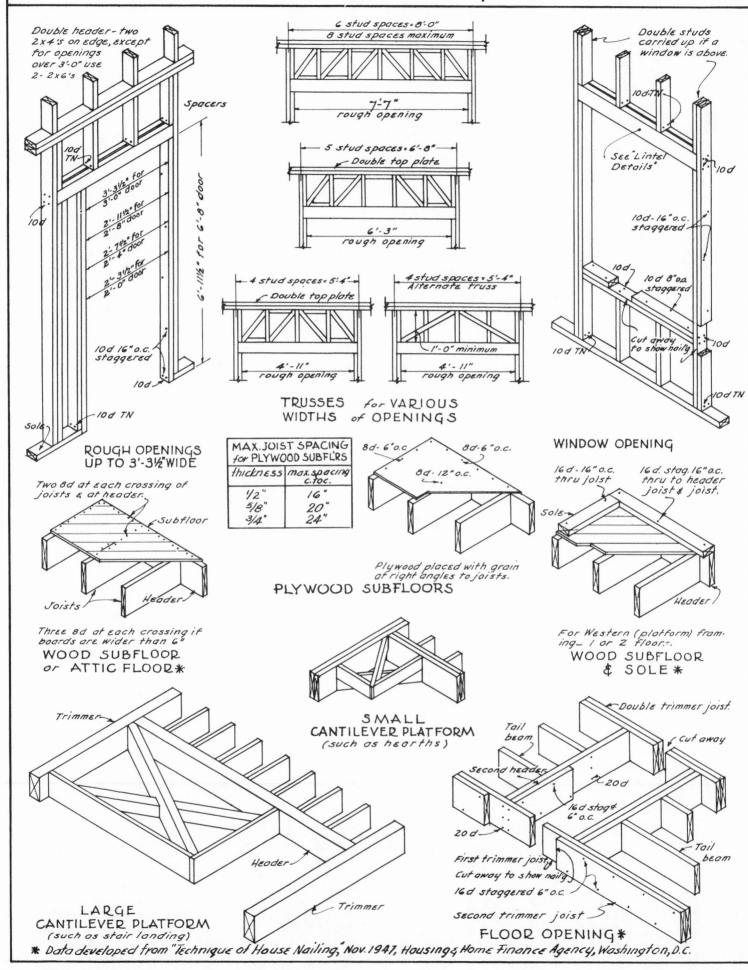

Double header– two 2×4's on edge, except for openings over 3'-0" use 2- 2×6's

Spacers

10d TN

3'-3½" for 3'-0" door
2'-11½" for 2'-8" door
2'-7½" for 2'-4" door
2'-3½" for 2'-0" door

6'-11½" for 6'-8" door

10d

10d 16" o.c. staggered

10d

Sole

10d TN

ROUGH OPENINGS UP TO 3'-3½" WIDE

6 stud spaces=8'-0"
8 stud spaces maximum

7'-7" rough opening

5 stud spaces=6'-8"
Double top plate

6'-3" rough opening

4 stud spaces=5'-4"
Double top plate

4'-11" rough opening

4 stud spaces=5'-4"
Alternate truss

1'-0" minimum

4'-11" rough opening

TRUSSES for **VARIOUS WIDTHS** of **OPENINGS**

Double studs carried up if a window is above.

10d TN

See "Lintel Details"

10d

10d-16" o.c. staggered

10d

10d 8" o.c. staggered

Cut away to show nail'g

10d TN

10d

10d TN

WINDOW OPENING

Max. JOIST SPACING for PLYWOOD SUBFLRS	
thickness	max. spacing c. to c.
½"	16"
⅝"	20"
¾"	24"

Two 8d at each crossing of joists & at header.

Subfloor

Joists   Header

Three 8d at each crossing if boards are wider than 6"

WOOD SUBFLOOR or ATTIC FLOOR ✳

8d- 6" o.c.   8d-6" o.c.

8d- 12" o.c.

Plywood placed with grain at right angles to joists.

PLYWOOD SUBFLOORS

16 d-16" o.c. thru joist

16d. stag. 16" o.c. thru to header joist & joist.

Sole

Header

For Western (platform) framing– 1 or 2 floors.

WOOD SUBFLOOR & SOLE ✳

Trimmer

LARGE CANTILEVER PLATFORM (such as stair landing)

Header

Trimmer

SMALL CANTILEVER PLATFORM (such as hearths)

Double trimmer joist

Tail beam

Cut away

Second header

20d

16d stag'd 6" o.c.

20d

First trimmer joist

Cut away to show nail'g

16d staggered 6" o.c.

Second trimmer joist

Tail beam

FLOOR OPENING ✳

✳ Data developed from "Technique of House Nailing," Nov. 1947, Housing & Home Finance Agency, Washington, D.C.

LIGHT WOOD FRAMING DETAILS

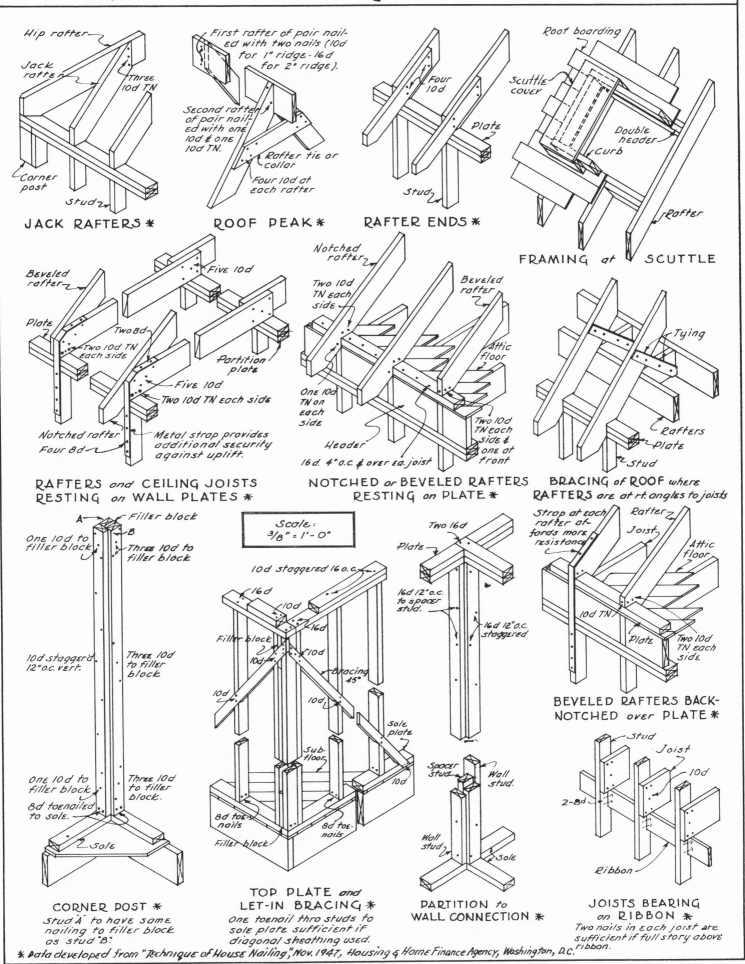

JACK RAFTERS *

Hip rafter

Jack rafter

Three 10d TN

Corner post

stud

ROOF PEAK *

First rafter of pair nailed with two nails (10d for 1" ridge - 16d for 2" ridge).

Second rafter of pair nailed with one 10d & one 10d TN.

Rafter tie or collar

Four 10d at each rafter

RAFTER ENDS *

Four 10d

Plate

stud

FRAMING at SCUTTLE

Roof boarding

Scuttle cover

Double header

Curb

Rafter

RAFTERS and CEILING JOISTS RESTING on WALL PLATES *

Beveled rafter

Plate

Five 10d

Two 8d

Two 10d TN each side

Partition plate

Five 10d

Two 10d TN each side

Notched rafter

Four 8d

Metal strap provides additional security against uplift.

NOTCHED or BEVELED RAFTERS RESTING on PLATE *

Notched rafter

Two 10d TN each side

Beveled rafter

Attic floor

One 10d TN on each side

Two 10d TN each side & one at front

Header

16d. 4" o.c. & over ea. joist

BRACING of ROOF where RAFTERS are at rt. angles to joists

Tying

Rafters

Plate

stud

Scale: 3/8" = 1'-0"

CORNER POST *

A
Filler block
B

One 10d to filler block

Three 10d to filler block

10d stagger'd 12" o.c. vert.

Three 10d to filler block

One 10d to filler block

Three 10d to filler block

8d toenailed to sole.

Sole

Stud "A" to have same nailing to filler block as stud "B".

TOP PLATE and LET-IN BRACING *

10d staggered 16 o.c.

16d

10d

16d

Filler block

10d

10d

10d

Bracing 45°

10d

Sub-floor

Sole plate

10d

8d toe nails

8d toe nails

Filler block

One toenail thro studs to sole plate sufficient if diagonal sheathing used.

PARTITION to WALL CONNECTION *

Two 16d

Plate

16d 12" o.c. to spacer stud.

16d 12" o.c. staggered

Spacer stud

Wall stud.

Wall stud.

Sole

BEVELED RAFTERS BACK-NOTCHED over PLATE *

Strap at each rafter affords more resistance

Rafter

Joist

Attic floor

10d TN

Plate

Two 10d TN each side

JOISTS BEARING on RIBBON *

stud

Joist

10d

2-8d

Ribbon

Two nails in each joist are sufficient if full story above ribbon.

* Data developed from "Technique of House Nailing", Nov. 1947, Housing & Home Finance Agency, Washington, D.C.

LIGHT WOOD FRAMING DETAILS

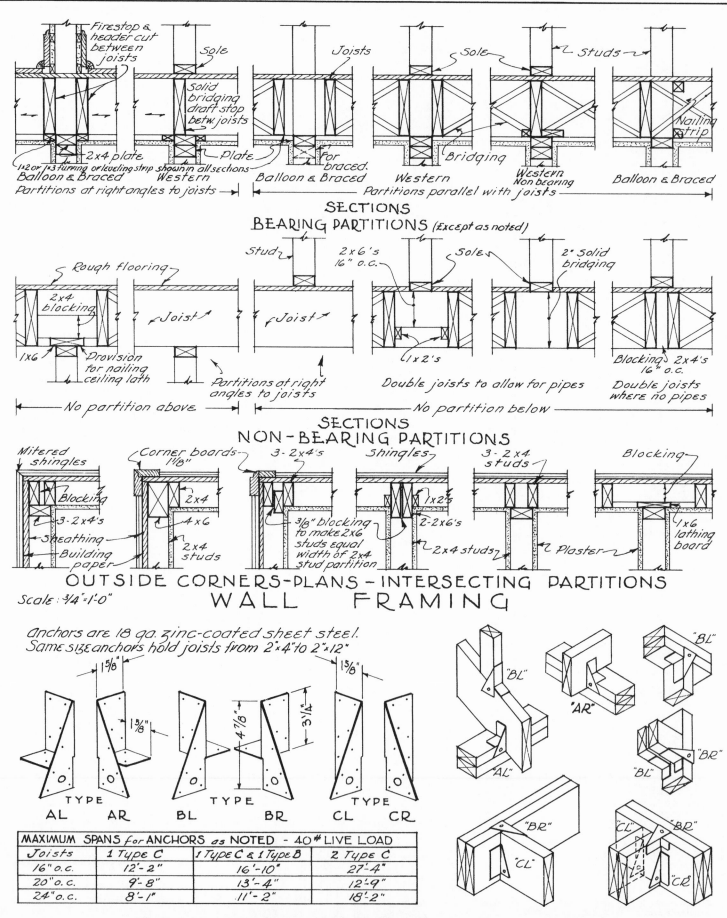

Firestop & header cut between joists

Sole

Joists

Sole

Studs

Solid bridging draft stop betw. joists

Nailing strip

2x4 plate

Plate

For braced

Bridging

1x2 or 1x3 furring or leveling strip shown in all sections

Balloon & Braced   **Western**   **Balloon & Braced**   **Western**   **Western** Non bearing   **Balloon & Braced**

← Partitions at right angles to joists →   ← Partitions parallel with joists →

SECTIONS
BEARING PARTITIONS (Except as noted)

Rough flooring

Stud

2x6's 16" o.c.

Sole

2" solid bridging

2x4 blocking

Joist

Joist

1x6

Provision for nailing ceiling lath

Partitions at right angles to joists

1x2's

Double joists to allow for pipes

Blocking 2x4's 16" o.c.

Double joists where no pipes

← No partition above →   ← No partition below →

SECTIONS
NON-BEARING PARTITIONS

Mitered shingles

Corner boards 1⅛"

3-2x4's

Shingles

3-2x4 studs

Blocking

Blocking

2x4

3-2x4's

4x6

Sheathing

2x4 studs

Building paper

3/8" blocking to make 2x6 studs equal width of 2x4 stud partition

1x2's

2-2x6's

2x4 studs

Plaster

1x6 lathing board

OUTSIDE CORNERS—PLANS—INTERSECTING PARTITIONS
WALL FRAMING

Scale: ¾" = 1'-0"

Anchors are 18 ga. zinc-coated sheet steel.
Same size anchors hold joists from 2"x4" to 2"x12"

1⅝"   1⅝"

1⅝"   4⅞"   3¼"

TYPE AL AR   **TYPE** BL BR   **TYPE** CL CR

"BL"

"AR"

"BL"

"AL"

"BR"

"BL"

"BR"

"BR"

"CL"

"CL"

"BR"

"CR"

MAXIMUM SPANS for ANCHORS as NOTED - 40# LIVE LOAD			
Joists	1 Type C	1 Type C & 1 Type B	2 Type C
16" o.c.	12'-2"	16'-10"	27'-4"
20" o.c.	9'-8"	13'-4"	12'-9"
24" o.c.	8'-1"	11'-2"	18'-2"

TECO TRIP-L-GRIP FRAMING ANCHORS
Data checked by Timber Engineering Co., Washington, D.C.

LIGHT WOOD FRAMING DETAILS

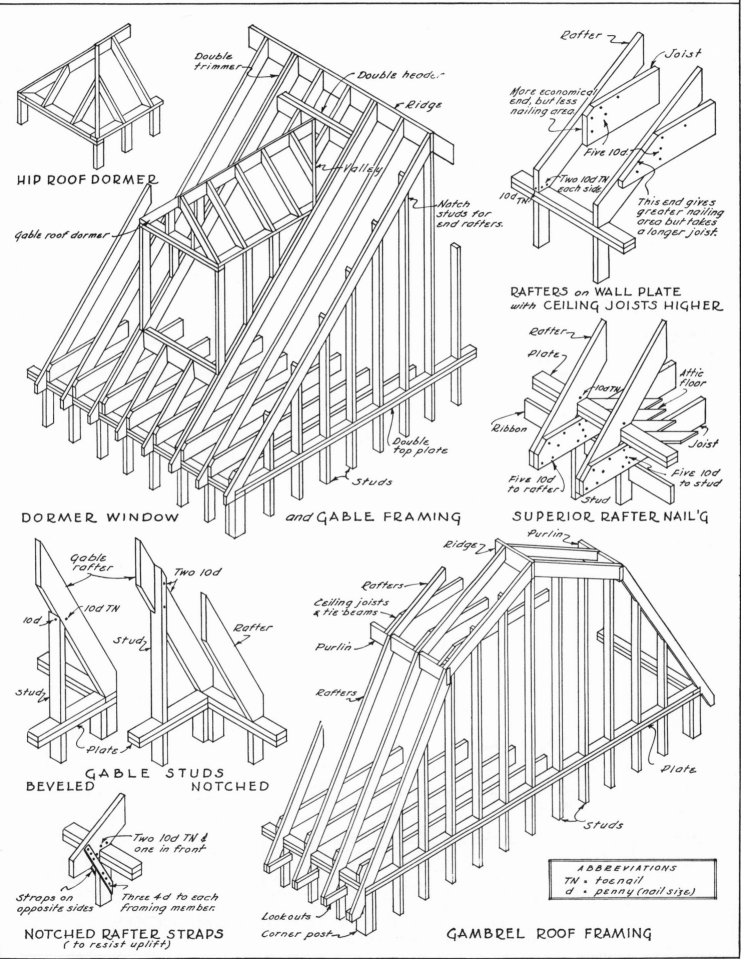

HIP ROOF DORMER

Gable roof dormer

Double trimmer

Double header

Ridge

Valley

Notch studs for end rafters.

Double top plate

Studs

DORMER WINDOW and **GABLE FRAMING**

Rafter

Joist

More economical end, but less nailing area.

Five 10d.

Two 10d TN each side.

10d TN

This end gives greater nailing area but takes a longer joist.

RAFTERS on WALL PLATE with CEILING JOISTS HIGHER

Rafter

Plate

Attic floor

10d TN

Ribbon

Five 10d to rafter

Joist

Five 10d to stud

Stud

SUPERIOR RAFTER NAIL'G

Gable rafter

Two 10d

10d

10d TN

Stud

Rafter

Stud

Plate

BEVELED   GABLE STUDS   NOTCHED

Two 10d TN & one in front

Straps on opposite sides

Three 4d to each framing member.

NOTCHED RAFTER STRAPS
(to resist uplift)

Ridge

Purlin

Rafters

Ceiling joists & tie beams

Purlin

Rafters

Plate

Studs

Lookouts

Corner post

GAMBREL ROOF FRAMING

ABBREVIATIONS
TN = toenail
d = penny (nail size)

PLANK and BEAM FRAMING for RESIDENCES

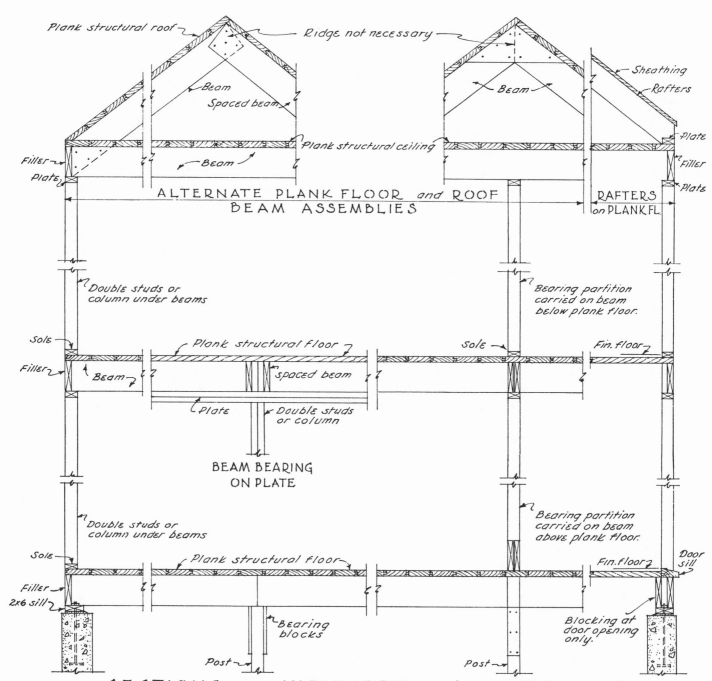

Plank structural roof — Ridge not necessary —

Beam
Spaced beam

Sheathing
Rafters

Plank structural ceiling

Filler
Plate

Beam

Beam

Plate
Filler
Plate

ALTERNATE PLANK FLOOR and ROOF BEAM ASSEMBLIES
RAFTERS on PLANK FL.

Double studs or column under beams

Bearing partition carried on beam below plank floor.

Sole

Plank structural floor

Sole

Fin. floor

Filler

Beam

spaced beam

Plate   Double studs or column

BEAM BEARING ON PLATE

Double studs or column under beams

Bearing partition carried on beam above plank floor.

Sole

Plank structural floor

Fin. floor

Door sill

Filler
2x6 sill

Bearing blocks

Blocking at door opening only.

Post

Post

SECTIONS showing VARIOUS DETAILS and ALTERNATIVES
(For exterior studs, bracing and sheathing, see page on "Western Framing")

Plank and beam structural floor and/or roof system is the use of a plank sub-floor or roof decking with supporting beams spaced up to 7 feet apart, instead of the usual boards for sub-floor or roof decking with joists or rafters spaced 12 to 24 inches. It may be employed in a building having joist construction for other floors or for the roof, and it is possible to utilize the advantageous features of both types by selecting that which is the more suitable for each part of the structure. Its adaptation to small house construction is a relatively new development. Compared with 2x8 joists spaced 16"o.c., 2" plank continuous over two 7'-0" spans gives the same stiffness as 2x8 joists with an 11'-4" span and the same strength as 2x8 joists with a 10'-4" span. 2x6 or 2x8 well-seasoned plank should be used; and, if serving as exposed ceiling of rooms below, Nº 1 Common or other tight-knotted material, selected for good appearance, should be used. Finish flooring should be laid at right angles with the plank of sub-floor. When a 25/32" thickness of flooring is used, and the underside of plank exposed as finish ceiling, finish floor nails should not be longer than 1¾".
  Properly designed plank spans up to 7'-0" are practical for the fulfilling of the requirements of the Federal Housing Administration for residences.

SCALE: 3/8" = 1'-0"

Adapted from data by the National Lumber Manufacturers' Association

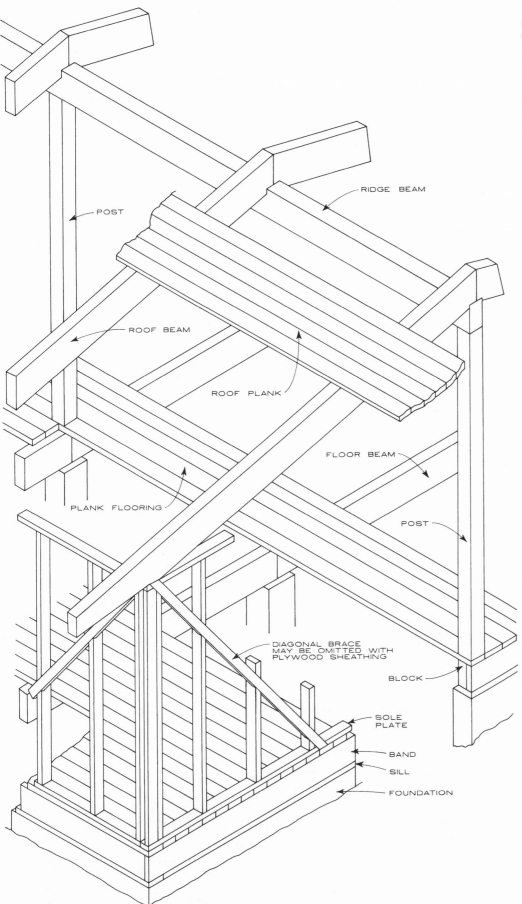

TYPICAL PLANK AND BEAM FRAMING FOR ONE STORY HOUSE

Labels within illustration: POST, RIDGE BEAM, ROOF BEAM, ROOF PLANK, FLOOR BEAM, PLANK FLOORING, POST, DIAGONAL BRACE MAY BE OMITTED WITH PLYWOOD SHEATHING, BLOCK, SOLE PLATE, BAND, SILL, FOUNDATION

Joseph A. Wilkes, AIA; Wilkes and Faulkner; Washington, D. C.

DESCRIPTION

Use of two inch nominal thickness plank for subfloors or roofs supported on beams spaced 6 to 8 feet apart.

PRINCIPLES OF DESIGN

Two inch plank used more efficiently when continuous over more than one span.

Uses standard lumber lengths such as 12, 14 and 16 feet with beams 6, 7 or 8 feet apart.

Design permitting, end joints between supports allows use of random lengths.

ADVANTAGES OF SYSTEM

Architectural effect provided by exposed plank and beam ceiling. Added effective height of ceiling at no increase in wall height.

Fewer members permits savings in labor.

Cross-bridging not required.

LIMITATIONS OF SYSTEM

Bearing partitions and heavy loads such as bathtubs, refrigerators etc., may require additional framing. Concealment must be provided for wiring, piping and duct work.

Insulation value of two inch deck may be adequate, but where additional insulation is required it may be attached below deck or as rigid insulation above deck under roofing.

CONSTRUCTION DETAILS AND FASTENING

Members of built-up beams should be securely spiked together from both outside faces. Spaced beams should be blocked at frequent intervals, and each member should be securely nailed to blocking. Where planks butt over a single member, a nominal beam width of three or more inches is necessary to provide a suitable bearing and nailing surface for the planks. Planks should be both blind and face-nailed to the beam. In this construction posts (rather than studs) carry the loads, which are concentrated and must be designed for conditions, but not smaller than 4 x 4 inches. Built-up posts should be spiked together.

When solid beams butt at a column, a nominal column dimension of 6 or more inches parallel to direction of beam is recommended to provide suitable bearing. Spike bearing blocks to column where necessary to increase bearing surface.

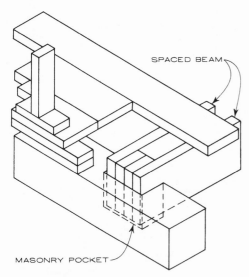

FIRST FLOOR FRAMING AT EXTERIOR WALL BEAM SET IN FOUNDATION

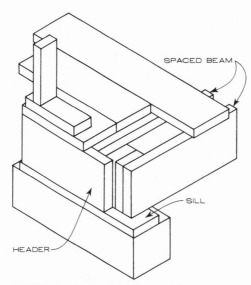

FIRST FLOOR FRAMING AT EXTERIOR WALL BEAM BEARING ON SILL

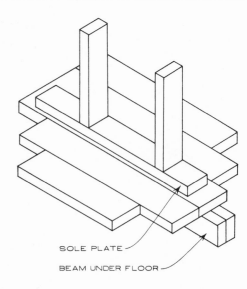

NON-BEARING PARTITION PAR-ALLEL TO PLANK SUPPORTED BY BEAM UNDER FLOOR

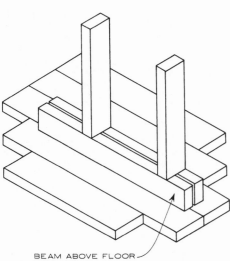

NON-BEARING PARTITION PARALLEL TO PLANK SUPPORTED BY BEAM ABOVE FLOOR

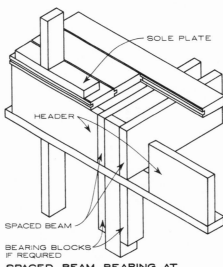

SPACED BEAM BEARING AT EXTERIOR WALL

The details in this column are preferable from the standpoint of equalizing shrinkage of horizontal lumber partition supports.

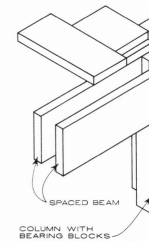

SPACED BEAM BEARING OVER BASEMENT SUPPORT

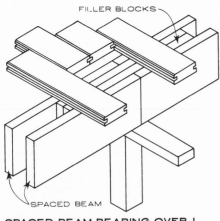

SPACED BEAM BEARING OVER 1 INTERIOR POST

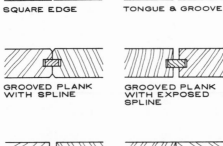

SQUARE EDGE

TONGUE & GROOVE

GROOVED PLANK WITH SPLINE

GROOVED PLANK WITH EXPOSED SPLINE

GROOVED PLANK MOULDED SPLINE

RABBETED PLANK BATTEN INSERT

JOINT TYPES IN EXPOSED PLANK CEILINGS

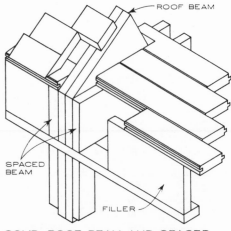

SOLID ROOF BEAM AND SPACED FLOOR BEAM BEARING ON EXTERIOR WALL

Joseph A. Wilkes, AIA; Wilkes and Faulkner; Washington, D. C.

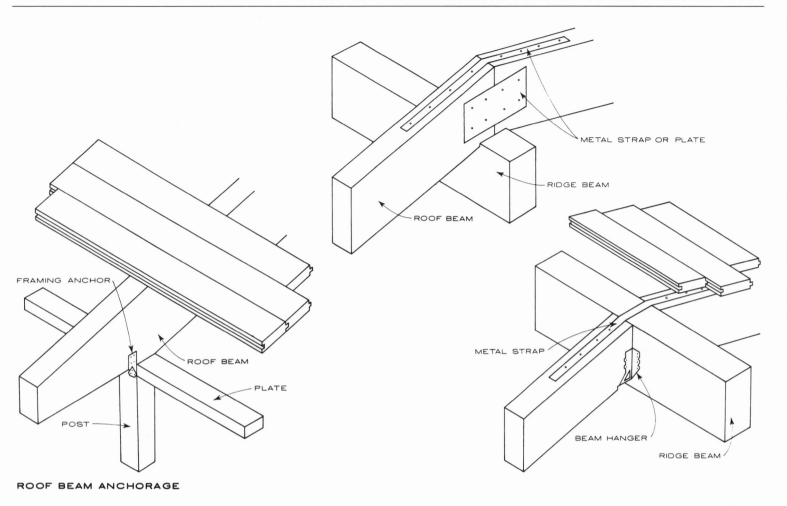

ROOF BEAM ANCHORAGE

DESIGN TABLE FOR NOMINAL TWO-INCH PLANK

Required values for fiber stress in bending (f) and modulus of elasticity (E) to support safely a live load of 20, 30, or 40 pounds per square foot within a deflection limitation of $1/300$. See tables on pages for "Lumber Grades and Allowable Stresses".

SPAN IN FEET	LIVE LOAD psf	TYPE A f (psi)	TYPE A E (psi)	TYPE B f (psi)	TYPE B E (psi)	TYPE C f (psi)	TYPE C E (psi)	TYPE D f (psi)	TYPE D E (psi)
6	20	310	570,000	310	230,000	250	30,000	310	40,000
	30	410	850,000	410	350,000	330	450,000	410	600,000
	40	510	1,130,000	510	470,000	410	600,000	510	800,000
7	20	420	900,000	420	370,000	330	480,000	420	640,000
	30	560	1,350,000	560	560,000	450	710,000	560	950,000
	40	700	1,800,000	700	750,000	560	950,000	700	1,270,000
8	20	543	1,340,000	543	557,000	434	707,000	543	948,000
	30	724	2,010,000	724	835,000	580	1,060,000	724	1,422,000
	40	906	2,670,000	906	1,110,000	720	1,410,000	906	1,890,000

Joseph A. Wilkes, AIA; Wilkes and Faulkner; Washington, D. C.

PLANK and BEAM FRAMING DETAILS

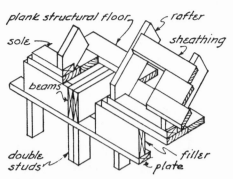

plank structural floor · rafter
sole
sheathing
beams
double studs
filler plate

BEAM on PLATE, RAFTER on
SOLE on PLANK STRUCT! FL.

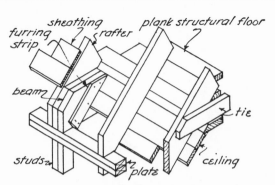

sheathing
furring strip · rafter
plank structural floor
beam
tie
studs
plate
ceiling

BEAM and RAFTER on
WALL PLATE

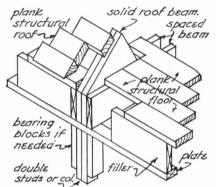

plank structural roof
solid roof beam
spaced beam
plank structural floor
bearing blocks if needed
double studs or col.
filler
plate

SPACED FL. & SOLID ROOF BEAMS

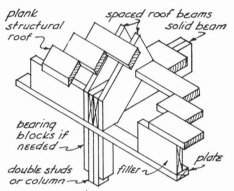

plank structural roof
spaced roof beams
solid beam
bearing blocks if needed
double studs or column
filler
plate

SOLID FL. & SPACED ROOF BEAMS

BEARING at WALL PLATE

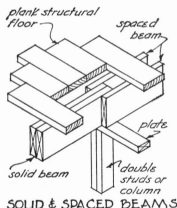

plank structural floor
spaced beam
plate
solid beam
double studs or column

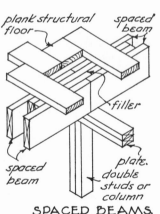

plank structural floor
spaced beam
filler
spaced beam
plate. double studs or column

SOLID & SPACED BEAMS.
BEARING at SECOND FLOOR – INTERIOR

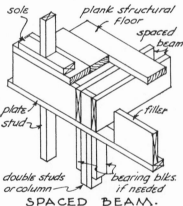

sole
plank structural floor
spaced beam
plate stud
filler
double studs or column
bearing blks. if needed

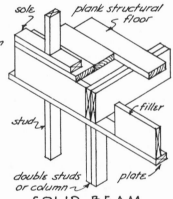

sole
plank structural floor
stud
filler
double studs or column
plate

SPACED BEAM.   SOLID BEAM.
BEARING at SECOND FLOOR – EXTERIOR

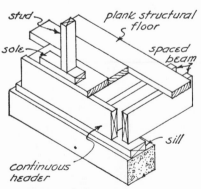

stud
plank structural floor
sole
spaced beam
sill
continuous header

BEAM BEARING on SILL.

stud
plank structural floor
sole
spaced beam
sill
blocking
foundation wall

BEAM BEARING on WALL.

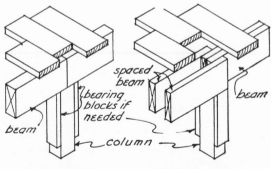

spaced beam
bearing blocks if needed
beam
beam
column

SOLID BEAM.   SPACED BEAM.
BEARING over BASEMENT POST

Adapted from data by the National Lumber Manufacturers Association

Scale : $\frac{3}{8}$" = 1'-0"

PLANK and BEAM CONSTRUCTION

PLANK-AND-BEAM FRAMING

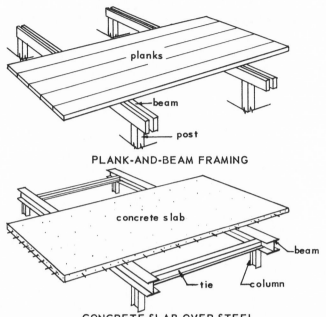

PLANK-AND-BEAM FRAMING

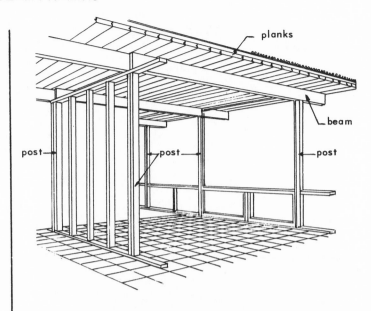

PLANK-AND-BEAM FRAMING

CONCRETE SLAB OVER STEEL

To show its characteristics more clearly, plank-and-beam wood framing can be compared to standard steel framing, which is very similar in principle.

PLANK-AND-BEAM FRAMING

Full benefit of this system is obtained in residential work with an open plan and a modular panel treatment such as 4'-0" dry-wall units and large glass areas.

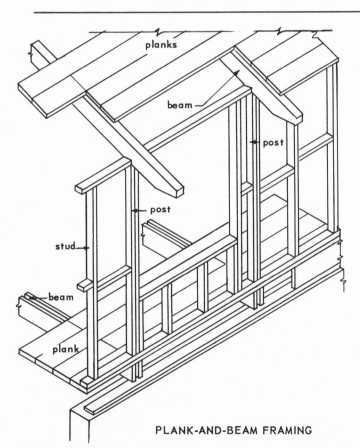

PLANK-AND-BEAM FRAMING

In this construction, a few large members replace the many small members used in typical wood framing. This results in a saving in the number of members, and, due to rapid site assembly, makes possible a saving in erection labor costs.

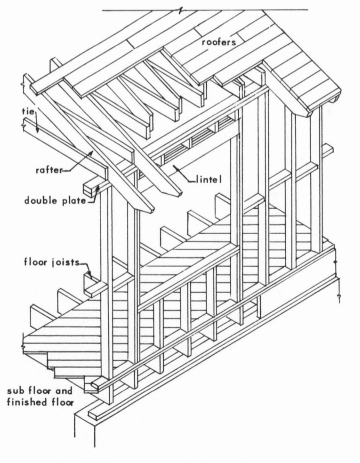

CONVENTIONAL WOOD FRAMING

Compiled from "Plank-and-Beam Systems for Residential Construction" — Housing and Home Finance Agency.

PLANK and BEAM CONSTRUCTION

ADVANTAGES OF THE PLANK-AND-BEAM FRAMING SYSTEM

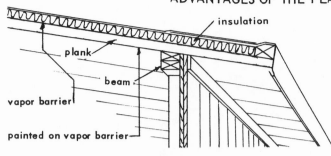

PLANK-AND-BEAM

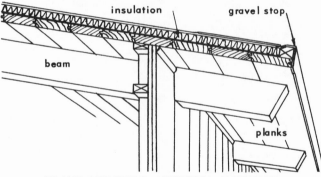

PLANK-AND-BEAM

Lath and plaster may be eliminated by placing the insulation on top of the planks and finishing their undersides or by affixing exposed insulation to the lower side of the plank members.

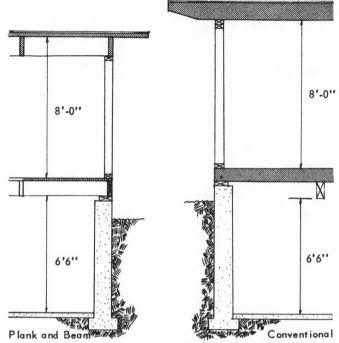

HEIGHT SAVING OF PLANK-AND-BEAM CONSTRUCTION

Plank-and-beam framing saves on building height, making it possible to use shorter wall studs and shallower basement foundation walls.

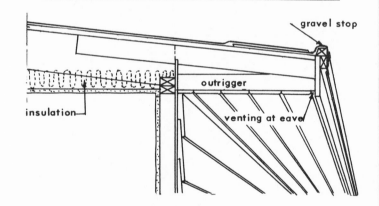

PLANK-AND-BEAM — EXPOSED OVERHANG

Overhang planks can be left exposed without marring the exterior appearance of the building, saving special soffit treatment, fascia and molds.

CONVENTIONAL BOXED OVERHANG

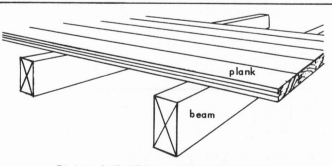

PLANK-AND-BEAM — ROOF OR FLOOR

One thickness of heavy planks, finished on both sides and supported on beams, may form the entire floor construction, replacing the usual finished flooring, subflooring, paper, framing, bridging, and plaster ceiling.

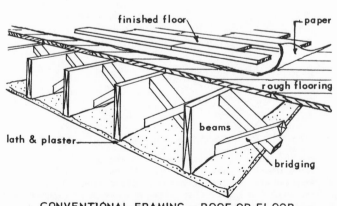

CONVENTIONAL FRAMING — ROOF OR FLOOR

Compiled from "Plank-and-Beam Systems for Residential Construction" — Housing and Home Finance Agency

PLANK and BEAM CONSTRUCTION

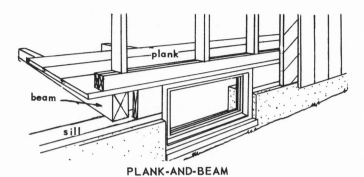

PLANK-AND-BEAM

Basement windows may be placed higher, making it unnecessary to use areaways.

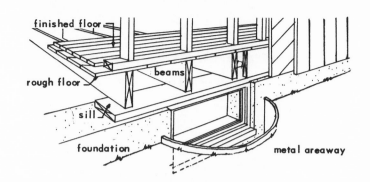

finished floor

rough floor

beams

sill

foundation   metal areaway

CONVENTIONAL

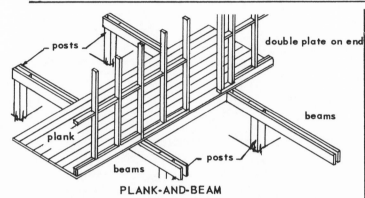

posts

double plate on end

plank

beams

beams

posts

PLANK-AND-BEAM

Additional framing is necessary under concentrated loads such as partitions and bathtubs. Cross beams or double plates can be used to take care of these conditions.

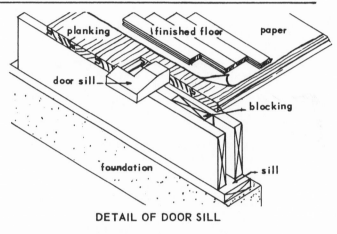

planking   finished floor   paper

door sill

blocking

foundation   sill

DETAIL OF DOOR SILL

PLANK AND BEAM FRAMING

MECHANICAL AND ELECTRICAL CONSIDERATIONS OF PLANK-AND-BEAM FRAMING.

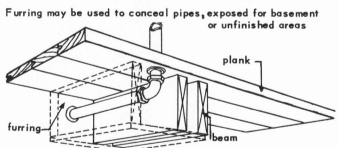

Furring may be used to conceal pipes, exposed for basement or unfinished areas

plank

furring

beam

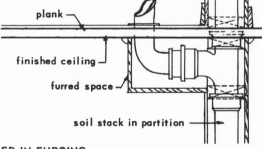

plank

finished ceiling

furred space

soil stack in partition

PLUMBING CONCEALED IN FURRING

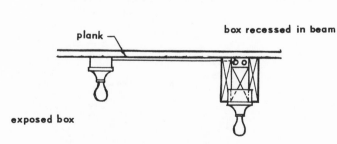

plank

box recessed in beam

exposed box

CEILING FIXTURES

Electrical layouts for plank-and-beam framing should indicate actual locations of runs and details of installation. Conduits left exposed on the ceiling become less conspicuous if they are run along the top side of beams or along the joints of the planking. In some cases the conduit may be concealed in a built-up beam.

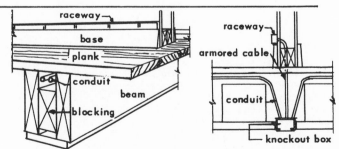

raceway

base

plank

conduit

beam

blocking

raceway

armored cable

conduit

knockout box

SURFACE MOUNTED RACEWAY

Elimination of ceiling lighting fixtures simplifies this problem. However, when desired, they may be left exposed or they may be recessed in the beam.

Surface mounted plug-in strips may be used in place of base receptacles and over kitchen counters to reduce wiring costs.

Compiled from "Plank-and-Beam System for Residential Construction" — Housing and Home Finance Agency

PLANK and BEAM CONSTRUCTION

Plank-and-beam framing may produce economy in construction if its design is carefully studied. In all cases local building codes must be consulted.

Following is a summary of possible economies in this construction.

1. Fewer different lengths and sizes of lumber are handled and placed.
2. Such items as bridging, subflooring, plastered ceilings, fascias, moldings, etc., can be completely eliminated.
3. Increased insulation is provided without extra cost.
4. Shorter wall studs and shallower basement foundation walls are required.
5. Areaways can be eliminated.

CONSTRUCTION DETAILS AND FASTENINGS

The members of built-up beams should be securely spiked together from both outside faces. When beam members are spaced, they should be blocked at frequent intervals, and each member should be securely nailed to the blocking.

Where planks butt over a single member beam, a nominal beam width of three or more inches is necessary to provide a suitable bearing and nailing surface for the planks. Planks should be both blind and face-nailed to the beam.

Beams should not be notched unless additional section is added.

At the first floor exterior, a sill may be used, or the beam may bear directly on the foundation wall.

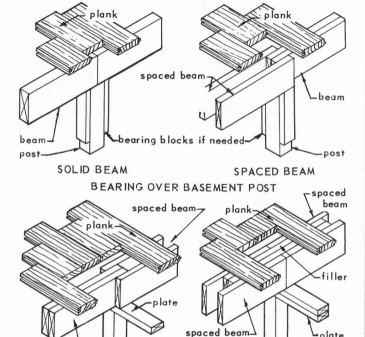

SOLID BEAM   SPACED BEAM
BEARING OVER BASEMENT POST

SOLID SPACED BEAMS   SPACED BEAMS
BEARING AT SECOND FLOOR INTERIOR

Adopted from data by the National Lumber Manufactures' Assoc.

At the exterior wall, solid blocking (box plate) should be provided between beams and between members of built-up beams. The plank flooring should extend over the blocking and studs should rest on a plate placed on top of the planking. The beams should bear on solid or built-up posts which are adequate to support the load.

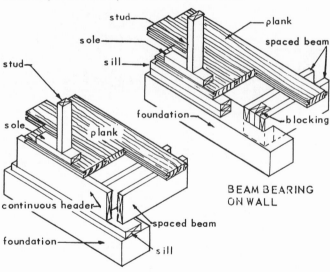

BEAM BEARING
ON WALL

BEAM BEARING ON SILL

Adopted from data by the National Lumber Manufacturers Assoc.

In this construction posts (rather than studs) carry the loads, which are concentrated; therefore they must be individually designed for each condition. Column ends should be squared to provide uniform bearing for the beams. Posts, either free-standing or in a partition, should not be smaller than 4 x 4 in section, and when they are built up, the members should be securely spiked together.

When solid beams butt at a column, a nominal column dimension of 6 or more inches parallel to the direction of the beams is recommended to provide suitable bearing for the beams. It may be necessary to spike bearing blocks to the column to increase the bearing surface. Columns should not be notched unless extra section is provided.

In two story plank-and-beam construction it is best to cut the studs at the second floor and cap them with a plate to provide bearing for the second-floor beams.

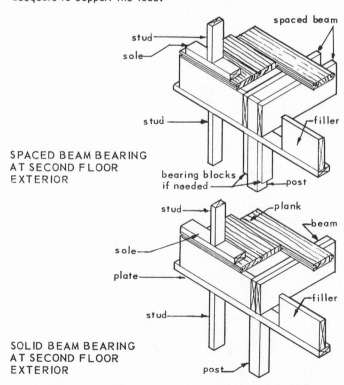

SPACED BEAM BEARING
AT SECOND FLOOR
EXTERIOR

SOLID BEAM BEARING
AT SECOND FLOOR
EXTERIOR

Adopted from data by the National Lumber Manufacturers' Assoc.

Compiled from "Plank-and-Beam System for Residential Construction" — Housing and Home Finance Agency

PLANK and BEAM CONSTRUCTION

It is necessary to have secure connections between the roof beams (or rafters) and the ceiling beams where they converge at the exterior wall.

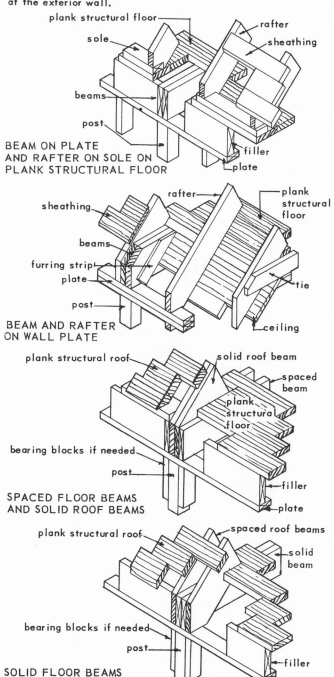

BEAM ON PLATE
AND RAFTER ON SOLE ON
PLANK STRUCTURAL FLOOR

BEAM AND RAFTER
ON WALL PLATE

SPACED FLOOR BEAMS
AND SOLID ROOF BEAMS

SOLID FLOOR BEAMS
AND SPACED ROOF BEAMS

Adopted from data by the National Lumber Manufacturers. Assoc.

Where the ceiling beam serves as a tie, it must be considered as a continuous member in tension. Where these tie beams butt together, they should lap or be spliced together and spiked securely.

Because plank-and-beam framing utilizes larger members, each carrying larger and more highly concentrated loads than members in conventional frame construction, it is absolutely necessary that the connections and fastenings between these larger members be designed accordingly. Structural members must be securely nailed to each other to provide a well integrated structure. It is advised that all connections in a plank-and-beam framing system be thoroughly checked for strength.

Compiled from "Plank-and-Beam System for Residential Construction" — Housing and Home Finance Agency.

INSULATION AND CONDENSATION

Much more study is necessary to select the proper amount and type of insulation and vapor barriers which are to be used in plank-and-beam framing than would be necessary for conventional framing where the insulation is concealed between joists or rafters. In plank-and-beam framing the insulation is either exposed to view on the ceiling, or installed over the planks and under the roofing.

Insulation used on roofs should be sturdy enough to support the weight of men working on it. Since small leaks will develop in any roof, it is best to use an insulation which will not rot, deteriorate, or fall apart when slightly wet, and one whose resistance to the flow of heat is not appreciably lowered by slight wetting.

Condensation on walls and ceilings is caused when moisture-laden warm air comes in contact with a cold surface. This generally occurs in the winter months when there is a great temperature difference between outside and inside.

Warm air can hold more moisture, by weight, than cold air. When warm moist air hits cold air or a cold surface the warm air is cooled to a dew point where it can no longer hold all of its moisture and thus drops particles of its moisture in the form of droplets called condensation.

Therefore, if the moisture in a house is kept to a minimum by exhausting moist air created from such activities as cooking, bathing, laundering, etc. through the use of exhaust fans, this condensation is much less apt to take place since the warm air in the house will contain less moisture.

A dwelling vented in this manner need not have an inside relative humidity of more than 40 or 45 percent at a design temperature of 70 degrees F. If such a condition is achieved vapor barriers may be omitted.

Uncontrolled condensation in a plank-and-beam roof may cause paint to peel, planks to rot, or a blistered and leaky roof.

Insulation installed above roof planks should be thick enough to keep the vapor barrier between the insulation and the roof planks warm enough so that the dew point is reached at the point of the barrier.

If the temperature of the roof planks can be kept close to the air temperature in the room, condensation will not occur. As an additional safeguard it is recommended that a vapor barrier be placed between the roof planks and the insulation to keep the moisture in the warm air from penetrating the insulation.

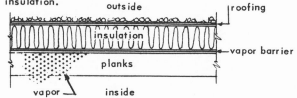

INSULATION AND VAPOR BARRIER

An additional vapor barrier on the underside of the ceiling will prevent the moisture-laden air from penetrating the wood. This additional protection can be provided by applying various finishing materials to the planks. Several types of paint and "natural" wood finishes are to a high degree impervious to vapor. However, ruptures in this protection may occur from the expansion and contraction of the planks.

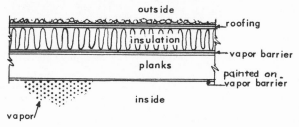

INSULATION AND VAPOR BARRIER

PLANK and BEAM FRAMING

THEORY FOR DESIGN OF PLANKING

All planking computations are based on the use of 2x6 or 2x8 members, tongue-and-grooved or splined, laid flat, and blind and face-nailed. Four jointing types are shown below.

For a good job, well-milled, well-seasoned, straight planks with a moisture content of not more than 14 to 19 percent should be used. Planks should be primed as soon as they are on the job with whatever finish is to be used. After installation of the planking, insulation and roofing should be applied as soon as possible.

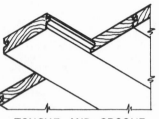

TONGUE-AND-GROOVE

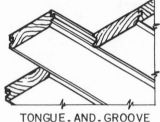

TONGUE-AND-GROOVE WITH V-JOINT

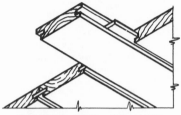

GROOVED AND SPLINED WITH EXPOSED SPLINE

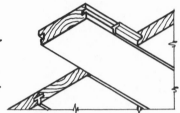

GROOVED PLANK WITH MOLDED SPLINE INSERT

PLANK JOINTING TYPES

Design factors to consider are:
1. Strength of the planks to carry an evenly distributed live load plus an allowance of 10 lbs. per sq. ft. dead load, or weight of the materials.
2. Stiffness to overcome objectionable deflections.

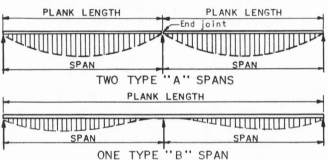

TWO TYPE "A" SPANS

ONE TYPE "B" SPAN

DEFLECTION DIAGRAMS FOR EVENLY DISTRIBUTED LOADS

Plank-and-beam framing becomes structurally more efficient when continuous spans are used to develop extra strength.

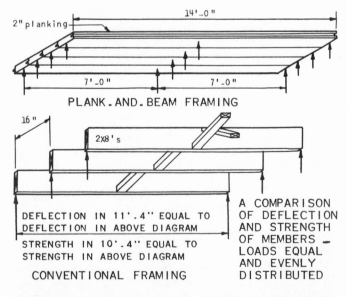

PLANK-AND-BEAM FRAMING

DEFLECTION IN 11'-4" EQUAL TO DEFLECTION IN ABOVE DIAGRAM

STRENGTH IN 10'-4" EQUAL TO STRENGTH IN ABOVE DIAGRAM

CONVENTIONAL FRAMING

A COMPARISON OF DEFLECTION AND STRENGTH OF MEMBERS — LOADS EQUAL AND EVENLY DISTRIBUTED

Beams designed as continuous must be built as such or serious failure of members will result. It is recommended that careful inspection of construction be made in all cases where plank-and-beam framing is used.

For any number of spans desired the planking can be laid out in one of the following ways.

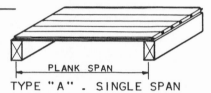

TYPE "A" - SINGLE SPAN

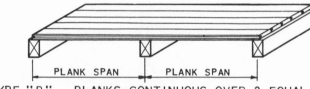

TYPE "B" - PLANKS CONTINUOUS OVER 2 EQUAL SPANS (Nearly 2½ times as stiff as Type "A")

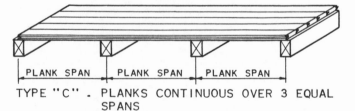

TYPE "C" - PLANKS CONTINUOUS OVER 3 EQUAL SPANS

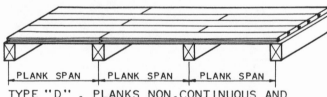

TYPE "D" - PLANKS NON-CONTINUOUS AND STAGGERED OVER 3 EQUAL SPANS

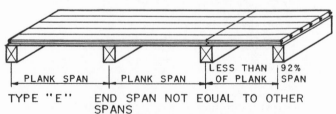

TYPE "E"   END SPAN NOT EQUAL TO OTHER SPANS

PLANK SPANNING TYPES

If the end span is less than 92% of other plank spans, TYPE E should be used. If the end span is greater than 92%, TYPE D should be used.

Compiled from "Plank-and-Beam System for Residential Construction" — Housing and Home Finance Agency

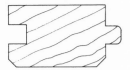

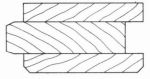

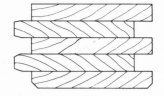

TONGUE & GROOVE

SIZES

NOMINAL	ACTUAL
2 × 6	1⁵/₈ × 5 FACE
2 × 8	1⁵/₈ × 7 FACE

V GROOVE

SIZES

NOMINAL	ACTUAL
3 × 6	2⁵/₈ × 5¹/₄ FACE
4 × 6	3¹/₂ × 5¹/₄ FACE

STRIATED

LAMINATED

SIZES

NOMINAL	ACTUAL
3 × 6,8,10	2¹/₄ × 5¹/₂,7¹/₂,9¹/₂
3(SUPER THICK) × 6,8	2⁵/₈ × 5¹/₂,7¹/₂
4 × 6,8	3¹/₁₆ × 5¹/₂,7¹/₂
5 × 6,8	3¹³/₁₆ × 5¹/₂,7¹/₂

TYPES OF WOOD DECKING

INSULATION FACTORS (U) BTU/HR., SQ. FT., DEGREE F.

SPECIES	DECK THICKNESS		INSULATION THICKNESS				
	NOM.	ACT.	O	1/2"	1"	11/2"	2"
INLAND RED CEDAR	3"	2¹/₄"	.24	.18	.14	.12	.10
	3" (super)	2⁵/₈"	.22	.16	.13	.12	.10
	4"	3¹/₁₆"	.19	.15	.12	.11	.09
	5"	3¹³/₁₆"	.15	.13	.11	.09	.08
SOUTHERN YELLOW PINE DOUGLAS FIR/LARCH	3"	2¹/₄"	.30	.21	.16	.13	.11
	3" (super)	2⁵/₈"	.27	.20	.15	.12	.10
	4"	3¹/₁₆"	.24	.18	.14	.12	.10
	5"	3¹³/₁₆"	.20	.15	.13	.11	.10
WHITE FIR IDAHO WHITE PINE	3"	2¹/₄"	.27	.19	.15	.12	.11
	3" (super)	2⁵/₈"	.24	.18	.14	.12	.11
	4"	3¹/₁₆"	.21	.16	.13	.11	.10
	5"	3¹³/₁₆"	.17	.14	.12	.10	.09

2 SPIKES PER PLANK AT BEAM

LAMINATED-SLANT NAILED 45° 30" O.C.

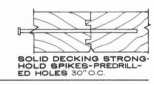

SOLID DECKING STRONG-HOLD SPIKES-PREDRILL-ED HOLES 30"O.C.

NAILING DECKING

WOOD DECKING DESIGN CHART—ALLOWABLE UNIFORMLY DISTRIBUTED TOTAL ROOF LOADS-PSF

THICKNESS	SPAN IN FEET	INLAND RED CEDAR E=1,200,000PSI F=950				IDAHO WHITE FIR INLAND WHITE FIR E=1,500,000PSI F=950				DOUGLAS FIR/LARCH SOUTHERN YELLOW PINE E=1,800,000PSI F=1635			
		BENDING		DEFLECTION		BENDING		DEFLECTION		BENDING		DEFLECTION	
		SIMPLE	CONTIN.	SIMPLE 1/240	CONTIN. 1/240	SIMPLE	CONTIN.	SIMPLE 1/240	CONTIN. 1/240	SIMPLE	CONTIN.	SIMPLE 1/240	CONTIN. 1/240
3"	10	62	52	30	45	62	52	37	52	106	88	44	67
	11	51	42	22	34	51	42	28	42	88	73	33	50
	12	43	36	17	26	43	36	22	33	74	61	26	39
	13	37	30	13	20	37	30	17	25	63	52	20	30
	14	31	26	11	16	31	26	13	20	54	45	16	24
	15	27	23	9	13	27	23	11	17	47	39	13	20
3" (superthick)	10	85	71	47	71	85	71	59	71	147	122	71	107
	11	70	59	36	54	70	59	44	59	121	101	53	80
	12	59	50	27	41	59	50	34	50	102	85	41	62
	13	51	42	22	33	51	42	27	40	87	72	32	49
	14	44	36	17	26	44	36	22	33	75	62	26	39
	15	38	31	14	21	38	31	18	27	65	54	21	32
	16	33	28	12	17	33	28	14	23	57	48	17	26
4"	10	114	96	74	96	114	96	93	96	197	164	111	164
	11	95	78	56	78	95	78	70	78	163	136	84	126
	12	80	67	43	65	80	67	53	67	137	114	64	97
	13	68	56	34	51	68	56	43	56	116	97	51	77
	14	58	48	27	41	58	48	34	48	100	84	41	61
	15	51	42	22	33	51	42	28	42	87	73	33	50
	16	44	38	18	27	44	38	23	34	77	64	27	41
	17	40	33	15	23	40	33	19	28	68	57	23	34
	18	35	29	13	19	35	29	16	24	61	51	19	29
	19	31	27	11	16	31	27	13	21	55	45	16	25
5"	10	178	150	144	150	178	150	178	150	307	256	215	256
	11	148	123	108	123	148	123	135	123	254	212	162	212
	12	124	104	83	104	124	104	104	104	213	178	125	178
	13	106	88	65	88	106	88	82	88	182	152	98	148
	14	91	76	52	76	91	76	66	76	157	131	79	119
	15	79	66	43	64	79	66	53	66	137	114	64	96
	16	69	59	35	53	69	59	44	59	120	100	53	79
	17	62	52	29	44	62	52	37	52	106	89	44	66
	18	56	45	25	37	56	45	31	45	95	79	37	56
	19	49	42	21	32	49	42	26	39	85	71	31	47
	20	44	37	18	27	44	37	23	34	77	64	27	41

Joseph A. Wilkes, AIA; Wilkes and Faulkner; Washington, D. C.

STANDARD MILL CONSTRUCTION

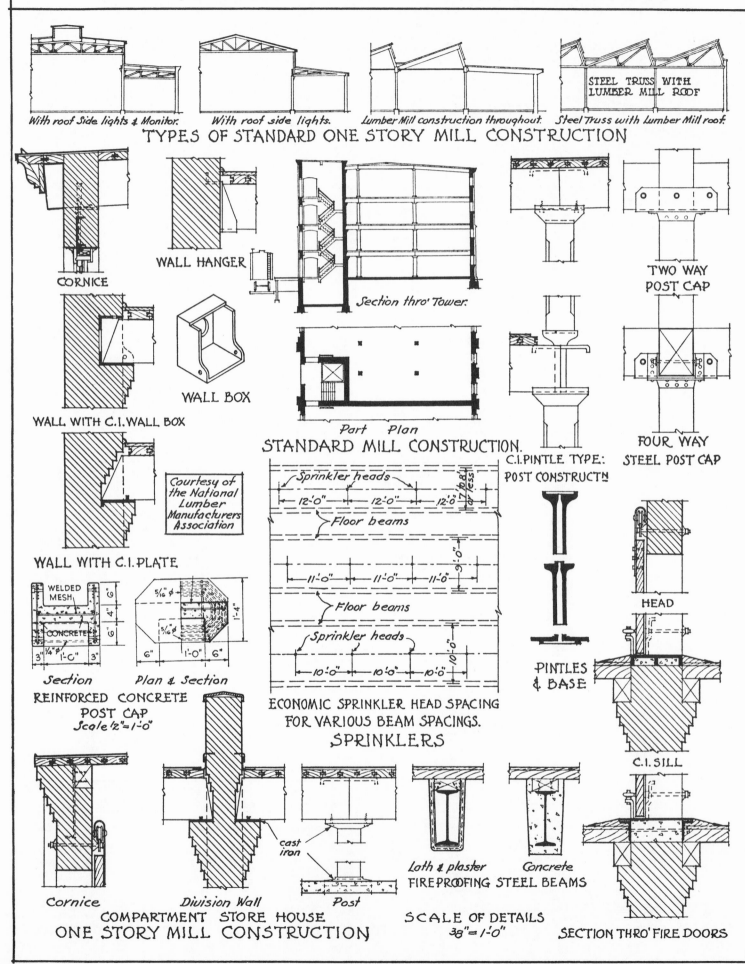

With roof Side lights & Monitor.   With roof side lights.   Lumber Mill construction throughout.   Steel Truss with Lumber Mill roof.

STEEL TRUSS WITH LUMBER MILL ROOF

TYPES OF STANDARD ONE STORY MILL CONSTRUCTION

CORNICE

WALL HANGER

Section thro' Tower.

TWO WAY POST CAP

WALL WITH C.I. WALL BOX

WALL BOX

Part   Plan

STANDARD MILL CONSTRUCTION.

FOUR WAY STEEL POST CAP

Courtesy of the National Lumber Manufacturers Association

WALL WITH C.I. PLATE

C.I. PINTLE TYPE: POST CONSTRUCT'N

HEAD

WELDED MESH
CONCRETE

Section   Plan & Section

REINFORCED CONCRETE POST CAP
Scale 1½"=1'-0"

Sprinkler heads
12'-0"   12'-0"   12'-0"   17 to 8' or less
Floor beams
11'-0"   11'-0"   11'-0"   9'-0"
Floor beams
Sprinkler heads
10'-0"   10'-0"   10'-0"   10'-0"

ECONOMIC SPRINKLER HEAD SPACING FOR VARIOUS BEAM SPACINGS.

SPRINKLERS

PINTLES & BASE

C.I. SILL

Cornice   Division Wall   Post
cast iron

Loth & plaster   Concrete
FIREPROOFING STEEL BEAMS

COMPARTMENT STORE HOUSE

SCALE OF DETAILS
3/8"=1'-0"

ONE STORY MILL CONSTRUCTION

SECTION THRO' FIRE DOORS

STANDARD MILL CONSTRUCTION

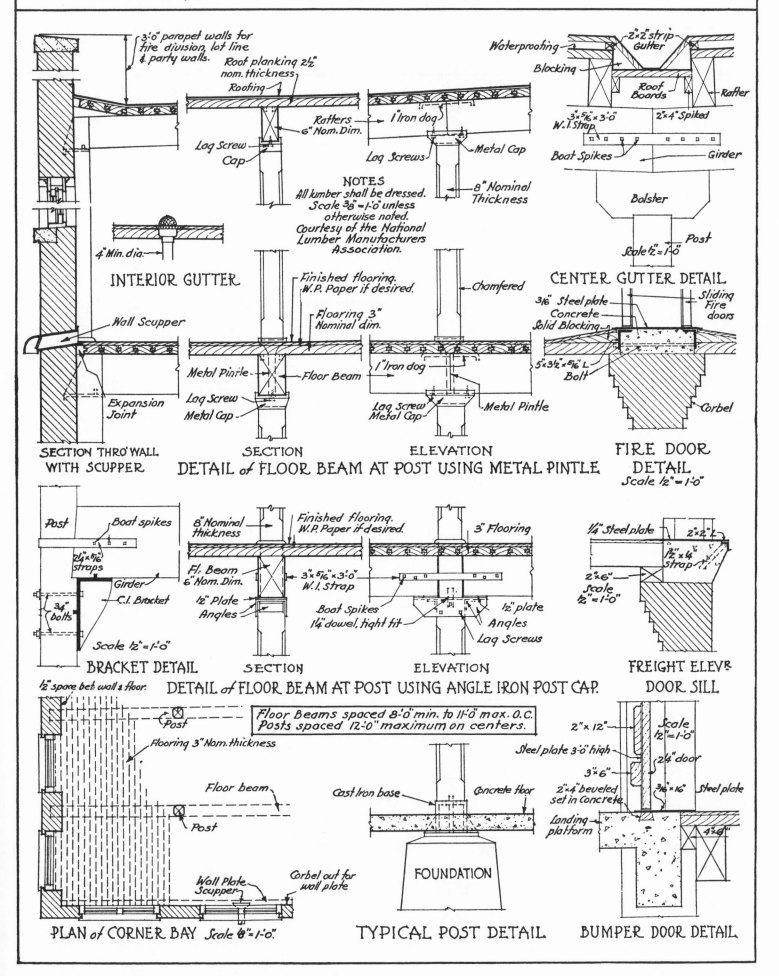

3'-0" parapet walls for fire division, lot line & party walls.

Roof planking 2½" nom. thickness

Roofing

Waterproofing

2"x2" strip Gutter

Blocking

Roof Boards

Rafter

Rafters 6" Nom. Dim.

1" Iron dog

3"x5/16"x3'-0" W.I. Strap

2"x4" Spiked

Lag Screw Cap

Metal Cap

Boat Spikes

Girder

Lag Screws

8" Nominal Thickness

Bolster

NOTES
All lumber shall be dressed.
Scale ⅜" = 1'-0" unless otherwise noted.
Courtesy of the National Lumber Manufacturers Association.

Scale ½" = 1'-0"

Post

4" Min. dia.

INTERIOR GUTTER

Finished flooring. W.P. Paper if desired.

Chamfered

CENTER GUTTER DETAIL

3/16" Steel plate

Sliding Fire doors

Wall Scupper

Flooring 3" Nominal dim.

Concrete

Solid Blocking

Metal Pintle

Floor Beam

1" Iron dog

5"x3½"x5/16" L

Bolt

Lag Screw
Metal Cap

Expansion Joint

Lag Screw
Metal Cap

Metal Pintle

Corbel

SECTION THRO' WALL WITH SCUPPER

SECTION

ELEVATION

FIRE DOOR DETAIL
Scale ½" = 1'-0"

DETAIL of FLOOR BEAM AT POST USING METAL PINTLE

Post

Boat spikes

8" Nominal thickness

Finished flooring. W.P. Paper if desired.

3" Flooring

¼" Steel plate

2"x2" L

2¼"x5/16" straps

Fl. Beam 6" Nom. Dim.

3"x5/16"x3'-0" W.I. Strap

1½"x4" strap

Girder

½" Plate Angles

C.I. Bracket

Boat Spikes

1¼" dowel, tight fit

2"x6"

Scale ½" = 1'-0"

¾" bolts

½" plate Angles

Lag Screws

Scale ½" = 1'-0"

BRACKET DETAIL

SECTION

ELEVATION

FREIGHT ELEV.R DOOR SILL

DETAIL of FLOOR BEAM AT POST USING ANGLE IRON POST CAP.

½" space bet. wall & floor.

Floor Beams spaced 8'-0" min. to 11'-0" max. O.C.
Posts spaced 12'-0" maximum on centers.

Post

2"x12"

Scale ½" = 1'-0"

Flooring 3" Nom. thickness

Steel plate 3'-0" high

2¼" door

Floor beam

3"x6"

Post

Cast Iron base

Concrete floor

2"x4" beveled set in Concrete

3/16"x16"

Steel plate

Landing platform

Wall Plate Scupper

Corbel out for wall plate

4"x6"

PLAN of CORNER BAY Scale 6" = 1'-0"

TYPICAL POST DETAIL

FOUNDATION

BUMPER DOOR DETAIL

SEMI-MILL CONSTRUCTION

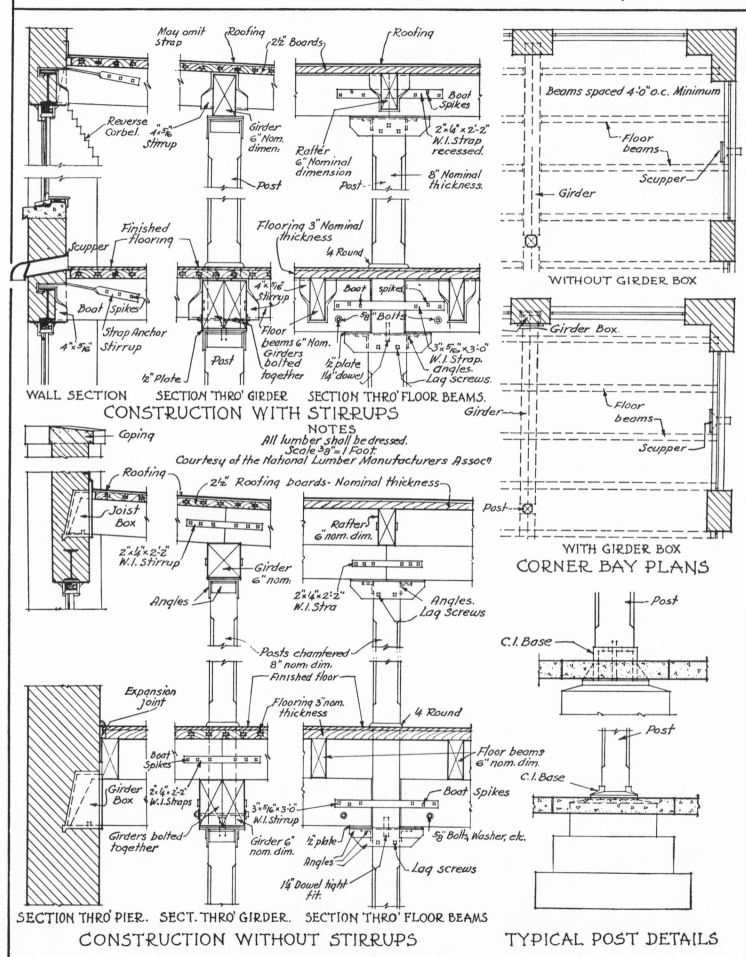

May omit strap

Roofing

2½" Boards

Roofing

Boat Spikes

2"×4"×2'-2" W.I.Strap recessed.

Reverse Corbel.

4"×5/16" Stirrup

Girder 6" Nom. dimen.

Rafter 6" Nominal dimension

8" Nominal thickness.

Post

Post

Finished flooring

Flooring 3" Nominal thickness

4 Round

Scupper

Boat spikes

Boat Spikes

4"×5/16" Stirrup

⅝" Bolts

Strap Anchor Stirrup

Floor beams 6" Nom.

3"×5/16"×3'-0" W.I.Strap.

4"×5/16"

Girders bolted together

½ plate 1¼" dowel

Angles. Lag screws.

½" Plate

Post

WALL SECTION   **SECTION THRO' GIRDER**   **SECTION THRO' FLOOR BEAMS.**

CONSTRUCTION WITH STIRRUPS

NOTES
All lumber shall be dressed.
Scale ⅜" = 1 Foot.
Courtesy of the National Lumber Manufacturers Assocⁿ.

Coping

Roofing

2½" Roofing boards - Nominal thickness

Joist Box

Rafter 6" nom. dim.

2"×4"×2'-2" W.I.Stirrup

Girder 6" nom.

Angles

2"×4"×2'-2" W.I. Stra

Angles. Lag Screws

Posts chamfered 8" nom. dim.

Finished floor

Expansion Joint

Flooring 3" nom. thickness

4 Round

Boat Spikes

Floor beams 6" nom. dim.

Girder Box

2"×4"×2'-2" W.I.Straps

3"×5/16"×3'-0" W.I.Shirrup

Boat Spikes

Girders bolted together

Girder 6" nom. dim.

½ plate

⅝" Bolts, Washer, etc.

Angles

Lag screws

1¼" Dowel tight fit.

SECTION THRO' PIER.   SECT. THRO' GIRDER.   SECTION THRO' FLOOR BEAMS

CONSTRUCTION WITHOUT STIRRUPS

Beams spaced 4'-0" o.c. Minimum

Floor beams

Scupper

Girder

WITHOUT GIRDER BOX

Girder Box.

Floor beams

Scupper

Girder

Post

WITH GIRDER BOX

CORNER BAY PLANS

Post

C.I. Base

Post

C.I. Base

TYPICAL POST DETAILS

LAMINATED MILL CONSTRUCTION

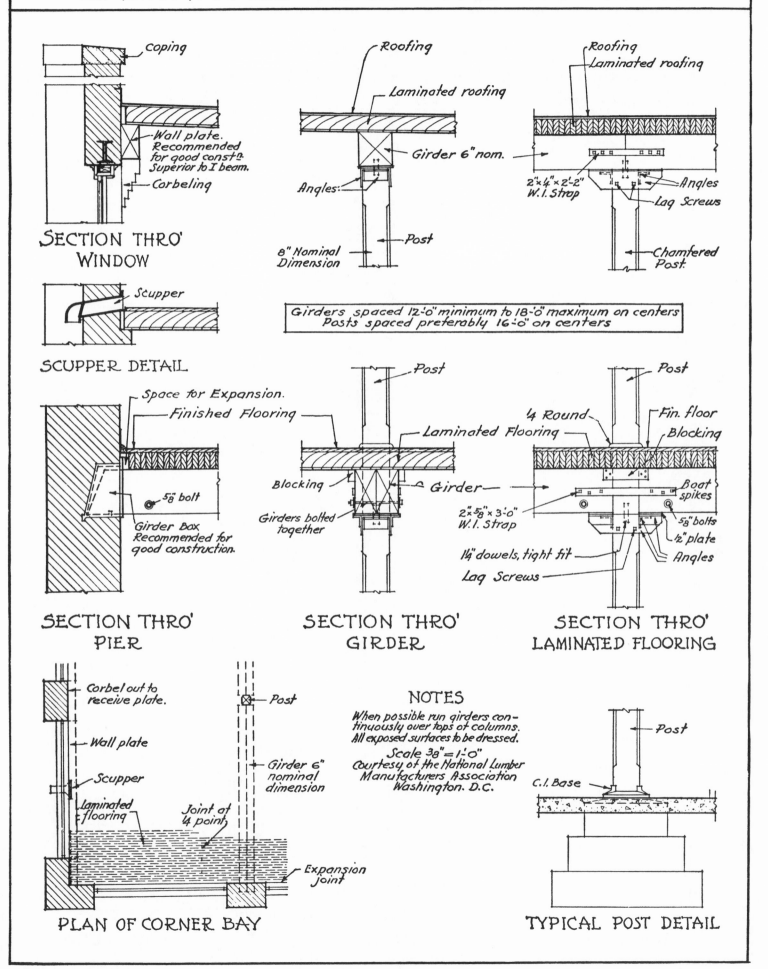

coping

Wall plate.
Recommended
for good constn.
Superior to I beam.

Corbeling

**SECTION THRO'
WINDOW**

Roofing

Laminated roofing

Girder 6" nom.

Angles:

Post

8" Nominal
Dimension

Roofing
Laminated roofing

2"x4"x2'-2"
W.I. Strap

Angles

Lag Screws

Chamfered
Post.

Scupper

SCUPPER DETAIL

Girders spaced 12'-0" minimum to 18'-0" maximum on centers
Posts spaced preferably 16'-0" on centers

Space for Expansion.
Finished Flooring

⅝" bolt

Girder Box
Recommended for
good construction.

**SECTION THRO'
PIER**

Post

Laminated Flooring

Blocking

Girder

Girders bolted
together

**SECTION THRO'
GIRDER**

Post

¼ Round

Fin. floor

Blocking

Boat
spikes

2"x⅝"x3'-0"
W.I. Strap

⅝"bolts

1¼" dowels, tight fit

½" plate

Lag Screws

Angles

**SECTION THRO'
LAMINATED FLOORING**

Corbel out to
receive plate.

Wall plate

Scupper

Laminated
flooring

Post

Girder 6"
nominal
dimension

Joint at
¼ point

Expansion
joint

PLAN OF CORNER BAY

NOTES

When possible run girders continuously over tops of columns.
All exposed surfaces to be dressed.

Scale ⅜"=1'-0"
Courtesy of the National Lumber
Manufacturers Association
Washington. D.C.

Post

C.I. Base

TYPICAL POST DETAIL

FRAME WALLS

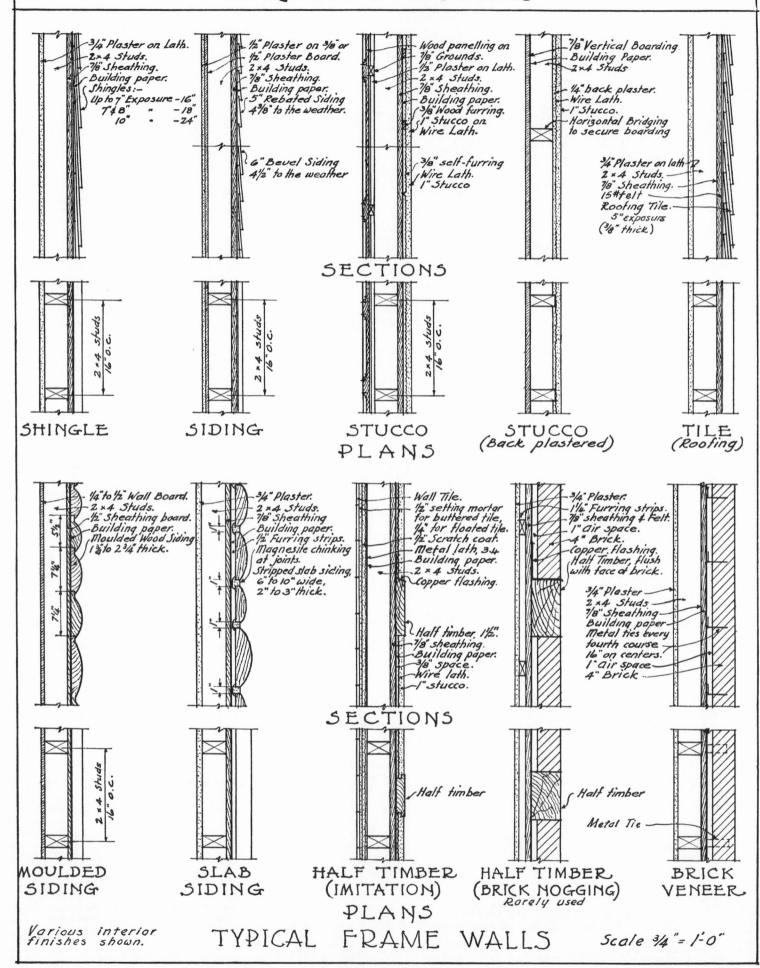

SECTIONS

¾" Plaster on Lath.
2×4 Studs.
⅞" Sheathing.
Building paper.
Shingles:–
  Up to 7" Exposure –16"
  7&8"   "   –18"
  10"   "   –24"

½" Plaster on ⅜ or
½" Plaster Board.
2×4 Studs.
⅞" Sheathing.
Building paper.
5" Rebated Siding
4⅜" to the weather.

6" Bevel Siding
4½" to the weather

Wood panelling on
⅞" Grounds.
½" Plaster on Lath.
2×4 Studs.
⅞" Sheathing.
Building paper.
⅜" Wood furring.
1" Stucco on
Wire Lath.

⅜" self-furring
Wire Lath.
1" Stucco

⅞" Vertical Boarding.
Building Paper.
2×4 Studs

¼" back plaster.
Wire Lath.
1" Stucco.
Horizontal Bridging
to secure boarding

¾" Plaster on lath.
2×4 Studs.
⅞" Sheathing.
15# felt
Roofing Tile.
  5" Exposure
  (⅜" thick)

PLANS

2×4 Studs
16" O.C.

2×4 Studs
16" O.C.

2×4 Studs
16" O.C.

SHINGLE   SIDING   STUCCO   STUCCO   TILE
                                                 (Back plastered) (Roofing)

SECTIONS

¼" to ½" Wall Board.
2×4 Studs.
½" Sheathing board.
Building paper.
Moulded Wood Siding
1¾" to 2¾" thick.

5½"
7¼"
7¼"

¾" Plaster.
2×4 Studs.
⅞" Sheathing
Building paper.
½" Furring strips.
Magnesite chinking
at joints.
Stripped slab siding,
6" to 10" wide,
2" to 3" thick.

Wall Tile.
½" setting mortar
for buttered tile,
¼" for floated tile.
½" Scratch coat.
Metal lath, 3.4.
Building paper.
2×4 Studs.
Copper flashing.

Half timber, 1½".
⅞" sheathing.
Building paper.
⅜" space.
Wire lath.
1" stucco.

¾" Plaster.
1¼" Furring strips.
⅞" sheathing & felt.
1" Air space.
4" Brick.
Copper flashing.
Half Timber, flush
with face of brick.

¾" Plaster
2×4 Studs.
⅞" Sheathing
Building paper.
Metal ties every
fourth course
16" on centers.
1" air space
4" Brick.

PLANS

2×4 Studs
16" O.C.

Half timber

Half timber

Metal Tie

MOULDED   SLAB   HALF TIMBER   HALF TIMBER   BRICK
SIDING   SIDING   (IMITATION)   (BRICK NOGGING)   VENEER
                                                    Rarely used

Various interior   TYPICAL FRAME WALLS   Scale ¾"= 1'-0"
finishes shown.

SHEATHING on WOOD FRAMING

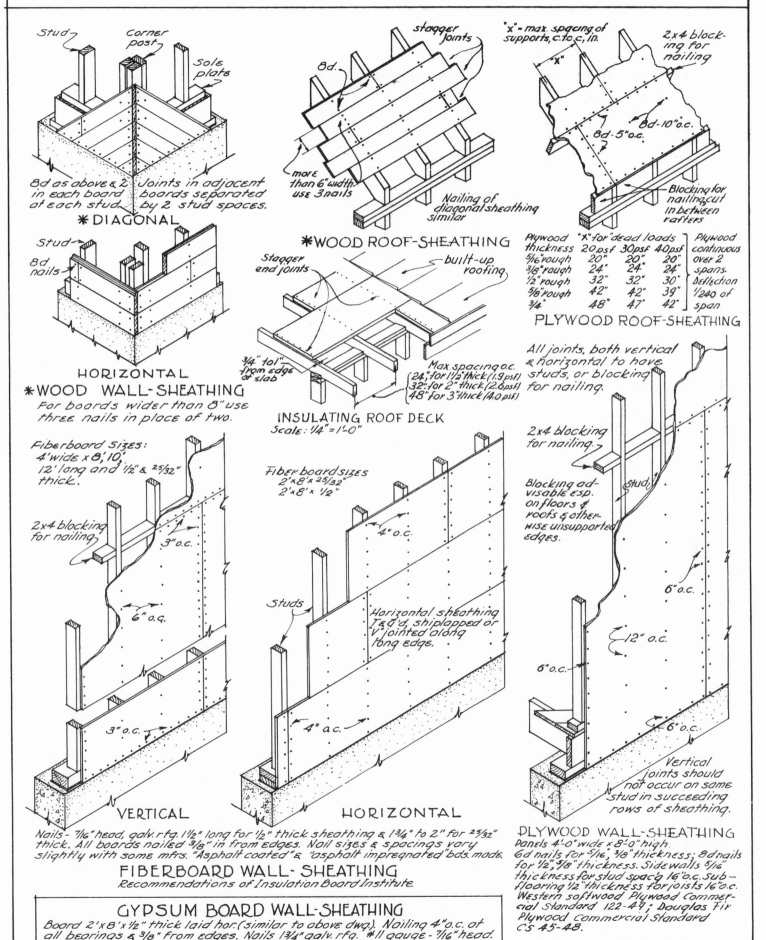

8d as above & 2 in each board at each stud. Joints in adjacent boards separated by 2 stud spaces.

*DIAGONAL

Nailing of diagonal sheathing similar

more than 6" width use 3 nails

*WOOD ROOF-SHEATHING

"x" = max. spacing of supports, c. to c., in.

2x4 blocking for nailing

8d-10" o.c.

8d-5" o.c.

Blocking for nailing, cut in between rafters

Plywood thickness	"x" for dead loads			Plywood
	20 psf	30 psf	40 psf	continuous over 2 spans.
5/16 rough	20"	20"	20"	Deflection 1/240 of span
3/8 rough	24"	24"	24"	
1/2 rough	32"	32"	30"	
5/8 rough	42"	42"	39"	
3/4	48"	47"	42"	

PLYWOOD ROOF-SHEATHING

HORIZONTAL

*WOOD WALL-SHEATHING

For boards wider than 8" use three nails in place of two.

Stagger end joints

built-up roofing

3/4" to 1" from edge of slab

Max. spacing o.c. 24" for 1½" thick (1.9 psf) 32" for 2" thick (2.6 psf) 48" for 3" thick (4.0 psf)

INSULATING ROOF DECK
Scale: ¼"=1'-0"

All joints, both vertical & horizontal to have studs, or blocking for nailing.

Fiberboard Sizes: 4' wide x 8', 10', 12' long and ½" & 25/32" thick.

2x4 blocking for nailing

3" o.c.

6" o.c.

3" o.c.

Fiber board sizes 2'x8'x 25/32" 2'x8'x ½"

Studs

4" o.c.

4" o.c.

Horizontal sheathing T & G'd, shiplapped or "V"-jointed along long edge.

2x4 blocking for nailing.

Blocking advisable esp. on floors & roofs & otherwise unsupported edges.

6" o.c.

12" o.c.

6" o.c.

6" o.c.

Vertical joints should not occur on same stud in succeeding rows of sheathing.

VERTICAL

HORIZONTAL

PLYWOOD WALL-SHEATHING
Panels 4'-0" wide x 8'-0" high. 6d nails for 5/16, 3/8 thickness; 8d nails for ½", 5/8 thickness. Sidewalls 5/16 thickness for stud spacg 16" o.c. Subflooring ½" thickness for joists 16" o.c. Western softwood Plywood Commercial Standard 122-49; Douglas Fir Plywood Commercial Standard CS 45-48.

Nails - 7/16" head, galv. rfg. 1½" long for ½" thick sheathing & 1¾" to 2" for 25/32" thick. All boards nailed 3/8" in from edges. Nail sizes & spacings vary slightly with some mfrs. "Asphalt coated" & "asphalt impregnated" bds. made.

FIBERBOARD WALL-SHEATHING
Recommendations of Insulation Board Institute

GYPSUM BOARD WALL-SHEATHING
Board 2'x8'x½" thick laid hor. (similar to above dwg.). Nailing 4"o.c. at all bearings & 3/8" from edges. Nails 1¾" galv. rfg. #11 gauge - 7/16" head.

Data checked by Insulation Board Institute - Scale; 3/8"=1'-0" except as noted.
*Data developed from "Technique of House Nailing, Nov. 1947, Housing & Home Finance Agency, Washington, D.C.

WOOD SIDING

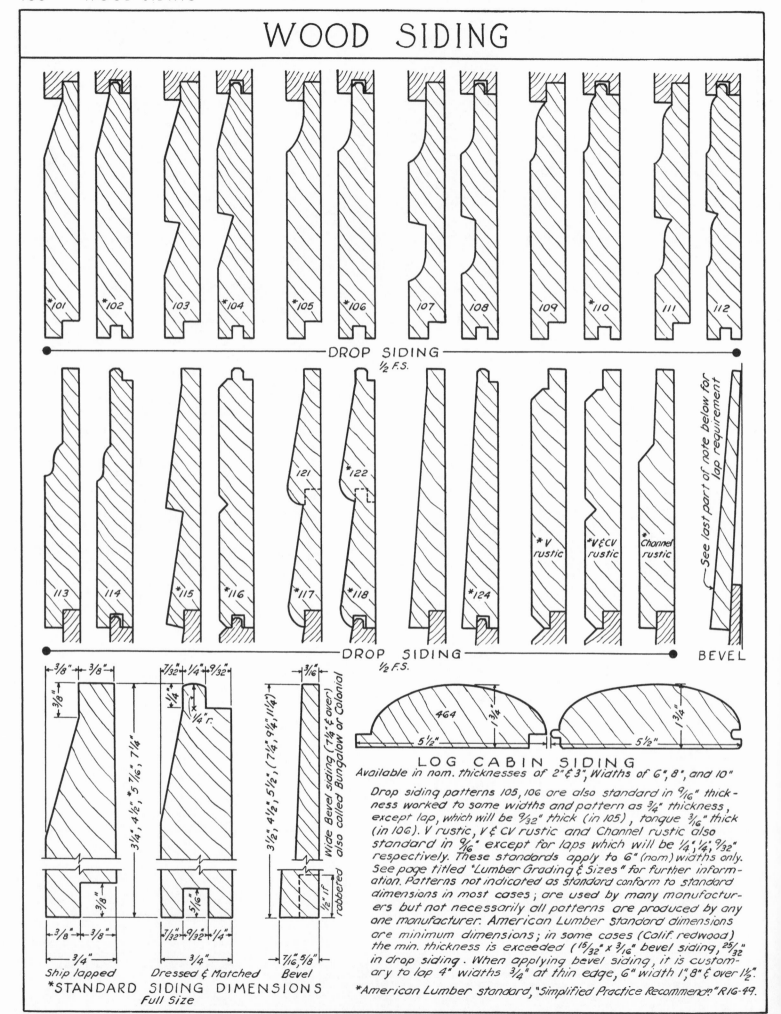

DROP SIDING
1/2 F.S.

*101 *102 103 *104 105 *106 107 108 109 *110 111 112

DROP SIDING
1/2 F.S.

113 114 *115 *116 *117 *118 *124 *V rustic *V & CV rustic *Channel rustic

121 122

See last part of note below for lap requirement

BEVEL

Ship lapped   Dressed & Matched   Bevel

*STANDARD SIDING DIMENSIONS
Full Size

Wide Bevel siding (7 1/4" & over) also called Bungalow or Colonial

LOG CABIN SIDING
Available in nom. thicknesses of 2" & 3", Widths of 6", 8", and 10"

Drop siding patterns 105, 106 are also standard in 9/16" thickness worked to same widths and pattern as 3/4" thickness, except lap, which will be 9/32" thick (in 105), tongue 3/16" thick (in 106). V rustic, V & CV rustic and Channel rustic also standard in 9/16" except for laps which will be 1/4", 1/4", 9/32" respectively. These standards apply to 6" (nom) widths only. See page titled "Lumber Grading & Sizes" for further information. Patterns not indicated as standard conform to standard dimensions in most cases; are used by many manufacturers but not necessarily all patterns are produced by any one manufacturer. American Lumber standard dimensions are minimum dimensions; in some cases (Calif. redwood) the min. thickness is exceeded (15/32" x 3/16" bevel siding, 25/32" in drop siding. When applying bevel siding, it is customary to lap 4" widths 3/4" at thin edge, 6" width 1", 8" & over 1 1/2".

*American Lumber standard, "Simplified Practice Recommend?" R16-49.

WOOD DOORS and FRAMES - STOCK

STANDARD SIZES
INTERIOR DOORS

Ponderosa Pine:

- 1'-6" × {6'-6", 6'-8"}
- {2'-0", 2'-4", 2'-6", 2'-8"} × {6'-0", 6'-6", 6'-8", 7'-0"}
- 3'-0 × {6'-8", 7'-0"}

Douglas Fir:

- {1'-6", 1'-8", 1'-10"} × {6'-6", 6'-8", 7'-0"}
- {2'-0", 2'-4", 2'-6", 2'-8", 2'-10, 3'-0} × {6'-0", 6'-6", 6'-8", 6'-10", 7'-0"}
- 2'-6" × 6'-4"
- {3'-4", 3'-6"} × 7'-0"

EXTERIOR DOORS

Ponderosa Pine:

- {2'-8", 3'-0", 3'-4"} × {6'-8", 7'-0"}

Douglas Fir:

- 2'-6" × 6'-6"
- 2'-8" × 6'-8"
- 2'-10" × 6'-10"
- 3'-0" × 7'-0"

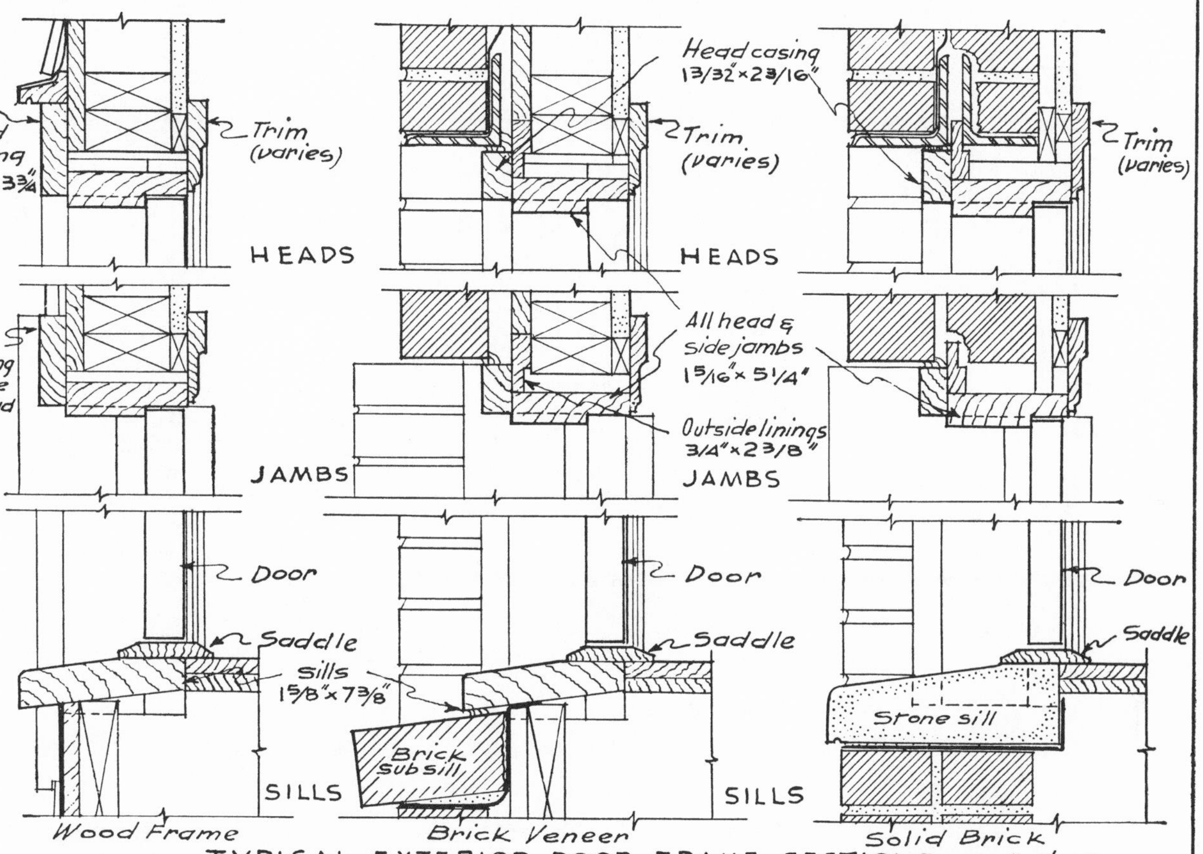
Head casing 13/32"×33/4"
Trim (varies)
HEADS
Side casing same as head
JAMBS
Door
Saddle
Sills 15/8"×73/8"
SILLS
Wood Frame
Head casing 13/32"×23/16"
Trim (varies)
HEADS
All head & side jambs 15/16"×51/4"
Outside linings 3/4"×23/8"
JAMBS
Door
Saddle
Brick sub sill
SILLS
Brick Veneer
Trim (varies)
Door
Saddle
Stone sill
Solid Brick

TYPICAL EXTERIOR DOOR FRAME SECTIONS 1½"=1'-0"

STD. THICKNESS INTERIOR DOORS
All 1⅜" & 1¾" except pine doors 2'-4" wide & less which are 1⅜"
EXTERIOR DOORS
All 1⅜" & 1¾" except pine 3'-4" wide = 1¾" only. Storm screen & combination = 1⅛"

Insert frame
I N T E R I O R D O O R S

Pine (CS 120-49)	# 99		# 100		# 101		# 102		# 106		# 107		# 108*		# 111*	
Fir (CS 73-49)		# 33		# 20		# 1		# 82		# 44		# 5		# 66		# 2080
Stile & Top Rail	4¾"	4 9/16"	4¾	4 9/16	4¼•"	4 9/16"	4¾"	4 9/16"	4¾"	4 9/16"	4¾	4 9/16"	4¾"	4 9/16"	4¾"	Entrance door sizes only
Lock Rail							8"	8"	8"	8"			8"	8"	8"	
Intermed. Rails	4⅝"	4½"									4⅝"	4½"	3⅞"	4½"	3⅞"	
Muntins (Vert.)									4⅝"	4½"			3⅞"	4½"	3⅞"	
Bottom Rail	9⅝"	9⅜"	9⅝"	9⅜"	9¼•" & 9½"	9⅜"	9⅝"	9⅜"	9⅝"	9⅜"	9⅝"	9⅜"	9⅝"	9⅜"	9⅝"	

•Face measure * also exterior #(110, 112)

ENTRANCE DOORS

Stock standard types in pine & fir. Thickness 1¾" only. Heights: 6'-8" & 7'-0". Pine widths 2'-8", 3'-0" & 3'-4", Fir 3'-0". Other standard types available. Std. thickness 1¾"

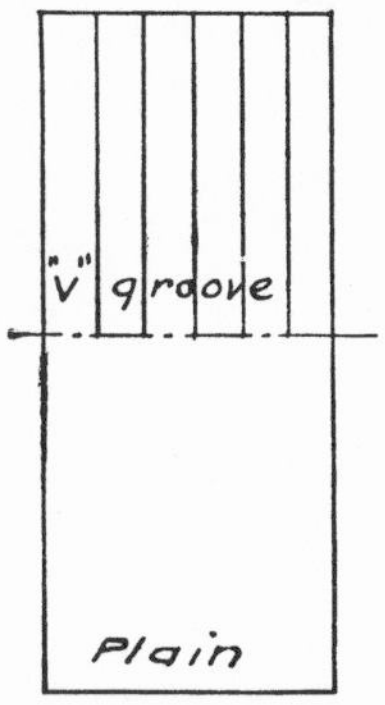
"V" groove
Plain

FLUSH DOORS

1¾" thick & in all exterior and interior sizes

EXTERIOR DOORS

Typical standard types in pine and fir. Various other types stocked.

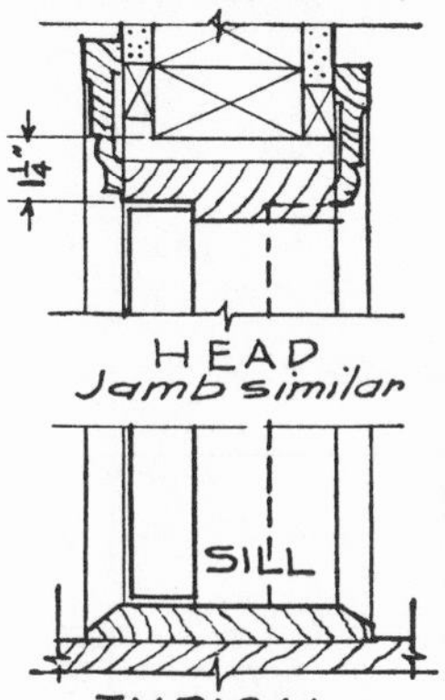
1¼"
HEAD
Jamb similar
SILL

TYPICAL INTERIOR DOOR FRAME

WOOD WINDOW & DOOR DETAILS

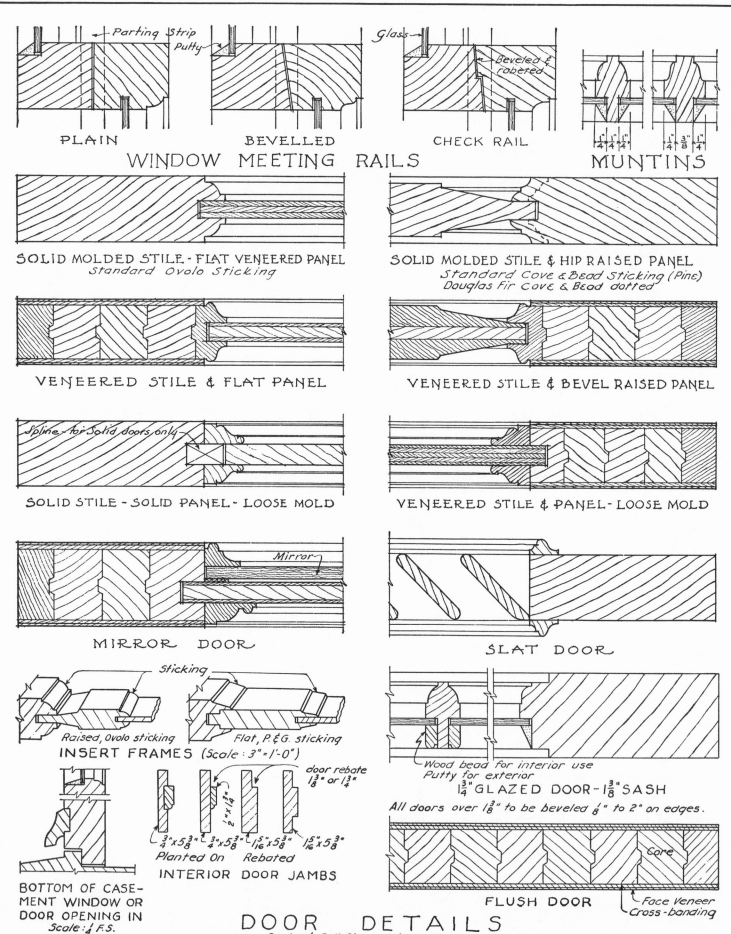

PLAIN   BEVELLED   CHECK RAIL

Parting Strip
Putty
Glass
Beveled & rebeted

WINDOW MEETING RAILS   MUNTINS

SOLID MOLDED STILE - FLAT VENEERED PANEL
Standard Ovolo Sticking

SOLID MOLDED STILE & HIP RAISED PANEL
Standard Cove & Bead Sticking (Pine)
Douglas Fir Cove & Bead dotted

VENEERED STILE & FLAT PANEL

VENEERED STILE & BEVEL RAISED PANEL

Spline - for Solid doors only

SOLID STILE - SOLID PANEL - LOOSE MOLD

VENEERED STILE & PANEL - LOOSE MOLD

Mirror

MIRROR DOOR

SLAT DOOR

Sticking

Raised, Ovolo sticking   *Flat, P.&G. sticking*

INSERT FRAMES *(Scale : 3" = 1'-0")*

Wood bead for interior use
Putty for exterior
1 3/4" GLAZED DOOR - 1 3/8" SASH

All doors over 1 3/8" to be beveled 1/8" to 2" on edges.

door rebate
1 3/8" or 1 3/4"
1" x 1 3/4"
2" x 1 3/4"
3/4" x 5 3/8"   3/4" x 5 3/8"   5/16" x 5 3/8"   1 1/2" x 5 3/8"
Planted On   *Rebated*
INTERIOR DOOR JAMBS

Core

BOTTOM OF CASE-
MENT WINDOW OR
DOOR OPENING IN
Scale : 1/4 F.S.

FLUSH DOOR

Face Veneer
Cross-banding

DOOR DETAILS
Scale : 1/2 Full Size, Unless Noted

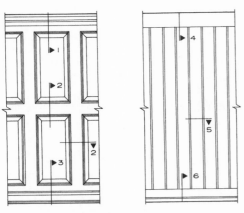

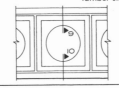

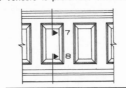

NOTES

1. For flush plywood paneling refer to interior plywood pages.
2. For fire protection refer to local and state building codes. Fire retardant classifications determined by tunnel test (ASTM #-84) and flame spread are considered the most important:
   Class I   (A)   0-25.
   Class II   (B)   26-75.
   Class III (C)   76-200.
   Since treated lumber can discolor considerably, treated core veneered construction with untreated face veneers is preferred. Conventional nitrocellu-lose lacquers increase flame spread. Conversion varnish or a similar catalyzed finish is neutral in flame spread.
3. For acoustics refer to acoustical pages. Generally, slats have higher sound absorption coefficients than flat panels.
4. For specification of architectural woodwork refer to Architectural Woodworking Institute (AWI) Quality Standard: lumber grades, section 100; standing and running trim, section 300; stile and rail paneling, section 500c; finishing, section 1500.
5. Shape and size of various elements vary with individual design as well as with the availability of lumber size.

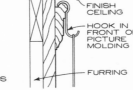

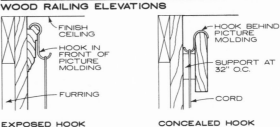

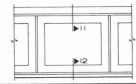

WOOD PANELING ELEVATIONS

WOOD RAILING ELEVATIONS

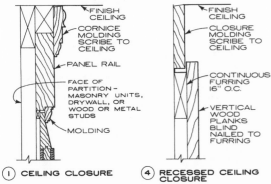

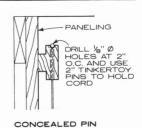

PICTURE MOLDING DETAILS

EXPOSED HOOK   CONCEALED HOOK   CONCEALED PIN

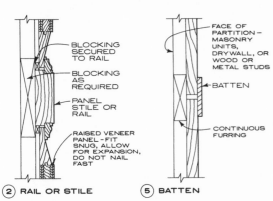

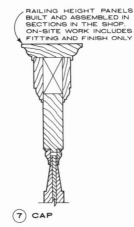

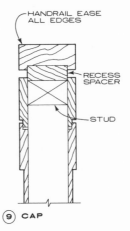

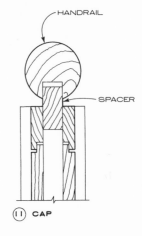

② RAIL OR STILE   ⑤ BATTEN   ⑦ CAP   ⑨ CAP   ⑪ CAP

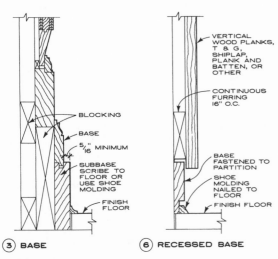

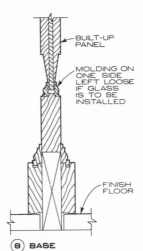

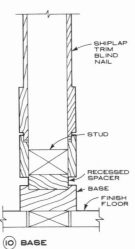

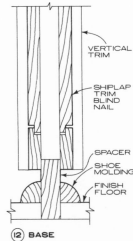

③ BASE   ⑥ RECESSED BASE   ⑧ BASE   ⑩ BASE   ⑫ BASE

SECTIONS

SECTIONS

WOOD PANELING DETAILS

WOOD RAILING DETAILS

Charles Szoradi, AIA; Washington, D.C.

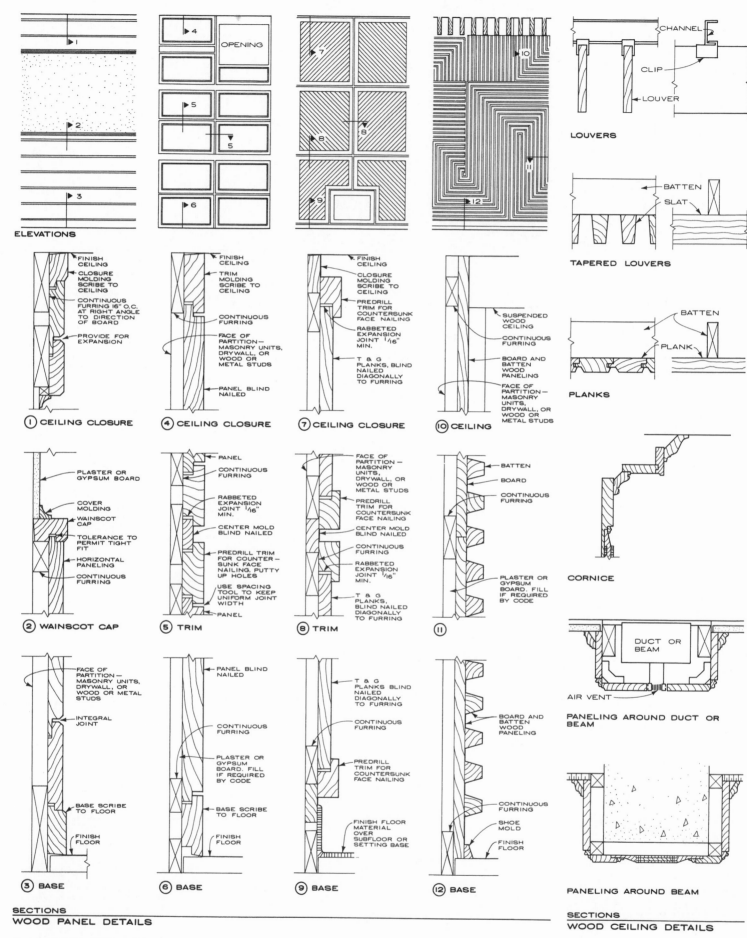

ELEVATIONS

① CEILING CLOSURE

FINISH CEILING

CLOSURE MOLDING SCRIBE TO CEILING

CONTINUOUS FURRING 16" O.C. AT RIGHT ANGLE TO DIRECTION OF BOARD

PROVIDE FOR EXPANSION

② WAINSCOT CAP

PLASTER OR GYPSUM BOARD

COVER MOLDING

WAINSCOT CAP

TOLERANCE TO PERMIT TIGHT FIT

HORIZONTAL PANELING

CONTINUOUS FURRING

③ BASE

FACE OF PARTITION — MASONRY UNITS, DRYWALL, OR WOOD OR METAL STUDS

INTEGRAL JOINT

BASE SCRIBE TO FLOOR

FINISH FLOOR

④ CEILING CLOSURE

FINISH CEILING

TRIM MOLDING SCRIBE TO CEILING

CONTINUOUS FURRING

FACE OF PARTITION — MASONRY UNITS, DRYWALL, OR WOOD OR METAL STUDS

PANEL BLIND NAILED

⑤ TRIM

PANEL

CONTINUOUS FURRING

RABBETED EXPANSION JOINT 1/16" MIN.

CENTER MOLD BLIND NAILED

PREDRILL TRIM FOR COUNTER-SUNK FACE NAILING, PUTTY UP HOLES

USE SPACING TOOL TO KEEP UNIFORM JOINT WIDTH

PANEL

⑥ BASE

PANEL BLIND NAILED

CONTINUOUS FURRING

PLASTER OR GYPSUM BOARD. FILL IF REQUIRED BY CODE

BASE SCRIBE TO FLOOR

FINISH FLOOR

⑦ CEILING CLOSURE

FINISH CEILING

CLOSURE MOLDING SCRIBE TO CEILING

PREDRILL TRIM FOR COUNTERSUNK FACE NAILING

RABBETED EXPANSION JOINT 1/16" MIN.

T & G PLANKS, BLIND NAILED DIAGONALLY TO FURRING

⑧ TRIM

FACE OF PARTITION — MASONRY UNITS, DRYWALL, OR WOOD OR METAL STUDS

PREDRILL TRIM FOR COUNTERSUNK FACE NAILING

CENTER MOLD BLIND NAILED

CONTINUOUS FURRING

RABBETED EXPANSION JOINT 1/16" MIN.

T & G PLANKS, BLIND NAILED DIAGONALLY TO FURRING

⑨ BASE

T & G PLANKS BLIND NAILED DIAGONALLY TO FURRING

CONTINUOUS FURRING

PREDRILL TRIM FOR COUNTERSUNK FACE NAILING

FINISH FLOOR MATERIAL OVER SUBFLOOR OR SETTING BASE

⑩ CEILING

SUSPENDED WOOD CEILING

CONTINUOUS FURRING

BOARD AND BATTEN WOOD PANELING

FACE OF PARTITION — MASONRY UNITS, DRYWALL, OR WOOD OR METAL STUDS

⑪

BATTEN

BOARD

CONTINUOUS FURRING

PLASTER OR GYPSUM BOARD. FILL IF REQUIRED BY CODE

⑫ BASE

BOARD AND BATTEN WOOD PANELING

CONTINUOUS FURRING

SHOE MOLD

FINISH FLOOR

SECTIONS
WOOD PANEL DETAILS

Charles Szoradi, AIA; Washington, D.C.

LOUVERS

CHANNEL

CLIP

LOUVER

TAPERED LOUVERS

BATTEN

SLAT

PLANKS

BATTEN

PLANK

CORNICE

PANELING AROUND DUCT OR BEAM

DUCT OR BEAM

AIR VENT

PANELING AROUND BEAM

SECTIONS
WOOD CEILING DETAILS

TYPES OF HARDWOOD PLYWOOD

Technical	Fully waterproof bond—approx. equal strength in two directions
Type 1 (ext.)	Fully waterproof bond—full weather exposure, resist organisms
Type 11 (int.)	Water resistant bond
Type 111 (int.)	Moisture—resistant bond

GRADES OF HARDWOOD PLYWOOD

Premium Grade (A)	Slight imperfections
Good Grade (1)	For natural finishes, no sharp contrasts
Sound Grade (2)	For smooth painted surfaces
Utility Grade (3)	Open defects permitted but limited in size, species not selected, no matching
Backing Grade (4)	Many flaws permitted, species not selected. No matching
Specialty Grade (SP)	Nonconforming for special uses, matching, etc. Grade and type by agreement

NUMBER OF PLIES

Odd number in pairs on opposite sides of core. For Technical Type, plies parallel to finish plies provide 40–60% of total thickness.

SOME POPULAR SPECIES OF HARDWOOD VENEERS

DENSE: white ash, yellow birch, black maple, red oak, rosewood, teak.
MEDIUM DENSE: black ash, gum, African mahogany, red maple, prima vera, American walnut.
LOW DENSITY: aspen, American basswood, American chestnut, yellow poplar.

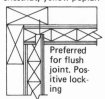

Preferred for flush joint. Positive locking

INSIDE CORNER

Usually used. Joint is glued

OUTSIDE CORNER

Spline usually 1/4" x 5/8". Dowels 6" to 12" o.c.

DOWEL AND SPLINE

Tongue usually 1/4" wide, 5/16" deep. Dowels sometimes added

TONGUE AND GROOVE

2 1/2" TO 3"

Glue spirals No. 8–10 dowels approx. 3/8"

DOWEL

VENEER EXPOSED PLYWOOD SPLINE

2 nails, 1 face hole, colored putty. Screws hidden by joint preferred for possible removal of panels. #10 or #12 size usual

NAILS AND SCREWS RECOMMENDED

3" x 2" clips 16" o.c. Allow 1" at ceiling to drop panel into place

METAL CLIPS

MATCHING HARDWOOD END

CONCEALED CROSSBAND

VENEER EDGEBAND

PANEL EDGES

DETAILS FOR QUALITY INTERIOR HARDWOOD PLYWOOD PANELING
LUMBER CORE PLYWOOD SHOWN

Foster C. Parriott; James M. Hunter & Associates; Boulder, Colorado

BOOK SLIP DIAMOND REV. DIAMOND "V"

CHECKER-BOARD 4W.CTR. AND BUTT HERRING-BONE BOX REV.BOX

VERT.BUTT HORIZ.BOOK LOT CENTER BALANCE RANDOM

VENEER MATCHING

STANDARD SIZES AND THICKNESSES OF HARDWOOD PLYWOOD

WIDTHS: 48"	Tolerance ± 1/32"
LENGTHS: 84", 96", 120"	Tolerance ± 1/32"
THICKNESSES: 1/8" to 3/4"	

Tolerances: Unsanded panels: ± 1/32"
Sanded panels: + 0" – 1/32" except that
1/4" or more wall panels + 0" – 3/64"

Data supplied by Hardwood Plywood Manufacturers' Association and by Champion Building Products, Division of Champion International

ROTARY

FLAT SLICING

QUARTER SLICING

HALF ROUND

RIFT CUT

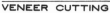
BACK CUT

VENEER CUTTING

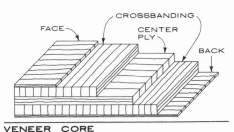

FACE CROSSBANDING CENTER PLY BACK

VENEER CORE

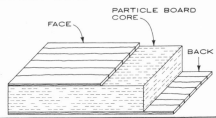

FACE PARTICLE BOARD CORE BACK

PARTICLE BOARD CORE

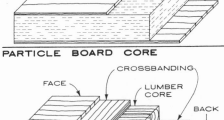

FACE CROSSBANDING LUMBER CORE BACK

LUMBER CORE

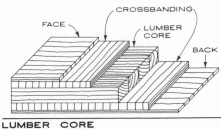

1 x 2 FURRING STRIPS WITH EXP. BOLTS, CONC. NAILS, OR EXPLOSIVE FASTENERS 18" O.C. ±

BLOCK ALL UNSUPPORTED EDGES

WITH GLUE – 3/4" NO. 19 BRADS 8" O.C.

WITHOUT GLUE – FIN. NAILS 6" O.C. AT EDGES, 12" O.C. INTERIOR

1/4" x 2" THIN PLYWOOD STRIPS

MASONRY **FRAME**

INTERIOR WALL AND FURRING APPLICATION

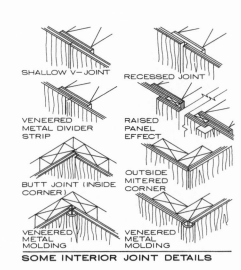

SHALLOW V–JOINT RECESSED JOINT

VENEERED METAL DIVIDER STRIP RAISED PANEL EFFECT

BUTT JOINT (INSIDE CORNER) OUTSIDE MITERED CORNER

VENEERED METAL MOLDING VENEERED METAL MOLDING

SOME INTERIOR JOINT DETAILS

LAMINATED HARDWOOD BLOCK FLOORING

Standard size	9" x 9" x 1/2"	
Grades	Prime	finished or unfinished
	Standard	
Species listed in accordance with hardness and wearing capacity	(1) Pecan (2) Hard maple (3) Oak (red and white) (4) Birch (5) Ash (6) Beech (7) Walnut (8) Cherry	
Plies	Three at right angles; tongue on corresponding groove on each of four edges	
Application	Laid in mastic over concrete or other suitable subflooring	

NOTE: Samples tested under ANSI—010.2-1975.

WOOD JOINTS

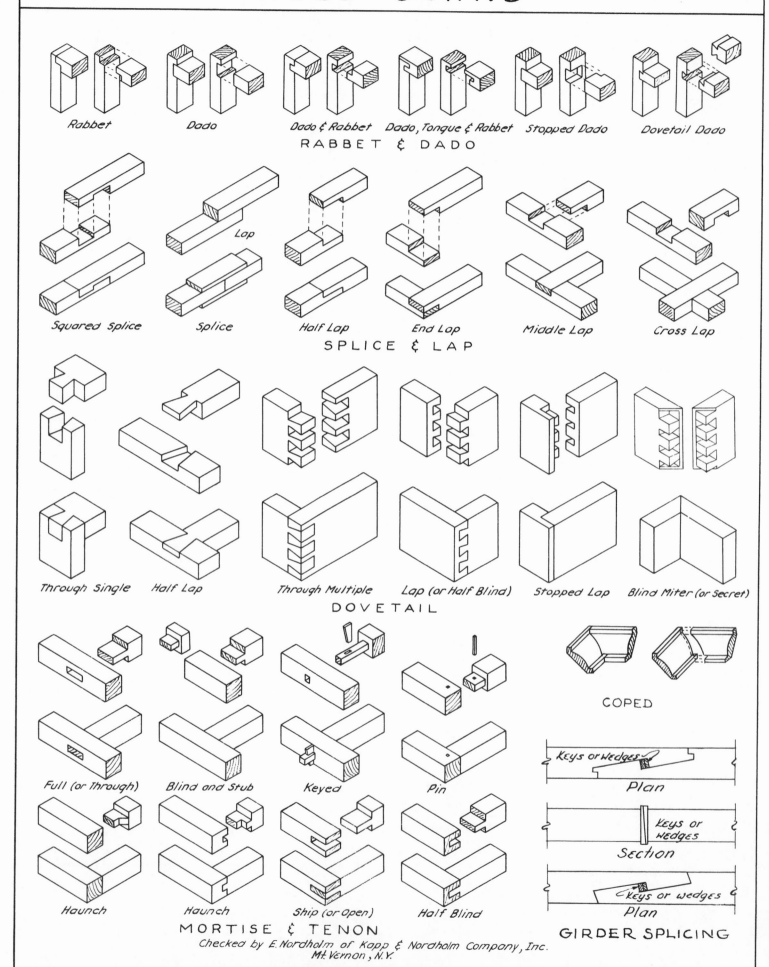

Rabbet　　Dado　　Dado & Rabbet　　Dado, Tongue & Rabbet　　Stopped Dado　　Dovetail Dado

RABBET & DADO

Squared Splice　　Splice　　Lap　　Half Lap　　End Lap　　Middle Lap　　Cross Lap

SPLICE & LAP

Through Single　　Half Lap　　Through Multiple　　Lap (or Half Blind)　　Stopped Lap　　Blind Miter (or Secret)

DOVETAIL

Full (or Through)　　Blind and Stub　　Keyed　　Pin

Haunch　　Haunch　　Ship (or Open)　　Half Blind

MORTISE & TENON

COPED

Keys or Wedges
Plan

Keys or Wedges
Section

Keys or Wedges
Plan

GIRDER SPLICING

Checked by E. Nordholm of Kapp & Nordholm Company, Inc.
Mt. Vernon, N.Y.

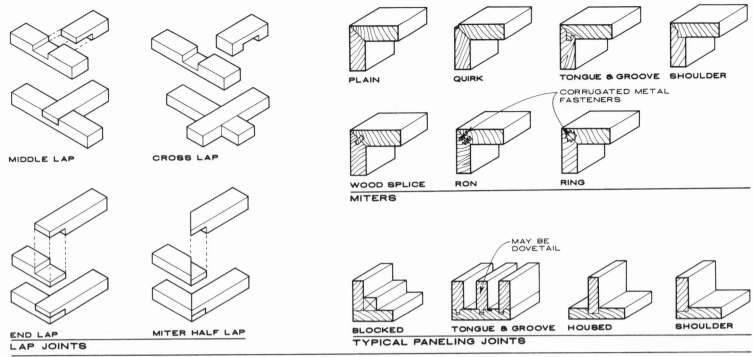

MIDDLE LAP

CROSS LAP

END LAP

MITER HALF LAP

LAP JOINTS

RIGHT ANGLE JOINTS

PLAIN

QUIRK

TONGUE & GROOVE

SHOULDER

CORRUGATED METAL FASTENERS

WOOD SPLICE

RON

RING

MITERS

MAY BE DOVETAIL

BLOCKED

TONGUE & GROOVE

HOUSED

SHOULDER

TYPICAL PANELING JOINTS

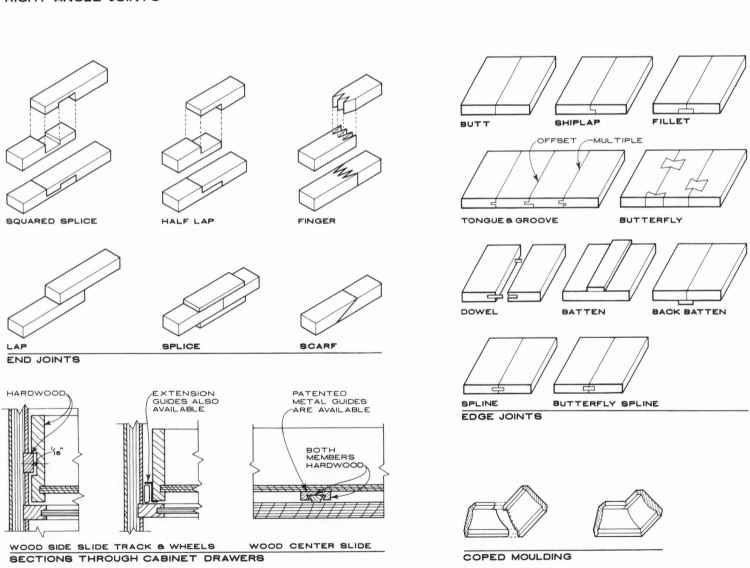

SQUARED SPLICE

HALF LAP

FINGER

LAP

SPLICE

SCARF

END JOINTS

HARDWOOD

1/16"

EXTENSION GUIDES ALSO AVAILABLE

PATENTED METAL GUIDES ARE AVAILABLE

BOTH MEMBERS HARDWOOD

WOOD SIDE SLIDE TRACK & WHEELS

WOOD CENTER SLIDE

SECTIONS THROUGH CABINET DRAWERS

BUTT

SHIPLAP

FILLET

OFFSET   MULTIPLE

TONGUE & GROOVE

BUTTERFLY

DOWEL

BATTEN

BACK BATTEN

SPLINE

BUTTERFLY SPLINE

EDGE JOINTS

COPED MOULDING

JOINTS in WOODWORK ~ PANELING

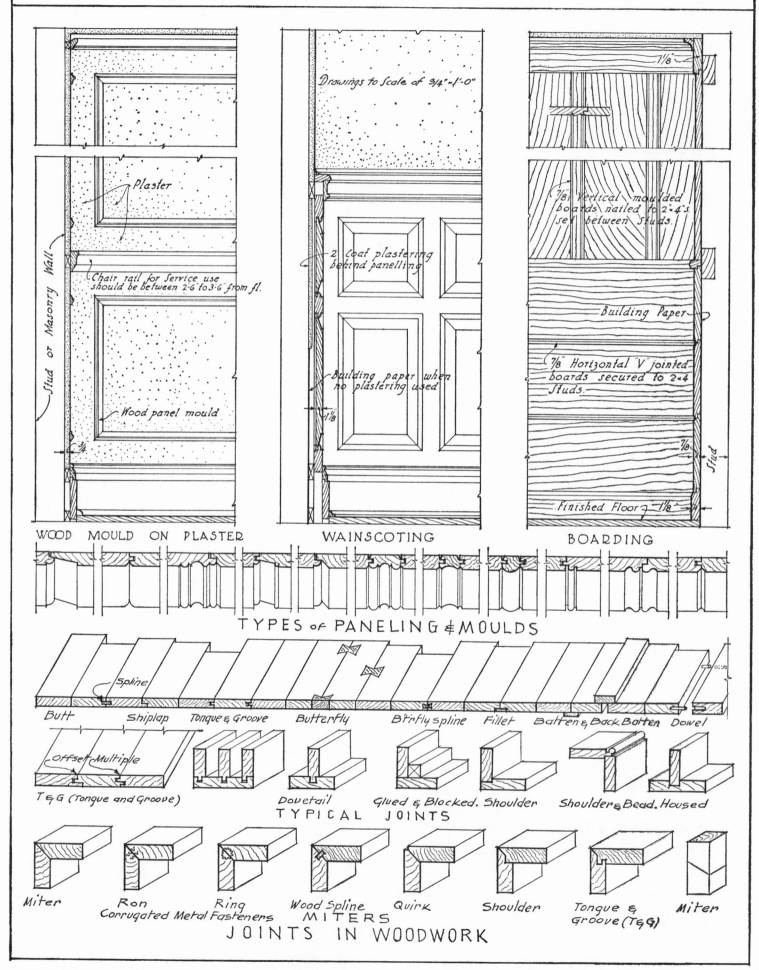

Plaster

Stud or Masonry Wall

Chair rail for Service use should be between 2′-6″ to 3′-6″ from fl.

Wood panel mould

3/4

WOOD MOULD ON PLASTER

Drawings to Scale of 3/4″=1′-0″

2 Coat plastering behind panelling

Building paper when no plastering used

1/8

WAINSCOTING

1/8

7/8″ Vertical moulded boards nailed to 2-4′s set between studs.

Building Paper

7/8″ Horizontal 'V' jointed boards secured to 2-4 Studs.

Stud

7/8

Finished Floor 1/8

BOARDING

TYPES of PANELING & MOULDS

Spline

Butt   Shiplap   Tongue & Groove   Butterfly   B'tr'fly spline   Fillet   Batten & Back Batten   Dowel

Offset — *Multiple*

T & G (Tongue and Groove)   Dovetail   Glued & Blocked. Shoulder   Shoulder & Bead. Housed

TYPICAL JOINTS

Miter   Ron   Ring   Wood Spline   Quirk   Shoulder   Tongue & Groove (T&G)   Miter
        Corrugated Metal Fasteners   **MITERS**

JOINTS IN WOODWORK

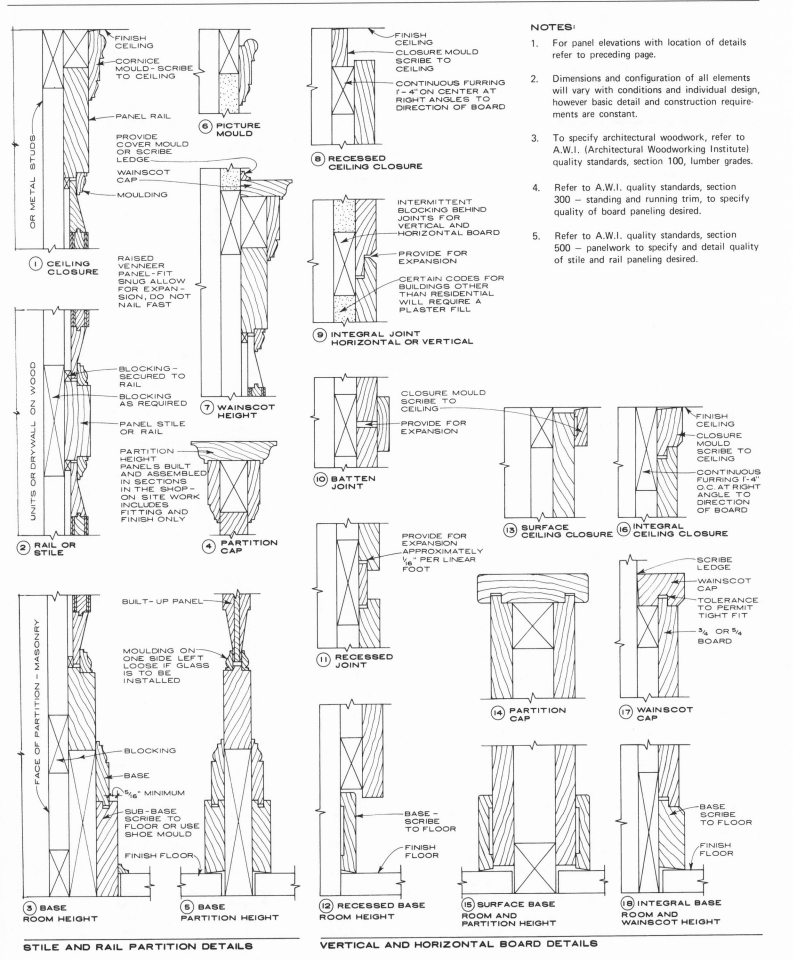

NOTES:

1. For panel elevations with location of details refer to preceding page.

2. Dimensions and configuration of all elements will vary with conditions and individual design, however basic detail and construction requirements are constant.

3. To specify architectural woodwork, refer to A.W.I. (Architectural Woodworking Institute) quality standards, section 100, lumber grades.

4. Refer to A.W.I. quality standards, section 300 — standing and running trim, to specify quality of board paneling desired.

5. Refer to A.W.I. quality standards, section 500 — panelwork to specify and detail quality of stile and rail paneling desired.

1 CEILING CLOSURE
FINISH CEILING
CORNICE MOULD- SCRIBE TO CEILING
PANEL RAIL
PROVIDE COVER MOULD OR SCRIBE LEDGE
WAINSCOT CAP
MOULDING
OR METAL STUDS

6 PICTURE MOULD

8 RECESSED CEILING CLOSURE
FINISH CEILING
CLOSURE MOULD SCRIBE TO CEILING
CONTINUOUS FURRING 1'-4" ON CENTER AT RIGHT ANGLES TO DIRECTION OF BOARD

7 WAINSCOT HEIGHT
RAISED VENNEER PANEL- FIT SNUG ALLOW FOR EXPANSION, DO NOT NAIL FAST

2 RAIL OR STILE
BLOCKING - SECURED TO RAIL
BLOCKING AS REQUIRED
PANEL STILE OR RAIL
UNITS OR DRYWALL ON WOOD

4 PARTITION CAP
PARTITION HEIGHT PANELS BUILT AND ASSEMBLED IN SECTIONS IN THE SHOP- ON SITE WORK INCLUDES FITTING AND FINISH ONLY

9 INTEGRAL JOINT HORIZONTAL OR VERTICAL
INTERMITTENT BLOCKING BEHIND JOINTS FOR VERTICAL AND HORIZONTAL BOARD
PROVIDE FOR EXPANSION
CERTAIN CODES FOR BUILDINGS OTHER THAN RESIDENTIAL WILL REQUIRE A PLASTER FILL

10 BATTEN JOINT
CLOSURE MOULD SCRIBE TO CEILING
PROVIDE FOR EXPANSION

13 SURFACE CEILING CLOSURE

16 INTEGRAL CEILING CLOSURE
FINISH CEILING
CLOSURE MOULD SCRIBE TO CEILING
CONTINUOUS FURRING 1'-4" O.C. AT RIGHT ANGLE TO DIRECTION OF BOARD

3 BASE ROOM HEIGHT
BUILT- UP PANEL
MOULDING ON ONE SIDE LEFT LOOSE IF GLASS IS TO BE INSTALLED
BLOCKING
BASE
$5/16$" MINIMUM
SUB-BASE SCRIBE TO FLOOR OR USE SHOE MOULD
FINISH FLOOR
FACE OF PARTITION - MASONRY

5 BASE PARTITION HEIGHT

11 RECESSED JOINT
PROVIDE FOR EXPANSION APPROXIMATELY $1/16$" PER LINEAR FOOT

14 PARTITION CAP

17 WAINSCOT CAP
SCRIBE LEDGE
WAINSCOT CAP
TOLERANCE TO PERMIT TIGHT FIT
$3/4$ OR $5/4$ BOARD

12 RECESSED BASE ROOM HEIGHT
BASE - SCRIBE TO FLOOR
FINISH FLOOR

15 SURFACE BASE ROOM AND PARTITION HEIGHT
BASE - SCRIBE TO FLOOR
FINISH FLOOR

18 INTEGRAL BASE ROOM AND WAINSCOT HEIGHT
BASE SCRIBE TO FLOOR
FINISH FLOOR

STILE AND RAIL PARTITION DETAILS

VERTICAL AND HORIZONTAL BOARD DETAILS

H. E. Heidtmann and R. Paccone; Sargent, Webster, Crenshaw & Folley; Syracuse, New York

MULTI-USE WOOD FRAME MEMBER

The following details illustrate how one single wood mill-member may be used to form all parts of the frames for windows, doors, panels and glass, including their heads, jambs, sills, mullions and posts.

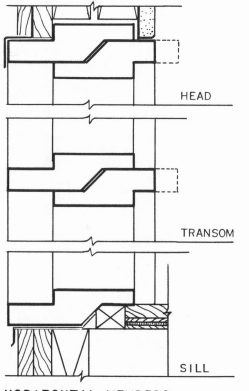

HEAD

TRANSOM

SILL

HORIZONTAL MEMBERS

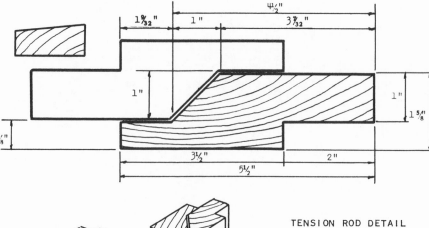

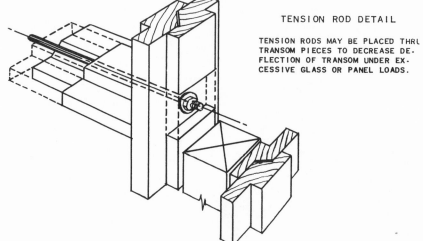

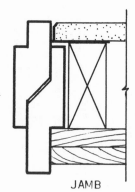

TENSION ROD DETAIL

TENSION RODS MAY BE PLACED THRU TRANSOM PIECES TO DECREASE DE-FLECTION OF TRANSOM UNDER EX-CESSIVE GLASS OR PANEL LOADS.

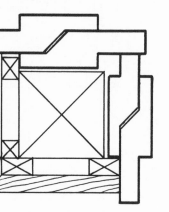

CORNER POST

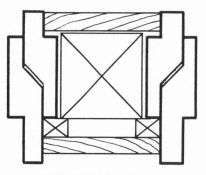

STRUCTURAL POST

MULLION

JAMB

VERTICAL MEMBERS

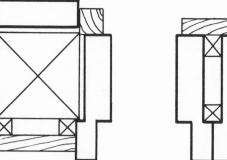

CORNER POST

MULLION

STRUCTURAL POST

JAMB

ALTERNATE VERTICAL MEMBERS

MULTI-USE WOOD FRAME MEMBER

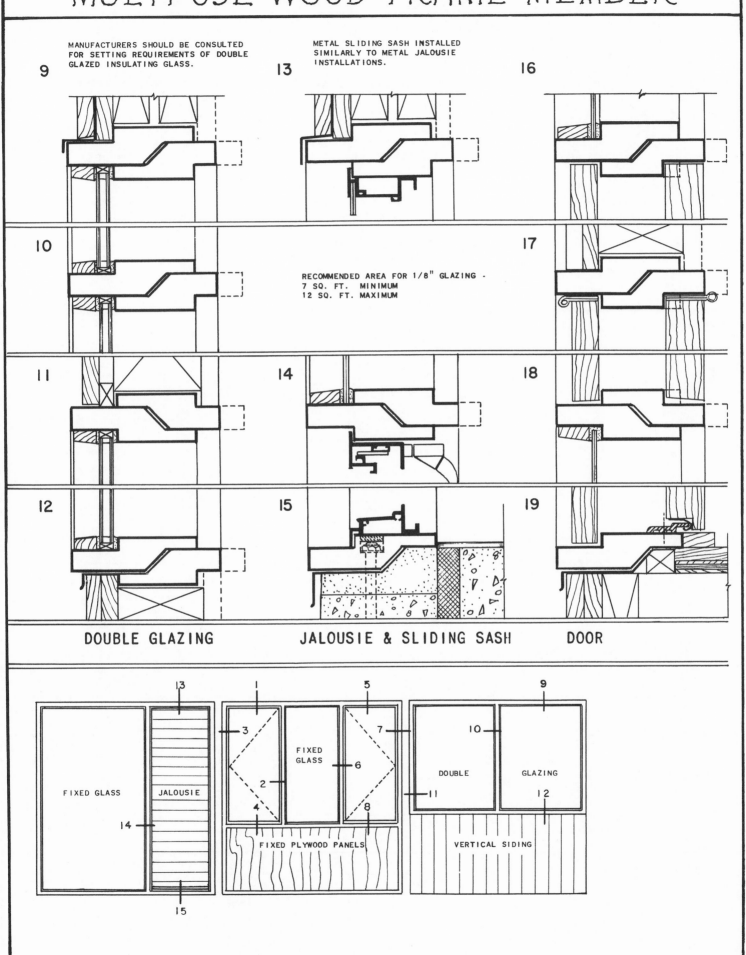

9 — MANUFACTURERS SHOULD BE CONSULTED FOR SETTING REQUIREMENTS OF DOUBLE GLAZED INSULATING GLASS.

13 — METAL SLIDING SASH INSTALLED SIMILARLY TO METAL JALOUSIE INSTALLATIONS.

16

10

RECOMMENDED AREA FOR 1/8" GLAZING -
7 SQ. FT. MINIMUM
12 SQ. FT. MAXIMUM

17

11

14

18

12

15

19

DOUBLE GLAZING   **JALOUSIE & SLIDING SASH**   **DOOR**

FIXED GLASS   JALOUSIE   FIXED GLASS   FIXED PLYWOOD PANELS   DOUBLE   GLAZING   VERTICAL SIDING

EAVES and WATERTABLES

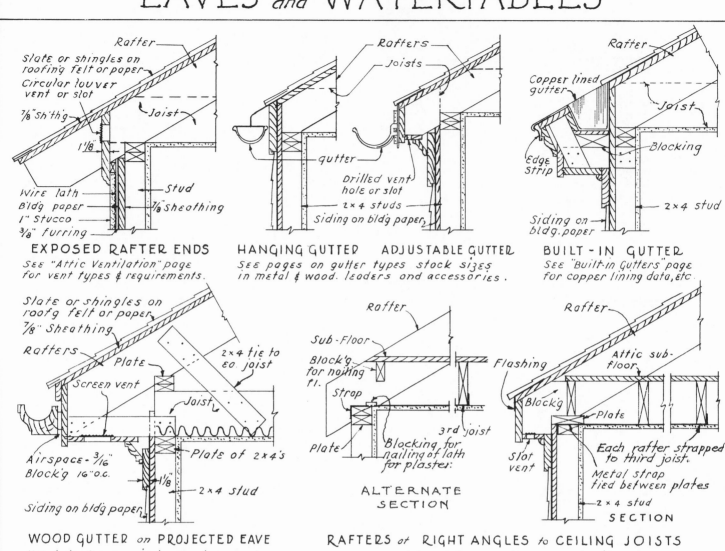

EXPOSED RAFTER ENDS
See "Attic Ventilation" page for vent types & requirements.

HANGING GUTTER   ADJUSTABLE GUTTER
See pages on gutter types, stock sizes in metal & wood. leaders and accessories.

BUILT-IN GUTTER
See "Built-in Gutters" page for copper lining data, etc.

WOOD GUTTER on PROJECTED EAVE
Used to keep windows at normal elevation when overhang is large.

RAFTERS at RIGHT ANGLES to CEILING JOISTS
Means used to anchor roof where design necessitates construction of this type. (Infrequently encountered).

EAVE DETAILS for PITCHED ROOFS

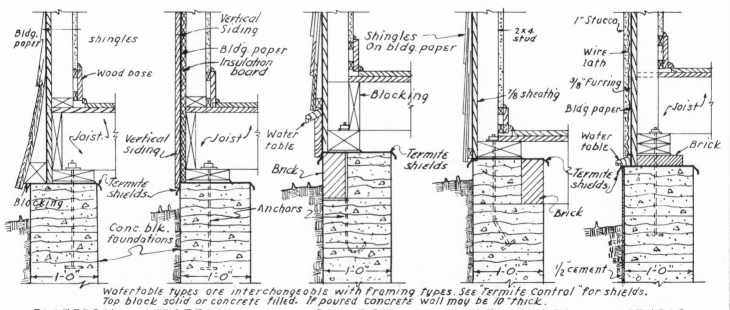

Watertable types are interchangeable with framing types. See Termite Control " for shields.
Top block solid or concrete filled. If poured concrete wall may be 10" thick.

PLATFORM or WESTERN FRAMING

BALLOON or BRACED

WITH JOISTS BELOW GRADE

STUCCO FINISH

SILLS and WATERTABLES
Scale 3/4" = 1'-0"

EAVES and OVERHANGS

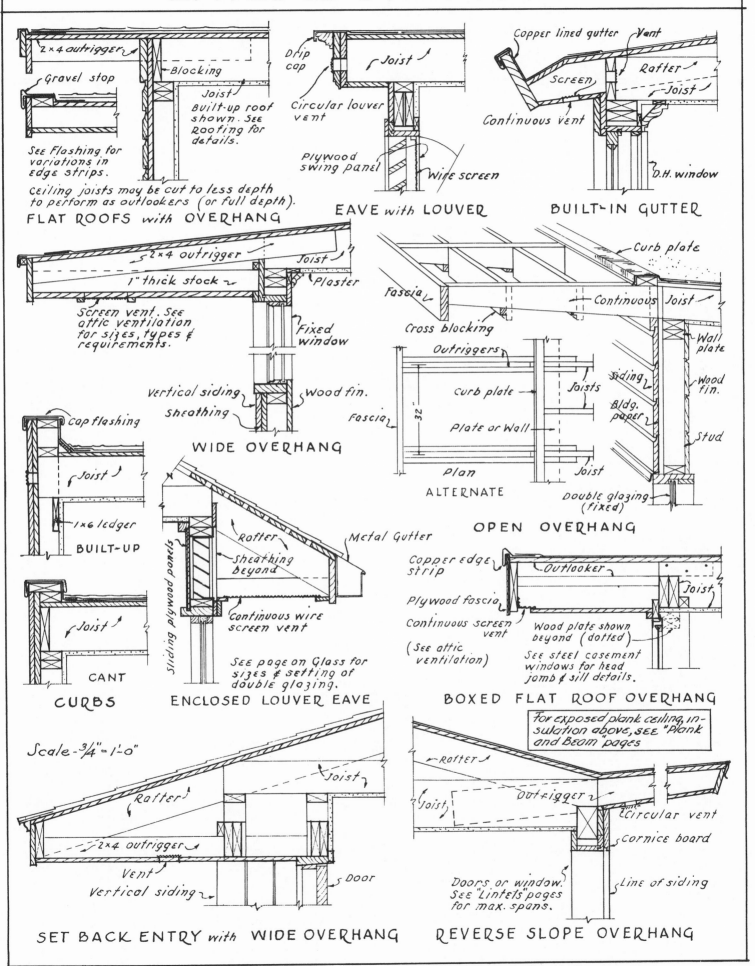

FLAT ROOFS with OVERHANG

2×4 outrigger
Gravel stop
Blocking
Joist
Built-up roof shown. See Roofing for details.
See Flashing for variations in edge strips.
Ceiling joists may be cut to less depth to perform as outlookers (or full depth).

EAVE with LOUVER

Drip cap
Joist
Circular louver vent
Plywood swing panel
Wire screen

BUILT-IN GUTTER

Copper lined gutter
Vent
Screen
Rafter
Joist
Continuous vent
D.H. window

WIDE OVERHANG

2×4 outrigger
Joist
1" thick stock
Plaster
Screen vent. See attic ventilation for sizes, types & requirements.
Fixed window
Vertical siding
Sheathing
Wood fin.

OPEN OVERHANG

Curb plate
Fascia
Continuous Joist
Cross blocking
Wall plate
Siding
Wood fin.
Bldg. paper
Stud
Double glazing (fixed)

ALTERNATE

Outriggers
Curb plate
Joists
Fascia
Plate or Wall
Plan
Joist
32

CURBS

Cap flashing
Joist
1×6 ledger
BUILT-UP

Joist
CANT

ENCLOSED LOUVER EAVE

Rafter
Sheathing beyond
Metal Gutter
Sliding plywood panels
Continuous wire screen vent
See page on Glass for sizes & setting of double glazing.

BOXED FLAT ROOF OVERHANG

Copper edge strip
Outlooker
Joist
Plywood fascia
Continuous screen vent
(See attic ventilation)
Wood plate shown beyond (dotted)
See steel casement windows for head jamb & sill details.

For exposed plank ceiling, insulation above, see "Plank and Beam" pages

Scale - ¾" = 1'-0"

SET BACK ENTRY with WIDE OVERHANG

Rafter
Joist
2×4 outrigger
Vent
Vertical siding
Door

REVERSE SLOPE OVERHANG

Rafter
Joist
Outrigger
Circular vent
Cornice board
Line of siding
Doors or window. See "Lintels" pages for max. spans.

WOOD BOOK SHELVES

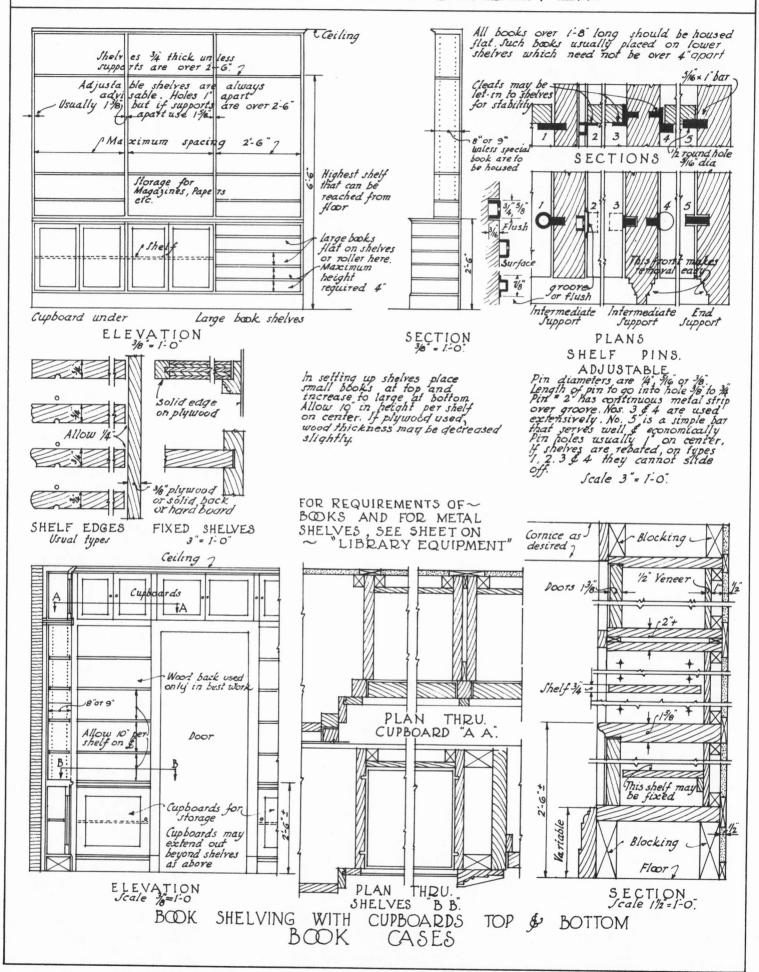

Ceiling

Shelves ¾ thick unless supports are over 2-6".

Adjustable shelves are always advisable. Holes 1" apart. Usually 1⅛" but if supports are over 2-6" apart use 1⅜".

Maximum spacing 2-6".

Storage for Magazines, Papers etc.

Shelf

Highest shelf that can be reached from floor

Large books flat on shelves or roller here. Maximum height required 4"

Cupboard under   Large book shelves

ELEVATION
3/8" = 1-0"

All books over 1-8" long should be housed flat. Such books usually placed on lower shelves which need not be over 4" apart

5/16 × 1" bar

Cleats may be let-in to shelves for stability

8" or 9" unless special book are to be housed

SECTIONS

½ round hole 5/16 dia

3", 5/8
¾
3/16
Flush

Surface

⅛"
groove or flush

Intermediate Support   Intermediate Support   End Support

PLANS
SHELF PINS.
ADJUSTABLE

Pin diameters are ¼", 5/16" or 3/8". Length of pin to go into hole 3/8" to ¾". Pin #2 has continuous metal strip over groove. Nos. 3 & 4 are used extensively. No. 5 is a simple bar that serves well & economically. Pin holes usually 1" on center. If shelves are rebated, on types 1, 2, 3 & 4 they cannot slide off.

Scale 3" = 1-0"

SECTION
3/8" = 1-0"

¾
Allow ¼"
¾
¾

Solid edge on plywood

3/8" plywood or solid back or hard board

SHELF EDGES
Usual types

FIXED SHELVES
3" = 1-0"

In setting up shelves place small books at top and increase to large at bottom. Allow 10" in height per shelf on center. If plywood used, wood thickness may be decreased slightly.

FOR REQUIREMENTS OF ~ BOOKS AND FOR METAL SHELVES, SEE SHEET ON ~ "LIBRARY EQUIPMENT"

Ceiling

A
Cupboards
A

Wood back used only in best work

8" or 9"

Allow 10" per shelf on ℄

B   B

Cupboards for storage

Cupboards may extend out beyond shelves as above

Door

2-6"±

ELEVATION
Scale 3/8 = 1-0

PLAN THRU.
CUPBOARD "A A."

PLAN THRU.
SHELVES "B B."

Cornice as desired

Blocking

½" Veneer

Doors 1⅜"

1" ½"

2"±

Shelf ¾"

1⅝"

This shelf may be fixed

2-6"±

Variable

Blocking

Floor

½"

½"

SECTION
Scale 1½" = 1-0".

BOOK SHELVING WITH CUPBOARDS TOP & BOTTOM

BOOK CASES

6 THERMAL AND MOISTURE PROTECTION

THERMAL COMFORT

Human thermal comfort is determined by the body's ability to dissipate the heat and moisture that are produced continuously by metabolic action. The rate of heat production varies with the size, age, sex, and degree of activity of the individuals whose comfort is under consideration. For men of average size, seated and doing light work, the metabolic rate is about 450 Btu/hr; for women under similar circumstances the comparable rate is about 385 Btu/hr. For a 155 lb man seated and doing moderate to heavy work, the rate ranges from 650 to 800 Btu/hr; standing and walking about while doing moderately heavy work will raise the rate to 1000 Btu/hr while the hardest sustained work will result in a metabolic rate of 2000 to 2400 Btu/hr. For an office with the usual complement of men and women, an average metabolic rate will range from 400 to 450 Btu/hr per person.

Thermal comfort is attained when the environment surrounding the individual can remove the bodily heat and moisture at the rate at which they are being produced. The removal, accomplished by convection, evaporation, and radiation, is regulated by the dry bulb temperature, the vapor pressure, and rate of movement of the air and the mean radiant temperature (MRT) of the surrounding surfaces. MRT is defined by ASHRAE as the temperature of an imaginary black enclosure in which the individual experiences the same rate of radiant heat exchange as in the actual environment. (See 1977 ASHRAE Handbook of Fundamentals, Chapter 8, for more information on MRT and human comfort.)

Heat and moisture removal are also strongly affected by the nature and amount of clothing being worn and by its insulating value. This quality can be evaluated in terms of a thermal resistance unit designated by clo, where 1 clo = 0.88°F/(Btu/hr · sq ft). Typical masculine office attire, complete with warm jacket and light trousers, has an insulating value of 1.12 clo while a woman's office dress is rated at 0.73 clo. Values for other combinations are given in the ASHRAE reference cited above, page 8.7, Tables 1-C and 1-D. Uncomfortably low ambient air temperatures can be made tolerable by putting on more and heavier clothing, thus increasing the clo value; the converse, unfortunately, is not true.

The properties of atmospheric air-water vapor mixtures in the temperature range normally experienced by the human body can be shown effectively on psychrometric charts, which can take many different forms. The most familiar is that put forth by Willis H. Carrier, who is generally regarded as the originator of the air-conditioning industry in the U.S.A. On the Carrier-type chart, shown in modified form in Fig. 1, the humidity ratio of moist air, in pounds or grains (1 lb = 7000 grains) of water vapor per pound of dry air, is plotted against the dry bulb temperature of the air. Significant psychrometric data are given in the table at temperature intervals of 5°F from 50 to 90°F.

The relative humidity of moist air is the ratio, expressed as a percentage, of the amount of water vapor actually present in a given quantity of that air to the amount that the same quantity of air could contain if it were completely saturated at the same temperature and pressure. The uppermost curved line on the chart, called the saturation line, denotes 100% relative humidity. The wet bulb temperature, measured by a thermometer with a water wetted sensor over which the air-vapor

mixture is flowing rapidly (800 to 900 fpm) is used in combination with the dry bulb temperature to find the % RH at conditions other than saturation. For example, at 75°F dry bulb and 60°F wet bulb the relative humidity is seen to be 40%.

The humidity ratio at this condition is 53 grains/lb of dry air while the dew point temperature, found by following the horizontal line of constant humidity ratio to its intersection with the saturation line, is 50°F.

The relatively restricted range of conditions within which most lightly clothed sedentary adults in the U.S.A. will experience thermal comfort is shown by the cross-hatched area on Fig. 1. Known as the ASHRAE comfort zone (also called "comfort envelope"), this area on the psychrometric chart represents the combinations of dry bulb temperature and relative humidity, which, when combined with an air movement of 45 fpm or less, will meet the thermal needs of most adults. For this chart, MRT = dry bulb temperature.

The effective temperature lines shown on Fig. 1 represent combinations of dry bulb temperature and relative humidity that will produce the same rate of heat and moisture dissipation by radiation, convection, and evaporation as an individual would experience in a black enclosure at the specified temperature and 50% relative humidity. As the % RH rises, the dry bulb temperature must be slightly reduced to produce the same feeling of comfort; as the % RH falls toward the 10 to 20% level experienced in desert climates, the dry bulb temperature may rise slightly without inducing discomfort.

The 65°F indoor temperature mandated by federal regulations for winter operation of public buildings is seen to be well below the normal comfort zone. Addition of clothing (higher clo values) may help to offset the discomfort that most occupants will experience at 65°F, regardless of the % RH, but extremities (fingers and toes) will be uncomfortably cold.

The upper range of the comfort zone is close to the 78°F effective temperature line, and so the 78°F dry bulb temperature that is mandated for summer operation of public buildings will be tolerable for most lightly clothed adults until the relative humidity rises above 60 to 65%. At that condition, discomfort will be experienced by many building occupants because of their inability to dissipate metabolic moisture. Increases in air velocity are beneficial under these conditions, but velocities above about 70 fpm will generally result in unpleasant working conditions because of drafts, blowing papers, and so on.

Figure 2 shows another version of the psychrometric chart in which wet bulb temperatures are plotted against dry bulb temperatures, with straight lines of constant % RH running upward from lower left to upper right. The effect of air velocity and clothing thermal resistance (expressed as clo units) is shown by the curved lines near the center of each diagram.

For these conditions, in which the mean radiant temperature equals the dry bulb temperature, relative humidity has only a small effect. As the activity level of the room occupants is lowered, reducing the metabolic rate, the comfortable air temperature range moves upward; as the activity level is increased, cooler air is required.

The effects of radiant energy transfer between individuals and the surfaces surrounding them can have significant influence on sensations of comfort or discomfort. An increase of 1°F in MRT is approximately equivalent to a 1.5°F increase in ambient air temperature. The use of radiant heating from moderately warm surfaces can help to offset the discomfort caused by air temperatures that are significantly below the ASHRAE comfort zone. Conversely, discomfort can be caused by large heated areas, such as sun warmed windows. An excessively high MRT can require a significant reduction in air temperature to create comfort. For an individual exposed to direct sunshine entering through an unshaded window, discomfort is almost certain to result.

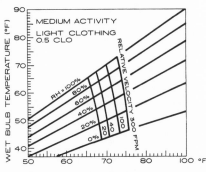

AIR TEMPERATURE = MEAN RADIANT TEMPERATURE

FIGURE 2

NOTE: Modified comfort chart for men, medium activity = 750 Btu/hr, thermal resistance of "light-clothing" = 0.5 clo.

MODIFIED COMFORT CHART

PROPERTIES OF WATER VAPOR AND SATURATED AIR

TEMPERATURE (°F)	VAPOR PRESSURE (IN. HG)	HUMIDITY RATIO (GRAINS/LB)	ENTHALPY (BTU/LB)	SPECIFIC VOLUME (CU FT/LB)
50	0.362	53.6	20.30	13.00
55	0.436	64.6	23.32	13.16
60	0.522	80.4	26.46	13.33
65	0.622	92.8	30.06	13.50
70	0.739	110.7	34.09	13.69
75	0.875	131.7	38.61	13.88
80	1.032	156.31	43.69	14.09
85	1.214	184.9	49.43	14.31
90	1.422	218.3	55.93	14.55

///// ASHRAE COMFORT ZONE

FIGURE 1

PSYCHROMETRIC CHART

John I. Yellott, P. E., Professor Emeritus, College of Architecture, Arizona State University; Tempe, Arizona

DEFINITIONS AND SYMBOLS

BRITISH THERMAL UNIT (Btu): The quantity of heat required to raise the temperature of one pound of water one degree Fahrenheit (specifically, from 59°F to 60°F).

DEGREE DAYS (DD): A temperature-time unit used in estimating building heating requirements. For any given day, the number of DD equals the difference between the reference temperature, usually 65°F, and the mean temperature of the outdoor air for that day. DD per month or per year are the sum of the daily DD for that period.

DEWPOINT TEMPERATURE: The temperature corresponding to 100% relative humidity for an air-vapor mixture at constant pressure.

EMITTANCE (e): The ratio of the radiant energy emitted by a surface to that emitted by a perfect radiator (a black body) at the same temperature.

HUMIDITY, ABSOLUTE: The weight of water vapor contained in a unit volume of an air-vapor mixture.

HUMIDITY RATIO: The ratio of the mass of water vapor to the mass of dry air in a given air-vapor mixture.

HUMIDITY, RELATIVE (RH): The ratio of the partial pressure of the water vapor in a given air-vapor mixture to the saturation pressure of water at the existing temperature.

ISOTHERM: A line on a graph or map joining points of equal temperature.

OVERALL HEAT TRANSFER COEFFICIENT (U or $1/R_T$): The rate of heat transfer under steady state conditions through a unit area of a building component caused by a difference of one degree between the air temperatures on the two sides of the component. In U.S. practice, the units are Btu/sq ft · hr · °F.

PERM: Unit of water vapor transmission through a material, expressed in grains of vapor per hour per inch of mercury pressure difference (7000 grains = 1 lb).

REFLECTANCE: The ratio of the radiant energy reflected by a surface to the energy incident upon the surface.

SURFACE HEAT TRANSFER COEFFICIENT (h): The rate of heat transfer from a unit area of a surface to the adjacent air and environment caused by a temperature difference of one degree between the surface and the air. In U.S. practice, the units are Btu/sq ft · hr · °F.

THERM: A unit of thermal energy equal to 100,000 Btu.

THERMAL CONDUCTANCE (C or 1/R): Time rate of heat flow through unit area of a material when a temperature difference of one degree is maintained across a specified thickness of the material. In U.S. practice, the units are Btu/hr · sq ft · °F.

THERMAL CONDUCTIVITY (k): Time rate of heat flow through unit area and unit thickness of a homogeneous material when a temperature of gradient of one degree is maintained in the direction of heat flow. In U.S. practice, the units are: Btu/hr · sq ft · (F/in.) or, when thickness is measured in feet, Btu/hr · ft · °F.

THERMAL RESISTANCE (R): Unit of resistance to heat flow, expressed as temperature difference required to cause heat to flow through a unit area of a building component or material at the rate of one heat unit per hour. In U.S. practice, the units are F/Btu/hr · ft^2).

TOTAL THERMAL RESISTANCE (R_t): The total resistance to heat flow through a complete building section or construction assembly, generally expressed as the temperature difference in °F needed to cause heat to flow at the rate of 1 Btu per hour per sq ft of area.

VAPOR BARRIER: A moisture impervious layer applied to surfaces enclosing a humid space to prevent moisture migration to a point where it may condense because of reduced temperature.

VAPOR PERMEABILITY: The property of a material that permits migration of water vapor under the influence of a difference in vapor pressure across the material.

VAPOR PERMEANCE: The ratio of the water vapor flow rate, in grains per hour, through a material of any specified thickness to the vapor pressure difference between the two surfaces of the material, expressed in inches of mercury. The unit is the perm.

VAPOR PRESSURE (P_v): The partial pressure of the water vapor in an air-vapor mixture. It is determined by the dewpoint temperature or by the drybulb temperature and the relative humidity of the mixture. The units are psi or inches of mercury.

VAPOR RESISTANCE: The resistance of a material or an assembly to the passage of water vapor when a vapor pressure difference exists between the two surfaces of the material or assembly. The unit is the rep, which is the reciprocal of the perm.

THERMAL TRANSMISSION

Problems in the performance of building construction materials and assemblies are frequently associated with undesirable flow of heat, moisture, or both. The heat transfer characteristics of most building materials are published in standard references such as the ASHRAE Handbook of Fundamentals. While the published data are subject to manufacturing and testing tolerances and judgment must be used in applying them, they may generally be used with confidence for design purposes.

Heat transmission coefficients are generally expressed as conductivities, k, for which the thickness unit is 1 in., or in conductances, C, for a specified thickness. The resistance to heat flow through a material, R, is the reciprocal of the conductance. For a homogeneous material of thickness L in., the thermal resistance R = L/k.

For a surface or an airspace, where the heat flows by both radiation and convection, combined coefficients are used, symbolized by h with a subscript to designate which particular surface or airspace is being considered. Thermal resistances at surfaces and across airspaces are again designated by R with an appropriate subscript, where R = 1/h. Such R values are strongly influenced by the nature and orientation of the surfaces.

To estimate the rate of heat flow through a building section, the total resistance (R_t) of that section is found by reference to published standard value or by adding the resistances of the individual components of the section. The overall coefficient U is then found as the reciprocal of the total resistance: $U = 1/R_t$. The rate of heat flow Q (Btu/hr) through a wall section of exposed area A sq ft is the product of the overall coefficient U, the area A and the temperature difference $(t_i - t_o)$: $Q = U \times A \times (t_i - t_o)$. This heat flow may be inward or outward, depending on t_i and t_o. The general procedure for finding the total thermal resistance and the U value for a given building section on which the sun is not shining is as follows:

1. Select the design outdoor conditions of air temperature (dry bulb), wind speed, and wind direction from local Weather Service records or ASHRAE recommendations. From this information select an outer surface coefficient h_o which will generally be 4.0 Btu/sq ft · hr · °F for summer and 6.0 for winter. Determine the indoor surface coefficient h_i which will be 1.46 Btu/sq ft · hr · °F under most conditions unless forced airflow exists along the wall of the window. Convert these to resistances with $R_o = 1/h_o$ and $R_i = 1/h_i$.
2. List all of the component elements of the section and determine the thermal resistance of each element by dividing the actual (not the nominal) thickness by its thermal conductivity k, except for airspaces. For airspaces, the thickness is taken into account in the conductance h_{as} and the thermal resistance R_{as} is the reciprocal of the conductance.
3. The total resistance of the building section is simply the sum of the individual resistances (make sure that every component is included properly). The U value of the section is then found from: $U = 1/R_t$. The U x A product is often needed to simplify the calculation of the total heat flow into or out of the building's envelope, as well as for the computations used to determine compliance with building energy performance standards.
4. For such building components as windows, skylights, and doors, U values may be found in standard references, for example, the ASHRAE Handbook of Fundamentals. Thermal resistances for a wide variety of common building materials are given in the table presented later in this section.

GENERAL NOTES

The foregoing does not include consideration of heat losses or gains due to ventilation air in large buildings or to infiltration of outdoor air through openings, cracks around windows and doors, construction imperfections, and so on. The energy required to heat this air in winter or to cool and dehumidify it in summer must be carefully estimated by methods given in the ASHRAE Handbook of Fundamentals. During both summer and winter, effects of the sun on both walls and windows must be taken into account.

The solution to the basic problem of attaining acceptable heat flow rates involves the selection of materials that are appropriate for the intended service and the incorporation of enough insulation within the building section to reduce the inward or outward heat flow to the desired rate. Since the indoor-outdoor temperature difference is one of the essential factors in the heat flow equation, the indoor temperature must be selected to comply with the pertinent code or other restriction. Temperatures from 65 to 72°F are generally used in winter while 75 to 78°F are typical summer values.

Selection of the outdoor design values involves careful consideration of the number of hours per year during which exceptionally low or high temperatures are encountered. National Weather Service temperature data are available for most locations in the United States and similar data exist for principal cities throughout the world. For winter design purposes, dry bulb temperatures are usually listed, which are exceeded by 99 and 97.5% of the total hours (2160) in December, January, and February. The 97.5% value is generally used for designing. Since the 54 hr (approximately) during which the outdoor air temperature will be lower than the stated value are experienced at intervals throughout the winter months. These temperatures are usually encountered in the early morning hours before sunrise, so that winter design heating loads tend to ignore solar effects. In summer, solar loads tend to dominate the air-conditioning picture.

Thermal conductances for walls, roofs, doors, and windows are combined in many of the energy conservation building standards to give a weighted average U value, designated as U_o. Allowable values for U_o depend on the building type and size and the number of heating degree days experienced at the building's location.

$$U_o = \frac{U_{xw} \times A_w + U_f \times A_f + U_d \times A_d}{A_w + A_f + A_d}$$

where the subscripts w, f, and d designate walls, fenestration, and door, respectively.

Allowable U_o values are specified in the ASHRAE Standard 90-75, which has been adopted by many states or other jurisdictions. For commercial buildings higher than three stories, U_o may range from 0.47 to 0.28 as the number of degree days per year increases from 500 to 8000. For commercial and institutional buildings of three stories or less, U_o ranges downward from 0.38 to 0.20 as degree days increase from 500 to 10,000. Estimation of summer cooling loads is also accomplished by using the U x A products as determined above, to which solar loads from fenestration must be added. Thermal resistances may be slightly higher in summer than in winter for the same building section because of variations in surface and airspace coefficients. By far the largest factor in most building heat gains is the load imposed by solar radiation entering through fenestration. Cooling load is also increased by internal heat sources within the structure including lighting, miscellaneous electrical loads, and the people in the building. Latent heat loads from moisture removal must also be considered. Properly qualified consultants should be called in to give advice in this field even before the orientation and fenestration of a proposed new building are fixed.

The energy conservation standards mentioned above also include provisions dealing with summer cooling requirements, which are set primarily by the latitude of the city in which the structure will be erected. The mass of the proposed building in terms of weight per square foot of wall area is also introduced to compensate in part for time lags caused by the thermal capacity of building components. It should be noted that cooling, a year-round requirement in many large buildings with high internal loads, is more costly in terms of energy consumption and cost than is heating. The internal heat gains that are helpful in winter are harmful in summer, since they can add greatly to the building's cooling load.

John I. Yellott, P. E.; College of Architecture; Arizona State University; Tempe, Arizona

MATERIAL & DESCRIPTION	AVERAGE TEMP.	DENSITY (lb per cu ft)	RESISTANCE (R)[a] Per inch thickness (1/k)	RESISTANCE (R)[a] For thickness listed (1/C)
BUILDING BOARDS, PANELS, FLOORING, ETC.				
Asbestos-cement board		120	0.25	—
Asbestos-cement board 1/8 in.		120	—	0.033
Gypsum or plaster board 3/8 in.		50	—	0.32
Gypsum or plaster board 1/2 in.		50	—	0.45
Plywood		34	1/25	—
Sheathing, wood fiber (impreg. or coated) 25/32"		20		2.06
		22	2.44	—
		25	2.27	—
Wood fiber board, lam. or homogeneous		26	2.38	—
		33	1.82	—
Wood fiber, hardboard type		65	0.72	—
Wood fiber, hardboard type 1/4 in.		65	—	0.18
Wood subfloor 25/32 in.		—	—	0.98
Wood, hardwood finish 3/4 in.		—	—	0.68
BUILDING PAPER				
Vapor-permeable felt		—	—	0.06
Vapor-seal, 2 layers of mopped 15 lb felt		—	—	0.12
Vapor-seal, plastic film		—	—	Negl.
FINISH FLOORING MATERIALS				
Carpet and fibrous pad		—	—	2.08
Carpet and rubber pad		—	—	1.23
Cork tile 1/8 in.		—	—	0.28
Terrazzo 1 in.		—	—	0.08
Tile-asphalt, linoleum, vinyl, rubber		—	—	0.05
INSULATING MATERIALS				
Blanket and Batt[b]				
Mineral wool, fibrous form processed from rock, slag, or glass		0.5	3.12	—
		1.5—4.0	3.70	—
Wood fiber		3.2—3.6	4.00	—
Boards and Slabs				
Cellular glass	90°F	9	2.44	—
	60°F		2.56	—
	30°F		2.70	—
	0°F		2.86	—
	−30°F		3.00	—
Corkboard	90°F	6.5—8.0	3.57	—
	60°F		3.70	—
	30°F		3.85	—
	0°F		4.00	—
	90°F	12	3.22	—
	60°F		3.33	—
	30°F		3.45	—
	0°F		3.57	—
Glass fiber	90°F	4—9	3.85	—
	60°F		4.17	—
	30°F		4.55	—
	0°F		4.76	—
	−30°F		5.26	—
Expanded rubber (rigid)	75°F	4.5	4.55	—
Expanded polyurethane (R-11 blown)	100°F	1.5—2.5	5.56	—
(Thickness 1 in. & greater)	75°F		5.88	—
	50°F		6.25	—
	25°F		5.88	—
	0°F		5.88	—
Expanded polystyrene, extruded	75°F	1.9	3.85	—
	60°F		4.00	—
	30°F		4.17	—
	0°F		4.55	—
	−60°F		5.26	—
Expanded polystyrene, molded beads	75°F	1.0	3.57	—
	30°F		3.85	—
	0°F		4.17	—
Mineral wool with resin binder	90°F	15	3.45	—
	60°F		3.57	—
	30°F		3.70	—
	0°F		4.00	—
Mineral fiberboard, wet felted				
Core or roof insulation		16—17	2.94	—
Acoustical tile		18	2.86	—
Acoustical tile		21	2.73	—
Mineral fiberboard, wet molded				
Acoustical tile[c]		23	2.38	—
Wood or can fiberboard				
Acoustical tile[c] 1/2 in.		—	—	1.19
Acoustical tile[c] 3/4 in.		—	—	1.78
Interior finish (plank, tile)		15	2.86	—

MATERIAL & DESCRIPTION		DENSITY (lb per cu ft)	RESISTANCE (R)[a] Per inch thickness (1/k)	RESISTANCE (R)[a] For thickness listed (1/C)
INSULATING MATERIALS				
Boards and Slabs (continued)				
Insulating roof deck				
Approximately 1-1/2 in.		—	—	4.17
Approximately 2 in.		—	—	5.56
Approximately 3 in.		—	—	8.33
Wood shredded (cemented, preformed slabs)		22	1.67	—
Loose Fill				
Mineral wool	90°F	2.0—5.0	3.33	—
(glass, slag, or rock)	60°F		3.70	—
	30°F		4.00	—
	0°F		4.35	—
Perlite (expanded)	90°F	5.0—8.0	2.63	—
	60°F		2.78	—
	30°F		2.94	—
	0°F		3.12	—
Vermiculite (expanded)	90°F	7.0—8.2	2.08	—
	60°F		2.18	—
	30°F		2.27	—
	0°F		2.38	—
	90°F	4.0—6.0	2.22	—
	60°F		2.33	—
	30°F		2.50	—
	0°F		2.63	—
Roof Insulation[d]				
Preformed, for use above deck				
Approximately 1/2 in.		—	—	1.39
Approximately 1 in.		—	—	2.78
Approximately 1-1/2 in.		—	—	4.17
Approximately 2 in.		—	—	5.26
Approximately 2-1/2 in.		—	—	6.67
Approximately 3 in.		—	—	8.33
Cellular glass		—	2.56	—
MASONRY MATERIALS - CONCRETES				
Cement mortar		116	0.20	—
Gypsum-fiber concrete, 87-1/2% gypsum, 12-1/2% wood chips		51	0.60	—
Lightweight aggregates including		120	0.19	—
expanded shale, clay or slate;		100	0.28	—
expanded slags; cinders; pumice;		80	0.40	—
perlite; vermiculite; also		60	0.59	—
cellular concretes		40	0.86	—
		30	1.11	—
		20	1.43	—
Sand & gravel or stone aggregate (oven dried)		140	0.11	—
Sand & gravel or stone aggregate (not dried)		140	0.08	—
Stucco		116	0.20	—
MASONRY UNITS				
Brick, common[d]		120	0.20	—
Brick, face[e]		130	0.11	—
Clay tile, hollow: 1 cell deep 3 in.		—	—	0.80
1 cell deep 4 in.		—	—	1.11
2 cells deep 6 in.		—	—	1.52
2 cells deep 8 in.		—	—	1.85

GLASS FIBER INSULATION BOARD

Conductivity $k = 0.25$ Btuh

Resistance $R = \dfrac{1}{k} = \dfrac{1}{0.25} = 4.0$

(4 in. in this example)

Conductance $C = \dfrac{k}{x} = \dfrac{0.25}{4} = 0.063$ Btuh

Resistance $R = \dfrac{x}{k} = \dfrac{4}{0.25} = 16.0$

SAND AND GRAVEL CONCRETE

Conductivity $k = 12$ Btuh

Resistance $R = \dfrac{1}{k} = \dfrac{1}{12} = 0.083$

(4 in. in this example)

Conductance $C = \dfrac{k}{x} = \dfrac{12}{3} = 3$ Btuh

Resistance $R = \dfrac{x}{k} = \dfrac{4}{12} = 0.33$

NOTE: Standard unit of area 1 sq ft. Standard unit temperature differential 1°F.

Owen L. Delevante, AIA; Glen Rock, New Jersey

E. C. Shuman, P. E.; Consulting Engineer; State College, Pennsylvania

MATERIAL & DESCRIPTION		DENSITY (lb per cu ft)	RESISTANCE (R)[a]	
			Per inch thickness (1/k)	For thickness listed (1/C)
MASONRY UNITS				
Concrete blocks, three oval core:				
Sand & gravel aggregate	4 in.	–	–	0.71
	8 in.	–	–	1.11
	12 in.	–	–	1.28
Cinder aggregate	3 in.	–	–	0.86
	4 in.	–	–	1.11
	8 in.	–	–	1.72
	12 in.	–	–	1.89
Lightweight aggregate	3 in.	–	–	1.27
(expanded shale, clay, slate	4 in.	–	–	1.50
or slag; pumice)	8 in.	–	–	2.00
	12 in.	–	–	2.27
Concrete blocks, rectangular core:				
Sand & gravel aggregate				
2 core, 8 in. 36 lb. g		–	–	1.04
Lightweight aggregate (expanded shale, clay, slate or slag; pumice)				
3 core, 6 in. 19 lb. g	45 F	–	–	1.65
2 core, 8 in. 24 lb. g	45 F	–	–	2.18
3 core, 12 in. 38 lb. g	45 F	–	–	2.48
Granite, marble		150–175	0.05	
Stone, lime or sand		–	0.08	
Gypsum partition tile:				
3 × 12 × 30 in. solid		–	–	1.26
3 × 12 × 30 in. 4-cell		–	–	1.35
4 × 12 × 30 in. 3-cell		–	–	1.67
METALS				
Aluminum		159–175	0.0007	
Brass, red		524–542	0.0014	
Brass, yellow		524–542	0.0014	
Copper, cast rolled		550–555	0.0004	
Iron, gray cast		438–445	0.0030	–
Iron, pure		474–493	0.0023	–
Lead		704	0.0040	–
Steel, cold drawn		490	0.0032	
Steel, stainless, type 304			0.0055	
Zinc, cast			0.0013	
PLASTERING MATERIALS				
Cement plaster, sand aggregate		116	0.20	–
Sand aggregate	1/2 in.	–	–	0.10
Sand aggregate	3/4 in.	–	–	0.15
Gypsum plaster:				
Lightweight aggregate	1/2 in.	45	–	0.32
Lightweight aggregate	5/8 in.	45	–	0.39
Lightweight aggregate, on metal lath	3/4 in.	–	–	0.47
Perlite aggregate		45	0.67	–
Sand aggregate		105	0.18	–
Sand aggregate	1/2 in.	105	–	0.09
Sand aggregate	5/8 in.	105	–	0.11
Sand aggregate, on metal lath	3/4 in.	–	–	0.1
Vermiculite aggregate		45	0.59	–
ROOFING				
Asbestos-cement shingles		120	–	0.21
Asphalt roll roofing		70	–	0.15
Asphalt shingles		70	–	0.44
Built-up roofing	3/8 in.	70	–	0.33
Slate	1/2 in.	–	–	0.05
SIDING MATERIALS				
(On Flat Surface)				
Shingles:				
Asbestos-cement		120	–	0.21
Wood, 16 in., 7-1/2 in. exposure		–	–	0.87
Wood, double, 16 in., 12 in. exposure		–	–	1.19
Wood, plus insul. backer board, 5/16 in.		–	–	1.40
Siding:				
Asbestos-cement, 1/4 in., lapped		–	–	0.21
Asphalt insulating siding (1/2 in. bd.)		–	–	1.46
Wood, drop, 1 × 8 in.		–	–	0.79
Wood, bevel, 1/2 × 8 in., lapped		–	–	0.81
Wood, bevel, 3/4 × 10 in., lapped		–	–	1.05
Architectural glass		–	–	0.10

Owen L. Delevante, AIA; Glen Rock, New Jersey

E. C. Shuman, P. E.; Consulting Engineer; State College, Pennsylvania

MATERIAL & DESCRIPTION		DENSITY (lb per cu ft)	RESISTANCE (R)[a]	
			Per inch thickness (1/k)	For thickness listed (1/C)
WOODS				
Maple, oak, and similar hardwoods		45	0.91	–
Fir, pine, and similar softwoods		32	1.25	–
Fir, pine, and similar softwoods				
	25/32 in.	32	–	0.98
	1 1/2 in.	32	–	1.89
	2 1/2 in.	32	–	3.12
	3 1/2 in.	32	–	4.35
Door, 1-3/4 in. thick solid wood core				1.96

STEEL DOORS (NOMINAL THICKNESS 1 3/4 IN.)

Mineral fiber core		–	–	1.69
Solid urethane foam core*		–	–	5.26
Solid polystyrene core*		–	–	2.13

*With thermal break.

AIR SURFACES

Position of Surface	Direction of Heat Flow	Type of Surface		
		Non-Reflective Materials	Reflective Aluminum Coated Paper	Highly Reflective Foil
		Resistance (R)	Resistance (R)	Resistance (R)
STILL AIR				
Horizontal	Upward	0.61	1.10	1.32
45° slope	Upward	0.62	1.14	1.37
Vertical	Horizontal	0.68	1.35	1.70
45° slope	Down	0.76	1.67	2.22
Horizontal	Down	0.92	2.70	4.55
MOVING AIR (any position)				
15 mph wind	Any	0.17 W	–	–
7-1/2 mph wind	Any	0.25 S	–	–

AIR SPACES

Position of Air Space and Thickness (inches)		Heat Flow Dir.	Sea-son	Types of Surfaces on Opposite Sides		
				Both Surfaces Non-Reflective Materials	Aluminum Coated Paper/ Non-Reflective Materials	Foil/ Non-Reflective Materials
				Resistance (R)	Resistance (R)	Resistance (R)
Horizontal	3/4	Up	W	0.87	1.71	2.23
	3/4		S	0.76	1.63	2.26
	4		W	0.94	1.99	2.73
	4		S	0.80	1.87	2.75
45° slope	3/4	Up	W	0.94	2.02	2.78
	3/4		S	0.81	1.90	2.81
	4		W	0.96	2.13	3.00
	4		S	0.82	1.98	3.00
Vertical	3/4	Down	W	1.01	2.36	3.48
	3/4		S	0.84	2.10	3.28
	4		W	1.01	2.34	3.45
	4		S	0.91	2.16	3.44
45° slope	3/4	Down	W	1.02	2.40	3.57
	3/4		S	0.84	2.09	3.24
	4		W	1.08	2.75	4.41
	4		S	0.90	2.50	4.36
Horizontal	3/4	Down	W	1.02	2.39	3.55
	1-1/2		W	1.14	3.21	5.74
	4		W	1.23	4.02	8.94
	3/4		S	0.84	2.08	3.25
	1-1/2		S	0.93	2.76	5.24
	4		S	0.99	3.38	8.08

GLASS. GLASS BLOCK AND PLASTIC SHEET

MATERIAL AND DESCRIPTION	OVERALL HEAT TRANSMISSION COEFFICIENT (U)	SEASONS	RESISTANCE (R)
VERTICAL PANELS—EXTERIOR			
Flat Glass			
Single glass	1.10	Winter	0.91
	1.04	Summer	0.96
Insulating glass, two lights of glass			
3/16 in. airspace	0.62	Winter	1.61
	0.65	Summer	1.54
1/4 in. airspace	0.58	Winter	1.72
	0.61	Summer	1.64
1/2 in. airspace	0.49	Winter	2.04
	0.56	Summer	1.79
Insulating glass, three lights of glass			
1/4 in. airspaces	0.39	Winter	2.56
	0.44	Summer	2.22
1/2 in. airspaces	0.31	Winter	3.23
	0.39	Summer	2.56
1/2 in. airspaces, low emittance coating			
e = 0.20	0.32	Winter	3.13
	0.38	Summer	2.63
e = 0.40	0.38	Winter	2.63
	0.45	Summer	2.22
e = 0.60	0.43	Winter	2.33
	0.51	Summer	1.96
Storm windows			
1–4 in. airspace	0.50	Winter	2.00
	0.50	Summer	2.00
Glass Block			
6 x 6 x 4 in. thick (nom.)	0.60	Winter	1.67
	0.57	Summer	1.76
8 x 8 x 4 in. thick (nom.)	0.56	Winter	1.79
	0.54	Summer	1.85
With cavity divider	0.48	Winter	2.08
	0.46	Summer	2.17
12 x 12 x 4 in. thick (nom.)	0.52	Winter	1.92
	0.50	Summer	2.00
With cavity divider	0.44	Winter	2.27
	0.42	Summer	2.38
12 x 12 x 2 in. thick (nom.)	0.60	Winter	1.67
	0.57	Summer	1.76
Single Plastic Sheet			
1/8 in. thick (nom.)	1.06	Winter	0.94
	0.98	Summer	1.02
1/4 in. thick (nom.)	0.96	Winter	1.04
	0.89	Summer	1.12
HORIZONTAL PANELS—EXTERIOR			
Flat Glass			
Single glass	1.23	Winter	0.81
	0.83	Summer	1.20
Insulating glass, two lights of glass			
3/16 in. airspace	0.70	Winter	1.43
	0.57	Summer	1.75
1/4 in. airspace	0.65	Winter	1.54
	0.54	Summer	1.85
1/2 in. airspace	0.59	Winter	1.69
	0.49	Summer	2.04
Glass Block			
11 x 11 x 3 in. thick with cavity divider	0.53	Winter	1.89
	0.35	Summer	2.86
12 x 12 x 4 in. thick with cavity divider	0.51	Winter	1.96
	0.34	Summer	2.94
Plastic Bubbles[k]			
Single walled	1.15	Winter	0.87
	0.80	Summer	1.25
Double walled	0.70	Winter	1.43
	0.46	Summer	2.17

NOTES

The thermal conductivity of glass is relatively high (k = 7.5), and, for single glazing, most of the thermal resistance is imposed at the indoor and outdoor surfaces. Indoors, approximately two-thirds of the heat flows by radiation to the room surfaces and only one-third flows by convection. This can be materially affected by the use of forced airflow from induction units, for example. The inner surface coefficient of heat transfer, h_i, can be substantially reduced by applying a low emittance metallic film to the glass.

For glazing with airspaces, the U value can be reduced to a marked degree by the use of low emittance films. This process imparts a variable degree of reflectance to the glass, thereby reducing its Shading Coefficient. Manufacturers' literature should be consulted for more details on this important subject. Also consult Chapter 26 of the 1977 ASHRAE Handbook of Fundamentals.

FOOTNOTES

a. Resistances are representative values for dry materials and are intended as design (not specification) values for materials in normal use. Unless shown otherwise in descriptions of materials, all values are for 75°C mean temperature.

b. Includes paper backing and facing if any. In cases where insulation forms a boundary (highly reflective or otherwise) of an airspace, refer to appropriate table for the insulating value of the airspace. Some manufacturers of batt and blanket insulation mark their products with R value, but they can ensure only the quality of the material as shipped.

c. Average values only are given, since variations depend on density of the board and on the type, size, and depth of perforations.

d. Thicknesses supplied by different manufacturers may vary depending on the particular material.

e. Values will vary if density varies from that listed.

f. Data on rectangular core concrete blocks differ from the data for oval core blocks because of core configuration, different mean temperature, and different unit weight. Weight data on oval core blocks not available.

g. Weight of units approx. 7⅝ high by 15⅝ long are given to describe blocks tested. Values are for 1 sq ft area.

h. Thermal resistance of metals is so low that in building constructions it is usually ignored. Values shown emphasize relatively easy flow of heat along or through metals so that they are usually heat leaks, inward or outward.

i. Spaces of uniform thickness bounded by moderately smooth surfaces.

j. Values shown not applicable to interior installations of materials listed.

k. Winter is heat flow up; summer is heat flow down.

l. Based on area of opening, not on total surface area.

Based on data from ASHRAE Handbook of Fundamentals, 1977, Chapter 22.

John I. Yellott, P. E.; College of Architecture; Arizona State University; Tempe, Arizona

SOLAR GAINS THROUGH SUNLIT FENESTRATION

Heat gains through sunlit fenestration constitute major sources of cooling load in summer. In winter, discomfort is often caused by excessive amounts of solar radiation entering through south facing windows. By contrast, passive solar design depends largely on admission and storage of the radiant energy falling on south facing and horizontal surfaces. Admission takes place both by transmission through glazing and by inward flow of absorbed energy. With or without the sun, heat flows through glazing, either inwardly or outwardly, whenever there is a temperature difference between the indoor and outdoor air. These heat flows may be calculated in the following manner.

The solar heat gain is estimated by a two-step process. The first step is to find, either from tabulated data or by calculation, the rate at which solar heat would be admitted under the designated conditions through a single square foot of double strength ($1/8$ in.) clear sheet glass. This quantity, called the solar heat gain factor (SHGF), is set by (a) the local latitude; (b) the date, hence the declination; (c) the time of day (solar time should be used); (d) the orientation of the window.

Tabulated values of SHGF are given in the 1977 ASHRAE Handbook of Fundamentals, Chapter 26, for latitudes from $0°$ (the equator) to $64°$ N by $8°$ increments and for orientations around the compass from N to NNW, by $22.5°$ increments. Selected values from the $40°$ table are given in an adjacent column.

Each individual fenestration system, consisting of glazing and shading devices, has a unique ability to admit solar heat. This property is evaluated in terms of its shading coefficient (SC), which is the ratio of the amount of solar heat admitted by the system under consideration to the solar heat gain factor for the same conditions. In equation form, this becomes:

$$\text{solar heat gain (Btu/sq ft} \cdot \text{hr)} = SC \times SHGF$$

Values of the shading coefficient are given in Chapter 26 of the 1977 ASHRAE Handbook of Fundamentals for the most widely used glazing materials alone and in combination with internal and external shading devices. Selected values for single and double glazing are given below:

SHADING COEFFICIENT FOR SELECTED GLAZING SYSTEMS

TYPE OF GLASS	SOLAR TRANSMISSION	SHADING COEFFICIENT, SC
Clear		
$1/8$ in.	0.86	1.00
$1/4$ in.	0.78	0.94
Heat absorbing		
$1/8$ in.	0.64	0.83
$1/4$ in.	0.46	0.69
Insulating glass, clear both lights		
$1/8 + 1/8$ in.	0.71	0.88
$1/4 + 1/4$ in.	0.61	0.81
Heat absorbing out		
Clear in, $1/4$ in.	0.36	0.55

For combinations of glazing and shading devices, see the ASHRAE chapter cited above.

The heat flow due to temperature difference is found by multiplying the U-value for the specified fenestration system by the area involved and by the applicable temperature difference:

$$Q = A \times [SC \times SHGF + U \times (t_o - t_i)]$$

The same equation is used for both summer and winter, with appropriate U-values, but in winter the conduction heat flow is usually outward because the outdoor air is colder than the indoor air.

Example: find the total heat gain, in Btu/sq ft $\cdot$ hr, for 1000 sq ft of unshaded $1/4$ in. heat absorbing single glass, facing west, in Denver ($40°$N latitude) at 4:00 P.M. solar time on October 21. Indoor air temperature is $70°$F; outdoor air temperature is $40°$F.

Solution: from the accompanying table, for 4:00 P.M. on October 21 find the SHGF for west facing fenestration on October 21 to be 173 Btu/sq ft $\cdot$ hr. For $1/4$ in. heat absorbing glass, SC = 0.69 and U for winter conditions is 1.10 Btu/sq ft $\cdot$ hr $\cdot$ $°$F.

$$Q = 1000 \times [0.69 \times 173 + 1.10 \times (40 - 70)]$$
$$= 1000 \times (119.4 - 33.0) = 86,400 \text{ Btu/hr}$$

Even though the outdoor air is $30°$ cooler than the indoor air, the net heat gain through the window in question would be equivalent to 7.2 tons of refrigeration.

For the same window area in summer, on August 21 at 4:00 P.M. solar time, SHGF = 216, and the air temperatures may be taken as $95°$F outdoors and $78°$F indoors. The total heat gain will be:

$$Q = 1000 \times [0.69 \times 216 + 1.04 \times (95 - 78)]$$
$$= 1000 \times (149.0 + 17.7) = 166,700 \text{ Btu/hr}$$
$$= 13.9 \text{ tons of refrigeration}$$

The cooling load can be reduced by selecting a fenestration system with lower shading coefficient and U-value. Under the same conditions, a double glazed window with two lights of $1/4$ in. clear glass and a highly reflective translucent inner shading device would have U = 0.52 and SC = 0.37. The cooling load would then be reduced to 88,760 Btu/hr or 7.4 tons of refrigeration.

SOL-AIR TEMPERATURE

When the opaque surfaces of a structure are struck by solar radiation, much of the energy is absorbed by the irradiated surface, raising its temperature and increasing the rate of heat flow into the roof or wall. The time lag between the onset of irradiation and the resulting rise in the indoor surface temperature depends on the thickness and mass per unit area of the building element and on the thermal conductivity, specific heat, and density of the materials. The time lag is negligible for an uninsulated metal roof, but it can be a matter of hours for a massive concrete or masonry wall.

Heat flow through sunlit opaque building elements is estimated by using the sol-air temperature, t_{sa}, defined as an imaginary outdoor temperature that, in the absence of sunshine, would give the same rate of heat flow as actually exists at the specified time under the combined influence of the incident solar radiation and the ambient air temperature.

$$t_{sa} = I \times Abs./h_o$$

where I = solar irradiance (Btu/sq ft $\cdot$ hr)

Abs. = surface absorptance, dimensionless

h_o = outer surface coefficient (Btu/sq ft $\cdot$ hr $\cdot$ $°$F)

Surface absorptances range from as low as 0.30 for a white surface to 0.95 for a black built-up roof. Values of h_o range from the conventional 4.0 for summer with an assumed wind speed of 7.5 mph to a still air value of 3.0.

Example: find the rate of heat flow through a 1000 sq ft uninsulated black built-up roof, U = 0.3, under strong summer sunshine, I = 300 Btu/sq ft $\cdot$ hr, still air with $100°$F outdoors, $78°$F indoors.

Solution: the sol-air temperature is found from

$$t_{sa} = 300 \times \frac{0.95}{3.0} + 100 = 195°F$$

The rate of heat flow, neglecting the time lag, is

$$Q = 1000 \times 0.3 \times (195 - 78) = 35,100 \text{ Btu/hr}$$

With no sunshine on the roof, the heat flow is

$$\text{heat flow} = 1000 \times 0.3 \times (100 - 78) = 6600 \text{ Btu/hr}$$

The effect of the solar radiation is thus to increase the heat flow rate by 88%. A more massive roof with a lower U-value would show considerably less effect of the incoming solar radiation.

SOLAR INTENSITY AND SOLAR HEAT GAIN FACTORS FOR 40°N LATITUDE

DATE	SOLAR TIME (A.M.)	DIRECT NORMAL (BTUH/SQ FT)	SOLAR HEAT GAIN FACTORS (BTUH/SQ FT)					SOLAR TIME (P.M.)
			N	E	S	W	HOR	
Jan 21	8	142	5	111	75	5	14	4
	10	274	16	124	213	16	96	2
	12	294	20	21	254	21	133	12
Feb 21	8	219	10	183	94	10	43	4
	10	294	21	143	203	21	143	2
	12	307	24	25	241	25	180	12
Mar 21	8	250	16	218	74	16	85	4
	10	297	25	153	171	25	186	2
	12	307	29	31	206	31	223	12
Apr 21	6	89	11	88	5	5	11	6
	8	252	22	224	41	21	123	4
	10	286	31	152	121	31	217	2
	12	293	34	36	154	36	252	12
May 21	6	144	36	141	10	10	31	6
	8	250	27	220	29	25	146	4
	10	277	34	148	83	34	234	2
	12	284	37	40	113	40	265	12
June 21	6	155	48	151	13	13	40	6
	8	246	30	216	29	27	153	4
	10	272	35	145	69	35	238	2
	12	279	38	41	95	41	267	12
Jul 21	6	138	37	137	11	11	32	6
	8	241	28	216	30	26	145	4
	10	269	35	146	81	35	231	2
	12	276	38	41	109	41	262	12
Aug 21	6	81	12	82	6	5	12	6
	8	237	24	216	41	23	122	4
	10	272	32	150	116	32	214	2
	12	280	35	38	149	38	247	12
Sep 21	8	230	17	205	71	17	82	4
	10	280	27	148	165	27	180	2
	12	290	30	32	200	32	215	12
Oct 21	8	204	11	173	89	11	43	4
	10	280	21	139	196	21	140	2
	12	294	25	27	234	27	177	12
Nov 21	8	136	5	108	72	5	14	4
	10	268	16	122	209	16	96	2
	12	288	20	21	250	21	132	12
Dec 21	8	89	3	67	50	3	6	4
	10	261	14	113	146	14	77	2
	12	285	18	19	253	19	113	12
			N	W	S	E	HOR	PM

John I. Yellott, P.E., Professor Emeritus; College of Architecture, Arizona State University; Tempe, Arizona

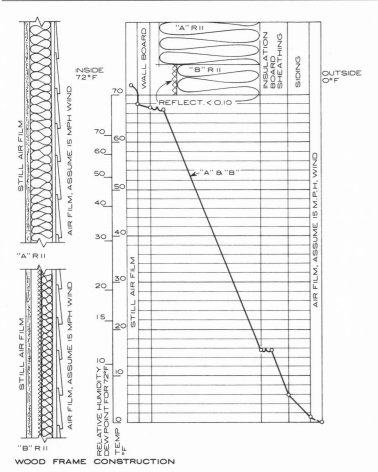

WOOD FRAME CONSTRUCTION

	WALL "A"			WALL "B"		
	R F/Btu*	°F Diff. Due to R*	Temp °F*	R F/Btu*	°F Diff Due to R*	Temp °F*
Indoor room air			72.0			72.0
Still air film (indoor)	0.68	3.2		0.68	3.2	
Indoor face of wall board			68.8			68.8
Gypsum or plaster board (1/2 in.)	0.45	2.1		0.45	2.1	
Back face of wall board			66.7			66.7
Stud air space remaining	negl.	—				
Inner face of insulation			66.7			66.7
Thermal insulation, R11-wo/refl.	11.00	51.37				
-w/refl.				11.00	51.37	
Outer face of insulation			15.3			15.3
Inner face of sheathing			15.3			15.3
Sheathing, 25/32 in., 20 lb.	2.06	9.6		2.06	9.6	
Outer face of sheathing			5.7			5.7
Inner face of siding			5.7			5.7
Siding, wood, 3/4 x 10, lapped	1.05	4.9		1.05	4.95	
Outer face of siding			0.8			0.8
Outdoor air film (15 mph wind)	0.17	0.80		0.17	0.80	
Outdoor air			0			0
TOTALS	15.41	72.0		15.41	72.0	

Heat Loss/sf = $\dfrac{\text{Temp. Diff., Room to Outdoors}}{\text{Total Resistance, R}}$ = $\dfrac{72-0}{15.41}$ = 4.7 Btu/hr. applies to insulated areas

only; studs and other materials are heat paths which increase heat loss.

Wall "A"—Full thick fibrous insulation R11, non-reflective faces, air spaces insufficient to provide any significant resistance.

Wall "B"—Reflective faced fibrous insulation, R11 with the facing; air space 3/4 in. or more in width required with the facing to provide R11; that space must not be counted a second time.

Insulation thicknesses are not specified but only the R value of the material as manufactured; proper installation is implied.

*
Decimals are used to check calculations only — fractional Btu's are usually of no consequence.

MASONRY CAVITY WALL CONSTRUCTION

	WALL "A"			WALL "B"		
	R F/Btu*	°F Diff. Due to R*	Temp °F*	R F/Btu*	°F Diff. Due to R*	Temp °F*
Indoor room air			72.0			72.0
Still air film (indoor)	0.68	10.55		0.68	4.16	
Indoor face of wall board			61.45			67.84
Gypsum or plaster board (1/2 in.)	0.45	6.98		0.45	2.76	
Back face of wall board			54.47			65.08
Furring air space (3/4 in.)	0.90	13.95		0.90	5.52	
Inner face of concrete block			40.52			59.56
Concrete block, 8 in., 3 oval core sand & gravel	1.11	17.10		1.11	6.80	
Outer face of concrete block			23.42			52.76
"A" cavity, 2 in. air space	0.90	13.95		—	—	
"B" cavity, filled w/insulation R8	—	—		8.0	49.04	
Inner face of face brick			9.47			3.72
Face brick, nom. 4 in.	0.44	6.83		0.44	2.70	
Outer face of face brick			2.64			1.02
Outdoor air film (15 mph wind)	0.17	2.63		0.17	1.04	
Outdoor air			0			0
TOTALS	4.65	72.01		11.75	72.02	

Heat Loss/sf = $\dfrac{\text{Temp. Diff., Room to Outdoors}}{\text{Total Resistance, R}}$ = $\dfrac{72-0}{4.65}$ = 15.5 Btu/hr. $\dfrac{72-0}{11.75}$ = 6.13 Btu/hr.

Wall "A"—2 in. open cavity

Wall "B"—2 in. cavity filled with insulation R8. (Verify if water-repellent type is required) R value is for material as manufactured; proper installation is implied.

*Decimals are used to check calculations only—fractional Btu's are usually of no consequence.

NOTE: In tabulation the considerable difference between the temperatures of inside surfaces of the two walls. Occupants of conventional rooms with Wall "A" will be less comfortable than with Wall "B" because of colder inside surface temperature; 61°F vs. 68°F.

Owen L. Delevante, AIA; Glen Rock, New Jersey

E. C. Shuman, P. E.; Consulting Engineer; State College, Pennsylvania

WINTER WEATHER DATA AND DESIGN CONDITIONS FOR THE UNITED STATES AND CANADA

STATE OR PROVINCE	CITY	LATITUDE (° ')	LONGITUDE (° ')	ELEVATION (FT)	WINTER DESIGN TEMP.*	AVE. WINTER TEMP.†	SEPT	OCT	NOV	DEC	JAN	FEB	MAR	APR	MAY	TOTAL
Ala.	Birmingham	33 3	86 5	61	21	54.2	6	93	363	555	592	462	363	108	9	2551
	Mobile	30 4	88 1	119	29	59.9	0	22	213	357	415	300	211	42	0	1560
Alaska	Fairbanks	64 5	147 5	436	-47	6.7	642	1203	1833	2254	2359	1901	1739	1068	555	14,279
	Juneau	58 2	134 4	17	1	32.1	483	725	921	1135	1237	1070	1073	810	601	9075
Ariz.	Flagstaff	35 1	111 4	6973	4	35.6	201	558	867	1073	1169	991	911	651	437	7152
	Tucson	32 1	111 0	2584	32	58.1	0	25	231	406	471	344	242	75	6	1800
Ark.	Little Rock	34 4	92 1	257	20	50.5	9	127	465	716	756	577	434	126	9	3219
Calif.	Bakersfield	35 2	119 0	495	32	55.4	0	37	282	502	546	364	267	105	19	2122
	Sacramento	38 3	121 3	17	32	54.4	0	62	312	533	561	392	310	173	76	2419
	San Diego	32 4	117 1	19	44	59.5	21	43	135	236	298	253	214	135	90	1458
	San Francisco	37 5	122 3	52	40	55.1	102	118	231	388	443	336	319	279	239	3001
Colo.	Alamosa	37 3	105 5	7536	-6	29.7	279	639	1065	1420	1476	1162	1020	696	440	8529
	Denver	39 5	104 5	5283	1	37.6	117	428	819	1035	1132	938	887	558	288	6283
Conn.	Hartford	41 1	73 1	7	9	37.3	117	394	714	1101	1190	1042	908	519	205	6235
Del.	Wilmington	39 4	75 3	78	14	42.5	51	270	588	927	980	874	735	387	112	4930
D.C.	Washington	38 5	77 0	14	17	45.7	33	217	519	834	871	762	626	288	74	4224
Fla.	Miami	25 5	80 2	7	47	71.1	0	0	0	65	74	56	19	0	0	214
	Tallahassee	30 2	84 2	58	30	60.1	0	28	198	360	375	286	202	36	0	1485
Ga.	Atlanta	33 4	84 3	1005	22	51.7	18	124	417	648	636	518	428	147	25	2961
	Savannah	32 1	81 1	52	27	57.8	0	47	246	437	437	353	254	45	0	1819
Hawaii	Honolulu	21 2	158 0	7	63	74.2	0	0	0	0	0	0	0	0	0	0
Idaho	Boise	43 3	116 1	2842	10	39.7	132	415	792	1017	1113	854	722	438	245	5809
Ill.	Chicago	42 0	87 5	658	-4	35.8	117	381	807	1166	1265	1086	939	534	260	6639
	Springfield	39 5	89 4	587	2	40.6	72	291	696	1023	1135	935	769	354	136	5429
Ind.	Indianapolis	39 4	86 2	793	2	39.6	90	316	723	1051	1113	949	809	432	177	5699
Iowa	Des Moines	41 3	93 4	948	-5	35.5	96	363	828	1225	1370	1187	915	438	180	6588
Kan.	Goodland	39 2	101 4	3645	0	37.8	81	381	810	1073	1166	955	884	507	236	6141
	Topeka	39 0	95 4	877	4	41.7	57	270	672	980	1122	893	722	330	124	5182
Ky.	Lexington	38 0	84 4	979	8	43.8	54	239	609	902	946	818	685	325	105	4683
La.	New Orleans	30 0	90 2	3	33	61.8	0	12	165	291	344	241	177	24	0	1254
	Shreveport	32 3	93 5	252	25	56.2	0	47	297	477	552	426	304	81	0	2184
Me.	Portland	43 4	70 2	61	-1	33.0	195	508	807	1215	1339	1182	1042	675	372	7511
Md.	Baltimore	39 1	76 4	146	13	43.7	48	264	585	905	936	820	679	327	90	4654
Mass.	Boston	42 2	71 0	15	9	40.0	60	316	603	983	1088	972	846	513	208	5634
Mich.	Detroit	42 2	83 0	633	6	37.2	87	360	738	1088	1181	1058	936	522	220	6232
	Escanaba	45 4	87 0	594	-7	29.6	243	539	924	1293	1445	1296	1203	777	456	8481
Minn.	Duluth	46 5	92 1	1426	-16	23.4	330	632	1131	1581	1745	1518	1355	840	490	10,000
	Minneapolis	44 5	93 1	822	-12	28.3	189	505	1014	1454	1631	1380	1166	621	288	8322
Miss.	Jackson	32 2	90 1	330	25	55.7	0	65	315	502	546	414	310	87	0	2239
Mo.	Columbia	39 0	92 2	778	4	42.3	54	251	651	967	1076	875	716	324	121	5046
Mont.	Billings	45 5	108 3	3367	-10	34.5	186	487	897	1135	1296	1100	970	570	285	7049
	Missoula	46 5	114 1	3200	-6	31.5	303	651	1035	1287	1420	1120	970	621	391	8125
Neb.	North Platte	41 1	100 4	2779	-4	35.5	123	440	885	1166	1271	1039	930	519	248	6684
	Omaha	41 2	95 5	978	-3	35.6	105	357	828	1175	1355	1126	939	465	208	6612
Nev.	Las Vegas	36 1	115 1	2162	28	53.5	0	78	387	617	688	487	335	111	6	2709
	Reno	39 3	119 5	4404	10	39.3	204	490	801	1026	1073	823	729	510	357	6332
N.H.	Concord	43 1	71 3	339	-3	33.0	177	505	822	1240	1358	1184	1032	636	298	7383
N.J.	Trenton	40 1	74 5	144	14	42.4	57	264	576	924	989	885	753	399	121	4980
N.M.	Albuquerque	35 0	106 4	5310	16	12.0	12	229	642	868	930	703	595	288	81	4348
N.Y.	Buffalo	43 0	78 4	705	6	34.5	141	440	777	1156	1256	1145	1039	645	329	7062
	New York	40 5	74 0	132	15	42.8	30	233	540	902	986	885	760	408	118	4871
N.C.	Charlotte	35 0	81 0	735	22	50.4	6	124	438	691	691	582	481	156	22	3191
	Wilmington	34 2	78 0	30	26	54.6	0	74	291	521	546	462	357	96	0	2347
N.D.	Bismarck	46 5	100 5	1647	-19	26.6	222	577	1088	1463	1708	1442	1203	645	329	8851
Ohio	Cleveland	41 2	81 5	777	5	37.2	105	384	738	1088	1159	1047	918	552	260	6351
	Columbus	40 0	82 5	812	5	39.7	84	347	714	1039	1088	949	809	426	171	5660
Okla.	Oklahoma City	35 2	97 4	1280	13	48.3	15	164	498	766	868	664	527	189	34	3725
	Tulsa	36 1	95 5	650	13	47.7	18	158	522	787	893	683	539	213	47	3860
Ore.	Salem	45 0	123 0	195	23	45.4	111	338	594	729	822	647	611	417	273	4754
Pa.	Pittsburgh	40 3	80 1	1137	5	38.4	105	375	726	1063	1119	1002	874	480	195	5987
	Williamsport	41 1	77 0	527	7	38.5	111	375	717	1073	1122	1002	856	468	177	5934
R.I.	Providence	41 4	71 3	55	9	38.8	96	372	660	1023	1110	988	868	534	236	5954
S.C.	Columbia	34 0	81 1	217	24	54.0	0	84	345	577	570	470	357	81	0	2484
S.D.	Rapid City	44 0	103 0	3165	-7	33.4	165	481	897	1172	1333	1145	1051	615	326	7345
Tenn.	Nashville	36 1	86 4	577	14	48.9	30	158	495	732	778	644	512	189	40	3578
Texas	Brownsville	25 5	97 3	16	39	67.6	0	0	66	149	205	106	74	0	0	600
	Dallas	32 5	96 5	481	22	55.3	0	62	321	524	601	440	319	90	6	2363
	El Paso	31 5	106 2	3918	24	52.9	0	84	414	648	685	445	319	105	0	2700
	Houston	29 4	95 2	50	32	61.0	0	6	183	307	384	288	192	36	0	1396
Utah	Salt Lake City	40 5	112 0	4220	8	38.4	81	419	849	1082	1172	910	763	459	233	6052
Vt.	Burlington	44 3	73 1	331	7	29.4	207	539	891	1349	1513	1333	1187	714	353	8269
Va.	Lynchburg	37 2	79 1	947	16	46.0	51	223	540	822	849	731	605	267	78	4166
Wash.	Seattle	47 4	122 2	14	27	46.9	129	329	543	657	738	599	577	396	242	4424
W. Va.	Charleston	38 2	81 4	939	11	44.8	63	254	591	865	880	770	648	300	96	4476
Wisc.	Green Bay	44 3	88 1	683	-9	30.3	174	484	924	1333	1494	1313	1141	654	305	8029
Wyo.	Casper	42 5	106 3	5319	-5	33.4	192	524	942	1169	1290	1084	1020	651	381	7410
CANADA																
Alta.	Edmonton	53 34	113 31	2219	-25	—	411	738	1215	1603	1810	1520	1330	765	400	10,268
B.C.	Vancouver	49 11	123 10	16	19	—	219	456	657	787	862	723	676	501	310	5515
Man.	Winnipeg	49 54	97 14	786	-27	—	322	683	1251	1757	2008	1719	1465	813	405	10,679
N.S.	Halifax	44 39	63 34	83	5	—	180	457	710	1074	1213	1122	1030	742	487	7361
Ont.	Toronto	43 41	79 38	578	-1	—	151	439	760	1111	1233	1119	1013	616	298	6827
Que.	Montreal	45 28	73 45	98	-10	—	165	521	882	1392	1566	1381	1175	684	316	8203

*Based on 97.5% Design Dry-Bulb values found in ASHRAE Handbook of Fundamentals, 1977.
†October–April, inclusive. ASHRAE Systems Handbook, 1976.
‡Based on the period 1931–1960, inclusive. ASHRAE Systems Handbook, 1976.

BUILT-UP ROOFING and ROLL ROOFING

BUILT-UP FLAT ROOF WITH SLAG or GRAVEL FINISH

Max. slopes
asphalt 2" to 4" in 12"
tarred ½" to 4" in 12"
Scale 1"=1'-0"

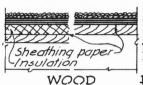
Sheathing paper
Insulation
WOOD

Insulation
POURED & PRECAST CONC. & POURED GYPSUM

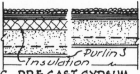
Insulation   Purlin
PRECAST GYPSUM

Insulation   Purlin
INSULATED STEEL DECK

BUILT-UP STEEP ROOF WITH MINERAL SURFACE FINISH

Min. slope 3" in 12"
Max. slope 5" in 12"
Scale 1"=1'-0"

Insulation
Lay sheathing paper on boards
WOOD

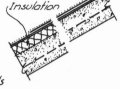
Insulation
POURED & PRECAST CONC.

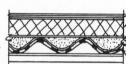
Insulation
POURED GYPSUM

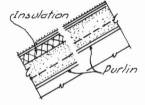
Insulation
Purlin
PRECAST GYPSUM

SPECIAL BUILT-UP ROOFS

Cement finish
Concrete fill
Gravel or slag
Built-up roof-4 ply
Slab
CEMENT FINISH

Gravel or slag
Asphalt or pitch
Gravel or slag
Built-up roof-4 ply
Slab
SPRAY POND

Built-up roof-4 ply
Insulation
Asbestos felt
Granulated fill
Asphalt or pitch
Corr. asbestos roof
CORRUGATED ASBESTOS

TILE ROOFS-FLAT

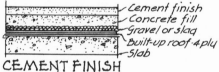

Tile finish - ⅜" or ½" jts.
In pitch or asphalt In cement
WOOD ROOF CONC. ROOF

½" setting bed
Built-up roof 4 or 5 ply
Slab   Slab

Tile finish   Shrinkage mesh
Built-up roof 4 or 5 ply
Cinder fill -1½ min.
Slab
Built-up roof under fill. Built-up roof over fill.
CONCRETE SLABS with FILL

Herringbone method using 8"×4" or 6"×3" tile.

Most economical - using any oblong shape tile.

Materials:

Quarry (Promenade) tiles are usually used but other floor tile may be used. Standard sizes are: Square, 9", 8", 6", 4", 2¾". Oblong: 9"×6", 8"×4", 8"×3¾", 6"×2¾". Provide expansion joint every 12'-0" in both directions for tiles set in cement. Max. slope ¼" in 12".

Roll roofing is best for structures where long maintenance free service is not important. Permanence may be achieved where appearance not a consideration by applying asphalt coatings at intervals of 5 to 10 years.

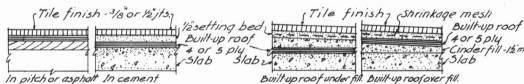

Headlap 3" min.
Wood deck
9" wide starter strips covered with asphalt cement.
Nails 4" apart & staggered.
Roofing to overhang rake & eaves ¼" to ⅜"
6" sidelap
Asphalt cement, quicksetting
Min. pitch 12" 2"
CONCEALED NAIL METHOD - ROLL ROOFING

Non-corroding metal drip
Nails
Roofing to overhang eaves & rake ¼" to ⅜"
Selvage
Exposure
Starter strip of 19" selvage
Quick-setting asphalt cement
Min. pitch 12" 1"
DOUBLE COVERAGE ROLL ROOFING

3'
17" 140#
DOUBLE COVERAGE, 19" SELVAGE

Wts. per 100 a'
5'
MINERAL SURF. 90#
SMOOTH SURFACE 45#, 55# & 65#
ASPHALT ROLL ROOFING

Data from the Asphalt Roofing Industry Bureau

ASPHALT SHINGLES

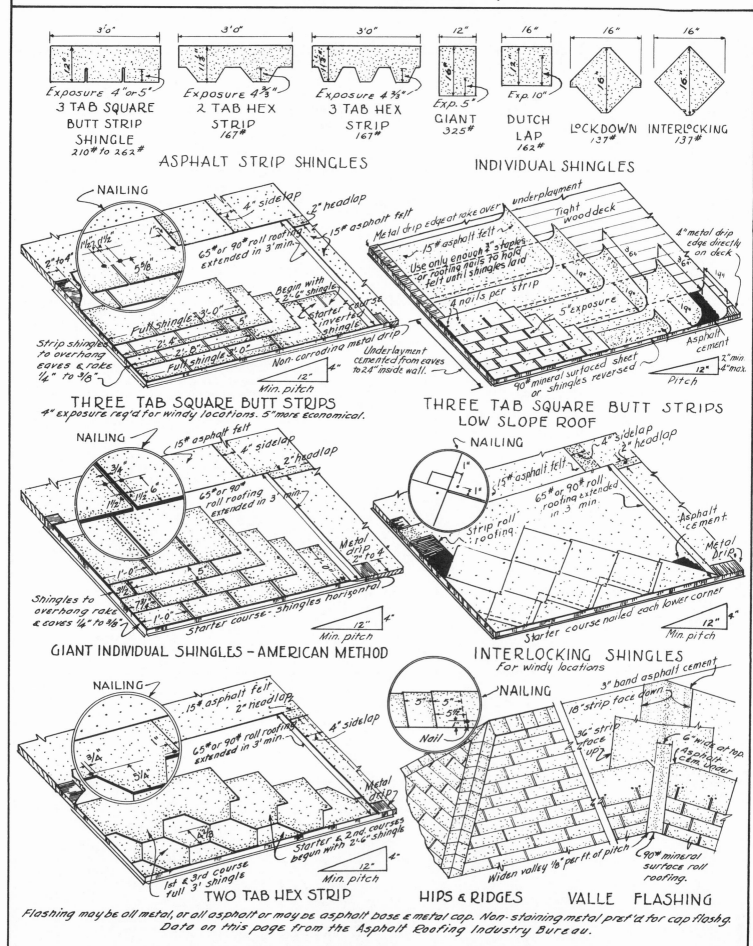

ASPHALT STRIP SHINGLES

- 3 TAB SQUARE BUTT STRIP SHINGLE 210# to 262# — Exposure 4" or 5"
- 2 TAB HEX STRIP 167# — Exposure 4⅜"
- 3 TAB HEX STRIP 167# — Exposure 4⅜"

INDIVIDUAL SHINGLES

- GIANT 325# — Exp. 5"
- DUTCH LAP 162# — Exp. 10"
- LOCKDOWN 137#
- INTERLOCKING 137#

THREE TAB SQUARE BUTT STRIPS
4" exposure req'd for windy locations. 5" more economical.

THREE TAB SQUARE BUTT STRIPS LOW SLOPE ROOF

GIANT INDIVIDUAL SHINGLES – AMERICAN METHOD

INTERLOCKING SHINGLES
For windy locations

TWO TAB HEX STRIP

HIPS & RIDGES   VALLEY FLASHING

Flashing may be all metal, or all asphalt or may be asphalt base & metal cap. Non-staining metal pref'd for cap flashg.
Data on this page from the Asphalt Roofing Industry Bureau.

ALUMINUM ROOFING and SIDING

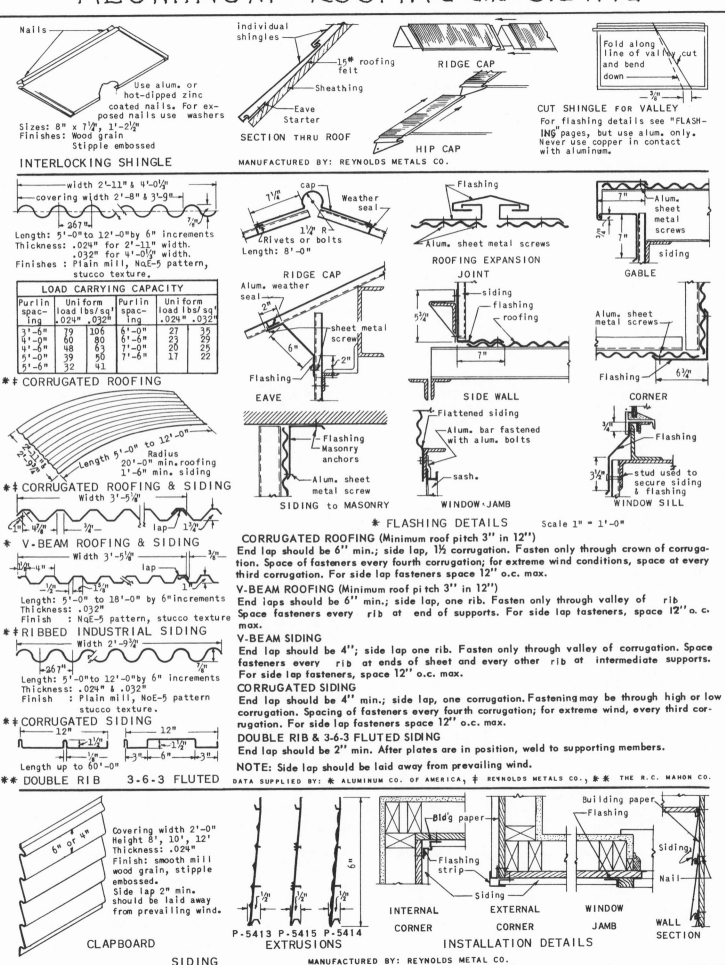

Nails

Use alum. or hot-dipped zinc coated nails. For exposed nails use washers

Sizes: 8" x 7¼", 1'-2½"
Finishes: Wood grain
Stipple embossed

INTERLOCKING SHINGLE

individual shingles — 15# roofing felt — Sheathing — Eave Starter

SECTION THRU ROOF

RIDGE CAP

HIP CAP

MANUFACTURED BY: REYNOLDS METALS CO.

Fold along line of valley cut and bend down — 3/8"

CUT SHINGLE FOR VALLEY

For flashing details see "FLASH-ING" pages, but use alum. only. Never use copper in contact with aluminum.

---

width 2'-11" & 4'-0⅓"
covering width 2'-8" & 3'-9"
267"   7/8"

Length: 5'-0"to 12'-0"by 6" increments
Thickness: .024" for 2'-11" width.
.032" for 4'-0⅓" width.
Finishes : Plain mill, NoE-5 pattern, stucco texture.

LOAD CARRYING CAPACITY

Purlin spacing	Uniform load lbs/sq' .024"	.032"	Purlin spacing	Uniform load lbs/sq' .024"	.032"
3'-6"	79	106	6'-0"	27	35
4'-0"	60	80	6'-6"	23	29
4'-6"	48	63	7'-0"	20	25
5'-0"	39	50	7'-6"	17	22
5'-6"	32	41			

*‡ CORRUGATED ROOFING

cap   7¼"   Weather seal
1½" R
Rivets or bolts
Length: 8'-0"

RIDGE CAP

Alum. weather seal   2"   6"   2"
sheet metal screw
Flashing

EAVE

Flashing
Masonry anchors
Alum. sheet metal screw

SIDING to MASONRY

Flashing
Alum. sheet metal screws

ROOFING EXPANSION JOINT

siding
flashing
roofing
7"
5¾"

SIDE WALL

Flattened siding
Alum. bar fastened with alum. bolts
sash.

WINDOW JAMB

7"   Alum. sheet metal screws
3/4"   7"
siding

GABLE

Alum. sheet metal screws
Flashing
6¾"

CORNER

3/4"   Flashing
3½"   stud used to secure siding & flashing

WINDOW SILL

Length 5'-0" to 12'-0"
2'-11" & 2'-9¾"
Radius 20'-0" min. roofing 1'-6" min. siding

*‡ CORRUGATED ROOFING & SIDING

Width 3'-5⅛"
1" 4⅞" 3/4" lap 1 3/8"

* V-BEAM ROOFING & SIDING

Width 3'-5⅛"   3/8"
1½" 4" 1/2" 1 5/8" lap

Length: 5'-0" to 18'-0" by 6"increments
Thickness: .032"
Finish : NoE-5 pattern, stucco texture

**‡ RIBBED INDUSTRIAL SIDING

Width 2'-9¾"
267"   7/8"

Length: 5'-0"to 12'-0"by 6" increments
Thickness: .024" & .032"
Finish : Plain mill, NoE-5 pattern stucco texture.

**‡ CORRUGATED SIDING

12"   12"
1½"   1½"
1/8"   3" 6" 3"

Length up to 60'-0"

** DOUBLE RIB   3-6-3 FLUTED

* FLASHING DETAILS   Scale 1" = 1'-0"

CORRUGATED ROOFING (Minimum roof pitch 3" in 12")
End lap should be 6" min.; side lap, 1½ corrugation. Fasten only through crown of corrugation. Space of fasteners every fourth corrugation; for extreme wind conditions, space at every third corrugation. For side lap fasteners space 12" o.c. max.

V-BEAM ROOFING (Minimum roof pitch 3" in 12")
End laps should be 6" min.; side lap, one rib. Fasten only through valley of rib Space fasteners every rib at end of supports. For side lap fasteners, space 12" o. c. max.

V-BEAM SIDING
End lap should be 4"; side lap one rib. Fasten only through valley of corrugation. Space fasteners every rib at ends of sheet and every other rib at intermediate supports. For side lap fasteners, space 12" o.c. max.

CORRUGATED SIDING
End lap should be 4" min.; side lap, one corrugation. Fastening may be through high or low corrugation. Spacing of fasteners every fourth corrugation; for extreme wind, every third corrugation. For side lap fasteners space 12" o.c. max.

DOUBLE RIB & 3-6-3 FLUTED SIDING
End lap should be 2" min. After plates are in position, weld to supporting members.

NOTE: Side lap should be laid away from prevailing wind.

DATA SUPPLIED BY: * ALUMINUM CO. OF AMERICA, ‡ REYNOLDS METALS CO., ** THE R.C. MAHON CO.

6" or 4"

Covering width 2'-0"
Height 8', 10', 12'
Thickness: .024"
Finish: smooth mill wood grain, stipple embossed.
Side lap 2" min. should be laid away from prevailing wind.

CLAPBOARD

1/2"   1/2"   1/2"
6"

P-5413 P-5415 P-5414

EXTRUSIONS

Bld'g paper
Flashing strip
Siding

INTERNAL CORNER

Building paper
Flashing
Siding

EXTERNAL CORNER

WINDOW JAMB

Siding
Nail

WALL SECTION

INSTALLATION DETAILS

SIDING

MANUFACTURED BY: REYNOLDS METAL CO.

GALVANIZED STEEL ROOFING and SIDING

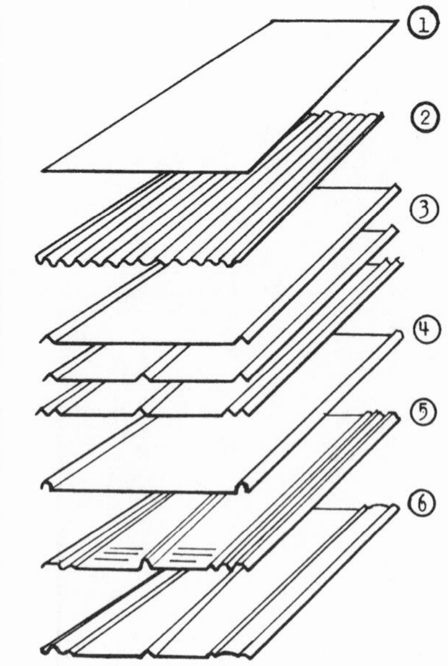

1
2
3
4
5
6

STANDARD SHEET SIZES						
USE	TYPES	MFG*	GAUGES	WIDTH	LENGTH‡	TO WEATHER
Roofing & siding	(1) PLAIN SHEET					
	26½" wide sheet	R B	24 & lighter 26 to 29	26½" 26½"	50' 50'**	24" 24"
	(2) CORRUGATED SHEET					
	1¼" Corrugations	R B	20 & lighter 20 to 29	26" or 27½" 25" or 26"	5'-12' 6'-12'	24" 24"
	2½" Corrugations	R B	16 & lighter 14 to 29	26" or 27½" 26" or 27½"	5'-12' 6'-12'	24" 24"
	(3) V-CRIMP SHEETS					
	2 V-crimped	R	26 to 29	25⅛"	6'-12'	24"
	3 V-crimped	R	26 to 29	25"	6'-12'	24"
	5 V-crimped	R B	26 to 29 26 thru 29	26" 26"	6'-12' 6'-12'	24" 24"
	(4) PRESSED STANDING SEAM SHEET					
		R	24 & lighter	24"+	5'-12'	24"
	(5) TRIPLE-DRAIN SHEET					
		R	26, 28, 29		5'-12'	24"
	(6) STORMPROOF SHEET					
		B	26, 28, 29	26⅛"	6'-12'	24"

* R = Republic Steel Corporation * B = Bethlehem Steel Company
‡ Lengths are restricted to multiples of 1 ft.
** Made up of 4 sheets with double cross lock seams

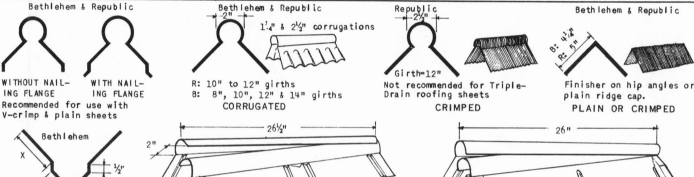

Bethlehem & Republic

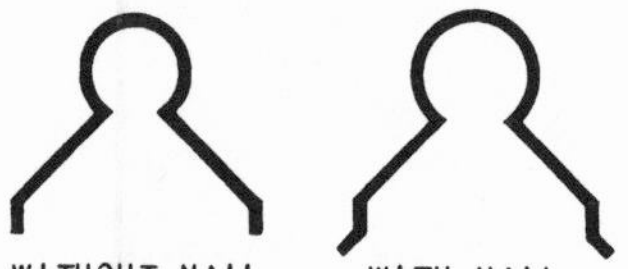

WITHOUT NAILING FLANGE WITH NAILING FLANGE
Recommended for use with V-crimp & plain sheets

Bethlehem & Republic

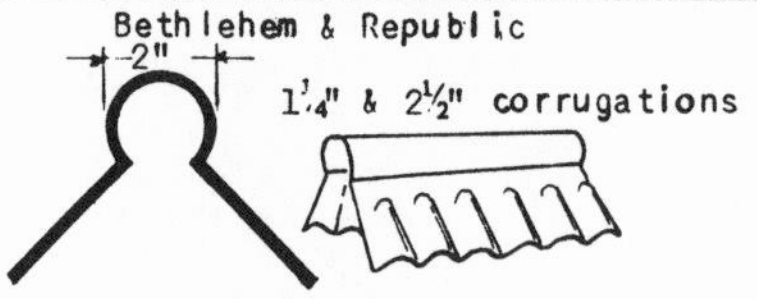

2"
1¼" & 2½" corrugations

R: 10" to 12" girths
B: 8", 10", 12" & 14" girths
CORRUGATED

Republic

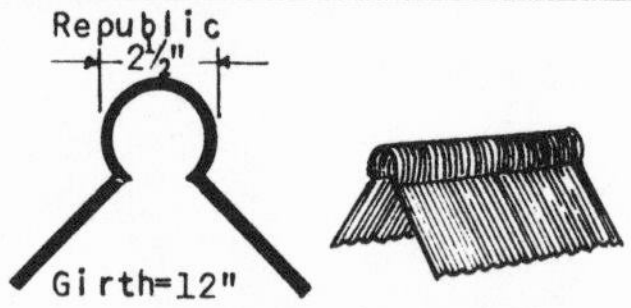

2½"
Girth=12"

Not recommended for Triple-Drain roofing sheets
CRIMPED

Bethlehem & Republic

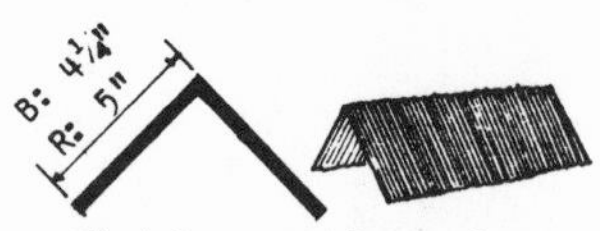

B: 4¼"
R: 5"

Finisher on hip angles or plain ridge cap.
PLAIN OR CRIMPED

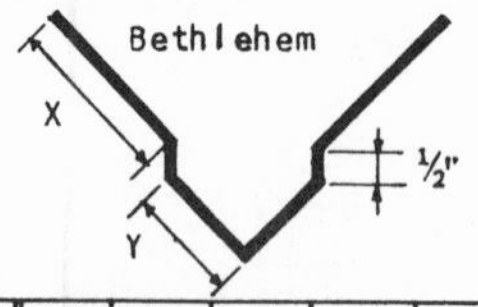

Bethlehem
X
Y
½"

X	3"	3½"	4"	4½"	5½"
Y	1½"	2"	2½"	3"	4"

Girths: 10",12",14",16" & 20"
FORMED VALLEY
NOTE: Rolled valley available in 50' length, girths 8" to 30"

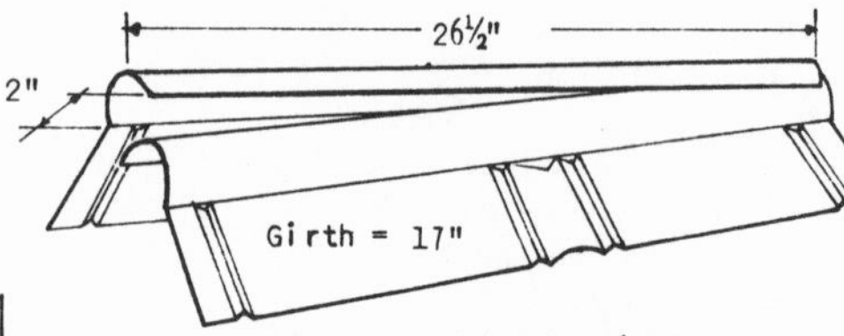

26½"
2"
Girth = 17"

Gauges: 26,28 & 29
FOR STORMPROOF ROOFING SHEETS

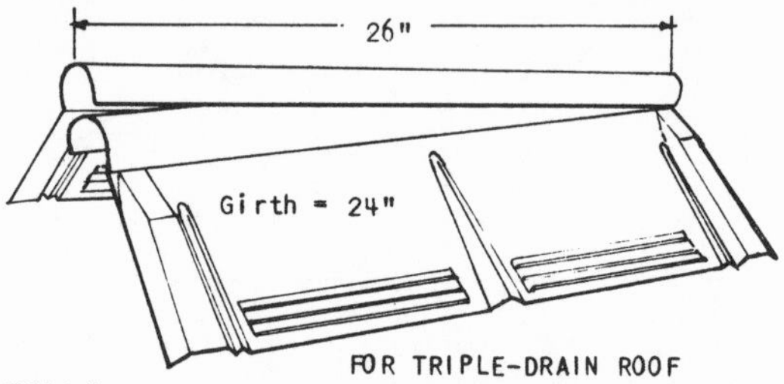

26"
Girth = 24"

FOR TRIPLE-DRAIN ROOF

2-PIECE ADJUSTABLE RIDGE ROLLS

FORMED RIDGE ROLLS

NOTE: The girth is the width of sheet required to form the shape.

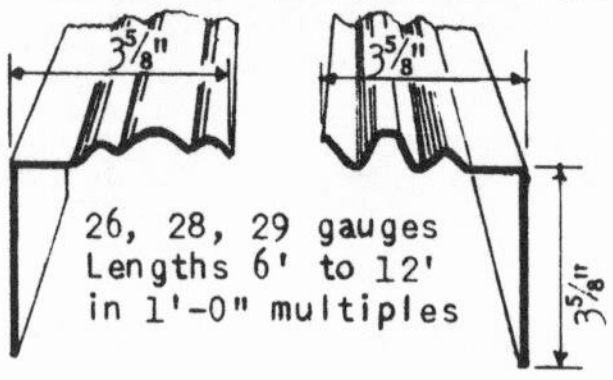

3⅝"
3⅝"
3⅝"

26, 28, 29 gauges
Lengths 6' to 12' in 1'-0" multiples

GABLE-END FINISHER GABLE-END STARTER

26,28 & 29 gauges
Lengths 6'-12'

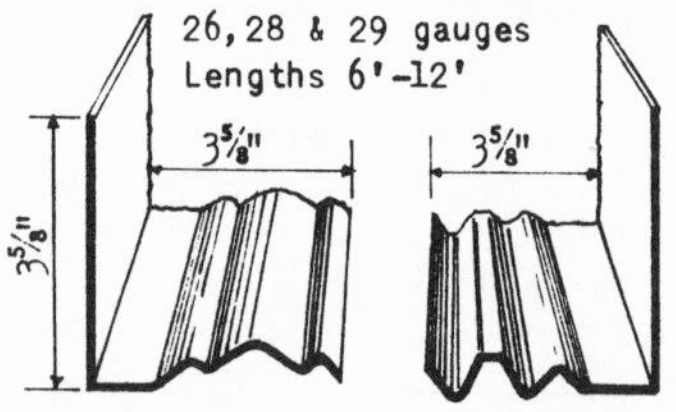

3⅝"
3⅝"
3⅝"

SIDE-WALL FINISHER SIDE-WALL STARTER

STORMPROOF

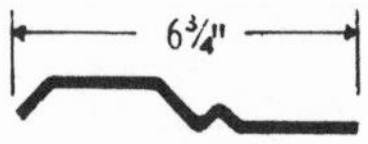

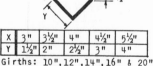

6¾"

GABLE-END FINISHER

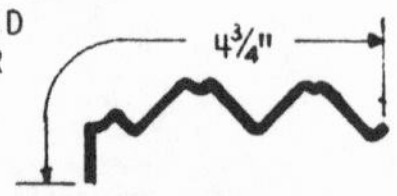

4¾"

GABLE-END STARTER

NOTE: Finisher laps over roofing sheet. Starter goes under roofing sheet.

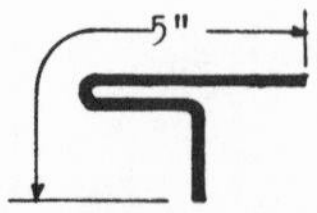

5"

OVERHANGING EAVES DRIP

TRIPLE-DRAIN

STORMPROOF & TRIPLE-DRAIN ACCESSORIES

Bethlehem & Republic

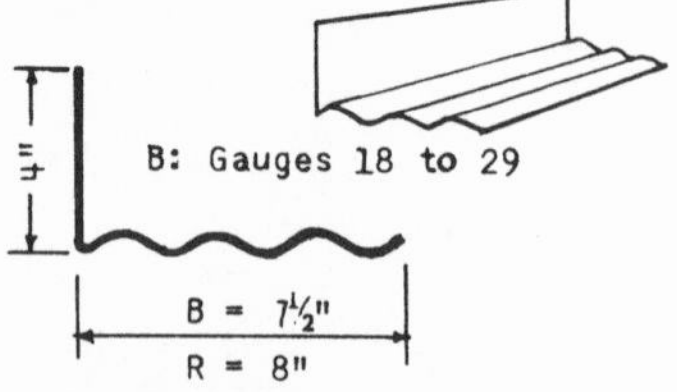

4"
B: Gauges 18 to 29
B = 7½"
R = 8"

CORRUGATED SIDE-WALL FLASHING

Bethlehem & Republic

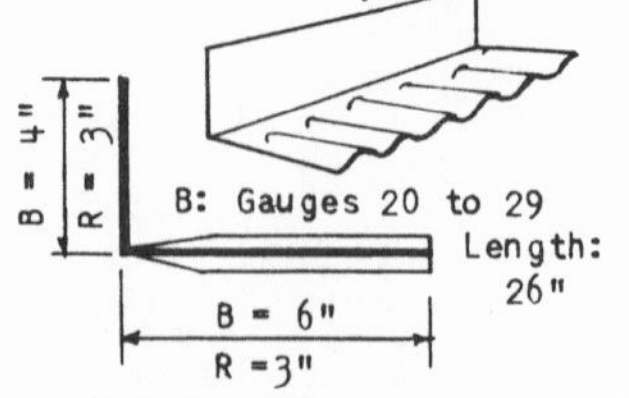

B = 4"
R = 3"
B: Gauges 20 to 29
Length: 26"
B = 6"
R = 3"

CORRUGATED END-WALL FLASHING

CORRUGATED SHEET ACCESSORIES

NOTE: Bethlehem ridge rolls, valley, and corrugated side-wall flashing available in lengths up to 10'-0".

NOTE:
For plain roll roofing details see "Zinc Roofing".
For construction details of corrugated and other types of sheet roofing see "Protected Metal Roofing & Siding".

DATA CHECKED BY REPUBLIC STEEL CORPORATION & BETHLEHEM STEEL COMPANY

PROTECTED METAL ROOFING and SIDING

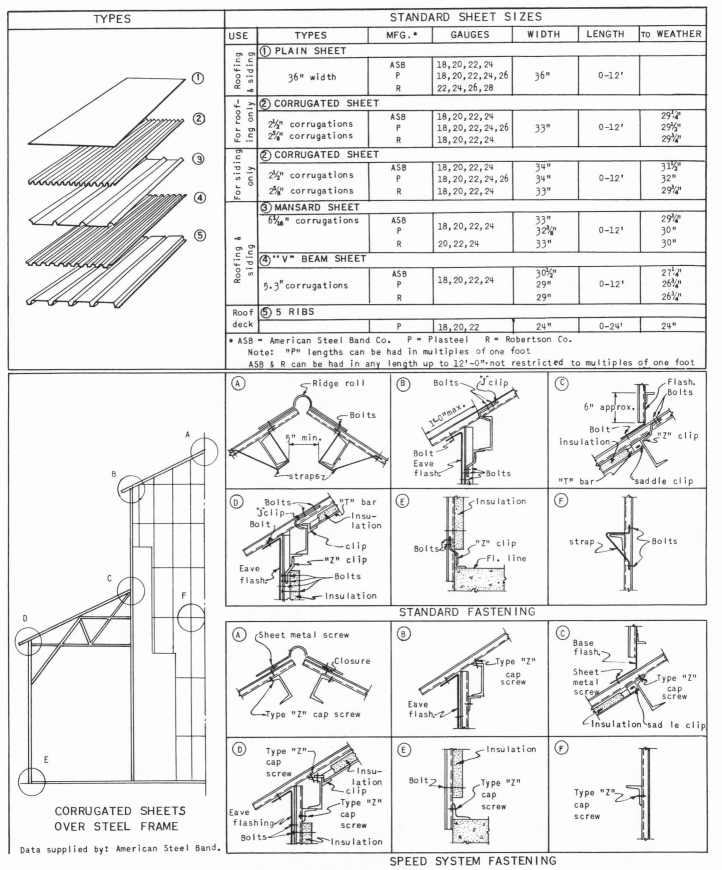

TYPES

STANDARD SHEET SIZES

USE	TYPES	MFG.*	GAUGES	WIDTH	LENGTH	TO WEATHER
Roofing & siding	① PLAIN SHEET 36" width	ASB P R	18,20,22,24 18,20,22,24,26 22,24,26,28	36"	0-12'	
For roofing only	② CORRUGATED SHEET 2½" corrugations 2⅝" corrugations	ASB P R	18,20,22,24 18,20,22,24,26 18,20,22,24	33"	0-12'	29¼" 29½" 29¾"
For siding only	② CORRUGATED SHEET 2½" corrugations 2⅝" corrugations	ASB P R	18,20,22,24 18,20,22,24,26 18,20,22,24	34" 34" 33"	0-12'	31½" 32" 29¾"
Roofing & siding	③ MANSARD SHEET 6¹⁄₁₆" corrugations	ASB P R	18,20,22,24 20,22,24	33" 32⅜" 33"	0-12'	29¾" 30" 30"
Roofing & siding	④ "V" BEAM SHEET 5.3" corrugations	ASB P R	18,20,22,24	30½" 29" 29"	0-12'	27¼" 26¾" 26¾"
Roof deck	⑤ 5 RIBS	P	18,20,22	24"	0-24'	24"

* ASB = American Steel Band Co.   P = Plasteel   R = Robertson Co.
Note: "P" lengths can be had in multiples of one foot
ASB & R can be had in any length up to 12'-0" not restricted to multiples of one foot

STANDARD FASTENING

SPEED SYSTEM FASTENING

CORRUGATED SHEETS OVER STEEL FRAME

Data supplied by: American Steel Band.

CONSTRUCTION DETAILS

Note: The principles of correct detailing of protected metal roofing are in general similar to those which apply to galvanized iron and aluminum roofing with the exception that bolts and nuts are used in place of rivets. For details of sandwich (insulation type) and V crimp roofings see pages on galvanized iron and aluminum roofings.

COPPER ROOFING

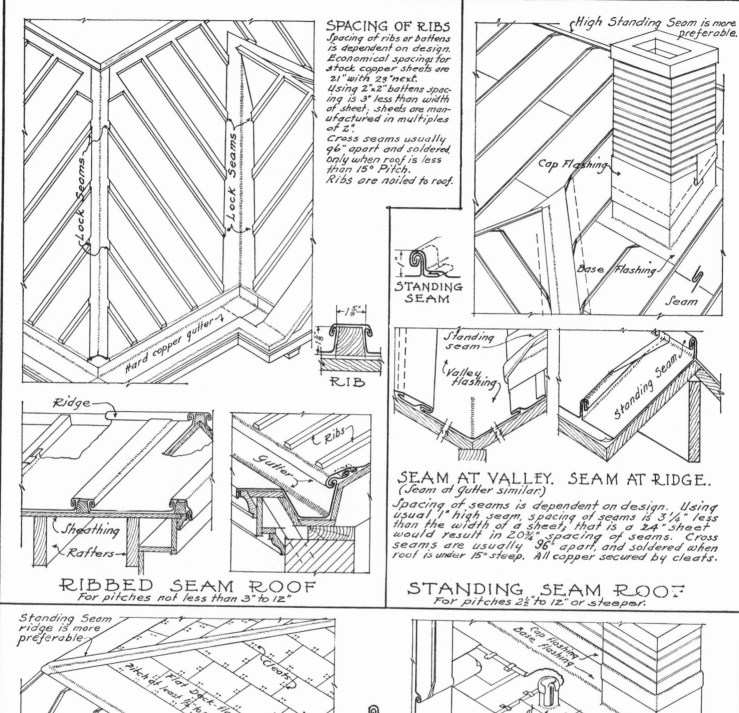

SPACING OF RIBS
Spacing of ribs or battens is dependent on design. Economical spacings for stock copper sheets are 21" with 23" next.
Using 2"x2" battens spacing is 3" less than width of sheet; sheets are manufactured in multiples of 2".
Cross seams usually 96" apart and soldered only when roof is less than 15° Pitch.
Ribs are nailed to roof.

Lock Seams

Lock Seams

Hard copper gutter

$1\frac{5}{8}$"

$1\frac{5}{8}$"

RIB

High Standing Seam is more preferable.

Cap Flashing

Base Flashing

Seam

STANDING SEAM

Ridge

Gutter

Sheathing

Rafters

Ribs

RIBBED SEAM ROOF
For pitches not less than 3" to 12"

Standing seam

Valley flashing

Standing Seam

Standing Seam

SEAM AT VALLEY. SEAM AT RIDGE.
(Seam at Gutter similar.)

Spacing of seams is dependent on design. Using usual 1" high seam, spacing of seams is $3\frac{1}{4}$" less than the width of a sheet; that is a 24" sheet would result in $20\frac{3}{4}$" spacing of seams. Cross seams are usually 96" apart, and soldered when roof is under 15° steep. All copper secured by cleats.

STANDING SEAM ROOF
For pitches $2\frac{1}{2}$" to 12" or steeper.

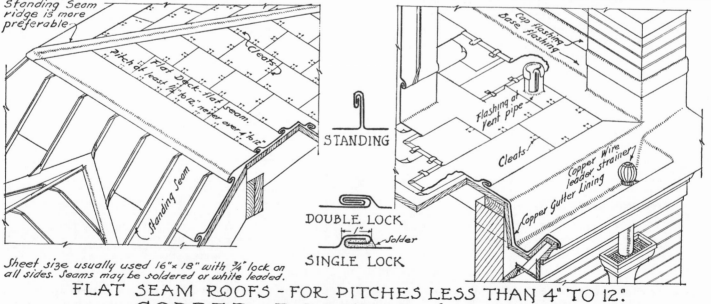

Standing Seam ridge is more preferable.

Cleats

Pitch at least $\frac{1}{2}$" to 12", never over 4" to 12"

Flat Deck-flat seam.

Standing Seam

STANDING

DOUBLE LOCK

1" Solder

SINGLE LOCK

Cap Flashing
Base Flashing

Flashing at Vent pipe

Cleats

Copper Wire leader strainer

Copper Gutter Lining

Sheet size usually used 16"x 18" with $\frac{3}{4}$" lock on all sides. Seams may be soldered or white leaded.

FLAT SEAM ROOFS - FOR PITCHES LESS THAN 4" TO 12".
COPPER ROOFING (16 & 20 OZ. COPPER)
Methods recommended by the Copper and Brass Research Association.

COPPER ROOFING & FLASHING

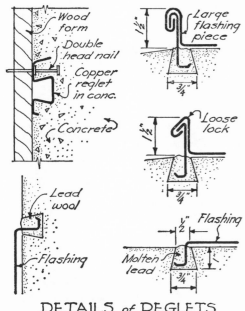

Wood form
Double head nail
Copper reglet in conc.
Concrete
Lead wool
Flashing

DETAILS of REGLETS
3" = 1'-0"

Lead caulking need not be continuous nor filled to very top of reglet. Lead plugs may be driven in at 12" intervals, space intervening & reglet top filled with elastic cem.

Large flashing piece

Loose lock

Flashing
Molten lead

UNSOLDERED (loose lap)
When loose lap seams are used on slopes amt. of lap determined by pitch.

SOLDERED
Pretin edge of sheet for solder, ½" min. wider than fin. seam. 1" lap for 20 oz., 1¼" for 20 to 24.

HEAVY SHEETS RIVETED

LAP SEAMS

HOOK LOCK
Pieces hooked together & joint malleted down.

FLAT LOCK
Developed from hook seam by use of grooving iron. Used where not room enough for hook lock.

DOUBLE LOCK
Virtually standing seam bent flat. Used to avoid soldering or to allow expansion & contraction

LOCK SEAMS

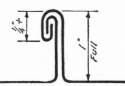

STANDING SEAM
This seam allows for expansion & contraction

DEVELOPMENT of DOUBLE LOCK or STANDING SEAM

Point driven into sheathing on new roofs. Slate butts rest against loop

For slate roofs already laid. Hook over upper edge of slate.

For old roofs. Also soldered to copper roofs.

Spacing: Approx. 18" staggered in both directions
COPPER WIRE SNOW GUARDS (3 or 4 rows)

ADJUSTABLE BRACKET & PIPE SNOW GUARD
Spacing of brackets 6' max. Brass pipe & bronze plate fastening & brackets.
Also made with 3 pipes.

STANDARD SIZES of SHEET COPPER, SOFT & COLD-ROLL

WEIGHT Oz. per ft.²	WIDTH Inches			LENGTH Inches
32	24	30	36	96
24	24	30	36	96
20	24	30	36	96
18	24	30	36	96
16	24	30	36	96, 120
14	24	30	36	96

STANDARD SIZES of STRIP COPPER

WEIGHT Oz. per ft.²	SIZE Inches	WEIGHT Oz. per ft.²	SIZE Inches
32	20 × 96	16	15 × 96
24	20 × 96	16	14 × 96
20	20 × 96	16	12 × 96
18	20 × 96	16	10 × 96
16	20 × 120	14	20 × 96
16	20 × 96	10	16 × 72

NOTE: The above weights & sizes are generally preferred, but additional weights & sizes are available. Strip is also generally available in rolls of 16 oz. copper in widths varying from 6" to 20" & from about 50' to 100' in length, depending on width, weighing between 80 & 100 lbs.

TEMPER & WEIGHT of COPPER SHEET & SHAPES FOR VARIOUS USES

NOTE: CR = cold rolled; S = Soft; * Membrane flashing

WHERE USED	TEMPER & WEIGHT Oz. per ft.²	WHERE USED	TEMPER & WEIGHT Oz. per ft.²	WHERE USED	TEMPER & WEIGHT Oz. per ft.²	WHERE USED	TEMPER & WEIGHT Oz. per ft.²
Cant Strips	16 CR	–Jambs	3* or 6 S	Gutters, Built-in – Apron	16 CR	–Batten Covers	16 CR
Chimneys	16 CR	–Sills	16 CR	–Lining	Varies	–Lock Strips	16 CR
Dormer Roofs	16 or 20 CR	Gable Ends	20 CR	–Lock Strip	Varies	–Valleys	16 CR
Dowels, Rods, Struts	16 or 20 CR	Hips	20 CR	–Half Round, Hanging	16 CR	–Standing Seam – Pan	16 or 20 CR
Edge Strips	16 to 32 CR	Hips, Saddle	16 CR	–Molded (or Box)	16 CR	–Roll	16 or 20 CR
Flashings:		Masonry Veneer	10 S	–Pole	16 CR	–Small Hse.	10 CR
Base, Low	16 CR	Ridges	16 CR	Leaders	16 CR	–Valleys	16 CR
Base, High	20 CR	Thro-Wall – Concealed	6 or 10 S	Leader Heads	16 or 20 CR	–Flat Seam – Cleats	20 CR
Belt Courses, Stone	20 CR	–Exposed, Wide	16 S	Leader Straps	16 CR	–Sheets	20 CR
Cap (Counter)	16 CR	–Exposed, Narrow	10 S	Louvres – Frame Covering	16 S	–Corrugated-Sheets	20 CR
Cavity Wall	10 S	Valleys, Closed-Slate or Tile	20 CR	–Slats	20 CR	Scuppers	20 CR
Copings	20 CR	–Wood	16 CR	Outlets-Gutter	16 to 24 CR	Siding –Standing Seam	20 CR
Cornices, Stone	20 CR	Valleys, Open-Slate or Tile	24 CR	–Roof	16 to 32 CR	–Flat Seam	20 CR
Cornices, Wood	16 CR	–Wood	16 CR	Roofing-Batten Seam-20"pans	16 CR	–Corrugated	16 CR
Door & Window – Heads	3* or 6 S	Gravel Stops	16 or 20 CR	–24"pans	20 CR	Vents & Ventilators	16 or 20 CR

Recommendation of Copper & Brass Research Association

LEAD ROOFING and PRECAST ROOFING

Weight per □'	Thickness in inches	Use for which it is recommended	Lengths
2½#	1/24	Cap & base flashg. Batten roofing if less than 24"o.c.	For cap flashing, batten caps, gutter lining 8'-0"
3#	3/64	Other roofing, cornice flashing, gutter lining.	for all other purposes. ————— 4'-0"
4#	1/16	Special roofing conditions	
6#	3/32	Scalloped edgings. Ornaments	Stock widths are rolled 24", 30" & 36" wide
8#	1/8	" " " & shower pans.	Do not use steel near lead.

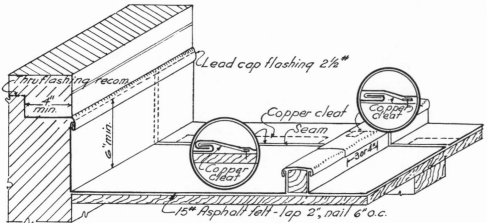

Thru flashing recom.
1¼"
4" min.
Lead cap flashing 2½#
6" min.
Copper cleat
Copper cleat
Seam
Copper cleat
3 or 4
15# Asphalt felt - lap 2", nail 6" o.c.

LEAD ROOFING

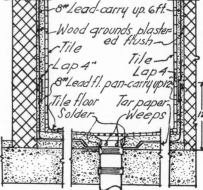

Secure top of lead w.p. with cleats
8# Lead - carry up. 6ft.
Wood grounds plastered flush
Tile
Lap 4"
Tile
Lap 4
8# Lead fl. pan - carry up 12"
Tile floor
Tar paper
Solder
Weeps
12"

WATERPROOFING SHOWER STALL

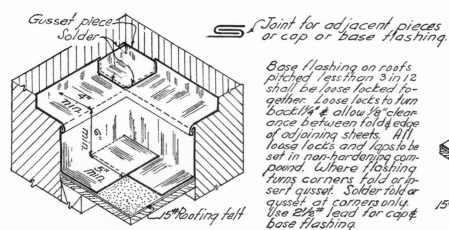

Gusset piece
Solder
4" min.
6" min.
5" min.
15# Roofing felt

FLASHING INTERIOR CORNER

⌇ Joint for adjacent pieces or cap or base flashing.

Base flashing on roofs pitched less than 3 in 12 shall be loose locked together. Loose locks to turn back 1¼" & allow ⅛" clearance between fold & edge of adjoining sheets. All loose locks and laps to be set in non-hardening compound. Where flashing turns corners fold or insert gusset. Solder fold or gusset at corners only. Use 2½# lead for cap & base flashing.

Solder
4" min.
6" min.
15# Roofing felt
Solder
Gusset piece

FLASHING EXTERIOR CORNER

Never nail lead, but secure with lead, copper or lead-coated copper cleats which are nailed with two hard copper wire nails. Secure lead to masonry with cleats or lead cap flashing strip. All cleats to be approx. 10" o.c. On steep roofs run cleats continuously in horizontal plane and secure them 12" o.c. Do not solder loose lock seams. Lap all vertical joints 3" min. Vertical surfaces over 18" high to have seams 18" apart. Lead expands but does not contract. Max. expansion is .02/ft. 12 lbs. of lead per 100□' is usual for lead-ctd. copper. Where lead is in contact with masonry coat with asphaltum.

LEAD (HARD) ROOFING, FLASHING & W.P.
Data checked by Lead Industries Association.

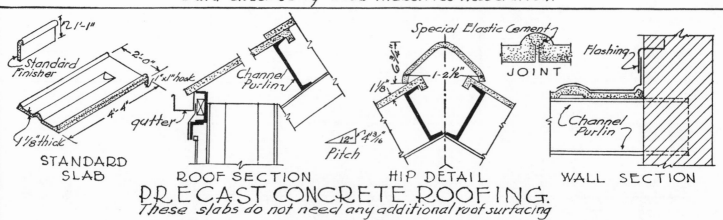

2"-1"
Standard Finisher
2'-0"
1"x1" hook
Channel Purlin
gutter
Special Elastic Cement
3¾"
1-2½"
1⅛"
4³⁄₁₆"
12"
Pitch
Flashing
JOINT
Channel Purlin
1⅛" thick
4'-4"

STANDARD SLAB   ROOF SECTION   HIP DETAIL   WALL SECTION

PRECAST CONCRETE ROOFING.
These slabs do not need any additional roof surfacing

MONEL ROOFING

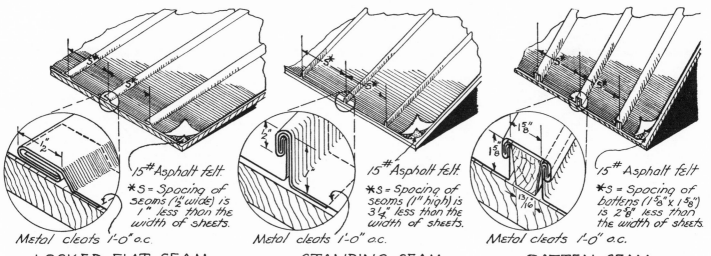

15# Asphalt felt.

*S = Spacing of seams (1½" wide) is 1" less than the width of sheets.

Metal cleats 1'-0" o.c.

LOCKED FLAT SEAM
For pitches less than 3 to 12

15# Asphalt felt.

*S = Spacing of seams (1" high) is 3¼" less than the width of sheets.

Metal cleats 1'-0" o.c.

STANDING SEAM
For pitches 3 to 12 or over

15# Asphalt felt

*S = Spacing of battens (1⅝" x 1⅝") is 2⅝" less than the width of sheets.

Metal cleats 1'-0" o.c.

BATTEN SEAM
For large pitches 3 to 12 or over.

The following maximum sheet widths are recommended to insure against buckling:
For No. 26 gauge; 20" wide. For No. 25 gauge & heavier; 24" wide.
Scale ¼" = 1'-0". Details at ½ full size.

TYPES of SEAMS

SHEET WEIGHTS & SIZES

U.S.S. GAUGE	MAX. WIDTH & LENGTH*	THICKNESS	WGT. #/▢'	U.S.S. GAUGE	MAX. WIDTH & LENGTH*	THICKNESS	WGT. #/▢'
Most commonly used gauges.				No. 21	36"x120"	.034	1.58
No. 26	36"x 96"	.018"	0.86	" 20	36"x120"	.037	1.73
" 25	36"x120"	.021"	1.01	" 19	36"x120"	.043	2.02
" 24	36"x120"	.025"	1.15	" 18	36"x120"	.050	2.30
Other available gauges.				" 17	36"x120"	.056	2.59
No. 23	36"x120"	.028"	1.30	" 16	36"x120"	.062	2.88
" 22	36"x120"	.031"	1.44	*St'd widths are 24", 30" & 36" St'd lengths; 96" & 120"			

Notes: Do not nail through roofing sheets. Use monel clips, cleats and nails for attachment. All bends and seams should be made with a radius at least equal to twice the thickness of the sheet. Cleats should be spaced 10"-12" o.c. The strongest joints can be obtained by lock-seaming, spot welding, or other means. Joints should allow for expansion of metal. For flashing, see pages on flashing.

RECOMMENDED GAUGES for SPECIFIC USES

USE	U.S.S. GAUGE	USE	U.S.S. GAUGE	USE	U.S.S. GAUGE
BATTEN SEAM ROOFING		(cont.) base, over 10" wide	#25	(cont.) frame covering	#26
24" wide	#25	base, 10" and under	26	louver slats (under 6'-0")	25
valleys	26	EAVES FLASHINGS	26	louver slats (over 6'-0")	24
eaves	24	EXPANSION JOINTS		vertical strips	24
cover strips	26	exterior walls	26	SIDINGS (BULKHEADS - ELEVATOR PENTHOUSES, & STAIRCASE SHAFTS.)	
CLEATS	26	roof curbs	25		
COPING COVER		"V" cover and floors	26		
edge strips on wood copings	24	FLAT SEAM ROOFING	25	crimped, keyed, and corrugated sheets	26
edge strips on stone copings	22	GRAVEL STOPS		flat sheets	25
standing seam	26	stops	25	SKYLIGHTS	
flat sheet coping	25	edge strips	24	caps	25
CORNICES & BELT COURSES		GUTTERS		condensation gutter	26
edge strip on wood cornices	24	gutter linings		STANDING SEAM ROOFING	
		36" girth & smaller	25	24" wide	25
edge strip on stone cornices	22	36" to 48" girth	24	valleys	26
belt courses	22	48" girth & larger	22	eaves	24
flat covering	25	molded gutters	25	THRU WALL FLASHING	
COUNTER, BASE & CAP FLASHINGS		hung gutters	26	flashings	26
		gutter expansion joints	26	VALLEY FLASHINGS	
		LEADERS		with wood or asphalt shingles	26
counter flashings	26	downspouts	26		
cap flashings	26	heads	26	with slate or tile roofing	24
		straps	26		
		LOUVERS (STATIONARY)			

Data on this sheet submitted by the International Nickel Company, Inc.

TIN ROOFING

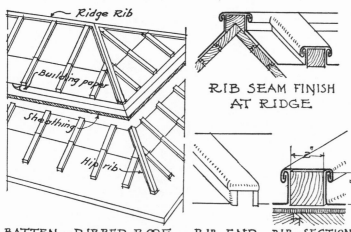

RIB SEAM FINISH AT RIDGE

BATTEN or RIBBED ROOF.   RIB END   RIB-SECTION.

See "Zinc" and Copper Roofing sheets for full details. All plates secured to ribs 1'-0" apart by cleats. Ribs nailed to sheathing. All cross seams to be flat locked and soldered. No nails to be driven thro' sheets. Ribs may be of any size desired but 2"x 2" is usual size. Sheets 20"x 28" or other standard sizes — See below

BATTEN or RIBBED SEAM ROOF.

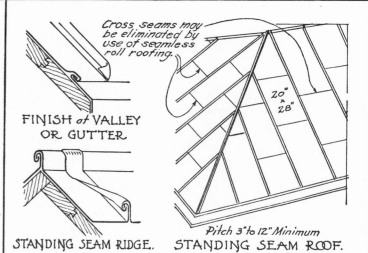

FINISH of VALLEY OR GUTTER

STANDING SEAM RIDGE.   STANDING SEAM ROOF.

Pitch 3" to 12" Minimum

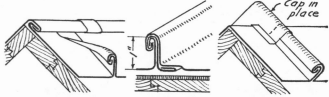

RIDGE COMB finished   STANDING SEAM   SEAM CAPPED
WITH FLAT SEAL.   DOUBLE LOCKED   RIDGE

For use on steep roofs; slope must be not less than 3" to 12". Sheet size usually used is 20"x 28", seam takes 2¾" from width of sheet. Cleats secure sheets to roof and are spaced 12" o.c. maximum.
Cross seams to be flat locked and soldered. Use 2-⅛" nails to a cleat and space 8" apart. Nailing tin directly is not advised.

STANDING SEAM ROOF.

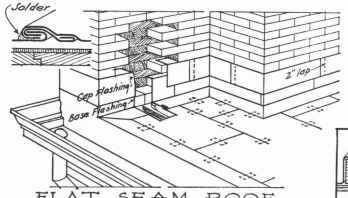

FLAT SEAM ROOF
(For Pitches less than 3" to 12")

Pitch roof not less than ½" to 12". Sheets are 14"x 12" and allow 1½" on both dimensions for seams. Attach to roof (narrow way) with cleats - two to 14". Solder with half & half solder after malleting seams flat.

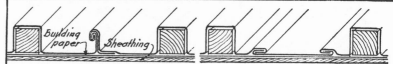

STANDING SEAM   FLAT SEAM
AND RIB SEAM.   AND RIB SEAM.
COMBINATION TYPES OF ROOFS.

Notes
Lay tin on 6# waterproof paper, free of tar. If this is not done paint underside with non oxide and oil. both may be done for safety. Prime top with same paint and finish with 2 coats lead & oil. For Flashing and Leaders & Gutters see sheets of those titles.

	Weights and Gauges of Tin Plate (Terne Plate) – without Tin finish –				
Gauge No.	Weight per □' in ounces	Weight per □' in pounds	Thickness	Stock Sizes	Recommended Use
IC (30)	9.	.56	.0122	14"x 20", 20"x 28", 14"x 96", 20"x 96", 24"x 96", 28"x 96", 28"x 120"	For flat seams, but IX is better.
IX (28)	11.1	.69	.0155		All roofs, flashings, built in gutters.
28 26 24 }	No longer available.			50 ft. rolls of IC & IX gauge seamless Terne roofing available in 14" 24" & 28" widths from Follansbee Steel Corp.	

Expansion of Tin .825" per 100' per 100°. Coating is:- mixture of lead & tin. Weights from 20 to 40 lbs per box (112 sheets 20"x 28"). The term "long terne" applies to the 40 lb. 40# is the best to use for good work. Copper steel alloy base is proving successful in prolonging life of this metal. Roofs should be repainted every 3 or 4 years.

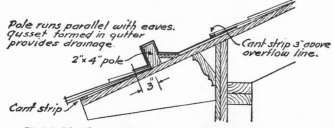

Pole runs parallel with eaves. Gusset formed in gutter provides drainage.
2"x 4" pole
Cant strip 3" above overflow line.
Cant strip

POLE GUTTER in SHINGLE ROOF.

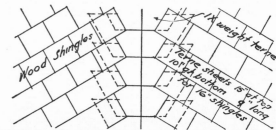

Wood shingles
IX weight terne
Terne sheets 15" at top & 10" at bottom for 16" shingles

FLASHING CLOSE VALLEY SHINGLE ROOF.

ZINC ROOFING

Note: Standard battens are 1-5/8" high for slope 4" to 12" or more.

For slopes less than 4" to 12" battens should be 2-5/8" high to avoid water leakage.

In the batten system metal is laid between parallel wooden batten strips which run from ridge to eave.

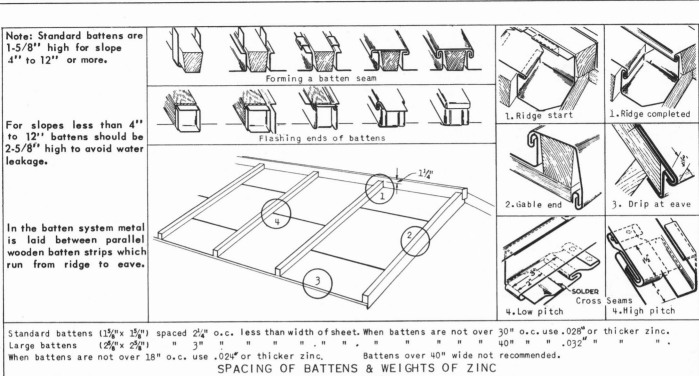

Forming a batten seam

Flashing ends of battens

1. Ridge start

1. Ridge completed

2. Gable end

3. Drip at eave

4. Low pitch

4. High pitch

SOLDER

Cross Seams

Standard battens (1⅝"x 1⅝") spaced 2¼" o.c. less than width of sheet. When battens are not over 30" o.c. use .028" or thicker zinc.
Large battens (2⅝"x 2⅝") " 3" " " " " " " " " " " " " " 40" " .032" " " " .
When battens are not over 18" o.c. use .024" or thicker zinc. Battens over 40" wide not recommended.

SPACING OF BATTENS & WEIGHTS OF ZINC
BATTEN SEAM

Note: Used on roofs with slopes of 4" to 12" or more.

Use a minimum of .024' zinc in narrow strips. Standard width 20".

Zinc may be had in either sheets or coils, the latter to be cut into lengths of not more than 8'. Seams 17½" oc. All sheets are secured by clips 1"x3" long nailed to roof 8" to 10" o.c.

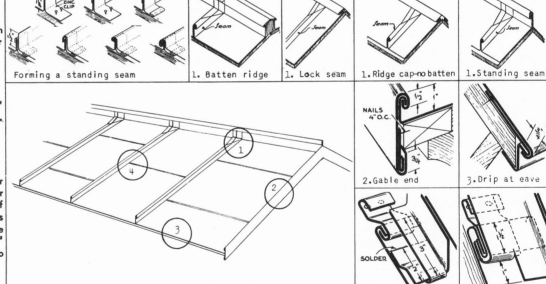

ZINC CLIP

Forming a standing seam

1. Batten ridge

1. Lock seam

1. Ridge cap-no batten

1. Standing seam

NAILS 4" O.C.

2. Gable end

3. Drip at eave

4. Low pitch

SOLDER

Cross Seams

4. High pitch

STANDING SEAM

ZINC GAUGES

Note: Specify decimal thickness to be used as too thin a metal will not give satisfactory service. .024" or thicker is recommended for roofing while .020" or thicker is used for flashing, leaders & gutters etc. Weight of zinc 20% less than weight of copper.

Ga. No.	Ounces per sq. ft.	Thickness in inches	Ga. No.	Ounces per sq. ft.	Thickness in inches
9	10.72	.018	17	29.92	.050
10	12.00	.020	18	32.96	.055
11	14.40	.024	19	36.00	.060
12	16.80	.028	20	41.92	.070
13	19.20	.032	21	48.00	.080
14	21.60	.036	22	53.92	.090
15	24.00	.040	23	60.00	.100
16	26.88	.045	24	75.20	.125

Note: Zinc can be used safely in direct contact with lead, tin & aluminum. With other metals insulation is required because of electrolysis. Zinc is not affected in contact with most lumber. When used with redwood or red cedar it should be coated with asphaltum paint. Do not use zinc where acid fumes occur. Zinc expands ¼" per 10' sheet in temperature change from 0° to 120°. Always use hot-dipped gal. nails with zinc and a glossy, saturated & coated paper under it. May be painted immediately after installation if zinc metallic paint is used.

Zinc Sizes = Sheets (.018" or thicker)-up to 5' wide, 8' long-Standard 3'x8'. Strips (.018" or thicker) to 1'8" wide; flat lengths to 12; coils, any size.

For FLASHING, LEADERS & GUTTERS see pages of those titles

DATA SUPPLIED BY AMERICAN ZINC INSTITUTE

SLATE ROOFING

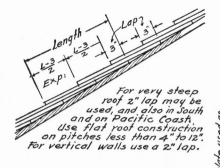

For very steep roof 2" lap may be used, and also in South and on Pacific Coast. Use flat roof construction on pitches less than 4" to 12". For vertical walls use a 2" lap.

LAP and EXPOSURE
Terms
"Textural" is a rough textured slate roof with uneven butts and a variation of thickness or size; generally not applied to slate over 3/8" thick.
"Graduated" Roof is a textural roof of large size slates, and more variation in thickness, size and colour.

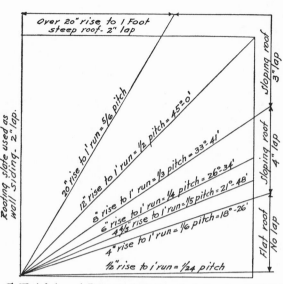

Over 20" rise to 1 Foot steep roof- 2" lap

Roofing slate used as wall siding- 2" lap.

20" rise to 1' run = 5/6 pitch
12" rise to 1' run = 1/2 pitch = 45°0'
8" rise to 1' run = 1/3 pitch = 33°41'
6" rise to 1' run = 1/4 pitch = 26°34'
4½" rise to 1' run = 1/5 pitch = 21°48'
4" rise to 1' run = 1/6 pitch = 18°-26'
½" rise to 1' run = 1/24 pitch

Sloping roof 3" lap
Sloping roof 4" lap
Flat roof No lap

DIAGRAM of PROPER LAP for PITCHES

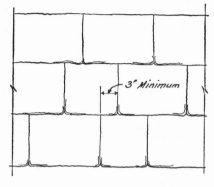

3" Minimum

PROPER JOINTING
Felt
With Commercial Standard Slate use 15# saturated Felt.
With Textural roofs use 30# Felt.
With Graduated roofs use 30# for 3/4 slates and 45#, 55# or 65# prepared roll roofing for heavier.

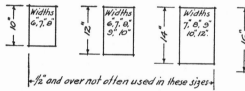

| Widths 6,7,8 | Widths 6,7,8, 9,10 | Widths 7,8,9 10,12 | Widths 8,9,10, 12 | Widths 9,10,11 12 | Widths 10,11 12,14 | Widths 11,12, 14 | Widths 12 & 14 |

10" 12" 14" 16" 18" 20" 22" 24"

½" and over not often used in these sizes

Random widths usually used.

LENGTHS AND WIDTHS OF SLATES-STANDARD
The above Slates are all split in these thicknesses:- 3/16", 1/4", 3/8", 1/2", 3/4", 1", 1¼", 1½", 1¾" and 2".

Commercial Standard is the Quarry run of 3/16" thickness and includes tolerable variations above and below 3/16". "Full 3/16" Slate" or "3/16" or "not less than 3/16" indicates hand picked selection with minimum variation. On other sizes reasonable plus tolerances only are permissable; thus a ½" slate must be full ½" or slightly thicker.

A Square of Roofing Slate means a sufficient number of slates of any size to cover 100 Square Feet with 3" lap. For Flat Roofs a square would cover more than 100 Square Feet.

STANDARD NOMENCLATURE FOR SLATE COLOR.

| Black | Gray | Purple | Green | Red |
| Blue Black | Blue gray | Mottled Purple & Green | Purple Variegated. | |

The above should be preceded by the word "Unfading" or "Weathering."
Other colors and combinations are termed specials.

Thickness for Flat Roofs
Ordinary and light service 3/16" thick. For Promenade or Heavy Service 1/4" to 3/8". For Special Terraces, Walks etc. 3/4" to 1¼" may be used & set in cement. (Editors' Note) The above sizes & recommendations are Dept. of Commerce Simplified Practice Recommendations R-14-28.

8" by 6,8,9
10" by 6,7,8
12" by 6,7,8

SIZE OF SLATE FOR FLAT ROOF

    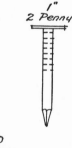 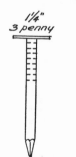

1" 2 Penny   1¼" 3 penny   1½" 4 Penny   1¾" 5 Penny   2" 6 Penny

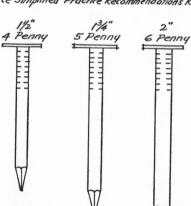

COPPER WIRE NAIL.
Similar to steel wire nail, used for flashing but not for slate.

LARGE FLAT HEAD COPPER WIRE NAIL.
Usual type for good work.

REGULAR CUT COPPER NAIL.
Not good for slate.

LARGE FLAT HEAD CUT COPPER ROOFING NAIL.
This type not good.

Nails should be of copper or yellow metal. In dry climates hot dip galvanized may be used. Use nail 1" longer than thickness of slate.

TYPES OF NAILS.   SIZES OF NAILS.
NAILS FOR USE WITH SLATE ROOFING.
STANDARD SLATE SIZES-ROOFING NAILS-COLORS & LAP OF SLATE ROOFS.
Standards recommended by the National Slate Association.

SLATE ROOFING

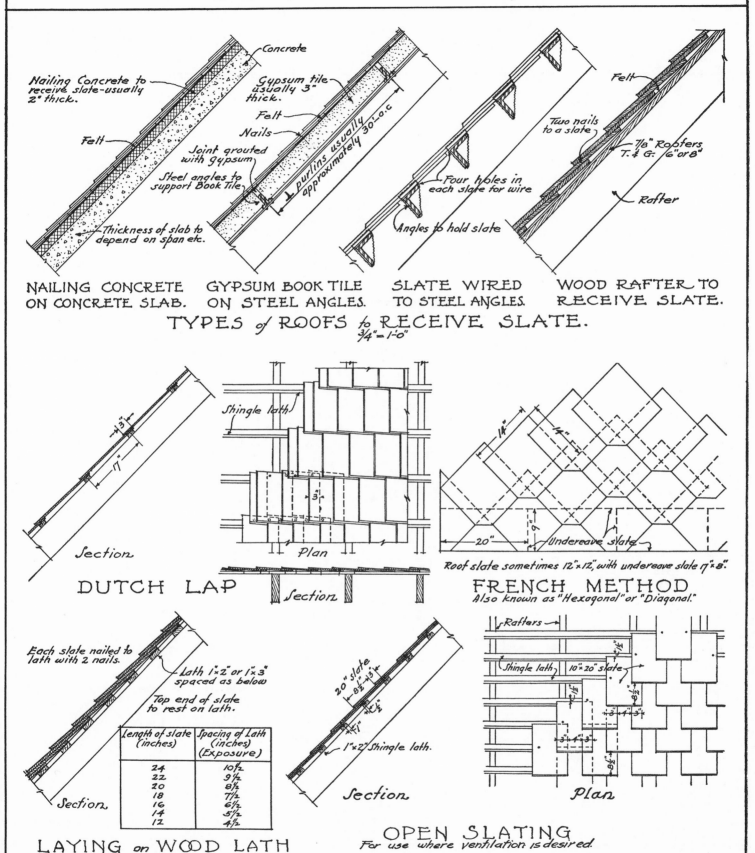

Concrete

Nailing Concrete to receive slate-usually 2" thick.

Felt

Thickness of slab to depend on span etc.

NAILING CONCRETE ON CONCRETE SLAB.

Gypsum tile usually 3" thick.

Felt

Nails

Joint grouted with gypsum

Steel angles to support Book Tile

1' purlins usually approximately 30' o.c.

GYPSUM BOOK TILE ON STEEL ANGLES.

Four holes in each slate for wire

Angles to hold slate

SLATE WIRED TO STEEL ANGLES.

Felt

Two nails to a slate

7/8" Roofers T. & G. 6" or 8"

Rafter

WOOD RAFTER TO RECEIVE SLATE.

TYPES of ROOFS to RECEIVE SLATE.
3/4" = 1'-0"

Shingle lath

3"

17"

Section

3"

Plan

Section

DUTCH LAP

14"

14"

20"

9"

Undereave slate

Roof slate sometimes 12"x12", with undereave slate 17"x8".

FRENCH METHOD
Also known as "Hexagonal" or "Diagonal."

Each slate nailed to lath with 2 nails.

Lath 1"x2" or 1"x3" spaced as below

Top end of slate to rest on lath.

Length of slate (inches)	Spacing of Lath (inches) (Exposure)
24	10½
22	9½
20	8½
18	7½
16	6½
14	5½
12	4½

Section

LAYING on WOOD LATH

20" slate
8½" 13"
6½"
1"

1"x2" Shingle lath.

Section

OPEN SLATING
For use where ventilation is desired.

Rafters

Shingle lath

10"x 20" slate

8½"

3" 4" 3"

3" 4" 3"

8½"

Plan

VARIOUS METHODS OF LAYING SLATE.
1/2" = 1'-0"
See "Roof Construction" sheet

TYPES of ROOFS to RECEIVE SLATE and LAYING SLATE ROOFS.
Methods recommended by the National Slate Association in "Slate Roofs."

SLATE ROOFING

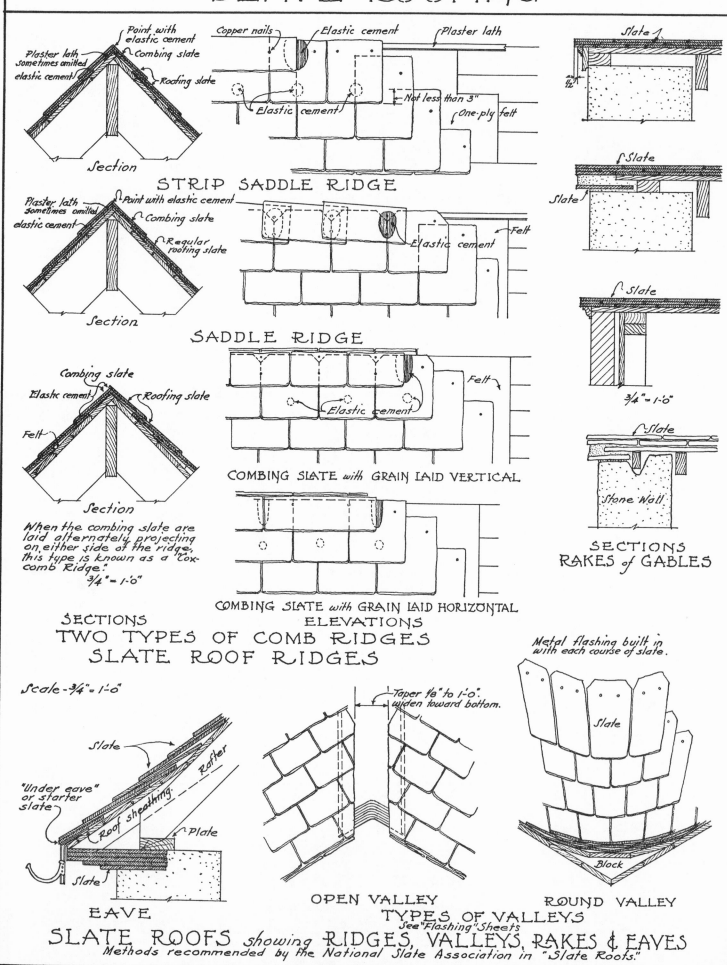

Point with elastic cement

Plaster lath sometimes omitted

elastic cement

Combing slate

Roofing slate

Section

Copper nails

Elastic cement

Plaster lath

Not less than 3"

Elastic cement

One-ply felt

STRIP SADDLE RIDGE

Plaster lath sometimes omitted

elastic cement

Point with elastic cement

Combing slate

Regular roofing slate

Section

Elastic cement

Felt

SADDLE RIDGE

Combing slate

Elastic cement

Roofing slate

Felt

Section

When the combing slate are laid alternately projecting on either side of the ridge, this type is known as a "Cox-comb Ridge."

3/4" = 1'-0"

Elastic cement

Felt

COMBING SLATE with GRAIN LAID VERTICAL

COMBING SLATE with GRAIN LAID HORIZONTAL
ELEVATIONS

SECTIONS
TWO TYPES OF COMB RIDGES
SLATE ROOF RIDGES

Slate

1/2"

Slate

Slate

Slate

3/4" = 1'-0"

Slate

Stone Wall

SECTIONS
RAKES of GABLES

Scale - 3/4" = 1'-0"

Slate

"Under eave" or starter slate

Rafter

Roof sheathing

Plate

Slate

EAVE

Taper 1/8" to 1'-0" widen toward bottom.

OPEN VALLEY

Metal flashing built in with each course of slate.

Slate

Block

ROUND VALLEY

TYPES OF VALLEYS
See "Flashing" Sheets

SLATE ROOFS *showing* **RIDGES, VALLEYS, RAKES & EAVES**
Methods recommended by the National Slate Association in "Slate Roofs."

SLATE ROOFING

Bevelled strip, or one or two plaster lath sometimes omitted. Hip slates are sometimes smaller slates. On less expensive work strip saddle hips are laid with butt joints which do not always join with roof courses.

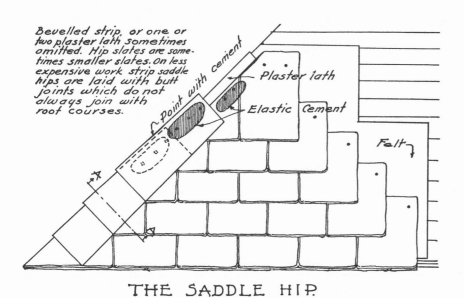

Plaster lath

Elastic Cement

Point with cement

Felt

THE SADDLE HIP

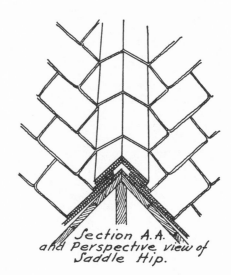

Section A.A.
and Perspective view of
Saddle Hip.

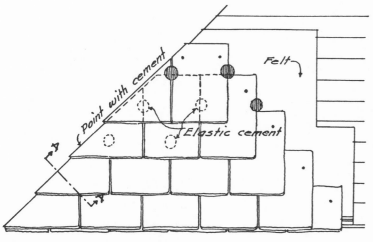

Point with cement

Felt

Elastic cement

THE MITRED HIP

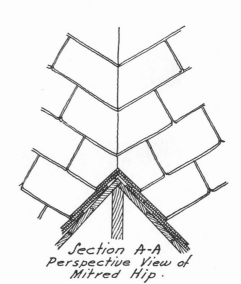

Section A-A
Perspective View of
Mitred Hip.

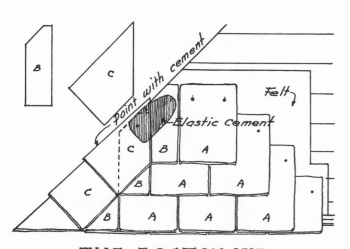

Point with cement

Felt

Elastic Cement

B

C

C   B   A

C   B   A

C   B   A

A   A   A

THE BOSTON HIP

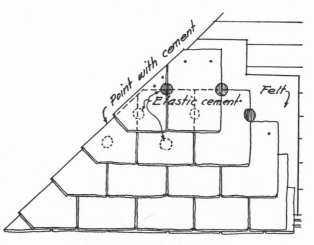

Point with cement

Elastic cement

Felt

THE FANTAIL HIP

SLATE ROOF HIPS
Methods recommended by the National Slate Association in "Slate Roofs.

CLAY TILE ROOFING

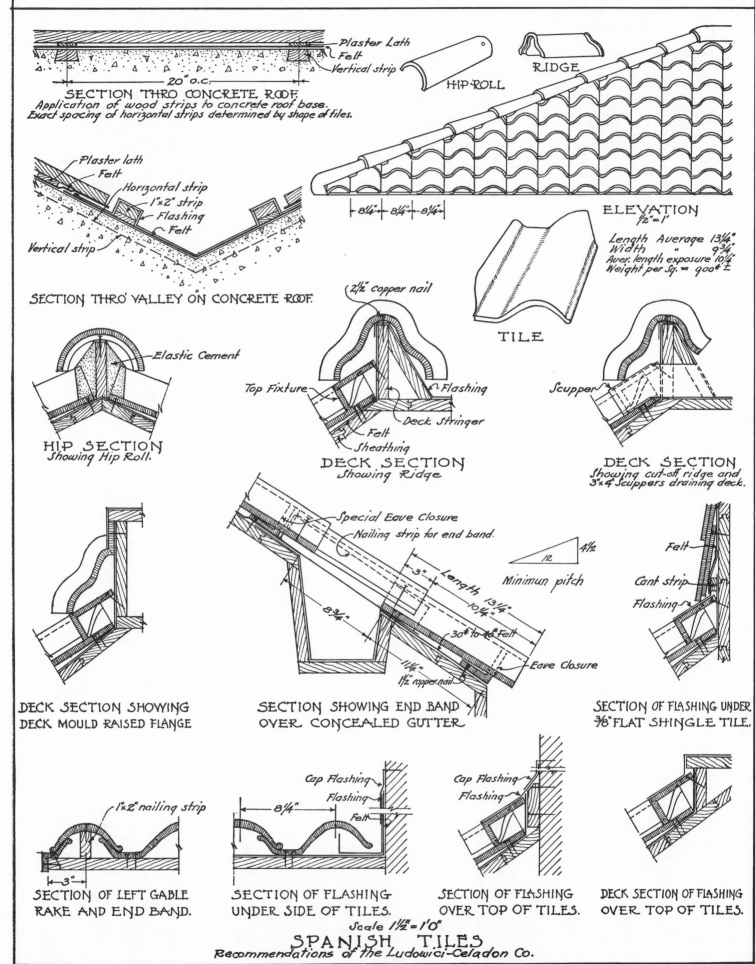

SECTION THRO CONCRETE ROOF
Application of wood strips to concrete roof base.
Exact spacing of horizontal strips determined by shape of tiles.

Plaster Lath
Felt
Vertical strip
20" o.c.

HIP ROLL   RIDGE

Plaster lath
Felt
Horizontal strip
1"x2" strip
Flashing
Felt
Vertical strip

SECTION THRO' VALLEY ON CONCRETE ROOF.

ELEVATION
½"=1'

Length Average 13¼"
Width   "   9¾"
Aver. length exposure 10¼"
Weight per Sq. = 900# ±

8¼" 8¼" 8¼"

TILE

Elastic Cement

HIP SECTION
Showing Hip Roll.

2½" copper nail
Top Fixture
Flashing
Deck Stringer
Felt
Sheathing

DECK SECTION
Showing Ridge

Scupper

DECK SECTION
Showing cut-off ridge and 3"x4" Scuppers draining deck.

DECK SECTION SHOWING DECK MOULD RAISED FLANGE

Special Eave Closure
Nailing strip for end band.
3"
Length 13¼"
10¼"
8¾"
30# to 45# Felt
1¼" copper nail
1½" copper nail
Eave Closure

4½
12
Minimum pitch

SECTION SHOWING END BAND OVER CONCEALED GUTTER

Felt
Cant strip
Flashing

SECTION OF FLASHING UNDER ⅜" FLAT SHINGLE TILE.

1"x2" nailing strip
3"

SECTION OF LEFT GABLE RAKE AND END BAND.

8¼"
Cap Flashing
Flashing
Felt

SECTION OF FLASHING UNDER SIDE OF TILES.

Cap Flashing
Flashing

SECTION OF FLASHING OVER TOP OF TILES.

DECK SECTION OF FLASHING OVER TOP OF TILES.

Scale 1½"=1'0"

SPANISH TILES
Recommendations of the Ludowici-Celadon Co.

CLAY TILE ROOFING

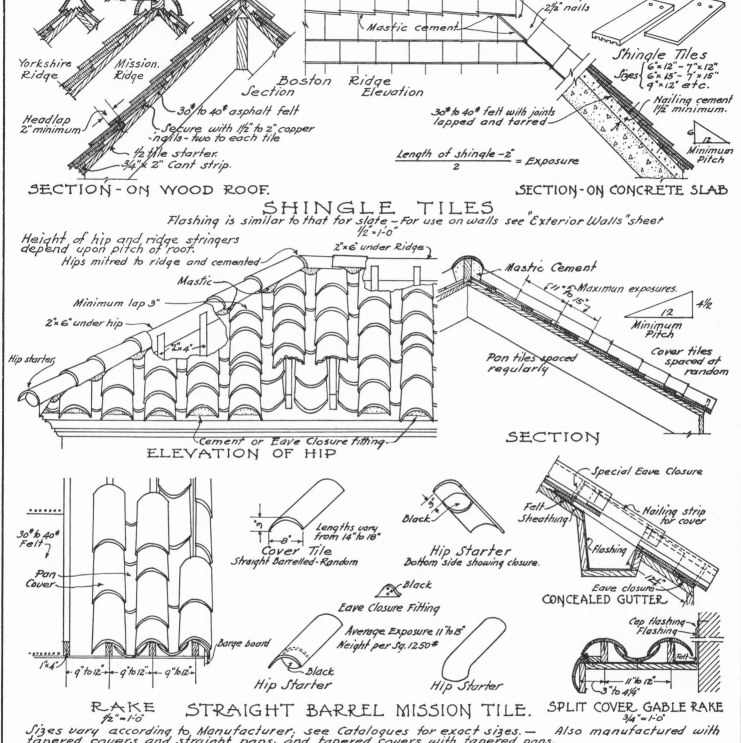

Set in Mastic cement
2"×2"

Boston Hip
2½" nails

Shingle Tiles
Sizes { 6"×12" - 7"×12"
6"×15" - 7"×15"
9"×12" etc.

Yorkshire Ridge   Mission Ridge

Mastic cement

Boston Ridge Section   Ridge Elevation

Nailing cement 1½" minimum.

Headlap 2" minimum

30# to 40# asphalt felt

Secure with 1½" to 2" copper nails - two to each tile

½ tile starter.
¾"× 2" Cant strip.

30# to 40# felt with joints lapped and tarred

$$\frac{\text{Length of shingle} - 2"}{2} = \text{Exposure}$$

Minimum Pitch

SECTION - ON WOOD ROOF.

SECTION - ON CONCRETE SLAB

SHINGLE TILES
Flashing is similar to that for slate - For use on walls see "Exterior Walls" sheet
½"=1'-0"

Height of hip and ridge stringers depend upon pitch of roof.
Hips mitred to ridge and cemented
Mastic
2"×6" under Ridge

Mastic Cement

Minimum lap 3"
2"×6" under hip

2"×4"

Maximum exposures.
11" to 15"

Minimum Pitch

Hip starter

Pan tiles spaced regularly

Cover tiles spaced at random

Cement or Eave Closure fitting

ELEVATION OF HIP

SECTION

30# to 40# Felt

Pan
Cover

3"
8"

Cover Tile
Straight Barrelled - Random

Lengths vary from 14" to 18"

Black

Hip Starter
Bottom side showing closure.

Special Eave Closure

Felt Sheathing

Nailing strip for cover

Flashing

Eave closure

CONCEALED GUTTER

Black

Eave Closure Fitting

Average Exposure 11" to 15"
Weight per Sq. 1250#

Black

Barge board

1"×4"   9"to 12"   9"to 12"   9"to 12"

Hip Starter

Hip Starter

Cap flashing Flashing

Felt

11" to 12"
3" to 4¼"

RAKE
½"=1'-0"

STRAIGHT BARREL MISSION TILE.

SPLIT COVER GABLE RAKE
¾"=1'-0"

Sizes vary according to Manufacturer: see Catalogues for exact sizes. — Also manufactured with tapered covers and straight pans; and tapered covers with tapered pans.

CLAY ROOFING TILES

For flashing of clay tile roof, see pages on Flashing

For other tile roofs such as promenade or quarry tile, see page "Built-up roofing"

CLAY TILE ROOFING

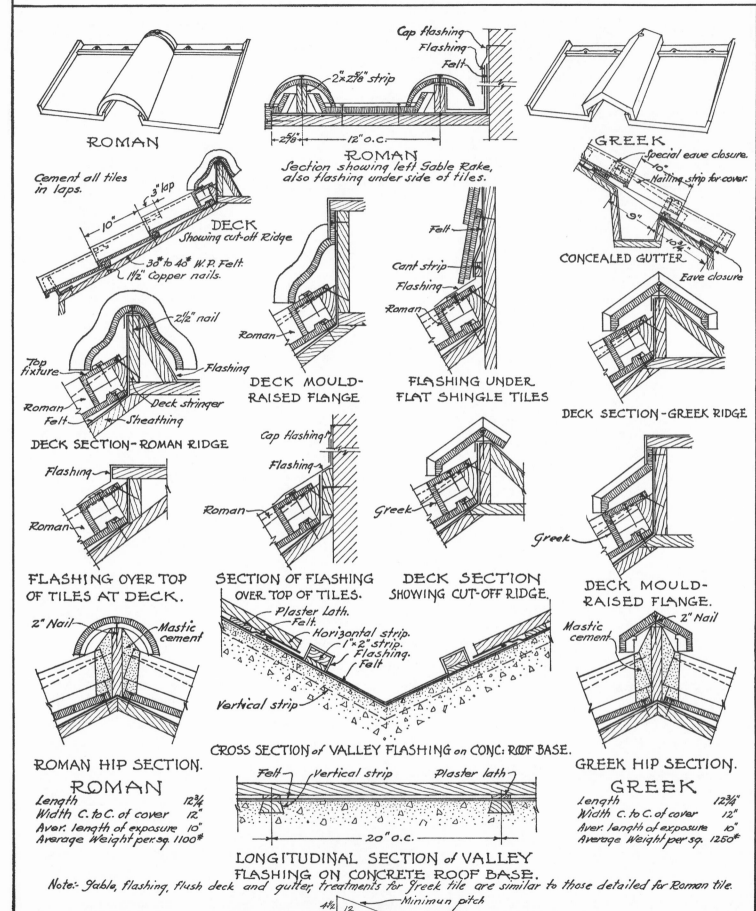

ROMAN

Cap flashing
Flashing
Felt
2"x 2⅝" strip
2⅝"   12" o.c.

ROMAN
Section showing left Gable Rake,
also flashing under side of tiles.

GREEK
Special eave closure.
Nailing strip for cover.
9"

CONCEALED GUTTER
Eave closure

Cement all tiles
in laps.
3" lap
10"

DECK
Showing cut-off Ridge
30# to 40# W.P. Felt.
1½" Copper nails.

Felt
Cant strip
Flashing
Roman

FLASHING UNDER
FLAT SHINGLE TILES

DECK SECTION-GREEK RIDGE

2½" nail
Top fixture
Roman
Felt
Deck stringer
Sheathing
Flashing

DECK SECTION-ROMAN RIDGE

DECK MOULD-
RAISED FLANGE

Flashing
Roman

FLASHING OVER TOP
OF TILES AT DECK.

Cap flashing
Flashing
Roman

SECTION OF FLASHING
OVER TOP OF TILES.

Greek

DECK SECTION
SHOWING CUT-OFF RIDGE.

2" Nail
Mastic
cement
Greek

DECK MOULD-
RAISED FLANGE.

2" Nail
Mastic
cement

ROMAN HIP SECTION.

Plaster Lath.
Felt.
Horizontal strip.
1"x 2" strip.
Flashing.
Felt.
Vertical strip

CROSS SECTION of VALLEY FLASHING on CONC. ROOF BASE.

GREEK HIP SECTION.

ROMAN

Length	12¾"
Width C. to C. of cover	12"
Aver. length of exposure	10"
Average Weight per sq.	1100#

Felt   Vertical strip   Plaster lath
20" o.c.

LONGITUDINAL SECTION of VALLEY
FLASHING ON CONCRETE ROOF BASE.

GREEK

Length	12¾"
Width C. to C. of cover	12"
Aver. length of exposure	10"
Average Weight per sq.	1250#

Note:- Gable, flashing, flush deck and gutter, treatments for Greek tile are similar to those detailed for Roman tile.

4½ / 12   Minimum pitch

ROMAN and GREEK TYPES of ROOFING TILES
Recommendations of the Ludowici Celadon Co.

1½" = 1'-0"

CLAY TILE ROOFING

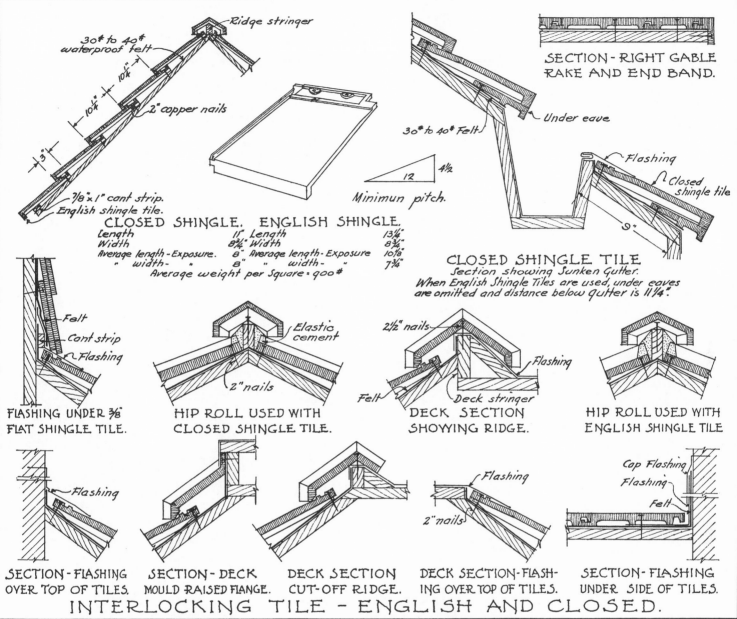

Ridge stringer

30# to 40# waterproof felt

10¼"
10¼"
10¼"
3"

2" copper nails

⅞" x 1" cant strip.
English shingle tile.

Minimum pitch.
12 4½

SECTION - RIGHT GABLE RAKE AND END BAND.

Under eave

30# to 40# Felt

Flashing

Closed shingle tile

9"

CLOSED SHINGLE TILE
Section showing Sunken Gutter.
When English Shingle Tiles are used, under eaves
are omitted and distance below gutter is 11¼"

CLOSED SHINGLE.   ENGLISH SHINGLE.

Length	11"	Length	13¼"
Width	8½"	Width	8¾"
Average length - Exposure.	8"	Average length - Exposure	10⅛"
" width - "	8"	" width - "	7¾"
	Average weight per Square - 900#		

Felt
Cant strip
Flashing

FLASHING UNDER ⅜
FLAT SHINGLE TILE.

Elastic cement

2" nails

HIP ROLL USED WITH
CLOSED SHINGLE TILE.

2½" nails

Flashing

Felt

Deck stringer

DECK SECTION
SHOWING RIDGE.

HIP ROLL USED WITH
ENGLISH SHINGLE TILE

Flashing

SECTION - FLASHING
OVER TOP OF TILES.

SECTION - DECK
MOULD RAISED FLANGE.

DECK SECTION
CUT-OFF RIDGE.

Flashing

2" nails

DECK SECTION - FLASH-
ING OVER TOP OF TILES.

Cap Flashing
Flashing
Felt

SECTION - FLASHING
UNDER SIDE OF TILES.

INTERLOCKING TILE - ENGLISH AND CLOSED.

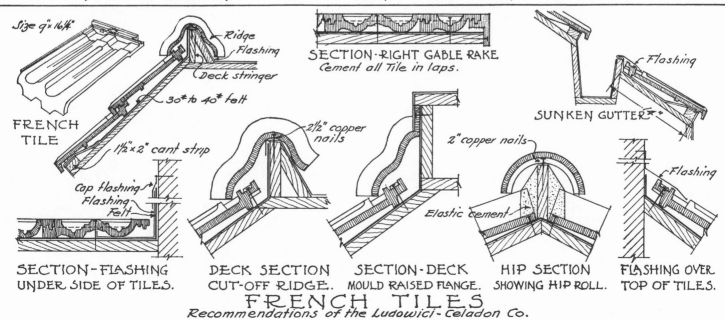

Size 9" x 16¼"

FRENCH
TILE

Ridge
Flashing
Deck stringer

30# to 40# felt

1½" x 2" cant strip

Cap flashing
Flashing
Felt

SECTION-FLASHING
UNDER SIDE OF TILES.

2½" copper nails

DECK SECTION
CUT-OFF RIDGE.

SECTION-RIGHT GABLE RAKE
Cement all Tile in laps.

Elastic cement

SECTION-DECK
MOULD RAISED FLANGE.

2" copper nails

HIP SECTION
SHOWING HIP ROLL.

Flashing

SUNKEN GUTTER

Flashing

FLASHING OVER
TOP OF TILES.

FRENCH TILES
Recommendations of the Ludowici-Celadon Co.

CORRUGATED WIRE GLASS

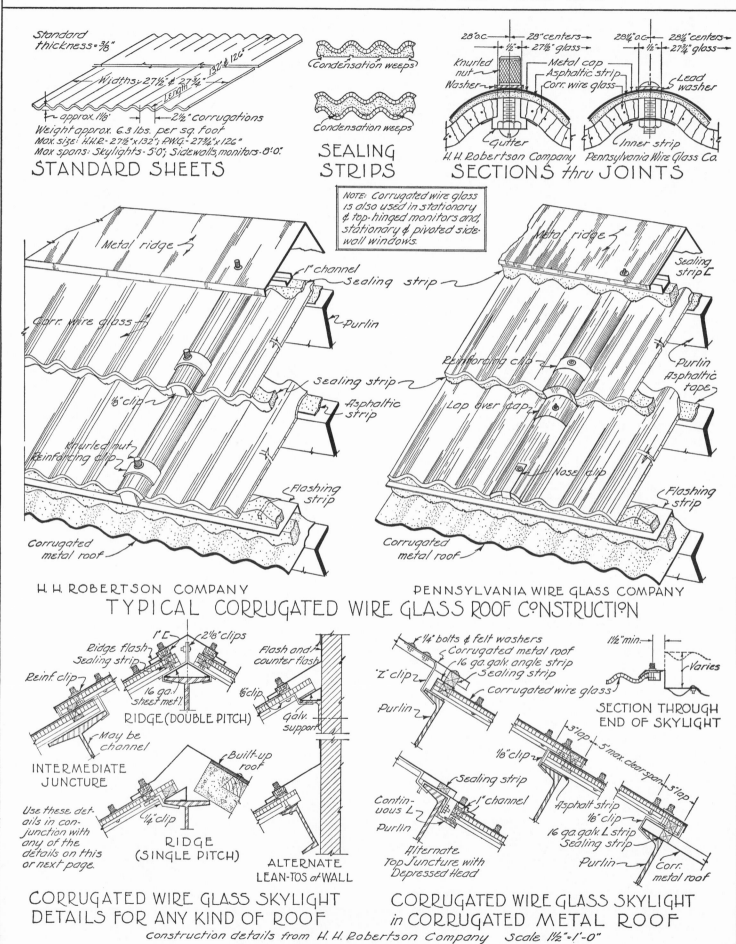

Standard thickness = 3/8"

Widths - 27½" & 27¾"

Length 132" & 126"

approx. 1⅛"   2½" corrugations

Weight approx. 6.3 lbs. per sq. foot
Max. size: H.H.R. - 27½" x 132"; P.W.G. - 27¾" x 126"
Max. spans: Skylights - 5'0"; Sidewalls, monitors - 8'0".

STANDARD SHEETS

Condensation weeps

Condensation weeps

SEALING STRIPS

28"o.c.   28" centers
½"   27½" glass
Knurled nut   Metal cap
Washer   Asphaltic strip
          Corr. wire glass
Gutter
H. H. Robertson Company

28¼"o.c.   28¼" centers
½"   27¾" glass
          Lead washer
          Inner strip
Pennsylvania Wire Glass Co.

SECTIONS thru JOINTS

NOTE: Corrugated wire glass is also used in stationary & top-hinged monitors and stationary & pivoted sidewall windows.

Metal ridge
1" channel
Sealing strip
Corr. wire glass
Purlin
Sealing strip
⅛" clip
Asphaltic strip
Knurled nut
Reinforcing clip
Flashing strip
Corrugated metal roof

Metal ridge
Sealing strip
Reinforcing clip
Purlin
Asphaltic tape
Lap over lap
Nose clip
Flashing strip
Corrugated metal roof

H. H. ROBERTSON COMPANY   PENNSYLVANIA WIRE GLASS COMPANY
TYPICAL CORRUGATED WIRE GLASS ROOF CONSTRUCTION

1" L   2⅛" clips
Ridge flash
Sealing strip
Reinf. clip
16 ga. sheet met'l.
RIDGE (DOUBLE PITCH)

May be channel
INTERMEDIATE JUNCTURE

Flash and counter flash
⅛"clip
Galv. support

Use these details in conjunction with any of the details on this or next page.

Built-up roof
¼" clip
RIDGE (SINGLE PITCH)

ALTERNATE LEAN-TOS of WALL

¼" bolts & felt washers
Corrugated metal roof
16 ga. galv. angle strip
Sealing strip
Corrugated wire glass
"Z" clip
Purlin

1½"min.
Varies
SECTION THROUGH END OF SKYLIGHT

⅛"clip
Sealing strip
1" channel
Continuous L
Purlin
Alternate Top Juncture with Depressed Head

3"lap   5"max. clear span   3"lap
⅛"clip
Asphalt strip
⅛" clip
16 ga. galv. L strip
Sealing strip
Purlin
Corr. metal roof

CORRUGATED WIRE GLASS SKYLIGHT DETAILS FOR ANY KIND OF ROOF

CORRUGATED WIRE GLASS SKYLIGHT in CORRUGATED METAL ROOF

Construction details from H. H. Robertson Company   Scale 1½"=1'-0"

CORRUGATED WIRE GLASS

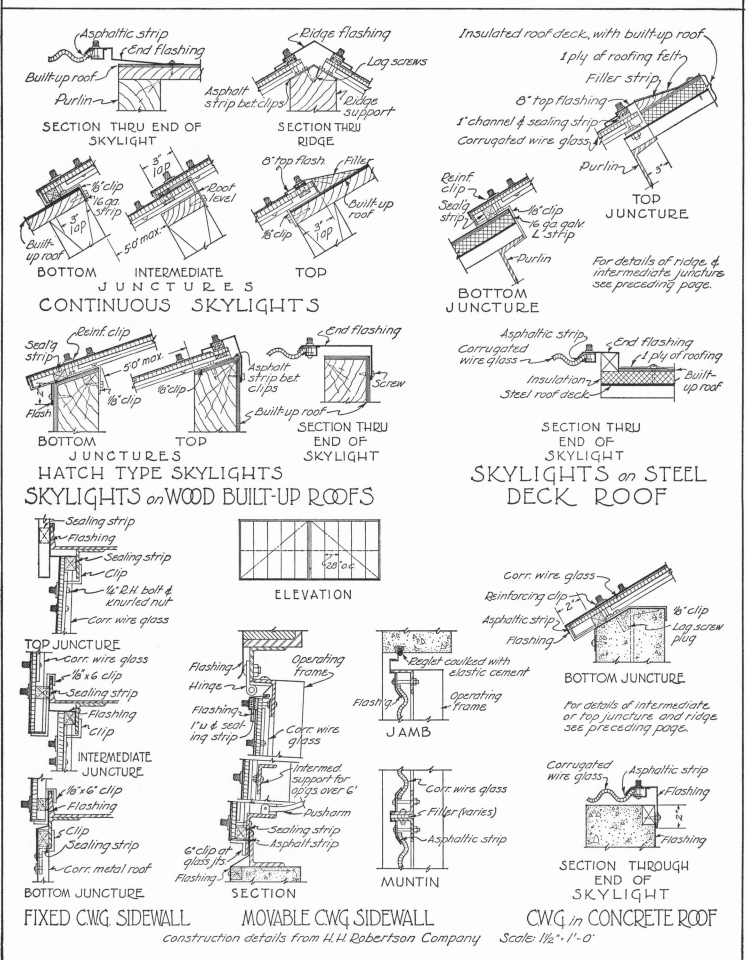

SECTION THRU END OF SKYLIGHT

Asphaltic strip
End flashing
Built-up roof
Purlin

SECTION THRU RIDGE

Ridge flashing
Lag screws
Asphalt strip bet. clips
Ridge support

Insulated roof deck, with built-up roof
1 ply of roofing felt
Filler strip
8" top flashing
1" channel & sealing strip
Corrugated wire glass
Purlin
3"

TOP JUNCTURE

BOTTOM — INTERMEDIATE — TOP
J U N C T U R E S

⅛" clip
16 ga. strip
3" lap
Root level
3" lap
Built-up roof
5'-0" max.
8" top flash.
Filler
⅛" clip
3" lap
Built-up roof

CONTINUOUS SKYLIGHTS

Reinf. clip
Seal'g strip
⅛" clip
16 ga. galv. L strip
Purlin

BOTTOM JUNCTURE

For details of ridge & intermediate juncture see preceding page.

BOTTOM — TOP
J U N C T U R E S

Seal'g strip
Reinf. clip
5'-0" max.
⅛" clip
Asphalt strip bet. clips
⅛" clip
Flash
Built-up roof

End flashing
Screw
Built-up roof

SECTION THRU END OF SKYLIGHT

HATCH TYPE SKYLIGHTS
SKYLIGHTS on WOOD BUILT-UP ROOFS

Asphaltic strip
Corrugated wire glass
End flashing
1 ply of roofing
Insulation
Steel roof deck
Built-up roof

SECTION THRU END OF SKYLIGHT

SKYLIGHTS on STEEL DECK ROOF

Sealing strip
Flashing
Sealing strip
Clip
¼" R.H. bolt & knurled nut
Corr. wire glass

TOP JUNCTURE

Corr. wire glass
⅛" x 6 clip
Sealing strip
Flashing
Clip

INTERMEDIATE JUNCTURE

⅛" x 6" clip
Flashing
Clip
Sealing strip
Corr. metal roof

BOTTOM JUNCTURE

ELEVATION

28" o.c.

Flashing
Hinge
Flashing
1"u & sealing strip
Operating frame
Corr. wire glass
Intermed. support for op'gs. over 6'
Pusharm
Sealing strip
Asphalt strip
6" clip at glass jts.
Flashing

SECTION

Reglet caulked with elastic cement
Flash'g.
Operating frame

JAMB

Corr. wire glass
Filler (varies)
Asphaltic strip

MUNTIN

Corr. wire glass
Reinforcing clip
Asphaltic strip
Flashing
2"
⅛" clip
Lag screw plug

BOTTOM JUNCTURE

For details of intermediate or top juncture and ridge see preceding page.

Corrugated wire glass
Asphaltic strip
Flashing
2"
Flashing

SECTION THROUGH END OF SKYLIGHT

FIXED C.W.G. SIDEWALL   MOVABLE C.W.G. SIDEWALL   C.W.G. in CONCRETE ROOF

Construction details from H. H. Robertson Company   Scale: 1½" = 1'-0"

WOOD SHINGLES

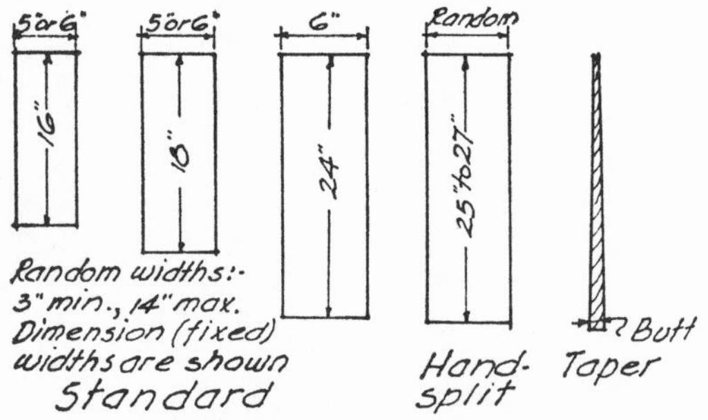
5"or6"
5"or6"
6"
Random
16"
18"
24"
25"to27"
Random widths:- 3" min., 14" max. Dimension (fixed) widths are shown
Standard
Hand-split
Butt
Taper

THICKNESSES & NAILS		
16" long	5 butts = 2"	3d
18" "	5 butts = 2¼"	3d
24" "	4 butts = 2"	4d
25" to 27"	1 butt = ½"	5 or 6d
25" to 27"	1 " = ⅝" to 1¼"	7 or 8d

EXPOSURE for ROOFING				
Shingle length	16"	18"	24"	27"
Pitch 5-12 or steeper	5"	5½"	7½"	8"
Pitch 3-12 or 4-12	3¾"	4¼"	5¾"	

EXPOSURE for SIDING				
Shingle length	16"	18"	24"	27"
Single course	7½"	8½"	11½"	12"
Double course	12"	14"	16"	16½"
Exposures shown are max.				

For double-coursing, use small-headed 5d nails. Always use hot zinc-dip nails. 3-12 is min. pitch recommended for roofs with wood shingles.

SHINGLE SIZES, EXPOSURES, AND NAILING

Durable woods for shingles: Tidewater Red Cypress-No 1, Bests, Primes, Economy or Clipper grade. Red Cedar-Certigrade No 1, No 2 & No 3. Redwood No 1, No 2 VG or No 3 MG grade. For longer life, shingles should be painted with creosote stain. Some shingles are pre-dipped in stain. Siding shingles may be treated as above, or with house paint.

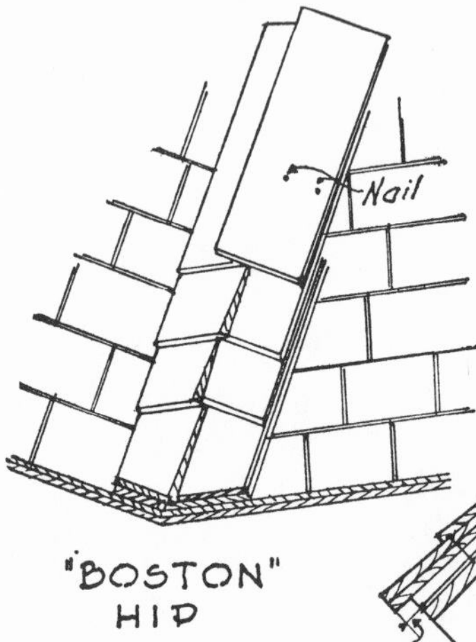
Nail
"BOSTON" HIP

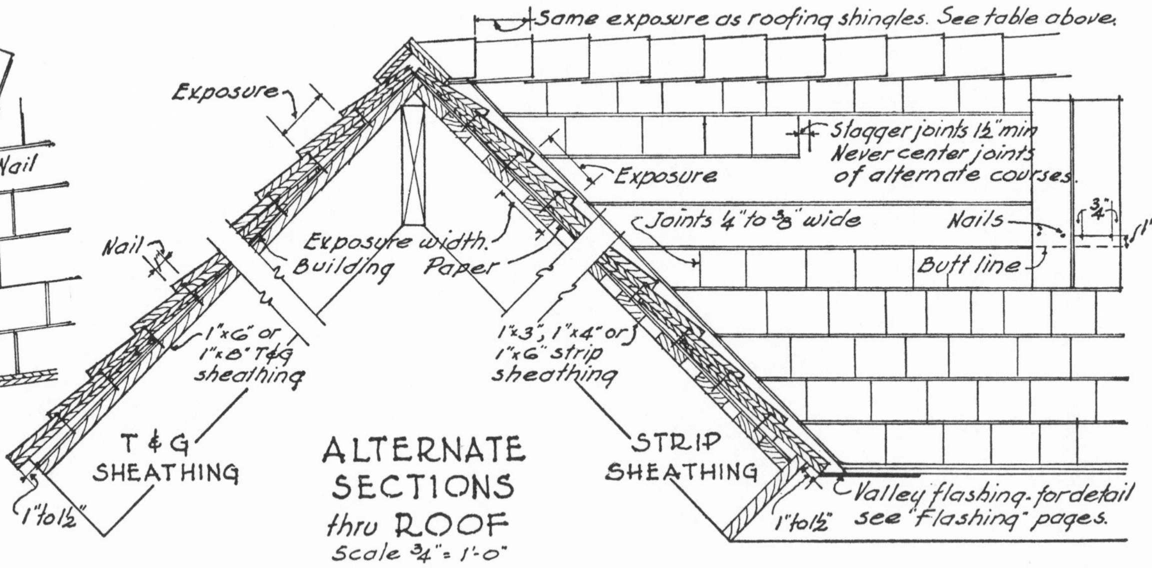
Same exposure as roofing shingles. See table above.
Exposure
Stagger joints 1½" min. Never center joints of alternate courses.
Exposure
Joints ¼" to ⅜" wide
Nails
¾"
1"
Butt line
Nail
Exposure width.
Building Paper
1"x6" or 1"x8" T&G sheathing
1"x3", 1"x4" or 1"x6" strip sheathing
T&G SHEATHING
ALTERNATE SECTIONS thru ROOF
Scale ¾" = 1'-0"
STRIP SHEATHING
1" to 1½"
1" to 1½"
Valley flashing-for detail see "Flashing" pages.

WOOD SHINGLE ROOFS

For exposures see table at top of page.

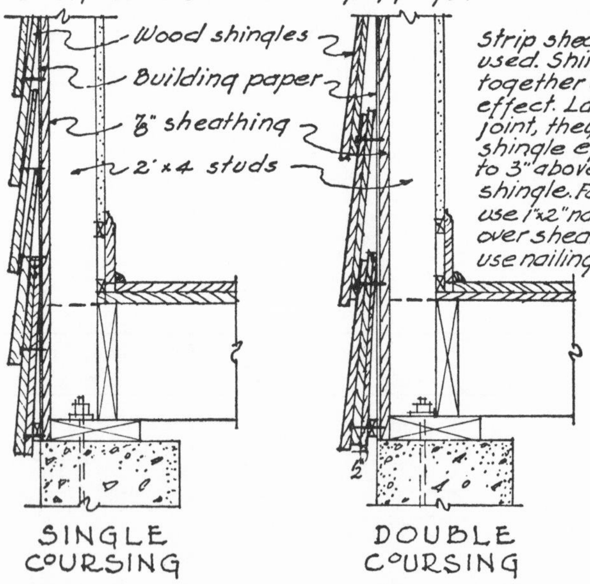
Wood shingles
Building paper
⅞" sheathing
2"x4" studs
SINGLE COURSING
DOUBLE COURSING

Strip sheathing may be used. Shingles laid close together give continuous effect. Laid with ⅛" to ⅜" joint, they give individual shingle effect. Nail 2" to 3" above butt of outside shingle. For fibre board sheath'g. use 1"x2" nailing strips horizontal over sheathing. For gypsum use nailing strips or E-5 nail.

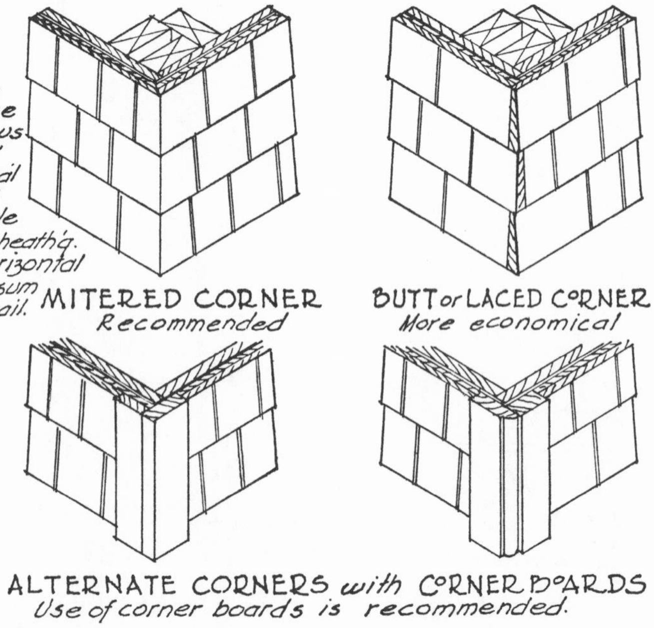
MITERED CORNER
Recommended
BUTT or LACED CORNER
More economical
ALTERNATE CORNERS with CORNER BOARDS
Use of corner boards is recommended.

WOOD SHINGLE SIDING

Scale ¾" = 1'-0"

FLASHING

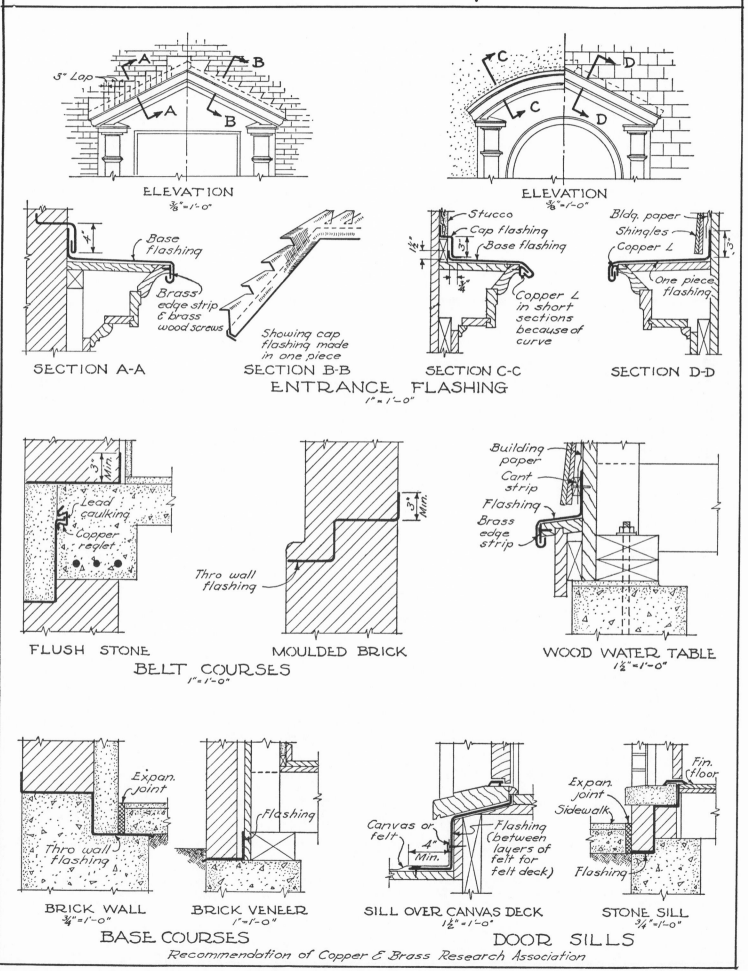

ELEVATION
3/8"=1'-0"

ELEVATION
3/8"=1'-0"

3" Lap

Base flashing

Brass edge strip & brass wood screws

Showing cap flashing made in one piece

SECTION A-A

SECTION B-B

Stucco
Cap flashing
Base flashing

Copper L in short sections because of curve

SECTION C-C

Bldg. paper
Shingles
Copper L

One piece flashing

SECTION D-D

ENTRANCE FLASHING
1"=1'-0"

3" Min.

Lead caulking
Copper reglet

FLUSH STONE

Thro wall flashing

3" Min.

MOULDED BRICK

BELT COURSES
1"=1'-0"

Building paper
Cant strip
Flashing
Brass edge strip

WOOD WATER TABLE
1½"=1'-0"

Expan. joint

Thro wall flashing

BRICK WALL
3/4"=1'-0"

Flashing

BRICK VENEER
1"=1'-0"

BASE COURSES

Canvas or felt

4" Min.

Flashing (between layers of felt for felt deck)

SILL OVER CANVAS DECK
1½"=1'-0"

Expan. joint
Sidewalk

Fin. floor

Flashing

STONE SILL
3/4"=1'-0"

DOOR SILLS

Recommendation of Copper & Brass Research Association

FLASHING

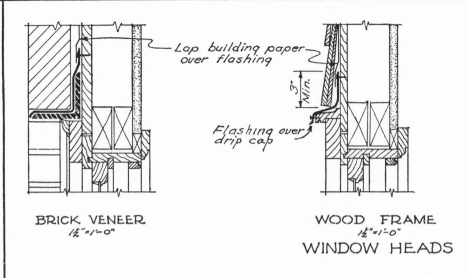

Lap building paper over flashing

3" Min.

Flashing over drip cap

BRICK VENEER
1½"=1'-0"

WOOD FRAME
1½"=1'-0"

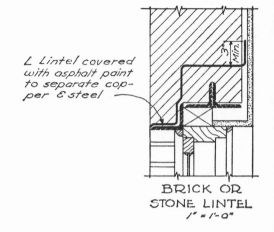

L Lintel covered with asphalt paint to separate copper & steel

3" Min.

BRICK OR STONE LINTEL
1"=1'-0"

WINDOW HEADS

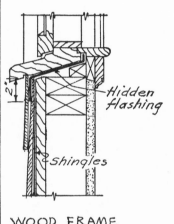

2"

Hidden Flashing

Shingles

WOOD FRAME

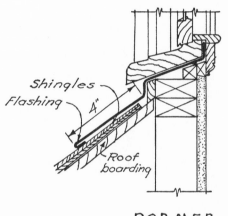

Shingles
Flashing

4"

Roof boarding

DORMER WINDOW SILLS
1½"=1'-0"

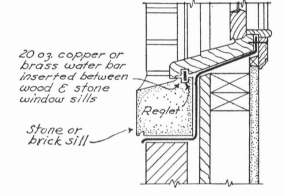

20 oz. copper or brass water bar inserted between wood & stone window sills

Reglet

Stone or brick sill

BRICK VENEER

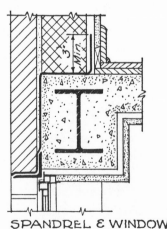

3" Min.

SPANDREL & WINDOW HEAD FLASHING

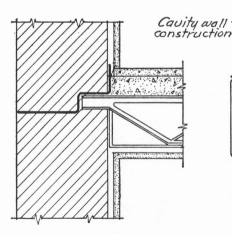

Cavity wall construction

OPEN WEB JOIST

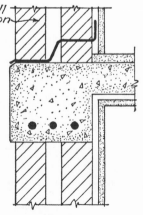

SPANDREL BEAM

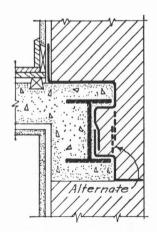

Alternate

OPEN WEB SPANDREL

SPANDRELS
1"=1'-0"

Recommendation of Copper & Brass Research Association.

FLASHING

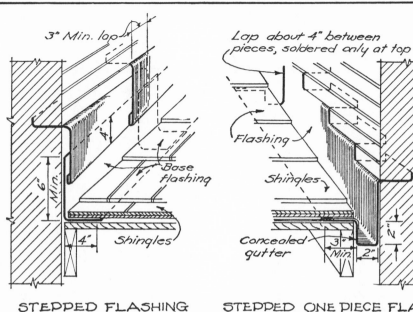

3" Min. lap

Lap about 4" between pieces, soldered only at top

Where roof slope is steep flashing may be made in one piece

Base flashing

Flashing

Shingles

Base flashing 20 oz. cleat 12" o.c.

Shingles

Concealed gutter

3" Min. 2"

Shingles 4"

Same method used for flashing shingled wall. Flashing in one piece carried up under bottom row of shingles 4" min.

STEPPED FLASHING   **STEPPED ONE PIECE FLASHING**   **TOP OF ROOF FLASHING**

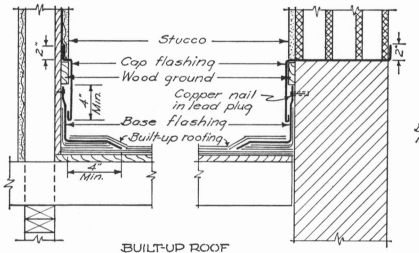
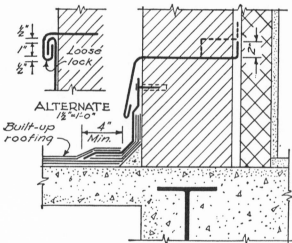
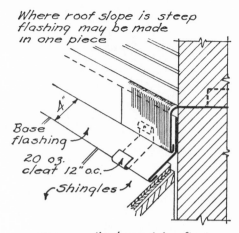

Stucco
Cap flashing
Wood ground
Copper nail in lead plug
Base flashing
Built-up roofing

Loose lock

ALTERNATE 1½"=1'-0"

Built-up roofing

4" Min.

BUILT-UP ROOF

STUCCO ON WOOD WALL   STUCCO ON MASONRY WALL   THRO WALL FLASHING

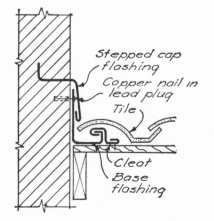
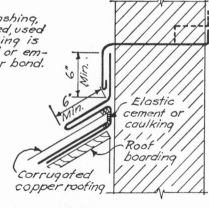

Stepped cap flashing
Copper nail in lead plug
Tile
Cleat
Base flashing

Stepped flashing, shown dotted, used when flashing is not ribbed or embossed for bond.
Built-up roofing

Elastic cement or caulking
Roof boarding
Corrugated copper roofing

TILE ROOF   **FIREWALL FLASHING**   **CORRUGATED COPPER ROOF**

FLASHING AT JUNCTURES OF ROOFS & WALLS
1"=1'-0"
Recommendation of Copper & Brass Research Association

FLASHING

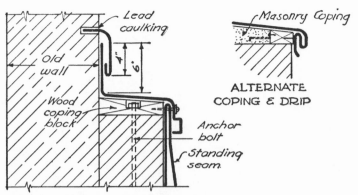

Lead caulking
Old wall
Wood coping block
Anchor bolt
Standing seam

NEW WALL BELOW EXISTING WALL

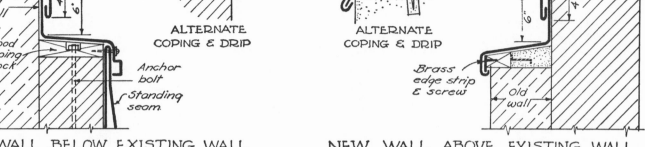

Masonry Coping

ALTERNATE COPING & DRIP

ALTERNATE COPING & DRIP

Brass edge strip & screw
Old wall

NEW WALL ABOVE EXISTING WALL

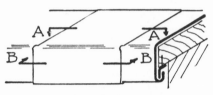

A   A
B   B

LOOSE LOCK
EXPANSION CAP
Located every 30 ft.

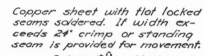
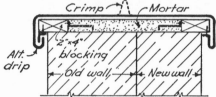

Copper sheet with flat locked seams soldered. If width exceeds 24" crimp or standing seam is provided for movement.

Crimp   Mortar
Alt. drip
2"x4" blocking
Old wall   New wall

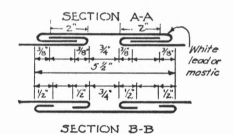

SECTION A-A
2"   2"
3/8   3/8   3/4   3/8   3/8
5 1/2"
White lead or mastic
1/2   1/2   3/4   1/2   1/2

SECTION B-B

NEW WALL LEVEL WITH EXISTING WALL

FLASHING BETWEEN OLD & NEW WALLS
1"=1'-0"

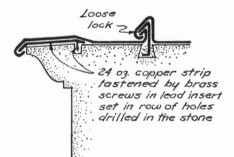

Loose lock

24 oz. copper strip fastened by brass screws in lead insert set in row of holes drilled in the stone

STONE CORNICE
1"=1'-0"

Large sheets are not caulked directly into reglets as movement from temperature changes will tear them. Use auxiliary strips set in reglets.

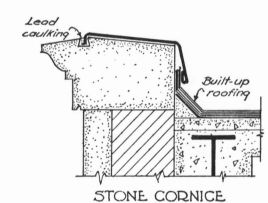

Lead caulking
Built-up roofing

STONE CORNICE
1"=1'-0"

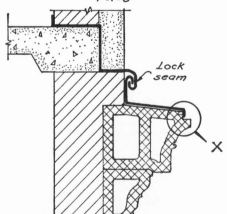

Lock seam

X

TERRA COTTA CORNICE
3/4"=1'-0"

DETAIL AT X

ALTERNATE
DRIP A

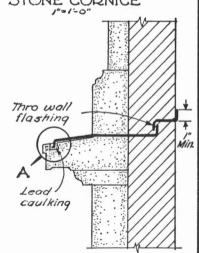

Thro wall flashing
1" Min.
A
Lead caulking

STONE CORNICE
3/8"=1'-0"

CORNICE FLASHING
Recommendation of Copper & Brass Research Association.

FLASHING

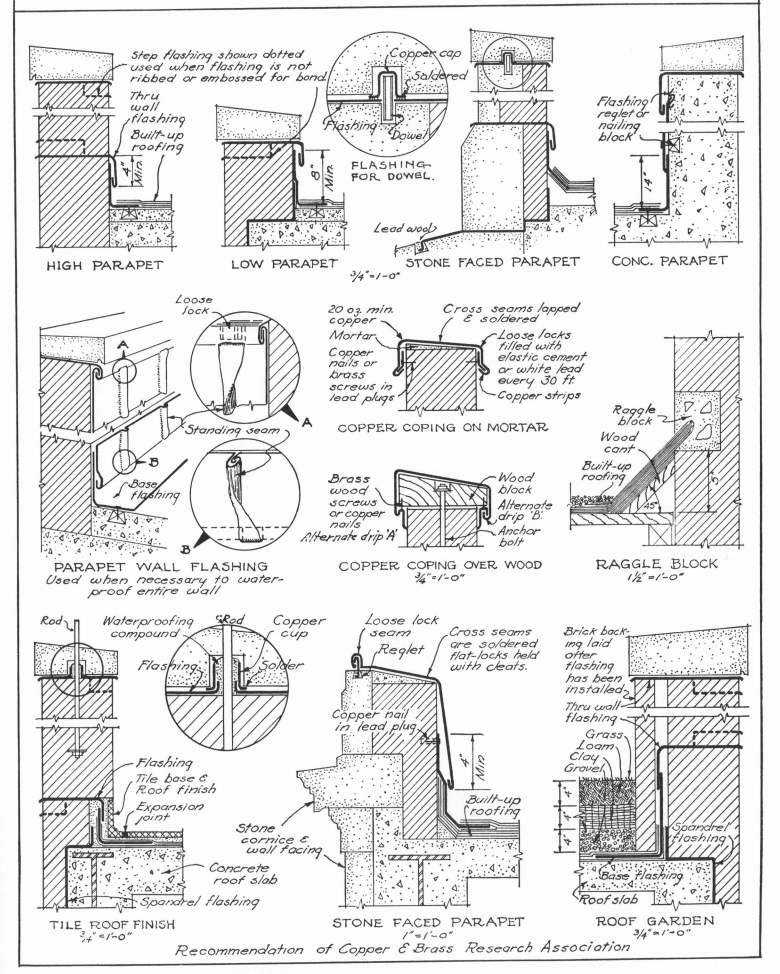

HIGH PARAPET

Step flashing shown dotted used when flashing is not ribbed or embossed for bond.
Thru wall flashing
Built-up roofing
4" Min.

LOW PARAPET

8" Min.

FLASHING FOR DOWEL.

Copper cap
Soldered
Flashing
Dowel

STONE FACED PARAPET

Lead wool

3/4"=1'-0"

CONC. PARAPET

Flashing reglet or nailing block
14"

PARAPET WALL FLASHING
Used when necessary to waterproof entire wall

Loose lock
A
B
Standing seam
Base flashing

COPPER COPING ON MORTAR

20 oz. min. copper
Mortar
Copper nails or brass screws in lead plugs
Cross seams lapped & soldered
Loose locks filled with elastic cement or white lead every 30 ft.
Copper strips

COPPER COPING OVER WOOD
3/4"=1'-0"

Brass wood screws or copper nails
Alternate drip 'A'
Wood block
Alternate drip 'B'.
Anchor bolt

RAGGLE BLOCK
1½"=1'-0"

Raggle block
Wood cant
Built-up roofing
5"
45°

TILE ROOF FINISH
3/4"=1'-0"

Rod
Waterproofing compound
Flashing
Rod
Copper cup
Solder
Flashing
Tile base & Roof finish
Expansion joint
Concrete roof slab
Spandrel flashing

STONE FACED PARAPET
1"=1'-0"

Loose lock seam
Reglet
Cross seams are soldered flat-locks held with cleats.
Copper nail in lead plug
4" Min.
Built-up roofing
Stone cornice & wall facing

ROOF GARDEN
3/4"=1'-0"

Brick backing laid after flashing has been installed
Thru wall flashing
Grass
Loam
Clay
Gravel
4"
4"
4"
4"
Spandrel flashing
Base flashing
Roof slab

Recommendation of Copper & Brass Research Association

FLASHING

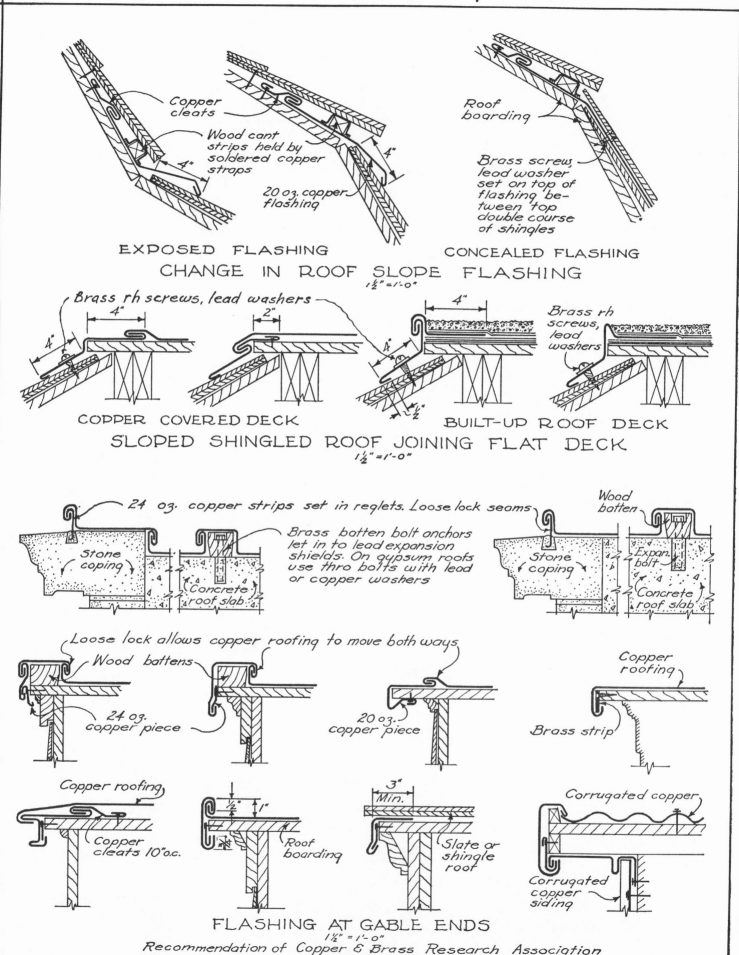

Copper cleats

Wood cant strips held by soldered copper straps

4"

20 oz. copper flashing

EXPOSED FLASHING

Roof boarding

Brass screw, lead washer set on top of flashing between top double course of shingles

4"

CONCEALED FLASHING

CHANGE IN ROOF SLOPE FLASHING
$1\frac{1}{2}" = 1'\text{-}0"$

Brass rh screws, lead washers

4"   4"   2"   4"   4"

COPPER COVERED DECK

Brass rh screws, lead washers

BUILT-UP ROOF DECK

SLOPED SHINGLED ROOF JOINING FLAT DECK
$1\frac{1}{2}" = 1'\text{-}0"$

24 oz. copper strips set in reglets. Loose lock seams

Stone coping

Concrete roof slab

Brass botten bolt anchors let in to lead expansion shields. On gypsum roofs use thro bolts with lead or copper washers

Wood batten

Stone coping

Expan. bolt

Concrete roof slab

Loose lock allows copper roofing to move both ways

Wood battens

24 oz. copper piece

20 oz. copper piece

Copper roofing

Brass strip

Copper roofing

Copper cleats 10" o.c.

½"   1"

Roof boarding

3" Min.

Slate or shingle roof

Corrugated copper

Corrugated copper siding

FLASHING AT GABLE ENDS
$1\frac{1}{2}" = 1'\text{-}0"$

Recommendation of Copper & Brass Research Association

FLASHING

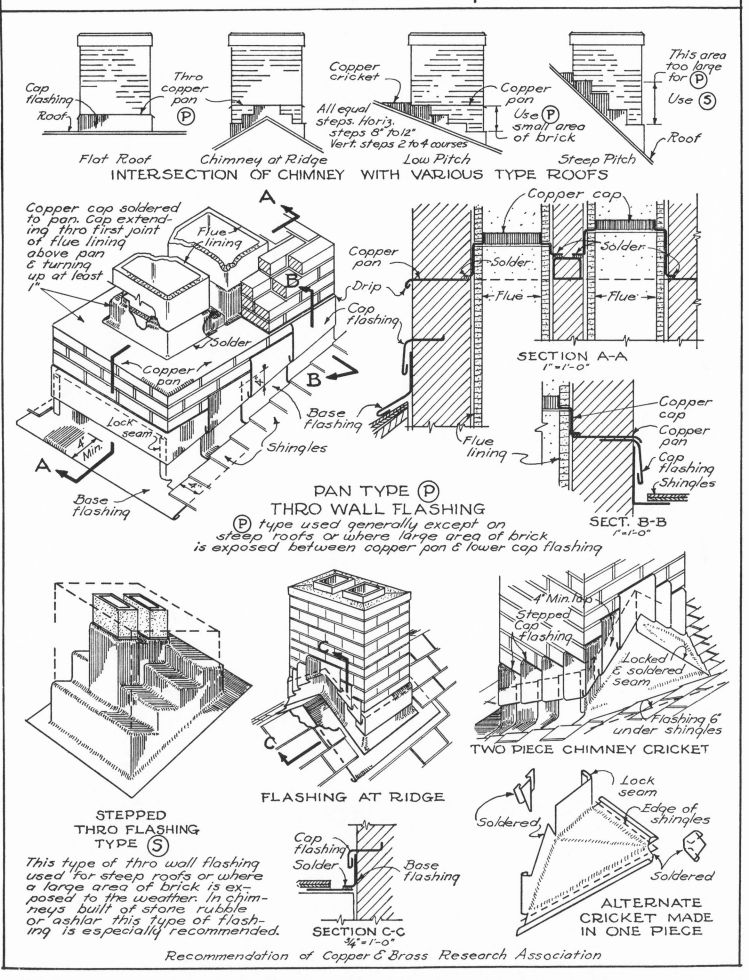

INTERSECTION OF CHIMNEY WITH VARIOUS TYPE ROOFS

Cap flashing — Roof — Flat Roof

Thro copper pan ⓟ — Chimney at Ridge

Copper cricket — All equal steps. Horiz. steps 8" to 12" Vert. steps 2 to 4 courses — Low Pitch

Copper pan — Use ⓟ small area of brick — This area too large for ⓟ Use ⓢ — Roof — Steep Pitch

Copper cap soldered to pan. Cap extending thro first joint of flue lining above pan & turning up at least 1"

Flue lining

Copper pan

Solder

Copper pan

Lock seam

4" Min.

Base flashing

Copper pan

Drip

Cap flashing

Base flashing

Shingles

4"

4"

Copper cap

Solder

Solder

Flue

Flue

Flue lining

SECTION A-A
1" = 1'-0"

Copper cap

Copper pan

Cap flashing

Shingles

SECT. B-B
1" = 1'-0"

PAN TYPE ⓟ
THRO WALL FLASHING

ⓟ type used generally except on steep roofs or where large area of brick is exposed between copper pan & lower cap flashing

STEPPED THRO FLASHING TYPE ⓢ

This type of thro wall flashing used for steep roofs or where a large area of brick is exposed to the weather. In chimneys built of stone rubble or ashlar this type of flashing is especially recommended.

Cap flashing

Solder

Base flashing

SECTION C-C
¾" = 1'-0"

FLASHING AT RIDGE

4" Min. lap

Stepped Cap flashing

Locked & soldered seam

Flashing 6" under shingles

TWO PIECE CHIMNEY CRICKET

Lock seam

Soldered

Edge of shingles

Soldered

ALTERNATE CRICKET MADE IN ONE PIECE

Recommendation of Copper & Brass Research Association

FLASHING

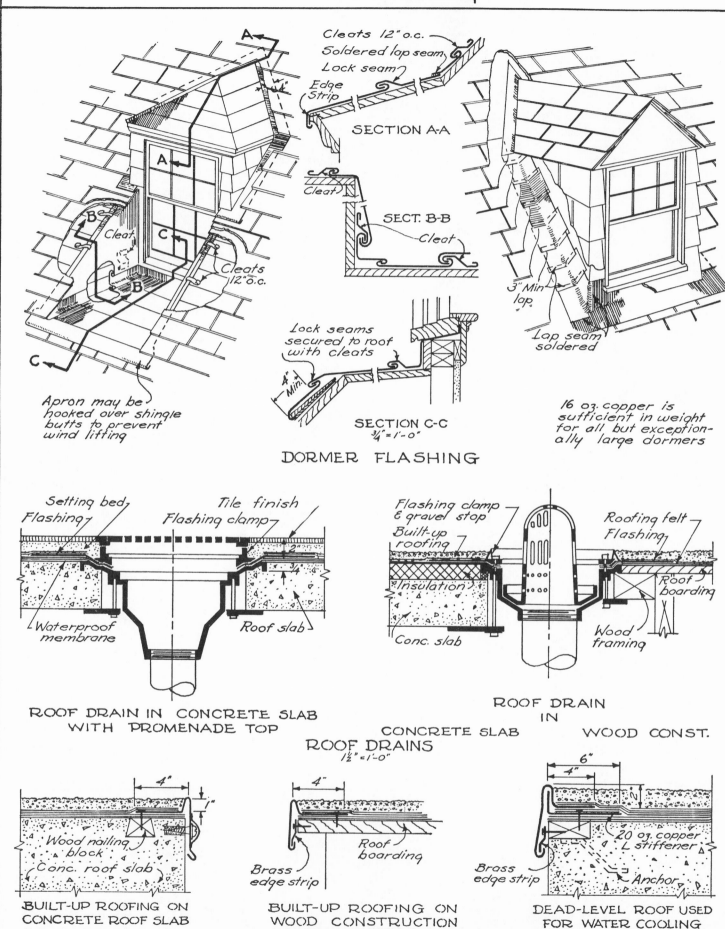

Cleats 12" o.c.
Soldered lap seam
Lock seam
Edge Strip

SECTION A-A

Cleat

SECT. B-B
Cleat

A

A

B

Cleat

C

B

Cleats 12" o.c.

C

Apron may be hooked over shingle butts to prevent wind lifting

Lock seams secured to roof with cleats

4" Min.

SECTION C-C
3/4"=1'-0"

DORMER FLASHING

3" Min lap.

Lap seam soldered

16 oz. copper is sufficient in weight for all but exceptionally large dormers

Setting bed
Flashing
Tile finish
Flashing clamp

Waterproof membrane

Roof slab

ROOF DRAIN IN CONCRETE SLAB WITH PROMENADE TOP

Flashing clamp & gravel stop
Built-up roofing
Insulation
Conc. slab

Roofing felt Flashing
Roof boarding
Wood framing

ROOF DRAIN IN CONCRETE SLAB

ROOF DRAIN IN WOOD CONST.

ROOF DRAINS
1½"=1'-0"

4"

Wood nailing block
Conc. roof slab

BUILT-UP ROOFING ON CONCRETE ROOF SLAB

4"

Brass edge strip

Roof boarding

BUILT-UP ROOFING ON WOOD CONSTRUCTION

GRAVEL STOPS
1½"=1'-0"

6"
4"

Brass edge strip

20 oz. copper L stiffener
Anchor

DEAD-LEVEL ROOF USED FOR WATER COOLING

Recommendation of Copper & Brass Research Ass'n.

FLASHING

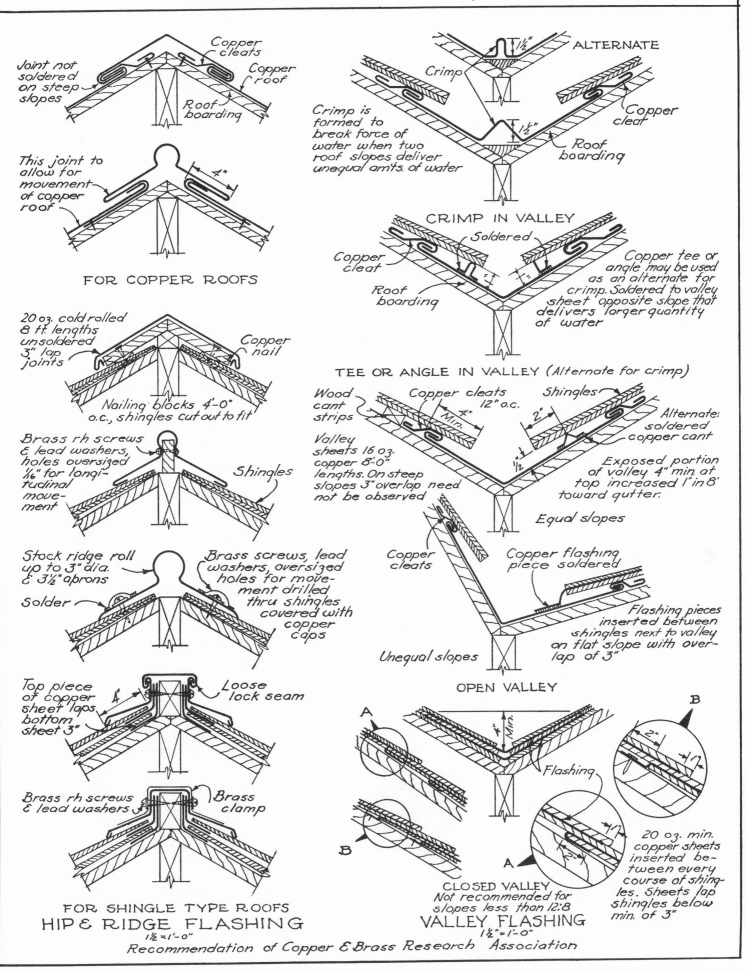

Joint not soldered on steep slopes

Copper cleats

Copper roof

Roof boarding

This joint to allow for movement of copper roof

4"

FOR COPPER ROOFS

20 oz. cold rolled 8 ft. lengths unsoldered 3" lap joints

Copper nail

Nailing blocks 4'-0" o.c., shingles cut out to fit

Brass rh screws & lead washers, holes oversized 1/16" for longitudinal movement

Shingles

Stock ridge roll up to 3" dia. & 3½" aprons

Solder

Brass screws, lead washers, oversized holes for movement drilled thru shingles covered with copper caps

Top piece of copper sheet laps bottom sheet 3"

4"

Loose lock seam

Brass rh screws & lead washers

Brass clamp

FOR SHINGLE TYPE ROOFS
HIP & RIDGE FLASHING
1½"=1'-0"

ALTERNATE

1½"

Crimp

Copper cleat

Roof boarding

1½"

Crimp is formed to break force of water when two roof slopes deliver unequal amts. of water

CRIMP IN VALLEY

Soldered

Copper cleat

Roof boarding

Copper tee or angle may be used as an alternate for crimp. Soldered to valley sheet opposite slope that delivers larger quantity of water

TEE OR ANGLE IN VALLEY (Alternate for crimp)

Wood cant strips

Copper cleats 12" o.c.

Shingles

4" Min.

2"

1½"

Alternate: soldered copper cant

Valley sheets 16 oz. copper 8'-0" lengths. On steep slopes 3" overlap need not be observed

Exposed portion of valley 4" min. at top increased 1" in 8' toward gutter.

Equal slopes

Copper cleats

Copper flashing piece soldered

Flashing pieces inserted between shingles next to valley on flat slope with overlap of 3"

Unequal slopes

OPEN VALLEY

A

B

4" Min.

Flashing

2"

1"

B

A

2"

1"

CLOSED VALLEY
Not recommended for slopes less than 12:8

20 oz. min. copper sheets inserted between every course of shingles. Sheets lap shingles below min. of 3"

VALLEY FLASHING
1½"=1'-0"

Recommendation of Copper & Brass Research Association

FLASHING

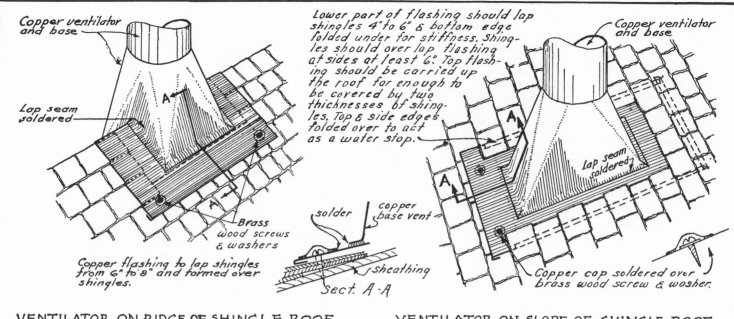

Copper ventilator and base

Lap seam soldered

Brass wood screws & washers

Copper flashing to lap shingles from 6" to 8" and formed over shingles.

Lower part of flashing should lap shingles 4" to 6" & bottom edge folded under for stiffness. Shingles should over lap flashing at sides at least 6". Top flashing should be carried up the roof far enough to be covered by two thicknesses of shingles. Top & side edges folded over to act as a water stop.

solder   copper base vent

Sect. A-A   sheathing

Copper ventilator and base

Lap seam soldered

Copper cap soldered over brass wood screw & washer.

VENTILATOR ON RIDGE OF SHINGLE ROOF.   **VENTILATOR ON SLOPE OF SHINGLE ROOF.**

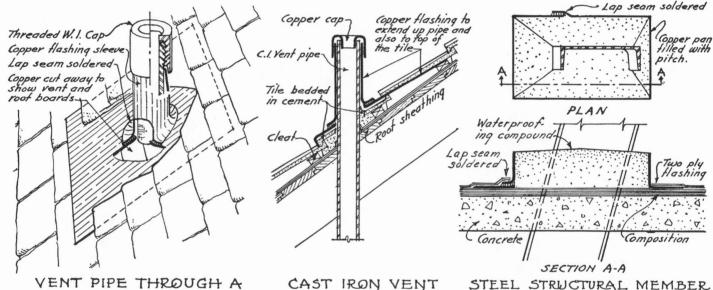

Threaded W.I. Cap
Copper flashing sleeve
Lap seam soldered
Copper cut away to show vent and roof boards

Copper cap
C.I. Vent pipe
Tile bedded in cement
Cleat

Copper flashing to extend up pipe and also to top of the tile
Roof sheathing

Lap seam soldered
Copper pan filled with pitch.

PLAN

Waterproofing compound
Lap seam soldered
Two ply flashing
Concrete
Composition

SECTION A-A

VENT PIPE THROUGH A SLOPING SHINGLE ROOF.   **CAST IRON VENT THRO' CONCRETE TILE**   **STEEL STRUCTURAL MEMBER THROUGH CONCRETE.**

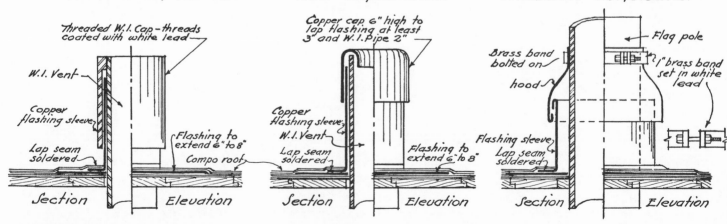

Threaded W.I. Cap - threads coated with white lead
W.I. Vent
Copper flashing sleeve
Lap seam soldered
Flashing to extend 6" to 8"
Compo roof
Section   Elevation

Copper cap 6" high to lap flashing at least 3" and W.I. Pipe 2"
Copper flashing sleeve
W.I. Vent
Lap seam soldered
Flashing to extend 6" to 8"
Section   Elevation

Flag pole
Brass band bolted on
hood
1" brass band set in white lead
Flashing sleeve
Lap seam soldered
Section   Elevation

FLASHING FOR IRON VENT with SCREW CAP   **FLASHING FOR IRON VENT with COPPER CAP**   **FLASHING for FLAG POLE**

COPPER FLASHING for ROOF VENTS, VENTILATORS, FLAG POLES ETC.
Methods recommended by the Copper and Brass Research Association.

LEADER & GUTTER ~ SIZE REQUIREMENTS

WIDTHS of RECTANGULAR GUTTERS (For level gutters. If slope exceeds 2%, gutter is narrowed & deepened.)

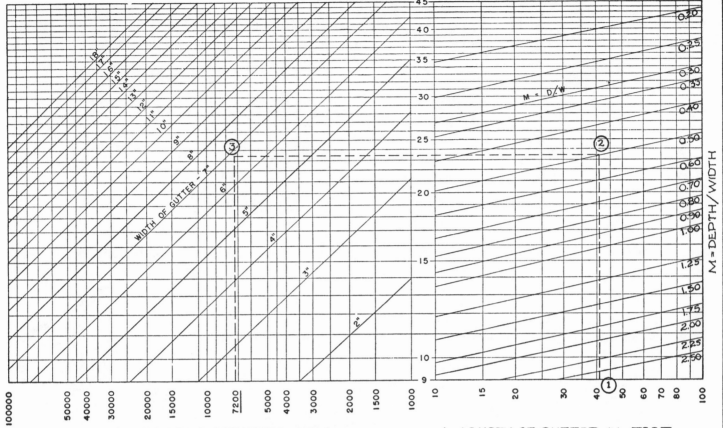

IA = RAINFALL INTENSITY × AREA   **L = LENGTH OF GUTTER IN FEET**

EXAMPLE: To design rectangular gutter in Atlanta. Roof 20'×40'. Gutter assumed width is ½ depth (M=0.5). From Rainfall Table Intensity I = 9"/hr. Area drained A = 800 sq. ft. IA = 7200. Start at ① on Rect. Gutter Graph using L = 40' for Gutter length & follow vertically to intersection ② with oblique line M=0.5. Follow horiz. to intersection ③ with vert. line IA = 7200. Point of intersection occurs between gutter widths of 6" & 7". Required width is 7" & depth is 3½".
EXAMPLE: To design semi-circular gutter in Buffalo. Roof Area = 800 sq. ft. From Rainfall table Intensity = 10"/hr. Using Semi-Circ. Gutter graph find intersection of 800 sq. ft. & 10"/hr. to be 8" which is required gutter width.
EXAMPLE: To design leader in Knoxville. Roof Area drained per leader = 3000 sq. ft. From Rainfall Table 1 sq. in. of leader serves 200 sq. ft. of roof area. Therefore 15 sq. in. is required. From Leader Dimensions Table select either 5" round, octagonal or square or 4"×5" rectangular. (NOTE: Gutter design is for large Buildings.)

RAINFALL DATA & DRAINAGE FACTORS

CITIES	MAXIMUM RECORD STORMS		CITIES	MAXIMUM RECORD STORMS	
NOTE: Roof drainage data based on assumption that for intensity of 8"/Hr. 1 sq.in. of leader drains 150 sq.ft.	Intensity in In./Hr. lasting for 5 minutes	Sq.ft. of roof drained per sq. in. of leader area.		Intensity in In./Hr. lasting for 5 minutes	Sq.ft. of roof drained per sq. in. of leader area.
Albany, N.Y.	7	175	New Orleans, La.	8	150
Atlanta, Ga.	9	130	New York, N.Y.	9	130
Boston, Mass.	7	175	Norfolk, Va.	8	150
Buffalo, N.Y.	10	120	Philadelphia, Pa.	8	150
Chicago, Ill.	7	175	Pittsburg, Pa.	7	175
Detroit, Mich.	7	175	St. Louis, Mo.	11	110
Duluth, Minn.	7	175	St. Paul, Minn.	8	150
Kansas City, Mo.	10	120	San Francisco, Cal.	3	400
Knoxville, Tenn.	6	200	Savannah, Ga.	8	150
Louisville, Ky.	8	150	Seattle, Wash.	2	600
Memphis, Tenn.	10	120	Washington, D.C.	8	150
Montgomery, Ala.	7	175			

DIMENSIONS of LEADERS

TYPE	AREA sq. in.	NOM. SIZE
Plain Round	7.07	3"
	12.57	4"
	19.63	5"
	28.27	6"
Corrugated Round	5.94	3"
	11.04	4"
	17.72	5"
	25.97	6"
Polygon Octagonal	6.36	3"
	11.30	4"
	17.65	5"
	25.40	6"
Square Corrugated	3.80	2"
	7.73	3"
	11.70	4"
	18.75	5"
Plain Rectangular	3.94	1¼"×2¼"
	6.00	2"×3"
	8.00	2"×4"
	12.00	3"×4"
	20.00	4"×5"
	24.00	4"×6"

WIDTHS of SEMI-CIRC. GUTTERS

(graph with AREA SQ.FT. vertical axis and RAINFALL INTENSITY IN./HR. horizontal axis)

Recommendation of Copper & Brass Research Assn.

GUTTERS & LEADERS

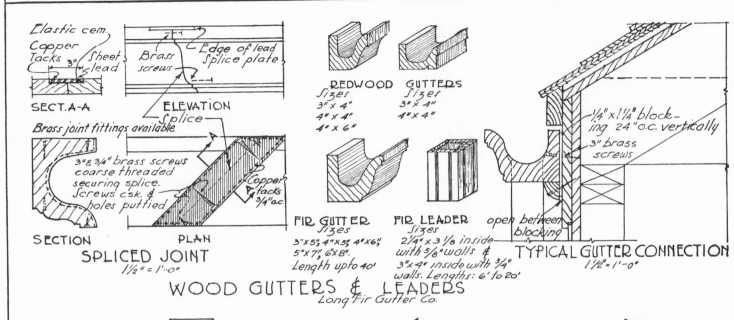

Elastic cem.
Copper Tacks
3"
Sheet lead

SECT. A-A

Brass screws
Edge of lead
Splice plate

ELEVATION
Splice

Brass joint fittings available

3" & 3/4" brass screws
coarse threaded
securing splice.
Screws csk. &
holes puttied

Copper tacks
3/4" o.c.

SECTION   PLAN

SPLICED JOINT
1 1/2" = 1'-0"

REDWOOD   GUTTERS
Sizes   Sizes
3" x 4"   3" x 4"
4" x 4"   4" x 4"
4" x 6"

FIR GUTTER
Sizes
3" x 5", 4" x 5", 4" x 6",
5" x 7", 6" x 8".
Length up to 40'

FIR LEADER
Sizes
2 1/4" x 3 1/8 inside
with 5/8" walls &
3" x 4" inside with 3/4"
walls. Lengths: 6' to 20'

open between
blocking

1/4" x 1 1/4" block-
ing 24" o.c. vertically
3" brass
screws

TYPICAL GUTTER CONNECTION
1 1/2" = 1'-0"

WOOD GUTTERS & LEADERS
Long Fir Gutter Co.

Single-bead
lap joint

Single-bead
slip joint

Double-bead
lap joint

Double-bead
slip joint

HALF ROUND GUTTERS
Copper: All above types in 4" to 10" diam.
Stainless Steel: Single bead in 4" to 10" diam.
Aluminum: Single bead lap joint in 5" diam.
Galv. Iron: All above types in 3 1/2" to 8" diam.
Lengths 10'. Double bead is stiffer
than single bead and permits wider
hanger spacing. But is more difficult to
line inside bead against roof. With considerable slope lengths may be lapped
3" and left unsoldered.

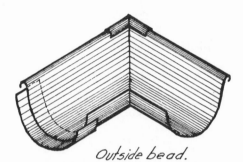

SLIP JOINT CONNECTION
Set 30' apart to pro-
vide for expansion &
contraction in long runs
of lap gutters.
Joints between are lap-
ped & soldered. Slip
joint not soldered.

Outside bead.

Inside bead.

GUTTER MITRES-SINGLE BEAD
Available without slip joint connection & in double bead or box gutter
type.

GUTTER DESIGN for SMALL RESIDENTIAL WORK
Avoid gutters under 4" wide.
Min. slope 1/16" per ft. required.
Min. depth equal to 1/2 & max.
depth not over 3/4 of width.
If leader spacing is less than
20' use a gutter same size
as leader. If leader spacing
is over 20' add 1" to leader dia.
for every add'l 30' on peak roofs,
1" for every add'l 40' on flat.

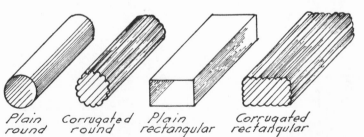

Plain
round

Corrugated
round

Plain
rectangular

Corrugated
rectangular

METAL LEADERS (downspouts)
Copper: See Leader Dimension Table on other page
Galvanized Iron: Same sizes as Copper.
Stainless Steel: 2" to 6" round & 2" to 5" rect. plain & corrug.
Aluminum: 3" round & 2 3/8" x 3 1/4" rect. plain & corrug.
Lengths 10'. General rule: 1 sq. in. of leader to 100 sq. ft.
of roof area drained. Corrugated resists bursting
from freezing best.

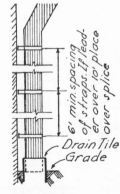

6" min. spacing
of straps. If lead-
er over 10' place
over splice

Drain Tile
Grade

LEADER WITH TILE SHOE

WEIGHTS of SHEET METAL		
Metal	for Leader	for Gutter
Aluminum	23 ga.	25 ga.
Zinc	11-13 ga.	12-13 ga.
Galv. Iron	24-26 ga	24-26 ga.
Tin on Steel	1 X	1 X
Lead, hard	4-8 lbs.	4-8 lbs.
Stain. Steel	28 ga.	28 ga.
Copper	16 oz.	16 oz.
Monel	26 ga	25-26 ga

The above metals are ar-
ranged in order of galvanic
activity.
Do not place metal far a-
part on this table in contact with each other.

GUTTER & LEADER ACCESSORIES

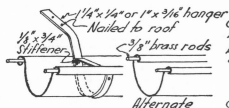

1¼"x¼" or 1"x³/₁₆" hanger
Nailed to roof
⅛"x¾" Stiffener
³/₈" brass rods
Alternate

FIXED STRAP HANGER OF BRASS – SPECIAL
(For the best class of residence) Space hangers 3'-0"o.c. for 1"x³/₁₆" hanger and 3'-6" o.c. for 1¼"x¼" hanger.

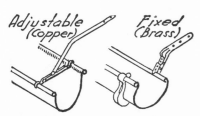

Adjustable (Copper)   Fixed (Brass)

STOCK STRAP HANGERS COPPER & BRASS
Spaced not over 2'-6" o.c. Blocking between bldg. & gutter essential to provide for overflow.

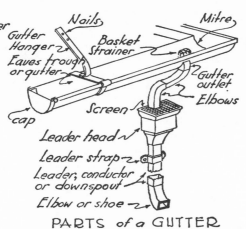

Nails
Gutter Hanger
Basket Strainer
Mitre
Eaves trough or gutter
Gutter outlet
Elbows
Screen
cap
Leader head
Leader strap
Leader, conductor or downspout
Elbow or shoe

PARTS of a GUTTER

Dash line indicates roof slope
Pitch 12-12   12-7   12-5   12-0
¼"   ½"   ¾"   1"
Gutters

Gutters should be placed below slope line so that snow & ice can slide clear. Steeper pitch requires less clearance.

PLACING of GUTTERS

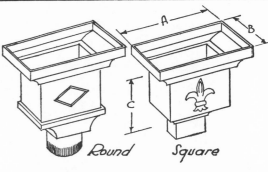

Round   Square

STOCK LEADER HEADS					
SIZE	OUTLET		A	B	C
	Square	Round			
Small	2"x3"	3"	9"	5½"	7½"
	3"x4"	4"	10"	6"	7½"
Large	2"x3"	3"	10"	6"	9"
	3"x4"	4"	11"	6½"	9"

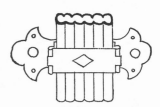

Wired

BRONZE LEADER STRAPS
Set 6'-0" apart min.

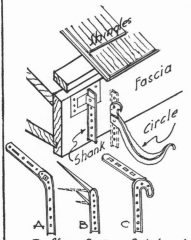

Shingles
Fascia
circle
Shank
A   B   C
Rafter   Spike   Subshingle

BRONZE HANGERS
A Nailed to side of rafter
B Spiked into rafter or fascia
C Adjustable, nailed under Shingles. Others available

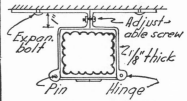

Expan. bolt   Adjustable screw   2¹/₈" thick
Pin   Hinge

HINGED LEADER STRAP–BRONZE.
Loose pin in left side permits removal of leader without taking strap off wall. Also made for round leaders.

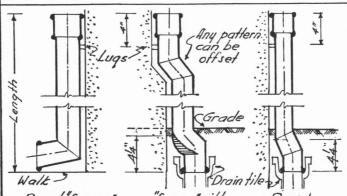

COPPER ELBOWS and SHOES

① 45°   ② 60°   ③ 75°   ④ 90°
Side Views

			Dia. or Size			
Elbows	Round	Plain & corrugated #1,2,3,4	2"	3"	5"	6"
	Square	" "	2"	3"	5"	
Shoes	Round	" " #3	2"	3"	5"	6"
	Square	Corrugated only #3	2"	3"	5"	

CAST IRON DOWNSPOUT SHOES

Lugs
Length
Any pattern can be offset
4"
Grade
Walk
Drain tile
Round, "Square" (or rectangular)   "Square" with Round Outlet   Round

Available lengths from 12" to 72" in increments of 6 inches; Plain, fluted or panel designs.

Copper Wire   Cast Bronze

BASKET STRAINERS
Copper wire type also made in square form to fit standard gutter outlets. Cast Bronze made 3,4,5,6, 7,8, in. round. 2"x3"; 3"x4" sq.

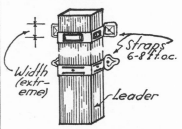

Straps 6-8 ft. o.c.
Width (extreme)
Leader

COPPER LEADER STRAPS
Variety of ornamentation available. Lengths 13" to 20". Widths 1½"-4³/₈"

SQUARE & RECTANGULAR							ROUND		
Spout size	2"x2"	2"x3"	3"x3"	3"x4"	4"x4"	4"x5"	4"x6"	Spout dia.	3"	4"	5"
Outlet dia.	3"	3"	4"	4"	4"	4"	5"	Outlet dia.	3"	4"	5"

Contractor's Foundry, Inc.
Data by Coppers Brass Research Association

BUILT-IN GUTTERS

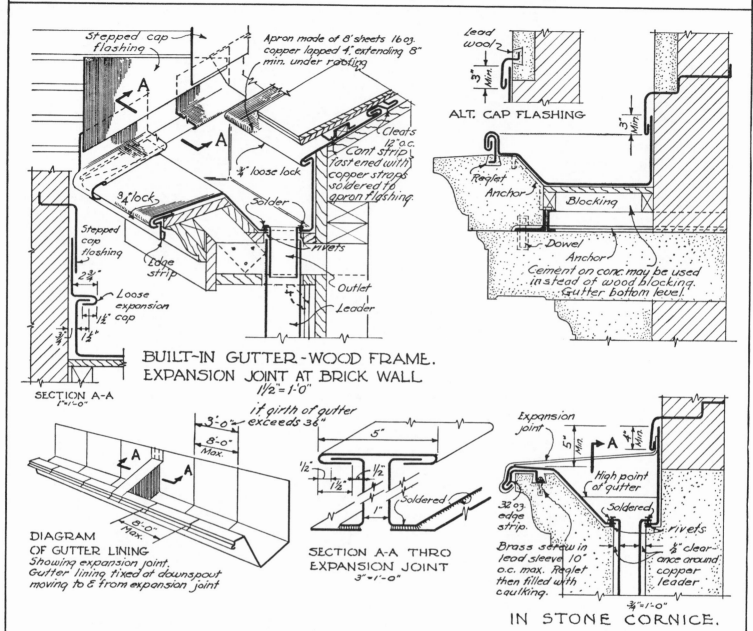

BUILT-IN GUTTER -WOOD FRAME.
EXPANSION JOINT AT BRICK WALL
1½" = 1'-0"

SECTION A-A 1"=1'-0"

ALT. CAP FLASHING

DIAGRAM OF GUTTER LINING
Showing expansion joint. Gutter lining fixed at downspout moving to & from expansion joint

SECTION A-A THRO EXPANSION JOINT 3"=1'-0"

IN STONE CORNICE. ¾"=1'-0"

*DETERMINATION OF GAUGE and EXPANSION JOINT LOCATION for COPPER GUTTER LININGS

Weight of Cold Rolled Copper in Ounces	Width of Gutter Bottom	Max. distance between Exp. Joint & Downspout, in ft. Angle of Gutter Sides					Weight of Cold Rolled Copper in Ounces	Width of Gutter Bottom	Max. distance between Exp. Joint & Downspout, in ft. Angle of Gutter Sides				
		90° 45°	90° 60°	90° 90°	60° 60°	45° 45°			90° 45°	90° 60°	90° 90°	60° 60°	45° 45°
16	6	18'-6"	19'-6"	21'-6"	17'-6"	15'-0"	20	6	24'-0"	26'-0"	29'-0"	23'-0"	20'-0"
	8	16'-0"	17'-6"	19'-0"	15'-0"	13'-0"		8	20'-6"	22'-0"	24'-6"	19'-6"	17'-0"
	10	14'-0"	15'-0"	16'-6"	13'-0"	11'-0"		10	18'-0"	19'-6"	21'-6"	17'-0"	15'-0"
24	8	26'-0"	28'-0"	31'-0"	25'-0"	22'-0"	32	10	40'-6"	43'-6"	47'-6"	39'-0"	34'-6"
	10	23'-0"	25'-0"	27'-0"	22'-0"	19'-6"		12	37'-6"	39'-6"	43'-0"	35'-6"	31'-6"
	12	21'-0"	22'-6"	24'-6"	20'-0"	17'-6"		14	34'-6"	36'-6"	40'-0"	32'-6"	29'-0"

Gutter linings must be unrestrained, except at downspouts. Built-in gutters are lined with cold rolled Copper. Sheets of 16 & 20 oz. are joined by ¾" wide locked & soldered seams. Sheets of 24 & 32 oz. are joined by 1½" wide lapped, riveted & soldered seams. Rivets are copper ³⁄₁₆" dia. with burrs under peened heads. Rivets spaced 3" o.c., two rows staggered.

BUILT-IN GUTTERS
Recommendation of Copper & Brass Research Association
*Data recommendation of Revere Copper & Brass Incorporated

ATTIC and CRAWL SPACE VENTILATION

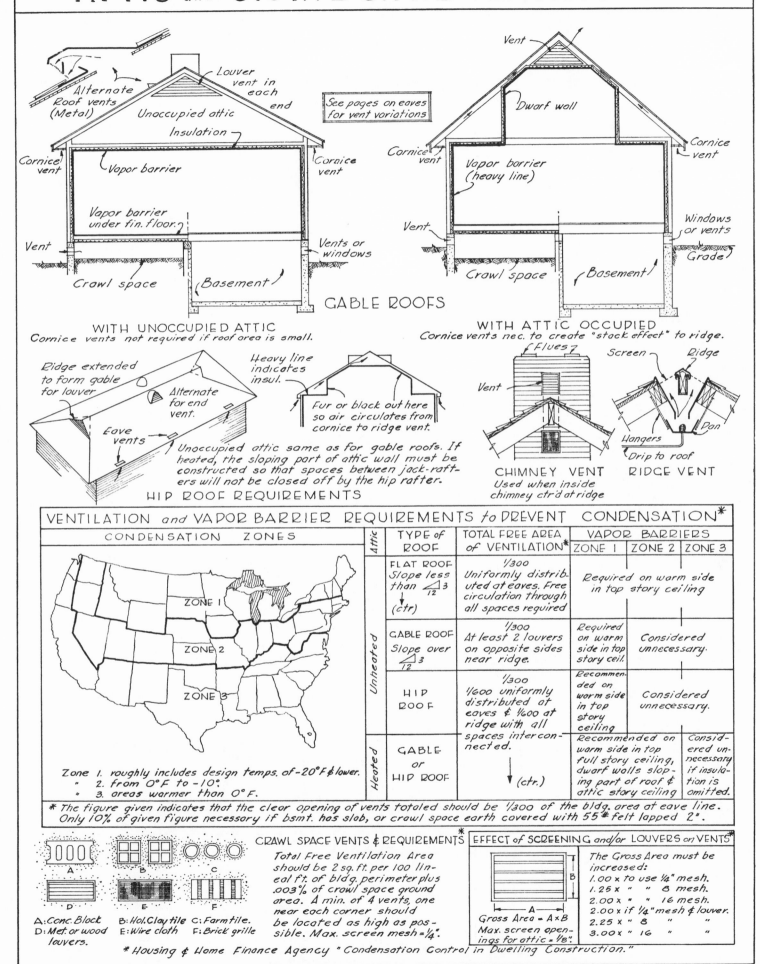

Alternate Roof vents (Metal)

Louver vent in each end

Unoccupied attic

Insulation

Vapor barrier

Cornice vent

Cornice vent

Vapor barrier under fin. floor.

Vent

Crawl space

Basement

Vents or windows

See pages on eaves for vent variations

Vent

Dwarf wall

Cornice vent

Vapor barrier (heavy line)

Cornice vent

Vent

Windows or vents

Grade

Crawl space

Basement

GABLE ROOFS

WITH UNOCCUPIED ATTIC
Cornice vents not required if roof area is small.

WITH ATTIC OCCUPIED
Cornice vents nec. to create "stack effect" to ridge.

Ridge extended to form gable for louver

Alternate for end vent.

Eave vents

Heavy line indicates insul.

Fur or block out here so air circulates from cornice to ridge vent.

Unoccupied attic same as for gable roofs. If heated, the sloping part of attic wall must be constructed so that spaces between jack-rafters will not be closed off by the hip rafter.

HIP ROOF REQUIREMENTS

Flues

Vent

CHIMNEY VENT
Used when inside chimney ctr'd at ridge

Screen

Ridge

Hangers

Pan

Drip to roof

RIDGE VENT

VENTILATION and VAPOR BARRIER REQUIREMENTS to PREVENT CONDENSATION*

CONDENSATION ZONES	Attic	TYPE of ROOF	TOTAL FREE AREA of VENTILATION*	VAPOR BARRIERS		
				ZONE 1	ZONE 2	ZONE 3
	Unheated	FLAT ROOF Slope less than △3/12 (ctr)	1/300 Uniformly distributed at eaves. Free circulation through all spaces required	Required on warm side in top story ceiling		
	Unheated	GABLE ROOF Slope over △3/12	1/300 At least 2 louvers on opposite sides near ridge.	Required on warm side in top story ceil.	Considered unnecessary.	
	Unheated	HIP ROOF	1/300 1/600 uniformly distributed at eaves & 1/600 at ridge with all spaces interconnected. (ctr.)	Recommended on warm side in top story ceiling	Considered unnecessary.	
	Heated	GABLE or HIP ROOF		Recommended on warm side in top full story ceiling, dwarf walls sloping part of roof & attic story ceiling		Considered unnecessary if insulation is omitted.

Zone 1. roughly includes design temps. of -20°F & lower.
" 2. from 0°F to -10°.
" 3. areas warmer than 0°F.

ZONE 1

ZONE 2

ZONE 3

* The figure given indicates that the clear opening of vents totaled should be 1/300 of the bldg. area at eave line. Only 10% of given figure necessary if bsmt. has slab, or crawl space earth covered with 55# felt lapped 2".

CRAWL SPACE VENTS & REQUIREMENTS*

A: Conc. Block   B: Hol. Clay tile   C: Farm tile.
D: Met. or wood louvers.   E: Wire cloth   F: Brick grille

Total Free Ventilation Area should be 2 sq. ft. per 100 lineal ft. of bldg. perimeter plus .003% of crawl space ground area. A min. of 4 vents, one near each corner should be located as high as possible. Max. screen mesh = 1/4".

EFFECT of SCREENING and/or LOUVERS on VENTS*

Gross Area = A x B
Max. screen openings for attic = 1/8".

The Gross Area must be increased:
1.00 x to use 1/4" mesh.
1.25 x " " 8 mesh.
2.00 x " " 16 mesh.
2.00 x if 1/4" mesh & louver.
2.25 x " 8 " "
3.00 x " 16 " "

* Housing & Home Finance Agency "Condensation Control in Dwelling Construction."

VENTILATION *of* RESIDENCES

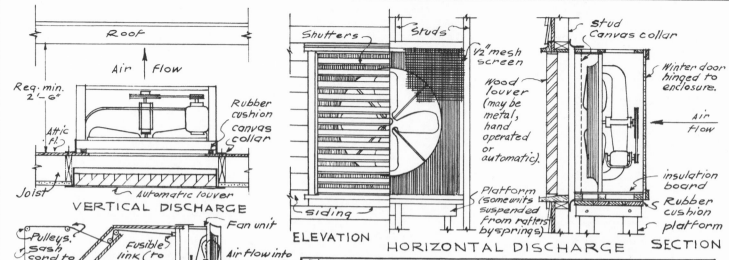

VERTICAL DISCHARGE

Roof

Air Flow

Req. min. 2'-6"

Attic fl.

Rubber cushion canvas collar

Joist — Automatic louver

Pulleys. Sash cord to closet on lower floor

Fusible link (to close door in case of fire)

Fan unit

Air flow into attic

Resilient pad

Trap door

Automatic shutter (if used)

Canvas boot

Joist

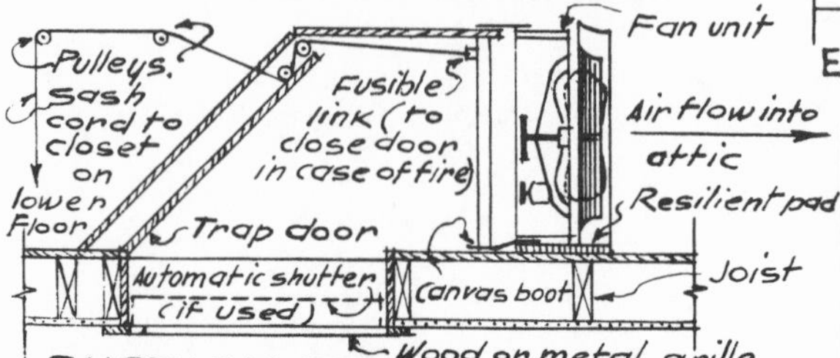

SUCTION BOX
Automatic closing shutter may be used instead.

Wood or metal grille

Shutters   Studs   Stud Canvas collar

½" mesh screen

Wood louver (may be metal, hand operated or automatic).

Platform (some units suspended from rafters by springs)

Winter door hinged to enclosure.

Air Flow

insulation board

Rubber cushion platform

siding

ELEVATION

HORIZONTAL DISCHARGE

SECTION

Discharge of fans exhausting directly to outside should be with prevailing winds. Fans discharging into attic space should be centrally located over area to be ventilated. Horizontally discharging fans usually installed in outside wall if attic is finished, in a penthouse if b'ldg has flat roof, or on the attic floor with a plenum chamber (suction box) if attic is unfinished. Vertical discharge fans are installed in attic floor when attic is unfinished or penthouse if roof is flat.

TYPICAL VENTILATING INSTALLATIONS

RECOMMENDED VENTILATION & SIZES of DISCHARGE OPENINGS

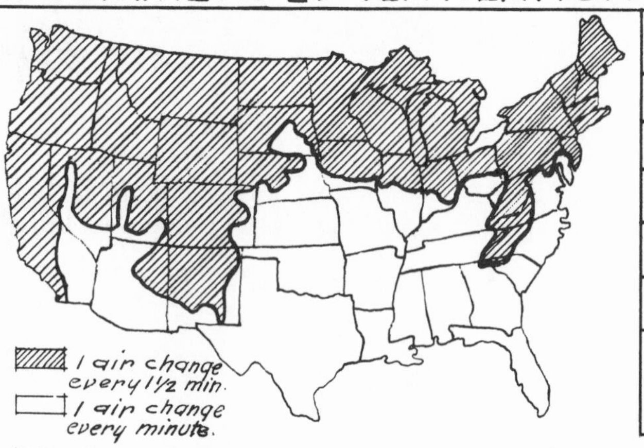

MINIMUM GROSS OUTLET AREAS for ATTIC FAN DISCHARGE OPENING

Type of Opening	Gross Area per 1000 CFM Free Air Fan Delivery
Wood louvers with ½" hardware cloth. 40% minimum free area.	2,27 sq. ft.
Metal louvers with ½" hardware cloth. 50% minimum free area.	1.82 sq. ft.
Plain opening covered with ½" hardware cloth 80% minimum free area.	1.14 sq. ft.
Automatic or manual shutters, 90% minimum free area.	1.01 sq. ft.

NOTE: If opening is covered with #16 mesh screen, double the gross area of opening or construct a box-like frame behind the opening or louver with a screen surface twice the area of the opening or louver.

▨ 1 air change every 1½ min.
☐ 1 air change every minute.

RECOMMENDED AIR CHANGE ZONES and CFM of FAN REQUIRED { Cubical contents of b'ldg ÷ 1 min. or { Cubical contents of b'ldg ÷ 1½ min.

TYPICAL AVERAGE FAN SIZES and SPECIFICATIONS

	CAPACITY CFM		MOTOR	FAN	FAN	DIMENSIONS	
	Free Air	0.1" SP	H.P.	SPEED	DIA	A	B
VERTICAL MOUNTING	5100	3800	1/6	580	24"	34"	14⅜"
	7500	5500	1/4	430	30"	42¼"	15¾"
	11400	8300	1/3	375	36"	48¼"	16¼"
	16000	12000	1/2	355	42"	54¼"	19¾"
	20000	14200	1/2	295	48"	60¼"	19¾"
	22500	18400	3/4	330	48"	60¼"	19¾"
HORIZONTAL	5000	3700	1/6	580	24"	27	15"
	7000	5000	1/4	465	30"	36	15"
	10500	8000	1/3	375	36"	42	15"
	16000	12000	1/2	340	42"	48	21"

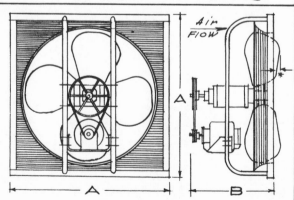

Air Flow

A   B

CFM ratings vary with mfrs. according to H.P. of motor, pulley sizes & design. DIA. of blades are considered stand- and up to 48". Dimensions vary and are approximate. Not all sizes made by all mfrs. * Projection of blades varies from 0" to 1¾"

Data checked by Mongitore & Moesel

GENERAL NOTES

Building attics, crawl spaces, and basements must be ventilated to remove moisture and water vapor resulting from human activity within the building. Moisture in basements and crawl spaces can occur, in addition, from water in the surrounding soil. The quantity of water vapor depends on building type (e.g., residence, school, hospital), activity (e.g., kitchen, bathroom, laundry), and air temperature and relative humidity. Proper ventilation and insulation must be combined so that the temperature of the ventilated space does not fall below the dew point; this is especially critical with low outdoor temperatures and high inside humidity. Inadequate ventilation will cause condensation and eventual deterioration of framing, insulation, and interior finishes.

The vent types shown allow natural ventilation of roofs and crawl spaces. Mechanical methods (e.g., power attic ventilators, whole house fans) can combine living space and attic ventilation, but openings for natural roof ventilation must still be provided. Protect all vents against insects and vermin with metal or fiberglass screen cloth. Increase net vent areas as noted in table.

VENTILATION REQUIREMENTS TO PREVENT CONDENSATION

SPACE	ROOF TYPE	TOTAL NET AREA OF VENTILATION	REMARKS
Joist (ceiling on underside of joists)	Flat	1/300. Uniformly distributed at eaves	Vent each joist space at both ends. Provide at least 1½'' free space above insulation for ventilation
	Sloped	Ditto	Ditto. On gable roofs, drill 1'' diameter holes through ridge beam in each joist space to provide through-ventilation to both sides of roof
Attic (unheated)	Gable	1/300. At least two louvers on opposite sides near ridge	
	Hip	1/300. Uniformly distributed at eaves. Provide additional 1/600 at ridge, with all vents interconnected	Ridge vents create stack effect from eaves; both are recommended over eaves vents alone

Total net vent area = 1/300 of building area at eaves line. With screens increase net area by: 1/4'' screen, 1.0; #8 screen, 1.25; #16 screen, 2.00.

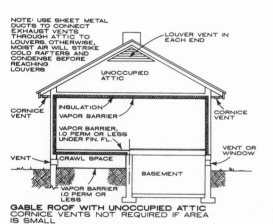

GABLE ROOF WITH UNOCCUPIED ATTIC
CORNICE VENTS NOT REQUIRED IF AREA IS SMALL

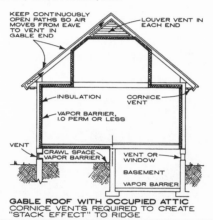

GABLE ROOF WITH OCCUPIED ATTIC
CORNICE VENTS REQUIRED TO CREATE "STACK EFFECT" TO RIDGE

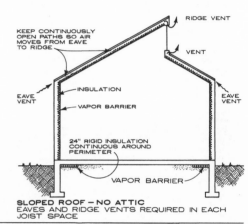

SLOPED ROOF — NO ATTIC
EAVES AND RIDGE VENTS REQUIRED IN EACH JOIST SPACE

TYPICAL ATTIC AND CRAWL SPACE VENTILATION APPLICATIONS

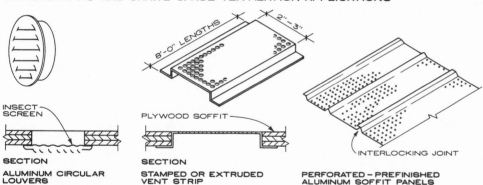

ALUMINUM CIRCULAR LOUVERS
1 INCH — 3 INCH DIAMETER

STAMPED OR EXTRUDED VENT STRIP

PERFORATED — PREFINISHED ALUMINUM SOFFIT PANELS
10'' × 10'-0'' LONG. ALSO IN ROLLS

EAVES VENTILATING MATERIALS

NOTE

Vapor barriers minimize moisture migration to attics and crawl spaces; their use is required for all conditions. Always locate vapor barriers on the warm (room) side of insulation. Provide ventilation on the cold side; this permits cold/hot weather ventilation while minimizing heat gain/loss.

CRAWL SPACES VENTILATION

Crawl spaces under dwellings where earth is damp and uncovered require a high rate of ventilation. Provide at least one opening per side, as high as possible. Calculate total net area by the formula:

$$a = \frac{2L}{100} + \frac{A}{300}$$

where

L = crawl space perimeter (linear ft)

A = crawl space area (sq ft)

a = total net vent area (sq ft)

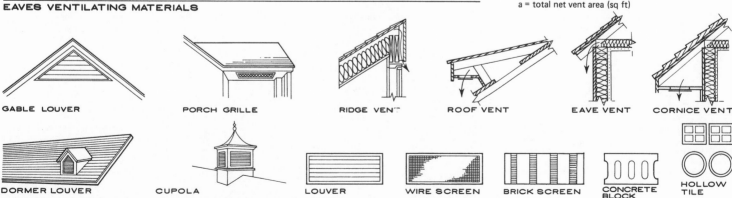

GABLE LOUVER   PORCH GRILLE   RIDGE VENT   ROOF VENT   EAVE VENT   CORNICE VENT

DORMER LOUVER   CUPOLA   LOUVER   WIRE SCREEN   BRICK SCREEN   CONCRETE BLOCK   HOLLOW TILE

TYPICAL ATTIC AND CRAWL SPACE VENT OPENINGS

David Metzger, Architect, CSI; Wilkes and Faulkner Associates; Washington, D.C.

WATER VAPOR MIGRATION

Water is present as vapor in indoor and outdoor air and as absorbed moisture in many building materials. Within the range of temperatures encountered in buildings water may exist in the liquid, vapor, or solid states. Moisture related problems may arise from changes in moisture content, from the presence of excessive moisture, or from the effects of changes of state such as freezing within wall insulation.

In the design and construction of buildings the behavior of moisture must be considered, including particularly the change from vapor to liquid (condensation). Such problems generally arise when moisture in relatively humid indoor air comes in contact with a cold surface such as a window or when the moisture migrates under the influence of vapor pressure differences through walls to enter a region of relatively low temperature where condensation can occur.

Moisture problems in residences generally occur in winter when the outdoor temperature and vapor pressure are low and there are many indoor vapor sources. These may include cooking, laundering, bathing, breathing, and perspiration from the occupants, as well as automatic washers and driers, dishwashers and humidifiers. All of these sources combine to cause vapor pressure indoors to be much higher than outdoors, so that the vapor tends to migrate outward through the building envelope. Vapor cannot permeate glazed windows or metal doors, but most other building materials are permeable to some extent. Walls are particularly susceptible to this phenomenon, and such migration must be prevented or at least minimized by the use of low permeability membranes known as vapor barriers, which should be installed as close as possible to the indoor surface of the building.

Water vapor migration is relatively independent of air motion within the building, since such migration depends primarily on vapor pressure differences. Migration always takes place from regions of higher vapor pressure toward spaces such as wall cavities where the vapor pressure will be lower. When surfaces below the local dewpoint temperature are encountered, condensation will occur and moisture droplets will form. If the local drybulb temperature is at or below 32°F, freezing will occur, which may lead to permanent structural damage.

Moisture in building materials usually increases their thermal conductance to a significant and unpredictable extent. Porous materials that become saturated with moisture lose most of their insulating capability and may not regain it when they dry out. Dust, which usually settles in airspaces, may become permanently affixed to originally reflective surfaces. Moisture migration by evaporation, vapor flow, and condensation can transport significant quantities of latent heat, particularly through fibrous insulating materials.

Positive steps should be taken to prevent migration of moisture in the form of vapor and accumulation in the form of water or ice within building components. Vapor barriers, correctly located near the source of the moisture, are the most effective means of preventing such migration. Venting of moisture laden air from bathrooms, laundry rooms, and kitchens will reduce indoor vapor pressure, as will the introduction of outdoor air with low moisture content.

PERMEANCE AND PERMEABILITY OF MATERIALS TO WATER VAPOR

MATERIAL	PERMEANCE (PERM)	MATERIAL	PERMEANCE (PERM)
MATERIALS USED IN CONSTRUCTION		**BUILDING PAPERS, FELTS, ROOFING PAPERS[3]**	
Concrete (1:2:4 mix)	3.2[5]	Duplex sheet, asphalt laminated, aluminum foil one side (43)[4]	0.176
Brick-masonry (4 in. thick)	0.8–1.1	Saturated and coated roll roofing (326)[4]	0.24
Concrete masonry (8 in. cored, limestone aggregate)	2.4	Kraft paper and asphalt laminated, reinforced 30-120-30 (34)[4]	1.8
Asbestos-cement board (0.2 in. thick)	0.54	Asphalt-saturated, coated vapor-barrier paper (43)[4]	0.6
Plaster on metal lath (3/4 in.)	15	Asphalt-saturated, not coated sheathing paper (22)[4]	20.2
Plaster on plain gypsum lath (with studs)	20	15-lb asphalt felt (70)[4]	5.6
Gypsum wallboard (3/8 in. plain)	50	15-lb tar felt (70)[4]	18.2
Structural insulating board (sheathing quality)	20–50[5]	Single kraft, double infused (16)[4]	42
Structural insulating board (interior, uncoated, 1/2 in.)	50–90	**LIQUID APPLIED COATING MATERIALS**	
Hardboard (1/8 in. standard)	11	Paint—two coats	
Hardboard (1/8 in. tempered)	5	Aluminum varnish on wood	0.3–0.5
Built-up roofing (hot mopped)	0.0	Enamels on smooth plaster	0.5–1.5
Wood, fir sheathing, 3/4 in.	2.9	Primers and sealers on interior insulation board	0.9–2.1
Plywood (Douglas fir, exterior glue, 1/4 in.)	0.7	Miscellaneous primers plus one coat flat oil paint on plastic	1.6–3.0
Plywood (Douglas fir, interior, glue, 1/4 in.)	1.9	Flat paint on interior insulation board	4
Acrylic, glass fiber reinforced sheet, 56 mil	0.12	Water emulsion on interior insulation board	30–85
Polyester, glass fiber reinforced sheet, 48 mil	0.05	Paint—three coats	
THERMAL INSULATIONS		Exterior paint, white lead and oil on wood siding	0.3–1.0
Cellular glass	0.0[5]	Exterior paint, white lead-zinc oxide and oil on wood	0.9
Mineral wool, unprotected	29.0	Styrene-butadiene latex coating, 2 oz/sq ft	11
Expanded polyurethane (R-11 blown)	0.4–1.6[5]	Polyvinyl acetate latex coating, 4 oz/sq ft	5.5
Expanded polystyrene—extruded	1.2[5]		
Expanded polystyrene—bead	2.0–5.8[5]	Asphalt cutback bastic	
PLASTIC AND METAL FOILS AND FILMS[2]		1/16 in. dry	0.14
Aluminum foil (1 mil)	0.0	3/16 in. dry	0.0
Polyethylene (4 mil)	0.08	Hot melt asphalt	
Polyethylene (6 mil)	0.06	2 oz/sq ft	0.5
Polyethylene (8 mil)	0.04	3.5 oz/sq ft	0.1
Polyester (1 mil)	0.7		
Polyvinylchloride, unplasticized (2 mil)	0.68		
Polyvinylchloride, plasticized (4 mil)	0.8–1.4		

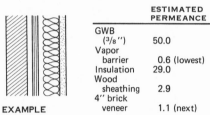

	ESTIMATED PERMEANCE
GWB (3/8")	50.0
Vapor barrier	0.6 (lowest)
Insulation	29.0
Wood sheathing	2.9
4" brick veneer	1.1 (next)

EXAMPLE

In this example the vapor barrier transmits 1 grain of moisture per square foot per hour for each unit of vapor pressure difference, and nothing else transmits less. However, since the cold brick veneer is nearly as low in permeance it is advisable to make certain that the vapor barrier is expertly installed, with all openings at pipes and with outlet boxes or joints carefully fitted or sealed. Alternatively, the brick veneer may have open mortar joints near the top and bottom to serve both as weep holes and as vapor release openings. They will also ventilate the wall and help to reduce heat gain in summer.

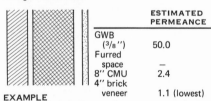

	ESTIMATED PERMEANCE
GWB (3/8")	50.0
Furred space	—
8" CMU	2.4
4" brick veneer	1.1 (lowest)

EXAMPLE

Vapor (under pressure) would easily pass through the interior finish, be slowed up by the concrete masonry unit, and be nearly stopped by the cold brick veneer. Unless this design is radically improved, the masonry will become saturated and may cause serious water stains or apparent "leaks" in cold weather. In addition, alternating freezing and thawing of condensation within the masonry wall can physically damage the construction.

- List the materials, without surface films or airspaces, in the order of their appearance in the building section, beginning with the inside surface material and working to the outside.
- Against each material list the permeance (or permeability) value from the table or a more accurate value if available from tests or manufacturers' data. Where a range is given, select an average value or use judgment in assigning a value based on the character and potential installation method of the material proposed for use.
- Start at the top of the list and note any material that has less permeance than the materials above it on the list. At that point the possibility exists that vapor leaking through the first material may condense on the second, provided the dew point (condensation point) is reached and the movement is considerable. In that case, provide ventilation through the cold side material or modify the design to eliminate or change the material to one of greater permeance.

NOTES

1. The vapor transmission rates listed will permit comparisons of materials, but selection of vapor barrier materials should be based on rates obtained from the manufacturer or from laboratory tests. The range of values shown indicates variation among mean values for materials that are similar but of different density. Values are intended for design guidance only.
2. Usually installed as vapor barriers. If used as exterior finish and elsewhere near cold side, special considerations are required.
3. Low permeance sheets used as vapor barriers. High permeance use elsewhere in construction.
4. Bases (weight in lb/500 sq ft).
5. Permeability (PERM-in.).

Based on data from "ASHRAE Handbook of Fundamentals," 1977, Chapter 20.

Owen J. Delevante, AIA; Glen Rock, New Jersey

E. C. Shuman, P.E.; Consulting Engineer; State College, Pennsylvania

BUILDING SECTION ANALYSIS FOR POTENTIAL CONDENSATION

Any building section may be analyzed by simple calculations to determine where condensation might occur and what might be done in selecting materials or their method of assembly to eliminate that possibility. The section may or may not contain a vapor barrier or it may contain a relatively imperfect barrier; the building section may include cold side materials of comparatively high resistance to the passage of vapor (which is highly undesirable and is to be avoided). With few exceptions, the vapor resistance at or near the warm surface should be five times that of any components. The table above gives permeances and permeability of building and vapor barrier materials. These values can be used in analyzing building sections by the following simple method:

7 DOORS AND WINDOWS

RESIDENTIAL STEEL CASEMENT WINDOWS and DOORS

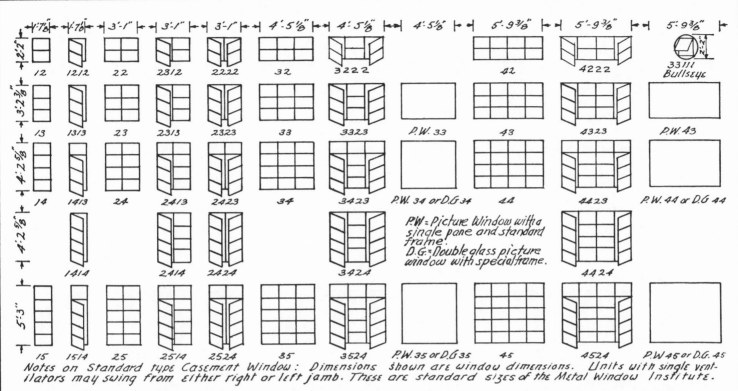

Notes on Standard type Casement Window: Dimensions shown are window dimensions. Units with single vent-ilators may swing from either right or left jamb. These are standard sizes of the Metal Window Institute.

Notes on Special Items (not standard): For size of masonry opening or for wood rebate dimensions, in usual construction, add ¼" to the above sizes. This may not hold for special wood or metal surrounds. See mfrs. catalogs for such dimensions. If several units are assembled with vertical mullions add ⅛" or ¼" (this di-mension varies with mfrs.) for each mullion. If units are assembled over each other, add ⅛" for each horizontal mullion. See fol. p. for types and sizes available for the Pacific Coast, Southwest and Rocky Mountain areas. Tee or pipe type vertical mullions and Tee horizontal mullions join combinations of units. Screens and/or storm sash, wood fins, steel fins wood and/or metal surrounds are available. In ventilators, any or all muntins may be omit-ted. Vertical muntins may be added. Inside metal trim and casings available. Operator types: Rotary, lever, or under-screen. Apartment Casements are standard Residence Casements equipped with Simplex locking handles and friction hinges on orders of 300 or more units. Sizes of glass vary fractionally with mfrs.

RESIDENTIAL CASEMENT WINDOWS

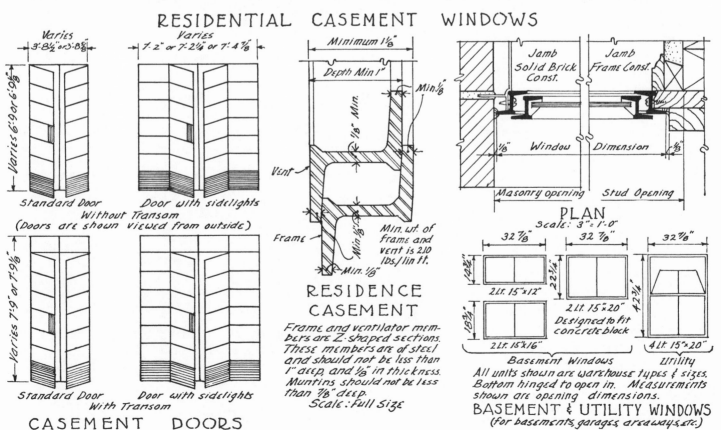

RESIDENTIAL STEEL CASEMENT WINDOWS, SHINGLES on FRAME

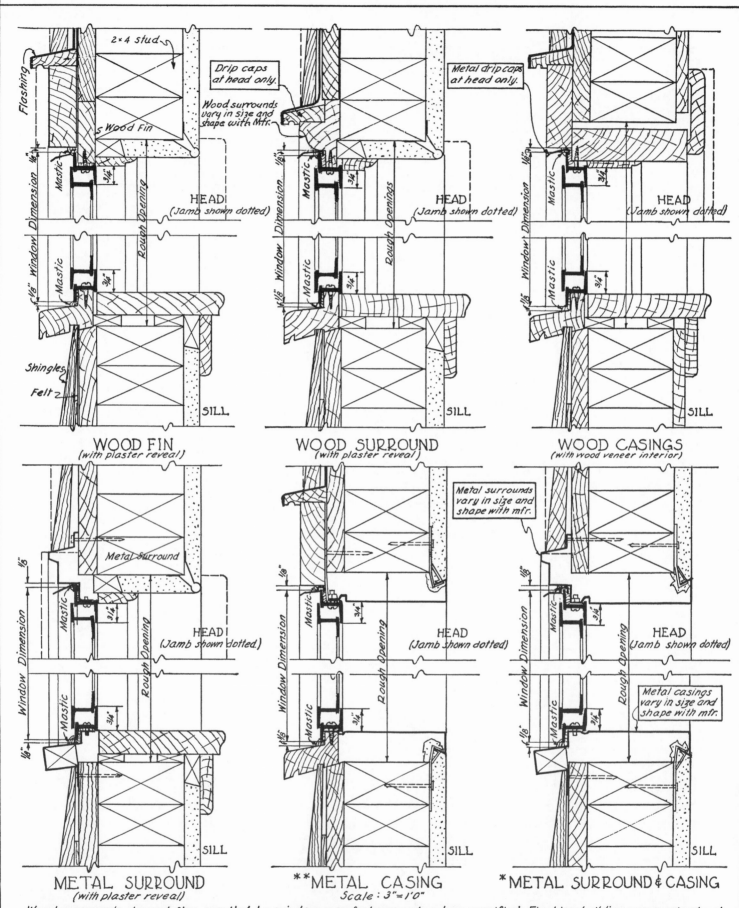

WOOD FIN
(with plaster reveal)

WOOD SURROUND
(with plaster reveal)

WOOD CASINGS
(with wood veneer interior)

METAL SURROUND
(with plaster reveal)

**METAL CASING
Scale: 3"=1'0"

*METAL SURROUND & CASING

*Wood surrounds & wood fins supplied by window manufacturers only when specified. Flashing, building paper, structural lintels, blocking, woodstops, stools, aprons, inside trim, etc., are not generally supplied by window mfr. *Metal surrounds may also be used with wood casings. ** Metal casings may also be used with wood surrounds.*

RESIDENTIAL STEEL CASEMENT WINDOWS, BRICK VENEER

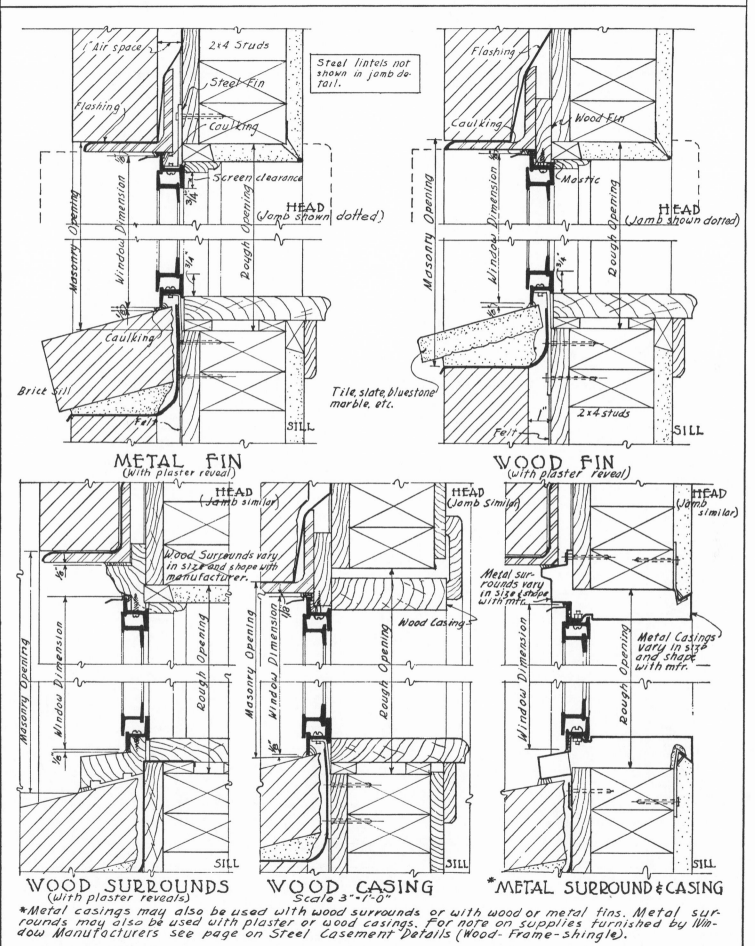

Steel lintels not shown in jamb detail.

METAL FIN
(With plaster reveal)

WOOD FIN
(with plaster reveal)

WOOD SURROUNDS
(with plaster reveals)

WOOD CASING
Scale 3"=1'-0"

*METAL SURROUND & CASING

*Metal casings may also be used with wood surrounds or with wood or metal fins. Metal surrounds may also be used with plaster or wood casings. For note on supplies furnished by Window Manufacturers see page on Steel Casement Details (Wood-Frame-shingle).

RESIDENTIAL STEEL CASEMENT WINDOWS, STUCCO on BLOCK and FRAME

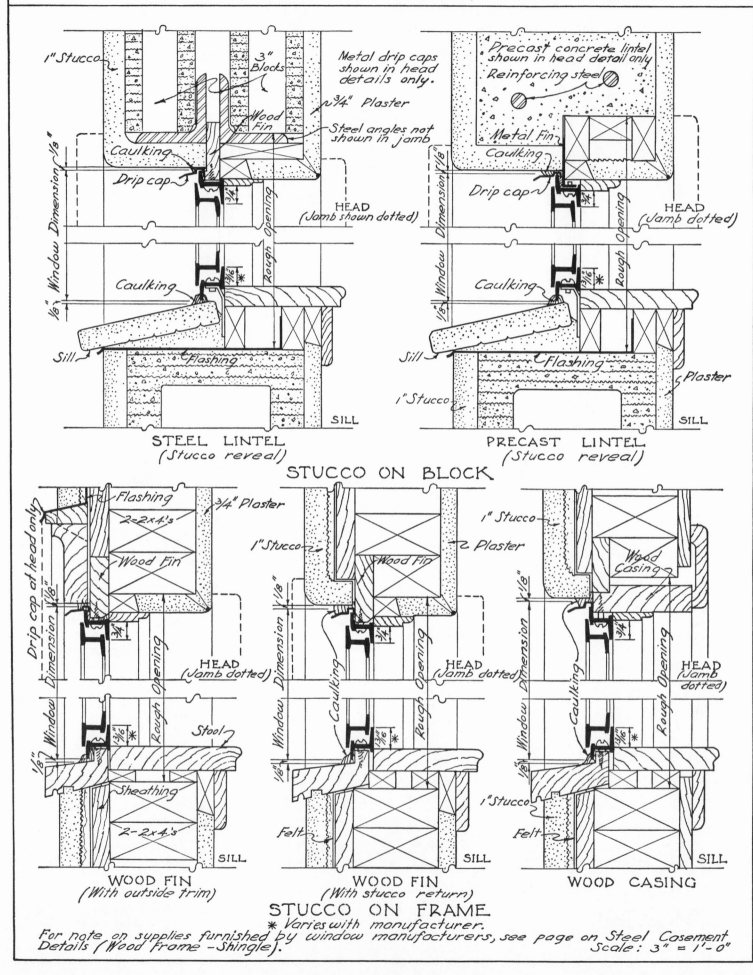

1" Stucco

3" Blocks

Metal drip caps shown in head details only.

¾" Plaster

Wood Fin

Steel angles not shown in jamb

Caulking

Drip cap

¾"

⅛" Window Dimension

Window Dimension ⅛"

Rough Opening

HEAD (Jamb shown dotted)

Caulking

3/16"

Sill

Flashing

SILL

STEEL LINTEL
(Stucco reveal)

Precast concrete lintel shown in head detail only

Reinforcing steel

Metal Fin

Caulking

Drip cap

¾"

Window Dimension ⅛"

Rough Opening

HEAD (Jamb dotted)

Caulking

3/16" *

Sill

1" Stucco

Flashing

Plaster

SILL

PRECAST LINTEL
(Stucco reveal)

STUCCO ON BLOCK

Flashing

¾" Plaster

2-2x4's

Wood Fin

Drip cap at head only

⅛"

¾"

Window Dimension ⅛"

Rough Opening

HEAD (Jamb dotted)

3/16" *

Stool

Sheathing

2-2x4's

SILL

WOOD FIN
(With outside trim)

1" Stucco

Wood Fin

Plaster

⅛"

Caulking

¾"

Window Dimension

⅛"

Rough Opening

HEAD (Jamb dotted)

3/16" *

Felt

1" Stucco

SILL

WOOD FIN
(With stucco return)

1" Stucco

Wood Casing

⅛"

Caulking

¾"

Window Dimension

⅛"

Rough Opening

HEAD (Jamb dotted)

3/16" *

Felt

SILL

WOOD CASING

STUCCO ON FRAME
* Varies with manufacturer.

For note on supplies furnished by window manufacturers, see page on Steel Casement Details (Wood Frame –Shingle).

Scale: 3" = 1'-0"

RESIDENTIAL STEEL CASEMENT WINDOWS, SOLID BRICK WALLS

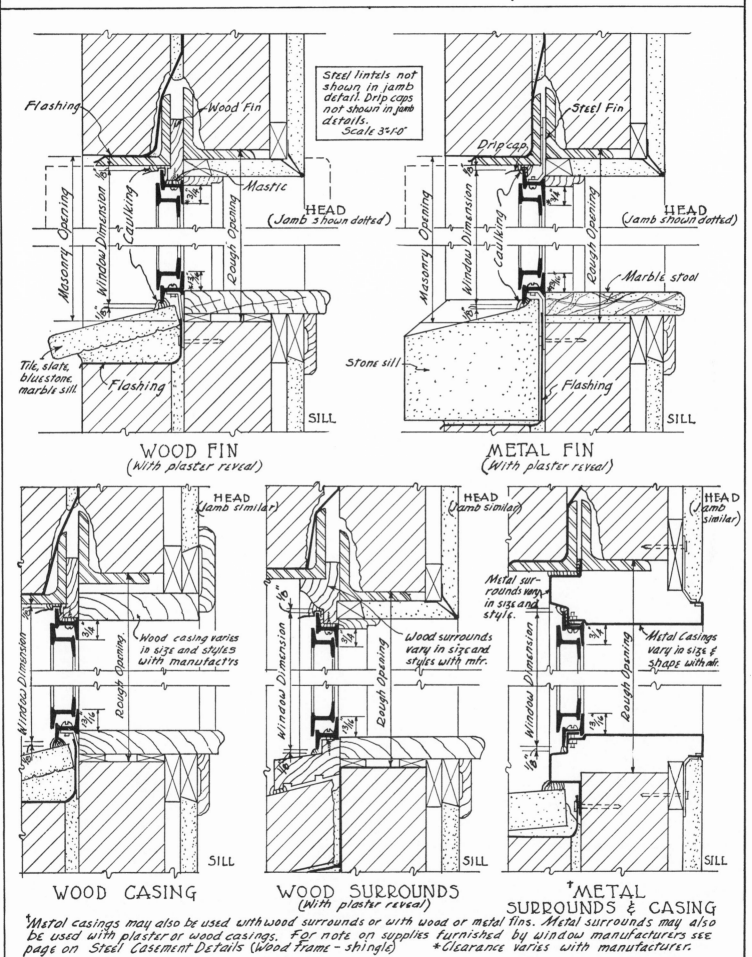

Steel lintels not shown in jamb detail. Drip caps not shown in jamb details.
Scale 3"=1'-0"

WOOD FIN
(With plaster reveal)

METAL FIN
(With plaster reveal)

WOOD CASING

WOOD SURROUNDS
(With plaster reveal)

†METAL SURROUNDS & CASING

†Metal casings may also be used with wood surrounds or with wood or metal fins. Metal surrounds may also be used with plaster or wood casings. For note on supplies furnished by window manufacturers see page on Steel Casement Details (Wood frame – shingle)   *Clearance varies with manufacturer.

RESIDENTIAL STEEL CASEMENT WINDOWS, MASONRY WALLS

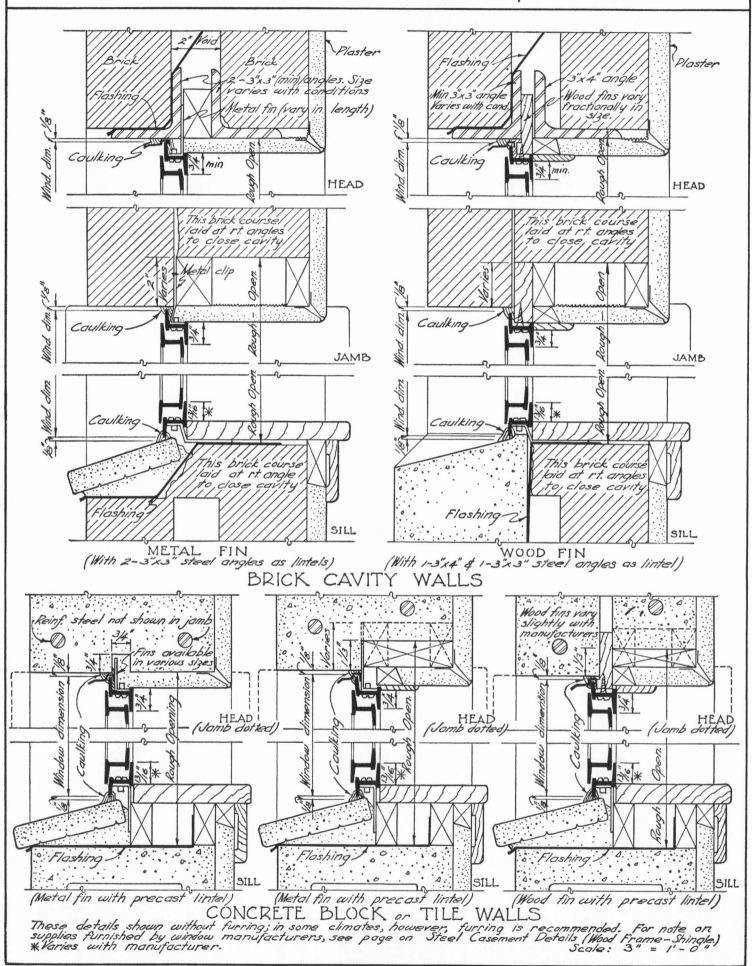

2" Void

Brick

Plaster

Brick

Flashing

2-3"x3"(min) angles. Size varies with conditions

Metal fin (vary in length)

Wind. dim. 1/8"

Caulking

3/4" min

Rough Open.

HEAD

Flashing

Plaster

Min 3"x3" angle Varies with cond.

3"x4" angle

Wood fins vary fractionally in size.

Wind. dim. 1/8"

Caulking

3/4" min.

Rough Open.

HEAD

This brick course laid at rt. angles to close cavity

Varies

Metal clip

Wind. dim. 1/8"

Caulking

2"

3/4"

Rough Open.

JAMB

This brick course laid at rt. angles to close cavity

Varies

Wind. dim. 1/8"

Caulking

3/4"

Rough Open.

JAMB

1/8" Wind. dim.

Caulking

13/16" *

Rough Open.

This brick course laid at rt. angle to close cavity

Flashing

SILL

1/8" Wind. dim.

Caulking

13/16" *

Rough Open.

This brick course laid at rt. angles to close cavity

Flashing

SILL

METAL FIN
(With 2-3"x3" steel angles as lintels)

WOOD FIN
(With 1-3"x4" & 1-3"x3" steel angles as lintel)

BRICK CAVITY WALLS

Reinf. steel not shown in jamb

3/4"

1/8"

3/4"

Fins available in various sizes

Window dimension

Caulking

3/4"

Rough Opening

HEAD
(Jamb dotted)

13/16" *

1/8"

Flashing

SILL

(Metal fin with precast lintel)

1/8"

Varies

1/8"

Window dimension

Caulking

3/4"

Rough Open.

HEAD
(Jamb dotted)

13/16" *

1/8"

Flashing

SILL

(Metal fin with precast lintel)

Wood fins vary slightly with manufacturers

1/8"

1/8"

Window dimension

Caulking

3/4"

Rough Open.

HEAD
(Jamb dotted)

13/16" *

1/8"

Flashing

SILL

(Wood fin with precast lintel)

CONCRETE BLOCK or TILE WALLS

These details shown without furring; in some climates, however, furring is recommended. For note on supplies furnished by window manufacturers, see page on Steel Casement Details (Wood Frame-Shingle.)

* Varies with manufacturer.

Scale: 3" = 1'-0"

RESIDENTIAL STEEL CASEMENT, BAY WINDOWS

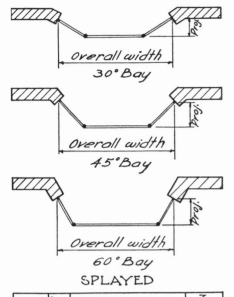

Overall width
30° Bay

Overall width
45° Bay

Overall width
60° Bay

SPLAYED

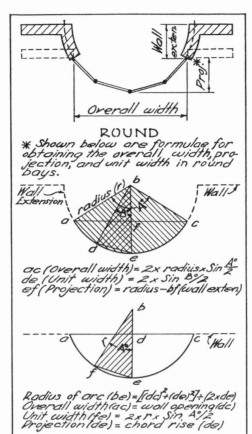

Overall width

ROUND

* Shown below are formulae for obtaining the overall width, projection, and unit width in round bays.

$$ac \text{ (Overall width)} = 2 \times radius \times \sin\frac{A°}{2}$$
$$de \text{ (Unit width)} = 2 \times \sin\frac{B°}{2}$$
$$ef \text{ (Projection)} = radius - bf \text{ (wall exten)}$$

Radius of arc $(be) = [(dc)^2 + (de)^2] \div (2 \times de)$
Overall width $(ac) = $ wall opening (dc)
Unit width $(fe) = 2 \times r \times \sin A°/2$
Projection $(de) = $ chord rise (de)

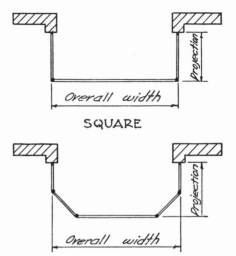

Overall width
SQUARE

Projection

Overall width
SQUARE-SPLAYED

ANGLE of BAY	Lights in Return	OVERALL WIDTH Lights in Front Section			PROJECTION
		*2	3	4	
30°	1	6'-1⅛"	7'-5¼"	8'-9½"	10"
	2	8'-8⅛"	10'-0¼"	11'-4½"	1'-6⅞"
45°	1	5'-7¼"	6'-11⅜"	8'-3⅝"	1'-2¼"
	2	7'-8½"	9'-0⅝"	10'-4⅞"	2'-2⅞"
60°	1	4'-11¼"	6'-3⅜"	7'-7⅝"	1'-5½"
	2	6'-5⅛"	7'-9¼"	9'-1½"	2'-9"

ANGLE of BAY	Lights in return	OVERALL WIDTH Lights in Front Section			PROJECTION
		*2	3	4	
SQUARE	1	3'-4"	4'-8⅛"	6'-0⅜"	1'-8¾"
	2	3'-4"	4'-8⅛"	6'-0⅜"	3'-2⅝"
SQUARE SPLAYED	1	5'-8¼"	7'-0⅜"	8'-4⅝"	2'-10⅞"
	2	7'-9½"	9'-1⅝"	10'-5⅞"	5'-5⅜"

* Dimensions based on single vent in returns & double (2) vented units in front.

Residence casements may be combined to form bay windows as suggested above. Such combinations require the use of bearing or non-bearing mullions. T-bar mullions cannot be used. Standard non-bearing mullions are generally supplied by the window manufacturer. These mullions are not designed to support any building construction. Structural angle shown below is only bearing mullion shown.

STANDARD BAY COMBINATIONS

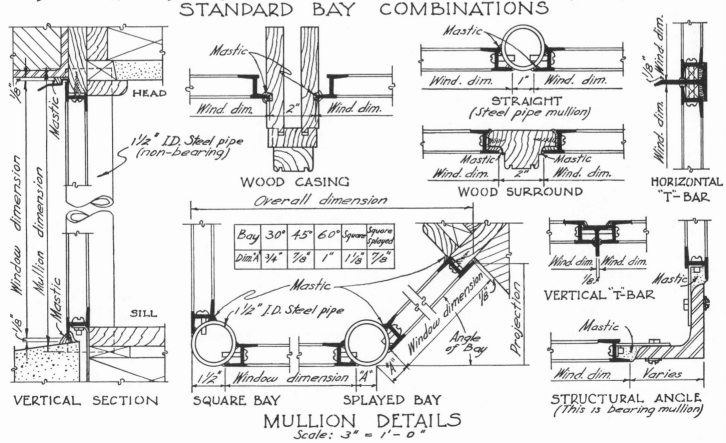

HEAD

1½" I.D. Steel pipe (non-bearing)

Window dimension

Mullion dimension

SILL

VERTICAL SECTION

WOOD CASING

Mastic
Wind. dim. — 2" — Wind. dim.

Mastic
Wind. dim. — 1" — Wind. dim.
STRAIGHT (Steel pipe mullion)

Mastic   Mastic
Wind. dim. — 2" — Wind. dim.
WOOD SURROUND

HORIZONTAL "T"-BAR

Overall dimension

Bay	30°	45°	60°	Square	Square Splayed
Dim. "A"	¾"	⅞"	1"	1⅛"	⅞"

Mastic
1½" I.D. Steel pipe

1½" Window dimension "A"
SQUARE BAY

Window dimension
Angle of Bay
Projection
SPLAYED BAY

VERTICAL "T"-BAR

Mastic
Wind. dim. — Varies
STRUCTURAL ANGLE
(This is bearing mullion)

MULLION DETAILS
Scale: 3" = 1'-0"

STEEL COMMERCIAL PROJECTED WINDOWS

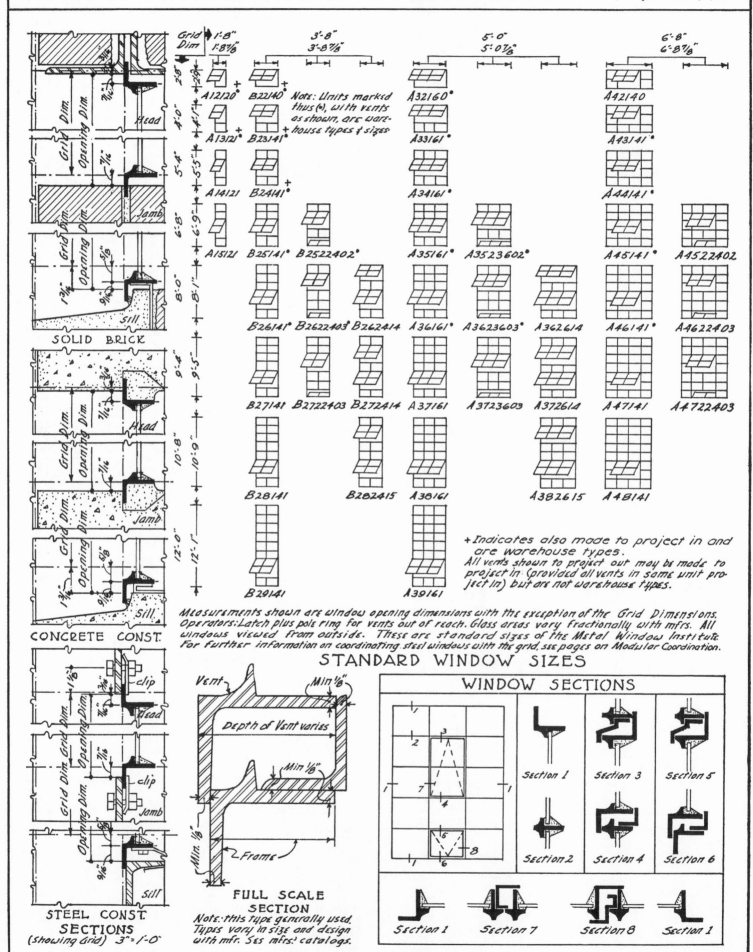

SOLID BRICK

CONCRETE CONST.

STEEL CONST.
SECTIONS
(showing Grid) 3"= 1'-0"

Note: Units marked thus (•), with vents as shown, are warehouse types & sizes

+Indicates also made to project in and are warehouse types.
All vents shown to project out may be made to project in (provided all vents in same unit project in) but are not warehouse types.

Measurements shown are window opening dimensions with the exception of the Grid Dimensions.
Operators: Latch plus pole ring for vents out of reach. Glass areas vary fractionally with mfrs. All windows viewed from outside. These are standard sizes of the Metal Window Institute. For further information on coordinating steel windows with the grid, see pages on Modular Coordination.

STANDARD WINDOW SIZES

FULL SCALE SECTION
Note: this type generally used. Types vary in size and design with mfr. See mfrs'. catalogs.

WINDOW SECTIONS

Section 1   Section 3   Section 5

Section 2   Section 4   Section 6

Section 1   Section 7   Section 8   Section 1

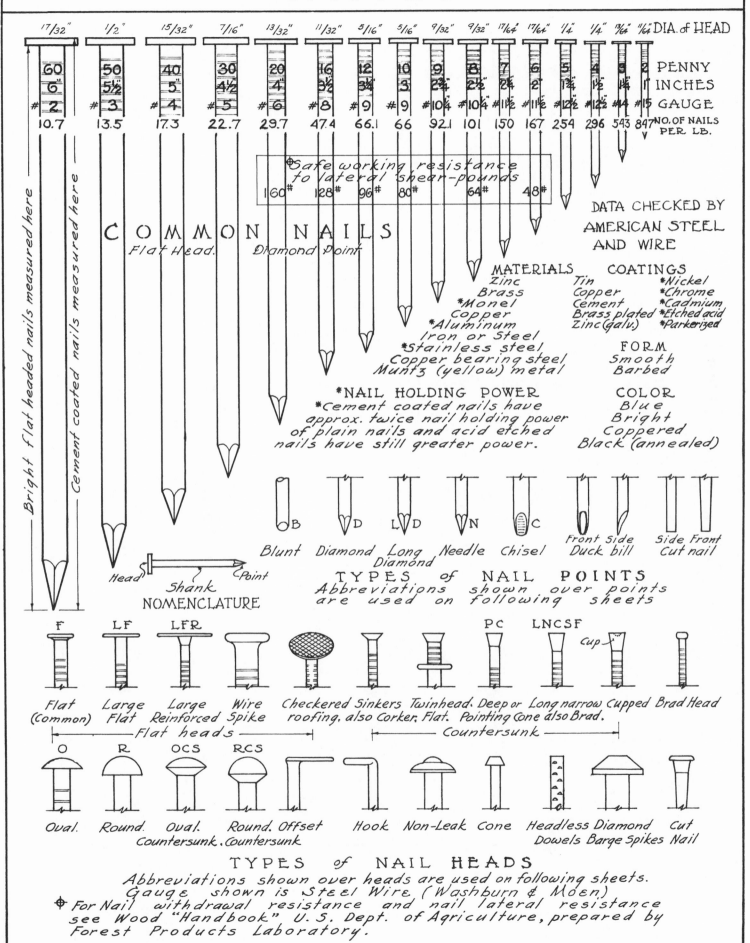

N A I L S

Sizes and types are taken from U.S. Federal Specification IV FF-N-101 (Part 5) unless marked *
For abbreviation for heads and points see other "Nails" sheet

NAIL TYPE	Shown 4d (1½") unless noted otherwise	SIZES	SPECIFICATION
F #14 gauge D	Barbed nails	¼" to 1½"	Cement coated, brass, steel
L CS.N #14 gauge D	Casing nails	2d to 40d / 6d to 10d *Alum.	Bright & cement coated *Cupped heads available
O #5 to #10 gauge D *Also flat head CS.	Cement nails also called concrete nails & hardened nails	½" to 3"	Smooth, bright *Oil quenched
L.N.F. Common brad Cup head available #15 to #2 ga.		2d to 60d	Bright " — may be secured with cupped head Cement coated { usually made in heavy gauges
F	Cut common	2d to 60d	Steel or Iron *Plain & zinc coated
Slightly smaller gauge than bright common	Copper-clad common nails	2d to 60d	Also used for shingle nails
F D Light gauge .095" Heavy .120"	Common brass wire nails	Light gauge Heavy "	*½, 1" to 3½" ¾ to 6"	Brass, Alum.
F D .109 (about 12 gauge)	Common copper wire nails; Alum.	*5/8" to 6"	Also used for shingle nails
	Standard cut nails (non-ferrous)	5/8" to 6"	Copper, muntz metal, or zinc
F 2" Long D #11½ gauge	Double headed	*1¾, 2", *2¼, 2½", *2¾ 3", 3½", *4", *4½"	Bright & cement coated made in several designs
Made in 5 diameters D Cupped head available Dowel Pins		5/8" to 2"	Barbed_*may have cupped head
O Made in 3 gauges D	Escutcheon Pins	¼" to 2"	Bright steel, brass plated, brass *also nickel-silver & copper & alum.
F 6d – 2" D #10 gauge	Fence nails	5d to 20d	Smooth; bright & cement coated (Gauge are heavier than common)
L N F #15 gauge D	Finishing nail, wire	2d to 20d	Smooth; *Cupped heads available (Smaller gauge than usual common brads)
	Finishing nails Cut iron & steel	Standard—3d to 20d Fine — 6d to 10d	
* 3d – 1⅛" #15 & 16 gauge	*Fine nails	*2d & 2d Ex. Fine *3d & 3d Ex. Fine	*Bright— Smaller gauge & heads than common nails
P.C. #14 gauge B	Flooring nails (Also with D point)	*3d to *20d 6d to 20d	*Bright & cement coated (different gauge) *Cupped heads available
L.N.CS. #11 gauge D or Blunt D 6d – 2"	Flooring brad	6d to 20d	Smooth; bright & cement coated Cupped heads available
N.CS.F. #15 gauge N 1⅛" Long	Parquet flooring nail or brad	1", 1⅛", 1¼"	Smooth or barbed
2"	Flooring nails Cut iron or steel	4d to 20d	Iron or steel
Oval ¼" Heavy chisel _ also CS. head	Hinge nails	Heavy—¼" to 3/8" dia. Light—3/16" to ¼" dia.	1½" to 4" Long	Smooth; bright or annealed
Oval 3/16" Light Long D	Hinge nails	Heavy—¼" dia. Light— 3/16" dia.	1½" to 3" also to *4"	Smooth; bright or annealed
F #15 gauge D 3d – 1⅛"	Lath nails (wood)	2d, 2d Light, 3d 3d Light, 3d heavy, 4d	Bright, (not recommended) blued or cement coated
Hook 1⅛" #12 gauge	Lath nails (Metal lath) staples #14,15 gauge	1⅛" Staples 1" to 1½"	Bright, blued, zinc coated, annealed
*Offset F #10 gauge D	*Lath offset head nails (For self furring metal lath)	*1¼" to *1¾"	Bright, zinc coated

NAILS

Sizes and types are taken from U.S. Federal Specification IV FF-N-101 (Part 5) unless marked *
For abbreviation for heads and points see other "Nails" sheet

NAIL TYPE	Shown 4d (1½") unless noted otherwise	SIZES	SPECIFICATION
 needle N.C.S.F. #14 gauge	Molding nails (brads)	⅞" to 1¼"	Smooth; bright or cement coated
 D ½ #9 or 10 gauge	Plaster-board nails Used also for wall board Rock Lath (5/16" head) →	1" to 1¾" 1⅛" to 1½" →	Smooth; bright or cement coated Blued *Aluminum
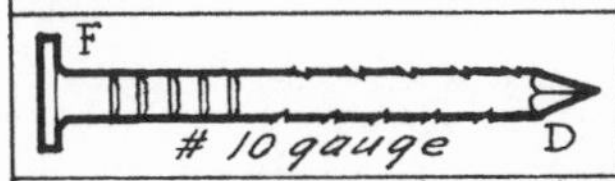 F D #10 gauge	Roofing nails (standard)	¾" to 2"	Bright, cement coated, zinc coated Barbed
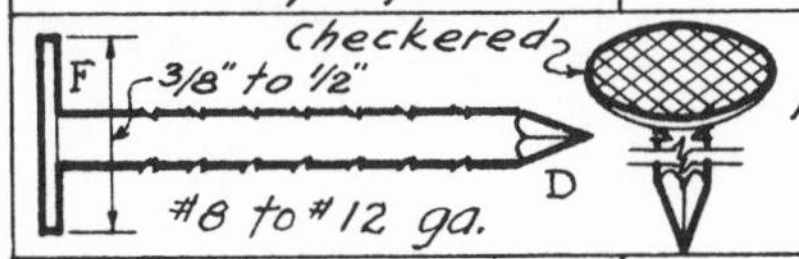 F 3/8" to ½" Checkered #8 to #12 ga. D	Roofing nails Large head	¾" to 1¾" also *2" ¾" to 2½" →	Barbed; bright or zinc coated Checkered available Aluminum (etched), neoprene washer opt'n'l.
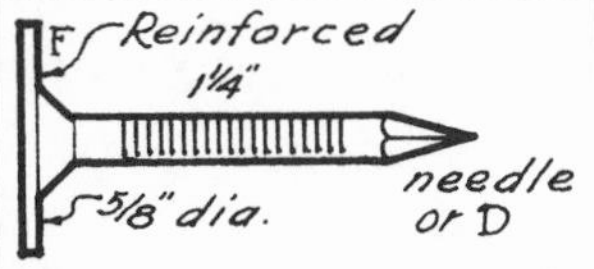 F Reinforced 1¼" 5/8" dia. needle or D	Roofing nails for prepared roofing	¾" to 1¼" #11 to #12 ga. *also #10 gauge	Bright or zinc coated
 Sheathing nails Cut copper or muntz M.		¾" to 3"	Copper or muntz metal
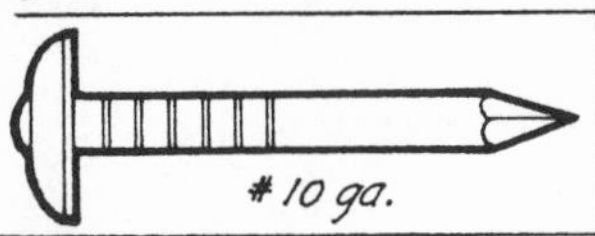 #10 ga.	*Non-leaking roofing nails	*1¾" to 2"	*Zinc coated—also with lead heads
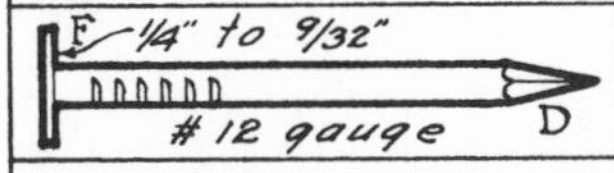 F ¼" to 9/32" #12 gauge D	Shingle nails Large headed also available 5/16" dia.	3d to 6d 2d to 6d →	Smooth; bright or zinc coated, cement coated, light & heavy *Aluminum
 *Shingle nails Cut iron or steel		2d to 6d	Plain or zinc coated

Shingle nails, copper wire are the same as common copper wire nails
Shingle nails, copper clad, are the same as copper clad common wire nails

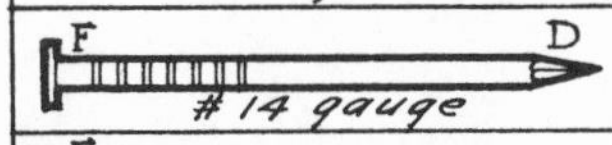 F D #14 gauge	Siding nails	2d to 40d 6d to 10d →	Smooth; bright or cement coated Smaller diameter than common nails *Aluminum
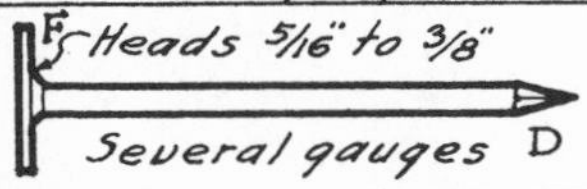 F Heads 5/16" to 3/8" Several gauges D	Slating nails—3/8" head 1" to 2" Slating nails—small heads 1" to 2" Slating nails—copper wire 7/8" to 1½"		Zinc coated Bright; cement coated and copper clad, copper
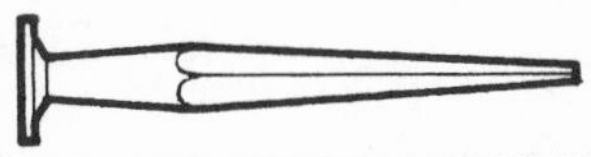 Cut slating nails non-ferrous		1¼" to 2"	Copper or muntz metal or zinc

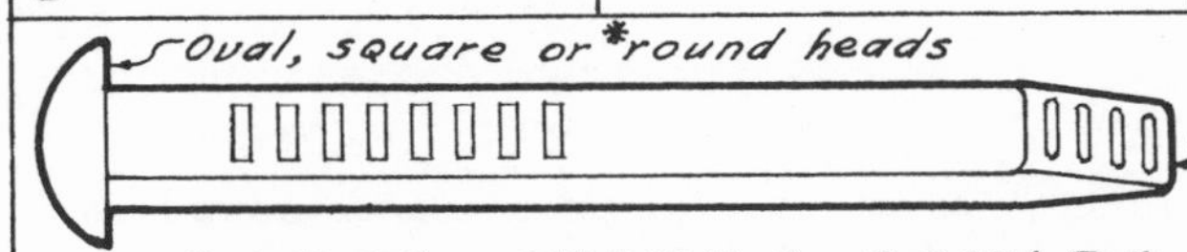

Oval, square or *round heads   Square or diamond heads

Chisel

BARGE SPIKES, SQUARE
¼" to 5/8" sq. 3" to 12" long, *also 16"

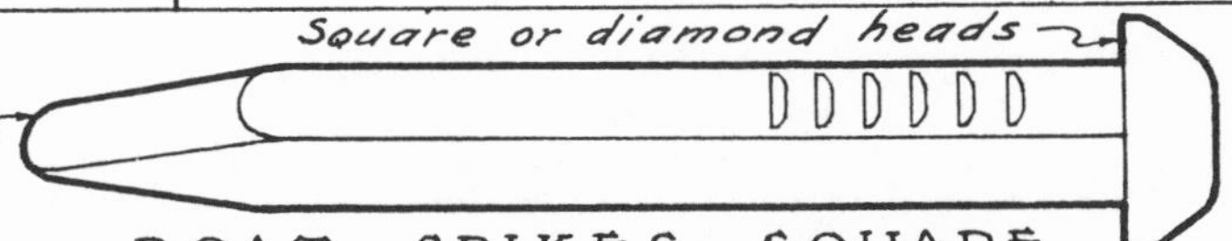

BOAT SPIKES, SQUARE
¼" to 5/8" sq. 3" to 12" long, heads from 7/32" to 1⅛" dia.

These spikes are usually used for hard wood, made plain and zinc coated

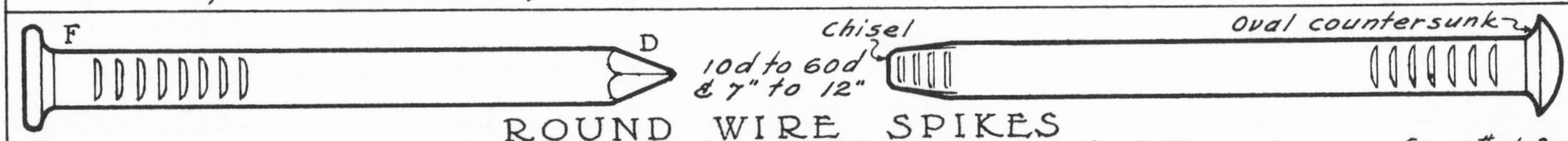

F   D   Chisel   Oval countersunk

10d to 60d & 7" to 12"

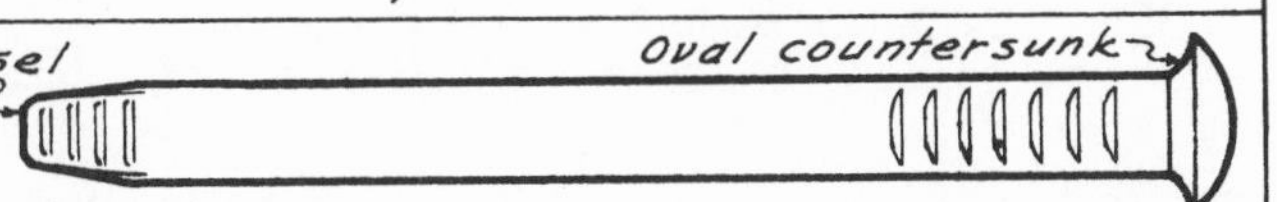

ROUND WIRE SPIKES
*May be secured up to 16" long. Smooth; bright or zinc coated. Gauges vary from #6 to 3/8"

Gutter Spikes — 5½" to 10½", ¼" dia. oval head; chisel point; or flat head diamond point. Bright or zinc coated

Common cut iron or steel spikes — 20d to 100d (4" to 8") Plain or zinc coated

Fetter Ring	Spirally grooved (helical)

NAIL USES

USE (All wood sizes are nominal)	SIZE PENNY	INCHES	TYPE, MATERIAL & FINISH NOTES ETC.[†]
CARPENTRY-WOOD-ROUGH			
1" Thick stock	8d	2½"	—Common nails
2" Thick stock	16d to 20d	3½" or 4"	—Common nails
3" Thick stock	40d to 60d	5" or 6"	—Common nails or spikes
Concrete Forms	variable		—Common or double headed nails
Framing generally—Sizes to fit conditions	10d, 16d, 20d, 60d	3", 3½", 4", 6"	—Common nails or spikes for large members
Toe nailing studs, joists, etc.	10d	3"	—Common nails
Spiking usual plates & sills	16d	3½"	—Common nails
Toe nailing rafters & plates	10d	3"	—Common nails
Sheathing: roof & wall	8d	2½"	—Common nails, may be zinc coated
Rough flooring			
CARPENTRY-WOOD-FINISHING			
Moldings—Size as required		⅞", 1", 1⅛", 1¼"	—Molding nails (brads)
Carpet strips, shoes	8d	2½"	} Finishing or casing nails
Door & window stops & members ¼" to ½" thick	4d	1½"	
Ceiling, trim, casing, picture mold, base balusters and members ½" to ¾" thick	6d	2"	—Finishing or casing nails
Ceiling, trim, casing, base, jambs, trim and members ¾" to 1" thick	8d	2½"	—Finishing or casing nails
Door & window trim, boards and other members 1" to 1¼" thick	10d	3"	—Finishing or casing nails
Drop siding, 1" thick	*7d or ▫9d	*2¼" or ▫2¾"	*Siding nails ——▫Casing nails
Bevel siding, ½" thick	*6d or ▫8d	*2" or ▫2½"	▫Finishing —— *Siding
FLOORING WOOD	See wood flooring sheet for sizes & types recommended		Cut steel, wire, finishing, wire casing, flooring brads, parquet, flooring nails
LATHING			
Wood lath	3d	1¼"	—Blued lath nail
Gypsum lath	3d	1¼"	—Blued common
Fiber lath			
Metal lath, interior		1"	—Blued lath nails, staples or offset head nails
Metal lath, exterior	*3d	*1¼"	—Self furring nails (double heads). Staples or cement coated
SHEATHING or SIDING			
Asbestos 3/8" thick		1¼"	} Galvanized roofing nail, 7/16" dia. head. See "Sheathing on Wood Framing" for spacing etc.
Fiber board ½" & 25/32"		1½" to 2"	
Gypsum board ½"		1¾"	
Plywood 5/16" & 3/8" thick	6d	2"	—Common
Plywood ½" & 5/8" "	8d	2½"	—Common
ROOFING & SHEET METAL			
Aluminum roofing		1¾" to 2½"	—Aluminum nail, neoprene washer optional
Asbestos, corrugated or sheets	Depends on thickness		—Leak proof roofing nails
Asbestos shingles		1" to 2"	—See "Asbestos Cement Roofing & Siding." Large head roofing, galv.
Asphalt shingles			
Copper cleats & flashing to wood			—Copper wire or cut slating nails
" " " " to prevent joints			—Barbed copper nails
Clay tile	4d to 6d	1½" to 2"	—See clay tile Roofing Sheets. Use copper
Prepared felt roofing		1" to 1¼"	Roofing nails or large head roofing nails; barbed preferred—Heads may be reinforced. Zinc
Shingles, wood	3d to 4d 4d to 8d for heavy butts	usual	See "Wood Shingles, Roof'g & Sid'g" for sizes Zinc coated, copper wire shingle, copper clad shingle, cut iron or cut steel
Slate	Use nails 1" larger than thickness of slate		Copper wire slating nail (large head) In dry climates zinc coated or copper clad nails may be used
Tin, Zinc roofing			—Zinc coated nails—Roofing or slating
Monel roofing			—Monel nail.
Nailing to sheet metal			—Self tapping screws, helical drive-screws
NAILING TO CONCRETE & CEMENT MORTAR			Concrete or cement nails (hardened) or helical drive nails or drive bolts

[†]Note: For further data on nail uses see pages on specific material involved.

SCREWS, BOLTS and NUTS

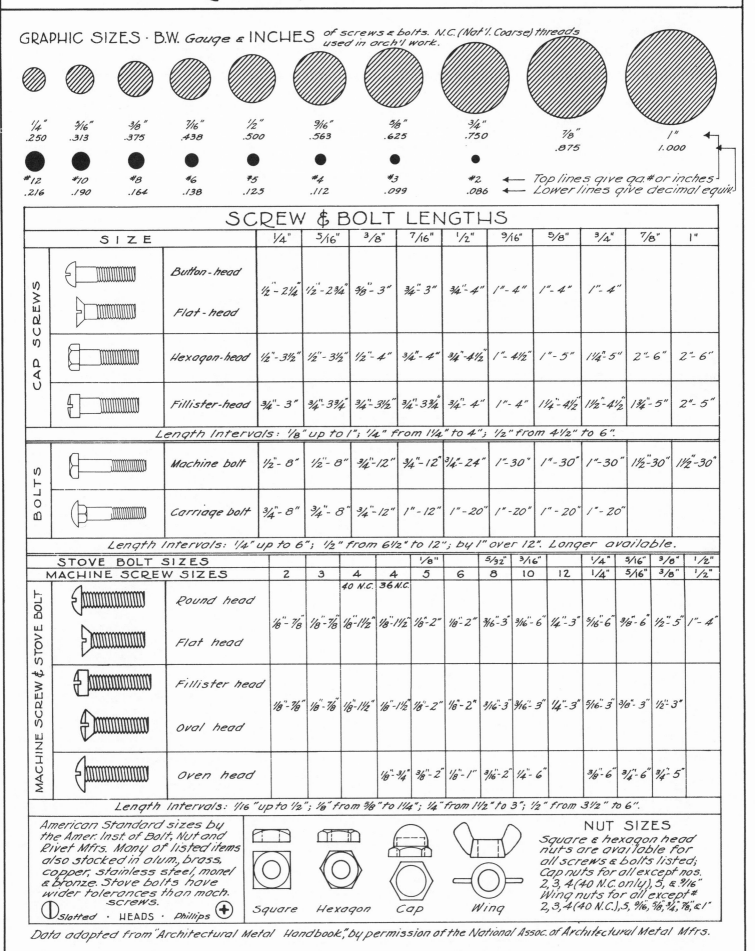

GRAPHIC SIZES · B.W. Gauge & INCHES of screws & bolts. N.C. (Nat'l. Coarse) threads used in arch'l work.

| 1/4" .250 | 5/16" .313 | 3/8" .375 | 7/16" .438 | 1/2" .500 | 9/16" .563 | 5/8" .625 | 3/4" .750 | 7/8" .875 | 1" 1.000 |

| #12 .216 | #10 .190 | #8 .164 | #6 .138 | #5 .125 | #4 .112 | #3 .099 | #2 .086 |

← Top lines give ga.# or inches
← Lower lines give decimal equiv.

SCREW & BOLT LENGTHS

	SIZE	1/4"	5/16"	3/8"	7/16"	1/2"	9/16"	5/8"	3/4"	7/8"	1"
CAP SCREWS	Button-head / Flat-head	1/2"-2 1/4"	1/2"-2 3/4"	5/8"-3"	3/4"-3"	3/4"-4"	1"-4"	1"-4"	1"-4"		
	Hexagon-head	1/2"-3 1/2"	1/2"-3 1/2"	1/2"-4"	3/4"-4"	3/4"-4 1/2"	1"-4 1/2"	1"-5"	1 1/4"-5"	2"-6"	2"-6"
	Fillister-head	3/4"-3"	3/4"-3 3/4"	3/4"-3 1/2"	3/4"-3 3/4"	3/4"-4"	1"-4"	1 1/4"-4 1/2"	1 1/2"-4 1/2"	1 3/4"-5"	2"-5"

Length Intervals: 1/8" up to 1"; 1/4" from 1 1/4" to 4"; 1/2" from 4 1/2" to 6".

	SIZE	1/4"	5/16"	3/8"	7/16"	1/2"	9/16"	5/8"	3/4"	7/8"	1"
BOLTS	Machine bolt	1/2"-8"	1/2"-8"	3/4"-12"	3/4"-12"	3/4"-24"	1"-30"	1"-30"	1"-30"	1 1/2"-30"	1 1/2"-30"
	Carriage bolt	3/4"-8"	3/4"-8"	3/4"-12"	1"-12"	1"-20"	1"-20"	1"-20"	1"-20"		

Length Intervals: 1/4" up to 6"; 1/2" from 6 1/2" to 12"; by 1" over 12". Longer available.

STOVE BOLT SIZES						1/8"		5/32"	3/16"		1/4"	5/16"	3/8"	1/2"
MACHINE SCREW SIZES		2	3	4	4	5	6	8	10	12	1/4"	5/16"	3/8"	1/2"
				40 N.C.	36 N.C.									
MACHINE SCREW & STOVE BOLT Round head / Flat head		1/8"-7/8"	1/8"-7/8"	1/8"-1 1/2"	1/8"-1 1/2"	1/8"-2"	1/8"-2"	3/16"-3"	3/16"-6"	1/4"-3"	5/16"-6"	3/8"-6"	1/2"-5"	1"-4"
Fillister head / Oval head		1/8"-7/8"	1/8"-7/8"	1/8"-1 1/2"	1/8"-1 1/2"	1/8"-2"	1/8"-2"	3/16"-3"	3/16"-3"	1/4"-3"	5/16"-3"	3/8"-3"	1/2"-3"	
Oven head					1/8"-3/4"	3/8"-2"	1/8"-1"	3/16"-2"	1/4"-6"		3/8"-6"	3/4"-6"	3/4"-5"	

Length Intervals: 1/16" up to 1/2"; 1/8" from 5/8" to 1 1/4"; 1/4" from 1 1/2" to 3"; 1/2" from 3 1/2" to 6".

American Standard sizes by the Amer. Inst. of Bolt, Nut and Rivet Mfrs. Many of listed items also stocked in alum., brass, copper, stainless steel, monel & bronze. Stove bolts have wider tolerances than mach. screws.

Slotted · HEADS · Phillips

Square   Hexagon   Cap   Wing

NUT SIZES
Square & hexagon head nuts are available for all screws & bolts listed; Cap nuts for all except nos. 2, 3, 4 (40 N.C. only), 5, & 9/16" Wing nuts for all except # 2, 3, 4 (40 N.C.), 5, 9/16", 5/8", 3/4", 7/8", & 1"

Data adapted from "Architectural Metal Handbook," by permission of the National Assoc. of Architectural Metal Mfrs.

SCREWS, BOLTS, ETC.

WOOD SCREWS

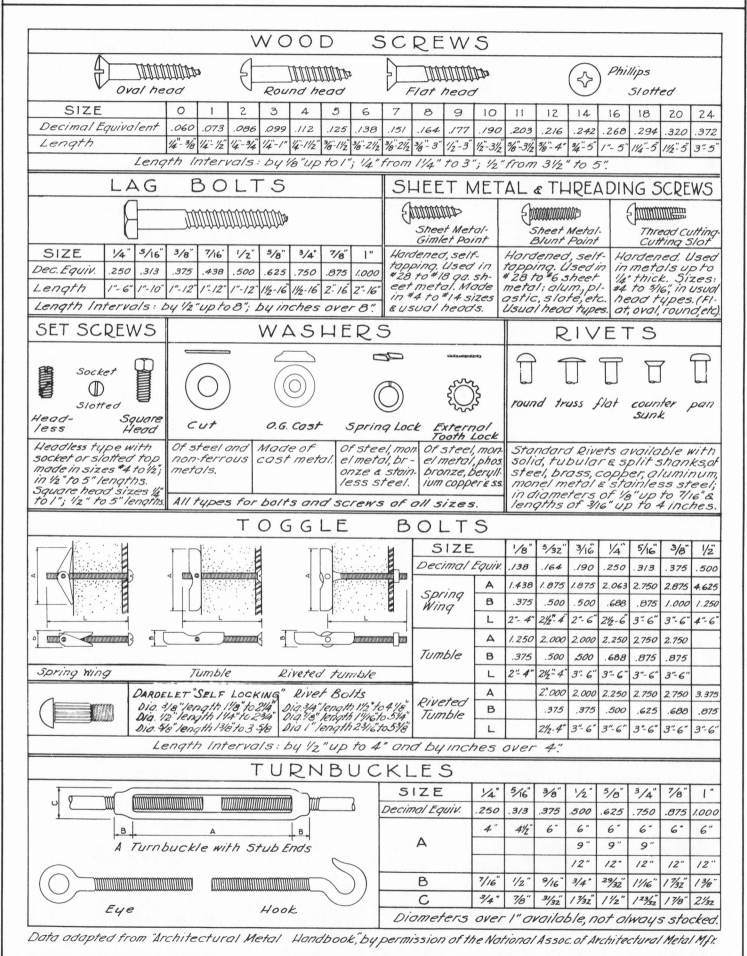

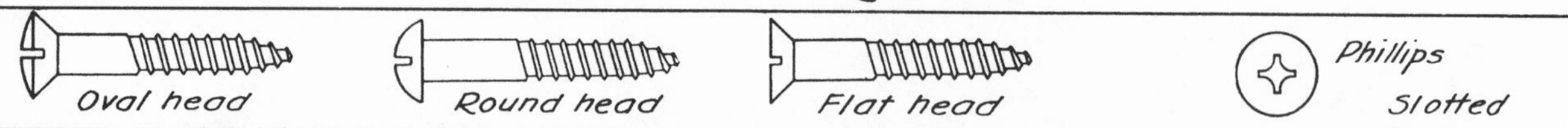
Oval head
Round head
Flat head
Phillips
Slotted

SIZE	0	1	2	3	4	5	6	7	8	9	10	11	12	14	16	18	20	24
Decimal Equivalent	.060	.073	.086	.099	.112	.125	.138	.151	.164	.177	.190	.203	.216	.242	.268	.294	.320	.372
Length	1/4"-3/8"	1/4"-1/2"	1/4"-3/4"	1/4"-1"	1/4"-1 1/2"	3/8"-1 1/2"	3/8"-2 1/2"	3/8"-2 1/2"	3/8"-3"	1/2"-3"	1/2"-3 1/2"	5/8"-3 1/2"	5/8"-4"	3/4"-5"	1"-5"	1 1/4"-5"	1 1/2"-5"	3"-5"

Length Intervals: by 1/8" up to 1"; 1/4" from 1 1/4" to 3"; 1/2" from 3 1/2" to 5".

LAG BOLTS

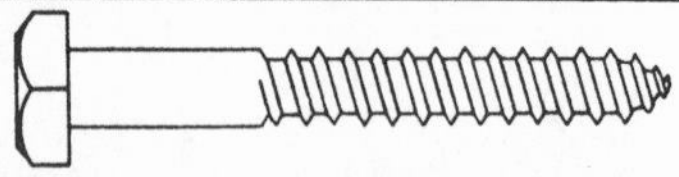

SIZE	1/4"	5/16"	3/8"	7/16"	1/2"	5/8"	3/4"	7/8"	1"
Dec. Equiv.	.250	.313	.375	.438	.500	.625	.750	.875	1.000
Length	1"-6"	1"-10"	1"-12"	1"-12"	1"-12"	1 1/2-16"	1 1/2-16"	2"-16"	2"-16"

Length Intervals: by 1/2" up to 8"; by inches over 8".

SHEET METAL & THREADING SCREWS

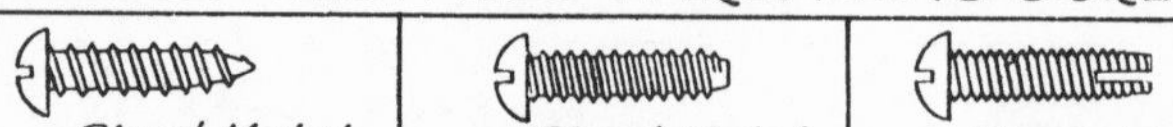

Sheet Metal-Gimlet Point	Sheet Metal-Blunt Point	Thread Cutting-Cutting Slot
Hardened, self-tapping. Used in #28 to #18 ga. sheet metal. Made in #4 to #14 sizes & usual heads.	Hardened, self-tapping. Used in #28 to #6 sheet metal; alum., plastic, slate, etc. Usual head types.	Hardened. Used in metals up to 1/4" thick. Sizes: #4 to 5/16", in usual head types. (Flat, oval, round, etc.)

SET SCREWS

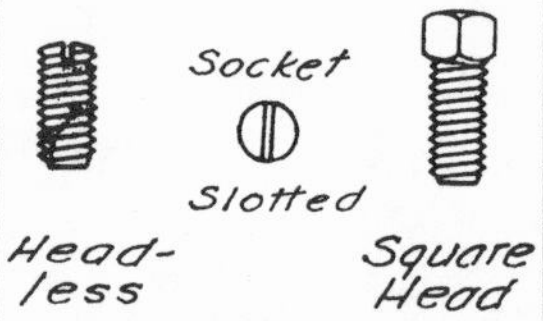
Socket
Slotted
Head-less
Square Head

Headless type with socket or slotted top made in sizes #4 to 1/2"; in 1/2" to 5" lengths. Square head sizes 1/4" to 1"; 1/2" to 5" lengths.

WASHERS

Cut	O.G. Cast	Spring Lock	External Tooth Lock
Of steel and non-ferrous metals.	Made of cast metal.	Of steel, monel metal, bronze & stainless steel.	Of steel, monel metal, phos. bronze, beryllium copper & s.s.

All types for bolts and screws of all sizes.

RIVETS

round
truss
flat
counter sunk
pan

Standard Rivets available with solid, tubular & split shanks, of steel, brass, copper, aluminum, monel metal & stainless steel; in diameters of 1/8" up to 7/16" & lengths of 3/16" up to 4 inches.

TOGGLE BOLTS

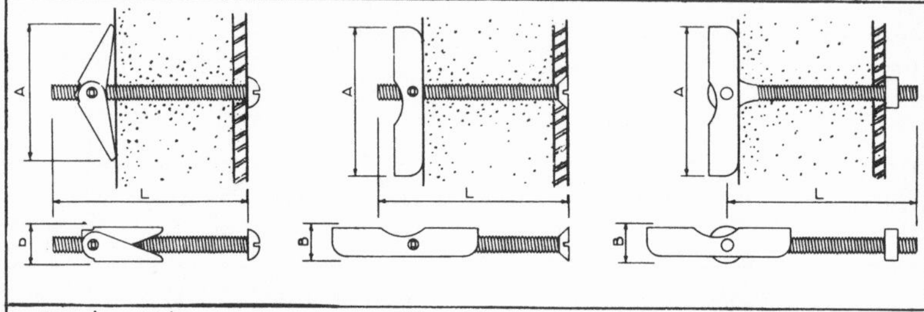
A
L
B
D

Spring wing — Tumble — Riveted tumble

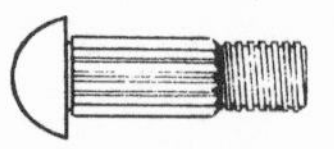

DARDELET "SELF LOCKING" Rivet Bolts
Dia. 3/8" length 1 1/8" to 2 1/4" — Dia. 3/4" length 1 1/2" to 4 1/8"
Dia. 1/2" length 1 1/4" to 2 3/4" — Dia. 7/8" length 1 9/16" to 5 1/4"
Dia. 5/8" length 1 3/8" to 3 5/8" — Dia 1" length 2 3/16" to 5 3/8"

SIZE		1/8"	5/32"	3/16"	1/4"	5/16"	3/8"	1/2"
Decimal Equiv.		.138	.164	.190	.250	.313	.375	.500
Spring Wing	A	1.438	1.875	1.875	2.063	2.750	2.875	4.625
	B	.375	.500	.500	.688	.875	1.000	1.250
	L	2"-4"	2 1/2"-4"	2"-6"	2 1/2-6"	3"-6"	3"-6"	4"-6"
Tumble	A	1.250	2.000	2.000	2.250	2.750	2.750	
	B	.375	.500	.500	.688	.875	.875	
	L	2"-4"	2 1/2"-4"	3"-6"	3"-6"	3"-6"	3"-6"	
Riveted Tumble	A		2.000	2.000	2.250	2.750	2.750	3.375
	B		.375	.375	.500	.625	.688	.875
	L		2 1/2-4"	3"-6"	3"-6"	3"-6"	3"-6"	3"-6"

Length Intervals: by 1/2" up to 4" and by inches over 4".

TURNBUCKLES

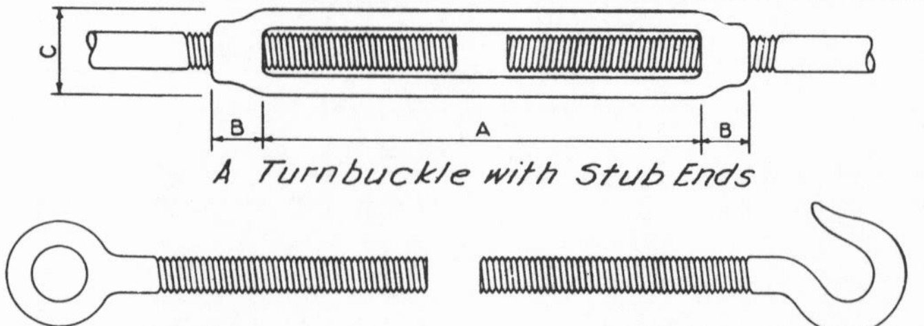
C
B
A
B

A Turnbuckle with Stub Ends

Eye — Hook

SIZE	1/4"	5/16"	3/8"	1/2"	5/8"	3/4"	7/8"	1"
Decimal Equiv.	.250	.313	.375	.500	.625	.750	.875	1.000
A	4"	4 1/2"	6"	6"	6"	6"	6"	6"
				9"	9"	9"		
				12"	12"	12"	12"	12"
B	7/16"	1/2"	9/16"	3/4"	29/32"	1 1/16"	1 7/32"	1 3/8"
C	3/4"	7/8"	31/32"	1 7/32"	1 1/2"	1 23/32"	1 7/8"	2 1/32

Diameters over 1" available, not always stocked.

Data adapted from "Architectural Metal Handbook," by permission of the National Assoc. of Architectural Metal Mfr.

SHIELDS and ANCHORS

MACHINE-BOLT ANCHORS and SHIELDS

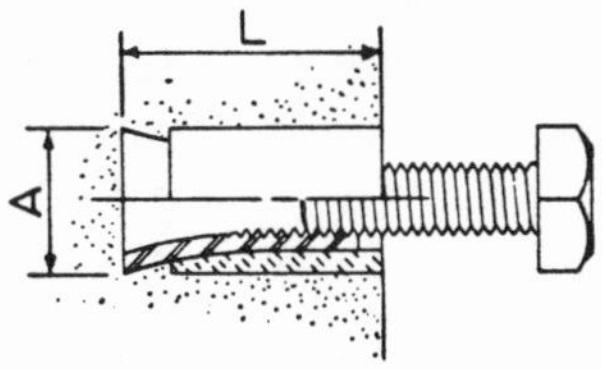

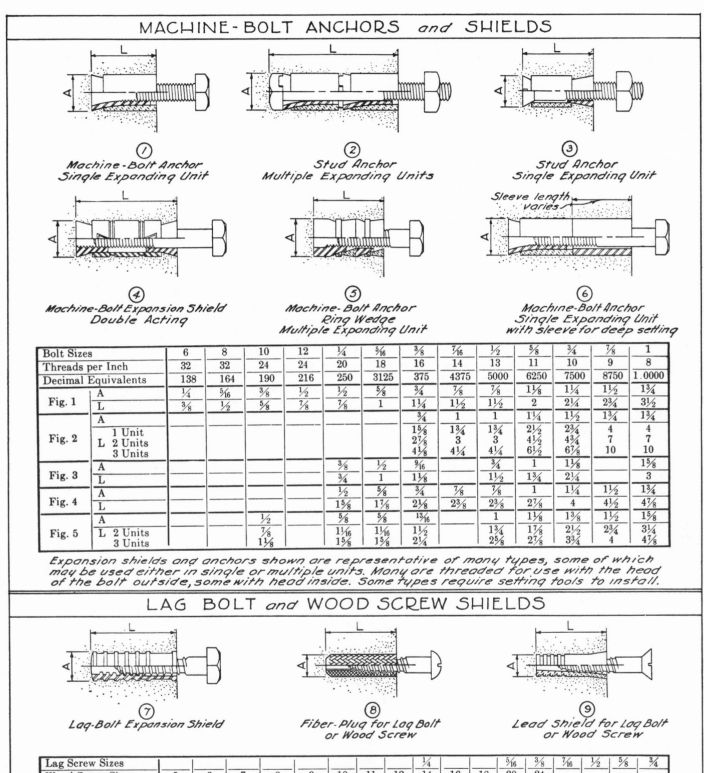

(1) *Machine-Bolt Anchor Single Expanding Unit*

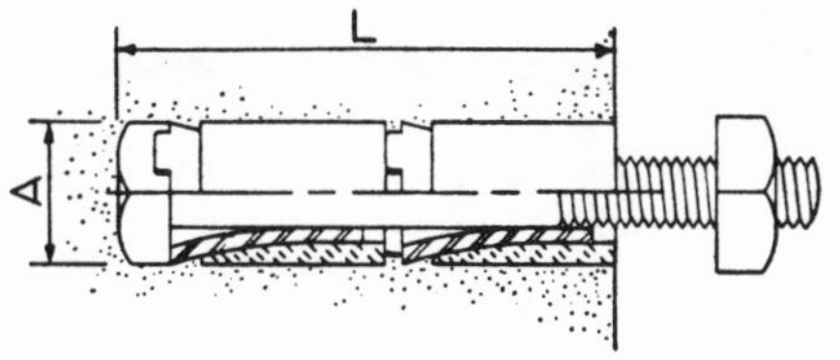

(2) *Stud Anchor Multiple Expanding Units*

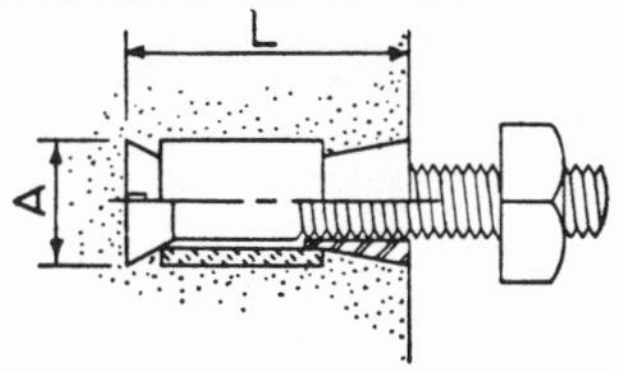

(3) *Stud Anchor Single Expanding Unit*

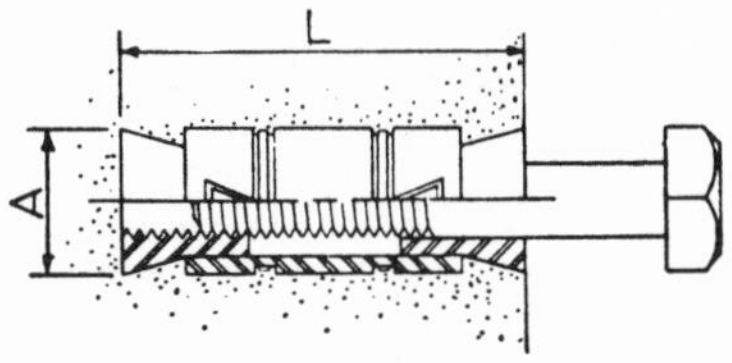

(4) *Machine-Bolt Expansion Shield Double Acting*

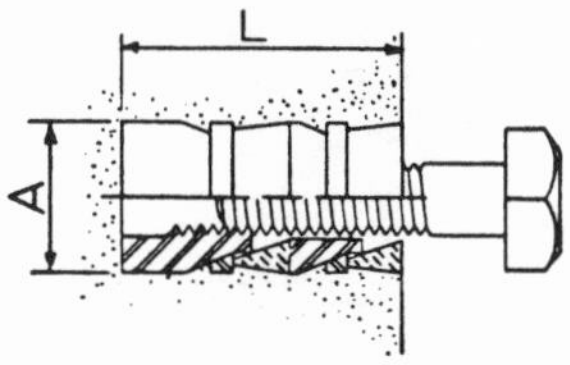

(5) *Machine-Bolt Anchor Ring Wedge Multiple Expanding Unit*

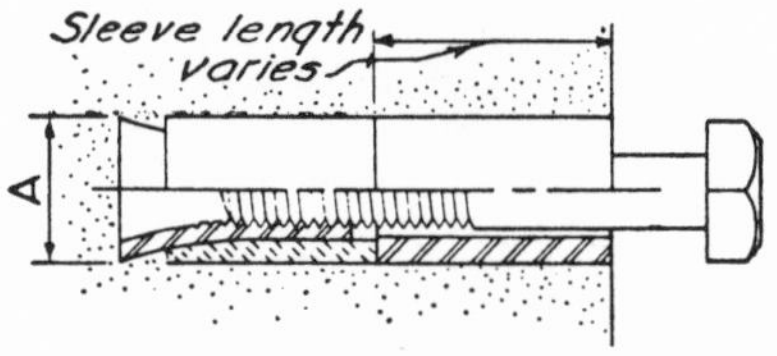

(6) *Machine-Bolt Anchor Single Expanding Unit with sleeve for deep setting*

Bolt Sizes		6	8	10	12	1/4	5/16	3/8	7/16	1/2	5/8	3/4	7/8	1
Threads per Inch		32	32	24	24	20	18	16	14	13	11	10	9	8
Decimal Equivalents		138	164	190	216	250	3125	375	4375	5000	6250	7500	8750	1.0000
Fig. 1	A	1/4	5/16	3/8	1/2	1/2	5/8	3/4	7/8	7/8	1 1/8	1 1/4	1 1/2	1 3/4
	L	3/8	1/2	5/8	7/8	7/8	1	1 1/4	1 1/2	1 1/2	2	2 1/4	2 3/4	3 1/2
Fig. 2	A							3/4	1	1	1 1/4	1 1/2	1 3/4	1 3/4
	L 1 Unit 2 Units 3 Units							1 5/8 2 7/8 4 1/8	1 3/4 3 4 1/4	1 3/4 3 4 1/4	2 1/2 4 1/2 6 1/2	2 3/4 4 3/4 6 7/8	4 7 10	4 7 10
Fig. 3	A					3/8	1/2	9/16		3/4	1	1 1/8		1 5/8
	L					3/4	1	1 1/8		1 1/2	1 3/4	2 1/4		3
Fig. 4	A					1/2	5/8	3/4	7/8	7/8	1	1 1/4	1 1/2	1 3/4
	L					1 5/8	1 7/8	2 1/8	2 3/8	2 3/8	2 7/8	4	4 1/2	4 7/8
Fig. 5	A			1/2		5/8	5/8	13/16		1	1 1/8	1 3/8	1 1/2	1 5/8
	L 2 Units 3 Units			7/8 1 1/8		1 1/16 1 5/8	1 1/16 1 5/8	1 1/2 2 1/4		1 3/4 2 5/8	1 7/8 2 7/8	2 1/2 3 3/4	2 3/4 4	3 1/4 4 7/8

Expansion shields and anchors shown are representative of many types, some of which may be used either in single or multiple units. Many are threaded for use with the head of the bolt outside, some with head inside. Some types require setting tools to install.

LAG BOLT and WOOD SCREW SHIELDS

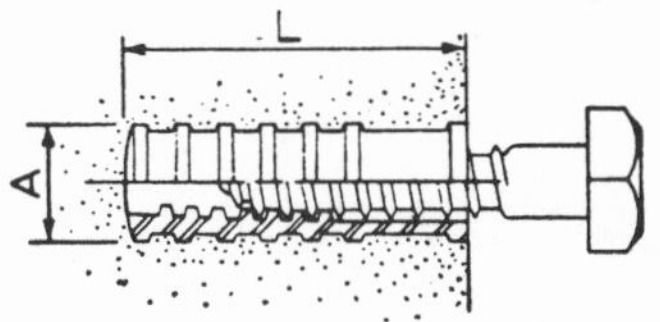

(7) *Lag-Bolt Expansion Shield*

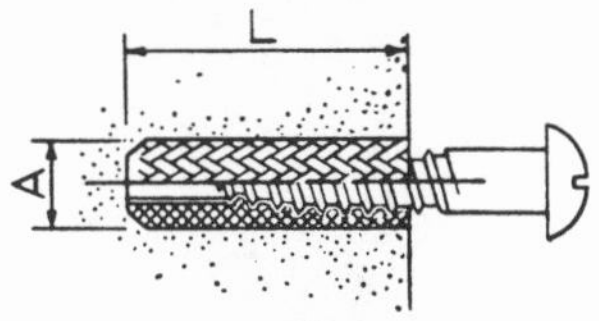

(8) *Fiber-Plug for Lag Bolt or Wood Screw*

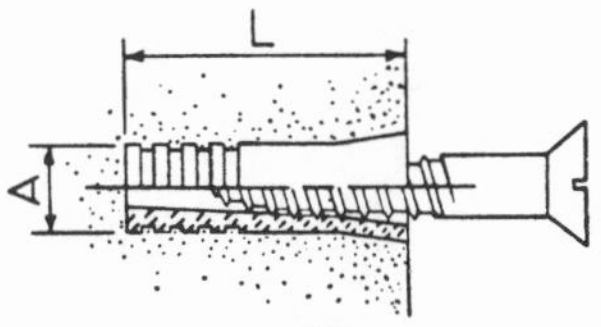

(9) *Lead Shield for Lag Bolt or Wood Screw*

Lag Screw Sizes										1/4			5/16	3/8	7/16	1/2	5/8	3/4
Wood Screw Sizes		5	6	7	8	9	10	11	12	14	16	18	20	24				
Decimal Equivalents		.125	.138	.151	.164	.177	.190	.203	.216	.242	.268	.294	.320	.372	.4375	.5000	.6250	.7500
Fig. 7	A									1/2			1/2	5/8		3/4	7/8	1
	L Short Long									1" 1 1/2"			1 1/4" 1 3/4"	1 3/4" 2 1/2"		2" 3"	2" 3 1/2"	2" 3 1/2"
Fig. 8	A	5/32	5/32	11/64	11/64	3/16	3/16	1/4	1/4	9/32	5/16	5/16	3/8	7/16	1/2	5/8	3/4	
	L	5/8" to 1"	5/8" to 1"	5/8" to 1 1/2"	5/8" to 1 1/2"	3/4" to 1 1/2"	3/4" to 1 1/2"	3/4" to 1 1/2"	3/4" to 1 1/2"	1" to 2"	1" to 2"	1" to 2"	1" to 2"	1 1/2" to 3"	1 1/2" to 3"	2" to 3"	2 1/2" to 3 1/2"	
Fig. 9	A	1/4	1/4	1/4	1/4	5/16	5/16	5/16	3/8	3/8	7/16	7/16	9/16	9/16	11/16	3/4	7/8	
	L	1/2" to 1 1/2"	1/2" to 1 1/2"	1/2" to 1 1/2"	1/2" to 1 1/2"	1/2" to 1 1/2"	1/2" to 1 1/2"	1/2" to 1 1/2"	3/4" to 1 1/2"	3/4" to 1 1/2"	1" to 1 1/2"	1" to 1 1/2"	1" to 2"	1" to 2"	2"	2"	2" to 3 1/2"	

Data adapted from "Architectural Metals Handbook" by permission of the National Assoc. of Architectural Metal Manufacturers.

HARDWARE

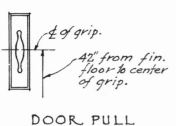

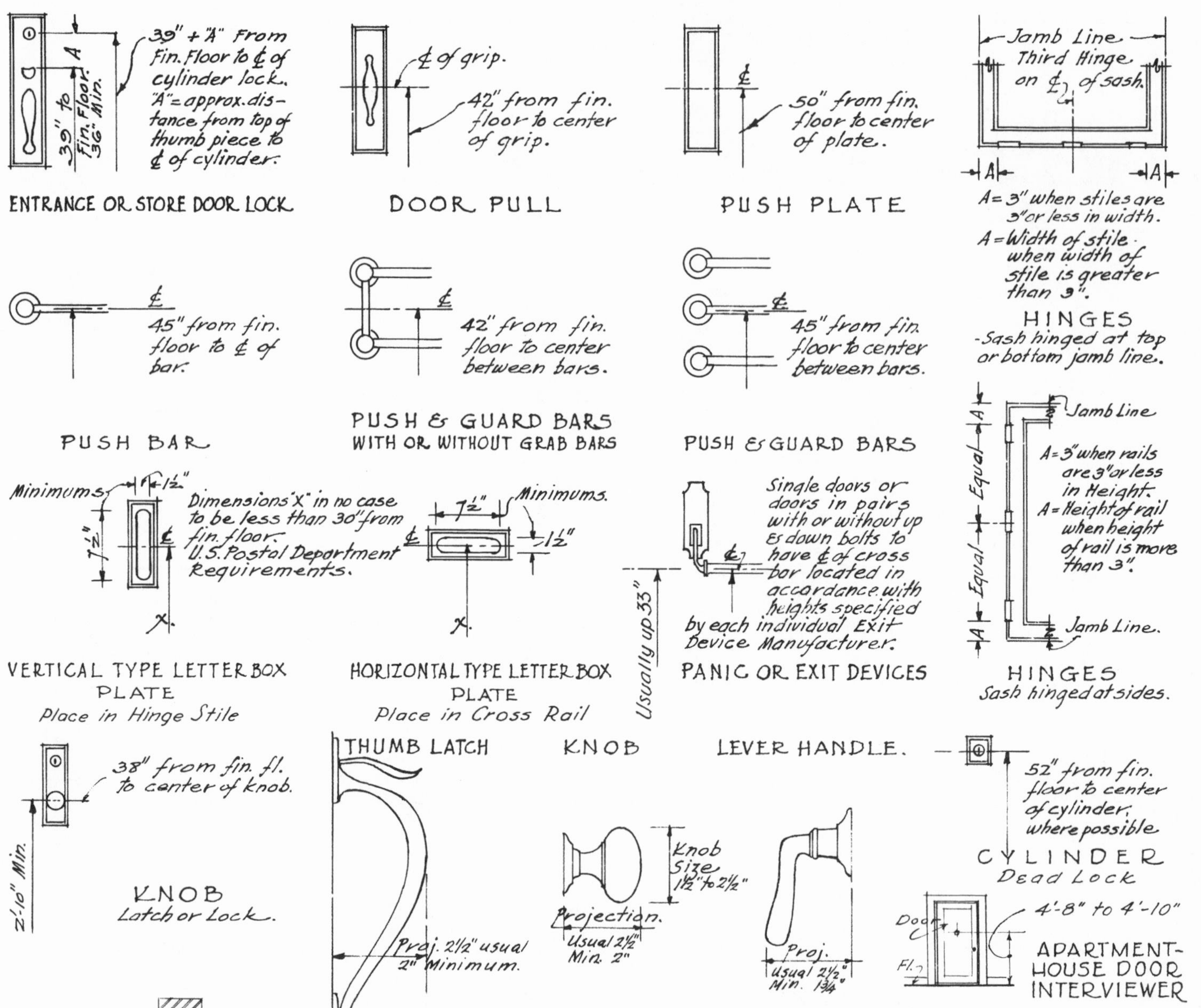

39" + "A" From Fin. Floor to ₵ of cylinder lock. "A"= approx. distance from top of thumb piece to ₵ of cylinder.

39" to Fin. Floor. 36" Min.

ENTRANCE OR STORE DOOR LOCK

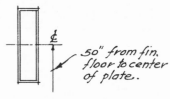

₵ of grip.

42" from fin. floor to center of grip.

DOOR PULL

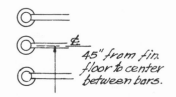

₵

50" from fin. floor to center of plate.

PUSH PLATE

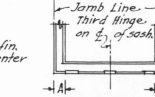

Jamb Line Third Hinge on ₵ of sash.

A

A=3" when stiles are 3" or less in width.
A=Width of stile when width of stile is greater than 3".

HINGES
-Sash hinged at top or bottom jamb line.

₵

45" from fin. floor to ₵ of bar.

PUSH BAR

₵

42" from fin. floor to center between bars.

PUSH & GUARD BARS WITH OR WITHOUT GRAB BARS

₵

45" from fin. floor to center between bars.

PUSH & GUARD BARS

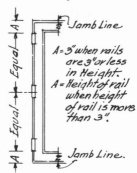

Jamb Line

A=3" when rails are 3" or less in Height.
A=Height of rail when height of rail is more than 3".

Jamb Line

Equal / A / Equal / Equal / A

HINGES
Sash hinged at sides.

Minimums
1" to 1½"
7½"

Dimensions "X" in no case to be less than 30" from fin. floor. U.S. Postal Department Requirements.

X

VERTICAL TYPE LETTER BOX PLATE
Place in Hinge Stile

7½"
Minimums.
1½"
₵
X

HORIZONTAL TYPE LETTER BOX PLATE
Place in Cross Rail

Single doors or doors in pairs with or without up & down bolts to have ₵ of cross bar located in accordance with heights specified by each individual Exit Device Manufacturer.

Usually up 33"

PANIC OR EXIT DEVICES

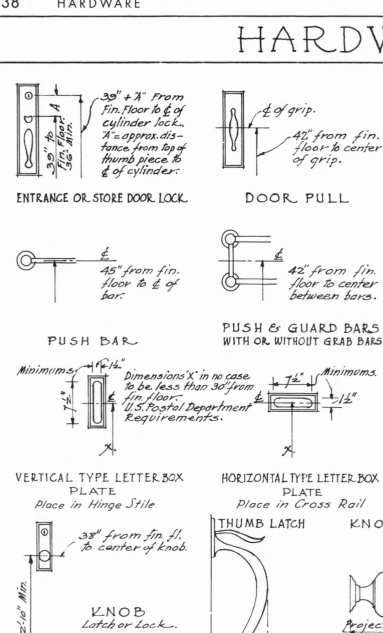

38" from fin. fl. to center of knob.

2'-10" Min.

KNOB
Latch or Lock.

THUMB LATCH

Proj. 2½" usual 2" Minimum.

KNOB

Knob Size 1½" to 2½"
Projection. Usual 2½" Min. 2"

LEVER HANDLE.

Proj. Usual 2½" Min. 1¾"

52" from fin. floor to center of cylinder, where possible.

CYLINDER
Dead Lock

Door / Fl.

4'-8" to 4'-10"

APARTMENT-HOUSE DOOR INTERVIEWER

CLEARANCE FOR KNOBS, LEVER HANDLES & THUMB LATCHES
The above projections govern rebate widths for storm doors, screen & louver doors, etc.

7½" to 3½" Long

Elevation

1¾"□ in 5, 6, 7, 8 #
2"□ & 2¼"□ in 7, 8, 9, 10 #

1¾" to 2⅛" diam.

Plans

Cast iron

SASH WEIGHTS
Pocket for sash weights generally 2¼" for residential work, 2½" for larger size weights.

Data checked by:
American Society of Architectural Hardware Consultants.

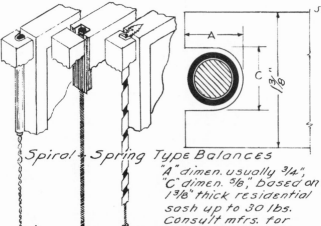

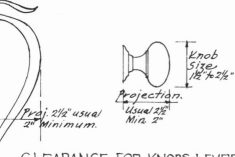

A
C
13/8"

Spiral-Spring Type Balances
"A" dimen. usually ¾", "C" dimen. ⅝", based on 1⅜" thick residential sash up to 30 lbs. Consult mfrs. for other sizes.

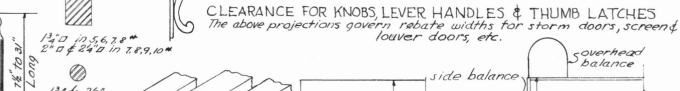

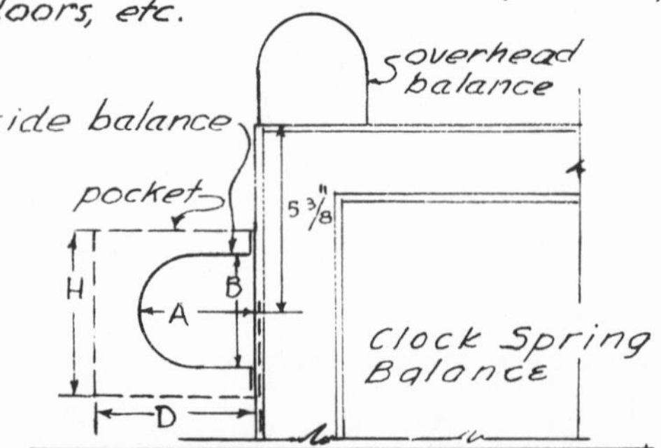

overhead balance
side balance
pocket
5⅜"
H
A
B

Clock Spring Balance

D

POCKET SIZES				
For Sash Wt. Lbs.	A	B	D	H
4 to 26	3"	3"	3¼"	3½"
6 to 35	3⅜"	3⅜"	3⅝"	3⅞"
23 to 50	3⁵⁄₁₆"	3⁵⁄₁₆"	4¼"	4½"
10 to 50	4⅜"	4⁷⁄₁₆"		

SPRING, SPIRAL and CLOCK-SPRING BALANCES

HARDWARE

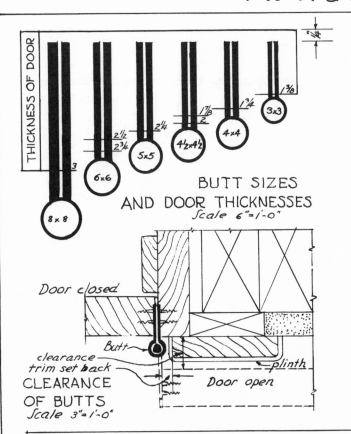

BUTT SIZES AND DOOR THICKNESSES
Scale 6"=1'-0"

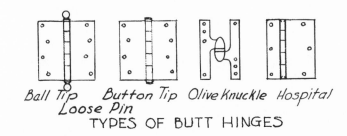

Ball Tip   Button Tip   Olive Knuckle   Hospital
Loose Pin
TYPES OF BUTT HINGES

CLEARANCE OF BUTTS
Scale 3"=1'-0"

Door closed

clearance
trim set back
Butt
plinth
Door open

CLEARANCE OF BUTTS AND SET BACK OF TRIM

STANDARD BUTT HINGE				EXTRA HEAVY BUTT HINGE							
Door Thick.	Butt Size	Max. Clear.	Set Back	Door Thick.	Butt Size	Max. Clear.	Set Back	Door Thick.	Butt Size	Max. Clear.	Set Back
1⅜	3×3	¾	⅜	1¾	4×4	1	⅜	2¼	5×5	1	½
	3½×3½	1¼	⅜		4½×4½	1½	½		6×6	2	⅝
	4×4	1¾	⅜		5×5	2	½		6×8	4	⅝
					6×6	3	⅝				
1¾	4×4	1	⅜	1⅞	4½×4½	1¼	½	2½	5×5	¾	½
	4½×4½	1½	½		5×5	1¾	½		6×6	1¾	⅝
	5×5	2	½		6×6	2¾	⅝		6×8	3¾	⅝
	6×6	3	½					2¾	6×6	1¼	⅝
									6×8	3¼	⅝
1⅞	4½×4½	1¼	½	2	4½×4½	1	½	3	6×6	¾	⅝
	5×5	1¾	½		5×5	1½	½		6×8	2¾	⅝
	6×6	2¾	⅝		6×6	2½	⅝		8×6	¾	⅝
									8×8	2¾	⅝

Extra heavy butts recommended for metal doors & much used doors
All dimensions given in inches

SIZES OF BUTT HINGES

THICKNESS (in inches)	WIDTH OF DOORS OR HEIGHT OF TRANSOMS	SIZE OF BUTT HINGE (in inches)
¾ to 1⅛ cabinet doors	To 24	2½ × 2½
⅞ and 1⅛ screen or combination doors	To 36	3 × 3
1⅛ doors	To 36	3½ × 3½
1¼ and 1⅜ doors	To 32 over 32 to 37	3½ × 3½ 4 × 4
1¾ and 1⅞ doors	To 32 over 32 to 37 over 37 to 43 over 43 to 50	4½ × 4½ 5 × 5 5×5 extra heavy 6×6 extra heavy
2, 2¼ and 2½ doors	To 37 over 37 to 43 over 43 to 50	5 × 5 5×5 extra heavy 6×6 extra heavy
1¼ and 1⅜ transoms	To 20 over 20 to 36	2½ × 2½ 3 × 3
1½, 1¾, and 1⅞ transoms	To 20 over 20 to 36	3 × 3 3½ × 3½

Width of butt hinges as necessary to clear trim.   Doors to 60" high inclusive require 2 butt hinges; over 60" to 90" high inclusive, 3 butt hinges; over 90" to 120" high inclusive, 4 butt hinges.

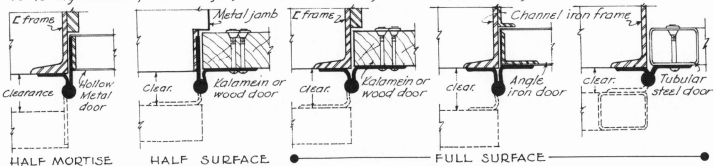

L frame   Metal jamb   L frame 2   Channel iron frame

Clearance — Hollow Metal door   Clear. — Kalamein or wood door   clear. — Kalamein or wood door   clear. — Angle iron door   clear. — Tubular steel door

HALF MORTISE   HALF SURFACE •————————— FULL SURFACE —————————•

TYPICAL APPLICATION of BUTT HINGES

Full Mortise shown in wood jamb near top of page. For clearance of butts & trim set-back, see table.
Data checked by: American Society of Architectural Hardware Consultants.

DOOR HARDWARE REQUIREMENTS

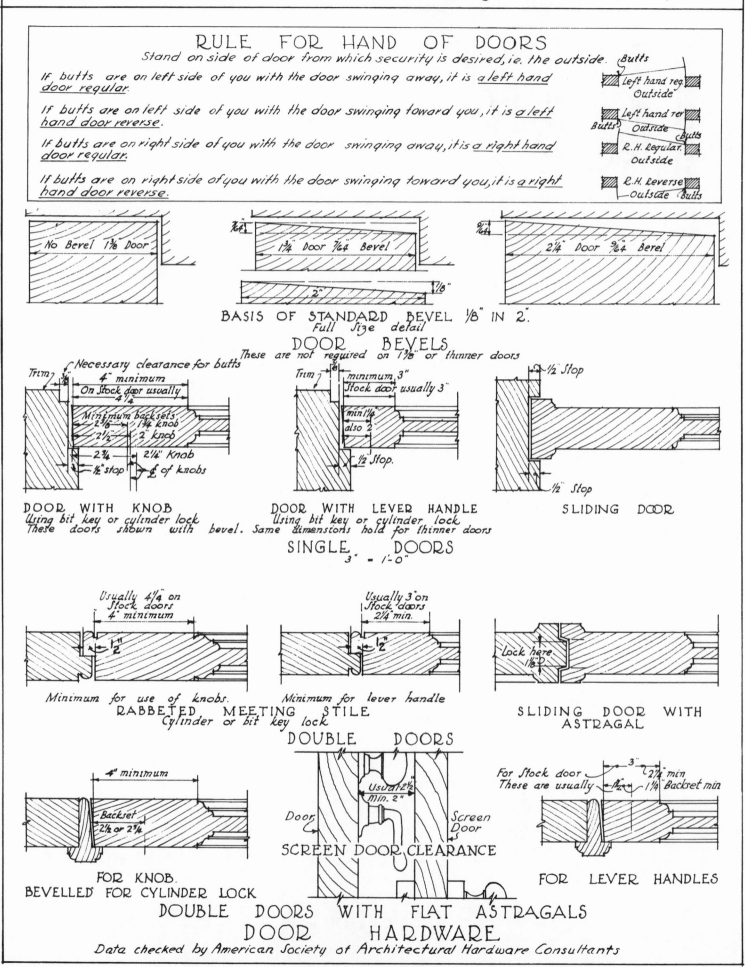

RULE FOR HAND OF DOORS

Stand on side of door from which security is desired, ie. the outside.

If butts are on left side of you with the door swinging away, it is a left hand door regular.

If butts are on left side of you with the door swinging toward you, it is a left hand door reverse.

If butts are on right side of you with the door swinging away, it is a right hand door regular.

If butts are on right side of you with the door swinging toward you, it is a right hand door reverse.

Butts
Left hand reg. Outside
Left hand rev. Outside   Butts
R.H. Regular Outside
R.H. Reverse Outside   Butts

No Bevel 1⅜ Door

1¾ Door ⁷⁄₆₄ Bevel   ⁷⁄₆₄   2"   ⅛"

2¼ Door ⁹⁄₆₄ Bevel   ⁹⁄₆₄

BASIS OF STANDARD BEVEL ⅛" IN 2".
Full Size detail
DOOR BEVELS
These are not required on 1⅜" or thinner doors

Necessary clearance for butts
Trim ¾"   4" minimum   On Stock door usually 4¼"
Minimum backsets — 2⅜" 1¾ knob, 2½" 2" knob, 2¾" 2¼" Knob
½" stop   ℄ of knobs

Trim ⅛   minimum 3"   Stock door usually 3"
min 1¼, also 2   ½" Stop.

½" Stop   ½" Stop

DOOR WITH KNOB
Using bit key or cylinder lock

DOOR WITH LEVER HANDLE
Using bit key or cylinder lock

SLIDING DOOR

These doors shown with bevel. Same dimensions hold for thinner doors
SINGLE DOORS
3" = 1'-0"

Usually 4¼ on Stock doors   4" minimum   ½"

Usually 3" on Stock doors   2¼" min.   ½"

Lock here. 1⅛

Minimum for use of knobs.
RABBETED MEETING STILE
Cylinder or bit key lock

Minimum for lever handle

SLIDING DOOR WITH ASTRAGAL

DOUBLE DOORS

4" minimum
Backset 2½ or 2¾

Door   Usual 2½ min. 2"   Screen Door

SCREEN DOOR CLEARANCE

For Stock door These are usually   3"   2¼" min 1½   1¼ Backset min

FOR KNOB.
BEVELLED FOR CYLINDER LOCK

DOUBLE DOORS WITH FLAT ASTRAGALS

FOR LEVER HANDLES

DOOR HARDWARE
Data checked by American Society of Architectural Hardware Consultants

DOOR HARDWARE REQUIREMENTS

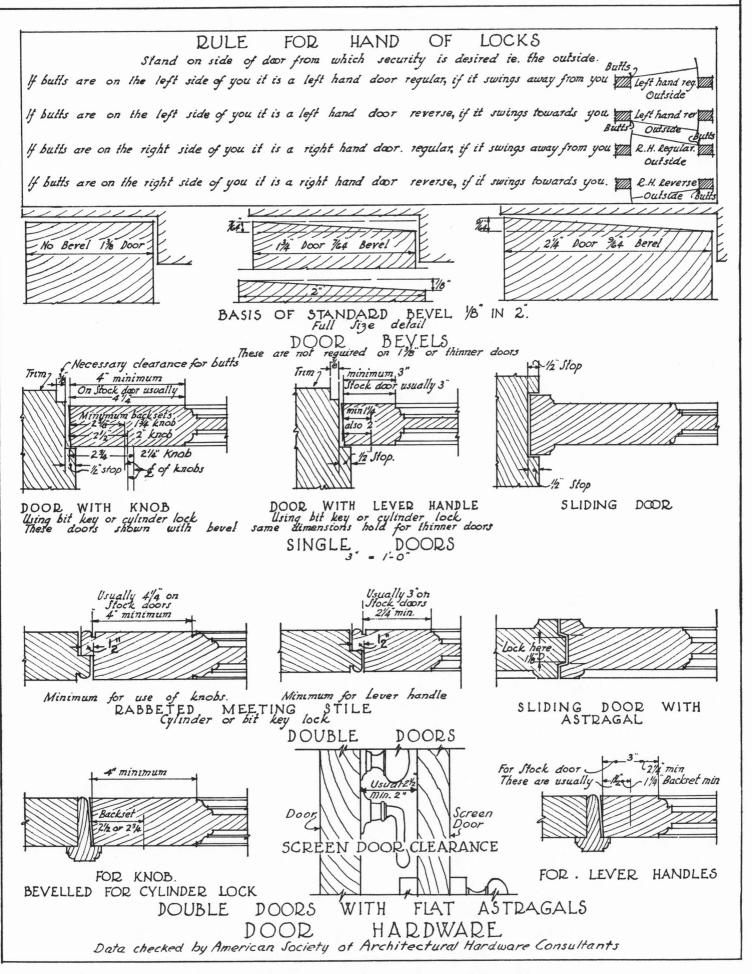

RULE FOR HAND OF LOCKS

Stand on side of door from which security is desired ie. the outside.

If butts are on the left side of you it is a left hand door regular, if it swings away from you — Left hand reg. Outside Butts

If butts are on the left side of you it is a left hand door reverse, if it swings towards you — Left hand rev. Outside Butts

If butts are on the right side of you it is a right hand door. regular, if it swings away from you — R.H. Regular. Outside Butts

If butts are on the right side of you it is a right hand door reverse, if it swings towards you. — R.H. Reverse Outside Butts

No Bevel 1⅜ Door

1¾ Door ⁷⁄₆₄ Bevel

2¼ Door ⁹⁄₆₄ Bevel

BASIS OF STANDARD BEVEL ⅛" IN 2"
Full Size detail

DOOR BEVELS
These are not required on 1⅜ or thinner doors

DOOR WITH KNOB
Using bit key or cylinder lock
These doors shown with bevel

DOOR WITH LEVER HANDLE
Using bit key or cylinder lock
same dimensions hold for thinner doors

SLIDING DOOR

SINGLE DOORS
3' = 1'-0

RABBETED MEETING STILE
Cylinder or bit key lock
Minimum for use of knobs.
Minimum for Lever handle

SLIDING DOOR WITH ASTRAGAL

DOUBLE DOORS

FOR KNOB.
BEVELLED FOR CYLINDER LOCK

SCREEN DOOR CLEARANCE

FOR . LEVER HANDLES

DOUBLE DOORS WITH FLAT ASTRAGALS

DOOR HARDWARE
Data checked by American Society of Architectural Hardware Consultants

WINDOW HARDWARE REQUIREMENTS

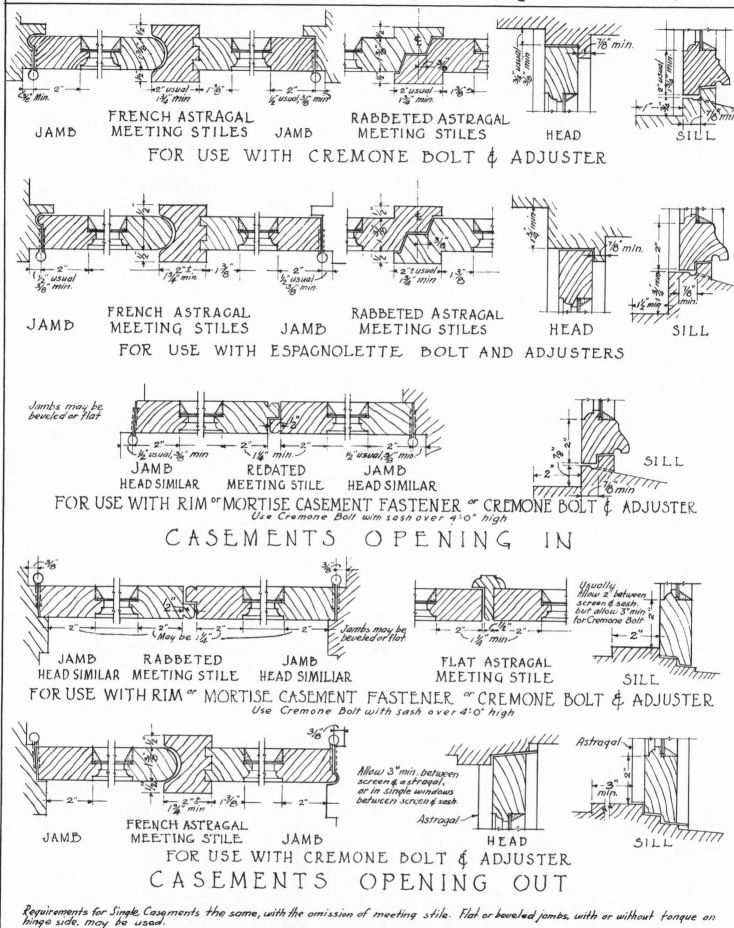

JAMB — FRENCH ASTRAGAL MEETING STILES — JAMB — RABBETED ASTRAGAL MEETING STILES — HEAD — SILL

FOR USE WITH CREMONE BOLT & ADJUSTER

JAMB — FRENCH ASTRAGAL MEETING STILES — JAMB — RABBETED ASTRAGAL MEETING STILES — HEAD — SILL

FOR USE WITH ESPAGNOLETTE BOLT AND ADJUSTERS

Jambs may be beveled or flat

JAMB HEAD SIMILAR — REBATED MEETING STILE — JAMB HEAD SIMILAR — SILL

FOR USE WITH RIM or MORTISE CASEMENT FASTENER or CREMONE BOLT & ADJUSTER
Use Cremone Bolt with sash over 4'-0" high

CASEMENTS OPENING IN

JAMB HEAD SIMILAR — RABBETED MEETING STILE — JAMB HEAD SIMILIAR — FLAT ASTRAGAL MEETING STILE — SILL

(May be 1¼")

Jambs may be beveled or flat.

Usually Allow 2" between screen & sash. but allow 3" min. for Cremone Bolt

FOR USE WITH RIM or MORTISE CASEMENT FASTENER or CREMONE BOLT & ADJUSTER
Use Cremone Bolt with sash over 4'-0" high

Allow 3" min. between screen & astragal, or in single windows between screen & sash.

Astragal

JAMB — FRENCH ASTRAGAL MEETING STILE — JAMB — HEAD — SILL

FOR USE WITH CREMONE BOLT & ADJUSTER

CASEMENTS OPENING OUT

Requirements for Single Casements the same, with the omission of meeting stile. Flat or beveled jambs, with or without tongue on hinge side, may be used.

3" = 1'-0"

Data checked by American Society of Architectural Hardware Consultants

WOOD CASEMENT HARDWARE

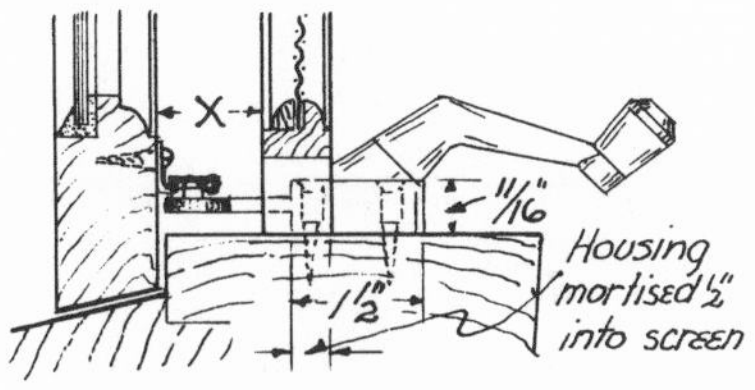
X
11/16
Housing mortised 1/2" into screen
1 1/2"

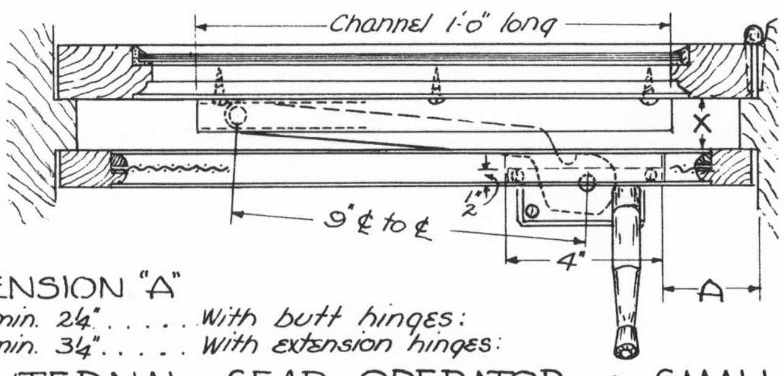
Channel 1'-0" long
X
1/2"
9" ¢ to ¢
4"
A

Standard operators are furnished with 9" arms for use with butt hinges to fit sash 14" to 20" wide; with extension hinges to fit sash 16" to 20" wide. Channel must be 15" long if extension hinges are used. Use of these operators on sash over 1'-8" wide or 3'-2" high is not recommended. Special operators are furnished with shorter arms for use with butt hinges to fit sash from 11" wide; with extension hinges to fit sash from 14" wide.

DIMENSION "X"		DIMENSION "A"	
min. 1";	max. 4"	min. 2¼"	With butt hinges:
min. 1";	max. 1½"	min. 3¼"	With extension hinges:

ANGULAR DRIVE-EXTERNAL GEAR OPERATOR *for* SMALL WOOD CASEMENTS

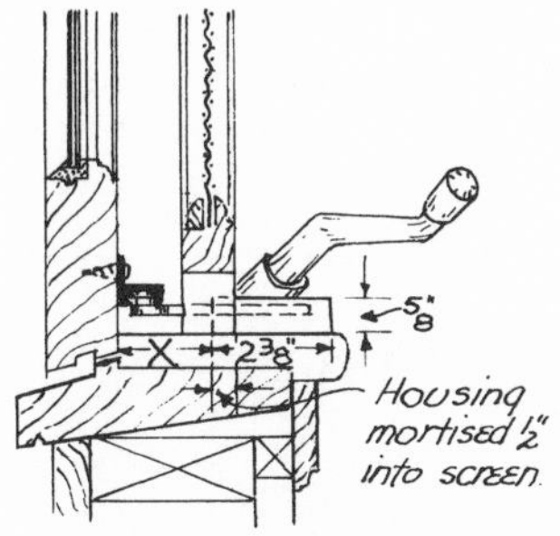
5/8"
X
2 3/8"
Housing mortised 1/2" into screen.

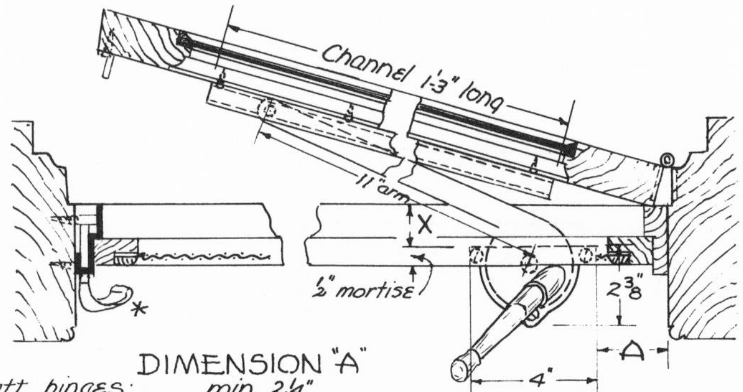
Channel 1'-3" long
11" arm
X
1/2" mortise
2 3/8"
A
4"
*

Standard operators are furnished with 11" arms for use with butt hinges to fit sash 16" to 30" wide; with extension hinges to fit sash 19" to 30" wide. Use of these operators on casements over 2'-6" wide or 6'-0" high is not recommended. Special operators can be furnished with shorter arms for use with butt hinges to fit sash from 11" wide; with extension hinges to fit sash from 17" wide. Operators may be equipped with a removable crank handle, or with a pole hook for remote operation by winding brace pole to fit special conditions.

DIMENSION "X"			DIMENSION "A"
min. 1⅛"	max. 4½"	With butt hinges:	min. 2¼"
min. 1⅛"	max. 3"	With extension hinges:	min. 4"

ANGULAR DRIVE-INTERNAL GEAR OPERATOR *for* LARGE WOOD CASEMENTS

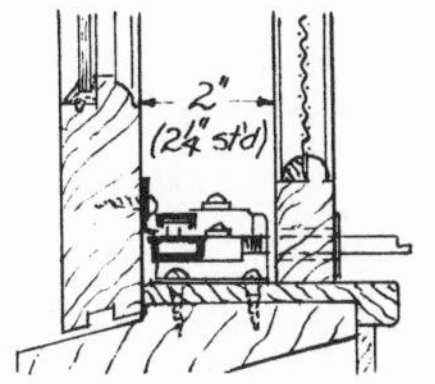
2"
(2¼" std)

ABOVE-STOOL INSTALLATION

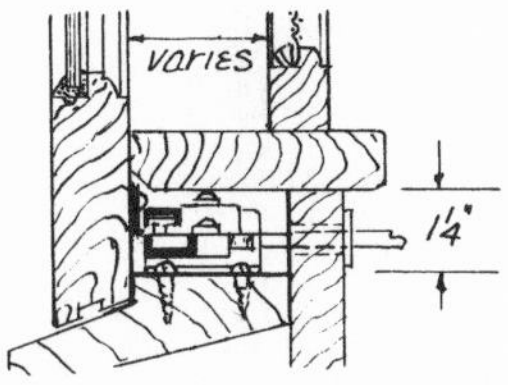
varies
1¼"

UNDER-STOOL INSTALLATION

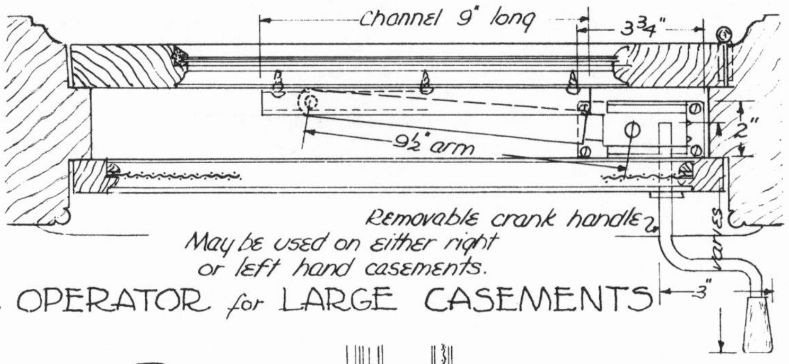
Channel 9" long
3 3/4"
9½" arm
2"
Removable crank handle
2
varies
3"

May be used on either right or left hand casements.

HORIZONTAL DRIVE-EXTERNAL GEAR OPERATOR *for* LARGE CASEMENTS

All rabbets on meeting rails should be eliminated as a standard practice. Where unavoidable, a one-half inch square rabbet, not bevelled, should be used.

The term "French Window" should be applied to glazed, narrow-stile openings, hinged at the side, which do not extend to the floor. The face width of stiles for such openings should be not less than two inches.

The term "French Door" should be applied to glazed, narrow-stile openings which extend to the floor. The face width of the stiles for such openings should be not less than three inches.

DETAILS AFFECTING HARDWARE

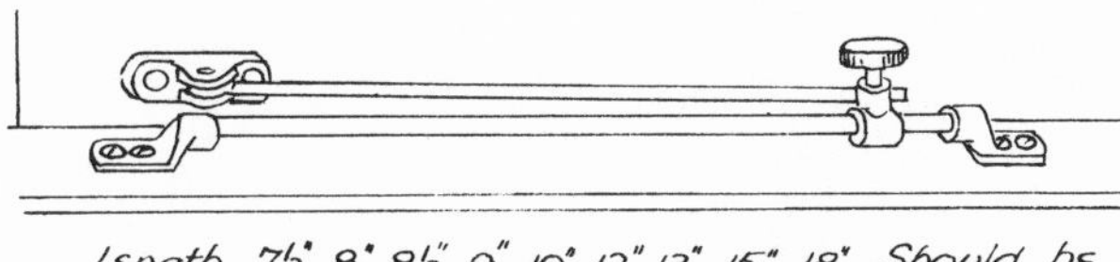

Length 7½", 8", 8½", 9", 10", 12", 13", 15", 18". Should be ⅔ of casement width. Design varies with m'f'r.

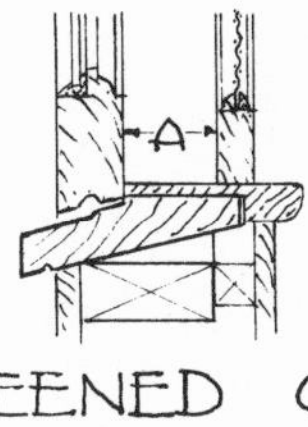
A

DIMENSION "A"
With butt hinges:
min. 1¼"; max. 3½"
With extension hinges:
min. 1½"; max. 3½"

SILL

SLIDE ADJUSTER *for* NON-SCREENED CASEMENTS

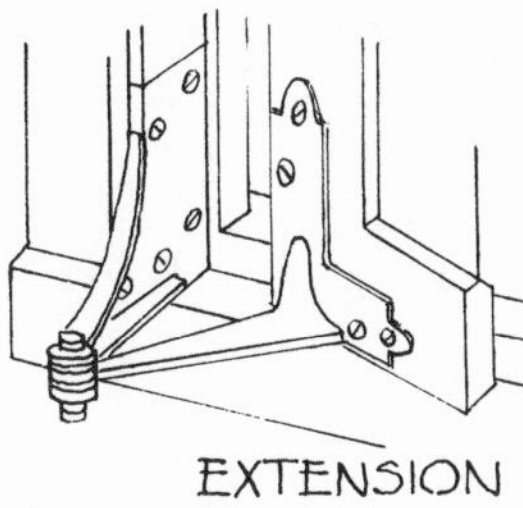

EXTENSION

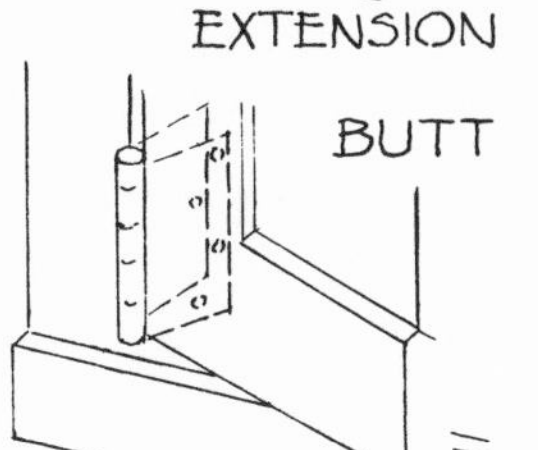

BUTT

HINGES.

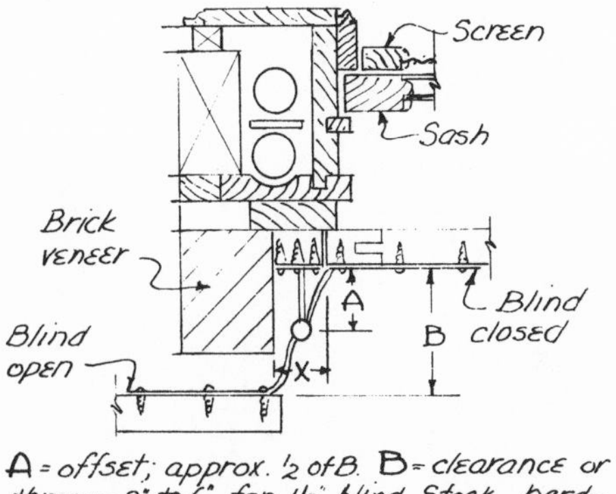
Screen
Sash
Brick veneer
A
B
Blind closed
Blind open
X

A = offset; approx. ½ of B. B = clearance or throw = 2" to 6" for 1⅛" blind. Stock hardware to fit jamb dimension X from 1½" to 3".

BLIND REQUIREMENTS

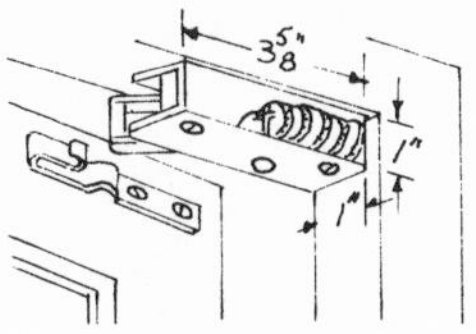
3 5/8"
1"
1"

CLOSER

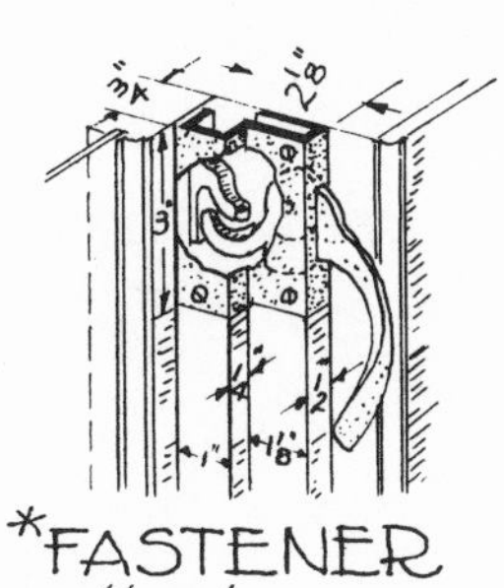
3/4"
2 1/8"
1"
1 1/8"

*FASTENER

Data checked by: American Society of Architectural Hardware Consultants.

SPRING HINGES, DOOR CHECKS (CLOSERS), STOPS *and* HOLDERS

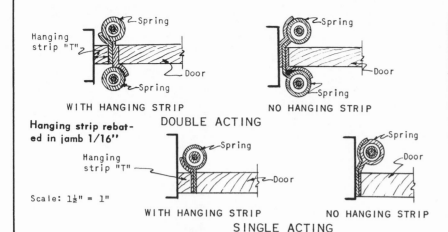

Spring

Hanging strip "T"

Door

Spring

Spring

Door

Spring

WITH HANGING STRIP

NO HANGING STRIP

DOUBLE ACTING

Hanging strip rebated in jamb 1/16''

Hanging strip "T"

Spring

Door

Spring

Door

Scale: 1½" = 1"

WITH HANGING STRIP

NO HANGING STRIP

SINGLE ACTING

SPRING BUTT HINGES

SPRING BUTT HINGE SIZES

Hinge Sizes	Door Thickness Min.–Max.*	Max. Door Width	Max. Door Weight	Depth Hanging Strip (T)
3"	¾"–1"	2'– 2"	30#	½"
4"	⅞"–1¼"	2'– 4"	42#	⅝"
5"	1" –1½"	2'– 6"	56#	⅝"
6"	1⅛"–1¾"	2'– 8"	72#	¾"
7"	1¼"–2"	2'– 9"	90#	⅞"
8"	1½"–2¼"	2'–10"	110#	1"
10"	1¾"–2½"	3'– 0"	150#	1⅛"
12"	2¼"–3"	3'– 2"	190#	1¼"

*Max. sizes shown are for wood doors; deduct 1/8'' for metal doors. Use min. thickness only for light wood doors. Check mfrs. for exact data.

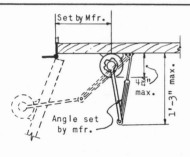

Set by Mfr.

4¼" max.

1'–3" max.

Angle set by mfr.

Max. 4½"

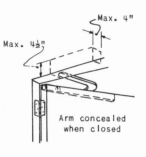

Max. 4"

Arm concealed when closed

Pivot

6¼" max.

Allow 1'–5½"

PLAN

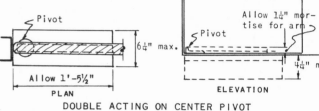

Allow 1¼" mortise for arm

Pivot

4¼" max.

ELEVATION

DOUBLE ACTING ON CENTER PIVOT

Cylinder may be mounted on door, or either side of door head. Corner mount permits full 180° opening but reduces effective power of check for closing. For exact dimensions check with mfr., and when ordering specify max. op. angle

OVERHEAD EXPOSED

Allow 1'–1"

Max. 6¼"

Sliding shoe

Rail

PLAN

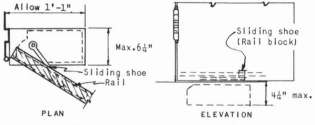

Sliding shoe (Rail block)

4¼" max.

ELEVATION

SINGLE ACTING ON BUTT HINGES

set by mfr.

Projected 1¾"

Requires approximately 1½" mortise in metal door, 1¾" in wood

OVERHEAD SEMI-CONCEALED

Scale: ½" = 1"

Max. 4"

Max. 4½"

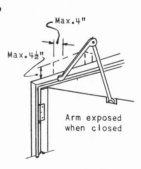

Arm exposed when closed

OVERHEAD CONCEALED

Arm

Pivot

Max. 6¼"

Allow 1'–1"

PLAN

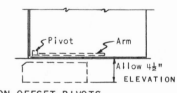

Pivot

Arm

Allow 4½"

ELEVATION

SINGLE ACTING ON OFFSET PIVOTS

FLOOR CLOSERS

DOOR CHECKS (CLOSERS)

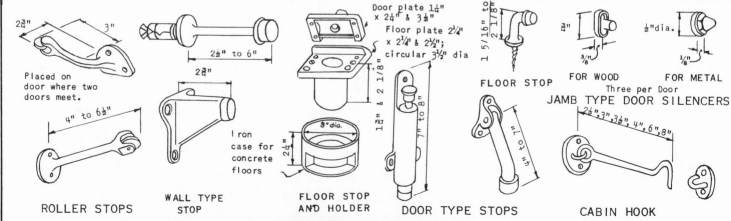

2¾"   3"

Placed on door where two doors meet.

4" to 6½"

ROLLER STOPS

2½" to 6"

2¾"

WALL TYPE STOP

Door plate 1¼" x 2¼" & 3½"

Floor plate 2¼" x 2¼" & 2½"; circular 3½" dia

1¾" & 2 1/8"

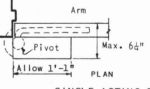

3" dia.

2¾"

Iron case for concrete floors

FLOOR STOP AND HOLDER

1 5/16" to 2 1/8"

7" to 8"

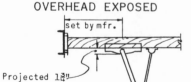

4" to 11"

DOOR TYPE STOPS

FLOOR STOP

¾"

3/8"

FOR WOOD

½" dia.

1/8"

FOR METAL

Three per Door

JAMB TYPE DOOR SILENCERS

2½",3",3½",4",6",8"

CABIN HOOK

DOOR STOPS AND HOLDERS

DATA BY THE AMERICAN SOCIETY OF ARCHITECTURAL HARDWARE CONSULTANTS

8 INTERIOR STAIRS AND STAIRWELLS

STAIR TREAD-RISER PROPORTION FORMULAE

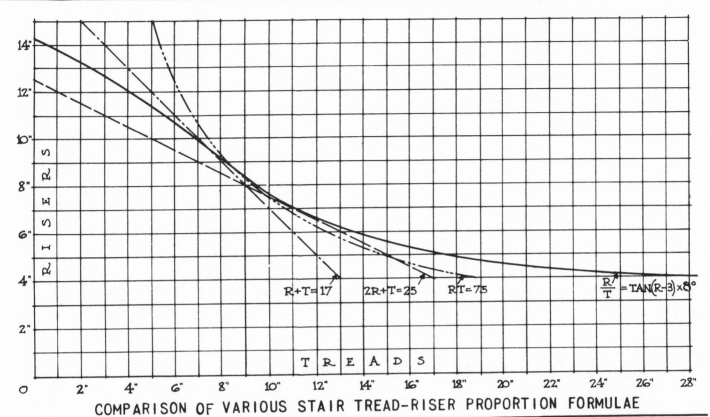

R+T=17   2R+T=25   RT=75 $\frac{R}{T} = TAN(R-3) \times 8°$

R I S E R S

T R E A D S

COMPARISON OF VARIOUS STAIR TREAD-RISER PROPORTION FORMULAE

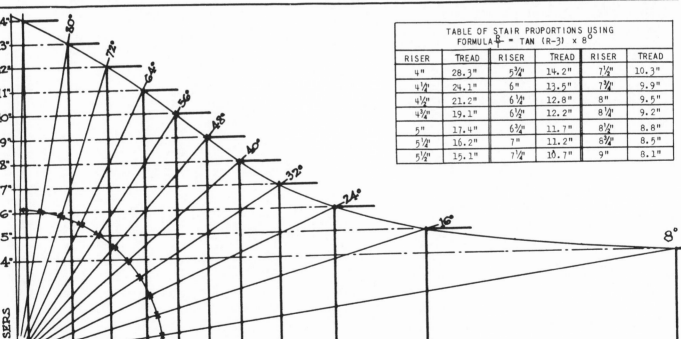

TABLE OF STAIR PROPORTIONS USING FORMULA $\frac{R}{T}$ = TAN (R-3) x 8°

RISER	TREAD	RISER	TREAD	RISER	TREAD
4"	28.3"	5¾"	14.2"	7½"	10.3"
4¼"	24.1"	6"	13.5"	7¾"	9.9"
4½"	21.2"	6¼"	12.8"	8"	9.5"
4¾"	19.1"	6½"	12.2"	8¼"	9.2"
5"	17.4"	6¾"	11.7"	8½"	8.8"
5¼"	16.2"	7"	11.2"	8¾"	8.5"
5½"	15.1"	7¼"	10.7"	9"	8.1"

TREADS   8.1" 9.5" 11.2" 13.5" 17.4"   28.3"

EXAMPLE: Assuming riser height of 8", find size of tread necessary for proper stair proportion.

Formula $\frac{R}{T}$=TAN. (R-3) x 8°

$\frac{8}{T} = \frac{TAN.(8-3) \times 8°}{1} = \frac{TAN. 5 \times 8°}{1} = \frac{TAN. 40°}{1}$

(in logarithm tables, tan. 40° = .83910)

$\frac{8}{T} = \frac{.83910}{1}$

.83910T = 8

$T = \frac{8}{.83910} = 9.5340"$

Tread = 9½"

STAIR PROPORTIONS USING FORMULA $\frac{R}{T}$ = TAN (R-3)8° OR T=R×COT(R-3)8°

FORMULA BY JAMIESON PARKER. A.I.A.

STAIR DATA

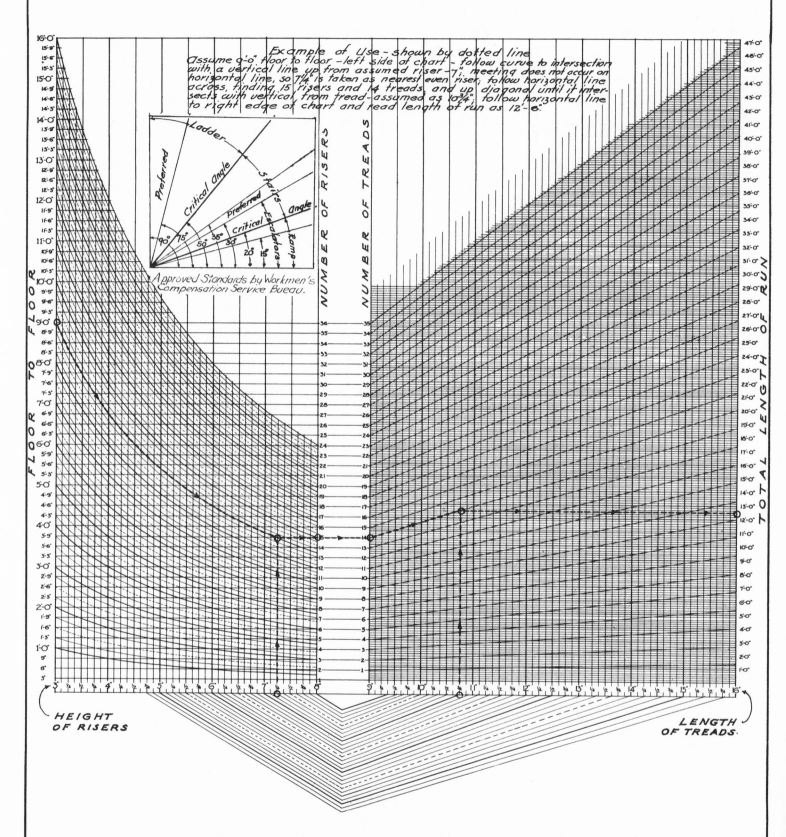

Example of Use - shown by dotted line
Assume 9'-0" floor to floor - left side of chart - follow curve to intersection with a vertical line up from assumed riser-7"; meeting does not occur on horizontal line, so 7¼" is taken as nearest even riser; follow horizontal line across, finding 15 risers and 14 treads, and up diagonal until it intersects with vertical from tread-assumed as 10¾", follow horizontal line to right edge of chart and read length of run as 12'-6".

Approved Standards by Workmen's Compensation Service Bureau.

NUMBER OF RISERS

NUMBER OF TREADS

FLOOR TO FLOOR

TOTAL LENGTH OF RUN

HEIGHT OF RISERS

LENGTH OF TREADS.

Lines connecting treads & risers are based on product of tread & riser =75 (about); these lines may be disregarded & any other rule substituted. They do not apply to exterior stairs.
Another rule commonly used is: run & riser =17'2; run equals tread less nosing.
Recommendations: minimum width of tread with nosing =11", except stairs with open risers. Maximum width of tread with nosing =15". Maximum height of riser = 7¾", min. 6"

Conceived by Frederick L. Ackerman, Architect.

NOTES

1. Codes and standards used on this page:
   ANSI = American National Standards Institute.
   BOCA = Building Officials and Code Administrators.
   NBC = National Building Code.
   SBCC = Southern Building Code Congress.
   UBC = Uniform Building Code.
2. T = tread; R = riser.
3. Maximum height between landings is 12 ft (most codes).

RULE-OF-THUMB FORMULAS

INTERIOR STAIRS

1. Riser + tread = 17 or $17\frac{1}{2}$ in.; $7\frac{1}{2}$ in. R + 10 in. T = $17\frac{1}{2}$ in.
2. Riser x tread = 70 or 75; thus 7.5 in. R x 10 in. T = 75 in.
3. 2(riser) + tread $\geq$ 24 in. $\leq$ 25 in.
4. Within any flight $\frac{3}{16}$ in. max. variation in riser or tread height or width is permitted.

EXTERIOR STAIRS

Exterior stairs generally are not as steep as interior stairs, since space for wider treads and lower risers is usually available outdoors. Also, more dangerous conditions exist (ice, snow, rain). Wider treads and lower risers make exterior steps safer. The following formula has been devised by Thomas Church in "Gardens Are For People": 2(riser) + tread = 26 in.; thus for a 6 in. riser, 6 x 2 = 12 in., subtracted from 26 = 14 in. tread.

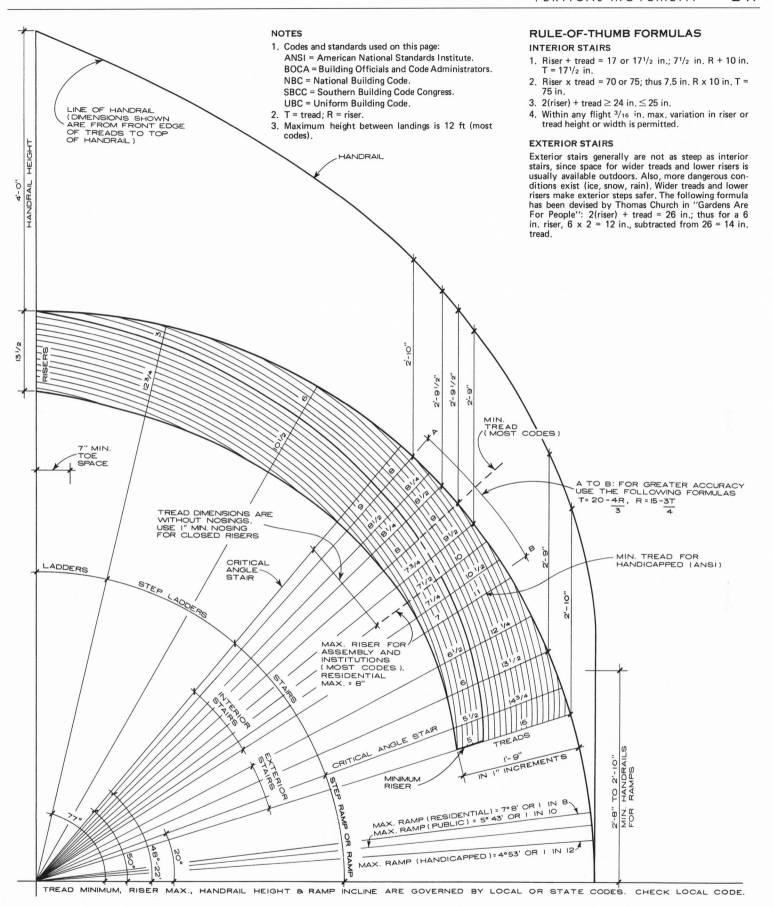

TREADS AND RISERS

Paul Vaughan, AIA; Charleston, West Virginia

SCISSOR STAIRS

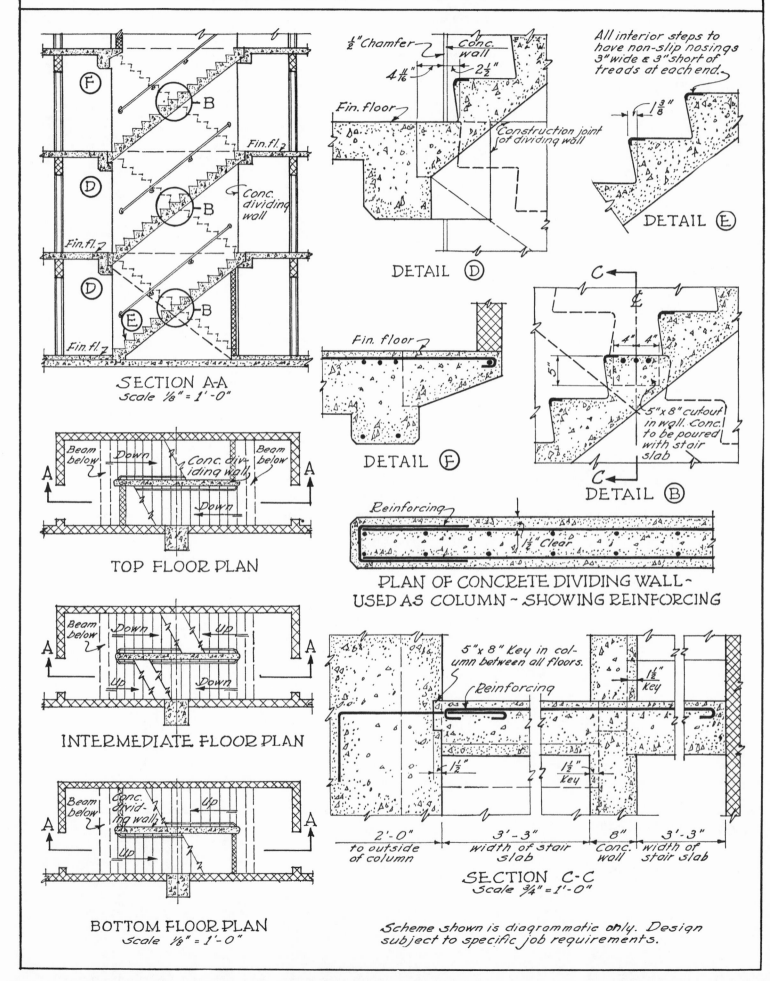

All interior steps to have non-slip nosings 3" wide & 3" short of treads at each end.

½" Chamfer

Conc. wall

4 11/16"   2½"

Fin. floor

Construction joint of dividing wall

DETAIL D

1 3/8"

DETAIL E

SECTION A-A
scale ⅛" = 1'-0"

Conc. dividing wall

Fin. fl.

Fin. floor

DETAIL F

C

4"   4"

5"

5"x 8" cutout in wall. Conc. to be poured with stair slab

DETAIL B

Beam below

Down

Conc. dividing wall

Beam below

Down

TOP FLOOR PLAN

Reinforcing

1½" Clear

PLAN OF CONCRETE DIVIDING WALL ~
USED AS COLUMN ~ SHOWING REINFORCING

Beam below

Down   Up

Up   Down

INTERMEDIATE FLOOR PLAN

5"x 8" Key in column between all floors.

Reinforcing

1½" Key

1½"

1½" Key

Beam below

Conc. dividing wall

Up

Up

BOTTOM FLOOR PLAN
Scale ⅛" = 1'-0"

2'-0"
to outside of column

3'-3"
width of stair slab

8"
Conc. wall

3'-3"
width of stair slab

SECTION C-C
Scale ¾" = 1'-0"

Scheme shown is diagrammatic only. Design subject to specific job requirements.

NOTE:
SEE PAGE ON STAIR DIAMENSIONS FOR CODE REQUIREMENTS FOR STAIRS

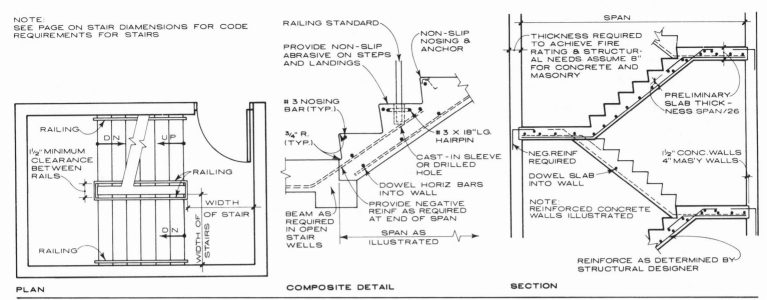

RAILING STANDARD

NON-SLIP NOSING & ANCHOR

PROVIDE NON-SLIP ABRASIVE ON STEPS AND LANDINGS

3 NOSING BAR (TYP.)

3/4" R. (TYP.)

3 X 18"LG. HAIRPIN

CAST-IN SLEEVE OR DRILLED HOLE

DOWEL HORIZ BARS INTO WALL

PROVIDE NEGATIVE REINF AS REQUIRED AT END OF SPAN

BEAM AS REQUIRED IN OPEN STAIR WELLS

SPAN AS ILLUSTRATED

SPAN

THICKNESS REQUIRED TO ACHIEVE FIRE RATING & STRUCTURAL NEEDS. ASSUME 8" FOR CONCRETE AND MASONRY

PRELIMINARY SLAB THICKNESS SPAN/26

NEG. REINF REQUIRED

DOWEL SLAB INTO WALL

1½" CONC. WALLS 4" MAS'Y WALLS

NOTE:
REINFORCED CONCRETE WALLS ILLUSTRATED

REINFORCE AS DETERMINED BY STRUCTURAL DESIGNER

RAILING

1½" MINIMUM CLEARANCE BETWEEN RAILS

RAILING

WIDTH OF STAIR

WIDTH OF STAIRS

RAILING

PLAN   **COMPOSITE DETAIL**   **SECTION**

"U" TYPE CONCRETE STAIRS

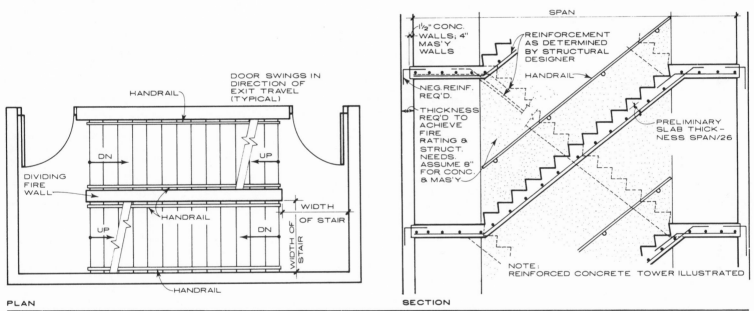

DOOR SWINGS IN DIRECTION OF EXIT TRAVEL (TYPICAL)

HANDRAIL

DIVIDING FIRE WALL

HANDRAIL

HANDRAIL

WIDTH OF STAIR

WIDTH OF STAIR

1½" CONC. WALLS; 4" MAS'Y WALLS

REINFORCEMENT AS DETERMINED BY STRUCTURAL DESIGNER

NEG. REINF. REQ'D.

THICKNESS REQ'D TO ACHIEVE FIRE RATING & STRUCT. NEEDS. ASSUME 8" FOR CONC. & MAS'Y

HANDRAIL

PRELIMINARY SLAB THICKNESS SPAN/26

NOTE:
REINFORCED CONCRETE TOWER ILLUSTRATED

PLAN   **SECTION**

SCISSOR TYPE CONCRETE STAIRS

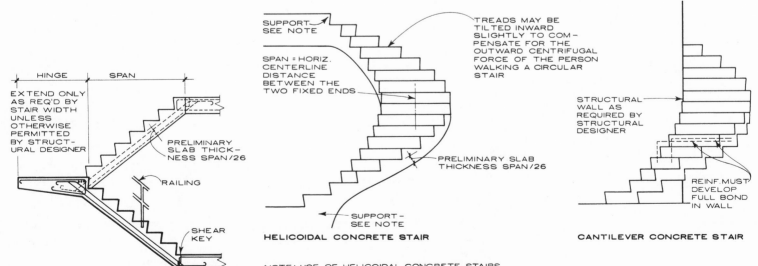

HINGE   SPAN

EXTEND ONLY AS REQ'D BY STAIR WIDTH UNLESS OTHERWISE PERMITTED BY STRUCTURAL DESIGNER

PRELIMINARY SLAB THICKNESS SPAN/26

RAILING

SHEAR KEY

FREE STANDING CONCRETE STAIR

SUPPORT - SEE NOTE

SPAN = HORIZ. CENTERLINE DISTANCE BETWEEN THE TWO FIXED ENDS

TREADS MAY BE TILTED INWARD SLIGHTLY TO COMPENSATE FOR THE OUTWARD CENTRIFUGAL FORCE OF THE PERSON WALKING A CIRCULAR STAIR

PRELIMINARY SLAB THICKNESS SPAN/26

SUPPORT - SEE NOTE

HELICOIDAL CONCRETE STAIR

NOTE: USE OF HELICOIDAL CONCRETE STAIRS DEPEND ON VERY STIFF FIXED ENDS SUPPORT AND SMALL SUPPORT DEFLECTION

STRUCTURAL WALL AS REQUIRED BY STRUCTURAL DESIGNER

REINF. MUST DEVELOP FULL BOND IN WALL

CANTILEVER CONCRETE STAIR

Irvin Bruce Schafer; Peoria, Illinois

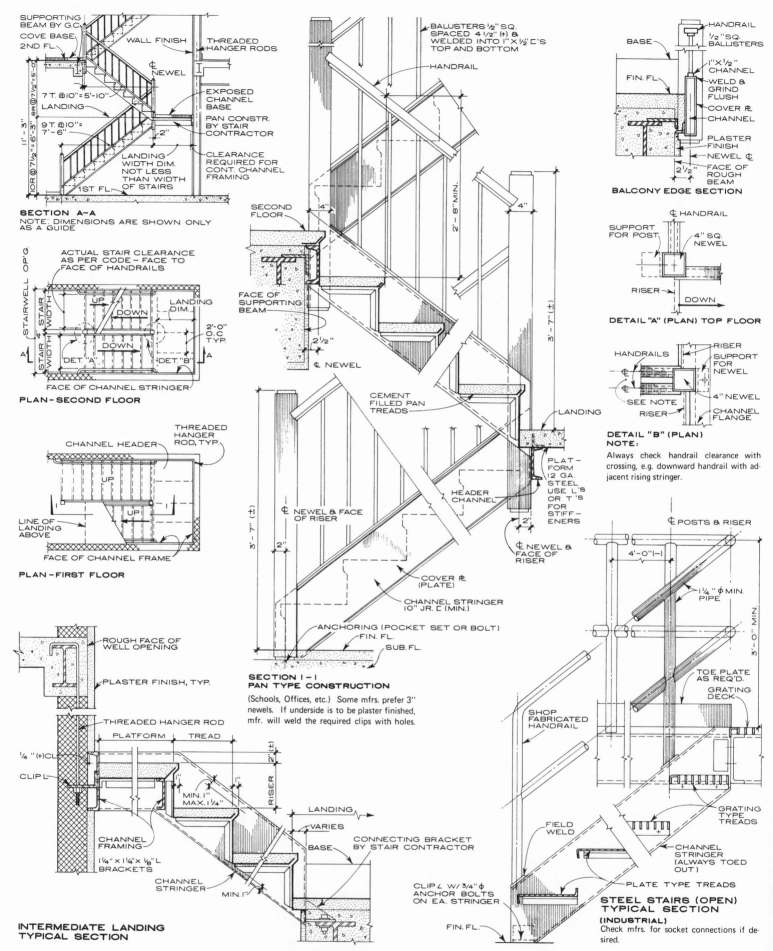

SECTION A-A
NOTE: DIMENSIONS ARE SHOWN ONLY AS A GUIDE

SUPPORTING BEAM BY G.C.
COVE BASE
2ND FL.
WALL FINISH
THREADED HANGER RODS
¢ NEWEL
7 T. @ 10" = 5'-10"
LANDING
9 T. @ 10" = 7'-6"
EXPOSED CHANNEL BASE
PAN CONSTR. BY STAIR CONTRACTOR
CLEARANCE REQUIRED FOR CONT. CHANNEL FRAMING
LANDING WIDTH DIM. NOT LESS THAN WIDTH OF STAIRS
1ST FL.

PLAN - SECOND FLOOR

ACTUAL STAIR CLEARANCE AS PER CODE - FACE TO FACE OF HANDRAILS
STAIRWELL OP'G
STAIR WIDTH
LANDING DIM.
UP
DOWN
DOWN
2'-0" O.C. TYP.
DET. "A"
DET. "B"
FACE OF CHANNEL STRINGER

PLAN - FIRST FLOOR

CHANNEL HEADER
THREADED HANGER ROD, TYP.
UP
UP
LINE OF LANDING ABOVE
FACE OF CHANNEL FRAME

INTERMEDIATE LANDING TYPICAL SECTION

ROUGH FACE OF WELL OPENING
PLASTER FINISH, TYP.
THREADED HANGER ROD
PLATFORM   TREAD
1/4" (+) CL.
CLIP L
RISER 2' (±)
MIN. 1" MAX. 1 1/4"
CHANNEL FRAMING
1 1/4" x 1 1/4" x 1/8" L BRACKETS
CHANNEL STRINGER
MIN. 1"
LANDING
VARIES
BASE
CONNECTING BRACKET BY STAIR CONTRACTOR

Paul R. Schieve, Sr. and Joseph Hornyak; Tippetts, Abbett, McCarthy, Stratton; New York, New York

BALUSTERS 1/2" SQ. SPACED 4 1/2" (±) & WELDED INTO 1" X 1/2" C'S TOP AND BOTTOM
HANDRAIL
SECOND FLOOR
4"
2'-8" MIN.
FACE OF SUPPORTING BEAM
2 1/2"
¢ NEWEL
4"
3'-7" (±)
LANDING
CEMENT FILLED PAN TREADS
HEADER CHANNEL
PLAT-FORM 12 GA. STEEL USE L'S OR T'S FOR STIFF-ENERS
¢ NEWEL & FACE OF RISER
2"
¢ NEWEL & FACE OF RISER
3'-7" (±)
2"
COVER PL (PLATE)
CHANNEL STRINGER 10" JR. C (MIN.)
ANCHORING (POCKET SET OR BOLT)
FIN. FL.
SUB. FL.

SECTION 1-1
PAN TYPE CONSTRUCTION

(Schools, Offices, etc.) Some mfrs. prefer 3" newels. If underside is to be plaster finished, mfr. will weld the required clips with holes.

HANDRAIL
BASE
1/2" SQ. BALUSTERS
FIN. FL.
1" X 1/2" CHANNEL
WELD & GRIND FLUSH
COVER PL.
CHANNEL
PLASTER FINISH
NEWEL ¢
2 1/2"
FACE OF ROUGH BEAM

BALCONY EDGE SECTION

¢ HANDRAIL
SUPPORT FOR POST
4" SQ. NEWEL
RISER
DOWN

DETAIL "A" (PLAN) TOP FLOOR

HANDRAILS
¢
¢
SEE NOTE
RISER
RISER
SUPPORT FOR NEWEL
4" NEWEL
CHANNEL FLANGE

DETAIL "B" (PLAN)
NOTE:

Always check handrail clearance with crossing, e.g. downward handrail with adjacent rising stringer.

¢ POSTS & RISER
4'-0" (–)
1 1/4" ⌀ MIN. PIPE
3'-0" MIN.
TOE PLATE AS REQ'D.
GRATING DECK
SHOP FABRICATED HANDRAIL
GRATING TYPE TREADS
FIELD WELD
CHANNEL STRINGER (ALWAYS TOED OUT)
PLATE TYPE TREADS
CLIP L W/ 3/4" ⌀ ANCHOR BOLTS ON EA. STRINGER
FIN. FL.

STEEL STAIRS (OPEN) TYPICAL SECTION
(INDUSTRIAL)
Check mfrs. for socket connections if desired.

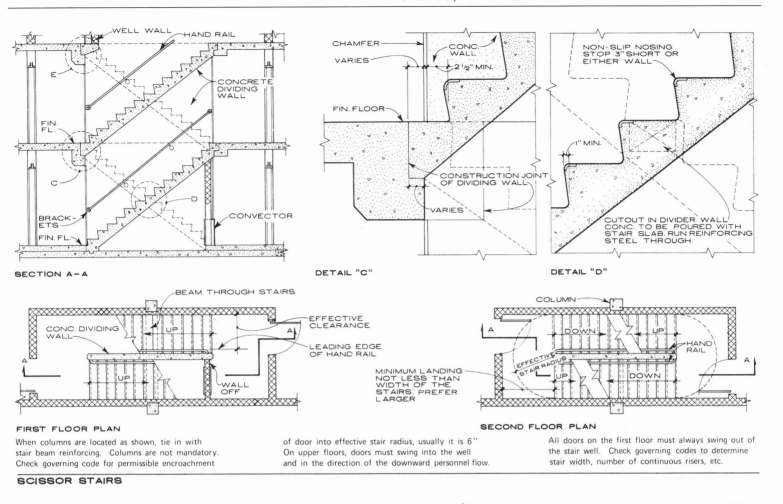

SECTION A-A

DETAIL "C"

DETAIL "D"

FIRST FLOOR PLAN

SECOND FLOOR PLAN

When columns are located as shown, tie in with stair beam reinforcing. Columns are not mandatory. Check governing code for permissible encroachment

of door into effective stair radius, usually it is 6" On upper floors, doors must swing into the well and in the direction of the downward personnel flow.

All doors on the first floor must always swing out of the stair well. Check governing codes to determine stair width, number of continuous risers, etc.

SCISSOR STAIRS

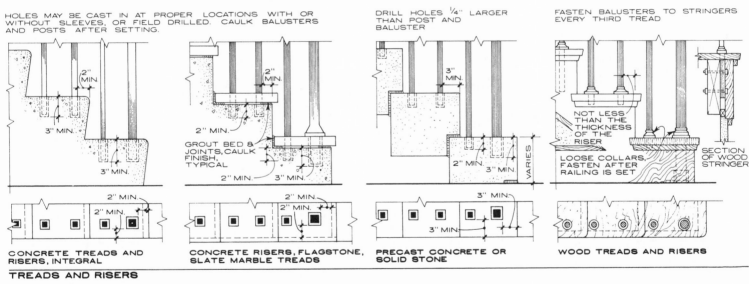

CONCRETE TREADS AND RISERS, INTEGRAL

CONCRETE RISERS, FLAGSTONE, SLATE MARBLE TREADS

PRECAST CONCRETE OR SOLID STONE

WOOD TREADS AND RISERS

TREADS AND RISERS

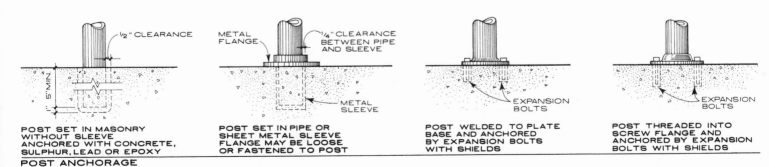

POST SET IN MASONRY WITHOUT SLEEVE ANCHORED WITH CONCRETE, SULPHUR, LEAD OR EPOXY

POST SET IN PIPE OR SHEET METAL SLEEVE FLANGE MAY BE LOOSE OR FASTENED TO POST

POST WELDED TO PLATE BASE AND ANCHORED BY EXPANSION BOLTS WITH SHIELDS

POST THREADED INTO SCREW FLANGE AND ANCHORED BY EXPANSION BOLTS WITH SHIELDS

POST ANCHORAGE

Paul R. Schieve, Sr. and Constantine Economou; Tippetts, Abbett, McCarthy, Stratton; New York, New York

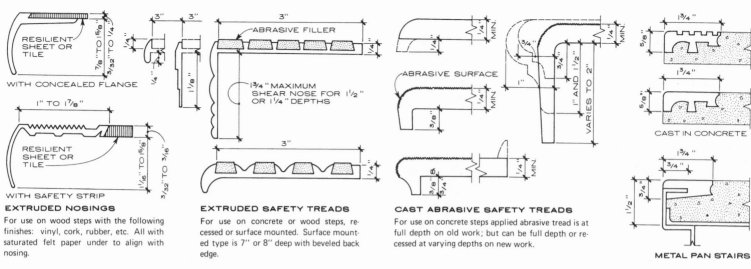

EXTRUDED NOSINGS

For use on wood steps with the following finishes: vinyl, cork, rubber, etc. All with saturated felt paper under to align with nosing.

EXTRUDED SAFETY TREADS

For use on concrete or wood steps, recessed or surface mounted. Surface mounted type is 7" or 8" deep with beveled back edge.

CAST ABRASIVE SAFETY TREADS

For use on concrete steps applied abrasive tread is at full depth on old work; but can be full depth or recessed at varying depths on new work.

1. Extruded types: Aluminum and aluminum with abrasive filler in lengths; as required up to 12'– 0".
2. Cast Types: Iron, aluminum, or bronze, and are made to order to exact size.
3. Types shown are used on new or old work. Old work: Fill worn surfaces to level.
4. Nosings and treads come with factory drilled countersunk holes, or with riveted strap anchors, or with wing type anchors.
5. Wood Application: Secure with wood screws.
6. Concrete Application: Secure with adhesive shields and screws, or with strap or wing anchors.
7. Nosings for concrete stairs: steel, bronze, brass and aluminum rolled, drawn or extruded cast abrasive.

NOSINGS FOR CONCRETE STAIRS

STANDARD EXTRUDED NOSINGS, STANDARD EXTRUDED & CAST ABRASIVE SAFETY TREADS & NOSINGS FOR CONCRETE STAIRS

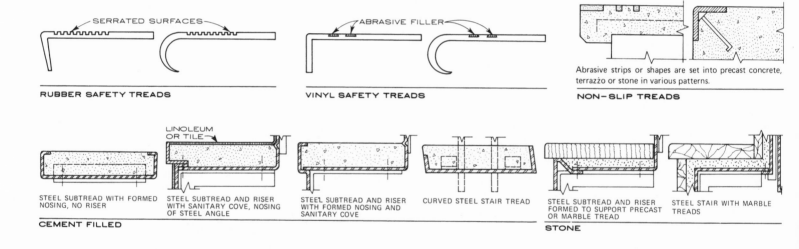

RUBBER SAFETY TREADS

VINYL SAFETY TREADS

NON–SLIP TREADS

Abrasive strips or shapes are set into precast concrete, terrazzo or stone in various patterns.

STEEL SUBTREAD WITH FORMED NOSING, NO RISER

STEEL SUBTREAD AND RISER WITH SANITARY COVE, NOSING OF STEEL ANGLE

STEEL SUBTREAD AND RISER WITH FORMED NOSING AND SANITARY COVE

CURVED STEEL STAIR TREAD

STEEL SUBTREAD AND RISER FORMED TO SUPPORT PRECAST OR MARBLE TREAD

STEEL STAIR WITH MARBLE TREADS

CEMENT FILLED

STONE

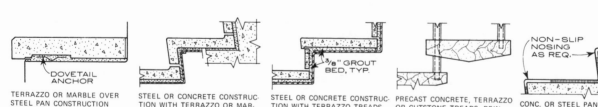

TERRAZZO OR MARBLE OVER STEEL PAN CONSTRUCTION WITH STEEL RISER

STEEL OR CONCRETE CONSTRUCTION WITH TERRAZZO OR MARBLE RISERS

STEEL OR CONCRETE CONSTRUCTION WITH TERRAZZO TREADS AND RISERS

PRECAST CONCRETE, TERRAZZO OR CUTSTONE TREADS, REINFORCED

CONC. OR STEEL PAN CONST.

WOOD CONSTRUCTION

Thin-set terrazzo risers and treads set and finished in place on concrete or steel pan construction.

PRECAST

THIN – SET

EXTRUDED ALUMINUM TREAD WITH WELDED END BARS BOLTED TO STRING

CAST ALUMINUM GRATING TREAD WITH ABRASIVE NOSING

STEEL GRATING TREAD

EXPANDED METAL TREAD WITH ANGLE NOSING FLAT

Back bars and end bars bolted to string.

ABRASIVE TREADS CAST INTEGRALLY WITH LUGS OR BOLTED TO CLIP ANGLE.

Lugs or clips angle bolted to structural member (stronger) on each side.

TYPICAL RISER & TREAD DETAILS

Paul R. Schieve, Sr. and Joseph Hornyak; Tippetts, Abbett, McCarthy, Stratton; New York, New York

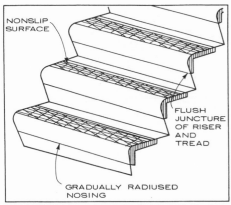

NONSLIP SURFACE

FLUSH JUNCTURE OF RISER AND TREAD

GRADUALLY RADIUSED NOSING

TREAD SIZE

Riser and tread dimensions must be uniform for the length of the stair. ANSI specifications recommend a minimum tread dimension of 11 in., nosing to nosing, and a riser height of 5 to 7 in. for maximum secure footing. Stairs with tread dimensions of less than 9 in. must be open riser stairs. These are a hazard for persons with leg braces, however, and should be used only where another stair, elevator, or ramp that complies with the standards is available.

TREAD COVERING

OSHA standards require finishes to be "reasonably slip resistant" with nosings of nonslip finish. Treads without nosings are acceptable provided that the tread is serrated or is of definite nonslip design. Uniform color and texture are recommended for clear delineation of edges.

NOSING DESIGN

ANSI specifications recommend nosings without abrupt edges which project no more than $1\frac{1}{2}$ in. beyond the edge of the riser. A "safe stair" will use a slightly rounded, abrasive nosing, firmly anchored to the tread, with no overhangs and a clearly visible edge.

RAILINGS

Handrails should be mounted at height 32 to 34 in. above the nosings and should be graspable for their entire length. A $1\frac{3}{4}$ to 2 in. diameter rounded handrail is recommended. It should extend 1 ft to 1 ft 6 in. beyond the top and bottom of the stair.

LIGHTING

Illumination of the stair with directional lighting from the lower landing will increase the visibility of the tread edge.

DESIGN OF A "SAFE" STAIR, USABLE BY THE PHYSICALLY HANDICAPPED

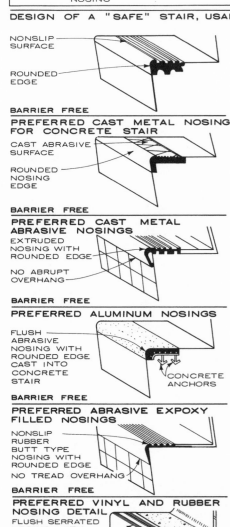

NONSLIP SURFACE

ROUNDED EDGE

BARRIER FREE

PREFERRED CAST METAL NOSING FOR CONCRETE STAIR

CAST ABRASIVE SURFACE

ROUNDED NOSING EDGE

BARRIER FREE

PREFERRED CAST METAL ABRASIVE NOSINGS

EXTRUDED NOSING WITH ROUNDED EDGE

NO ABRUPT OVERHANG

BARRIER FREE

PREFERRED ALUMINUM NOSINGS

FLUSH ABRASIVE NOSING WITH ROUNDED EDGE CAST INTO CONCRETE STAIR

CONCRETE ANCHORS

BARRIER FREE

PREFERRED ABRASIVE EXPOXY FILLED NOSINGS

NONSLIP RUBBER BUTT TYPE NOSING WITH ROUNDED EDGE

NO TREAD OVERHANG

BARRIER FREE

PREFERRED VINYL AND RUBBER NOSING DETAIL

FLUSH SERRATED NOSING WITH ROUNDED EDGE

GRADUAL RETURN

BARRIER FREE

PREFERRED STEEL SUBTREAD DETAIL

ABRASIVE STRIPS

ROUNDED EDGE

MARBLE RISER

MARBLE TREAD

BARRIER FREE

PREFERRED STONE TREAD DETAIL

Olga Barmine; Darrel Rippeteau, Architect; Washington, D.C.

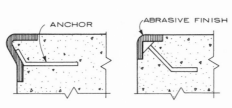

ANCHOR

ABRASIVE FINISH

SERRATED METAL NOSING

WOOD OR CONCRETE

METAL PAN INSTALLATION

OTHER CAST METAL NOSINGS

TREAD FINISH

LAP TYPE NOSING

BUTT TYPE NOSING

OTHER EXTRUDED ALUMINUM NOSINGS

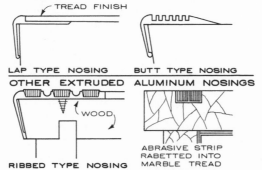

WOOD

RIBBED TYPE NOSING

ABRASIVE STRIP RABETTED INTO MARBLE TREAD

OTHER ALUMINUM NOSINGS WITH ABRASIVE FILLER

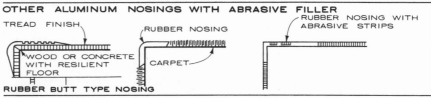

TREAD FINISH

WOOD OR CONCRETE WITH RESILIENT FLOOR

RUBBER BUTT TYPE NOSING

RUBBER NOSING

CARPET

RUBBER NOSING WITH ABRASIVE STRIPS

OTHER NONSLIP VINYL AND RUBBER NOSINGS

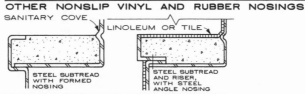

SANITARY COVE

LINOLEUM OR TILE

STEEL SUBTREAD WITH FORMED NOSING

STEEL SUBTREAD AND RISER, WITH STEEL ANGLE NOSING

OTHER CEMENT FILLED STEEL SUBTREADS

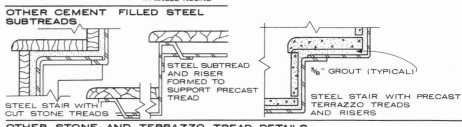

STEEL STAIR WITH CUT STONE TREADS

STEEL SUBTREAD AND RISER FORMED TO SUPPORT PRECAST TREAD

$\frac{3}{8}$" GROUT (TYPICAL)

STEEL STAIR WITH PRECAST TERRAZZO TREADS AND RISERS

OTHER STONE AND TERRAZZO TREAD DETAILS

NOTE

Cast nosings for concrete stairs are iron, aluminum, or bronze, custom made to exact size. Nosings and treads come with factory drilled countersunk holes or riveted strap anchors, or with wing type anchors.

CAST METAL ABRASIVE STRUCTURAL TREAD TYPES

NOTE

Abrasive materials are used as treads, nosings, or inlay strips for new work, and also as surface mounted replacement treads for old work. A homogeneous epoxy abrasive is cured on an extruded aluminum base for a smoother surface or is used as filler between aluminum ribs.

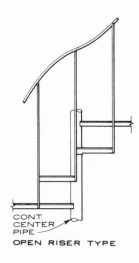

CONT. CENTER PIPE

OPEN RISER TYPE

CONT. CENTER PIPE

CLOSED RISER TYPE

GENERAL NOTES:

1. C.I., stl, or alum. stairs are identified by treads. When al. treads are specified all parts are alum.

2. Center pipe may terminate at platform, or be capped above well rail, or be extended and secured to clg.

3. Balusters: 1 Per tread. 3/4" bar or 3/4" O.D. for stl/al, 15/16" for C.I. At quarter points- 1 1/4" O.D. for C.I.

4. Formed steel floor plate tread is welded to steel collar and web for cantilever type, or to steel collar and riser assembly for open riser type.

5. Cantilever treads are secured and held in position by set screws in the hub, or welded.

6. Plated screw and bolt fasteners for stl and C.I. stairs. SST fasteners for al. stairs.

7. Platform sizes are 1" larger than stair radius and anchored to suit well opening construction.

8. Design refence must be made to state or local laws and ordinances.

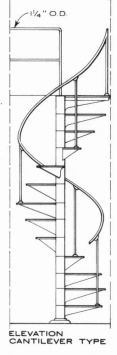

WELL OPENING

1¼" O.D.

ELEVATION CANTILEVER TYPE

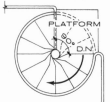

PLATFORM

DN.

PLAN
SQUARE WELL
LEFT HAND STAIR
RAILING ON LEFT
GOING UP

PLATFORM

DN.

PLAN
SQUARE WELL
RIGHT HAND STAIR
RAILING ON RIGHT
GOING UP

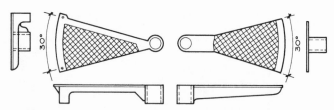

OPEN RISER TREADS			CANTILEVER TREADS	
TREAD DEGREE	NO. OF TREADS IN A CIRCLE	RISER SIZE	HEAD◊ ROOM	REMARKS
22°–30'	16	7"	7'-0"	Narrowest treads, Lowest riser
28°– 0'	12–13	7 5/8"–7 3/4"	6'-9"	
30°– 0'	12–13	8 3/8"–9"	6'-9"	Widest treads, Highest riser

◊ Head room calculated on a basis of 3/4 of a circle.

Surfaces of treads and platforms

Cast Iron:
Raised diamond abrasive

Steel:
Checkered plate abrasive,
expanded metal grating,
bar grating

Aluminum:
Checkered plate, abrasive
bar grating

Special:
Wood or rubber cemented to steel tread,
or plywood treads for carpeting

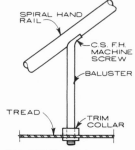

SPIRAL HAND RAIL

C.S. F.H. MACHINE SCREW

BALUSTER

TREAD

TRIM COLLAR

BALUSTER DETAIL

STANDARD SIZES OF STAIRS, PLATFORMS AND WELLS

*DIA. OF STAIR (IN)	CENTER PIPE, O.D. (IN)		PLATFORM SIZE (IN) SQ/ 1/4 CIRCLE	WELL OPEN'G (IN) SQ/CIRCU-LAR
	C.I.	STL/AL		
42	3 1/2	3 1/2	22	44
48 +	3 1/2	3 1/2	25	50
54 +	4 1/2	3 1/2	28	56
60 +	4 1/2	3 1/2	31	62
66	4 1/2	5	34	68
72	4 1/2	5	37	74

*Also available in 78" 84" 90" & 98" - special sizes.
+Most residential stairs - with 28° treads, larger dia.
Residential stairs usually 22°–30'

SPIRAL STAIRS OF CAST IRON, STEEL OR ALUMINUM

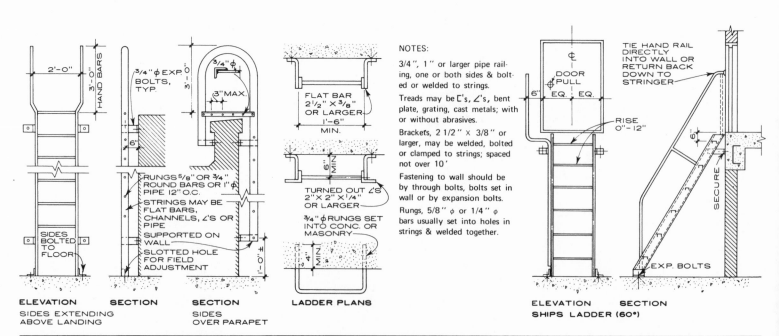

2'-0"

HAND BARS

3'-0"

3/4"ø EXP. BOLTS, TYP.

3/4"ø

3'-1"

3" MAX.

6"

RUNGS 5/8" OR 3/4" ROUND BARS OR 1" ø PIPE 12" O.C.

STRINGS MAY BE FLAT BARS, CHANNELS, ∠'S OR PIPE

SUPPORTED ON WALL

SLOTTED HOLE FOR FIELD ADJUSTMENT

SIDES BOLTED TO FLOOR

FLAT BAR 2½" X 3/8" OR LARGER 1'-6" MIN.

6" MIN.

TURNED OUT ∠'S 2" X 2" X ¼" OR LARGER

3/4"ø RUNGS SET INTO CONC. OR MASONRY

4" MIN.

ELEVATION
SIDES EXTENDING ABOVE LANDING

SECTION
SIDES OVER PARAPET

SECTION

LADDER PLANS

NOTES:

3/4", 1" or larger pipe railing, one or both sides & bolted or welded to strings.

Treads may be ['s, ∠'s, bent plate, grating, cast metals; with or without abrasives.

Brackets, 2 1/2" x 3/8" or larger, may be welded, bolted or clamped to strings; spaced not over 10'

Fastening to wall should be by through bolts, bolts set in wall or by expansion bolts.

Rungs, 5/8" ø or 1/4" ø bars usually set into holes in strings & welded together.

DOOR PULL

6" EQ. EQ.

RISE 0"- 12"

TIE HAND RAIL DIRECTLY INTO WALL OR RETURN BACK DOWN TO STRINGER

6"

SECURE

EXP. BOLTS

ELEVATION

SECTION
SHIPS LADDER (60°)

VERTICAL AND SHIPS LADDERS

Paul R. Schieve, Sr. and Joseph Hornyak; Tippetts, Abbett, McCarthy, Stratton; New York, New York

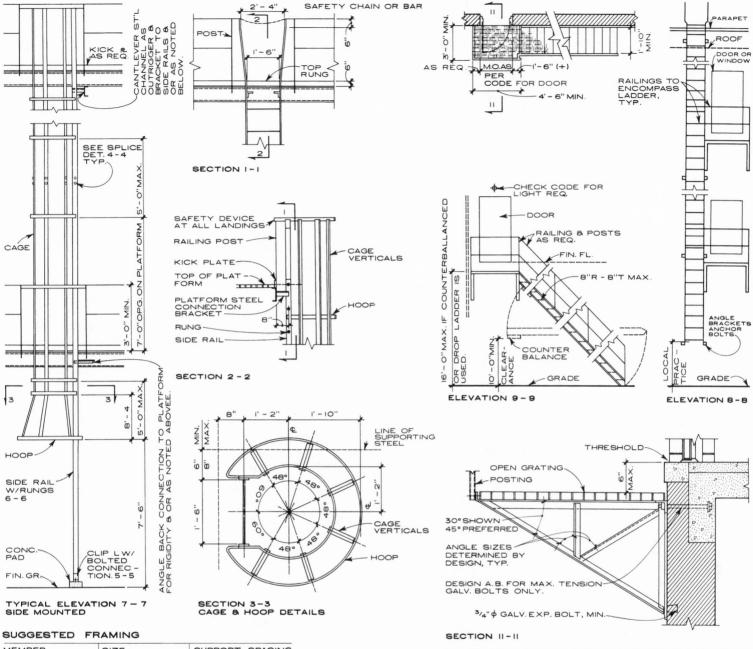

SECTION I-I

SECTION 2-2

TYPICAL ELEVATION 7-7 SIDE MOUNTED

SECTION 3-3 CAGE & HOOP DETAILS

ELEVATION 9-9

ELEVATION 8-8

SECTION II-II

TYPICAL FIRE ESCAPE DETAILS

SUGGESTED FRAMING

MEMBER	SIZE	SUPPORT SPACING
LADDER SIDE RAILS	2 1/2" x 3/8"	8'-0" Maximum
	3" x 3/8"	12'-0" Maximum
	3 1/2" x 3/8"	16'-0" Maximum
CAGE HOOP	5" x 3/8"	20'-0" Maximum top & bottom
	2" x 3/8"	All intermediates
CAGE VERTICALS	2" x 3/8"	See section 3-3 above
LADDER RUNGS	3/4"φ Plug welded into side rails.	

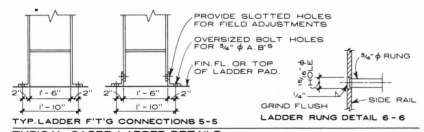

TYP. LADDER F'T'G CONNECTIONS 5-5

LADDER RUNG DETAIL 6-6

TYPICAL CAGED LADDER DETAILS
CONSULT LOCAL CODE FOR POSSIBLE VARIATIONS

GENERAL NOTES: 4 BASIC TYPES

1. Vertical ladders with platforms at exit door & windows. This type used only for industrial buildings of low height.
2. Stairways supported on brackets attached to building walls with platforms at exits. This type used for any height building permitted by code. Lowest section may be counterbalanced or drop ladder. Fire escape stairs may be used as required means of exit only in existing buildings, subject to provisions of occupancy chapter applying....."not more than 50 percent of required exit cpaacity in any case." (NFPA 1.01 Life Safety Code 1966). (5—9111)
3. Free-standing stairways independently supported on steel columns, with platforms & walk-ways at exits. This type used on buildings where the construction cannot be attached to.
4. Chute-fire escapes, used chiefly for buildings where persons are under institutional care.

  A—On all fire escapes, design reference must be made to state or local laws & ordinances.
  B—Frames for platforms may be angles as shown, or channels bolted to brackets; grating can be bolted, welded to or set in frame loose. Alternate bracket may be round or square steel, usually 1" or 1 1/4".

Paul R. Schieve, Sr. and Joseph Hornyak; Tippetts, Abbett, McCarthy, Stratton; New York, New York

STAIR FRAMING

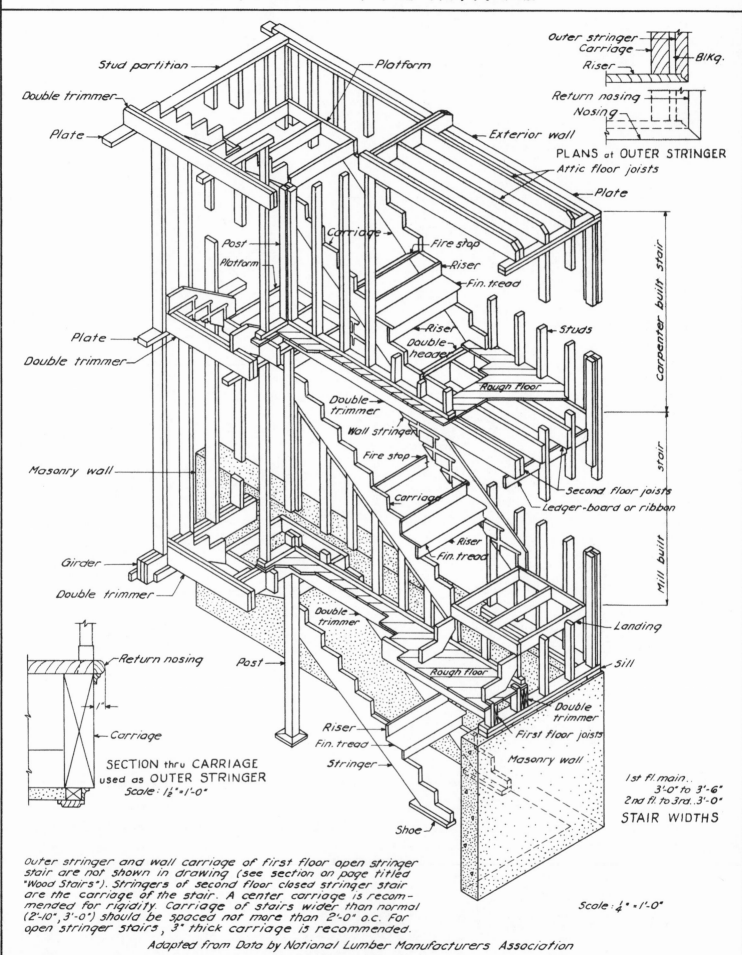

Stud partition

Double trimmer

Plate

Platform

Outer stringer

Carriage

BlKg.

Riser

PLANS at OUTER STRINGER

Return nosing

Nosing

Exterior wall

Attic floor joists

Plate

Carriage

Post

Platform

Fire stop

Riser

Fin. tread

Carpenter built stair

Riser

Double header

Studs

Plate

Double trimmer

Rough Floor

Double trimmer

Wall stringer

Fire stop

stair

Masonry wall

Carriage

Second floor joists

Ledger-board or ribbon

Riser

Fin. tread

Mill built

Girder

Double trimmer

Double trimmer

Post

Landing

Sill

Return nosing

Post

Rough floor

1"

Double trimmer

First floor joists

Carriage

Riser

Fin. tread

Masonry wall

Stringer

SECTION thru CARRIAGE
used as OUTER STRINGER
Scale: 1½" = 1'-0"

Shoe

1st fl. main..
3'-0" to 3'-6"
2nd fl. to 3rd..3'-0"

STAIR WIDTHS

Scale: ¼" = 1'-0"

Outer stringer and wall carriage of first floor open stringer
stair are not shown in drawing (see section on page titled
"Wood Stairs"). Stringers of second floor closed stringer stair
are the carriage of the stair. A center carriage is recommended for rigidity. Carriage of stairs wider than normal
(2'-10", 3'-0") should be spaced not more than 2'-0" o.c. For
open stringer stairs, 3" thick carriage is recommended.

Adapted from Data by National Lumber Manufacturers Association

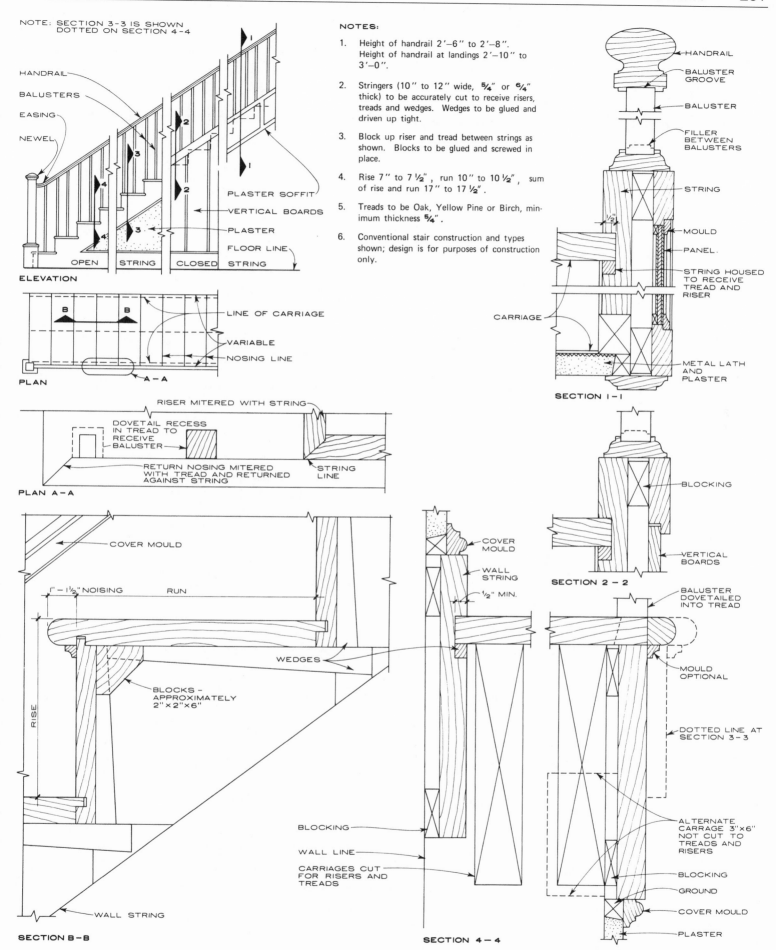

NOTE: SECTION 3-3 IS SHOWN DOTTED ON SECTION 4-4

HANDRAIL
BALUSTERS
EASING
NEWEL

PLASTER SOFFIT
VERTICAL BOARDS
PLASTER
FLOOR LINE

OPEN   STRING   CLOSED   STRING

ELEVATION

LINE OF CARRIAGE
VARIABLE
NOSING LINE

PLAN   A — A

RISER MITERED WITH STRING
DOVETAIL RECESS IN TREAD TO RECEIVE BALUSTER
RETURN NOSING MITERED WITH TREAD AND RETURNED AGAINST STRING
STRING LINE

PLAN A–A

COVER MOULD
1"–1½" NOSING   RUN
RISE
BLOCKS – APPROXIMATELY 2"x2"x6"
WEDGES
WALL STRING

SECTION B–B

COVER MOULD
WALL STRING
½" MIN.
WEDGES
BLOCKING
WALL LINE
CARRIAGES CUT FOR RISERS AND TREADS

SECTION 4–4

NOTES:

1. Height of handrail 2'–6" to 2'–8".
   Height of handrail at landings 2'–10" to 3'–0".

2. Stringers (10" to 12" wide, ⁵⁄₄" or ⁶⁄₄" thick) to be accurately cut to receive risers, treads and wedges. Wedges to be glued and driven up tight.

3. Block up riser and tread between strings as shown. Blocks to be glued and screwed in place.

4. Rise 7" to 7½", run 10" to 10½", sum of rise and run 17" to 17½".

5. Treads to be Oak, Yellow Pine or Birch, minimum thickness ⁵⁄₄".

6. Conventional stair construction and types shown; design is for purposes of construction only.

HANDRAIL
BALUSTER GROOVE
BALUSTER
FILLER BETWEEN BALUSTERS
STRING
MOULD
PANEL
STRING HOUSED TO RECEIVE TREAD AND RISER
CARRIAGE
METAL LATH AND PLASTER

SECTION 1–1

BLOCKING
VERTICAL BOARDS

SECTION 2–2

BALUSTER DOVETAILED INTO TREAD
MOULD OPTIONAL
DOTTED LINE AT SECTION 3-3
ALTERNATE CARRIAGE 3"x6" NOT CUT TO TREADS AND RISERS
BLOCKING
GROUND
COVER MOULD
PLASTER

H. E. Heidtmann and R. Paccone; Sargent, Webster, Crenshaw & Folley; Syracuse, New York

WOOD STAIRS

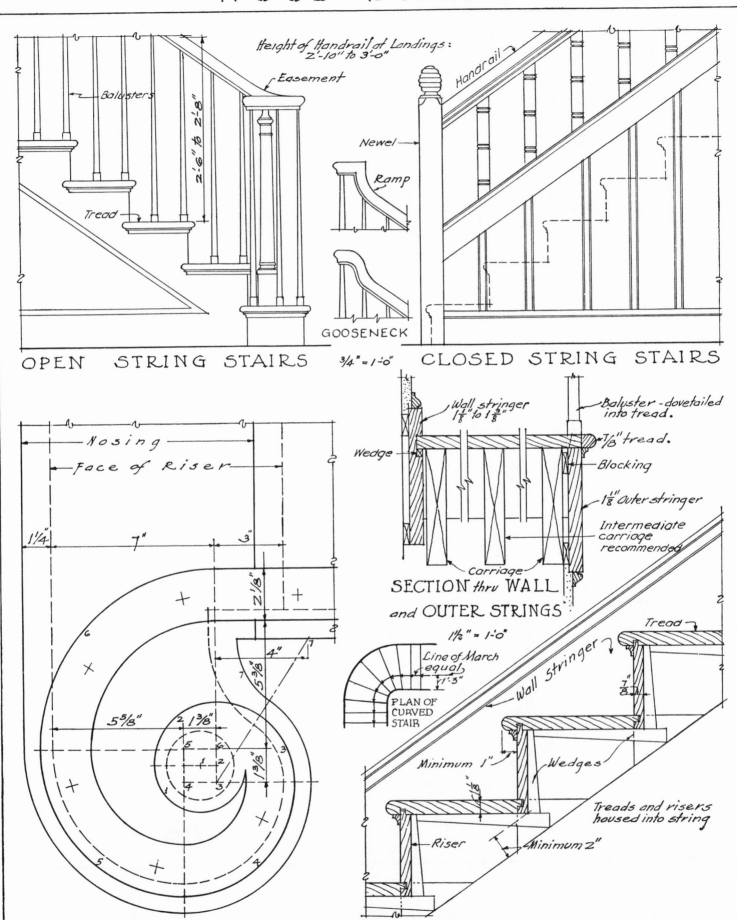

Height of Handrail at Landings: 2'-10" to 3'-0"

Easement

Balusters

2'-6" to 2'-8"

Tread

OPEN STRING STAIRS

Handrail

Newel

Ramp

GOOSENECK

3/4" = 1'-0"

CLOSED STRING STAIRS

Nosing

Face of Riser

1 1/4"   7"   3"

2 1/8"

5 5/8"   4"

5 5/8"   1 3/8"   7"

1 3/8"

DETAIL of a SIMPLE VOLUTE

3" = 1'-0"

Wall stringer 1 1/8" to 1 3/8"

Baluster - dovetailed into tread.

Wedge

1 1/8" tread.

Blocking

1 1/8" Outer stringer

Intermediate carriage recommended

Carriage

SECTION thru WALL and OUTER STRINGS

1 1/2" = 1'-0"

Line of March equal 1'-3"

PLAN OF CURVED STAIR

Tread

Wall Stringer

7/8"

Minimum 1"

1/8"

Wedges

Riser

Minimum 2"

Treads and risers housed into string

SECTION thru TREADS and RISERS

1 1/2" = 1'-0"

9 SPECIALTIES

FIREPLACES

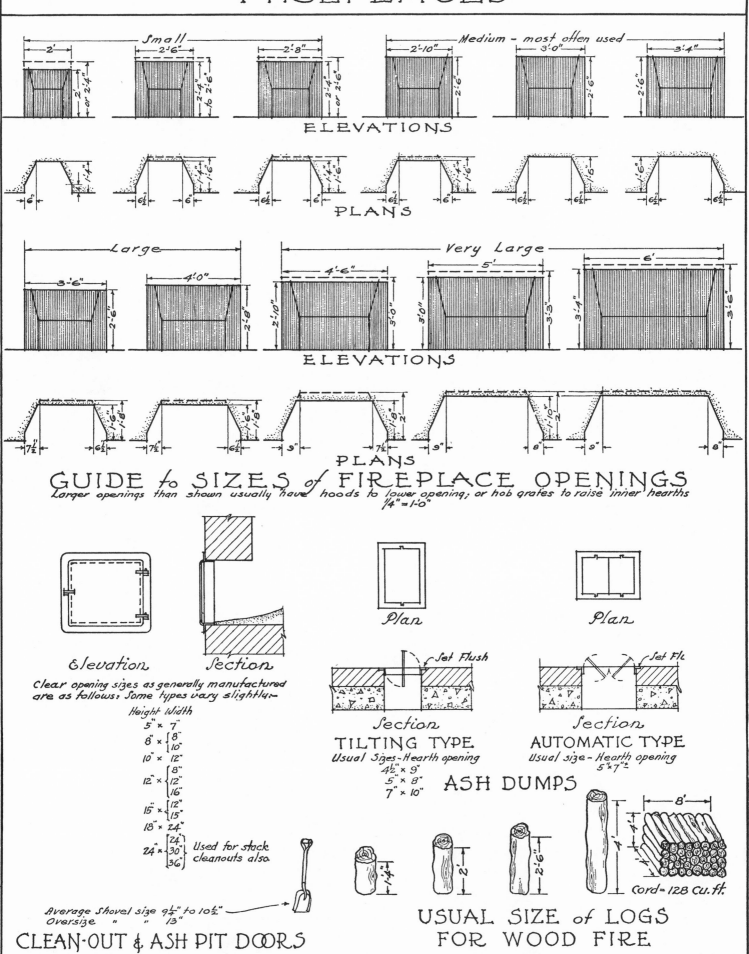

ELEVATIONS

PLANS

ELEVATIONS

PLANS

GUIDE to SIZES of FIREPLACE OPENINGS

Larger openings than shown usually have hoods to lower opening; or hob grates to raise inner hearths
1/4" = 1'-0"

Elevation   Section

Clear opening sizes as generally manufactured are as follows: Some types vary slightly:-

Height	Width
5" ×	7"
8" ×	8" 10"
10" ×	12"
12" ×	8" 12" 16"
15" ×	12" 15"
18" ×	24"
24" ×	24" 30" 36"

Used for stack cleanouts also.

Plan   Plan

Set Flush   Set Fl

Section   Section

TILTING TYPE
Usual Sizes - Hearth opening
4½" × 9"
5" × 8"
7" × 10"

AUTOMATIC TYPE
Usual size - Hearth opening
5" × 7½"

ASH DUMPS

Average Shovel size 9½" to 10½"
Oversize   "   "   13"

Cord = 128 cu.ft.

CLEAN-OUT & ASH PIT DOORS

USUAL SIZE of LOGS FOR WOOD FIRE

FIREPLACES

Effective Flue size 1/10 to 1/12 area of Fireplace opening. See sheet titled "Flues"

Minimum Flues:- Round 10
Rectangular 8½" × 13"
" (Modular) 7½ × 15½"

May set back to 4" Minimum

Fire Clay Flue Lining

Flue should center over Fireplace

* Flue lining to start at throat of Fireplace

Angle 30° or 1/5

Steel Smoke chamber shown

Throat area always more than Flue area

4" Min. 5½" Max.

If brick is used cut bricks flush.

4" Min. 5½" Max.

* Wood trim to be kept away from opening - Minimum

Lintel

4"

6" to 8"

4"

Not over 30

Allow 2" for soapstone set in Cement.

Fireplace opening. For heights generally used see Sheet Preceding

1'-4" Min: 2' Max: except for special conditions.

See Sheet Preceding

Approx. 8", never over ½ height of opening

Ash chute

ELEVATION

SECTION
Fireplace without Damper

SECTION
Fireplace with Damper

Fire stop here with incombustible material

8" Minimum 12" if exterior wall

* 4" to wood studs or joists

* 4" Minimum

* 2" to wood studs or joists

* 4" Minimum. 8" if no flue lining is used

Fire clay Flue Lining

Fire clay Flue Lining

* 4" Minimum; 8" if no Flue lining is used.

6"×9" Cast Iron Ash Dump & Frame. or 6"×15"

Back hearth of Brick, Soapstone, cement or Briquettes

* 2" to wood studs or joists

Minimum Linings:- Firebrick 4"
Briquettes & cem: backing 2"
Soapstone " " 2"

Usually 4", may be less

* Limit for wood trim

8"

splay

About 4½" to Foot of depth

1'-0"*

Width of opening 2' to 7' See Sheet Preceding

1'-8"*

Front Hearth of Marble, Tile, Soapstone, Stone, Brick, Cement or Briquettes.

PLAN

* National Board of Fire Underwriters recommendation

3/4" = 1'

FIREPLACES

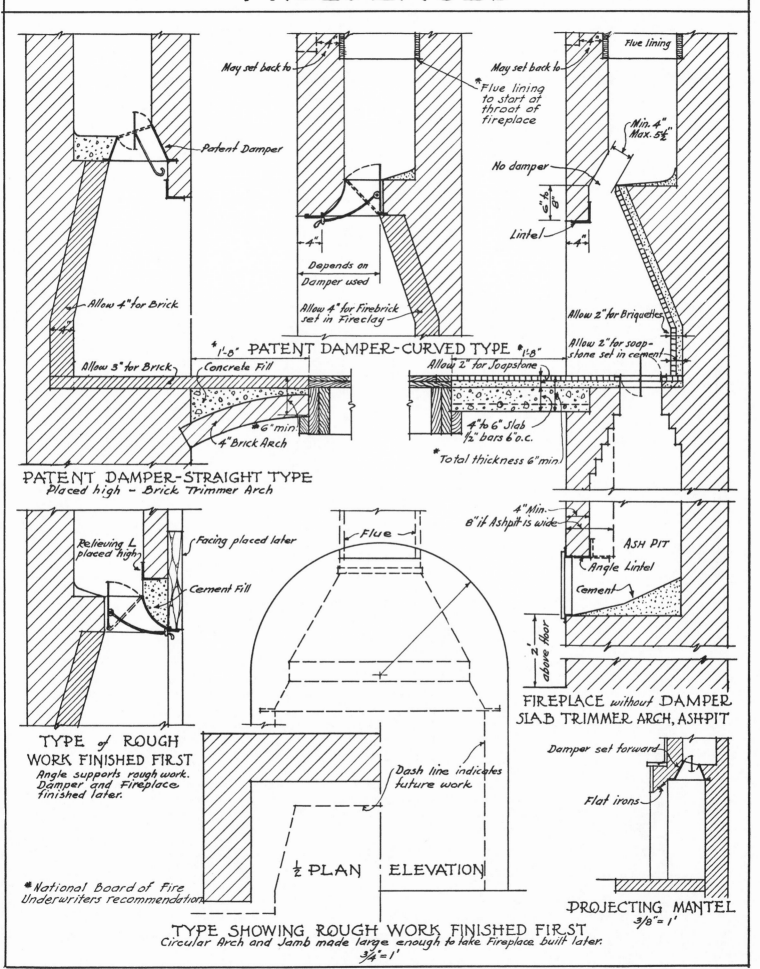

May set back to -

Patent Damper

Allow 4" for Brick

4"

Allow 3" for Brick

Concrete Fill

6" min.

4" Brick Arch

PATENT DAMPER-STRAIGHT TYPE
Placed high - Brick Trimmer Arch

May set back to -

* Flue lining to start at throat of fireplace

4"

Depends on Damper used

Allow 4" for Firebrick set in Fireclay

1'-8" **PATENT DAMPER-CURVED TYPE** *1'-8"*

Allow 2" for Soapstone

4" to 6" Slab ½" bars 6" o.c.

* Total thickness 6" min.

Flue lining

May set back to -

Min. 4"
Max. 5½"

No damper

6" to 8"

Lintel

4"

Allow 2" for Briquettes

Allow 2" for soapstone set in cement

Relieving L placed high

Facing placed later

Cement Fill

TYPE of ROUGH WORK FINISHED FIRST
Angle supports rough work. Damper and Fireplace finished later.

* *National Board of Fire Underwriters recommendation*

Flue

Dash line indicates future work

½ PLAN   ELEVATION

TYPE SHOWING ROUGH WORK FINISHED FIRST
Circular Arch and Jamb made large enough to take Fireplace built later.
¾" = 1'

4" Min.
8" if Ashpit is wide

ASH PIT

Angle Lintel

Cement

2' above floor

FIREPLACE without DAMPER SLAB TRIMMER ARCH, ASHPIT

Damper set forward

Flat irons

PROJECTING MANTEL
3/8" = 1'

CHIMNEYS

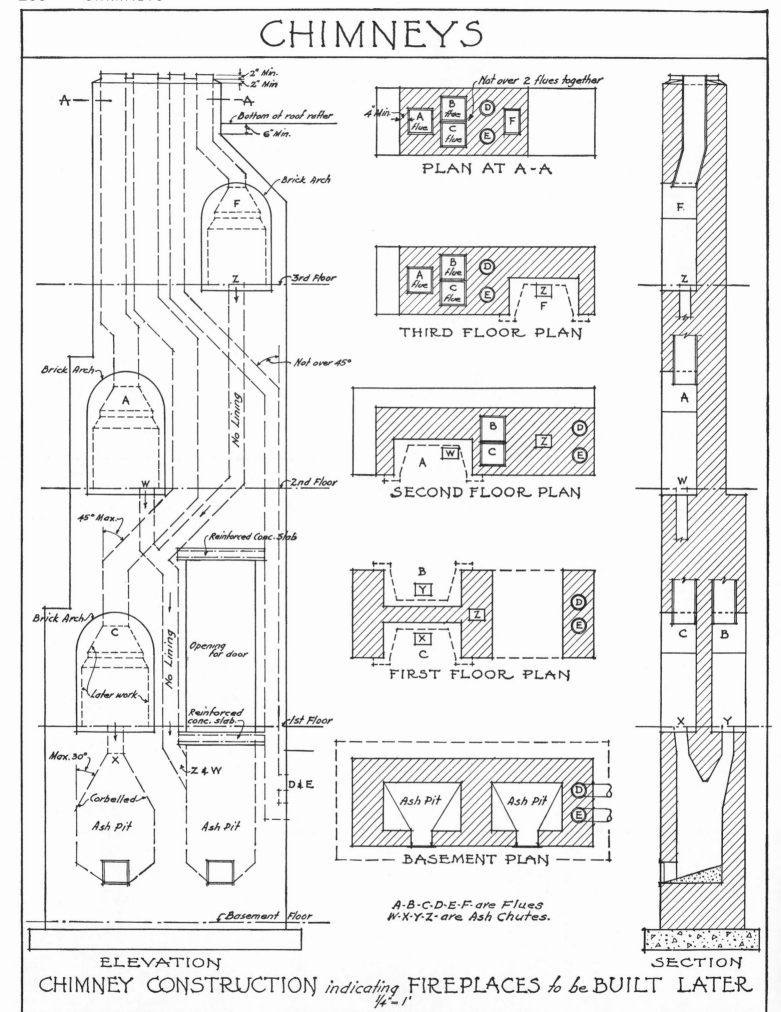

2" Min.
2" Min
Bottom of roof rafter
6" Min.

Brick Arch

F

3rd Floor

Brick Arch

Not over 45°

No Lining

A

W

2nd Floor

45° Max.

Reinforced Conc. Slab

Brick Arch

C

No Lining

Opening for door

Later work

Reinforced conc. slab.

1st Floor

Max. 30°

Z & W

D & E

Corbelled

Ash Pit

Ash Pit

Basement Floor

ELEVATION

A   A

PLAN AT A-A

Not over 2 flues together

4" Min.

A flue   B flue   D   F
          C flue   E

THIRD FLOOR PLAN

A flue   B flue   D
          C flue   E
                    Z
                    F

SECOND FLOOR PLAN

B   D
C   Z   E
A   W

FIRST FLOOR PLAN

B
Y
Z
X
C
D
E

BASEMENT PLAN

Ash Pit   Ash Pit   D
                      E

A·B·C·D·E·F· are Flues
W·X·Y·Z· are Ash Chutes.

SECTION

F.
Z
A
W
C   B
X   Y

CHIMNEY CONSTRUCTION *indicating* FIREPLACES *to be* BUILT LATER

¼"=1'

CHIMNEYS

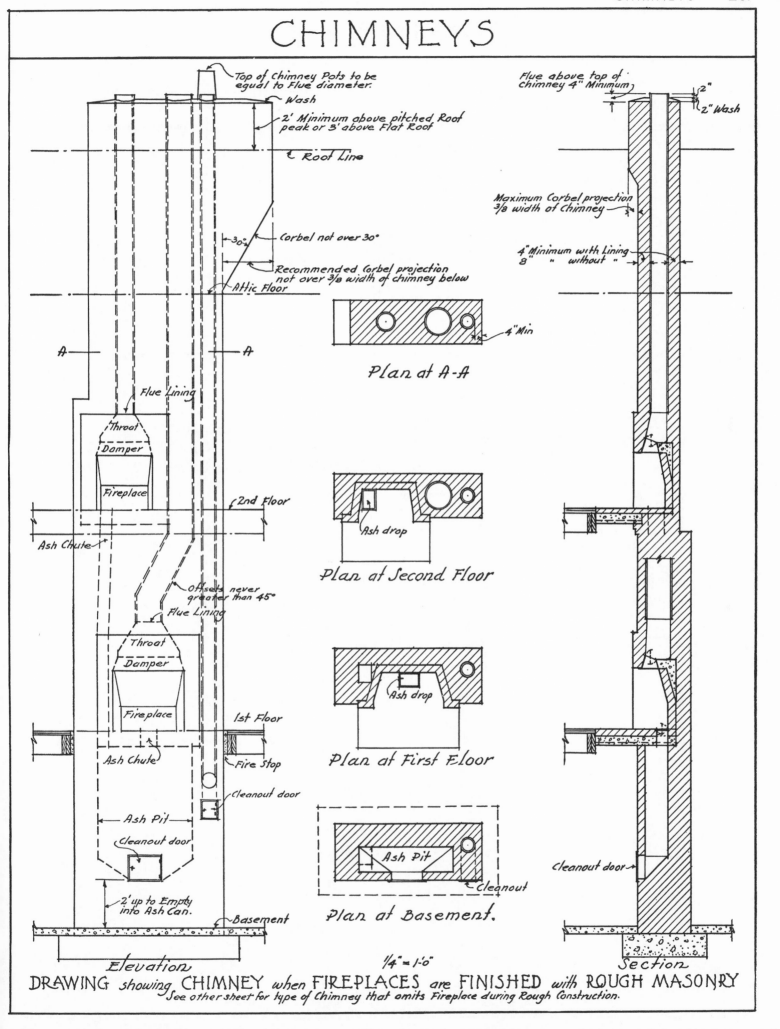

Top of Chimney Pots to be equal to Flue diameter.

Wash

2' Minimum above pitched Roof peak or 3' above Flat Roof

Roof Line

Corbel not over 30°

30°

Recommended Corbel projection not over ⅜ width of chimney below

Attic Floor

A — — A

Flue Lining

Throat

Damper

Fireplace

2nd Floor

Ash Chute

Offsets never greater than 45°

Flue Lining

Throat

Damper

Fireplace

1st Floor

Ash Chute

Fire Stop

Cleanout door

Ash Pit

Cleanout door

2' up to Empty into Ash Can.

Basement

Elevation

Flue above top of chimney 4" Minimum

2"

2" Wash

Maximum Corbel projection ⅜ width of Chimney

4" Minimum with Lining
8"   "   without "

Plan at A-A

4" Min

Ash drop

Plan at Second Floor

Ash drop

Plan at First Floor

Ash Pit

Cleanout

Plan at Basement.

Section

Cleanout door

¼" = 1'-0"

DRAWING showing CHIMNEY when FIREPLACES are FINISHED with ROUGH MASONRY

See other sheet for type of Chimney that omits Fireplace during Rough Construction.

CHIMNEYS

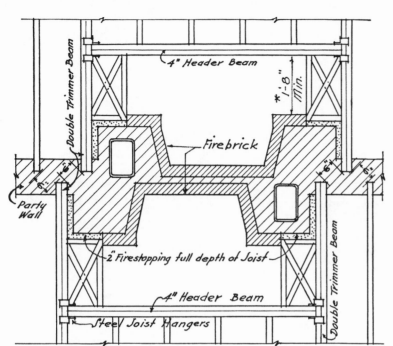

*FIREPLACES BACK TO BACK IN PARTY WALL
SHOWING SPACING BETWEEN JOISTS
3/8"=1'-0"

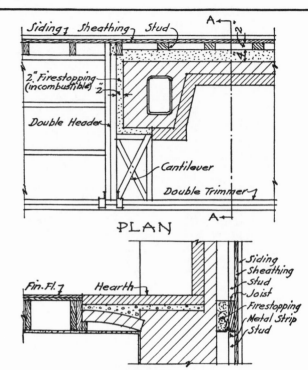

PLAN

SECTION A·A
**FIREPLACE IN EXTERIOR FRAME
WALL– BRICKWORK CONCEALED
3/8"=1'-0"

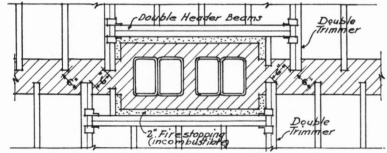

*CHIMNEY IN PARTY WALL SHOWING SPACING
BETWEEN JOISTS AND FIRESTOPPING
3/8"=1'-0"

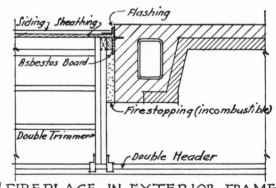

**FIREPLACE IN EXTERIOR FRAME
WALL – BRICKWORK EXPOSED.
3/8"=1'-0"

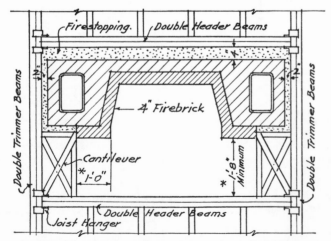

*FIREPLACE FRAMING & FIRESTOPPING
3/8"=1'-0"

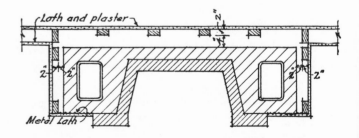

*FIREPLACE IN FRAME PARTITION
3/8"=1'-0"

CHIMNEYS & FIREPLACES *showing* FRAMING & FIRESTOPPING *in* WOOD CONSTᴺ

* Recommendations of the National Board of Fire Underwriters.
** Recommendations of National Lumber Manufacturers Association.

FLUES

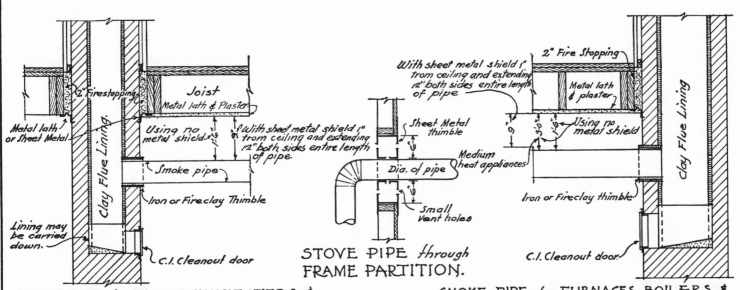

SMOKE PIPE for STOVES, H.W.HEATERS &
SMALL RANGES—CONNECTIONS & CLEARANCES.

STOVE PIPE *through*
FRAME PARTITION.

SMOKE PIPE *for* FURNACES, BOILERS &
LARGE RANGES—CONNECTIONS & CLEARANCES.

SMOKE PIPE CONNECTIONS and CLEARANCES

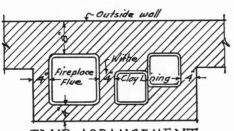

FLUE ARRANGEMENT,
OUTSIDE BRICK WALL

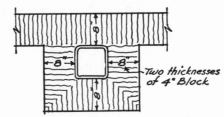

FLUE LINING IN OUTSIDE
HOLLOW TILE WALL.
*Not to be used except in
connection with HollowTile Wall.*

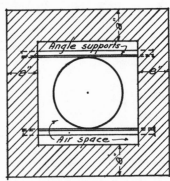

STEEL STACK
SURROUNDED *with* BRICK
Used for large Boilers

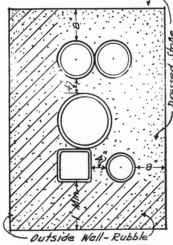

FLUE ARRANGEMENTS
IN STONE CHIMNEY

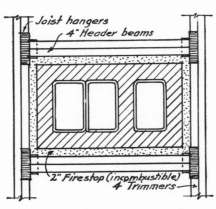

FRAMING (WOOD)
AROUND CHIMNEY

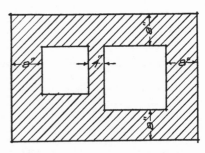

REQUIRED PROTECTION
AROUND UNLINED FLUES

Sheet copper– min. #24 U.S. ga.
Galv. iron– min. #20 U.S. ga.

*For runs directly thru
roof or ext. walls to outer
air. Clearances thru
combustible material
as for smoke pipe.*

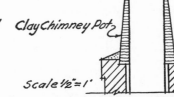

1" clearance from
combustible material.

Approved Type "B" vent

FLUE FROM GAS BURNING EQUIPMENT.
May be without masonry

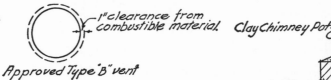

Clay Chimney Pot

Cement Wash

Scale ½"=1'

SETTING *of* CHIMNEY POT

Recommendations of the National Board of Fire Underwriters.

FLUES and CHIMNEYS

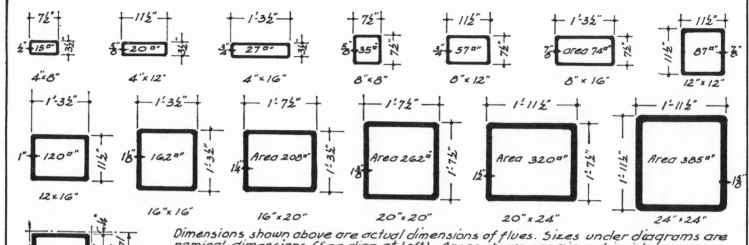

4"×8"   4"×12"   4"×16"   8"×8"   8"×12"   8"×16"   12"×12"

12×16"   16"×16"   16"×20"   20"×20"   20"×24"   24"×24"

Dimensions shown above are actual dimensions of flues. Sizes under diagrams are nominal dimensions. (See diag. at left). Areas shown are min. net inside areas. Wall thicknesses shown are min. req'd. Outside corner radius shall be no more than one-fourth the smallest distance between outside of walls. Modular rectangular flues are 2'-0" long. For proper flue size for fireplaces see page titled: "Modular Flue Sizes for Fireplaces."

MODULAR RECTANGULAR FLUE LININGS

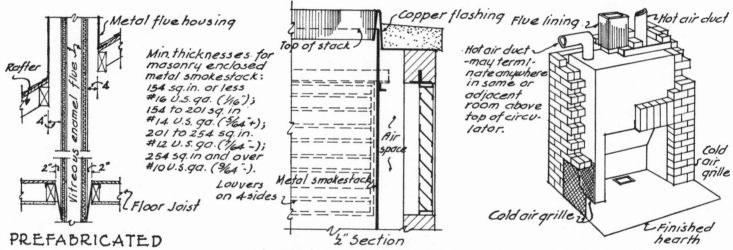

Min. thicknesses for masonry enclosed metal smokestack:
154 sq. in. or less #16 U.S. ga. (1/16");
154 to 201 sq. in. #14 U.S. ga. (5/64"+);
201 to 254 sq. in. #12 U.S. ga. (7/64"−);
254 sq. in. and over #10 U.S. ga. (9/64"−).

Louvers on 4 sides

Hot air duct may terminate anywhere in same or adjacent room above top of circulator.

PREFABRICATED "VITROLINER" FLUE

TOP of METAL SMOKESTACK with BRICK SURROUNDS

HEAT CIRCULATOR within FIREPLACE

Drawings below apply to reinforced conc., as well as to solid masonry.

Dwell'gs-4" other bldgs-8" For stone masonry 12" min.

Chimneys for stoves, cooking ranges, warm air, hot water & low pressure steam heating furnaces, low heat industrial appliances, portable type incinerators, fireplaces.

Chimneys for high pressure steam boilers, smoke houses, and other medium heat appliances other than incinerators. Continue fire-brick up 25' min.

Chimneys for cupolas, brass furnaces, porcelain baking kilns, and other high heat appliances.

For non-fuel fired incinerators where grate of combustion chamber does not exceed 9□'

For fuel & non-fuel fired incinerators where grate of combustion chamber exceeds 9□'. Continue fire brick up 30' above roof of combustion chamber for non-fuel; 40' for fuel.

For residence bldgs., institutional bldgs., churches, schools & restaurants.

LOW HEAT APPLIANCES — **MEDIUM HEAT APPLIANCES** — **HIGH HEAT APPLIANCES** — **CHIMNEYS for NON-PORTABLE INCINERATORS**

MINIMUM CHIMNEY REQUIREMENTS
Recommendations of the National Board of Fire Underwriters

FLUES – NON·MODULAR

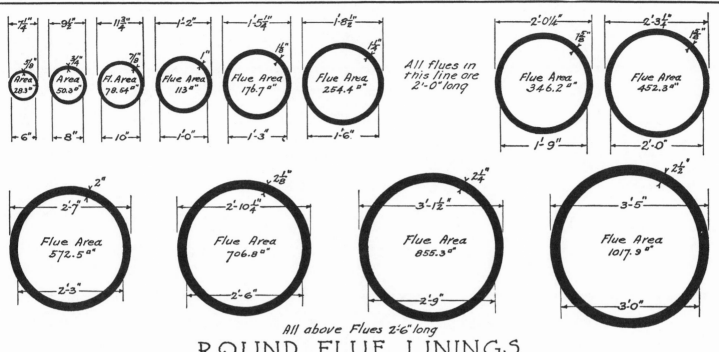

All flues in this line are 2'-0" long

All above Flues 2'-6" long

ROUND FLUE LININGS
Nominal Flue Sizes for Round Flues is interior diameter

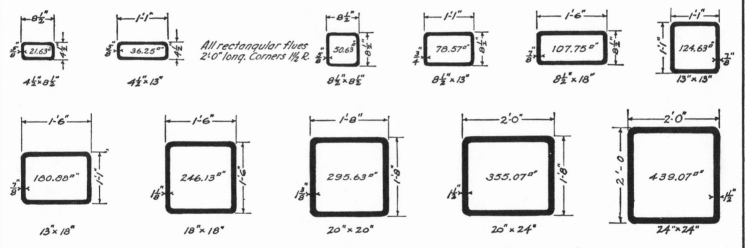

All rectangular flues 2'-0" long. Corners 1½ R.

RECTANGULAR FLUE LININGS
Nominal Flue size for Rectangular Flues is Exterior Dimension — Interior Areas only are shown.

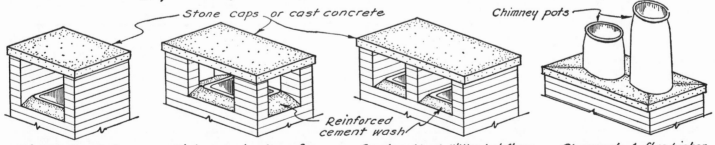

Stone caps or cast concrete

Chimney pots

Reinforced cement wash

Chimney hoods to prevent downdraft due to adjoining hills, buildings, trees, etc.

Water protection for seldom used flue.

Best method: Withe bet. flues

Cheapest: 1 flue higher

METHODS of PREVENTING SMOKE from ONE FLUE GOING DOWN an UNUSED FLUE

Open two sides of chimney hood must be larger than flue area.

CHIMNEY HOODS & POTS

Fireplace Flue Sizes:- 1/10 Area of Fireplace opening recommended. Absolute minimum size:- 1/12 area of Fireplace opening. Flues should never be less than 70 square inches inside area.
Flues for Stoves and Ranges and Room Heaters:- 39 Sq. In. minimum using Rectangular flue, or 6" dia. (inside) using Round Flue.
Flues for Gas Furnaces, Boilers and Automatic Water Heaters to be same size as for Coal.
Vents for other Gas fired equipment may be smaller, but should never be less than 10 square inches.

Fire Clay Flue Linings Standardized by National Clay Pipe Manufacturers Inc.

MODULAR FLUE SIZES *for* FIREPLACES

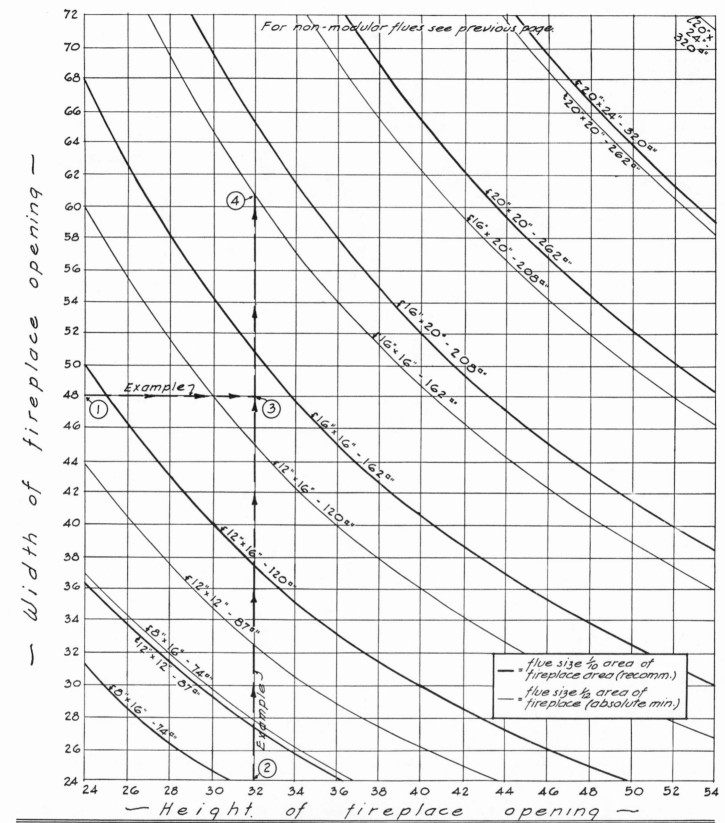

For non-modular flues see previous page.

~ Width of fireplace opening ~

~ Height of fireplace opening ~

Legend:
— = flue size 1/10 area of fireplace area (recomm.)
— = flue size 1/12 area of fireplace (absolute min.)

__Problem__ : Find proper modular flue size (@ 1/12 fireplace area) for fireplace 48" wide and 32" high.
__Solution__: ① Find 48" fireplace width at left of chart.
② Find 32" fireplace height at bottom of chart.
③ Follow width line across and height line up until they intersect.
④ Proper flue size will be nearest curve indicating 1/12 fireplace area above intersection (16"x 16").
Modular flues only made in rectangular sizes. If round flue is desired for modular chimney, use non-modular round flue.
Chart based on net flue areas. If flue is less than 20' high it is advisable to use next larger flue size
unless the intersection ③ falls well below the fireplace area curve.

NON-MODULAR FLUE SIZES for FIREPLACES

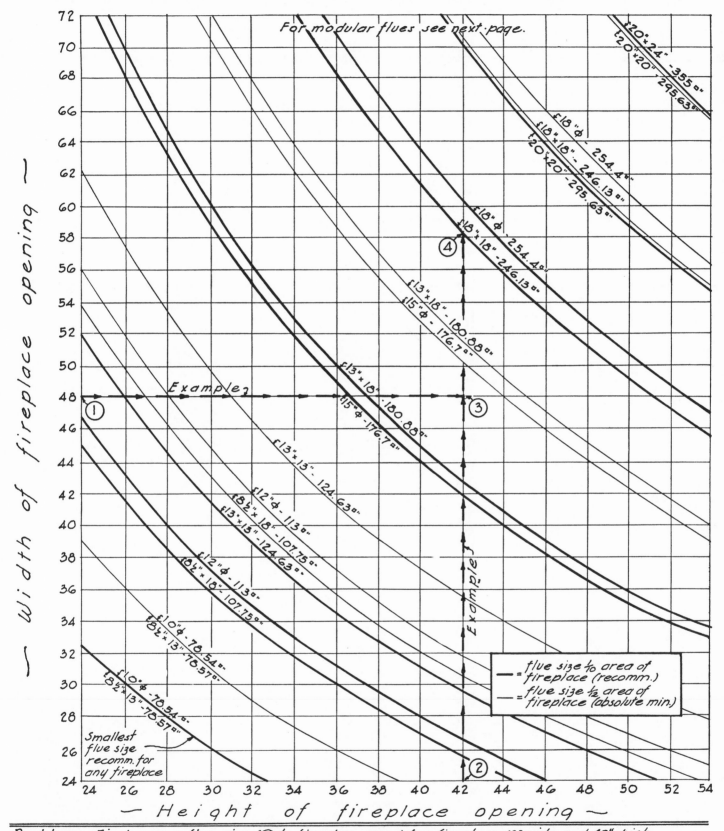

For modular flues see next page.

Width of fireplace opening ~

~ *Height of fireplace opening* ~

Legend:
— = flue size 1/10 area of fireplace (recomm.)
— = flue size 1/12 area of fireplace (absolute min.)

Smallest flue size recomm. for any fireplace

Problem: Find proper flue size (@ 1/10 fireplace area) for fireplace 48" wide and 42" high.

Solution:
① Find 48" fireplace width at left of chart.
② Find 42" fireplace height at bottom of chart.
③ Follow width line across and height line up until they intersect.
④ Proper flue size will be nearest curve indicating 1/10 fireplace area above intersection (18"x18").

For round flue, continue up from intersection ③ to nearest round flue curve for 1/10 fireplace area (18"∅).
Chart is based on net inside flue areas. If flue is less than 20' high, it is advisable to use next larger flue size unless the intersection falls well below the fireplace area curve.

ROUND FLUE LININGS

AREA (sq. in.)	A	T	LENGTH
26	6"	5/8"	2'-0"
47	8"	3/4"	2'-0"
74.5	10"	7/8"	2'-0"
108	12"	1"	2'-0"
171	15"	1 1/8"	2'-0"
240	18"	1 1/4"	2'-0"
298	20"	1 3/8"	2'-0"
433	24"	1 5/8"	2'-0"
551	27" *	2"	2'-6"
683	30" *	2 1/8"	2'-6"
829	33" *	2 1/4"	2'-6"
989.5	36" *	2 1/2"	2'-6"

* Not available in some localities

Areas shown are net inside areas.

Wall thicknesses shown are minimum required.

Nominal flue sizes for round flues is interior diameter, outside dimensions for non-modular rectangular flues. Nominal dimensions for modular flue linings are actual dimensions plus 1/2".

Verify with local manufacturers for available types and sizes of flue linings.

RECTANGULAR FLUE LININGS
STANDARD

AREA (sq. in.)	A	B	T
22	4 1/2"	8 1/2"	5/8"
36	4 1/2"	13"	5/8"
51	8 1/2"	8 1/2"	5/8"
79	8 1/2"	13"	3/4"
108	8 1/2"	18"	7/8"
125	13"	13"	7/8"
168	13"	18"	7/8"
232	18"	18"	1 1/8"
279	20"	20"	1 3/8"
338	20"	24"	1 1/2"
420	24"	24"	1 1/2"

All flue linings listed above are 2'-0" long.

Fireplace flue sizes: 1/10 area of fireplace opening recommended. 1/12 area is minimum.

Flue area should never be less than 70 sq. in. for fireplace of 840 sq. in. opening or smaller.

Flues for stoves and ranges and room heaters: 39 sq. in. minimum using rectangular flue, or 6" dia. (inside) using round flue.

RECTANGULAR FLUE LININGS
MODULAR

AREA (sq. in.)	A	B	T
15	4"	8"	1/2"
20	4"	12"	5/8"
27	4"	16"	3/4"
35	8"	8"	5/8"
57	8"	12"	3/4"
74	8"	16"	7/8"
87	12"	12"	7/8"
120	12"	16"	1"
162	16"	16"	1 1/8"
208	16"	20"	1 1/4"
262	20"	20"	1 3/8"
320	20"	24"	1 1/2"
385	24"	24"	1 5/8"

All flue linings listed above are 2'-0" long, also available, on request, in 12" lengths.

For proper flue sizes for fireplaces using modular flue linings see page titled: Modular Flue Sizes for Fireplaces.

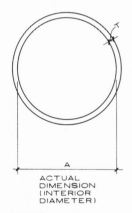

ACTUAL DIMENSION (INTERIOR DIAMETER)

ROUND

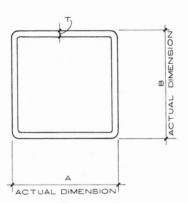

ACTUAL DIMENSION

STANDARD

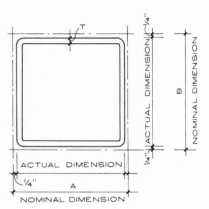

ACTUAL DIMENSION

NOMINAL DIMENSION

Cross section of flue lining shall fit within rectangle of dimension corresponding to nominal size.

MODULAR

CLAY FLUE LININGS

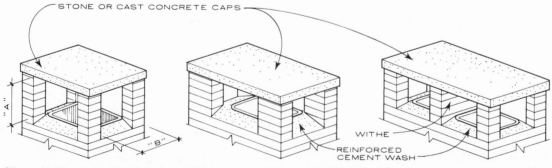
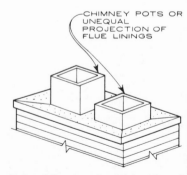

Chimney hoods to prevent downdraft due to adjoining hills, buildings, trees, etc.

"A" should be 1/4 greater than "B" in all hooded chimneys.

Chimney hoods also serve as water protection for seldom used flues.

Withe between flues is the best method of preventing downdraft.

Unequal projection of flues above the stack is a safeguard against smoke pouring out of one flue and down the other.

CHIMNEY HOODS & POTS

Robert B. Martin, AIA; Lincoln City, Oregon

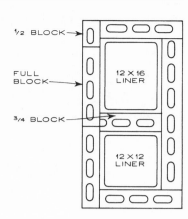

Recommended by the International Conference of Building Officials as required by the Uniform Building Code.

Internally mixed brick red color.

8 1/2" × 12 1/2"

1" SHELL

8 1/2" × 16 1/2"

12 1/2" × 12 1/2"

12 1/2" × 16 1/2"

11-5/8"

EXPANDED SHALE FLUE LININGS

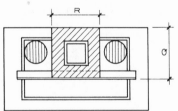

PLAN ABOVE HEATSAVER

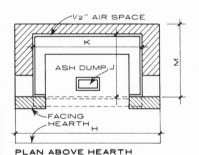

PLAN ABOVE HEARTH

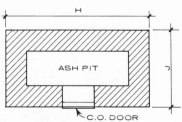

PLAN BELOW HEARTH

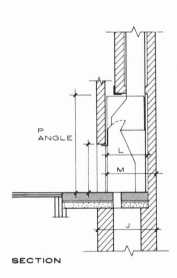

SECTION

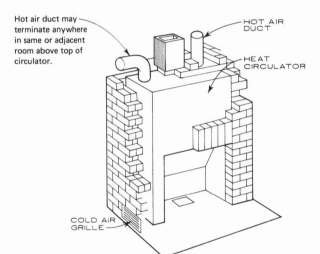

Hot air duct may terminate anywhere in same or adjacent room above top of circulator.

ROUGH MASONRY DIMENSIONS IN INCHES

NO.	H	J	K	L	M	N	P	STANDARD FLUE	MODULAR FLUE
28	52	32	36	24	28	26 2/3	56	13 x 13	12 x 12
32	56	32	40	24	28	26 2/3	56	13 x 13	12 x 12
36	60	32	44	24	28	26 2/3	56	13 x 13	12 x 12
40	72	32	56	24	28	29 1/3	66 2/3	13 x 13	12 x 16
48	80	32	64	24	28	29 1/3	66 2/3	13 x 13	12 x 16
60	92	36	76	28	32	32	80	13 x 18	16 x 20

NOTES : Figures given are nominal sizes to conform to modular dimensions. The thickness of facing will vary with material used. The wall back of the Heatsaver as shown is 4" thick. If this is an exterior wall it should be 8", and dimension M increased 4".

Q and R measurements can be determined by adding wall thickness to flue size dimensions. Since wall thickness can vary, Q and R are not given in the table. Minimum wall thickness is 4". On the 28" unit only, the R measurement cannot be more than 20", or the warm air opening through the casing, as shown on the drawing, will be distorted.

HEAT CIRCULATOR FIREPLACE

Robert B. Martin, AIA; Lincoln City, Oregon

SPECIAL FIREPLACES and DAMPERS

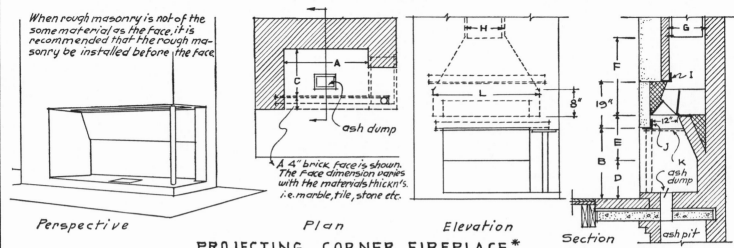

When rough masonry is not of the some material as the face, it is recommended that the rough masonry be installed before the face.

Perspective

A 4" brick face is shown. The face dimension varies with the materials thickn's. i.e. marble, tile, stone etc.

ash dump

Plan

Elevation

Section

ash pit

PROJECTING CORNER FIREPLACE *

| A | B | C | D | E | F | Non-Modular Flue | | Modular Flue Size | | L | Donley Damper | upper angle | lower angle | plate lintel | Corner Post |
						G	H	G	H			I	J	K	
32"	29"	16"	14"	20"	32"	13"	13"	12"	16"	40"	#532	42"	42"	11"x16"	29"
36"	29"	16"	14"	20"	32"	13"	18"	16"	16"	44"	#536	48"	48"	11"x16"	29"
40"	29"	16"	14"	20"	35"	13"	18"	16"	20"	48"	#540	54"	54"	11"x16"	29"
48"	32"	20"	14"	24"	40"	13"	18"	16"	20"	56"	#548	60"	60"	11"x16"	32"

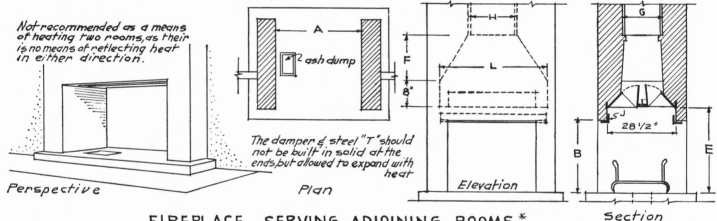

Not recommended as a means of heating two rooms, as their is no means of reflecting heat in either direction.

Perspective

ash dump

The damper & steel "T" should not be built in solid at the ends, but allowed to expand with heat

Plan

Elevation

Section

28½"

FIREPLACE SERVING ADJOINING ROOMS *

Width of Opening A	Ht. of Opening B	Damper Height E	Smoke Chamber F	Non-Modular Flue		Modular Flue Size		Angle J	L	Tee	Donley Damper
				G	H	G	H				
32"	29"	35"	21"	13"	18"	16"	16"	42"	40"	39"	#532
36"	29"	35"	21"	13"	18"	16"	20"	42"	44"	43"	#536
40"	29"	35"	27"	18"	18"	16"	20"	48"	48"	47"	#540
48"	32"	37"	32"	18"	18"	20"	20"	54"	56"	55"	#548

The above information obtained from "Book of Successful Fireplaces, How to Build Them", the Donley Bros. Co.

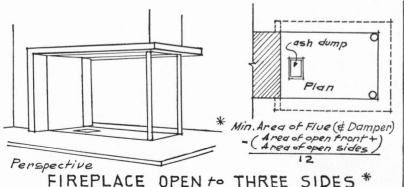

Perspective

ash dump

Plan

* Min. Area of Flue (& Damper) =

$$\frac{(\text{Area of open front} +)(\text{Area of open sides})}{12}$$

FIREPLACE OPEN to THREE SIDES *

| Max. Fin. Opening | | Max. Fin. Opening | | Max. Fin. Opening | |
Height	Width	Height	Width	Height	Width
25"	24"	24½"	24"	24"	26"
25"	30"	25½"	30"	28"	30"
26"	33"	25 7/8"	33"	28"	34"
29"	41"	27½"	36"	30"	42"
32"	47"	31 3/8"	42"	30"	48"
32"	59"	33"	48"	34"	54"
36"	71"	36"	60"	34"	60"
Heatform		Heatilator		Heatsaver	

PRE. FAB. STEEL UNIT FIREPLACES

These units, built in to the fireplace, provide additional heat by convection, via ducts & grilles, to spaces adjacent to fireplace. Consult manufacturer for details.

GENERAL NOTE :

Based on advice of the late Frederick N. Whitley, fireplace and chimney specialist.

The open floor plan makes useful multi-opening and free standing fireplaces. Design requirements for such fireplaces vary from those of conventional fireplaces. The following rules of thumb are given to aid in achieving proper function of these newer fireplaces.

Trouble factors encountered in the design for most fireplaces are:
1. Flue too small
2. Damper throat too narrow
3. Omission of smoke shelf
4. Smoke chamber inadequate in volume

Proper functioning of fireplaces is dependent not only on fireplace and flue design, but also on the following:

1. Height of flue and its projection above various types of roof.
2. Neighboring and adjoining conditions, such as terrain, trees and buildings.
3. Wind directions and climate

Certain cross draft conditions within a room may cause the following types of fireplace to smoke without regard to the design of chimney or fireplace.
1. Fireplace open front and side
2. Fireplace open front and back
3. Fireplace open three sides (one long and two short sides)
4. Fireplace open three sides (two long and one short side)
5. Fireplace open four sides.

Rules of thumb design data follow, below and to right:

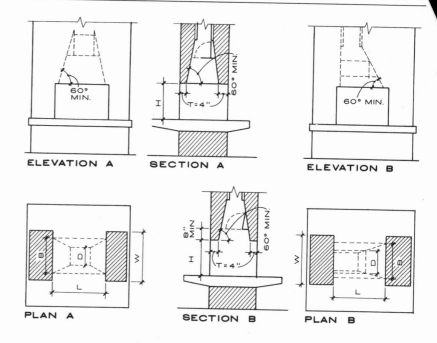

ELEVATION A   SECTION A   ELEVATION B

PLAN A   SECTION B   PLAN B

FIREPLACE OPEN FRONT AND BACK

H   height from top of hearth to bottom of facing

B   (depth of burning area) $5/6$ H minus 8", but never less than 24"

W   (width of fireplace) = B plus T plus T

D   (damper at bottom of flue, Section A) = free area of flue

D   (damper closer to fire, Section B) = twice free area of flue. Set damper a minimum 8" (preferably 12") from bottom of smoke chamber. Operatable part of damper when open should extend entire length of smoke chamber as shown.

FLUE : free area (i.e., inside dimensions of flue) = $1/2$ of H x (L plus W)

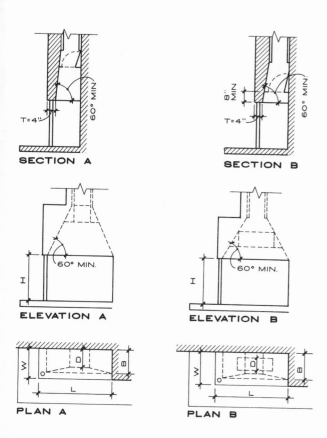

SECTION A   SECTION B

ELEVATION A   ELEVATION B

PLAN A   PLAN B

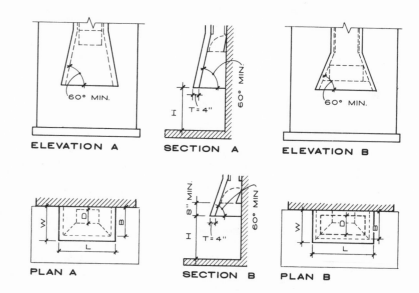

ELEVATION A   SECTION A   ELEVATION B

PLAN A   SECTION B   PLAN B

FIREPLACE OPEN FRONT AND SIDE

H   height from top of hearth to bottom of facing

B   (depth of burning area) $2/3$ H minus 4"

W   (width of fireplace) B plus T

D   (damper at bottom of flue, Section A) = free area of flue

D   (damper closer to fire, Section B) = twice the free area of the flue Set damper a minimum 8" (preferably 12") from bottom of smoke chamber as shown.

FLUE : free flue area = $1/2$ of H x (L + W)

Robert B. Martin, AIA; Lincoln City, Oregon

FIREPLACE OPEN THREE SIDES (ONE LONG AND TWO SHORT SIDES)

H   height from top of hearth to bottom of facing

B   (depth of burning area) = $2/3$ H minus 4"

W   (width of fireplace) = B plus T

D   (damper at bottom of flue, Section A) = free area of flue

D   (damper closer to fire, Section B) = twice free area of flue. Set damper a minimum 8" (preferably 12") from bottom of smoke chamber. Operatable part of damper when open should extend entire length of smoke chamber as shown.

FLUE : free area = $1/12$ of H x (L plus 2W)

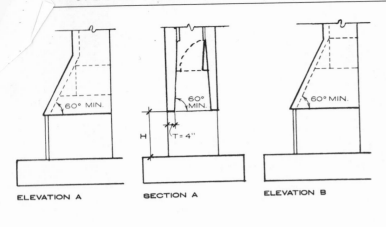

ELEVATION A SECTION A ELEVATION B

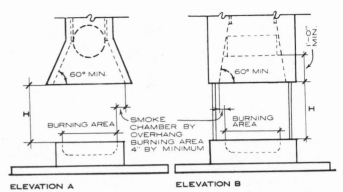

ELEVATION A ELEVATION B

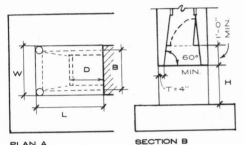

PLAN A SECTION B PLAN B

FIREPLACE OPEN THREE SIDES
(TWO LONG AND ONE SHORT SIDE)

1. H = height from top of hearth to bottom.
2. B (depth) of burning area) = $^5/_6$ H minus 8", but never less than 24".
3. W (width of fireplace) = B plus T plus T.
4. D (damper at bottom of flue, Sect. A) = free area of flue.
5. D (damper closer to fire, Sect. B) = twice free area of flue. Set damper a minimum of 12" from bottom of smoke chamber. Operatable part of damper when open should extend entire length of smoke chamber, as shown.
6. Flue: free area = $^1/_{12}$ of H x (2L plus W).

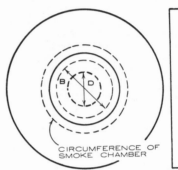

PLAN A PLAN B

FIREPLACE OPEN FOUR SIDES

1. H (height from top of hearth to bottom of facing) must never exceed the longest dimension of the burning area. It is recommended that H never exceed 28".
2. B (burning area, circular fireplace, Elev. A) = 32" minimum diameter.
3. B (burning area, square or rectangular fireplace) = 24" minimum dimension.
4. D (damper at bottom of flue, Elev. A) = area of flue.
5. D (damper closer to fire, Elev. B) = twice flue area. Set damper a minimum of 12" from bottom of smoke chamber. Operatable part of damper when open should extend entire length of smoke chamber, as shown.
6. Flue, circular fireplace: free area = $^1/_{12}$ of H x 3.14 x (B plus 8").
7. Flue, square or rectangular fireplace: free area = $^1/_{12}$ of H x (2L plus 2W).

GENERAL NOTES:

In addition to proper damper and flue size, the flue height and fresh air necessary to support combustion are factors which should not be overlooked in fireplace design. The following rules of thumb make allowance for these factors:

1. In a one story flat roofed building the flue should extend 8'–0" above the roof.
2. In a flat roofed building of two or more stories the flue should extend 6'–0" above the roof.
3. In a one story pitched roof building the flue should extend 4'–0" above the roof ridge.
4. In a pitched roof building of two stories or more the flue should extend 4'–0" above the roof ridge.
5. Fresh air to support combustion and proper draft is often supplied by crack leagage around doors and windows. It can also be supplied by leaving a space between the floor and the bottoms of doors in the room where the fireplace is located. However, in air-conditioned buildings, where cracks and crevices are weather-stripped and insulated, it is more of a problem to supply the proper quantity of fresh air. The following formulas indicate the quantities of fresh air necessary for the various fireplaces. Letters shown in formulas are on the diagrams for each fireplace.

Fireplace open front and side: cubic feet per minute of fresh air = (L plus W) x H x 60. Fireplace open front and back: c.f.m. fresh air = 2L x H x 60.

Fireplace open three sides (one long and two short sides): c.f.m. fresh air = (L plus 2W) x H x 60.

Fireplace open three sides (two long and one short side): c.f.m. fresh air = (2L plus W) x H x 60.

Fireplace open four sides:
Circular: c.f.m. fresh air = 3.14 x (B plus 8") x H x 60.

Square or rectangular: c.f.m. fresh air = (2L plus 2W) x H x 60.

NOTE:

Consult local building codes on all details of fireplace construction and chimney heights.

This and the following pages show examples of special fireplaces. Variations in design may be achieved by use of different dampers.
1. Low dampers with separate lintels and more elaborate masonry work. Two dampers often required.
2. High dampers with integral lintels and a minimum of masonry work.
Relative costs will vary with each condition.

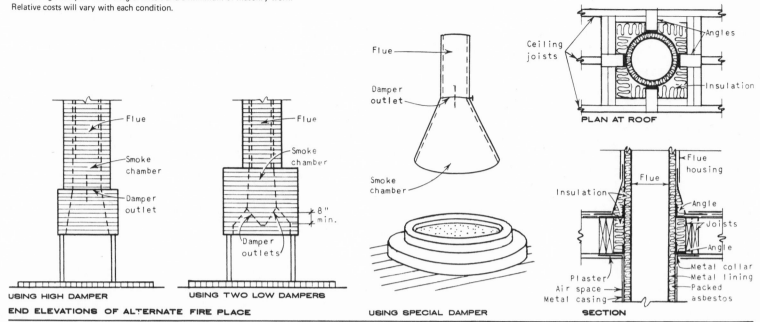

USING HIGH DAMPER **USING TWO LOW DAMPERS**
END ELEVATIONS OF ALTERNATE FIRE PLACE **USING SPECIAL DAMPER** **SECTION**

FIREPLACE OPEN FOUR SIDES

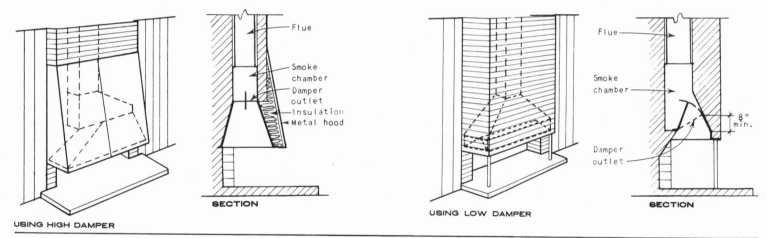

USING HIGH DAMPER **SECTION** **USING LOW DAMPER** **SECTION**

FIREPLACE OPEN THREE SIDES
(ONE LONG AND TWO SHORT SIDES)

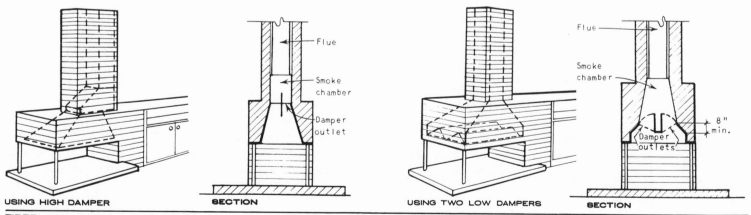

USING HIGH DAMPER **SECTION** **USING TWO LOW DAMPERS** **SECTION**

FIREPLACE OPEN THREE SIDES
(TWO LONG AND ONE SHORT SIDE)

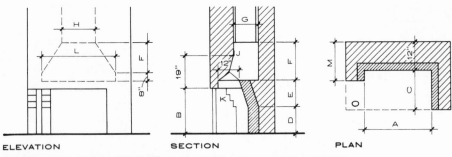

ELEVATION **SECTION** **PLAN**

NOTE:

Back flange of damper must be fully supported on masonry to protect from heat.

Do not build in solidly at ends; allow for expansion.

Facing allowed for 4"; this will vary with material used.

All dampers on this page: Donley Bros. Co.

LINTEL ANGLE SIZE FOR COLUMN "J" BELOW:

A: 3" x 3" x $^3/_{16}$"

B: 3 $^1/_2$" x 3" x $^1/_4$"

FIREPLACE OPEN FRONT AND SIDE (PROJECTING CORNER)

DAMPER NO.	A	B	C	D	E	F	OLD FLUE SIZE G	OLD FLUE SIZE H	NEW FLUE SIZE G	NEW FLUE SIZE H	L	M	ANGLE J (2 REQD)	PLATE LINTEL K	CORNER POST HEIGHT
528	28	26½	16	14	20	29⅓	13	13	12	12	36	16	A-36	11 X 16	26½
532	32	26½	16	14	20	32	13	13	12	16	40	16	A-42	11 X 16	26½
536	36	26½	16	14	20	35	13	13	12	16	44	16	A-48	11 X 16	26½
540	40	29	16	14	20	35	13	18	16	16	48	16	B-54	11 X 16	29
548	48	29	20	14	24	43	13	18	16	16	56	20	B-60	11 X 16	29
554	54	29	20	14	23	45	13	18	16	16	62	20	B-72	11 X 16	29
560	60	29	20	14	23	51	13	18	16	20	68	20	B-78	11 X 16	29

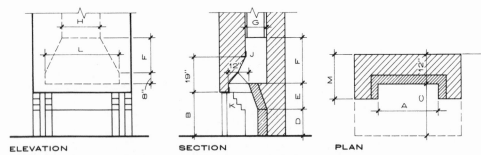

ELEVATION **SECTION** **PLAN**

NOTE:

Support back flange of damper on masonry. Do not build solidly at ends

LINTEL ANGLE SIZE FOR COLUMN "J" BELOW:

A: 3" x 3" x $^3/_{16}$"

B: 3 $^1/_2$" x 3" x $^1/_4$"

FIREPLACE OPEN THREE SIDES: (TWO SHORT, ONE LONG)

DAMPER NO.	A	B	C	D	E	F	OLD FLUE SIZE G	OLD FLUE SIZE H	NEW FLUE SIZE G	NEW FLUE SIZE H	L	M	ANGLE J (2 REQD.)	PL. LINTEL K (2 REQD.)	CORNER POST HT. (2 REQD.)
528	28	26½	20	14	18	27	13	13	12	16	36	20	A-42	11 X 16	26½
532	32	26½	20	14	18	32	13	13	16	16	40	20	A-48	11 X 16	26½
536	36	26½	20	14	18	32	13	18	16	16	44	20	A-48	11 X 16	26½
540	40	29	20	14	21	35	13	18	16	16	48	20	B-54	11 X 16	29
548	48	29	20	14	21	40	13	18	16	20	56	20	B-60	11 X 16	29
554	54	29	20	14	23	45	18	18	16	20	62	20	B-72	11 X 16	29
560	60	29	20	14	23	51	18	18	16	20	68	20	B-78	11 X 16	29

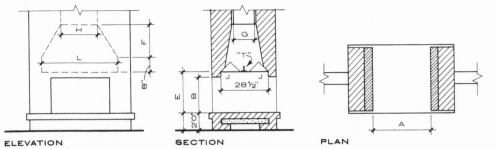

ELEVATION **SECTION** **PLAN**

NOTE:

Tee and damper not to be built in solidly at ends.

LINTEL ANGLE SIZE FOR COLUMN "J" BELOW:

A: 3" x 3" x $^3/_{16}$"

B: 3 $^1/_2$" x 3" x $^1/_4$"

FIREPLACE OPEN FRONT AND BACK (FIREPLACE OPEN THREE SIDES—ONE SHORT, TWO LONG—SIMILAR TO THIS)

DAMPER NO. (2 REQUIRED)	A	B	E	F	OLD FLUE SIZE G	OLD FLUE SIZE H	NEW FLUE SIZE G	NEW FLUE SIZE H	ANGLE J (2 REQUIRED)	L	TEE LENGTH
528	28	24	35	19	13	13	12	16	A-36	36	35
532	32	29	35	21	13	18	16	16	A-40	40	39
536	36	29	35	21	13	18	16	20	A-42	44	43
540	40	29	35	35	18	18	16	20	A-48	48	47
548	48	32	37	37	18	18	20	20	B-54	56	55

Robert B. Martin, AIA; Lincoln City, Oregon

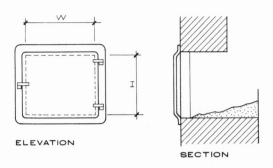

ELEVATION

SECTION

CLEANOUT OR ASHPIT DOORS

OPENING SIZES

W		H	W		H
4"	x	8"	12"	x	10"
5"	x	8"	12"	x	12"
8"	x	8"	12"	x	18"
8"	x	10"	18"	x	24"
10"	x	10"	24"	x	24"
12"	x	8"			

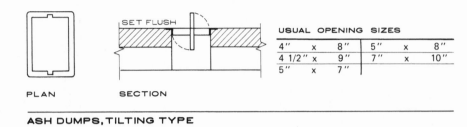

PLAN   SECTION

USUAL OPENING SIZES

4"	x	8"	5"	x	8"
4 1/2"	x	9"	7"	x	10"
5"	x	7"			

ASH DUMPS, TILTING TYPE

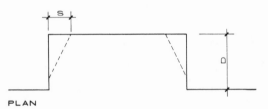

ELEVATION

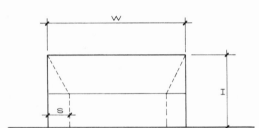

PLAN

FIREPLACE OPENING SIZES

W	H	D	S
2'-0"	1'-6" to 1'-9"	1'-4" to 1'-6"	
2'-6"	1'-9" to 1'-10 1/2"	1'-6" to 1'-7"	
2'-8"	1'-9" to 2'-0"	1'-6" to 1'-8"	
2'-10"	2'-0"	1'-8"	
3'-0"	2'-0"	1'-8"	6 1/2"
3'-4"	2'-0"	1'-8"	6 1/2"
3'-6"	2'-0"	1'-8"	6"
4'-0"	2'-1 1/2"	1'-9"	6"
4'-6"	2'-3" to 2'-6"	1'-10" to 2'-0"	9"
5'-0"	2'-6" to 2'-9"	2'-0" to 2'-2"	9"
6'-0"	2'-9" to 3'-0"	2'-2" to 2'-4"	9"

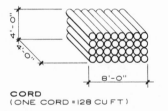

CORD
(ONE CORD = 128 CU FT)

LOGS

USUAL LOG LENGTHS

1'-4", 2'-0", 2'-6" and 4'-0"

TO SELECT LOGS:

Allow 3" minimum clearance between log and each side of fireplace. Smaller logs thus used with splay.

NOTE:

Larger openings than those shown may have hoods to lower openings or hobs to raise inner hearth.

Robert B. Martin, AIA; Lincoln City, Oregon

TOWER CLOCKS and BELLS

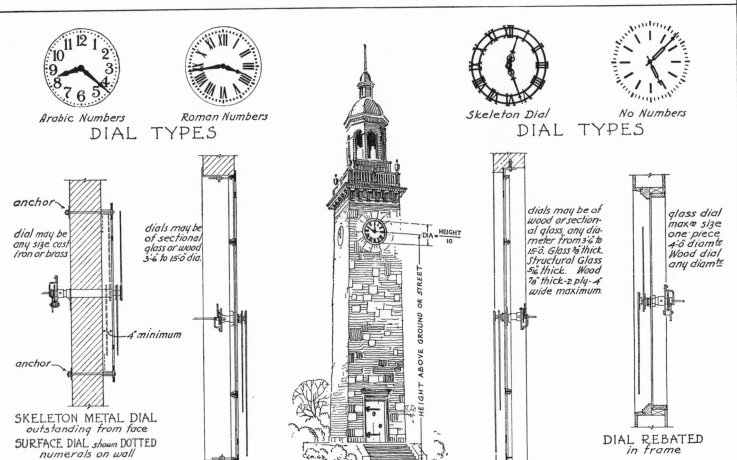

Arabic Numbers   **Roman Numbers**

DIAL TYPES

Skeleton Dial   **No Numbers**

DIAL TYPES

anchor

dial may be any size cast iron or brass

4" minimum

anchor

SKELETON METAL DIAL
outstanding from face
SURFACE DIAL shown **DOTTED**
numerals on wall

dials may be of sectional glass or wood 3'-6" to 15'-0" dia.

FLUSH DIAL
in masonry

SECTIONS thro' DIALS

HEIGHT ABOVE GROUND OR STREET

DIA = HEIGHT / 10

SIZE of CLOCK RELATIVE TO HEIGHT ABOVE GRADE
Standard dials made up to 15'-0" dia. and specials up to 50'-0".

dials may be of wood or sectional glass, any diameter from 3'-6" to 15'-0". Glass ⅜" thick. Structural Glass 5/16" thick. Wood ⅞" thick-2 ply-4" wide maximum.

DIAL REBATED
in masonry

glass dial maxᵐ size one piece 4'-0" diamᵗʳ. Wood dial any diamᵗʳ.

DIAL REBATED
in frame

SECTIONS thro' DIALS
Standard dials made in multiples of 6"

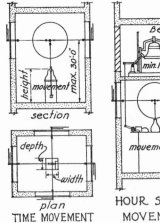

height   movement   max. 30'-0"

section

depth

width

plan

TIME MOVEMENT

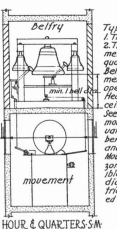

Belfry

min. 1 bell dia.

movement   max. 30'-0"

HOUR STRIKE MOVEMENT

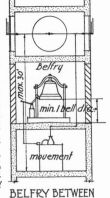

Belfry

min. 1 bell dia.

movement

HOUR & QUARTERS·S·M·

Types of clocks =
1. Time movement.
2. Time & strike movement. 3. Time-strike-&-quarter-strike movement Belfry. Place over movement if practical. Make openings max. size. Head of opening near ceiling & sill near floor. See Mfrs. Cat. for exact movement sizes, which vary according to number of dials, size of dials, and type of clock. Movements-Many horizontal locations possible; directly behind dial is preferable. Electric movement indicated & now largely used.

max. 30'

Belfry

min. 1 bell dia.

movement

BELFRY BETWEEN DIAL & MOVEMENT

movement height   movement

CLOCK OVER BELFRY

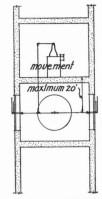

movement

maximum 20'

MOVEMENT ABOVE CLOCK

DIAGRAMMATIC ARRANGEMENTS and RECOMMENDATIONS – CLOCK TOWER ELEMENTS

CHURCH BELL DATA

Medium Tone	Weight lbs	Size Diameter	Size Height	Mounting Outside Frame	Mounting Dia. Wheel
D	400 lbs	2'-3"	1'-10"	3'-5" × 3'-8"	4'-4"
C sharp	450 lbs	2'-4"	2'-0"	3'-5" × 3'-8"	4'-4"
C	500 lbs	2'-5"	2'-0"	3'-5" × 3'-8"	4'-4"
B	600 lbs	2'-7"	2'-1"	3'-8" × 3'-11"	4'-9"
B flat	700 lbs	2'-9"	2'-3"	3'-11" × 4'-2"	4'-9"
B flat	800 lbs	2'-10"	2'-4"	3'-11" × 4'-2"	5'-6"
A	900 lbs	3'-0"	2'-5"	4'-2" × 4'-6"	5'-9"
A	1000 lbs	3'-1"	2'-7"	4'-2" × 4'-6"	5'-9"
A flat	1200 lbs	3'-3"	2'-9"	4'-8" × 4'-9"	6'-3"
G	1500 lbs	3'-6"	3'-0"	4'-10" × 4'-10"	6'-6"

CHURCH BELL DATA

Medium Tone	Weight lbs	Size Diameter	Size Height	Mounting Outside Frame	Mounting Dia. Wheel
F sharp	1800 lbs	3'-9"	3'-1"	5'-5" × 5'-7"	7'-0"
F	2000 lbs	3'-10"	3'-3"	5'-5" × 5'-7"	7'-0"
E	2500 lbs	4'-2"	3'-5"	5'-9" × 6'-0"	7'-0"
E flat	3000 lbs	4'-5"	3'-7"	6'-4" × 6'-8"	7'-8"
D	3500 lbs	4'-8"	3'-9"	6'-4" × 6'-8"	7'-8"
C sharp	4000 lbs	4'-10"	3'-11"	7'-4" × 7'-2"	8'-6"
C	4500 lbs	5'-1"	4'-1"	7'-4" × 7'-2"	8'-6"
C	5000 lbs	5'-3"	4'-2"	7'-4" × 7'-2"	8'-6"
B	6000 lbs	5'-7"	4'-5"	7'-4" × 7'-2"	8'-6"
B flat	7000 lbs	5'-9"	4'-8"	8'-11" × 9'-2"	9'-6"

10 CONVEYING SYSTEMS

PNEUMATIC TUBES

Pneumatic tube systems provide very rapid Transmission of small articles, paper and liquids in "carriers" to and from predetermined stations. Also any office paper which can be folded to a 5½" x 2⅜" size (see dwg. below) may act as its own carrier. One end of the folded paper is turned up, acting as a sail, and the air in the system carries the paper to its destination. The power may be either vacuum or pressure.

Tube size may be selected from 1½" to 3" x 12" and the system used will vary with the articles to be carried and the service demanded

Pneumatic tube systems have proved useful not only in long accepted uses such as in department stores, post offices, mills and hospitals, but in many industries, especially in product control, and in building types as listed below.

CARRIER

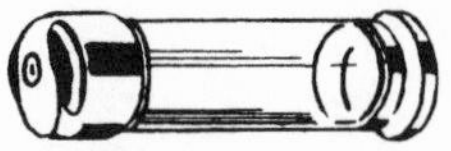

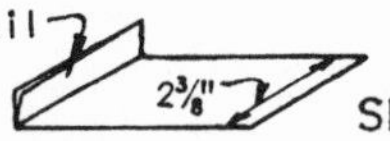

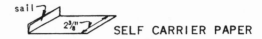

SELF CARRIER PAPER

INSTALLATION

Installation may be exposed in furred space, in floor slabs, outside of the building or underground.

Exposed lines and lines through refrigerated space must be protected to prevent condensation on the interior of the tube.

Underground tube should be placed below frost line in conduit and the interior of conduit and space around tubes filled with tar.

The minimum radius of the tubes as indicated on the following table must be considered in determining the location where tubes will be run as their minimum radii vary from 18" to 5'-0".

SELECTION OF SIZES

BUILDING TYPE	CARRIER INSIDE			TUBE	
	DIA., SIZE	LENGTH	CU. IN.	SIZE	RADII
Office	1 3/8"	6"	8.9	2¼"	18"
	1 7/16"	6½" 8½"			24" 36"
	1 3/8"	9" 10"	13.36 14.85		42" 48"
	7 15/16"	10" 12"	29.5 35.38	3"	48"
	1¾" x 4½"	12"		3" x 6"	48"
	10 11/16" x 2 11/16"	15"	430.83	3" x 12"	60"
Dept. Stores & Banks	1 3/8"	6" 9" 10"	8.9 13.36 14.85	2¼"	18" 42" 48"
	5 9/16" x 2 9/16"	12"	154.14	4" x 7"	48"
Railroad Yard install.	7 15/16"	12"	35.38	3"	48"
	2 11/16"	12"	68.0	4"	48"
	5 9/16" x 2 9/16"	12" 14"	154.14 179.83	4" x 7"	48" 60

BUILDING TYPE	CARRIER INSIDE			TUBE	
	DIA., SIZE	LENGTH	CU. IN.	SIZE	RADII
Telegraph & Post Office	1 3/8"	6"	8.9	2¼"	42"
	5 9/16" x 2 9/16"	12" 14"	154.14 179.83	4" x 7"	48" 60"
Mills	1 15/16"	10" 12"	29.5 35.38	3"	48" 48"
	2½"	5½"		4"	48"
M.F.G. Co.	10 11/16" x 2 11/16"	15"	430.83	3" x 12"	60"
Product Contr.	2 3/16"	7½"		4"	38"
Laboratory	1 15/16"	10" 12"	29.5 35.38	3"	48" 48"
	2 11/16"	12" 14"	68.0 69.0	4"	48" 60"
Hospitals	2 11/16"	12" 14"	68.0 69.0	4"	48" 60"
	5 9/16" x 2 9/16"	14"	179.83	4" x 7"	60"
Blue print	1 7/8"	24"		3"	60"

The table indicates that offices may use a variety of carrier sizes and the specific size selected will depend on the article to be transported. This applies also to mills and laboratories to a lesser degree, when the carrier size is determined the tube size is indicated as well as the minimum radius of a bend of the tube.

Data supplied by: Standard Conveyor Co. and Lamson Co.

3" x ½" tube for self carrier paper form is well adapted in Hospitals, Banks, Stock markets, Offices, Restaurants, Telegraph Exchange

The radius of the tube is 12" (flat bend) or 30" (edge bend)

Data supplied by: International Standard Trading Corporation

POWER UNITS TO PROVIDE AIR POWER (for vacuum or pressure type)

The air power to transmit the carriers may be generated by:

1. Turbo blower and exhauster (centrifugal type power units)
2. Positiverotary type.

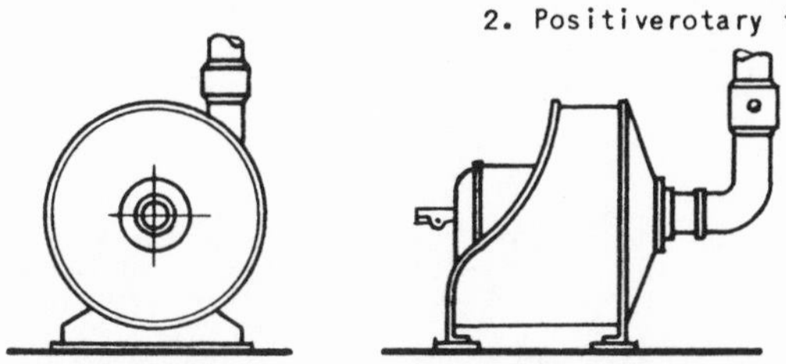

Front view Side view

1 - CENTRIFUGAL TYPE POWER UNIT

The centrifugal type power units are quiet, may be set in almost any location inside or outside and operates on suction or combination of suction and pressure. Are recommended generally except where extremely long lines are to be used.

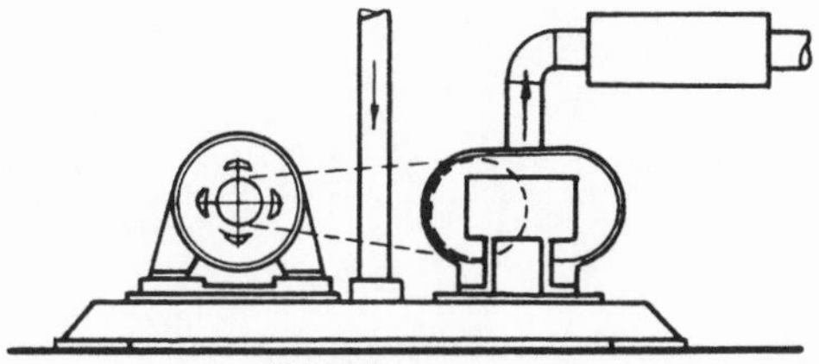

Side view

2 - POSITIVE TYPE POWER UNIT

The positive rotary type power unit operates equally well on pressure or suction or combinations of the two. This unit is recommended for use where long lines are to be used and reversible action is desirable. The unit may be located any place inside or outside.

Data supplied by: The Spencer Turbine Co.

GENERAL NOTES:

Pneumatic Tube Systems: Use of pneumatic tube systems, under vacuum or pressure, allows transmission of paper, small articles and liquids in "carrier" tubes to and from predetermined stations.

Applicable systems are commercial offices and stores; industrial plants, warehouses and air and rail stations;

banks; hospitals and laboratories. Care should be taken in the latter instances to exclude services in areas where centrifuge action in transmitted liquids is undesirable.

Installation of Systems: Systems can be placed anywhere in or about the area served, exposed or furred in structure, outside or underground. Lines exposed to weather or

through refrigerated spaces must be protected and insulated to prevent condensation in the system. Subsurface installations should be placed in corrugated pipe below the frost line, and tubing should be mill wrapped and joints welded and protected with mill wrap tape and pressure tested.

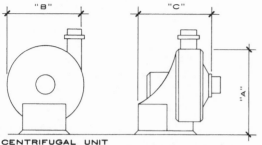

CENTRIFUGAL UNIT

CENTRIFUGAL EXHAUSTERS AND BLOWERS (This chart shows only extremes for each case.)

VACUUM	RPM	HP	A	B	C	VACUUM	RPM	HP	A	B	C
12 oz.	3500	1 min.	30	29	20	20 oz.	3500	1 1/2 min.	36	35	20
		5 max.	36	35	27			15 max.	46	41	42
	1750	7 1/2 min.	54	54	34		1750	7 1/2 min.	54	54	38
		50 max.	93	79	54			60 max.	80	67	60
16 oz.	3500	1 min.	30	29	20	24 oz.	3500	1 1/2 min.	36	35	22
		10 max.	42	42	31			25 max.	59	54	46
	1750	7 1/2 min.	54	54	30		1750	7 1/2 min.	54	54	36
		75 max.	92	80	60			75 max.	80	67	60

Used indoor or outside, centrifugal types operate on vacuum or vacuum and pressure combinations. Quieter than most types, they are recommended except where

long lines are to be used or where reversible action is required. Sizes vary with horsepower of motor, vacuum and r.p.m.

POWER UNITS FOR VACUUM OR PRESSURE

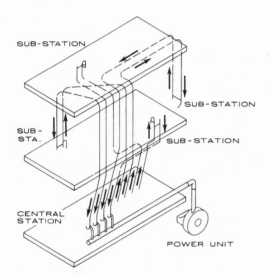

VACUUM TYPE
INDEPENDENT TWIN LINE

This system may dispatch carriers from all stations simultaneously with continuous, nearly unlimited transaction. It may have any number of stations since independent lines run to and from all stations. It is considered to be most efficient, low in maintenance cost, and is the quietest system.

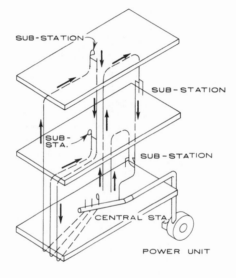

VACUUM TYPE
COMBINATION LINE

This system may dispatch carriers from the central station to all sub-stations via separate lines, but return lines are common. Where intermittent service is satisfactory, such as in mail order houses and industrial plants, this system may be used to advantage.

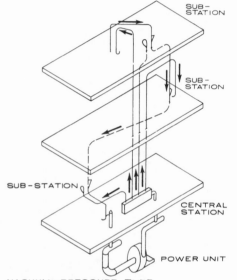

VACUUM-PRESSURE TYPE
COMBINATION LINE

This system utilizes both vacuum and pressure. It is economical of power and of length of return lines. It is necessary that the number of open ends be the same for the vacuum as for the pressure lines. Provides quick service. Its use is restricted to mercantile houses, drug, grocery and meat packing plants, and similar types of buildings.

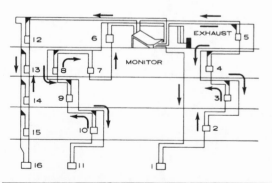

NOTE:

This system operates automatically once the carrier's adjustable ring is set for the proper destination. Within seconds electromechanical switching carries the carrier to the correct station. First, the carrier travels by vacuum to the central station where it is automatically tested to determine the correct line and station. This is done by relays and selectors which establish the path the carrier is to follow to reach its destination. If the carrier is set by mis-

take for a nonexistent station, it will be discharged into a "reject" tube at the central station. A signal light and bell will indicate an error. This system provides for quicker delivery with less chance of error. It yields economy of length of line. Typical buildings which might find this type suitable are hotels, airline terminals, railroad stations, hospitals, industry.

AUTOMATIC SELECTIVE SYSTEM

LWH; King and King; Syracuse, New York

CARRIER STATISTICS

SIZE	FIGURE	DESCRIPTION	BODY MATERIAL	CLEAR INSIDE LENGTH	CLEAR INSIDE DIMENSIONS	MINIMUM RADIUS BEND
1 1/2"	1	Message	Fiber	5 1/8"	15/16"	15"
	2	Cash	Brass	3 15/16"	1 5/8"	14"
	3	Telegram	Plastic	4 1/4"	1 3/8"	14"
	4	Message	Plastic	6"	1 3/8"	24"
2 1/4" O.D.	4	Message	Plastic	9"	1 3/8"	42"
	4	Message	Plastic	10"	1 3/8"	42"
	6	Utility	Rubber	6"	1 3/8"	24"
	6	Utility	Rubber	9"	1 3/8"	42"
	6	Utility	Rubber	10"	1 3/8"	42"
	5	Message	Plastic	9"	2"	30"
	5	Message	Plastic	10"	2"	48"
	5	Message	Plastic	11"	2"	48"
3" O.D.	6	Utility	Rubber	9"	1 15/16"	30"
	6	Utility	Rubber	10"	1 15/16"	48"
	6	Utility	Rubber	11"	1 15/16"	48"
	7	Test Piece	Steel	3 1/2"	2"	48"
	15	Message	Fiberglass	11"	1 3/4"	48"
	5	Message	Plastic	10"	2 3/4"	48"
	5	Message	Plastic	12"	2 3/4"	48"
	5	Message	Plastic	14"	2 3/4"	60"
	6	Message	Rubber	10"	2 11/16"	48"
	6	Message	Rubber	12"	2 11/16"	48"
4" O.D.	6	Message	Rubber	14"	2 11/16"	60"
	7	Test Piece	Steel	Varies	Varies	48"
	8	Punch Card	Alum.	Varies	3 3/8"	48"
	9	Blueprint	Alum.	42"	2 3/8"	SPCL.
	13	Bottle	Leather	Varies	Varies	48"
	16	Message	Plastic	12"	2 13/16"	48"
	16	Message	Plastic	12 1/2"	2 13/16"	60"
	17	X-ray	Plastic	14 1/2"	2"	48"
6" O.D.	11	Utility	Plastic	15 1/2"	4 5/8"	72"
	14	Message	Plastic	14 3/4"	4 1/2"	48"
4" x 7"	12	Message	Plastic	14 5/16"	2 9/16" x 5 9/16"	48"
	18	Message	Plastic	14 5/16"	2 1/2" x 5 9/16"	48"
4" x 12"	10	Utility	Alum.	15"	2 9/16" x 10 7/16"	60"
5" x 13"	10	Utility	Alum.	15 7/8"	3" x 11"	60"

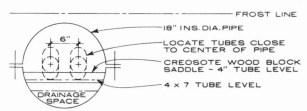

DETAIL OF PIPE BELOW GROUND

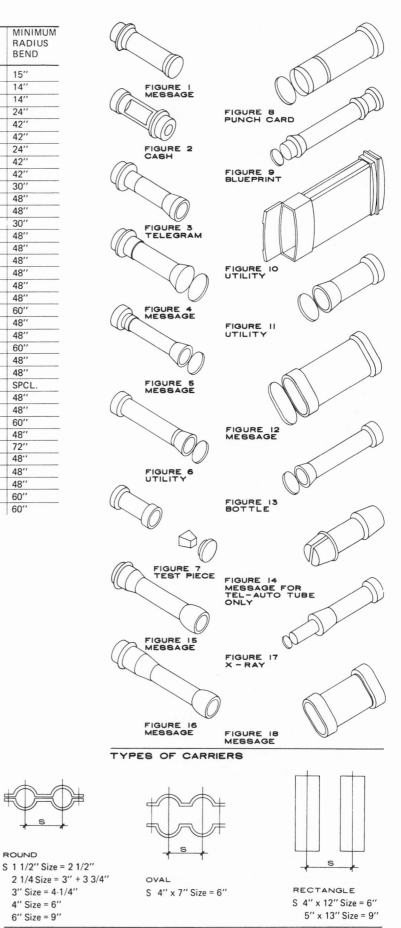

FIGURE 1 MESSAGE
FIGURE 2 CASH
FIGURE 3 TELEGRAM
FIGURE 4 MESSAGE
FIGURE 5 MESSAGE
FIGURE 6 UTILITY
FIGURE 7 TEST PIECE
FIGURE 8 PUNCH CARD
FIGURE 9 BLUEPRINT
FIGURE 10 UTILITY
FIGURE 11 UTILITY
FIGURE 12 MESSAGE
FIGURE 13 BOTTLE
FIGURE 14 MESSAGE FOR TEL-AUTO TUBE ONLY
FIGURE 15 MESSAGE
FIGURE 16 MESSAGE
FIGURE 17 X-RAY
FIGURE 18 MESSAGE

TYPES OF CARRIERS

TUBE STANDARDS

SIZE TUBE O.D.	MAT.L.	NET WGT. PER FOOT Lbs.	STAND LENGTH	WALL THICKNESS GA.	DIM.
1 1/2"	Steel	.55	15'-0"	20	.035"
2 1/4"	Steel	.85	15'-0"	20	.035"
3"	Steel	1.36	15'-0"	19	.042"
4"	Steel	2.75	15'-0"	16	.065"
6"	Steel	4.00	15'-0"	16	.065"
4" x 7"	Steel	4.54	15'-0"	16	.065"
4" x 12"	Steel	9.00	10'-0"	14	.078"
5" x 13"	Steel	13.15	10'-0"	12	.109"

LWH & RWL; King and King; Syracuse, New York

ROUND
S 1 1/2" Size = 2 1/2"
2 1/4 Size = 3" + 3 3/4"
3" Size = 4-1/4"
4" Size = 6"
6" Size = 9"

OVAL
S 4" x 7" Size = 6"

RECTANGLE
S 4" x 12" Size = 6"
5" x 13" Size = 9"

STANDARD TUBE SPACING

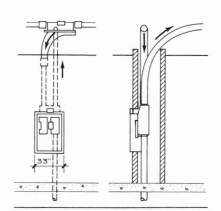

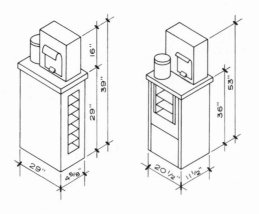

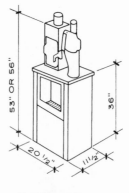

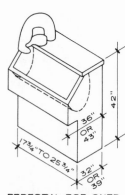

PEDESTAL FOR DOWN DISCHARGE CLOSED RECEIVER TERMINAL

PEDESTAL FOR OVER DELIVERY CARRIER RECEIVING STATION

DOWN DISCHARGE TERMINALS

GENERAL NOTES:

A carrier, placed in the sending side of the loop at any one of 16 sending-receiving stations shown at right, will be conveyed swiftly and directly to any one of the other 15. No human element enters to delay or impede the carrier's transit. An Automatic Monitor, in a matter of seconds, transfers the carrier to its correct receiving tube . . . then, an electrically controlled deflector in the receiving tube, delivers the carrier into its ordered station. Such a system has much to recommend it to any user. First, an Automatic System eliminates operating personnel at a Central Station. Not only does this automatic device speed carrier delivery but also permits 24 hour a day communications service, 7 days a week without supervision. Second, by grouping sending-receiving sub-stations along one or more twin-tube loops, 2 airtubes can service all 5 sub-stations as illustrated. The same 2 airtubes could service all 10 sub-stations if that maximum number were located on a given loop. This design effects a tangible saving in space, materials and labor. It also sharply reduces problems encountered when installing a system in existing structures.

PEDESTALS FOR 2¼" PNEUMATIC TERMINALS

Down Discharge Terminals can be recessed in walls with only dispatching and receiving doors exposed. Can be used for all automatic selective systems.

Pedestal for 2¼" Pneumatic terminals have steel cabinet bases with carrier storage under top. Sending inlet on opposite end.

Pedestals for Down Discharge closed receiver terminals for conventional or sutomatic systems are supplied with base units 20½" wide, 11½" deep, 36" to countertop and an overall height of 53" on 2¼" and 3" systems or an overall height of 56" on 4" systems.
conventional or automatic systems are supplied with base

Pedestal for Over delivery carrier receiving stations have belt sling type pocket sizes available for 2¼", 3" and 4" two station systems. 2¼" and 3" system pedestals are 18" wide and 36" deep; 4" system pedestals are 26" wide by 43" deep.

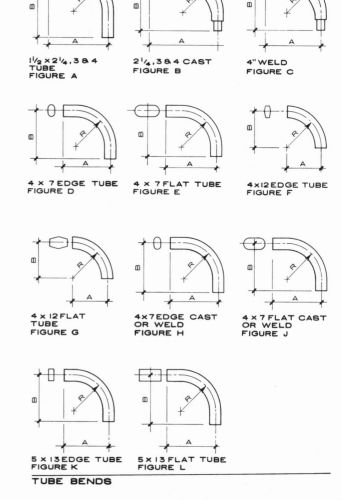

1½ x 2¼, 3 & 4 TUBE
FIGURE A

2¼, 3 & 4 CAST
FIGURE B

4" WELD
FIGURE C

4 x 7 EDGE TUBE
FIGURE D

4 x 7 FLAT TUBE
FIGURE E

4 x 12 EDGE TUBE
FIGURE F

4 x 12 FLAT TUBE
FIGURE G

4 x 7 EDGE CAST OR WELD
FIGURE H

4 x 7 FLAT CAST OR WELD
FIGURE J

5 x 13 EDGE TUBE
FIGURE K

5 x 13 FLAT TUBE
FIGURE L

TUBE BENDS

TUBE BENDS: CARRIER LENGTHS AND TYPES

SIZE		FIG.	12	A	B	MAT'L.	GA.	CARRIER LENGTH AND TYPE
1 1/2"		A	15	21	21	Steel	20	5 1/8" Type #1
2 1/4"		A	14	19	20	Steel	20	Varies, Types #2 and 3
		A	18	22	26	Steel	20	Varies, Types #2 and 3
		A	24	30	33	Steel	20	6" Type 4 and 6
		A	42	50	50	Steel	20	10" Type 4 and 6
		B	7 1/2	8 3/8	8 3/8	Cast		Varies, Types #2 and 3
		B	15	17 3/4	17 3/4	Cast		9" Type 4 and 6
3"		A	30	36	36	Steel	19	9" Type 5 and 6
		A	48	54	56	Steel	19	11" Type 5, 6 and 15
		B	24	28	28	Cast		11" Type 5, 6 and 15
4"		A	48	54	86	Steel	16	10" and 12" Types 5, 6, 13
		A	60	65	80	Steel	16	14" Type 5, 6, 13
		B	24	28	28	Cast		14" Type 5, 6, 8, 13 + 16
		C	23	32 1/2	32 1/2	Weld		14" Type 5, 6, 8, 13 + 16
6"		A	48			Steel	16	14 3/4" Type 14
		A	72			Steel	16	15 1/2" Type 11
4 X 7	Edge	D	60	72	74	Steel	16	14 5/16" Type 12 + 18
	Flat	E	60	72	74	Steel	16	14 5/16" Type 12 + 18
	Edge	H	24	29	29	Cast		14 5/16" Type 12 + 18
	Flat	J	24	29	29	Cast		14 5/16" Type 12 + 18
	Edge	H	24	32	32	Weld		14 5/16" Type 12 + 18
	Flat	J	24	32	32	Weld		14 5/16" Type 12 + 18
4 X 12	Edge	F	60	60	60	Steel	14	15" Type 10
	Flat	G	60	60	60	Steel	14	15" Type 10
5 X 13	Edge	K	60	66	66	Steel	12	15 7/8" Type 10
	Flat	L	60	66	66	Steel	12	15 7/8" Type 10

LWH; King and King; Syracuse, New York

11 ELECTRICAL

LIGHTNING PROTECTION

Following are based on:"Code for Protection against Lightning", Parts I & II - U.S. Department of Commerce National Bureau of Standards Handbook H 40; approved as A.S.A. Standard C-5.2-1937. also the same as National Fire Codes for Bldg. Const. & Equipment published by National Fire Protection Association 1944. If Underwriters Laboratories Master Label is required, include; "Install complete lightning protection system as required by the Underwriters Laboratories in accord with the Installation Requirements for a Master Label Lightning Protection System. Upon completion attach a Master's Label to Building."

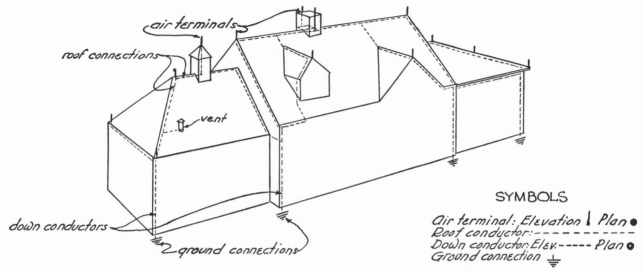

air terminals

roof connections

vent

down conductors

ground connections

SYMBOLS

Air terminal: Elevation | Plan ●
Roof conductor: ─ ─ ─ ─ ─
Down conductor: Elev. ----- Plan ◉
Ground connection ⏚

GENERAL LAYOUT *for* RESIDENTIAL BUILDING

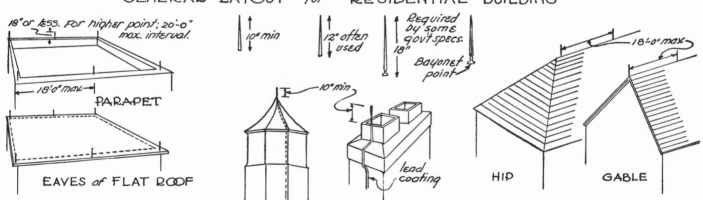

18" or less. For higher point; 20'-0" max. interval.

18'-0" max.

PARAPET

EAVES of FLAT ROOF

10" min

12" often used

Required by some gov't specs. 18"

Bayonet point

10" min

lead coating

18'-0" max.

HIP

GABLE

Height of air terminal above top of structure min 10" to max. 5'-0" for flat roofs. Air terminals required on decks, skylights, dormers, chimneys, vents, flagpoles, spires, steeples, towers, silos. Terminal must be within 2'-0" of object or corner. No terminals required for metal projections such as ventilator, stacks; but they shall be bonded to conductors.

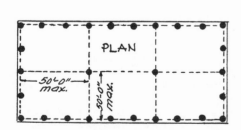

PLAN

50'-0" max.

50'-0" max.

LARGE FLAT or SLIGHTLY
SLOPING ROOFS
Divide surface into rectangles not exceeding 50'-0" in length or width.

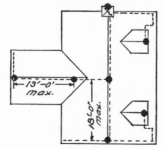

13'-0" max.

18'-0" max.

GABLE or HIP ROOF
with DORMERS and
CHIMNEY

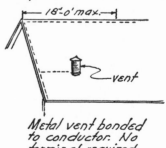

18'-0" max.

vent

Metal vent bonded to conductor. No terminal required.

Min. bend of conductor.

Roof conductors to form an enclosing network to join each air terminal to all the rest in system. For ground connections see next page.

For ground connections see next page.

AIR TERMINALS & ROOF CONDUCTORS

LIGHTNING PROTECTION

Symbol for down conductor ●

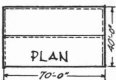

PLAN

Plan 110'-0" or less in perimeter; minimum of 2 down conductors. If over 110'-0" in perimeter, add 1 for each additional 50'-0" or fraction thereof.

perimeter 110'-0" or less.

Plan 300'-0" or less in perimeter; minimum of 2 down conductors. If over 300'-0" in perimeter add 1 for each additional 100'-0" or fraction thereof.

PLAN

perimeter 300'-0" or less.

PLAN

70'-0"
40'-0"

EXAMPLE
Perimeter 220'-0"
110'-0" perimeter; Two ●
220'-0"-110'-0" = 110'-0"
110/50 = 2+1 = Three ●
Total = Five ●

EXAMPLE
Perimeter 410'-0"
300'-0" perimeter; Two ●
410'-0"-300'-0" = 110'-0"
110/100 = 1+1 = Two ●
Total = Four ●

PLAN

60'-0"
125'-0"

GABLE, GAMBREL, or HIPPED ROOFS
Scale: 1/64" = 1'-0"

FLAT, FRENCH or SAW TOOTH ROOFS

DOWN CONDUCTORS
REQUIRED for SQUARE or RECTANGULAR SHAPED STRUCTURES

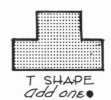

ELL SHAPE
Add one ●

T SHAPE
Add one ●

H SHAPE
Add two ●

WING TYPE
Add one ● per wing

In addition to the above requirements; On irregular shaped structures, the total number of down conductors shall be sufficient to make the average distance between them along the perimeter not greater than 100'-0".

EXTRA DOWN CONDUCTORS REQUIRED for IRREGULAR SHAPED STRUCTURES

PERSPECTIVE

80'-0"

If structure is over 60'-0" high; add one down conductor for each additional 60'-0" or fraction thereof, but not so as to cause down conductors placed about perimeter at intervals of less than 50'-0".

EXAMPLE
Flat roof; perimeter 340'-0"
By plan: 3 down conductors required. By elevation: 1 extra required because of height.
By plan: Three ●
By elevation: One ●
Total Four ●

70'-0"
100'-0"
PLAN

Extra down conductors are not required if distance between is less than 50'-0". This plan does not have conductors at less than 50'-0" intervals, so none can be omitted.

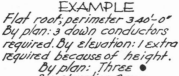

Dead end

This is required as an extra down conductor.

Over 16'-0"

Existing

Install extra down conductors wherever it becomes necessary to avoid dead ends, or branch conductors ending at air terminals, which exceed 16'-0" in length, except that single down conductors descending flagpoles, spires & similar structures which are adjuncts of buildings shall not be regarded as dead ends, but shall be treated as air terminals.

EXTRA DOWN CONDUCTORS
REQUIRED for STRUCTURES OVER 60'-0" HIGH

DEAD ENDS

Requirements for metal roofed or clad buildings, if sections are insulated from one another, are same as for buildings composed of non-conductive materials. When metal is continuous, terminals and conductors, if used, shall be bonded to it and grounded. Structures of steel frame or reinforced concrete construction need no protection if steel is connected and grounded.

LIGHTNING PROTECTION

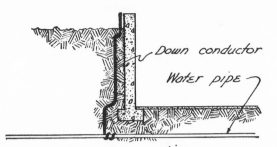

Ground connection
to metal water pipe.

GROUNDING to PIPE

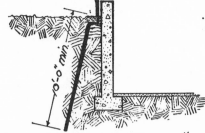

In moist clay or other soil
of similar character as to
electrical resistivity, extend
rod into soil not less than 10'-0".

GROUNDING to DEEP SOIL

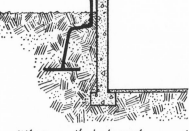

When soil is largely sand,
gravel, or stones, enlarge
electrodes by addition of
rods, strips, or plates.

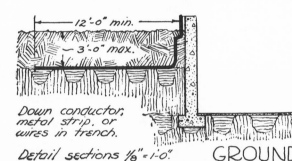

12'-0" min.

3'-0" max.

Down conductor,
metal strip, or
wires in trench.

Detail sections 1/8" = 1'-0".

Rock at least 1'-0" under grade.
Maximum required trench depth 3'-0".
Minimum 1'-0". If trench cannot
be dug over 1'-0" in depth (because of rock), encircle building
with a buried conductor and
connect to all down conductors.

Connection to down conduct.

GROUNDING to SHALLOW SOIL

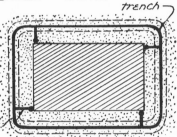

trench

Plan 1/32" = 1'-0".

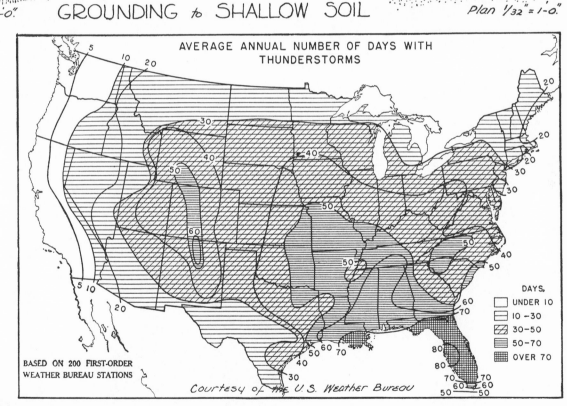

**AVERAGE ANNUAL NUMBER OF DAYS WITH
THUNDERSTORMS**

BASED ON 200 FIRST-ORDER
WEATHER BUREAU STATIONS

Courtesy of the U.S. Weather Bureau

DAYS.
☐ UNDER 10
▤ 10 - 30
▨ 30 - 50
▥ 50 - 70
▦ OVER 70

lead covering 25'-0"

uncovered conductor

6'-0"

guard

2'-0"

SMOKE STACK

Terminals on highest parts.
Main conductor down trunk.

Radial conductor in trench
1'-0" deep. Required: 3 for
every main conductor. Need
shallow network to prevent
damage to roots.

Encircling conductor.
Average 10'-0" to 25'-0".

TREE PROTECTION

Maximum protection; cone ABC. Minimum; ABD.
Vertical conductor assumed to divert strikes
which might fall in conical space. Cone of
influence is not a zone of complete protection

CONE of INFLUENCE

LIGHTNING PROTECTION

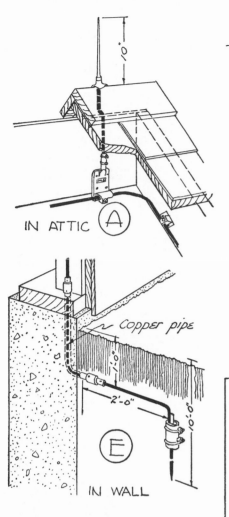

IN ATTIC (A)

IN WALL (E)

Copper pipe

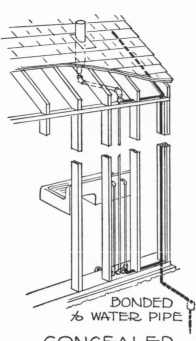

BONDED to WATER PIPE

CONCEALED TYPE
This type installed during construction.

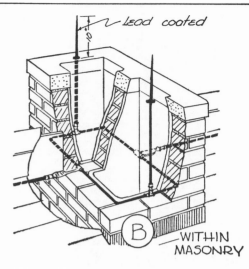

Lead coated

WITHIN MASONRY (B)

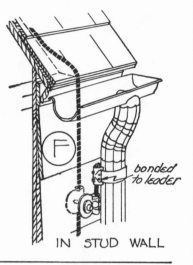

bonded to leader

IN STUD WALL (F)

KEY to DETAILS

UNDER EAVE (A)

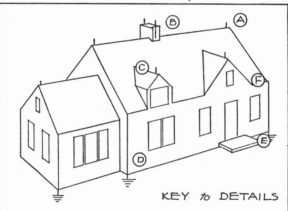

Lead coated

(B)

UNDER EAVE (C)

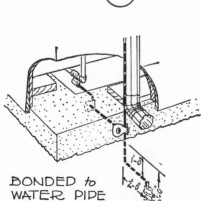

BONDED to WATER PIPE (D)

SEMI-CONCEALED TYPE

All details on this sheet are applicable to residential buildings. Heavy solid lines indicate lightning conductors exposed to view. Heavy dotted lines indicate lightning conductors hidden from view.

Courtesy of West Dodd Lightning Conductor Corp.

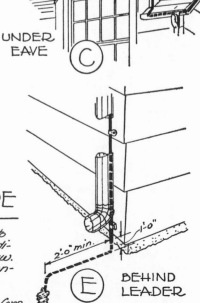

2-0" min.

BEHIND LEADER (E)

LIGHTNING PROTECTION

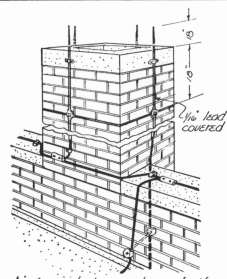

Air terminals & connections to the
top of coping conductor Terminals
must be within 2'-0" of each corner.
LARGE CHIMNEY

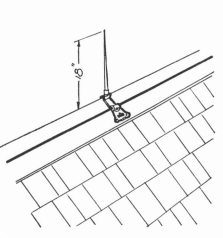

Air terminal and
ridge conductor.
ROOF RIDGE

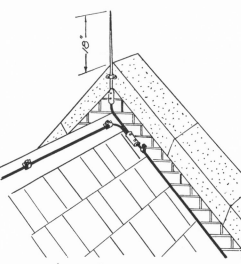

Air terminal & connections
to the roof conductor.
STONE GABLE

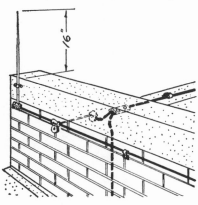

conductor from
air terminal.
BELOW COPING

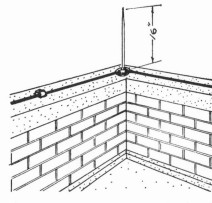

Conductor with corner air terminal.
Terminals must be within 2'-0" of corner.
TOP of COPING

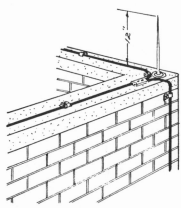

Conductor with corner air
terminal & down conductor.
TOP of COPING

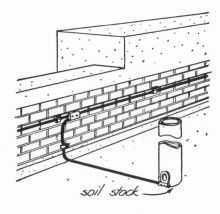

soil stack

Parapet & conductor to soil stack.
BOND from INSIDE

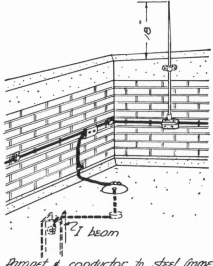

I beam

Parapet & conductor to steel frame.
BOND from INSIDE

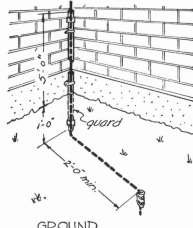

guard

GROUND
CONNECTION

EXPOSED TYPE

Details on this sheet are mainly applicable to commercial bld'gs.
Heavy solid lines indicate lightning conductors exposed to view.
Heavy dotted lines indicate lightning conductors hidden from view.

Courtesy of West Dodd Lightning Conductor Corp.

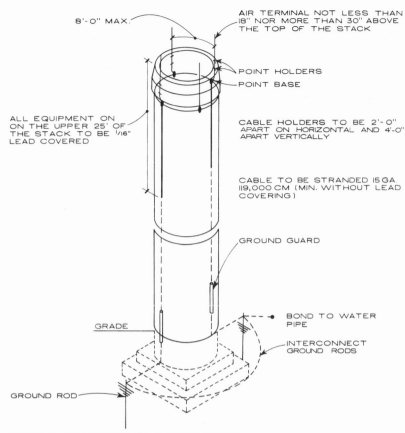

8'-0" MAX.

AIR TERMINAL NOT LESS THAN 18" NOR MORE THAN 30" ABOVE THE TOP OF THE STACK

POINT HOLDERS

POINT BASE

ALL EQUIPMENT ON ON THE UPPER 25' OF THE STACK TO BE 1/16" LEAD COVERED

CABLE HOLDERS TO BE 2'-0" APART ON HORIZONTAL AND 4'-0" APART VERTICALLY

CABLE TO BE STRANDED 15 GA. 119,000 CM (MIN. WITHOUT LEAD COVERING)

GROUND GUARD

GRADE

BOND TO WATER PIPE

INTERCONNECT GROUND RODS

GROUND ROD

TYPICAL SMOKESTACK INSTALLATION

If stack is partly or entirely of reinforced concrete, reinforcing shall be made electrically continuous and bonded to system top and bottom.

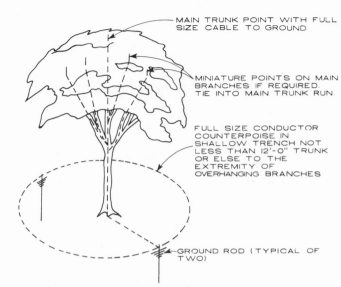

MAIN TRUNK POINT WITH FULL SIZE CABLE TO GROUND

MINIATURE POINTS ON MAIN BRANCHES IF REQUIRED. TIE INTO MAIN TRUNK RUN.

FULL SIZE CONDUCTOR COUNTERPOISE IN SHALLOW TRENCH NOT LESS THAN 12'-0" TRUNK OR ELSE TO THE EXTREMITY OF OVERHANGING BRANCHES

GROUND ROD (TYPICAL OF TWO)

TYPICAL TREE INSTALLATION

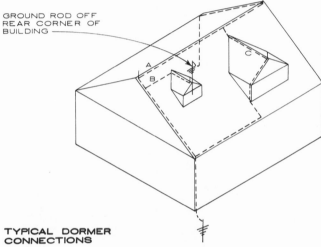

GROUND ROD OFF REAR CORNER OF BUILDING

TYPICAL DORMER CONNECTIONS

A. No dead ends on main ridge or dormers as high or higher than main ridge.

B. Total conductor less than 16' –0'' (dead end allowable).

C. Conductor exceeds 16' thus requiring continuation to ground.

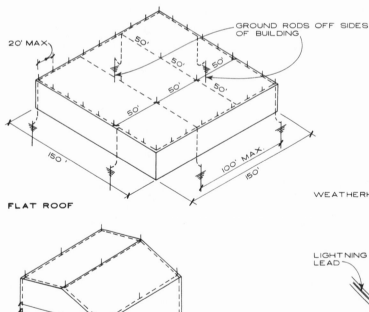

GROUND RODS OFF SIDES OF BUILDING

20' MAX.

50' 50' 50' 50' 50' 50' 50'

150'   100' MAX.   150'

FLAT ROOF

PITCHED ROOF

TYPICAL AIR TERMINAL & CONDUCTOR LAYOUTS

A = 40' or less and 1/8 pitch or less.
B = more than 40' and 1/4 pitch or less.

R. W. Lindquist; Thompson Lightning Protection; St. Paul, Minnesota

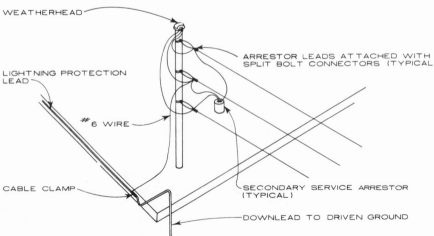

WEATHERHEAD

ARRESTOR LEADS ATTACHED WITH SPLIT BOLT CONNECTORS (TYPICAL)

LIGHTNING PROTECTION LEAD

#6 WIRE

CABLE CLAMP

SECONDARY SERVICE ARRESTOR (TYPICAL)

DOWNLEAD TO DRIVEN GROUND

TYPICAL SECONDARY ELECTRICAL SERVICE ARRESTOR

12 ENERGY AND ENVIRONMENTAL DESIGN

ORIENTATION

Altitude of Sun ~ June ~

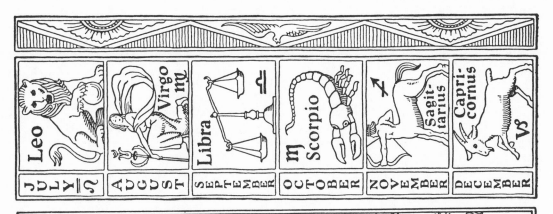

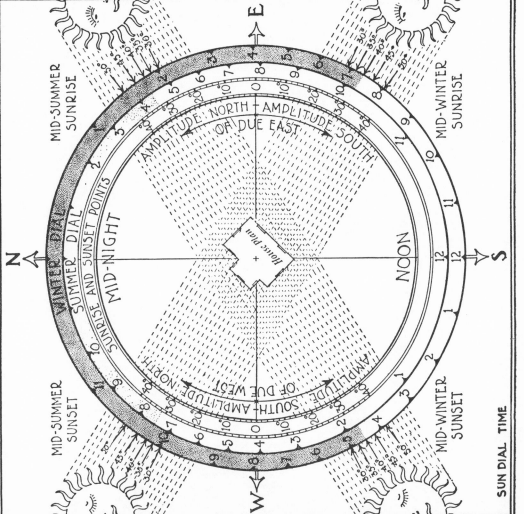

Orientation Chart

Directions for use

Pin cut-out of small scale plan at center and revolve same until sun strikes at desired angles.
Outer dial indicates Midwinter and black indicates darkness.
Second dial indicates Summer and grey indicates darkness.
Third dial shows degrees North and South of due East and West, for locating rising and setting sun.
Degree markings at end of arrows pointing to outer perimeter indicate corrections for latitudes other than 40° of North latitude for which chart is made; this is line through Philadelphia, Denver and Reno.

Courtesy of House Beautiful and American Face Brick Association.

Altitude of Sun ~ December ~

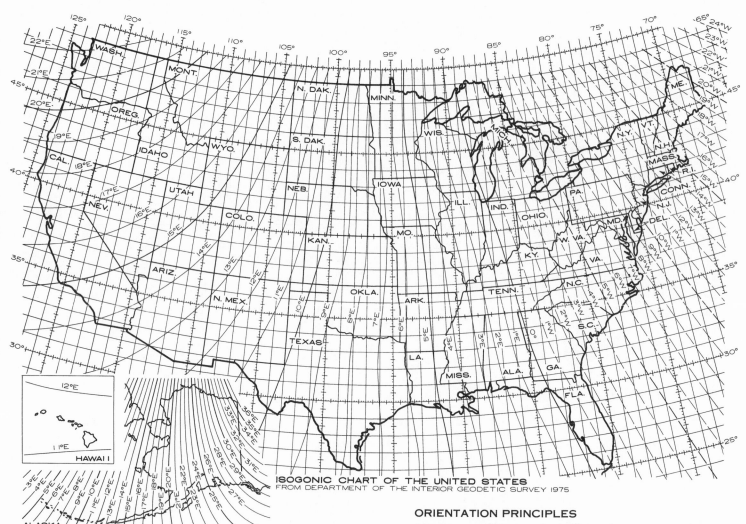

ISOGONIC CHART OF THE UNITED STATES
FROM DEPARTMENT OF THE INTERIOR GEODETIC SURVEY 1975

COMPASS ORIENTATION

The above map is the isogonic chart of the United States. The wavy lines from top to bottom show the compass variations from the true north. At the lines marked E the compass will point east of true north; at those marked W the compass will point west of true north. According to the location, correction should be done from the compass north to find the true north.

EXAMPLE: On a site in Wichita, Kansas, find the true north.

STEP 1.   Find the compass orientation on the site.

STEP 2.   Locate Wichita on the map. The nearest compass variation is the 10°E line.

STEP 3.   Adjust the orientation correction to true north.
The graphical example illustrates a building which lies 25° east with its axis from the compass orientation.

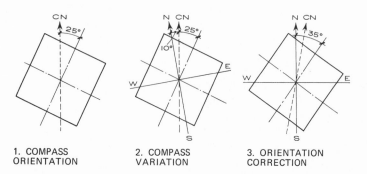

1. COMPASS ORIENTATION   2. COMPASS VARIATION   3. ORIENTATION CORRECTION

Victor Olgyay, AIA; Associate Professor; School of Architecture, Princeton University; Princeton, New Jersey

ORIENTATION PRINCIPLES

Orientation in architecture encompasses a large segment of different considerations. The expression "total orientation" refers both to the physiological and psychological aspects of the problem.

At the physiological side the factors which affect our senses and have to be taken into consideration are: the thermal impacts—the sun, wind, and temperature effects acting through our skin envelope; the visible impacts—the different illumination and brightness levels affecting our visual senses; the sonic aspects—the noise impacts and noise levels of the surroundings influencing our hearing organs. In addition, our respiratory organs are affected by the smoke, smell, and dust of the environs.

On the psychological side, the view and the privacy are aspects in orientation which quite often override the physical considerations.

Above all, as a building is only a mosaic unit in the pattern of a town organization, the spatial effects, the social intimacy, and its relation to the urban representative directions—aesthetic, political, or social—all play a part in positioning a building.

THERMAL FORCES INFLUENCING ORIENTATION

The climatic factors such as wind, solar radiation, and air temperature play the most eminent role in orientation. The position of a structure in northern latitudes, where the air temperature is generally cool, should be oriented to receive the maximum amount of sunshine without wind exposure. In southerly latitudes, however, the opposite will be desirable; the building should be turned on its axis to avoid the sun's unwanted radiation and to face the cooling breezes instead.

At right the figure shows these regional requirements diagrammatically.

Adaptation for wind orientation is not of great importance in low buildings, where the use of windbreaks and the arrangement of openings in the high and low pressure areas can help to ameliorate the airflow situation. However, for high buildings, where the surrounding terrain has little effect on the upper stories, careful consideration has to be given to wind orientation.

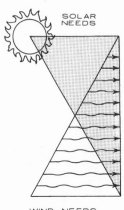

SOLAR NEEDS

WIND NEEDS

NOTES

To visualize the thermal impacts on differently exposed surfaces four locations are shown approximately at the 24°, 32°, 40° and 44° latitudes. The forces are indicated on average clear winter and summer days. The air temperature variation is indicated by the outside concentric circles. Each additional line represents a 2°F difference from the lowest daily temperature. The direction of the impact is indicated according to the sun's direction as temperatures occur. (Note the low temperatures at the east side, and the high ones in westerly directions.)

The total (direct and diffuse) radiation impact on the various sides of the building is indicated with arrows. Each arrow represents 250 Btu/sq ft · day radiation. At the bottom of the page the radiations are expressed in numerical values.

The values show that in the upper latitudes the south side of a building receives nearly twice as much radiation in winter as in summer. This effect is even more pronounced at the lower latitudes, where the ratio is about one to four. Also, in the upper latitudes, the east and west sides receive about 2½ times more radiation in summer than in winter. This ratio is not as large in the lower latitudes; but it is noteworthy that in summer these sides receive two to three times as much radiation as the south elevation. In the summer the west exposure is more disadvantageous than the east exposure, as the afternoon high temperatures combine with the radiation effects. In all latitudes the north side receives only a small amount of radiation, and this comes mainly in the summer. In the low latitudes, in the summer, the north side receives nearly twice the impact of the south side. The amount of radiation received on a horizontal roof surface exceeds all other sides.

Experimental observations were conducted on the thermal behavior of building orientation at Princeton University's Architectural Laboratory. Below are shown the summer results of structures exposed to the cardinal directions. Note the unequal heat distribution and high heat impact of the west exposure compared to the east orientation. The southern direction gives a pleasantly low heat volume, slightly higher, however, than the north exposure.

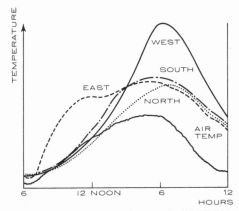

ROOM TEMPERATURE IN DIFFERENTLY ORIENTED HOUSES

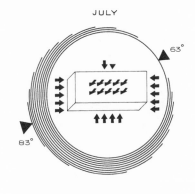

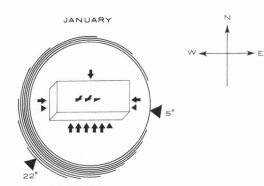

JANUARY   JULY

MINNEAPOLIS, MINN.

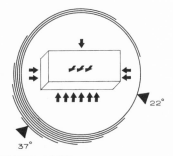
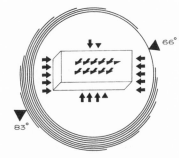

NEW YORK AREA

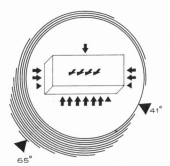
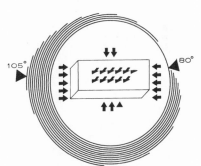

PHOENIX, ARIZ.

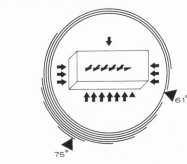
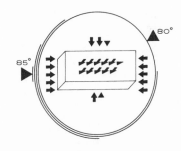

MIAMI, FLA.

ORIENTATION: CONCLUSIONS

1. The optimum orientation will lie near the south; however, will differ in the various regions, and will depend on the daily temperature distribution.
2. In all regions an orientation eastward from south gives a better yearly performance and a more equal daily heat distribution. Westerly directions perform more poorly with unbalanced heat impacts.
3. The thermal orientation exposure has to be correlated with the local wind directions.

Victor Olgyay, AIA; Associate Professor; School of Architecture, Princeton University; Princeton, New Jersey

TOTAL DIRECT AND DIFFUSED RADIATION (BTU/SQ FT · DAY)

LATITUDE	SEASON	EAST	SOUTH	WEST	NORTH	HORIZONTAL
44° LATITUDE	WINTER	416	1374	416	83	654
	SUMMER	1314	979	1314	432	2536
40° LATITUDE	WINTER	517	1489	517	119	787
	SUMMER	1277	839	1277	430	2619
32° LATITUDE	WINTER	620	1606	620	140	954
	SUMMER	1207	563	1207	452	2596
24° LATITUDE	WINTER	734	1620	734	152	1414
	SUMMER	1193	344	1193	616	2568

UNIVERSAL SUN CHART

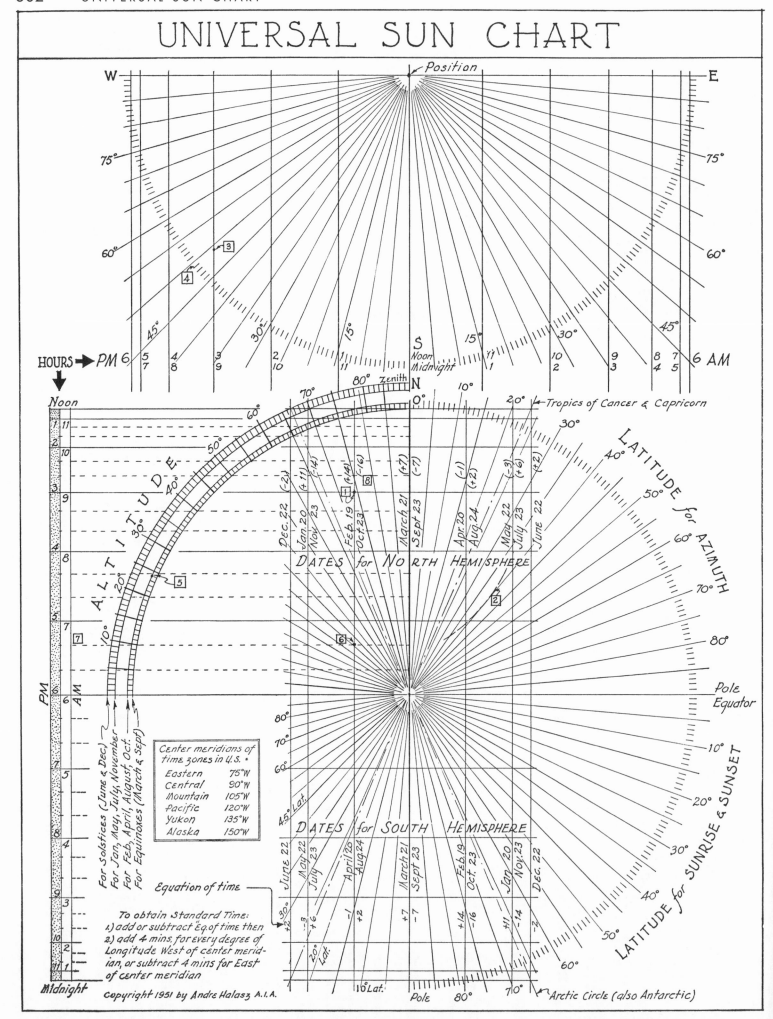

Center meridians of time zones in U.S.:

Eastern	75°W
Central	90°W
Mountain	105°W
Pacific	120°W
Yukon	135°W
Alaska	150°W

For Solstices (June & Dec.)
For Jan., May, July, November
For Feb., April, August, Oct.
For Equinoxes (March & Sept.)

Equation of time

To obtain Standard Time:
1.) add or subtract "Eq. of time" then
2.) add 4 mins. for every degree of Longitude West of center meridian, or subtract 4 mins for East of center meridian

UNIVERSAL SUN CHART - APPLICATION

The UNIVERSAL SUN CHART is mathematically true for any hour of any day of the year, for any place on the globe. It may be interpolated by eye for any intermediate value, and is as accurate as the reading taken, i.e. better than 1°. To use, follow EXAMPLE.

EXAMPLE: Find the direction of the Sun's rays at Columbus, Ohio (Lat. 40°N, Long. 83°W) at 3 PM, February 19th. Start with lower chart. From intersection of vertical DATE line (North Hemisphere, Feb. 19) and Horizontal HOUR line (3 PM) [1] measure with dividers to inclined LATITUDE for AZIMUTH line (40°). For accuracy, swing dividers in tangent arc as shown [2]. Lay off this distance in upper chart along 3 PM vertical HOUR line, [3], starting at top, and read: [4] azimuth = 49° West of South. * [Azimuth is angle of Sun's rays in plan.] Now measure distance from "azimuth point" [3] to POSITION and lay off in lower chart, horizontally to left of vertical ¢ until distance intersects ALTITUDE circle for February [5] (not along 3 PM hour line; move dividers up & down keeping distance horizontal; or lay off distance along any hour line and project vertically to February ALTITUDE circle). Read: altitude = 24° [Altitude is true angle of Sun's rays with the horizontal, see sketch below].

For noon altitude, steps [3] & [4] may be omitted because noon azimuth = 0° To find time of Sunrise & Sunset, find the intersection of vertical DATE line with inclined LATITUDE for SUNRISE & SUNSET [6] and read time by HOUR lines [7]: Sunrise = 6:40 AM. Sunset = 5:20 PM. To find azimuth of sunrise & sunset, repeat steps [2] & [3] from point [6]

Time shown is Sun Time. If desired to convert to Local Standard Time, 2 steps are necessary:
Step 1 = add the small figure "equation of time" on DATE line [8]: 3 PM +14 mins = 3:14 PM.
Step 2: add 4 mins for each degree West of Standard Time Meridian: 8 x 4 = 32; 3:14+32= 3:46 PM Standard Time. (This is a maximum case; more often the two corrections cancel out or are negligible.)

* When [2] is clockwise from [1] as in example, AZIMUTH is measured from the SOUTH; if counter-clockwise, AZIMUTH is from the North (reverse for Southern Hemisphere).

TO CONSTRUCT SHADOWS with TRUE POSITION of SUN=

For Plan & Elevations:
① Lay out Azimuth in Plan with respect to Compass.
② Lay out Altitude upon Azimuth.
Follow steps 3, 4, 5, 6, to obtain Elevations of Sun-Ray.
Proceed as in conventional Shades & Shadows.

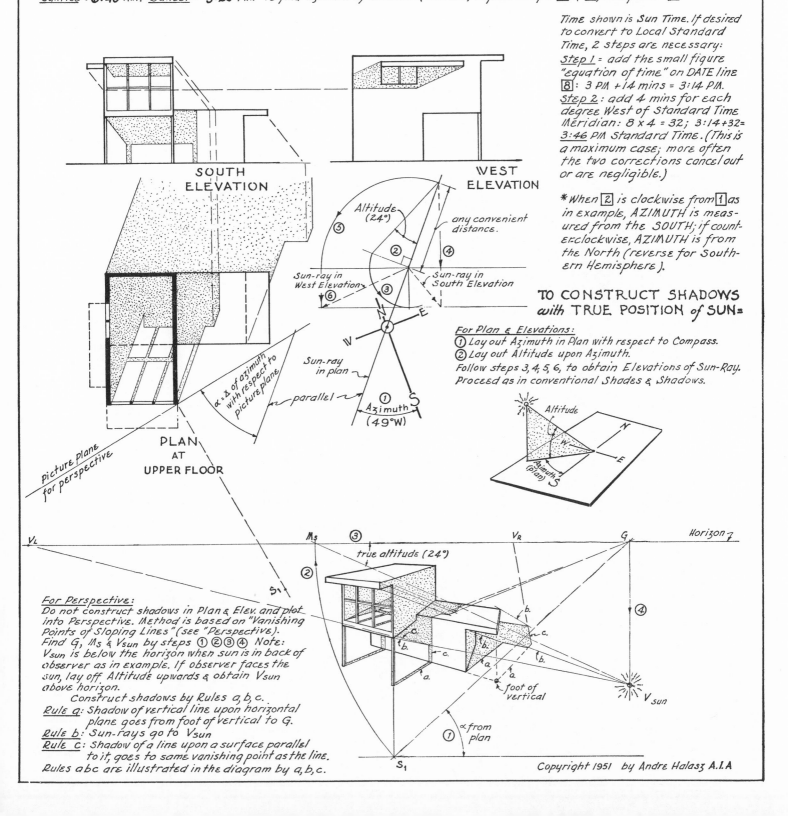

SOUTH ELEVATION

WEST ELEVATION

Altitude (24°)
any convenient distance.
Sun-ray in West Elevation
Sun-ray in South Elevation
Sun-ray in plan
α = ∠ of azimuth with respect to picture plane
parallel
Azimuth (49°W)
picture plane for perspective
PLAN AT UPPER FLOOR
Altitude
Azimuth (plan)
true altitude (24°)

For Perspective:
Do not construct shadows in Plan & Elev. and plot into Perspective. Method is based on "Vanishing Points of Sloping Lines" (see "Perspective").
Find G, Ms & Vsun by steps ①②③④ Note: Vsun is below the horizon when sun is in back of observer as in example. If observer faces the sun, lay off Altitude upwards & obtain Vsun above horizon.
Construct shadows by Rules a, b, c.
Rule a: Shadow of vertical line upon horizontal plane goes from foot of vertical to G.
Rule b: Sun-rays go to Vsun
Rule c: Shadow of a line upon a surface parallel to it, goes to same vanishing point as the line.
Rules abc are illustrated in the diagram by a, b, c.

Horizon
foot of vertical
α from plan

EXPLANATION of TABLES for SUN SHADES

EXPLANATION OF TABLES

The following 3 pages of tables give factors for shading of windows and depth that the sun will enter a room.
(a) By use of solid overhang. (b) By use of solid vertical shading device such as a fence, wall, or planting.
(c) Depth of penetration of sun through wall openings not covered by shading device.

EXPLANATION OF FACTORS

Numbers shown on tables are factors (F) in feet and 1/10 ths. of a foot. They are projections required to cast 1 foot of shade on a vertical plane, measured down from bottom of overhanging eave.

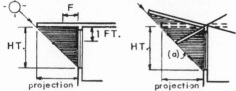

Note:
To find projection of horizontal overhang required to cast a specific shade below bottom of eave of overhang, multiply height required (HT. in feet) by factor F.

To find projection of sloping overhang required, solve as for a horizontal overhang. Take a section thru wall of your building and lay off calculated horizontal projection. Draw a line "a" through bottom of eave of overhang and bottom of shade. Where roof slope intersects this line, required overhang can be measured.

USE OF TABLES TO FIND FACTOR F

Step 1. Find the latitude of building site from the SUN SHADE MASTER MAP which follows tables.
(a) Select from TABLES OF SUN SHADE FACTORS the latitude nearest to site latitude.

Step 2. Directly under latitude select hours, A.M. to P.M. when shade is wanted. Hours & months when shade is wanted depend on the site, climate, use of building, if air conditioned, etc. Time shown is "Sun Time." at center of each hourly time zone. Find time zone of site from the SUN SHADE MASTER MAP which follows. To find Sun Time from Standard Time use the procedure outlined on the MASTER MAP.

Step 3. Select month or months when shade is wanted.

Step 4. Select from orientation diagrams below the one most similar to your building.

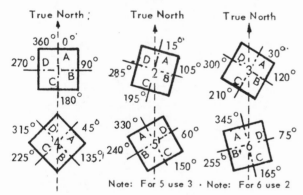

Note: For 5 use 3 · Note: For 6 use 2

Angles shown read clockwise from True North 0° or 360°. East is 90°, South is 180°, West is 270°. Make correction from magnetic North for site deviation.
(a) Note that sides of diagram are labeled A, B, C, D. Decide which sides of your bldg. will require shade.
(b) Turn to table under month or months selected, find the orientation you selected — 1, 2, 3, or 4.
Note: (1) If your orientation is 5 use 3 in the chart.
If your orientation is 6 use 2 in the chart.
(2) Also change times as follows: For times,

4 P. M. of orientation 5 or 6 use time 8 A. M. of 3 or 2
3 P. M. of orientation 5 or 6 use time 9 A. M. of 3 or 2
2 P. M. of orientation 5 or 6 use time 10 A. M. of 3 or 2
10 A. M. of orientation 5 or 6 use time 2 P. M. of 3 or 2
9 A. M. of orientation 5 or 6 use time 3 P. M. of 3 or 2
8 A. M. of orientation 5 or 6 use time 4 P. M. of 3 or 2
For noon do not substitute.

Step 5. Follow down under month & orientation number until the latitude and time rows previously selected are intersected. Here select sides (indicated as A, B, C, D) which you decided to shade and use factors following the letters.
(a) When a side (letter) does not appear it is because sun does not shine on it at that time.
(b) When selecting factors for several hours and for several months use the largest factor.

Step 6. Find projection of overhang required. (See note under EXPLANATION OF FACTORS).

Step 7. If length "x" is desired assume plane "a" perpendicular to end of window & calculate for its overhang.

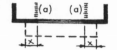

EXAMPLES

Problem "A":
1. Assume building is at Lat. 40° 16'. Use 40° Lat.
2. Shading wanted 9 A.M. to 3 P.M.
3. This shading wanted April 20th to Sept. 23rd.
4. Center of building is on an axis 61° East of North. Use Orientation No. 5. Bldg. on site 60° East of North.
5. On side C shade entire window to 5' below overhang eave. On side D shade entire window to 4' below overhang eave.

Solution
1. Interchange orientation No. 5 to orientation No. 3. For 3 P.M. of orientation No. 5 substitute 9 A.M. for No. 3 etc.
2. Largest factor for side C orientation No. 3, 40° Lat. between 9 A.M. & 3 P.M., April 20th to Sept 23rd, is factor 1.4' at 9 A.M. on Sept. 23rd (3 P.M. on table before conversion). Multiply 1.4' by 5' height = 7' projection.
3. Largest factor for side D is .69'. Multiply .69' by 4' height = 2.76' projection.

Problem B
1. To find height of vertical shading device. Known:
D — Distance from plane to be shaded to shading device.
H — Height from fl. to top of window or side to be shaded.
G — Height from floor to grade at shading device.
H' — Portion of shading device needed to shade H, (H'=H)

Unknown: Y height of vertical device above finished grade.

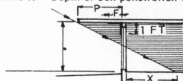

Solution: Find factor F as in preceding problem.
1. Formula for Y = D/F + H ± G (in ft. and fractions of ft.),
2. If the height of the device is fixed and the distance D is sought the formula becomes D = F (Y − H ± G)
Note: If grade is below floor use − G ⎰ Differs from
If grade is above floor use + G ⎱ diagram

Problem C
1. To find depth of penetration of sun through wall opening. (Generally used to calculate penetration of winter sun).
Known: P — Projection of shading device.
Known: H — Height from bottom of eave of shading device to finished floor.
Unknown: X — Depth of sun penetration into room.

Solution: Find factor F from table as in Problem A except select time & months you wish to know depth of sun penetration.
1. Formula for X = FH − P (in feet and fractions of feet.)

Sun Shade data prepared in consultation with Andre Halasz A.I.A.

TABLES for SUN SHADES

Date	Orientation	26° N. Latitude 8 AM	26° 9	26° 10	26° 12	26° 2 PM	26° 3	26° 4	30° N. Latitude 8 AM	30° 9	30° 10	30° 12	30° 2 PM	30° 3	30° 4	32° N. Latitude 8 AM	32° 9	32° 10	32° 12	32° 2 PM	32° 3	32° 4	34° N. Latitude 8 AM	34° 9	34° 10	34° 12	34° 2 PM	34° 3	34° 4
DEC. 22	1	B3.4	B1.6	B.85	C1.2	C1.3	C1.6	C2.4	B4.0	B1.7	B .9	C1.3	C1.5	C1.8	C2.9	B4.3	B1.8	B.96	C1.4	C1.6	C1.9	C3.2	B4.6	B1.9	B1.0	C1.5	C1.7	C2.1	C3.5
		C2.4	C1.6	C1.3	-	D.85	D1.6	D3.4	C2.9	C1.8	C1.5	-	D .9	D1.7	D4.0	C3.2	C1.9	C1.6	-	D.96	D1.8	D4.3	C3.5	C2.1	C1.7	-	D1.0	D1.9	D4.6
	2	B3.9	B1.9	B1.2	B .3	C1.5	C1.9	C3.2	B4.6	B2.1	B1.3	B.34	C1.7	C2.1	C3.8	B5.0	B2.2	B1.3	B .4	C1.8	C2.3	C4.2	B5.4	B2.4	B1.4	B .4	C1.9	C2.5	C4.6
		C1.5	C1.1	C1.1	C1.1	D.49	D1.1	D2.6	C1.8	C1.3	C1.2	C1.3	D .5	D1.2	D3.0	C2.0	C1.4	C1.3	C1.4	D.51	D1.3	D3.4	C2.2	C1.5	C1.4	C1.5	D.53	D1.3	D3.6
	3	B4.2	B2.1	B1.4	B.57	C1.6	C2.1	C3.8	B4.9	B2.4	B1.5	B.66	C1.7	C2.4	C4.5	B5.4	B2.5	B1.6	B.71	C1.9	C2.6	C5.0	B5.8	B2.7	B1.7	B .8	C2.0	C2.8	C5.3
		C .4	C.56	C.71	C1.	D.08	D.56	D1.1	C.53	C .7	C.84	C1.1	D.03	D.57	D2.0	C.61	C.75	C.90	C1.2	D.03	D .6	D2.2	C.68	C.85	C.98	C1.3	D .0	D.63	D2.3
	4	A.68	-	B1.5	B.81	B.32	C2.2	C4.1	A.74	B2.5	B1.7	B.94	B.41	B.06	C4.8	A.80	B2.6	B1.8	B1.0	B.45	B.08	C5.3	A.83	B2.9	B1.9	B1.1	B.50	B.11	C5.7
		B4.1	B2.2	C.32	C.81	C1.5		D.68	B4.8	C.06	C.41	C.94	C1.7	C2.5	D.74	B5.3	C.08	C.45	C1.0	C1.8	C2.6	D.80	B5.7	C.11	C.50	C1.1	C1.9	C2.9	D.83
JAN. 20 NOV. 23	1	B3.2	B1.5	B.81	C1.	C1.2	C1.4	C2.1	B3.7	B1.6	B.89	C1.2	C1.4	C1.6	C2.5	B4.3	B1.8	B.93	C1.3	C1.5	C1.7	C2.9	B4.7	B1.9	B.97	C1.4	C1.6	C1.9	C3.2
		C2.1	C1.4	C1.2	-	D.81	D1.5	D3.2	C2.5	C1.6	C1.4	-	D.89	D1.6	D3.7	C2.9	C1.7	C1.5	-	D.93	D1.8	D4.3	C3.2	C1.9	C1.6	-	D.97	D1.9	D4.7
	2	B3.6	B1.8	B1.1	B.27	C1.3	C1.7	C2.8	B4.3	B2.0	B1.2	B .3	C1.6	C2.0	C3.4	B4.9	B2.1	B1.3	B.33	C1.7	C2.1	C3.9	B5.4	B2.3	B1.3	B.35	C1.8	C2.3	C4.3
		C1.2	C.95	C.92	C1.	D.48	D1.1	D2.5	C1.5	C1.1	C1.1	C1.2	D .5	D1.2	D3.0	C1.7	C1.2	C1.2	C1.2	D.52	D1.2	D3.4	C1.9	C1.4	C1.3	C1.3	D.53	D1.3	D3.7
	3	B3.8	B2.0	B1.3	B.52	C1.4	C1.9	C3.4	B4.6	B2.2	B1.5	B.59	C1.6	C2.2	C4.0	B5.1	B2.4	B1.5	B.64	C1.7	C2.4	C4.6	B5.7	B2.6	B1.6	B.68	C1.8	C2.6	C5.1
		C.20	C.45	C.61	C .9	D.11	D.60	D1.7	C.31	C.56	C.73	C1.0	D.08	D.62	D2.0	C.38	C.63	C.80	C1.1	D.07	D.64	D2.2	C.45	C.70	C.86	C1.2	D.09	D.67	D2.4
	4	A.78	A.07	B1.4	B.73	B.25	C2.0	C3.7	A.93	A.03	B1.6	B.84	B.33	C2.3	C4.4	A.96	A 0	B1.7	B .9	B.37	C2.5	C5.1	A1.0	B2.7	B1.8	B.97	B.41	B.01	C5.6
		B3.7	B2.0	C.25	C.73	C1.4	D.07	D.78	B4.4	B2.3	C.33	C.84	C1.6	D.03	D.93	B5.1	B2.5	C.37	C .9	C1.7	D .0	D.96	B5.6	C.01	C.41	C.97	C1.8	C2.7	D1.0
FEB. 19 OCT. 23	1	B2.5	B1.3	B.72	C.75	C 81	C.91	C1.2	B2.8	B1.4	B.75	C.87	C.93	C1.0	C1.4	B2.9	B1.4	B.78	C.93	C1.0	C1.1	C1.5	B3.0	B1.5	B.81	C1.	C1.1	C1.2	C1.6
		C1.2	C.91	C.81	-	D.72	D1.3	D2.5	C1.4	C1.0	C.93	-	D.75	D1.4	D2.8	C1.5	C1.1	C1.0	-	D.78	D1.4	D2.9	C1.6	C1.2	C1.1	-	D.81	D1.5	D3.0
	2	B2.7	B1.5	B.90	B.19	C.97	C1.2	C1.8	B3.0	B1.6	B.97	B.22	C1.1	C1.4	C2.0	B3.2	B1.7	B1.0	B.24	C1.2	C1.5	C2.2	B3.3	B1.8	B1.1	B.25	C1.3	C1.6	C2.3
		C.48	C.54	C.60	C.75	D.48	D1.0	D2.1	C.62	C.65	C.70	C.84	D.48	D1.1	D2.3	C.69	C.72	C.77	C.90	D.50	D1.1	D2.4	C.77	C.77	C.83	C.95	D.50	D1.1	D2.5
	3	A.23	B1.6	B1.0	B.37	C1.1	C1.4	C2.3	A-17	B1.7	B1.1	B.43	C1.2	C1.6	C2.6	A.15	B1.8	B1.2	B.46	C1.3	C1.7	C2.8	A.12	B1.9	B1.2	B .5	C1.3	C1.8	C2.9
		B2.7	C.14	C.34	C.65	D.21	D.66	D1.6	B3.1	C.21	C.43	C.75	D.18	D.67	D1.7	B3.3	C.26	C.48	C.80	D.17	D.68	D1.8	B3.4	C.29	C.52	C.86	D.16	D.69	D1.8
	4	A.93	A.26	B1.1	B.53	B.06	C1.6	C2.6	A.96	A.23	B1.2	B.62	B.12	C1.7	C2.9	A.99	A.21	B1.3	B.66	B.15	C1.8	C3.1	A1.0	A.20	B1.3	B .7	B.18	C1.9	C3.3
		B2.6	B1.6	C.06	C.53	C1.1	D.26	D.93	B2.9	B1.7	C.12	C.62	C1.2	D.23	D.96	B3.1	B1.8	C.15	C.66	C1.3	D.21	D.99	B3.3	B1.9	C.18	C .7	C1.3	D.20	D1.0
MAR. 21 SEPT. 23	1	B1.9	B1.1	B.63	C.49	C.49	C.50	C.50	B2.1	B1.1	B.65	C.57	C.58	C.58	C.60	B2.1	B1.2	B.67	C.61	C.62	C.63	C.65	B2.1	B1.2	B.68	C.67	C.67	C.67	C .7
		C.50	C.50	C.49	-	D.63	D1.1	D1.9	C.60	C.58	C.58	-	D.65	D1.1	D2.1	C.65	C.63	C.62	-	D.67	D1.2	D2.1	C .7	C.67	C.67	-	D.68	D1.2	D2.1
	2	A.01	B1.2	B.73	B.12	C.63	C.76	C1.0	B2.1	B1.3	B.78	B.14	C.73	C.86	C1.1	B2.2	B1.3	B.81	B.15	C.77	C.91	C1.2	B2.2	B1.3	B.83	B.17	C.82	C.96	C1.2
		B2.0	C.19	C.31	C.47	D.48	D.93	D1.8	C.05	C.27	C.39	C.55	D.48	D.94	D1.8	C.08	C.31	C.43	C.59	D.48	D.95	D1.9	C.12	C.34	C.47	C.64	D.48	D.97	D1.9
	3	A.54	A.12	B.79	B.24	C.76	C.98	C1.4	A.50	A.06	B.86	B.28	C.83	C1.1	C1.6	A.48	A.03	B.89	B .3	C.87	C1.1	C1.6	A.45	A 0	B.93	B.33	C.92	C1.2	C1.7
		B1.9	B1.2	C.11	C.42	D.30	D.70	D1.4	B2.1	B1.3	C.17	C.50	D.27	D.69	D1.5	B2.1	B1.3	C.20	C.53	D.26	D.68	D1.5	B2.2	B1.4	C.24	C.58	D.25	D.68	D1.5
	4	A1.0	A.42	A.09	B.34	C.79	C1.1	C1.7	A1.0	A.38	A.05	B .4	C.87	C1.2	C1.9	A1.0	A.37	A.03	B.43	B.03	C1.3	C1.9	A1.0	A.35	A 0	B.47	B 0	C1.3	C2.0
		B1.7	B1.1	B.79	C.34	D.09	D.42	D1.0	B1.9	B1.2	B.87	C .4	D.05	D.38	D1.0	B1.9	B1.3	B.91	C.43	C.91	D.37	D1.0	B2.0	B1.3	B.96	C.47	C.96	D.35	D1.0
APR. 20 AUG. 24	1	B1.7	B.98	B.57	C.26	C.23	C.18	C.07	B1.7	B1.0	B.58	C.33	C.31	C.25	C.15	B1.7	B1.0	B.59	C.37	C.35	C.29	C.19	B1.7	B1.0	B.60	C.42	C.39	C.33	C.23
		C.07	C.18	C.23	-	D.57	D.98	D1.7	C.15	C.25	C.31		D.58	D1.0	D1 7	C.19	C.29	C.35	-	D.59	D1.0	D1.7	C.23	C.33	C.39	-	D.60	D1.0	D1.7
	2	A.35	A.07	B.62	B.06	C.37	C.43	C.50	A.29	A 0	B.64	B.08	C.45	C.50	C.58	A.25	B1.1	B.66	B.09	C.49	C.54	C.62	A.21	B1.1	B.68	B.10	C.53	C.58	C.66
		B1.6	B.99	C.07	C.25	D.49	D.90	D1.6	B1.7	B1.0	C.15	C.32	D.48	D.90	D1.6	B1.6	C.02	C.18	C.36	D.48	D.90	D1.6	B1.7	C.05	C.22	C.40	D.48	D.89	D1.6
	3	A.76	A.33	A.08	B.13	C.49	C.64	C.89	A.71	A.27	A.03	B.16	C.56	C.72	C.97	A.68	A.25	B.69	B.18	C.60	C.76	C1.0	A.65	A.21	B.71	B.21	C.64	C.79	C1.1
		B1.5	B.94	B.61	C.22	D.38	D.76	D1.4	B1.5	B.99	B.66	C.28	D.36	D.73	D1.4	B1.6	B1.0	C 0	C.32	D.34	D.72	D1.4	B1.6	B1.0	C.03	C.36	D.32	D.71	D1.4
	4	A1.1	A.56	A.24	B.18	C.57	C.82	C1.2	A1.1	A.52	A.20	B.23	C.63	C.89	C1.3	A1.1	A.50	A.17	B.26	C.67	C.92	C1.3	A1.0	A.48	A.14	B.29	C.70	C.95	C1.4
		B1.2	B.82	B.57	C.18	D.24	D.56	D1.1	B1.3	B.89	B.63	C.23	D.20	D.52	D1.1	B1.3	B.92	B.67	C.26	D.17	D.50	D1.1	B1.4	B.95	B.70	C.29	D.14	D.48	D1.0
MAY 22 JULY 23	1	A.19	A.02	B.53	C.1	C.05	A.02	A.19	A.10	B .9	B.54	C.17	C.12	C.04	A.10	A.06	B.89	B.54	C.21	C.16	C.08	A.06	A.03	B.90	B.54	C.24	C.20	C.12	A.03
		B1.5	B.88	C.05	-	D.53	D.88	D1.5	B1.4	C.04	C.12		D.54	D .9	D1.4	B1.4	C.08	C.16	-	D.54	D.89	D1.4	B1.4	C.12	C.20	-	D.54	D.90	D1.4
	2	A.56	A.25	A.08	B.02	C.19	C .2	C.19	A.47	A.18	A.01	B.04	C.26	C.27	C.26	A.43	A.14	B.56	B.05	C.29	C.31	C.30	A.40	A.11	B.57	B.06	C.33	C.35	C.33
		B1.4	B.84	B.53	C .1	D .5	D.86	D1.5	B1.4	B.88	B.55	C.17	D.48	D.85	D1.4	B1.4	B.88	C.01	C.20	D.47	D.84	D1.4	B1.4	B.90	C.05	C.24	D.47	D.83	D1.4
	3	A.89	A.46	A.22	B.05	C.31	C.42	C.56	A.81	A.40	A.15	B.08	C.38	C.49	C.62	A.77	A.37	A.12	B.10	C.41	C.52	C.65	A.74	A.34	A.09	B.12	C.44	C.55	C.68
		B1.2	B.75	B.49	C.09	D.43	D.77	D1.4	B1.2	B .8	B.53	C.15	D.40	D.75	D1.3	B1.2	B.81	B.55	C.18	D.38	D.73	D1.3	B1.2	B.84	B.56	C.21	D.36	D.72	D1.3
	4	A1.2	A.64	A.34	B.07	C.42	C .6	C.89	A1.1	A.60	A.29	B.12	C.47	C.66	C.94	A1.1	A.57	A.26	B.15	C.49	C.69	C.96	A1.0	A.55	A.24	B.17	C.52	C.72	C.98
		B.89	B .6	B.42	C.07	D.34	D.64	D1.2	B.94	B.66	B.47	C.12	D.29	D.60	D1.1	B.96	B.69	B.49	C.15	D.26	D.57	D1.1	B.98	B.72	B.52	C.17	D.24	D.55	D1.0
JUNE 22	1	A.27	A.09	A 0	C.04	A 0	A.09	A.27	A.19	A.02	B.51	C.11	C.06	A.02	A.19	A.16	B.88	B.52	C.15	C.09	C.01	A.16	A.12	B.85	B.52	C.18	C.13	C.04	A.12
		B1.4	B.89	B.51	-	D.51	D.89	D1.4	B1.4	B.88	C.06	-	D.51	D.88	D1.4	B1.3	C.01	C.09	-	D.52	D.88	D1.3	B1.3	C.04	C.13	-	D.52	D.85	D1.3
	2	A.61	A.32	A.13	B.01	C.12	C.13	C.09	A.53	A.25	A.07	B.03	C.19	C.20	C.16	A .5	A.21	A.04	B.03	C.22	C.23	C.18	A.46	A.17	A 0	B.04	C.26	C.26	C.22
		B1.2	B.83	B.49	C.04	D.50	D.89	D1.4	B1.3	B.84	B.51	C.11	D.48	D.86	D1.4	B1.3	B.85	B.53	C.14	D.41	D.85	D1.3	B1.3	B.83	B.53	C.18	D.46	D.81	D1.3
	3	A.91	A.53	A.26	B.02	C.25	C.36	C.44	A.84	A.46	A.20	B.05	C.31	C.42	C.50	A.81	A.43	A.17	B.07	C.34	C.45	C.52	A.77	A.38	A.14	B.09	C.37	C.46	C.55
		B1.0	B.72	B.44	C.04	D.45	D.82	D1.3	B1.1	B.75	B.48	C.10	D.41	D.77	D1.3	B1.1	B.77	B.50	C.13	D.40	D.76	D1.2	B1.1	B.76	B.51	C.16	D.38	D.71	D1.2
	4	A1.2	A.70	A.36	B.03	C.36	C.56	C.77	A1.1	A.65	A.32	B.08	C.41	C.60	C.81	A1.1	A.61	A.30	B.10	C.43	C.63	C.83	A1.0	A.57	A.27	B.13	C.46	C.63	C.85
		B.77	B.56	B.36	C.03	D.36	D.70	D1.2	B.81	B.60	B.41	C.08	D.32	D.64	D1.1	B.83	B.63	B.43	C.10	D.30	D.61	D1.1	B.85	B.63	B.46	C.13	D.27	D.57	D1.0

TABLES for SUN SHADES

Date	Orientation	36° N. Latitude 8 AM	9	10	12	2 PM	3	4	38° N. Latitude 8 AM	9	10	12	2 PM	3	4
Dec. 22	1	B5.1	B2.1	B1.1	C1.7	C1.8	C2.3	C3.8	B6.0	B2.3	B1.1	C1.8	C2.0	C2.6	C4.6
		C3.8	C2.3	C1.8	-	D1.1	D2.1	D5.1	C4.6	C2.6	C2.0	-	D1.1	D2.3	D6.0
	2	B5.9	B2.6	B1.5	B.43	C2.0	C2.7	C5.0	B7.0	B2.9	B1.6	B.46	C2.3	C3.1	C6.0
		C2.4	C1.7	C1.5	C1.6	D.54	D1.4	D3.9	C2.9	C1.9	C1.7	C1.7	D.57	D1.5	D4.6
	3	B6.3	B2.9	B1.8	B.83	C2.1	C3.0	C5.8	B7.5	B3.3	B2.0	B.90	B.03	C3.4	C7.0
		C.77	C.93	C1.1	C1.4		D.50	D2.5	C1.0	C1.1	C1.2	C1.6	C2.3	D.70	D2.9
	4	A.87	B3.1	B2.0	B1.2	B.54	B.14	C6.3	A1.0	B3.4	B2.2	B1.3	B.63	B.19	C7.5
		B6.3	C.14	C.54	C1.2	C2.0	C3.1	D.87	B7.5	C.19	C.63	C1.3	C2.2	C3.4	D1.0
Jan. 20 / Nov. 23	1	B5.2	B2.0	B1.0	C1.5	C1.7	C2.1	C3.6	B6.2	B2.1	B1.1	C1.6	C1.8	C2.2	C4.4
		C3.6	C2.1	C1.7	-	D1.0	D2.0	D5.2	C4.4	C2.2	C1.8	-	D1.1	D2.1	D6.2
	2	B5.9	B2.5	B1.4	B.38	C1.9	C2.5	C4.8	B7.1	B2.6	B1.5	B.41	C2.1	C2.7	C5.8
		C2.2	C1.5	C1.4	C1.4	D.55	D1.4	D4.1	C2.6	C1.6	C1.5	C1.5	D.58	D1.5	D4.9
	3	B6.3	B2.8	B1.7	B.74	C1.9	C2.8	C5.7	B7.5	B3.0	B1.9	B .8	C2.1	C3.	C6.9
		C.54	C.77	C.93	C1.3	D.04	D.70	D2.7	C.67	C.86	C1.0	C1.4	D.03	D.73	D3.2
	4	A1.1	B2.9	B1.9	B1.	B.46	B.03	C6.2	A1.3	B3.1	B2.1	B1.1	B.51	B.06	C7.5
		B6.2	C.03	C.46	C1.	C1.9	C2.9	D1.1	B7.5	C.06	C.51	C1.1	C2.1	C3.1	D1.3
Feb. 19 / Oct. 23	1	B3.2	B1.5	B.84	C1.1	C1.2	C1.3	C1.7	B3.4	B1.6	B.89	C1.2	C1.3	C1.4	C1.9
		C1.7	C1.3	C1.2	-	D.84	D1.5	D3.2	C1.9	C1.4	C1.3	-	D.89	D1.6	D3.4
	2	B3.5	B1.8	B1.1	B.27	C1.3	C1.6	C2.5	B3.7	B1.9	B1.2	B.29	C1.4	C1.8	C2.7
		C.83	C.84	C.89	C1.	D.51	D1.2	D2.0	C.92	C.92	C.97	C1.1	D.53	D1.2	D2.8
	3	A.10	B2.0	B1.3	B.53	C1.4	C1.9	C3.1	A.07	B2.1	B1.4	B.57	C1.5	C2.0	C3.3
		B3.6	C.34	C.57	C.92	D.15	D.69	D1.9	B3.9	C.39	C.63	C.99	D.14	D.71	D2.
	4	A1.0	A.18	B1.4	B.75	B.22	C2.0	C3.5	A1.1	A.16	B1.5	B.81	B.25	C2.1	C3.7
		B3.5	B2.0	C.22	C.75	C1.4	D.18	D1.0	B3.7	B2.1	C.25	C.81	C1.5	D.16	D1.1
Mar. 21 / Sept 23	1	B2.2	B1.2	B .7	C.71	C.72	C.73	C.75	B2.3	B1.3	B.72	C.77	C.77	C.79	C.82
		C.75	C.73	C.72	-	D .7	D1.2	D2.2	C.82	C.79	C.77	-	D.72	D1.3	D2.3
	2	B2.3	B1.4	B.87	B.18	C.88	C1.0	C1.3	B2.4	B1.4	B.90	B.20	C.93	C1.1	C1.4
		C.16	C.39	C.52	C.69	D.49	D.99	D1.9	C.20	C.44	C.56	C.74	D.49	D1.0	D2.0
	3	A.43	B1.4	B.97	B.35	C.98	C1.3	C1.7	A.42	B1.5	B1.0	B.38	C1.0	C1.3	C1.8
		B2.3	C.02	C.27	C.62	D.24	D.69	D1.5	B2.4	C.05	C.31	C.67	D.23	D.69	D1.6
	4	A1.0	A.34	B1.0	B .5	B.01	C1.4	C2.1	A1.0	A.33	B1.1	B.54	B.03	C1.5	C2.2
		B2.1	B1.4	C.01	C .5	C1.0	D.34	D1.0	B2.2	B1.5	C.03	C.54	C1.1	D.33	D1.0
Apr. 20 / Aug. 24	1	B1.7	B1.0	B.60	C.45	C.42	C.36	C.27	B1.7	B1.0	B.61	C.49	C.46	C.41	C.31
		C.27	C.36	C.42	-	D.60	D1.0	D1.7	C.31	C.41	C.46	-	D.61	D1.0	D1.7
	2	A.18	B1.1	B.69	B.11	C.56	C.61	C.70	A.14	B1.1	B.71	B.12	C.61	C.66	C.75
		B1.7	C.09	C.25	C.44	D.47	D.89	D1.6	B1.8	C.13	C.29	C.48	D.47	D.88	D1.6
	3	A.62	A.19	B.73	B.22	C.67	C.82	C1.1	A.59	A.15	B.76	B.24	C.71	C.87	C1.1
		B1.6	B1.1	C.06	C.39	D.31	D.70	D1.4	B1.7	B1.1	C.09	C.43	D.29	D.68	D1.3
	4	A1.0	A.46	A.12	B.32	C.72	C.98	C1.4	A1.0	A.43	A.10	B.35	C.76	C1.0	C1.5
		B1.4	B.98	B.72	C.32	D.12	D.46	D1.0	B1.5	B1.0	B.76	C.35	D.10	D.43	D1.0
May 22 / July 23	1	B1.4	B.90	B.54	C.27	C.23	C.15	D1.4	B1.4	B.90	B.55	C.31	C.27	C.19	C.03
		-	C.15	C.23	-	D.54	D.90	-	C.03	C.19	C.27	-	D.55	D.90	D1.4
	2	A.36	A.08	B.58	B.07	C.36	C.38	C.36	A.33	A.04	B.60	B.08	C.40	C.42	C.40
		B1.4	B.91	C.08	C.26	D.46	D.83	D1.4	B1.4	B.92	C.12	C.30	D.46	D.82	D1.4
	3	A.70	A.31	A.07	B.13	C.47	C.58	C.70	A.68	A.28	A.03	B.15	C.51	C.61	C.74
		B1.2	B.86	B.59	C.24	D.35	D.70	D1.2	B1.3	B.88	B.61	C.27	D.34	D.68	D1.2
	4	A1.0	A.52	A.22	B.19	C.55	C.74	C1.0	A.98	A.49	A.19	B.22	C.58	C.77	C1.0
		B1.0	B.74	B.55	C.19	D.22	D.52	D1.0	B1.0	B.77	B.58	C.22	D.19	D.49	D.98
June 22	1	A.08	B.85	B.52	C.22	C.16	C.08	A.08	A.05	B.86	B.53	C.26	C.20	C.12	A.05
		B1.3	C.08	C.16	-	D.52	D.85	D1.3	B1.3	C.12	C.20	-	D.53	D.86	D1.3
	2	A.42	A.14	B.54	B.05	C.29	C.29	C.26	A.39	A.10	B.56	B.06	C.34	C.34	C.29
		B1.3	B.84	C.02	C.21	D.46	D.80	D1.3	B1.3	B.86	C.06	C.25	D.45	D.80	D1.3
	3	A.74	A.35	A.11	B.11	C.40	C.49	C.59	A.70	A.32	A.08	B.13	C.44	C.53	C.61
		B1.1	B.77	B.53	C.19	D.36	D.69	D1.2	B1.1	B.80	B.56	C.22	D.35	D.68	D1.2
	4	A1.0	A.54	A.25	B.15	C.48	C.65	C.87	A.97	A.52	A.22	B.18	C.52	C.69	C.90
		B.87	B.65	B.48	C.15	D.25	D.54	D1.0	B.90	B.69	B.52	C.18	D.22	D.52	D.97

Date	Orientation	40° N. Latitude 8 AM	9	10	12	2 PM	3	4	41° N. Latitude 8 AM	9	10	12	2 PM	3	4
Dec. 22	1	B7.6	B2.4	B1.2	C1.9	C2.2	C2.7	C5.8	B8.3	B2.6	B1.3	C2.0	C2.3	C2.9	C6.4
		C5.8	C2.7	C2.2	-	D1.2	D2.4	D7.6	C6.4	C2.9	C2.3	-	D1.3	D2.6	D8.3
	2	B8.8	B3.1	B1.8	B.49	C2.5	C3.3	C7.6	B9.6	B3.2	B1.9	B.52	C2.6	C3.5	C8.3
		C3.6	C2.0	C1.8	C1.9	D.60	D1.6	D5.8	C4.0	C2.2	C1.9	C2.0	D.63	D1.7	D6.3
	3	B9.4	B3.5	B2.2	B.95	B.05	C3.6	C8.8	B10.	B3.7	B2.3	B1.0	B.05	C3.8	C9.6
		C1.2	C1.2	C1.3	C1.7	C2.5	D.72	D3.6	C1.4	C1.3	C1.4	C1.7	C2.7	D.77	D3.9
	4	A1.2	B3.6	B2.4	B1.4	B.70	B.22	C9.4	A1.3	B3.9	B2.6	B1.4	B.74	B.25	C10.
		B9.4	C.22	C.70	C1.4	C2.4	C3.6	D1.2	B10.	C.25	C.74	C1.4	C2.6	C3.9	D1.3
Jan. 20 / Nov. 23	1	B7.2	B2.2	B1.2	C1.7	C2.0	C2.4	C5.1	B7.8	B2.3	B1.2	C1.8	C2.0	C2.5	C5.5
		C5.1	C2.4	C2.0	-	D1.2	D2.2	D7.2	C5.5	C2.5	C2.0	-	D1.2	D2.3	D7.8
	2	B8.2	B2.8	B1.6	B.44	C2.2	C2.9	C6.7	B8.9	B2.9	B1.7	B.46	C2.3	C3.0	C7.3
		C3.0	C1.7	C1.6	C1.7	D .6	D1.6	D5.6	C3.3	C1.8	C1.7	C1.7	D.62	D1.6	D5.8
	3	B8.7	B3.1	B2.0	B.86	C2.3	C3.2	C8.0	B9.5	B3.2	B2.0	B .9	C2.4	C3.3	C8.7
		C.80	C.93	C1.1	C1.5	D.02	D.75	D3.7	C.88	C.98	C1.2	C1.6	D 0	D.76	D3.9
	4	A1.5	B3.3	B2.2	B1.2	B.57	B.09	C8.6	A1.6	B3.4	B2.3	B1.3	B.60	B.11	C9.4
		B8.6	C.09	C.57	C1.2	C2.2	C3.3	D1.5	B9.4	C.11	C.60	C1.3	C2.3	C3.4	D1.6
Feb. 19 / Oct. 23	1	B3.6	B1.7	B.93	C1.2	C1.3	C1.5	C2.0	B3.8	B1.7	B.94	C1.3	C1.4	C1.5	C2.1
		C2.0	C1.5	C1.3	-	D.93	D1.7	D3.6	C2.1	C1.5	C1.4	-	D.94	D1.7	D3.8
	2	B4.0	B2.0	B1.2	B.31	C1.5	C1.9	C2.9	B4.2	B2.1	B1.3	B.33	C1.6	C1.9	C3.0
		C1.0	C.99	C1.1	C1.2	D.55	D1.3	D3.0	C1.1	C1.0	C1.1	C1.2	D.55	D1.3	D3.1
	3	A.05	B2.2	B1.5	B.61	C1.6	C2.1	C3.6	A.05	B2.3	B1.5	B.64	C1.7	C2.2	C3.7
		B4.2	C.43	C.69	C1.1	D.14	D.72	D2.0	B4.3	C.45	C.71	C1.1	D.12	D.72	D2.2
	4	A1.1	A.15	B1.6	B.87	B.28	C2.2	C4.0	A1.2	A.14	B1.6	B .9	B.30	C2.3	C4.2
		B4.0	B2.2	C.28	C.87	C1.6	D.15	D1.1	B4.2	B2.3	C.30	C .9	C1.6	D.14	D1.2
Mar. 21 / Sept 23	1	B2.4	B1.3	B.74	C.83	C.83	C.85	C.90	B2.4	B1.3	B.75	C.86	C.86	C.88	C.92
		C.90	C.85	C.83	-	D.74	D1.3	D2.4	C.92	C.88	C.86	-	D.75	D1.3	D2.4
	2	B2.5	B1.5	B.92	B.21	C1.0	C1.2	C1.5	B2.5	B1.5	B.95	B.22	C1.0	C1.2	C1.5
		C.26	C.49	C.61	C .8	D .5	D1.0	D2.0	C.27	C.51	C.64	C.83	D .5	D1.0	D2.1
	3	A.39	B1.6	B1.1	B.41	C1.1	C1.4	C2.0	A.38	B1.6	B1.1	B.43	C1.1	C1.4	C2.0
		B2.5	C.09	C.35	C.72	D.22	D.69	D1.6	B2.5	C.10	C.37	C.74	D.23	D.69	D1.6
	4	A1.0	A.30	B1.1	B.58	B.06	C1.5	C2.3	A1.0	A.30	B1.1	B .6	B.08	C1.6	C2.3
		B2.3	B1.5	C.06	C.58	C1.1	D.30	D1.0	B2.3	B1.6	C.08	C .6	C1.1	D.30	D1.0
Apr. 20 / Aug. 24	1	B1.8	B1.1	B.63	C.54	C.51	C.44	C.35	B1.8	B1.1	B.63	C.56	C.53	C.47	C.37
		C.35	C.44	C.51	-	D.63	D1.1	D1.8	C.37	C.47	C.53	-	D.63	D1.1	D1.8
	2	A.12	B1.1	B.74	B.14	C.65	C.71	C.79	A.10	B1.2	B.75	B.14	C.68	C.73	C.81
		B1.8	C.16	C.33	C.52	D.47	D.90	D1.6	B1.8	C.18	C.35	C.54	D.47	D.90	D1.6
	3	A.58	A.13	B.80	B.27	C.75	C.92	C1.2	A.57	A.12	B.82	B.28	C.78	C.94	C1.2
		B1.7	B1.1	C.12	C.47	D.29	D.68	D1.4	B1.7	B1.2	C.14	C.48	D.28	D.68	D1.4
	4	A1.0	A.42	A.08	B.38	C.80	C1.1	C1.5	A1.0	A.41	A.07	B.39	C.82	C1.1	C1.5
		B1.5	B1.1	B.80	C.38	D.08	D.42	D1.0	B1.5	B1.1	B.82	C.39	D.07	D.41	D1.0
May 22 / July 23	1	B1.4	B.90	B.55	C.35	C.30	C.22	C.06	B1.4	B.91	B.55	C.38	C.32	C.24	C.08
		C.06	C.22	C.30	-	D.55	D.90	D1.4	C.08	C.24	C.32	-	D.55	D.91	D1.4
	2	A.30	A.01	B.61	B.09	C.43	C.45	C.43	A.28	B.94	B.62	B.09	C.46	C.47	C.45
		B1.4	B.93	C.15	C.34	D.45	D.81	D1.4	B1.4	-	C.17	C.36	D.45	D.81	D1.4
	3	A.65	A.25	A.01	B.17	C.54	C.64	C.77	A.64	A.24	B.64	B.19	C.56	C.66	C.79
		B1.3	B.89	B.63	C.31	D.32	D.67	D1.2	B1.3	B.91	C 0	C.33	D.31	D.66	D1.2
	4	A.96	A.48	A.17	B.25	C.60	C.80	C1.1	A.95	A.47	A.16	B.26	C.62	C.81	C1.1
		B1.1	B.80	B.60	C.25	D.17	D.48	D.96	B1.1	B.81	B.62	C.26	D.16	D.47	D.95
June 22	1	A.01	B.85	B.53	C.29	C.24	C.15	A.01	B1.3	B.86	B.53	C.31	C.26	C.17	C 0
		B1.3	C.15	C.24	-	D.53	D.85	D1.3	C 0	C.17	C.26	-	D.53	D.86	D1.3
	2	A.35	A.07	B.57	B.07	C.37	C.36	C.32	A.33	A.05	B.58	B.08	C.39	C.38	C.34
		B1.3	B.86	C.09	C.28	D.44	D.78	D1.3	B1.3	B.87	C.11	C.30	D.44	D.78	D1.3
	3	A.67	A.29	A.05	B.14	C.47	C.55	C.64	A.65	A.28	A.03	B.15	C.49	C.59	C.66
		B1.1	B.81	B.58	C.25	D.33	D.66	D1.2	B1.1	B.83	B.59	C.27	D.33	D.65	D1.1
	4	A.94	A.49	A.20	B.20	C.54	C.71	C.92	A.93	A.48	A.19	B.22	C.56	C.72	C.93
		B.92	B.71	B.54	C.20	D.20	D.49	D.94	B.93	B.72	B.56	C.22	D.19	D.48	D.93

TABLES for SUN SHADES

Column groups (orientation 1, 2, 3, 4 under each date):

Date group	Orientations
DEC. 22	1, 2, 3, 4
JAN. 20 / NOV. 23	1, 2, 3, 4
FEB. 19 / OCT. 23	1, 2, 3, 4
MAR. 21 / SEPT. 23	1, 2, 3, 4
APR. 20 / AUG. 24	1, 2, 3, 4
MAY 22 / JULY 23	1, 2, 3, 4
JUNE 22	1, 2, 3, 4

Within each latitude block the columns are the times of day: **8 AM, 9, 10, 12, 2 PM, 3, 4**. Rows are the Date/Orientation combinations listed above.

46° N. LATITUDE

Date/Orient.	8 AM	9	10	12	2 PM	3	4
DEC 22 – 1	B18.	B3.2	B1.6	B1.6	C3.0	C3.7	C14.
DEC 22 – 2	C14.	C3.7	C3.0	C3.0	D1.6	D3.2	D18.
DEC 22 – 3	B21.	B4.1	B2.3	B2.3	C3.3	C4.4	C18.-
DEC 22 – 4	C8.9	C2.8	C2.5	B.64	D.76	D2.1	D14.
JAN 20 – 1	B23.	B4.7	B2.9	B2.9	B.11	C4.8	C21.
JAN 20 – 2	C3.2	C1.6	C1.8	B1.2	C3.4	D.91	D8.5
JAN 20 – 3	A2.7	B4.9	B3.2	B1.8	B.98	B.37	C23.
JAN 20 – 4	B23.	C.37	C.98	C1.8	C3.2	C4.9	D2.7
FEB 19 – 1	B12.	B2.9	B2.9	C2.2	C2.6	C3.2	C8.8
FEB 19 – 2	C8.8	C3.2	C2.6	C2.6	D1.5	D2.9	D12.
FEB 19 – 3	B14.	B3.6	B2.1	B2.1	C2.9	C3.8	C12.
FEB 19 – 4	C5.4	C2.3	C2.1	C2.1	D.72	D2.0	D9.6
MAR 21 – 1	B15.	B4.1	B2.5	B2.5	B.03	C4.2	C14.
MAR 21 – 2	C1.5	C1.3	C1.5	B1.1	C2.9	D.93	D6.2
MAR 21 – 3	A2.4	B4.3	B2.8	B1.6	B.79	D.82	D2.7
MAR 21 – 4	B15.	C.19	C.79	C1.9	B.28	C2.7	C5.2
APR 20 – 1	B4.7	B1.4	B1.7	C1.0	C1.6	C1.8	C2.7
APR 20 – 2	C2.7	C1.1	C1.0	C1.0	D1.1	D2.0	D4.7
APR 20 – 3	B5.2	B1.7	B1.5	B1.1	C1.9	C2.3	C3.8
APR 20 – 4	C1.4	C.64	C1.3	C1.3	D.60	D1.4	D3.8
MAY 22 – 1	B5.4	B2.6	B1.8	B1.7	C1.8	C2.6	C4.7
MAY 22 – 2	C.02	C.19	C.48	C.48	D.10	D.82	D2.7
MAY 22 – 3	A1.4	A.27	B1.3	B1.3	B.40	C2.7	C5.2
MAY 22 – 4	A1.1	B1.8	B1.9	B.72	B.15	D.13	D1.4
JUNE 22 – 1	B5.2	B2.7	B2.7	C.40	C1.9	D.13	D1.4
JUNE 22 – 2	B2.6	B1.4	B1.1	C.81	C1.0	C1.1	C1.1
JUNE 22 – 3	C1.1	C1.1	C1.0	C1.0	D.81	D1.4	D2.6
JUNE 22 – 4	C.39	C.64	C.78	B.26	C1.2	C1.4	D1.7

44° N. LATITUDE

Date/Orient.	8 AM	9	10	12	2 PM	3	4
DEC 22 – 1	B12.	B2.8	B1.4	C2.3	C2.7	C3.3	C9.3
DEC 22 – 2	C9.3	C3.3	C2.7	-	D1.4	D2.8	D12.
DEC 22 – 3	B14	B3.6	B2.1	B.58	C2.9	C3.9	C12.
DEC 22 – 4	C5.9	C2.4	C2.2	C2.2	D.69	D1.9	D9.1
JAN 20 – 1	B15.	B4.1	B2.6	B1.1	B.08	C4.3	C14.
JAN 20 – 2	C2.1	C1.4	C1.6	C2.0	C3.0	D.90	D5.7
JAN 20 – 3	A1.9	B4.3	B2.9	B1.6	B.86	B.30	C15
JAN 20 – 4	B15	C.30	C.86	C1.6	C2.9	C4.3	D1.9
FEB 19 – 1	B10.	B2.7	B1.4	C2.	C2.4	C3.0	C7.4
FEB 19 – 2	C7.4	C3.	C2.4	-	D1.4	D2.7	D10.
FEB 19 – 3	B12.	B3.4	B1.9	B.52	C2.6	C3.6	C9.8
FEB 19 – 4	C4.5	C2.2	C1.9	C2.	D.69	D1.9	D8.0
MAR 21 – 1	B13.	B3.8	B2.4	B1.0	B.01	C3.9	C12.
MAR 21 – 2	C1.2	C1.2	C1.4	C1.8	C2.7	D.87	D5.2
MAR 21 – 3	A2.1	B4.0	B2.6	B1.4	B.72	B.16	C13
MAR 21 – 4	B13	C.16	C.72	C1.4	C2.6	C4.0	D2.1
APR 20 – 1	B2.5	B1.4	B1.0	C1.4	C1.5	C1.7	C2.3
APR 20 – 2	C2.5	C.98	C1.5	-	D.99	D1.9	D4.3
APR 20 – 3	B4.8	B1.6	B1.3	B.37	C1.7	C2.1	C3.3
APR 20 – 4	C1.3	C.59	C1.2	C1.4	D.58	D1.4	D3.5
MAY 22 – 1	C1.3	B1.7	B1.7	B.71	C1.8	C2.4	C4.3
MAY 22 – 2	A O	B2.5	C.81	C1.2	D.11	D.76	D2.5
MAY 22 – 3	B4.9	C.54	C1.2	C1.2	B.36	C2.5	C4.8
MAY 22 – 4	A1.3	A.11	B2.6	B1.4	C1.8	C2.1	D1.3
JUNE 22 – 1	B4.8	B2.5	B1.8	C1.	C1.8	D.11	D1.3
JUNE 22 – 2	B2.5	B1.7	C.36	C.67	C1.2	C1.2	D1.2
JUNE 22 – 3	C1.0	B1.1	B.78	C.96	C.96	C.98	C1.0
JUNE 22 – 4	C1.1	C.43	C.59	C.44	C.59	D1.4	D2.5

43° N. LATITUDE

Date/Orient.	8 AM	9	10	12	2 PM	3	4
DEC 22 – 1	B11.	B2.7	B1.4	C2.2	C2.5	C3.1	C8.3
DEC 22 – 2	C8.3	C3.1	C2.5	-	D1.4	D2.7	D11.
DEC 22 – 3	B12.	B3.5	B2.0	B.56	C2.8	C3.7	C11.
DEC 22 – 4	C5.2	C2.3	C2.1	C2.1	D.66	D1.8	D8.1
JAN 20 – 1	B13.	B3.9	B2.4	B1.1	B.07	C4.1	C13
JAN 20 – 2	C1.8	C1.4	C1.5	C1.9	C2.9	D.85	D5.1
JAN 20 – 3	A1.7	B4.2	B2.7	B1.5	B.81	B.28	C13
JAN 20 – 4	B13.	C.28	C.81	C1.5	C2.7	C4.2	D1.7
FEB 19 – 1	B9.4	B2.6	B1.3	C1.9	C2.3	C2.8	C6.7
FEB 19 – 2	C6.7	C2.8	C2.3	-	D1.3	D2.6	D9.4
FEB 19 – 3	B11.	B3.3	B1.8	B.5	C2.5	C3.4	C8.9
FEB 19 – 4	C4.0	C2.1	C1.8	C1.9	D.66	D1.8	D7.3
MAR 21 – 1	B11.	B3.7	B2.3	B.97	C2.6	C3.8	C11.
MAR 21 – 2	C1.1	C.51	C1.3	C1.7	B O	D.85	D4.8
MAR 21 – 3	A1.9	B3.9	B2.5	B1.4	C2.6	B.15	C11.
MAR 21 – 4	B11.	C.15	C.68	C1.4	B.68	C3.9	D1.9
APR 20 – 1	B2.4	B1.4	B.99	C1.4	C1.5	C1.7	C2.3
APR 20 – 2	C.97	C.95	C.94	-	D.99	D1.8	D4.1
APR 20 – 3	B4.5	B1.6	B1.3	B.35	C1.7	C2.1	C3.3
APR 20 – 4	C1.2	C.56	C1.2	C1.3	D.57	D1.3	D3.3
MAY 22 – 1	A.01	B1.7	B1.6	B.68	C1.8	C2.4	C4.1
MAY 22 – 2	B4.7	C.51	C.78	C1.2	D.11	D.76	D2.4
MAY 22 – 3	A1.2	A.12	B1.8	B.97	C2.6	C2.5	C4.5
MAY 22 – 4	A1.0	B2.5	B2.5	C.97	B.34	C2.5	C4.3
JUNE 22 – 1	B2.4	B1.4	B1.4	C1.4	C.94	D.12	D1.2
JUNE 22 – 2	C.97	C.51	C.56	C.65	C1.2	C.28	C2.4
JUNE 22 – 3	B2.6	B1.6	B1.6	C.94	D.78	D1.3	D1.0
JUNE 22 – 4	C.32	C.22	C.34	C.44	C.94	C.95	C.97

42° N. LATITUDE

Date/Orient.	8 AM	9	10	12	2 PM	3	4
DEC 22 – 1	B9.5	B2.6	B1.3	C2.1	C2.4	C3.0	C7.4
DEC 22 – 2	C7.4	C3.0	C2.4	-	D1.3	D2.6	D9.5
DEC 22 – 3	B12.	B3.3	B1.9	B.54	C2.7	C3.6	C9.6
DEC 22 – 4	C4.7	C2.2	C2.0	C2.0	D.64	D1.8	D7.3
JAN 20 – 1	B12.	B3.8	B2.3	B1.0	B.06	C3.9	C11.
JAN 20 – 2	C1.6	C1.4	C1.4	C1.8	C2.7	D.77	D4.6
JAN 20 – 3	A1.5	B4.0	B2.6	B1.5	B.77	B.26	C12.
JAN 20 – 4	B12.	C.26	C.77	C1.5	C2.6	C4.0	D1.5
FEB 19 – 1	B8.5	B2.4	B1.2	C1.9	C2.1	C2.6	C6
FEB 19 – 2	C6	C2.6	C2.1	D1.2	D1.3	D2.4	D8.5
FEB 19 – 3	B9.8	B3.0	B1.8	B.48	C2.4	C3.1	C8
FEB 19 – 4	C3.6	C1.9	C1.9	C.64	D1.7	D1.7	D6.6
MAR 21 – 1	B10.	B3.4	B2.1	B.93	C2.5	C3.5	C9.5
MAR 21 – 2	C.97	C1.0	C1.2	C1.6	-	D.79	D4.3
MAR 21 – 3	A1.7	B3.5	B2.4	B1.3	C1.1	B.12	C10.
MAR 21 – 4	B10.	C.12	C.64	C1.3	C2.4	C3.5	D1.7
APR 20 – 1	B3.9	B1.8	B.95	C1.3	C1.4	C1.6	C2.2
APR 20 – 2	C2.2	C1.6	C1.4	-	D.95	D1.8	D3.9
APR 20 – 3	B4.4	B2.1	B1.3	B.34	C1.6	C2.0	D3.2
APR 20 – 4	C1.1	C1.1	C1.1	C1.3	D.55	D1.3	D3.2
MAY 22 – 1	A.04	B2.3	B1.6	B.66	C1.7	C2.3	C3.9
MAY 22 – 2	B4.5	C.49	C.75	C1.1	D.14	D.73	D2.3
MAY 22 – 3	A1.2	A.12	B3.7	B.93	B.32	C2.4	C4.3
MAY 22 – 4	A2.4	B1.6	B.32	C.93	C1.7	C2.4	D1.2
JUNE 22 – 1	B2.4	B1.3	B.56	C.58	C.55	C.49	C.39
JUNE 22 – 2	C.39	C.49	C.55	-	D.63	D1.1	D1.8
JUNE 22 – 3	A.08	A.03	B.76	B.15	C1.1	D1.1	D1.6
JUNE 22 – 4	C.29	C.27	C.54	C.67	C.86	C1.2	C2.0

MASTER MAP *for* SUN SHADES

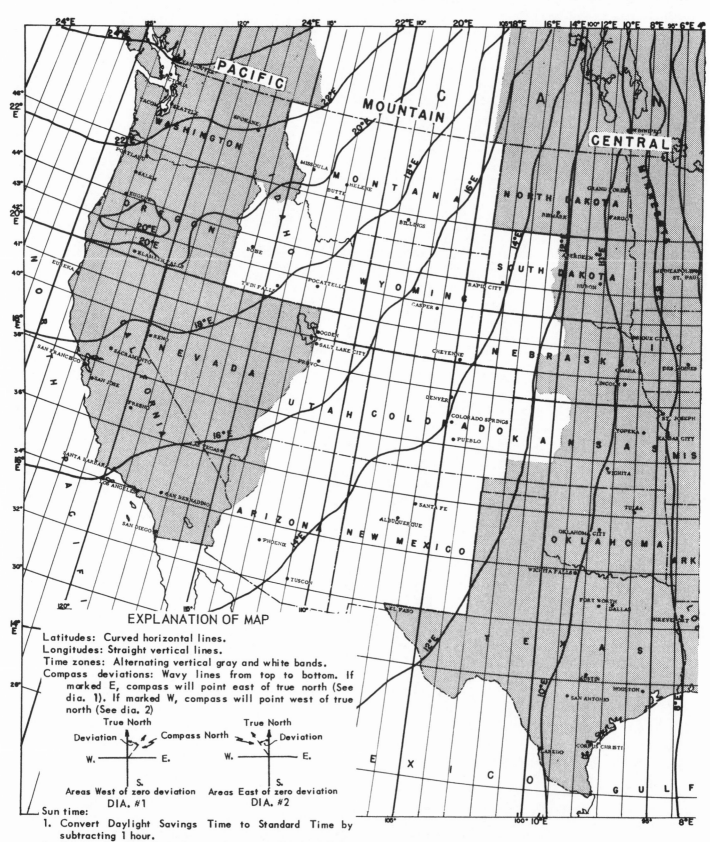

EXPLANATION OF MAP

Latitudes: Curved horizontal lines.
Longitudes: Straight vertical lines.
Time zones: Alternating vertical gray and white bands.
Compass deviations: Wavy lines from top to bottom. If marked E, compass will point east of true north (See dia. 1). If marked W, compass will point west of true north (See dia. 2)

Areas West of zero deviation
DIA. #1

Areas East of zero deviation
DIA. #2

Sun time:

1. Convert Daylight Savings Time to Standard Time by subtracting 1 hour.

2. Correct Standard Time for site location: Subtract 4 minutes for every degree of longitude that site is west of central longitude or add 4 mins. for every degree of longitude site is east of central longitude. Central longitudes of Time zones are:

Eastern Time Zone 75°	Mountain Time Zone 105°
Central Time Zone 90°	Pacific Time Zone 120°

3. Correct for time variations for day and month: Add or subtract minutes as follows:

Jan. 20 −11 min.	May 22 +3 min.	Sept. 23 + 7 min.
Feb. 19 +14 min.	June 22 −2 min.	Oct. 23 +16 min.
Mar. 21 − 7 min.	July 23 −6 min.	Nov. 23 +14 min.
Apr. 20 + 1 min.	Aug. 24 −2 min.	Dec. 22 + 2 min.

MASTER MAP *for* SUN SHADES

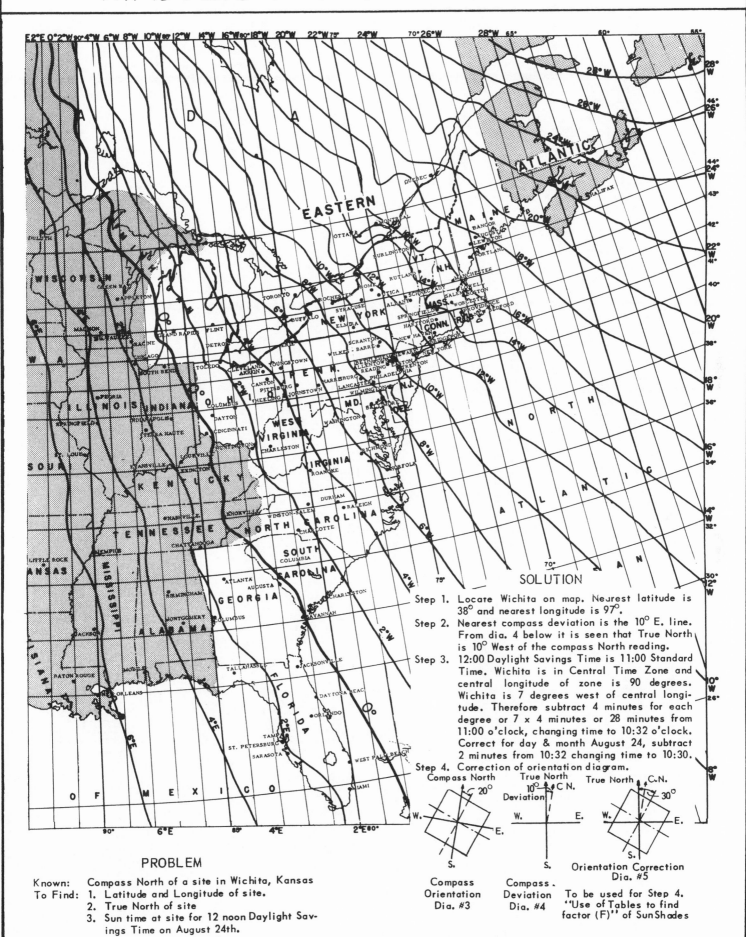

SOLUTION

Step 1. Locate Wichita on map. Nearest latitude is 38° and nearest longitude is 97°.

Step 2. Nearest compass deviation is the 10° E. line. From dia. 4 below it is seen that True North is 10° West of the compass North reading.

Step 3. 12:00 Daylight Savings Time is 11:00 Standard Time. Wichita is in Central Time Zone and central longitude of zone is 90 degrees. Wichita is 7 degrees west of central longitude. Therefore subtract 4 minutes for each degree or 7 x 4 minutes or 28 minutes from 11:00 o'clock, changing time to 10:32 o'clock. Correct for day & month August 24, subtract 2 minutes from 10:32 changing time to 10:30.

Step 4. Correction of orientation diagram.

Compass North   True North   True North

Compass   Compass.
Orientation   Deviation
Dia. #3   Dia. #4   Orientation Correction
                                           Dia. #5
                                           To be used for Step 4.
                                           "Use of Tables to find
                                           factor (F)" of Sun Shades

PROBLEM

Known: Compass North of a site in Wichita, Kansas
To Find: 1. Latitude and Longitude of site.
          2. True North of site
          3. Sun time at site for 12 noon Daylight Savings Time on August 24th.

LOUVER SPACING *for* SUN SHADING OVERHANGS

LOUVER SPACING FOR OVERHANGS

The preceding sheets on sunshades show how to calculate the width of a solid overhang. The following shows a method for calculating the spacing or height of vertical and sloping louvers that run parallel to the building, to provide complete shade.

Step 1. Find the width of the projection as in steps one through six on sun shade pages. This width was based on the lowest angle of the sun.

Step 2. The calculations for the spacing of the louvers, however, are determined from the highest angle of the sun. Thus we must now use the smallest "F" factor found in step one to solve the problem of spacing.

PROBLEM

Known. "F" smallest factor obtained in step one. This is a pure number, related to one unit.

"H" height in inches (assumed vertical height of louver; for sloping louvers the desired angle of the louver and the width of board to be used should be laid out on paper and "H" measured vertically between highest and lowest corners.

Unknown. "D" distance between louvers in inches.

Vertical louvers: horizontal distance between inside faces of Louvers.
Sloping louvers: horizontal distance from top inside corner of one louver to bottom inside corner of second.

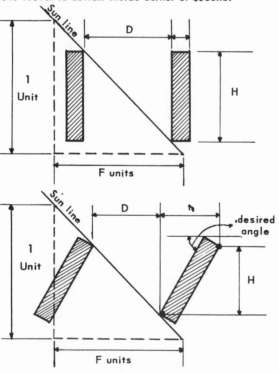

Solution. Substitute in the following formula the various dimensions obtained and solve to find the distance between louvers, "D"

$$D = \frac{F H}{I} \text{ (D \& H in inches)}$$

or

$$H = \frac{D}{F} \text{ (D \& H in inches)}$$

Unknown. "D" horizontal distance in inches for vertical or sloping louvers on a pitched roof.

Solution. Lay out to scale the triangle "I" to "F" to determine sun line. Then superimpose the roof pitch across sun line.

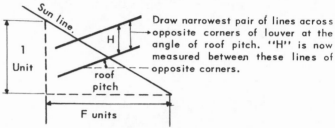

Draw narrowest pair of lines across opposite corners of louver at the angle of roof pitch. "H" is now measured between these lines of opposite corners.

At points of intersection of roof pitch and sun line lay out the desired vertical or sloping louvers with the "points of opposite corners touching these intersections. Then measure "D" for distance required.

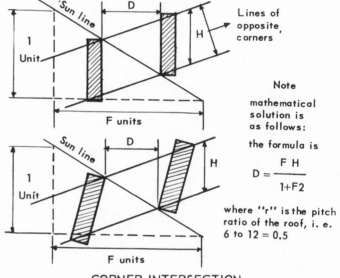

Note

mathematical solution is as follows:

the formula is

$$D = \frac{F H}{1+F^2}$$

where "r" is the pitch ratio of the roof, i. e. 6 to 12 = 0.5

CORNER INTERSECTION

If it is desired to shade two walls by the use of louvered overhangs, the procedure to find the overhangs is the same for both walls as outlined above. The corner joining of the two may be made in either of the following ways:

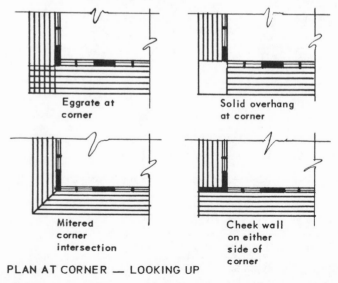

Eggrate at corner

Solid overhang at corner

Mitered corner intersection

Cheek wall on either side of corner

PLAN AT CORNER — LOOKING UP

data prepared in consultation with Andre Halasz A.I.A.

SUN-SHADING DEVICES

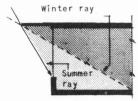

SOLID ROOF OVERHANG - FLAT AND PITCHED: effective primarily on South wall. Length of overhang can be calculated to eliminate summer sun's rays completely and to allow desirable winter rays to enter. Prevents free air movement. Darkens room on overcast days.

CONTROL OF REFLECTED LIGHT FROM GROUND ADJACENT TO GLASS AREA: light-colored concrete, cement, gravel or tile negate use of overhang by reflecting sun's rays into room. Grass, flagging or dark paving absorb or diffuse light.

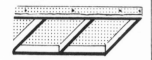

OVERHANGING BEAMS WITH REMOVABLE FABRIC: eliminates summer sun's rays. Removable to allow entry of winter rays. Hinders free air movement.

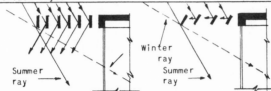

LOUVERED OVERHANG: eliminates direct rays of sun. Spacing of louvers and projection of overhang should be calculated if louvers are fixed. Permits free air movement and entry of diffused light.

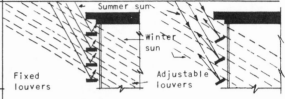

ADJUSTABLE HORIZONTAL LOUVERS: adjustable to control direct sun's rays and glare. View is broken by horizontal lines. Operation is questionable in northern climate.

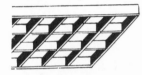

EGGCRATE OVERHANG: more effective than louvers as it eliminates oblique rays of sun. Permits free air movement and entry of diffused light. Expensive.

OVERHANG WITH HINGED SHADES: adjustable to eliminate summer sun's rays and to permit entry of winter rays. Interferes with view and free air movement.

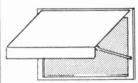

AWNING: adjustable to eliminate summer rays and to permit entry of winter rays. Interferes with view and free air movement. Expensive upkeep.

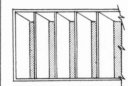

VERTICAL LOUVERS: On South, eliminates low rays. Use with overhang to eliminate all sun. Interferes with view. For Southern use.

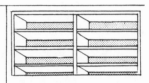

HORIZONTAL VERTICAL LOUVERS: On South, eliminates all sun's rays and glare. Interferes with view. For Southern Use.

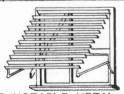

ADJUSTABLE METAL LOUVERED AWNING: controls sun at any angle. Operation doubtful in cold climate.

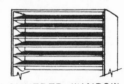

LOUVERED WINDOW UNIT OR JALOUSIE: adjustable to control direct sun's rays and glare. View is broken by horizontal louvers.

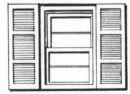

OPERATING SHUTTERS: eliminates sun's rays when closed. Interferes with view.

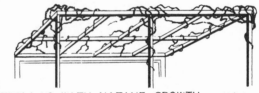

TRELLIS WITH NATIVE GROWTH: a thick growth eliminates sun's rays; some diffused light will penetrate. Allows sun penetration through bare vines in winter. Air moves freely around leaves.

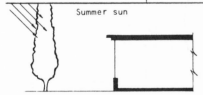
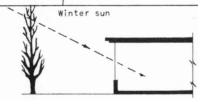

DECIDUOUS TREES (adjacent to South wall): eliminate or diffuse sun's rays in summer, allow sun penetration through bare branches in winter.

FENCE, HEDGE, WALL OR GROWTH ON LATTICE: eliminates low East and West rays of sun during summer. If growth is used, it allows sun penetration through bare vines in winter.

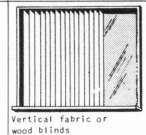

Fabric shades

Vertical fabric or wood blinds

Venetian blinds

INTERIOR DEVICES: easily installed and economical. Eliminate direct rays. However, heat gain through glass is high.

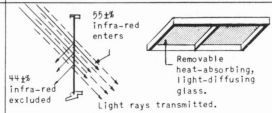

HEAT-ABSORBING GLASS: reduces amount of solar heat which enters room. Almost 1/2 of the sun's infra-red rays are excluded.

OVERHANG DETAILS *for* SUN SHADING

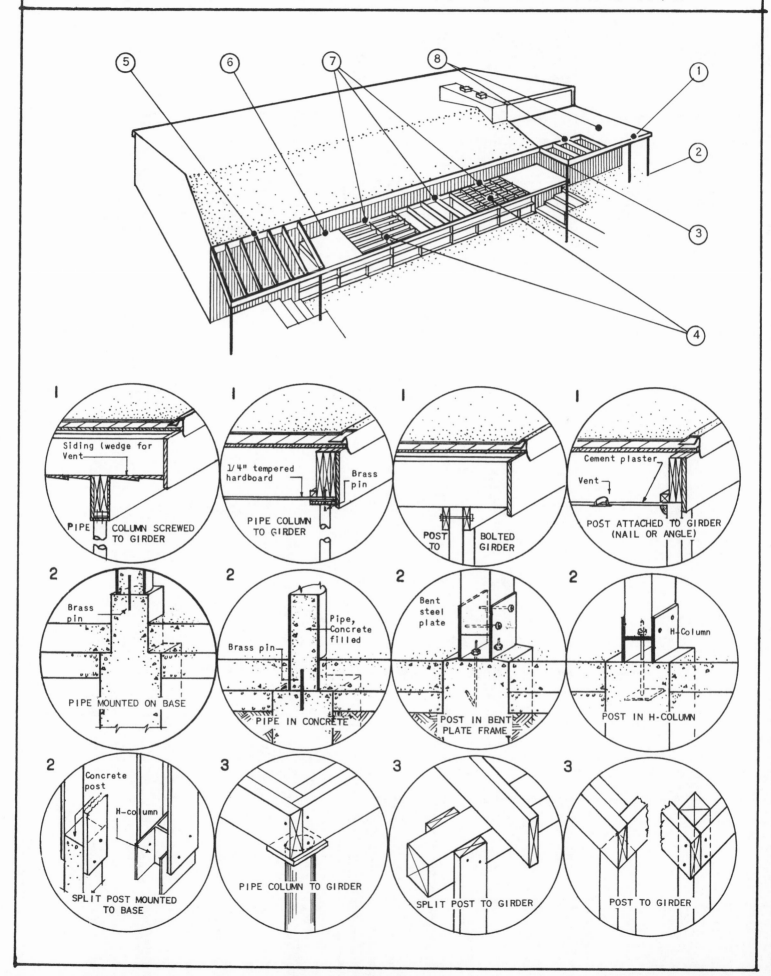

Siding (wedge for Vent)

PIPE COLUMN SCREWED TO GIRDER

1/4" tempered hardboard

Brass pin

PIPE COLUMN TO GIRDER

POST TO BOLTED GIRDER

Cement plaster

Vent

POST ATTACHED TO GIRDER (NAIL OR ANGLE)

Brass pin

PIPE MOUNTED ON BASE

Pipe, Concrete filled

Brass pin

PIPE IN CONCRETE

Bent steel plate

POST IN BENT PLATE FRAME

H-Column

POST IN H-COLUMN

Concrete post

H-column

SPLIT POST MOUNTED TO BASE

PIPE COLUMN TO GIRDER

SPLIT POST TO GIRDER

POST TO GIRDER

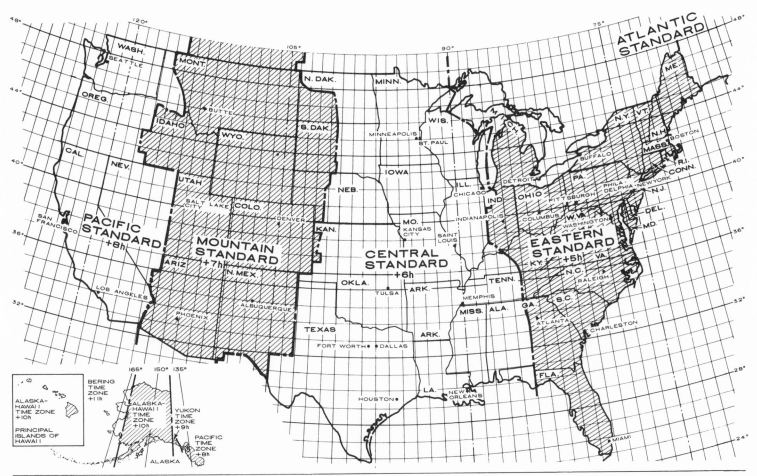

STANDARD TIME ZONES OF THE UNITED STATES
NOTE: Greenwich Standard Time is 0 h.

SOLAR TIME

Solar time generally differs from local standard or daylight saving time, and the difference can be significant, particularly when DST is in effect.

Because the sun appears to move at the rate of 360°/24 hr, its apparent motion is 4 min/1° of longitude. The procedure for finding AST (apparent solar time), explained in detail in the references cited previously, is

$$AST = LST + ET + 4(LSM - LON)$$

where ET = equation of time (min)
  LSM = local standard time meridian (degrees of arc)
  LON = local longitude, degrees of arc
  4 = minutes of time required for 1.0° rotation of earth

The longitudes of the six standard time meridians that affect the United States are: eastern ST, 75°; central ST, 90°; mountain ST, 105°; Pacific ST, 120°; Yukon ST, 135°; Alaska-Hawaii ST, 150°.

The equation of time is the measure, in minutes, of the extent by which solar time, as told by a sundial, runs faster or slower than civil or mean time, as determined by a clock running at a uniform rate. The table below gives values of the declination and the equation of time for the 21st day of each month of a typical year (other than a leap year). This date is chosen because of its significance on four particular days: (a) the winter solstice, December 21, the year's shortest day, $\delta = -23°$ 27 min; (b) the vernal and autumnal equinoxes, March 21 and September 21, when the declination is zero and the day and night are equal in length; and (c) the summer solstice, June 21, the year's longest day, $\delta = +23°$ 27 min.

EXAMPLES

Find AST at noon, local summer time, on July 21 for Washington, D.C., longitude = 77°; and for Chicago, longitude = 87.6°.

SOLUTIONS

In summer, both Washington and Chicago use daylight saving time, and noon, local summer time, is actually 11:00 a.m., local standard time. For Washington, in the eastern time zone, the local standard time meridian is 75° east of Greenwich, and for July 21, the equation of time is -6.2 min. Thus noon, Washington summer time, is actually

$$11:00 - 6.2\ min + 4 \times (75 - 77) = 10:46\ a.m.$$

For Chicago, in the central time zone, the local standard time meridian is 90°. Chicago lies 2.4° east of that line, and noon, Chicago summer time, is

$$11:00 - 6.2\ min + 4 \times 2.4 = 11:03\ a.m.$$

The hour angle, H, for these two examples would be

for Washington: H = 0.25 × (12:00 - 10:46)
    = 0.25 × 74 = 18.8° east

for Chicago: H = 0.25 × (12:00 - 11:03)
    = 14.25° east

YEAR DATE, DECLINATION, AND EQUATION OF TIME FOR THE 21ST DAY OF EACH MONTH; WITH DATA* (A, B, C) USED TO CALCULATE DIRECT NORMAL RADIATION INTENSITY AT THE EARTH'S SURFACE

MONTH	JAN.	FEB.	MAR.	APR.	MAY	JUNE	JULY	AUG.	SEPT.	OCT.	NOV.	DEC.
Day of the year†	21	52	80	111	141	173	202	233	265	294	325	355
Declination, (δ) degrees	-19.9	-10.6	0.0	+11.9	+20.3	+23.45	+20.5	+12.1	0.0	-10.7	-19.9	-23.45
Equation of time (min)	-11.2	-13.9	-7.5	+1.1	+3.3	-1.4	-6.2	-2.4	+7.5	+15.4	+13.8	+1.6
Solar noon	Late			Early			Late			Early		
A: Btuh/sq ft	390	385	376	360	350	345	344	351	365	378	387	391
B: 1/m	0.142	0.144	0.156	0.180	0.196	0.205	0.207	0.201	0.177	0.160	0.149	0.142
C: dimensionless	0.058	0.060	0.071	0.097	0.121	0.134	0.136	0.122	0.092	0.073	0.063	0.057

*A is the apparent solar irradiation at air mass zero for each month; B is the atmospheric extinction coefficient; C is the ratio of the diffuse radiation on a horizontal surface to the direct normal irradiation.
†Declinations are for the year 1964.

John I. Yellott, P.E.; College of Architecture; Arizona State University; Tempe, Arizona

DIAGRAM		A EXCLUDES DIRECT SUN RAYS	B RE-RADIATES HEAT	C CONTROLS SKY GLARE	D CONTROLS GROUND GLARE & HEAT	E EFFECTIVE ORIENTATION	F RESTRICTS VIEW	G HINDERS FREE AIR MOVEMENT	H CONTROLS WINTER RAYS	I MAINTENANCE (NOT CLEANING)
1. OVERHANG	Length of overhang calculated to eliminate summer sun.	Seasonal	No	No	No	South	No	Yes	Yes	Minimum unless otherwise noted
2. VERTICAL SCREEN (WITH OVERHANG)	Length of louver calculated to eliminate summer sun. Length of louver for sky glare dependent on amount of control desired on exterior conditions and occupants normal eye level.	Optional: Completely or seasonal.	Minimal	Yes	Some—amount varies with design.	Any direction. depends on design.	Yes— If opaque blade in louver. No— if tinted glass blade.	Slight	Depends on design	High for louver.
3. VERTICAL SCREEN (WITHOUT OVERHANG)	Length of louver or glass panel calculated to eliminate summer sun. Length of louver for sky glare dependent on amount of control desired on exterior conditions and occupants normal eye level.	Optional: Completely or seasonal.	Minimal	Yes	Some—amount varies with design.	Any direction. depends on design.	Yes— If opaque blade in louver. No— if tinted glass blade.	No— if louvers. Yes— if glass panel unless vent slats are provided.	Depends on design	Low for glazing
4. ADJUSTABLE EXTERIOR HORIZONTAL LOUVERS	Louvers can be adjusted to control direct rays of sun.	Optional	Minimal	No	Yes	Any direction. South is least restrictive to view.	Yes	No	Depends on design	Varies—depending on scale and materials used.
5A. OVERHANG VERTICALLY LOUVERED	Length of overhang calculated to eliminate summer sun.	Seasonal	No	Yes	No	South	No	No	Yes	Varies—depends on material used.
5B. OVERHANG ANGLE LOUVERED	Length of overhang and pitch of louvers calculated to eliminate summer sun and permit winter rays full penetration.	Seasonal	No	No	No	No	No	No	Yes—with louvers as shown, can permit maximum winter sun if desired.	Varies—depends on material used.
6. EXTERIOR VERTICAL LOUVERED	If fixed louvers can be set so as to eliminate low angle sun rays for predetermined orientation. If operable, maximum control any orientation but with various amount of view interference.	Optional: Completely or seasonal depending on orientation or other factors.	Minimal	Some	Some	East or west, south with adequate overhang.	Yes	No	Depends on design	Moderate
		As desired.	Minimal	Can be good see J	Some	Any	Yes	No	Yes	High
7. SPEC. GLAZING (GLASS, PLASTIC, COATED GLASS)	Heat absorbing glazing controls solar heat gain. Heat absorbing and low transmission glazing controls heat gain and sky glare. Sandwich of glass and fixed louvers can control direct sun rays and sky glare and admits greater amounts of useful daylight.	No— reduces— depending on glazing material.	Can be substantial unless double glazing used	Yes— ideal if darker sheets used in upper portion of window.	Yes	Any	No	See K	Yes— more than others	Low
		Seasonal	Low to minimal.	Yes	Same	Any	Yes	See K	Less than 7A	Low

J. Stanley Sharp, AIA; Handren, Sharp and Associates; New York, New York

J	K	L
EFFECT ON INTERIOR LIGHTING	**CAUTIONS**	**VARIATIONS**
Harsh without ideal exterior conditions, or with no glare control in glass or interior control devices.	Tends to trap warm air. High sash if open may let heat into building.	Overhang with light & heat transmission glass. Overhang with open framing with removable material (fabric, fiber glass). Trellis with plant material—permits entry of winter sun. Fixed awning—similar characteristics, except maintenance is high. Operable awning—also similar, plus lower sun angle control (west), restricts view when down.
Good	Check clearance for operating sash and window cleaning.	Addition of vertical member may be used to cut off low angle oblique rays. Adjustable vertical blinds or awnings afford good control for low sun, or glare from beach or water, without permanent restriction of view. Maintenance is high.
Good	Check clearance for operating sash and window cleaning.	Addition of vertical member may be used to cut off low angle oblique rays. Adjustable vertical blinds or awnings afford good control for low sun, or glare from beach or water, without permanent restriction of view. Maintenance is high.
Good—could be used for darkening device.		Exterior operating shutters have similar characteristics, and can be opened when not required but with loss of sky glare control.
Diffused reflected light from louvers improves quality of daylighting by reducing contrast between interior ceiling and bright sky.		Egg crate overhang instead of louvers to control oblique sun rays. Adjustable louvered awnings (questionable in cold climates) require high maintenance.
Diffused reflected light from louvers improves quality of daylighting by reducing contrast between interior ceiling and bright sky.		Egg crate overhang instead of louvers to control oblique sun rays. Adjustable louvered awnings (questionable in cold climates) require high maintenance.
Varies depending on position in room.	Check clearance for operating sash and window cleaning.	Narrow windows with adequate side reveals or projecting blades have similar sun and glare control.
Good—if a limited view is acceptable.		When used with adequate overhang on south will eliminate all sun in summer months.
Good (see C) w/high levels of artificial light, interior visual comfort is improved as reduces contrast between work surfaces and window area. Good—combine w/7A for ideal sky glare control w/a restricting eye level view.	Open sash may defeat sun & glare control, but is appropriate for a/c buildings. Replacement delay is probable. Open sash may defeat sun & glare control, but is appropriate for a/c buildings.	Allow only storm sash to be tinted to eliminate problem noted under B. Louvered screen placed in front of glazing would control sun but restricts view, maintenance factor if movable, and sky glare control is lost.

J. Stanley Sharp, AIA; Handren, Sharp and Associates; New York, New York

GENERAL NOTES

Uncontrolled glare, generated by the sun's rays, can become uncomfortable in winter; in summer, this glare plus solar heat can be intolerable. Glare can be effectively controlled by either interior or exterior devices, but solar heat gain is best controlled by interception outside the building. Tinted glass and/or interior devices such as shades, horizontal blinds, vertical blinds, as well as various screening methods may be used to control sky glare and glare from the direct rays of the sun. However, they do little to reduce interior air temperature because the sun rays have been allowed to enter the room. Do not use any form of translucent glass where sun will fall directly on it because this will produce glare similar to the dirty windshield of a car. Objectionable glare (i.e., a brightness ratio in excess of 10:1 between peripheral vision and the immediate area of vision) can occur at any orientation, including north, through indirect sources, by reflection from various surfaces. For example, light from a slightly overcast sky or from patches of white clouds can be 30 to 300 times greater than the light reflected from a well-lighted work surface. Provisions for shielding these secondary sources are particularly important to good vision when occupants of a space must remain in relatively fixed positions.

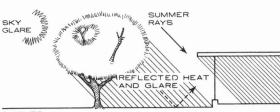

SUMMER
SUN AND GLARE AND HEAT CONTROLLED; I.E. EXCLUDED

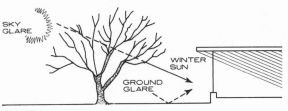

WINTER
SUN ACCEPTED—GLARE CAN BE A PROBLEM (SNOW IN PARTICULAR). CLOSELY SPACED LIMBS CAN CONTROL SKY GLARE.

SOUTH EXPOSURE

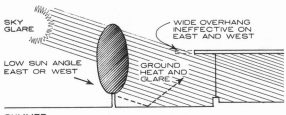

SUMMER
SUN GLARE AND HEAT CONTROLLED

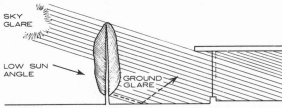

WINTER
LOW SUN ANGLE NOW ACCEPTED; GLARE CONTROLLED BY DENSE BRANCH STRUCTURE; HEAT CAN BE REASONABLY CONTROLLED AS DESIRED BY INSIDE DEVICES (SHADES, BLINDS, OR DRAPES).

EAST AND WEST EXPOSURE

APPLICATIONS IN CONJUNCTION WITH PLANTING

EXAMPLES OF HOW BASIC CONTROL DEVICES CAN BE USED IN CONJUNCTION WITH NATURAL FEATURES TO ACHIEVE GOOD SEASONAL RESULTS

NOTE

For more positive sky glare control in winter and summer, coniferous trees should be used.

SOLAR ANGLES

The position of the sun in relation to specific geographic locations, seasons, and times of day can be determined by several methods. Model measurements, by means of solar machines or shade dials, have the advantage of direct visual observations. Tabulative and calculative methods have the advantage of exactness. However, graphic projection methods are usually preferred by architects, as they are easily understood and can be correlated to both radiant energy and shading calculations.

SOLAR PATH DIAGRAMS

A practical graphic projection is the solar path diagram method. Such diagrams depict the path of the sun within the sky vault as projected onto a horizontal plane. The horizon is represented as a circle with the observation point in the center. The sun's position at any date and hour can be determined from the diagram in terms of its altitude (β) and azimuth (ϕ). (See figure on right.) The graphs are constructed in equidistant projection. The altitude angles are represented at 10° intervals by equally spaced concentric circles; they range from 0° at the outer circle (horizon) to 90° at the center point. These intervals are graduated along the south meridian. Azimuth is represented at 10° intervals by equally spaced radii; they range from 0° at the south meridian to 180° at the north meridian. These intervals are graduated along the periphery. The solar bearing will be to the east during morning hours, and to the west during afternoon hours.

(CONTINUED NEXT PAGE)

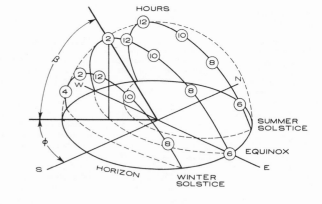

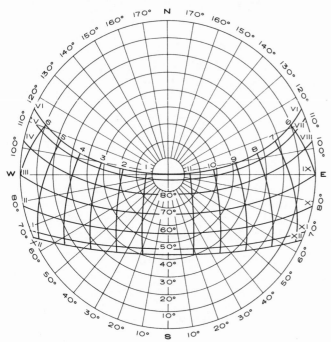

24°N LATITUDE

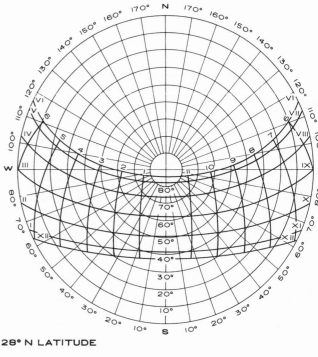

28°N LATITUDE

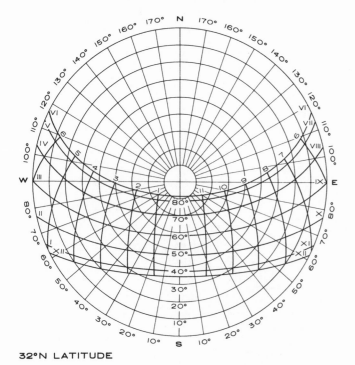

32°N LATITUDE

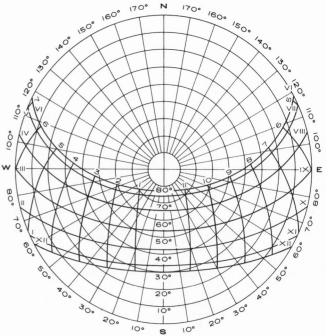

36°N LATITUDE

Victor Olgyay, AIA; Associate Professor; School of Architecture, Princeton University; Princeton, New Jersey

SOLAR PATH DIAGRAMS (CONTINUED)

The earth's axis is inclined 23°27' to its orbit around the sun and rotates 15° hourly. Thus, from all points on the earth, the sun appears to move across the sky vault on various parallel circular paths with maximum declinations of ±23°27'. The declination of the sun's path changes in a cycle between the extremes of the summer solstice and winter solstice. Thus the sun follows the same path on two corresponding dates each year. Due to irregularities between the calendar year and the astronomical data, here a unified calibration is adapted. The differences, as they do not exceed 41', are negligible for architectural purposes.

DECLINATION OF THE SUN

DATE	DECLINATION	CORRESP. DATE	DECLINATION	UNIFIED CALIBR.
June 21	+23°27'			+23°27'
May 21	+20°09'	July 21	+20°31'	+20°20'
Apr. 21	+11°48'	Aug. 21	+12°12'	+12°00'
Mar. 21	+0°10'	Sep. 21	+0°47'	+0°28'
Feb. 21	−10°37'	Oct. 21	−10°38'	−10°38'
Jan. 21	−19°57'	Nov. 21	−19°53'	−19°55'
Dec. 21	−23°27'			−23°27'

The elliptical curves in the diagrams represent the horizontal projections of the sun's path. They are given on the 21st day of each month. Roman numerals designate the months. A cross grid of curves graduate the hours indicated in arabic numerals. Eight solar path diagrams are shown at 4° intervals from 24°N to 52°N latitude.

EXAMPLE

Find the sun's position in Columbus, Ohio, on February 21, 2 P.M.:

STEP 1. Locate Columbus on the map. The latitude is 40°N.

STEP 2. In the 40° sun path diagram select the February path (marked with II), and locate the 2 hr line. Where the two lines cross is the position of the sun.

STEP 3. Read the altitude on the concentric circles (32°) and the azimuth along the outer circle (35°30'W).

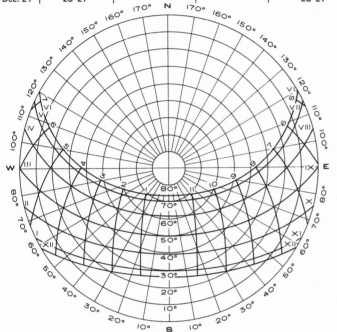

40°N LATITUDE

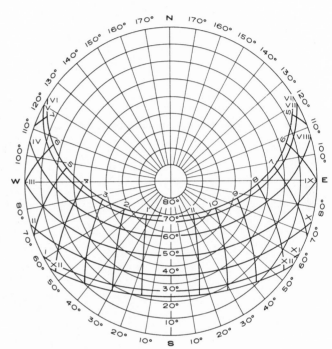

44°N LATITUDE

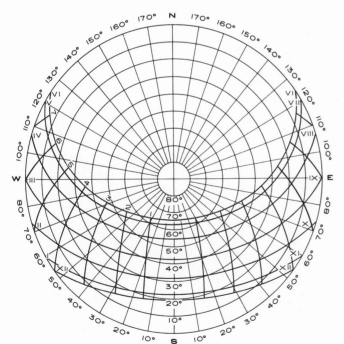

48°N LATITUDE

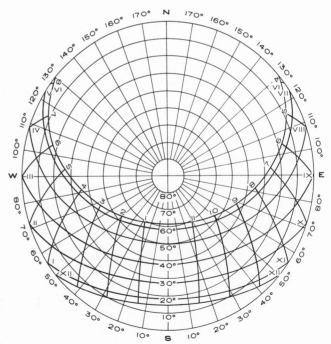

52°N LATITUDE

Victor Olgyay, AIA; Associate Professor; School of Architecture, Princeton University; Princeton, New Jersey

SHADING DEVICES

The effect of shading devices can be plotted in the same manner as the solar path was projected. The diagrams show which part of the sky vault will be obstructed by the devices and are projections of the surface covered on the sky vault as seen from an observation point at the center of the diagram. These projections also represent those parts of the sky vault from which no sunlight will reach the observation point; if the sun passes through such an area the observation point will be shaded.

SHADING MASKS

Any building element will define a characteristic form in these projection diagrams, known as "shading masks." Masks of horizontal devices (overhangs) will create a segmental pattern; vertical intercepting elements (fins) produce a radial pattern; shading devices with horizontal and vertical members (eggcrate type) will make a combinative pattern. A shading mask can be drawn for any shading device, even for very complex ones, by geometric plotting. As the shading masks are geometric projections they are independent of latitude and exposed directions, therefore they can be used in any location and at any orientation. By overlaying a shading mask in the proper orientation on the sun-path diagram, one can read off the times when the sun rays will be intercepted. Masks can be drawn for full shade (100% mask) when the observation point is at the lowest point of the surface needing shading; or for 50% shading when the observation point is placed at the halfway mark on the surface. It is customary to design a shading device in such a way that as soon as shading is needed on a surface the masking angle should exceed 50%. Solar calculations should be used to check the specific loads. Basic shading devices are shown below, with their obstruction effect on the sky vault and with their projected shading masks.

SHADING MASK PROTRACTOR

The half of the protractor showing segmental lines is used to plot lines parallel and normal to the observed vertical surface. The half showing bearing and altitude lines is used to plot shading masks of vertical fins or any other obstruction objects. The protractor is in the same projection and scale as the sun-path diagrams (see pages on solar angles); therefore it is useful to transfer the protractor to a transparent overlay to read the obstruction effect.

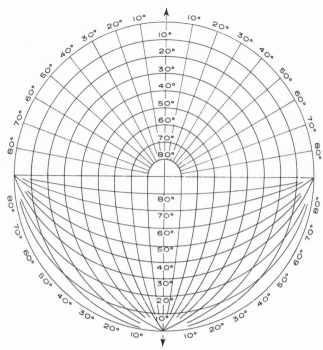

SHADING MASK PROTRACTOR

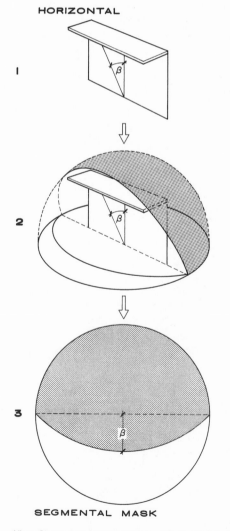

HORIZONTAL

SEGMENTAL MASK

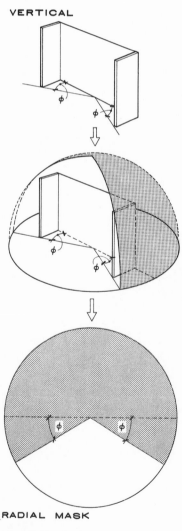

VERTICAL

RADIAL MASK

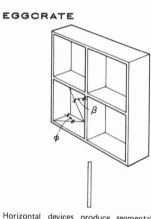

EGGCRATE

Horizontal devices produce segmental obstruction patterns, vertical fins produce radial patterns, and eggcrate devices produce combination patterns.

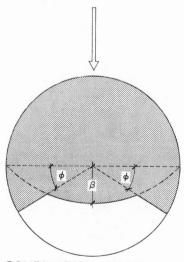

COMBINATION MASK

Victor Olgyay, AIA; Associate Professor; School of Architecture, Princeton University; Princeton, New Jersey

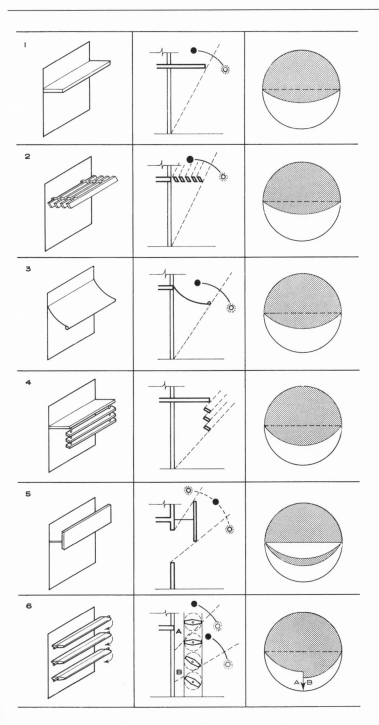

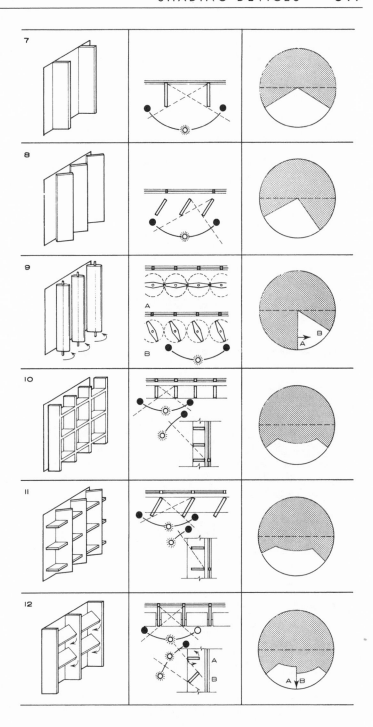

EXAMPLES OF VARIOUS TYPES OF SHADING DEVICES

The illustrations show a number of basic types of devices, classified as horizontal, vertical, and eggcrate types. The dash lines shown in the section diagram in each case indicate the sun angle at the time of 100% shading. The shading mask for each device is also shown, the extent of 100% shading being indicated by the gray area.

General rules can be deduced for the types of shading devices to be used for different orientations. Southerly orientations call for shading devices with segmental mask characteristics, and horizontal devices work in these directions efficiently. For easterly and westerly orientations vertical devices serve well, having radial shading masks. If slanted, they should incline toward the north, to give more protection from the southern positions of the sun. The eggcrate type of shading device works well on walls facing southeast, and is particularly effective for southwest orientations. Because of this type's high shading ratio and low winter head admission; its best use is in hot climate regions. For north walls, fixed vertical devices are recommended; however, their use is needed only for large glass surfaces, or in hot regions. At low latitudes on both south and north exposures eggcrate devices work efficiently.

Whether the shading devices be fixed or movable, the same recommendations apply in respect to the different orientations. The movable types can be most efficiently utilized where the sun's altitude and bearing angles change rapidly: on the east, southeast, and especially, because of the afternoon heat, on the southwest and west.

Victor Olgyay, AIA; Associate Professor; School of Architecture, Princeton University; Princeton, New Jersey

HORIZONTAL TYPES 1. Horizontal overhangs are most efficient toward south, or around southern orientations. Their mask characteristics are segmental. 2. Louvers parallel to wall have the advantage of permitting air circulation near the elevation. Slanted louvers will have the same characteristics as solid overhangs, and can be made retractable. 4. When protection is needed for low sun angles, louvers hung from solid horizontal overhangs are efficient. 5. A solid, or perforated screen strip parallel to wall cuts out the lower rays of the sun. 6. Movable horizontal louvers change their segmental mask characteristics according to their positioning.

VERTICAL TYPES 7. Vertical fins serve well toward the near east and near west orientations. Their mask characteristics are radial. 8. Vertical fins oblique to wall will result in asymmetrical mask. Separation from wall will prevent heat transmission. 9. Movable fins can shade the whole wall, or open up in different directions according to the sun's position.

EGGCRATE TYPES 10. Eggcrate types are combinations of horizontal and vertical types, and their masks are superimposed diagrams of the two masks. 11. Solid eggcrate with slanting vertical fins results in asymmetrical mask. 12. Eggcrate device with movable horizontal elements shows flexible mask characteristics. Because of their high shading ratio, eggcrates are efficient in hot climates.

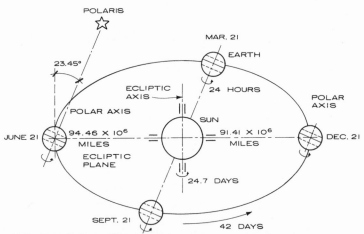

NOTE: THE TILT OF THE EARTH'S AXIS WITH RESPECT TO THE ECLIPTIC AXIS CAUSES THE CHANGING SEASONS AND THE ANNUAL VARIATIONS IN NUMBER OF HOURS OF DAYLIGHT AND DARKNESS.

ANNUAL MOTION OF THE EARTH ABOUT THE SUN

NOTE: Q DESIGNATES THE SUN'S POSITION SO OQ IS THE EARTH–SUN LINE WHILE OP' IS THE NORMAL TO THE TILTED SURFACE AND OP IS PERPENDICULAR TO THE INTERSECTION, OM, BETWEEN THE TILTED SURFACE AND THE HORIZONTAL PLANE.

SOLAR ANGLES WITH RESPECT TO A TILTED SURFACE

SOLAR CONSTANT

The sun is located at one focus of the earth's orbit, and we are only 147.2 million km (91.4 million miles) away from the sun in late December and early January, while the earth-sun distance on July 1 is about 152.0 million km (94.4 million miles).

Solar energy approaches the earth as electromagnetic radiation at wavelengths between 0.25 and 5.0 μm. The intensity of the incoming solar irradiance on a surface normal to the sun's rays beyond the earth's atmosphere, at the average earth-sun distance, is designated as the solar constant, I_{sc}. Although the value of I_{sc} has not yet been precisely determined by verified measurements made in outer space, the most widely used value is 429.2 Btu/sq ft · hr (1353 W/sq m) and the current ASHRAE values are based on this estimate. More recent measurements made at extremely high altitudes indicate that I_{sc} is probably close to 436.6 Btu/sq ft · hr (1377 W/sq m). The unit of radiation that is widely used by meteorologists is the langley, equivalent to one kilogram calorie/square centimeter. To convert from langleys/day to Btu/sq ft · day, multiply Ly/day by 369. To convert from W/sq m to Btu/sq ft · hr, multiply the electrical unit by 0.3172.

SOLAR ANGLES

At the earth's surface the amount of solar radiation received and the resulting atmospheric temperature vary widely, primarily because of the daily rotation of the earth and the fact that the rotational axis is tilted at an angle of 23.45° with respect to the orbital plane. This tilt causes the changing seasons with their varying lengths of daylight and darkness. The angle between the earth-sun line and the orbital plane, called the solar declination, d, varies throughout the year, as shown in the following table for the 21st day of each month.

JAN -19.9° APR +11.9° JUL +20.5° OCT -10.7°
FEB -10.6° MAY +20.3° AUG +12.1° NOV -19.9°
MAR   0.0°   JUN +23.5° SEP   0.0° DEC -23.5°

Very minor changes in the declination occur from year to year, and when more precise values are needed the almanac for the year in question should be consulted.

The earth's annual orbit about the sun is slightly elliptical, and so the earth-sun distance is slightly greater in summer than in winter. The time required for each annual orbit is actually 365.242 days rather than the 365 days shown by the calendar, and this is corrected by adding a 29th day to February for each year (except century years) that is evenly divisible by 4.

To an observer standing on a particular spot on the earth's surface, with a specified longitude, LON, and latitude, L, it is the sun that appears to move around the earth in a regular daily pattern. Actually it is the earth's rotation that causes the sun's apparent motion. The position of the sun can be defined in terms of its altitude β above the horizon (angle HOQ) and its azimuth ϕ, measured as angle HOS in the horizontal plane.

At solar noon, the sun is, by definition, exactly on the meridian that contains the south-north line, and consequently the solar azimuth ϕ is 0.0°. The noon altitude β is:

$$= 90° - L + \delta$$

Because the earth's daily rotation and its annual orbit around the sun are regular and predictable, the solar altitude and azimuth may be readily calculated for any desired time of day as soon as the latitude, longitude, and date (declination) are specified.

SHADOW CONSTRUCTION WITH TRUE SUN ANGLES

Required information: angle of orientation in relation to north-south axis (C), azimuth ϕ, and altitude angle β of the sun at the desired time (Figure 1).

STEP 1. Lay out building axis, true south and azimuth ϕ of sun in plan (Figure 2).

STEP 2. Lay out altitude β upon azimuth ϕ. Construct any perpendicular to ϕ. From the intersection of this perpendicular and ϕ project a line perpendicular to elevation plane (building orientation). Measure distance x along this line from elevation plane. Connect the point at distance x from elevation plane to center to construct sun elevation β (Figure 2).

STEP 3. Use sun plan $\phi + C$ and sun elevation β to construct shadows in plan and elevation in conventional way (Figure 3).

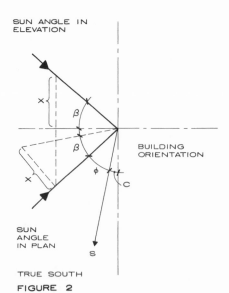

FIGURE 1

SUN ANGLE IN ELEVATION

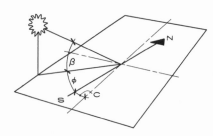

BUILDING ORIENTATION

SUN ANGLE IN PLAN

TRUE SOUTH

FIGURE 2

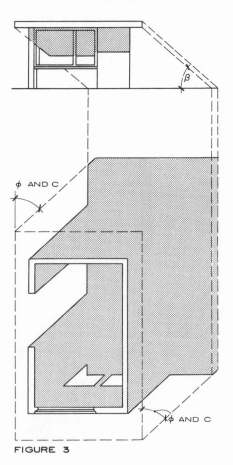

FIGURE 3

John I. Yellot, P.E.; College of Architecture; Arizona State University; Tempe, Arizona

CALCULATION OF SOLAR POSITION

The sun's altitude above the horizontal plane, A, and the solar azimuth, B, as measured toward the north from the south-north line in the horizontal plane, can be calculated accurately for any location, date, and time of day by using the following formulas:

$$\sin A = \cos L \cos d \cos H + \sin L \sin d$$

$$\cos B = \frac{\sin A \sin L - \sin d}{\cos A \cos L}$$

where

d = solar declination (angle between earth-sun line and equatorial plane)

H = hour angle of the sun = 15° x number of hours from local solar noon

Example: find solar altitude and azimuth for L = 40° north; local solar time = 2:00 P.M., H = 30°; date = March 21, d = 0.0°

$$\sin A = 0.766 \times 1.00 \times 0.866 + 0.643 \times 0.00$$

$$= 0.663$$

$$A = \text{arc sin } 0.663 = 41.53°$$

$$\cos B = \frac{0.663 \times 0.643 - 0.00}{0.749 \times 0.766} = 0.743$$

$$B = \text{arc cos } 0.743 = 41.98°$$

CALCULATION OF SOLAR IRRADIATION

The amount of solar radiation falling on exposed surfaces must be known before the importance of shading can be properly evaluated. Because shading devices protect surfaces primarily from the sun's direct irradiation, a method is given below for estimating this component of the total irradiation on clear days, for surfaces with varying orientation. For additional details, see 1977 ASHRAE Handbook of Fundamentals, p. 26.26. The intensity of direct solar irradiation depends on the solar altitude, the amount of water vapor in the atmosphere, and the earth-sun distance. When these factors are taken into account in accordance with the ASHRAE procedure, the following values are found for the direct normal irradiance (I_{DN}) in Btu/sq ft · hr:

Solar altitude (degrees)									
5	10	15	20	25	30	35	45	60	90

June 21, declination = +23.45°

| 33 | 106 | 156 | 189 | 212 | 229 | 241 | 258 | 272 | 281 |

March 21, September 21, declination = 0.00°

| 55 | 142 | 195 | 228 | 250 | 266 | 277 | 293 | 306 | 314 |

December 21, declination = -23.45°

| 77 | 173 | 226 | 258 | 279 | 294 | 305 | 320 | 332 | 339 |

At any given solar altitude, I_{DN} is significantly higher in winter than in summer because of the reduced water vapor content of the atmosphere and the shortened earth-sun distance. The direct irradiation $I_{D\theta}$ received by a particular surface is the product of the direct normal irradiance and the cosine of the angle of incidence θ between the solar rays and a line perpendicular to the surface:

$$I_{D\theta} = I_{DN} \cos \theta$$

For horizontal surfaces, the incident angle θ_H is the complement of the solar altitude ($\theta_H = 90 - A$), so:

$$I_{DH} = I_{DN} \times \sin A$$

For vertical surfaces, the incident angle θ_V is found from:

$$\cos \theta_V = \cos A \cos G$$

where the surface-solar azimuth G is the angle between the solar azimuth and the surface azimuth. Then:
$$I_{DV} = I_{DN} \cos A \cos G.$$

SOLAR-SURFACE ANGLES

The direction of the earth-sun line OQ is defined by the solar altitude A (angle HOQ) and the solar azimuth B (angle HOS). These can be calculated when the location (latitude), date (declination), and time of day (hour angle) are known. The surface azimuth S is the angle SOP between the south-north line SON and the normal to the surface OP. The surface-solar azimuth G is the angle HOP.

The angle of incidence θ depends on the orientation and tilt of the irradiated surface. For a horizontal surface, θ_H is the angle QOV between the earth-sun line OQ and the vertical line OV. For the vertical surface shown above as facing SSE, the angle of incidence θ_V is the angle QOP between the earth-sun line OQ and the normal to the surface, OP. For surfaces such as solar collectors, which are generally tilted at some angle T upward from the horizontal, the incident angle θ_T may be found from the equation:

$$\cosine\ \theta_T = \cosine\ A\ \cosine\ S\ \sine\ T + \sine\ A\ \cosine\ T$$

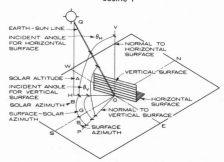

EARTH - SUN LINE
INCIDENT ANGLE FOR HORIZONTAL SURFACE
NORMAL TO HORIZONTAL SURFACE
VERTICAL SURFACE
SOLAR ALTITUDE
INCIDENT ANGLE FOR VERTICAL SURFACE
HORIZONTAL SURFACE
SOLAR AZIMUTH
NORMAL TO VERTICAL SURFACE
SURFACE-SOLAR AZIMUTH
SURFACE AZIMUTH

SOLAR ANGLE DIAGRAM

In the tables below, calculated values of the solar position angles in degrees and the direct irradiation values in Btu/sq ft · hr are shown for six vertical orientations and for horizontal surfaces, from 26°N to 46°N latitude by 4° intervals. The values are given for the summer and winter solstices and the spring and fall equinoxes.

26°N LATITUDE

JUNE 21

AM		ALT	AZM	S	SE	E	NE	N	SW	HOR
						BTU/SQ FT · HR				
6	6	10.05	111.30		42	98	96	38		19
7	5	22.82	105.97		91	180	164	52		79
8	4	35.93	101.15		110	193	164	38		143
9	3	49.24	96.45		107	171	134	19		199
10	2	62.69	91.17		87	126	91	3		243
11	1	76.15	82.61	9	53	66	41			271
12		87.45	0.00	13	9				9	281
	PM			S	SW	W	NW	N	SE	HOR

MARCH/SEPTEMBER 21

AM		ALT	AZM	S	SE	E	NE	N	SW	HOR
6	6	0.00	90.00							
7	5	13.45	83.30	21	138	175	109			42
8	4	26.71	75.80	56	196	222	117			115
9	3	39.46	66.33	88	205	202	80			181
10	2	51.11	52.79	114	186	150	25			233
11	1	60.25	31.43	130	148	79			36	266
12		64.00	0.00	135	95				95	277
	PM			S	SW	W	NW	N	SE	HOR

DECEMBER 21

AM		ALT	AZM	S	SE	E	NE	N	SW	HOR
7	5	2.23	62.48	5	10	9	3			
8	4	13.76	54.88	120	206	171	36			51
9	3	24.12	45.30	177	252	179	1			113
10	2	32.66	33.01	212	248	138			53	162
11	1	38.46	17.65	232	216	74			112	194
12		40.55	0.00	239	169				169	204
	PM			S	SW	W	NW	N	SE	HOR

30°N LATITUDE

JUNE 21

AM		ALT	AZM	S	SE	E	NE	N	SW	HOR
						BTU/SQ FT · HR				
6	6	11.48	110.59		50	113	110	42		25
7	5	23.87	104.30		97	184	163	47		84
8	4	36.60	98.26		117	194	157	28		146
9	3	49.53	91.79		117	171	125	5		200
10	2	62.50	83.46	14	99	126	79			243
11	1	75.11	67.48	27	66	66	27			270
12		83.45	0.00	32	23				23	279
	PM			S	SW	W	NW	N	SE	HOR

MARCH/SEPTEMBER 21

AM		ALT	AZM	S	SE	E	NE	N	SW	HOR
6	6	0.00	90.00							
7	5	12.95	82.37	23	137	170	104			40
8	4	25.66	73.90	63	199	218	110			109
9	3	37.76	63.43	100	212	200	71			173
10	2	48.59	49.11	128	196	148	14			223
11	1	56.77	28.19	147	159	79			48	254
12		60.00	0.00	153	108				108	265
	PM			S	SW	W	NW	N	SE	HOR

DECEMBER 21

AM		ALT	AZM	S	SE	E	NE	N	SE	HOR
7	5	0.38	62.40							
8	4	11.44	54.15	110	185	152	30			38
9	3	21.27	44.12	177	246	171			4	96
10	2	29.28	31.73	217	248	134			59	143
11	1	34.64	16.77	240	221	72			119	173
12		36.55	0.00	247	175				175	183
	PM			S	SW	W	NW	N	SE	HOR

Gary L. Powell; College of Architecture; Arizona State University; Tempe, Arizona

34°N LATITUDE

JUNE 21

AM		ALT	AZM	S	SE	E	NE	N	SW	HOR
5	7	1.47	117.57							
6	6	12.86	109.78		57	126	121	45		
7	5	24.80	102.54		103	188	162	42		34
8	4	37.07	95.28		125	195	151	18		99
9	3	49.49	87.10	9	127	171	115			158
10	2	61.79	76.00	31	111	125	67			205
11	1	73.17	55.10	46	79	66	14			234
12		79.45	0.00	51	36				36	244
	PM			S	SW	W	NW	N	SE	HOR

MARCH/SEPTEMBER 21

AM		ALT	AZM	S	SE	E	NE	N	SW	HOR
6	6	0.00	90.00							
7	5	12.39	81.48	25	134	165	99			37
8	4	24.49	72.11	69	201	215	103			103
9	3	35.89	60.79	110	217	197	61			163
10	2	45.89	45.92	142	204	147	3			211
11	1	53.21	25.60	163	170	78			60	241
12		56.00	0.00	169	120				120	251
	PM			S	SW	W	NW	N	SE	HOR

DECEMBER 21

AM		ALT	AZM	S	SE	E	NE	N	SW	HOR
8	4	9.08	53.57	93	155	126	23			25
9	3	18.38	43.12	173	236	162			8	79
10	2	25.86	30.65	219	246	130			63	123
11	1	30.81	16.05	245	223	70			123	152
12		32.55	0.00	253	179				179	162
	PM			S	SW	W	NW	N	SE	HOR

38°N LATITUDE

JUNE 21

AM		ALT	AZM	S	SE	E	NE	N	SW	HOR
5	7	3.32	117.42		3	9	10	5		1
6	6	14.18	108.87		64	137	130	47		37
7	5	25.60	100.70		109	190	160	36		93
8	4	37.33	92.25		133	195	144	8		149
9	3	49.13	82.47	23	137	171	105			199
10	2	60.58	69.06	48	122	125	55			238
11	1	70.61	45.67	64	92	66	1			262
12		75.45	0.00	70	50				50	270
	PM			S	SW	W	NW	N	SE	HOR

MARCH/SEPTEMBER 21

AM		ALT	AZM	S	SE	E	NE	N	SW	HOR
6	6	0.00	90.00							
7	5	11.77	80.63	26	130	158	93			33
8	4	23.20	70.43	75	202	210	96			96
9	3	33.86	58.38	120	222	194	53			153
10	2	43.03	43.16	155	212	145			7	198
11	1	49.57	23.52	177	180	77			71	227
12		52.00	0.00	185	131				131	236
	PM			S	SW	W	NW	N	SE	HOR

DECEMBER 21

AM		ALT	AZM	S	SE	E	NE	N	SW	HOR
8	4	6.69	53.12	69	114	92	16			13
9	3	15.44	42.30	164	221	149			10	61
10	2	22.40	29.74	216	240	124			66	103
11	1	26.96	15.45	246	222	68			126	130
12		28.55	0.00	255	180				180	139
	PM			S	SW	W	NW	N	SE	HOR

42°N LATITUDE

JUNE 21

AM		ALT	AZM	S	SE	E	NE	N	SW	HOR
5	7	5.15	117.16		11	31	33	16		3
6	6	15.44	107.87		70	147	137	47		43
7	5	26.28	98.78		115	192	157	30		96
8	4	37.38	89.19	3	140	196	136			150
9	3	48.45	77.96	36	146	170	95			196
10	2	58.95	62.79	64	133	125	43			233
11	1	67.64	38.62	82	105	66			12	256
12		71.45	0.00	88	63				63	263
	PM			S	SW	W	NW	N	SE	HOR

MARCH/SEPTEMBER 21

AM		ALT	AZM	S	SE	E	NE	N	SW	HOR
6	6	0.00	90.00							
7	5	11.09	79.84	27	126	151	87			30
8	4	21.81	68.88	79	201	205	89			88
9	3	31.70	56.21	128	225	191	45			142
10	2	40.06	40.79	166	218	143			16	184
11	1	45.88	21.82	190	188	76			81	211
12		48.00	0.00	198	140				140	220
	PM			S	SW	W	NW	N	SE	HOR

DECEMBER 21

AM		ALT	AZM	S	SE	E	NE	N	SW	HOR
8	4	4.28	52.82	35	58	46	8			4
9	3	12.46	41.63	148	197	131			12	44
10	2	18.91	29.00	209	229	116			66	82
11	1	23.09	14.96	242	217	65			125	107
12		24.55	0.00	253	179				179	115
	PM			S	SW	W	NW	N	SE	HOR

46°N LATITUDE

JUNE 21

AM		ALT	AZM	S	SE	E	NE	N	SW	HOR
5	7	6.97	116.78		20	56	60	29		8
6	6	16.63	106.77		76	155	142	47		48
7	5	26.82	96.80		121	194	154	23		99
8	4	37.22	86.15	13	147	195	129			149
9	3	47.47	73.66	50	155	169	85			192
10	2	56.95	57.25	80	144	124	31			226
11	1	64.40	33.33	99	116	65			24	248
12		67.45	0.00	106	75				75	255
	PM			S	SW	W	NW	N	SE	HOR

MARCH/SEPTEMBER 21

AM		ALT	AZM	S	SE	E	NE	N	SW	HOR
6	6	0.00	90.00							
7	5	10.36	79.09	27	120	142	81			26
8	4	20.32	67.45	83	199	199	82			80
9	3	29.42	54.27	134	227	187	37			130
10	2	36.98	38.75	175	223	140			24	169
11	1	42.14	20.43	201	195	75			89	194
12		44.00	0.00	210	148				148	203
	PM			S	SW	W	NW	N	SE	HOR

DECEMBER 21

AM		ALT	AZM	S	SE	E	NE	N	SW	HOR
8	4	1.86	52.65	3	5	4	1			
9	3	9.46	41.12	122	162	107			11	27
10	2	15.41	28.41	194	212	105			63	61
11	1	19.23	14.56	232	207	60			122	84
12		20.55	0.00	244	173				173	92
	PM			S	SW	W	NW	N	SE	HOR

Gary L. Powell; Arizona State University; Tempe, Arizona

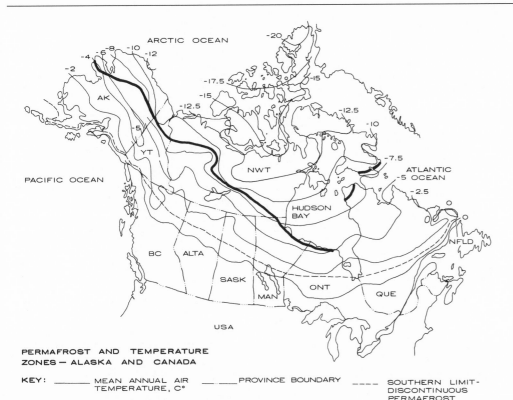

PERMAFROST AND TEMPERATURE
ZONES — ALASKA AND CANADA

KEY: _____ MEAN ANNUAL AIR   — __ — PROVINCE BOUNDARY   ———— SOUTHERN LIMIT-
                  TEMPERATURE, C°   DISCONTINUOUS
                                                                                         PERMAFROST

         _____ SOUTHERN LIMIT   —···—···— COUNTRY BOUNDARY
                  CONTINENTAL
                  PERMAFROST

PERMAFROST, ICE WEDGES AND LENSES, AND FROST HEAVE

DEFINITION OF PERMAFROST: Ground of any kind that stays colder than the freezing temperature of water throughout several years.

TERMS

ACTIVE LAYER: Top layer of ground subject to annual freezing and thawing.

FROST HEAVING: Lifting or heaving of soil surface created by the freezing of subsurface frost susceptible material.

FROST SUSCEPTIBLE SOIL: Soil that has enough permeability and capillary action (wickability) to expand upon freezing.

ICE LENSE (TABER ICE): Pocket of ice.

ICE WEDGE: Wedge shaped mass of ice within the soil. Wedges range up to 3 or 4 wide and 10 deep.

PERELETOK: Frozen layer at the base of the active layer that remains unthawed during cold summers.

RESIDUAL THAW ZONE: Layer of unfrozen ground between the permafrost and active layer. This layer does not exist when annual frost extends to the permafrost, but is present during warm winters.

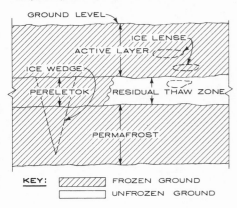

KEY: ▨▨▨ FROZEN GROUND
       ▢▢▢ UNFROZEN GROUND

CCC/HOK; Anchorage, Alaska

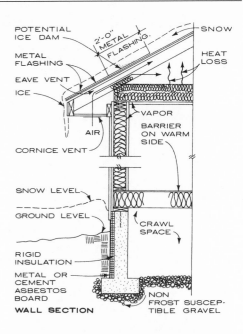

WALL SECTION

EAVE AND FOUNDATION DETAILING IN COLD CLIMATES

Snow buildup on the roof is warmed by heat loss from the building. The melting snow flows down the roof and is refrozen at the eave because of the eave's cold condition. The use of a cornice vent and insulation to create a "cold roof" helps to reduce the problem of ice damming. When an ice dam is created, the water backs up, leaking under roofing materials. The placement of metal flashing on the roof at least 2 ft 0 in. up from the wall line causes the snow and ice to slide off and also prevents moisture penetration.

All vapor barriers in cold and arctic conditions must be on the warm side to avoid condensation in the insulation. Use of rigid insulation on the exterior of the foundation wall (with a metal or cement asbestos board cover for protection) creates a heat bank and keeps the utility space from freezing.

PILES

In the arctic, piles are popular because they are a simple way of providing thermal isolation of heated structures, minimize disturbance of existing thermal regime, permit flow of flood waters, and prevent the buildup of drifting snow. However, frost heaving can force the piles upward during the freeze season without allowing the piles to return to the original level when the soil thaws.

Solutions to the problem of pile heaving:

1. Anchor the pile against uplift by placing anchors or notches on the pile within the permafrost zone.

2. Break the bond in the active layer. (Use bond breaking plastic wrap or grease pile in the active layer.)

3. To aviod thaw of the surrounding soil, use one of the three main one-way heat extractors: (a) The gaseous flow system or, (b) the liquid system, containing tubes with "Venturi" funnels to allow warm liquid to rise and cold liquid to sink, and (c) a mechanical refrigeration system. The designer must be careful not to allow heat to be transferred from the building to the pile (thus avoiding thawing the permafrost).

CONDITIONS OF BUILDING ON PERMAFROST

CONDITION 1: Building elevated on piles allows for the dissipation of building heat to help prevent the ground from thawing. Added benefits include winter refreezing of ground by cold winter air and prevention of snowdrift buildup.

CONDITION 2: Building elevated on nonfrost susceptible gravel pad. Benefits include lessening of snowdrift problems and retardation of permafrost thaw. Existing ground cover can remain as insulation. Rigid insulation can also be used.

UTILITIES IN COLD CLIMATE AND ARCTIC CONDITIONS

Utilidors or utiliducts are the most common way to provide protection, easy access, and insulation of utility lines to avoid disturbance to the permafrost.

Human waste at isolated facilities may be handled by compost privies (waterless toilets) and chemical toilets, which are commonly referred to as "honey buckets." Disposal systems include incineration and sewage lagoons.

LOCATION

Generally the hot-dry regions of North America are in the SW corner of the United States and the NW corner of Mexico, below the snow line. They consist of valleys and deserts below 3000 ft in elevation with an annual temperature above 65°F.

HOT—DRY REGION OF THE U.S.

CLIMATE SUMMARY

Some part of every day or night throughout the year is totally comfortable and pleasant; the balance of the time the climate is usually excessively hot or cold. The 3 to 5 months of summer are the most demanding and establish the critical design parameters; preventing heat gain is the objective. Winter nights are cold but winter days are comfortable. Lack of cloud cover means maximum solar radiation (above 80% annual possible sunshine), little rainfall (average less than 10 in./yr), and high evaporation rate (over 100 in./yr). Summer cooling loads are larger than winter heating loads for all building types.

CLIMATE CHARACTERISTICS

EXCESSIVE RADIATION

Solar radiation and thermal reradiation of heat stored in materials are the prime sources of discomfort. Daily temperature highs average over 100°F from mid-May into September. Clear night skys absorb summer heat but cause heavy frosts every winter.

LOW HUMIDITY

Precipitation averages under 10 in./yr. Infrequent rains are often heavy; resulting runoff produces flash floods. Evaporation rates average over 100 in./yr, resulting in very low relative humidities. Occasional dust storms are encountered.

HIGH DIURNAL TEMPERATURE VARIATION

Range between daily maxima and minima may exceed 50°F. However, in late summer, night temperatures may not drop below 80°F.

HIGH SEASONAL TEMPERATURE VARIATION

Winter lows and summer highs may vary as much as 100°F.

SIGNIFICANT MICROCLIMATES

Both natural and manmade microclimatic variations can occur in a relatively short distance: elevation and landscaping are the major influences.

PLANNING AND SITING

PLANNING

Encourage high density and compact planning; use party or common walls, concentrate development for mutual shading and insulation. Mixed land uses reduce travel time and the need for frequent travel.

PEDESTRIANS

Provide tight, protected circulation; encourage short pedestrian paths. Shading is necessary for pedestrians—use arcades, narrow alleyways, awnings, tree canopies, trellises.

LANDSCAPING

Vegetation is desirable for psychological and evap-transpiration cooling. Prefer native types: riparian near buildings, desert varieties in open areas. Cluster non-native materials for maximum effect through engineered watering systems; use oasis concepts. Deciduous plants provide a sense of seasons and also winter sun penetration. Vegetative ground cover can reduce ground reflectance, shade the earth, and reduce air temperatures. Include rain holding and percolation areas in site shaping.

Professor Jeffrey Cook; College of Architecture; Arizona State University; Tempe, Arizona

BUILDING FORM

ORIENTATION

Minimize exposure to W. Ideal orientation for openings is S. However, orientations from S to 25°E of S can provide appropriate shading control. Northerly orientations for openings are also desirable. Avoid swimming pools on W or N of building.

SHAPE

Compact building forms elongated on an E-W axis are preferable. Design forms to maximize self-shading. Generally keep volume-to-surface ratio high. Avoid courtyard and patio schemes except where building volume/surface ratio is large, or perimeter walls have maximum thermal resistance. Earth contact designs and underground approaches desirable.

MICROCLIMATE

Respond to existing microclimate conditions. Design adjacent microclimates on all sides. Landscape shields on E and W can temper sun and heat impact on buildings. Major elements can direct prevailing cooling breezes. Walled-in gardens and yards can hold cool air pools. Consider water features and heavy vegetation for cooling effect, but watch the costs of water.

FUNCTIONAL ZONING

Use varying construction strategies in a single building. High mass construction is recommended for day use or 24 hr use functions; light, highly insulated low mass construction preferred for occasional use or night use functions; use screened porches, exposed decks, and sheltered terraces for controlled outdoor uses, occupied on time-of-day or season basis.

THERMAL ZONING

Place noninhabited spaces on the W to buffer heat. Isolate heat producing activities. Use vestibules or lobbies in public spaces to provide thermal transitions.

NATURAL LIGHTING

Day lighting (diffuse solar radiation) of work spaces is recommended especially from N. All daylight sources (windows and skylights) should be self-shaded on the exterior. Since smaller window openings are preferred, natural lighting requires special design attention. Use light colored interiors to distribute daylight.

COLOR/TEXTURE

Use light reflective colors on roof and E, S, and W walls to reject summer heat. A greater range of choice is possible on N elevations. Avoid specular reflective surfaces (mirror finishes) because of their focusing nature. Use medium or darker colors adjacent to openings to avoid reflections into interiors. Bright colors are preferable for visual contrast in the bright sunshine of the region; colors in the shadows, such as eaves and soffits, are especially effective.

DESIGN STRATEGIES

Design for cooling by evaporation by considering vegetation, pools, fountains, roof ponds, sprays, landscape watering systems, and so on. Mechanical evaporation cooling systems are effective.

Provide heavy interior thermal mass protected by insulation from exterior temperatures for thermal conservation, combine high mass and low mass in a

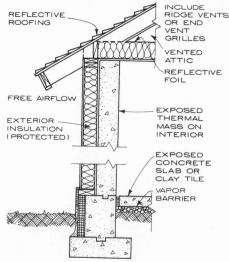

RESIDENTIAL CONSTRUCTION DETAIL

single structure for different times of use.

Use transitional zones both in construction (i.e., thick wall assemblies) and in planning (i.e., intermediate or transitional areas and seasonal spaces).

Design microclimates using both architectural and landscape materials and forms to modify climate and temper the natural extremes.

BUILDING ELEMENTS

FOUNDATIONS

Use masonry or concrete in earth contact; slab on grade, basement, or earth-bermed structures. Insulation necessary above grade.

EXTERIOR WALLS

Walls should be seasonally shaded whenever possible. In hot climates shading strategies are critical.

ROOFS

The roof is the most effective location for both shading and insulation. Roof surfaces should be reflective. Overhead insulation values should be approximately 1.5 times thermal resistance of walls. Vented attics are the common method of reducing overhead radiant heat gain. Double roofs, roof ponds, or sprayed roofs are also effective. Roof sprays are more effective than ponds and can bring down surface temperatures approximately 50°F; however, the process is very hard on materials.

THERMAL CAPACITY

Both capacity insulation and resistance insulation materials are important. Heat capacity construction is recommended in excess of 70 lb of heat absorbing building materials per cu ft of space. An ideal strategy is a minimum of a 10 hr heat lag.

THERMAL RESISTANCE

Minimum recommended thermal resistance in roofs is R30 and in walls, R19. Together with caulking, vapor barriers are recommended also to reduce infiltration.

WEATHERING

Masonry, concrete, and ceramic clay products can last indefinitely. Masonry construction requires frequent wetting during setting and curing. Adobe requires maintenance but can have an extended life. Generally, exposed metals show little weathering. Excessive heat and ultraviolet radiation are destructive of many materials such as wood and plastics.

OPENINGS

Doors, windows, and other openings should be selectively shaded according to season. Closures should be tightly fitted and should include weather stripping. Double glazing is cost effective for all elevations. Generally, ratio of opening to floor space should be small (12% or less). Provide for seasonal natural cross-ventilation. Partially movable shading may provide seasonal control. Shading devices should be self-venting by free convection to avoid heat buildup.

EQUIPMENT

EQUIPMENT CHOICES

Select equipment that minimizes heat production.

EVAPORATIVE COOLING

Above 1500 ft elevation conventional evaporative coolers can provide complete comfort more than 90% of the time. Below 1500 ft they can be effective more than 50% of the time. Systems require complete air changes every 2 to 3 min. They provide total comfort if the wet bulb temperature is below 70°F; reasonable comfort when wet bulb temperature is between 70 and 74°F. For wet-bulb temperature above 74°F evaporation coolers only produce relief. Duct sizes must allow air at 1600 ft/min, preferably 1200 ft/min for silence and efficiency.

AIR CONDITIONERS

Heat pumps are a good choice although the cooling load determines sizing. In these climates equipment must operate consistently at higher outdoor air temperatures (115°F and above). Conventional refrigerated air conditioners and heat pumps are normally rated at operating temperatures of 82 and 95°F. Equipment sizing should accommodate load operating conditions.

HEAT SINKS

Generally stable earth temperatures range from 68 to 75°F, thus the earth offers poor cooling sources. Clear night skies can offer 25% conductive/convective, 25% radiative, 50% evaporative cooling potential. Evaporative sprays are the most effective heat sinks; mechanical evaporation systems probably have the most potential.

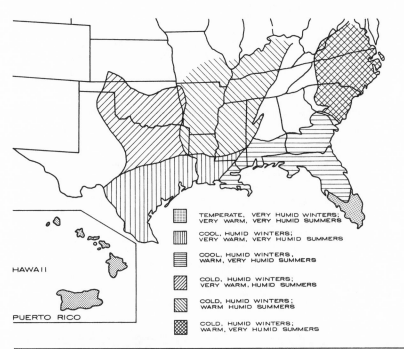

TEMPERATE, VERY HUMID WINTERS;
VERY WARM, VERY HUMID SUMMERS

COOL, HUMID WINTERS;
VERY WARM, VERY HUMID SUMMERS

COOL, HUMID WINTERS;
WARM, VERY HUMID SUMMERS

COLD, HUMID WINTERS;
VERY WARM, HUMID SUMMERS

COLD, HUMID WINTERS;
WARM HUMID SUMMERS

COLD, HUMID WINTERS;
WARM, VERY HUMID SUMMERS

HAWAII

PUERTO RICO

WARM – HUMID REGIONS OF THE UNITED STATES

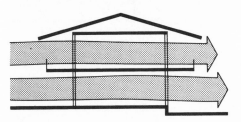

Suburban or rural, single family, where land is plentiful.

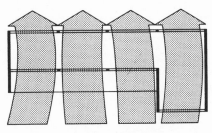

L-shaped plan allows a narrower frontage, screens and doors need perforation and careful attention to detail.

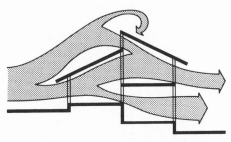

Double banked split level buildings generally stifle air motion, but can allow adequate cross ventilation through careful design.

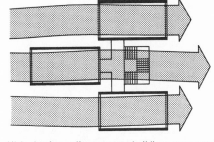

High density, tall apartment buildings must provide maximum external walls for two generous openings per habitable room.

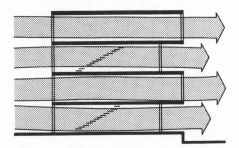

Maisonettes and split-levels can be economical solutions with access balconies, terraces, and corridors assisting in air movement and shading.

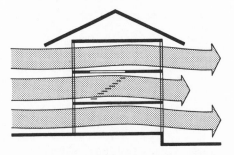

Multistory row development in medium density areas permits cross ventilation when deep room single banked plans are employed.

BUILDING FORM UNDER NATURAL CONDITIONS

Arthur Bowen, RIBA; Professor of Architecture & Planning; University of Miami; Coral Gables, Florida

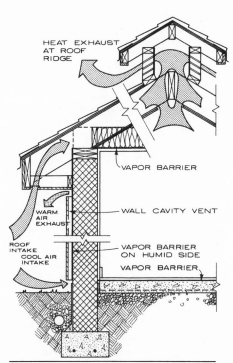

HEAT EXHAUST
AT ROOF
RIDGE

VAPOR BARRIER

WARM
AIR
EXHAUST

WALL CAVITY VENT

ROOF
INTAKE
COOL AIR
INTAKE

VAPOR BARRIER
ON HUMID SIDE

VAPOR BARRIER

TYPICAL VENTILATION PATTERNS IN WALL SECTION

WARM-HUMID CONSTRUCTION

Characteristics of warm-humid climates are moist air, above average rainfall, variable air movement, damp ground, and air temperatures seldom exceeding skin temperature. Hot humid areas do not exist in the United States.

ORIENTATION

Under all conditions in overheated areas, the building structure must be vented for cooling. Human comfort may be achieved, when natural conditions prevail, by convective cooling of interior space and human skin. Building orientation must accomplish these needs; solar radiation response is of secondary concern as several methods are available to overcome this. When mechanical comfort conditions are employed, solar radiation considerations dominate orientation. Generally, all habitable rooms must have at least two external openings; bathrooms, stores, and kitchens should be placed in the leeward areas of buildings. Stack vents should be used to release heat from kitchens. Corridors, balconies, and terraces assist lateral air movement, while stairwells and elevators encourage vertical motion. Roofs should be pitched because of rainfall, unless needed for activities.

MATERIALS AND CONSTRUCTION METHODS

Diurnal temperatures vary by 10–15°F, so that thermal mass with a long time lag is unnecessary and may be undesirable under certain conditions. Appropriate materials should be poor conductors—wood, plastics, aluminum. Well ventilated structures are essential to prevent mildew or rotting of materials. Regular cleaning of fly screens will allow continuous airflow and control vermin that can be abundant in these regions. Exterior finishes should be of a light color.

SITE AND LANDSCAPE PLANNING

Airflow in and around buildings and urban areas is essential in warm-humid regions. Under natural conditions, single banked buildings should be staggered to achieve this. When mechanically controlled, cooling of the building envelope, only, need be assured. Generous employment of landscaped areas in and around buildings promotes cooling.

BUILDING FORM UNDER MECHANICALLY CONTROLLED CONDITIONS

Envelope must be ventilated with a pitched roof unless it is used for another purpose. Interior volume must be minimal with a low surface/volume ratio. Airflow through the building's interior must be prohibited.

NATURAL VENTILATION IN AND AROUND BUILDINGS

Airflow may be gainfully employed in and around buildings for the following tasks:

1. To provide essential air exchange for hygienic purposes—for health and for odor removal.
2. To cool human skin by accelerating conductive and evaporative loss when this is needed.
3. To cool interior space when this is desirable.
4. To cool building fabric in overheated conditions.
5. To remove undesirable moisture from the building's fabric, surfaces, and interior spaces.

GLOBAL AND LOCAL WIND SYSTEMS

Global air movement is governed by three forces: pressure gradient, coriolis, and friction. Local conditions of topography, continentality, and urbanization modify or even supersede prevailing regional systems. Seasonal and diurnal changes are recorded throughout the United States, and this information may be obtained from the National Climate Center, Asheville, North Carolina, and the "Climatic Atlas of the United States" published by the United States Government Printing Office. A wind rose, wedge or matrix, should be compiled for each site, establishing the velocity, frequency, direction, and temperatures that affect it. (Figure 1.)

AIRFLOW PATTERNS

Air will flow from higher (+ve) to a lower (–ve) pressure zone. These pressures exist at a building's boundary and between exterior and interior air. (Figure 2.) Pressures may be manipulated in and around buildings by location and size of openings. Where air velocity is low, it will be accelerated when inlets are smaller than outlets. Where steady, desirable, prevailing winds occur in warm-humid conditions, restricted openings hinder comfort and both inlets and outlets should be large.

Wind flowing against a building causes a high pressure area on the windward side and a low pressure area or wind shadow on the leeward side.

Incoming airstreams may change direction several times, resulting in a decrease in velocities, but promoting turbulence that will improve air movement in areas where stagnation may otherwise occur. Velocities decrease when partitions are located close to the inlet but improve when located nearer the outlet.

CROSS VENTILATION PATTERNS

Partition perpendicular to initial flow alters pattern; back room supplied at cooling speed. (Figure 3.)

Flow is intercepted by partitions; blocking slows flow effect to considerable extent. Cooling effect becomes meager. (Figure 4.)

Partitions parallel to initial flow splits pattern but result remains at adequate high speeds. (Figure 5.)

High inlet and outlet produces poor air movement at body level. (Figure 6.)

Low inlet and outlet produces desirable low level airflow across human body. (Figure 7.)

Poor patterns result when low and high inlets alternate on opposite walls. (Figure 8.)

Louvers can direct airflow upward or downward. (Figure 9.)

Canopies produce an upward airstream that can be corrected by separating the projection from the wall or piercing the canopy. (Figures 10 and 11.)

External barriers reduce air movement through building. (Figure 12.)

Inlet and outlet size and locations radically affect airflow patterns in partitioned rooms. (Figures 13 and 14.)

EFFECTS OF SITE AND LANDSCAPE PLANNING

The building can be exposed or protected from air motion as determined by regional and local conditions. Orientation, shape, and the prudent selection and setting of landscape materials can provide optimum conditions at the building's boundary. Building materials and live plantings may be used individually and in various combinations to create wind barriers or wind scoops in harmony with building needs. Arbors of large canopy trees may reduce ambient temperatures 4–6°F and encourage cool, dense air to flow toward buildings. (Figure 15.)

Arthur Bowen, RIBA; Professor of Architecture & Planning; University of Miami; Coral Gables, Florida

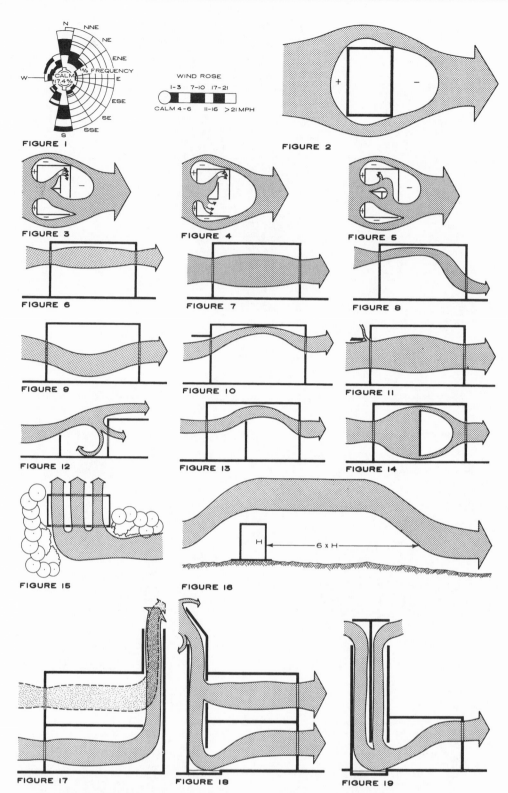

FIGURE 1

WIND ROSE
1-3 7-10 17-21
CALM 4-6 11-16 >21 MPH

FIGURE 2

FIGURE 3

FIGURE 4

FIGURE 5

FIGURE 6

FIGURE 7

FIGURE 8

FIGURE 9

FIGURE 10

FIGURE 11

FIGURE 12

FIGURE 13

FIGURE 14

FIGURE 15

FIGURE 16

FIGURE 17

FIGURE 18

FIGURE 19

For winds up to 5 mph, a wind shadow is created on the leeward side of buildings, in depth approximately six times the height or width, whichever is the lesser dimension. The depth of the shadow increases with increasing wind velocity. (Figure 16.)

SOLAR INDUCED VENTILATION

Three categories of thermal chimneys can generate airflow: (1) anabatic or "stack effect," which is a conventional method of hot air release from interior space (Figure 17); (2) pressure or "down draft" chimney, which functions efficiently when predictable direction and velocity prevailing winds occur (Figure 18); and (3) "katabatic" or "cold draft" chimneys, which will only function efficiently when large diurnal temperature differences occur (Figure 19).

WALL OPENINGS

Wall openings traditionally are windows and doors. Pivoted and awning windows provide good ventilation. Sliding glass doors and windows provide only 50% of available opening unless rolled back completely. Adjustable louvered doors and windows provide privacy and good ventilation. A louvered "Caribbean" hood provides good rain protection and ventilation at the same time.

DAYLIGHTING

Ample daylight is available throughout North America for lighting interior spaces during a large portion of the working day. This light is thought by many to be psychologically desirable, and there is some evidence that it has biological benefits. Its variability through the day provides some beneficial visual exercise. Its use in place of, or in conjunction with, other light sources can conserve energy. Daylight carries with it significant quantities of heat which, in properly designed buildings, may be used to conserve energy. Daylight produces less interior heat per unit of illumination, however, than do most forms of electric light.

The principles of good lighting apply equally to daylight and electric light. The difference is in the location of the light source, its color spectrum, and its variability.

SOURCE

Daylight comes directly from the sun, from the diffuse sky and clouds, and is reflected from the ground and other surrounding objects. Direct sun penetrating into interior workspaces may cause excessive luminance contrasts. Direct sun should be controlled by proper orientation of the building, or by louvers, overhangs, shades, blinds, or other devices. Diffuse light from the sky may cause excessive luminance contrasts when viewed by eyes concentrating on an interior task. In such cases, the sky should be filtered or shielded from view or the view of the task should be oriented away from the windows. As much as half the light entering a space can be reflected from the ground.

DESIGN GUIDELINES

ROOM DEPTH

The level of illumination will be shallower in the interior than near the window. A rule of thumb is that daylighting can be effective for task illumination up to about 20 to 24 ft away from the windows, but this depends on the size and location of the windows. A window high in the fenestration wall will deliver light deeper into the interior than a low window of the same size. Venetian blinds may be used to reflect daylight against the ceiling and into more remote areas of the space while preventing the penetration of direct sunlight and view of excessively luminous areas on the exterior. The cross-sectional diagrams below show how the depth of the room affects daylight.

FINISHES

Finishes of interior surfaces are important in the control of light and luminous ratios. Light colored surfaces, diffusely reflecting, will aid in the distribution of light and reduce luminance ratios. The diagrams below show how room surfaces affect daylight from a window. The ceiling is the most effective surface for reflecting light and should be very light in color (preferably white). The floor is one of the least significant, and it is here that the designer has the greatest opportunity for use of darker colors, such as those found in carpets, although very dark colors may cause excessive luminance differences.

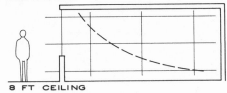

8 FT CEILING

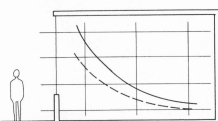

12 FT CEILING

The higher and larger the window, the more light there will be in the interior. The dashed illumination curve for the 8 ft ceiling can be compared with the solid curve for the 12 ft ceiling. Window areas below the level of the work surface are not effective in providing light on the task.

WINDOW HEIGHT

Benjamin H. Evans, AIA; Blacksburg, Virginia

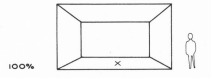

100%

All room surfaces are white, and the illumination level at point x is 100%.

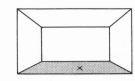

68%

With the floor painted black the illumination level is 68% of the all-white room.

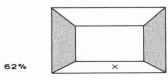

62%

With the sidewalls painted black.

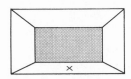

50%

The back wall has been painted black, and the illumination level at point x is only 50% of that in the all-white room.

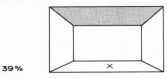

39%

With the ceiling painted black.

SURFACE FINISHES

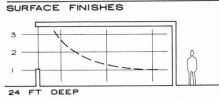

24 FT DEEP

The dashed curve indicates the illumination distribution for a typical 24 ft deep room.

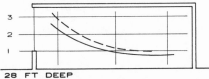

28 FT DEEP

The solid curve indicates the illumination level for a 28 ft deep room and can be compared with the dashed curve from the top diagram.

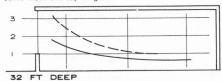

32 FT DEEP

The solid curve indicates the illumination level for a 32 ft deep room and can be compared with the dashed curve from the top diagram.

ROOM DEPTH

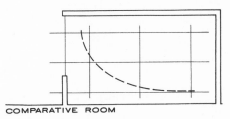

COMPARATIVE ROOM

A particular room produces a distribution of daylight as indicated by the dashed curve (repeated below).

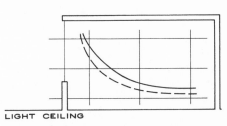

LIGHT CEILING

When the reflectivity of the ceiling is increased (painted white) the illumination level increases as indicated by the solid curve. The distribution curve flattens somewhat, since the increased ceiling reflectance increases illumination most toward the back wall.

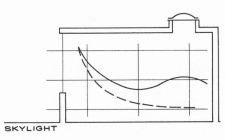

SKYLIGHT

The introduction of a skylight near the back wall increases the illumination in that area. (A clerestory, or a high window in the back wall, would produce similar results.)

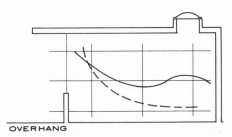

OVERHANG

An overhang can be used to reduce the illumination near the windows to a greater degree than in the back of the room. Another way to do this is with horizontal louvers on the exterior of the window wall or with interior venetian blinds.

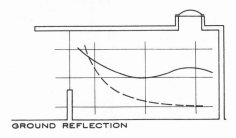

GROUND REFLECTION

Increasing the ground reflectivity (e.g., with a concrete walk) outside the window will increase the general level of interior illumination.

DAYLIGHTING METHODS

TERMS COMMONLY USED IN LIGHTING DESIGN

ENGLISH	SI	MEASURE OF
Candlepower	Candlepower	Intensity
Lumen	Lumen	Light flux
Footcandle (ft-c)	Lux	Density-lumen/ft^2 (lux/m^2)
Reflectance (R)	Reflectance	$R = \dfrac{\text{ft-c (reflected)}}{\text{ft-c (incident)}}$
Transmission (T)		$T = \dfrac{\text{ft-c (transmitted)}}{\text{ft-c (incident)}}$
Footlambert (ft-L)	Candlepower/m^2	Luminance ft-L = ft-c x R

SUBJECTIVE IMPRESSION APPEARS TO BE AFFECTED BY:

Visual clarity	Peripheral wall brightness
	Luminance in the center of the room
	Cool color light source and continuous spectrum output
Spaciousness	Peripheral lighting (not affected by color)
Relaxation	Nonuniform, peripheral (wall) lighting
Attention	Intensity of light and contrast
	Recommended contrast ratios:
	2/1: subliminal differences
	10/1: minimum for significant focal contrast
	100/1: dominating contrast
Privacy, intimacy	Lighting of background and/or inanimate objects (centerpieces)
Gaiety, playfulness	Visual noise and "clutter" such as sparkle, random patterns
Somberness	Dimness and diffusion of light

SEEING

Although many of the characteristics of quality seeing conditions are known, it is a difficult area to define precisely. Research continues in an effort to uncover knowledge of how people see and what kind of lighting conditions are most desirable for every situation.

RECOGNITION OF TASKS

The human ability to recognize detail generally varies with respect to (1) contrast between the details of a task and its immediate surround, (2) luminance (or brightness) of the task, (3) size of the task, and (4) time of viewing.

Maximum visibility is attained when the luminance contrast of details against their background is greatest (e.g., black ink on white paper). Significant savings of electric energy can occur when the task contrast is maximized because the level of illumination needed is reduced. The same opportunity occurs with task size (e.g., large size type on a typewriter saves on the need for illumination). The luminance of the task depends on the amount of incident illumination and the reflectivity of the task. A small amount of light on white paper may be as effective for seeing as a large amount of illumination on dark cloth. With increased time available for viewing, illumination levels can be reduced (e.g., when speed is not critical).

VEILING REFLECTIONS

Substantial losses in contrast, hence in visibility and visual performance, can result when light is reflected from specular visual tasks (the task is "veiled"). This is perhaps the most significant factor in poor seeing conditions. Three factors govern these veiling reflections: (1) the nature of the task, (2) the observer's

Benjamin H. Evans, AIA; Blacksburg, Virginia

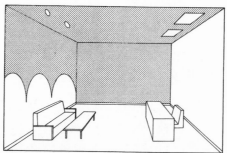

LIGHTING CAN DEFINE A CHANGE OF MOOD BETWEEN DESK AND MORE RELAXED SEATING AREA

LUMINAIRE PATTERNS THAT CONFLICT WITH STRUCTURE CAN DESTROY HARMONY OF SPACE

ILLUMINATION

Proper illumination depends on the establishment of design goals that define the desired environment, rather than on the equipment needed. Lighting is the most expressive tool available for setting the tone for perception of the environment. It should be thought of as a design tool and not as an "add on" to provide light, and its consideration should be fundamental to any design effort.

Light should be considered to be what we "see by" and not that which we actually see. We do not see footcandles (the measure of quantity). We see luminance as a result of reflected or direct light. (When perceived rather than measured, it is called brightness.) The footlambert is the unit of measurement of brightness.

Of course, there must be enough light. (The unit of measure is the footcandle.) The quantities of illumination necessary for various visual tasks have been

orientation and viewing angle, and (3) the lighting system.

THE TASK

The luminance of the task (e.g., writing or printing on paper) depends on both the amount of light being reflected from it and the bright object or surface (e.g., luminaire) that may be reflected in it. Diffusing or matte papers and inks tend to reduce veiling reflections.

THE OBSERVER

If the eye is in such a position that the rays of light from the "offending zone" are reflected toward it, veiling reflections will occur. This situation can usually be observed in a space by placing a sheet of clear acetate or some other glossy surface over the task

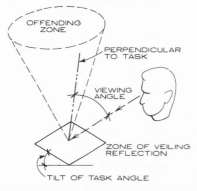

TASK LIGHTING

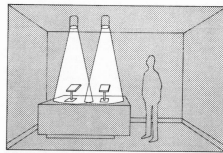

DOWNLIGHTS FOCUS ATTENTION ON OBJECT

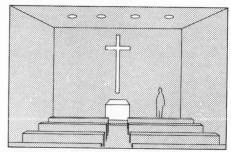

LIGHT CAN DIRECT ATTENTION TO A SPECIFIC FOCAL POINT BY A SHARP CONTRAST OF LIGHT AND DARK SURFACES

recommended by the Illuminating Engineering Society (IES) based on research. But the quantity of illumination needed on walls, floors, ceilings, and so on, for the creation of a beautiful and functional environment is very much left to the designer's logic, experience, and intuition. The proper lighting of all tasks, whether functional or esthetic, is vital to a total design, and recommended footcandle levels should be considered only as targets.

PURPOSE

Lighting can define the intended use of a space by focusing on points of attention and subduing less important areas. It can be used to express structural concepts by silhouetting beams, arches, and columns or to emphasize unusual contours. Mechanical equipment can be made to visually recede with dark paint and the absence of light. Light can help to define space use changes through brightened ceiling areas or changes of light patterns on walls.

(such as a book or paper with writing or printing) and observing the reflections (if any). Sources of light in this offending zone should be minimized for best seeing conditions.

LIGHTING SYSTEMS

The worst condition is a highly concentrated, bright source, above and forward, directed at the task. Paradoxically, it is also the condition under which the worker can most easily escape veiling reflections by tilting or reorienting the task so that the reflected rays do not reach the eye (e.g., as in turning the back so the light comes over the shoulder). Placement of lighting equipment and fenestrations in the general area above and forward of the task (or desk) should be avoided. When the nature of the tasks and their location are known, luminaires can be located to avoid the offending zone. When task locations are not known and flexibility is necessary, as for speculative office space, general low level ambient lighting, which tends to negate the effects of veiling reflections, and task lighting can be provided by plug-in units at the discretion of the tenant.

EQUIVALENT SPHERE ILLUMINATION (ESI)

ESI is a unit adopted by the IES for measuring the visibility potential of a particular task at a particular location and with a specific lighting system. It is a unit of measurement just as is the meterstick. It is not a standard of quality, but a way of taking into consideration those elements by which quality is judged. ESI cannot be measured over the area of a room as simply as raw footcandles, because ESI depends on a task, a location, an orientation, and a lighting system. A task has 50 ESI when it is as visible as it would be when illuminated by 50 ft-c of illuminance produced by a photometric sphere.

TASK AMBIENT LIGHTING

Task ambient (T/A) lighting systems have become popular because they provide higher intensity illumination on the task only and lower levels of ambient light for general circulation, thereby reducing electric energy usage. T/A systems are designed to give localized desk (or task) lighting and, usually, to project some percentage of illumination toward the ceiling for ambient (general purpose) lighting. A T/A lighting system generally requires fewer watts per square foot of floor space (as little as 1.5 W/sq ft) than does the conventional ceiling lighting system (up to 4 or 5 W/sq ft) and thus can be a significant energy saver. However, the principles of good lighting still apply, and not all T/A lighting systems provide sufficient task illumination without producing excessive ceiling reflections. Luminaires should be glarefree; the light source should not be visible from the working position. Direct glare from the normal passing position should be avoided. The downlight should illuminate the back panel of the work station as evenly as possible. A T/A system should not produce excessively bright spots of light on low ceilings and adjacent walls. Poor distribution of illumination on room surfaces can be visually disturbing to occupants.

LUMINAIRE SELECTION PARAMETERS

In selecting a luminaire that will create good seeing conditions several factors should be considered:

1. DIRECT GLARE is produced by excessive luminances in the visual field that affect the visual systems as the individual looks around the environment. It is usually associated with the luminaire zone from 45° to 90°. To minimize direct glare, the luminous intensity should be kept out of the 45° to 90° zone.

2. VISUAL COMFORT PROBABILITY (VCP) is the indicator used to evaluate the direct glare zone area of luminance. Luminaries are given a VCP rating, which indicates the percent of people who, if seated in the most undesirable location, will be expected to find the luminaire acceptable from the standpoint of direct glare (excessive luminances in the visual field).

3. Direct glare may not be a problem if all three of the following conditions are satisfied: (a) The VCP is 70 or more; (b) the ratio of maximum-to-average luminance does not exceed 5 to 1 at 45°, 55°, 65°, 75°, and 85° from nadir crosswise and lengthwise; (c) maximum luminaire luminances do not exceed:

2250 ft-L at 45°
1620 ft-L at 55°
1125 ft-L at 65°
750 ft-L at 75°
495 ft-L at 85°

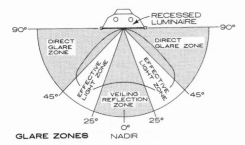

GLARE ZONES

ASHRAE STANDARD 90-75

The American Society for Heating, Refrigeration, and Air Conditioning Engineers has established a procedure for determining a "Lighting Power Budget," which has been adopted in some areas as a mechanism for determining how much electrical energy will be allowed for lighting purposes in new buildings. The lighting power budget is intended only as a mechanism for encouraging energy conservation in lighting and is not a design tool. Once the budget has been established, the designer is free to design the lighting system to achieve the best quality lighting within the budget and for the circumstances. Much can be done to conserve energy while staying within the lighting budget.

MAINTENANCE AND DEPRECIATION

All elements of the building that affect light need to be kept clean. Luminaires, diffusers, lenses, window glass, louvers, blinds, wall surfaces, and so on, tend to collect dust, which reduces their light-controlling efficiency. In the lighting formulas below a Luminaire Dirt Depreciation (LDD) factor is used to account for collected dust and dirt. The LDD figure used will depend on the type of atmosphere in the room and the frequency of cleaning. Also, lamps depreciate with time, with their effective lumen output reduced, which is accounted for in the calculations with the application of the Lamp Lumen Depreciation (LLD) factor.

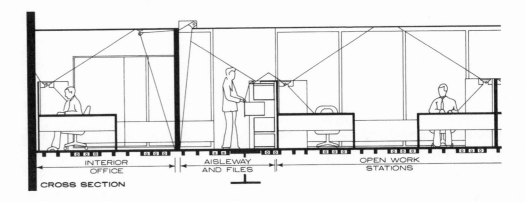

CROSS SECTION — INTERIOR OFFICE | AISLEWAY AND FILES | OPEN WORK STATIONS

SOME USEFUL FORMULAS FOR GENERAL LIGHTING DESIGN

$$\text{NUMBER OF LUMINAIRES} = \frac{\text{footcandles desired} \times \text{room area}}{\text{CU} \times \text{LLD} \times \text{LDD} \times \text{lamps/luminaire} \times \text{lumens/lamps}}$$

$$\text{AVERAGE FOOTCANDLES} = \frac{\text{lumens/lamp} \times \text{lamps/luminaire} \times \text{CU} \times \text{LLD} \times \text{LDD}}{\text{area of room (sq ft)}}$$

$$\text{TOTAL ILLUMINATION (W/sq ft)} = \frac{\text{footcandles desired}}{\text{overall lumens/watt} \times \text{CU} \times \text{LLD} \times \text{LDD}}$$

where   CU = Coefficient of Utilization
LLD = Lamp Lumen Depreciation
LDD = Luminaire Dirt Depreciation

NOTE

See manufacturer's photometric tables or the Lighting Handbook of the Illuminating Engineering Society for tables giving values of CU, LLD, LDD, lumens/lamps, and so on.

TYPICAL EXAMPLES

Room size 25 x 40 ft; ceiling height 9 ft; office area 70 ft-c; 2 x 4 ft recessed troffers with 4–40 W T12 lamps (3100 lm) each. From IES tables, Room Index = E and CU = 0.67 (plastic lens):

$$\text{NUMBER OF FIXTURES} = \frac{70 \times 25 \times 40}{0.67 \times 0.7 \times 4 \times 3100} = 8.4 \text{ (use 8 luminaires)}$$

$$\text{TOTAL ILLUMINATION (W/sq ft)} = \frac{8 \times 200 \text{ W/luminaire}}{25 \times 40} = 1.6 \text{ W/sq ft}$$

IES RECOMMENDED ILLUMINATION LEVELS (ESI AT THE TASK)

5 FT-C	10 FT-C	20 FT-C	30 FT-C	50 FT-C	70 FT-C	100 FT-C	150 FT-C	200 FT-C
Exits, at floor	Restaurant	Cleaning	Classrooms	Inspection	Commercial kitchen	Garage repair	Rough drafting	Fine drafting
TV viewing	Parking garages	Hospital room	Waiting rooms	Rough factory assembly	General writing and reading	Office reading	Accounting	Engraving
Theater foyer	Hotel bath	Stairways	Restrooms	Bank lobby	Dormitory desk	Sewing	Office fine work	Color printing inspection
	General residential	Hotel bedroom	Entrance foyers	Church pulpit	Handicraft	Merchandising areas	Proofreading	Critical seeing tasks
			Laundry	Checking and sorting				
			Reading printed material					

Benjamin H. Evans, AIA; Blacksburg, Virginia

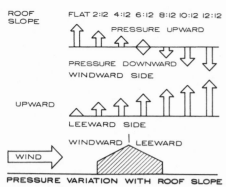

PRESSURE VARIATION WITH ROOF SLOPE

Wind resistant construction requires that roof, wall, floor, and foundation structures be tied together, thus acting in unison to withstand the wind forces acting on the entire structure.

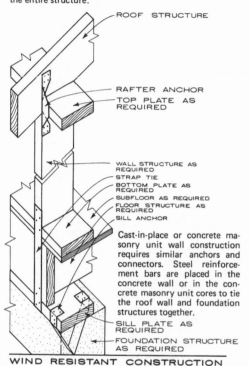

Cast-in-place or concrete masonry unit wall construction requires similar anchors and connectors. Steel reinforcement bars are placed in the concrete wall or in the concrete masonry unit cores to tie the roof wall and foundation structures together.

WIND RESISTANT CONSTRUCTION

MINIMUM DESIGN WIND LOADS

SOUTHERN STD. BLDG. CODE			UNIFORM CODE	
HEIGHT ZONE	HORIZONTAL LOADS		HEIGHT ZONE	HORIZONTAL LOADS
FT	LB/SQ FT		FT	LB/SQ FT
	INLAND REGION	COASTAL REGION		
0-30	10	25	0-60	15
31-50	20	35	60 up	20
51-99	24	45		
100-199	28	50	Coastal region is the area lying within 125 miles of the coast.	
200-299	30	50		
300-399	32	50		
Over 400	40	50		

MINIMUM WIND LOADS ON PITCHED, OR GABLE, ROOFS

1. For roof slopes less than 30°; design to withstand loads acting outward normal to the surface equal to 1¼ times the horizontal loads specified for the corresponding height zone in which the roof is located.
2. For roof slopes greater than 30°; design to withstand loads acting inward normal to the surface equal to those specified for zone, with load applied to windward slope.

Douglas R. Coonley, CHI Housing, Inc.; Hanover, New Hampshire

Protection is provided on the leeward side of hills and in valleys oriented away from prevailing wind directions. Vegetation and trees serve to filter or deflect wind, thus reducing wind loads. Man-made structures provide similar protection to natural forms. However, built structures are usually more angular than trees or hills, causing less predictable and more turbulent airflow.

Proper site planning can substantially increase energy output from wind collector systems. Windward hill crests, open fields, high points of land, valleys oriented in line with prevailing winds, and edges of open bodies of water provide favorable wind collector locations. Increased height above ground level usually gives smoother and faster airflow because of reduced ground interference. Built structures can retard the performance of wind systems if they obstruct the free flow of air. Careful planning, measurement, and expert consultation are necessary to ensure proper design with wind. On-site data collection and analysis are often required to realize a successful and integrated wind design.

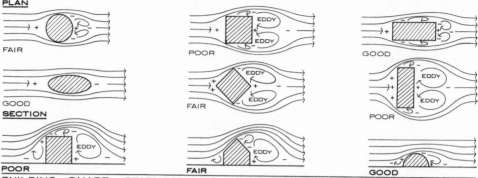

BUILDING SHAPE, ORIENTATION, AND AIRFLOW

Passive wind systems use wind directly without discrete conversion, storage, or distribution systems. Windows, vents, louvers, and roof vents are examples of passive wind systems. Active wind systems use wind indirectly to produce mechanical or electrical energy.

An active wind system includes collector, converter, orientation device, support, storage, distribution, and control. The collector intercepts the wind and drives a converter which changes the collector's motion into a more usable energy form (such as electricity). Generators, gear trains, mechanical linkages, and pumps are examples of converters. An orientation device keeps the wind collector pointed in the proper direction. Tail vanes, gear drives, and collectors are examples of orientation devices. Vertical axis collectors usually do not require an orientation device because of their multidirectional character. The collector system is held aloft by a support structure which may be a tower, post, guy wire, or building (such as a Dutch windmill). A distribution system transmits the energy to places where it is to be used through electric lines, mechanical linkages, or water lines. Energy storage may be provided by batteries, fuel cells, water tanks, or reservoirs. A control system monitors and coordinates these components to provide proper operation and performance of the wind collector system.

Energy output from active collectors depends on wind velocity, collector type, and distribution system. Consult local wind data and wind system distributors for specific information. Active wind systems require shutdown during extreme wind conditions (usually in winds above 40 mph), and usually do not produce energy in winds below 5 mph. The useful working range varies with different wind collector systems and must be coordinated with site conditions to achieve proper performance.

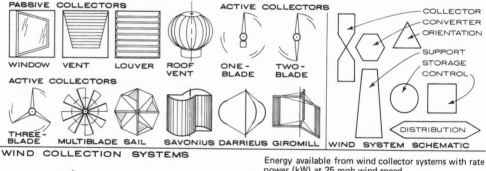

WIND COLLECTION SYSTEMS

Energy available from wind collector systems with rate power (kW) at 25 mph wind speed.

▨	3750-5000 KWH/KW
▩	2250-3750 KWH/KW
☐	750-2250 KWH/KW

Estimated energy output in kWh/kW at 100 ft elevation.

Wind varies greatly in both velocity and direction from one site to another. Thus specific site evaluation is critical in determining potential energy output from each wind site. Average annual wind direction is not very useful because wind direction varies widely on an hourly, daily, monthly, and seasonal basis.

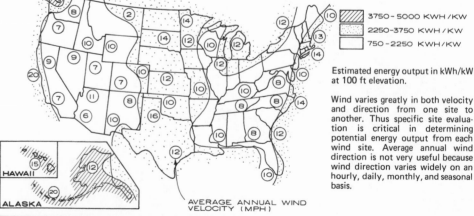

AVERAGE ANNUAL WIND VELOCITY (MPH)

ANNUAL AVERAGE WIND VELOCITY AND AVAILABLE ENERGY IN U.S.A.

APPENDIX

ARCHITECTURAL SYMBOLS

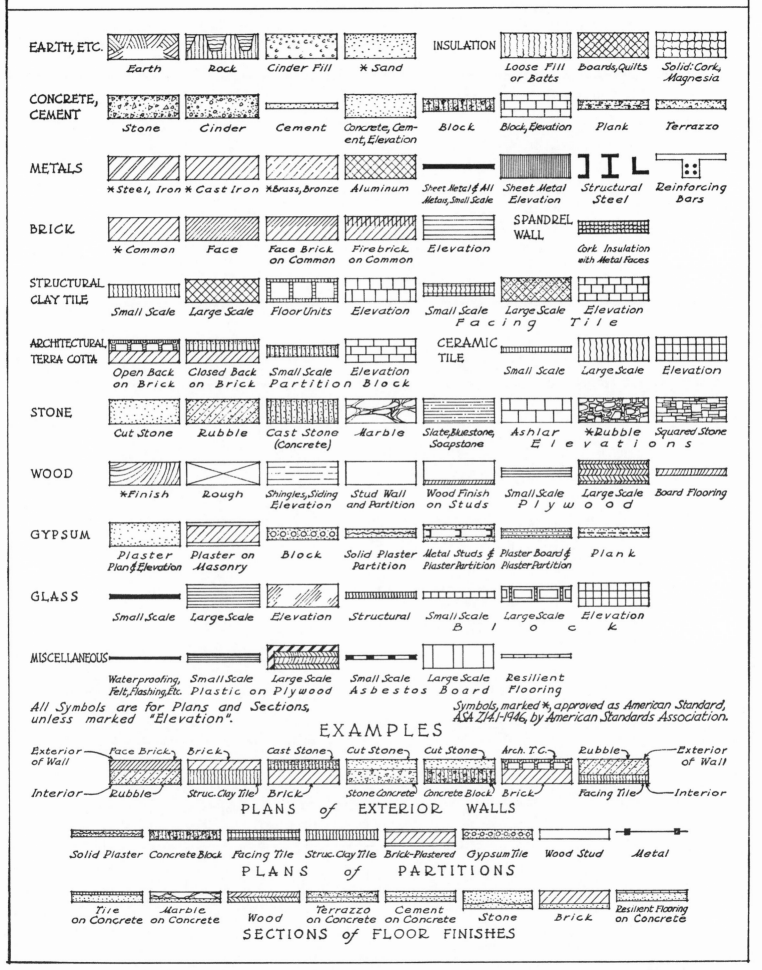

EARTH, ETC. — Earth | Rock | Cinder Fill | *Sand | **INSULATION** — Loose Fill or Batts | Boards, Quilts | Solid: Cork, Magnesia

CONCRETE, CEMENT — Stone | Cinder | Cement | Concrete, Cement, Elevation | Block | Block, Elevation | Plank | Terrazzo

METALS — *Steel, Iron | *Cast Iron | *Brass, Bronze | Aluminum | Sheet Metal & All Metals, Small Scale | Sheet Metal Elevation | Structural Steel | Reinforcing Bars

BRICK — *Common | Face | Face Brick on Common | Firebrick on Common | Elevation | SPANDREL WALL | Cork Insulation with Metal Faces

STRUCTURAL CLAY TILE — Small Scale | Large Scale | Floor Units | Elevation | Small Scale | Large Scale | Elevation — Facing Tile

ARCHITECTURAL TERRA COTTA — Open Back on Brick | Closed Back on Brick | Small Scale Partition Block | Elevation | CERAMIC TILE — Small Scale | Large Scale | Elevation

STONE — Cut Stone | Rubble | Cast Stone (Concrete) | Marble | Slate, Bluestone, Soapstone | Ashlar | *Rubble | Squared Stone — Elevations

WOOD — *Finish | Rough | Shingles, Siding Elevation | Stud Wall and Partition | Wood Finish on Studs | Small Scale | Large Scale — Plywood | Board Flooring

GYPSUM — Plaster Plan & Elevation | Plaster on Masonry | Block | Solid Plaster Partition | Metal Studs & Plaster Partition | Plaster Board & Plaster Partition | Plank

GLASS — Small Scale | Large Scale | Elevation | Structural | Small Scale | Large Scale | Elevation — Block

MISCELLANEOUS — Waterproofing, Felt, Flashing, Etc. | Small Scale | Large Scale — Plastic on Plywood | Small Scale | Large Scale — Asbestos Board | Resilient Flooring

All Symbols are for Plans and Sections, unless marked "Elevation".

Symbols, marked *, approved as American Standard, ASA Z14.1-1946, by American Standards Association.

EXAMPLES

Exterior of Wall — Face Brick | Brick | Cast Stone | Cut Stone | Cut Stone | Arch. T.C. | Rubble — Exterior of Wall

Interior — Rubble | Struc. Clay Tile | Brick | Stone Concrete | Concrete Block | Brick | Facing Tile — Interior

PLANS of EXTERIOR WALLS

Solid Plaster | Concrete Block | Facing Tile | Struc. Clay Tile | Brick-Plastered | Gypsum Tile | Wood Stud | Metal

PLANS of PARTITIONS

Tile on Concrete | Marble on Concrete | Wood | Terrazzo on Concrete | Cement on Concrete | Stone | Brick | Resilient Flooring on Concrete

SECTIONS of FLOOR FINISHES

CONVENTIONS

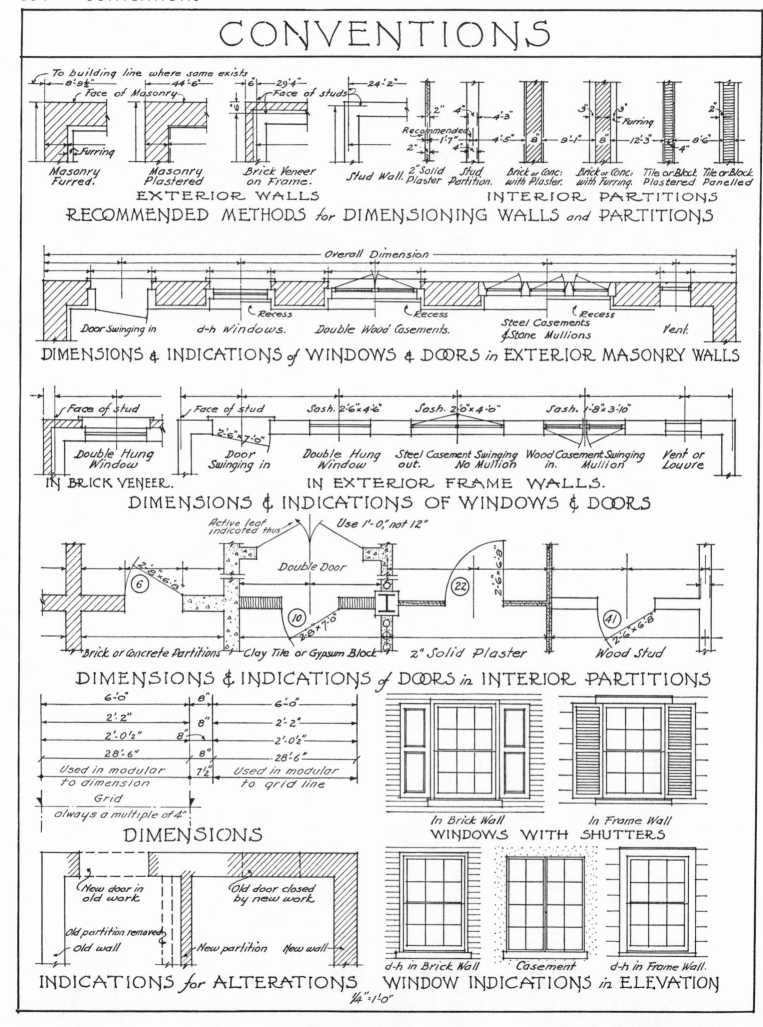

RECOMMENDED METHODS for DIMENSIONING WALLS and PARTITIONS

EXTERIOR WALLS — INTERIOR PARTITIONS

Masonry Furred. Masonry Plastered. Brick Veneer on Frame. Stud Wall. 2" Solid Plaster. Stud Partition. Brick or Conc. with Plaster. Brick or Conc. with Furring. Tile or Block Plastered. Tile or Block Panelled.

DIMENSIONS & INDICATIONS of WINDOWS & DOORS in EXTERIOR MASONRY WALLS

Door Swinging in — d-h Windows. — Double Wood Casements. — Steel Casements & Stone Mullions — Vent.

DIMENSIONS & INDICATIONS OF WINDOWS & DOORS

IN BRICK VENEER. — IN EXTERIOR FRAME WALLS.

Double Hung Window — Door Swinging in — Double Hung Window — Steel Casement Swinging out. No Mullion — Wood Casement Swinging in. Mullion — Vent or Louvre

DIMENSIONS & INDICATIONS of DOORS in INTERIOR PARTITIONS

Brick or Concrete Partitions — Clay Tile or Gypsum Block — 2" Solid Plaster — Wood Stud

DIMENSIONS

Used in modular to dimension Grid always a multiple of 4"

Used in modular to grid line

WINDOWS WITH SHUTTERS

In Brick Wall — In Frame Wall

INDICATIONS for ALTERATIONS

New door in old work — Old door closed by new work — Old partition removed — Old wall — New partition — New wall

WINDOW INDICATIONS in ELEVATION

d-h in Brick Wall — Casement — d-h in Frame Wall.

¼" = 1'-0"

WELDING SYMBOLS

SUMMARY OF STANDARD WELDING SYMBOLS

◆ AMERICAN WELDING SOCIETY ◆

IDENTIFICATION OF ARROW SIDE AND OTHER SIDE OF JOINT AND ARROW-SIDE AND OTHER-SIDE MEMBER OF JOINT

(Diagrams labeled: ARROW OF WELDING SYMBOL, OTHER SIDE OF JOINT, ARROW SIDE OF JOINT, ARROW-SIDE MEMBER OF JOINT, OTHER-SIDE MEMBER OF JOINT)

LOCATION OF ELEMENTS OF A WELDING SYMBOL

- FINISH SYMBOL
- CONTOUR SYMBOL
- ROOT OPENING; DEPTH OF FILLING FOR PLUG AND SLOT WELDS
- GROOVE ANGLE; INCLUDED ANGLE OF COUNTERSINK FOR PLUG WELDS
- LENGTH OF WELD
- PITCH (CENTER TO CENTER SPACING) OF WELDS
- SIZE; SIZE OR STRENGTH FOR RESISTANCE WELDS
- REFERENCE LINE
- SPECIFICATION, PROCESS, OR OTHER REFERENCE
- TAIL (OMIT WHEN REFERENCE IS NOT USED)
- BASIC WELD SYMBOL OR DETAIL REFERENCE
- ARROW CONNECTING REFERENCE LINE TO ARROW SIDE OR ARROW-SIDE MEMBER OF JOINT
- FIELD WELD SYMBOL
- WELD-ALL-AROUND SYMBOL
- NUMBER OF SPOT OR PROJECTION WELDS

(Letters shown: F A R S T L-P (N); BOTH SIDES / ARROW SIDE / OTHER SIDE)

BASIC WELD AND GAS WELDING SYMBOLS / RESISTANCE WELDING SYMBOLS

LOCATION SIGNIFICANCE	BEAD	FILLET	PLUG OR SLOT	SQUARE	GROOVE V	GROOVE BEVEL	GROOVE U	GROOVE J	PROJECTION	SPOT	SEAM	FLASH OR UPSET
ARROW SIDE										NOT USED	NOT USED	NOT USED
OTHER SIDE			NOT USED							NOT USED	NOT USED	NOT USED
BOTH SIDES	NOT USED		NOT USED							NOT USED	NOT USED	NOT USED
NO ARROW-SIDE OR OTHER SIDE SIGNIFICANCE		NOT USED	NOT USED									

TYPICAL WELDING SYMBOLS

BEAD WELD SYMBOL INDICATING BEAD TYPE BACK WELD
- ANY APPLICABLE SINGLE GROOVE WELD SYMBOL

DUAL BEAD WELD SYMBOL INDICATING BUILT-UP SURFACE
- SIZE (HEIGHT OF DEPOSIT) OMISSION INDICATES NO SPECIFIC HEIGHT DESIRED
- ORIENTATION, LOCATION AND ALL DIMENSIONS OTHER THAN SIZE ARE SHOWN ON THE DRAWING

DOUBLE-FILLET WELDING SYMBOL
- SIZE (LENGTH OF LEG)
- SPECIFICATION, PROCESS OR OTHER REFERENCE

CHAIN-INTERMITTENT-FILLET WELDING SYMBOL
- SIZE (LENGTH OF LEG)
- LENGTH OF INCREMENTS
- PITCH (DISTANCE BETWEEN CENTERS) OF INCREMENTS

STAGGERED INTERMITTENT-FILLET WELDING SYMBOL
- SIZE (LENGTH OF LEG)
- LENGTH OF INCREMENTS
- PITCH (DISTANCE BETWEEN CENTERS) OF INCREMENTS

SINGLE-V GROOVE WELDING SYMBOL
- SIZE (DEPTH OF CHAMFERING) OMISSION INDICATES DEPTH OF CHAMFERING EQUAL TO THICKNESS OF MEMBERS
- ROOT OPENING
- GROOVE ANGLE

SINGLE-V GROOVE WELDING SYMBOL INDICATING ROOT PENETRATION
- SIZE (DEPTH OF CHAMFERING PLUS ROOT PENETRATION)
- ROOT OPENING
- GROOVE ANGLE

DOUBLE-BEVEL GROOVE WELDING SYMBOL
- OMISSION OF SIZE DIMENSION INDICATES A TOTAL DEPTH OF CHAMFERING EQUAL TO THICKNESS OF MEMBERS
- GROOVE ANGLE
- ARROW POINTS TOWARD MEMBER TO BE CHAMFERED

WELDING SYMBOLS FOR COMBINED WELDS

PLUG WELDING SYMBOL
- SIZE (DIA. OF HOLE AT ROOT)
- INCLUDED ANGLE OF COUNTERSINK
- PITCH (DISTANCE BETWEEN CENTERS) OF WELDS
- DEPTH OF FILLING IN INCHES OMISSION INDICATES FILLING IS COMPLETE

SLOT WELDING SYMBOL
- DEPTH OF FILLING IN INCHES OMISSION INDICATES FILLING IS COMPLETE
- ORIENTATION, LOCATION AND ALL DIMENSIONS OTHER THAN DEPTH OF FILLING ARE SHOWN ON THE DRAWING

SPOT WELDING SYMBOL
- SIZE (DIA. OF WELD) OR MIN. ACCEPTABLE SHEAR STRENGTH IN LB. PER WELD MAY BE USED INSTEAD
- NUMBER OF WELDS
- PITCH (DISTANCE BETWEEN CENTERS) OF WELDS

PROJECTION WELDING SYMBOL
- SIZE (MIN. ACCEPTABLE SHEAR STRENGTH IN LB. PER WELD) DIA. OF WELD MAY BE USED INSTEAD
- PITCH (DISTANCE BETWEEN CENTERS) OF WELDS
- NUMBER OF WELDS

SEAM WELDING SYMBOL
- SIZE (WIDTH OF WELD) MIN. ACCEPTABLE SHEAR STRENGTH IN LB. PER LINEAR INCH MAY BE USED INSTEAD
- LENGTH OF WELDS OR INCREMENTS; OMISSION INDICATES THAT WELD EXTENDS BETWEEN ABRUPT CHANGES IN DIRECTION OR AS DIMENSIONED
- PITCH (DISTANCE BETWEEN CENTERS) OF INCREMENTS

FLASH OR UPSET WELDING SYMBOL

BRAZING, FORGE, THERMIT, INDUCTION AND FLOW WELDING SYMBOL
- PROCESS REFERENCE MUST BE USED TO INDICATE PROCESS DESIRED

SUPPLEMENTARY SYMBOLS USED WITH WELDING SYMBOLS

WELD-ALL-AROUND SYMBOL
- WELD-ALL-AROUND SYMBOL INDICATES THAT WELD EXTENDS COMPLETELY AROUND THE JOINT

FIELD WELD SYMBOL
- FIELD WELD SYMBOL INDICATES THAT WELD IS TO BE MADE AT A PLACE OTHER THAN THAT OF INITIAL CONSTRUCTION

FLUSH-CONTOUR SYMBOL
- FLUSH-CONTOUR SYMBOL INDICATES FACE OF WELD TO BE MADE FLUSH. WHEN USED WITHOUT A FINISH SYMBOL INDICATES WELD TO BE MADE FLUSH WITHOUT SUBTRACTIVE FINISHING
- FINISH SYMBOL (USER'S STD) INDICATES METHOD OF OBTAINING SPECIFIED CONTOUR BUT NOT DEGREE OF FINISH

CONVEX-CONTOUR SYMBOL
- CONVEX-CONTOUR SYMBOL INDICATES FACE OF WELD TO BE CONVEX. CONTOUR
- FINISH SYMBOL (USER'S STD) INDICATES METHOD OF OBTAINING SPECIFIED CONTOUR BUT NOT DEGREE OF FINISH

Approved as American Standard, A.S.A. Z32.2.1-1949 by American Standards Association

PLUMBING SYMBOLS

PLUMBING FIXTURE SYMBOLS

Roll Rim	Corner	Recessed	Sitz	Angle tub	Shower Stalls	Shower Head	Overhead Gang Shower
			SB			Plan Elev.	Plan / Elev.

— BATHS — / — SHOWERS —

LT	No Tank (Flush Valve)	B		Pedestal Type	Wall Type	Corner Type	Stall Type	Trough Type	PL	WL	L	ML	DL	DW
Low Tank									Pedestal	Wall	Corner	Manicure or Medical	Dental	Dishwasher

WATER CLOSETS — BIDET — URINALS — LAVATORIES

S	Kitchen, R&L Drain Board	Kitchen, L.H. Drain Board	Combination Sink & Dishwasher	Combination Sink & Laundry Tray	S T	SS	Wash (Wall Type)	Wash (Free-standing)	HWT	WH
Plain Kitchen					Service				* HWT / Tank	Heater

— SINKS — / HOT WATER —

DF	DF	O O O	M	HR	*HF HB	R	G	D	G	O	O L
Pedestal Type	Wall Type	Trough Type	METER	HOSE RACK	HOSE BIBS OR FAUCET	GAS RANGE	Gas Vacuum OUTLETS	DRAIN	Grease SEPARATORS	Oil	*LEADER

DRINKING FOUNTAINS

C/O CO	Garage	Floor, with Backwater Valve	ROOF SUMP	SUMP *PIT	FAI On Sidewalk / FAI On Building	MH	LH	L	DW	RB	YDI
Floor *Pipe					FRESH AIR *INTAKE	Man Hole	Lamp Hole Drain	Leader Drain	Dry Well	Receiving Basin	Yard Drain Inlet

CLEANOUTS — DRAINS — / *DRAINAGE / SYMBOLS

WM	AW	IM	D	D	D	LT	L T		
Wringer Type	Automatic	*IRONING MACHINE	Centri-fugal	Cabinet	Rack	*Single	Double	Built-In	Surface
*WASHING MACHINES			— DRYERS —			LAUNDRY TRAYS		*IRONING BOARDS	

PIPING SYMBOLS

PLUMBING

Soil, Waste or Leader (Above Grade)	————————
Soil, Waste or Leader (Below Grade)	— — — — —
Vent	- - - - - - -
Cold Water	————————
Hot Water	– – – – – –
Hot Water Return	———————
Fire Line	—F———F—
Gas	—G———G—
Acid Waste	—ACID—
Drinking Water Flow	– – – – – –
Drinking Water Return	———————
Vacuum Cleaning	—V———V—
Compressed Air	———A———

SPRINKLERS

Main Supplies	———S———
Branch and Head	—O———O—
Drain	—S———S—

PNEUMATIC TUBES

Tube Runs	═══════

DRAINAGE*

Sewer—Cast Iron	——S-CI——
Sewer—Clay Tile, Bell & Spigot	——S-CT——
Drain—Clay Tile, Bell & Spigot	————————
Drain—Open Tile or Agricultural Tile	— — — — —

All Symbols, except those marked ✱, *approved as American Standard, ASA Z32.2.3-'49 by American Standards Association.*

PIPING & HEATING & VENTILATING SYMBOLS

PIPING   SYMBOLS

HEATING

High Pressure Steam

Medium Pressure Steam

Low Pressure Steam

High Pressure Return

Medium Pressure Return

Low Pressure Return

Boiler Blow Off

Condensate or Vacuum Pump Discharge

Feedwater Pump Discharge

Make Up Water

Air Relief Line

Fuel Oil Flow — FOF

Fuel Oil Return — FOR

Fuel Oil Tank Vent — FOV

Compressed Air — A

Hot Water Heating Supply

Hot Water Heating Return

AIR CONDITIONING

Refrigerant Discharge — RD

Refrigerant Suction — RS

Condenser Water Flow — C

Condenser Water Return — CR

Circulating Chilled or Hot Water Flow — CH

Circulating Chilled or Hot Water Return — CHR

Make Up Water

Humidification Line — H

Drain — D

Brine Supply — B

Brine Return — BR

HEATING & VENTILATING SYMBOLS

Heat Transfer Surface, Plan

Wall Radiator, Plan

Wall Radiator on Ceiling, Plan

RADIATORS & CONVECTORS, PLANS — for Architectural Drawings.

For Radiator — If Convector is used instead of Radiator, substitute CONV. for RAD.

*Exposed — RAD

*Recessed — RAD

*Enclosed, Flush — RAD ENCL

*Enclosed, Projecting — RAD ENCL

Unit Heater (Propeller), Plan

Unit Heater (Centrifugal Fan), Plan

Unit Ventilator, Plan

TRAPS

Thermostatic

Blast Thermostatic

Float and Thermostatic

Float

Boiler Return

VALVES

Reducing Pressure

Air Line

Lock and Shield

Diaphragm

Air Eliminator

Strainer

Thermometer

Thermostat

All Symbols, except those marked *, approved as American Standard, ASA Z32.2-1941, by American Standards Association.

DUCTWORK SYMBOLS

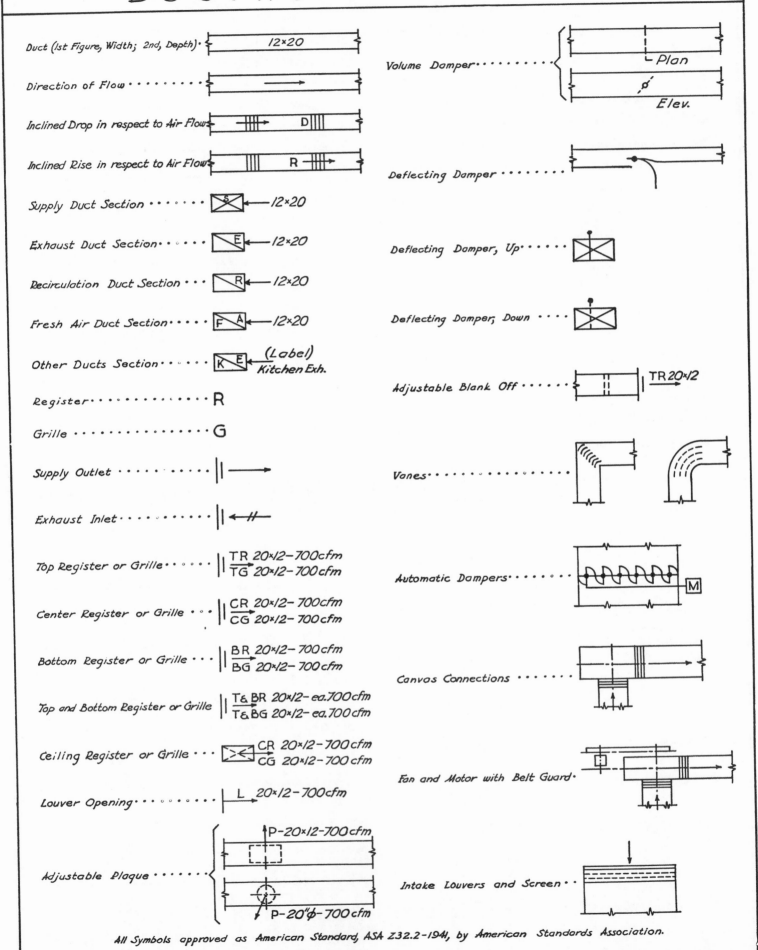

Duct (1st Figure, Width; 2nd, Depth)· 12×20

Direction of Flow · · · · · · · · · ·

Inclined Drop in respect to Air Flow · · · · · · · D

Inclined Rise in respect to Air Flow · · · · · · · R

Supply Duct Section · · · · · · · S ← 12×20

Exhaust Duct Section · · · · · E ← 12×20

Recirculation Duct Section · · · R ← 12×20

Fresh Air Duct Section · · · · F A ← 12×20

Other Ducts Section · · · · · K E (Label) Kitchen Exh.

Register · · · · · · · · · · · · · R

Grille · · · · · · · · · · · · · · · G

Supply Outlet · · · · · · · · · · →

Exhaust Inlet · · · · · · · · · · ←

Top Register or Grille · · · · · · TR 20×12–700cfm TG 20×12–700cfm

Center Register or Grille · · · · CR 20×12–700cfm CG 20×12–700cfm

Bottom Register or Grille · · · BR 20×12–700cfm BG 20×12–700cfm

Top and Bottom Register or Grille · · · T&BR 20×12–ea.700cfm T&BG 20×12–ea.700cfm

Ceiling Register or Grille · · · CR 20×12–700cfm CG 20×12–700cfm

Louver Opening · · · · · · · · · L 20×12–700cfm

Adjustable Plaque · · · · · · · P–20×12–700cfm P–20"φ–700cfm

Volume Damper · · · · · · · · · Plan Elev.

Deflecting Damper · · · · · · ·

Deflecting Damper, Up · · · · ·

Deflecting Damper, Down · · · ·

Adjustable Blank Off · · · · · · TR 20×12

Vanes · · · · · · · · · · · · · · ·

Automatic Dampers · · · · · · · M

Canvas Connections · · · · · · ·

Fan and Motor with Belt Guard ·

Intake Louvers and Screen · · ·

All Symbols approved as American Standard, ASA Z32.2–1941, by American Standards Association.

HEAT-POWER APPARATUS & REFRIGERATING SYMBOLS

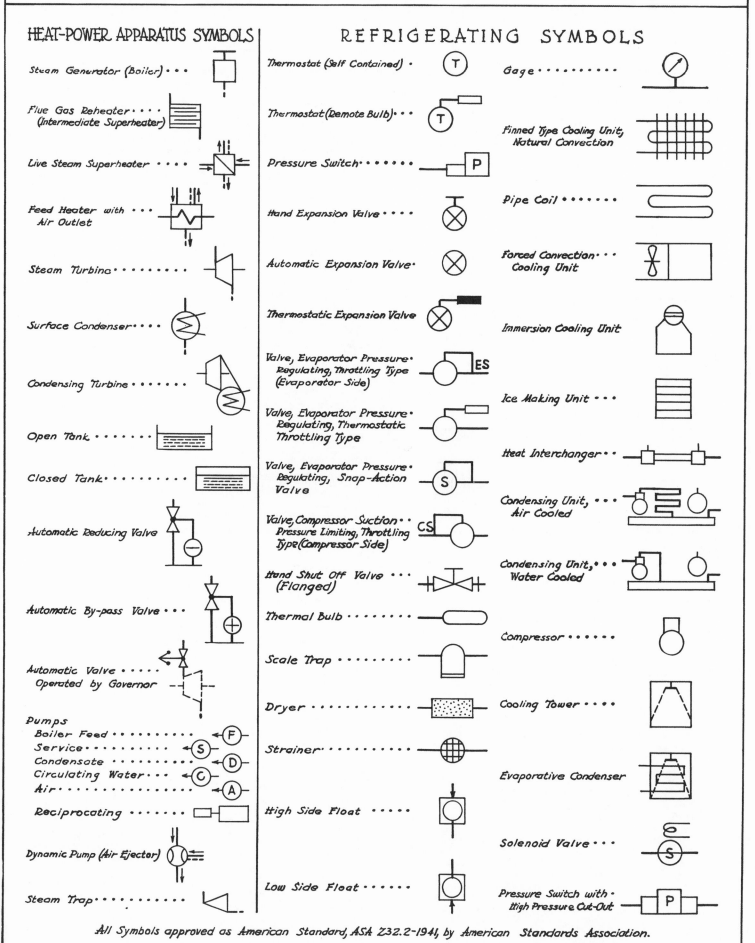

HEAT-POWER APPARATUS SYMBOLS

Steam Generator (Boiler) · · ·

Flue Gas Reheater · · · ·
(Intermediate Superheater)

Live Steam Superheater · · · ·

Feed Heater with · · ·
Air Outlet

Steam Turbine · · · · · · · ·

Surface Condenser · · · ·

Condensing Turbine · · · · · · ·

Open Tank · · · · · · · ·

Closed Tank · · · · · · · · ·

Automatic Reducing Valve

Automatic By-pass Valve · · ·

Automatic Valve · · · · ·
Operated by Governor

Pumps
  Boiler Feed · · · · · · · ·
  Service · · · · · · · · ·
  Condensate · · · · · · · ·
  Circulating Water · · ·
  Air · · · · · · · · · ·

Reciprocating · · · · · · · ·

Dynamic Pump (Air Ejector) ·

Steam Trap · · · · · ·

REFRIGERATING SYMBOLS

Thermostat (Self Contained) ·

Thermostat (Remote Bulb) · · ·

Pressure Switch · · · · · · ·

Hand Expansion Valve · · · ·

Automatic Expansion Valve ·

Thermostatic Expansion Valve

Valve, Evaporator Pressure ·
Regulating, Throttling Type
(Evaporator Side)

Valve, Evaporator Pressure ·
Regulating, Thermostatic
Throttling Type

Valve, Evaporator Pressure ·
Regulating, Snap-Action
Valve

Valve, Compressor Suction · ·
Pressure Limiting, Throttling
Type (Compressor Side)

Hand Shut Off Valve · · ·
(Flanged)

Thermal Bulb · · · · · · · ·

Scale Trap · · · · · · · · ·

Dryer · · · · · · · · · · ·

Strainer · · · · · · · · · ·

High Side Float · · · · ·

Low Side Float · · · · · ·

Gage · · · · · · · · · ·

Finned Type Cooling Unit,
Natural Convection

Pipe Coil · · · · · · ·

Forced Convection · · ·
Cooling Unit

Immersion Cooling Unit

Ice Making Unit · · ·

Heat Interchanger · ·

Condensing Unit, · · ·
Air Cooled

Condensing Unit, · · ·
Water Cooled

Compressor · · · · · ·

Cooling Tower · · · ·

Evaporative Condenser

Solenoid Valve · · ·

Pressure Switch with ·
High Pressure Cut-Out

All Symbols approved as American Standard, ASA Z32.2-1941, by American Standards Association.

ELECTRICAL SYMBOLS

GENERAL OUTLETS

CEILING WALL

O	—O	Outlet
Ⓑ	—Ⓑ	Blanked Outlet
Ⓓ		Drop Cord
Ⓔ	—Ⓔ	Electrical Outlet; for use only when circle used alone might be confused with columns, plumbing symbols, etc.
Ⓕ	—Ⓕ	Fan Outlet
Ⓙ	—Ⓙ	Junction Box
Ⓛ	—Ⓛ	Lamp Holder
ⓁPS	—ⓁPS	Lamp Holder with Pull Switch
Ⓢ	—Ⓢ	Pull Switch
Ⓥ	—Ⓥ	Outlet for vapor Discharge Lamp
Ⓧ	—Ⓧ	Exit Light Outlet
Ⓒ	—Ⓒ	Clock Outlet (Specify Voltage)

CONVENIENCE OUTLETS

⊖	Duplex Convenience Outlet
⊖1,3	Convenience Outlet other than Duplex 1 = Single, 3 = Triplex, etc.
⊖WP	Weatherproof Convenience Outlet
⊖R	Range Outlet
⊖S	Switch and Convenience Outlet
⊖R	Radio and Convenience Outlet
●	Special Purpose Outlet (Describe in Spec.)
⊙	Floor Outlet

SWITCH OUTLETS

S	Single Pole Switch
S2	Double Pole Switch
S3	Three Way Switch
S4	Four Way Switch
SD	Automatic Door Switch
SE	Electrolier Switch
SK	Key Operated Switch
SP	Switch and Pilot Lamp
SCB	Circuit Breaker
SWCB	Weatherproof Circuit Breaker
SMC	Momentary Contact Switch
SRC	Remote Control Switch
SWP	Weatherproof Switch
SF	Fused Switch
SWF	Weatherproof Fused Switch

SPECIAL OUTLETS

Oa,b,c etc.	Any Standard Symbol as given above with the addition of a lower
⊖a,b,c etc.	case subscript letter may be used to designate some special
S a,b,c etc.	variation of Standard Equipment of particular interest in a specific set of Architectural Plans. When used they must be listed in the key of Symbols on each drawing and if necessary further described in the Specifications.

PANELS, CIRCUITS & MISCELLANEOUS

▬	Lighting Panel
▨	Power Panel
——	Branch Circuit; Concealed in ceiling or wall
—.—	Branch Circuit Concealed in floor
----	Branch Circuit; Exposed
→→	Home Run to Panel Board. Indicate number of Circuits by number of arrows. Note : Any circuit without further designation indicates a two-wire circuit. For a greater number of wires indicate as follows : —⧓— (3 wires) —⧓⧓— (4 wires), etc.
▬▬	Feeders. Note: Use heavy lines and designate by number corresponding to listing in Feeder Schedule.
▭	Under floor Duct and Junction Box. Triple System. Note: For double or single Systems eliminate one or two lines. This symbol is equally adaptable to auxiliary system layouts.
Ⓖ	Generator
Ⓜ	Motor
Ⓘ	Instrument
Ⓣ	Power Transformer. (Or draw to scale)
⊠	Controller
⊟	Isolating Switch

AUXILIARY SYSTEMS

⊡	Push Button
⊐	Buzzer
⊐o	Bell
◇	Annunciator
◀	Outside Telephone
◁	Interconnecting Telephone
▷◁	Telephone Switchboard
Ⓣ	Bell Ringing Transformer
Ⓓ	Electric Door Opener
Ⓕo	Fire Alarm Bell
Ⓕ	Fire Alarm Station
⊠	City Fire Alarm Station
FA	Fire Alarm Central Station
FS	Automatic Fire Alarm Device
W	Watchman's Station
[W]	Watchman's Central Station
H	Horn
N	Nurse's Signal Plug
M	Maid's Signal Plug
R	Radio Outlet
SC	Signal Central Station
▭	Interconnection Box
⫴⫴	Battery
– – – – –	Auxiliary System Circuits Note: Any line without further designation indicates two-wire system. For a greater number of wires designate with numerals in manner similar to ———12-No. 18 W-¾" C., designate by number corresponding to listing in Schedule.
⬜a,b,c, etc.	Special Auxiliary Outlets Subscript letters refer to notes on plans or detailed description in Specifications.

American Standard Graphical Electrical Symbols for Architectural Plans, Z32.9-1943

ABBREVIATIONS

Standardized abbreviations are marked with reference numbers [1] to [7] incl. and these refer to the following:

[1] American Standard ABBREVIATIONS FOR SCIENTIFIC & ENGINEERING TERMS. ASA Z10.1-1941
[2] Lumber Standards.
[3] American Standard GRAPHIC SYMBOLS FOR USE ON DRAWINGS IN MECHANICAL ENGINEERING. ASA Z32.2-1941 (abbreviations used with symbols).
[4] American Standard GRAPHIC ELECTRICAL SYMBOLS FOR ARCHITECTURAL PLANS. Z32.9-1943 (abbreviations used with symbols).
[5] Hardware. Approved by the American Society of Hardware Consultants & National Contract Hardware Association 1949.
[6] American Standard ABBREVIATIONS FOR USE ON DRAWINGS. ASA Z32.13-1946
[7] American Standards GRAPHICAL PLUMBING SYMBOLS FOR USE ON DRAWINGS. ASA Z32.2.3-1949 (abbreviations used with symbols).

The non-standardized abbreviations are generally based on the following:
(a) Same abbreviation for singular and plural.
(b) Periods used only to avoid misinterpretation.
(c) Spaces between letters used for clarity only.
(d) Capitals used generally in view of the fact that
    most of these abbreviations are for use on drawings.

Recommendations

Where two or more standardized abbreviations are shown for the same item: for drawings use reference numbers [3], [4], [6] or [7]. and for text use reference numbers [1], [2], or [5].

Include an abbreviation list on each set of drawings.

Abbreviations for Texts: It is usual to capitalize only when the letter stands for a proper noun. Signs such as " # * are not recommended.

abbreviation................ABBREV	American Society of Mechanical Engineers....A.S.M.E.	asphalt tile....................AT
access area.......................AA	American Society of Refrigerating Engineers.....ASRE	asphalt tile base............ATB[6]
access door.......................AD	American Society for Testing Materials.......A.S.T.M.	assemble....................ASSEM[6]
access panel.....................AP[6]	American Standard.........AMER STD	assembly....................ASSY[6]
acoustic........................ACST[6]	American Standards Association....................ASA	associate....................ASSOC[6]
acoustical plaster.......ACST PLAS	American Water Works Association.................AWWA	Associate Royal Institute of British Architects.A.R.I.B.A.
acoustical tile..................AT	American Welding Society.......AWS	association.........ASSN[6] or ASSOC
acre.............ACRE[1] (spell out)	American Wire Gauge...........AWG[6]	Association of American Railroads....................AAR
actual..........................ACT.[6]	amount.........................AMT[6]	at.............................@
addendum.......................ADD.[6]	ampere...............amp or AMP[6]	atmospheric pressure.....ATM PRESS
addition.......................ADD.[6]	anchor bolt......................AB[6]	automatic....................AUTO[6]
adhesive.......................ADH[6]	angle...........................∠	automatic washing machine......AWM
aggregate......................AGGR[6]	annunciator...................ANN[6]	avenue........................AVE[6]
air conditioning........AIR COND[6]	apartment.......................APT.[6]	average........avg[1] or av[2] or AVG[6]
alarm..........................ALM[6]	approved......................APPD[6]	axis............................AX
alcove...........................A	approximate..................APPROX[6]	back feed.......................BF[6]
alternating current....a-c[1] or AC[6]	architect......................ARCH	backset........................BS[5]
altitude........................ALT[6]	architectural..................ARCH	back water valve...............BWV[6]
aluminum........................AL[6]	architectural terra cotta......ATC	bag.............................BG
American Concrete Institute ...ACI	area...........................A[6]	barrel................bbl[1] or BBL[6]
American Gas Association.......AGA	area drain.......................AD	basement......................BSMT[6]
American Institute of Architects..............A.I.A.	article.........................ART	bathroom.........................B
American Institute of Electrical Engineers........AIEE	asbestos......................ASB[6]	bath tub........................BT
American Institute of Steel Construction....AISC or A.I.S.C.	asbestos board..................AB	beaded one side................BIS[2]
American Society of Civil Engineers.............ASCE	asbestos millboard............AMB[6]	beam...........................BM[6]
American Society of Heating & Ventilating Engineers A.S.H.V.E.	asbestos roof shingles........ARS[6]	bedroom........................BR[6]
	asphalt.......................ASPH[6]	bell and flange................B&F[6]
		bell and spigot................B&S[6]
		benchboard................BNCHBD[6]
		bench mark.....................BM[6]

ABBREVIATIONS

bending moment....................M[6]
better................BTR or Btr[2]
between..................BET.[6]
beveled...................Bev[2]
bidet....................B[3],[7]
block......................BL
blocking..................BLKG
blower....................BLO[6]
blow-off..................BO[6]
blueprint.................BP[6]
bluestone..................BS
board................bd[2] or BD[6]
board foot.........fbm[1] or bd ft[2]
board measure...........b.m.[2]
boiler....................BLR[6]
boiler feed...............BF[6]
boiler house..............BH[6]
boiler room...............BR
bolts.....................BT
book shelves............BK SH
borrowed light...........BLT[6]
bottom...................BOT[6]
boulevard................BLVD
boundary.................BDY[6]
bracket..................brkt
brass....................BRS[6]
brass steeple tips.......BST[5]
brazing..................BRZG[6]
breadth...................B[6]
brick....................BRK[6]
brine return(pipe).......BR[3]
brine supply(pipe).......B[3]
British thermal
    units.........B[1] or BTU[6] or Btu
bronze...................BRZ[6]
broom closet.............BC
Brown and Sharpe
    gauge........B&S[6] or B&S ga
building.................BLDG[6]
building line............BL[6]
built-in.................BLT-IN
bulb angle...............BA
bulkhead.................BHD[6]
bullet tips..............BLT[5]
bulletin board..........BB
bundle..............bdl[2] or BDL[6]
Bureau of Standards......BS[6]
burglar alarm............BA
button...................BUT.[6]
buzzer...................BUZ[6]
by (as 6' x8').............X[2]
by-pass..................BP[6]
cabinet..................CAB.[6]
cadmium..................Cd[6]
cadmium plate............Cd PL[6]
calcimine.................C
calking..................CLKG[6]
candlepower..............CP[6]
carpenter................CARP.[6]
casing...................CSG
cast (used with other materials)C[6]
cast box strike..........CBX[5]
cast brass...............CB
cast concrete............C CONC
cast iron................CI[6]

cast iron pipe...........CIP[6]
cast steel...............CS[6]
cast stone................CS
casting..................CSTG[6]
catch basin..............CB[6]
ceiling............Clg[2] or CLG[6]
cellar...................CEL
cement...................CEM[6]
cement asbestos..........CEM A[6]
cement asbestos board....CEM AB[6]
cement floor.............CEM FL[6]
cement mortar............CEM MORT[6]
cement plaster...........CEM PLAS[6]
cement water paint.......CEM P
cent.....................c or ¢
center...................CTR
center line...........℄ or CL[6]
center matched...........CM[2]
centers on...............OC
center to center...c to c[1] or C to C[6]
ceramic..................CER[6]
cesspool.................CP[6]
chalk board..............Ch B
chamfer..................CHAM[6]
change...................CHG[6]
channel..........CHAN[6] or [or]
channel iron frame.......CIF[5]
check valve..............CV[6]
china cabinet............CH CAB
chromium plate...........Cr PL[6]
cinder block.............CIN BL
circle...................CIR[6]
circuit..................CKT[6]
circuit breaker..........CIR BKR
circular...........cir[1] or CIR[6]
circular mils.....cir mils[1] or CM[6]
circulating chilled or
    hot water flow.......CH[3]
circulating chilled or hot
    hot water return.....CHR[3]
circulating water pump...CWP[6]
circumference............CIRC[6]
class....................CL[6]
cleanout.................CO[3],[6],[7]
cleanout and deck plate....CO & DP
cleanout door............COD
clear..............Clr[2] or CLR[6]
clearance................CL[6]
clear glass..............CL GL
clear wire glass.........CL W GL
clock outlet..............C[4]
closet...........C or CL or CLO[6]
clothes line hook.........CLH
clothes pole.............CP
coal bin.................CB
coat closet..............CC
coat hook................CH[6]
coated...................CTD[6]
coefficient..........COEF[6] or C
cold rolled steel........CRS[6]
cold water...............CW[6]
column...................COL[6]
combination..............COMB.[6]
commercial projected window...CPW[6]
Commercial Standard..............CS

common.............Com[2] or COM[6]
company..................CO[6]
compartment..............COMPT[6]
compressed air line......A[3]
concrete.................CONC[6]
concrete block...........CONC B[6]
Concrete Ceiling.........CONC C[6]
concrete floor...........CONC F[6]
condenser water flow.....C[3]
condenser water return...CR[3]
conductance, thermal.....C
conductivity, thermal....k
conductor................COND[6]
conduit..................CND[6]
cone tips................CT[5]
connection...............CONN
construction.............CONST[6]
continuous or continue...CONT
contract.................CONTR[6]
contractor...............CONTR[6]
convector................CONV
convector enclosure......CONV ENCL
copper...................COP
copper covered...........COP COV
cork tile................CT
corner...................COR[6]
corner guards............CG
counter..................CTR[6]
counter flashing.........CFLG[6]
countersink..............CSK[6]
countersunk screw........CS
countersunk wood screw....CWS
courses..................C[6]
cover....................COV[6]
cover plate..............COV PL
cross section............X-SECT[6]
cubic..............cu[1] or CU[6]
cubic foot......cu ft[1],[2] or CU FT[6]
cubic feet per minute..cfm[1] or CFM[6]
cubic inch......cu in.[1] or CU IN.[6]
cubic yard........cu yd[1] or CU YD[6]
current..................CUR[6]
curtain rod..............C R
cut out..................CO[6]
cycle....................CY[6]
cycles per minute........CPM[6]
cycles per second........CPS[6]
cylinder...........cyl[1] or CYL[6]
cylinder lock............CYL L[6]
damper...................DMPR[6]
dampproofing.............DP
decibel............db[1] or DB[6]
degree.............(°)[1],[6] or DEG[6]
degree centigrade........C[1]
degree Fahrenheit........F[1]
department...............DEPT[6]
detail...................DET[6]
diagram..................DIAG[6]
diameter........diam[1] or DIA[6] or φ
dimension...........dim[2] or DIM[6]
dinette..................Dt
dining alcove............D A
dining room..............D R
direct current........d-c[1] or DC[6]
disconnect...............DISC[6]

ABBREVIATIONS

dishwasher	DW[7]	
distance	DIST[6]	
distributed	DIST	
ditto	" or DO.[6]	
division	DIV[6]	
double acting	DA	
double glass	DG[6]	
double hung window	DHW[6]	
dovetail	DVTL[6]	
dowel	DWL[6]	
down	DN[6] or D	
downspout	DS[6]	
dozen	doz[1] or DOZ[6]	
drain	D[3.7] or DR[6]	
drain board	DB	
drawing	DWG[6]	
dressed(lumber)	DRS[6]	
dressed and matched	D&M[2]	
dressing table	DR T	
drinking fountain	DF[3.6.7]	
drop cord (outlet)	D[4]	
dryer	D	
dry well	DW	
duct section, exhaust	E[3]	
duct section, fresh air	FA[3]	
duct section, recirculation	R[3]	
duct section, supply	S[3]	
dumbwaiter	DW[6]	
duplex	DX[6]	
duplicate	DUP[6]	
each	EA[6]	
each face	EF[6]	
east	E[6]	
east northeast	ENE	
east by north	EbN	
edge	E[2]	
edge grain	E G[2]	
elbow	ELL[6]	
electric	elec[1] or ELEC[6]	
electric panel	EP	
elevation	el[1] or EL[6]	
elevator	Elev	
emergency	EMER[6]	
enamel	E	
enclose	ENCL[6]	
enclosure	ENCL	
end to end	E to E[6]	
engineer	ENGR[6]	
entrance	ENT[6]	
equipment	EQUIP.[6]	
equivalent square feet	E□[1]	
equivalent direct radiation	EDR[6]	
escutcheon	ESC[6]	
estimate	EST[6]	
excavate	EXC[6]	
executive	EXEC[6]	
exhaust duct section	E[3]	
existing	EXIST.[6]	
exit light outlet	X[4]	
expansion bolt	EXP BT	
expansion joint	EXP JT[6]	
extension	EXT[6]	
exterior	EXT[6]	
external	EXT[6]	
extinguisher, fire	F EXT	

extra heavy	X HVY[6] or XH	
extrude	EXTR[8]	
fabricate	FAB[6]	
face to face	F to F[6]	
facing tile	FT	
factory	FCTY	
fan (outlet)	F[4]	
Federal	FED.[6]	
Federal Specifications	FS[6]	
feeder	FDR[6]	
feed water	FW[6]	
feet	(')[6] or FT[6]	
feet board measure	FBM[6] or ft b m[2]	
feet per minute	FPM[6]	
feet per second	FPS[6]	
feet surface measure	FTSM	
Fellow American Institute of Architects	F.A.I.A.	
Fellow Royal Institute of British Architects	F.R.I.B.A.	
figure	FIG.[6]	
fillet	FIL[6]	
finish	FIN.[6]	
finished floor	Fin FI	
firebrick	FBRK	
Fire Department Connection	FDC[6]	
fire door	F DR[6]	
fire extinguisher	F EXT	
fire hose	FH[6]	
fire hose cabinet	FHC[6]	
fire hose rack	FHR[6]	
fire hydrant	FHY[6]	
fire line	F[3]	
fire main	FM[6]	
fire place	FP[6]	
fireproof	FPRF[6]	
fireproof self closing	FPSC	
fire standpipe	FSP	
fitting	FTG[6]	
fixture	FIX.[6]	
flame proof	FP[6]	
flange	FLG[6]	
flashing	FL[6]	
flat finish	F	
flat grain	F G[2]	
flat head	FH[6]	
flat headed screw	FHS	
flat headed wood screw	FHWS	
floor	FL[6]	
floor cabinet	FL CAB	
floor drain	FD[6]	
flooring	Flg[2] or FLG[6]	
fluorescent	FLUOR[6]	
flush	FL[6]	
flush metal saddle	FMS	
flush metal threshold	FMT[6]	
flush threshold	FT[6]	
foot	ft[1.2] or (')[2.6] or FT[6]	
foot bath	FB[3.7]	
foot-candle	FT-C or ft-c[1]	
foot-Lambert	FT-L or ft-L[1]	
foot pound	ft lb[1] or FT LB[6]	
footing	FTG[6]	
foundation	FND[6]	
frame	FR[6]	

framework	FRWK[6]	
framing	Frm[2]	
free-on-board	fob[1]	
freezing point	fp[1] or FP[6]	
frequency	FREQ[6]	
fresh air duct section	FA[3]	
fresh air intake(or inlet)	FAI	
front	FR[6]	
fuel oil	FO[6]	
fuel oil flow (pipe)	FOF[3]	
fuel oil return (pipe)	FOR[3]	
fuel oil tank vent (pipe)	FOV[3]	
full size	FS	
furnish	FURN[6]	
furred ceiling	FC	
gallery	GALL[6]	
gallon	gal[1] or GAL[6]	
gallons per Acre per Day	GPAD[6]	
gallons per hour	GPH[6]	
gallons per minute	gpm[1] or GPM[6]	
gallons per second	gps[1] or GPS[6]	
galvanized	GALV[6]	
galvanized iron	GI[6]	
galvanized steel	GS[6] or galv S	
games room	GR	
gas range	G[7]	
gas line or outlet	G[3.7]	
gate valve	GTV[6]	
gauge	GA[6]	
general contract	GEN CONT	
generator	G[4] or GEN[6]	
glass	GL[6]	
glass block	GL BL	
glaze	GL[6]	
government	GOVT[6]	
grade	GR[6]	
grade line	GL[6]	
grand master keyed	GMK[5]	
granite	G	
grating	GRTG[6]	
gravity	G[6]	
grease trap	GT[6]	
grease separator	G[3.7]	
green	GRN[6]	
grid (modular)	G[6]	
grille	G[3]	
grille, bottom	BG[3]	
grille, ceiling	CR[3]	
grille, center	CG[3]	
grille, top	TG[3]	
grille, top & bottom	T&BG[3]	
guard	GD[6]	
gypsum	GYP[6]	
half-round	H RD[6]	
handhole	HH[6]	
hanging closet	H CL	
hardware	HDW[6]	
hardwood	HDWD or Hdwd[2]	
head	HD[6]	
heartwood	hrtwd[2]	
heater	H	
heater, water	WH[3.6]	
heater room	HR	
height	HGT[6] H or HT	

ABBREVIATIONS

hexagonal.....HEX[6]
high point.....H PT[6]
high-pressure.....H-PRESS[6]
hollow metal.....HM
hollow metal door.....HMD[5]
hollow metal frame.....HMF[5]
horizon.....H
horizontal.....HOR[6]
horsepower.....hp[1] or HP[6]
hose bibb.....HB[7] or HF[3]
hose cabinet.....H CAB
bose faucet.....HF[3] or HB[7]
hose rack.....HR[3,7]
hospital.....HOSP[6]
hot rolled steel.....HRS[6]
hot water.....HW[6]
hot water, circulating.....HW C[6]
hot water heater.....HWH or WH[3]
hot water tank.....HWT[1,7]
hour.....hr[1] or HR[6]
house.....HSE[6]
humidification line.....H[3]
hundred.....C
I beam.....I
Illuminating Engineering Society.....IES
inch.....(")[1,2,6] or in[1,2] or IN[6]
include.....INCL[6]
incorporated.....INC[6]
indicated horsepower.....IHP[6]
information.....INFO[6]
inlet.....IN[6]
inlet manhole.....IMH[6]
inside diameter.....ID[1,6]
inside pipe size.....IPS
instantaneous.....INST[6]
insulate.....INS[6]
insulation.....INS
interior.....INT[6]
intermediate.....INTER[6]
internal.....int[1] or INT[6]
invert.....INV[6]
iron.....I[6]
ironing machine.....IM
iron-pipe size.....IPS[6]
jamb-template machine screws.....JTMS[5]
janitor's closet.....J CL
joint.....JT[6]
junction box (outlet).....J[4]
kalamein.....KAL[6]
kalamein door.....KD[5]
kalamein frame.....KF[5]
kalsomine.....K
keyed alike.....KA[5]
keyed alike & master keyed.....KAMK[5]
keyed alike & grand master keyed.....KAGMK[5]
kick plate.....KP[6]
kiln-dried.....KD[2,6]
kilo.....K[6]
kilocycle.....KC[6]
kilogram.....KG[6]
kilometer.....km[1] or KM[6]
kilowatt.....kw[1] or KW[6]
kilowatthour.....kwhr[1]
kip (1000 lb).....K[6]

kitchen.....K
kitchen sink.....KS or S[7]
knocked down.....k.d.[2] or KD[6]
laboratory.....LAB[6]
ladder.....LAD.[6]
lamphole.....LH
landing.....LDG[6]
lath.....Lth[2] or LTH
latitude.....LAT[6] or ϕ
laundry.....LAU[6]
laundry chute.....LC[6]
laundry trays.....LT[3,7]
lavatory.....Lav[3] or LAV[6] or L[7]
lavatory, dental.....DL[7]
lavatory, medical.....ML[3]
lavatory, pedestal.....PL[3]
lavatory, wall.....WL[3,7]
lead and oil.....LO
lead covered.....LC[6]
leader.....L
leader drain.....LD
left.....L[6]
left hand.....LH[5]
left hand reverse.....LHR[5]
length.....lgth[2] or LG[6] or L
length overall.....LOA[6]
level.....LEV
library.....LIB
light.....LT[6]
light weight concrete.....LWC[6]
light weight insulating concrete.....LWIC[6]
limestone.....LS
line.....L[6]
linear feet.....lin ft[1,2]
linen chute.....L CH
linen closet.....L CL
lining.....Lng[2] or LN
linoleum.....Lino
linoleum base.....LB[6]
linoleum floor.....LF[6]
living room.....LR[6]
locker.....LKR[6]
locker room.....LKR R
long.....LG[6]
louver.....LV
louver opening.....LVO or L[3]
louvered door.....LVD
low frequency.....LF
low point.....LP
low pressure.....LP
low tension.....LT
lumber.....lbr[2] or LBR[6]
lumen.....L[6]
machine.....MACH[6]
machine room.....MACH R
magnesia block.....MB
mail chute.....MC
main.....MN[6]
malleable iron.....MI[6]
malleable iron pipe.....MIP[6]
manhole.....MH[6]
manufacture.....MFR[6]
manufacturer.....MFR
marble.....MR[6]

mark.....MK[6]
masonry opening.....MO
master keyed.....MK[5]
material.....MATL[6]
maximum.....max[1] or MAX[6]
mean high tide.....MHT[6]
mean sea level.....MSL[6]
measurement.....MST
mechanic.....MEC
mechanical.....MECH[6]
medical lavatory.....ML[3]
medicine cabinet.....MC
medium.....MED
membrane.....MEMB[6]
Men's rest room.....MRR
Men's toilet.....MT
Men's wash room.....MWR
merchantable.....Merch[2]
metal.....MET.[6] or M
metal base.....MB
metal covered wood.....MCW
meter (instrument of measure).....M[3,6,7]
meter (measure).....m[1]
mezzanine.....MEZZ[6]
millimeter.....mm[1]
minimum.....min or MIN[6]
minute.....min[1]
minute (angular measure).....(')[1]
miscellaneous.....MISC[6]
model.....MOD[6]
modern tips.....MT[5]
modular.....MOD
modulus of elasticity.....E
monitor.....MON[6]
monument.....MON[6]
moment, bending.....M
motor.....M[4]
motor generator.....MG[6]
moulding.....Mldg[2] or MLDG[6]
mounting.....MTG[6]
movable partition.....M PART
nail.....N
national.....NATL[6]
National Board of Fire Underwriters.....NBFU
National Bureau of Standards.....NBS
National Electric Code.....NEC[1]
National Electrical Manufacturers Assoc.....NEMA
National Fire Protection Association.....NFPA
National Lumber Manufacturers Association.....NLMA
nickel.....NI[6]
nickel-silver.....NI-SIL[6]
nipple.....NIP[6]
nominal.....NOM[6]
non-removable pin (set screw in barrel).....NRP
non-slip.....NS
normal.....NOR[6]
north.....N[6]
north-northwest.....NNW
Not in Contract.....NIC
number.....No[2] or NO.[6] or #

ABBREVIATIONS

oak..............................O
octagon........................OCT[6]
octagonal......................OCT
office..........................OFF[6]
on center.......................OC[6]
one thousand feet board
    measure.....................MBM[6]
opening........................OPNG[6]
opposite.......................OPP[6]
ornament.......................ORN[6]
ounce........................oz[1] or OZ[6]
out to out...................O to O[6]
outlet.........................OUT[6]
outside diameter.............OD[1,6]
oval headed screw.............OHS
oval headed wood screw........OHWS
overall........................OA[6]
overflow.......................OVFL[6]
overhead.......................OVHD[6]
overload.......................OVLD[6]
page............................PG[6]
painted.......................PTD[6]
pair............................PR[6]
panel..........................PNL[6]
pantry.........................PAN.[6]
parallel.......................PAR[6]
parkway........................PKWY[6]
part............................PT[6]
partition.....................PARTN[6]
parts per million..............ppm
passage.......................PASS.[6]
passenger.....................PASS.[6]
pedestal.......................PED[6]
pedestal lavatory...............PL[3]
penny (nail size)..............d[1,6]
per.............................../
percent......................% or p c
perpendicular.................PERP[6]
pet cock........................P C
phase...........................PH[6]
pi (ratio of circ. to
    dia. of a circle)............π
piece...........................PC[6]
pint............................pt[1]
pipe shaft......................P S
pipe sleeve....................P SL[6]
place............................PL
plain sawed....................Pln[2]
plaster.................PLAS[6] or PL
plastic.......................PLSTC[6]
plate (steel)............PL[6] or ₤
plate glass...................PL GL
platform.......................PLAT
plumbing.......................PLMB[6]
plumbing stack..................ST
point...........................PT[6]
point of tangent................PT
polish.........................POL[6]
polished plate glass...........PPGL
polished wire glass............PWGL
porch............................P
portable......................PORT.[6]
position.......................POS
pound...............# or lb[1] or LB[6]

pounds per cubic foot............
    .lb per cu ft[1] or LB/CU FT or LBS/FT[3]
pounds per square foot.........
    ....PSF[6] or #/☐' or LB/FT[2]
pounds per square inch.........
    ....PSI[6] or #/☐" or LB/SQ IN
powder room......................PR
power..........................PWR[6]
power house.....................PH[6]
precast.......................PRCST[6]
prefabricated................PREFAB[6]
premolded....................PRMLD[6]
pressure reducing valve.......PRV[6]
property........................Prop
proposed......................PROP[6]
Protected cast box strike....PCBX[5]
protected strike...............PX[5]
protected wrought box strike.PWBX[5]
pull chain..................P or PC
push button.....................PB[6]
quantity.......................QTY[6]
quarry.........................QRY[6]
quarry tile base...............QTB[6]
quarry tile floor..............QTF[6]
quarry tile roof...............QTR[6]
quart.......................qt[1] or QT[6]
quartered......................Qtd[2]
radial.........................RAD[6]
radiator (exposed & recessed).RAD[6]
radiator enclosed.........RAD ENCL
radiator recess...........RAD REC
radio............................R[4]
radius.....................r or R[6]
random.........................rdm[2]
range.............................R
range, gas.......................R[7]
receiving basin..................RB
receptacle....................RECP[6]
recirculate..................RECIRC[6]
recirculation duct section......R[3]
rectangle.....................RECT[6]
reducer........................RED[6]
reflective.....................REFL
reflector.....................REFL[6]
refrigerator....................REF
refrigerant discharge (pipe)...RD[3]
refrigerator suction...........RS[3]
register.......................REG[6]
register, bottom................BR[3]
register, ceiling...............CR[3]
register, center................CR[3]
register, top...................TR[3]
register, top & bottom.......T&BR[3]
regulator......................REG[6]
reinforce or reinforcing.....REINF
relative humidity...............RH[6]
relief valve....................RV
remote control..................RC[6]
remove.........................REM[6]
repair.........................REP[6]
required......................REQD[6]
resin emulsion...................RE
return.........................RET[6]
revision.......................REV
revolutions per minute.rpm[1] or RPM[6]
revolutions per second..rps[1] or RPS[6]

right...........................RT[6]
right hand......................RH[6]
right hand reverse............RHR[5]
riser............................R[6]
rivet..........................RIV[6]
road............................RD[6]
roof............................RF[6]
roof drain......................RD[6]
roofing.............Rfg[2] or RFG[6]
room....................RM[6] or R
rough..........................RGH[6]
rough wire glass..............RWGL
round...............rnd[2] or RD[6]
roundheaded screw..............RHS
Royal Architectural
    Institute of Canada......R.A.I.C.
rubber.........................RUB[6]
saddle...................SDL[6] or S
safe working pressure........SWP[6]
safety.........................SAF[6]
safety valve....................SV[6]
sapwood........................Sap[2]
scale............................SC
schedule.......................SCH[6]
screw..........................SCR[6]
screwed (piping)...............scd
scupper.......................SCUP[6]
scuttle..........................S[6]
seamless......................SMLS[6]
second...............SEC[6] or sec[1]
second (angular measure)......(")[1]
section.......................SECT[6]
select.................Sel[2] or SEL[6]
self-closing.....................SC
service........................SERV[6]
set screw.......................SS[6]
sewer.........................SEW.[6]
sewer, cast iron pipe.........S-CI
sewer, clay tile..............S-CT
sheathing...................SHTHG[6]
sheet...........................SH[6]
shelves (as 2 shelves)........2 SH
shiplap.......................Shlp[2]
shower..........................SH[6]
shut off valve................SOV[6]
siding...............Sdg[2] or SDG[6]
sill-cock........................S-C
Simplified Practice
    Recommendations............SPR
sink..................SK[6] or S[3,7]
sink and laundry tray.......S & T[3]
sink, service.................SS[3,7]
sitz bath.......................SB[7]
slate...........................SL[6]
sleeve.........................SLV[6]
slop sink or service sink.......SS
socket.........................SOC[6]
soil pipe.......................SP[6]
solder.........................SLD[6]
south............................S[6]
south by west..................SbW
southwest........................SW
speaker.......................SPKR[6]
specifications................SPEC[6]
sprinkler......................SPR[5]
square..........Sq[2] or SQ[6] or ☐
square edge...................Sq E[2]

ABBREVIATIONS

square foot	sq ft[1] or □'
square inch	sq in[1] or □"
stained	stnd[2] or STN
stained-waxed	SW
stainless steel	SST[6]
stairs	ST
stairway	STWY[6]
stanchion	STAN[6]
standard	std[1] or Std[2] or STD[6]
standard wire gauge	S.W.G.
standpipe	SP[6]
static pressure	SP[6]
station	STA[6]
steam working pressure	ST WP[6]
steel	STL[6]
steel partition	ST PART
steel saddle	ST S
steel steeple tips	SST[5]
sterilizer	STER[6]
stiffener	STIFF.[6]
stirrup	STIR.[6]
stock	stk or STK[6]
stone	STN[6]
storage	STG[6]
storage closet	ST CL
storm water	ST W[6]
street	ST[6]
strike only-template machine screws	STMS[5]
string	STR[6]
structural	STR[6]
substitute	SUB[6]
sump pit	SP
superintendent	SUPT[6]
supersede	SUPSD[6]
supplement	SUPP[6]
supplementary	SUPPY
supply	SUP[6]
supply duct section	S[3]
support	SUPT[6]
surface	SUR[6]
surface area	A or S
surface foot	SF
surfaced and matched	S&M
surfaced four sides	S4S
surfaced one side and one edge	S1S1E
surface measure	SM
suspend	SUSP[6]
suspended ceiling	SUSP CEIL
switch	SW[6] or S[4]
switch, automatic door	SD[4]
switchboard	SWBD[6]
switch, key operated	SK[4]
symbol	SYM[6]
system	SYS[6]
tangent	tan[1] or TAN[6]

technical	TECH[6]
tee	T[6]
telegraph	TLG[6]
telephone	TEL[6]
telephone booth	TB
temperature	temp[1] or TEMP[6]
template	TEMP[6]
template-machine screws	TMS[5]
tensile strength	TS[6]
terminal	TERM.[6]
terrazzo	TER[6]
terra cotta	TC[6]
thermal conductance	C
thermal conductivity	k
thermometer	THERM[6]
thermostat	THERMO[6]
thick or thickness	THK[6] or T
thousand	M[2,6]
thousand pounds	kip[1] or KIP[6]
thread	THD[6]
threaded	THR
toilet	T
tongue and groove	T&G[2,6]
top, bottom and sides	TB&S[2]
transformer, power	T[4] or TRANS[6]
transom	T
tray	T
tread	T[6] or TR
trimmed opening	TO
trough urinal	TU[3]
turnbuckle	TRNBKL[6]
typewriter	TYPW
typical	TYP[6]
ultimate	ULT[6]
Underwriters Laboratories	UL
unfinished	UNFIN
United States Standard	USS[6]
U.S. Standard Gauge	USSG
unit heater	UH[6]
up	U
urinal	UR[6]
urinal, trough type	TU[3]
utility room	UR
vacuum	VAC[6]
vacuum cleaning line	V[3]
valve box	VB[6]
vanishing point	VP
vapor proof	VAP PRF[6]
variable	VAR[6]
varnish	VARN[6]
velocity	VEL[6]
vent	V
vent duct	VD
vent pipe	VP[6]
vent shaft	VS
vent stack	VS[6]
ventilate	VENT.[6]

ventilation	VENT
ventilator	V
vertical	VERT[6]
vertical grain	VG
vestibule	VEST.[6]
vitreous	VIT[6]
volt	V[6] or v[1]
volume	VOL[6] or V
wall	W[6]
wall cabinet	W CAB
wall lavatory	WL[3,7]
wall paint flat	WF
wall paint gloss	WG
wall paint semi gloss	WSG
wall vent	WV
warehouse	WHSE[6]
Washburn and Moen gauge	W&M GA
washing machine	WM
washroom	WR[6]
water	W[6]
watercloset	WC[6]
water cooler	WCR[6]
water heater	WH[6]
water line	WL[6]
waterproof or waterproofing	WP
watertight	WT[6]
watt	W[6] or w[1]
watthour	WHR[6]
waxed	W
weather stripping	WS[6]
weatherproof	WP[6]
weephole	WH
weight	wt[1,2] or WT[6]
west	W[6]
wide flange (steel)	WF
width	Wth[2] or W[6]
window	WDW
wire	W[6]
wire glass	W GL
with	W/
with (hardware)	X
without	W/O
women's rest room	WRR
women's toilet	WT
wood	WD[6]
wood door	WD[5]
wood frame	WF[5]
working pressure	WP[6]
wringer-washing machine	WWM
wrought	WRT[6]
wrought iron	WI[6]
yard	yd[1] or YD[6]
yard drain inlet	YDI
year	yr[1] or YR[6]
yellow	YEL[6]
zinc	Z[6]

For reference numbers see first page of abbreviations.

LETTERING

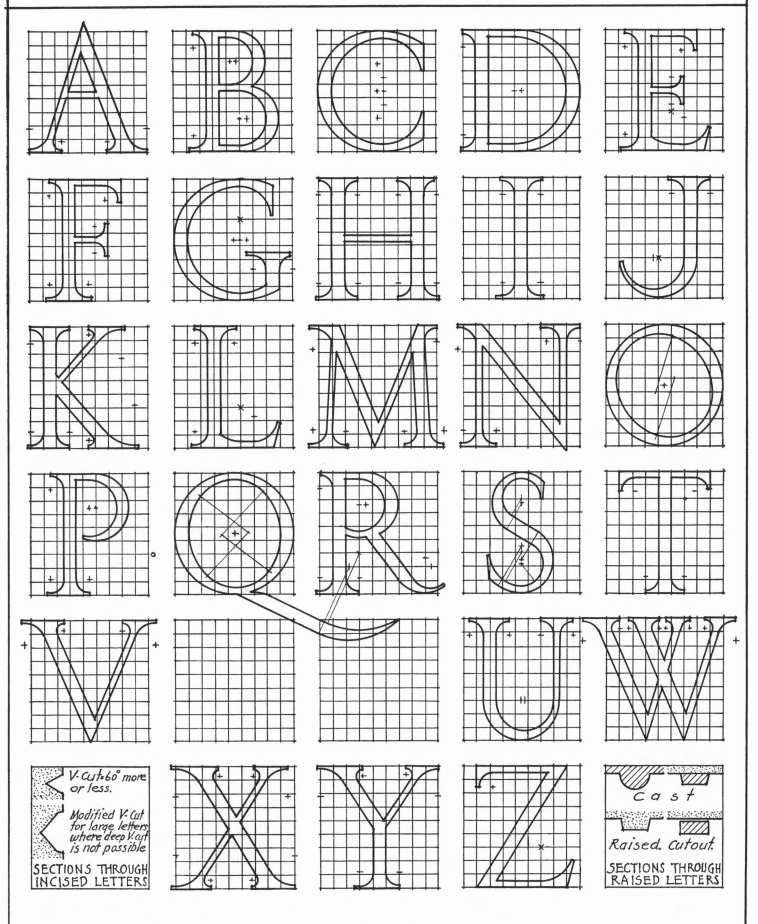

V-Cut=60° more or less.

Modified V-Cut for large letters where deep V-cut is not possible.

SECTIONS THROUGH INCISED LETTERS

Cast

Raised. Cutout.

SECTIONS THROUGH RAISED LETTERS

LETTERING

ABCDEFGHIJKLMN
OPQRSTUVWXYZ &
USED FOR TITLES

ABCDEFGHIJKLMNOPQRSTUVWXYZ
ABCDEFGHIJKLMNOPQRSTUVWXYZ

ABCDEFGHIJKLMNOPQRSTUVWXYZ
ABCDEFGHIJKLMNOPQRSTUVWXYZ

abcdefghijklmnopqrstuvwxyz
abcdefghijklmnopqrstuvwxyz
used for subtitles as Plan · Elevation

ABCDEFGHIJKLMNOPQRSTUVWXYZ - PLAN - POOL
PLAN TRANSVERSE SECTION ELEVATION

ABCDEFGHIJKLMNOPQRSTUVWXYZ-1234567890
THIS · IS · ANOTHER · TYPE · USED · FOR · SUB-TITLES
ABCDEFGHIJKLMNOPQRSTUVWXYZ - SLOPING

abcdefgghijklmnopqrstuvwxyz   *This type is often used for notes*
abcdefghijklmnopqrstuvwxyz,   *an upright variation of the foregoing*

ABCDEFGHIJKLMNOPQRSTUVWXYZ - NOTES OR SMALL SCALE TITLES
ABCDEFGHIJKLMNOPQRSTUVWXYZ - A SLOPING VARIATION OF ABOVE

abcdefghijklmnopqrstuvwxyz   *an upright type of lettering which may be used for notes*
abcdefghijklmnopqrstuvwxyz   *Type of lettering used throughout this book for notes etc.*

SPELLING & ROMAN NUMERALS

ROMAN NUMERALS

ARABIC =	1	5	10	50	100	500	1000	50,000
ROMAN =	I	V	X	L	C	D	M	$\overline{\text{L}}$

RULES:

1. If no letter precedes a letter of greater value, add the number represented by the letters.
   Example: XXX represents 30, VI represents 6

2. If a letter precedes a letter of greater value, subtract the smaller from the greater, add the remainder or the remainders thus obtained to the numbers represented by the other letters.
   Example: IV represents 4; XL represents 40; CXLV represents 145

3. A bar placed over a letter multiplies value by 1000.

OTHER ILLUSTRATIONS =	9	13	14	42	55	96	1601	4240
	IX	XIII	XIV	XLII	LV	XCVI	MDCI	$\overline{\text{IV}}$CCXL

SPELLING

(See Index for spelling of other words.)

Where two spellings are given, the first is preferred.

abbreviations
abutment, abutted, abutting
baluster, balustrade
bat or batt
bathroom (one word)
bathtub (one word)
bedroom (one word)
bevel, beveled or bevelled, beveling or bevelling
brickwork
bridging
bulletin
calk, caulk
cantilever
car-port (or two words)
center, centre (latter usually in England)
colonnade
cupola
dampproofing
datum (singular), data (plural, but may be used as singular)
dining room (two words)
downstairs
drafting, draughting, (latter seldom used)
draftsman, draughtsman (latter seldom used)
enclose, inclose (latter preferable for land)
enclosure, inclosure (latter preferable for land)
entasis
equivalent
escalator
escutcheon
Fahrenheit

faience (tile)
fascia
flagstone (one word)
focus (singular), foci or focuses (plural)
games room (two words)
gauge or gage
grill (to cook on)
grille or grill (grating)
gymnasium (singular), gymnasiums or gymnasia (plural)
hanger (a hanging device)
hangar (a garage for planes)
integral
kalamein
kalsomine or calcimine
lanai (a Hawaiian veranda)
lean-to-roof
level, leveled or levelled, leveling or levelling
lien (mechanics)
living room
louver (Louvre is a building in Paris)
mantel, mantle (latter is also a cloak)
marquee
mat (finish, Matt is a name)
miter, or mitre, mitered or mitred
modillion
mould or mold
mortgage
movable
oriel (oriole is a bird)
paneled or panelled, paneling or panelling
parallel

permanent, permanency
permeable
plaster-work
playroom (one word)
practice (practice of Architecture)
precede, preceding
program or programme
rabbet (pronounced like the animal) or rebate (commonly pronounced like rabbet but may be pronounced as spelled) rabbetted
raggle or reglet (a groove in masonry. The Dictionary defines "reglet" as a narrow flat moulding)
receptacle
remove, removable
sheet metal
spackle or sparkle (usually pronounced like latter. Several other spellings used but none in dictionaries)
stile (of a door. Style of Architecture)
supersede (not supercede)
template or templet
terrazzo
theater (in England often theatre)
through or thru (latter not in some dictionaries)
transept
upstairs
wainscot
wallboard (one word)
waterproofing
weephole (one word)
underpinning

MODULAR COORDINATION

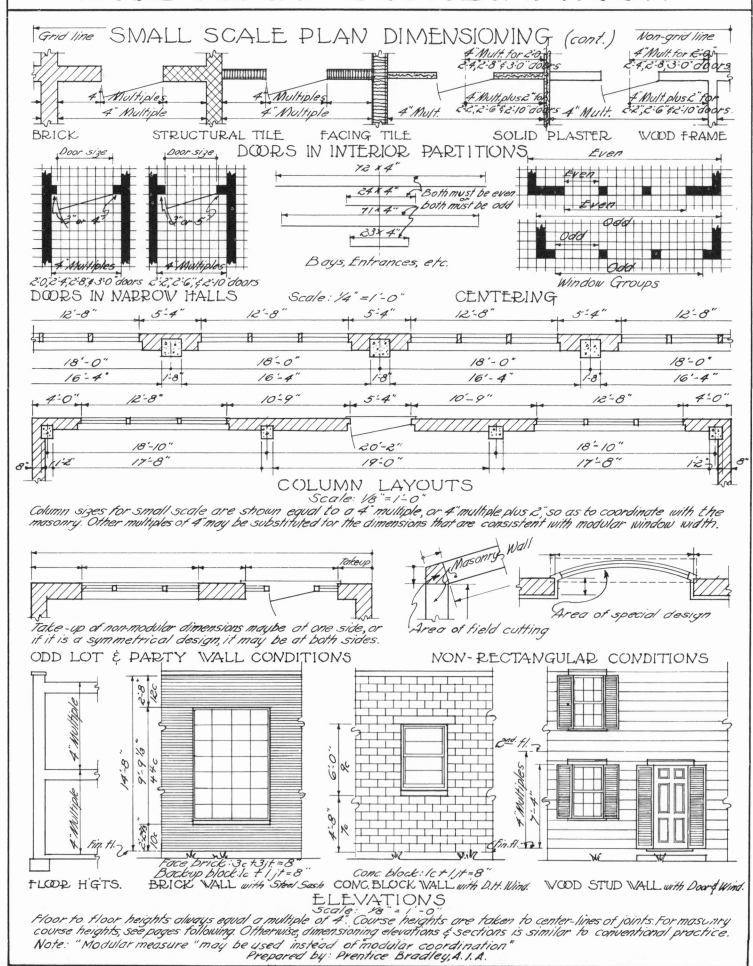

SMALL SCALE PLAN DIMENSIONING (cont.)

Grid line   Non-grid line

4" Mult. for 2-0"   4" Mult. for 2-0"
2-4, 2-8 & 3-0 doors   2-4, 2-8, 3-0 doors

4" Multiples   4" Multiples   4" Mult. plus 2" for   4" Mult. plus 2" for
4" Multiple   4" Multiple   4" Mult.   2-2, 2-6 & 2-10 doors   2-2, 2-6 & 2-10 doors
                                                         4" Mult.

BRICK   STRUCTURAL TILE   FACING TILE   SOLID PLASTER   WOOD FRAME

DOORS IN INTERIOR PARTITIONS

Door size   Door size   Even

72 x 4"   Even

2" or 4"   2" or 5"   24 x 4"   } Both must be even
                                  71 x 4"   } or both must be odd   Even

                                  23 x 4"   Odd

4" Multiples   4" Multiples   Odd

                              Bays, Entrances, etc.   Odd

2-0, 2-4, 2-8 & 3-0 doors   2-2, 2-6 & 2-10 doors   Window Groups

DOORS IN NARROW HALLS   Scale: 1/4" = 1'-0"   CENTERING

12'-8"   5'-4"   12'-8"   5'-4"   12'-8"   5'-4"   12'-8"

18'-0"   18'-0"   18'-0"   18'-0"
16'-4"   1'-8"   16'-4"   1'-8"   16'-4"   1'-8"   16'-4"

4'-0"   12'-8"   10'-9"   5'-4"   10'-9"   12'-8"   4'-0"

8"   1'-2"   18'-10"   20'-2"   18'-10"   1'-2"   8"
          17'-8"   19'-0"   17'-8"

COLUMN LAYOUTS
Scale: 1/8" = 1'-0"

Column sizes for small scale are shown equal to a 4" multiple, or 4" multiple plus 2", so as to coordinate with the masonry. Other multiples of 4" may be substituted for the dimensions that are consistent with modular window width.

Takeup   Masonry Wall

                          Area of field cutting   Area of special design

Take-up of non-modular dimensions maybe at one side, or if it is a symmetrical design, it may be at both sides.

ODD LOT & PARTY WALL CONDITIONS   NON-RECTANGULAR CONDITIONS

2'-8"   12c
14'-8"   9'-9 1/3"   4" Multiple   9'-9 1/3"   44c   6'-0"   9c   2nd fl.
2'-2 2/3"   10c   4'-8"   7c   4" Multiples   7'-4"
4" Multiple   fin. fl.
fin. fl.   fin. fl.

Face brick: 3c + 3jt = 8"
Backup block: 1c + 1jt = 8"   Conc. block: 1c + 1jt = 8"

FLOOR HGTS.   BRICK WALL with Steel Sash   CONC. BLOCK WALL with D.H. Wind.   WOOD STUD WALL with Door & Wind.

ELEVATIONS
Scale: 1/8" = 1'-0"

Floor to floor heights always equal a multiple of 4". Course heights are taken to center-lines of joints. For masonry course heights, see pages following. Otherwise, dimensioning elevations & sections is similar to conventional practice.
Note: "Modular measure" may be used instead of "modular coordination"
Prepared by: Prentice Bradley, A.I.A.

MODULAR COORDINATION

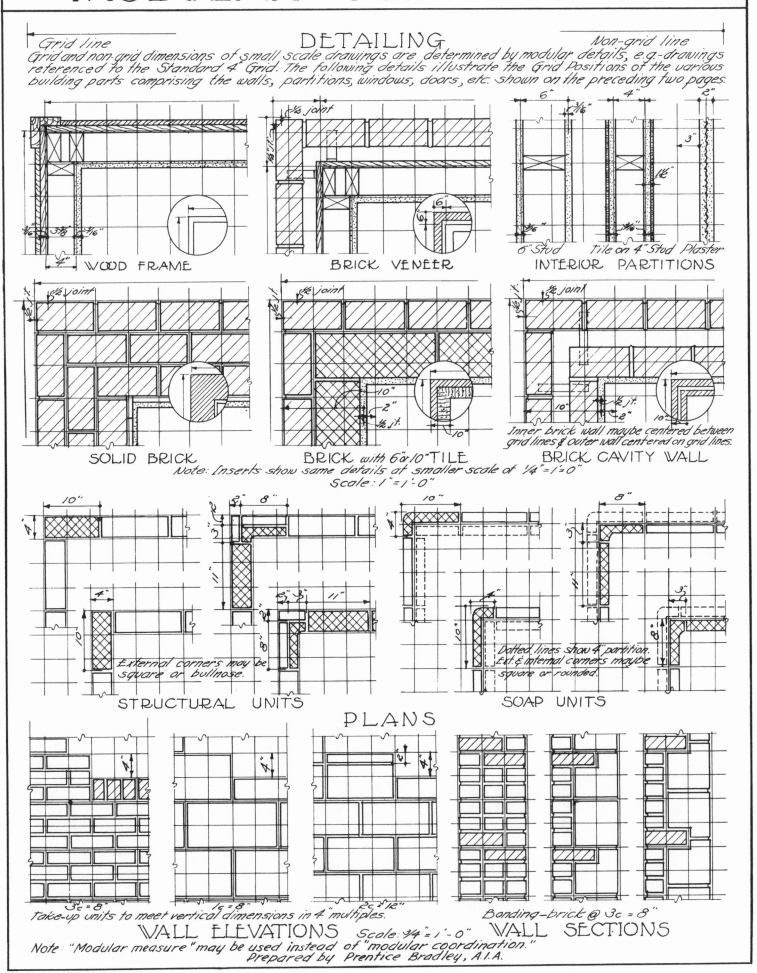

DETAILING

Grid line   Non-grid line

Grid and non-grid dimensions of small scale drawings are determined by modular details, e.g. drawings referenced to the Standard 4" Grid. The following details illustrate the Grid Positions of the various building parts comprising the walls, partitions, windows, doors, etc. shown on the preceding two pages.

WOOD FRAME   BRICK VENEER   INTERIOR PARTITIONS

6" Stud   Tile on 4" Stud   Plaster

SOLID BRICK   BRICK with 6" or 10" TILE   BRICK CAVITY WALL

Inner brick wall maybe centered between grid lines & outer wall centered on grid lines.

Note: Inserts show same details at smaller scale of ¼"=1'-0"
Scale: 1"=1'-0"

External corners may be square or bullnose.

STRUCTURAL UNITS

Dotted lines show 4" partition. Ext. & Internal corners maybe square or rounded.

SOAP UNITS

PLANS

Take-up units to meet vertical dimensions in 4" multiples.

Bonding-brick @ 3c = 8"

WALL ELEVATIONS   Scale: ¼"=1'-0"   WALL SECTIONS

Note: "Modular measure" may be used instead of "modular coordination."
Prepared by Prentice Bradley, A.I.A.

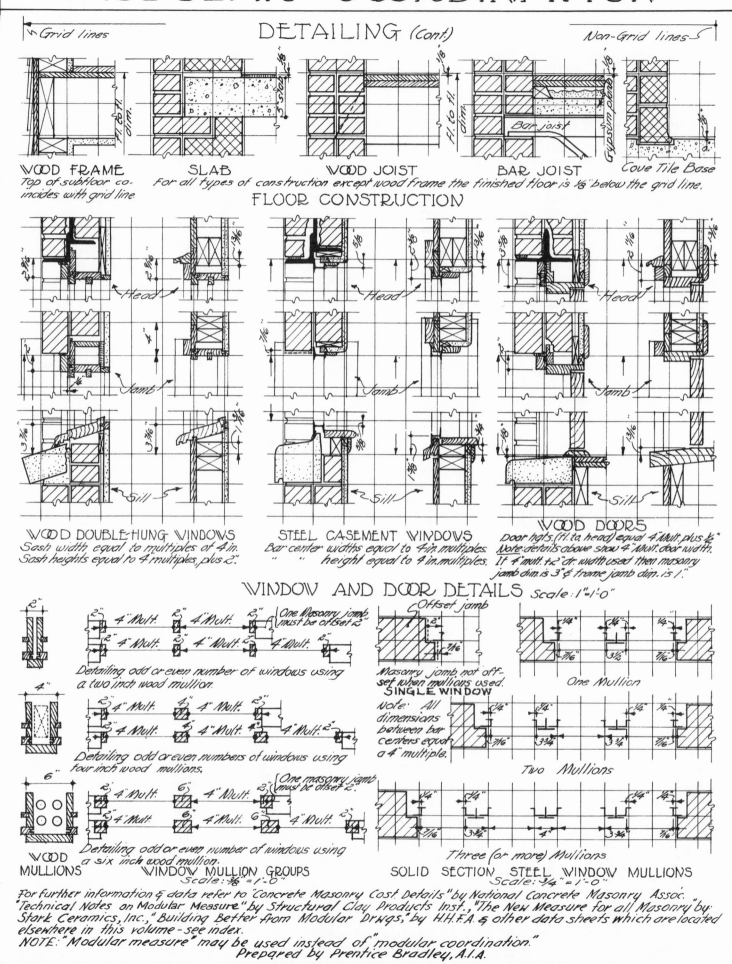

MODULAR COORDINATION

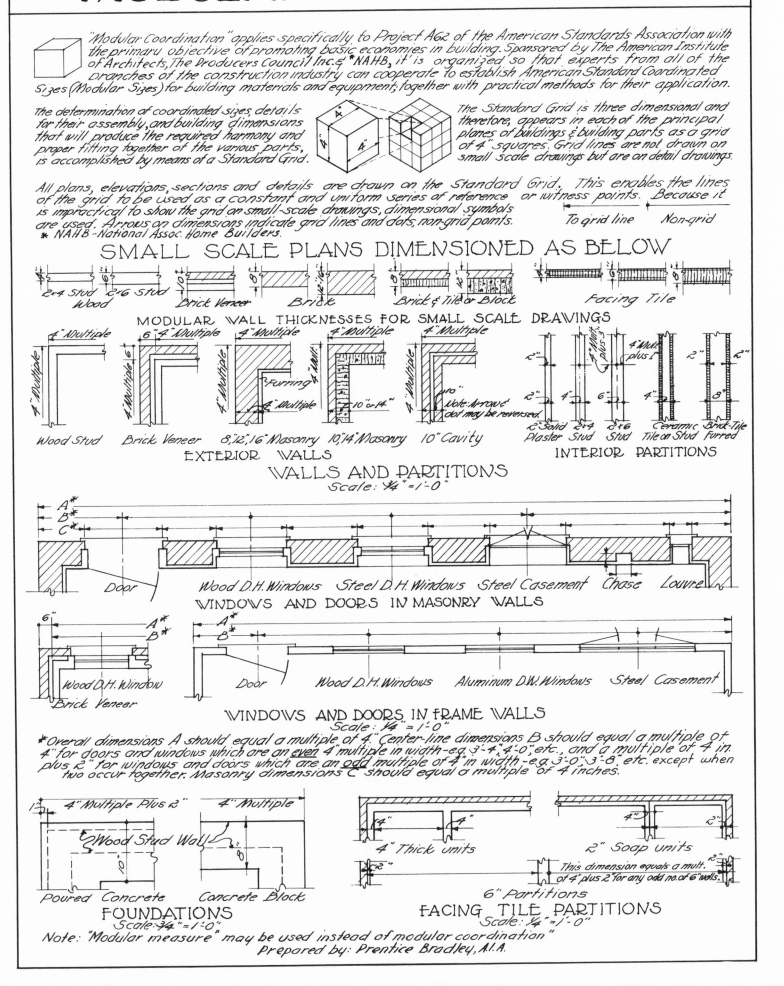

"Modular Coordination" applies specifically to Project A62 of the American Standards Association with the primary objective of promoting basic economies in building. Sponsored by The American Institute of Architects, The Producers Council Inc.& *NAHB, it is organized so that experts from all of the branches of the construction industry can cooperate to establish American Standard Coordinated Sizes (Modular Sizes) for building materials and equipment, together with practical methods for their application.

The determination of coordinated sizes, details for their assembly, and building dimensions that will produce the required harmony and proper fitting together of the various parts, is accomplished by means of a Standard Grid.

The Standard Grid is three dimensional and therefore, appears in each of the principal planes of buildings & building parts as a grid of 4" squares. Grid lines are not drawn on small scale drawings but are on detail drawings.

All plans, elevations, sections and details are drawn on the Standard Grid. This enables the lines of the grid to be used as a constant and uniform series of reference or witness points. Because it is impractical to show the grid on small-scale drawings, dimensional symbols are used. Arrows on dimensions indicate grid lines and dots, non-grid points.

To grid line   Non-grid

* NAHB - National Assoc. Home Builders.

SMALL SCALE PLANS DIMENSIONED AS BELOW

2x4 Stud   2x6 Stud   Brick Veneer   Brick   Brick & Tile or Block   Facing Tile
Wood

MODULAR WALL THICKNESSES FOR SMALL SCALE DRAWINGS

Wood Stud   Brick Veneer   8,"12,"16" Masonry   10,'14' Masonry   10" Cavity   2" Solid   2x4   2x6   Ceramic   Brick-Tile
                                                                                       Plaster   Stud   Stud   Tile on Stud   furred
EXTERIOR WALLS   INTERIOR PARTITIONS

WALLS AND PARTITIONS
Scale: ¼" = 1'-0"

Door   Wood D.H. Windows   Steel D.H. Windows   Steel Casement   Chase   Louvre

WINDOWS AND DOORS IN MASONRY WALLS

Wood D.H. Window   Door   Wood D.H. Windows   Aluminum D.W. Windows   Steel Casement
Brick Veneer

WINDOWS AND DOORS IN FRAME WALLS
Scale: ¼" = 1'-0"

*Overall dimensions A should equal a multiple of 4" Center-line dimensions B should equal a multiple of 4" for doors and windows which are an even 4" multiple in width - e.g. 3'-4", 4'-0", etc., and a multiple of 4 in. plus 2" for windows and doors which are an odd multiple of 4" in width - e.g. 3'-0", 3'-8" etc. except when two occur together. Masonry dimensions C should equal a multiple of 4 inches.

4" Multiple Plus 2"   4" Multiple
Wood Stud Wall

4" Thick units   2" Soap units

Poured Concrete   Concrete Block   6" Partitions
                                                            This dimension equals a mult. of 4 plus 2 for any odd no. of 6" walls.

FOUNDATIONS   FACING TILE PARTITIONS
Scale: ¾"=1'-0"   Scale: ¼"=1'-0"

Note: "Modular measure" may be used instead of modular coordination"
Prepared by: Prentice Bradley, A.I.A.

PARALINE DRAWING includes pictorial types in which parallel lines of the object are parallel in the drawing. The most important of these are isometric, dimetric, and oblique drawings.

ORTHOGRAPHIC DRAWING includes all drawing types in which the projectors are perpendicular to the plane of projection. The most common are multi-view, isometric, dimetric, and trimetric.

AXONOMETRIC DRAWING includes paraline types on which measurements can usually be made only on axis direction lines. Widely used axonometric drawings are isometric and dimetric.

OBLIQUE DRAWING has one set of planes parallel to the plane of projection. The parallel projectors are at an oblique angle to show three dimensions of the object. Measurements can be made in any direction on planes parallel to the plane of projection.

AXIS LINES are the three mutually perpendicular lines which meet at the corner of a box shape and all lines parallel to them.

SOME TYPES OF DRAWINGS

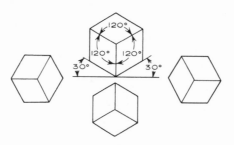

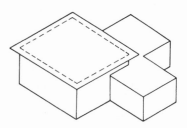

THE THREE ISOMETRIC AXIS must be kept 120° apart since they are required to be at the same angle to the plane of projection in order to be foreshortened equally and to be at the same scale. When one axis is horizontal or vertical the other two axes can be drawn with the 30° x 60° triangle on the T—square. These four positions are illustrated above. The vertical position of one axis is widely used. It allows the top or bottom of the object to be shown. The axes can be at any angle if they are kept 120° apart.

ADVANTAGES of isometric drawing: Use of one scale on the three axes; use of a standard triangle; fairly easy to dimension; and looks neat when dimension lines, arrows, and numerals are kept in isometric forms.

DISADVANTAGES: Equal importance is given to each of the three visible planes. There is no opportunity to emphasize complex and important areas and subordinate blank unimportant ones. Only one picture effect is possible with the three visible planes and unsatisfactory line relations cannot be avoided.

ISOMETRIC DRAWING — MEASURE ON AXES ONLY — ONE SCALE

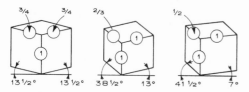

DIMETRIC SCALES—ANGLES FORMULA

$$\cos a = \frac{-\sqrt{2H^2 - V^2}}{2H}$$ In this formula:

a = one of two equal angles between the projection of axes. H = one of two equal scales. V = third scale. A = a — 90° = angle with horizontal of two equal axes of symmetrical dimetric. A = one angle with the horizontal of unsymmetrical dimetric. B = 90° — 2A = second angle with horizontal of unsymmetrical dimetric.

THE FORMULA ABOVE can be used to work out the various combinations of scales and angles for dimetric drawing. Three of the most useful of these scales and angles are given on the diagrams of cubes above. The scales are relative ones with the larger scales given as 1 and the smaller ones as fractions.

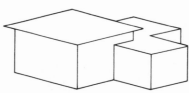

SYMMETRICAL DIMETRIC DRAWING is very useful to reduce the top or bottom area of the object which may be large and blank in an isometric. Only the setup having a common fractional scale relation which can be found on standard scales is illustrated here. When it is desired to make the top or bottom area of a symmetrical dimetric larger than in isometric, it may be found that plan oblique drawing is better for the purpose. Symmetrical dimetric gives equal emphasis to the two wall areas. When one wall area should be emphasized in a paraline drawing, either unsymmetrical dimetric or elevation oblique drawing can be used.

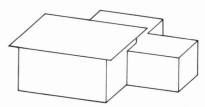

UNSYMMETRICAL DIMETRIC DRAWING allows emphasis on one or two of the three planes represented and subordination of the other two or one. It allows for a great deal of variation in the relative importance of the three sets of areas for best pictorial effect. This type of paraline drawing is for many objects the most natural and best in its pictorial effect. A symmetrical dimetric setup of scales and angles can be turned with one of the two equal axes in a vertical position for unsymmetrical dimetric. When the two equal scale axes are turned to produce equal angles with the horizontal the setup is symmetrical.

DIMETRIC DRAWING — MEASURE ON AXES ONLY — TWO SCALES ARE REQUIRED

CAVALIER OBLIQUE   **GENERAL OBLIQUE**   **CABINET OBLIQUE**

OBLIQUE DRAWINGS ARE CLASSIFIED according to scale used on the receding lines as Cavalier Oblique Drawings, General Oblique Drawings, and Cabinet Oblique Drawings. Cavalier Oblique is easy to draw since the one scale is used on all axes. However the receding lines appear too long. Cabinet Oblique uses one half scale on receding lines which appear too short. General Oblique drawing uses a scale in between full and half scale to obtain better proportions which give a more satisfactory representation of the appearance of the object. Two thirds and three fourths scale give good proportions and either may be used on the receding lines.

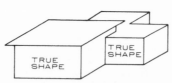

IN ELEVATION OBLIQUE DRAWING a set of vertical planes is parallel to the picture plane and has lines and areas drawn true shape. Any angle can be chosen for the receding lines which are drawn from the true shape areas. It is therefore possible to show top or bottom and either side of the object attached to the front in varying amounts. A low angle of receding lines shows more of the side and less top or bottom while a large angle with the horizontal will show more of the top or bottom and less of the side. Some irregular wall plane shapes are explained better in oblique drawing than in other types of pictorial drawing.

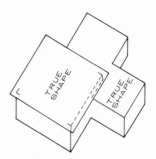

PLAN OBLIQUE DRAWING has plan planes true shape. Turn the plan of the object to a satisfactory angle and then draw verticals, which are the receding lines. The plan can be turned at any angle. Therefore both wall planes can be given equal emphasis, or one can be subordinated.

OBJECTS WITH IRREGULAR or unusual plan shapes sometimes explain more clearly in plan oblique than any other type of pictorial drawing.

OBLIQUE DRAWINGS—MEASURE ON AXES OF RECEDING AREAS—ANY DIRECTION ON TRUE SHAPES

C. Leslie Martin; University of Cincinnati; Cincinnati, Ohio

PERSPECTIVE

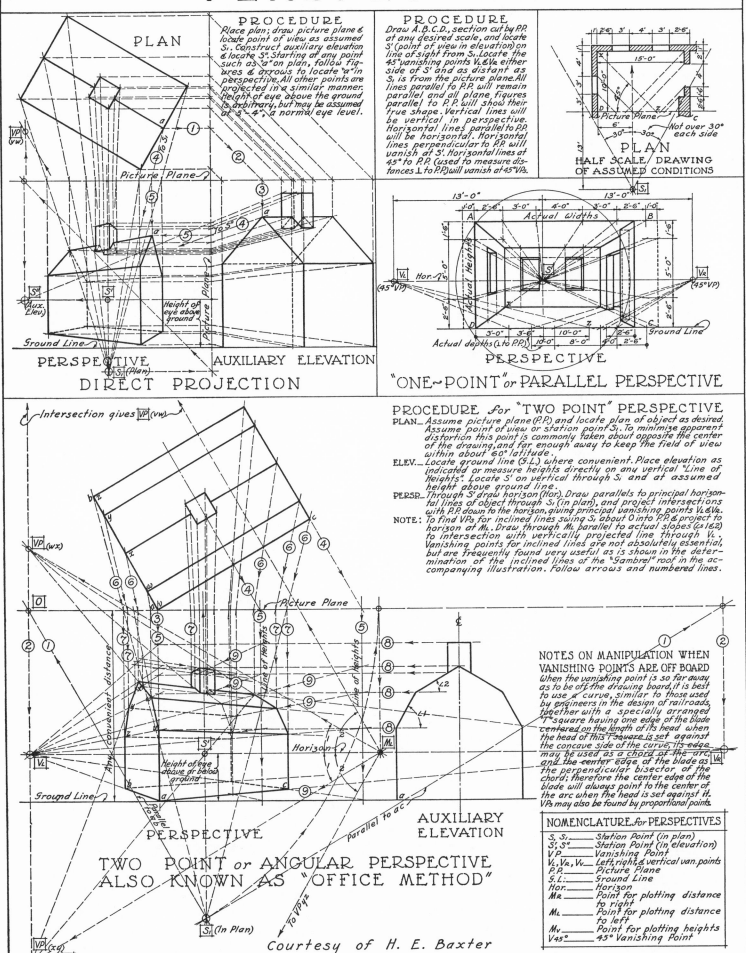

PLAN

PROCEDURE
Place plan; draw picture plane & locate point of view as assumed S_1. Construct auxiliary elevation & locate S''. Starting at any point such as "a" on plan, follow figures & arrows to locate "a" in perspective. All other points are projected in a similar manner. Height of eye above the ground is arbitrary, but may be assumed at 5'-4", a normal eye level.

PROCEDURE
Draw A.B.C.D., section cut by P.P. at any desired scale, and locate S' (point of view in elevation) on line of sight from S_1. Locate the 45° vanishing points V_L & V_R either side of S' and as distant as S_1 is from the picture plane. All lines parallel to P.P. will remain parallel and all plane figures parallel to P.P. will show their true shape. Vertical lines will be vertical in perspective. Horizontal lines parallel to P.P. will be horizontal. Horizontal lines perpendicular to P.P. will vanish at S'. Horizontal lines at 45° to P.P. (used to measure distances ⊥ to P.P.) will vanish at 45° VPs.

PLAN
HALF SCALE DRAWING OF ASSUMED CONDITIONS

PERSPECTIVE   **AUXILIARY ELEVATION**
DIRECT PROJECTION

PERSPECTIVE
"ONE-POINT" or PARALLEL PERSPECTIVE

PROCEDURE for "TWO POINT" PERSPECTIVE
PLAN — Assume picture plane (P.P.) and locate plan of object as desired. Assume point of view or station point S_1. To minimize apparent distortion this point is commonly taken about opposite the center of the drawing, and far enough away to keep the field of view within about 60° latitude.

ELEV. — Locate ground line (G.L.) where convenient. Place elevation as indicated or measure heights directly on any vertical "Line of Heights". Locate S' on vertical through S_1 and at assumed height above ground line.

PERSP. — Through S' draw horizon (Hor.). Draw parallels to principal horizontal lines of object through S_1 (in plan), and project intersections with P.P. down to the horizon, giving principal vanishing points V_L & V_R.

NOTE: To find VPs for inclined lines swing S_1 about O into P.P. & project to horizon at M_L. Draw through M_L parallel to actual slopes (∠s 1&2) to intersection with vertically projected line through V_L. Vanishing points for inclined lines are not absolutely essential, but are frequently found very useful as is shown in the determination of the inclined lines of the "Gambrel" roof in the accompanying illustration. Follow arrows and numbered lines.

NOTES ON MANIPULATION WHEN VANISHING POINTS ARE OFF BOARD
When the vanishing point is so far away as to be off the drawing board, it is best to use a curve, similar to those used by engineers in the design of railroads, together with a specially arranged "T" square having one edge of the blade centered on the length of its head. When the head of this "T" square is set against the concave side of the curve, its edge may be used as a chord of the arc, and the center edge of the blade as the perpendicular bisector of the chord; therefore the center edge of the blade will always point to the center of the arc when the head is set against it. VPs may also be found by proportional points.

PERSPECTIVE   **AUXILIARY ELEVATION**

TWO POINT or ANGULAR PERSPECTIVE
ALSO KNOWN AS "OFFICE METHOD"

Courtesy of H. E. Baxter

NOMENCLATURE for PERSPECTIVES
S, S_1	Station Point (in plan)
$S'; S''$	Station Point (in elevation)
V P	Vanishing Point
V_L, V_R, V_V	Left, right, & vertical van. points
P.P.	Picture Plane
G.L.:	Ground Line
Hor.	Horizon
M_R	Point for plotting distance to right
M_L	Point for plotting distance to left
M_V	Point for plotting heights
$V_{45°}$	45° Vanishing Point

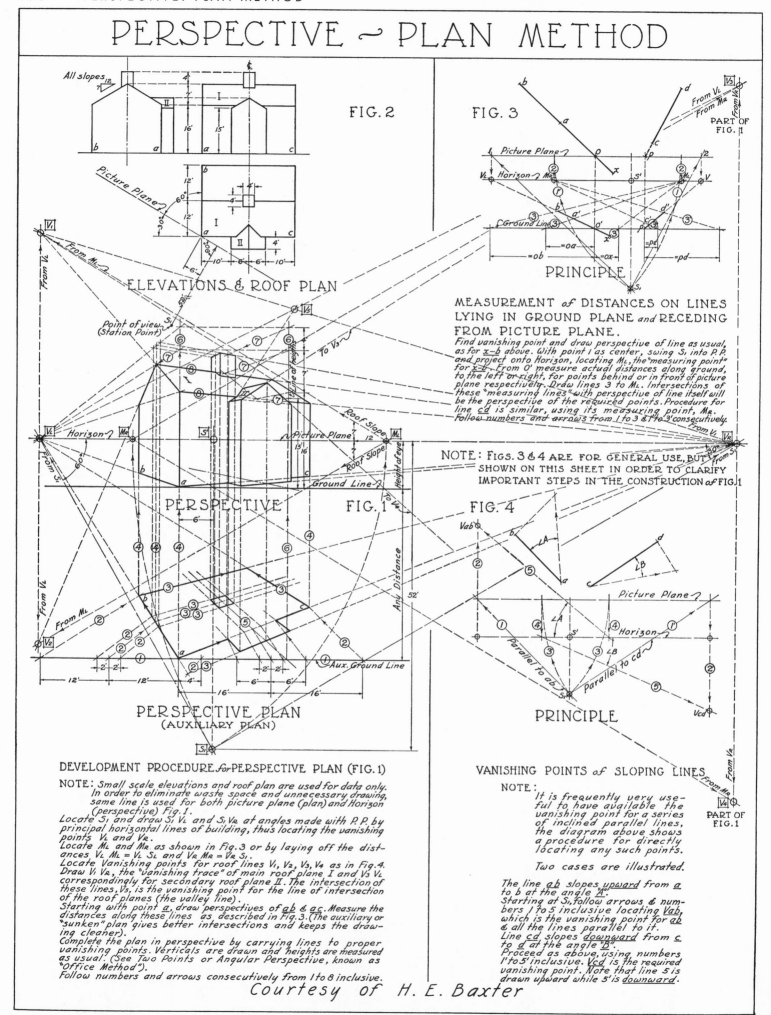

PERSPECTIVE ~ THREE POINT

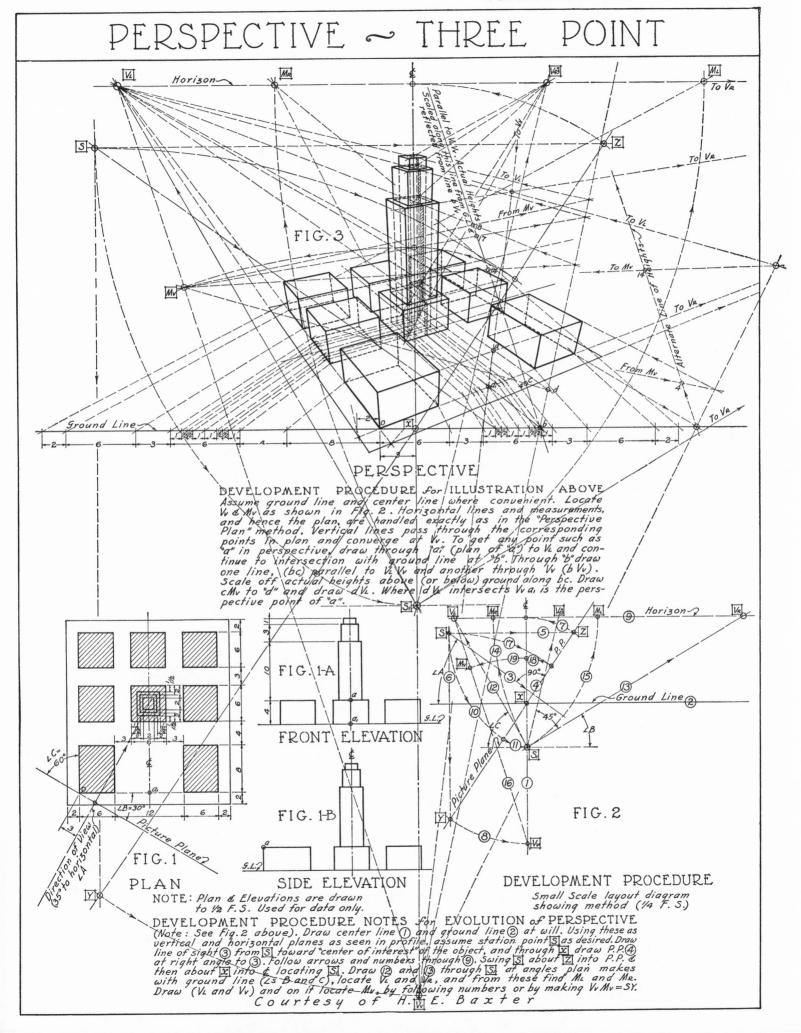

FIG.3

PERSPECTIVE

DEVELOPMENT PROCEDURE *for* ILLUSTRATION ABOVE
Assume ground line and center line where convenient. Locate Vv & Mv as shown in Fig. 2. Horizontal lines and measurements, and hence the plan, are handled exactly as in the "Perspective Plan" method. Vertical lines pass through the corresponding points in plan and converge at Vv. To get any point such as "a" in perspective, draw through "a" (plan of "a") to VL and continue to intersection with ground line at "b". Through "b" draw one line, (bc) parallel to VL Vv and another through Vv (b Vv). Scale off actual heights above (or below) ground along bc. Draw cMv to "d" and draw dVL. Where dVL intersects Vv a, is the perspective point of "a".

FIG. 1-A

FRONT ELEVATION

FIG. 1-B

SIDE ELEVATION

FIG. 1

PLAN

NOTE: *Plan & Elevations are drawn to ½ F.S. Used for data only.*

FIG. 2

DEVELOPMENT PROCEDURE
Small Scale layout diagram showing method (¼ F.S.)

DEVELOPMENT PROCEDURE NOTES *for* EVOLUTION *of* PERSPECTIVE
(Note: See Fig. 2 above). Draw center line ① and ground line ② at will. Using these as vertical and horizontal planes as seen in profile, assume station point S as desired. Draw line of sight ③ from S toward "center of interest" of the object, and through X draw P.P. ④ at right angle to ③. Follow arrows and numbers through ⑨. Swing S about Z into P.P. & then about X into ₵ locating S. Draw ⑫ and ⑬ through S at angles plan makes with ground line (∠s B and C), locate VL and VR, and from these find ML and MR. Draw (VL and Vv) and on it locate Mv by following numbers or by making Vv Mv = SY.

Courtesy of H. E. Baxter

MATHEMATICS: AREAS, VOLUMES, SURFACES

AREAS of PLANE FIGURES

FORM	NAME	AREA	FORM	NAME	AREA (Note: $\pi = 3.1416$)
	TRIANGLE	Either side × ½ altitude (Altitude perpendicular distance to opposite vertex or corner)		CIRCLE	πr^2 0.7854 × diam.² 0.0796 × circumference²
	TRAPEZIUM (irregular quadrilateral)	Divide by a diagonal into two triangles and proceed as above		SECTOR of circle	$\frac{\alpha°}{360°} \times \pi r^2$ Or: Length of arc × ½ radius
	PARALLEL-OGRAM	Either side × altitude (Altitude = perpendicular distance to opposite side)		SEGMENT of circle	$\frac{r^2}{2}\left(\frac{\alpha}{180°} - \sin\alpha\right)$ Or: Subtract triangle from sector
	TRAPEZOID	½ sum of parallel sides × altitude		ELLIPSE	Major axis × minor axis × 0.7854
	REGULAR POLYGON	½ sum of all sides × inside radius		PARABOLA	Base × ⅔ altitude

VOLUMES of TYPICAL SOLIDS

ANY PRISM OR CYLINDER RIGHT OR OBLIQUE REGULAR OR NOT

VOLUME = AREA of BASE × ALTITUDE
(Altitude = distance between parallel bases, measured perpendicular to the bases. When bases are not parallel: Altitude = perp. distance from one base to center of other).

ANY PYRAMID OR CONE RIGHT OR OBLIQUE REGULAR OR NOT

VOLUME = AREA of BASE × ⅓ ALTITUDE

(Altitude = distance from base to apex, measured perpendicular to base).

ANY FRUSTUM OR TRUNCATED PORTION OF THE ABOVE SOLIDS

h = altitude of cut-off
H = altitude of whole

VOLUME = From the volume of the whole solid if complete, subtract the volume of the portion cut off.
Note: The altitude of the cut-off part must be measured perpendicular to its own base.

SURFACES OF THE ABOVE SOLIDS

The area of the surface is best found by adding together the areas of all the faces. The area of a right cylindrical surface = perimeter of base × length of elements (average length if other base is oblique). The area of a right conical surface = perimeter of base × ½ length of elements. There is no simple rule for the area of an oblique conical surface, or for a cylindrical one where neither base is perpendicular to the elements. Best method is to construct a development, as if for making a paper model, and measure its area by method given on next page.

VOLUMES and SURFACES of DOUBLE-CURVED SOLIDS

SPHERE

VOLUME = 4/3 πr^3 = 0.5236 d^3

SURFACE = $4\pi r^2$ = 3.14159265 d^2

ELLIPSOID

VOLUME = ⅙ πabc

No simple rule for the surface.

SECTOR OF SPHERE

VOLUME = ⅔ $\pi r^2 b$

SURFACE = ½ $\pi r (4b + c)$

(or: Segment + Cone).

PARABOLOID of REVOLUTION

VOLUME = Area of circular base × ½ altitude

No simple rule for the surface

SEGMENT OF SPHERE

VOLUME = ⅓ $\pi b^2 (3r - b)$

(or: Sector − Cone)

SURFACE = $2\pi rb$

(not including the circle)

VOLUME = Area of section × $2\pi R$

SURFACE = Perimeter of section × $2\pi R$

Note: consider the section on one side of axis only.

R = distance from axis of ring to true center of section.

CIRCULAR RING OF ANY SECTION

Compiled by Prof. Andre Halasz A.I.A.

MATHEMATICS: IRREGULAR AREAS & VOLUMES

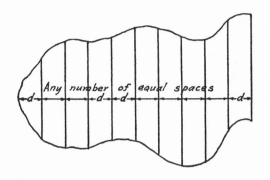

1. Divide the figure into parallel strips by equally spaced parallel lines.
2. Measure the length of each of the parallel lines.
3. Obtain a summation of the unit areas by one of the three "rules" given:

   a. "_Trapezoid Rule_". Add together the lengths of the parallels, taking the first and last at ½ value, and mutiply by the interval "d".

   b. "_Simpson's Rule_". Add the parallels, taking the first & last at full value; the second, fourth, sixth, etc., from _each end_, at 4 x full value; and the third, 5th etc. from _each end_, at 2 x full value; multiply by ⅓ d.
     Note: Simpson's works only with an _even number of intervals_.

   c. "_Durand's Rule_". Add the parallels, taking the first & last at 5/12 value; the second from each end at 13/12 value; & all others at full value; multiply by d.

a. is sufficiently accurate for estimating & other ordinary purposes.
b. is very accurate for areas bounded by smooth curves, but note limitations.
c. is most accurate for very irregular shapes.

   Note: A _Planimeter_ is a simple instrument with which irregular areas can be directly read off.

AREAS OF IRREGULAR PLANE FIGURES

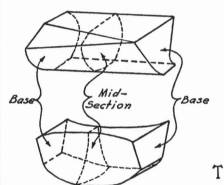

This formula is quite accurate for any solid with two bases, connected by a surface of straight line elements (upper figure), or smooth simple curves (lower figure). Construct a section midway between the bases; then

VOLUME = Areas of two bases + 4 x area of mid-section; multiply the sum by ⅙ perp. distance between bases.

THE PRISMATOID FORMULA for IRREGULAR SOLIDS

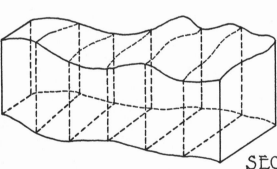

This method in general use for estimating quantities of earth work, etc.
1. Construct a series of _equally spaced_ sections ("profiles").
2. Determine the area of each section by methods given above (preferably with a planimeter).
3. Apply either of the three summation "rules" given above, to determine total volume.

SECTIONING METHOD for VERY IRREGULAR VOLUMES

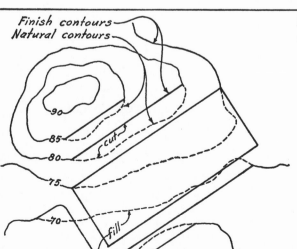

This method more rapid than the sectioning method, and is sufficiently accurate for estimating purposes, and for balancing cut and fill.
1. Draw "natural" and "finish" contours on same contour map.
2. Measure the differential areas between new and old contours, at each contour; enter in parallel columns according to whether cut or fill.
3. Where a cut or fill ends right on a contour level, use ½ value.

EXAMPLE

Contour	Cut	Fill
85—	——— 300	
80—	——— 960	
75—	2,460÷2=1,230	3,800÷2=1,900
70—	——— 20	———2,200
Totals—	———9,200	———6,800
	x5=46,000 cu.ft.	34,000 cu.ft.

4. Add up each column & multiply by the contour interval, to get volume in cu.ft.

The closer the contour interval, the greater the accuracy.

TO OBTAIN VOLUME of CUT & FILL DIRECT from CONTOUR PLAN

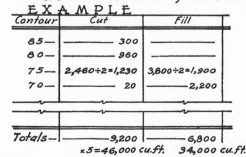

Compiled by Prof. Andre Halasz A.I.A.

TRIANGLES, ARCS & CHORDS

OBLIQUE TRIANGLES

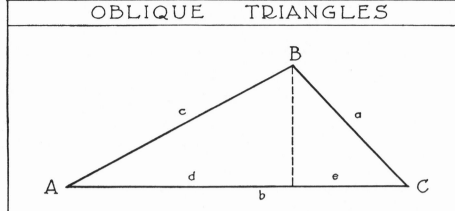

FIND	GIVEN	SOLUTION
a	ABb	$b \sin A \div \sin B$
	ABc	$c \sin A \div \sin(A+B)$
	ACb	$b \sin A \div \sin(A+C)$
	ACc	$c \sin A \div \sin C$
	BCb	$b \sin(B+C) \div \sin B$
	BCc	$c \sin(B+C) \div \sin C$
	Abc	$\sqrt{b^2 + c^2 - 2bc \cdot \cos A}$
b	ABa	$a \sin B \div \sin A$
	ABc	$c \sin B \div \sin(A+B)$
	ACa	$a \sin(A+C) \div \sin A$
	ACc	$c \sin(A+C) \div \sin C$
	BCa	$a \sin B \div \sin(B+C)$
	BCc	$c \sin B \div \sin C$
	Bac	$\sqrt{a^2 + c^2 - 2ac \cdot \cos B}$
c	ABa	$a \sin(A+B) \div \sin A$
	ABb	$b \sin(A+B) \div \sin B$
	ACa	$a \sin C \div \sin A$
	ACb	$b \sin C \div \sin(A+C)$
	BCa	$a \sin C \div \sin(B+C)$
	BCb	$b \sin C \div \sin B$
	Cab	$\sqrt{a^2 + b^2 - 2ab \cdot \cos C}$
$\frac{1}{2}(B+C)$	Abc	$90° - \frac{1}{2}A$
$\frac{1}{2}(B-C)$		$\tan = [(b-c)\tan(90° - \frac{1}{2}A)] \div (b+c)$
$\frac{1}{2}(A+C)$	Bac	$90° - \frac{1}{2}B$
$\frac{1}{2}(A-C)$		$\tan = [(a-c)\tan(90° - \frac{1}{2}B)] \div (a+c)$
$\frac{1}{2}(A+B)$	Cab	$90° - \frac{1}{2}C$
$\frac{1}{2}(A-B)$		$\tan = [(a-b)\tan(90° - \frac{1}{2}C)] \div (a+b)$

FIND	GIVEN	SOLUTION
A	abcs	$\sin \frac{1}{2}A = \sqrt{(s-b)(s-c) \div bc}$
		$\cos \frac{1}{2}A = \sqrt{s(s-a) \div bc}$
		$\tan \frac{1}{2}A = \sqrt{(s-b)(s-c) \div s(s-a)}$
	Bab	$\sin A = a \sin B \div b$
	Bac	$\frac{1}{2}(A+C) + \frac{1}{2}(A-C)$
	Cab	$\frac{1}{2}(A+B) + \frac{1}{2}(A-B)$
	Cac	$\sin A = a \sin C \div c$
B	abcs	$\sin \frac{1}{2}B = \sqrt{(s-a)(s-c) \div s(s-a)}$
		$\cos \frac{1}{2}B = \sqrt{s(s-b) \div ac}$
		$\tan \frac{1}{2}B = \sqrt{(s-a)(s-c) \div s(s-b)}$
	Aab	$\sin B = b \sin A \div a$
	Abc	$\frac{1}{2}(B+C) + \frac{1}{2}(B-C)$
	Cab	$\frac{1}{2}(A+B) - \frac{1}{2}(A-B)$
	Cac	$\sin B = b \sin C \div c$
C	abcs	$\sin \frac{1}{2}C = \sqrt{(s-a)(s-b) \div ab}$
		$\cos \frac{1}{2}C = \sqrt{s(s-c) \div ab}$
		$\tan \frac{1}{2}C = \sqrt{(s-a)(s-b) \div s(s-c)}$
	Aac	$\sin C = c \sin A \div a$
	Abc	$\frac{1}{2}(B+C) - \frac{1}{2}(B-C)$
	Bac	$\frac{1}{2}(A+C) - \frac{1}{2}(A-C)$
	Bbc	$\sin C = c \sin B \div b$
Area	abc	$\sqrt{s(s-a)(s-b)(s-c)}$
	Cab	$\frac{1}{2}ab \sin C$
s	abc	$a + b + c \div 2$
d	abcs	$(b^2 + c^2 - a^2) \div 2b$
e	abcs	$(a^2 + b^2 - c^2) \div 2b$

RIGHT TRIANGLES

FIND	GIVEN	SOLUTION
A	ab	$\tan A = a \div b$
	ac	$\sin A = a \div c$
	bc	$\cos A = b \div c$
B	ab	$\tan B = b \div a$
	ac	$\cos B = a \div c$
	bc	$\sin B = b \div c$
a	Ab	$b \tan A$
	Ac	$c \sin A$
b	Aa	$a \div \tan A$
	Ac	$c \cos A$
c	Aa	$a \div \sin A$
	Ab	$b \div \cos A$
Area	ab	$ab \div 2$

ARC

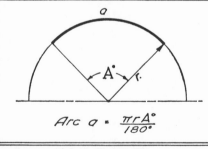

$$\text{Arc } a = \frac{\pi r A°}{180°}$$

CHORD

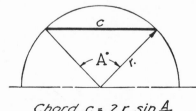

$$\text{Chord } c = 2r \sin \frac{A}{2}$$

Formulae checked by Ralph Eberlin C.E.

ELLIPSES

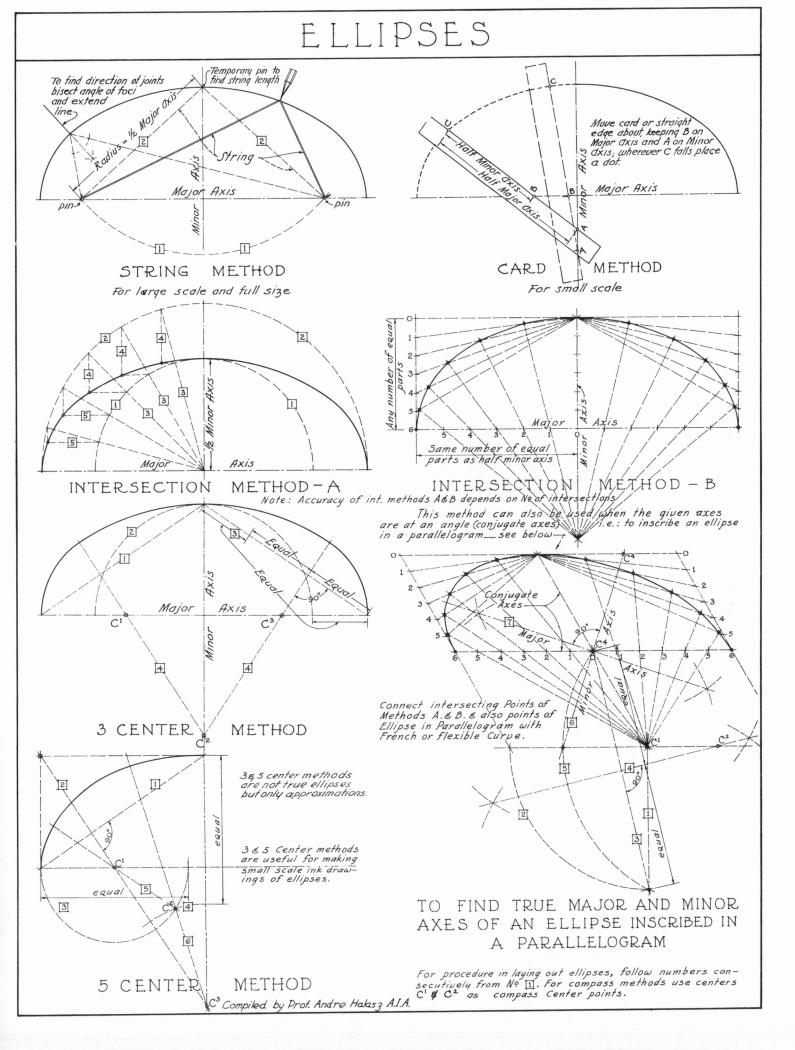

STRING METHOD

For large scale and full size

To find direction of joints bisect angle of foci and extend line

Temporary pin to find string length

Radius = ½ Major Axis

String

Major Axis

Minor Axis

pin   pin

CARD METHOD

For small scale

Move card or straight edge about, keeping B on Major axis and A on Minor axis; wherever C falls place a dot.

Half Minor axis

Half Major axis

Major Axis

Minor Axis

INTERSECTION METHOD - A

½ Minor Axis

Major   Axis

INTERSECTION METHOD - B

Any number of equal parts

Major Axis

Minor Axis

Same number of equal parts as half minor axis

Note: Accuracy of int. methods A & B depends on Nº of intersections.

This method can also be used when the given axes are at an angle (conjugate axes) i.e.: to inscribe an ellipse in a parallelogram — see below —

3 CENTER METHOD

Equal   Equal   Equal

90°

Major   Axis

Minor   Axis

C¹   C³

C²

Conjugate Axes

Major   Axis

Minor   Axis

90°

C⁴

C⁴

C¹

C²

Connect intersecting Points of Methods A & B. & also points of Ellipse in Parallelogram with French or flexible Curve.

3 & 5 center methods are not true ellipses but only approximations.

3 & 5 Center methods are useful for making small scale ink drawings of ellipses.

5 CENTER METHOD

90°

equal

equal

C¹

C²

C³

TO FIND TRUE MAJOR AND MINOR AXES OF AN ELLIPSE INSCRIBED IN A PARALLELOGRAM

For procedure in laying out ellipses, follow numbers consecutively from Nº 1. For compass methods use centers C¹ & C² as compass Center points.

Compiled by Prof. Andre Halasz A.I.A.

PARABOLA & ENTASIS

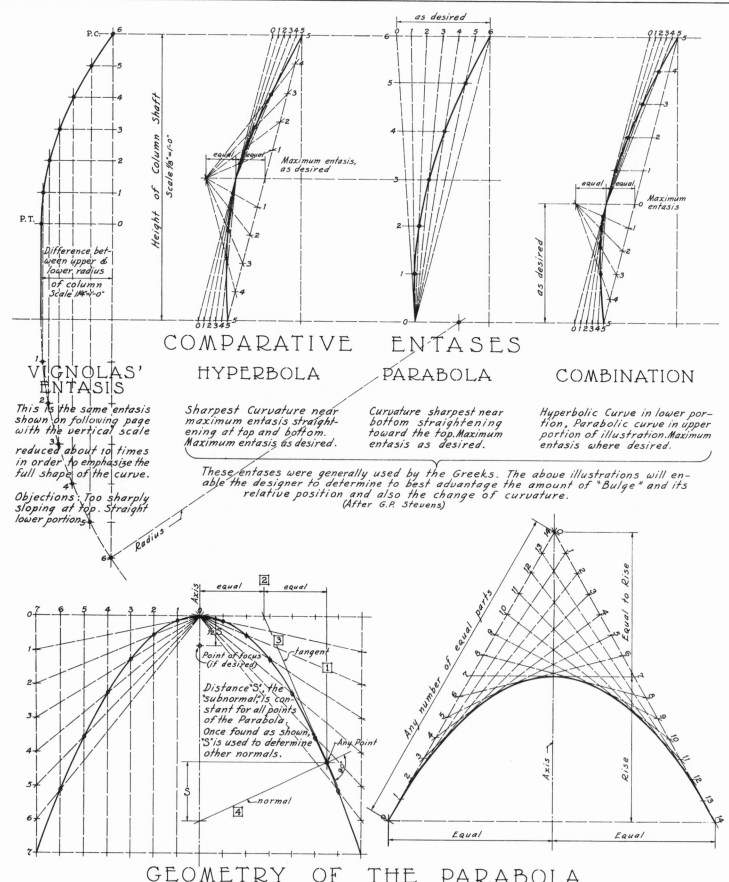

COMPARATIVE ENTASES

VIGNOLAS' ENTASIS

This is the same entasis shown on following page with the vertical scale reduced about 10 times in order to emphasize the full shape of the curve.

Objections: Too sharply sloping at top. Straight lower portions.

HYPERBOLA

Sharpest Curvature near maximum entasis straightening at top and bottom. Maximum entasis as desired.

PARABOLA

Curvature sharpest near bottom straightening toward the top. Maximum entasis as desired.

COMBINATION

Hyperbolic Curve in lower portion, Parabolic curve in upper portion of illustration. Maximum entasis where desired.

These entases were generally used by the Greeks. The above illustrations will enable the designer to determine to best advantage the amount of "Bulge" and its relative position and also the change of curvature.
(After G.P. Stevens)

Difference between upper & lower radius of column Scale 1¼"=1'-0"

Height of Column Shaft Scale 1/8"=1'-0"

Maximum entasis, as desired

GEOMETRY OF THE PARABOLA

INTERSECTION METHOD ~ TANGENT & NORMAL

This is comparable to the intersection method for the ellipse shown on previous page, & is equally good for inscribing a parabola in a parallelogram.

Point of focus (if desired)

Distance "S", the "subnormal", is constant for all points of the Parabola. Once found as shown, "S" is used to determine other normals.

tangent

Any Point

normal

ENVELOPE METHOD

This method does not give points on the curve, but a series of tangents which outline the parabola directly.

Any number of equal parts

Equal to Rise

Axis

Rise

Equal   Equal

Compiled by Prof. Andre Halasz A.I.A.

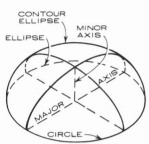

OBLATE SPHEROID

An ellipse rotated about its minor axis.

NOTES:

1. The dome shapes shown above are SURFACES OF POSITIVE CUR—VATURE, that is, the centers of both principal radii of curvature are on the same side of the surface.

2. SURFACES OF NEGATIVE CURVATURE (saddle shapes) such as those shown below, are surfaces in which the centers of the two principal radii of curvature are on opposite sides of the surface.

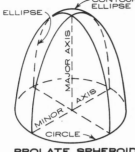

PROLATE SPHEROID

An ellipse rotated about its major axis.

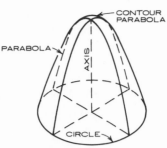

PARABOLOID OF REVOLUTION

A parabola rotated about its axis.

The elliptic paraboloid is similar, but its plan is an ellipse instead of circle, and vertical sections are varying parabolas.

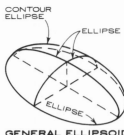

GENERAL ELLIPSOID

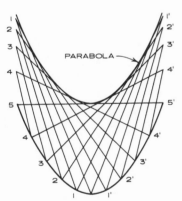

HYPERBOLIC PARABOLOID

(STRAIGHT LINE BOUNDARIES)
This shape and the hyperboloid of one sheet are the only two doubly ruled curved surfaces.

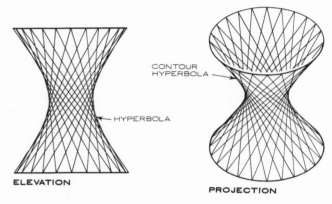

ELEVATION

PROJECTION

CONTOUR HYPERBOLA

HYPERBOLA

CIRCLE

NOTE:

This shape is a doubly ruled surface, which can also be drawn with ellipses as plan sections instead of the circles shown.

PLAN
HYPERBOLOID OF REVOLUTION
(OR HYPERBOLOID OR ONE SHEET)

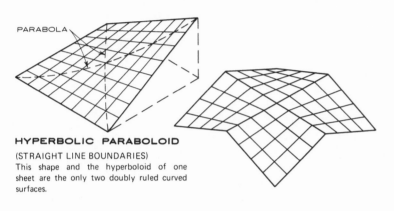

SECTION A-A

SECTION B-B

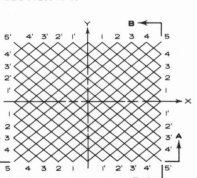

PLAN
HYPERBOLIC PARABOLOID
(PARABOLA BOUNDATIONS)

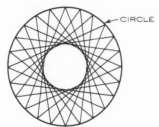

PROJECTION

HYPERBOLA
PARABOLA
PARABOLA
HYPERBOLA

SECTION

ELEVATION

RULINGS IN PARALLEL PLANES

PLAN
CONOID
(SINGLY RULED SURFACE)

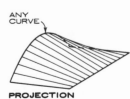

ANY CURVE

PROJECTION

AREA & CUBE NOMOGRAPH

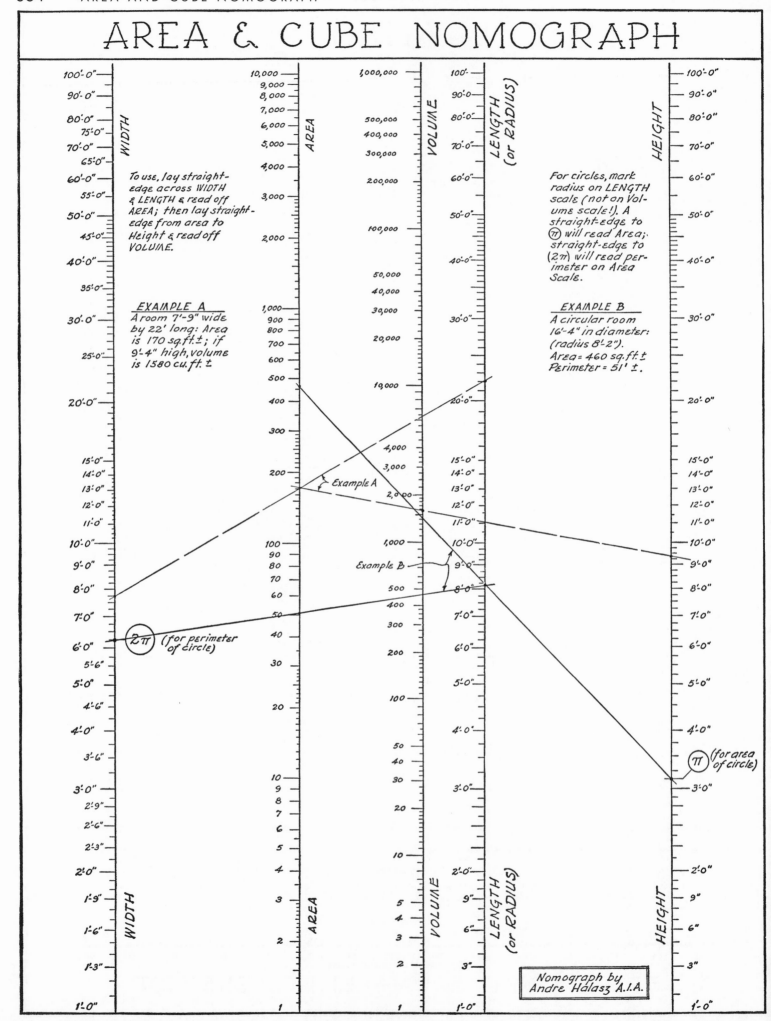

WIDTH

AREA

VOLUME

LENGTH (or RADIUS)

HEIGHT

To use, lay straight-edge across WIDTH & LENGTH & read off AREA; then lay straight-edge from area to Height & read off VOLUME.

EXAMPLE A
A room 7'-9" wide by 22' long: Area is 170 sq.ft.±; if 9'-4" high, volume is 1580 cu.ft. ±

For circles, mark radius on LENGTH scale (not on Volume scale!). A straight-edge to (π) will read Area; straight-edge to (2π) will read perimeter on Area Scale.

EXAMPLE B
A circular room 16'-4" in diameter: (radius 8'-2").
Area = 460 sq.ft.±
Perimeter = 51' ±

Example A

Example B

2π (for perimeter of circle)

π (for area of circle)

Nomograph by Andre Halasz A.I.A.

MISCELLANEOUS DATA

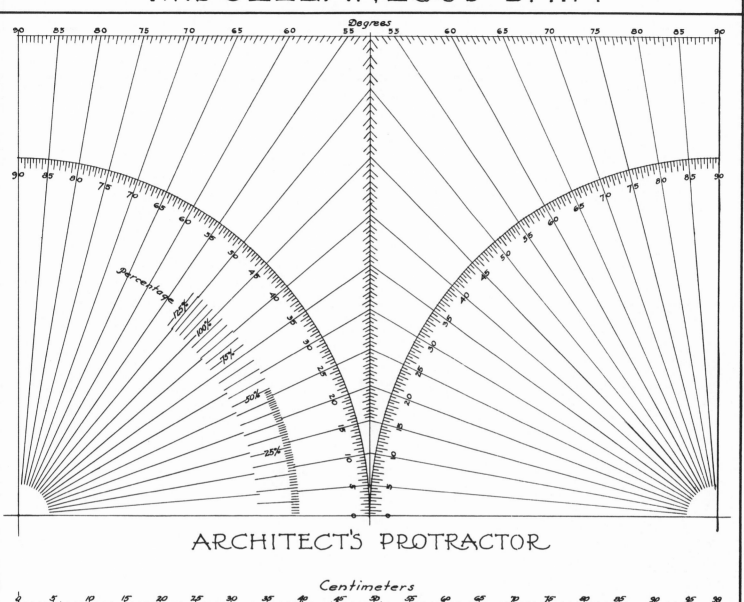

ARCHITECT'S PROTRACTOR

Centimeters

Inches

Conversion Formula
1 c. = 0.3937 inches

Conversion Formula
1 Inch = 2.540 c.

CENTIMETERS to INCHES

Meters

Feet

Conversion Formula
1 m. = 3.281 ft.

Conversion Formula
1 ft. = 0.3048 m.

METERS to FEET

Inches

Hundredths of one Foot

DECIMAL EQUIVALENTS of ONE FOOT

Inches

Fractions of one Foot

FRACTIONAL EQUIVALENTS of ONE FOOT

MISCELLANEOUS DATA

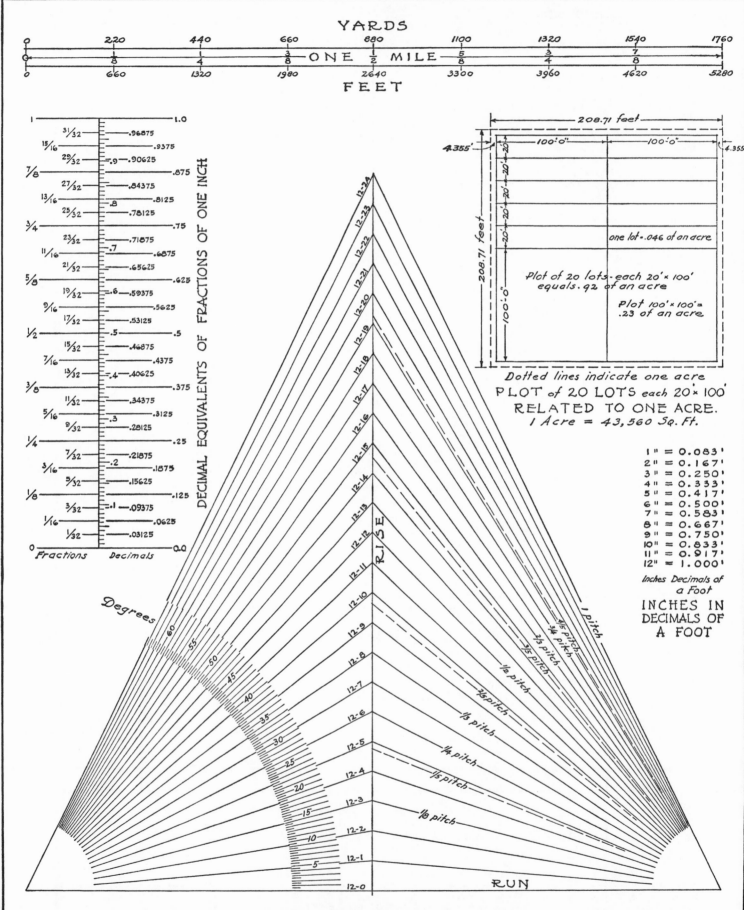

YARDS

| 0 | 220 | 440 | 660 | 880 | 1100 | 1320 | 1540 | 1760 |

ONE ½ MILE

| 0 | 1/8 | 1/4 | 3/8 | 1/2 | 5/8 | 3/4 | 7/8 |

| 0 | 660 | 1320 | 1980 | 2640 | 3300 | 3960 | 4620 | 5280 |

FEET

DECIMAL EQUIVALENTS OF FRACTIONS OF ONE INCH

Fractions		Decimals	
1		1.0	1.0
	31/32		.96875
15/16		.9375	.9375
	29/32	=.9	.90625
7/8			.875
	27/32		.84375
13/16		.8	.8125
	25/32		.78125
3/4			.75
	23/32		.71875
11/16		.7	.6875
	21/32		.65625
5/8			.625
	19/32	=.6	.59375
9/16			.5625
	17/32		.53125
1/2		.5	.5
	15/32		.46875
7/16			.4375
	13/32	=.4	.40625
3/8			.375
	11/32		.34375
5/16		.3	.3125
	9/32		.28125
1/4			.25
	7/32		.21875
3/16		.2	.1875
	5/32		.15625
1/8			.125
	3/32	=.1	.09375
1/16			.0625
	1/32		.03125
0		0.0	0.0

Fractions   Decimals

Degrees: 60, 55, 50, 45, 40, 35, 30, 25, 20, 15, 10, 5

RISE: 12-24, 12-23, 12-22, 12-21, 12-20, 12-19, 12-18, 12-17, 12-16, 12-15, 12-14, 12-13, 12-12, 12-11, 12-10, 12-9, 12-8, 12-7, 12-6, 12-5, 12-4, 12-3, 12-2, 12-1, 12-0

RUN

Pitches: 1 pitch, 4/5 pitch, 3/4 pitch, 2/3 pitch, 1/2 pitch, 2/5 pitch, 1/3 pitch, 1/4 pitch, 1/5 pitch, 1/6 pitch

208.71 feet

4.355'   100'-0"   100'-0"   4.355'

one lot=.046 of an acre

Plot of 20 lots-each 20'× 100' equals .92 of an acre

Plot 100'×100'= .23 of an acre

208.71 feet   100'-0"   100'-0"

Dotted lines indicate one acre

PLOT of 20 LOTS each 20'× 100'
RELATED TO ONE ACRE.
1 Acre = 43,560 Sq. Ft.

1"	=	0.083'
2"	=	0.167'
3"	=	0.250'
4"	=	0.333'
5"	=	0.417'
6"	=	0.500'
7"	=	0.583'
8"	=	0.667'
9"	=	0.750'
10"	=	0.833'
11"	=	0.917'
12"	=	1.000'

Inches Decimals of a Foot

INCHES IN DECIMALS OF A FOOT

ROOF SLOPES in RUN & RISE, PITCHES and DEGREES

DECIMAL EQUIVALENTS

DECIMALS OF A FOOT						DECIMALS OF AN INCH	
FRACTION	DECIMAL	FRACTION	DECIMAL	FRACTION	DECIMAL	FRACTION	DECIMAL
1/16	0.0052	4-1/16	0.3385	8-1/16	0.6719	1/64	0.015625
1/8	0.0104	4-1/8	0.3438	8-1/8	0.6771	1/32	0.03125
3/16	0.0156	4-3/16	0.3490	8-3/16	0.6823	3/64	0.046875
1/4	0.0208	4-1/4	0.3542	8-1/4	0.6875	1/16	0.0625
5/16	0.0260	4-5/16	0.3594	8-5/16	0.6927	5/64	0.078125
3/8	0.0313	4-3/8	0.3646	8-3/8	0.6979	3/32	0.09375
7/16	0.0365	4-7/16	0.3698	8-7/16	0.7031	7/64	0.109375
1/2	0.0417	4-1/2	0.3750	8-1/2	0.7083	1/8	0.125
9/16	0.0469	4-9/16	0.3802	8-9/16	0.7135	9/64	0.140625
5/8	0.0521	4-5/8	0.3854	8-5/8	0.7188	5/32	0.15625
11/16	0.0573	4-11/16	0.3906	8-11/16	0.7240	11/64	0.171875
3/4	0.0625	4-3/4	0.3958	8-3/4	0.7292	3/16	0.1875
13/16	0.0677	4-13/16	0.4010	8-13/16	0.7344	13/64	0.203125
7/8	0.0729	4-7/8	0.4063	8-7/8	0.7396	13/32	0.21875
15/16	0.0781	4-15/16	0.4115	8-15/16	0.7448	15/64	0.234375
1-	0.0833	5-	0.4167	9-	0.7500	1/4	0.250
1-1/16	0.0885	5-1/16	0.4219	9-1/16	0.7552	17/64	0.265625
1-1/8	0.0938	5-1/8	0.4271	9-1/8	0.7604	9/32	0.28125
1-3/16	0.0990	5-3/16	0.4323	9-3/16	0.7656	19/64	0.296875
1-1/4	0.1042	5-1/4	0.4375	9-1/4	0.7708	5/16	0.3125
1-5/16	0.1094	5-5/16	0.4427	9-5/16	0.7760	21/64	0.328125
1-3/8	0.1146	5-3/8	0.4479	9-3/8	0.7813	11/32	0.34375
1-7/16	0.1198	5-7/16	0.4531	9-7/16	0.7865	23/64	0.359375
1-1/2	0.1250	5-1/2	0.4583	9-1/2	0.7917	3/8	0.375
1-9/16	0.1302	5-9/16	0.4635	9-9/16	0.7969	25/64	0.390625
1-5/8	0.1354	5-5/8	0.4688	9-5/8	0.8021	13/32	0.40625
1-11/16	0.1406	5-11/16	0.4740	9-11/16	0.8073	27/64	0.421875
1-3/4	0.1458	5-3/4	0.4792	9-3/4	0.8125	7/16	0.4375
1-13/16	0.1510	5-13/16	0.4844	9-13/16	0.8177	29/64	0.453125
1-7/8	0.1563	5-7/8	0.4896	9-7/8	0.8229	15/32	0.46875
1-15/16	0.1615	5-15/16	0.4948	9-15/16	0.8281	31/64	0.484375
2-	0.1667	6-	0.5000	10-	0.8333	1/2	0.500
2-1/16	0.1719	6-1/16	0.5052	10-1/16	0.8385	33/64	0.515625
2-1/8	0.1771	6-1/8	0.5104	10-1/8	0.8438	17/32	0.53125
2-3/16	0.1823	6-3/16	0.5156	10-3/16	0.8490	35/64	0.546875
2-1/4	0.1875	6-1/4	0.5208	10-1/4	0.8542	9/16	0.5625
2-5/16	0.1927	6-5/16	0.5260	10-5/16	0.8594	37/64	0.578125
2-3/8	0.1979	6-3/8	0.5313	10-3/8	0.8646	19/32	0.59375
2-7/16	0.2031	6-7/16	0.5365	10-7/16	0.8698	39/64	0.609375
2-1/2	0.2083	6-1/2	0.5417	10-1/2	0.8750	5/8	0.625
2-9/16	0.2135	6-9/16	0.5469	10-9/16	0.8802	41/64	0.640625
2-5/8	0.2188	6-5/8	0.5521	10-5/8	0.8854	21/32	0.65625
2-11/16	0.2240	6-11/16	0.5573	10-11/16	0.8906	43/64	0.671875
2-3/4	0.2292	6-3/4	0.5625	10-3/4	0.8958	11/16	0.6875
2-13/16	0.2344	6-13/16	0.5677	10-13/16	0.9010	45/64	0.703125
2-7/8	0.2396	6-7/8	0.5729	10-7/8	0.9063	23/32	0.71875
2-15/16	0.2448	6-15/16	0.5781	10-15/16	0.9115	47/64	0.734375
3-	0.2500	7-	0.5833	11-	0.9167	3/4	0.750
3-1/16	0.2552	7-1/16	0.5885	11-1/16	0.9219	49/64	0.765625
3-1/8	0.2604	7-1/8	0.5938	11-1/8	0.9271	25/32	0.78125
3-3/16	0.2656	7-3/16	0.5990	11-3/16	0.9323	51/64	0.796875
3-1/4	0.2708	7-1/4	0.6042	11-1/4	0.9375	13/16	0.8125
3-5/16	0.2760	7-5/16	0.6094	11-5/16	0.9427	53/64	0.828125
3-3/8	0.2813	7-3/8	0.6146	11-3/8	0.9479	27/32	0.84375
3-7/16	0.2865	7-7/16	0.6198	11-7/16	0.9531	55/64	0.859375
3-1/2	0.2917	7-1/2	0.6250	11-1/2	0.9583	7/8	0.875
3-9/16	0.2969	7-9/16	0.6302	11-9/16	0.9635	57/64	0.890625
3-5/8	0.3021	7-5/8	0.6354	11-5/8	0.9688	29/32	0.90625
3-11/16	0.3073	7-11/16	0.6406	11-11/16	0.9740	59/64	0.921875
3-3/4	0.3125	7-3/4	0.6458	11-3/4	0.9792	15/16	0.9375
3-13/16	0.3177	7-13/16	0.6510	11-13/16	0.9844	61/64	0.953125
3-7/8	0.3229	7-7/8	0.6563	11-7/8	0.9896	31/32	0.96875
3-15/16	0.3281	7-15/16	0.6615	11-15/16	0.9948	63/64	0.984375
4-	0.3333	8-	0.6667	12-	1.0000	1"	1.000

Reprinted from "Wood Structural Design Data", Vol.1, courtesy of the National Lumber Manufacturers Assoc.

WEIGHTS & MEASURES

VOLUME

MEASURES

VOLUME
1 cord of wood   = 128 cu. ft.
1 perch of masonry = 16½ " ".
(In most localities). Standard is 24¾ cubic feet.

LIQUID
4 gills = 1 pint = 16 fluid oz.
2 pints = 1 quart = 32 " ".
4 quarts = 1 gallon = 128 fl. oz.

APOTHECARY
1 fluid oz. = 8 drams = 480 minims = 2 tablespoons = 6 teaspoons = 1.805 cu. in. = 29.58 cu. cm. = ¹⁄₁₂₈th gallon.

DRY
2 pints = 1 quart = 67.2 cu. in.
4 quarts = 8 pints = 268.8 " ".
1 peck = 16 pints = 537.6 " ".
4 pecks = 1 bushel = 2150.42 " ".
1 standard barrel (for fruit

DRY (continued)
& veg.) = 7056 cu. in. = 105 dry quarts. "Struck barrel" is 20" dia, 28½" high.

BOARD
1 board foot = 144 sq. in. = a volume of board 1 ft. sq. & 1" thick. No. of board feet in a log = ¼(d"-4)²L, where d = smaller dia. of log; L = length of log in feet; 4 = deduction allowance for slab.

MISCELLANEOUS
1 ton round timber = 40 cu. ft.
1 ton hewn timber = 50 " ".
All dressed stock is measured as "Strip Count." i.e., the full size of rough material in manufacture.

WEIGHT

MEASURES

NOTE: Unit of grain is same in all.

AVOIRDUPOIS
16 drams = 437.5 grains = 1 ounce
16 ounces = 7000 grains = 1 pound
100 lbs. = 1 hundredweight = 1 cental
2000 lbs. = 20 = 1 short ton
28 lbs. = 2 stones = 1 quarter
4 quarters (long unit) = 112 lbs.
2240 lbs. = 20 hundredwt. = 1 long ton
1 standard lime bbl. small = 180 # net.
1 " " " large = 280 # ".
1 standard bag lime = 80 # net.
1 " " cement = 94 # ".

TROY
24 grains = 1 pennyweight (dwt.)
20 dwts. = 480 grains = 1 ounce
1 assay ton = 29,167 milligrams
1 carat (for weighing diamonds) = 3.086 grains = 200 grams.

APOTHECARY
20 grains = 1 scruple ℈
3 scruples = 60 grains = 1 dram ℨ
8 drams (drachms) = 1 ounce ℥

METRIC
10 milligrams = 1 centigram
10 centigrams = 1 decigram
10 decigrams = 1 gram
10 grams = 1 decagram
10 decagrams = 1 hectogram
10 hectograms = 1 kilogram

IRON & LEAD
14 pounds = 1 stone
21½ stones = 1 pig
8 pigs = 1 fother

EQUIVALENTS

Cubic inches	Cubic feet	Cubic yards	U.S. Apothecary ounces	U.S. Quarts Liquid	U.S. Quarts Dry	U.S. Gallons Liquid	U.S. Gallons Dry	U.S. Bushels	Liters
1	0.0₂5787	0.0₄2143	0.5541	0.01732	0.01488	0.0₂4329	0.0₂3720	0.0₃4650	0.01639
1728	1	0.03704	957.5	29.92	25.71	7.4805	6.429	0.8036	28.32
46656	27	1	25853	807.9	694.3	202.0	173.6	21.70	764.6
1.805	0.001044	0.0₄3868	1	0.03125	0.02686	0.007813	0.006714	0.0₃8392	0.02957
57.75	0.03342	0.001238	32	1	0.8594	0.25	0.2148	0.02686	0.9464
67.20	0.03889	0.001440	37.24	1.164	1	0.2909	0.25	0.03125	1.101
231	0.1337	0.004951	128	4	3.437	1	0.8594	0.1074	3.785
268.8	0.1556	0.005761	148.9	4.655	4	1.164	1	0.125	4.405
2150	1.244	0.04609	1192	37.24	32	9.309	8	1	35.25
61.02	0.03531	0.001308	33.81	1.057	0.9081	0.2642	0.2270	0.02838	1

EQUIVALENTS

Kilograms	Grains	Ounces Troy & Apoth'y	Ounces Avoirdupois	Pounds Troy & Apoth'y	Pounds Avoirdupois	Tons Short	Tons Long	Tons Metric
1	15,432	32.15	35.27	2.6792	2.205	0.0₂1102	0.0₂9842	0.001
0.0₂6480	1	0.0₂2083	0.0₂2286	0.0₃1736	0.0₃1429	0.0₇7143	0.0₆6378	0.0₆6480
0.03110	480	1	1.09714	0.08333	0.06857	0.0₄3429	0.0₄3061	0.0₄3110
0.02835	437.5	0.9115	1	0.07595	0.0625	0.0₄3125	0.0₄2790	0.0₄2835
0.3732	5,760	12	13.17	1	0.8229	0.0₃4114	0.0₃3673	0.0₃3732
0.4536	7,000	14.58	16	1.215	1	0.0005	0.0₃4464	0.0₃4536
907.2	14.0₆	29,167	320₃	2,431	2,000	1	0.8929	0.9072
1,016	15680₄	32,667	35,840	2,722	2,240	1.12	1	1.016
1,000	15,432,356	32,151	35,274	2,679	2,205	1.102	0.9842	1

LINEAR

MEASURES

LENGTH
4 inches = 1 hand
9 inches = 1 span
12 inches = 1 foot
3 feet = 1 yard
5½ yds = 16½ feet = 1 rod = 1 pole = 1 perch.
40 poles = 220 yds. = 1 furlong
8 furlongs = 1,760 yds = 5,280 feet = 1 mile.
3 miles (U.S. Naut.) = 1 league

NAUTICAL
6,080.27 feet = 1 nautical mile
1.15156 statute mi. = " "
1 nautical mi. per hr. = 1 knot
6 feet = 1 fathom
120 fathoms = 1 cable length

SURVEYOR OR GUNTHER
7.92 inches = 1 link
100 links = 66 ft. = 4 rods = 1 chain
80 chains = 1 mile
1 vara (Texas) = 33⅓ in. = 2¾ ft.

EQUIVALENTS

Centimeters	Inches	Feet	Yards	Meters	Chains	Kilometers	Miles
1	0.3937	0.03281	0.01094	0.01	0.0₃4971	0.0₄1	0.0₅6214
2.540	1	0.0833	0.02778	0.0254	0.001263	0.0₄254	0.0₄1578
30.48	12	1	0.3333	0.3048	0.01515	0.0₃3048	0.0₃1894
91.44	36	3	1	0.9144	0.04545	0.0₃9144	0.0₃5682
100	39.37	3.281	1.0936	1	0.04971	0.001	0.0₃6214
2012	792	66	22	20.12	1	0.02012	0.0125
100,000	39,370	3,281	1,093.6	1,000	49.71	1	0.6214
160,935	63,360	5,280	1,760	1,609	80	1.609	1

Subscripts after any figure, 0₂, 0₃ etc, mean that that figure is to be repeated the indicated number of times, i.e, 0.0₃27 = 0.00027

LUMBER ~ SIZES & WEIGHTS

Nominal Size inches	Dressed Size inches	Area of Section sq. in.	Weight per ft. lbs.	Wt. of Beams or Studs 16" o.c. (lbs./sq.')	Nominal Size inches	Dressed Size inches	Area of Section sq. in.	Weight per ft. lbs.
2 x 4	1⅝x3⅝	5.89	1.64	1.23	4 x 8	3⅝x7½	27.2	7.55
2 x 6	1⅝x5⅝	9.14	2.54	1.91	4 x 10	3⅝x9½	34.4	9.57
2 x 8	1⅝x7½	12.2	3.39	2.54	4 x 12	3⅝x11½	41.7	11.6
2 x 10	1⅝x9½	15.4	4.29	3.22	4 x 14	3⅝x13½	48.9	13.6
2 x 12	1⅝x11½	18.7	5.19	3.89	6 x 6	5½x5½	30.3	8.4
3 x 4	2⅝x3⅝	9.52	2.64	1.98	6 x 8	5½x7½	41.3	11.4
3 x 6	2⅝x5⅝	14.8	4.10	3.08	6 x 10	5½x9½	52.3	14.5
3 x 8	2⅝x7½	19.7	5.47	4.10	6 x 12	5½x11½	63.3	17.5
3 x 10	2⅝x9½	24.9	6.93	5.31	8 x 8	7½x7½	56.3	15.6
3 x 12	2⅝x11½	30.2	8.39	6.29	8 x 10	7½x9½	71.3	19.8
4 x 4	3⅝x3⅝	13.1	3.65	2.74	8 x 12	7½x11½	86.3	23.9
4 x 6	3⅝x5⅝	20.4	5.66	4.25	8 x 14	7½x13½	101.3	28.0

Weights based on 40 lbs. per cu. foot.

HYDROSTATICS for PLUMBING

1 cu. ft. water weighs 62.5 lbs.   1 cu. in. water = .003617 gals.
1 cu. in. " " .03617 lbs.   Gallons x 0.16 = cubic ft.
1 gallon " " 8.338 lbs.

To find water pressure: Head (ft.) x 0.434 = Pressure (#/□")
Example: 125' x 0.434 = 54.25 #/□"

To find water head: $\frac{Pressure (\#/\square")}{0.434}$ = Head (feet)

Example: $\frac{54.25 \#/\square"}{0.434}$ = 125' $\frac{}{0.434}$

WEIGHTS of MATERIALS

WEIGHTS OF MATERIAL

WEIGHTS GIVEN ARE AVERAGE

SOILS, MASONRY & CONCRETE MATERIALS
LBS. per CU. FT.

Cement, dry --------------------- 90
Cinders or ashes ------------- 40-45
Clay, damp & plastic ---------- 110
Clay, dry --------------------- 63
Clay & gravel, dry ------------ 100
Earth, dry & loose ------------- 76
Earth, dry & packed ------------ 95
Earth, moist & loose ---------- 78
Earth, moist & packed --------- 96
Earth, mud, packed ------------ 115
Granite, without mortar ---- 158-168
Limestone, marble, without
    mortar --------------------- 165
Sand or gravel, dry & loose -90-105
Sand or gravel, dry & packed
    100-120
Sand or gravel, dry & wet -- 118-120
Sandstone, bluestone, with
    mortar --------------------- 147
Slate ------------------------- 175

METALS
Aluminum, cast ---------------- 165
Brass, red -------------------- 546
Brass, yellow, extruded bronze- 528
Bronze, commercial ------------ 552
Bronze, statuary -------------- 509
Copper, cast or rolled -------- 556
Iron, cast gray --------------- 450
Iron, wrought ----------------- 485
Lead -------------------------- 710
Monel metal ---------------- 552-556
Nickel ------------------------ 555
Stainless steel, rolled ----- 492-510
Steel, rolled ----------------- 490
Zinc, rolled or cast ---------- 440

FUELS & LIQUIDS
Coal, piled, anthracite ------ 47-58
Coal, piled, bituminous ------ 40-54
Gasoline ---------------------- 75
Water, at 4° C ------------- 62.43

WOOD (12% MOISTURE CONTENT)
Birch, red oak ---------------- 44
Cedar, northern white --------- 22
Cedar, western red ------------ 23
Cypress, southern ------------- 32
Douglas fir, (coast region) ----- 34
Fir, commercial white; idaho
    white pine ----------------- 27
Hemlock --------------------- 28-29
Maple, hard (black & sugar) ----- 42
Oak, white -------------------- 47
Pine, long-leaf southern ------- 29
Pine; northern white sugar ----- 25
Pine, ponderosa; spruce; eastern
    & sitka -------------------- 28

LBS. per CU. FT.

Pine, short leaf, southern ------ 36
Poplar, yellow; redwood --------- 28
Walnut, black ----------------- 38

CONCRETE (See Floor Materials, Flooring & Roof Slabs)
Cinder, concrete fill ---------- 60
Cinder, reinforced -------- 100-115
Slag, plain ------------------- 130
Stone, plain ------------------ 144
Stone, reinforced ------------- 150

BRICK MASONRY (INCLUDING MORTAR)
Cell type --------------------- 115
Common ------------------------ 120
Pressed ----------------------- 140
Soft -------------------------- 100

STONE ASHLAR MASONRY (INCLUDING MORTAR)
Granite -------------------- 155-162
Limestone, marble ------------- 150
Sandstone, bluestone ---------- 130
    For rubble masonry deduct
    10 lbs. from the above

MORTAR & PLASTER
Cement, portland -------------- 144
Mortar, masonry --------------- 116
Plaster ----------------------- 96

EXTERIOR WALLS & WALL MATERIALS
Masonry (Incl. mortar; no plaster unless noted)
LBS. per SQ. FT.

2" Solid architectural T. C. ---- 22
4" Solid architectural T. C. ---- 37
4" brickwork ------------------ 35
8" brickwork ------------------ 74
12" brickwork ----------------- 115
4" brick veneer on wood, with
    sheathing & plaster -------- 45
4" brick with 6" concrete block
    backup ----------------- 75-88
4" brick with 8" concrete block
    backup --------------- 90-100
4" brick with 6" hollow clay
    tile backup ------------ 70-74
4" brick with 8" hollow clay
    tile backup ------------ 74-82
Cavity wall 4" brick & 4" brick- 70
(Brick assumed at 4.5 lbs. each laid
    with 1/2" joints. Weight of brick
    varies from 4 lbs. to 6 lbs. each.)
8" concrete, reinforced stone or
    gravel -------------------- 100
10" concrete, reinforced stone or
    gravel -------------------- 125
12" concrete, reinforced stone or
    gravel -------------------- 150
4" concrete block, stone or
    gravel ------------------ 27-33

LBS. per SQ. FT.

6" concrete block, stone or
    gravel ------------------ 35-48
8" concrete block, stone or
    gravel ------------------ 50-60
12" concrete block, stone or
    gravel ------------------ 74-85
2" granite with 1/2" parging- 29-30
4" granite with 1/2" parging- 58-60
4" glass block ---------------- 20
4" hollow clay tile (load bearing)
    21-24
6" hollow clay tile (load bearing)
    30-34
8" hollow clay tile (load bearing)
    34-42
12" hollow clay tile (load bearing)
    49-66
4" limestone facing, 1/2" parging
    55
4" limestone, 8" brick backing- 134
4" limestone, 8" hollow concrete
    block backing ---------- 105-115
4" limestone, 8" hollow clay tile
    backing ----------------- 89-97
4" sandstone or bluestone facing,
    1/2" parging -------------- 49
1" mortar ------------------ 10-12

Wood Frame
Normal standard dead load for wood frame house, lbs. per sq. ft. per tier. For wood joists, bridging, flooring, and underflooring, lath & plaster on walls and ceilings-17
4" wood studs, wood sheathing,
    lath & plaster ------------ 10
1" wood sheathing, 1/4" asbestos
    board -------------------- 2.5
1/2" gypsum sheathing or gypsum
    board -------------------- 2.2
1/2" wood fiber sheathing or
    insulation board --------- 0.8
Wood siding, asphalt siding ----- 2
Asbestos cement siding -------- 1.8
Plaster ----------------------- 4-5
2" wood furring, lath & plaster 7.5

Miscellaneous
#20 gauge corrugated iron siding- 2
Corrugated asbestos siding --- 3.5-4
Corrugated glass, 2 1/2"O.C. --- 6.5
Fenestra type "C" insulated panel
    aluminum ------------------ 3
Fenestra type "C" insulated panel
    steel --------------------- 6.5

Precast Bldg. Sections
    (Atterbury) 8" stone concrete- 50
    (Atterbury) 8" light weight
    concrete ------------------ 38

WEIGHTS of MATERIALS (cont'd)

FLOOR MATERIAL & FLOORING & ROOF SLABS

LBS. per CU. FT.

Concrete, Aerocrete	50-80
Concrete, cinder fill	60
Concrete, Haydite	100
Concrete, Nailcode	75
Concrete, Perlite	35-50
Concrete, Porete, light weight	25-80
Concrete, pumice	60-90
Concrete, Vermiculite	20-40
For other Concrete - See "Basic Materials"	

LBS. per SQ. FT.

Cement finish, 1" thick	12
Fenestra bldg. systems, variable for depth (1 1/2"-7 1/2") & gauges	4-11
Fill, cinder concrete, per 1" thickness	5
Flexicore, 6" precast light weight concrete	30
Flexicore, 6" precast stone concrete	40
Flooring, hardwood, 25/32"	4
Flooring or underflooring, soft wood	2.5-3
Flooring, wood block, 3"	15
Joist, floor, 2" x 8", 16" o.c. with subflooring	6
Joist, floor, 2" x 10", 16" o.c. with subflooring	6.5
Joist, floor, 2" x 12", 16" o.c. with subflooring	7
Marble & setting bed	25-30
Plywood, 1/2" subflooring	1.5
Pyrofill, per 1" thickness	5
Terrazzo, 2", 3"	24, 36
Tile, ceramic & setting bed	15-23

FLOORING MATERIAL & FLOORING & ROOF SLABS

Metal tile & joists 20" wide pans & 5" joists

4" deep plus 2 1/2" topping	45
6" " " " " "	50
8" " " " " "	56
10" " " " " "	64
12" " " " " "	69

One way clay tile - 16" wide tile & 4" joists

4" deep with no topping	27
5" " " " "	31
6" " " " "	37
7" " " " "	42
8" " " " "	46
9" " " " "	50
10" " " " "	54

Two way slag block - 16" x 16" blocks & 4" joists

4 1/2" deep with no topping	39
6" " " " "	49

7" deep with no topping	54
8" " " " "	59
9" " " " "	67
10" " " " "	74
10" " " 1" "	86

Two way clay tile & joist - 16" x 16" Blocks & 4" Joists

4" deep with no topping	31
4 1/2" deep with no topping	35
5" " " " "	39
6" " " " "	45
7" " " " "	52
8" " " " "	60
9" " " " "	68
10" " " " "	77

ROOFING & ROOFING MATERIALS

Acoustical Tile (without supports) per 1/2"	5-.8
Built up	5-6.5
Cemesto roof deck, 1 9/16"	4.8
Copper	1.5-2.5
Corrugated asbestos	3.5-4
Corrugated glass	6.3
Corrugated iron	1.27-1.75
Deck, steel roof, without finish or insulation	2.25-3.6
Galvanized iron	1.25-1.75
Gypsum tile, roof, 3"	17
Hung ceiling	8-10
Kalo insulating tile, roofing	2.6-5
Lead, 1/8"	6-8
Monel metal	1.25-1.5
Plank, cinder concrete, 2"	15
Plank, Durisol roof, 3 1/4" & 4 1/4"	14, 17
Plank, gypsum, 2"	12
Plank, Porex, 3 1/4"	14
Shingles, asbestos cement	2.5-2.8
Shingles, asphalt	1.7-2.8
Shingles, wood	2-3
Skylights, glass & frame	10-12
Slab, Porex per 1"	2.4
Slab, precast concrete, light weight channel, 3 1/2"	12-14
Slate, 3/16" to 1/4"	7-9.5
Slate, 3/8" & 1/2"	14, 18
Stainless steel	2.5
Tile, cement flat	13.5
Tile, cement ribbed	16
Tile, clay flat with setting bed	15-20
Tile, clay mission	13.5
Tile, clay shingle type	8-16

FOR CONCRETE & COMBINATION ROOF SLABS SEE FLOORING SLABS

PARTITIONS

Building board, wall board (wood fibre) 1/2" thick	8
4" Concrete partition block, light weight, plaster 2S	27-34

LBS. per SQ. FT.

6" Concrete partition block, light weight, plaster 2S	34-45
3" Gypsum block, plaster 2S	21
4" Gypsum block, plaster 2S	25
6" Gypsum block, plaster 2S	31
Gypsum board, 1/2" thick	2.1
Johns-Manville, Universal & Imperial Partitions	4, 11
Kalo partitions, 1" & 1 3/4"	2.2, 3.75
Lath & plaster, 2" x 4" wood studs	14-16
Movable, steel (office type)	4-8
Plaster	4-5
Plywood, 1/2" thick	1.5
2" Solid plaster partition	18
3" Solid plaster partition	27
2" Facing tile, structural	16-17
4" Facing tile, structural	27-30
6" Facing tile, structural	41
3" Hollow clay tile, with plaster 2S	24
4" Hollow clay tile, with plaster 2S	25
6" Hollow clay tile, with plaster 2S	32

INSULATION

Bats, blankets, per 1" thickness	.1-.4
Boards, vegetable fibre	1.5-2
Cork board	.75
Fiber glass	1.3
Foam glass	1.

MISCELLANEOUS

C.I. 4", extra heavy (per lin.ft.)	13
C.I. radiator, per sq. ft. of radiation	7
Glass: double strength & single strength	1.6, 1.2
Glass, single strength	1.2
Glass, 1/4" plate	3.27
Plastics, 1/4" acrylic	1.5

LIVE LOADS

In general. See building codes for specific requirements.

Dwellings, apts. hotels, clubs, hospitals, prisons	40
Factories & workshops, etc. variable, see Bldg. Code	
Office buildings: office space	50
corridors & public space	100
Schools: class rooms	40, 50 or 60
corridors	100
Sidewalks	250 & 300
Theater lobbies, gyms, grandstands, stages, places of assembly with no fixed seats	100
Theaters, auditoriums with fixed seats	50-100
Stairs & fire escapes, except private residences	100

REFERENCES AND ACKNOWLEDGEMENTS

STRUCTURAL CLAY TILE: "TILE ENGINEERING. HANDBOOK OF DESIGN" BY HARRY C. PLUMMER & E. F. WANNER. BRICKWORK: "BRICK ENGINEERING. HANDBOOK OF DESIGN" BY HARRY C. PLUMMER & LESLIE J. REARDON. STEEL & OTHER METAL: "MANUAL OF THE AMERICAN INSTITUTE OF STEEL CONSTRUCTION", "ARCHITECTURAL METAL HANDBOOK" - NATL. ASSOC. OF ORNAM. METAL MFGRS. SOLID PLASTER PARTITIONS: "THE PARTITION HANDBOOK" BY ERDWIN M. LURIE. METAL LATH MFGRS. ASSOC. FLOORING & ROOFING SYSTEMS & SLAB WEIGHTS: "DESIGN. DATA BOOK FOR CIVIL ENGINEERS" BY ELWYN E. SEELYE. CONCRETE BLOCK: PORTLAND CEMENT ASSOCIATION

WEIGHTS of MATERIALS

WEIGHTS OF MATERIAL

WEIGHTS GIVEN ARE AVERAGE

SOILS, MASONRY & CONCRETE MATERIALS

LBS. per CU. FT.

Cement, dry---------------------94
Cinders or ashes-------------40-45
Clay, damp & plastic-----------110
Clay, dry-----------------------63
Clay & gravel, dry-------------100
Earth, dry & loose--------------76
Earth, dry & packed-------------95
Earth, moist & loose-----------78
Earth, moist & packed----------96
Earth, mud, packed-------------115
Granite, without mortar----158-168
Limestone, marble, without
   mortar-----------------150-165
Sand or gravel, dry & loose-90-105
Sand or gravel, dry & packed
                          100-120
Sand or gravel, dry & wet--118-120
Sandstone, bluestone, with
   mortar-----------------------147
Slate--------------------------175

METALS

Aluminum, cast-----------------165
Brass, red---------------------546
Brass, yellow, extruded bronze-528
Bronze, commercial-------------552
Bronze, statuary---------------509
Copper, cast or rolled---------556
Iron, cast gray----------------450
Iron, wrought------------------485
Lead---------------------------710
Monel metal----------------552-556
Nickel---------------------555-565
Stainless steel, rolled-----492-510
Steel, rolled------------------490
Zinc, rolled or cast-----------440

FUELS & LIQUIDS

Coal, piled, anthracite------47-58
Coal, piled, bituminous------40-54
Gasoline-----------------------75
Water, at 4° C--------------62.43

WOOD (12% MOISTURE CONTENT)

Birch, red oak-----------------44
Cedar, northern white----------22
Cedar, western red-------------23
Cypress, southern--------------32
Douglas fir, (coast region)-----34
Fir, commercial white; idaho
   white pine------------------27
Hemlock----------------------28-29
Maple, hard (black & sugar)-----42
Oak, white---------------------47
Pine, long-leaf southern-------29
Pine, northern white sugar-----25
Pine, ponderosa; spruce; eastern
   & sitka---------------------28

LBS. per CU. FT.

Pine, short leaf, southern------36
Poplar, yellow; redwood----------28
Walnut, black-------------------38

CONCRETE (See Floor Materials, Flooring & Roof Slabs)

Cinder, concrete fill-----------60
Cinder, reinforced---------100-115
Slag, plain--------------------130
Stone, plain-------------------144
Stone, reinforced--------------150

BRICK MASONRY (INCLUDING MORTAR)

Cell type----------------------115
Common-------------------------120
Pressed------------------------140
Soft---------------------------100

STONE ASHLAR MASONRY (INCLUDING MORTAR)

Granite--------------------155-162
Limestone, marble--------------150
Sandstone, bluestone-----------130
   For rubble masonry deduct
   10 lbs. from the above

MORTAR & PLASTER

Cement, portland---------------144
Mortar, masonry----------------116
Plaster------------------------96

EXTERIOR WALLS & WALL MATERIALS

Masonry (Incl. mortar; no plaster unless noted)   LBS. per SQ. FT.

2" Solid architectural T. C.----16
4" Solid architectural T. C.----32
4" brickwork-------------------35
8" brickwork-------------------74
12" brickwork------------------115
4" brick veneer on wood, with
   sheathing & plaster----------45
4" brick with 6" concrete block
   backup---------------------75-88
4" brick with 8" concrete block
   backup--------------------90-100
4" brick with 6" hollow clay
   tile backup---------------70-74
4" brick with 8" hollow clay
   tile backup---------------74-82
Cavity wall 4" brick & 4" brick--70
(Brick assumed at 4.5 lbs. each laid
   with 1/2" joints. Weight of brick
   varies from 4 lbs. to 6 lbs. each.)
8" concrete, reinforced stone or
   gravel----------------------100
10" concrete, reinforced stone or
   gravel----------------------125
12" concrete, reinforced stone or
   gravel----------------------150
4" concrete block, stone or
   gravel--------------------27-33

LBS. per SQ. FT.

6" concrete block, stone or
   gravel--------------------35-48
8" concrete block, stone or
   gravel--------------------50-60
12" concrete block, stone or
   gravel--------------------74-85
2" granite with 1/2" parging-29-30
4" granite with 1/2" parging-58-60
4" glass block-----------------20
4" hollow clay tile (load bearing)
                              21-24
6" hollow clay tile (load bearing)
                              30-34
8" hollow clay tile (load bearing)
                              34-42
12" hollow clay tile (load bearing)
                              49-66
4" limestone facing, 1/2" parging
                              55
4" limestone, 8" brick backing-134
4" limestone, 8" hollow concrete
   block backing------------105-115
4" limestone, 8" hollow clay tile
   backing-------------------89-97
4" sandstone or bluestone facing,
   1/2" parging----------------49
1" mortar-------------------10-12

Wood Frame

Normal standard dead load for wood
frame house, lbs. per sq. ft. per
tier. For wood joists, bridging,
flooring, and underflooring, lath
& plaster on walls and ceilings-17
4" wood studs, wood sheathing,
   lath & plaster---------------10
1" wood sheathing, 1/4" asbestos
   board-----------------------2.5
1/2" gypsum sheathing or gypsum
   board-----------------------2.2
1/2" wood fiber sheathing or
   insulation board------------0.8
Wood siding, asphalt siding----- 2
Asbestos cement siding---------1.8
Plaster------------------------4-5
2" wood furring, lath & plaster7.5

Miscellaneous

#20 gauge corrugated iron siding-2
Corrugated asbestos siding---3.5-4
Corrugated glass, 2 1/2"O.C.---6.5
Fenestra type "C" insulated panel
   aluminum---------------------3
Fenestra type "C" insulated panel
   steel-----------------------6.5
Precast Bldg. Sections
   (Atterbury) 8" stone concrete-50
   (Atterbury) 8" light weight
   concrete--------------------38

COMPARATIVE GAUGES

GAUGE NO. (These run from #0,000,000 to #40)	GRAPHIC SIZES (Based on U.S. Std gauge)	U S STD REVISED (Manufact'rs thickness weight ga.) For hot and cold rolled steel sheets.		UNITED STATES STANDARD (USS) For stainless steel & monel metal sheets.		AMERICAN STEEL WIRE or WASHBURN & MOEN (W&M) For iron and steel wire.		BROWN AND SHARP (B&S) or AMERICAN WIRE (AW) For aluminum, copper, brass, bronze & nickel silver strip & wire and small sizes copper & brass tubing.		BIRMINGHAM WIRE (BWG) or STUBS IRON WIRE for hot and cold rolled steel strip. Flat steel wire. Steel, aluminum, bronze, monel, stainless steel tubing & larger size copper and brass tubing.		MACHINE AND WOOD SCREWS For ferrous & non-ferrous metals.		GRAPHIC SIZES (Based on B&S gauge)	GAUGE NO. (These run from #0,000,000 to #40)
		Decimal	Fract?	Decimal	Fract?	Decimal	Fract?	Decimal	Fract?	Decimal	Fract?	Decimal	Fract?		
000		.3750"	3/8"	.3750"	3/8"	.3625"	23/64	.4096"	13/32+	.425"	27/64"	Graphic sizes do not apply to this column			000
00		.3437"	11/32	.3437"	11/32	.3310"	21/64+	.3648"	23/64+	.380"	3/8+				00
0		.3125"	5/16	.3125"	5/16	.3065"	5/16–	.3249"	21/64–	.340"	11/32–	.060"	1/16–		0
1		.2812"	9/32	.2812"	9/32	.2830"	9/32+	.2893"	19/64–	.300"	19/64+	.073"	5/64–		1
2		.2656"	17/64	.2656"	17/64	.2625"	17/64–	.2576'	1/4+	.284"	9/32+	.086"	3/32–		2
3		.2391"	15/64+	.2500"	1/4"	.2437"	1/4–	.2294"	15/64–	.259"	17/64–	.099"	3/32+		3
4		.2242"	7/32+	.2344"	15/64	.2253"	7/32+	.2043"	13/64+	.238"	15/64+	.112"	7/64+		4
5		.2092"	13/64+	.2187"	7/32	.2070"	13/64+	.1819"	3/16–	.220"	7/32+	.125"	1/8		5
6		.1943"	3/16+	.2031"	13/64	.1920"	3/16+	.1620"	5/32+	.203"	13/64	.138"	9/64–		6
7		.1793"	11/64+	.1875"	3/16	.1770"	11/64+	.1443"	9/64+	.180"	3/16–	.151"	5/32–		7
8		.1644"	11/64–	.1719"	11/64	.1620"	5/32+	.1285"	1/8+	.165"	11/64–	.164"	11/64–		8
9		.1495"	5/32–	.1562"	5/32	.1483"	9/64+	.1144"	7/64+	.148"	9/64+	.177"	11/64+		9
10		.1345"	9/64–	.1406"	9/64	.1350"	9/64–	.1019"	7/64–	.134"	9/64–	.190"	3/16+		10
11		.1196"	1/8–	.1250"	1/8	.1205"	1/8–	.0907"	3/32–	.120"	1/8–	.203"	13/64		11
12		.1046"	7/64–	.1094"	7/64	.1055"	7/64–	.0808"	5/64+	.109"	7/64	.216"	7/32–		12
13		.0897"	3/32–	.0938"	3/32	.0915"	3/32–	.0719"	5/64–	.095"	3/32+	–	–		13
14		.0747"	5/64–	.0781"	5/64	.0800"	5/64+	.0640"	1/16+	.083"	5/64+	.242"	1/4–		14
15		.0673"	1/16+	.0703"	5/64–	.0720"	5/64–	.0571"	1/16–	.072"	5/64–	–	–		15
16		.0598"	1/16–	.0625"	1/16	.0625"	1/16	.0508"	3/64+	.065"	1/16+	.268"	17/64+		16
17		.0538"	3/64+	.0562"	1/16–	.0540"	3/64+	.0452"	3/64–	.058"	1/16–	–	–		17
18		.0478"	3/64+	.0500"	3/64+	.0475"	3/64–	.0403"	3/64–	.049"	3/64+	.294"	19/64–		18
19		.0418"	3/64–	.0437"	3/64–	.0410"	3/64–	.0359"	1/32+	.042"	3/64–	–	–		19
20		.0359"	1/32+	.0375"	1/32+	.0348"	1/32+	.0320"	1/32+	.035"	1/32+	.320"	5/16+		20
21		.0329"	1/32+	.0344"	1/32+	.0317"	1/32+	.0285"	1/32–	.032"	1/32+	–	–		21
22		.0299"	1/32–	.0312"	1/32	.0286"	1/32–	.0253"	1/32–	.028"	1/32–	–	–		22
23		.0269"	1/32–	.0281"	1/32–	.0258"	1/32–	.0226"	1/64+	.025"	1/32–	–	–		23
24		.0239"	1/32–	.0250"	1/32–	.0230"	1/64+	.0201"	1/64+	.022"	1/64+	.372"	3/8–		24
25		.0209"	1/64+	.0219"	1/64+	.0204"	1/64+	.0179"	1/64+	.020"	1/64+	–	–		25
26		.0179"	1/64+	.0187"	1/64+	.0181"	1/64+	.0159"	1/64+	.018"	1/64+	–	–		26
27		.0164"	1/64+	.0172"	1/64+	.0173"	1/64+	.0142"	1/64+	.016"	1/64+	–	–		27
28		.0149"	1/64–	.0156"	1/64	.0162"	1/64+	.0126"	1/64–	.014"	1/64–	–	–		28
29		.0135"	1/64–	.0141"	1/64–	.0150"	1/64–	.0112"	1/64–	.013"	1/64–	–	–		29
30		.0120"	1/64–	.0125"	1/64–	.0140"	1/64–	.0100	1/64–	.012"	1/64–	.450"	29/64–		30

LAND MEASUREMENT

When estimating area available for lots on large scale site developments it is safe to assume that 20% of entire area will be in streets.

To estimate number lots of a given size which a site will yield, using the above percentage for streets, use the following formula.

Note: 80% of 1 acre = 34,848 sq. ft.

$$\text{No. of lots} = \frac{\text{Total site area, (acres) x 34,848}}{\text{Width of lots x Depth of lots}}$$

Example: Site 50 acres
Lots are 60 ft. x 120 ft.

$$\text{or} = \frac{50 \text{ acres} \times 34,848}{60 \text{ ft.} \times 120 \text{ ft.}} = 242 \text{ lots}$$

USUAL LOT SIZES

a = acres
□' = sq. ft.

			FRONT OR WIDTH OF LOT						
			20'	40'	50'	60'	75'	80'	100'
DEPTH OF LOT	100'	□'	2,000	4,000	5,000	6,000	7,500	8,000	10,000
		a	.0459	.0718	.1148	.1377	.1722	.1837	.2296
	110'	□'	2,200	4,400	5,500	6,600	8,250	8,800	11,000
		a	.0505	.1010	.1263	.1515	.1894	.2021	.2525
	120'	□'	2,400	4,800	6,000	7,200	9,000	9,600	12,000
		a	.0551	.1102	.1377	.1653	.2066	.2204	.2755
	130'	□'	2,600	5,200	6,500	7,800	9,750	10,400	13,000
		a	.0597	.1194	.1492	.1791	.2238	.2388	.2984
	140'	□'	2,800	5,600	7,000	8,400	10,500	11,200	14,000
		a	.0643	.1286	.1607	.1929	.2411	.2571	.3214
	150'	□'	3,000	6,000	7,500	9,000	11,250	12,000	15,000
		a	.0689	.1377	.1722	.2066	.2582	.2755	.3444

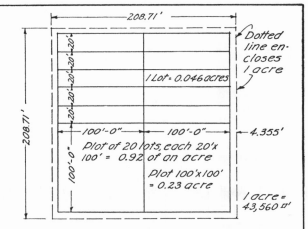

1 Lot = 0.046 acres

Dotted line encloses 1 acre

Plot of 20 lots, each 20'x 100' = 0.92 of an acre

Plot 100'x100' = 0.23 acre

1 acre = 43,560 □'

PLOT OF 20 LOTS, each 20'x100' in RELATION to ONE ACRE

CONVERSION TABLE – SQ.FT. TO ACRES

SQ.FT.	ACRES	SQ.FT.	ACRES	SQ.FT.	ACRES	SQ.FT.	ACRES	SQ.FT.	ACRES	SQ.FT.	ACRES
10 =	.0002	600 =	.0138	11,000 =	.2525	25,000 =	.5739	39,000 =	.8953	435,600 =	10.0000
20 =	.0005	700 =	.0161	12,000 =	.2755	26,000 =	.5969	40,000 =	.9183	479,160 =	11.0000
30 =	.0007	800 =	.0184	13,000 =	.2984	27,000 =	.6198	41,000 =	.9412	522,720 =	12.0000
40 =	.0009	900 =	.0207	14,000 =	.3214	28,000 =	.6428	42,000 =	.9642	566,280 =	13.0000
50 =	.0011	1,000 =	.0230	15,000 =	.3444	29,000 =	.6657	43,000 =	.9871	609,840 =	14.0000
60 =	.0014	2,000 =	.0459	16,000 =	.3673	30,000 =	.6887	43,560 =	1.0000	653,400 =	15.0000
70 =	.0016	3,000 =	.0689	17,000 =	.3903	31,000 =	.7117	87,120 =	2.0000	696,960 =	16.0000
80 =	.0018	4,000 =	.0918	18,000 =	.4132	32,000 =	.7346	130,680 =	3.0000	740,520 =	17.0000
90 =	.0021	5,000 =	.1148	19,000 =	.4362	33,000 =	.7576	174,240 =	4.0000	784,080 =	18.0000
100 =	.0023	6,000 =	.1377	20,000 =	.4591	34,000 =	.7805	217,800 =	5.0000	827,640 =	19.0000
200 =	.0046	7,000 =	.1607	21,000 =	.4821	35,000 =	.8035	261,360 =	6.0000	871,200 =	20.0000
300 =	.0069	8,000 =	.1837	22,000 =	.5051	36,000 =	.8264	304,920 =	7.0000	914,760 =	21.0000
400 =	.0092	9,000 =	.2066	23,000 =	.5280	37,000 =	.8494	348,480 =	8.0000	958,320 =	22.0000
500 =	.0115	10,000 =	.2296	24,000 =	.5510	38,000 =	.8724	392,040 =	9.0000	1,001,880 =	23.0000

AREA EQUIVALENTS

NOTE

Subscripts after any figure, 0_4, 0_5, etc. mean that that figure is to be repeated the indicated number of times.

EXAMPLE:

$0{,}0_4 2551 = 0{,}00002551$

SQUARE METERS	SQUARE INCHES	SQUARE FEET	SQUARE YARDS	SQUARE RODS	SQUARE CHAINS	RODS	ACRES	SQ.MILES OR SECTIONS
1	1550	10.76	1.196	0.0395	0.002471	$0{,}0_3 9884$	$0{,}0_2 2471$	$0{,}0_6 3861$
$0{,}0_3 6452$	1	0.006944	$0{,}0_3 7716$	$0{,}0_4 2551$	$0{,}0_5 1594$	$0{,}0_6 6377$	$0{,}0_6 1594$	$0{,}0_9 2491$
0.09290	144	1	0.1111	0.003673	$0{,}0_3 2296$	$0{,}0_4 9184$	$0{,}0_4 2296$	$0{,}0_7 3587$
0.8361	1296	9	1	0.03306	0.002066	$0{,}0_3 8264$	$0{,}0_3 2066$	$0{,}0_6 3228$
25.29	39204	272.25	30.25	1	0.0625	0.02500	0.00625	$0{,}0_5 9766$
404.7	627264	4356	484	16	1	0.4	0.1	$0{,}0_3 1562$
1012	1568160	10890	1210	40	2.5	1	0.25	$0{,}0_3 3096$
4047	6272640	43560	4840	160	10	4	1	0.001562
$2589{,}8$	....	27878400	3097600	102400	6400	2560	640	1

OTHER AREA MEASURES:

1 are = a square 10 meters x 10 meters = 100 sq. meters.

1 hectare = 100 ares = 10,000 centiares

1 section of Gov't. surveyed land = 1 sq. mile = 640 acres

1 acre (Texas) = 5645 sq. varas

1 square (Architects' measure) = 100 sq. ft.

compiled by Ralph Eberlin, C.E.

ROMAN ORDERS of ARCHITECTURE

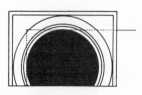

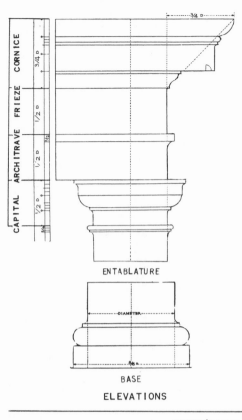

ENTABLATURE

BASE

ELEVATIONS

CAPITAL

BASE

PLANS

TUSCAN

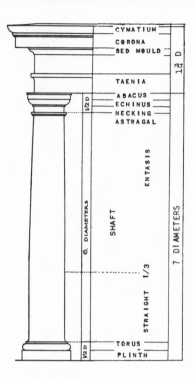

COMPLETE ORDER

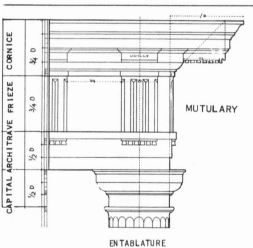

MUTULARY

ENTABLATURE

DENTICULATED

ENTABLATURE

ELEVATIONS

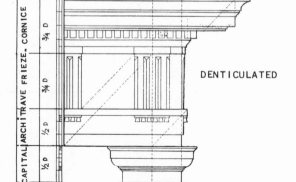

PLAN   CAPITAL

ELEVATION

PLAN   BASE

DORIC

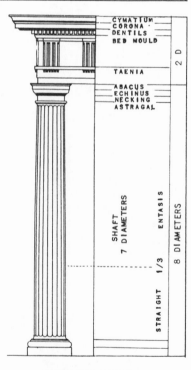

COMPLETE ORDER

ROMAN ORDERS of ARCHITECTURE

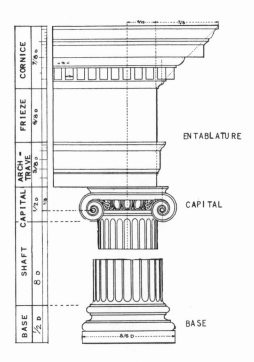

CORNICE	7/8 D		
FRIEZE	6/8 D	
ARCH-TRAVE	5/8 D	
CAPITAL	1/2 D	1/3
SHAFT	8 D	
BASE	1/2 D	

ENTABLATURE

CAPITAL

BASE

ELEVATIONS

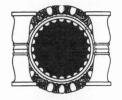

CAPITAL

BASE

PLANS

IONIC

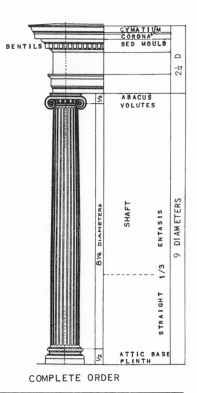

CYMATIUM
CORONA
BED MOULD
DENTILS

ABACUS
VOLUTES

SHAFT   ENTASIS

8½ DIAMETERS   9 DIAMETERS

STRAIGHT   1/3

ATTIC BASE
PLINTH

COMPLETE ORDER

CORNICE	
FRIEZE	3/4 D
ARCHI-TRAVE	3/4 D
CAPITAL	7/6 D
SHAFT	8 1/3 D
BASE	1/2 D

ENTABLATURE

CAPITAL

BASE

ELEVATIONS

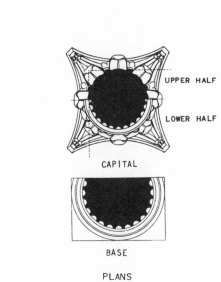

UPPER HALF

LOWER HALF

CAPITAL

BASE

PLANS

CORINTHIAN

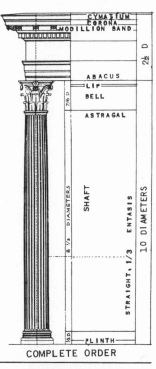

CYMATIUM
CORONA
MODILLION BAND

ABACUS
LIP
BELL
ASTRAGAL

SHAFT   ENTASIS

8 1/3 DIAMETERS   10 DIAMETERS

STRAIGHT, 1/3

PLINTH

COMPLETE ORDER

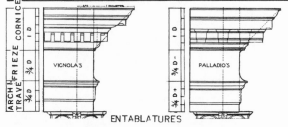

	CORNICE	1 D
FRIEZE	3/4 D
ARCHI-TRAVE	3/4 D

VIGNOLA'S

PALLADIO'S

ENTABLATURES

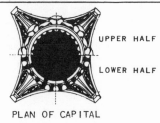

UPPER HALF

LOWER HALF

PLAN OF CAPITAL

COMPOSITE

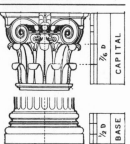

CAPITAL

BASE

ENTASIS, VOLUTE, RAKE MOULDS and POLYGONS

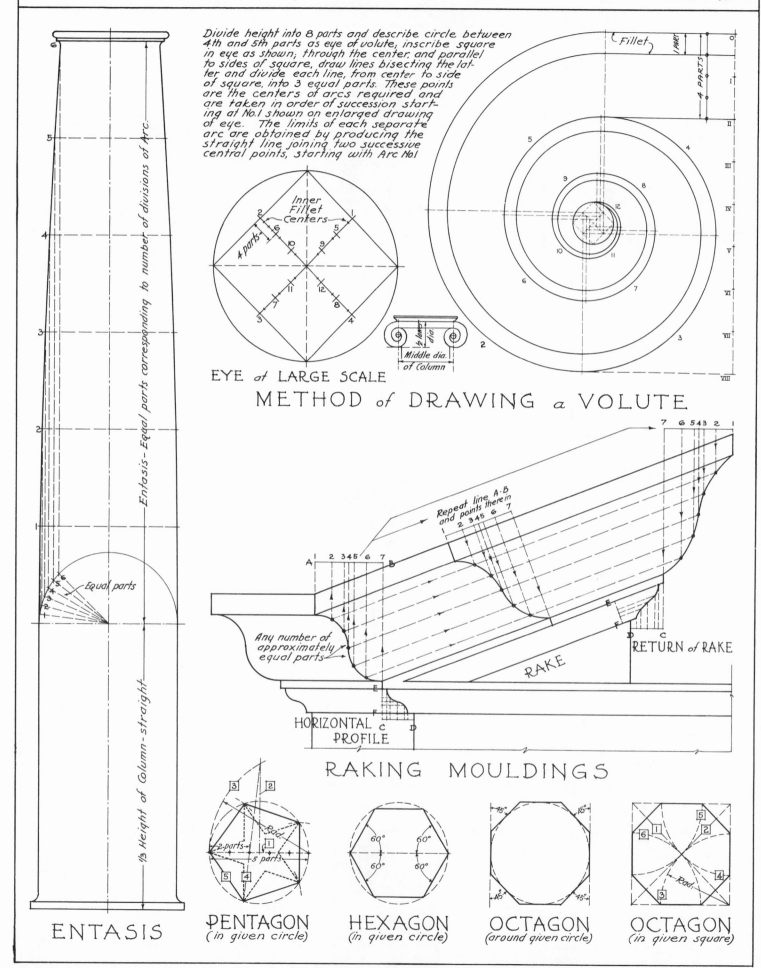

Divide height into 8 parts and describe circle between 4th and 5th parts as eye of volute, inscribe square in eye as shown; through the center, and parallel to sides of square, draw lines bisecting the latter and divide each line, from center to side of square, into 3 equal parts. These points are the centers of arcs required and are taken in order of succession starting at No.1 shown on enlarged drawing of eye. The limits of each separate arc are obtained by producing the straight line joining two successive central points, starting with Arc No.1

Inner Fillet Centers

4 parts

EYE at LARGE SCALE

½ lower dia.
Middle dia. of Column

METHOD of DRAWING a VOLUTE

Fillet
1 PART
4 PARTS

Repeat line A-B and points therein

Any number of approximately equal parts

RAKE

RETURN of RAKE

HORIZONTAL PROFILE

RAKING MOULDINGS

Entasis-Equal parts corresponding to number of divisions of Arc.

Equal parts

⅓ Height of Column-straight.

ENTASIS

PENTAGON
(in given circle)

Rad.
2 parts
5 parts

HEXAGON
(in given circle)

60° 60°
60° 60°

OCTAGON
(around given circle)

45° 45°
45° 45°

OCTAGON
(in given square)

Rad.

SI METRIC BACKGROUND DATA

The metric system originated in France as a product of the French Revolution, and gained gradual acceptance in Europe and in the French and Spanish colonies. In 1875 the United States joined 16 other countries in signing the Treaty of the Meter. The work of the General Conference of Weights and Measures resulted in a revised metric system in 1960, named Système International d'Unités (SI). It is this SI metric system that is referenced in the US Metric Act of 1975, and is presented in this chapter.

The Metric Conversion Act, Public Law 94-168, calls for a voluntary conversion process, and established the US Metric Board. In 1972 the American National Metric Council (ANMC) was formed under the sponsorship of the American National Standards Institute (ANSI). Involving more than 300 trade, professional, labor, consumer, and government organizations and more than 400 major corporations, the American National Metric Council has organized the voluntary conversion process. The ANMC Construction Industries Coordinating Committee (CICC) has prepared a conversion plan for adoption by the industry.

ANSI/ASTM Metric Standards are developed under the jurisdiction of ASTM Committee E-6 on Performance of Building Constructions. Subcommittee E 06.62 on Coordination of Dimensions for Building Materials and Systems has responsibility for such ANSI/ASTM Standards as E621-78 "Metric (SI) Units in Building Design and Construction." In addition, the Center for Building Technology of the National Bureau of Standards has published a number of Technical Notes and other special publications concerning metric conversion and dimensional coordination. The American Institute of Architects, with the cooperation of the ANMC, and the Center for Building Technology, has produced the "AIA Metric Building and Construction Guide." This chapter is based on information contained in that publication.

THE SI SYSTEM

Although the metric (SI) system applies to all measurement related systems, this chapter concerns the application of the SI System to construction. Concepts of dimensional coordination, although not restricted to the metric system, are seen as an essential part of a smooth transition of the construction industry to the use of the metric (SI) system.

MATERIALS AND COMPONENTS FOR METRIC BUILDING IN THE TRANSITIONAL PERIOD—SUGGESTED ADAPTATION IN DESIGN AND CONSTRUCTION FOR VARIOUS PRODUCT CATEGORIES*

CATEGORY	COMPLEXITY OF ADAPTATION	TYPICAL EXAMPLES OF MATERIALS AND COMPONENTS	ADAPTIVE ACTION IN DESIGN	ADAPTIVE ACTION IN CONSTRUCTION
A. DIMENSIONAL COORDINATION NOT REQUIRED				
A.1	No change in materials—no problems foreseen	Formless or plastic materials: water, paint, mastics, tar; sand, cement, lime, dry mortar mix, loose-fill insulation; read-mixed concrete, pre-mixed masonry mortar	Specify in metric units. Develop necessary site guidelines	Weigh or measure in metric quantities. Use metric data on coverage, mix ratios, etc.
A.2	Customary sizes usable—interim "soft conversion"	Structural steel sections, reinforcing bars, pipes, tubes, hardware, fixtures, fittings	Specify metric equivalents or show permissible substitutions. Select preferred "free" dimensions such as length or centerlines	Order or cut to metric length; set out to coordinated centerlines
B. MINOR SITE ADJUSTMENTS TO COORDINATE WITH PREFERRED DIMENSIONS				
B.1	Modification in one direction to fit in with preferred dimensions	a. Adjustment by trimming: lumber studs and joists, laminates, roofing, gutters b. Adjustment by lapping: shingles, tar felt, underlay, sheathing, waterproof membranes c. Adjustment by change in joint width: bricks, blocks, ceramic tiles	Specify preferred metric dimensions to expedite the transition. Indicate construction adjustments in drawings or instructions	Set out project in preferred building dimensions and adjust products accordingly
C. DIMENSIONAL COORDINATION REQUIRED				
C.1	Purpose-made items—no difficulties foreseen	Precast panels and slabs, door assemblies, window assemblies, fabricated metalwork, built-in units	Specify rationalized metric sizes	Order or fabricate components in rationalized metric sizes
C.2	Reshaping of customary dimensions possible	Glazing, plywood, gypsum wallboard, sheathing, lath, rigid insulation materials	Investigate supply in rationalized metric sizes and specify	Order rationalized metric sizes. Cut off site or on site
C.3	Reshaping of customary dimensions difficult, costly, or impossible	Windows, doors, metal partitions, metal roof decking, fluorescent fixture, metal cladding panels, stainless steel sections and sinks, large ceramic panels, distribution boards and panels, fixed appliances and cabinets, lockers	Preorder preferred sizes before job commencement. Discuss trial batches with manufacturers. Use adaptive design and detailing	Adapt during the interim period until preferred metric sizes emerge. Construct suitable openings or spaces for non-coordinated components and assemblies

*The list may be expanded or modified to suit particular market conditions.

LINEAR MEASURE—EQUIVALENTS

MILLIMETERS	CENTIMETERS	DECIMETERS	METERS	DECAMETERS	HECTOMETERS	KILOMETERS	YARDS
1	0.1	0.01	0.001	0.0001	0.00001	0.000001	
10	1	0.1	0.01	0.001	0.0001	0.00001	
100	10	1	0.1	0.01	0.001	0.0001	
1,000	100	10	1	0.1	0.01	0.001	1.0936
10,000	1,000	100	10	1	0.1	0.01	
100,000	10,000	1,000	100	10	1	0.1	
1,000,000	100,000	10,000	1,000	100	10	1	
			.9144				1

AREA MEASURE—EQUIVALENTS

SQUARE MILLIMETERS	SQUARE CENTIMETERS	SQUARE DECIMETERS	SQUARE METERS	ARES	HECTARES	SQUARE KILOMETERS	ACRES
1	0.01	0.0001	0.000001				
100	1	0.01	0.0001	0.000001			
10,000	100	1	0.01	0.0001	0.000001		
1,000,000	10,000	100	1	0.01	0.0001	0.000001	
	1,000,000	10,000	100	1	0.01	0.0001	
		1,000,000	10,000	100	1	0.01	2.471
			1,000,000	10,000	100	1	247.1
				40.47	.4047		1

SI UNITS AND RULES FOR USE

Specific rules for use, type style, and punctuation have been established by the General Conference on Weights and Measures (CGPM); the National Bureau of Standards (NBS) is responsible for determining preferred usage in the United States.

Standard, lowercase type is used for unit names and symbols, except when the symbols are derived from proper names, such as newton (N) or pascal (Pa). There is one exception to this in the use of the capital letter L as the symbol for liter. This is because the lowercase "l" was thought by the U.S. Department of Commerce to be easily confused with the numeral "1." Symbols are not followed by a period or a full stop, except at the end of a sentence. The symbols for all quantities, such as length, mass, and time, are printed in italic (l, k, s, . . .). In typewriting and longhand, underlining is an acceptable substitute for italic letters. Unit names are used in the plural to express numerical values greater than 1, equal to 0, or less than −1. All other values take the singular form of the unit name, thus 100 meters, 1.1 meters, 0 degrees Celsius, −4 degrees Celsius, 0.5 meter, ¹/₂ liter, −0.2 degree Celsius, −1 degree Celsius. The plural of unit names is formed by adding an "s." Exceptions are hertz, lux, and siemens, which remain unchanged, and henry, which becomes henries. Symbols are the same in both singular and plural.

Prefixes denoting decimal multiples and submultiples (allowing SI units to express magnitudes from the sub-atomic to the astronomic) are governed by the same rules concerning capitalization and punctuation.

It is important to note that mega, giga, and tera (M, G, T) are capitalized in symbol form to avoid confusion with established unit symbols, but they maintain the lowercase form when spelled out in full. No space is left between the prefix and the letter for the unit name, thus mL (milliliter), mm (millimeter), kA (kiloampere).

Preference is given to the use of decimal multiples that are related to the basic units by multiples of 1000. As far as possible, prefixes denoting magnitudes of 100, 10, 0.1, and 0.01 should be limited. Certain multiples of SI units, not likely to be extensively used, have been given special names (Table 4).

The prefix symbol is considered to be part of the unit symbol and is attached to it without a space or dot, thus km not k m, k-m, or k.m.

A space is left between a numeral and the unit name or symbol to which it refers, thus 20 mm, 10⁶ N. In angle measure no space is left between the numeral and the degree symbol, thus 27°. The symbol for degree Celsius °C is an inseparable symbol with no space between the two parts; it is also preferable to leave no space between the numeral and the unit, thus 20°C.

When a quantity is used as an adjective, it is preferable to use a hyphen instead of a space between the number and the unit name or between the number and the symbol; thus a 3-meter pole, a 35-mm film.

In the United States and Canada, the decimal point is a dot on the line, but in some other countries a comma or a raised dot is used.

Decimal notation is preferred with metric measurements, but simple fractions are acceptable (except on engineering drawings), such as those where the denominator is 2, 3, 4, 5, 8, and 10.

Examples: 0.5 g, 1.75 kg, and 0.7 L are preferred; ¹/₂ g, 1³/₄ kg, and ⁷/₁₀ L are acceptable (except on engineering drawings).

A zero before the decimal point should be used in numbers between 1 and −1 to prevent the possibility that a faint decimal point will be overlooked.

Example: The oral expression "point seven five" is written 0.75.

Since the comma is used as the decimal marker in many countries, a comma should not be used to separate groups of digits. Instead, the digits should be separated into groups of three, counting both to the left and to the right from the decimal point, and a space used to separate the groups of three digits. The space should be of fixed width, equal to that formerly occupied by the comma.

Examples: 4 720 525   0. 528 75

If there are only four digits to the left or right of the decimal point, the space is acceptable but is not preferred.

Examples: 6875 or 6 875
0.1234 or 0.123 4

However, in a column with other numbers that show the space and are aligned on the decimal point, the space is necessary.

Example:
```
      14.8
   3 780
 +12 100
  15 894.8
```

Compound units are those formed by combining simple units by means of the mathematical signs for multiplication and division and by the use of exponents.

When writing symbols for units such as square centimeter or cubic meter, the symbol for the unit should be written followed by the superscript ² or ³, respectively, thus 26 cm² and 14 m³.

For a compound unit that is a quotient, "per" should be used to form the name (kilometer per hour) and a slash (/) to form the symbol (km/h). There is no space before or after the slash. Compound units that are quotients may also be written by using negative exponents (km · h⁻¹).

For everyday rounding of metric values obtained by converting untoleranced customary values, the following simplified rules are suggested:

1. If the customary value is expressed by a combination of units such as feet and inches, or pounds and ounces, first express it in terms of the smaller unit.
   Example: 14 ft 5 in. = 173 in.
2. When the digits to be discarded begin with a 5 or more, increase by one unit the last digit retained.
   Example: 8.3745, if rounded to three digits, would be 8.37; if rounded to four digits, 8.375.
3. Multiply the customary value by the conversion factor. If the first significant digit of the metric value is equal to or larger than the first significant digit of the customary value, round the metric value to the same number of significant digits as there are in the customary value.
   Examples: 11 mi x 1.609 km/mi = 17.699 km, which rounds to 18 km

   61 mi x 1.609 km/mi = 98.149 km, which rounds to 98 km
4. If smaller, round to one more significant digit.
   Examples: 66 mi x 1.609 km/mi = 106.194 km, which rounds to 106 km

   8 ft x 0.3048 m/ft = 2.4384 m, which rounds to 2.4 m
   Exceptions: It is sometimes better to round to one less digit than specified above. For example, according to the foregoing, 26 pounds per square inch air pressure in an automobile tire would be converted as follows:

   26 psi* x 6.895 kPa/psi = 179.27 kPa

   which rounds to 179 kPa

   but kPa, where the zero is not a significant digit, would usually be better because tire pressures are not expected to be very precise. The rules do not apply to conversion of °F to °C.
5. Where a customary value represents a maximum or minimum limit that must be respected, the rounding must be in the direction that does not violate the original limit.

TABLE 1. SI BASE UNITS

PHYSICAL QUANTITY	UNIT	SYMBOL
Length	Meter	m
Mass	Kilogram	k
Time	Second	s
Electric current	Ampere	A
Thermodynamic temperature	Kelvin	K
Luminous intensity	Candela	cd
Amount of substance	Mole	mol

TABLE 2. SI SUPPLEMENTARY UNITS

PHYSICAL QUANTITY	UNIT	SYMBOL
Plane angle	Radian	rad
Solid angle	Steradian	sr

TABLE 3. DERIVED UNITS WITH COMPOUND NAMES

PHYSICAL QUANTITY	UNIT	SYMBOL
Area	Square meter	m²
Volume	Cubic meter	m³
Density	Kilogram per cubic meter	kg/m³
Velocity	Meter per second	m/s
Angular velocity	Radian per second	rad/s
Acceleration	Meter per second squared	m/s²
Angular acceleration	Radian per second squared	rad/s²
Volume rate of flow	Cubic meter per second	m³/s
Moment of inertia	Kilogram meter squared	kg · m²
Moment of force	Newton meter	N · m
Intensity of heat flow	Watt per square meter	W/m²
Thermal conductivity	Watt per meter Kelvin	W/m · K
Luminance	Candela per square meter	cd/m²

TABLE 4. MULTIPLES OF SI UNITS WITH SPECIAL NAMES

PHYSICAL QUANTITY	NAME	SYMBOL	MAGNITUDE
Volume	Liter	L	10⁻³ m³ = 0.0001 m³
Mass	Megagram (metric ton)	Mg(t)	10³ kg = 1000 kg
Area	Hectare	ha	10⁴ m² = 10 000 m²
Pressure	Millibar*	mbar*	10² Pa = 100 Pa

*Used for meteorological purposes only.

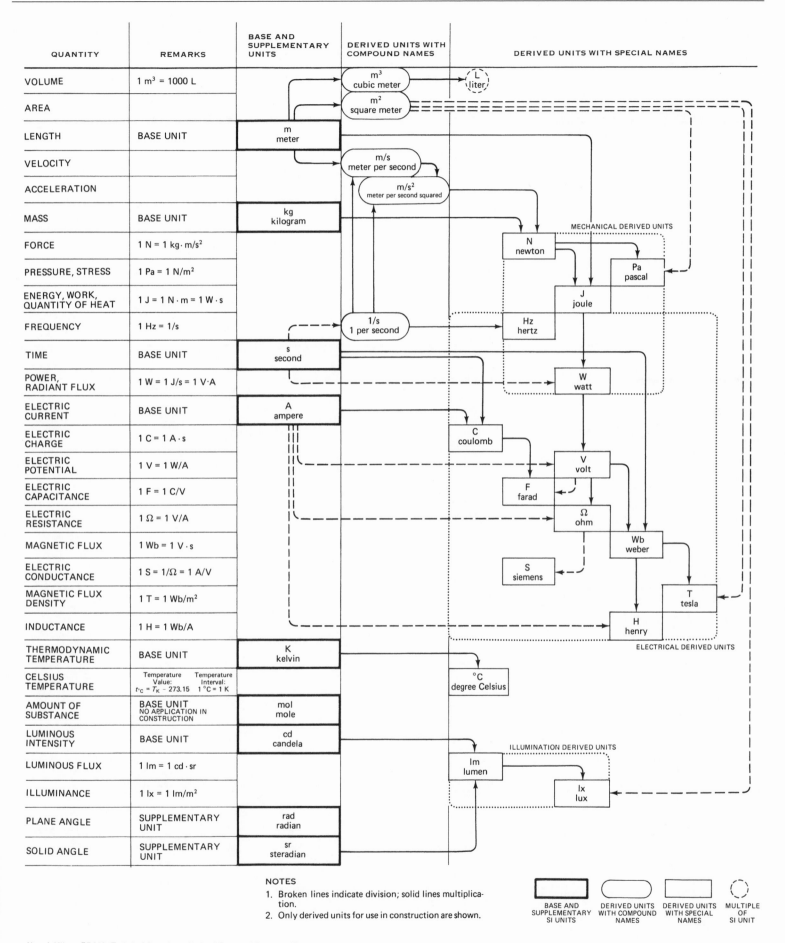

QUANTITY	REMARKS	BASE AND SUPPLEMENTARY UNITS	DERIVED UNITS WITH COMPOUND NAMES	DERIVED UNITS WITH SPECIAL NAMES
VOLUME	$1\ m^3 = 1000\ L$		m^3 cubic meter	L liter
AREA			m^2 square meter	
LENGTH	BASE UNIT	m meter		
VELOCITY			m/s meter per second	
ACCELERATION			m/s^2 meter per second squared	
MASS	BASE UNIT	kg kilogram		
FORCE	$1\ N = 1\ kg \cdot m/s^2$			N newton
PRESSURE, STRESS	$1\ Pa = 1\ N/m^2$			Pa pascal
ENERGY, WORK, QUANTITY OF HEAT	$1\ J = 1\ N \cdot m = 1\ W \cdot s$			J joule
FREQUENCY	$1\ Hz = 1/s$		1/s 1 per second	Hz hertz
TIME	BASE UNIT	s second		
POWER, RADIANT FLUX	$1\ W = 1\ J/s = 1\ V \cdot A$			W watt
ELECTRIC CURRENT	BASE UNIT	A ampere		
ELECTRIC CHARGE	$1\ C = 1\ A \cdot s$			C coulomb
ELECTRIC POTENTIAL	$1\ V = 1\ W/A$			V volt
ELECTRIC CAPACITANCE	$1\ F = 1\ C/V$			F farad
ELECTRIC RESISTANCE	$1\ \Omega = 1\ V/A$			Ω ohm
MAGNETIC FLUX	$1\ Wb = 1\ V \cdot s$			Wb weber
ELECTRIC CONDUCTANCE	$1\ S = 1/\Omega = 1\ A/V$			S siemens
MAGNETIC FLUX DENSITY	$1\ T = 1\ Wb/m^2$			T tesla
INDUCTANCE	$1\ H = 1\ Wb/A$			H henry
THERMODYNAMIC TEMPERATURE	BASE UNIT	K kelvin		
CELSIUS TEMPERATURE	Temperature Value: $t_C = T_K - 273.15$ Temperature Interval: $1\ °C = 1\ K$			°C degree Celsius
AMOUNT OF SUBSTANCE	BASE UNIT NO APPLICATION IN CONSTRUCTION	mol mole		
LUMINOUS INTENSITY	BASE UNIT	cd candela		
LUMINOUS FLUX	$1\ lm = 1\ cd \cdot sr$			lm lumen
ILLUMINANCE	$1\ lx = 1\ lm/m^2$			lx lux
PLANE ANGLE	SUPPLEMENTARY UNIT	rad radian		
SOLID ANGLE	SUPPLEMENTARY UNIT	sr steradian		

MECHANICAL DERIVED UNITS

ELECTRICAL DERIVED UNITS

ILLUMINATION DERIVED UNITS

NOTES
1. Broken lines indicate division; solid lines multiplication.
2. Only derived units for use in construction are shown.

BASE AND SUPPLEMENTARY SI UNITS

DERIVED UNITS WITH COMPOUND NAMES

DERIVED UNITS WITH SPECIAL NAMES

MULTIPLE OF SI UNIT

Hans J. Milton, FRAIA, Technical Consultant, National Bureau of Standards; Gaithersburg, Maryland

MEASUREMENT OF LENGTH

The basic SI unit of length is the meter. Fractions or multiples of the base unit are expressed with prefixes, only some of which are recommended for construction. In order to be clear, avoid those prefixes that are not specifically recommended for construction.

Common SI units for length as used in construction are:

UNIT NAME	SYMBOL	COMMENT	COMPUTER SYMBOL
Meter	m	Also spelled metre	M
Millimeter	mm	0.001 meter	MM
Kilometer	km	1000 meters	KM
Micrometer	um	0.000 001 meter	UM

Note: Centimeter is not recommended for construction.

The recommended unit for dimensioning buildings is the millimeter. The use of the meter would be limited to large dimensions, such as levels, overall dimensions, and engineering computations. Meters are also used for estimating and land surveying. On architectural drawings, dimensions require no symbol if millimeters are consistently used.

Kilometers are used for transportation and surveying. Micrometers would be used for thicknesses of materials, such as coatings.

Conversion factors for length are shown below:

METRIC	CUSTOMARY
1 meter	3.280 84 feet or 1.093 61 yards
1 millimeter	0.039 370 1 inch
1 kilometer	0.621 371 mile or 49.709 6 chains
1 micrometer	0.000 393 7 inch or 0.3937 mils

CUSTOMARY	METRIC
1 mile	1.609 344 km
1 chain	20.1168 m
1 yard	0.9144 m
1 foot	0.3048 m 304.8 mm
1 inch	25.4 mm

(1 U.S. survey foot = 0.304 800 6 m.)

The recommended linear basic module for construction is 100 mm in the United States. See page on dimensional coordination for application of this basic module. This is very close to the 4 in. module in general use for light construction. Scales of drawing relate to units of length. Use meters on all drawings with scale ratios between 1:200 and 1:2000. Use millimeters on drawings with scale ratios between 1:1 and 1:200.

MEASUREMENT OF AREA

There are no basic SI metric units for area. Rather, area units are derived from units for length, as follows:

UNIT NAME	SYMBOL	COMMENT
Square meter	m²	1 m² = 10⁶ mm²
Square millimeter	mm²	
Square kilometer	km²	Land area
Hectare	ha	1 ha = 10 000 m²

Note that the hectare, although not an SI unit, is acceptable as a supplemental unit. It is used for surface measurement of land and water only.

At times, area is expressed by linear dimensions such as 40 mm x 90 mm; 300 x 600. Normally the width is written first and depth or height second.

The square centimeter is not recommended for construction. Such measurements may be converted to millimeters (1 cm² = 100 mm²) or to meters (1 cm² = 10⁻⁴ m² = 0.0001 m²).

Conversion factors for area are shown below.

METRIC	CUSTOMARY
1 km²	0.386 101 mile² (U.S. Survey)
1 ha	2.471 04 acre (U.S. Survey)
1 m²	10.7639 ft² 1.195 99 yd²
1 mm²	0.001 550 in.²

CUSTOMARY	METRIC
1 mile² (U.S. Survey)	2.590 00 km²
1 acre (U.S. Survey)	0.404 687 ha 4046.87 m²
1 yd²	0.836 127 m²
1 ft²	0.092 903 m²
1 in.²	645.16 mm²

MEASUREMENT OF VOLUME AND SECTION MODULUS

There are no basic SI metric units for volume, but these are derived from units for length as well as non-SI units that are acceptable for use.

UNIT NAME	SYMBOL	COMMENT
Cubic meter	m³	1 m³ = 1000 L
Cubic millimeter	mm³	
Liter	L	Volume of fluids
Milliliter	mL	1 mL = 1 cm³
Cubic centimeter	cm³	1 cm³ = 1000 mm³

In construction, the cubic meter is used for volume and capacity of large quantities of earth, concrete, sand, and so on. It is preferred for all engineering purposes.

The section modulus is also expressed as unit of length to the third power (m³ and mm³).

Conversion factors are listed below.

VOLUME, MODULUS OF SECTION

METRIC	CUSTOMARY
1 m³	0.810 709 x 10³ acre ft 1.307 95 yd³ 35.3147 ft³ 423.776 board ft
1 mm³	61.0237 x 10⁻⁶ in.³

CUSTOMARY	METRIC
1 acre ft	1233.49 m³
1 yd³	0.764 555 m³
100 board ft	0.028 316 8 m³
1 ft³	16.387 1 mm³ 28 3168 1 (cm³)
1 in.³	16.3871 mL(cm³)

LIQUID, CAPACITY

METRIC	CUSTOMARY
1 L	0.035 3147 ft³ 0.264 172 gal (U.S.) 1.056 69 qt (U.S.)
1 mL	0.061 023 7 in.³

CUSTOMARY	METRIC
1 gal (U.S. liquid)	3.785 41 L
1 qt (U.S. liquid)	946.353 mL
1 pt (U.S. liquid)	473.177 mL
1 fl oz (U.S.)	29.5735 mL

NOTE: 1 gal (U.K.) = approximately 1.2 gal (U.S.).

MEASUREMENT OF MASS

The SI metric system recommends the use of the word mass in place of the more common word weight, because weight refers specifically to the pull of gravity, which can vary in different locations. The SI system also separates the concept of mass from that of force.

SI metric units and other acceptable units for mass are:

UNIT NAME	SYMBOL	COMMENT
Kilogram	kg	Most used
Gram	g	
Metric ton	t	1 t = 1000 kg

The kilogram is based on a prototype, and unlike other SI units cannot be derived without reference to the international prototype kilogram maintained under specified conditions at the International Bureau of Weights and Measures (BIPM) near Paris, France.

Conversion factors are listed below.

METRIC	CUSTOMARY
1 kg	2.204 62 lb (avoirdupois) 35.2740 02 oz (avoirdupois)
1 metric ton	1.102 31 ton (short, 2000 lb) 2204.62 lb
1 g	0.035 274 oz 0.643 015 pennyweight

CUSTOMARY	METRIC
1 ton (short)	0.907 185 metric ton (megagram) 907.185 kg
1 lb	0.453 592 kg
1 oz	28.3495 9 g
1 pennyweight	1.555 17 g

NOTE: A long ton (2240 lb) = 1016.05 kg or 1.016 05 metric ton.

TIME

The SI unit for time is the second, from which other units of time are derived. In construction measurements, such as flow rates, the use of minutes is not recommended, so that cubic meters per second, liters per second, or cubic meters per hour would be normally used. Time symbols are as follows:

Second	s
Minute	min
Hour	h
Day	d
Month	—
Year	a (365 days or 31 536 000 seconds)

For clarity, international recommendations for writing time and dates are as follows:

Time   Express by hour/minute/second on a 24 hour day:

03:20:30
16:45

Dates   Express by year/month/day:

1978-06-30
1978 06 30 (second preference)
19780630 (computer entry)

MEASUREMENT OF TEMPERATURE

The SI base unit of temperature is the Kelvin, which is a scale based on absolute zero. The allowable unit Celsius is equal to the Kelvin unit except that 0° Celsius is the freezing point of water. Thus a temperature listed in degrees Celsius plus 275.15 degrees is the temperature in degrees Kelvin. Celsius is in common use for construction, not Kelvin.

CUSTOMARY	METRIC
1°F	0.555 556°C 5/9° C or 5/9 K

METRIC	CUSTOMARY
1°C	1 K 1.8°F

NOTE: Centigrade is not recognized as part of the SI system.

PLANE ANGLE

While the SI unit for plane angle is the radian, the customary units degree (°), minute ('), and second ('') of arc will be retained in most applications in construction, engineering, and land surveying.

CUSTOMARY	METRIC
1°	(π/180) rad

ENERGY RELATIONSHIP

SI metric units provide a direct, coherent relationship between mechanical, thermal, and electrical energy.

The ampere (A) (SI base unit) is that constant current which, if maintained in two straight, parallel conductors of infinite length and of negligible cross section, placed 1 meter apart in a vacuum, would produce between these conductors a force equal to 2×10^{-7} newton per meter of length.

One newton (N) is that force which gives to a mass of 1 kilogram (kg) an acceleration of 1 meter per second squared (m/s^2). Hence $1.0 \, N = 1.0 \, kg \cdot m/s^2$.

One joule (J) is the work done when the point of application of a force of 1 newton moves a distance of 1 meter along the line of action of the force. Hence $1.0 \, J = 1.0 \, N \cdot m$.

A watt (W) is the power which in 1 second gives rise to the energy of 1 joule. Conversely, a joule is a watt-second.

Since the customary coherent relationships with other electrical quantities will still prevail, the observations made above in respect to work, energy, quantity of heat, and power may be summarized, from a "units" point of view as follows:

$N \cdot m = J \quad J/s = W \quad J = W \cdot s \quad W = A \cdot V \quad J = A \cdot V \cdot s$

MASS

The preferred unit multiples of mass are milligram, gram, kilogram, and megagram (or metric ton), which are written respectively as:

mg   g   kg   Mg   (or t)

Weight is predominantly a concept of the customary "gravitational" system. Since SI is an absolute system dealing with mass and with the forces related to the acceleration of a mass, there is no special name for a unit of weight in SI.

Weight in a particular force due solely to gravitational attraction on a mass.

FORCE

Since SI is a coherent system and since the fundamental law of physics (F α ma) states that force is dependent solely on mass and on acceleration,

1.0 kg accelerated at 1.0 m/s^2

$\longrightarrow$ 1.0 force unit

$\longrightarrow$ 1.0 newton (1.0 N)

The use of the name "newton" for the unit of force should fix in the mind the full significance of the distinctions between mass and force.

Normally a mass to be supported or moved will be specified or labeled in terms of kilograms (kg), but all forces acting on structure, either gravitationally or laterally (including wind, sway, and impact), should be specified or determined ultimately in terms of newtons (N).

Based on customary gravitational usage:

Mass: 1.0 slug   32.17 lb   14.59 kg
        1.488 kgf/(m/s^2)

Force: 1.0 lbf   32.17 pdl   4.448 N
        0.4536 kgf

Based on SI usage:

Mass: 1.0 kg   2.205 lb   0.068 52 slug
        0.1020 kgf/(m/s^2)

Force: 1.0 N   7.233 pdl   0.2248 lbf
        0.1020 kgf

The force definitions are as follows:

The "newton" is the force required to accelerate 1 kilogram mass at the rate of 1.0 m/s^2.

The "poundal" is the force required to accelerate 1 pound of mass at the rate of 1.0 ft/s^2.

The "pound force" is the force required to accelerate 1 pound of mass at the rate of 32.1740 ft/s^2.

The related definitions for the derived mass units are:

The "slug" is that mass which, when acted upon by 1 pound-force, will be accelerated at the rate of 1.0 ft/s^2.

The gravitational metric unit of mass is that unit of mass which, when acted upon by 1 kilogram-force, will be accelerated at 1.0 m/s^2. There seems to be no generally accepted name or symbol for this gravitational unit of mass, except the inference to the kilogram.

The "kilogram" and the "pound" are base units, not derived units as are the slug and the gravitational metric unit of mass. The kilogram and the pound relate directly to an artifact of mass which, by convention, is regarded as dimensionally independent—thus the name "base unit."

DERIVED UNITS WITH SPECIAL NAMES

PHYSICAL QUANTITY	UNIT	SYMBOL	DERIVATION
Frequency	Hertz	Hz	s^{-1}
Force	Newton	N	$kg \cdot m/s^2$
Pressure, stress	Pascal	Pa	N/m^2
Work, energy, quantity of heat	Joule	J	$N \cdot m$
Power	Watt	W	J/s
Electric charge	Coulomb	C	$A \cdot s$
Electric potential	Volt	V	W/A
Electric capacitance	Farad	F	C/V
Electric resistance	Ohm	O	V/A
Electric conductance	Siemens	S	Ω^{-1}
Magnetic flux	Weber	Wb	$V \cdot s$
Magnetic flux density	Tesla	T	Wb/m^2
Inductance	Henry	H	Wb/A
Celsius temperature	Degree Celsius	°C	K
Luminous flux	Lumen	lm	$cd \cdot sr$
Illumination	Lux	lx	lm/m^2
Activity	Becquerel	Bq	s^{-1}
Absorbed dose	Gray	Gy	J/kg

COMPARISON OF UNIT SYSTEMS

QUANTITY	MASS LENGTH, TIME (ABSOLUTE)		FORCE, LENGTH, TIME (GRAVITATIONAL)		CUSTOMARY COMBINED SYSTEM
	SI	ENGLISH	METRIC	ENGLISH	
Mass	kg	lb	kgf/(m/s^2)	lbf/(ft/s^2) (slug)	lb (alt: lbm)
Force	$kg \, m/s^2$ N (newton)	$lb \, ft/s^2$ 1 dp (poundal)	kgf (alt:kp)	lbf	lbf
Coherence factor	1.0	1.0	1.0	1.0	1/32.17

COMPARATIVE ANALYSIS OF SOME APPROXIMATE PHYSICAL PROPERTIES[a] FOR REPRESENTATIVE ENGINEERING MATERIALS

IN TERMS OF U.S. CUSTOMARY UNITS							IN TERMS OF PREFERRED SI UNITS						
COEFFICIENT OF LINEAR EXPANSION α (10^6 IN./ IN °F)	ALLOWABLE STRESSES (LBF/IN.^{2} x 10^3)			ELASTIC MODULUS (LBF/IN.^{2} x 10^6)		WEIGHT DENSITY W (LB/FT^3)	MATERIAL	MASS DENSITY ρ (KG/M^3)	ELASTIC MODULUS (GPA = GN/M^2)		ALLOWABLE STRESSES (MPA = MN/M^2)			COEFFICIENT OF LINEAR EXPANSION α μM/(M · K)
	σ_f^b	σ_c^c	τ_s	E	G				E	G	σ_f^b	σ_c^c	τ_s	
6.5	20	20	10	30	12	490	Mild steel	7850	200	80	140	140	70	11.7
6.9	24	24	15	30	12	490	High-strength steel	7850	200	80	165	165	100	12.4
6.0	3	10	2	15	6	450	Cast iron	7200	100	40	20	70	15	10.8
9.3	8	8	5	17	6.4	560	Copper	8960	120	45	55	55	35	16.7
10.4	12	8	6	13	5	520	Brass	8300	90	35	80	55	40	18.7
13.0	16	15	8	10.3	4	170	Aluminum	2700	70	27	110	100	55	23.4
							Timber							
1.7	1.3	0.8	0.05	1.2	—	27	Softwood	430	9	—	9.6	5.5	0.3	3.1
2.5	1.8	1.2	0.10	1.6	—	48	Hardwood	770	12	—	12.4	8.3	0.7	4.5
6.2	1.2	1.0	0.15	2.5	—	150	Concrete (reinf.)	2400	17	—	8.3	6.9	1.0	11.2
—	—	0.03	—	—	—	105	Soil	1680	—	—	—	0.2	—	—
4.4	—	0.3	—	—	—	165	Rock	2640	—	—	—	2.0	—	7.9
	—	—	—	—	—	62.4	Water	1000	—	—	—	—	—	

NOTE: Values given are rounded in each system and are not direct conversions.

[a] For use only for comparing representative values in the respective unit systems; not intended for design. For design purposes see other standard references such as ANSI, AISC, ACI, and IFI.

[b] Extreme fiber bending.

[c] Short compression block; in timber, parallel to grain.

UNITS FOR USE IN HEAT TRANSFER CALCULATIONS

QUANTITY NAME	SI UNIT	UNIT NAME	CONVERSION FACTOR	
Energy, quantity of heat (E, Q)	J(W · s)	joule	1 Btu (int.)	= 1.055 056 kJ
			1 kWh	= 3.6 MJ
			1 therm	= 105.5056 MJ
Heat flow rate (P, q)	W(J/s)	watt	1 Btu/h	= 0.293 071 W
			1 Btu/s	= 1.055 056 kW
			1 ton (refrig.)	= 3.516 800 kW
Specific energy, calorific value (mass basis)	J/kg	joule per kilogram	1 Btu/lb	= 2.326 kJ/kg
Irradiation, intensity of heat flow, heat loss from surfaces	W/m²	watt per square meter	1 Btu/ft² · h	= 3.152 481 W/m²
			1 W/ft²	= 10.763 91 W/m²
			1 Btu/ft² · s	= 11.348 93 kW/m²
Specific heat capacity (mass basis)	J/(kg · K)	joule per kilogram kelvin	1 Btu/lb · °F	= 4.1868 kJ/(kg · K)
Thermal conductivity (k-value)	W/(m · K)	watt per meter kelvin	1 Btu · in/h · ft² · °F	= 0.144 228 W/(m · K)
			1 Btu · in/s · ft² · °F	= 519.2204 W/(m · K)
			1 Btu/h · ft · °F	= 1.730 73 W/(m · K)
Thermal conductance, coefficient of heat transfer (c, U-value)	W/(m² · K)	watt per square meter kelvin	1 Btu/h · ft² · °F	= 5.678 26 W/(m² · K)
Thermal resistance, thermal insulance (R)	m² · K/W	square meter kelvin per watt	1 °F · h · ft²/Btu	= 0.176 110 m² · K/W

HEAT TRANSFER IN BUILDINGS

Heat transfer calculations, involving heat loss, heat gain, or thermal insulating properties of materials, will be simplified in SI because of the coherent relationships between units used. Heat transfer units are generally derived from the unit for temperature (kelvin or degree Celsius), the unit for energy and quantity of heat (joule), the unit for heat transfer rate (watt), and the units for time (second), length (meter), areas (square meter), and mass (kilogram).

TEMPERATURE

The Celsius temperature scale, for which the zero reference is the freezing point of water, will also be used for ambient temperatures.

TIME

Use of the hour (h), as in 5 km/h, and the day (d), as in m³/d, will occur in special cases, but the use of the minute (min) will be deemphasized in favor of the second (s).

HEATING DEGREE-DAYS

For heating design purposes and the determination of suitable insulation, the concept of heating degree-days, founded on a base temperature of 65°F (18.33°C), will possibly be revised to use a base temperature of 18°C (64.4°F).

In heat transfer through a composite element, such as a building wall, a sequence of conduction and convection coefficients may be involved. As in other "series type" problems the approach to determining the combined or "overall" coefficient U is based on the sum of the resistances, which is the sum of the reciprocals of the conductances in the path of the heat transfer.

The following definitions can be used to identify the coefficients:

K = thermal conductance;

$$K = \frac{kA}{L} \frac{W}{m \cdot K} \times \frac{m^2}{m} = W/K$$

R = thermal resistance;

$$R = \frac{L}{kA} \frac{m \cdot K}{W} \times \frac{m}{m^2} = K/W$$

Frequently, these factors may be stated in terms of unit areas. Any data taken from reference tables should be checked carefully.

The overall heat transfer relationship can be stated as:

$$q = U \cdot A \cdot \Delta T$$

where q = heat transfer rate
 A = cross-sectional area of heat, W(=J/s) transfer path, m²
 ΔT = overall temperature differential, K
 U = overall heat transfer coefficient, W/(m · K)

To determine U is often necessary to use the relationship:

$$\frac{1}{U} = R_1 + R_2 + R_3, \text{ etc.}; \qquad \frac{1}{U} = R_1$$

Alternatively, this may be stated as:

$$R_1 = \frac{1}{h_i} + \frac{L_2}{k_2} + \frac{L_3}{k_3} + \frac{1}{h_c}$$

EXAMPLE CALCULATION OF HEAT LOSS THROUGH A WALL

An exterior building wall consists of 100 mm of brick, 200 mm of dense concrete, and 20 mm of gypsum plaster, for which the thermal conductivities are, respectively, k = 0.50, 1.50, and 1.20 W/(m · K). The surface heat transfer (film) coefficients are as follows: (interior) h_i = 8.1 and (exterior) h_c = 19.0 W/(m² · K). What is the heat loss through a 2400 mm (2.4 m) by 6000 mm (6.0 m) panel of this wall when there is a temperature difference of 30°C (30°K)?

THERMAL CONDUCTIVITY

The thermal conductivity, or k-value, of a material is defined as the amount of heat energy conducted through a unit area of unit thickness in unit time with unit temperature difference between the two faces. In SI the unit W/(m · K) replaces Btu · in/h · ft² · °F, but if unit time is considered useful, the alternative expression is J/(s · m · K), because 1 W = 1 J/s. Unit thickness has been canceled out against unit area; otherwise the expression should be J · m/(s · m² · K), which directly resembles the customary expression in terms of constituent units.

OVERALL HEAT TRANSFER

Conductivity generally increases with the level of absolute temperature. Some typical thermal conductivities (k-values) at 300 K are:

MATERIAL OR SUBSTANCE	K = W/m · K
Copper	386
Aluminum	202
Steel	55
Concrete	0.9-1.4
Glass	0.8-1.1
Brick	0.4-0.7
Water	0.614
Mineral wool	0.04
Air	0.0262

Computation of thermal resistance:

$$R_T = \frac{1}{8.1} + \frac{0.100}{0.50} + \frac{0.200}{1.50} + \frac{0.020}{1.20} + \frac{1}{19.0}$$

$$= 0.5261 \ m^2 \cdot K/W$$

$$U = \frac{1}{R_T}; \qquad U = 1.901 \ W/(m^2 \cdot K)$$

$$q = U \cdot A \cdot \Delta T$$

$$q = 1.901(2.4 \times 6.0)30$$

$$= 821 \ W = 821 \ J/s$$

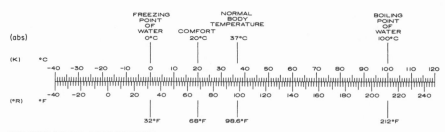

TEMPERATURE CONVERSION

ENERGY VALUES FOR ALTERNATIVE ENERGY SOURCES

ENERGY SOURCE AND QUANTITY	VALUE (MEGAJOULES, MJ)
1 kg of dry wood (8600 Btu/lb)	20
1 kg of bituminous coal (25 800 000 Btu/ton)	30
1 L of kerosene (135 000 Btu/gal)	37.6
1 L of crude oil (5 800 000 Btu/barrel)	38.5
1 m³ of natural gas (1050 Btu/ft³)	39
1 kWh of electricity	3.6
1 therm (100,000 Btu)	105.5

MOMENT BENDING, TORSIONAL

Bending moment and torsional moment are concepts of statics. Both involve the production of a force and a perpendicular distance, the latter being termed the moment arm. Thus the primary SI unit is the newton-meter, which may be symbolized as N · m, kN · m, and so on.

TORQUE

When rotation occurs as a result of an applied moment the condition is one requiring the application of the principles of dynamics. In such cases the key factor is torque, which is based on a product of force and distance moved along the line of action of the force. This product is expressed in newton-meters per radian (N · m/rad), which is equal to joules per radian (J/rad). The radian may be omitted where only complete revolutions are of concern or where dynamic conditions are equated instantaneously with static conditions.

PRESSURE, STRESS, ELASTIC MODULUS

These may be stated directly either in pascals (Pa) or in newtons per square meter (N/m²). Common multiples are kPa, MPa, GPa or kN/m², MN/m², GN/m². Occasionally stress is expressed in newtons per square millimeter (N/mm²).

MOMENT OF INERTIA

The mass moment of inertia of any body relating to rotation about a given axis is the second moment of the particles of that mass about the given axis and as such is given generally in kilogram-square meters per radian squared (kg · m²/rad²). The radius of gyration is normally given in meters per radian (m/rad). The radian may be omitted where only complete revolutions are of concern or where dynamic conditions are equated instantaneously with static conditions.

Second moment of area (1) and section modulus (S) of the cross-section of structural sections or machine parts are usually preferred in terms of 10^6 mm⁴ and 10^3 mm³, respectively, for consistency with other dimensions of sections, which usually will be given in millimeters.

ANGULAR MEASURE

The "radian" (rad), although not a base unit, is specifically identified as a "supplementary unit" and as such is the preferred unit for measurement of plane angles. The customary units of degrees, minutes, and seconds of angular measure are considered to be outside SI, but are acceptable where there is a specific practical reason to use them, as in cartography. If degrees are to be used, a statement of parts of degrees in decimals is preferred. The SI unit of solid angle is the "steradian" (sr).

FLUID MECHANICS

Fluid mechanics utilizes the physical concepts of density (mass per unit volume), dynamic viscosity, kinematic viscosity, surface tension, potential energy, and pressure in dealing with the flow of relatively incompressible fluids at constant temperatures. There is a proper SI expression for each of these quantities, derived from base units in accordance with applicable physical relationships. Metric considerations in fluid mechanics are discussed in other engineering metric reference sources.

UNITS OUTSIDE SI NOT RECOMMENDED FOR USE

UNIT NAME	SYMBOL	VALUE IN SI UNITS	
dyne	dyn	10^{-5} N	(or 10 uN)
bar	bar	10^5 Pa	(or 100 kPa)
erg	erg	10^{-7} J	(or 100 nJ)
poise	P	10^{-1} Pa · s	(or 100 mPa · s)
stokes	St	10^{-4} m²/s	(or 100 mm²/s)
gauss	Gs, (G)	10^{-4} T	(or 100 uT)
maxwell	Mx	10^{-8} Wb	(or 10 nWb)
stilb	sb	10^4 cd/m²	(or 10 kcd/m²)
phot	ph	10^4 lx	(or 10 klx)
kilogram-force	kgf	9.806 65 N	
calorie (int.)	cal	4.1868 J	
kilocalorie (int.)	kcal	4.1868 kJ	
torr	torr	133.322 Pa	
oersted	Oe	79.5775 A/m	

ROUNDING OF NUMBERS

Conversion from one measuring system to another requires rounding of numbers. For example, a quantity rounded to the nearest meter has an implied precision of ±0.5 m, while a quantity rounded to the nearest foot has an implied precision of ±0.5 ft. The two are quite different. If a quantity in feet (to the nearest foot) is to be converted to meters, any rounding should be to the nearest 0.3 m.

In making the changeover to SI, critical decisions about new rounded values will be required for many factors widely used in technical work.

SIGNIFICANT DIGITS

In general, the result of any multiplication, division, addition, or subtraction cannot be given in more significant digits than are present in any one component of the original data. This condition pertains regardless of the number of decimal places in which a conversion factor is given.

In reference tables conversion factors should be stated to a substantial number of decimal places to cover a wide range of uses. It is the responsibility of the user

SINGLE LINE, DUAL SCALE CHARTS

Conversions also can be interpreted on a single line, dual scale, graphical representation.

METERS TO FEET   (CONVERSION FACTORS I M = 3.281 FT, I FT = 0.3048 M)

ACOUSTICS

SI units have been applied in acoustics to define frequency (hertz), sound power (watt), sound intensity (watt per square meter), and sound pressure level (pascal).

The reference quantities for the dimensionless logarithmic unit decibel (dB) are also expressed in SI units.

1. Sound power reference quantity: 1 pW = 10^{-12} W; therefore

$$\text{sound power level (dB)} = 10 \log_{10} \frac{\text{actual power (W)}}{10^{-12}}$$

2. Sound intensity reference quantity: 1 pW/m² = 10^{-12} W/m2; therefore

sound intensity level (dB)

$$= 10 \log_{10} \frac{\text{actual intensity (W/m}^2)}{10^{-12}}$$

3. Sound pressure reference quantity: 20 Pa = 2 x 20×10^6 Pa; therefore

sound pressure level (dB)

$$= 20 \log_{10} \frac{\text{actual pressure (Pa)}}{20 \times 10^6}$$

ELECTRICITY AND MAGNETISM

Electrical engineering, for many years, has used metric (SI) units as practical electrical units. These units are all coherent in that they are formed directly from SI base and derived units on a unity (one-to-one) basis.

to interpret the resultant decimal number to the extent applicable.

Example: What is the equivalent of 3 miles in terms of kilometers?

CONVERSION FACTOR	DIRECT MULTIPLICATION	SIGNIFICANT EQUIVALENT	
miles to kilometers = 1.609	3 mi = 4.827 km	3 mi	5 km
Or, in reverse form: kilometers to miles = 0.6214	5 km = 3.107 mi	5 km	3 mi

ABANDONED UNITS

For various reasons many derived and specialized units will fall into disuse as the changeover to SI progresses. Some, like British thermal unit (Btu) and horsepower (hp), will be dropped because they are based on the inch-pound (English) system.

Former metric units, of the c.g.s. variety, are no longer recommended. In addition a number of traditional metric units are outside SI, and their use is to be avoided.

The only changes involved the use of the term "siemens" (S) for electrical conductance, instead of the previous name "mho," and the replacement of the cycle per second with the SI unit hertz (Hz).

The kilowatt-hour (kWh) is not an SI unit but will probably be retained for the measurement of electrical energy consumption because of its long history and extensive use. The recalibration of existing electricity meters from kilowatt-hours to megajoules (MJ), on the basis of 1 kWh = 3.6 MJ, hardly seems justified at this time. However, the kilowatt-hour should not be introduced into new areas.

ILLUMINATION ENGINEERING

The SI units for luminous intensity, the candela (cd), and for luminous flux, the lumen (lm), are already in general use in the United States.

Illuminance (luminous flux per unit area) will be expressed in the derived SI unit lux (lx), which is a special name for the lumen per square meter (lm/m²). The lux (lx) and kilolux (klx) replace the footcandle, which is also known as the lumen per square foot.

Similarly, the SI unit of luminance, the candela per square meter (cd/m²), replaces the candela per square foot, the lambert, and the footlambert.

Conversion factors are:

1 lx =	0.092 footcandle
1 footcandle =	10.7639 lx
1 klx =	92.903 footcandles
1 cd/m² =	0.092 903 cd/ft²
=	0.291 964 footlambert
1 cd/ft² =	10.7639 cd/m²
1 footlambert =	3.426 259 cd/m²

UNITS FOR ELECTRICITY AND MAGNETISM

QUANTITY	UNIT NAME	SYMBOL	DERIVATION	REMARKS
Electric current	ampere	A		SI base unit
Current density	ampere per square meter	A/m²		
Magnetic field strength	ampere per meter	A/m		
Electric charge quantity of electricity	coulomb	C	(A · s)	
Electric charge density	coulomb per cubic meter	C/m³		
Electric potential, electromotive force	volt	V	(W/A)	
Electric field strength	volt per meter	V/m		1 V/m = 1 N/C
Electric capacitance	farad	F	(C/V)	
Permittivity	farad per meter	F/m		
Electric resistance	ohm	Ω	(V/A)	
Electric conductance	siemens	S	(A/V)	Replaces "mho"; also equals 1/Ω
Electric power	watt	W	(V · A)	Also equals J/s
Magnetic flux	weber	Wb	(V · s)	
Magnetic flux density	tesla	T	(Wb/m²)	1 T = 1 V · s/m²
Inductance	henry	H	(Wb/A)	1 H = 1 V · s/A
Permeability	henry per meter	H/m		

METRIC DRAWINGS

Metric drawing sizes are those set by the International Standards Organization (ISO), "A" Series, with a $1:\sqrt{2}$ aspect ratio. These sizes are suitable for reduction using a 35 mm microfilm frame. Metric drawing scales are comparable to U.S. customary scales, as shown in the table. The metric system favors the use of ratios to define slopes, and a table comparing this with pitches and percentages is shown. Other recommended metric drawing practices are similar to customary standard drawing practices.

DRAWING SHEET DIMENSIONS (MM)

SIZE	SHEET SIZE	TOP AND BOTTOM	BINDING MARGIN	RIGHT BORDER	NET SIZE
A0	1189 x 841	20	40	16	1133 x 801
A1	841 x 594	14	28	12	801 x 566
A2	594 x 420	10	20	8	566 x 400
A3	420 x 297	7	20	6	394 x 283
A4*	210 x 297	7	20	6	184 x 283
B1	1000 x 707	14	28	12	960 x 679

*The filing edge of A4 size sheets is the long edge.

COMPARISON OF DRAWING SCALES

METRIC SCALES	CUSTOMARY RATIO	CUSTOMARY SCALES
1:5	1:4	3'' = 1'0''
1:10	1:18	1½'' = 1'0''
	1:12	1'' = 1'0''
1:20	1:16	¾'' = 1'0''
	1:24	½'' = 1'0''
1:50	1:48	¼'' = 1'0''
1:100	1:96	⅛'' = 1'0''
1:200	1:92	1/16'' = 1'0''
1:500	1:384	1/32'' = 1'0''
	1:480	1'' = 40'0''
	1:600	1'' = 50'0''
1:1000	1:960	1'' = 80'0''
	1:1200	1'' = 100'0''
1:2000	1:2400	1'' = 200'0''
1:5000	1:4800	1'' = 400'0''
	1:6000	1'' = 500'0''
1:10 000	1:10 560	6'' = 1 mi
	1:12 000	1'' = 1000'0''
1:25 000	1:21 120	3'' = 1 mi
	1:24 000	1'' = 2000'0''
1:50 000	1:63 360	1'' = 1 mi
1:100 000	1:126 720	½'' = 1 mi

EXPRESSION OF SLOPE

RATIO Y/X	ANGLE	ANGLE (RAD)	PERCENTAGE (%)
Shallow slopes			
1:100	0°34'	0.0100	1
1:67	0°52'	0.0150	1.5
1:57	1°	0.0175	1.75
1:50	1°09'	0.0200	2
1:40	1°26'	0.0250	2.5
1:33	1°43'	0.0300	3
1:29	2°	0.0349	3.5
1:25	2°17'	0.0399	4
1:20	2°52'	0.0499	5
1:19	3°	0.0524	5.25
Slight slopes			
1:17	3°26'	0.0599	6
1:15	3°48'	0.0664	6.7
1:14.3	4°	0.0698	7
1:12	4°46'	0.0832	8.3
1:11.4	5°	0.0873	8.75
1:10	5°43'	0.0998	10
1:9.5	6°	0.1047	10.5
1:8	7°07'	0.1245	12.5
1:7.1	8°	0.1396	14
1:6.7	8°32'	0.1490	15
1:6	9°28'	0.1652	16.7
1:5.7	10°	0.1745	17.6
1:5	11°19'	0.1975	20
1:4.5	12°30'	0.2182	22.2
1:4	14°02'	0.2450	25
Medium slopes			
1:3.7	15°	0.2618	25.8
1:3.3	16°42'	0.2915	30
1:3	18°26'	0.3217	33.3
1:2.75	20°	0.3491	36.4
1:2.5	21°48'	0.3805	40
1:2.4	22°30'	0.3927	41.4
1:2.15	25°	0.4363	46.6
1:2	26°34'	0.4537	50
1:1.73	30°	0.5326	57.5
1:1.67	30°58'	0.5405	60
1:1.5	33°42'	0.5880	67
1:1.33	36°52'	0.6434	75
1:1.2	40°	0.6981	84
1:1	45°	0.7854	100
Steep slopes			
1.19:1	50°	0.8727	119
1.43:1	55°	0.9599	143
1.5:1	56°19'	0.9827	150
1.73:1	60°	1.0472	173
2:1	63°26'	1.1071	200
2.15:1	65°	1.1345	215
2.5:1	68°12'	1.1903	250
2.75:1	70°	1.2217	275
3:1	71°34'	1.2491	300
3.73:1	75°	1.3090	373
4:1	75°58'	1.3253	400
5:1	78°42'	1.3735	500
5.67:1	80°	1.3963	567
6:1	80°32'	1.4056	600
11.43:1	85°	1.4835	1143
∞	90°	1.5708	∞

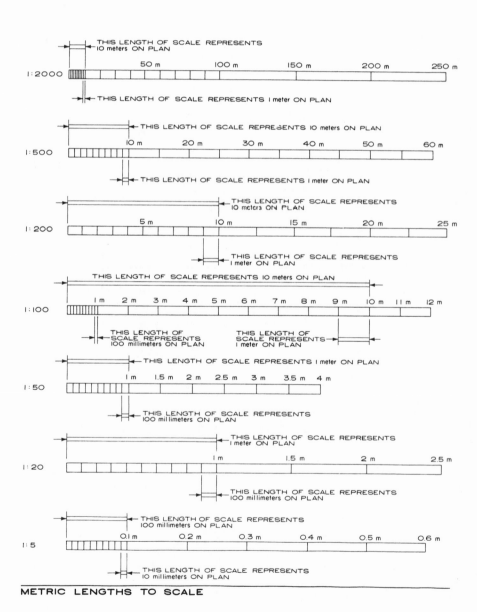

METRIC LENGTHS TO SCALE

The Basic Module for the construction industry is 100 mm. This is an internationally accepted value. The basic module should apply to building components as well as entire buildings.

Multimodules, if carefully selected, can be coordinated with the controlling dimensions for a building, thus minimizing component sizes.

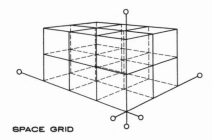

SPACE GRID

In a dimensional reference system the reference space grid is made up of the horizontal and vertical planes used to define the locations of points, lines, or surfaces in space.

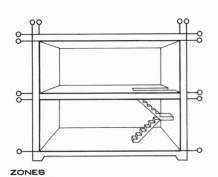

ZONES

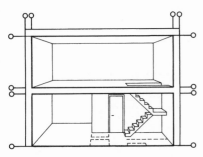

ACTIVITY SPACES

Zones and usable spaces: Zones are the spaces between controlling planes. They may be occupied but not always filled by one or more components. Finishes should be contained within the zone, although on occasion they may be placed outside as long as this does not inhibit the use of other coordinated components.

The space between zones can be referred to as an activity space. This is the space in which human or mechanical activities take place. In turn it may contain components such as partitions or stairs.

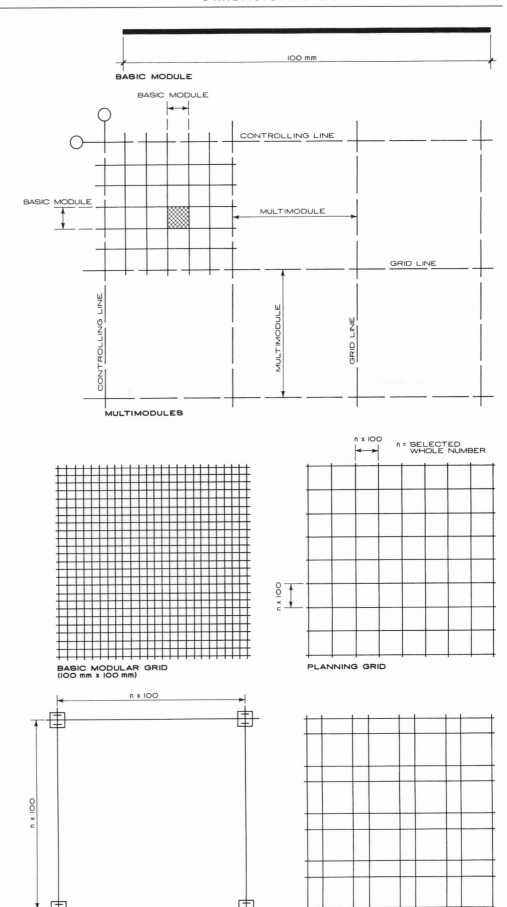

BASIC MODULE

MULTIMODULES

BASIC MODULAR GRID (100 mm x 100 mm)

PLANNING GRID

STRUCTURAL GRID

TARTAN GRID: 1:2 RATIO OF BANDWIDTHS

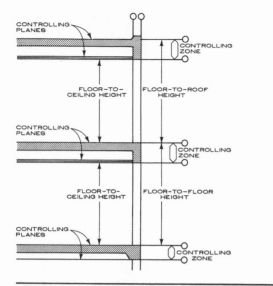

VERTICAL CONTROLLING DIMENSIONS

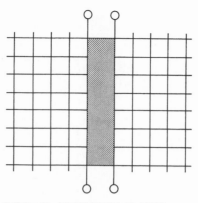

PARALLEL REFERENCE PLANES

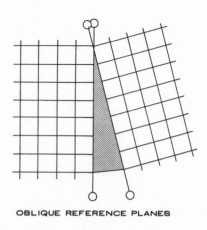

OBLIQUE REFERENCE PLANES

Neutral zones are nonmodular interruptions of a modular reference grid to accommodate intermediate building elements, such as walls or floors, or parts of a building placed at an angle with a separate grid for each portion.

NEUTRAL ZONES

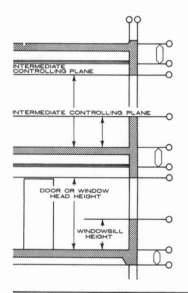

INTERMEDIATE CONTROLLING PLANES

CONTROLLING DIMENSIONS IN BUILDING DESIGN

The application of dimensional coordination in building design involves the use of horizontal and vertical controlling dimensions, either axial or face-to-face, between the major reference planes for structural elements. Enclosing elements, or "solids," are assigned controlling zones, such as floors, roofs, structural walls, or columns. Controlling lines normally coincide with the space reference system. To permit maximum flexibility and interchangeability of building components, controlling dimensions should bear a direct relationship to the coordinating sizes of building products.

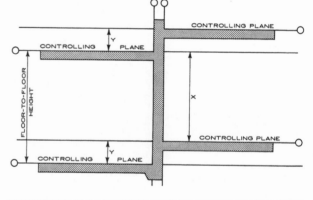

CHANGE OF LEVEL FOR FLOORS AND ROOFS

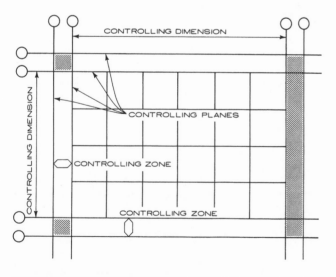

BOUNDARY CONTROLLING PLANES

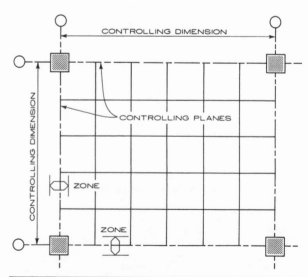

AXIAL CONTROLLING PLANES

HORIZONTAL CONTROLLING DIMENSIONS (mm)

DIMENSIONS	MULTIPLES OF MULTIMODULES 300	600	1200	3000	6000	MOST PRE-FERRED VALUES
300	x					
600	x	x				x
900	x					
1 200	x	x	x			x
1 500	x					
1 800	x	x				x
2 100	x					
2 400	x	x	x			x
2 700	x					
3 000	x	x		x		x
3 300	x					
3 600	x	x	x			x
4 200		x				
4 800		x	x			x
5 400		x				
6 000		x	x	x	x	x
6 600		x				
7 200		x	x			x
7 800		x				
8 400		x	x			x
9 000		x		x		x
9 600		x	x			x
10 800			x			
12 000			x	x	x	x
13 200			x			
14 000			x			
15 000				x		
15 600			x			
16 800			x			
18 000			x	x	x	x
19 200			x			
20 400			x			
21 000				x		
21 600			x			
22 800			x			
24 000			x	x	x	x
25 200			x			
26 400			x			
27 000				x		
27 600			x			
30 000			x	x	x	x

NOMINAL AND COORDINATING DIMENSIONS FOR CLAY MASONRY: FULL SIZE UNITS

NOMINAL HEIGHT (mm)	COORDINATING HEIGHT (mm)	COORDINATING LENGTH (mm)
50	2 courses to 100	300
67	3 courses to 200	200 300
75	4 courses to 300	200 300
80	5 courses to 400	200 300
100	100	200 300 400
133	3 courses to 400	200 300 400
150	2 courses to 300	300 400
200	200	200 300 400
300	300	300

Note: For horizontal flexibility and/or to maintain bond patterns, the following supplementary lengths may be required:

NOMINAL LENGTH (mm)	SUPPLEMENTARY LENGTHS (mm)
200	100
300	100, 150, 200, 250
400	100, 200, 300

PREFERRED SIZES FOR BUILDING COMPONENTS AND ASSEMBLIES

CATEGORY	EXAMPLES	PREFERRED SIZES (mm) 1ST	2ND
Small (under 500 mm)	Brick block, tile, paving units	100 200 300 400	25 50 75 150 250
Medium (under 1 500 mm)	Panels, partitions, doorsets, windows, slabs	600 800 900 1 200	500 700 1 000 1 400 — See Note 1
Large (under 3 600 mm)	Precast floor and wall units, panels, doors, windows, stairs	1 800 2 400 3 000 3 600	(n x 300): 1 500 2 100 2 700 3 300 — (n x 200): 1 600 2 000 2 200 2 600 2 800 3 200 3 400 — See Note 2
Very Large (over 3 600 mm)	Prefabricated building elements, precast floor and roof sections	4 800 6 000 7 200 8 400 9 500 10 800 12 000	(n x 600): 4 200 6 600 7 800 9 000 10 200 11 400 — (n x 1 500): 4 500 7 500 10 500 — See Note 3

NOTES

1. For the purposes of rationalization, those multiples of 100 mm, above 1 000 mm, that are prime numbers (e.g., 1 100, 1 300) constitute a lower order of preferences when special requirements exist.
2. Alternative second preferences are shown; for vertical dimensions the use of multiples of 200 mm may sometimes be more appropriate than the use of multiples of 300 mm, as with masonry materials.
3. Alternative second preferences are shown; for some projects it will be more appropriate to size large components or assemblies in multiples of 1 500 mm.

PRODUCTS FOR USE IN THE VERTICAL PLANE: MASONRY PANELS

VERTICAL (mm)	HORIZONTAL (mm) 600 x n	300 x n	200 x n
600 x n	1	2	3
220 x n	2	3	3
100 x n	3	3	

GENERAL NOTES

Preferred sizes and dimensions allow better coordination between manufactured components, design, and construction operations. The tables are presented to allow an open system of selection compatible with dimensional coordination concepts presented on the preceding pages. Preferred dimensions in building are selected multimodules for horizontal and vertical applications derived from the basic 100 mm module.

The preferred dimension concept is similar to the customary 4 in. module concept presently in use in the construction industry. As an example, preferred horizontal controlling dimensions similar to the customary 1, 2, or 4 ft multimodule in metric terms may be stated this way:

up to 3600 mm : 300 mm

up to 9600 mm : 600 mm

above 9600 mm : 1200 mm

For large dimensions, 6000 mm may be more useful or, as a second preference, 3000 mm.

Certain numbers are preferred because they are divisible by 2 or 3. Such numbers are 600, 1200, 1800, 2400 mm, as indicated in the table. The long history of using such multimodules is incorporated in the conversion plans to SI metric.

Refer to standards and manufacturer's data for application of the preferred SI metric sizes and dimensions.

PREFERRED DIMENSIONS FOR PANELS AND PLANKS

TYPE	PREFERENCE	WIDTH (mm)	LENGTH (mm)
Panels	First	1 200	2 400
	Second	600	2 400 3 000
		1 200	1 200 1 800 3 000 3 600
	Third	1 200	2 100 2 700
Planks	First	400	2 400
	Second	400	3 000 3 600

PREFERRED DOOR SIZES

HEIGHT (mm)	SINGLE WIDTH 700*	800	900	1 000	DOUBLE WIDTH 1 200	1 500	1 800
2 100	2	2	1	2	1	1	1
2 200	2	2	2	1	2	2	1
2 400	2	1	1	1	2	2	1

*Too narrow for wheelchair use.

PREFERRED SIZES FOR WINDOWS

HEIGHT (mm)	WIDTH (mm) 600	900	1200	1500	1800	2100	2400	2700	3000
600	1	2	1	2	1	2	1	2	1
800	2	3	2	3	2	3	2	3	2
900	2	3	2	3	2	3	2	3	2
1000	2	3	2	3	2	3	2	3	2
1200	1	2	1	2	1	2	1	2	1
1400	2	3	2	3	2	3	2	3	2
1500	2	3	2	3	2	3	2	3	2
1600	2	3	2	3	2	3	2	3	2
1800	1	2	1	2	1	2	1	2	1
2000	2	3	2	3	2	3	2	3	2
2100	2	3	2	3	2	3	2	3	2
2400	1	2	1	2	1	2	1	2	1
2700	2	3	2	3	2	3	2	3	2
3000	1	2	1	2	1	2	1	2	1

Note: In some construction, widths of 1000, 1400, 1600, and 2000 mm may be required for brick or block sizes and, combined with first preference heights, may be substituted as a third preference series of sizes.

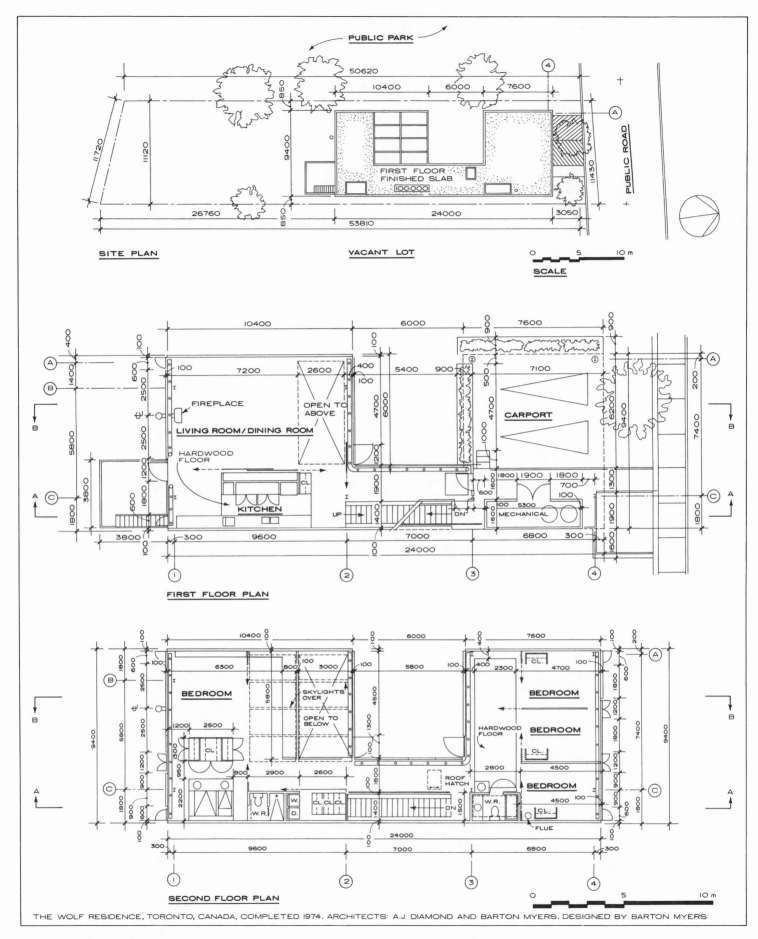

SITE PLAN   VACANT LOT

SCALE

FIRST FLOOR PLAN

SECOND FLOOR PLAN

THE WOLF RESIDENCE, TORONTO, CANADA, COMPLETED 1974. ARCHITECTS: A.J. DIAMOND AND BARTON MYERS. DESIGNED BY BARTON MYERS

Robert Hill, Barton Myers Associates; Toronto, Canada

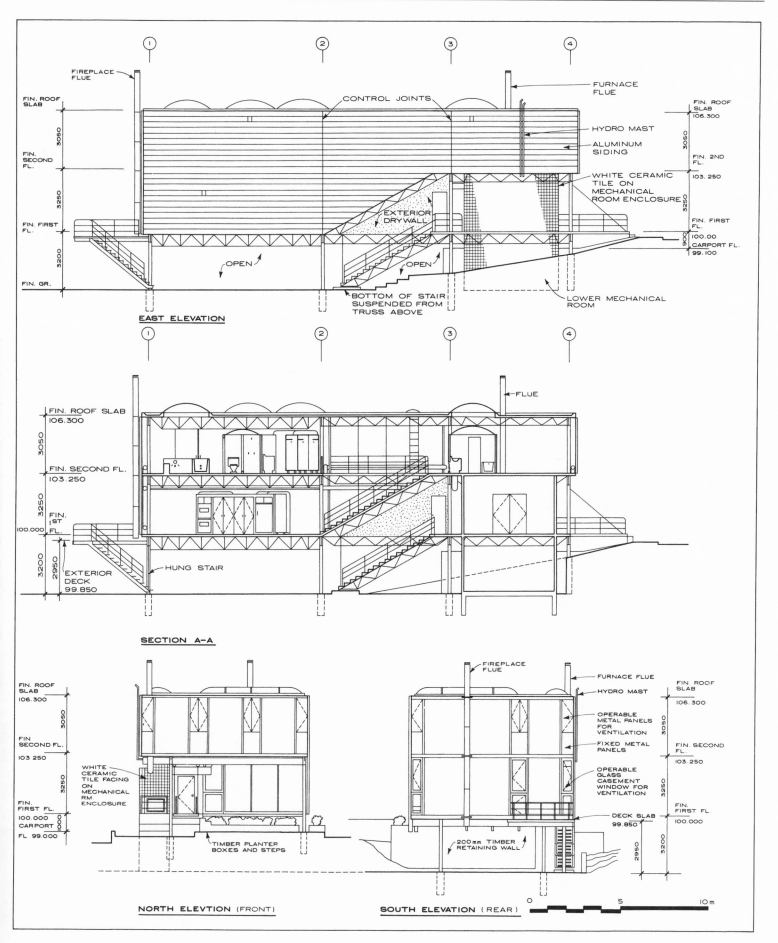

EAST ELEVATION

SECTION A-A

NORTH ELEVTION (FRONT)

SOUTH ELEVATION (REAR)

Robert Hill, Barton Myers Associates; Toronto, Canada

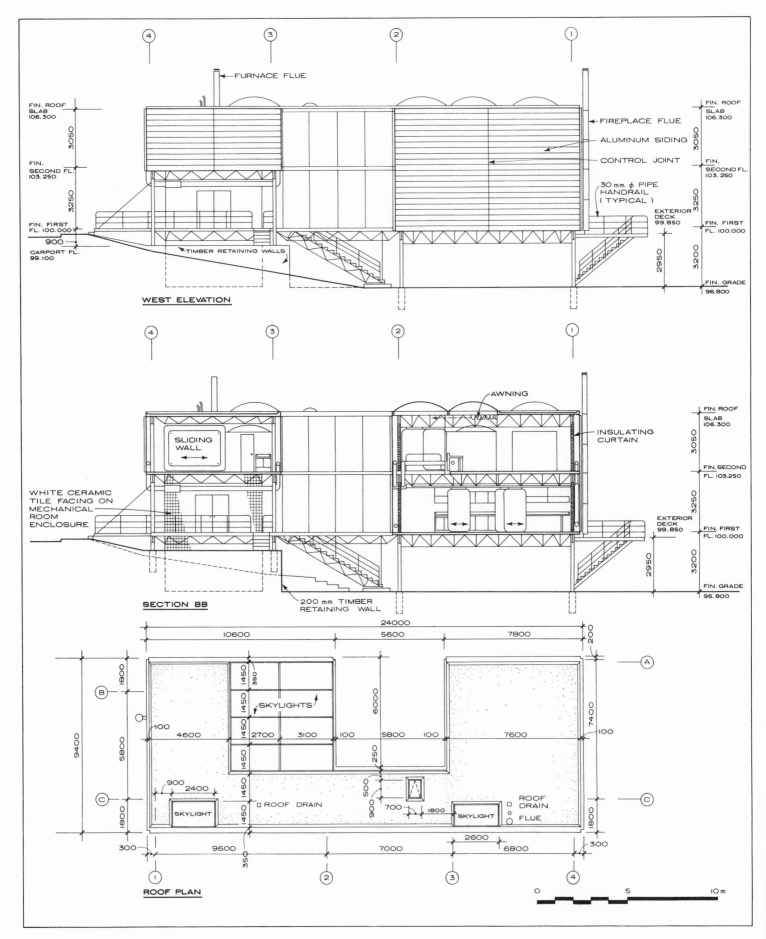

FURNACE FLUE

FIN. ROOF
SLAB
106.300

3050

FIN.
SECOND FL.
103.250

3250

FIN. FIRST
FL. 100.000

900

CARPORT FL.
99.100

TIMBER RETAINING WALLS

WEST ELEVATION

FIREPLACE FLUE

ALUMINUM SIDING

CONTROL JOINT

30 mm. φ PIPE
HANDRAIL
(TYPICAL)

EXTERIOR
DECK
99.850

FIN. ROOF
SLAB
106.300

3050

FIN.
SECOND FL.
103.250

3250

FIN. FIRST
FL. 100.000

2950

3200

FIN. GRADE
96.800

AWNING

SLIDING
WALL

INSULATING
CURTAIN

WHITE CERAMIC
TILE FACING ON
MECHANICAL
ROOM
ENCLOSURE

SECTION BB

200 mm TIMBER
RETAINING WALL

FIN. ROOF
SLAB
106.300

3050

FIN. SECOND
FL. 103.250

3250

EXTERIOR
DECK
99.850

FIN. FIRST
FL. 100.000

2950

3200

FIN. GRADE
96.800

24000

10600   5600   7800   200

1800

9400

5800

1800

300   9600   350   7000   2600   6800   300

100

4600   2700   3100   100   5800   100   7600

1450
350

1450

1450

1450

1450

1450

SKYLIGHTS

6000

250

500

900

700   1800

900
2400

SKYLIGHT

ROOF DRAIN

ROOF
DRAIN

FLUE

SKYLIGHT

7400   100

1800

A

B

C

C

1   2   3   4

ROOF PLAN

0   5   10 m

Robert Hill, Barton Myers Associates; Toronto, Canada

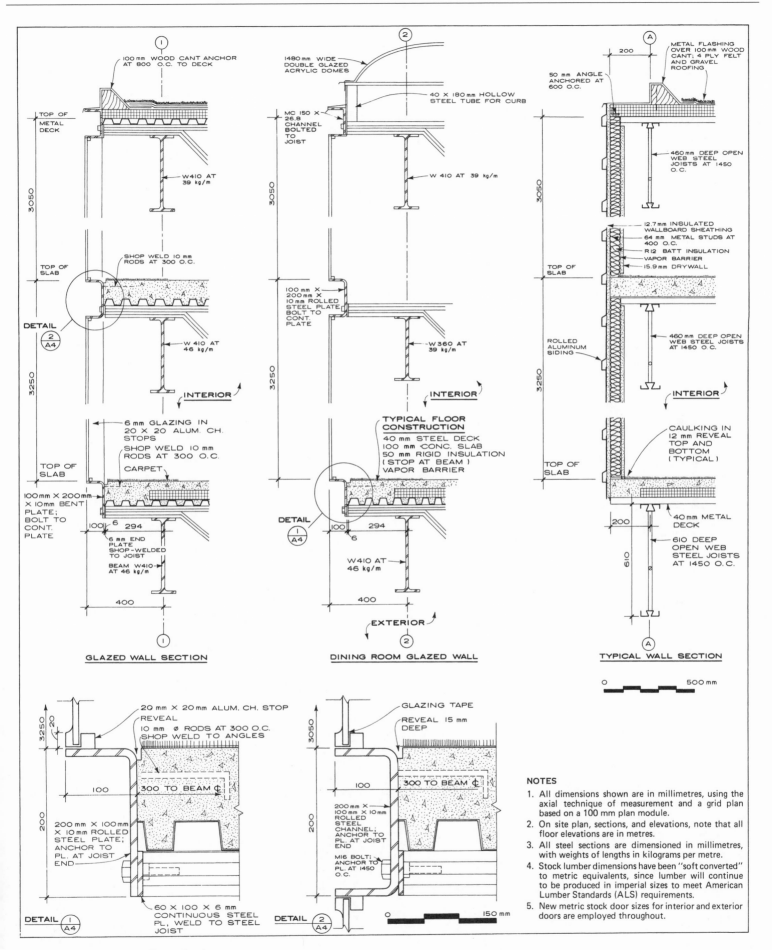

GLAZED WALL SECTION

DINING ROOM GLAZED WALL

TYPICAL WALL SECTION

NOTES

1. All dimensions shown are in millimetres, using the axial technique of measurement and a grid plan based on a 100 mm plan module.
2. On site plan, sections, and elevations, note that all floor elevations are in metres.
3. All steel sections are dimensioned in millimetres, with weights of lengths in kilograms per metre.
4. Stock lumber dimensions have been "soft converted" to metric equivalents, since lumber will continue to be produced in imperial sizes to meet American Lumber Standards (ALS) requirements.
5. New metric stock door sizes for interior and exterior doors are employed throughout.

Robert Hill, Barton Myers Associates; Toronto, Canada

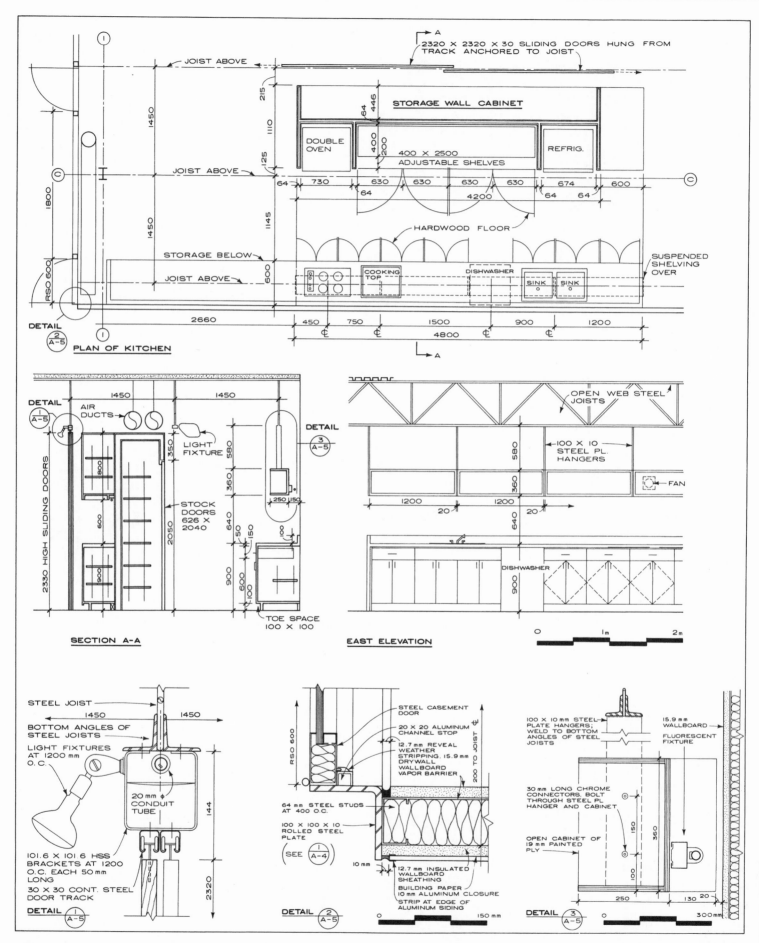

PLAN OF KITCHEN

SECTION A-A

EAST ELEVATION

Robert Hill, Barton Myers Associates; Toronto, Canada

INCHES AND FRACTIONS TO MILLIMETERS (1 IN. = 25.4 mm)

INCHES	0	1	2	3	4	5	6	7	8	9	10	11
						MILLIMETERS (mm)						
0	...	25.40	50.80	76.20	101.60	127.00	152.40	177.80	203.20	228.60	254.00	279.40
1/16	1.59	26.99	52.39	77.79	103.19	128.59	153.99	179.39	204.79	230.19	255.59	280.99
1/8	3.18	28.58	53.98	79.38	104.78	130.18	155.58	180.98	206.38	231.78	257.18	282.58
3/16	4.76	30.16	55.56	80.96	106.36	131.76	157.16	182.56	207.96	233.36	258.76	284.16
1/4	6.35	31.75	57.15	82.55	107.95	133.35	158.75	184.15	209.55	234.95	260.35	285.75
5/16	7.94	33.34	58.74	84.14	109.54	134.94	160.34	185.74	211.14	236.54	261.94	287.34
3/8	9.53	34.93	60.33	85.73	111.13	136.53	161.93	187.33	212.73	238.13	263.53	288.93
7/16	11.11	36.51	61.91	87.31	112.71	138.11	163.51	188.91	214.31	239.71	265.11	290.51
1/2	12.70	38.10	63.50	88.90	114.30	139.70	165.10	190.50	215.90	241.30	266.70	292.10
9/16	14.29	39.69	65.09	90.49	115.89	141.29	166.69	192.09	217.49	242.89	268.29	293.69
5/8	15.88	41.28	66.68	92.08	117.48	142.88	168.28	193.68	219.08	244.48	269.88	295.28
11/16	17.46	42.86	68.26	93.66	119.06	144.46	169.86	195.26	220.66	246.06	271.46	296.86
3/4	19.05	44.45	69.85	95.25	120.65	146.05	171.45	196.85	222.25	247.65	273.05	298.45
13/16	20.64	46.04	71.44	96.84	122.24	147.64	173.04	198.44	223.84	249.24	274.64	300.04
7/8	22.23	47.63	73.03	98.43	123.83	149.23	174.63	200.03	225.43	250.83	276.23	301.63
15/16	23.81	49.21	74.61	100.01	125.41	150.81	176.21	201.61	227.01	252.41	277.81	303.21

FEET AND INCHES TO MILLIMETERS (1 FT = 304.8 mm; 1 IN. = 25.4 mm)

INCHES	0	1	2	3	4	5	6	7	8	9	10	11
MILLIMETERS	...	25	51	76	102	127	152	178	203	229	254	279

FEET	0	1	2	3	4	5	6	7	8	9
						MILLIMETERS (mm)				
0	...	305	610	914	1 219	1 524	1 829	2 134	2 438	2 743
10	3 048	3 353	3 658	3 962	4 267	4 572	4 877	5 182	5 486	5 791
20	6 096	6 401	6 706	7 010	7 315	7 620	7 925	8 230	8 534	8 839
30	9 144	9 449	9 754	10 058	10 363	10 668	10 973	11 278	11 582	11 887
40	12 192	12 497	12 802	13 106	13 411	13 716	14 021	14 326	14 630	14 935
50	15 240	15 545	15 850	16 154	16 459	16 764	17 069	17 374	17 678	17 983
60	18 288	18 593	18 898	19 202	19 507	19 812	20 117	20 422	20 726	21 031
70	21 336	21 641	21 946	22 250	22 555	22 860	23 165	23 470	23 774	24 079
80	24 384	24 689	24 994	25 298	25 603	25 908	26 213	26 518	26 882	27 127
90	27 432	27 737	28 042	28 346	28 651	28 956	29 261	29 566	29 870	30 175
100	30 480	30 785	31 090	31 394	31 699	32 004	32 309	32 614	32 918	33 223
110	33 528	33 833	34 138	34 442	34 747	35 052	35 357	35 662	35 966	36 271
120	36 576	36 881	37 186	37 490	37 795	38 100	38 405	38 710	39 014	39 319
130	39 624	39 929	40 234	40 538	40 843	41 148	41 453	41 758	42 062	42 367
140	42 672	42 977	43 282	43 586	43 891	44 196	44 501	44 806	45 110	45 415
150	45 720									

FEET TO METERS (1 FT = 0.304 8 m)

FEET	0	1	2	3	4	5	6	7	8	9
						METERS (m)				
0	...	0.305	0.610	0.914	1.219	1.524	1.829	2.134	2.438	2.743
10	3.048	3.353	3.658	3.962	4.267	4.572	4.877	5.182	5.486	5.791
20	6.096	6.401	6.706	7.010	7.315	7.620	7.925	8.230	8.534	8.839
30	9.144	9.449	9.754	10.058	10.363	10.668	10.973	11.278	11.582	11.887
40	12.192	12.497	12.802	13.106	13.411	13.716	14.021	14.326	14.630	14.935
50	15.240	15.545	15.850	16.154	16.459	16.764	17.069	17.374	17.678	17.983
60	18.288	18.593	18.898	19.202	19.507	19.812	20.117	20.422	20.726	21.031
70	21.336	21.641	21.946	22.250	22.555	22.860	23.165	23.470	23.774	24.079
80	24.384	24.689	24.994	25.298	25.603	25.908	26.213	26.518	26.822	27.127
90	27.432	27.737	28.042	28.346	28.651	28.956	29.261	29.566	29.870	30.175
100	30.480	30.785	31.090	31.394	31.699	32.004	32.309	32.614	32.918	33.223
110	33.528	33.833	34.138	34.442	34.747	35.052	35.357	35.662	35.966	36.271
120	36.576	36.881	37.186	37.490	37.795	38.100	38.405	38.710	39.014	39.319
130	39.624	39.929	40.234	40.538	40.843	41.148	41.453	41.758	42.062	42.367
140	42.672	42.977	43.282	43.586	43.891	44.196	44.501	44.806	45.110	45.415
150	45.720	46.025	46.330	46.634	46.939	47.244	47.549	47.854	48.158	48.463
160	48.768	49.073	49.378	49.682	49.987	50.292	50.597	50.902	51.206	51.511
170	51.816	52.121	52.426	52.730	53.035	53.340	53.645	53.950	54.254	54.559
180	54.864	55.169	55.474	55.778	56.083	56.388	56.693	56.998	57.302	57.607
190	57.912	58.217	58.522	58.826	59.131	59.436	59.741	60.046	60.350	60.655
200	60.960									

MILES TO KILOMETERS (1 MI = 1.609 344 km)

MILES	0	1	2	3	4	5	6	7	8	9
					KILOMETERS (km)					
0	. . .	1.609	3.219	4.828	6.437	8.047	9.656	11.265	12.875	14.484
10	16.093	17.703	19.312	20.921	22.531	24.140	25.750	27.359	28.968	30.578
20	32.187	33.796	35.406	37.015	38.624	40.234	41.843	43.452	45.062	46.671
30	48.280	49.890	51.499	53.108	54.718	56.327	57.936	59.546	61.155	62.764
40	64.374	65.983	67.592	69.202	70.811	72.420	74.030	75.639	77.249	78.858
50	80.467	82.077	83.686	85.295	86.905	88.514	90.123	91.733	93.342	94.951
60	96.561	98.170	99.779	101.389	102.998	104.607	106.217	107.826	109.435	111.045
70	112.654	114.263	115.873	117.482	119.091	120.701	122.310	123.919	125.529	127.138
80	128.748	130.357	131.966	133.576	135.185	136.794	138.404	140.013	141.622	143.232
90	144.841	146.450	148.060	149.669	151.278	152.888	154.497	156.106	157.716	159.325
100	160.934	162.544	164.153	165.762	167.372	168.981	170.590	172.200	173.809	175.418
110	177.028	178.637	180.247	181.856	183.465	185.075	186.684	188.293	189.903	191.512
120	193.121	194.731	196.340	197.949	199.559	201.168	202.777	204.387	205.996	207.605
130	209.215	210.824	212.433	214.043	215.652	217.261	218.871	220.480	222.089	223.699
140	225.308	226.918	228.527	230.136	231.746	233.355	234.964	236.574	238.183	239.792
150	241.402	243.011	244.620	246.230	247.839	249.448	251.058	252.667	254.276	255.866
160	257.495	259.104	260.714	262.323	263.932	265.542	267.151	268.760	270.370	271.979
170	273.588	275.198	276.807	278.417	280.026	281.635	283.245	284.854	286.463	288.073
180	289.682	291.291	292.901	294.510	296.119	297.729	299.338	300.947	302.557	304.166
190	305.775	307.385	308.994	310.603	312.213	313.822	315.431	317.041	318.650	320.259
200	321.869									

SQUARE INCHES TO SQUARE MILLIMETERS (1 IN.^{2} = 645.16 mm^2)

SQUARE INCHES	0	1	2	3	4	5	6	7	8	9
					SQUARE MILLIMETERS (mm^2)					
0	. . .	0.645	1.290	1.935	2.581	3.226	3.781	4.516	5.161	5.806
10	6.452	7.097	7.742	8.387	9.032	9.677	10.323	10.968	11.613	12.258
20	12.903	13.548	14.194	14.839	15.484	16.129	16.774	17.419	18.064	18.710
30	19.355	20.000	20.645	21.290	21.935	22.581	23.226	23.871	24.516	25.161
40	25.806	26.452	27.097	27.742	28.387	29.032	29.677	30.323	30.968	31.613
50	32.258	32.903	33.548	34.193	34.839	35.484	36.129	36.774	37.419	38.064
60	38.710	39.355	40.000	40.645	41.290	41.935	42.581	43.226	43.871	44.516
70	45.161	45.806	46.452	47.097	47.742	48.387	49.032	49.677	50.322	50.968
80	51.613	52.258	52.903	53.548	54.193	54.839	55.484	56.129	56.774	57.419
90	58.064	58.710	59.355	60.000	60.645	61.290	61.935	62.581	63.226	63.871
100	64.516	65.161	65.806	66.451	67.097	67.742	68.387	69.032	69.677	70.322
110	70.968	71.613	72.258	72.903	73.548	74.193	74.839	75.484	76.129	76.774
120	77.419	78.064	78.710	79.355	80.000	80.645	81.290	81.935	82.580	83.226
130	83.871	84.516	85.161	85.806	86.451	87.097	87.742	88.387	89.032	89.677
140	90.322	90.968	91.613	92.258	92.903					

SQUARE FEET TO SQUARE METERS (1 FT^2 = 0.0929 m^2)

SQUARE FEET	0	1	2	3	4	5	6	7	8	9
SQUARE METER	. . .	0.09	0.19	0.28	0.37	0.46	0.56	0.65	0.74	0.84

SQUARE FEET	0	10	20	30	40	50	60	70	80	90
					SQUARE METERS (m^2)					
0	. . .	0.93	1.86	2.79	3.72	4.65	5.57	6.50	7.43	8.36
100	9.29	10.22	11.15	12.08	13.01	13.94	14.86	15.79	16.72	17.65
200	18.58	19.51	20.44	21.37	22.30	23.23	24.15	25.08	26.01	26.94
300	27.87	28.80	29.73	30.66	31.59	32.52	33.45	34.37	35.30	36.23
400	37.16	38.09	39.02	39.95	40.88	41.81	42.74	43.66	44.59	45.52
500	46.45	47.38	48.31	49.24	50.17	51.10	52.03	52.95	53.88	54.81
600	55.74	56.67	57.60	58.53	59.46	60.39	61.32	62.25	63.17	64.10
700	65.03	65.96	66.89	67.82	68.75	69.68	70.61	71.54	72.46	73.39
800	74.32	75.25	76.18	77.11	78.04	78.97	79.90	80.83	81.75	82.68
900	83.61	84.54	85.47	86.40	87.33	88.26	89.19	90.12	91.04	91.97
1000	92.90	93.83	94.76	95.69	96.62	97.55	98.48	99.41	100.34	101.26
1100	102.19	103.12	104.05	104.98	105.91	106.84	107.77	108.70	109.63	110.55
1200	111.48	112.41	113.34	114.27	115.20	116.13	117.06	117.99	118.92	119.84
1300	120.77	121.70	122.63	123.56	124.49	125.42	126.35	127.28	128.21	129.14
1400	130.06	130.99	131.92	132.85	133.78	134.71	135.64	136.57	137.50	138.43
1500	139.35									

ACRES TO HECTARES (1 ACRE = 0.404 685 6 ha)

ACRES	0	1	2	3	4	5	6	7	8	9
HECTARES	...	0.40	0.81	1.21	1.62	2.02	2.43	2.83	3.24	3.64

	0	10	20	30	40	50	60	70	80	90
ACRES					HECTARES (ha)					
0	...	4.05	8.09	12.14	16.19	20.23	24.28	28.33	32.37	36.42
100	40.47	44.52	48.56	52.61	56.66	60.70	64.75	68.80	72.84	76.89
200	80.94	84.98	89.03	93.08	97.12	101.17	105.22	109.27	113.31	117.36
300	121.41	125.45	129.50	133.55	137.59	141.64	145.69	149.73	153.78	157.83
400	161.87	165.92	169.97	174.01	178.06	182.11	186.16	190.20	194.25	198.30
500	202.34	206.39	210.44	214.48	218.53	222.58	226.62	230.67	234.72	238.76
600	242.81	246.86	250.91	254.95	259.00	263.05	267.09	271.14	275.19	279.23
700	283.28	287.33	291.37	295.42	299.47	303.51	307.56	311.61	315.65	319.70
800	323.75	327.80	331.84	335.89	339.94	343.98	348.03	352.08	356.12	360.17
900	364.22	368.26	372.31	376.36	380.40	384.45	388.50	392.55	396.59	400.64
1000	404.69									

CUBIC FEET TO CUBIC METERS (1 FT^3 = 0.0283 m^3)

CUBIC FEET	0	1	2	3	4	5	6	7	8	9
					CUBIC METERS (m^3)					
0	...	0.028	0.057	0.085	0.113	0.142	0.170	0.198	0.227	0.255
10	0.283	0.311	0.340	0.368	0.396	0.425	0.453	0.481	0.510	0.538
20	0.566	0.595	0.623	0.651	0.680	0.708	0.736	0.765	0.793	0.821
30	0.850	0.878	0.906	0.934	0.963	0.991	0.019	1.048	1.076	1.104
40	1.133	1.161	1.189	1.218	1.246	1.274	1.303	1.331	1.359	1.386
50	1.416	1.444	1.472	1.501	1.529	1.557	1.586	1.614	1.642	1.671
60	1.699	1.727	1.756	1.784	1.812	1.841	1.869	1.897	1.926	1.954
70	1.982	2.010	2.034	2.067	2.095	2.124	2.152	2.180	2.209	2.237
80	2.265	2.293	2.322	2.350	2.379	2.407	2.435	2.464	2.492	2.520
90	2.549	2.577	2.605	2.633	2.662	2.690	2.718	2.747	2.775	2.803
100	2.832	2.860	2.888	2.917	2.945	2.973	3.002	3.030	3.058	3.087
110	3.115	3.143	3.171	3.200	3.228	3.256	3.285	3.313	3.341	3.370
120	3.398	3.426	3.455	3.483	3.511	3.540	3.568	3.596	3.625	3.653
130	3.681	3.710	3.738	3.766	3.794	3.823	3.851	3.879	3.908	3.936
140	3.964	3.993	4.021	4.049	4.078	4.106	4.134	4.163	4.191	4.219
150	4.248	4.276	4.304	4.332	4.361	4.389	4.417	4.446	4.474	4.502
160	4.531	4.559	4.587	4.616	4.644	4.672	4.701	4.729	4.757	4.786
170	4.814	4.482	4.870	4.899	4.927	4.955	4.984	5.012	5.040	5.069
180	5.097	5.125	5.154	5.182	5.210	5.239	5.267	5.295	5.234	5.352
190	5.380	5.409	5.437	5.465	5.493	5.522	5.550	5.578	5.606	5.635
200	5.663									

NOTE: 1 cubic meter (m^3) equals 1000 liters (L). Cubic feet can be converted to liters by shifting the decimal point three places to the right; for example, 125 cubic feet = 3.540 m^3 = 3540 L.

GALLONS TO LITERS (1 GAL [U.S.] = 3.785 41L)

GALLONS	0	1	2	3	4	5	6	7	8	9
					LITERS (L)					
0	...	3.79	7.57	11.36	15.14	18.93	22.71	26.50	30.28	34.07
10	37.85	41.64	45.42	49.21	53.00	56.78	60.57	64.35	68.14	71.92
20	75.71	79.49	83.28	87.06	90.85	94.64	98.42	102.21	105.99	109.78
30	113.56	117.35	121.13	124.92	128.70	132.49	136.27	140.06	143.85	147.63
40	151.42	155.20	158.99	162.77	166.56	170.34	174.13	177.91	181.70	185.49
50	189.27	193.06	196.84	200.63	204.41	208.20	211.98	215.77	219.55	223.34
60	227.12	230.91	234.70	238.48	242.27	246.05	249.84	253.62	257.41	261.19
70	264.98	268.76	272.55	276.34	280.12	283.91	287.69	291.48	295.26	299.05
80	302.83	306.62	310.40	314.19	317.97	321.76	325.55	329.33	333.12	336.90
90	340.69	344.47	348.26	352.04	355.83	359.61	363.40	367.18	370.97	374.76

	0	10	20	30	40	50	60	70	80	90
100	378.5	416.4	454.2	492.1	530.0	567.8	605.7	643.5	681.4	719.2
200	757.1	794.9	832.8	870.6	908.5	946.4	984.2	1022.1	1059.9	1097.8
300	1135.6	1173.5	1211.3	1249.2	1287.0	1324.9	1362.7	1400.6	1438.5	1476.3
400	1514.2	1552.0	1589.9	1627.7	1665.6	1703.4	1741.3	1779.1	1817.0	1854.9
500	1892.7	1930.6	1968.4	2006.3	2044.1	2082.0	2119.8	2157.7	2195.5	2233.4
600	2271.2	2309.1	2347.0	2384.8	2422.7	2460.5	2498.4	2536.2	2574.1	2611.9
700	2649.8	2687.6	2725.5	2763.4	2801.2	2839.1	2876.9	2914.8	2952.6	2990.5
800	3028.3	3066.3	3104.0	3141.9	3179.7	3217.6	3255.5	3293.3	3331.2	3369.0
900	3406.9	3444.7	3482.6	3520.4	3558.3	3596.1	3634.0	3671.8	3709.7	3747.6
1000	3785.4									

POUNDS TO KILOGRAMS (1 LB = 0.453 592 kg)

POUNDS	0	1	2	3	4	5	6	7	8	9
					KILOGRAMS (kg)					
0	...	0.45	0.91	1.36	1.81	2.27	2.72	3.18	3.63	4.08
10	4.54	4.99	5.44	5.90	6.35	6.80	7.26	7.71	8.16	8.62
20	9.07	9.53	9.98	10.43	10.89	11.34	11.79	12.25	12.70	13.15
30	13.61	14.06	14.52	14.97	15.42	15.88	16.33	16.78	17.24	17.69
40	18.14	18.60	19.05	19.50	19.96	20.41	20.87	21.32	21.77	22.23
50	22.68	23.13	23.59	24.04	24.49	24.95	25.40	25.85	26.31	26.76
60	27.22	27.67	28.12	28.58	29.03	29.48	29.94	30.39	30.84	31.30
70	31.75	32.21	32.66	33.11	33.57	34.02	34.47	34.93	35.38	35.83
80	36.29	36.74	37.19	37.65	38.10	38.56	39.01	39.46	39.92	40.37
90	40.82	41.28	41.73	42.18	42.64	43.09	43.54	44.00	44.45	44.91
100	45.36	45.81	46.27	46.72	47.17	47.63	48.08	48.53	48.99	49.44
110	49.90	50.35	50.80	51.26	51.71	52.16	52.62	53.07	53.52	53.98
120	54.43	54.88	55.34	55.79	56.25	56.70	57.15	57.61	58.06	58.51
130	58.97	59.42	59.87	60.33	60.78	61.24	61.69	62.14	62.60	63.05
140	63.50	63.96	64.41	64.86	65.32	65.77	66.22	66.68	67.13	67.59
150	68.04	68.49	68.95	69.40	69.85	70.31	70.76	71.21	71.67	72.12
160	72.57	73.03	73.48	73.94	74.39	74.84	75.30	75.75	76.20	76.66
170	77.11	77.56	78.02	78.47	78.93	79.38	79.83	80.29	80.74	81.19
180	81.65	82.10	82.55	83.01	83.46	83.91	84.37	84.82	85.28	85.73
190	86.18	86.64	87.09	87.54	88.00	88.45	88.90	89.36	89.81	90.26
200	90.72									

U.S. SHORT TONS (2000 LB) TO METRIC TONS (1 TON = 0.907 185 t)

SHORT TONS	0	1	2	3	4	5	6	7	8	9
					METRIC TONS (t)					
0	...	0.907	1.814	2.722	3.629	4.536	5.443	6.350	7.257	8.165
10	9.072	9.979	10.886	11.793	12.701	13.608	14.515	15.422	16.329	17.237
20	18.144	19.051	19.958	20.865	21.772	22.680	23.587	24.494	25.401	26.308
30	27.216	28.123	29.030	29.937	30.844	31.751	32.659	33.566	34.473	35.380
40	36.287	37.195	38.102	39.009	39.916	40.823	41.731	42.638	43.545	44.452
50	45.359	46.266	47.174	48.081	48.988	49.895	50.802	51.710	52.617	53.524
60	54.431	55.338	56.245	57.153	58.060	58.967	59.874	60.781	61.689	62.596
70	63.503	64.410	65.317	66.225	67.132	68.039	68.946	69.853	70.760	71.668
80	72.575	73.482	74.389	75.296	76.204	77.111	78.018	78.925	79.832	80.739
90	81.647	82.554	83.461	84.368	85.275	86.183	87.090	87.997	88.904	89.811
100	90.718									

NOTE: 1 metric ton (t) equals 1000 kilograms (kg). U.S. short tons can be converted to kilograms by shifting the decimal point three places to the right; for example, 48 short tons = 43.545 t = 43.545 kg (rounded to the nearest kilogram).

POUNDS PER CUBIC FOOT TO KILOGRAMS PER CUBIC METER (1 LB/FT^3 = 16.018 46 kg/m^3)

POUNDS PER CUBIC FOOT	0	1	2	3	4	5	6	7	8	9
					KILOGRAMS PER CUBIC METER (kg/m^3)					
0	...	16.0	32.0	48.1	64.1	80.1	96.1	112.1	128.1	144.2
10	160.2	176.2	192.2	208.2	224.3	240.3	256.3	272.3	288.3	304.4
20	320.4	336.4	352.4	368.4	384.4	400.5	416.5	432.5	448.5	464.5
30	480.6	496.6	512.6	528.6	544.6	560.6	576.7	592.7	608.7	624.7
40	640.7	656.8	672.8	688.8	704.8	720.8	736.8	752.9	768.9	784.9
50	800.9	816.9	833.0	849.0	865.0	881.0	897.0	913.1	929.1	945.1
60	961.1	977.1	993.1	1009.2	1025.2	1041.2	1057.2	1073.2	1089.3	1105.3
70	1121.3	1137.3	1153.3	1169.3	1185.4	1201.4	1217.4	1233.4	1249.4	1265.5
80	1281.5	1297.5	1313.5	1329.5	1345.6	1361.6	1377.6	1393.6	1409.6	1425.6
90	1441.7	1457.7	1473.7	1489.7	1505.7	1521.8	1537.8	1553.8	1569.8	1585.8
100	1601.8	1617.9	1633.9	1649.9	1665.9	1681.9	1698.0	1714.0	1730.0	1746.0
110	1762.0	1778.0	1794.1	1810.1	1826.1	1842.1	1858.1	1874.2	1890.2	1906.2
120	1922.2	1938.2	1954.3	1970.3	1986.3	2002.3	2018.3	2034.3	2050.4	2066.4
130	2082.4	2098.4	2114.4	2130.5	2146.5	2162.5	2178.5	2194.5	2210.5	2226.6
140	2242.6	2258.6	2274.6	2290.6	2306.7	2322.7	2338.7	2354.7	2370.7	2386.8
150	2402.8	2418.8	2434.8	2450.8	2466.8	2482.9	2498.9	2514.9	2590.9	2546.9
160	2563.0	2579.0	2595.0	2611.0	2627.0	2643.0	2659.1	2675.1	2691.1	2707.1
170	2723.1	2739.2	2755.2	2771.2	2787.2	2803.2	2819.2	2835.3	2851.3	2867.3
180	2883.3	2899.3	2915.4	2931.4	2947.4	2963.4	2979.4	2995.4	3011.5	3027.5
190	3043.5	3059.5	3075.5	3091.6	3107.6	3123.6	3139.6	3155.6	3171.7	3187.7
200	3203.7									

POUNDS-FORCE PER SQUARE INCH (PSI) TO MEGAPASCALS (MPa) (1 PSI = 0.006 895 MPa)

POUNDS-FORCE PER SQUARE INCH	0	10	20	30	40	50	60	70	80	90
					MEGAPASCALS (MPa)					
0	...	0.069	0.138	0.207	0.276	0.345	0.414	0.483	0.552	0.621
100	0.689	0.758	0.827	0.896	0.965	1.034	1.103	1.172	1.241	1.310
200	1.379	1.448	1.517	1.586	1.655	1.724	1.793	1.862	1.931	1.999
300	2.068	2.137	2.206	2.275	2.344	2.413	2.482	2.551	2.620	2.689
400	2.758	2.827	2.896	2.965	3.034	3.103	3.172	3.241	3.309	3.378
500	3.447	3.516	3.585	3.654	3.723	3.792	3.861	3.903	3.999	4.068
600	4.137	4.206	4.275	4.344	4.413	4.482	4.551	4.619	4.688	4.757
700	4.826	4.895	4.964	5.033	5.102	5.171	5.240	5.309	5.378	5.447
800	5.516	5.585	5.654	5.723	5.792	5.861	5.929	5.998	6.067	6.136
900	6.205	6.274	6.343	6.412	6.481	6.550	6.619	6.688	6.757	6.826
	0	100	200	300	400	500	600	700	800	900
1000	6.895	7.584	8.274	8.963	9.653	10.342	11.032	11.721	12.411	13.100
2000	13.790	14.479	15.168	15.858	16.547	17.237	17.926	18.616	19.305	19.995
3000	20.684	21.374	22.063	22.753	23.442	24.132	24.821	25.511	26.200	26.890
4000	27.579	28.269	28.958	29.647	30.337	31.026	31.716	32.405	33.095	33.784
5000	34.474	35.163	35.853	36.542	37.232	37.921	38.611	39.300	39.990	40.679
6000	41.369	42.058	42.747	43.437	44.126	44.816	45.505	46.195	46.884	47.574
7000	48.263	48.953	49.642	50.332	51.021	51.711	52.400	53.090	53.779	54.469
8000	55.158	55.848	56.537	57.226	57.916	58.605	59.295	59.984	60.674	61.363
9000	62.053	64.742	63.432	64.121	64.811	65.500	66.190	66.879	67.569	68.258
10 000	68.948									

NOTE: 1 megapascal (MPa) is equal to 1 meganewton per square meter (MN/m^2) and to 1 newton per square millimeter (N/mm^2).

POUNDS-FORCE PER SQUARE FOOT TO KILOPASCALS (kPa) = 0.047 88 kN/m^2

POUNDS-FORCE PER SQUARE FOOT	0	10	20	30	40	50	60	70	80	90
					KILOPASCALS (kPa = kN/m^2)					
0	—	0.479	0.958	1.436	1.915	2.394	2.873	3.352	3.830	4.309
100	4.788	5.267	5.746	6.224	6.703	7.182	7.661	8.140	8.618	9.097
200	9.576	10.055	10.534	11.013	11.491	11.970	12.449	12.928	13.406	13.886
300	14.364	14.843	15.322	15.800	16.279	16.758	17.237	17.716	18.195	18.673
400	19.152	19.631	20.110	20.589	21.067	21.546	22.025	22.504	22.983	23.461
500	23.910	24.419	24.898	25.377	25.855	26.334	26.813	27.292	27.771	28.249
600	28.728	29.207	29.686	31.165	30.643	31.122	31.601	32.080	32.559	33.037
700	33.516	33.995	34.474	34.953	35.431	35.910	36.389	36.868	37.347	37.825
800	38.304	38.783	39.262	39.741	40.219	40.698	41.177	41.656	42.135	42.613
900	43.092	43.571	44.050	44.529	45.007	45.486	45.965	46.444	46.923	47.401
1000	47.880									

NOTE: 1 kilopascal (kPa) is equal to 1 kilonewton per square meter (kN/m^2).

LUMENS PER SQUARE FOOT TO LUX (lm/m^2) AND KILOLUX (1 lm/FT^2 = 10.7639 lx)

LUMENS PER SQUARE FOOT	0	1	2	3	4	5	6	7	8	9
					LUX (lm/m^2)					
0	...	10.8	21.5	32.3	43.1	53.8	64.6	75.3	86.1	96.9
10	107.6	118.4	129.2	139.9	150.7	161.5	172.2	183.0	193.8	204.5
20	215.3	226.0	236.8	247.6	258.3	269.1	279.9	290.6	301.4	312.2
30	322.9	333.7	344.4	355.2	366.0	376.7	387.5	398.3	409.0	419.8
40	430.6	441.3	452.1	462.8	473.6	484.4	495.1	505.9	516.7	527.4
50	538.2	549.0	559.7	570.5	581.3	592.0	602.8	613.5	624.3	635.1
60	645.8	656.6	667.4	678.1	688.9	699.7	710.4	721.2	731.9	742.7
70	753.5	764.2	775.0	785.8	796.5	807.3	818.1	828.8	839.6	850.3
80	861.1	871.9	882.6	893.4	904.2	914.9	925.7	936.5	947.2	958.0
90	968.8	979.5	990.3	1001.0	1011.8	1022.6	1033.3	1044.1	1054.9	1065.6
	0	10	20	30	40	50	60	70	80	90
					KILOLUX (1000 lux)					
100	1.076	1.184	1.292	1.399	1.507	1.615	1.722	1.830	1.938	2.045
200	2.153	2.260	2.368	2.476	2.583	2.691	2.799	2.906	3.014	3.122
300	3.229	3.337	3.444	3.552	3.660	3.767	3.875	3.983	4.090	4.198
400	4.306	4.413	4.521	4.628	4.736	4.844	4.951	5.059	5.167	5.274
500	5.382	5.490	5.597	5.705	5.813	5.920	6.028	6.135	6.243	6.351
600	6.458	6.566	6.674	6.781	6.889	6.997	7.104	7.212	7.319	7.427
700	7.535	7.642	7.750	7.858	7.965	8.073	8.181	8.288	8.396	8.503
800	8.611	8.719	8.826	8.934	9.042	9.149	9.257	9.365	9.472	9.580
900	9.688	9.795	9.903	10.010	10.118	10.226	10.333	10.441	10.549	10.656
1000	10.764									

POUND-FORCE TO NEWTONS (1 lbf = 4.448 22 N)

POUND-FORCE	0	1	2	3	4	5	6	7	8	9
	NEWTONS (N)									
0	. . .	4.45	8.90	13.34	17.79	22.24	26.69	31.14	35.59	40.03
10	44.48	48.93	53.38	57.83	62.28	66.72	71.17	75.62	80.07	84.52
20	88.96	93.41	97.86	102.31	106.76	111.21	115.65	120.10	124.55	129.00
30	133.45	137.89	142.34	146.79	151.24	155.69	160.14	164.58	169.03	173.48
40	177.93	182.38	186.83	191.27	195.72	200.17	204.62	209.07	213.51	217.96
50	222.41	226.86	231.31	235.76	240.20	244.65	249.10	253.55	258.00	262.45
60	266.89	271.34	275.79	280.24	284.69	289.13	293.58	298.03	302.48	306.93
70	311.38	315.82	320.27	324.72	329.17	333.62	338.06	342.51	346.96	351.41
80	355.86	360.31	364.75	369.20	373.65	378.10	382.55	387.00	391.44	395.89
90	400.34	404.79	409.24	413.68	418.13	422.58	427.03	431.48	435.93	440.37

POUND-FORCE	0	10	20	30	40	50	60	70	80	90
100	444.8	489.3	533.8	578.3	622.8	667.2	711.7	756.2	800.7	845.2
200	889.6	934.1	978.6	1023.1	1067.6	1112.1	1156.5	1201.0	1245.5	1290.0
300	1334.5	1378.9	1423.4	1467.9	1512.4	1556.9	1601.4	1645.8	1690.3	1734.8
400	1779.3	1823.8	1868.3	1912.7	1957.2	2001.7	2046.2	2090.7	2135.1	2179.6
500	2224.1	2268.6	2313.1	2357.6	2402.0	2446.5	2491.0	2535.5	2580.0	2624.5
600	2668.9	2713.4	2757.9	2802.4	2846.9	2891.3	2935.8	2980.3	3024.8	3069.3
700	3113.8	3158.2	3202.7	3247.2	3291.7	3336.2	3380.6	3425.1	3469.6	3514.1
800	3558.6	3603.1	3647.5	3692.0	3736.5	3781.0	3835.5	3870.0	3914.4	3958.9
900	4003.4	4047.9	4092.4	4136.8	4181.3	4225.8	4270.3	4314.8	4359.3	4403.7
1000	4448.2	4492.7	4537.2	4581.7	4626.1	4670.6	4715.1	4759.6	4804.1	4848.6
1100	4893.0	4937.5	4982.0	5026.5	5071.0	5115.5	5159.9	5204.4	5248.9	5293.4
1200	5337.9	5382.3	5426.8	5471.3	5515.8	5560.3	5604.8	5649.2	5693.7	5738.2
1300	5782.7	5827.2	5871.7	5916.1	5960.6	6005.1	6049.6	6094.1	6138.5	6183.0
1400	6227.5	6272.0	6316.5	6361.0	6405.4	6449.9	6494.4	6538.9	6583.4	6627.8
1500	6672.3	6716.8	6761.3	6805.8	6850.3	6894.7	6939.2	6983.7	7028.2	7072.7
1600	7117.2	7161.6	7206.1	7250.6	7295.1	7339.6	7384.0	7428.5	7473.0	7517.5
1700	7562.0	7606.5	7650.9	7695.4	7739.9	7784.4	7828.9	7873.3	7917.8	7962.3
1800	8006.0	8051.3	8095.8	8140.2	8184.7	8229.2	8273.7	8318.2	8362.7	8407.1
1900	8451.6	8496.1	8540.6	8585.1	8629.5	8674.0	8718.5	8763.0	8807.5	8852.0
2000	8896.4									

NOTE: 1000 newtons (N) equal 1 kilonewton (1kN). The lower portion of the table could also have been shown in kilonewtons; for example, 4893.0 N = 4.8930 kN. The table can also be used for the conversion of kips (1000 lbf) to kilonewtons (kN), since a multiplier of 1000 applies to both measurements units.

INDEX

The number in parentheses preceding a page number indicates the edition from which that material was taken.

399